The AMERICAN HERITAGE®

Student
Thesaurus

Paul Hellweg
Joyce LeBaron
Susannah LeBaron

HOUGHTON MIFFLIN
Boston • New York

This book is dedicated to
Frankie J. and Robert D. Hellweg, Brendan I. Steinman

and is in loving memory of
Truellen Ruth Davis and Carlos Stannard LeBaron

Acknowledgments

Margery S. Berube, *Vice President and Director of Lexical Publishing,* who initiated the project and oversaw its development.

David R. Pritchard, *Senior Project Editor,* who also helped to get the book started and provided input for its development.

Beth Anderson, *Editor,* who served as overall Project Manager. Her supportive attitude and professional expertise make her one of the best editors any author could hope to work with.

Diane Fredrick, *Contributing Editor,* who worked extensively on every stage of the editorial process.

Jacquelyn Pope, *Associate Editor,* who reviewed page proofs.

Beth Rubè, *Production Supervisor,* who oversaw the book's design and composition.

Margaret Anne Miles, *Senior Art and Production Coordinator,* who compiled and coordinated the artwork for the Word Group Features.

In addition, the authors wish to acknowledge

Dorothy Barresi, Diane Dalbey, Diane Dever, Katharine Haake, Paula Harvey, Jan Higgins, Mary Leis, Larry Leis, Gary Leis, George D. Lindbeck, Bev Manassee, June/Mohler, Bob Oliver, D.R. Rockhold, Warren Steinman, George Welton, and the folks at Mary's Donut Depot.

The authors are indebted to all of the above.
Paul Hellweg
Joyce LeBaron
Susannah LeBaron

ISBN 0-618-28029-4

Book design by Victory Productions

Visit our website: www.houghtonmifflinbooks.com

Library of Congress Cataloging-in-Publication Data

Hellweg, Paul.
    The American heritage student thesaurus / by Paul Hellweg, Joyce LeBaron, and Susannah LeBaron.
        p.   cm.
    Summary: Provides synonyms, antonyms, Word Groups, parts of speech, and usage for 6000 entry words.
    ISBN 0-395-93026-X (hardcover)
    1. English language—Synonyms and antonyms Juvenile literature.
    [1. English language—Synonyms and antonyms.] I. LeBaron, Joyce.
II. LeBaron, Susannah. III. Title. IV. Title: Student thesaurus.
PE1591.H4434 1999
423'. 1—dc21   99-29829
                                                                              CIP

PICTURE CREDITS

<u>Cover photographs:</u> butterflies courtesy The Image Bank-Jody Dole/Getty Images

A-Z Text: aircraft Laurel Cook Lhowe **amphibian** © 1999 PhotoDisc, Inc. **artist** © 1999 PhotoDisc, Inc. **author** © 1999 PhotoDisc, Inc. **boat** Laurel Cook Lhowe **bottle** © School Division, Houghton Mifflin Company **button** © 1999 PhotoDisc, Inc. **canine** © Houghton Mifflin Company/Evelyn Shafer **castle** © 1999 PhotoDisc, Inc. **chair** © 1999 PhotoDisc, Inc. **constellation** Tech-Graphics **dinosaur** Tech-Graphics **document** © 1999 PhotoDisc, Inc. **envelope** © 1999 PhotoDisc, Inc. **feline** © 1999 PhotoDisc, Inc. **garden** © 1999 PhotoDisc, Inc. **guitar** © 1999 PhotoDisc, Inc. **hat** © 1999 PhotoDisc, Inc. **herb** Cecile Duray-Bito **insect** Cecile Duray-Bito **jewelry** © School Division, Houghton Mifflin Company **knife** © 1999 PhotoDisc, Inc. **legume** Laurel Cook Lhowe **lizard** Laurel Cook Lhowe **mammal** Laurel Cook Lhowe **music** Tech-Graphics **nail** Chris Costello **nut** © 1999 PhotoDisc, Inc. **oil** © 1999 PhotoDisc, Inc. **pasta** © School Division, Houghton Mifflin Company **poem** © 1999 PhotoDisc, Inc. **pottery** © 1999 PhotoDisc, Inc. **primate** Laurel Cook Lhowe **railroad** © 1999 PhotoDisc, Inc. **reptile** © 1999 PhotoDisc, Inc. **rodent** © 1999 PhotoDisc, Inc. **shoe** Albano Ballerini **song** Tech-Graphics **spider** © 1999 PhotoDisc, Inc. **theater** © 1999 PhotoDisc, Inc. **tree** Chris Costello **vegetable** © 1999 PhotoDisc, Inc.

Manufactured in the United States of America   DOW 10 9 8 7 6 5 4 3 2 1

Table of Contents

Index to Word Groups

You will find Word Group features at the following entries:

Introduction

You Are a Writer

You write papers and reports for school. Perhaps you send cards, letters, or e-mail to friends and relatives. Maybe you keep a journal or a diary. It is natural to want to record your experiences in writing. Perhaps you are interested in creative writing. People your age have written poems, short stories, even novels. Writing is a craft and you can learn it. Every craft has tools that are useful, and one of the most important tools that you as a writer can use is a thesaurus.

What Is a Thesaurus?

A thesaurus is a book of synonyms—words that share the same or nearly the same meaning. For example, **shine, beam, gleam, glimmer, radiate,** and **shimmer** are all synonyms for the verb **glow,** just as **clamor, din, racket, sound, tumult, uproar, hubbub,** and **pandemonium** are all synonyms for the noun **noise.** You will find all these and many more synonyms listed in this thesaurus.

Of course, not every word you can think of has a synonym. Words that don't have synonyms, such as *uncle* or *spaghetti* or *computer,* are not included in a thesaurus. But many words do have synonyms, and we have listed more than 6,000 of them as entries in this book, with approximately 100,000 synonyms in all.

Why Use a Thesaurus?

A writer uses a thesaurus to make his or her style more interesting. For example, if you have used the word *nice* three times already and are getting tired of it, you can look up **nice** in this thesaurus and choose from **agreeable, delightful, enjoyable, good, pleasant, pleasing, enchanting, wonderful, decent, kind, polite, thoughtful, courteous, proper, considerate,** or **cordial.**

A thesaurus can also be used to make your writing more precise. If you are writing about the Grand Canyon and would like to use a word to describe it that is more colorful and specific than the word *big,* you can look up **big** in your thesaurus and then choose from **immense, gigantic, colossal, enormous,** or **tremendous.**

How to Choose the Best Word

Another way to think of a thesaurus is as a book of *word choices.* But how do you choose the right word? Which is the best word to get your meaning across? Just because synonyms share the same meaning doesn't mean that they can always be substituted for each other. In any particular sentence, some synonyms will probably work better than others. That's why we have designed this thesaurus in a way that helps you find the best synonyms for your needs.

First, we include a typical example sentence for every meaning of every entry word in the book. This gives you a clear idea of how the word is commonly used in writing and speaking. Second, we have listed the synonyms in the order that they best fit the example sentence. Synonyms that closely fit the example sentence come first, while those that do not fit as well are listed last.

Remember, we have arranged the synonyms to fit the particular example sentence that is given in that entry. It's up to you to decide which synonyms fit best in your sentence.

The Main Entry

Here is an entry in this thesaurus:

The entry word is printed in blue type, making it easy to find. The part of speech is printed in italic letters, and if the entry word can be used as more than one part of speech, each one is treated separately. The word *land*, for instance, can be used as either a noun or a verb, and synonyms and an example sentence are provided for each. If the entry word has more than one meaning for a particular part of speech, each meaning is numbered.

> **land** *noun* **1.** ground, soil, earth, terrain, dirt, loam, turf This is good land for growing soybeans. **2.** region, country, nation, state, homeland, realm, territory America has been called "the land of opportunity." **3.** property, real estate, acreage, acres, grounds My grandmother owns land in Idaho. ◆ *verb* **1.** alight, set down, touch down, arrive, disembark Astronauts first landed on the moon on July 20, 1969. **2.** get, secure, win, gain, obtain, catch, procure My sister just landed the lead role in the school play. ● **Antonyms:** *verb* **1.** embark, take off **2.** lose, relinquish

In addition to synonyms, many English words also have antonyms—words that are opposite in meaning. We have included a varied selection of antonyms in this thesaurus, putting them after the entry word to which they refer. For example, you can see that the antonyms for **land** are

verb **1.** embark, take off **2.** lose, relinquish

Note that numbered lists of antonyms correspond to the numbered definitions in the main entry and may not always be in numerical sequence. Also, antonyms may not be given for all the parts of speech listed in the entry. At **land,** antonyms are listed for the verb, not the noun.

Homographs

Words with the same spelling but different meanings are called homographs. These are entered separately in the thesaurus, and each is followed by a small raised number, such as **present**[1] and **present**[2] on page 247.

Word Groups

We have included some entry words in this thesaurus that do not have actual synonyms but instead have a group of closely related words. For example, there are no words that mean the same thing as **hat.** There are, however, many words that refer to different types of hats, and we have put these related words in a Word Group box on page 149.

Some Word Group boxes point out the differences between related terms. For example, you can quickly learn the difference between an **archipelago** and an **atoll** at the Word Group for **island** on page 170.

Word groups are entered in the same alphabetical order as the main entry words. For example, you will find the Word Group for **hat** on page 149 between the entries for **hasty** and **hatch.**

A Final Word

This thesaurus will help you find the right words to express your thoughts and keep your writing lively, accurate, and interesting. Learning to use a thesaurus and a dictionary effectively will serve you well, not only while you are in school, but for the rest of your writing days. The writers, editors, and publishers of *The American Heritage® Student Thesaurus* want this book to be a useful tool in your writing efforts. We would enjoy hearing from students, teachers, and parents. If you have questions or comments, please contact us: Dictionary Department, Houghton Mifflin Company, 222 Berkeley Street, Boston, MA 02116.

Aa

abandon *verb* **1. desert, forsake, leave, discard, renounce, relinquish** The frustrated driver abandoned his broken-down car. **2. cease, discontinue, break off, leave off, give up, quit** We abandoned our chores to go swimming. ◆ *noun* **unrestraint, uninhibitedness, recklessness, wildness** The street revelers danced with abandon at Mardi Gras. ● **Antonyms:** *verb* **1. keep, claim 2. continue, maintain** ◆ *noun* **restraint, self-control**

abandoned **deserted, unoccupied, vacant, empty, forgotten, neglected** The abandoned house had broken windows and an overgrown lawn. ● **Antonyms: occupied, cared for**

abase *verb* **degrade, demean, debase, lower, cheapen, humiliate** Cheating on a test abases one's character. ● **Antonyms: uplift, raise**

abate *verb* **diminish, decrease, moderate, subside, slacken, lessen** The storm is expected to abate by morning. ● **Antonyms: increase, intensify**

abbey *noun* **cloister, priory, monastery, friary, nunnery, mission** The abbey had been home to the order of monks for 200 years.

abbreviate *verb* **contract, shorten, condense, abridge, reduce, compress** "Doctor" is commonly abbreviated as "Dr." ● **Antonyms: expand, extend, lengthen**

abdicate *verb* **relinquish, renounce, resign, give up, quit** In 1936 Edward VIII abdicated the British throne.

abduct *verb* **kidnap, seize, grab, carry off, snatch** The ambassador was abducted by terrorists.

aberration *noun* **anomaly, irregularity, abnormality, deviation, oddity** Any snowfall in Florida is an aberration. ● **Antonyms: normality, normalcy**

abhor *verb* **detest, loathe, hate, despise, execrate, disdain** I abhor being tickled. ● **Antonyms: love, like, adore**

abide *verb* **1. endure, tolerate, bear, stand, take, accept** African violets cannot abide direct sunlight. **2. reside, dwell, live, stay, remain** My family abides in an apartment downtown.

ability *noun* **1. capability, capacity, faculty, power, competence, might, potential** My computer has the ability to play a CD while I use other programs. **2. skill, talent, technique, expertise, craft, proficiency, adeptness** Kevin is taking guitar lessons to develop his ability as a musician. ● **Antonym: inability**

able *adjective* **competent, capable, good, skilled, skillful, proficient** My father considers himself an able mechanic. ● **Antonyms: incapable, unable**

abnormal *adjective* **irregular, unnatural, deviant, unusual, strange, weird** Claustrophobia is an abnormal fear of enclosed spaces. ● **Antonyms: normal, natural, ordinary**

abode *noun* **dwelling, residence, domicile, home, house** Some unusual abodes include windmills, boats, and lighthouses.

abolish *verb* **end, eliminate, eradicate, cancel, abrogate, disallow** The Thirteenth Amendment to the Constitution abolished slavery in the United States. ● **Antonyms: establish, keep, retain**

abominable *adjective* **1. detestable, despicable, contemptible, repugnant, vile** Genocide is an abominable crime. **2. unpleasant, disagreeable, miserable, bad, awful, terrible, horrible** The torrid weather last August was abominable. ● **Antonyms: 1. commendable, admirable 2. pleasant, agreeable**

about *adverb* **1. almost, nearly, approximately, roughly, close to, around** The school year is about over. **2. around, round, back, backward, backwards** A storm forced the small boat to turn about. ◆ *preposition* **1. concerning, regarding, relating to, dealing with, touching, involving** I am reading a book about the Korean War. **2. near, close to, approximately, nearly, roughly, almost** I have a cousin who is about my age.

above *adverb* **overhead, over, upstairs, aloft, up, upward, upwards** My best friend lives in the apartment above. ◆ *preposition* **1. over, higher than, on top of, on, upon** The plane flew above the clouds. **2. over, more than, greater, surpassing, beyond, exceeding** The Japanese emperor ranks above all his subjects. ● **Antonyms: below, beneath, under**

abrade *verb* **erode, wear down, wear away, rub, chafe, grate, smooth** The river abraded layers of sandstone, limestone, and shale to form the gorge.

abridge *verb* **shorten, condense, abbreviate, compress, cut, trim** The literary magazine abridged the author's latest novel. ❧ **Antonyms: lengthen, expand**

abroad *adverb* **1. overseas, touring, traveling, away, elsewhere** My family spent two weeks abroad last summer. **2. widely, broadly, everywhere, extensively** He circulated his petition abroad in the city's neighborhoods. ❧ **Antonyms: 1. home, stateside**

abrupt *adjective* **1. hasty, quick, rapid, sudden, hurried, unexpected** I made an abrupt stop when a dog ran in front of my bike. **2. steep, sharp, precipitous, sheer, sudden** In 1987, the stock market had an abrupt drop similar to that of 1929. **3. curt, blunt, brusque, short** The irritated customer was abrupt with the salesperson. ❧ **Antonyms: 1. expected, slow 2. gradual 3. civil, courteous, polite**

absence *noun* **1. nonattendance, nonappearance, absenteeism, truancy** My mother called the school to explain my absence. **2. deficiency, lack, shortage, need, dearth, scarcity** A prolonged absence of vitamin C in one's diet will cause scurvy. ❧ **Antonyms: 1. attendance, presence 2. abundance**

absent *adjective* **1. missing, not present, away, gone, out, lacking** Kiko was absent from choir today. **2. inattentive, preoccupied, distracted, absent-minded, oblivious, unaware** The tired traveler had an absent look on his face. ❧ **Antonyms: 1. present 2. attentive, aware**

absolute *adjective* **1. complete, total, utter, consummate, perfect, pure** My grandmother thinks that I am an absolute genius. **2. unlimited, unrestricted, unconditional, full, supreme, unreserved** Russian czars once ruled with absolute power. **3. positive, definite, certain, conclusive, exact, unambiguous, unequivocal** Absolute proof is required to convict a defendant of murder. ❧ **Antonyms: 1. incomplete, partial 2. conditional, limited 3. dubious, questionable**

absolutely *adverb* **completely, perfectly, totally, utterly, entirely, positively, definitely** My mother looks absolutely beautiful in her new dress. ❧ **Antonyms: somewhat, fairly, probably**

absorb *verb* **1. soak up, sop up, take up, retain, swallow, drink** I used a sponge to absorb the spilled milk. **2. take in, understand, assimilate, learn** It was difficult to absorb

the bad news. **3. captivate, engross, fascinate, hold, engage, involve** Andy was absorbed in the computer game and lost track of time. ❧ **Antonyms: 1. disperse, eliminate, 3. bore, distract**

absorbing *adjective* **engrossing, captivating, fascinating, interesting, intriguing, gripping** I watched an absorbing documentary about wolves. ❧ **Antonyms: boring, dull, uninteresting**

abstain *verb* **refrain, avoid, forgo, resist, keep from, eschew** People who wear braces should abstain from eating sticky foods. ❧ **Antonyms: indulge, partake**

abstract *adjective* **hypothetical, philosophical, theoretical, intellectual, indefinite** Socrates was a Greek philosopher who asked many abstract questions about the nature of morality. ◆ *noun* **summary, condensation, abridgment, synopsis, extract** The building developer submitted an abstract of his plans to the city council. ◆ *verb* **condense, shorten, abridge, summarize, epitomize, outline** I abstracted information from the encyclopedia for my report. ❧ **Antonyms:** *adjective* **concrete, specific**

absurd *adjective* **ridiculous, foolish, nonsensical, preposterous, ludicrous, idiotic, insane** I thought the horror movie was absurd. ❧ **Antonyms: reasonable, sensible**

abundance *noun* **profusion, wealth, excess, surplus, plenitude, plenty** The orchard produced an abundance of apples. ❧ **Antonyms: lack, scarcity**

abundant *adjective* **ample, plentiful, rich, bounteous, generous** Our dog has an abundant supply of tennis balls. ❧ **Antonyms: insufficient, scant, scarce**

abuse *verb* **1. misuse, mistreat, exploit, harm, hurt, misapply, damage** I abused my time by watching TV instead of doing my homework. **2. malign, belittle, insult, revile, assail, berate** The scathing review abused his poetry as drivel. ◆ *noun* **1. misuse, mistreatment, damage, harm, hurt** Sam's soccer shoes have taken a lot of abuse. **2. insults, invective, criticism, censure, obloquy** The comedian's abuse of motorcycle gangs made the audience laugh. ❧ **Antonyms:** *verb* **1. protect, respect 2. praise, extol** ◆ *noun* **2. praise, acclaim**

abyss *noun* **chasm, crevasse, fissure, gorge, hole, depth** The Mariana Trench is a 35,800-foot-deep abyss located in the Pacific Ocean.

academic *adjective* **1. scholastic, educational, scholarly, bookish, studious, intellectual** I am on the science team in my school's academic Olympics. **2. theoretical, abstract,**

speculative, conjectural, hypothetical, debatable, moot Her lecture on the origins of the planet Earth posed many academic questions. ➡ **Antonyms: 2. practical, realistic**

accelerate *verb* **speed, hasten, expedite, quicken, rush** Experiments have shown that some forms of classical music accelerate learning. ➡ **Antonyms: decelerate, slow**

accent *noun* **1. inflection, intonation, pronunciation, articulation, rhythm, tone** I didn't realize that I had an American accent until I went to England. **2. emphasis, stress, importance, significance, prominence** Thomas's clarinet teacher puts an accent on breath control. ◆ *verb* **accentuate, emphasize, highlight, feature, play up, stress** My parents always remind me to accent the good things in my life. ➡ **Antonyms:** *verb* **underplay, minimize**

accept *verb* **1. receive, take, acquire, welcome, get** Sharon happily accepted the ticket I offered her. **2. acknowledge, admit, believe, agree, hold, understand, approve** Is there anyone who does not accept that the world is round? **3. endure, abide, bear, stand, take, tolerate** Sometimes it is hard to accept criticism. ➡ **Antonyms: 1. refuse, reject 2. deny, repudiate 3. oppose, resist**

acceptable *adjective* **satisfactory, adequate, fair, suitable, sufficient, tolerable** My teacher said that I am making acceptable progress. ➡ **Antonyms: poor, unsatisfactory**

access *noun* **1. entrance, admission, entry, admittance, entrée, ingress** I gained access to the locker room through a side door of the gym. **2. approach, passage, route, path, road, way** The access to my uncle's farm is down a dirt road.

accessory *noun* **1. extra, adjunct, trimming, frill, component, attachment** Air conditioning is considered to be an accessory in an automobile. **2. accomplice, partner, assistant, associate, confederate, conspirator** The cashier was convicted as an accessory in the robbery.

accident *noun* **1. chance, fluke, fortune, luck, coincidence** She solved the puzzle quickly, but quite by accident. **2. mishap, crash, disaster, collision, wreck, mistake** Henry sprained his wrist in a skateboarding accident. ➡ **Antonyms: 1. design, plan**

accidental *adjective* **chance, lucky, unexpected, unintentional, unplanned, inadvertent** The farmer's accidental discovery of oil made him very rich. ➡ **Antonyms: intended, planned**

acclaim *verb* **praise, applaud, hail, commend, approve, laud** The new musical was acclaimed by all the critics.

◆ *noun* **praise, applause, approval, recognition, honor, commendation** The author was pleased by the great acclaim that her novel received. ➡ **Antonyms:** *verb* **criticize, denounce** ◆ *noun* **criticism, disapproval**

accommodate *verb* **1. oblige, indulge, please, assist, support, provide** Mom accommodated my request for macaroni and cheese. **2. hold, contain, house, lodge, put up, take in** Our cafeteria accommodates 400 students.

accompany *verb* **escort, chaperon, come along, lead, go along with, attend, follow** Several parents accompanied the students on the field trip.

accomplice *noun* **partner, confederate, conspirator, ally, associate** Margie and her cousin were accomplices in sneaking out to the mall.

accomplish *verb* **achieve, carry out, complete, attain, realize, reach** My mom accomplished a major goal last year when she graduated from college. ➡ **Antonyms: fail, forsake, give up**

accomplishment *noun* **achievement, feat, attainment, success, victory, effort** It is quite an accomplishment to read Tolstoy's lengthy novel *War and Peace*. ➡ **Antonym: failure**

accord *verb* **1. give, grant, confer, bestow, present, allow** The Constitution accords United States citizens many rights. **2. agree, coincide, concur, correspond, match, square** Frank's explanation does not accord with his sister's. ◆ *noun* **1. agreement, harmony, concurrence, concert, concord, congruence** Many students and teachers are in accord that summer vacation is too short. **2. agreement, arrangement, understanding, pact, treaty, deal, contract** The nations reached an accord about international trade. ➡ **Antonyms:** *verb* **1. withhold, deny 2. differ, disagree** ◆ *noun* **1. conflict, disagreement**

account *noun* **1. description, narrative, chronicle, report, history, story** Ahmed gave us a detailed account of the class field trip. **2. explanation, justification, reason, cause, basis, rationale, rationalization** My mother demanded an account for the extra charges on her phone bill. **3. ledger, register, statement, balance, books, tab** My parents examine the household accounts every month. **4. importance, worth, consideration, significance, value, consequence** Laurie holds her brother's opinion to be of little account. ◆ *verb* **1. consider, regard, deem, believe, judge, hold** King Solomon was accounted a fair and wise judge. **2. explain, clarify, justify, rationalize, elucidate, answer** No one could account for the missing cookies. ➡ **Antonyms:** *noun* **4. insignificance, worthlessness**

accumulate *verb* collect, assemble, gather, acquire, accrue, amass Paul has accumulated an impressive collection of arrowheads. ➡ **Antonyms:** scatter, disperse, dissipate

accuracy *noun* correctness, precision, exactness, accurateness, rightness My piano teacher emphasizes accuracy in fingering. ➡ **Antonyms:** imprecision, carelessness

accurate *adjective* correct, exact, precise, right, true, truthful I always double-check to make sure that my answers are accurate. ➡ **Antonym:** incorrect

accuse *verb* blame, charge, impute, attribute, arraign, denounce Amy accused her little brother of spying on her. ➡ **Antonyms:** acquit, clear

accustomed *adjective* usual, habitual, customary, normal, traditional, regular In France, the accustomed greeting is a kiss on the cheek. ➡ **Antonyms:** strange, unusual

ache *verb* **1.** hurt, throb, pain, be sore, smart My arm aches from playing tennis all afternoon. **2.** long, yearn, desire, pine, wish, want Yuliy aches to be reunited with his family. ◆ *noun* hurt, pain, soreness, discomfort, throbbing If that ache persists, you should see a doctor. ➡ **Antonyms:** *noun* comfort, relief

achieve *verb* accomplish, attain, fulfill, realize, reach, complete I recently achieved my goal of saving 300 dollars. ➡ **Antonyms:** fail, miss

achievement *noun* accomplishment, feat, triumph, attainment, victory, success His achievements in competitive swimming are impressive. ➡ **Antonyms:** defeat, failure

acid *adjective* **1.** dry, sour, tangy, tart, bitter, acrid, biting Lemons, oranges, and limes have an acid taste. **2.** sharp, biting, cutting, caustic, harsh Her acid remark hurt my feelings. ➡ **Antonyms:** 1. sweet, sugary 2. friendly, gentle, kind

acknowledge *verb* **1.** admit, concede, grant, allow, avow, own My friend acknowledges that I have the better CD collection. **2.** consider, recognize, deem, judge, regard, hold Her mathematical abilities are acknowledged to be superior. **3.** reply to, answer, respond to, react to, thank The musician acknowledged his fans' enthusiasm by performing an encore. ➡ **Antonyms:** 1. deny, refute, reject 2. & 3. ignore, neglect

acknowledgment *noun* **1.** answer, response, reply, gratitude, thanks, appreciation I mailed my acknowledgment of the invitation immediately. **2.** recognition, admis-

sion, concession, confession, affirmation, acceptance His acknowledgment of his mistake gained him our respect. ➡ **Antonym:** 2. denial

acquaint *verb* inform, introduce, present, advise, apprise, familiarize Our new neighbor acquainted us with her family history.

acquaintance *noun* **1.** familiarity, awareness, knowledge, understanding, grasp, experience Raising my puppy has given me an acquaintance with canine behavior. **2.** associate, colleague, companion, comrade, friend, contact I have many acquaintances, but only a few close friends. ➡ **Antonyms:** 1. ignorance, unawareness 2. stranger

acquiesce *verb* agree, yield, consent, accede, give in, capitulate My sister acquiesced to my request to change the channel. ➡ **Antonyms:** disagree, resist, rebel

acquire *verb* gain, obtain, procure, get, come by, secure My mother recently acquired a beautiful kachina doll for her collection. ➡ **Antonyms:** lose, relinquish

acquisition *noun* **1.** obtaining, gaining, procurement, acquirement, attainment His acquisition of Excalibur made young Arthur the king of Britain. **2.** possession, property, object, purchase, addition, accession The Huntington Library in Pasadena, California, has acquisitions that are famous worldwide.

acquit *verb* **1.** absolve, pardon, exonerate, vindicate, free, clear The jury acquitted the defendant when new evidence proved his innocence. **2.** behave, conduct, comport, act, perform Dad said that we acquitted ourselves very well at the wedding. ➡ **Antonyms:** 1. indict, convict, sentence

act *noun* **1.** deed, action, feat, performance, undertaking, stunt It was an act of stupidity not to study for my math final. **2.** pretense, show, deception, hoax, affectation, masquerade A gopher snake puts on an act to make predators think it is a rattlesnake. **3.** bill, decree, law, statute, legislation, ordinance National holidays must be approved by acts of Congress. ◆ *verb* **1.** serve, function, perform, labor, work, operate Our cat acted as a mother to an orphaned baby rabbit. **2.** behave, comport, carry, conduct, acquit The boy acted with great dignity when he received his Eagle Scout award. **3.** pretend, affect, simulate, fake, feign, put on My dad acted excited when he received yet another tie for Father's Day.

action *noun* **1.** deed, act, effort, performance, accomplishment, undertaking The lifeguard's swift action saved the drowning swimmer. **2.** behavior, conduct, comportment,

deportment, ways His kind action was that of a true gentleman. **3. activity, performance, operation, functioning, movement, working** The action of chewing is the first step of the digestive process. **4. battle, combat, fighting, conflict, clash** The action at Shiloh, Tennessee, was some of the bloodiest in the Civil War.

activate *verb* **actuate, initiate, turn on, start, energize, prompt** I adjusted the thermostat to activate the air conditioner. ⇒ **Antonyms: deactivate, stop**

active *adjective* **1. busy, brisk, dynamic, energetic, lively, spry, industrious** I had an active day at school. **2. functioning, working, operating, going, operative, running** Mount Saint Helens is an active volcano located in southwest Washington. ⇒ **Antonyms: idle, passive**

activity *noun* **1. pastime, pursuit, interest, hobby, avocation, undertaking** One of my favorite activities is playing computer games. **2. liveliness, action, movement, commotion, bustle, exercise** The teen center was filled with activity during the dance. ⇒ **Antonyms: 2. calm, inactivity, quiet**

actor *noun* **1. entertainer, performer, player, actress, thespian** My drama teacher said that I was a good actor. **2. player, participant, party, functionary, agent, operator** The scientists' discovery made them key actors in their field.

actual *adjective* **real, definite, true, genuine, factual, tangible** The actual number of planets in our solar system is a matter of debate. ⇒ **Antonyms: false, unreal**

actually *adverb* **in fact, really, genuinely, truly, literally, indeed** His birthday was actually on Friday, but we celebrated on Saturday.

acute *adjective* **1. keen, perceptive, powerful, sharp, strong, sensitive** Dogs have a very acute sense of smell. **2. sharp, intense, piercing, excruciating, fierce, severe** Migraine headaches can cause acute pain. **3. serious, critical, crucial, severe, urgent, dire, vital** Our school district has an acute shortage of funding. ⇒ **Antonyms: 1. dull, weak 2. mild 3. noncritical**

adage *noun* **proverb, saying, aphorism, maxim, motto, axiom** Benjamin Franklin coined the famous adage, "Early to bed and early to rise, makes a man healthy, wealthy, and wise."

adamant *adjective* **unyielding, resolute, firm, determined, uncompromising, obdurate** She is an adamant supporter of animal rights. ⇒ **Antonyms: flexible, yielding**

adapt *verb* **adjust, acclimate, conform, change, fit, accommodate** My cousin from the Philippines adapted quickly to our climate.

adaptable *adjective* **versatile, flexible, adaptive, pliant, accommodating, malleable** The actress was adaptable and could play a wide variety of roles. ⇒ **Antonyms: inflexible, rigid, set**

add *verb* **1. total, sum up, calculate, compute, tally, count** Today in math we learned how to add numbers on an abacus. **2. include, combine, join, supplement, append, attach** My mother always adds pickles to her potato salad. ⇒ **Antonyms: 1. deduct, subtract 2. eliminate, remove**

addict *noun* **fan, aficionado, devotee, enthusiast, fanatic, zealot** My grandmother is an Internet addict.

addiction *noun* **dependence, craving, dependency, need, fixation, enslavement** It is easy to develop an addiction to nicotine.

addition *noun* **1. adding up, summing, totaling, counting up, computing, reckoning** Addition and subtraction are basic math skills. **2. adding, including, attaching, joining, extending, combining** The addition of plants cheered up the room a great deal. **3. annex, extension, attachment, expansion, enlargement, wing** We built an addition onto our house. ⇒ **Antonyms: 1. subtraction 2. subtracting, removal**

additional *adjective* **extra, added, more, supplementary, further, increased** I bought some additional batteries for my portable stereo. ⇒ **Antonym: less**

address *verb* **1. speak to, talk to, lecture, discuss, greet, hail** The President will address Congress tomorrow. **2. devote, apply, dedicate, bend, concentrate, direct** I addressed myself to cleaning my room. ◆ *noun* **1. residence, location, place, dwelling, abode, street number** I have lived at the same address for many years. **2. speech, talk, oration, discourse, lecture, sermon** The President delivers the State of the Union address each January.

adept *adjective* **skilled, proficient, accomplished, deft, expert, masterful** My uncle is an adept carpenter. ⇒ **Antonyms:** *adjective* **unskilled, inept, amateurish**

adequate *adjective* **enough, sufficient, satisfactory, acceptable, tolerable, fair** It is important to get adequate nutrition through your diet. ⇒ **Antonym: insufficient**

adhere *verb* **1. attach, cling, fasten, hold, stick, bond** Some vines use little rootlike suckers to adhere to buildings. **2. follow, keep, heed, obey, observe, abide by** Success comes to those who adhere to their goals. ➤ **Antonyms: 1. detach, separate**

adjacent *adjective* **adjoining, alongside, close to, near, bordering, contiguous** The park is adjacent to the library. ➤ **Antonyms: distant, remote**

adjourn *verb* **recess, break up, interrupt, suspend, discontinue, stay, waive** The drama workshop adjourned for lunch. ➤ **Antonyms: convene, assemble**

adjust *verb* **1. modify, change, regulate, correct, fix, alter, set** I adjusted the volume on the TV. **2. adapt, conform, settle, accustom, acclimate, fit** Frank found it hard to adjust to his new schedule.

adjustment *noun* **1. alteration, change, modification, accommodation, improvement, tuning** I made adjustments to the strings as I tuned my guitar. **2. balance, order, alignment, stability, equilibrium, harmony** The gears on my bicycle slip out of adjustment easily.

administer *verb* **1. manage, direct, supervise, lead, head, run** The principal administers the school. **2. dispense, give, provide, apply, supply, furnish** Paramedics administered first aid to the injured person.

admirable *adjective* **excellent, praiseworthy, respectable, honorable, fine, good** Many people esteem Martin Luther King Jr. as an admirable man. ➤ **Antonyms: bad, contemptible**

admiration *noun* **esteem, regard, respect, approval, reverence, appreciation** I have great admiration for my grandmother's handmade quilts. ➤ **Antonyms: contempt, disdain**

admire *verb* **esteem, respect, laud, commend, revere** I admire my Uncle Joe for being fluent in four languages. ➤ **Antonyms: scorn, disdain**

admit *verb* **1. acknowledge, concede, confess, disclose, reveal, own** I must admit that I have forgotten your name. **2. accept, let in, allow, receive, take in, induct, welcome** My older sister was just admitted to college. ➤ **Antonyms: 1. deny, refute 2. exclude**

admonish *verb* **1. chastise, chide, rebuke, reprimand, scold** I was admonished for teasing my little sister. **2. advise, counsel, apprise, warn, caution, alert** My father admonished me to put on sunscreen at the beach. ➤ **Antonyms: 1. praise, commend**

adolescent *noun* **teen, teenager, youth, juvenile, minor** Most Olympic gymnasts are adolescents.

adopt *verb* **1. affect, acquire, take on, assume, embrace, appropriate, employ** After a summer in Georgia, I had adopted a Southern accent. **2. ratify, affirm, approve, pass, endorse, authorize** The members of my outdoor club adopted a new set of bylaws. ➤ **Antonyms: 1. reject, spurn 2. veto, disapprove**

adorable *adjective* **delightful, lovable, charming, likable, appealing, cute** Nicole alone thinks that her pet snake is adorable. ➤ **Antonyms: offensive, unlovable**

adore *verb* **love, revere, cherish, venerate, worship, idolize** I adore my mother because she is loving and wise. ➤ **Antonyms: despise, hate**

adorn *verb* **decorate, ornament, trim, embellish, garnish, bedeck** She adorned the old hat with ribbons and flowers.

adroit *adjective* **skillful, proficient, dexterous, facile, sharp, artful, clever** My brother is adroit at fly fishing. ➤ **Antonyms: awkward, clumsy**

adult *noun* **grown-up, man, woman, elder, parent** My Scout troop requires that an adult be present at all meetings and outings. ◆ *adjective* **mature, grown, developed, full-fledged, full-grown** Adult blue whales are the world's largest animals. ➤ **Antonyms:** *noun* **child** ◆ *adjective* **immature**

advance *verb* **1. move, proceed, progress, march, continue, go forward** The ticket line advanced slowly. **2. further, improve, promote, benefit, forward, boost** Marie Curie's discoveries advanced our knowledge of radioactivity. **3. propose, introduce, suggest, submit, present, put forward** My father advanced the idea that we go camping on our vacation. **4. promote, elevate, raise, upgrade, boost, rise** I was recently advanced to first chair in the trumpet section of the school band. ◆ *noun* **advancement, development, improvement, progress, gain, growth** Advances in technology have made computers faster and more powerful. ◆ *adjective* **prior, early, preceding, previous, first** We received advance notice that school would be closed today. ➤ **Antonyms:** *verb* **1. retreat, withdraw 2. hinder, impede 3. suppress, withhold 4. demote, lower** ◆ *noun* **reversal, setback** ◆ *adjective* **late**

advantage *noun* **1. asset, benefit, convenience, boon, edge, favor, superiority** Our science department has the advantage of a well-equipped laboratory. **2. benefit, profit, gain, interest, avail, use** It is to your advantage to turn your homework in on time. ◈ **Antonyms: 2. drawback, hindrance**

advantageous *adjective* **beneficial, useful, profitable, helpful, valuable** He finds it advantageous to sit near the front of the classroom. ◈ **Antonyms: unfavorable, harmful**

adventure *noun* **escapade, exploit, feat, venture, undertaking, enterprise** Going rafting on the Rogue River in Oregon is quite an adventure.

adventurous *adjective* **1. daring, intrepid, adventuresome, enterprising, bold, daredevil** John Muir was an adventurous outdoorsman. **2. dangerous, hazardous, perilous, risky, treacherous** Skydiving is an adventurous activity. ◈ **Antonyms: 1. cautious, timid 2. safe**

adversary *noun* **opponent, competitor, rival, foe, antagonist, enemy** The two friends can be fierce adversaries on the tennis court. ◈ **Antonyms: ally, partner**

adverse *adjective* **hostile, bad, unfavorable, unsatisfactory, disadvantageous, contrary** Adverse weather forced us to postpone our baseball game. ◈ **Antonyms: beneficial, favorable**

adversity *noun* **hardship, misfortune, affliction, difficulty, trouble, bad luck** Mother Teresa was dedicated to helping those suffering adversity. ◈ **Antonyms: good luck, ease**

advertise *verb* **promote, publicize, broadcast, promulgate, popularize, pitch** I advertised my dog-walking business in the local paper.

advertisement *noun* **ad, announcement, commercial, notice, promotion** I saw the advertisement for your dog-walking business in the newspaper.

advice *noun* **guidance, counsel, recommendation, suggestion, admonition** Sometimes it is difficult to follow good advice.

advise *verb* **1. counsel, recommend, suggest, urge, encourage** The doctor advised me to stay off my sprained ankle. **2. notify, inform, apprise, tell, warn, announce** The travel agent advised us that our flight had been changed.

advocate *verb* **recommend, urge, endorse, support, favor, back** The PTA is advocating a change to a year-round school schedule. ◆ *noun* **champion, proponent, patron,**

supporter, defender President Theodore Roosevelt was a great advocate of national parks. ◈ **Antonyms:** *verb* **oppose** ◆ *noun* **opponent, adversary**

affect[1] *verb* **1. alter, change, modify, impinge on, influence, sway** The airline strike affected our vacation plans. **2. move, stir, touch, impress, involve, reach** The movie affected me deeply.

affect[2] *verb* **pretend, put on, simulate, feign, fake** I affected confidence even though I was nervous.

affection *noun* **fondness, love, tenderness, warmth, feeling** My cousins and I have great affection for one another. ◈ **Antonyms: dislike, hate**

affectionate *adjective* **loving, fond, devoted, demonstrative, caring** My cockatiel is very affectionate and likes to ride on my shoulder. ◈ **Antonyms: cold, unfeeling**

affinity *noun* **1. inclination, penchant, liking, attraction, leaning** I have an affinity for math. **2. similarity, resemblance, correspondence, kinship, connection** The music of J. S. Bach has a great affinity with that of Antonio Vivaldi. ◈ **Antonyms: 1. aversion, antipathy 2. dissimilarity**

affirm *verb* **1. assert, aver, avow, hold, maintain, attest** The witness affirmed that he was telling the truth. **2. approve, support, sanction, validate, endorse, ratify** Dad affirmed my decision to give my old bike to charity. ◈ **Antonyms: 1. deny, refute 2. veto, reject**

affluent *adjective* **prosperous, rich, wealthy, moneyed, well-off, privileged** My affluent uncle is helping fund my college education. ◈ **Antonyms: poor, destitute**

afford *verb* **1. pay for, manage, bear, support, incur, sustain** I'll soon be able to afford a new skateboard. **2. furnish, give, provide, supply, extend, grant** Your party afforded me the excuse to buy a new outfit.

affront *verb* **offend, insult, annoy, anger, displease, miff** I was affronted by his rude remark. ◆ *noun* **insult, offense, slight, slur, discourtesy, indignity** That bumper sticker is an affront to good taste.

afraid *adjective* **1. fearful, frightened, scared, alarmed, apprehensive, intimidated** Ann is afraid of her neighbor's dog. **2. regretful, sorry, apologetic, unhappy, reluctant** I'm afraid that I won't be able to attend the play. ◈ **Antonyms: 1. courageous, fearless 2. happy, pleased**

after *preposition* following, subsequent to, later than, past, behind Dessert comes after the main course. ♦ *adverb* 1. afterward, afterwards, later, eventually, subsequently, thereafter, next, then You go on ahead, and I'll come after. 2. behind, following, last First came the mother swan, and then the cygnets came waddling after. ♦ *adjective* later, following, subsequent, ensuing, next, succeeding, successive In after years the garden was neglected and became overgrown with weeds. ♦ *conjunction* as soon as, once, when I can go to the movie after I've finished my chores. ➤ **Antonym: before**

aftermath *noun* consequence, effect, result, end product, outcome, issue As an aftermath of the earthquake, many buildings had to be repaired.

again *adverb* 1. once more, anew, over, another time He liked the book so much that he decided to read it again. 2. on the other hand, furthermore, moreover, additionally, besides, further, then I think you would like sushi, but then again you may not.

against *preposition* 1. into, versus, opposite to, toward, across, contrary to The plane had to fly against a strong headwind. 2. on, upon, alongside, next to, close to I propped the ladder against the wall.

age *noun* 1. maturity, life span, lifetime, years Of all the earth's mammals, human beings reach the greatest age. 2. epoch, era, period, time, phase, generation Curt loves to read about the age of the dinosaurs. ♦ *verb* ripen, mature, develop, grow, season Letting tomatoes age on the vine ensures good flavor. ➤ **Antonym:** *noun* 1. youth

aged *adjective* 1. elderly, old, senior, ancient, venerable My aged aunt still takes long walks every day. 2. ripe, mature, mellow, seasoned, grown, developed Aged duck eggs are considered a delicacy in China. ➤ **Antonyms: 1. young, youthful 2. unripe, immature**

agency *noun* 1. means, agent, instrument, mechanism, medium Our Scout troop is an agency of holiday cheer when we carol at the hospital. 2. bureau, business, company, firm, service, organization My mother works for a real estate agency.

agenda *noun* schedule, timetable, plan, program, roster, menu, list The club secretary handed out the agenda for the meeting.

agent *noun* 1. delegate, representative, broker, negotiator, operative, emissary A sports agent recruited the talented high-school football player. 2. instrument, vehicle, cause, force, mechanism, means Godzilla is an agent of destruction.

aggravate *verb* 1. intensify, worsen, exacerbate, inflame, magnify, complicate, increase Dampness aggravates my allergies. 2. irritate, annoy, bother, irk, provoke, bug My sister's constant use of the phone aggravates my parents. ➤ **Antonyms: 1. diminish, lessen 2. calm, soothe**

aggregate *noun* total, whole, sum, collection, conglomeration, mix, blend I have an aggregate of 150 books. ➤ **Antonyms:** *adjective* separate, individual

aggressive *adjective* 1. belligerent, combative, argumentative, quarrelsome, bellicose A wolverine is so aggressive it will take on a mountain lion or a bear. 2. bold, ambitious, vigorous, energetic, competitive, zealous The determined athlete followed an aggressive training schedule. ➤ **Antonyms: 1. peaceful, friendly 2. timid, apathetic**

aghast *adjective* shocked, horrified, distressed, appalled, stunned I was aghast to find that I had left my airline ticket at home.

agile *adjective* nimble, deft, quick, spry, facile, limber Mountain goats are extremely agile. ➤ **Antonyms: awkward, clumsy**

agitate *verb* 1. churn, stir, shake, rock, jiggle A washing machine agitates clothes to get the dirt out of them. 2. disturb, upset, provoke, perturb, bother, ruffle The speaker's controversial comments agitated the audience. ➤ **Antonyms: 2. calm, soothe**

agonize *verb* anguish, struggle, wrestle, worry, brood, suffer He agonized over the decision to euthanize his old dog.

agony *noun* anguish, distress, pain, torment, suffering, misery My brother and I went through agony when our parents divorced. ➤ **Antonyms: comfort, bliss**

agree *verb* 1. concur, coincide, match, harmonize, correspond, accord Our opinions about the movie did not agree. 2. consent, assent, allow, permit, accede Mom and Dad finally agreed to let me get a drum set. ➤ **Antonyms: 1. differ, disagree 2. deny, oppose**

agreement *noun* 1. accord, accordance, conformance, concurrence, harmony, concert My brother and I are usually in agreement about what to watch on TV. 2. bargain, deal, pact, arrangement, understanding My sister and I made an agreement not to tattle on each other. ➤ **Antonyms: 1. disagreement, discord**

ahead *adverb* 1. forward, in front, out in front, before, onward, on Eli pulled ahead just in time to win the race.

2. in advance, before, earlier, first, beforehand, before-time Mom called ahead and made reservations at the restaurant. ➡ **Antonyms: 1. behind 2. after**

aid *verb* **assist, help, support, abet, boost, relieve** We stopped to aid the stranded motorist. ◆ *noun* **help, assistance, support, cooperation, service** Dad enlisted my aid in making dinner. ➡ **Antonyms: 1. hinder, obstruct 2. hindrance, deterrent**

aide *noun* **assistant, helper, deputy, attendant, aide-de-camp, adjutant** My mother volunteers as a teacher's aide once a week.

ail *verb* **distress, trouble, bother, afflict, upset, worry** My stomach often ails me just before a big test.

ailment *noun* **disease, illness, sickness, affliction, disorder, indisposition** Pneumonia can be a serious ailment.

aim *verb* **1. point, direct, level, train, focus, sight** Hunting safety demands that one aim a gun at the ground when passing it to another person. **2. intend, plan, mean, propose, endeavor, strive** His aim was to finish his chores by noon. ◆ *noun* **purpose, goal, objective, intention, target, ambition, design, point, wish** The aim of the Red Cross is to provide relief to victims of war and natural disasters.

air *noun* **1. atmosphere, gasses, space, sky** The bat soared through the night air. **2. manner, demeanor, bearing, presence, mien, look** The young executive had an air of confidence. ◆ *verb* **1. ventilate, freshen, aerate, refresh, circulate, purify** I opened the windows to air the room. **2. express, voice, state, vent, communicate, tell** At the meeting, the workers were able to air their grievances. ➡ **Antonyms:** *verb* **2. conceal, hide**

Word Group

An **aircraft** is a machine or device that is capable of flying. **Aircraft** is a general term that has no true synonyms. Here are some common types of aircraft:

airliner, airplane, airship, glider, helicopter, jet, turbojet, turboprop

airport *noun* **airfield, airstrip, landing field, landing strip, airdrome** We drove to the airport to pick up my aunt and uncle.

aisle *noun* **corridor, lane, walkway, passageway, course** My little brother got lost in the aisles of the grocery store.

alarm *noun* **1. dismay, distress, fear, trepidation, anxiety, apprehension** The doctor assured me that tonsillitis is no cause for alarm. **2. alert, signal, warning, tocsin, bell, siren** When the fire alarm went off, we all had to go outside. ◆ *verb* **shock, startle, dismay, frighten, scare, upset** Maria alarmed her friends with her daredevil antics. ➡ **Antonyms:** *noun* **1. serenity, tranquility** ◆ *verb* **calm, reassure**

alcove *noun* **niche, nook, recess, inglenook, corner, compartment** Japanese homes often have an alcove called a *tokonoma* used to display flowers and art.

alert *adjective* **1. attentive, vigilant, watchful, observant, aware, wakeful** I find it difficult to stay alert when I am tired. **2. perceptive, intelligent, bright, clever, quick, sharp** He has an alert mind. ◆ *noun* **signal, warning, alarm, siren, tocsin** Everyone ran to the storm cellar when they heard the tornado alert. ◆ *verb* **advise, notify, warn, caution, inform, admonish** We were alerted to prepare for more flooding. ➡ **Antonyms:** *adjective* **1. inattentive, unwary 2. dull, slow**

alias *noun* **pseudonym, nom de plume, pen name, nickname, name** Karen Blixen wrote *Out of Africa* under the alias of Isak Dinesen.

Word Group

An **alibi** is a claim that a person was elsewhere when a crime took place. **Alibi** is a very specific term with no true synonyms. Here are some related words:

account, excuse, explanation, reason, report, statement, story, version

alien *adjective* **1. unfamiliar, strange, unusual, foreign, exotic, unnatural** When I traveled in Africa, I was enchanted by the alien landscape. **2. contradictory, opposed, different, unknown, unlike, inconsistent** Her chatter at the party was alien to her usually quiet personality. ◆ *noun* **foreigner, stranger, émigré, immigrant, nonnative, outsider** He had to register as an alien when he first came to this country. ➡ **Antonyms:** *adjective* **1. familiar, natural 2. consistent, compatible**

alienate *verb* **estrange, disaffect, turn off, distance, turn away, separate** The girl alienated her friends when she began using drugs.

alike *adjective* **identical, like, matched, similar, equivalent** No two snowflakes are exactly alike. ◆ *adverb* **identically, similarly, uniformly, evenly, equally, comparably** The twins dress alike when they want to confuse people. ⬧ **Antonyms:** *adjective* **different, opposite** ◆ *adverb* **differently**

alive *adjective* **1. living, live, breathing, existing, animate** William kept a baby hummingbird alive by feeding it with an eyedropper. **2. extant, active, viable, functioning, operative, running** I keep my goals alive by writing them down every day. **3. animated, alert, lively, vivacious, spirited, vigorous** My dog comes alive when I take her leash out of the drawer. ⬧ **Antonyms: 1. dead, lifeless 2. inactive, inoperative 3. lifeless, apathetic**

all *adjective* **complete, entire, whole, total** I spent all day in bed because I wasn't feeling well. ◆ *noun* **utmost, best, maximum, totality, entirety, everything** I gave the piano solo my all. ◆ *adverb* **wholly, entirely, completely, fully, thoroughly, totally** The garden is all watered. ⬧ **Antonyms:** *adjective* **partial** ◆ *noun* **nothing** ◆ *adverb* **partially**

allay *verb* **reduce, relieve, alleviate, assuage, ease, lessen** His calm manner helped to allay our fears. ⬧ **Antonyms: increase, intensify**

allege *verb* **assert, claim, charge, contend, declare, state** My brother alleges that I enter his room when he is gone. ⬧ **Antonyms: deny, disavow**

allegiance *noun* **loyalty, faithfulness, devotion, fidelity, fealty, respect** My dog gives her allegiance to anyone who feeds her. ⬧ **Antonyms: disloyalty, treachery**

allegory *noun* **fable, tale, story, moral, parable** *Pilgrim's Progress* is a 17th-century allegory in which the hero, Christian, journeys to the City of God.

alleviate *verb* **relieve, lessen, allay, assuage, ease, reduce** A night-light has alleviated my little sister's fear of the dark. ⬧ **Antonyms: aggravate, intensify**

alley *noun* **alleyway, passageway, path, passage, lane** We keep our trash cans in the alley behind our house.

alliance *noun* **union, coalition, partnership, confederation, league** Germany, Italy, and Japan formed an alliance during World War II.

allied *adjective* **1. combined, joined, united, aligned, confederated, joint** The dwarves and elves formed an allied army to defeat the goblin horde. **2. similar, related, affiliated, connected, like** Physics and mathematics are allied sciences.

allocate *verb* **allot, assign, designate, apportion, give** The English department allocates one thesaurus per student.

allot *verb* **allocate, allow, apportion, grant, assign** I allot myself an hour of TV every day.

allow *verb* **1. permit, let, consent, agree to, approve, authorize** I allow my cat to sleep on my bed. **2. allot, allocate, set aside, provide, spare** I always allow space for flowers in my vegetable garden. **3. admit, concede, acknowledge, grant, confess** My teacher allowed that he had miscalculated my test score. ⬧ **Antonyms: 1. forbid, prohibit 3. deny, refute**

allowance *noun* **allocation, allotment, portion, quota, ration, share** The dress pattern called for a ⅝-inch seam allowance.

allude *verb* **refer, mention, hint, suggest, imply, intimate** The teacher alluded to the possibility that we would have a quiz on Friday.

allure *verb* **attract, draw, lure, pull, entice, captivate** I was allured to the movie by the previews. ◆ *noun* **appeal, draw, charm, attraction, fascination, lure** That movie star has a great deal of allure. ⬧ **Antonyms:** *verb* **repel, alienate**

ally *verb* **join, unite, combine, align, collaborate** Some citizen groups ally themselves with the police to help reduce crime. ◆ *noun* **partner, associate, colleague, confederate, collaborator, accomplice** My friend and I were allies in the snowball fight. ⬧ **Antonyms:** *verb* **divide, separate** ◆ *noun* **enemy, foe, opponent**

almost *adverb* **nearly, about, practically, virtually, approximately, mostly** I almost missed the school bus. ⬧ **Antonyms: completely, entirely**

alone *adjective* **companionless, unaccompanied, unattended, isolated, solitary, secluded** Hillary spent the afternoon alone while her mom ran errands. ◆ *adverb* **independently, individually, separately, solitarily, by oneself** I prefer to study alone. ⬧ **Antonyms:** *adjective* **accompanied, attended** ◆ *adverb* **together, jointly**

aloof *adjective* **distant, withdrawn, detached, indifferent, reticent, reserved, haughty, unsociable** The actress Greta Garbo was aloof from society. ◆ *adverb* **apart, distant, remote, withdrawn, separate** The monastery stood aloof from the village. ⬧ **Antonyms:** *adjective* **friendly, open, warm**

aloud *adverb* **out loud, audibly, loudly, openly, distinctly** Gretchen enjoys reading aloud to her little brother. ⬧ **Antonyms: silently, inaudibly**

already *adverb* **before, earlier, previously, formerly, heretofore** I have seen that episode already. ⚫ **Antonyms: eventually, not yet**

also *adverb* **too, in addition, besides, additionally, likewise, further** Wherever I go, my brother wants to go also.

alter *verb* **modify, change, adjust, revise, transform, vary** The tailor altered my suit. ⚫ **Antonyms: continue, keep, maintain**

altercation *noun* **argument, dispute, fight, quarrel, spat, tiff, clash, squabble** We had an altercation over which of us owned the book. ⚫ **Antonyms: agreement, harmony, peace**

alter ego *noun* **twin, double, counterpart, mate, friend, other self** My friend and I are each other's alter ego.

alternate *verb* **switch, shift, rotate, oscillate, fluctuate** My cat alternates between sleeping and eating. ◆ *adjective* **1. alternating, every other, every second, recurring, recurrent** I mow the lawn on alternate Saturdays. **2. alternative, another, different, substitute, second** We took an alternate route to avoid traffic. ◆ *noun* **substitute, backup, standby, replacement, stand-in** My father couldn't go to the convention, so he sent an alternate.

alternative *noun* **choice, option, selection, possibility, recourse, substitute** There are so many alternatives that I can't decide which movie to rent.

altitude *noun* **elevation, height, loftiness, highness, tallness** The altitude of California's Mount Pinos is 8,831 feet.

altogether *adverb* **completely, entirely, absolutely, totally, perfectly** Our teacher warned us that we were being altogether too rowdy. ⚫ **Antonyms: partially, partly**

altruistic *adjective* **benevolent, beneficent, charitable, good-hearted, unselfish, generous** The Salvation Army is an altruistic organization. ⚫ **Antonyms: selfish, unkind**

always *adverb* **regularly, invariably, consistently, without exception, every time** I always brush my teeth before going to bed. **2. forever, eternally, constantly, perpetually, unceasingly, everlastingly** I will keep in touch with you always. ⚫ **Antonyms: never, rarely**

amass *verb* **accumulate, accrue, collect, garner, pile up, compile** I amass all my dirty laundry in one corner of my room. ⚫ **Antonyms: disperse, dispense**

amateur *noun* **nonprofessional, novice, dilettante, beginner, apprentice, neophyte** All the actors in the community theater production were amateurs. ◆ *adjective* **nonprofessional, inexpert, unskilled, amateurish, clumsy** I am an amateur golfer. ⚫ **Antonyms:** *noun* **expert, professional** ◆ *adjective* **skilled, competent**

amaze *verb* **astonish, astound, surprise, shock, impress, awe** Veida was amazed to beat her mother at chess.

amazement *noun* **astonishment, wonder, disbelief, surprise, shock, awe** I was struck with amazement the first time I saw the ocean.

ambassador *noun* **diplomat, envoy, emissary, minister, representative, consul** It is traditional for visiting ambassadors to present gifts to their hosts.

ambiguous *adjective* **unclear, vague, equivocal, uncertain, cryptic** The instructions were so ambiguous that even my dad couldn't build the model. ⚫ **Antonyms: clear, definite, distinct**

ambition *noun* **1. aim, goal, objective, desire, aspiration** Diane's ambition is to become a veterinarian. **2. drive, desire, energy, passion, zeal** Our lacrosse team has the ambition to win the championship this season.

ambitious *adjective* **1. aspiring, determined, eager, purposeful, zealous** The ambitious actor is working to land a starring role. **2. bold, daring, challenging, difficult, grandiose, demanding** The mayor unveiled her ambitious plan to build a new civic center. ⚫ **Antonyms: 1. aimless, lazy 2. modest, simple**

amble *verb* **stroll, ramble, saunter, wander, meander, walk** We enjoyed the sun as we ambled along the river bank.

ambush *noun* **ambuscade, trap, surprise attack, assault, offensive** The soldiers set up an ambush along the trail. ◆ *verb* **ambuscade, bushwhack, waylay, surprise, attack** In 480 B.C., Persian forces successfully ambushed the Spartan army at Thermopylae.

amend *verb* **1. improve, better, perfect, correct, fix, strengthen** I amended my term paper according to my teacher's suggestions. **2. change, revise, modify, reform, update, add to** The United States Constitution has been periodically amended. ⚫ **Antonyms: 1. worsen, weaken**

amiable *adjective* **friendly, good-natured, pleasant, congenial, sociable, agreeable** The new student seems very amiable. ⚫ **Antonyms: unfriendly, unsociable**

amiss *adverb* wrong, awry, wrongly, improperly, incorrectly My demonstration of how a volcano works went terribly amiss. ◆ *adjective* wrong, awry, faulty, defective, out of order Something is amiss with my computer, and it won't boot up. ➡ **Antonyms:** *adverb* properly, correctly ◆ *adjective* right, proper

among *preposition* amongst, amid, amidst, between, betwixt We walked among the trees.

amorous *adjective* loving, affectionate, romantic, ardent, fond, passionate My parents often give each other amorous looks. ➡ **Antonyms:** unloving, cold

amount *noun* 1. sum, total, aggregate, summation, totality, number The amount you owe for lunch is five dollars. 2. quantity, volume, measure, bulk, mass, magnitude My horse eats a large amount of oats. ◆ *verb* equal, total, reach, approach, constitute, correspond The money I have earned amounts to over four hundred dollars.

> **Word Group**
>
> An **amphibian** is a cold-blooded animal that has a backbone and moist skin. **Amphibian** is a general term with no true synonyms. Here are some common amphibians:
>
> **bullfrog, eft, frog, mud puppy, newt, salamander, toad, tree frog**

ample *adjective* 1. abundant, substantial, plentiful, voluminous, large, generous We had an ample amount of food for our barbecue. 2. enough, sufficient, adequate, satisfactory, suitable, decent There is ample room in the attic for storage. ➡ **Antonyms:** 1. small, meager 2. insufficient, inadequate

amplify *verb* 1. intensify, magnify, heighten, boost, strengthen A rabbit's large ears help to amplify its hearing. 2. augment, supplement, develop, expand, elaborate, add to The speaker amplified his lecture with visual aids. ➡ **Antonyms:** 1. diminish, reduce 2. decrease, curtail

amuse *verb* entertain, divert, delight, cheer, please Justine amused us with a song she wrote. ➡ **Antonyms:** bore, tire

amusement *noun* enjoyment, entertainment, diversion, fun, pleasure, distraction The circus provides amusement for people of all ages.

amusing *adjective* entertaining, funny, witty, diverting, interesting, humorous I tried to be amusing by hanging a spoon off my nose. ➡ **Antonyms:** boring, uninteresting, tiresome

analysis *noun* examination, study, investigation, review, inquiry My history class is doing an analysis of the causes of the Civil War.

analyze *verb* examine, evaluate, study, investigate, inspect, appraise The cytologist analyzed the blood sample.

anarchy *noun* disorder, confusion, chaos, turmoil, lawlessness, riot Anarchy often exists during times of war. ➡ **Antonyms:** order, control

ancestor *noun* 1. forebear, forefather, foremother, parent, progenitor Allen can trace his ancestors back to the Middle Ages. 2. forerunner, predecessor, antecedent, precursor, source Jazz is one of the ancestors of rock 'n' roll. ➡ **Antonyms:** 1. descendant, offspring

anchor *noun* mooring, stabilizer, mainstay, support, stability Religion is an anchor for many people. ◆ *verb* attach, fasten, secure, hold, fix, moor The bench was anchored to the sidewalk. ➡ **Antonyms:** *verb* detach, disconnect

ancient *adjective* prehistoric, old, early, aged, age-old, archaic The archaeologists explored the ruins of an ancient Mayan temple. ➡ **Antonyms:** modern, new, recent

anecdote *noun* story, tale, reminiscence, narrative, account, yarn I love to hear my dad's anecdotes about his college days.

anger *noun* rage, wrath, fury, irateness, outrage ire People often say things in anger that they later regret. ◆ *verb* incense, infuriate, outrage, upset, enrage, madden It angers me when my parents don't listen to my side of a story. ➡ **Antonyms:** *verb* calm, soothe

angle *noun* 1. vantage, position, direction, perspective, viewpoint, standpoint It is hard to see the TV screen from this angle. 2. aspect, facet, side, point, consideration, feature She considered her options from every angle. ◆ *verb* bend, curve, turn, twist, crook, arc The road angles to the left.

angry *adjective* mad, furious, irate, upset, incensed, irritated My mother was angry when I came home late.

anguish *noun* pain, suffering, despair, grief, torment I was filled with anguish when my best friend died in an accident. ➡ **Antonyms:** solace, comfort

animal *noun* **beast, creature, being, organism** As a mammal that lays eggs, the platypus is a strange animal.

animate *verb* **1. enliven, excite, energize, stimulate, vitalize, invigorate** The many different opinions animated our discussion. **2. inspire, motivate, stir, arouse, move, energize** Kim is animated by a desire to join the Peace Corps. ◆ *adjective* **live, living, alive, animated, moving, vital** The skillful puppeteer made the marionettes seem animate. ➡ **Antonyms:** *verb* **1. kill, extinguish 2. discourage, dampen** ◆ *adjective* **inanimate, dead, lifeless**

animated *adjective* **lively, spirited, dynamic, vivacious, energetic** I enjoy having animated conversations with my friends. ➡ **Antonyms: lifeless, sluggish, dull**

animosity *noun* **hatred, enmity, hostility, antagonism, ill will, bitterness** There was animosity between the warring nations. ➡ **Antonyms: amity, friendship**

annex *verb* **appropriate, seize, incorporate, add, attach, append** After World War II, the Soviet Union annexed parts of Poland. ◆ *noun* **addition, extension, branch, wing, ell** The museum built an annex to house the new exhibit. ➡ **Antonyms:** *verb* **detach, separate**

announce *verb* **1. report, tell, declare, proclaim, disclose, reveal** My older brother recently announced his engagement. **2. herald, signal, foretell, presage** The doorman announced us by telephone.

announcement *noun* **notice, notification, message, statement, declaration, proclamation** My older sister sent out graduation announcements to all our relatives.

annoy *verb* **bother, disturb, trouble, harass, pester, irritate** Please don't annoy me while I'm doing my homework. ➡ **Antonyms: comfort, soothe**

annul *verb* **nullify, cancel, void, revoke, rescind** People sometimes file for bankruptcy in order to annul their debts. ➡ **Antonyms: validate, confirm**

anomaly *noun* **aberration, abnormality, oddity, peculiarity, incongruity, irregularity** Many anomalies have been reported in the Bermuda Triangle.

anonymous *adjective* **unnamed, nameless, unsigned, unknown, secret, unidentified** An anonymous caller gave the police an important tip.

another *adjective* **1. additional, more, one more, added, supplemental, extra** The waitress asked if I wanted another glass of milk. **2. different, other, further, separate, new, distinct** I asked the clerk if the sweater came in another color.

answer *noun* **1. reply, response, acknowledgment, rejoinder, return** I mailed an answer to the invitation. **2. solution, resolution, key, explanation, determination, diagnosis** Arthur thinks that acquiring a taste for insects is the answer to world hunger. ◆ *verb* **1. reply, respond, react, rejoin, return, acknowledge** I don't know how to answer your question. **2. fulfill, meet, serve, satisfy, complete, suffice** Levi Strauss's canvas jeans answered prospectors' needs for durable clothing. ➡ **Antonyms:** *verb* **1. ask, inquire, question**

antagonism *noun* **hostility, animosity, enmity, ill will, friction, rancor** There is fierce antagonism between the long-time rivals. ➡ **Antonyms: amity, accord**

antagonist *noun* **adversary, opponent, competitor, enemy, foe, rival** Darth Vader is Luke Skywalker's antagonist in the movie *Star Wars*. ➡ **Antonyms: ally, supporter**

anthem *noun* **hymn, song, psalm, paean, ballad, refrain** In 1931, Congress adopted "The Star Spangled Banner" as our national anthem.

antic *adjective* **odd, ludicrous, bizarre, fantastic, far-fetched, grotesque** Many gothic cathedrals are decorated with antic gargoyles. ◆ *noun* **caper, prank, frolic, trick, stunt, shenanigan** We enjoyed the antics of the monkeys at the zoo. ➡ **Antonyms:** *adjective* **serious, solemn** ◆ *noun* **solemnity**

anticipate *verb* **1. foresee, predict, expect, envision, see, divine** The stockbroker anticipated the rise in soybean commodities. **2. expect, hope, hope for, long for, count on, look forward to** I'm anticipating a wonderful meal in this restaurant.

antidote *noun* **remedy, treatment, cure, corrective, neutralizer, antitoxin** A paste of baking soda and water is an old-fashioned antidote for bee stings.

antique *adjective* **old, old-fashioned, vintage, aged, old-time** My stepmom's hobby is restoring antique furniture. ◆ *noun* **heirloom, relic, antiquity, artifact** Our piano is an antique. ➡ **Antonyms:** *adjective* **new, modern, recent**

anxiety *noun* **apprehension, uneasiness, nervousness, concern, distress, worry** She felt some anxiety about giving her oral report. ➡ **Antonyms: confidence, assurance**

anxious *adjective* **1. worried, apprehensive, nervous, fearful, uneasy** I was anxious about my appointment with the orthodontist. **2. eager, impatient, desirous, keen, enthusiastic** I am anxious for you to meet my cousin. ◆ **Antonyms: 1. confident, relieved 2. hesitant, reluctant**

anyway *adverb* **nevertheless, anyhow, nonetheless, regardless, notwithstanding** I didn't feel well, but I went to school anyway.

apart *adverb* **away, removed, aside, distant, separately, clear** The goal posts stand 20 feet apart. ◆ **Antonyms: near, together**

apathetic *adjective* **uninterested, indifferent, unconcerned, incurious, impassive, uncaring** By the end of the day, the students were tired and apathetic. ◆ **Antonyms: concerned, interested**

apathy *noun* **indifference, disinterest, unconcern, incuriosity, inattention** Because of my apathy, I missed the deadline to audition for the school play. ◆ **Antonyms: concern, enthusiasm, interest**

ape *verb* **mimic, imitate, mock, parody, copy, impersonate** My older brother apes my mannerisms to tease me.

aperture *noun* **hole, opening, outlet, vent, slit, space** My dog got out of the yard through an aperture in the fence.

aphorism *noun* **motto, saying, adage, maxim, proverb, axiom** Many T-shirts have humorous aphorisms printed on them.

apocalyptic *adjective* **ominous, threatening, portentous, prescient, baneful, dire** I saw a movie about an apocalyptic vision of the ending of the world.

apogee *noun* **apex, height, peak, pinnacle, summit, top** The rock star died at the apogee of his career. ◆ **Antonyms: nadir, bottom**

apology *noun* **1. regrets, amends, confession, acknowledgment, repentance, atonement** Please accept my apology for being late. **2. defense, justification, vindication, explanation, plea, excuse** *Mein Kampf* is an apology of Adolph Hitler's political philosophy.

appall *verb* **shock, alarm, dismay, horrify, stun, outrage** I was appalled to learn that women weren't allowed to vote until 1921. ◆ **Antonyms: please, console**

apparatus *noun* **1. system, organization, bureaucracy, network, structure** The sheriff's department is the law enforcement apparatus in our community. **2. equipment,** **gear, machinery, appliance, device, mechanism** Our teacher set out the apparatus for the science experiment.

apparel *noun* **attire, clothing, clothes, garments, dress, garb** My dad buys his clothes at a store that sells apparel for tall men.

apparent *adjective* **1. obvious, clear, evident, plain, visible, noticeable** It is apparent that you don't feel like talking. **2. seeming, ostensible, presumable** It was an apparent victory, but the loser is demanding a recount of the ballots. ◆ **Antonyms: 1. doubtful, uncertain**

apparition *noun* **ghost, specter, spirit, phantom, wraith, shadow** The apparition of Marley visited Scrooge in Dickens's *A Christmas Carol.*

appeal *noun* **1. bid, call, entreaty, plea, request, supplication** The public TV station is making an appeal for contributions. **2. attraction, allure, charm, fascination, draw, lure** The appeal of a day at the beach was irresistible. ◆ *verb* **1. ask, apply, solicit, petition, request, implore** The flood victims appealed to the government for assistance. **2. interest, attract, fascinate, tempt, draw, excite** Windsurfing appeals to me. ◆ **Antonyms: *verb* 1. refuse, reject 2. repel, repulse**

appear *verb* **1. emerge, issue, materialize, show up, arise** The moon appeared from behind the clouds. **2. seem, look, act, feel, sound, be obvious** You appear to be enjoying that book. ◆ **Antonyms: 1. disappear, vanish**

appearance *noun* **1. arrival, emergence, coming, entrance, manifestation, materialization** We were thrilled by the sudden appearance of dolphins in front of the boat. **2. image, look, aspect, demeanor, mien, bearing** Ted always has a neat appearance. **3. semblance, impression, pretense, guise, pretext** Many people believe that glasses give one the appearance of intelligence. ◆ **Antonyms: 1. disappearance, vanishing**

appease *verb* **1. pacify, calm, soothe, quiet, placate, mollify** The mail carrier appeased the barking dog with a biscuit. **2. satisfy, relieve, assuage, content, allay, alleviate** The piece of candy appeased my craving for sugar. ◆ **Antonyms: 1. irritate, provoke 2. aggravate**

appellation *noun* **name, nickname, designation, epithet, sobriquet, label** My friend DeReese goes by the appellation of Corky.

append *verb* **attach, affix, fasten, add, annex, join** Mom sometimes appends a note to my lunch bag. ◆ **Antonyms: remove, detach, subtract**

appendix *noun* addendum, addition, attachment, supplement My math book has an appendix that lists answers to the self-test problems.

appetite *noun* 1. hunger, taste, stomach, thirst, relish I lose my appetite when I get nervous. 2. craving, desire, yen, fondness, liking, love I have an appetite for travel.

appetizing *adjective* appealing, inviting, pleasing, delicious, tasty, savory At dinnertime, our kitchen is filled with appetizing aromas. ➡ **Antonyms:** repugnant, unappetizing

applaud *verb* 1. clap, cheer, root, hail, hurrah, salute We applauded when the guest speaker was introduced. 2. praise, commend, compliment, laud, congratulate My teacher applauded our class's efforts to win the canned food drive. ➡ **Antonyms:** 1. boo, hiss 2. condemn, criticize

applause *noun* 1. clapping, ovation, plaudit, cheers, cheering, hand Mandy's cello recital earned her a great deal of applause. 2. praise, acclaim, commendation, kudos, accolades, compliments The musician's new album received much applause from the critics. ➡ **Antonyms:** 1. booing, hissing 2. condemnation, criticism

appliance *noun* apparatus, equipment, implement, device, machine, gadget Kitchen appliances range in size from can openers to refrigerators.

applicable *adjective* appropriate, suitable, fitting, proper, germane, pertinent Jake found his knowledge of fractions applicable to his woodworking project. ➡ **Antonyms:** inapplicable, inappropriate

application *noun* 1. function, purpose, use, value, employment A pocketknife has many practical applications. 2. relevance, bearing, pertinence, relevancy, suitability, applicability The study of chemistry has application to pharmacy. 3. diligence, assiduousness, industry, dedication, perseverance Her application to her chemistry studies won her a scholarship. 4. appeal, petition, request, requisition, entreaty, solicitation My older sister sent applications for entry to five different colleges.

apply *verb* 1. administer, put, spread, lay, give, place Mom applied aloe vera gel to my burn. 2. employ, exercise, use, utilize, engage, implement, practice He applied all of his strength to open the tightly sealed jar. 3. dedicate, devote, direct, address, bend, commit, concentrate My dad suggested that I apply myself to cleaning my room. 4. pertain, relate, fit, concern, bear, suit Honesty is a traditional value that still applies today.

appoint *verb* 1. designate, select, name, assign, delegate, commission I have been appointed to the student council. 2. set, fix, determine, establish, choose, arrange, settle, decide My parents have appointed 10:00 as my curfew. ➡ **Antonyms:** 1. discharge, dismiss

appointment *noun* 1. assignment, selection, designation, election, nomination My stepmother was pleased by her appointment to the research committee. 2. job, position, situation, post, place The young lawyer was hoping to get an appointment with a prestigious law firm. 3. date, engagement, meeting, rendezvous, booking Mom made an appointment for me to see the doctor.

appreciate *verb* 1. esteem, prize, treasure, value, cherish, like I appreciate my friends. 2. comprehend, perceive, understand, acknowledge, recognize, grasp I appreciate your argument, but I still disagree. ➡ **Antonyms:** 1. dislike, disdain

appreciation *noun* 1. gratitude, gratefulness, thankfulness, thanks She expressed her appreciation for the gift in her thank-you note. 2. awareness, perception, understanding, enjoyment, regard, liking I developed a new appreciation of music I after started singing lessons. ➡ **Antonyms:** 1. ingratitude, ungratefulness 2. ignorance, disregard

apprehend *verb* 1. capture, seize, arrest, nab, pick up The criminal was apprehended as he tried to leave the country. 2. understand, comprehend, grasp, know, fathom, follow, recognize Sometimes my homework is difficult to apprehend. ➡ **Antonym:** 2. misunderstand

apprehensive *adjective* anxious, uneasy, worried, concerned, afraid, nervous I was apprehensive about attending a new school. ➡ **Antonyms:** confident, secure, calm

apprentice *noun* student, beginner, novice, learner, pupil, assistant I am an apprentice cook. ➡ **Antonyms:** professional, master, expert

approach *verb* 1. near, reach, gain, come to, converge, advance, verge The racehorses increased their speed as they approached the finish line. 2. begin, start, initiate, undertake, take on Colleen approached organizing her desk with a positive attitude. ◆ *noun* 1. advance, coming, nearing, movement We could hear the approach of the train. 2. method, way, procedure, course, plan, means The best approach for achieving success is persistence. 3. avenue, passage, route, road, entrance The approach to the mansion was lined with tall oaks. ➡ **Antonyms:** *verb* 1. recede, withdraw 3. conclude, finish ◆ *noun* 1. departure 3. exit, outlet

appropriate *adjective* proper, correct, right, suitable, fitting Do you know the appropriate fork to use for salad? ◆ *verb* 1. allocate, allot, assign, authorize, designate Construction on the new school will begin once funds are appropriated. 2. seize, take, usurp, commandeer, assume, confiscate While King Richard I was fighting the Third Crusade, his brother John tried to appropriate the throne of England. ➡ **Antonyms:** *adjective* inappropriate, unfitting ◆ *verb* 1. withhold

approval *noun* 1. praise, admiration, respect, regard, approbation, commendation Our neighbor receives much approval for her prize-winning roses. 2. consent, sanction, authorization, permission, leave I gave my younger sister approval to wear my denim jacket. ➡ **Antonyms:** 1. disapproval, criticism 2. disapproval, denial

approve *verb* 1. authorize, sanction, ratify, confirm, allow, endorse My teacher approved my report topic. 2. commend, praise, respect, accept, appreciate, favor Jane's parents have always approved of her interest in sports. ➡ **Antonyms:** 1. disapprove, reject 2. disapprove, dislike

approximate *adjective* close, estimated, loose, rough, comparative, near This is the approximate location where I lost my earring. ◆ *verb* 1. resemble, approach, border on, rival, challenge, verge on, near My dad bought a car that approximates the one he had when he was 18. 2. estimate, guess, gauge, judge, reckon, put, set, figure She approximated the number of jelly beans in the jar. ➡ **Antonyms:** *adjective* accurate, exact, precise

approximately *adverb* about, almost, nearly, roughly, around, close to I am approximately two years younger than you. ➡ **Antonyms:** exactly, precisely

apt *adjective* 1. suitable, appropriate, becoming, befitting, correct, proper My godmother always chooses an apt gift for my birthday. 2. liable, likely, prone, inclined, disposed He is apt to be late because of the traffic. 3. bright, intelligent, clever, gifted, able, astute He is an apt chess player. ➡ **Antonyms:** 1. unsuitable, inappropriate 2. disinclined, unlikely 3. slow, dull

aptitude *noun* gift, talent, bent, flair, instinct, knack She has an aptitude for art history.

arbitrary *adjective* 1. chance, whimsical, capricious, subjective, random, impulsive It was an arbitrary choice to rent this video. 2. despotic, absolute, autocratic, dictatorial, totalitarian, tyrannical Peter the Great used his arbitrary rule to modernize Russian society. ➡ **Antonyms:** 1. objective, logical

arbitrate *verb* decide, settle, mediate, adjudge, determine, rule My mother arbitrated the dispute between my sister and me.

archaic *adjective* antiquated, ancient, old, dated, outdated, obsolete Latin and Sanskrit are examples of archaic languages. ➡ **Antonyms:** modern, recent, new

arctic *adjective* polar, frigid, freezing, icy, frozen, cold Arctic temperatures limit the variety of plant life in polar regions. ➡ **Antonyms:** hot, torrid, warm

ardent *adjective* passionate, fervent, enthusiastic, avid, impassioned I am an ardent fan of baseball. ➡ **Antonyms:** apathetic, indifferent, cool

ardor *noun* zeal, fervor, enthusiasm, fire, passion, excitement My math teacher has great ardor for her profession. ➡ **Antonyms:** apathy, indifference

area *noun* 1. region, zone, territory, locality, vicinity, section Pine trees grow best in areas that receive a lot of rain. 2. space, expanse, room, extent, size My bed and desk take up most of the area in my room. 3. field, sphere, realm, domain, subject, department My dad works in the area of medicine.

argue *verb* 1. debate, contend, plead, assert, reason, state My little brother argued his case for a later bedtime. 2. indicate, attest, point out, prove, suggest, demonstrate Your sneezing argues that you have a cold. 3. quarrel, disagree, dispute, bicker, feud, fight, squabble My sister and I used to argue over which one of us had longer hair.

argument *noun* 1. dispute, disagreement, debate, spat, altercation, quarrel, fight My friend and I resolved our argument by flipping a coin. 2. reason, case, grounds, justification, logic, defense Her argument for skipping chores was that she needed time to study.

arid *adjective* 1. dry, parched, waterless, bone-dry, sere, barren My grandfather moved to Arizona because its arid climate is good for his health. 2. lifeless, dull, drab, lackluster, unimaginative I couldn't wait to get away from their arid conversation. ➡ **Antonyms:** 1. moist, wet 2. exciting, lively

arise *verb* 1. appear, begin, start, emerge, originate, spring up, commence A disagreement arose when my friends and I tried to decide which movie to see. 2. rise, ascend, move upward, climb, lift We saw the smoke arise from the burning building. 3. result, proceed, derive, emanate, flow, issue, happen, occur Many scientific insights have arisen from observation of the physical world. ➽ **Antonyms: 1. stop, cease 2. descend, lower**

aristocrat *noun* **noble, patrician, peer, peeress, grandee, lord, lady** Many aristocrats lost their lives to the guillotine during the French Revolution. ➽ **Antonyms: commoner, proletarian**

arm[1] *noun* **1. branch, fork, offshoot, appendage, projection, extension** We went swimming in an arm of the Adriatic Sea. **2. agency, department, division, organ, wing, branch** The National Park Service is an arm of the Department of the Interior.

arm[2] *noun* **firearm, gun, weapon, ordnance, weaponry, armament** Paul Revere warned the Massachusetts Minutemen to ready their arms. ◆ *verb* **equip, provide, outfit, furnish, prepare, fortify** I armed myself with a calculator and five pencils for the math test.

army *noun* **1. military, armed force, troops, soldiers, infantry** After World War II, West Germany did not form an army until 1955. **2. horde, swarm, host, group, mass, crowd** An army of ants descended on the melted ice cream.

aroma *noun* **fragrance, smell, scent, bouquet, perfume, redolence, savor** I love the aroma of freshly baked bread.

aromatic *adjective* **fragrant, redolent, scented, perfumed** Our garden is bordered with aromatic herbs. ➽ **Antonyms: fetid, rank**

around *adverb* **1. about, everywhere, all over, over, throughout** I looked around until I found my missing shoe. **2. near, nearby, about, approximately, almost, nearly** Around fifty floats were in the parade. ◆ *preposition* **about, near, near to, close to** I'll be home around dinnertime. ➽ **Antonyms:** *adverb* **2. exactly, precisely**

arouse *verb* **1. awaken, awake, rouse, stir, wake, waken** The dog's barking aroused the neighborhood in the middle of the night. **2. stir, kindle, spark, stimulate, excite** Our work in geography class has aroused my interest in maps. ➽ **Antonyms: 2. repress, stifle**

arraign *verb* **charge, accuse, indict, summon, prosecute** The prisoner was arraigned on charges of grand larceny. ➽ **Antonyms: exonerate, absolve**

arrange *verb* **1. order, organize, place, position, sort, array, systematize** Our library arranges books by the Dewey decimal system. **2. plan, prepare, schedule, manage, lay out** My school arranged a field trip to the museum. **3. settle, work out, negotiate, set, decide, coordinate** The trustee arranged the sale of the estate.

arrangement *noun* **1. formation, layout, order, deployment, disposition, organization** All of my teachers have seating arrangements for their classes. **2. agreement, settlement, terms, deal, understanding** The arrangement in my house is that we all take turns setting the table. **3. plan, measure, preparation, provision, schedule, program** My parents made arrangements for me to visit my cousins.

array *verb* **1. arrange, deploy, dispose, order, organize, group** The soldiers arrayed themselves along the perimeter of the enemy's territory. **2. attire, deck out, dress up, clothe, bedeck** She was arrayed in jewels and furs. ◆ *noun* **1. display, exhibition, arrangement, formation, order, panoply** Customers wandered through the array of cars at the dealership. **2. attire, apparel, dress, clothing, clothes, finery, garments** My parents dressed in formal array when they attended the opera. ➽ **Antonyms:** *verb* **1. disarrange, disorder** ◆ *noun* **1. disarray, disorder**

arrest *verb* **1. detain, apprehend, capture, catch, seize, nab, pick up** Police officers arrested the robbery suspect. **2. check, stop, cease, discontinue, halt, stay** Cancer can often be arrested if detected early enough. **3. engage, catch, hold, occupy, absorb, engross, attract** Her fascinating story arrested my entire attention. ◆ *noun* **apprehension, capture, seizure, detention** The arrest was made by an undercover detective. ➽ **Antonyms:** *verb* **1. free, release 2. encourage, accelerate**

arrival *noun* **1. appearance, coming, advent, approach, entrance** My aunt's unexpected arrival was a wonderful surprise. **2. comer, visitor, guest, caller, newcomer** The late arrival took a seat in the back of the theater. ➽ **Antonyms: 1. departure, exit**

arrive *verb* **1. appear, show up, get in, come, reach, turn up** When does the next train arrive? **2. come, happen, take place, occur, return** The first day of school seems to arrive earlier each year. ➽ **Antonyms: 1. depart, leave, withdraw**

arrogant *adjective* **conceited, egotistical, haughty, proud, vain** My brother became arrogant after he was elected class president. ➽ **Antonyms: humble, modest**

art *noun* **craft, skill, technique, methods, profession, artistry, work** We are learning the art of calligraphy at school.

article *noun* **1. feature, piece, story, review, report** I wrote an article about the book fair for my school paper. **2. section, part, clause, provision, element, passage** There are seven articles to the Constitution of the United States. **3. item, object, piece, thing, product, entity** Shirts, socks, and jeans are all articles of clothing.

articulate *adjective* **1. clear, coherent, intelligible, comprehensible, understandable, lucid** The instructions were articulate and easy to follow. **2. eloquent, fluent, expressive, smooth-spoken, facile** Abraham Lincoln was an articulate statesman. ◆ *verb* **pronounce, enunciate, say, utter, vocalize** I had trouble articulating *r*'s when I first learned English.

artifice *noun* **1. device, stratagem, ruse, trick, ploy** In the movie *Tootsie,* the hero uses the artifice of dressing as a woman in order to get a job. **2. deception, trickery, cunning, guile, deceit, duplicity, chicanery** The conman used artifice to gain the trust of his victims. ◆ **Antonyms: 2. honesty, sincerity**

artificial *adjective* **1. fake, imitation, simulated, man-made, mock** Only an expert can tell artificial diamonds from real ones. **2. affected, feigned, pretended, contrived, phony, insincere** I spoke with an artificial accent in the school play. ◆ **Antonyms: 1. authentic, genuine, real 2. sincere, natural**

> **Word Group**
>
> An **artist** is a person who creates works of art. **Artist** is a general term with no true synonyms. Here are some different kinds of artists:
>
> artisan, choreographer, composer, illustrator, musician, painter, sculptor, songwriter, writer

ascend *verb* **climb, mount, rise, scale, lift, move** I ascended the stairs. ◆ **Antonym: descend**

ascent *noun* **1. ascension, climb, scaling, mounting, rising** My uncle has made a dozen ascents of California's Mount Whitney. **2. slope, rise, grade, gradient, incline** We trudged up the ascent to see the sweeping view of the valley. ◆ **Antonym: 1. descent**

ascertain *verb* **find, determine, verify, discover, establish, learn** I called the store to ascertain what time it closed.

ascetic *adjective* **austere, abstinent, abstemious, Spartan, puritanical, strict** Zen monks live an ascetic life. ◆ **Antonyms: self-indulgent, comfortable**

ashamed *adjective* **embarrassed, humiliated, mortified, abashed, sorry** He was ashamed that he had failed the spelling test. ◆ **Antonyms: proud, unashamed**

aside *adverb* **apart, away, out of the way, by** I set aside a piece of birthday cake for you.

asinine *adjective* **stupid, silly, foolish, ridiculous, senseless, idiotic** He told us an asinine joke at the party. ◆ **Antonyms: smart, clever, intelligent**

ask *verb* **1. inquire, query, question, quiz, examine, investigate** My brother asked if he could borrow my basketball. **2. request, solicit, seek, beg, appeal, plead, entreat** I asked my little sister to feed my rabbit while I was at camp. **3. invite, bid, summon, call, send for, beckon** My parents asked our neighbors over for dinner. **4. expect, demand, require, call for, entail, involve, necessitate** My hockey coach asks that we attend practice regularly. ◆ **Antonyms: 1. answer, reply, respond**

asleep *adjective* **1. sleeping, dozing, napping, slumbering, resting** My cat is asleep on the windowsill. **2. numb, insensible, unresponsive, deadened, inert, dead** My leg fell asleep during the long bus ride. ◆ **Antonym: 1. awake**

aspect *noun* **1. element, facet, feature, point, side, characteristic, angle** My favorite aspect of the concert was the piano solo. **2. appearance, look, manner, air, visage, image, shape** Our yard took on a whole new aspect when we replaced the lawn with wildflowers.

aspersion *noun* **slander, libel, smear, slur, deprecation, defamation** The actress sued the tabloid for casting aspersions on her character. ◆ **Antonyms: praise, commendation**

aspiration *noun* **goal, dream, desire, ambition, aim, objective** It is my aspiration to be an interior decorator.

aspire *verb* **desire, strive, seek, want, aim, hope, dream** Jane aspires to become a champion tennis player.

assail *verb* **attack, assault, set upon, strike, berate, blast** The rock stars were assailed by fans after their concert.

assailant *noun* **attacker, aggressor, assaulter, enemy, foe** The assailant was arrested after the victim identified his picture.

assassin *noun* **killer, executioner, murderer, slayer, homicide** The function of the Secret Service is to protect United States leaders from assassins.

assassinate *verb* **kill, slay, murder, slaughter, massacre** President Lincoln was assassinated five days after the Civil War ended.

assault *noun* **attack, strike, offensive, raid, advance, charge** The soldiers made an assault on the enemy camp. ◆ *verb* **attack, assail, have at, strike, charge, beat** Robert assaulted the overgrown grass with his lawnmower. ⏵ **Antonyms:** *noun* **retreat, withdrawal** ◆ *verb* **retreat, withdraw**

assemble *verb* **1. congregate, gather, collect, group, rally, meet** The football team assembled around the coach. **2. put together, construct, make, connect, build, fabricate** My stepdad helped me assemble my new kite. ⏵ **Antonyms: 1. disband, disperse 2. disassemble, dismantle**

assembly *noun* **1. gathering, meeting, convention, rally, conference, convocation** We had a school assembly to honor our retiring principal. **2. construction, connecting, fitting, making, fabricating** The directions said that some assembly would be required.

assent *verb* **agree, consent, accede, acquiesce, concur, approve** Everyone on the team assented to the new practice schedule. ◆ *noun* **agreement, consent, acquiescence, approval, concurrence, endorsement, sanction** My parents gave their assent for me to sleep at my friend's house. ⏵ **Antonyms:** *verb* **dissent, disagree** ◆ *noun* **dissent, disagreement**

assert *verb* **claim, insist, declare, maintain, contend, state, aver** My little sister asserted that she wanted to go home. ⏵ **Antonyms: deny, refute**

assertive *adjective* **bold, self-confident, forceful, aggressive, sure** Being a junior referee has helped me become more assertive. ⏵ **Antonyms: timid, hesitant**

assess *verb* **1. impose, levy, put, exact, tax, charge, fine** Congress has the power to assess taxes. **2. evaluate, appraise, estimate, gauge, judge, consider** He assessed the weather and took his umbrella.

asset *noun* **1. advantage, aid, benefit, resource, strength, help, plus** Aunt Truellen's huge vocabulary is a great asset when she plays word games. **2. property, possessions, capital, wealth, funds, resources** My dad's assets include two houses and a boat. ⏵ **Antonyms: 1. disadvantage, drawback**

assiduous *adjective* **diligent, industrious, sedulous, dedicated, determined, persistent** James Audubon was an assiduous observer of wildlife. ⏵ **Antonyms: lazy, indolent**

assign *verb* **1. appoint, post, station, charge, designate, name** Rick was assigned to be on hall duty for the week. **2. allot, allocate, give, dispense, distribute, hand out** I hope our teacher doesn't assign us any more book reports. **3. ascribe, attribute, accredit, consign, relegate** Music has been assigned the ability to communicate without words.

assignment *noun* **task, job, duty, chore, obligation, responsibility, position** The soldier's assignment was to stand guard.

assimilate *verb* **incorporate, absorb, integrate, accommodate, take in, digest** The Romans assimilated conquered peoples by giving them citizenship. ⏵ **Antonyms: reject, segregate**

assist *verb* **aid, help, serve, support, relieve, collaborate with** I like to assist my dad with the yard work. ◆ *noun* **boost, lift, aid, help, hand** My grandmother gave me an assist onto the horse. ⏵ **Antonyms:** *verb* **hamper, hinder**

assistance *noun* **aid, help, service, support, hand, relief, cooperation** Tristan gave his mother assistance in unloading the groceries.

assistant *noun* **aide, helper, subordinate, deputy, apprentice, colleague** My teacher has an assistant hand out papers. ◆ *adjective* **associate, deputy, auxiliary, subsidiary, supportive** Our school was just assigned a new assistant principal.

associate *verb* **1. identify, connect, affiliate, link, correlate, relate** Jack-o'-lanterns and haunted houses are associated with Halloween. **2. socialize, fraternize, mingle, mix, consort** My parents like to associate with a wide variety of people. ◆ *noun* **1. colleague, partner, coworker, fellow, peer** My mother's business associates came to our house for dinner. **2. friend, companion, comrade, chum, pal, buddy** My mom and my soccer coach are also tennis associates. ◆ *adjective* **assistant, adjunct, subordinate, secondary, auxiliary, ancillary** My father is an associate professor at the university. ⏵ **Antonyms:** *verb* **1. dissociate, separate** ◆ *adjective* **principal, major, unaffiliated**

association *noun* **1. club, group, organization, society, league** Margaret belongs to a national association for stamp collectors. **2. connection, relationship, correlation, affiliation, alliance, link** There is an association between the time I spend studying and my test grades.

assorted *adjective* **varied, various, mixed, diverse, miscellaneous, sundry** I gave my teacher a box of assorted chocolates for the holidays. ⏵ **Antonyms: identical, similar, uniform**

assortment *noun* collection, variety, selection, array, mixture I have an assortment of unmatched socks in my drawer.

assume *verb* 1. presume, believe, suppose, surmise, suspect, think I assume that you got my message. 2. undertake, incur, shoulder, tackle, take on, accept Keegan had to assume more responsibility at home when his brother left for college. 3. take, take over, appropriate, commandeer, usurp, expropriate, seize The vice president assumes control if the President is incapacitated. 4. feign, simulate, affect, put on, pretend A chameleon will assume the color of its surroundings in order to evade predators. ◆ **Antonyms:** 1. know 3. relinquish, abandon

assurance *noun* 1. guarantee, pledge, promise, vow, word He gave us his assurance the car would be ready Friday. 2. confidence, self-confidence, poise, self-assurance, certainty The politician's assurance was evident during his TV interview. ◆ **Antonyms:** 2. doubt, uncertainty, timidity

assure *verb* 1. guarantee, promise, reassure, vouch, swear The veterinarian assured us that our iguana would be fine. 2. ascertain, make sure, ensure, determine, verify We must assure that we lock the door when we leave.

astonish *verb* amaze, surprise, astound, stun, shock, flabbergast I astonished my parents by cleaning my room without being asked.

astonishment *noun* amazement, surprise, disbelief, wonder, awe, shock I gaped in astonishment as the bird flew into our car.

astound *verb* astonish, amaze, awe, dumbfound, flabbergast I was astounded to learn that Mount Everest is more than five miles high.

astute *adjective* shrewd, perspicacious, clever, sharp, perceptive, intelligent The fictional detective Sherlock Holmes is famous for his astute observations. ◆ **Antonyms:** obtuse, blind, dumb

athletic *adjective* muscular, powerful, robust, strong John is an athletic boy who loves to play soccer and lift weights. ◆ **Antonyms:** frail, weak, puny

atmosphere *noun* 1. air, sky, stratosphere, heavens It takes just a few minutes for a space shuttle to exit Earth's atmosphere. 2. ambiance, feeling, mood, environment, tone, surroundings I love the cozy atmosphere at this restaurant.

atrocious *adjective* 1. heinous, cruel, monstrous, shocking, vile, inhuman Many people feel that vivisection is an atrocious practice. 2. abominable, terrible, disgusting, offensive, repulsive, bad I think that racist jokes are atrocious. ◆ **Antonyms:** 1. humane, benevolent 2. good, fine

atrophy *noun* wasting away, degeneration, deterioration, decline, withering, shriveling A lack of calcium may cause an atrophy in bone mass. ◆ *verb* waste away, degenerate, deteriorate, wither, shrivel, shrink The muscles in my arm atrophied while I had it in a cast. ◆ **Antonyms:** *noun* growth, development ◆ *verb* regenerate, recover

attach *verb* 1. fasten, connect, secure, couple, tie, join Carrie attached a basket to her bicycle. 2. ascribe, put, place, assign, attribute I attach a lot of importance to good nutrition. ◆ **Antonyms:** 1. detach, disconnect

attachment *noun* 1. accessory, addition, supplement, extra, extension Our vacuum cleaner has an attachment for cleaning upholstery. 2. bond, tie, affection, devotion, love, fondness, connection Rebecca has a strong attachment to her best friend. ◆ **Antonyms:** 2. aversion, dislike, antipathy

attack *verb* 1. assault, charge, storm, strike, raid, beset, hit Attila the Hun invaded Italy, but he did not attack Rome. 2. criticize, fault, denounce, censure, berate, impugn During the debate, Carlos attacked his opponent's argument. 3. begin, start, commence, tackle, undertake I attacked my homework after dinner. ◆ *noun* 1. assault, offensive, raid, strike, charge, invasion The enemy launched their attack at dawn. 2. bout, spell, fit, seizure, spasm, stroke Hay fever gives me attacks of sneezing. ◆ **Antonyms:** *verb* 1. retreat, withdraw 2. praise, commend, defend ◆ *noun* 1. defense, retreat

attain *verb* accomplish, achieve, reach, realize, gain, win Kwan attained her goal of becoming captain of the cheerleading team. ◆ **Antonyms:** fail, lose, fall short

attempt *verb* try, endeavor, strive, struggle, venture, undertake I did not attempt to move the massive desk by myself. ◆ *noun* effort, try, endeavor, venture, go, bid She cleared six feet on her first attempt at the high jump.

attend *verb* 1. go to, appear at, be present, frequent, visit Marc attends hockey practice after school. 2. tend, care for, look after, minister to, serve, wait upon, assist The nurse attended her patient. 3. listen, heed, mind, note, hear Please attend to what I am saying. ◆ **Antonyms:** 1. miss, stay away 2. & 3. ignore, disregard

attendant *noun* assistant, helper, aide, associate, escort The zoo attendant was feeding the lions.

attention *noun* **1. care, concentration, attentiveness, heedfulness, alertness, vigilance** He pays careful attention to the details of his work. **2. consideration, notice, observance, heed, regard, awareness** I enjoy my father's attention when I visit him. ⏺ **Antonyms: disregard, inattention**

attentive *adjective* **1. alert, heedful, observant, intent, watchful, awake** The entire class was very attentive when the fire chief visited. **2. considerate, thoughtful, solicitous, courteous, polite, respectful** The attentive suitor brought flowers to his fiancée. ⏺ **Antonyms: 1. inattentive, unobservant 2. inconsiderate, thoughtless**

attire *verb* **dress, clothe, garb, array, bedeck, costume** He was attired in jeans and a sweatshirt. ◆ *noun* **apparel, clothing, garments, garb, clothes, dress** My mom wears comfortable attire to her yoga class.

attitude *noun* **1. outlook, point of view, perspective, approach, disposition, mood** Nick brings a positive attitude to everything he does. **2. position, stance, opinion, posture, pose, carriage** I have a neutral attitude toward vegetarianism.

attract *verb* **draw, lure, pull, appeal to, interest, bring** The jingle of car keys always attracts my dog's attention. ⏺ **Antonyms: repel, repulse**

attraction *noun* **appeal, draw, pull, allure, enticement, fascination, inducement** The baby elephants are the main attraction at our zoo. ⏺ **Antonym: repulsion**

attractive *adjective* **appealing, pleasing, becoming, pretty, fetching, handsome** That shirt is an attractive shade of green. ⏺ **Antonyms: unappealing, unattractive**

attribute *verb* **credit, ascribe, assign, charge, lay, attach** The saying "The game isn't over till it's over" is attributed to Yogi Berra. ◆ *noun* **quality, characteristic, trait, feature, property, aspect** Self-respect is an important attribute for a person to possess.

audacity *noun* **1. courage, resolution, boldness, daring, nerve, bravery** The soldier's audacity during the battle won him a medal. **2. gall, presumptuousness, brazenness, cheek, impertinence, presumption** My brother had the audacity to borrow my new CD without asking. ⏺ **Antonyms: 1. caution, cowardice 2. discretion, reticence**

audible *adjective* **perceptible, discernible, distinct, clear, detectable** In ancient Greek amphitheaters, even a whisper spoken on-stage was audible in the last row. ⏺ **Antonym: inaudible**

audience *noun* **1. onlookers, spectators, crowd, following, assembly, gathering** This street musician always attracts a large audience. **2. reception, interview, meeting, hearing, conference** The king granted an audience to the visiting dignitary.

audition *noun* **tryout, hearing, screening, reading, trial** The choir director held auditions for concert solos.

augment *verb* **increase, enlarge, expand, magnify, swell, amplify** My mother's salary augments our family income. ⏺ **Antonyms: decrease, diminish, reduce**

augury *noun* **divination, fortune telling, soothsaying, prophecy, omen** The shaman used augury to predict the weather.

august *adjective* **majestic, dignified, grand, regal, royal, magnificent** The actor was known for playing august roles such as Shakespeare's kings. ⏺ **Antonyms: common, lowly, uninspiring**

austere *adjective* **1. harsh, severe, hard, stern, strict, cold** Siberia has an austere landscape. **2. plain, bare, simple, ascetic, Spartan, abstinent** Mahatma Gandhi was a proponent of living an austere life. ⏺ **Antonyms: 1. cheerful, friendly 2. lavish, extravagant**

authentic *adjective* **genuine, real, actual, true, valid, accurate** Skip claims to have an authentic photograph of a UFO. ⏺ **Antonyms: fake, imitation, false**

Word Group The **author** of a written work is its original creator. **Author** is a general term with no true synonyms. Here are some different kinds of authors:

columnist, essayist, journalist, novelist, playwright, poet, scribe, scriptwriter

authoritarian *adjective* **despotic, dictatorial, tyrannical, totalitarian, strict, harsh** The authoritarian government was overthrown by the rebels. ⏺ **Antonyms: permissive, tolerant**

authority *noun* **1. authorization, control, power, right, jurisdiction, command** My parents gave me the authority to set my own bedtime. **2. expert, specialist, master, connoisseur, professional** Shannon is an authority on baseball cards. **3. credibility, plausibility, competence, prestige** The ranger spoke with authority about the region's geological features.

authorize *verb* **1. empower, enable, license, qualify, entitle** The Federal Trade Commission is authorized to curb unfair trade practices. **2. approve, sanction, endorse, allow, permit, countenance** The principal authorized the field trip. ➡ **Antonyms: 1. prohibit, prevent 2. disallow, forbid**

autocrat *noun* **authoritarian, despot, tyrant, dictator, totalitarian** Henry Ford was an autocrat who fired employees that he considered too independent.

autograph *noun* **signature, inscription, handwriting, mark, sign** I asked the basketball star for his autograph. ◆ *verb* **sign, endorse, inscribe** The symphony conductor autographed my program.

automatic *adjective* **1. self-operating, self-regulating, automated, self-acting, mechanical** Our iron has an automatic shutoff as a safety feature. **2. involuntary, reflexive, spontaneous, instinctive, unconscious, natural** Breathing is an automatic body function that is controlled by the medulla oblongata. ➡ **Antonyms: 1. manual 2. deliberate, intentional**

automation *noun* **mechanization, computerization, robot, machine, computer** Automation of the mail-sorting process increased the efficiency of the postal service.

automobile *noun* **car, auto, motor vehicle, motorcar, vehicle** Alternative fuels for automobiles are being developed.

autonomous *adjective* **independent, self-governing, sovereign, self-sufficient, self-reliant, free** Baby kangaroos become autonomous about 33 weeks after birth. ➡ **Antonyms: dependent, governed**

avail *noun* **use, benefit, advantage, account, gain** I tried to reach him to no avail; he was out.

available *adjective* **free, obtainable, open, accessible, ready, on hand** There were no parking spaces available. ➡ **Antonyms: unavailable, inaccessible**

avarice *noun* **greed, greediness, avariciousness, cupidity** King Midas was so full of avarice that he asked the gods to make it so everything he touched turned to gold. ➡ **Antonyms: generosity, munificence**

avenge *verb* **revenge, retaliate, punish, pay back, get even** Hamlet was instructed to avenge the murder of his father. ➡ **Antonyms: forgive, excuse**

avenue *noun* **1. boulevard, street, thoroughfare, road, drive** The main street of town is a tree-lined avenue.

2. route, path, means, way, line, course Drawing is my favorite avenue of personal expression.

average *noun* **mean, norm, par, standard, ordinary, typical** Clark's ability in English is far above the average. ◆ *adjective* **1. mean, middle, medium, par** The average age in our class is 13 years, 2 months. **2. ordinary, typical, usual, standard, common, regular** Did you know that the average candy bar has over 200 calories? ➡ **Antonyms:** *adjective* **2. exceptional, unusual**

aversion *noun* **abhorrence, hatred, loathing, repulsion, repugnance, dislike** I have a fierce aversion to snakes. ➡ **Antonyms: fondness, liking**

avid *adjective* **enthusiastic, ardent, zealous, keen, intense, passionate, eager, anxious** Everyone here is an avid sports fan. ➡ **Antonyms: apathetic, indifferent, reluctant**

avoid *verb* **elude, evade, sidestep, escape, bypass, circumvent** We went to the beach on Wednesday to avoid the weekend crowds. ➡ **Antonyms: confront, meet**

awake *verb* **1. awaken, wake up, waken, rouse, arouse, stir** I awoke to the sound of my clock radio. **2. spark, stimulate, kindle, incite, inspire, alert, excite** What awoke your interest in acting? ◆ *adjective* **1. wakeful, wide-awake, unsleeping, conscious** I was awake all night finishing my science work. **2. alert, vigilant, watchful, attentive, heedful, aware** The security guard was awake to any signs of suspicious activity. ➡ **Antonyms:** *verb* **1. sleep 2. repress** ◆ *adjective* **1. asleep 2. inattentive**

awaken *verb* **1. awake, wake up, waken, rouse, arouse, stir** The loud music awakened me from my nap. **2. spark, stimulate, kindle, bestir, incite, inspire** The winter Olympics awakened my interest in downhill skiing. ➡ **Antonyms: 1. sleep 2. repress, subdue**

award *verb* **give, bestow, confer, grant, present, reward** Joan's cherry jam was awarded a blue ribbon at the state fair. ◆ *noun* **prize, trophy, honor, tribute, medal, decoration** My brother received the award for best athlete. ➡ **Antonyms:** *verb* **disallow, deny**

aware *adjective* **cognizant, conscious, knowledgeable, mindful, informed** I wasn't aware that it was my turn to set the table. ➡ **Antonyms: unaware, uninformed**

awe *noun* **wonder, amazement, astonishment, reverence, respect** Seeing the Grand Canyon for the first time filled me with awe. ◆ *verb* **impress, dazzle, amaze,**

astound, astonish, stun, daunt I was awed to meet the President of the United States.

awesome *adjective* amazing, astonishing, impressive, inspiring, majestic, intimidating, daunting The faces carved on Mount Rushmore represent awesome feats of artistry and engineering.

awful *adjective* **1.** horrible, terrible, appalling, bad, ghastly, abominable Adrienne thinks that an onion milkshake would taste awful. **2.** fearsome, formidable, frightful, alarming, dire, dreadful Mount Everest is famous for its awful storms, which have killed dozens of climbers.

awfully *adverb* extremely, immensely, terribly, very, exceedingly Susan had an awfully hard time walking all three dogs at once.

awkward *adjective* **1.** clumsy, uncoordinated, unskilled, bungling, graceless, inept, ungainly Before I took tennis lessons, my serve was awkward. **2.** embarrassing, disconcerting, uncomfortable, mortifying, unpleasant, uneasy, confused Walking into the wrong restroom is an awkward mistake. **3.** cumbersome, difficult, unmanageable, unwieldy, bulky The large suitcase was awkward to carry.
● **Antonyms: 1.** coordinated, graceful **2.** comfortable **3.** easy, convenient

awry *adverb* amiss, wrong, askew, badly, astray, askance The performance went awry when the backdrop fell over.
● **Antonyms:** well, correctly, right

axiom *noun* rule, principle, law, precept, truism, theorem Isaac Newton formulated important axioms that form the basis of mechanical physics.

Bb

babble *verb* **chatter, prattle, jabber, blabber, talk** The girls babbled on about how much fun the party had been. ◆ *noun* **chatter, prattle, jabber, blabber, burble, murmur** My grandmother enjoys listening to my little brother's babble.

baby *noun* **infant, newborn, babe, neonate, toddler, tot** I had no hair when I was a baby. ◆ *verb* **coddle, pamper, dote on, indulge, spoil, cater to** I babied my hamster when it was sick.

back *noun* **1. spine, spinal column, backbone** My gymnastics coach says that I have a strong and flexible back. **2. rear, end, rear end, far end, stern, tail** My friends and I like to sit at the back of the bus. ◆ *verb* **1. retreat, move away, withdraw, recoil, backtrack, retire** I slowly backed away from the growling dog. **2. support, sponsor, aid, finance, endorse, help** The local hardware store is backing my brother's hockey team. ◆ *adjective* **1. rear, posterior, end, hind, tail** The back cover of my book got wet in the rain. **2. minor, outlying, obscure, out-of-the-way, remote, secluded** We drove on back roads in order to avoid traffic. **3. past, previous, earlier, prior** I collect back issues of my favorite comic books. ◆ *adverb* **backward, backwards, rearward, away** Mom moved the car back so she could open the garage door. ➡ **Antonyms:** *noun* **2. front** ◆ *verb* **1. advance, move forward 2. oppose, hinder** ◆ *adjective* **1. front, fore 2. major 3. current**

background *noun* **1. backdrop, setting, surroundings, landscape, distance** The art class painted the background for the set of the school play. **2. experience, training, education, qualifications, history** Our new music teacher has a strong background in jazz. ➡ **Antonym: 1. foreground**

backing *noun* **endorsement, encouragement, approval, support, sponsorship, aid** I have my friend's backing to run for class president. ➡ **Antonyms: discouragement, opposition**

backward *adjective* **1. backwards, rearward, reversed, behind, retrograde** My cat walked away from me without a backward glance. **2. undeveloped, deprived, disadvantaged, impoverished, depressed** The backward village had neither electricity nor running water. ◆ *adverb* **backwards, rearward, back, behind, around, about** I lost my balance and fell over backward. ➡ **Antonyms:** *adjective* **1. forward 2. advanced, developed** ◆ *adverb* **forward**

bad *adjective* **1. poor, inferior, unsatisfactory, awful, imperfect, defective** Our TV reception was bad until we got a satellite dish. **2. wrong, immoral, sinful, criminal, corrupt, evil, wicked** Stealing is bad. **3. disobedient, naughty, ill-behaved, mischievous, unruly** It was bad of me to stay out past my curfew. **4. inauspicious, unfavorable, unfortunate, adverse, unlucky** Missing the bus was a bad way to start the day. **5. disagreeable, nasty, unpleasant, offensive, repulsive, rotten** Rotten eggs have a bad odor. **6. damaging, harmful, hurtful, injurious, deleterious** Skiing without sunglasses can be bad for your eyes. **7. regretful, sorry, contrite, remorseful, upset, guilty, sad** I felt bad for having yelled at my sister. ➡ **Antonym: good**

badge *noun* **shield, insignia, emblem, identification, medallion** The police officer polished her badge.

badger *verb* **nag, pester, hound, bother, harass, torment** My little brother kept badgering me to take him to the park.

baffle *verb* **bewilder, confuse, mystify, perplex, confound, stymie** The computer programmer was baffled by the virus in the system.

bag *noun* **1. sack, tote bag, pouch, bundle** The clerk put our groceries into a paper bag. **2. baggage, luggage, suitcase, valise, satchel** The taxi driver put our bags in the trunk.

bait *noun* **lure, enticement, inducement, temptation, attraction** The store offered free samples as bait to attract customers. *verb* **taunt, harass, goad, heckle, provoke, tease, torment** It is traditional in baseball for opposing teams to bait one another.

balance *noun* **1. equilibrium, stability, steadiness, footing, poise** A tightrope walker needs to have excellent balance. **2. remainder, residue, rest, leftover, excess, surplus** I saved half my birthday money and spent the balance on a new computer game. **3. harmony, equilibrium, symmetry, parity, proportion, ratio** My science class is studying the ecological balance of tide pools. ◆ *verb* **1. stabilize, steady, poise, level, equalize** I balanced the coin on its edge. **2. compensate, offset, neutralize, counteract, contrast, compare** The team's strengths and weaknesses balance each other well.

bald *adjective* **1. bare, smooth, exposed, naked, open, hairless** The tires on my bike are worn almost bald. **2. obvious, flagrant, outright, blunt, plain, unadorned** She told a bald lie when she said she hadn't seen us. ➡ **Antonyms: 1. covered, hairy 2. concealed, elaborate**

baleful *adjective* **menacing, ominous, sinister, malevolent, threatening** The teacher gave me a baleful stare when I passed a note to my friend. ➡ **Antonyms: benevolent, good**

balk *verb* **hesitate, draw back, resist, shrink, refuse, demur, stop** My little brother balked at going on-stage at the kindergarten pageant.

ball¹ *noun* **globe, sphere, orb, spheroid** My mother taught me how to wind yarn into a ball.

ball² *noun* **dance, promenade, prom, reception, party** The governor and her husband attended the inaugural ball.

ban *verb* **forbid, prohibit, proscribe, bar, disallow, outlaw** The city council has banned smoking in public places. ◆ *noun* **prohibition, proscription, injunction, restriction, boycott** The ban against bringing weapons to school is strictly enforced. ➡ **Antonyms:** *verb* **allow, permit** ◆ *noun* **approval, permission**

banal *adjective* **trite, commonplace, overused, overworked, stale, dull** The disaster movie had a banal plot, but I loved the special effects. ➡ **Antonyms: original, new, fresh**

band¹ *noun* **strip, ribbon, sash, strap, stripe, belt, ring** The cowboy's hat was decorated with a leather band. ◆ *verb* **gird, girdle, belt, tie, bind, encircle** The shipping crate was banded with metal straps.

band² *noun* **1. gang, crew, group, pack, party, company, horde** A band of outlaws robbed the stagecoach. **2. ensemble, group, combo, orchestra, symphony** James plays bass guitar in a band with his friends. ◆ *verb* **join, unite, assemble, ally, combine, merge** My cousins and I banded together to harvest the vegetables in our grandmother's huge garden. ➡ **Antonyms:** *verb* **break up, split up**

bandit *noun* **outlaw, robber, thief, criminal, highwayman, desperado** The sheriff's posse caught the bandits that robbed the stagecoach.

bane *noun* **affliction, curse, scourge, plague, torment, nuisance** My sister thinks I am the bane of her social life.

bang *noun* **1. clap, crack, blast, boom, report, explosion** The angry woman slammed the door with a bang. **2. hit, thump, whack, blow, wallop, smack, knock** I got a bang on the head going through the low doorway. ◆ *verb* **1. beat, pound, strike, slam, whack, hammer** I banged my shoes together to knock off the dirt. **2. boom, clap, blast, crash, explode** We saw lightning and then heard thunder bang in the distance.

banish *verb* **exile, deport, eject, evict, expel, drive out** Napoleon was banished to the island of Elba in 1814.

bank¹ *noun* **1. shore, side, edge, slope, rise, shelf** The river overflowed its banks during the rainy season. **2. drift, mound, pile, heap, hill, mass** The children had fun flinging themselves in the snow bank. ◆ *verb* **gather, accumulate, amass, mass, mound, pile up** The clouds banking on the horizon presaged a storm.

bank² *noun* **repository, depository, stock, supply, reserve, store** The Red Cross maintains a large blood bank.

banner *noun* **pennant, streamer, flag, ensign, standard, colors** Banners and balloons announced the store's grand opening.

banquet *noun* **dinner, feast, meal, repast, fete, reception** The coach congratulated each player at the awards banquet.

bar *noun* **1. rod, shaft, pole, rail, spike, stick** The jewelry store has bars across its windows. **2. stripe, band, strip, ribbon, line, streak** A candy cane is characterized by its red and white bars. **3. obstacle, barrier, impediment, hindrance, obstruction, block** A lack of experience can be a bar to getting some jobs. **4. barroom, pub, saloon, tavern, lounge, nightclub** In most states you have to be at least 21 years old to enter a bar. ◆ *verb* **1. secure, lock, bolt, close, barricade** Did you remember to bar the gate to the horse corral? **2. block, obstruct, impede, hinder, thwart, check** A rockslide barred the road. **3. prevent, prohibit, restrict, ban, exclude, keep out** The public was barred from the beach during the hurricane. ➡ **Antonyms:** *noun* **3. aid, advantage** ◆ *verb* **1. unfasten, open 3. allow, permit**

bare *adjective* **1. barren, naked, bald, clear, blank, open, empty** There's a bare patch on the lawn where the wading pool sat. **2. fundamental, basic, essential, mere, scant, simple, plain** Sunglasses are among the bare essentials for backpacking. ◆ *verb* **expose, reveal, show, exhibit, display, disclose, uncover** The dog bared its teeth at the stranger. ➡ **Antonyms:** *verb* **conceal, cover**

barely *adverb* **just, hardly, scarcely, only, almost, scarce** The light snowfall barely covered the ground. ➡ **Antonyms: completely, fully**

bargain *noun* **1. agreement, arrangement, deal, pact, understanding, promise** My brother and I made a bargain to help each other clean our rooms. **2. buy, deal, good buy, value, discount, steal** Dad got a bargain on his new golf clubs. ◆ *verb* **negotiate, barter, haggle, deal, trade, compromise** My friends and I bargain with each other for baseball cards.

bark *noun* **woof, yap, yip, yelp, grunt, cry** Whenever someone knocks at the door, my dog gives a loud bark. ◆ *verb* **1. woof, yap, yip, yelp, bay, howl, cry** Our neighbor's dog sometimes barks all night long. **2. snap, snarl, bawl, bellow, holler, shout, yell** The drill instructor barked commands at the new recruits.

barrage *noun* **storm, deluge, shower, hail, fusillade, bombardment** The museum guide answered a barrage of questions from the students. ◆ *verb* **bombard, deluge, shower, rain, blitz, pour, pepper** My friends and I barraged one another with snowballs.

barrel *noun* **drum, cask, keg, tun, hogshead, vessel** Crude oil is sold by the barrel.

barren *adjective* **1. bare, empty, vacant, depleted, arid, void** We admired the open view as we hiked up the barren hillside. **2. infertile, sterile, unfruitful, childless, unproductive** The barren mare was unable to produce a foal. ➡ **Antonyms: 1. lush, fertile 2. fertile, productive**

barricade *noun* **barrier, obstruction, obstacle, roadblock, rampart, palisade** Road workers set up barricades to detour traffic. ◆ *verb* **block off, shut off, blockade, bar, obstruct, defend** Police barricaded the streets around the parade route.

barrier *noun* **obstacle, obstruction, impediment, hindrance, barricade, hurdle** The river was a barrier to the forest fire.

barter *verb* **exchange, swap, trade, bargain, replace, substitute** I bartered my comic books for my friend's baseball cards.

base¹ *noun* **1. bottom, foundation, foot, seat, support** The base of a pyramid is square, but the sides are triangular. **2. basis, essence, root, core, heart, fundamental** Many soups use chicken broth as a base. **3. installation, camp, headquarters, post, station, site** The nearby military base has just been closed. ◆ *verb* **1. found, ground, predicate, model, build, construct** The movie was based on a true story. **2. locate, situate, place, lodge, station, post** My dad's company is based in Boston. ➡ **Antonyms:** *noun* **1. top, summit**

base² *adjective* **dishonorable, contemptible, sordid, immoral, mean, vile, low** The prosecutor held that the defendant had base motives for committing the crime. ➡ **Antonyms: admirable, honorable, good**

basement *noun* **cellar, storm cellar, storeroom** Dad's workshop is down in the basement.

bash *verb* **smash, knock, pound, strike, slam, hit** The invaders bashed the castle gates with a battering ram.

bashful *adjective* **shy, timid, reticent, reserved, diffident, demure** I felt bashful on the first day at my new school. ➡ **Antonyms: outgoing, bold, confident**

basic *adjective* **essential, fundamental, integral, key, elementary, vital** Flour is one of the basic ingredients in a cake.

basis *noun* **cornerstone, source, root, reason, cause, justification** Her kindness is the basis of her popularity.

bat *noun* **club, mallet, cudgel, stick, cane** Baseball bats are made of either wood or metal. ◆ *verb* **hit, swat, knock, slam, smack, strike** The kitten batted at the fly.

batch *noun* **quantity, lot, bunch, group, assortment** Dad and I made a batch of peanut butter cookies.

bathe *verb* **wash, cleanse, clean, rinse, soak, wet** I bathe my dog in the bathtub.

bathroom *noun* **bath, restroom, washroom, lavatory, toilet, latrine** Our apartment has three bedrooms and two bathrooms.

baton *noun* **wand, staff, rod, stick, club, scepter** My sister practices twirling her baton in the backyard.

batter *verb* **buffet, hammer, pound, pummel, smash, beat, assault** High winds and waves battered the sailboat.

battle *noun* **1. combat, conflict, fight, war, engagement** The soldiers were armed and ready for battle. **2. dispute, argument, disagreement, debate, struggle, contest** My sister and I had a battle over what color to paint our room. ◆ *verb* **fight, combat, duel, skirmish, contest, struggle against** The champion boxer battled to defend his title.

bauble *noun* **trinket, gewgaw, gimcrack, trifle, ornament** The players' costumes glittered with baubles.

bawl *verb* **1. cry, wail, weep, sob, blubber** The little girl bawled when she couldn't find her teddy bear. **2. bellow, cry, call, shout, yell, roar, bark** The calf bawled for its mother.

bay¹ *noun* **cove, harbor, inlet, lagoon, gulf** The boat was anchored in a secluded bay.

bay² *noun* **hold, compartment, chamber, section, nook, recess** Cranes lowered freight into the ship's cargo bay.

bay[3] *verb* **howl, wail, yowl, cry, bark, yelp** The hounds bayed when they caught the fox's scent.

bazaar *noun* **1. marketplace, market, plaza, flea market, exchange** My uncle bought beautiful rugs at a bazaar in the Middle East. **2. sale, rummage sale, fair, show, exposition, carnival** I made potholders to sell at the church bazaar.

beach *noun* **shore, seashore, seaside, coast, seacoast, strand** I looked for seashells along the beach.

beacon *noun* **light, signal, sign, beam, guide, landmark** Skyscrapers have flashing red beacons to alert aircraft.

bead *noun* **drop, droplet, drip, globule, blob** A bead of water ran down the chilled glass.

beam *noun* **1. joist, rafter, timber, girder, trestle, brace, support** We hung herbs from the beam in our garden shed. **2. ray, shaft, gleam, glimmer, streak** The flashlight's beam dimmed as the batteries faded. ◆ *verb* **shine, blaze, gleam, glimmer, radiate** The light from the candle beamed.

bear *verb* **1. carry, tote, support, uphold, shoulder, transport** Camels can bear surprisingly heavy loads. **2. convey, deliver, transmit, tell, transfer, bring, move** The letter bore news of my acceptance to the Junior Symphony. **3. exhibit, display, show, manifest, demonstrate, reveal** Cucumbers bear a strong resemblance to zucchini. **4. produce, yield, generate, bring forth, give, make** Apple trees bear fruit in late summer and early fall. **5. abide, endure, stand, tolerate, suffer, brook, accept** Alene cannot bear to wear woolen sweaters. **6. relate, pertain, apply, concern, refer, correlate** The testimony of the witness bore directly on the case.

> ## Word Group
>
> A **beard** is the hair on a man's chin, cheeks, and throat. **Beard** is a very specific term with only one synonym (**whiskers**). Here are some common types of beards:
>
> A **goatee** ends in a point just below the chin. An **imperial** is grown from the lower lip and chin. **Muttonchops** are side whiskers separated by a shaven chin. Whiskers that grow down the side of the face, with the rest of the beard shaved off, are **sideburns**. A **vandyke** is a short, pointed beard.

bearing *noun* **1. deportment, manner, demeanor, presence, mien, air, style** The queen has a dignified bearing. **2. relevance, relationship, connection, application, pertinence, significance** Our sense of smell has a strong bearing on our sense of taste. **3. angle, course, heading, direction, orientation, track, way** The plane flew on a bearing of 270 degrees.

beast *noun* **1. animal, creature, critter, quadruped, mammal** The lion is said to be the king of beasts. **2. fiend, brute, monster, savage, barbarian, devil** Many people feel that Joseph Stalin was a beast.

beat *verb* **1. drum, pound, pummel, hit, strike, pulse, throb** The rain beating on the roof lulled me to sleep. **2. hammer, forge, form, shape, fashion, fabricate, stamp** Blacksmiths beat hot iron bars into horseshoes. **3. whip, whisk, blend, mix, stir, churn** Please beat these eggs and add them to the cake batter. **4. defeat, best, triumph over, overcome, surpass, conquer, vanquish** My friend usually beats me at tennis. ◆ *noun* **1. rhythm, pulse, tempo, cadence, throb** Everybody danced to the beat of the music. **2. route, circuit, round, territory, area** The police officer walked his beat.

beautiful *adjective* **attractive, lovely, pretty, stunning, gorgeous, comely** My aunt makes beautiful flower arrangements. ➡ **Antonyms: ugly, unattractive, unsightly**

beautify *verb* **adorn, decorate, ornament, improve, enhance, embellish** The newly planted trees beautified the downtown area.

beauty *noun* **attractiveness, loveliness, good looks, handsomeness, elegance, charm** Some cultures consider a tattoo a mark of beauty.

because *conjunction* **since, as, on account of, due to, for, considering** I can't go to the movies because I have to do my homework.

beckon *verb* **1. gesture, signal, wave, motion, flag, hail, bid** The traffic officer beckoned for the cars to move forward. **2. call, entice, draw, pull, attract, lure, invite** The summit beckoned to the mountaineers.

become *verb* **1. change into, turn into, develop into, metamorphose, grow into, convert to** Caterpillars become either moths or butterflies. **2. suit, flatter, enhance, befit, go with, agree, fit** Your new hairstyle becomes you.

becoming *adjective* **1. appropriate, suitable, befitting, proper, right, decent** The senator's vulgar behavior was not becoming. **2. attractive, flattering, pleasing, pretty, handsome** That dress is very becoming on you. ➡ **Antonyms: 1. inappropriate, improper, unsuitable 2. ugly, unattractive**

bedraggled *adjective* scruffy, unkempt, disheveled, messy, muddy, rundown The stray dog looked bedraggled. ➡ **Antonyms:** neat, clean, dry

before *adverb* already, previously, earlier, formerly, heretofore, beforehand I've read that book before. ◆ *preposition* prior to, ahead of, preceding, in front of I always wash my hands before dinner. ➡ **Antonyms:** after, following

beg *verb* beseech, entreat, implore, importune, plead, appeal I begged my parents to buy me a stereo.

beget *verb* 1. father, sire, parent, procreate, breed The stallion begat a number of prize-winning foals. 2. result in, cause, create, make, produce Regular exercise begets physical fitness.

beggar *noun* mendicant, pauper, panhandler, almsman, almswoman Some homeless people become beggars.

begin *verb* start, commence, open, initiate, originate, embark Our school begins on the first Tuesday after Labor Day. ➡ **Antonyms:** finish, stop

beginner *noun* novice, learner, neophyte, fledgling, student, amateur The ski resort has a bunny slope for beginners. ➡ **Antonyms:** master, expert

beginning *noun* 1. start, opening, commencement, outset, introduction, initiation We found our seats before the beginning of the concert. 2. inception, genesis, origin, conception, source, birth Many people believe that life on Earth had its beginning in the oceans. ➡ **Antonyms:** end, ending, finish

beguile *verb* 1. deceive, delude, fool, mislead, trick, dupe The con artist beguiled many people with his money-making scheme. 2. charm, delight, bewitch, captivate, enchant, entrance We were beguiled by the actor's performance.

behave *verb* 1. function, perform, operate, work, react, manage These tires behave well on snow and ice. 2. act, conduct oneself, comport oneself, acquit oneself Animals often behave strangely before an earthquake.

behavior *noun* conduct, manners, comportment, deportment, actions, performance Our teacher complimented us on our good behavior during the assembly.

behind *adverb* 1. late, behindhand, slow, belatedly, tardily It is important not to get behind in your schoolwork. 2. in the rear, in back of, aft, after, back, following I lagged behind my friends as we walked home. ◆ *preposition* in back of, at the rear of, after, beyond, following My little brother likes to hide behind the couch. ➡ **Antonyms:** *adverb* ahead, before ◆ *preposition* in front of

behold *verb* look at, gaze upon, observe, see, watch, witness The butterfly migration was magnificent to behold.

being *noun* 1. existence, actuality, reality, life, occurrence, presence The United States of America came into being on July 4, 1776. 2. individual, mortal, soul, person, creature, organism, human Do you believe that there are intelligent beings on other planets?

belief *noun* 1. conviction, feeling, opinion, position, view, theory It is my belief that honesty is the best policy. 2. trust, confidence, faith, reliance, dependence I have complete belief in your dependability. 3. creed, doctrine, faith, dogma, principle, ideology Many people prefer not to discuss their religious beliefs.

believe *verb* 1. accept, hold, trust, have faith in, credit, rely on A few people still believe that Earth is flat. 2. think, assume, suppose, presume, guess, imagine I believe that I will go to college. ➡ **Antonyms:** 1. disbelieve, doubt 2. know

belligerent *adjective* 1. truculent, contentious, quarrelsome, scrappy, unfriendly, nasty Some sports fans become belligerent when their team loses. 2. bellicose, hostile, aggressive, warring, militant, combative The belligerent nation attacked its neighbor. ➡ **Antonyms:** peaceful, friendly

bellow *verb* shout, yell, holler, bawl, roar, bark, call, cry I bellowed at my dog when he ran out of the yard. ◆ *noun* shout, roar, whoop, yell, howl, cry The crowd gave a bellow of approval on hearing the election results.

belly *noun* 1. abdomen, stomach, tummy, midriff, paunch, underside The cat crouched on its belly as it stalked the gopher. 2. interior, insides, recesses, depths, center, core The ship's belly was filled with cargo.

belongings *noun* possessions, property, goods, personal effects, things When my family moved, we packed all our belongings into boxes.

below *adverb* beneath, under, underneath, downwards When we stood on the hilltop we could see the town below. ◆ *preposition* 1. beneath, under, underneath I keep the fish food on the shelf below my fish tank. 2. lower than, less than, under, subordinate to, inferior to The temperature is five degrees below zero. ➡ **Antonym:** above

belt *noun* area, zone, tract, band, strip, circle A green belt of grass and trees surrounds the campus. ◆ *verb* 1. gird, ring, band, encompass, encircle, fasten I belted the old suitcase with a piece of rope. **2. hit, slug, slam, knock, strike, whack, smash** I belted the ball over the outfield fence.

bemused *adjective* **absent-minded, preoccupied, inattentive, faraway, bewildered** My cousin is so bemused that he is always getting lost.

bend *verb* **1. twist, flex, curve, turn, loop, coil, wind** To make his sculpture, the artist bends steel bars into various shapes. **2. yield, give in, submit, buckle, bow** The peasants refused to bend to the tyrant's demands. **3. modify, change, distort, contort, deviate** They will not bend the rules of the contest for you. ◆ *noun* **curve, turn, crook, twist, hook, angle** Our house is just past the bend in the road. ➤ **Antonym:** *verb* **1. straighten**

beneath *adverb* **below, under, underneath, lower down** You take the upper bunk, and I'll take the one beneath. ◆ *preposition* **below, under, underneath, lower than** My missing shoe was beneath the sofa.

beneficial *adjective* **helpful, useful, valuable, good, advantageous** Flashcards can be a beneficial study aid. ➤ **Antonyms: harmful, bad, useless**

benefit *noun* **advantage, asset, boon, help, aid, plus** The new library will be a great benefit to the community. ◆ *verb* **help, aid, assist, better, improve, serve, profit** Earthworms benefit plants by aerating the soil. ➤ **Antonyms:** *noun* **loss, disadvantage, damage**

benevolent *adjective* **kind, kindhearted, kindly, good, goodhearted, altruistic** I felt benevolent when I helped with the holiday toy drive. ➤ **Antonyms: malevolent, cruel, unkind**

benign *adjective* **1. benevolent, kind, kindhearted, goodhearted, gentle** The First Lady gave me a benign smile when I shook her hand. **2. temperate, mild, favorable, warm, fair, nice** Hawaii has a benign climate. **3. harmless, nonmalignant, innocuous, curable** We were relieved to hear that Grandfather's tumor was benign. ➤ **Antonyms: 1. unkind, malevolent 2. harsh, severe 3. malignant, bad**

bequeath *verb* **will, leave, bestow, pass on, hand down, give** My grandmother bequeathed a portion of her estate to her alma mater.

bequest *noun* **legacy, inheritance, bestowal, gift, settlement, endowment** My father has received a substantial bequest from his uncle.

berate *verb* **scold, upbraid, revile, castigate, rebuke** Don't berate yourself when you make a mistake.

beseech *verb* **implore, entreat, beg, supplicate, appeal** I beseeched my parents to let me go to the party.

beset *verb* **1. beleaguer, plague, trouble, harry, bother** Our train trip back to Chicago was beset by delays. **2. besiege, surround, assail, attack, assault, circle, hem in** The senator was beset by reporters questioning him on the new tax bill.

beside *preposition* **next to, alongside, with, compared to** Please sit beside me at lunch.

besides *adverb* **furthermore, moreover, also, in addition, too** I can't afford to go to the movie; besides, I have to study for a test.

best *adjective* **1. finest, greatest, principal, preeminent, top, favorite** My best friend and I love to shop together. **2. greater, better, larger, largest, biggest, most** I spent the best part of the day raking leaves. ◆ *adverb* **most, most of all, above all, extremely, fully, greatly** What kind of pizza do you like best? ◆ *noun* **finest, foremost, first, highest, top** I think that my school is the best. ◆ *verb* **defeat, beat, vanquish, trounce, overcome, surpass** The wrestler bested his opponent in just two minutes. ➤ **Antonyms:** *adjective* & *noun* **worst** ◆ *adverb* **least** ◆ *verb* **succumb, lose**

bestow *verb* **confer, award, present, grant, give, accord** The city bestowed a medal on the boy for rescuing a drowning child.

bet *noun* **wager, stake, gamble, venture, chance, risk** Mike and I have a bet as to which team will win the World Series. ◆ *verb* **wager, stake, gamble, challenge, chance, risk** I bet my dad that I could beat him at chess.

betray *verb* **1. deceive, double-cross, abandon, desert, fail, mislead** The spy refused to betray her country when she was captured. **2. reveal, expose, give away, disclose, divulge, show** I would never betray any of my best friend's secrets. ➤ **Antonyms: 2. conceal, hide, keep**

better *adjective* **1. superior, finer, worthier, stronger, preferable** My spelling is better now than it was last year. **2. greater, larger, largest, bigger, most, best, more** We spent the better part of the day cleaning the house. **3. healthier, well, fitter, improved, stronger, haler** I had the flu last week, but I feel better now. ◆ *adverb* **more, greater, finer, preferably, best** I like spaghetti better than meat loaf. ◆ *verb* **1. beat, exceed, surpass, outdo, pass, top, best** Julie bettered her own race time by a full second. **2. improve, enhance, help, raise, strengthen, advance** You can better your grade if you do extra work. ➡ **Antonyms:** *adjective* **1. worse, poorer 2. lesser, smaller ♦** *adverb* **less ♦** *verb* **2. worsen, lessen**

between *preposition* **betwixt, among, amid, amidst, connecting, joining** My friend and I can eat a whole pizza between us.

beverage *noun* **drink, liquid, refreshment, juice, fluid** My favorite beverage is lemonade.

beware *verb* **heed, mind, notice, regard, look out for, watch out for** Our camp counselor told us to beware of the poison ivy. ➡ **Antonym: ignore**

bewilder *verb* **baffle, confuse, mystify, perplex, puzzle** The story problem in my algebra class bewildered me.

beyond *preposition* **1. past, after, behind, farther than, across** The neighborhood park is just beyond that grove of trees. **2. later than, after, past, following, subsequent to** I'm not allowed to stay out beyond 10 p.m.

bias *noun* **leaning, prejudice, preference, slant, predilection** A referee should have no bias toward either team. **♦** *verb* **influence, prejudice, sway, slant, skew** Don't let my opinion bias your decision.

bicker *verb* **squabble, quarrel, quibble, argue, fight, wrangle** My brother and I bickered over which video game to play. ➡ **Antonyms: agree, concur**

bid *verb* **1. command, order, direct, charge, instruct, tell** My father bid me to clean my room. **2. invite, request, ask, summon, call** Our neighbors bid us to join them for a barbecue. **3. offer, propose, proffer, tender, submit** My stepmother bid 200 dollars for the antique table. **♦** *noun* **1. proposal, estimate, offer, offering** The job will go to the contractor who submits the lowest bid. **2. attempt, try, endeavor, effort, venture** I made a successful bid to become vice-president of the student council.

big *adjective* **1. large, enormous, gigantic, huge, immense, tremendous** Great Danes are big dogs. **2. older, grown, grown-up, mature, adult** My big brother is going away to college next fall. **3. important, prominent, influential, major, significant, notable, leading** Our soccer team practiced hard for the big tournament. ➡ **Antonyms: 1. little, small 2. younger, immature 3. minor, insignificant, unimportant**

bill[1] *noun* **1. check, tab, statement, invoice, charge, tally** The waiter brought the bill when we finished our meal. **2.**

act, draft, measure, proposal, law, statute** The new environmental protection bill was approved by Congress. **♦** *verb* **invoice, charge, debit** The department store billed us for our purchases.

bill[2] *noun* **visor, brim, projection, peak, beak, nose** The bill on my cap keeps the sun out of my eyes.

billow *noun* **cloud, surge, wave, swell** We raised billows of dust when we shook out the old rug. **♦** *verb* **surge, swell, roll, rise up, balloon, puff up** Black smoke billowed from the burning building.

bin *noun* **container, crate, box, chest, crib** Our school has recycling bins outside the lunchroom.

bind *verb* **1. tie, tie up, secure, wrap, knot, fasten, join** I bound the old newspapers together with twine. **2. bandage, dress, wrap, swathe, cover** The doctor used a strip of gauze to bind the wound. **3. compel, obligate, commit, require, charge, hold** Citizenship binds you to be loyal to a country. ➡ **Antonyms: 1. untie, unbind 3. free, release**

binge *noun* **spree, bout, fling** I went on a reading binge this summer and read 50 books.

birth *noun* **1. delivery, childbirth, parturition, bearing** Baby elephants weigh about 250 pounds at birth. **2. beginning, commencement, inception, dawn, start, origin, emergence** The bicentennial anniversary of the birth of the United States was celebrated in 1976. **3. ancestry, descent, extraction, blood, family, lineage** My grandfather is of Scandinavian birth. ➡ **Antonyms: 1. death 2. conclusion, end, finish**

bit *noun* **1. fragment, particle, piece, scrap, speck, whit** Bits of confetti floated through the air during the parade. **2. moment, second, instant, spell, while, time** We are leaving for the beach in just a bit.

bite *verb* **1. chomp, gnaw, gnash, nibble, munch, chew** I bit into the apple. **2. sting, nip, pierce, prick, wound, cut** I swatted at the mosquito that was trying to bite me. **♦** *noun* **1. sting, prick, puncture, nip, wound** Spider bites can be painful. **2. morsel, mouthful, bit, piece, crumb, nibble, taste** I'm so full that I can't eat another bite.

bitter *adjective* **1. acrid, biting, pungent, tart, unpleasant** He winced at the bitter taste of the medicine. **2. harsh, brutal, rough, severe, hard, intense** We had a bitter winter last year. **3. resentful, sullen, acrimonious, rancorous, spiteful, angry** His friend's deception made Ron bitter. ➡ **Antonyms: 1. sweet, sugary 2. mild, gentle 3. forgiving, friendly**

bizarre *adjective* **odd, strange, weird, unusual, crazy, fantastic** The clown was wearing a bizarre outfit made from umbrellas. ◆ **Antonyms: normal, ordinary**

black *adjective* **1. ebony, jet, onyx, raven** On Halloween I dressed as a vampire and wore a black cape. **2. dark, pitch-dark, inky, unlit, starless, gloomy** The inside of the cave was black. **3. evil, wicked, nefarious, bad, sinister, sinful** The Inquisition was a black time in European history. **4. angry, furious, hostile, malevolent, mean, sullen** News of the defeat put the general in a black mood. ◆ **Antonyms: 1. white 2. sunny, light, bright 3. good, moral 4. happy, cheerful, friendly**

blade *noun* **1. edge, cutter, knife, sword, cutting edge** My pocketknife has two blades. **2. leaf, leaflet, frond, lamina, spear, petal, needle** You can make a crude whistle from a blade of grass.

blame *verb* **accuse, charge, censure, criticize, fault** I blamed my sister for making us late to school. ◆ *noun* **accountability, responsibility, culpability, fault, guilt** My sister accepted the blame for making us late to school. ◆ **Antonyms:** *verb* **exonerate, absolve**

bland *adjective* **1. mild, calm, soothing, gentle, even, tranquil** The bland music soothed the crying baby. **2. tasteless, insipid, dull, boring, uninteresting, vapid, flat** My stepsister and I agree that oatmeal is bland. ◆ **Antonyms: 1. sharp, harsh 2. piquant, flavorful**

blank *adjective* **1. empty, bare, clear, unmarked, plain, open** I have three blank pages left in my sketchbook. **2. expressionless, vacant, void, deadpan, mindless, vacuous** His blank expression told me he hadn't gotten the punch line to the joke. ◆ *noun* **void, vacuum, emptiness, space, gap, vacancy, nothing** I drew a blank and could not answer the question. ◆ **Antonyms:** *adjective* **1. filled, full 2. alert**

blanket *noun* **layer, covering, cover, coating, mantle, carpet** A thick blanket of snow covered the countryside. ◆ *adjective* **comprehensive, general, all-inclusive, universal, overall, unconditional** Our school has a blanket rule against smoking on school grounds. ◆ *verb* **cover, bury, coat, overlay, cloak, conceal** The storm blanketed our yard with hailstones.

blast *noun* **1. gust, surge, rush, flurry, breeze, blow** A blast of humid air hit me when I opened the car window. **2. bang, boom, roar, explosion, thunder, detonation** The hunters heard the distant blast of a shotgun. ◆ *verb* **1. detonate, dynamite, explode, burst, blow** Miners blasted their way through the rock. **2. shatter, destroy, demolish, dash, defeat, ruin** Copernicus blasted the idea that Earth is the

center of the solar system. **3. blare, blow, boom, roar, thunder, wail, scream** The ambulance blasted its siren as it raced to the hospital.

blatant *adjective* **obvious, flagrant, conspicuous, glaring, clear, plain, overt** The jaywalker showed a blatant disregard for his personal safety. ◆ **Antonyms: subtle, inconspicuous, hidden**

blaze *noun* **1. fire, flames, conflagration, inferno, burning, holocaust** It took firefighters two hours to extinguish the blaze. **2. flare, flash, glare, gleam, beam, dazzle** A blaze of sunlight suddenly broke through the clouds. ◆ *verb* **burn, flame, flare, glow, beam, gleam, radiate, shine** The campfire blazed cheerfully.

bleach *verb* **lighten, whiten, blanch, wash out, fade** The sun has bleached my hair. ◆ **Antonym: darken**

bleak *adjective* **1. depressing, dismal, dreary, cheerless, forbidding, grim** The Great Depression was a bleak era in American history. **2. harsh, severe, stark, raw, hard, barren** Antarctica has a bleak climate. ◆ **Antonyms: 1. bright, sunny 2. warm, mild**

bleary *adjective* **blurry, fuzzy, indistinct, unclear, vague, cloudy** The rain on the window gave the landscape a bleary look. ◆ **Antonyms: clear, distinct**

blemish *verb* **mar, tarnish, detract from, flaw, spoil, harm** The gymnast's stumble blemished his otherwise perfect performance. ◆ *noun* **defect, flaw, imperfection, blotch, impurity** A blemish in the wood reduced the table's value. ◆ **Antonyms:** *verb* **improve, perfect**

blend *verb* **1. combine, mix, stir, scramble, unite, merge** I blended all the cookie ingredients in a large bowl. **2. go together, harmonize, coordinate, integrate, synthesize, unify** Our new sofa blends well with the chairs and carpet. ◆ *noun* **combination, mix, mixture, compound, fusion, union** This material is a blend of cotton and rayon. ◆ **Antonyms:** *verb* **1. divide, separate**

bless *verb* **1. consecrate, sanctify, anoint, dedicate, hallow** The priest blessed the animals on the Feast of Saint Francis. **2. grace, favor, endow, bestow, furnish, give** We were blessed with great weather for our vacation.

blight *noun* **affliction, bane, curse, scourge, plague, disease** The scandal was a blight on the politician's career. ◆ *verb* **wither, afflict, spoil, ruin, damage, mar** These crops have been blighted by the long drought. ◆ **Antonyms:** *noun* **blessing, boon** ◆ *verb* **aid, benefit, help**

blind *adjective* **1. sightless, visionless, unseeing, eyeless** My cat is blind in one eye. **2. ignorant of, unaware of, unperceptive, unknowing, naive** Many people are blind to the dangers of secondhand smoke. **3. concealed, hidden, unseen, unnoticeable** The mountain road had a lot of blind curves. ◆ *noun* **front, cover, screen, façade, camouflage, ruse** The little store was a blind for an illegal gambling operation. ◆ *verb* **daze, dazzle, bedazzle, stun, obscure** The camera's flash blinded me for a moment. ➹ **Antonyms:** *adjective* **2. perceptive, aware 3. obvious, visible**

bliss *noun* **rapture, ecstasy, happiness, joy, joyfulness, delight** It was bliss to go to the rock concert with my friends. ➹ **Antonyms: misery, sorrow, sadness**

blissful *adjective* **delightful, happy, ecstatic, joyous, rapturous** I spent a blissful afternoon lying by the pool. ➹ **Antonyms: unhappy, miserable**

blizzard *noun* **snowstorm, winter storm, flurry, storm, gale, tempest** The blizzard left huge snowdrifts in the streets.

bloat *verb* **distend, swell, puff up, expand, enlarge, inflate** Green hay is dangerous for cows as it causes their stomachs to bloat. ➹ **Antonyms: shrivel, shrink**

block *noun* **1. cube, chunk, piece, hunk, lump, brick** The ancient pyramids are constructed of huge blocks of sandstone. **2. blockage, obstruction, barrier, obstacle, impediment, clog** The jackknifed truck was a block to traffic. ◆ *verb* **1. obstruct, impede, stop, bar, jam, interfere** My coach will block me from playing if I don't improve my grades. **2. screen, shroud, shut off, obscure, hide, conceal** Clouds blocked our view of the city. ➹ **Antonyms:** *verb* **1. clear, open, unblock 2. reveal**

Word Group

A **blockade** is the closing off of an area by troops or warships to prevent people and supplies from going in and out. **Blockade** is a very specific term with no true synonyms. Here are some related words:

attack, barricade, barrier, encirclement, obstacle, obstruction, siege

---

blood *noun* **ancestry, birth, descent, heritage, lineage, family** My family is of Scandinavian blood.

bloom *noun* **blossom, flower, bud** The blooms on our magnolia tree are pink. ◆ *verb* **blossom, flower, flourish, thrive, grow, open, sprout** The rosebushes bloomed all summer long.

blossom *noun* **flower, bloom, bud** Cherry blossoms can be either pink or white. ◆ *verb* **1. flower, bloom, bud, open** Apple trees blossom in the springtime. **2. develop, grow, mature, ripen, flourish, thrive, prosper, succeed** The Italian Renaissance blossomed in the city-state of Florence. ➹ **Antonyms:** *verb* **2. wither, diminish, fade**

blot *noun* **blotch, smear, smudge, stain, spot, blemish** I used hairspray to remove the ink blot from my shirt. ◆ *verb* **stain, spot, mark, smudge, blemish, sully, tarnish** The tablecloth was blotted with spaghetti sauce.

blotch *noun* **spot, splotch, mark, blemish, smudge, stain** The mechanic's uniform had greasy blotches on it.

blow[1] *verb* **1. float, flutter, waft, swirl, move, sail, fly** The laundry on the clothesline was blowing in the wind. **2. breathe, puff, exhale, expel, pant, gasp** I blew on the campfire to get it going. **3. sound, blare, toot, whistle, honk, play** The referee blew her whistle to begin the game. **4. blast, burst, dynamite, explode, detonate, erupt** Work crews used dynamite to blow a tunnel through the mountain.

blow[2] *noun* **1. hit, jab, punch, stroke, clout, swat** I landed several good blows during the pillow fight with my brother. **2. shock, jolt, setback, misfortune, catastrophe, calamity** The stock market crash of 1929 dealt a crippling blow to the American economy.

bluff[1] *verb* **deceive, fool, mislead, trick, dupe** An opossum will play dead to bluff a predator. ◆ *noun* **deception, pretense, ruse, fraud, sham, fake, lie** I knew his threats were just a bluff.

bluff[2] *noun* **cliff, bank, escarpment, promontory, hill, precipice** We set up our camp near the top of the bluff.

blunder *noun* **error, mistake, slip, lapse, bungle** I made a blunder when I used salt instead of sugar in the cake batter. ◆ *verb* **stumble, bumble, bungle, flounder, stagger** I blundered around in the darkness trying to find the light switch.

blunt *adjective* **1. dull, unsharpened, round** The knife was blunt and would not cut the tomato. **2. candid, direct, abrupt, frank, tactless, brusque** My friend gave me a blunt answer when I asked her how I looked. ➹ **Antonyms: 1. sharp 2. subtle, tactful**

blur *verb* **1. cloud, dim, obscure, shroud, veil** The fog blurred our view of the landscape. **2. smear, smudge, spread, run, stain** Rain blurred the letters on the freshly painted sign.

blush *verb* **flush, redden, turn red, color, glow** My brother blushed when the instructor praised him. ♦ *noun* **flush, glow, reddening, redness, ruddiness, color, bloom** His compliment brought a blush to my cheeks.

board *noun* **1. plank, slat, lumber, timber, wood** I used pine boards and concrete blocks to make bookshelves. **2. keep, meals, food, fare, provisions** My aunt got a job that paid her room and board. **3. committee, council, panel, commission, cabinet, directorate** Our neighbor was recently elected to the board of education. ♦ *verb* **1. lodge, put up, house, quarter, billet, room** We are boarding an exchange student this year. **2. get on, enter, embark, catch, take** It's time to board the train.

boast *verb* **brag, vaunt, crow, flaunt, aggrandize** Some people like to boast about their accomplishments. ♦ *noun* **brag, vaunt, claim, assertion, avowal, bragging** The athlete made good on his boast that he would win the race.

Word Group A **boat** may be a large, seagoing vessel, but **boat** more commonly refers to a small, open craft for traveling on water. **Boat** is a very specific term with no true synonyms. Here are some common types of small, open boats:

bateau, canoe, catamaran, dinghy, dory, gondola, punt, rowboat, scull, skiff

bode *verb* **portend, presage, forebode, foreshadow, indicate, signify** The storm clouds did not bode well for our afternoon picnic.

body *noun* **1. physique, build, figure, frame, torso, trunk** Exercise is good for both body and mind. **2. corpse, cadaver, remains, carcass, skeleton, bones** Police found two bodies at the crime scene. **3. group, mass, unit, band, assembly** The main body of spectators stayed until the game was over. **4. substance, consistency, thickness, density, fullness, richness** Add a little flour to give the gravy more body.

bog *noun* **marsh, marshland, swamp, swampland, quagmire, fen** We wore rubber boots to explore the bog. ♦ *verb* **slow, stall, delay, impede, obstruct, hinder** Negotiations bogged down when both sides refused to compromise. ● **Antonyms:** *verb* **advance, progress**

bogus *adjective* **counterfeit, fake, phony, imitation, false, fraudulent** The man was arrested for passing bogus 20-dollar bills. ● **Antonyms: authentic, genuine, real**

boil *verb* **simmer, stew, cook, steam, bubble, parboil** I boiled the corn-on-the-cob for about five minutes.

boisterous *adjective* **rowdy, clamorous, noisy, loud, turbulent, wild** The students were boisterous as they exited gym class. ● **Antonyms: quiet, serene, orderly**

bold *adjective* **1. brave, courageous, valiant, intrepid, daring, heroic** The bold father quail chased the roadrunner away from his chicks. **2. audacious, brazen, brash, impudent, forward, presumptuous** I was sent to my room for making a bold remark at the dinner table. **3. vivid, pronounced, conspicuous, striking, colorful, loud** My new T-shirt is white with bold red stripes. ● **Antonyms: 1. cowardly, timid 2. deferential, polite 3. pale, dull**

bolt *noun* **1. screw, pin, catch, fastener, rod, bar** Turning the bolt under the bicycle seat adjusts its height. **2. dart, rush, run, sprint, bound, spring** The field mouse made a bolt for safety when it saw the hawk. ♦ *verb* **1. fasten, latch, lock, secure, bar** Please bolt the door and turn off the porch light. **2. dash, dart, fly, run, rush, sprint, jump** My dog bolted out of the yard when I opened the gate. **3. gobble, gulp, wolf, gorge, guzzle, swill** I bolted my breakfast because I was late for school.

bombard *verb* **beset, barrage, assail, attack, assault, bomb** I was bombarded with questions about my trip.

bombastic *adjective* **grandiloquent, grandiose, flowery, overblown, pompous** The senator's long, bombastic speech delayed the vote on the legislation. ● **Antonyms: restrained, simple, elegant**

bond *noun* **1. restraint, fetter, manacle, shackle, chain, handcuff** Houdini was famous for being able to escape elaborate bonds. **2. attachment, tie, link, connection, union, allegiance** My grandmother and I have always had a strong bond. ♦ *verb* **cement, glue, fuse, attach, fasten, adhere** I used glue to bond my broken sunglasses back together. ● **Antonyms:** *verb* **detach, separate**

bondage *noun* **servitude, subjugation, enslavement, serfdom, slavery** The Russian Emancipation Act of 1861 released serfs from bondage. ● **Antonyms: freedom, liberty**

bonus *noun* **reward, addition, extra, gift, prize** Because she was the top salesperson, Mom received a bonus.

boom *verb* **1. crash, roar, rumble, thunder, blast, roll** Thunder boomed in the distance. **2. flourish, burgeon, mushroom, increase, grow, prosper** Alaska's population boomed when oil was discovered. ♦ *noun* **1. clap, report,**

roar, rumble, thunder, blast A sonic boom shook our windows. **2. expansion, growth, upswing, gain, advance, boost** The advent of the personal computer brought a boom to the electronics industry.

boon *noun* **benefit, advantage, gain, blessing, godsend, gift** The discovery of penicillin was a boon to medicine.

boost *verb* **1. hoist, lift, raise, heft, push, shove** I boosted my little sister up onto her horse. **2. increase, raise, build up, elevate, improve, promote** Winning the first game of the season boosted our team's confidence. ◆ *noun* **1. lift, hoist, raise, push, shove, assist** My friend gave me a boost over the fence. **2. increase, hike, rise, upsurge, upturn, growth, jump** The company's new marketing campaign gave their sales a big boost. ▸ **Antonyms:** *verb* **lower, drop** ◆ *noun* **2. decrease, reduction**

booth *noun* **stall, stand, cubicle, box, compartment, enclosure** We must have visited every booth at the quilt show.

booty *noun* **loot, plunder, spoils, contraband, take, prize** The pirates buried their booty on a deserted island.

border *noun* **1. boundary, borderland, frontier, march, line, threshold** The Rio Grande River forms part of the border between the United States and Mexico. **2. edge, margin, perimeter, periphery, verge, limits** Mom had planted marigolds around the border of her vegetable garden. ◆ *verb* **1. abut, adjoin, neighbor, touch, meet, contact, join** Tennessee and Kentucky border one another. **2. edge, rim, surround, enclose, skirt** Our property is bordered with trees and lilac bushes. ▸ **Antonyms:** *noun* **2. center, middle**

bore[1] *verb* **burrow, drill, tunnel, penetrate, pierce, mine, dig** Boll weevil larvae bore into cotton plants.

bore[2] *verb* **tire, weary, fatigue, tax, annoy, irritate** Sometimes school bores me. ◆ *noun* **dull person, tiresome person, annoyance, nuisance, pest** I think a person who never says anything is a bore. ▸ **Antonyms:** *verb* **invigorate, stimulate, excite**

boring *adjective* **dull, uninteresting, dreary, tedious, tiresome, monotonous** I fell asleep during the boring movie. ▸ **Antonyms: interesting, exciting, stimulating**

borrow *verb* **1. use, get a loan, obtain, scrounge, sponge** May I borrow five dollars? **2. appropriate, adopt, steal, plagiarize, take, copy** The movie plot was borrowed from one of Jane Austen's novels.

boss *noun* **supervisor, employer, manager, director, chief, leader** My dad's boss is the company's founder. ◆ *verb*

order, direct, command, domineer, dominate, supervise My older brother sometimes tries to boss me around. ▸ **Antonyms:** *noun* **employee, subordinate**

bother *verb* **1. aggravate, annoy, disturb, irritate, pester, harass** The loud music bothered my concentration. **2. upset, dismay, disquiet, concern, worry, unsettle** It bothers me when my brother wears my shirts. ◆ *noun* **annoyance, nuisance, aggravation, irritant, irritation, problem** Telephone calls at dinnertime are a real bother.

Word Group

A **bottle** is a container, usually made of glass or plastic, having a mouth that can be corked or capped. **Bottle** is a very specific term with no true synonyms. Here are some common types of bottles:

A **carafe** is used for serving water or wine. A **cruet** is a small bottle for holding vinegar, oil, or other condiments. A **flask** has a flattened shape and is made to fit in a pocket. A **jar** is a cylinder with a wide mouth and usually no handles. A **jug** is a tall, often rounded vessel with a narrow mouth and a handle. A **magnum** holds about two fifths of a gallon of wine or liquor.

bottom *noun* **1. base, lowest point, foot, floor, ground, foundation** We rode our sled to the bottom of the hill. **2. core, heart, root, substance, essence, origin** We need to get to the bottom of this problem. ▸ **Antonyms: 1. top, tip, summit**

boulevard *noun* **avenue, thoroughfare, street, road, parkway, concourse** The city's main boulevard is lined with shade trees.

bounce *verb* **1. rebound, glance, ricochet, boomerang, recoil, carom** The basketball bounced off the backboard. **2. jump, spring, bound, leap, hop, skip, vault** We bounced up and down on the trampoline. ◆ *noun* **1. rebound, bound, hop, jump, skip, leap, spring** The shortstop caught the ball on the second bounce. **2. elasticity, springiness, resilience, resiliency, flexibility** A good tennis ball has lots of bounce.

bound[1] *verb* **hop, spring, leap, jump, skip, bounce, vault** The rabbit bounded away. ◆ *noun* **jump, leap, spring, hop, skip, vault** I cleared the stream in a single bound.

bound[2] *noun* **limit, boundary, border, confines, edge, perimeter** The rancher has two ponds within the bounds of his property. ◆ *verb* **border, edge, limit, restrict, confine, delimit** The United States is bounded on the north by Canada.

bound[3] *adjective* **1. obligated, obliged, committed, beholden, indebted, constrained** I am bound to do my chores before going out with my friends. **2. certain, sure, destined, fated, likely, apt** You're bound to get a good grade if you study hard.

boundary *noun* **border, borderline, frontier, bounds, edge, perimeter, limit** The boundary between North and South Korea runs along the 38th parallel.

boundless *adjective* **infinite, endless, limitless, unlimited, immeasurable, vast, enormous** Mary's enthusiasm for horseback riding is boundless. ▸ **Antonyms: limited, restricted, confined**

bountiful *adjective* **plentiful, abundant, bounteous, copious, generous, large** Our tomato crop was bountiful this summer. ▸ **Antonyms: sparse, scanty, small**

bounty *noun* **1. generosity, benevolence, aid, help, donations, gifts** The shelter for the homeless is dependent on the bounty of local citizens. **2. reward, payment, bonus, premium, prize, recompense** The FBI offered a bounty for the capture of the bank robbers.

bouquet *noun* **1. posy, arrangement, assortment, bunch, spray, nosegay** We gave Mom a bouquet of flowers on her birthday. **2. aroma, fragrance, scent, smell, redolence, perfume** Dad said that his wine had a fruity bouquet.

bout *noun* **1. match, competition, contest, encounter, engagement, fight** The championship bout will be televised nationally. **2. spell, interval, period, course, attack, siege** My grandfather suffers occasional bouts of arthritis.

bow[1] *noun* **prow, front, forecastle, foredeck** Dolphins like to swim in front of a ship's bow. ▸ **Antonyms: stern, back**

bow[2] *verb* **1. genuflect, curtsy, salaam, kowtow, kneel, stoop** The actors bowed to the audience after the play. **2. capitulate, submit, surrender, yield, succumb, bend** The government would not bow to the terrorists' demands. ◆ *noun* **obeisance, genuflection, salaam, kowtow, curtsy, nod** A bow is a sign of respect in many cultures.

bowl *noun* **1. dish, container, vessel, basin, tureen, pot** I had a bowl of cereal for breakfast. **2. outdoor theater, amphitheater, stadium, arena, coliseum, forum** The Hollywood Bowl is a famous landmark in Los Angeles.

box[1] *noun* **carton, case, crate, bin, container, package** Oranges and apples are often shipped in cardboard boxes. ◆ *verb* **pack, package, crate, case, encase, load** I helped box up the Christmas decorations after the holidays.

box[2] *noun* **punch, hit, strike, cuff, swat, whack** My friend gave me a playful box on the arm. ◆ *verb* **punch, hit, strike, cuff, swat, buffet** The kitten boxed at a toy stuffed with catnip.

boy *noun* **lad, youngster, youth, child, schoolboy, young man** My grandfather was a boy when he immigrated to America.

boycott *verb* **avoid, eschew, shun, spurn, reject, embargo, strike** The Olympic Games were boycotted by 62 nations in 1980. ◆ *noun* **protest, ban, prohibition, proscription, strike, embargo** Cesar Chavez organized a famous boycott against California's grape growers.

brace *noun* **1. prop, support, reinforcement, strut, underpinning, stay** The braces of the bridge were made of steel. **2. team, pair, couple, duo, twosome** The hunters returned with a brace of quail each. ◆ *verb* **shore up, reinforce, strengthen, support, fortify, steady** We used a board to brace the old fence.

brag *verb* **boast, vaunt, crow, gloat, exaggerate** My grandparents brag about me to their friends.

braid *verb* **plait, interweave, intertwine, weave, twist, interlace** I braid my hair to keep it out of my face when I play soccer.

brake *noun* **check, curb, constraint, restraint, control, rein** Higher interest rates serve to put a brake on inflation. ◆ *verb* **stop, halt, slow, slow down, decelerate, slacken, check** My bicycle tires left skid marks when I braked suddenly. ▸ **Antonyms:** *verb* **start, accelerate**

branch *noun* **1. limb, bough, arm, stem, offshoot, twig** The ice storm broke several branches from trees in our yard. **2. division, extension, department, office, bureau, chapter** My family uses the local branch of our county library. ◆ *verb* **divide, diverge, fork, part, subdivide, diversify** When the trail branched, we checked our map for the right route.

brand *noun* **1. brand name, kind, sort, type, make, variety** What's your favorite brand of cold cereal? **2. mark, sign, symbol, label, imprint, stamp, trademark** The rancher checked the steer's brand to discover its owner. ◆ *verb* **identify, label, mark, tag, characterize, stigmatize, discredit** Historians have branded Benedict Arnold a traitor.

brandish *verb* **flourish, wave, flash, exhibit, flaunt, wield** My sister brandished her new driver's license and offered to take me to a movie.

brash *adjective* **brazen, bold, forward, pushy, presumptuous, impudent** Reporters are often brash in the pursuit of a story. ➤ **Antonyms: respectful, polite, cautious**

bravado *noun* **swagger, bluff, bluster, boastfulness, bragging** The Cowardly Lion in *The Wonderful Wizard of Oz* was full of bravado.

brave *adjective* **courageous, fearless, heroic, valiant, gallant, intrepid** The brave astronauts of *Apollo 13* overcame severe difficulties during their mission. ◆ *verb* **meet, dare, defy, endure, bear, undergo, face** The pioneers braved many dangers in their westward journey. ➤ **Antonyms:** *adjective* **cowardly, fearful**

bravery *noun* **courage, courageousness, heroism, valor, intrepidity, pluck** The police officer was decorated for her bravery. ➤ **Antonyms: cowardice, timidity, fear**

break *verb* **1. shatter, splinter, fracture, destroy, crack, burst** The plate broke when I dropped it. **2. penetrate, pierce, breach, perforate, enter** The attacking soldiers broke through the enemy's lines. **3. end, halt, stop, cease, interrupt, discontinue, suspend** The heavy rains have broken the long drought. **4. renege, betray, violate, disregard, ignore, neglect** It is important not to break promises. **5. cripple, crush, destroy, ruin, overwhelm, tame** The long illness did not break the boy's spirit. **6. surpass, beat, exceed, outdo, top, better, eclipse** Roger Bannister was the first runner to break the four-minute mile. **7. disclose, reveal, divulge, tell, report, communicate** My parents broke the news that we were moving next summer. ◆ *noun* **1. opening, breach, gap, hole, crack, rift, fracture** The sun shone through a break in the clouds. **2. rest, respite, breather, recess, intermission** I took a break after mowing the lawn. **3. good luck, windfall, bargain, opportunity, chance** It was a break to find the computer I wanted on sale. ➤ **Antonyms:** *verb* **1. repair, fix 3. start, begin 4. keep, heed, obey 5. restore, increase 7. conceal, hide**

breathe *verb* **1. inhale, inspire, respire, draw in, exhale, expire** We breathed in the wonderful fragrances at the florist's. **2. utter, say, tell, speak, impart, whisper, confide** I was careful not to breathe his secret to anyone.

breed *verb* **1. procreate, reproduce, propagate, increase, multiply** Because they are sterile hybrids, mules cannot breed offspring. **2. raise, rear, grow, nurture, nourish, cultivate** My aunt breeds Siamese cats. **3. generate,** produce, promote, develop, cause, create The fable *The Fox and the Lion* teaches that familiarity breeds contempt. ◆ *noun* **species, strain, kind, sort, type, variety, manner** The border collie is my favorite breed of dog.

breeze *noun* **gentle wind, light wind, zephyr, draft, waft, air** An afternoon breeze ruffled our window curtains.

brevity *noun* **briefness, shortness, conciseness, succinctness, impermanence** William Shakespeare said that brevity is the soul of wit.

brew *verb* **1. steep, boil, cook, infuse, seethe, ferment** My mother brews a pot of tea each morning. **2. devise, concoct, contrive, hatch, scheme, foment** Computer hackers had brewed a plan to break into government files.

bridge *verb* **cross, cross over, span, go over, join, connect** A fallen tree bridged the stream.

brief *adjective* **1. fleeting, momentary, quick, fast, hasty** Our neighbor came over for a brief visit. **2. concise, short, succinct, terse, brusque, little** I sent my uncle a brief note to thank him for my birthday present. ◆ *verb* **inform, instruct, explain, apprise, advise, prime** Our teacher briefed us on what to study for the test. ➤ **Antonyms:** *adjective* **lengthy, long**

bright *adjective* **1. brilliant, dazzling, shining, blazing, luminous** Visitors to Las Vegas are usually dazzled by the city's bright lights. **2. brilliant, vivid, intense, radiant, shiny, lustrous** I painted my desk bright yellow. **3. brilliant, intelligent, smart, clever, competent, quick** The bright student was only 16 years old when she entered college. **4. happy, cheerful, cheery, sunny, gay, merry** The teacher greeted her class with a bright smile. **5. auspicious, propitious, promising, good, favorable** My school counselor says that I have a bright future ahead of me. ➤ **Antonyms: 1. dim, dark 2. dull, pale 3. slow, dumb, stupid 4. sad, glum, somber**

brilliant *adjective* **1. bright, gleaming, shining, sparkling, glittering, radiant** The motorcycle's chrome wheels had a brilliant shine. **2. bright, intense, vivid, colorful, rich, showy** The highway workers wore brilliant orange vests. **3. gifted, talented, bright, intelligent, smart, quick** Leonardo da Vinci was a brilliant artist, scientist, and inventor. **4. magnificent, outstanding, remarkable, splendid, superb** The composer's new opera is a brilliant success. ➤ **Antonyms: 1. dull, tarnished 2. dull, pale 3. unintelligent 4. poor, bad, mediocre**

brim *noun* **rim, lip, brink, edge, margin, periphery** I filled my glass to the brim with milk. ◆ *verb* **fill, fill up, overflow, run over, flood** Her eyes brimmed with tears.

bring *verb* **1. carry, tote, take, bear, transport, convey** She offered to bring the soda for the party. **2. result in, cause, create, generate, produce** These heavy rains could bring floods. **3. persuade, convince, compel, force, make, induce** Justin cannot bring himself to eat asparagus. **4. attract, draw, lure, entice, beckon, pull** What brings you here? ➻ **Antonyms: 2. prevent, suppress 3. dissuade 4. repulse, repel**

brink *noun* **verge, threshold, edge, borderline** The scientist was on the brink of a breakthrough in his research.

brisk *adjective* **1. energetic, vigorous, lively, strenuous, active, quick** I take my dog for a brisk walk every day. **2. bracing, crisp, invigorating, keen, sharp** The brisk wind made my ears ache. ➻ **Antonyms: 1. sluggish, lethargic, slow**

brittle *adjective* **friable, crumbly, breakable, delicate, crisp** The pages in this old book are brittle. ➻ **Antonyms: flexible, strong**

broach *verb* **bring up, raise, introduce, mention, put forth, advance** Many people find it difficult to broach the subject of AIDS.

broad *adjective* **1. wide, expansive, large, spacious** The explorers had to build a raft to cross the broad river. **2. full, plain, clear, obvious, open, unmistakable** I was so tired that I fell asleep in broad daylight. **3. comprehensive, extensive, far-ranging, overall, general** My friend has a broad range of interests. ➻ **Antonyms: 1. narrow 3. limited, restricted**

broadcast *verb* **1. televise, telecast, air, transmit, beam, show, play** The local cable station will broadcast our high school graduation. **2. spread, disseminate, relay, circulate, announce, advertise** My parents broadcast the happy news that they had adopted another child.

broken *adjective* **1. fractured, cracked, shattered, fragmented, separated, severed** The doctor put my broken arm in a cast. **2. defective, faulty, inoperable, out of order, imperfect** Dad fixed the broken lawn mower. **3. interrupted, discontinuous, intermittent, sporadic, disturbed** The dog's ceaseless barking made for a night of broken sleep. ➻ **Antonyms: 1. whole, intact 2. working, functioning 3. continuous, unbroken**

brood *noun* **clutch, chicks, young, offspring, litter, children** The mother hen clucked anxiously over her brood. ◆ *verb* **worry, fret, agonize, ponder, contemplate, deliberate** I try not to brood over my mistakes.

brook[1] *noun* **creek, stream, river, kill, rill, run** Brendan likes to fish in the brook near his home.

brook[2] *verb* **take, accept, stand, tolerate, abide, countenance** Some people cannot brook criticism.

browse *verb* **1. look through, scan, skim, glance at, survey** I browsed through a magazine while I waited at the dentist's office. **2. graze, eat, feed, pasture, crop, nibble** Deer were browsing in the meadow.

bruise *verb* **hurt, injure, wound, harm, damage, insult** The rugby player bruised his ribs during the game. ◆ *noun* **contusion, discoloration, mark, injury** Bruises sometimes turn green and yellow as they heal.

brush[1] *noun* **sweep, whisk, graze, skim, stroke** I knocked the crumbs from my shirt with a brush of my hand. ◆ *verb* **1. curry, groom, smooth, sweep, clean, polish** I need to brush my dog because she is shedding her winter coat. **2. graze, skim, touch, caress, kiss** A butterfly brushed my arm as it flew past.

brush[2] *noun* **underbrush, thicket, undergrowth, scrub, bushes** Quail build their nests in dense brush.

brush[3] *noun* **encounter, run-in, meeting, confrontation** We had a brush with disaster when a tornado damaged our garage.

brusque *adjective* **curt, abrupt, blunt, gruff, terse, short** I thought his brusque response was rude. ➻ **Antonyms: civil, polite, friendly**

brutal *adjective* **1. cruel, ruthless, merciless, vicious, savage, sadistic** War can bring out brutal behavior in people. **2. hard, harsh, bitter, rough, severe** We have had a brutal winter with abnormally low temperatures. ➻ **Antonyms: 1. gentle, kind, merciful 2. pleasant, mild**

brute *noun* **barbarian, savage, monster, beast, animal** History has characterized Genghis Khan as a brute. ◆ *adjective* **physical, bodily, senseless** I used brute force to open the jar of pickles.

buck *verb* **1. jump, leap, spring, bound, vault, jerk** Young foals like to run and buck. **2. oppose, resist, contest, dispute, challenge** My little brother bucks going to bed at 8 p.m.

bucket *noun* **pail, can, container, bucketful, pailful, tub** We had to use several buckets of water to fully extinguish the campfire.

buckle *noun* **clasp, catch, fastener, clamp, clip** My belt has a brass buckle. ◆ *verb* **1. fasten, hook, secure, latch, connect, attach** Please buckle your seat belt. **2. bend, sag, warp, twist, bulge, curl** The boards on the porch have buckled with age.

bud *noun* **bloom, blossom, flower, shoot, sprout, nucleus** The rosebushes are already showing a few buds. ◆ *verb* **bloom, blossom, flower, sprout, leaf, develop, grow** Most plants bud in the springtime.

buddy *noun* **friend, comrade, companion, chum, pal** Dad and his buddies play golf together most Saturdays.

budge *verb* **move, yield, shift, dislodge, dislocate** I pushed with all my strength, but the door wouldn't budge.

budget *noun* **allotment, allocation, amount, allowance, financial plan** Mom increases our grocery budget during the holidays. ◆ *verb* **allocate, apportion, allot, ration, plan, schedule** My busy schedule demands that I budget my time carefully.

buff *verb* **polish, shine, burnish, rub, smooth** I helped my dad buff the car.

buffet *verb* **batter, hammer, pound, strike, hit, beat** High winds and waves buffeted the seacoast.

build *verb* **1. construct, erect, put up, raise, make, assemble, fabricate** The city is building a new courthouse. **2. create, develop, fashion, form, increase, expand** The resourceful entrepreneur built her business with very little capital. ◆ *noun* **body, physique, frame, figure, shape, form** He has a good build for rock climbing. ◈ **Antonyms:** *verb* **1. demolish, disassemble 2. decrease, diminish**

building *noun* **structure, construction, edifice, erection** The new office building is 30 stories high.

bulge *noun* **lump, swelling, bump, protrusion, protuberance** The bulge under the blanket is our sleeping cat. ◆ *verb* **swell, balloon, distend, stick out, protrude** My suitcase bulged with the many clothes I had packed.

bulk *noun* **1. mass, size, largeness, volume, extent, weight, quantity** We were impressed by the elephant's enormous bulk. **2. main part, greater part, majority, preponderance, body, most** The businessman invested the bulk of his money in the stock market.

bulky *adjective* **1. massive, oversize, immense, large, heavy, stout** The chair was too bulky to fit into our car. **2. unwieldy, cumbersome, unmanageable, ungainly, awkward, clumsy** The mattress was lightweight, but bulky and difficult to maneuver. ◈ **Antonyms: 1. small, little 2. handy, manageable**

bulletin *noun* **report, announcement, message, statement, notice** A news bulletin interrupted the TV show.

bully *noun* **tormentor, persecutor, ruffian, tyrant, despot, intimidator** I stood up to the bully when he picked on my little brother. ◆ *verb* **intimidate, menace, threaten, domineer, hector, tyrannize** Self-confident people are difficult to bully.

bump *verb* **1. hit, collide, knock, crash, strike, carom** I bumped into the door while looking for the light switch. **2. bounce, jounce, jar, jolt, shake, jostle** My bicycle bumped along the rocky path. ◆ *noun* **1. jar, jolt, jounce, thump, shock, knock** We felt a slight bump as the airplane touched ground. **2. lump, swelling, bulge, knob, knot, nodule** A bump formed where the bee had stung me.

bunch *noun* **cluster, bundle, clump, batch, assortment, quantity, group** We bought a bunch of bananas at the market. ◆ *verb* **crowd, cluster, gather, huddle, mass, group** Antelope bunch together for safety when they see a lion. ◈ **Antonyms:** *verb* **disperse, scatter**

bundle *noun* **1. stack, pile, batch, bunch, lot** I carried a bundle of firewood into the house. **2. package, parcel, packet, carton, box, sack** Would you carry these bundles to the car? ◆ *verb* **tie, wrap, bind, truss, package, collect** We bundled up our newspapers for recycling.

burden *noun* **1. load, weight, cargo, freight, pack, payload** Elephants can carry a heavier burden than any other animal. **2. difficulty, hardship, strain, worry, cross** Friends can help lighten the burdens of life. ◆ *verb* **trouble, encumber, afflict, load, saddle, weight** It won't burden me at all to water your plants while you are away.

bureau *noun* **agency, department, office, service, commission, board** I made my vacation plans through our local travel bureau.

bureaucrat *noun* **civil servant, public servant, official, functionary, clerk** Bureaucrats handle the routine work of government.

burgeon *verb* **mushroom, expand, grow, increase, soar, swell** The marketing division reported that sales burgeoned when the new product line was introduced. ◈ **Antonyms: diminish, shrink, dwindle**

burglar *noun* **robber, thief, pilferer, crook, criminal, prowler** The loud alarm frightened away the burglars.

burly *adjective* **muscular, strong, brawny, strapping, hefty, stocky** The movie star had two burly bodyguards. ⬦ **Antonyms: puny, weak, skinny**

burn *verb* **1. blaze, flame, flare, smolder, incinerate, torch** The logs burned cheerfully in the fireplace. **2. char, scorch, sear, singe, blacken** I burned the toast. **3. shine, radiate, blaze, beam, glow, gleam, flash** The neon sign burned brightly all night long. **4. smart, sting, hurt, irritate** This smog is making my eyes burn. **5. fume, seethe, boil, churn** Our team is burning to win the championship.

burnish *verb* **polish, buff, rub, shine, brighten, gloss** I burnished the copper pot until it shone.

burrow *noun* **den, lair, tunnel, nest, warren, cavity, hole** The rabbit slept in its burrow. ⬦ *verb* **dig, tunnel, bore, excavate, trench** Chipmunks have burrowed all over our yard.

burst *verb* **1. explode, pop, blow up, break open, rupture, split** A potato will burst if you bake it without piercing the skin. **2. break out, erupt, gush, fly, rush, run** I burst into laughter when I heard the punch line. ⬦ *noun* **eruption, outbreak, gush, release, explosion** A burst of applause followed each of the magician's tricks.

bury *verb* **1. inter, lay to rest, entomb** I buried the dead bird in our backyard. **2. conceal, cover, hide, immerse, submerge** My history notes had buried the floppy disk I needed. ⬦ **Antonyms: 1. exhume, disinter 2. expose, uncover, reveal**

business *noun* **1. profession, trade, line, occupation, job, work** My dad is in the plumbing business. **2. free enterprise, commerce, trade, industry, manufacturing** Many people find international business an exciting field. **3. establishment, company, firm, enterprise, corporation** My uncle has his own business as a computer consultant. **4. merchandising, selling, transaction, commerce, dealing** This department store does most of its business during the holidays. **5. affair, concern, duty, responsibility, work, interest, matter** I make it my business to stay informed on world events.

bustle *verb* **hurry, hustle, rush, whirl, scurry, scamper** The busy waitress bustled from table to table. ⬦ *noun* **hubbub, commotion, activity, excitement, tumult, agitation** I was overwhelmed by the noisy bustle at the shopping mall during the holidays.

busy *adjective* **1. active, engaged, occupied, involved, absorbed** Homework and after-school activities keep me very busy. **2. full, hectic, hard, strenuous, cluttered, crowded** The marching band had a busy day at the tournament. ⬦ *verb* **occupy, engage, employ, involve, divert** The children busied themselves with making decorations for the Halloween party. ⬦ **Antonyms: *adjective* 1. idle, inactive 2. slow, lazy**

but *conjunction* **however, nevertheless, yet, although, though, except** I thought going to the museum would bore me, but I enjoyed it. ⬦ *preposition* **except, excepting, save, other than, barring, excluding, besides** Everybody in my family likes eggs but me. ⬦ *adverb* **only, merely, solely, just, simply** I couldn't bake a pie yesterday because there was but one apple left.

Word Group

A **button** is a disk or knob used to fasten edges together or to serve as a decoration. **Button** is a very specific term with no true synonyms. Here are some related words:

buckle, catch, clasp, hook, link, snap, stud, zipper

buy *verb* **purchase, pay for, acquire, get, obtain** I want my parents to buy me a horse. ⬦ *noun* **bargain, deal, value, purchase, investment, steal** At 40 dollars, that stereo is a good buy.

by *preposition* **1. near, next to, alongside, beside, close to** She placed a spoon by each bowl. **2. at, before, no later than** I have to be at school by 7 a.m. for swim team practice.

bypass *verb* **go around, skirt, circumvent, avoid, detour** I was able to bypass the line and board the train because I already had my ticket.

Cc

cab *noun* taxi, taxicab, hired car, limousine, hack Mom took a cab to the train station.

cabin *noun* 1. bungalow, cottage, chalet, hut, lodge, log cabin My family rented a lakeside cabin for vacation. 2. berth, compartment, room, stateroom, quarters The ship's steward showed us to our cabin.

cabinet *noun* 1. cupboard, closet, locker, sideboard, shelves, case We have birch cabinets in our kitchen. 2. advisory board, council, committee, advisers, counselors, ministry, bureau The prime minister consulted with her cabinet.

cable *noun* 1. wire, line, chain, rope, strand, guy, cord The cable was made up of many strands of woven wire. 2. cablegram, message, telegram, wire, radiogram My father received a cable from his sister in Germany.

cache *noun* hoard, reservoir, store, stock, inventory, reserve, stockpile, supply Pioneer farmers kept a cache of seed grain for spring planting. ◆ *verb* hide, conceal, secrete, store, lay away, stash, save, bury We watched a gray squirrel cache acorns around our yard.

cackle *verb* laugh, guffaw, chuckle, chortle, giggle, prattle, jabber The cartoon made me cackle. ◆ *noun* guffaw, laugh, laughter, chortle, giggle, chuckle, prattle Her cackle made the people around her laugh also.

café *noun* coffeehouse, coffee shop, restaurant, diner, snack bar, cafeteria, bistro My sister is a waitress in a café.

cage *noun* coop, enclosure, pen, cell, prison, trap, pound I keep my parrot in a large cage. ◆ *verb* confine, enclose, fence in, pen, shut in, wall in, immure, imprison At the San Diego Wild Animal Park, animals are not caged but are allowed to roam free. ◆ **Antonyms:** *verb* free, release

cajole *verb* coax, wheedle, persuade, inveigle, blandish, induce, entice I cajoled my mother into letting me use her makeup.

cake *noun* block, bar, lump, piece, chunk, cube, slab, loaf We keep a cake of hand soap by the bathroom sink. ◆ *verb* solidify, thicken, harden, coagulate, dry, congeal, consolidate, set The old truck's engine was caked with oil.

calamity *noun* disaster, misfortune, cataclysm, catastrophe, tragedy, scourge, trouble The drought was a calamity for the farmers. ◆ **Antonyms:** benefit, blessing

calculate *verb* 1. reckon, compute, determine, figure, add up, measure I calculated the cost of my skateboard and helmet to be 162 dollars. 2. evaluate, appraise, assess, estimate, gauge, judge, predict, surmise No one can truly calculate the effects of global warming. 3. design, intend, plan, devise, mean, fashion, aspire The mayor's speech was calculated to win approval for the school referendum.

caliber *noun* quality, class, grade, merit, stature, value, virtue, worth Her work is of the highest caliber.

call *verb* 1. cry, scream, shout, yell, hail, bawl, bellow, holler, roar I turned around when I heard someone call my name. 2. summon, bid, ask, command, order, hail, demand, require I have to go now because I hear Dad calling me. 3. name, designate, address, label, title, dub, term, tag, christen We call Carlos "Bunny" because he raises rabbits. 4. dial, phone, ring, telephone, call up, buzz Mom called Grandmother to tell her that we would be late. ◆ *noun* 1. cry, whoop, signal, outcry, shout, scream, hail, yell, holler I heard the call of the wild geese as they flew above. 2. attraction, appeal, fascination, allure, charm, draw, enchantment, enticement, lure Jack London's novel *The Call of the Wild* is the story of a dog's adventures during the Alaskan gold rush. 3. need, reason, cause, grounds, justification, occasion, excuse There is no call to worry until we know why they are late.

callous *adjective* unfeeling, unsympathetic, hard, insensitive, heartless, hardhearted, obdurate, tough The team thought the coach was a callous taskmaster. ◆ **Antonyms:** sympathetic, compassionate

calm *adjective* 1. composed, collected, cool, unruffled, possessed, detached, relaxed The class remained calm when the fire alarm went off. 2. motionless, undisturbed, still, quiet, placid, peaceful, serene, tranquil, smooth My friends and I enjoyed rowing on the calm lake. ◆ *noun* 1. tranquility, serenity, composure, self-control, equanimity, self-possession, The brain can emit chemicals that induce calm and well-being. 2. stillness, hush, lull, peace, placidity, quiet The calm of the evening was broken by sirens. ◆ *verb* pacify, quiet, relax, soothe, still, settle, placate, mollify I calm my horse by speaking quietly.

camouflage *noun* **concealment, cover, disguise, mask, screen, front, blind** The soldiers wore camouflage for their maneuvers in the jungle. ◆ *verb* **cloak, conceal, disguise, hide, cover, mask, screen, veil** The politician camouflages her feelings when she talks to reporters. ➡ **Antonyms:** *verb* **expose, reveal**

camp *noun* **campsite, bivouac, encampment, campground, tent, cabin, shelter** The hikers set up their camp near a small lake. ◆ *verb* **encamp, pitch camp, bivouac, quarter, rough it, shelter** We camped in the desert to study the stars.

campaign *noun* **1. operation, maneuver, offensive, action, attack, battle** George Washington's campaigns at Trenton and Princeton greatly boosted American morale. **2. drive, crusade, movement, push, project, effort** Brooke started a campaign to clean up the local park. ◆ *verb* **run, stump, crusade, push, compete, electioneer, contest** The senator is campaigning for reelection.

can *noun* **tin, canister, container, receptacle, vessel, jar** I had a can of vegetable soup for lunch today. ◆ *verb* **tin, jar, preserve, bottle, conserve, put up, keep** Grandmother decided to can most of her peach crop.

cancel *verb* **1. drop, stop, revoke, void, rescind, invalidate, call off, withdraw** Michael canceled his subscription to the dirt bike magazine. **2. offset, balance, negate, counteract, neutralize, nullify, erase** I canceled my low quiz score by doing extra credit. ➡ **Antonyms: 1. keep, maintain**

candid *adjective* **direct, frank, straightforward, open, honest, plainspoken, unreserved, straight, blunt** I was candid with him about his foolish actions. ➡ **Antonyms: evasive, dishonest**

candidate *noun* **contender, nominee, runner, aspirant, applicant, contestant** I am a candidate for class president.

cane *noun* **staff, stave, stick, walking stick, crook, crutch** He used a cane for a period after his knee surgery.

Word Group

A **canine** is a mammal belonging to the dog family. **Canine** is a general term with no true synonyms. Here are some common types of canines:

coyote, dingo, dog, fox, jackal, maned wolf, wolf

canny *adjective* **shrewd, astute, cagey, smart, clever, sharp, artful, careful** That was a canny move to invite both of them to the party. ➡ **Antonyms: inept, dumb, naive**

canon *noun* **code, rule, law, principle, precept, regulation, standard, maxim** The canon of the Old Testament was drawn up between A.D. 90 and 100 by an assembly of rabbis.

canopy *noun* **awning, covering, cover, hood, marquee** My little sister has a lace canopy over her bed.

cant[1] *noun* **slant, slope, pitch, tilt, gradient, incline, list, rake** The steep cant of the cabin's roof allows snow to slide off easily. ◆ *verb* **incline, lean, list, slant, slope, tilt, tip, heel, rake** The old barn cants to the north.

cant[2] *noun* **jargon, lingo, argot, dialect, language, idiom, terminology, vocabulary** Many words that used to be only computer cant have come into everyday use.

cantankerous *adjective* **cranky, cross, quarrelsome, grumpy, irritable, grouchy** My great-uncle says that his arthritis makes him cantankerous. ➡ **Antonyms: agreeable, pleasant**

canter *verb* **gallop, trot, run, lope, race** The horse cantered around the arena.

canvass *verb* **survey, poll, interview, question, scan** We canvassed the school on the issue of a dress code.

canyon *noun* **gorge, ravine, gulch, chasm** Idaho's Snake River has carved a canyon through black basalt.

cap *noun* **1. cover, seal, top, lid, stopper, cork** He twisted the cap off his bottle of water. **2. limit, limitation, restriction, maximum, quota, ceiling, top** Dad's company put a cap on salary increases. ◆ *verb* **cover, seal, top, close, protect, stopper, cork** Please cap the mustard jar when you are through. ➡ **Antonyms:** *verb* **open, unseal**

capability *noun* **ability, capacity, competence, talent, aptitude, potential** She has great capability in both mathematics and English.

capable *adjective* **able, competent, qualified, talented, skilled, fit, adept, expert** Capable teachers are always in demand. ➡ **Antonyms: incapable, incompetent**

capacity *noun* **1. volume, content, room, size, space, limit** The capacity of a typical oil barrel is 55 gallons. **2. talent, aptitude, ability, means, power, potential, strength, might** Lucille Ball had a great capacity for comedy.

cape¹ *noun* **cloak, mantle, wrap, poncho, serape** She wears her gray velvet cape on special occasions.

cape² *noun* **point, headland, promontory, peninsula, spit** Cape Horn is the southernmost tip of South America.

caper *noun* **1. leap, hop, skip, spring, gambol, prance, bound** We watched the capers of the children in the yard. **2. prank, antic, joke, trick, escapade, stunt, lark** Ted's caper was so elaborate it took a week to plan. ◆ *verb* **gambol, cavort, dance, frolic, prance, leap, skip, bound** The lambs capered about in the spring sunshine.

capital *noun* **wealth, assets, cash, funds, money, means, resources** Mom finally has enough capital to start her own business. ◆ *adjective* **excellent, first-rate, splendid, superb, superior, outstanding, extraordinary** That was a capital meal! ◈ **Antonyms:** *adjective* **inferior, poor, bad**

capitulate *verb* **concede, surrender, give in, yield, submit, bow, acquiesce, relent** I had to capitulate when my brother produced proof of his point.

caprice *noun* **whim, impulse, fancy, conceit, vagary, urge** On a caprice, we decided to drive to the ocean.

capricious *adjective* **changeable, erratic, inconsistent, variable, volatile, mercurial, fickle** A capricious wind scattered the leaves in all directions. ◈ **Antonyms: consistent, constant, regular**

capsize *verb* **overturn, turn over, topple, upset, roll, invert** Kayaks are easy to right once they have been capsized.

captain *noun* **head, leader, commander, chief, master, skipper, boss** Jorge is the captain of our football team. ◆ *verb* **command, direct, lead, head, pilot, control, manage** Laura's dream is to captain an airplane someday.

captivate *verb* **fascinate, charm, beguile, bewitch, entrance, dazzle, hypnotize** We were captivated by the laser light show. ◈ **Antonyms: repel, repulse, alienate**

captive *noun* **prisoner, hostage, detainee, slave, internee** Marco Polo spent three years as a captive in Genoa. ◆ *adjective* **confined, imprisoned, incarcerated, caged, bound** The captive tiger paced back and forth. ◈ **Antonyms:** *adjective* **free, unconfined**

capture *verb* **seize, take, grab, secure, win, apprehend, catch, arrest** Soviet troops captured Berlin on May 2, 1945. ◆ *noun* **apprehension, arrest, seizure, possession, occupation** The thief evaded capture for several days but was eventually arrested. ◈ **Antonyms:** *verb* **liberate, release** ◆ *noun* **liberation, release**

car *noun* **auto, automobile, motor vehicle, motorcar, vehicle** I can't wait till I'm old enough to drive a car.

caravan *noun* **cavalcade, convoy, procession, train, band, column** With our two sets of cousins, we formed a caravan to travel to the family reunion.

carcass *noun* **body, corpse, remains, cadaver, skeleton** The eagle carried the carcass of a rabbit in its talons.

cardinal *adjective* **chief, foremost, key, leading, main, major, primary** Wearing a seat belt is a cardinal rule of safety. ◈ **Antonyms: secondary, subordinate**

care *noun* **1. anxiety, worry, concern, burden, trouble, fear, stress** Karla's only care is getting good grades. **2. attention, caution, vigilance, regard, solicitude, heed** The surgeon worked with great care. **3. protection, supervision, charge, keeping, custody, trust, responsibility** Margie left her purse in my care when she went swimming. ◆ *verb* **1. mind, object, protest, disapprove, resent, fret** Would you care if we stopped at the drugstore before going home? **2. desire, like, want, wish, love, enjoy, prize, cherish** Would you care for more ice cream? **3. attend, look after, mind, protect, watch, tend, see to** My cousin is going to care for my cat while I am away. ◈ **Antonyms:** *noun* **2. carelessness, neglect** ◆ *verb* **2. dislike, reject 3. neglect**

career *noun* **profession, occupation, trade, vocation, work, job, business, livelihood** Keegan is planning a career in law enforcement.

carefree *adjective* **lighthearted, untroubled, easygoing, relaxed, cheerful, happy** I enjoyed a carefree day with my friends. ◈ **Antonyms: worried, unhappy, careworn**

careful *adjective* **1. prudent, cautious, wary, watchful, heedful, mindful, circumspect** I made a careful descent down the cluttered stairs. **2. thorough, conscientious, fastidious, meticulous, painstaking, precise** Ben made a careful check through his report for errors. **3. mindful, solicitous, tactful, thoughtful, considerate, sensitive** The usher was careful and gave the bride's grandmother a good seat. ◈ **Antonyms: 1. careless, reckless 2. sloppy 3. inconsiderate**

careless *adjective* **1. negligent, mindless, unthinking, remiss, lax, forgetful, heedless** I was careless and forgot to turn off the iron. **2. inconsiderate, irresponsible, casual,**

indifferent, uncaring, insensitive, tactless The clerk was careless in his attention to the customer. ⚫ **Antonyms: 1. careful, prudent 2. considerate, tactful**

caretaker *noun* **keeper, custodian, guardian, steward, warden, superintendent, attendant** My cousin enjoys her job as caretaker of the seals at the zoo.

cargo *noun* **freight, lading, load, shipment, payload, goods, merchandise** Cargo was loaded into the airplane's hold.

caricature *noun* **parody, satire, burlesque, mockery, cartoon, lampoon** The cartoonist was known for his caricatures of famous people.

carnival *noun* **fair, circus, festival, celebration, jubilee, jamboree, gala** When the carnival comes to town, I'm going to ride the Ferris wheel.

carpet *noun* **1. rug, mat, matting, throw rug, carpeting** We put a new carpet down in the family room. **2. cover, blanket, layer, covering, coat, sheet, mantle** The carpet of new snow showed the footprints of wild animals. ◆ *verb* **cover, coat, blanket, overlay, shroud, cloak, clothe** A thick layer of leaves carpeted our yard.

carriage *noun* **1. buggy, coach, cart, wagon, surrey** My family toured the city in a horse-drawn carriage. **2. posture, stance, bearing, attitude, demeanor, manner** My dancing teacher complimented me on my carriage.

carry *verb* **1. bear, convey, transport, lug, bring, tote, take, haul** I carry my books to school in my backpack. **2. transmit, conduct, convey, transfer, move** Air carries sound waves over long distances. **3. bear, maintain, support, sustain, uphold** In my family, I carry the responsibility of putting out the trash. **4. acquit, act, bear, behave, comport** I admire the way she carried herself through those difficult times. **5. furnish, have, provide, supply, keep, stock, offer, sell** I am looking for a store that carries gerbil food. **6. disseminate, communicate, report, print, broadcast, transmit, publish** This newspaper carries mostly local news.

cart *verb* **transport, haul, carry, convey, move, transfer, take** We can have this lumber for free if we cart it away.

carve *verb* **1. slice, cleave, cut up, split, divide, apportion, allot** The large estate was carved up into smaller parcels of land. **2. sculpt, whittle, cut, form, shape, fashion, engrave** Grandpa carves wooden animals and gives them as gifts.

case[1] *noun* **1. instance, occurrence, event, incident, occasion, situation, example** The police are investigating two cases of vandalism. **2. argument, point, reason, position, plea, cause, proof** You made a good case for getting a new computer.

case[2] *noun* **box, carton, container, crate, package, bin, chest** She bought a case of root beer for the picnic.

cash *noun* **currency, bills, change, coins, money, specie, legal tender** Our neighborhood market accepts only cash or personal checks.

cask *noun* **barrel, keg, vat, tun, drum, hogshead, vessel** At the vineyard, the wine is stored in casks.

cast *verb* **1. throw, hurl, toss, fling, heave, lob, pitch, propel** We need to cast the dice to see who goes first. **2. shed, project, give, send, radiate, throw, spread, sow, scatter** In the early morning, the sun casts long shadows. **3. turn, direct, aim, point, level, set, train** The dog cast a look in my direction but did not bark. **4. form, mold, shape, found, model, sculpt** Bells are usually cast from an alloy of copper and tin. ◆ *noun* **1. throw, toss, fling, heave, lob, hurl, pitch, launch** Lilly caught a fish on her first cast. **2. company, troupe, actors, players, performers** The entire cast attended tonight's rehearsal. **3. hue, shade, tinge, tint, tone** The rocks of the Southwest often have a pink or red cast. **4. impression, form, shape, mold, replica, model** The detectives made a plaster cast of the footprint found at the crime scene. **5. appearance, aspect, expression, look, set, form, quality** Her face had a sorrowful cast.

Word Group

A **castle** is a large building with strong walls and other defenses against attack. **Castle** is a very specific term with no true synonyms. Here are some related words:

bastion, chateau, citadel, donjon, fort, fortress, hold, keep, palace, stronghold, tower

casual *adjective* **1. accidental, spontaneous, unplanned, chance, unexpected, unforeseen, serendipitous** At the mall, I had a casual meeting with one of my friends. **2. unconcerned, nonchalant, cool, calm, blasé, offhand** She was very casual about the loss of her necklace. **3. informal, relaxed, easygoing, simple, familiar** My parents invited some friends over for a casual dinner. ⚫ **Antonyms: 1. planned, intentional 2. serious, concerned 3. formal, official**

casualty *noun* **victim, dead, fatality, injured, wounded, missing** There were over two hundred casualties in yesterday's airplane crash.

cataclysm *noun* **1. upheaval, convulsion, shock, earthquake, eruption, flood** The Great Rift Valley in Africa was formed by a cataclysm in the earth's surface. **2. disaster, calamity, catastrophe, tragedy, ruin** World War II was one of the greatest cataclysms of the 20th century.

catalog *noun* **directory, index, list, register, inventory, schedule, bulletin** Most universities publish catalogs that describe the courses they offer. ◆ *verb* **list, register, record, index, classify, categorize, inventory, file** Ellie cataloged all of the stamps in her collection.

catapult *verb* **hurl, launch, propel, shoot, pitch, fling, throw** I catapulted myself over a fence in my hurry to get home.

catastrophe *noun* **calamity, disaster, tragedy, cataclysm, misfortune, blow, failure** The sinking of *Titanic* was a great catastrophe.

catch *verb* **1. capture, grab, seize, get, take, snare, hold** My cat caught a mouse yesterday. **2. detect, discover, find out, surprise, find** My mother caught me reading by flashlight in bed. **3. contract, get, develop, come down with, acquire, take** I caught the chicken pox from my brother. **4. snag, lodge, stick, fasten, moor, secure, set** I caught my sweater on a branch. **5. attract, draw, pull, beckon, captivate, lure, entice** The display of photography books caught my eye. **6. apprehend, understand, comprehend, follow, get, grasp, see** I caught the meaning of my mother's warning. ◆ *noun* **1. grab, snatch, capture, grasp, seizure, apprehension** Holly made a spectacular catch playing softball today. **2. clasp, latch, bolt, fastener, hook, pin, clip** Dad put a new catch on the cupboard door. **3. pitfall, snag, drawback, hitch, gimmick, trick** The catch to our cheap seats was that they were in the last row. ➡ **Antonyms:** *verb* **1. release, loose 6. misunderstand, misinterpret**

category *noun* **class, group, classification, type, order, set, kind** Our local video store shelves movies by category.

catholic *adjective* **broad, wide, universal, general, inclusive, comprehensive, extensive** My parents' taste in music is catholic. ➡ **Antonyms: narrow, restricted**

cause *noun* **1. origin, source, basis, reason, stimulus, causation, root** Investigators are trying to determine the cause of the fire. **2. ideal, goal, principle, purpose, conviction, movement** My dad contributes time and money to support environmental causes. ◆ *verb* **create, generate, produce, make, effect, precipitate, engender** Yesterday's heavy rain caused some flooding. ➡ **Antonym:** *noun* **1. result**

caustic *adjective* **1. acidic, corrosive, destructive, burning, alkaline** A caustic cleaning agent should remove the stains from the sink. **2. sarcastic, biting, cutting, acerbic, stinging, trenchant** Politicians bore the brunt of the comedian's caustic wit.

caution *noun* **1. alertness, attention, care, carefulness, vigilance, prudence** Mom traversed the icy road with great caution. **2. warning, admonition, notice, alert, alarm, advice, counsel** I read the caution on the bottle of medicine. ◆ *verb* **advise, warn, alert, counsel, admonish, exhort, forewarn** My dance teacher cautions me always to stretch before I practice. ➡ **Antonyms:** *noun* **1. negligence, neglect, carelessness**

cautious *adjective* **alert, attentive, careful, wary, watchful, prudent, deliberate** Marcia was very cautious her first time on the uneven bars. ➡ **Antonyms: careless, rash**

cavalcade *noun* **procession, caravan, cortege, column, parade, train, file** The ambassador's cavalcade included motorcycles and a dozen limousines.

cave *noun* **cavern, grotto, cavity, hole, chamber, hollow, den** Caves are commonly formed by the action of rainwater on soluble rocks.

cavity *noun* **crater, hole, hollow, opening, pit, space, depression, pocket** Erosion from running water has left many small cavities in the soft rock.

cavort *verb* **frolic, play, romp, rollick, prance, caper, dance, gambol** We had fun cavorting on the beach.

cease *verb* **end, halt, quit, stop, terminate, discontinue, leave off, desist** The officer ordered his men to cease firing. ➡ **Antonyms: begin, start, continue**

celebrate *verb* **1. commemorate, honor, observe, keep, dedicate, remember** Passover celebrates the Jews' escape from Egypt and slavery. **2. praise, honor, extol, laud, exalt, glorify, proclaim** John Muir's writings celebrate the beauty of nature. **3. revel, make merry, feast, rejoice, carouse, fete, party** On New Year's Eve, some people celebrate all night long.

celebrated *adjective* **famous, renowned, prominent, eminent, illustrious, acclaimed** I interviewed the celebrated athlete for our school paper. ➡ **Antonyms: unknown, obscure**

celebration *noun* **party, fete, gala, festival, jubilee** We had a celebration when my brother graduated from college.

celebrity *noun* **1. star, superstar, dignitary, notable, hero, luminary, VIP** Allison hopes to see some celebrities when she visits Hollywood. **2. fame, renown, repute, prominence, eminence, notability, stardom, notoriety** He has achieved celebrity as our most popular local DJ. ➡ **Antonyms: 2. obscurity, oblivion**

celestial *adjective* **heavenly, divine, spiritual, sublime, transcendental** In his essays collected as *The American Crisis*, Thomas Paine calls freedom "a celestial article."

celibate *adjective* **chaste, virginal, abstinent, unwed, unmarried** She joined a religious order that requires its members to be celibate.

cell *noun* **room, chamber, compartment, cubicle, stall, niche, cage** The monks live in small cells in the monastery.

cellar *noun* **basement, storeroom, underground room, vault** We like to play board games in the cellar on rainy days.

cement *noun* **concrete, mortar, adhesive, glue** Dad used cement to anchor our basketball hoop. ◆ *verb* **1. bond, glue, fasten, fix, stick, set, bind, fuse** I cemented the lamp's broken pieces back together. **2. strengthen, solidify, reinforce, fortify, seal, stabilize** An annual reunion helps to cement our family bonds. ➡ **Antonyms: *verb* 1. disconnect, separate 2. weaken, loosen**

cemetery *noun* **burial ground, graveyard, resting place, catacomb, tomb** We went to the cemetery to visit my great-grandfather's grave.

censor *verb* **cut, edit, expurgate, remove, restrict, delete, suppress** The excessively violent movie was censored before release.

censure *noun* **criticism, disapproval, rebuke, reproof, castigation, remonstrance, condemnation** In Hawthorne's novel *The Scarlet Letter*, Hester Prynne suffers from the censure of the villagers. ◆ *verb* **criticize, condemn, rebuke, castigate, reprimand, upbraid, berate,** My coach censured me for being late to practice all week. ➡ **Antonyms: *noun* praise, admiration ◆ *verb* praise, commend**

center *noun* **1. core, inside, interior, middle, heart, nucleus** I prefer chocolate candies that have soft centers. **2. hub, focus, focal point, crux, cynosure, heart, soul** The farmers' market is a center of activity every Saturday. ◆ *verb* **focus, concentrate, converge, consolidate, gather, unite**

I centered my report on the evolution of early humans. ➡ **Antonyms: *noun* 1. exterior, outside**

central *adjective* **1. middle, midway, inside, interior, mid, equidistant, inner** Mom grew up on a farm in the central part of our state. **2. chief, main, prime, principal, key, leading, head** Our local librarian said that the central library has the book that I want. **3. essential, pivotal, principal, fundamental, basic, significant** A central principle of American government is the system of checks and balances. ➡ **Antonyms: 1. exterior, outside 2. & 3. ancillary, secondary, peripheral**

cerebral *adjective* **intellectual, analytical, thoughtful, thinking, mental** Chess and bridge are both considered to be cerebral games.

ceremonious *adjective* **formal, dignified, stately, solemn, majestic, proper** The crowning of Elizabeth II as queen of Great Britain was a very ceremonious occasion. ➡ **Antonyms: informal, unceremonious**

ceremony *noun* **1. celebration, rite, ritual, service, observance, tradition** I attended my uncle's wedding ceremony. **2. ceremoniousness, formality, propriety, pomp, solemnity, form** The graduates accepted their diplomas with ceremony.

certain *adjective* **1. established, definite, particular, precise, specific, set, fixed** There is a certain time of year that is best for planting sweet peas. **2. indisputable, undeniable, sure, doubtless, absolute, incontrovertible, irrefutable, unquestionable** It is certain that you have to be 16 before you can apply for a driver's license. **3. sure, definite, assured, guaranteed, inevitable, unerring, trustworthy** It is certain that we are going to have a test on Tuesday. **4. confident, positive, definite, sure, convinced, assured, fixed** I am absolutely certain that I do not want anchovies on my pizza. ➡ **Antonyms: 1. vague, uncertain 3. questionable 4. undecided, open**

certainly *adverb* **definitely, positively, surely, undoubtedly, absolutely, unquestionably** Juan said that he would certainly attend my birthday party.

certainty *noun* **1. sureness, certitude, conviction, confidence, assurance, faith, trust** Her certainty made me believe her story. **2. fact, reality, actuality, surety, verity, truth** It is a certainty that the sun rises every morning. ➡ **Antonyms: 1. doubt, skepticism 2. uncertainty**

certificate *noun* **voucher, document, deed, paper, authorization, affidavit** I received a gift certificate to my favorite clothing store.

certify *verb* confirm, verify, affirm, corroborate, substantiate, authenticate, guarantee, vouchsafe I had to certify my age with a copy of my birth certificate.

chafe *verb* 1. rub, irritate, inflame, burn, abrade, scrape My new shoes chafe my feet. 2. annoy, irritate, irk, aggravate, nettle, peeve, provoke It chafes me to have to go to bed when my little brother does. ◆ **Antonyms:** 1. soothe 2. mollify, pacify

chagrin *noun* embarrassment, discomposure, dismay, frustration, humiliation, shame, mortification He felt chagrin at raising his hand then forgetting the answer. ◆ *verb* embarrass, abash, upset, dismay, humiliate, mortify, disconcert I was chagrined to discover that my socks didn't match. ◆ **Antonyms:** *noun* satisfaction, gratification ◆ *verb* please, satisfy

chain *noun* 1. links, cable, braid, rope, leash, line He bought a length of chain to secure his bicycle. 2. sequence, series, line, string, succession, train, course The dog's entrance at the cat show started the unfortunate chain of events. 3. restraint, constriction, bond, fetter, manacle, shackle Education helps to break the chains of ignorance. ◆ *verb* fasten, hold, secure, tie, bind, moor, tether I chained my bicycle to a lamppost before going into the store. ◆ **Antonyms:** *verb* unfasten, untie, free

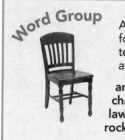

Word Group

A **chair** is a piece of furniture built for sitting on. **Chair** is a general term with no true synonyms. Here are some different kinds of chairs:

armchair, director's chair, easy chair, folding chair, highchair, lawn chair, love seat, recliner, rocker, stool, throne

chairperson *noun* chair, chairman, chairwoman, director, leader, head My mother is the chairperson of our town's school board.

challenge *noun* 1. dare, bid, call, invitation, defiance, threat Lauren accepted Austin's challenge to a rematch on the tennis court. 2. difficulty, problem, test, trial, struggle My cousin enjoys the challenges of rock climbing. ◆ *verb* 1. dare, bid, call, summon, invite, call out, provoke Sam challenged Michael to a game of chess after school. 2. question, dispute, contest, defy, take exception to I challenged my mother's decision not to let me go to the dance. 3. stimulate, spur, stir, arouse, excite, animate, test Putting the new jigsaw puzzle together challenged us for several hours.

chamber *noun* room, apartment, cell, antechamber, alcove, boudoir, cubicle We toured the chambers of the magnificent old castle.

champion *noun* winner, victor, conqueror, hero, leader, master, paragon The world champion earned three gold medals at the Olympics. ◆ *verb* defend, advocate, plead, uphold, back, endorse, support The lawyer championed his client's cause. ◆ *adjective* top, premier, first, best, chief, splendid, greatest, superior We raise champion poodles.

chance *noun* 1. accident, luck, coincidence, happenstance, fate, fortune, providence Wilhelm Roentgen discovered x-rays by chance. 2. likelihood, possibility, probability, prospect, odds There's a good chance that school will be canceled due to snow. 3. opportunity, moment, break, occasion, opening, time Please give me a call when you have a chance. 4. risk, gamble, danger, hazard, liability, jeopardy, peril Police officers must guard against taking unnecessary chances. ◆ *adjective* accidental, unplanned, spontaneous, random, inadvertent, unforeseen, lucky, fortunate I had a chance meeting with a friend at the grocery store. ◆ *verb* 1. happen, fall, occur, result, transpire, come I chanced upon my old report cards in a box in the attic. 2. attempt, hazard, risk, try, venture, dare, tackle, undertake Matt decided to chance skiing down the steep slope.

change *verb* 1. alter, modify, vary, adapt, adjust, reorganize, mutate I changed my mind about going out and decided to stay home. 2. exchange, replace, substitute, swap, trade, convert My friend asked us to wait while she changed her clothes. ◆ *noun* 1. alteration, modification, transition, shift, mutation, metamorphosis I couldn't find enough information, so I made a change in my report topic. 2. variation, break, difference, switch, variety, novelty, turnabout We wanted a vacation that was a change from camping. ◆ **Antonyms:** *verb* 1. keep, maintain, remain

channel *noun* 1. course, route, passage, streambed, waterway, trench, gutter The main channel of the Mississippi River is more than 2,300 miles long. 2. furrow, groove, trench, duct, conduit, passage, tube My dad used a router to make a channel in the wood. 3. means, way, course, path, route, vehicle, avenue The underground railroad was a channel to freedom for thousands of slaves. ◆ *verb* 1. abrade, erode, eat, wear, corrode, wear down A glacier can channel out a valley at the rate of 45 meters a day. 2. direct, guide, funnel, steer, route, send, conduct Traffic through the construction zone was channeled to one lane.

chant *noun* plainsong, hymn, psalm, melody, song, recitative The monks include chants as part of their morning service. ◆ *verb* **intone, vocalize, carol, sing** The warriors chanted to the beat of the drums.

chaos *noun* **confusion, disorder, tumult, turmoil, pandemonium, uproar, anarchy, bedlam** There is always chaos during a battle. ◗ **Antonyms: calm, order**

chaperon *noun* **escort, attendant, guardian, companion, overseer** Parents and teachers act as chaperons at our school dances. ◆ *verb* **escort, accompany, shepherd, attend, oversee, safeguard** My parents agreed to help chaperon our choir tour.

chapter *noun* **1. section, division, part, unit, portion, passage** The first chapter whetted my appetite for the rest of the book. **2. time, period, episode, phase, stage, era, age** The time we spent with our relatives in Italy was a memorable chapter in my life. **3. branch, group, unit, affiliate, division, member, subdivision** The Four-H Club has local chapters all over the country.

char *verb* **burn, scorch, singe, sear, torch, cook, heat** I charred the hamburgers by leaving them on the grill too long.

character *noun* **1. temperament, nature, personality, disposition, makeup, essence** Many psychologists believe that a person's character is formed before the age of 7. **2. honor, integrity, morality, principle, rectitude, respectability, courage** I think a political leader should be a person of strong character. **3. hero, heroine, antagonist, player, part, role** Petra will play one of the characters in the school play. **4. eccentric, oddball, personality, oddity, clown, freak, original** It's refreshing to talk to our neighbor because he is such a character.

characteristic *adjective* **distinctive, particular, specific, distinguishing, illustrative, individual, typical** Snow is characteristic of winter. ◆ *noun* **attribute, feature, quality, trait, property, trademark, idiosyncrasy** One characteristic of water is that it boils at 212°F (100°C). ◗ **Antonyms:** *adjective* **unusual, aberrant**

charge *verb* **1. assess, bill, ask, demand, require, invoice, debit** David charges a minimum of ten dollars for mowing a lawn. **2. attack, assault, storm, rush, set on, assail, beset** The troops charged the enemy from both the air and the sea. **3. accuse, cite, indict, blame, arraign** The suspect was charged with one count of armed robbery. **4. adjure, enjoin, exhort, bid, instruct, tell, direct** My science teacher charged me to bring my grade up this term. ◆ *noun* **1. cost, expense, fee, price, amount, payment, rate** There was no additional charge to have our new stove delivered. **2. control, care, custody, protection, responsibility, guardianship, jurisdiction** My brothers were in my charge for the afternoon.

3. duty, task, assignment, order, command, burden, obligation I was given the charge of returning the library books. **4. accusation, allegation, complaint, indictment, imputation, denunciation** The suspect was arrested on a charge of shoplifting. **5. assault, attack, rush, offensive, blitz, onslaught, raid** A cavalry charge routed the enemy soldiers. ◗ **Antonyms:** *verb* **2. retreat, withdraw 3. acquit, absolve** ◆ *noun* **5. retreat, withdrawal**

charity *noun* **1. goodwill, tolerance, kindness, benevolence, grace, generosity, magnanimity** Our neighbor treated us with charity despite the fact we had broken his window. **2. philanthropy, largesse, contribution, donation, alms, beneficence** The family's charity was well known in the community.

charm *noun* **1. appeal, allure, elegance, attractiveness, fascination, refinement** My uncle's log cabin is small, but it has a lot of charm. **2. magic spell, spell, magic, incantation, enchantment, sorcery, witchery** We recited a charm over the seeds to make them grow quickly. **3. amulet, talisman, good-luck piece, fetish, mascot, trinket** Horseshoes, four-leaf clovers, and rabbits' feet are all considered to be lucky charms. ◆ *verb* **captivate, delight, enthrall, fascinate, thrill, bewitch, hypnotize** The clown's antics charmed everyone. ◗ **Antonyms:** *verb* **repulse, repel**

charming *adjective* **attractive, engaging, delightful, captivating, enchanting winsome** Ellen has a charming smile. ◗ **Antonyms: unpleasant, offensive**

chart *noun* **table, graph, illustration, tabulation, outline, visual aid, map** We made a chart of student birthdays by month. ◆ *verb* **graph, plot, map, outline, show, record, project** The club treasurer charted the results of this year's fundraising efforts.

charter *noun* **grant, certificate, deed, agreement, contract, document, constitution, code** William Penn received charters from Charles II for what is now Pennsylvania and Delaware. ◆ *verb* **rent, hire, lease, engage, contract, employ** The company chartered a boat to carry employees to the annual picnic.

chase *verb* **1. run after, pursue, follow, trail, hunt, seek** My dog loves to chase tennis balls. **2. drive away, evict, oust, disperse, scatter, rout, dispel** The lady chased us away from her apple trees. ◆ *noun* **pursuit, race, quest, hunt, search** The police caught the car thief after a long, dangerous chase.

chasm *noun* **1. gorge, abyss, crevasse, fissure, cleft, breach, gulf** We marveled at the steepness and depth of the huge chasm. **2. schism, rift, breach, separation, split, difference, divergence** Our argument created quite a chasm between us.

chaste *adjective* **celibate, abstinent, virginal, virtuous, pure, innocent** Several of my friends and I have made a decision to remain chaste until we are married. ➡ **Antonyms: lewd, wanton**

chastise *verb* **criticize, scold, admonish, reprimand, rebuke, chasten, punish** My father chastised me for not letting him know I would be late. ➡ **Antonyms: praise, compliment, commend**

chat *verb* **converse, talk, chitchat, discuss, gossip, chatter, visit** My mom chatted with the clerk who rang up our order. ◆ *noun* **conversation, talk, discussion, gossip, dialogue, visit** Aunt Helene stopped by for a little chat.

chatter *verb* **prattle, jabber, babble, prate, gossip, blather** The children chattered happily as they played in the backyard. ◆ *noun* **chitchat, gossip, prattle, palaver, babble, blather** The busy café was filled with lunchtime chatter.

cheap *adjective* **1. inexpensive, low-cost, economical, reasonable, budget, sale** This restaurant has great meals at cheap prices. **2. unearned, undeserved, easy, facile, painless** I made a careless play and allowed my opponent a cheap victory. **3. inferior, mediocre, poor, shabby, shoddy, worthless, second-rate** This cheap pen keeps leaking ink. **4. stingy, miserly, mean, tight, parsimonious, niggardly, tightfisted** My friends thought I was being cheap, but I'm saving up to buy a computer. ➡ **Antonyms:** *adjective* **1. costly, expensive 2. hard, difficult 3. excellent, superior 4. generous**

cheat *verb* **1. swindle, trick, defraud, deceive, fool, mislead, bilk** The dishonest art dealer cheated his customers by selling them forgeries. **2. elude, escape, frustrate, thwart, foil, beat, defeat** You can't cheat fate. ◆ *noun* **swindler, charlatan, trickster, crook, knave, fake, impostor** The salesman turned out to be a cheat.

check *verb* **1. curb, halt, restrain, stop, impede, limit, prevent** A sandbag dike checked the rising floodwaters. **2. inspect, look over, examine, survey, review, compare, test** We checked our list to make sure we had not forgotten anything. **3. tick, mark, note, tally, record, register** The teacher checked off the names of the students as they arrived. **4. correspond, agree, match, conform, mesh, jibe, tally, coincide** Does the receipt check with the items we purchased? ◆ *noun* **1. control, restraint, harness, curb, limit, constraint, restriction** Elsie counts to ten when she's angry to keep her temper in check. **2. examination, inspection,**

investigation, search, review, scrutiny The security guard made a routine check of the building. **3. tick, mark, dash, score, line, cross, stroke** The scorekeeper made a check for every basket made. **4. bill, tab, receipt, statement, invoice, ticket, stub** The waiter brought our check when we had finished our meal. ➡ **Antonyms:** *verb* **1. accelerate, begin 2. ignore, overlook 4. contradict, disagree**

cheer *verb* **1. root, applaud, shout, yell, praise, hail, hurrah** The crowd cheered when the home team scored a goal. **2. gladden, hearten, comfort, console, encourage, buoy, uplift** My friend tried to cheer me when I was sick. ◆ *noun* **1. cry, shout, yell, applause, acclamation, hurrah** The audience broke into cheers when the band took the stage. **2. cheerfulness, delight, gladness, happiness, joy, merriment, liveliness** My cousin's visits always fill me with cheer. ➡ **Antonyms:** *verb* **2. depress, sadden** ◆ *noun* **2. sadness, gloom**

cheerful *adjective* **gay, glad, happy, joyful, merry, pleasant, lighthearted** All the students and teachers were in a cheerful mood on the last day of school. ➡ **Antonyms: depressed, sad**

cherish *verb* **adore, love, revere, treasure, value, appreciate, prize** I cherish my family more than anything else. ➡ **Antonyms: dislike, hate**

chest *noun* **1. breast, bosom, ribs, bust, trunk, thorax** My brother does pushups every day to strengthen his arms and chest. **2. box, crate, trunk, carton, container, coffer, bureau** My little brother keeps his toys in a large wooden chest.

chew *verb* **bite, chomp, gnaw, munch, nibble, champ, masticate** My puppy likes to chew on sticks.

chic *adjective* **stylish, fashionable, smart, swank, elegant, sophisticated** My mother wore a chic dress to the cocktail party. ➡ **Antonyms: passé, dowdy, shabby**

chide *verb* **scold, reproach, reprove, reprimand, admonish, criticize** It amuses me to hear my grandmother chide my mother. ➡ **Antonyms: praise, compliment**

chief *noun* **head, director, captain, leader, ruler, boss, supervisor** The chief of our local fire department gave us a talk on fire safety. ◆ *adjective* **1. head, leading, first, top, foremost, ranking** My dad talked to the chief mechanic about repairing our car. **2. key, essential, principal, main, primary, highest** Dad says that his chief concern is the welfare of our family. ➡ **Antonyms:** *noun* **subordinate, servant** ◆ *adjective* **1. subordinate 2. least, lowest**

chiefly *adverb* **essentially, mainly, mostly, primarily, especially, generally** Our house is made chiefly of wood.

child *noun* **1. juvenile, youngster, youth, toddler, tyke, kid, minor** Mozart first achieved fame when he was a 4-year-old child. **2. descendant, offspring, progeny, scion, heir, daughter, son** Francine is her parents' only child. ➽ **Antonyms: 1. adult, grownup 2. parent**

chill *noun* **cold, coldness, coolness, iciness, chilliness, nip** There was a chill in the cabin until we got a fire going. ◆ *adjective* **1. chilly, cold, cool, frigid, icy, numbing, chilling, raw** When autumn days turn chill, winter is close at hand. **2. unfriendly, aloof, cool, hostile, forbidding, stony** His unconvincing excuse received a chill reaction. ◆ *verb* **1. cool, refrigerate, freeze, ice, congeal** Pudding should be chilled before it is served. **2. frighten, scare, terrify, horrify, unnerve, disquiet** The scary ghost story chilled everyone. **3. cloud, dampen, depress, dash, dishearten, discourage** The audience's unfavorable response chilled the actor's enthusiasm. ➽ **Antonyms:** *noun* **heat, warmth** ◆ *adjective* **1. hot, warm 2. friendly, encouraging** ◆ *verb* **1. heat, warm 2. comfort, cheer**

chilly *adjective* **1. chill, cold, cool, icy, frigid, nippy** The day was chilly, so I wore a sweater to school. **2. unfriendly, distant, aloof, unresponsive, unreceptive, cold, remote, unenthusiastic** The tennis rivals gave each other a chilly greeting before the match began. ➽ **Antonyms: 1. hot, warm 2. friendly, cordial**

chime *verb* **ring, sound, peal, toll, jingle, strike, bong** The bell in the tower chimed the hour.

chintzy *adjective* **cheap, gaudy, garish, tacky, shabby, seedy** I know this shirt is chintzy, but I like the color. ➽ **Antonyms: elegant, expensive, stylish**

chip *noun* **1. fragment, piece, scrap, bit, flake, shaving, shard** I used some wood chips to start the fire. **2. dent, ding, scratch, gash, nick, notch** I used a wood filler to repair the chip in this table. ◆ *verb* **1. nick, notch, break, crack, damage** I accidentally chipped one of Mom's teacups. **2. chisel, carve, cut away, whittle, cut, flake, shape, hew** The sculptor carefully chipped the stone into the shape he wanted.

chirp *verb* **peep, cheep, tweet, twitter, warble, sing** Each morning I hear the birds chirping outside my window.

chisel *verb* **1. carve, sculpt, cut, hew, engrave, form, fashion** The names on these old tombstones were chiseled by hand. **2. swindle, deceive, cheat, bilk, trick, gyp, defraud** He tried to chisel money out of my grandmother with an insurance scam.

chivalrous *adjective* **gallant, honorable, noble, courageous, valiant, gentlemanly, true** My sister wants a boyfriend who is chivalrous. ➽ **Antonyms: rude, boorish, cowardly**

chivalry *noun* **gallantry, nobility, honor, courage, bravery, valor, virtuousness** The legendary King Arthur and his knights were renowned for their chivalry. ➽ **Antonyms: cowardice, rudeness, boorishness**

choice *noun* **pick, selection, preference, option, alternative, possibility, decision** You have your choice of apple or pumpkin pie for dessert. ◆ *adjective* **1. excellent, fine, select, special, first-class, superior, exceptional** We had choice seats for the concert. **2. careful, exact, deliberate, considered, select, appropriate, fitting** She stated her opinion in a few choice words. ➽ **Antonyms:** *adjective* **1. average, ordinary, common 2. careless, unfitting, random**

choke *verb* **1. strangle, smother, suffocate, stifle, throttle, asphyxiate, gag** I loosened my tie because I felt like it was choking me. **2. block, clog, congest, close, obstruct, plug, occlude** The freeway was choked with traffic. ➽ **Antonyms:** *verb* **2. clear, open**

choose *verb* **1. pick, select, decide, determine, elect, name** We need to choose sides before we can start the game. **2. prefer, want, wish, opt, decide, desire** I would choose chocolate cake, not fruit, for dessert. ➽ **Antonyms: 1. reject, refuse 2. forgo, forbear**

chop *verb* **cut, hack, sever, slice, split, mince, hew, fell** I chopped onions for the meatloaf. ◆ *noun* **blow, hit, punch, stroke, cut, whack, crack** The karate master broke a board with a single chop of his hand.

chore *noun* **1. duty, job, task, work, responsibility, housework** My daily chores include making my bed and setting the dinner table. **2. effort, drudgery, nuisance, burden, bother, grind** Weeding the garden can be a real chore. ➽ **Antonyms: 2. pleasure, indulgence**

chorus *noun* **1. choir, chorale, singing group, singers, ensemble, vocalists** Our women's chorus has 12 members. **2. refrain, chorale, verse, theme, melody, tune, song** We liked the chorus so much that we sang it again.

chronic *adjective* **1. constant, continual, persistent, enduring, lingering, abiding, protracted** His smoking habit has given him a chronic cough. **2. habitual, routine,**

confirmed, inveterate, frequent, perpetual She is a chronic complainer. ➻ **Antonyms: 1. brief, temporary 2. occasional, infrequent**

chronicle *noun* **record, history, report, narrative, journal, log** This book is a chronicle of the events that led to the American Revolution. ◆ *verb* **record, log, document, report, recount, narrate** My social studies report chronicles the significant political events of this decade.

chubby *adjective* **plump, fat, heavy, stocky, stout, pudgy, overweight** Our cat has grown chubby with age. ➻ **Antonyms: lean, thin, skinny**

chuckle *verb* **chortle, giggle, laugh, snicker, smile** She chuckled as she read the Sunday comics. ◆ *noun* **chortle, giggle, laugh, snicker, smile** I usually get a chuckle out of Grandpa's corny jokes.

chum *noun* **buddy, friend, pal, companion, crony, playmate** My dad has known several of his chums since grade school.

church *noun* **1. house of worship, cathedral, chapel, temple, tabernacle, synagogue, mosque** Melinda attends a Bible study class at her church. **2. religious order, religion, faith, denomination, sect, belief, order** The pope is the head of the Roman Catholic Church.

churn *verb* **stir, beat, whip, shake, agitate, toss, swirl, convulse** My great-grandmother used to churn her own butter.

chute *noun* **trough, slide, ramp, incline, shaft, channel, passageway** Our bags were sent down the luggage chute to be loaded onto the plane.

circle *noun* **1. ring, hoop, loop, disk, orbit, circuit, circumference** The teacher had us arrange our desks in a circle. **2. clique, set, coterie, group, crowd, gang, bunch, society** I really enjoy my circle of friends. ◆ *verb* **loop, ring, enclose, surround, encircle, belt** I circled the correct answers on my math test.

circuit *noun* **1. orbit, path, revolution, circle, circumference, ring** The moon takes 27.3 days to complete its circuit around Earth. **2. route, path, beat, round, district, region, course** The security guard walks the same circuit every night.

circular *adjective* **round, curved, arched, spherical, looped, coiled, globular** In some parts of the world, houses are circular in shape.

circulate *verb* **1. move, flow, swirl, turn, circle, rotate, spin** I turned on a fan to circulate the air. **2. distribute, pass, spread, disseminate, disperse** Victoria circulated a petition to change her school's dress code.

circulation *noun* **flow, motion, dispersal, distribution, dissemination, spread, rotation** Regular exercise promotes healthy circulation of the blood.

circumference *noun* **perimeter, circuit, periphery, boundary, bounds, limits, outline** We walked the entire circumference of the lake.

circumstance *noun* **fact, event, detail, factor, particular, context, condition** I tried to explain the circumstances under which I was given a detention.

circumstantial *adjective* **secondary, unessential, nonessential, extraneous, incidental, unimportant** These books are important to my report, but that one is circumstantial. ➻ **Antonyms: intrinsic, important**

circumvent *verb* **avoid, bypass, evade, escape, elude, detour, sidestep** I sneaked in the back door to circumvent comments on my late arrival. ➻ **Antonyms: face, confront**

citadel *noun* **fortress, stronghold, fort, bastion, keep** The villagers all took refuge in the citadel.

cite *verb* **1. quote, refer to, name, mention, allude to, note, specify, repeat** I cited Shakespeare twice during my speech. **2. commend, honor, recognize, acknowledge, laud, praise** Several students were cited for their volunteer activities in the community. ➻ **Antonyms: 2. condemn, criticize, ignore**

citizen *noun* **national, inhabitant, native, resident, subject, denizen, civilian** Are you a citizen of the United States? ➻ **Antonyms: foreigner, alien**

city *noun* **metropolis, municipality, town, megalopolis, borough, burg** I would rather live in a big city than a small town.

civic *adjective* **civil, communal, public, local, municipal, metropolitan, civilian** We attended the opening ceremonies at our new civic center.

civil *adjective* **1. civic, communal, public, civilian, political, national** In the United States, civil liberties are protected by law. **2. cordial, courteous, polite, kind, pleasant, decent** He gave a civil answer to the rude question. ➻ **Antonyms: 2. impolite, rude**

civilization *noun* **1. refinement, development, edification, humanization, cultivation, enlightenment** The ancient Greeks attained a high degree of civilization. **2. culture, society, community, nation, people, polity** My brother is taking a class in western civilization at the junior college. ➧ **Antonyms: 1. savagery, barbarism**

claim *verb* **1. demand, occupy, require, take, call for, deserve** My after-school activities claim much of my free time. **2. assert, declare, contend, maintain, profess, believe** My friend claims that one of her ancestors was an African king. ◆ *noun* **1. right, title, call, interest, stake, demand, suit** My brother made a claim for the last piece of pie. **2. assertion, allegation, declaration, statement, avowal** This product makes the claim that it can remove all fabric stains. ➧ **Antonyms: verb 2. deny, disavow ◆ noun 2. disavowal, denial**

clamor *noun* **commotion, din, noise, uproar, racket, disturbance** The clamor from our neighbor's party kept me awake. ◆ *verb* **bawl, holler, howl, roar, shout, yell, demand** The audience clamored for another song. ➧ **Antonyms: noun calm, quiet, tranquility**

clamp *noun* **clip, vice, clasp, brace, fastener, bracket, hold** A clamp held the two boards together until the glue had dried. ◆ *verb* **fasten, clasp, grip, make fast, clench, secure** I clamped a reading light onto my headboard.

clan *noun* **family, tribe, house, relatives, kin, lineage** Most Scottish clans have their own distinctive tartan.

clandestine *adjective* **secret, surreptitious, covert, hidden, furtive, unlawful** Romeo and Juliet were married in a clandestine ceremony. ➧ **Antonyms: open, overt, public**

clang *verb* **clank, ring, chime, jangle, resound, reverberate** The cowbells clanged as the cattle plodded towards the barn. ◆ *noun* **clank, ring, chime, clangor, clash, din** The wrench hit the garage floor with a loud clang.

clap *verb* **1. applaud, cheer, root, acclaim, approve** Everyone clapped wildly when the diver completed his daring 90-foot jump. **2. pat, slap, smack, strike, hit, whack** The whole team clapped Kyle on the back after he scored the winning touchdown. ◆ *noun* **1. peal, report, boom, crack, thunderclap** The thunder's loud clap came just seconds after the flash of lightning. **2. pat, slap, smack, thwack, hit** My friend gave me a clap on my shoulder. ➧ **Antonyms: verb 1. boo, hiss, heckle**

clarify *verb* **clear up, explain, elucidate, explicate, simplify, define** Seeing our looks of confusion, the coach clarified his instructions. ➧ **Antonyms: obscure, muddle, confuse**

clash *verb* **1. bang, clatter, jangle, rattle, crash, clang** The cymbals clashed loudly at the finale. **2. differ, disagree, conflict, argue, quarrel, battle** My dad and I sometimes clash over how I wear my hair. ◆ *noun* **1. disagreement, conflict, difference, discord, skirmish** There is sure to be a clash of opinions on that issue. **2. crash, clang, rattle, jangle, clatter, clangor** The cymbal's loud clash startled the audience. ➧ **Antonyms: verb 2. agree, concur ◆ noun 1. agreement, harmony**

clasp *noun* **1. hook, fastener, snap, catch, clip, clamp** Please fasten the clasp of my necklace for me. **2. grasp, grip, hold, embrace, hug, clutch** I held my little brother's hand in a firm clasp as we crossed the street. ◆ *verb* **1. fasten, hook, secure, hold, clip, pin, clamp** The door clasped shut behind me. **2. grasp, grip, embrace, hold, clench, hug, clutch** I clasped my nose and jumped off the dock into the water.

class *noun* **1. category, classification, order, set, division, kind, sort** Dinosaurs fall into two classes based on the shape of their hip bones. **2. rank, grade, level, stratum, caste, bracket, station** My family considers itself to be part of the middle class. **3. course, subject, session, grade, lecture, section** My favorite class is English. **4. style, refinement, elegance, flair, taste** The students conducted themselves with class at the school party. ◆ *verb* **arrange, categorize, classify, group, rank, sort** Whales and gorillas would be classed together as mammals.

classic *adjective* **exemplary, ideal, model, vintage, classical, typical** The Model T Ford is a classic early automobile. ◆ *noun* **masterpiece, masterwork, ideal, paragon, archetype, standard** Orson Welles's *Citizen Kane* is considered to be a motion-picture classic. ➧ **Antonyms: adjective poor, unknown, atypical**

classify *verb* **arrange, class, organize, rank, sort, divide** Diamonds are classified according to their quality.

clatter *verb* **rattle, clang, clank, clash, clink, bang, bump** The loose shutter clattered against the house in the wind. ◆ *noun* **rattling, jangling, rattle, jangle, clangor, racket** We could hear the clatter of dishes in the kitchen.

clause *noun* **article, stipulation, condition, term, item, specification** The contract contains a clause stating that there is no penalty for early payment.

clean *adjective* **1. unsoiled, spotless, cleansed, washed, fresh, neat** We changed into clean clothes after working on the car. **2. honorable, honest, virtuous, wholesome, upright** I try to lead a clean life. **3. entire, complete, total,**

thorough, absolute, decisive My dad decided to make a clean break and quit smoking. **4. polished, smooth, skillful, expert, adept, deft, adroit** The ice skater executed a clean triple axle. ◆ *adverb* **1. honestly, fairly, equitably, justly, sportingly** The coach always instructs us to play clean. **2. entirely, completely, absolutely, totally, thoroughly, utterly,** I clean forgot about our meeting. ◆ *verb* **cleanse, scrub, wash, neaten, tidy, launder** It was my turn to clean the bathroom. ➡ **Antonyms:** *adjective* **1. dirty, filthy 2. dishonest, wicked 3. partial** ◆ *adverb* **1. dirty, unfairly 2. partially** ◆ *verb* **dirty, soil, mess**

clear *adjective* **1. bright, cloudless, sunny, fair, unclouded, fine** On a clear day, you can see the mountains from here. **2. see-through, translucent, transparent, pellucid, limpid** Milk jugs are usually made of clear plastic. **3. open, free, unblocked, unobstructed, empty, vacant** The school bus driver had a clear view of the road ahead. **4. obvious, apparent, unambiguous, definite, evident, unequivocal** The doctor said I had a clear case of the mumps. **5. untroubled, peaceful, clean, pure, blameless, unblemished** His conscience was clear once he admitted he put the food coloring in the fish tank. ◆ *adverb* **1. distinctly, clearly, discernibly, starkly, understandably** I can hear you loud and clear. **2. entirely, completely, altogether, utterly, straight, clean** It rained clear through the night. ◆ *verb* **1. clean, tidy, remove, empty, open, free** Dad asked me to clear the back porch. **2. pass over, leap, jump, vault, hurdle, miss** The horse cleared the hurdles. **3. exonerate, absolve, acquit, free, release** New evidence has cleared him of the crime. **4. clarify, solve, resolve, make clear, elucidate, explain** A long talk helped my stepdad and me to clear up our misunderstandings. ➡ **Antonyms:** *adjective* **1. cloudy, hazy, foggy 2. opaque 3. blocked, obstructed 4. ambiguous, unclear 5. guilty, troubled** ◆ *verb* **1. load, soil 3. accuse 4. confuse, muddy**

clemency *noun* **mercy, leniency, charity, forgiveness, compassion, forbearance** The judge showed clemency in sentencing the prisoner. ➡ **Antonyms: cruelty, vengefulness**

clever *adjective* **1. bright, intelligent, sharp, smart, ingenious, resourceful** Many useful inventions are the result of a clever idea. **2. adroit, skillful, dexterous, facile, nimble, efficient** The juggler was very clever with his hands. ➡ **Antonyms: 1. dumb, stupid 2. clumsy, awkward**

client *noun* **customer, patron, buyer, shopper, consumer** A good accountant is likely to have many clients.

cliff *noun* **bluff, precipice, rock face, crag, escarpment, face** We saw a mountaineer climbing the steep cliff.

climate *noun* **1. clime, weather, temperature, atmosphere, nature** Southern Arizona has a hot climate. **2. attitude, environment, ambiance, mood, feeling, quality** The newly elected President brought a climate of change and enthusiasm with him.

climax *noun* **high point, turning point, zenith, peak, culmination, summit** The climax of the mystery was so exciting that I didn't hear Mom call me to dinner.

climb *verb* **1. ascend, go up, mount, scale, clamber, scramble, shinny, shin** Most expeditions to climb Mount Everest take several months. **2. soar, mount, lift, rise, arise, ascend** The airplane climbed steeply as it cleared the runway. ◆ *noun* **ascent, ascension, route, grade, incline, pitch** It's an easy climb to the top of that hill. ➡ **Antonyms:** *verb* **descend** ◆ *noun* **descent**

clinch *verb* **1. fasten, bolt, fix, secure, clamp, clasp** Dad clinched the trailer to the back of his truck. **2. confirm, seal, settle, conclude, complete, finalize** We clinched our agreement with a handshake.

cling *verb* **1. adhere, stick, bond, attach, fasten, affix** Rob's rain-soaked sweater clung to his body. **2. grasp, clasp, clutch, hold on, embrace, hug** We clung to each other during the scary movie.

clinical *adjective* **objective, dispassionate, unprejudiced, unbiased, open-minded, analytical** The director explained our mistakes in a clinical manner. ➡ **Antonyms: subjective, personal, biased**

clip[1] *verb* **1. cut, shear, snip, crop, trim, bob** My sister clipped my bangs for me. **2. strike, hit, slug, whack, swat, smack** My brother clipped me, so I hit him back. ◆ *noun* **1. cut, trim, snip, shortening, crop, bob** I stopped in at the barber's for a quick clip. **2. segment, portion, interval, extract, excerpt, bit** We viewed a film clip on amoebas in biology class. **3. blow, punch, hit, jab, sock, smack** A clip to the jaw made the boxer stagger. **4. pace, rate, speed, velocity** The horse finished the race at a fast clip.

clip[2] *noun* **1. clasp, fastener, pin, grip, clamp** A magnetic clip on our refrigerator holds paper for notes and lists. **2. pin, brooch, cameo, ornament, clasp** I received a beautiful antique clip from my great-aunt. ◆ *verb* **fasten, attach, fix, clasp, secure, hold** I clipped my hair into a ponytail. ➡ **Antonyms:** *verb* **unclip, unfasten**

cloak *noun* **1. cape, mantle, shawl, stole, robe, wrap** In early movies, the villain often wore a black cloak. **2. cover, screen, veil, mask, blanket, curtain** A cloak of fog kept us from seeing the boat. ◆ *verb* **conceal, cover, hide, screen, disguise, mask** The Stealth bomber has features that cloak it from enemy radar. ◆ **Antonyms:** *verb* **reveal, show, expose**

clog *noun* **obstruction, blockage, impediment, occlusion, clot, jam** A clog of vegetable peelings prevented the sink from draining. ◆ *verb* **block, obstruct, choke, occlude, bar, close** Traffic clogged the roads to the airport. ◆ **Antonyms:** *verb* **unclog, clear, free**

close *adjective* **1. approaching, imminent, impending, near, coming, nearby** As the wind freshened, I realized the storm was close. **2. intimate, friendly, attached, loyal, loving, affectionate** My sister and I are very close. **3. similar, equivalent, alike, comparable, like, equal** The test results in the two experiments were very close. **4. careful, firm, strict, tight, thorough, rigorous** The lioness kept a close watch over her cubs. **5. stuffy, airless, thick, dense, muggy, stifling, tight** Please open a window; this room is too close. ◆ *verb* **1. shut, fasten, lock, seal, secure, cover** I closed the garage door and locked it. **2. obstruct, block, plug, clog, occlude, choke** The leaves in the gutter had closed the downspout. **3. complete, conclude, end, finish, stop, wrap up** Our principal closed his speech with a funny story. ◆ *noun* **conclusion, end, closure, stop, termination, finish** Our conversation came to a close when Travis's bus pulled up. ◆ *adverb* **near, nearby, nigh** Don't sit too close to the TV. ◆ **Antonyms:** *adjective* **1. distant, far 2. estranged, cool 3. different 4. careless, casual** ◆ *verb* **1. open, unlock 2. clear, open 3. begin, start** ◆ *noun* **beginning, start**

clot *noun* **mass, coagulation, occlusion, gob, curd, lump** Heart attacks can be caused by clots in the blood. ◆ *verb* **coagulate, congeal, thicken, coalesce, jell, solidify** The blood clotted very quickly after I cut my hand.

Word Group

Cloth is fabric or material made by weaving, knitting, or matting fibers together. **Cloth** is a general term with no true synonyms. Here are some common types of cloth:

batik, brocade, calico, canvas, challis, chintz, corduroy, cotton, denim, felt, flannel, gabardine, gingham, jersey, khaki, lamé, linen, madras, muslin, nylon, organdy, plaid, poplin, rayon, sateen, satin, seersucker, silk, taffeta, terry, tricot, tweed, twill, velour, velvet, wool

---

clothing *noun* **clothes, apparel, attire, garments, garb, dress** My friends and I enjoy shopping at stores that sell used clothing.

cloud *noun* **1. plume, fog, vapor, haze, mist, puff** The geyser erupted with a cloud of steam. **2. shadow, pall, shroud, gloom, stain, taint** News of the accident threw a cloud over the entire school. ◆ *verb* **1. fog, mist, dim, obscure, conceal, blur** Steam clouded the bathroom mirror during my shower. **2. dull, impair, confuse, addle, discourage, deject** A lack of sleep last night has clouded my thinking today. **3. tarnish, sully, disgrace, stain, discredit, besmirch** His name had been clouded by the neighbors' accusations. ◆ **Antonyms:** *verb* **1. clear, reveal, brighten 2. clarify, cheer, uplift 3. exonerate, exalt**

cloudy *adjective* **1. overcast, gray, hazy, leaden, sunless, murky** It was cloudy in the morning, but the sun came out in the afternoon. **2. unclear, vague, obscure, ambiguous, confusing, muddy, uncertain** She gave a cloudy account of the events leading up to the accident. ◆ **Antonyms:** **1. bright, clear, sunny 2. clear, obvious, straightforward**

clown *noun* **1. comedian, comic, wit, jester, joker, prankster** I love watching the circus clowns perform their hilarious stunts. **2. buffoon, boor, oaf, dolt, bumpkin** Stop acting like a clown. ◆ *verb* **fool, play, joke, kid, caper, jest** My brother clowned around by imitating a monkey.

club *noun* **1. cudgel, truncheon, stick, nightstick, bat, staff** In England, most police officers carry clubs instead of guns. **2. association, group, organization, society, league, fellowship** Mother's bridge club is meeting at our house this afternoon. **3. center, facility, clubhouse, hall, country club, resort** I play tennis at the local athletic club. ◆ *verb* **beat, hit, pound, strike, batter, hammer** I clubbed the rug to get the dust out of it.

clue *noun* **lead, sign, trace, hint, evidence, indication, suggestion** Police said that the burglar left no clues.

clump *noun* **1. cluster, group, bunch, body, thicket, grove** Let's have our picnic near that clump of lilac bushes. **2. lump, mass, chunk, hunk, blob, glob** The snow turned into clumps of ice as the weather grew colder. **3. thud, tramp, stamp, clatter, bang, knock** We could hear the noisy clump of a raccoon on the roof. ◆ *verb* **1. stomp, stump, thump, tramp, plod, march** My little niece clumped through the house wearing my boots. **2. coagulate, solidify, thicken, congeal, clot** Gravy clumps if the flour is added too quickly.

clumsy *adjective* **1. awkward, uncoordinated, bumbling, fumbling, inept, graceless** I felt clumsy when I bumped into the door jamb. **2. unwieldy, cumbersome, unmanageable, ungainly, inconvenient, troublesome, bulky** The overstuffed chair was very clumsy to move. ◈ **Antonyms:** 1. agile, adroit, dexterous 2. manageable, handy

cluster *noun* batch, bunch, clump, bundle, group, set I bought some grapes and ate the entire cluster. ◆ *verb* bunch, assemble, collect, flock, gather, mass The chickens cluster around the farmer at feeding time. ◈ **Antonyms:** *verb* disperse, scatter

clutch *verb* grab, grasp, seize, grip, snatch, hold I clutched at my hat as the wind tried to tear it away. ◆ *noun* 1. clasp, grasp, grip, hold, clamp, embrace The hawk had a firm clutch on a small animal. 2. possession, control, power, custody, grasp, hands The soldiers had fallen into the clutches of the enemy. 3. crisis, pinch, emergency, crunch, exigency, plight, predicament In a clutch, we can call for help on our cellular phone. ◈ **Antonyms:** *verb* release, relinquish, free

clutter *noun* mess, litter, jumble, disorder, tangle, hodgepodge My room is a clutter of books, papers, and clothes. ◆ *verb* litter, strew, mess up, snarl, pile, heap The old man's backyard is cluttered with car parts. ◈ **Antonyms:** *noun* order, organization ◆ *verb* straighten, tidy, arrange

coach *noun* 1. carriage, stage, stagecoach, bus, omnibus The queen's coach was drawn by a team of six gray horses. 2. trainer, instructor, adviser, guide, manager, teacher My friend's father is my Little League coach. ◆ *verb* drill, instruct, teach, train, tutor, advise Mother coached my little brother on his part for our Passover ceremony.

coarse *adjective* 1. gritty, rough, sandy, scratchy, granular, grainy Sandpaper has a coarse texture. 2. offensive, crude, rude, vulgar, indelicate, boorish My parents do not approve of coarse humor. 3. inferior, low quality, second-rate, shoddy, tawdry, substandard This fabric is too coarse to use for a dress. ◈ **Antonyms:** 1. smooth, fine 2. polite, refined 3. superior, good

coast *noun* seacoast, seashore, seaside, shore, shoreline, seaboard, A lighthouse warns ships that the coast is near. ◆ *verb* glide, slide, drift, flow, roll, sail She coasted down the hill on her bicycle.

coat *noun* 1. jacket, overcoat, raincoat, windbreaker, wrap, topcoat I always wear a warm coat when I play in the snow. 2. fur, hair, pelt, wool, hide, skin, fleece A wolf's coat gets very thick in the winter. 3. coating, covering, layer, blanket, film, surface Last fall we gave our house a fresh coat of paint. ◆ *verb* cover, layer, spread, apply, glaze, smear The janitors coated the gym floor with wax over the winter vacation. ◈ **Antonyms:** *verb* remove, clear

coax *verb* persuade, urge, wheedle, cajole, influence, lure My friends coaxed me into going along to the park.

code *noun* law, regulation, rule, standard, system, canon The local fire code prohibits burning trash.

coerce *verb* force, compel, persuade, pressure, make, bully My sister coerced me into lending her my new sweater. ◈ **Antonyms:** allow, permit

coherent *adjective* logical, comprehensible, clear, lucid, rational, sound My teacher says I express myself in a very coherent manner. ◈ **Antonyms:** illogical, vague, confusing

coil *noun* roll, loop, reel, ring, spiral, twist The rancher bought a coil of barbed wire. ◆ *verb* curl, roll, twist, wind, wrap, turn The python coiled itself around a tree branch.

coin *noun* coinage, change, money, currency, cash My dad needs some more coins for the parking meter. ◆ *verb* create, devise, originate, concoct, invent, make up William Shakespeare is said to have coined over 1,700 new words.

coincide *verb* accord, agree, concur, correspond, match, square His opinion of the movie doesn't coincide with mine. ◈ **Antonyms:** disagree, differ

coincidence *noun* accident, chance, fluke, fate, luck, correspondence It is a coincidence that my best friend and I have the same last name. ◈ **Antonyms:** design, plan

cold *adjective* 1. chilly, cool, icy, frosty, chilled, frigid, frozen Cold lemonade tastes wonderful on a hot summer day. 2. unfriendly, icy, chill, reserved, cool, stony, aloof, haughty The losing contestant gave the judges a cold stare. 3. faint, weak, dim, faded, dead, old The trail was cold by the time the search and rescue team arrived. ◆ *adverb* completely, absolutely, entirely, promptly, immediately, abruptly My suggestion to order pizza was turned down cold. ◆ *noun* chill, coldness, coolness, iciness, frost, freeze I shivered in the cold without my jacket. ◈ **Antonyms:** *adjective* 1. hot, warm 2. friendly, cordial 3. strong, clear ◆ *adverb* partially ◆ *noun* heat, warmth

cold-blooded *adjective* emotionless, cruel, heartless, merciless, brutal, unfeeling Many criminals are described as being cold-blooded. ◈ **Antonyms:** sympathetic, humane, compassionate

collaborate *verb* cooperate, team up, work with, join, join forces, coauthor Owen Chamberlin and Emilio Segre collaborated in discovering the antiproton.

collapse *verb* **fall, disintegrate, crumple, fail, give way, buckle, topple** The bridge collapsed in the flood. ◆ *noun* **1. cave-in, failure, breakdown, disintegration, ruination, crash** Engineers are investigating the cause of the tunnel's sudden collapse. **2. prostration, exhaustion, debility, breakdown, seizure, stroke** The marathon runner's collapse was caused by heat exhaustion.

colleague *noun* **associate, coworker, confederate, partner, ally, comrade** Mom values her friendships with her colleagues at work.

collect *verb* **1. accumulate, amass, gather, garner, assemble, bring together** Our class collected food for the homeless shelter. **2. acquire, obtain, accrue, secure, amass, accumulate** Tommy collected two new fossils at an abandoned quarry. **3. compose, control, recover, calm, quiet, soothe** We collected ourselves after the minor earthquake. ● **Antonyms: 1. disperse, scatter 3. excite, agitate**

collection *noun* **1. gathering, collecting, accumulating, compilation, assembly** Every Thanksgiving, my school sponsors a drive for the collection of canned food. **2. accumulation, assortment, assembly, stockpile, mass, hoard** Many local museums have fine collections of Native American artifacts.

college *noun* **1. university, junior college, community college, school, academy, institute** I plan to attend a local college after I graduate from high school. **2. council, body, league, society, group, institute** The College of Cardinals of the Roman Catholic Church elects the pope.

collide *verb* **1. bump, hit, slam, run into, crash, smash** The basketball players collided. **2. clash, disagree, differ, deviate, conflict, diverge** My parents' and my opinions collided over the issue of my curfew. ● **Antonyms: 1. miss, avoid 2. agree, coincide**

collision *noun* **accident, crash, impact, smashup, wreck, blow** I swerved my bicycle to avoid a collision with a car.

collusion *noun* **conspiracy, plot, scheme, intrigue, complicity, pact** The corrupt council members were found to be in collusion.

colony *noun* **1. possession, dependency, outpost, settlement, territory, community** Jamestown was the first permanent British colony in North America. **2. flock, swarm, bevy, society, band, group** Some species of crows and ravens live in large colonies.

color *noun* **1. hue, shade, tint, value, tinge, tone, cast** My favorite color is yellow. **2. dye, pigment, dyestuff,** coloring, tint, paint, stain Will the color in this blouse fade if I wash it in hot water? **3. liveliness, drama, interest, vividness, vivacity, vigor** The debate coach said my speech had a lot of color. ◆ *verb* **1. dye, paint, stain, tint, adorn, wash** I colored two dozen eggs last Easter. **2. exaggerate, distort, twist, slant, embroider, prejudice** I admitted to coloring my account of my bad day at school. **3. blush, flush, redden, brighten, glow, flame** His cheeks color when he exercises. ● **Antonyms:** *noun* **3. dullness** ◆ *verb* **3. blanch, pale**

colorful *adjective* **1. bright, loud, vivid, gaudy, flashy, showy** Jason likes to wear colorful print shirts. **2. picturesque, distinctive, unusual, vivid, interesting, diverse** My grandfather was a very colorful character. ● **Antonyms: 1. drab, dull 2. humdrum, uninteresting**

colossal *adjective* **enormous, gigantic, tremendous, vast, giant, huge** Our school play was a colossal success. ● **Antonyms: small, tiny, miniature**

column *noun* **1. pillar, tower, cylinder, shaft, pilaster, pier** Trajan's column in Rome is both his tomb and a memorial to his achievements. **2. line, file, rank, tier, row, string, procession** The general reviewed the columns of troops.

comb *verb* **1. brush, untangle, straighten, adjust, smooth, style** I need to comb my hair, and then I'll be ready to go. **2. search, scour, ransack, rummage, hunt, sift** We combed the house looking for Dad's keys.

combat *verb* **battle, fight, struggle, oppose, attack, resist** Our mayor says that one of her top priorities is to combat poverty. ◆ *noun* **battle, war, conflict, action, fight, warfare** The air force's newest jet fighter has not been tested in combat. ● **Antonyms:** *noun* **peace, harmony, cooperation**

combatant *noun* **warrior, soldier, fighter, adversary, contestant, antagonist** All combatants were issued extra ammunition. ● **Antonym: civilian**

combative *adjective* **belligerent, militant, contentious, truculent, aggressive, quarrelsome** My sister was in a combative mood, so I avoided her. ● **Antonyms: cooperative, peaceable**

combine *verb* **blend, mix, commingle, merge, unite, join** If you combine blue and yellow paint, you'll get green. ● **Antonyms: divide, separate**

combustion *noun* **burning, flaming, ignition, kindling, incineration, blazing, fire** The combustion of gasoline vapor and air is what drives a car engine.

come *verb* **1. approach, proceed, move, advance, near, move toward** Please come to the front of the class when I call your name. **2. appear, arrive, show up, reach, materialize, surface** My school bus comes at 7 a.m. **3. occur, take place, transpire, happen, fall, develop** Christmas comes only once a year. **4. arise, issue, originate, hail, emanate, spring** My friend Kjell comes from Norway. ● **Antonyms: 1. & 2. depart, go, leave**

comedy *noun* **humor, wittiness, funniness, wit, fun, jesting** I like movies that have some comedy in them. ● **Antonym: tragedy**

comely *adjective* **pretty, lovely, fair, attractive, good-looking, winsome** The homecoming queen and her court are a group of comely girls. ● **Antonyms: ugly, homely, repulsive**

comfort *verb* **console, hearten, soothe, ease, pacify, relieve** Whenever I'm feeling bad, my friends try to comfort me. ◆ *noun* **1. ease, well-being, contentment, pleasure, satisfaction, luxury** My family is not rich, but we live in comfort. **2. solace, consolation, support, help, relief, aid** It's a comfort to have my sister home when Mom and Dad are out. ● **Antonyms:** *verb* **distress, worry, torment** ◆ *noun* **1. poverty, hardship 2. aggravation, irritation**

comfortable *adjective* **1. cozy, snug, pleasant, pleasurable, satisfying, agreeable** Cold winter nights make me appreciate my warm and comfortable bed. **2. calm, contented, relaxed, serene, at ease, happy** She didn't feel very comfortable her first day at the new school. **3. sufficient, enough, ample, adequate, plentiful, satisfactory** My fantasy is to live in the south of France with a comfortable income. ● **Antonyms: 1. uncomfortable 2. uneasy, nervous, tense 3. insufficient, inadequate**

comic *adjective* **funny, humorous, amusing, silly, droll, witty** We laughed at the comic antics of Marcia's kitten. ◆ *noun* **comedian, comedienne, wit, joker, jokester, clown, humorist** My cousin thinks he is a real comic. ● **Antonyms:** *adjective* **tragic, serious**

comical *adjective* **amusing, funny, humorous, laughable, ridiculous, droll** My puppy is comical when he chases his tail. ● **Antonyms: serious, solemn, tragic**

command *verb* **1. direct, order, summon, require, bid, demand** The drill instructor commanded his troops to do 50 pushups. **2. head, lead, control, govern, rule, supervise** A lieutenant commands a platoon of about forty soldiers. **3. deserve, merit, exact, inspire, prompt, motivate** The forces of nature command respect. ◆ *noun* **1. demand, direction,**

order, instruction, ultimatum, decree Sometimes my older brother's requests sound more like commands. **2. authority, charge, control, leadership, power, direction** A naval captain has command over both a ship and its crew. **3. mastery, control, grasp, knowledge, proficiency, comprehension** I admire your command of the English language. ● **Antonyms:** *verb* **1. beg, plead 2. follow 3. repel, discourage**

commemorate *verb* **celebrate, honor, remember, memorialize, salute, glorify** The town held a ceremony to commemorate the slain police officer. ● **Antonyms: ignore, forget, dishonor**

commence *verb* **begin, open, start, kick off, originate, initiate** The graduation ceremony will commence at 3:00. ● **Antonyms: end, finish**

commend *verb* **1. congratulate, compliment, honor, praise, applaud, acclaim** My teacher commended me on my excellent report. **2. entrust, commit, confer, transfer, consign, relegate** My brother commended his pet rabbit into my care when he went to camp. ● **Antonyms: 1. criticize, censure, deride**

comment *noun* **1. observation, remark, statement, opinion, mention, note** Dad made an appreciative comment about the cleaning I had done. **2. talk, gossip, rumor, commentary, conversation, discussion** The mayor's sudden resignation caused a lot of comment. ◆ *verb* **mention, remark, say, state, express, reflect** All of my friends commented on how hard the test had been.

commerce *noun* **business, trade, exchange, traffic, dealing, trading** Many American jobs depend on international commerce.

commission *noun* **1 mandate, mission, assignment, task, job, charge** The ambassador's commission is to represent the interests of his country. **2. board, committee, council, agency, delegation, commissioners** The Commission of Public Works is in charge of road repair in our city. **3. percentage, cut, allowance, dividend, fee, payment** A real estate agent gets a commission on every house she or he sells. ◆ *verb* **1. assign, charge, command, delegate, appoint, authorize** The mayor commissioned the police to set up a special task force. **2. hire, engage, contract, employ, charter, requisition** My parents commissioned an architect to redesign our kitchen.

commit *verb* **1. do, perpetrate, enact, effect, execute, perform, complete** The police do not know who committed the crime. **2. entrust, consign, transfer, hand over, deliver, give** I committed my earnings to my mother for safekeeping. **3. assign, confine, institutionalize, intern, immure, imprison** The schizophrenic was committed to a mental hospital for treatment. **4. devote, pledge, resolve, vow, promise, obligate** Our town is committed to building a new high school. ➡ **Antonyms: 2. withhold, withdraw, receive 3. release, free**

committee *noun* **commission, council, group, panel, board** I am on the committee that is planning our school's book fair.

commodity *noun* **merchandise, property, chattel, goods, object, product** That catalog sells commodities to agricultural businesses.

common *adjective* **1. public, general, universal, shared, joint, mutual** It is common knowledge that the dinosaurs are extinct. **2. widespread, general, prevalent, extensive, prevailing, pervasive** Dandelions are a common weed. **3. average, normal, ordinary, routine, simple, typical, usual** The doctor said that my type of knee injury is very common. **4. unrefined, vulgar, coarse, cheap, crass, low, commonplace** My mother thinks it is common to talk too loud in public. ➡ **Antonyms: 3. unique, unusual 4. polished, polite, cultured**

commonplace *adjective* **common, conventional, customary, familiar, mundane, ordinary** Going to the beach is commonplace for me. ◆ *noun* **platitude, banality, bromide, cliché, maxim, axiom, saying** "Too many cooks spoil the broth" is a commonplace. ➡ **Antonyms:** *adjective* **uncommon, rare, interesting**

commotion *noun* **disturbance, clamor, turmoil, racket, confusion, uproar** The raccoon that came in the pet door caused a big commotion in our house. ➡ **Antonyms: calm, quiet**

communal *adjective* **common, general, shared, joint, public, collective** There are communal showers in the locker rooms at our school gym. ➡ **Antonyms: private, personal**

communicate *verb* **1. convey, show, inform, relate, report, declare, state** Dogs communicate through behavior and body language. **2. transmit, convey, give, pass, spread, impart** Contagious diseases are easily communicated from one person to another.

community *noun* **1. city, town, neighborhood, population, public, residents** Our mayor hopes to involve the entire community in his anticrime campaign. **2. body, circle, bloc, society, brotherhood, culture, group** The scientific community feels that more money should be devoted to research.

commute *verb* **alleviate, curtail, decrease, mitigate, diminish, modify** The governor commuted the prisoner's death sentence to life imprisonment.

compact[1] *adjective* **1. dense, firm, hard, solid, compressed, concentrated** An igloo is made from very compact blocks of snow. **2. undersized, little, small, tiny, cramped, limited** My uncle's recreational vehicle has a compact kitchen. **3. brief, concise, terse, succinct, short, pithy** Mao Tse-tung is famous for his little red book of compact sayings. ◆ *verb* **compress, crush, consolidate, cram, pack, squeeze** We have an appliance that compacts trash into small bundles. ➡ **Antonyms:** *adjective* **1. loose, slack 2. spacious, roomy 3. long, rambling**

compact[2] *noun* **accord, understanding, pact, treaty, agreement, deal** The two nations signed a compact to help defend each other.

companion *noun* **1. comrade, friend, partner, attendant, escort, helper, guide** Dad says that it's safer to hike with a companion. **2. counterpart, complement, mate, twin, match** I found one glove but could not find its companion.

company *noun* **1. group, gathering, party, body, band, troupe** We traveled with a large company of people to Yellowstone Park this summer. **2. caller, guest, visitor, visitant, society, fellowship** Mother spruced up the house because she was expecting company. **3. companionship, fellowship, society, presence, comradeship, friendship** Grandpa says that he always enjoys my company. **4. business, establishment, firm, corporation, association, concern** Bonnie works for a company that sells appliances.

comparable *adjective* **similar, like, akin, equivalent, tantamount, alike** Turkey is comparable to chicken in nutritional value. ➡ **Antonyms: different, unrelated, dissimilar**

compare *verb* **1. liken, correspond, parallel, match, relate, associate** My aunt compares having a dog to having a small child. **2. contrast, juxtapose, consider, analyze, examine, balance** We compared the options and decided to travel to my grandmother's by car.

comparison *noun* **1. assessment, evaluation, appraisal, crosscheck, valuation, rating** A comparison of the two stereos revealed the one with better sound. **2. similarity, resemblance, correspondence, parity, connection, equivalence** To me, there's no comparison between a frozen pizza and a fresh one.

compartment *noun* **division, section, niche, part, space, place** My wallet has a compartment for loose change.

compassion *noun* empathy, concern, sympathy, tenderness, mercy, love Good doctors have compassion for their patients. ➶ **Antonyms:** cruelty, antipathy, disdain

compassionate *adjective* benevolent, empathetic, sympathetic, merciful, tenderhearted, humane Buddha is known as "The Compassionate One." ➶ **Antonyms:** heartless, merciless, unfeeling

compatible *adjective* agreeable, congenial, harmonious, congruous, sympathetic, adaptable My friends and I are compatible with one another. ➶ **Antonym:** incompatible

compel *verb* force, oblige, require, cause, make, drive Bad weather compelled us to change our plans.

compensate *verb* **1.** recompense, reimburse, repay, indemnify, pay, remunerate We compensated our neighbors for the plantings our goat ate. **2.** make up, balance, offset, equalize, counteract, counterbalance He compensates for his hearing loss by reading lips.

compensation *noun* recompense, benefit, remuneration, wages, earnings, reward My dad's company offers excellent compensation to its employees.

compete *verb* contend, strive, fight, combat, battle, vie I will compete in next Saturday's golfing tournament. ➶ **Antonyms:** yield, surrender

competent *adjective* proficient, skilled, skillful, expert, professional, good A competent typist rarely makes mistakes. ➶ **Antonyms:** incompetent, unskilled

competition *noun* **1.** rivalry, struggle, striving, competing, contention, battling The competition at the Olympics is intense. **2.** contest, tournament, event, match, game, meet The sixth grade class will have a spelling competition next week. **3.** opposition, rival, competitor, challenger, opponent, adversary My stepmom was disappointed to lose an important client to the competition.

compile *verb* accumulate, assemble, collect, gather, garner, amass Ingrid compiled a list of people she wanted to invite to her barbecue. ➶ **Antonyms:** scatter, disperse

complacent *adjective* confident, pleased, at ease, composed, unconcerned, self-satisfied I was complacent after the test because I had known all the answers. ➶ **Antonyms:** agitated, concerned, upset

complain *verb* grumble, protest, object, whine, gripe, denounce Last summer many people complained about the unrelenting heat. ➶ **Antonyms:** compliment, commend, praise

complaint *noun* **1.** objection, protest, criticism, dissatisfaction, lament, gripe My only complaint about our vacation was that it ended too soon. **2.** grievance, injustice, hardship, inequity, wrong, trouble With an absentee landlord, the tenants in the apartments have suffered many complaints. **3.** illness, ailment, disease, malady, sickness, affliction The doctor asked me to describe my complaint. ➶ **Antonyms:** **1.** compliment, commendation, approval **3.** remedy, balm, salve

complement *noun* **1.** accompaniment, supplement, augmentation, balance, completion, consummation This sauce is a delicious complement to the steamed asparagus. **2.** quota, sum, entirety, totality I now have a full complement of tools for my bicycle. ◆ *verb* complete, round out, consummate, fulfill, conclude, perfect I bought a necktie that complements my new shirt.

complete *adjective* **1.** intact, whole, entire, total, plenary, full When I dealt the cards, I discovered that the deck wasn't complete. **2.** finished, done, through, concluded, ended, fulfilled I worked all weekend, and now my art project is complete. **3.** absolute, perfect, thorough, thoroughgoing, utter, sheer Our picnic turned into a complete disaster when it poured rain. ◆ *verb* **1.** crown, culminate, round out, consummate, cap, perfect A visit to the Vietnam War memorial completed our tour of Washington, D.C. **2.** accomplish, finish, conclude, end, fulfill, perform I completed my book report two weeks before it was due. ➶ **Antonyms:** *adjective* **1.** incomplete **2.** unfinished ◆ *verb* **2.** begin, start

complex *adjective* complicated, difficult, intricate, elaborate, involved, convoluted A jigsaw puzzle with 5,000 pieces is too complex for my tastes. ◆ *noun* network, system, conglomerate, compound, composite, maze The office building was a confusing complex of corridors and hallways. ➶ **Antonyms:** *adjective* easy, simple

compliance *noun* concurrence, conformity, agreement, obedience, observance, acquiescence The company had three months to enter into compliance with the new regulations. ➶ **Antonyms:** nonconformity, resistance

complicate *verb* confuse, mix up, muddle, snarl, hamper, confound, involve Please don't complicate our game by adding new rules. ➶ **Antonyms:** simplify, clarify

complicated *adjective* complex, difficult, convoluted, elaborate, intricate, involved His directions are so complicated, I'm sure I'll get lost. ➶ **Antonyms:** easy, simple, clear

compliment *noun* praise, admiration, approval, flattery, commendation, acclaim Penny received many compliments on her dance performance. ◆ *verb* commend, praise, approve, flatter, salute, hail Ray was pleased when I complimented his artwork. ➤ **Antonyms:** *noun* insult, criticism, condemnation ◆ *verb* insult, criticize, denounce

comply *verb* abide by, obey, observe, respect, conform, follow We are expected to comply with the dress code at our school. ➤ **Antonyms:** disobey, resist

component *noun* part, piece, element, unit, factor, ingredient, constituent A modem and a sound card are optional components of a computer.

compose *verb* 1. constitute, form, make up, build, fashion Hydrogen and oxygen are the elements that compose water. 2. create, make, produce, devise, write, author Karen composed a poem in honor of her mother's birthday. 3. calm, collect, quiet, relax, settle, soothe The actor reserves time to compose himself before a performance. ➤ **Antonyms:** 3. excite, agitate, arouse

composite *noun* mix, amalgamation, blend, combination, compound, fusion My ancestry is a composite of several different nationalities.

composition *noun* 1. creation, invention, making, origination, composing, formulation After learning to play the guitar, I was inspired to attempt music composition. 2. work, opus, piece, exercise, creation, theme I enjoy listening to many of the compositions of Debussy and Chopin. 3. arrangement, organization, layout, formulation, makeup, content My mother enjoys planning the composition of her summer garden. 4. aggregate, conglomerate, combination, compound, mix, composite That house is a composition of several architectural styles.

compound *verb* 1. blend, combine, mix, join, link, amalgamate Tim compounds strawberry and raspberry jam for his peanut butter sandwiches. 2. increase, intensify, add to, amplify, augment, extend My attempt to justify my actions only compounded my parents' anger. ◆ *noun* blend, composite, combination, complex, union, mixture Calcium carbonate is an inorganic compound. ➤ **Antonyms:** *verb* 1. separate, divide 2. lessen, decrease

comprehend *verb* 1. grasp, perceive, understand, apprehend, fathom, know I know how to use my computer, but I don't really comprehend how it works. 2. include, comprise, have, encompass, take in, embrace The curriculum for our gym class comprehends aerobics and weight training. ➤ **Antonyms:** 1. misunderstand 2. exclude, omit

comprehensive *adjective* complete, full, thorough, inclusive, exhaustive This history book has a comprehensive index of all subjects covered. ➤ **Antonyms:** incomplete, partial

compress *verb* condense, reduce, squeeze, compact, press, cram My summer class in geography compressed a semester's work into six weeks. ➤ **Antonyms:** expand, stretch, enlarge

comprise *verb* contain, include, incorporate, constitute, consist of Japan comprises more than 3,500 islands.

compromise *noun* agreement, arrangement, understanding, settlement, accommodation, bargain My parents and I reached a compromise on the new figure for my allowance. ◆ *verb* 1. settle, agree, negotiate, adjust, accommodate My brother and I compromised by sharing the last piece of cake. 2. jeopardize, mar, ruin, imperil, risk, discredit Contamination of a research lab compromises the validity of the experiments. ➤ **Antonyms:** *noun* difference, dispute, contention ◆ *verb* 1. dispute, differ, contest

compulsory *adjective* mandatory, required, obligatory, imperative, requisite, necessary Wearing your seat belt is compulsory in most states. ➤ **Antonyms:** optional, voluntary

compute *verb* calculate, determine, figure, reckon, gauge, ascertain Maria computed the mean of 106, 111, 125, and 130. ➤ **Antonyms:** guess, suppose, approximate

comrade *noun* buddy, companion, friend, pal, crony, associate Dad has stayed in touch with many of his air force comrades. ➤ **Antonym:** stranger

conceal *verb* hide, secrete, camouflage, cover, mask, screen My cat conceals himself behind the couch whenever we have company. ➤ **Antonyms:** expose, reveal

concede *verb* 1. acknowledge, admit, confess, agree, grant, accept We conceded that we were lost and needed directions. 2. give up, surrender, yield, resign, cede, grant The losing candidate conceded the election before all the votes had been counted. ➤ **Antonyms:** 1. deny, refute, reject 2. win, defeat

conceit *noun* egotism, pride, self-importance, vanity, vainglory, arrogance Our neighbors are full of conceit over their two new cars. ➤ **Antonyms:** humility, modesty

conceited *adjective* arrogant, haughty, vain, cocky, self-important, smug The conceited artist claimed he was the best painter around. ➤ **Antonyms:** humble, modest

conceive *verb* **1. form, develop, originate, create, invent, devise** Sir Isaac Newton is said to have conceived the concept of gravity when he saw an apple fall. **2. envision, think, visualize, imagine, comprehend, realize** It's hard to conceive of how long there has been life on Earth.

concentrate *verb* **1. focus, heed, pay attention, attend, apply, dedicate, devote** I concentrated my attention on what the teacher was saying. **2. center, centralize, cluster, focus, collect, gather** The motion picture industry is concentrated in southern California. **3. condense, thicken, strengthen, distill, intensify, reduce** We boiled the fruit juice to concentrate it into syrup. ➡ **Antonyms: 2. scatter, spread, disperse 3. dilute, thin**

concept *noun* **conception, idea, notion, theory, thought, abstraction** Jules Verne wrote about the concept of space flight long before it became a reality.

concern *verb* **1. affect, interest, involve, pertain, influence, bear on** The principal planned to speak on a subject that concerns us all. **2. distress, disturb, trouble, worry, bother, disquiet** Grandfather's chronic cough concerns us. ◆ *noun* **1. affair, business, consideration, interest, matter, issue** Many people feel that religious beliefs are a private concern. **2. apprehension, anxiety, worry, care, trouble, solicitude** Amy keeps her kitten indoors out of concern for its safety. **3. business, firm, company, establishment, house, enterprise** There is a hardware concern in our town that was established in 1912.

concerning *preposition* **about, regarding, relative to, in relation to, in reference to, in respect to** The teacher talked to me concerning my grades.

concert *noun* **performance, program, recital, show** My friend will play a solo in next week's concert.

concession *noun* **allowance, compromise, surrender, adjustment, admission, grant** Germany had to make many concessions after World War I.

conciliatory *adjective* **appeasing, placating, compromising, reconciliatory, accommodating, friendly** My sister became quite conciliatory after she broke my favorite figurine. ➡ **Antonyms: antagonistic, hostile, belligerent**

concise *adjective* **brief, terse, succinct, short, condensed, summary** We were assigned to write a concise report of no more than one page. ➡ **Antonyms: wordy, verbose, long**

conclude *verb* **1. close, complete, end, finish, terminate, settle** The celebration concluded with a display of fireworks. **2. determine, infer, deduce, reason, judge, surmise** The doctor concluded that I was in excellent health. ➡ **Antonyms: 1. begin, start**

conclusion *noun* **1. close, end, ending, finish, termination, finale** The conclusion of the movie was very exciting. **2. decision, determination, judgment, deduction, verdict, opinion** The detective's conclusion was that the butler had committed the crime. ➡ **Antonyms: 1. beginning, start, inauguration**

conclusive *adjective* **decisive, definitive, irrefutable, convincing, determinative, incontrovertible** The evidence in the case is not conclusive. ➡ **Antonyms: inconclusive, tentative, questionable**

concoction *noun* **blend, synthesis, combination, mixture, contrivance, fabrication** Her story was a concoction of truth and fiction.

concord *noun* **1. concordance, agreement, accord, unity, harmony, peace** Traditionally it has been difficult for farmers and ranchers to live in concord. **2. treaty, compact, agreement, covenant, accord, pact** In 1998, Pakistan and India signed a concord regarding the limiting of nuclear arms. ➡ **Antonyms: 1. discord, dissent, conflict**

concrete *adjective* **actual, definite, real, firm, solid, tangible, specific** The prosecution did not have concrete evidence against the defendant. ➡ **Antonyms: vague, abstract, general**

concur *verb* **agree, assent, consent, accord, acquiesce, coincide** I concur with your opinion of the new movie. ➡ **Antonyms: disagree, object, dissent**

condemn *verb* **1. criticize, denounce, vilify, deplore, attack, blame** In last week's sermon, our minister condemned the use of illegal drugs. **2. convict, doom, sentence, punish, damn** During the Roman Empire, prisoners were frequently condemned to serve as galley slaves. ➡ **Antonyms: 1. admire, praise 2. acquit, pardon**

condense *verb* **1. concentrate, thicken, reduce, solidify, consolidate, boil down** Many commercial soups are condensed before canning. **2. abbreviate, abridge, reduce, shorten, curtail, cut** The publisher condensed the author's book by cutting out five chapters. ➡ **Antonyms: 1. dilute 2. expand, increase, amplify**

condescend *verb* **stoop, deign, vouchsafe, lower, humble, demean** I hope that the movie star will condescend to sign my autograph book. ➡ **Antonyms: scorn, disdain**

condescending *adjective* patronizing, disdainful, contemptuous, pompous, imperious, haughty Her condescending manner has made her unpopular. ● **Antonyms:** modest, unassuming, unpretentious

condition *noun* 1. form, order, repair, shape, state, status, standing We hope to find a used car that's in good condition. 2. ailment, disease, illness, malady, sickness, affliction My uncle needs medication for his heart condition. 3. circumstance, situation, environment, predicament, plight, case The heavy snowfall has created hazardous conditions. 4. qualification, provision, requirement, restriction, stipulation, proviso Dad said I could go to the movies on the condition that I do my homework first. ◆ *verb* 1. prepare, ready, shape, train, mold, strengthen The coach began to condition the team on the first day of practice. 2. acclimate, accustom, adapt, habituate, adjust, reconcile I had to condition myself to the high mountain altitudes.

condolence *noun* sympathy, commiseration, solace, consolation, comfort, pity I sent a note of condolence to my friend when her grandmother died.

condone *verb* excuse, forgive, pardon, overlook, ignore, disregard Our coach does not condone missing practice. ● **Antonyms:** condemn, punish, censure

conduct *verb* 1. direct, guide, lead, steer, supervise, pilot The guide conducted us on a tour of Mark Twain's house. 2. transmit, convey, transfer, exchange, channel, carry Water readily conducts sound. 3. acquit, act, behave, bear, carry, comport The children conducted themselves with restraint in the gift shop. ◆ *noun* 1. behavior, manner, comportment, deportment, attitude, actions Our school rewards good conduct with extra privileges. 2. direction, control, management, leadership, supervision, administration My dad is responsible for the conduct of his department.

confederate *noun* accomplice, associate, cohort, conspirator, collaborator, ally The two criminals were confederates in the bank robbery. ◆ *verb* align, unite, federate, combine, ally, league, join During the American Civil War, 11 southern states confederated to oppose the Union. ● **Antonyms:** *noun* enemy, rival, opponent ◆ *verb* secede, withdraw

confer *verb* 1. consult, deliberate, discuss, speak, talk, converse Dad conferred with his lawyer before signing the business contract. 2. bestow, award, give, grant, present, donate A special award was conferred on the hometown hero.

conference *noun* 1. consultation, discussion, interview, meeting, talk, seminar My parents will have a conference with my teacher next week. 2. league, association, organization, assembly, congress, convention We attended all the playoff games of the basketball conference.

confess *verb* acknowledge, admit, concede, disclose, reveal, confide Gillian confessed that she ate the last cupcake. ● **Antonyms:** deny, disavow, repudiate

confide *verb* disclose, reveal, tell, whisper, inform, admit My best friend confides in me because she knows I can keep a secret. ● **Antonyms:** deny, keep secret

confidence *noun* 1. self-confidence, self-reliance, assurance, poise, aplomb, self-possession Lori does her balance beam routine with great confidence. 2. faith, reliance, trust, belief, credence, conviction We have complete confidence in our family dentist. ● **Antonyms:** 1. uncertainty, diffidence, self-doubt 2. distrust, suspicion, doubt

confident *adjective* certain, positive, sure, assured, convinced, secure George is confident he will pass tomorrow's math test. ● **Antonyms:** doubtful, uncertain

confidential *adjective* classified, secret, personal, private, restricted, privileged The lawyer locks his confidential files when he leaves his office. ● **Antonyms:** public, open

configuration *noun* arrangement, order, formation, disposition, pattern, contour I changed the configuration of the furniture in my room.

confine *verb* 1. hold, limit, restrain, restrict, circumscribe, regulate We were told to confine our speeches to five minutes. 2. imprison, incarcerate, detain, contain, restrict, cage We built a fence to confine our dogs to the backyard. ● **Antonyms:** 1. extend, amplify 2. release, liberate, free

confirm *verb* 1. corroborate, authenticate, certify, support, uphold, verify The second doctor we consulted confirmed the original diagnosis. 2. reinforce, buttress, clinch, fix, fortify, strengthen His kind behavior only confirms my good opinion of him. ● **Antonyms:** 1. contradict, refute 2. weaken, diminish

confirmation *noun* 1. approval, ratification, validation, acceptance, endorsement, sanction Appointments of justices to the Supreme Court must receive the confirmation of Congress. 2. verification, corroboration, affirmation, authentication, substantiation, proof We received confirmation of our airline reservations. ● **Antonyms:** 1. veto, disapproval, refusal 2. denial

confiscate *verb* appropriate, seize, take, impound, expropriate, commandeer The teacher confiscated my skateboard. ⏵ **Antonyms: release, return**

conflict *noun* 1. fight, war, battle, combat, fray, encounter, warfare The Vietnam War was the longest military conflict in American history. 2. clash, disagreement, dispute, confrontation, argument, feud The President tried to stay out of the conflict that arose among his advisors. ◆ *verb* clash, contradict, differ, disagree, vary, oppose, diverge Jake's version of the incident conflicted with Dan's. ⏵ **Antonyms:** *noun* 1. peace, truce 2. agreement, concord ◆ *verb* harmonize, agree

conform *verb* agree, comply, correspond, follow, obey, observe We have to wear clothing that conforms to the school dress code. ⏵ **Antonyms: differ, disagree**

confound *verb* disconcert, unsettle, confuse, puzzle, bewilder, mystify I was confounded when my computer screen suddenly went blank. ⏵ **Antonym: enlighten**

confront *verb* accost, challenge, defy, encounter, face, meet I angrily confronted my brother when I found my favorite shirt in his room. ⏵ **Antonyms: avoid, evade, flee**

confrontation *noun* encounter, struggle, clash, conflict, battle, meeting The two rival football teams met in an exciting confrontation. ⏵ **Antonyms: avoidance, evasion**

confuse *verb* 1. baffle, bewilder, mystify, perplex, puzzle My friend's map confused me, and I got lost. 2. mistake, mix up, confound, jumble, misidentify I confused the salt and sugar and ruined the cake batter. ⏵ **Antonyms: 2. differentiate, clarify**

confusion *noun* chaos, disorder, turmoil, bewilderment, perplexity, bafflement There was much confusion when the plane landed in the wrong city. ⏵ **Antonyms: calm, order**

congeal *verb* coagulate, harden, solidify, gel, jell, thicken, set The hot bacon grease soon congealed in the frying pan. ⏵ **Antonyms: dissolve, melt, liquefy**

congenial *adjective* 1. kindred, compatible, agreeable, harmonious, like, congruous My mother and father are a congenial couple. 2. affable, friendly, amiable, genial, amicable, pleasant I think my friends are very congenial. ⏵ **Antonyms: 1. incompatible, dissimilar, 2. unfriendly, unpleasant**

congratulate *verb* applaud, cheer, hail, commend, compliment, praise We all congratulated Mary when she won the short-story contest. ⏵ **Antonyms: censure, condemn, criticize**

congregate *verb* gather, assemble, collect, convene, flock, meet My family congregates at my grandparents' for Thanksgiving. ⏵ **Antonyms: disperse, scatter, spread**

congregation *noun* 1. assembly, assemblage, collection, company, crowd, gathering There was a congregation of protesters in front of city hall. 2. flock, brethren, churchgoers, disciples, fellowship, laity The country church has a small but faithful congregation.

conjecture *noun* guess, inference, speculation, supposition, presumption, assumption It is my conjecture that he is late because he missed his train. ◆ *verb* speculate, infer, theorize, judge, surmise, guess I can only conjecture as to why she didn't come to the party. ⏵ **Antonyms:** *noun* certainty, knowledge ◆ *verb* know

connect *verb* 1. join, link, couple, attach, fasten, unite The Chunnel connects Great Britain and France. 2. associate, equate, identify, relate, correlate, link It was hard for me to connect names with faces when I first joined my scout troop. ⏵ **Antonyms: 1. detach, separate**

connection *noun* 1. attachment, coupling, junction, union, joint, link Our car wouldn't start because the battery connection was loose. 2. association, link, relation, relationship, relevance, bearing The police said there was no apparent connection between the two bank robberies.

connive *verb* collude, conspire, contrive, devise, intrigue, scheme, plot The gamblers connived to cheat the casino. ⏵ **Antonyms: resist, deplore, expose**

connoisseur *noun* expert, authority, judge, specialist, savant, adept My uncle is a connoisseur of Italian wines. ⏵ **Antonyms: amateur, novice, tyro**

connotation *noun* meaning, implication, significance, intent, import, sense Many words in the English language have multiple connotations.

conquer *verb* beat, defeat, overcome, subdue, triumph over, vanquish Rome conquered England during the first century A.D. ⏵ **Antonyms: lose, surrender, succumb**

conquest *noun* takeover, overthrow, subjugation, conquering, victory, triumph The Norman conquest of England occurred in 1066. ⏵ **Antonyms: failure, surrender, loss**

conscientious *adjective* **1. scrupulous, honest, just, honorable, moral, principled** He is one of the most conscientious people I know. **2. diligent, complete, thorough, careful, exacting, fastidious** Our teacher made a conscientious effort to learn everyone's name by the second day of school. ⟿ **Antonyms: 1. corrupt, immoral, dishonest 2. careless, sloppy**

conscious *adjective* **1. aware, knowledgeable, mindful, heedful, observant, alert** Dale gradually became conscious of having nodded off on the train ride home. **2. deliberate, intentional, planned, purposeful, calculated, willful** Jill is making a conscious effort to improve her grades. ⟿ **Antonyms: 1. unconscious, unaware 2. unintentional, impulsive**

consecutive *adjective* **successive, uninterrupted, subsequent, ensuing, succeeding, following** It rained for three consecutive days last week. ⟿ **Antonyms: interrupted, irregular**

consent *verb* **assent, agree, allow, approve, authorize, permit** I finally consented to let my brother ride my bike. ◆ *noun* **agreement, approval, assent, authorization, permission, leave** My neighbor gave his consent for me to cut through his backyard. ⟿ **Antonyms:** *verb* **object, deny, oppose** ◆ *noun* **veto, refusal, dissent**

consequence *noun* **1. aftermath, effect, outcome, result, product, upshot** I missed the bus and as a consequence had to walk to school. **2. importance, significance, value, import, influence, weight** One's high-school grades are of great consequence in deciding where to apply to college. ⟿ **Antonyms: 1. prelude, source, cause 2. insignificance, unimportance**

conservative *adjective* **discreet, conventional, reasonable, standard, traditional, moderate** Mom wore a conservative gray suit to her business meeting. ⟿ **Antonyms: liberal, radical**

conserve *verb* **preserve, save, spare, husband, keep, maintain** We were asked to conserve water during the long drought. ⟿ **Antonyms:** *verb* **consume, waste**

consider *verb* **1. contemplate, deliberate, ponder, reflect, think over, examine** I like to consider the options before I make a decision. **2. believe, judge, reckon, regard, view, account** Everyone in the class considers Greg to be the top student. **3. allow for, remember, heed, count, note** My cat is in excellent condition, especially when you consider her age. ⟿ **Antonyms: 1. & 3. ignore, overlook, neglect**

considerable *adjective* **1. extensive, substantial, great, much, large, significant** With considerable effort, we pushed the car out of the ditch. **2. important, significant, big, historic, meaningful, influential** The premiere of the new opera was a considerable event in the music world. ⟿ **Antonyms: insignificant, minor**

considerate *adjective* **thoughtful, kind, polite, courteous, attentive, friendly** It was very considerate of you to bring me some flowers from your garden. ⟿ **Antonyms: inconsiderate, thoughtless**

consideration *noun* **1. deliberation, reflection, study, thought, contemplation, debate** After much consideration, my parents have decided to buy a new house. **2. concern, factor, issue, point, circumstance, item** The weather is always a consideration when one plans a camping trip. **3. regard, respect, thoughtfulness, appreciation, courtesy, attention** She always shows consideration for other people's feelings. **4. fee, payment, recompense, remuneration, compensation, pay** I agreed to do my sister's chores for a small consideration. ⟿ **Antonyms: 1. & 3. disregard, neglect**

consist *verb* **1. comprise, contain, hold, have, include, incorporate** The vocabulary test consisted of 20 words. **2. lie, rest, exist, reside, abide, be, dwell** My idea of vacation consists in having fun and getting lots of sleep.

consistent *adjective* **steady, constant, unchanging, even, regular, predictable** The car ahead of us maintained a consistent speed. ⟿ **Antonyms: inconsistent, erratic, irregular**

consolation *noun* **solace, comfort, cheer, succor, relief, support** My parents bought me a puppy as consolation when my best friend moved away. ⟿ **Antonyms: discouragement, discomfort**

console *verb* **comfort, soothe, solace, succor, cheer, gladden** After my visit to the orthodontist, I consoled myself by purchasing a new CD. ⟿ **Antonyms: distress, perturb, upset**

consolidate *verb* **1. combine, join, link, merge, unite, centralize** The man consolidated his debts by getting one loan that covered everything. **2. strengthen, cement, fortify, reinforce, secure, enhance** We think the block party will consolidate the spirit of goodwill in our neighborhood. ⟿ **Antonyms: 1. divide, separate 2. weaken, diminish**

conspicuous *adjective* **1. noticeable, obvious, prominent, clear, evident, visible** A giraffe's long neck is its most conspicuous feature. **2. notable, striking, remarkable, unusual, eye-catching, flagrant** Flamingoes are conspicuous because of their pink feathers. **Antonyms: 1. inconspicuous, hidden 2. average, mundane**

conspiracy *noun* **intrigue, plot, scheme, collusion, plan, connivance** There was a conspiracy within the military to overthrow the country's government.

constant *adjective* **1. permanent, steady, regular, fast, unchanging, invariable** There is a saying that nothing is as constant as change. **2. persistent, continuous, continual, perpetual, incessant, endless** A newborn infant requires almost constant attention. **3. loyal, faithful, true, staunch, devoted, steadfast** Don Quixote had a constant companion named Sancho Panza. **Antonyms: 1. variable, changing 2. occasional, irregular 3. fickle, faithless**

Word Group

A **constellation** is a group of stars, especially one perceived as a design or mythological figure. **Constellation** is a specific term with no true synonyms. The 12 constellations of the zodiac (celestial band that contains the paths of the sun, moon, and principal planets) are

SCORPIUS

Aries, Taurus, Gemini, Cancer, Leo, Virgo, Libra, Scorpius, Sagittarius, Capricorn, Aquarius, Pisces

consternation *noun* **dismay, apprehension, alarm, fear, panic, indignation** We were filled with consternation when the airline lost our baggage. **Antonyms: composure, calm, equanimity**

constitute *verb* **1. compose, make up, establish, make** Do you know the ingredients that constitute a chocolate cake? **2. set up, establish, create, found, institute, originate** The Senate constituted a committee to investigate the Internal Revenue Service.

constrain *verb* **1. oblige, compel, force, obligate, pressure, coerce** I felt constrained to help with the yard work. **2. restrain, hold back, bridle, inhibit, confine, curb** We constrained our dog when his enthusiasm overwhelmed our visitors. **Antonyms: 1. ask, implore, plead 2. free, loose, release**

constrict *verb* **compress, narrow, contract, bind, squeeze, tighten** A pressure bandage slows bleeding by constricting the blood vessels. **Antonyms: expand, stretch, dilate**

construct *verb* **build, fabricate, make, erect, assemble, manufacture** I helped my dad construct our new garage.

consul *noun* **delegate, emissary, envoy, ambassador, agent, representative** The consul to Qatar spoke to our class about life in the Middle East.

consult *verb* **confer, deliberate, discuss, speak, talk, parley** Dad consulted with my mom and me before accepting an out-of-state transfer. **Antonyms: ignore, disregard**

consultation *noun* **conference, discussion, deliberation, council, counsel, session** The doctors held a consultation regarding the condition of their patient.

consume *verb* **1. devour, ingest, eat, swallow, down, digest** The giant anteater of South America can consume over thirty thousand ants in a day. **2. destroy, exhaust, finish, use up, waste, ravage** The forest fire consumed more than five hundred acres. **3. engross, preoccupy, absorb, immerse, dominate, fascinate** Lately, I have been consumed by my interest in tap dancing.

consummate *verb* **complete, conclude, wind up, wrap up, end, finish** A student art exhibit will consummate this semester's activities. ◆ *adjective* **1. complete, absolute, total, perfect, supreme, utter** My grandparents' arrival a day early was a consummate surprise. **2. skilled, polished, talented, gifted, able, matchless** We thoroughly enjoyed the pianist's consummate performance. **Antonyms:** *verb* **begin, start** ◆ *adjective* **1. incomplete, unfinished 2. mediocre, unskilled**

consumption *noun* **utilization, use, usage, consuming, assimilation, expenditure** The United States leads the world in consumption of fossil fuels. **Antonyms: conservation, preservation**

contact *noun* **1. encounter, touch, meeting, touching, connection, union** Our camp counselor warned us to avoid contact with poison ivy. **2. communication, touch, liaison, correspondence, association, closeness** I plan to keep in close contact with my friends after I move. **3. connection, source, help, associate, friend, acquaintance** My stepmom has a contact who got us tickets to a special movie premiere. ◆ *verb* **1. touch, meet, graze, brush, connect** I got an electric shock when my hand contacted the door knob. **2. communicate with, reach, call, converse, correspond, meet** Please leave a number where I can contact you.

contagious *adjective* **transmissible, communicable, catching, infectious, spreadable, transmittable** Diphtheria is a highly contagious disease.

contain *verb* **1. bear, carry, have, hold, include, accommodate** This computer disk contains all the reports I wrote this year. **2. check, control, limit, restrain, stop, suppress** Firefighters were able to contain the blaze quickly.

contaminate *verb* **foul, pollute, soil, dirty, spoil, taint, defile, infect** The oil spill contaminated several miles of shoreline. ➡ **Antonyms: purify, cleanse, purge**

contemplate *verb* **1. look at, gaze, view, behold, stare, eye** My dog contemplated the platter of cheeseburgers I had set on the counter. **2. consider, deliberate, ponder, reflect, study, think** My older sister is contemplating getting an apartment of her own.

contemporary *adjective* **1. contemporaneous, concurrent, concomitant, coexistent, parallel, synchronous** Chopin, Berlioz, Liszt, Schubert, and Wagner were contemporary composers during the romantic period. **2. current, modern, recent, late, new, present-day** There are several contemporary theories regarding functions of the brain. ➡ **Antonyms: 2. obsolete, antique, old-fashioned**

contempt *noun* **1. despite, disdain, disgust, disrespect, scorn, hatred** I felt contempt for her when I found out she had lied to me. **2. discredit, disgrace, dishonor, ignominy, disrepute, disfavor** Spies are commonly held in contempt. ➡ **Antonyms: admiration, respect**

contend *verb* **1. battle, combat, fight, duel, struggle against, wrestle** We had to contend with a lot of mosquitoes on our canoe trip. **2. compete, strive, contest, vie, challenge, struggle** The track team is contending for the state championship. **3. affirm, allege, assert, claim, declare, state** He contends that he is a better swimmer than I am. ➡ **Antonyms: 1. surrender, yield 3. deny, refute**

content[1] *noun* **1. ingredient, component, part, factor, section, piece** What are the contents of that sandwich? **2. subject, substance, text, theme, topic, thesis** The content of chapter three covers atoms and molecules.

content[2] *adjective* **contented, gratified, happy, pleased, satisfied, comfortable** Anyone who wasn't content with his or her grade could take the test again. ◆ *noun* **contentment, contentedness, happiness, pleasure, satisfaction, gratification** The man sighed with content after he finished dessert. ◆ *verb* **appease, placate, gratify, satisfy, delight, please** I couldn't go to the ball game and had to content myself with watching it on TV. ➡ **Antonyms:** *adjective* **discontented, unhappy** ◆ *noun* **dissatisfaction, unhappiness** ◆ *verb* **dissatisfy, disturb, offend**

contented *adjective* **content, gratified, happy, pleased, satisfied, comfortable** The contented baby fell asleep in her mother's arms. ➡ **Antonyms: discontented, fretful, uneasy**

contest *noun* **competition, match, tournament, championship, meet, game** She took first place in our school's spelling contest. ◆ *verb* **dispute, object to, challenge, oppose, resist, contend** The losing candidate contested the election results by calling for a recount. ➡ **Antonyms:** *verb* **accept, approve, support**

contestant *noun* **contender, competitor, participant, opponent, rival, entry** All the contestants have to be 16 or older.

continual *adjective* **constant, continuous, perpetual, persistent, incessant, steady** It's hard to study with these continual interruptions. ➡ **Antonyms: sporadic, intermittent, occasional**

continue *verb* **1. endure, go on, last, persist, remain, stay** The drought is expected to continue for the remainder of this year. **2. resume, carry on, pick up, renew, restart, reinstate** The speaker paused for a moment and then continued his lecture. ➡ **Antonyms: discontinue, stop**

continuous *adjective* **constant, continual, endless, nonstop, perpetual, uninterrupted** The human brain needs a continuous supply of oxygen-rich blood. ➡ **Antonyms: intermittent, periodic**

contort *verb* **twist, bend, convolute, distort, gnarl, knot** Our yoga instructor can contort herself into incredible positions. ➡ **Antonyms: straighten, smooth**

contour *noun* **outline, profile, silhouette, shape, form, curve** The fighter plane followed the contour of the landscape.

contract *noun* **agreement, arrangement, compact, bargain, deal, pact** My parents signed a contract when they leased a new car. ◆ *verb* **1. shorten, tighten, compress, decrease, reduce, shrink** Your muscles contract when you lift a heavy object. **2. engage, agree, pledge, promise, undertake, vow** The disposal company contracted to pick up our trash once a week. **3. acquire, catch, develop, get, incur, obtain** My uncle contracted malaria while traveling in Central America. ➡ **Antonyms:** *verb* **1. expand, lengthen**

contradict *verb* **challenge, refute, clash, conflict, controvert, disagree, oppose** The theories of Copernicus contradicted the then accepted belief that Earth was the center of the universe. ➡ **Antonyms: confirm, verify**

contradiction *noun* **1. opposition, disagreement, contrast, conflict, denial, dispute** The two books contain information that stands in contradiction. **2. difference, discrepancy, incongruity, inconsistency, dissimilarity, variation** There is a contradiction between the time on the clock and the time on my watch. ➤ **Antonyms: 1. support, corroboration, verification 2. similarity, resemblance**

contradictory *adjective* **dissimilar, inconsistent, contrary, counter, opposed, opposing** Her words are sometimes contradictory to her actions. ➤ **Antonyms: similar, consistent**

contrary *adjective* **1. contradictory, counter, opposing, opposite, different, other** Contrary to popular belief, wolves do not howl at the moon. **2. adverse, unfavorable, disagreeable, unpropitious, untoward, inauspicious** This has been a contrary day. **3. headstrong, obstinate, stubborn, perverse, wayward, disobedient** My contrary dog never comes when I call him. ➤ **Antonyms: 1. identical, consistent 2. favorable, propitious 3. compliant, submissive**

contrast *verb* **compare, distinguish, differentiate, balance, oppose, differ** My report contrasts the life of African Americans today with that of their ancestors. ◆ *noun* **difference, variation, variance, dissimilarity, divergence, counterpoint** The coolness of our basement was a refreshing contrast to the heat outside. ➤ **Antonyms:** *noun* **resemblance, similarity**

contribute *verb* **1. donate, give, grant, supply, bestow, confer** Ramona's class raised 120 dollars to contribute to a local charity. **2. aid, help, support, assist, reinforce, influence** The gold-medal gymnast said her parents' support contributed to her success. ➤ **Antonyms: 1. take, receive 2. curb, impede, detract**

contribution *noun* **donation, gift, offering, handout, present, payment** I made a five-dollar contribution to the American Red Cross.

contrite *adjective* **regretful, apologetic, repentant, remorseful, sorrowful, penitent** I was very contrite when I broke my neighbor's window. ➤ **Antonyms: unapologetic, unrepentant**

contrition *noun* **remorse, regret, compunction, contriteness, repentance, rue** Mom expressed contrition for having hurt my feelings.

contrive *verb* **1. scheme, plot, conspire, connive, plan, devise** My friend and I contrived a plan to sneak into a movie. **2. concoct, create, design, devise, improvise, form** I contrived a mousetrap out of a board and a tin can.

control *verb* **1. direct, govern, manage, dominate, supervise, administer** My dad controls all the operations of his business. **2. check, curb, restrain, subdue, suppress, repress** My dentist advised me to control my sweet tooth. ◆ *noun* **1. authority, command, direction, power, rule, management** The club's finances are under the treasurer's control. **2. check, curb, restraint, restriction, limitation, regulation** The mayor is trying to impose strict controls on public spending. **3. knob, dial, switch, button, lever, handle** I showed my parents how to use the controls on our new VCR.

controversy *noun* **contention, disagreement, debate, argument, dispute, quarrel** The President's plan to raise taxes caused much controversy. ➤ **Antonyms: agreement, accord**

convalescence *noun* **recovery, recuperation, rehabilitation, restoration, rejuvenation, improvement** I was able to return to school after a brief convalescence.

convene *verb* **assemble, congregate, gather, meet, get together, rally** The school board will convene next week. ➤ **Antonyms: adjourn, dismiss, dissolve**

convenience *noun* **advantage, benefit, amenity, ease, service, utility** The bank installed an ATM for the convenience of its customers. ➤ **Antonyms: inconvenience, disadvantage**

convenient *adjective* **advantageous, beneficial, helpful, handy, useful, expedient** Mom finds it convenient to live so near a supermarket. ➤ **Antonym: inconvenient**

convention *noun* **1. meeting, assembly, congress, convocation, conference, gathering** My mom has to attend a sales convention in San Diego. **2. custom, practice, tradition, standard, habit, formality** It is the convention in some families to have supper together every night.

conventional *adjective* **common, customary, normal, regular, standard, usual, traditional** My parents had a conventional wedding in a church. ➤ **Antonyms: uncommon, original, unusual**

conversation *noun* **chat, discussion, talk, conference, speech, tête-à-tête** I enjoyed our conversation very much.

converse[1] *verb* **chat, chitchat, speak, talk, confer, discuss** The two commuters spent the bus ride conversing about the weather.

converse[2] *adjective* **reversed, transposed, opposite, opposing, counter, inverse** The puzzle had words arranged in converse order. ◆ *noun* **opposite, reverse, antithesis, counter, contrary, antipodes** Hot is the converse of cold.

convert *verb* **alter, change, modify, switch, transform, turn** The old mansion has been converted into a museum. ◆ *noun* **believer, follower, recruit, disciple, adherent, devotee** He is a new convert to vegetarianism.

convey *verb* **1. bring, carry, transport, bear, move, transmit** The ancient Romans built aqueducts to convey water to their cities. **2. communicate, express, relate, state, disclose, impart** I searched for the right words to convey my thoughts.

convict *verb* **find guilty, sentence, condemn, judge, adjudge** The jury convicted the defendant on two counts of armed robbery. ◆ *noun* **inmate, prisoner, captive, outlaw, criminal, felon** Three convicts escaped from the state prison. ➡ **Antonyms:** *verb* **acquit, pardon**

conviction *noun* **belief, idea, opinion, position, sentiment, faith** Ann has strong convictions regarding civil rights.

convince *verb* **assure, persuade, satisfy, sway, impress, influence** Your story has convinced me that you are telling the truth. ➡ **Antonyms: dissuade, discourage, deter**

cook *verb* **prepare, do, make, heat, bake, broil, fry, grill, microwave, roast** It is my turn to cook dinner tonight.

cool *adjective* **1. chill, chilly, cold, icy, frigid, unheated** We rested in the cool shade of a big tree. **2. calm, collected, composed, serene, cool-headed, unexcited** The pilot remained cool when one of the plane's engines failed. **3. aloof, distant, remote, reserved, unfriendly, haughty** She seems cool to those who don't know her. ◆ *verb* **1. chill, refrigerate, ice, freeze, frost** We cooled our sodas by putting the bottles in the stream. **2. dampen, diminish, reduce, lessen, abate, moderate** Our enthusiasm for the hike cooled when the weather turned stormy. ➡ **Antonyms:** *adjective* **1. hot, warm 2. excited, agitated 3. friendly, warm** ◆ *verb* **1. heat, warm 2. increase, amplify**

cooperate *verb* **collaborate, work together, team up, associate, affiliate, coordinate** If we cooperate, we can clean out the garage in no time. ➡ **Antonyms: oppose, resist**

cooperation *noun* **collaboration, participation, teamwork, partnership, aid, help** Keeping the schoolyard free of litter requires the cooperation of all the students. ➡ **Antonyms: opposition, disagreement**

coordinate *adjective* **equal, equivalent, similar, alike, parallel, correlative** The two officers are coordinate in rank. ◆ *verb* **attune, adapt, conform, integrate, harmonize, synchronize** Good swimmers coordinate their breathing with their strokes. ➡ **Antonyms:** *adjective* **disparate, unequal** ◆ *verb* **disorganize, muddle**

cope *verb* **contend, deal, handle, manage, control** The baby-sitter had a tough time coping with five children at once.

copious *adjective* **abundant, ample, plentiful, bountiful, large, generous** There was a copious amount of food at the potluck. ➡ **Antonyms: skimpy, scant, meager**

copy *noun* **duplicate, reproduction, double, imitation, facsimile, replica** Medieval monks created beautiful copies of important manuscripts. ◆ *verb* **1. duplicate, reproduce, replicate, depict, simulate** Our teacher had us copy the vocabulary words from the chalkboard. **2. imitate, follow, emulate, mimic, model, ape** Many writers have copied the style of Ernest Hemingway. ➡ **Antonyms:** *noun* **original, archetype, prototype** ◆ *verb* **2. originate, create**

cord *noun* **line, strand, string, twine, rope, thread** Ethan used a length of cord to tie up the newspapers.

cordial *adjective* **courteous, friendly, congenial, nice, pleasant, warm** She received a cordial invitation to stay for dinner. ➡ **Antonyms: unfriendly, ungracious, cool**

core *noun* **1. kernel, seed, pit** We save our apple cores for the compost pile. **2. center, middle, interior, inside, heart, nucleus** Earth has a dense core of nickel and iron. **3. essence, crux, foundation, heart, root, basis** My teacher has identified the core of my difficulty in math.

corner *noun* **1. edge, angle, bend, end, point, nook** I folded the corner of a page to mark my place in the book. **2. intersection, junction, juncture, crossing, crossroads** Frank lives on the corner of First and Maple streets. **3. jam, predicament, dilemma, fix, impasse, plight, pickle** I was boxed into a corner by my conflicting obligations. **4. monopoly, domination, control, mastery, ownership, cartel** With a corner on the market, a company can control price and availability. ◆ *verb* **trap, entrap, snare, ensnare, capture, catch** Our hamster got out, and I finally cornered it behind the couch.

corporal *adjective* **bodily, physical, corporeal, fleshly, somatic** Whipping is a form of corporal punishment.

corporation *noun* **business, company, firm, establishment, enterprise, concern** She works for a corporation that develops computer software.

corps *noun* **unit, detachment, force, crew, outfit, company, body** The Civilian Conservation Corps was established in 1933 and provided work for men aged 18 to 25.

correct *verb* **1. fix, remedy, right, amend, rectify, adjust, repair** These eyeglasses will correct your vision. **2. discipline, chastise, chasten, reprove, reprimand, punish** I had to correct my dog when he tore the newspaper to bits. ◆ *adjective* **1. accurate, exact, precise, right, true, flawless** The correct spelling of most words can be found in a dictionary. **2. decent, proper, respectable, appropriate, fitting** The correct thing to do is to return a lost wallet to its rightful owner. ◆ **Antonyms:** *verb* **1. spoil, ruin, damage 2. condone, excuse** ◆ *adjective* **1. incorrect, false, wrong 2. improper, inappropriate**

correction *noun* **1. revision, improvement, remedy, alteration, emendation, adjustment** I made a lot of spelling corrections before I handed in my report. **2. discipline, punishment, penalty, chastisement, castigation, reproof** A person convicted of a minor crime may be sent to a house of correction.

correlate *verb* **equate, compare, associate, connect, coordinate, correspond** The results of the two independent experiments correlated perfectly. ◆ **Antonyms: contradict, oppose**

correlation *noun* **relationship, connection, interrelationship, correspondence, interconnection, interdependence** There is a correlation between getting adequate sleep and doing well in school.

correspond *verb* **1. accord, agree, match, jibe, fit, harmonize, equate** Theses facts do not correspond with what I saw on TV. **2. communicate, exchange letters, write, contact, pen** She corresponds regularly with her pen pal in Sweden. ◆ **Antonyms: 1. differ, disagree**

corridor *noun* **hall, hallway, aisle, passage, passageway, gallery** The principal's office is at the end of the main corridor.

corroborate *verb* **confirm, support, authenticate, prove, verify, affirm** Experiments have corroborated the theory that regular exercise promotes longevity. ◆ **Antonyms: disprove, repudiate**

corrode *verb* **eat away, wear away, erode, rust, oxidize, destroy** Acid rain corrodes railroad tracks, stone buildings, and statues.

corrupt *adjective* **1. bad, dishonest, unprincipled, immoral, wicked, depraved, debased** The corrupt boxer accepted a bribe to lose the fight. **2. inaccurate, erroneous, wrong, false, faulty, bad** The data was corrupt because the experiment had not been recorded accurately. ◆ *verb* **1. degrade, debase, warp, pervert, subvert, deprave** Greed has corrupted many people. **2. contaminate, spoil, defile, pollute, taint, foul** My computer's hard drive has been corrupted by a virus. ◆ **Antonyms:** *adjective* **1. virtuous, honorable 2. accurate, correct**

corruption *noun* **dishonesty, corruptness, crookedness, wrongdoing, vice, wickedness** The former city official went to prison for bribery and corruption. ◆ **Antonyms: honesty, integrity**

cost *noun* **1. charge, price, amount, expense, payment, outlay** If you buy these sunglasses, the case is included at no extra cost. **2. loss, sacrifice, toll, damage, injury, penalty, expense** The general said that the enemy had to be defeated at any cost. ◆ *verb* **1. sell for, go for, come to, amount to, fetch, bring** This book costs 17 dollars. **2. lose, sacrifice, injure, hurt, harm, damage** His mistake cost him the contract.

costly *adjective* **1. expensive, high-priced, high, dear, steep, valuable** I like this skateboard, but it is too costly. **2. harmful, damaging, injurious, disastrous, ruinous** Gail found out that cheating on the test was a costly mistake. ◆ **Antonyms: 1. inexpensive, reasonable, cheap**

costume *noun* **attire, clothing, clothes, apparel, dress, outfit, disguise** Most of the guests wore native costumes to the luau.

cottage *noun* **bungalow, cabin, chalet, lodge, hut, home** My grandparents own a summer cottage on Cape Cod.

council *noun* **assembly, board, cabinet, committee, panel, congress** The student council will meet today.

counsel *noun* **advice, guidance, recommendation, suggestion, direction, opinion** I asked my music teacher's counsel on which piece I should play for the recital. ◆ *verb* **advise, guide, direct, instruct, recommend, suggest** My advisor counseled me on selecting courses for next year.

counselor *noun* **adviser, consultant, attorney, counsel, advocate, guide, mentor** My stepfather is a mental health counselor.

count *verb* **1. add up, total, calculate, enumerate, tally, figure** The chaperon counted heads to make sure that everyone was present. **2. include, admit, consider, regard, impute, ascribe** Do you count your pets as members of the family? **3. regard, consider, believe, deem, hold, rate,**

reckon I count myself fortunate to have known him. **4. matter, concern, signify, import, weigh, affect** It is what you do that counts, not what you say. ◆ *noun* **sum, total, calculation, computation, tally, enumeration** The ballot count revealed that Michele had won the class election.

counter *adjective* **opposite, contrary, reverse, contradictory, antithetical, contrasting** The opinion polls were running counter to the politician's hopes. ◆ *verb* **oppose, answer, respond, return, parry, retort** Lindsey countered my suggestion that we get pizza by proposing hamburgers instead.

counterfeit *verb* **1. forge, falsify, imitate, copy, reproduce, mimic** They arrested the criminal who had been counterfeiting 20-dollar bills. **2. fake, pretend, affect, put on, simulate, feign** A good actress or actor can counterfeit any emotion. ◆ *adjective* **1. fake, forged, imitation, phony, false, fraudulent** These counterfeit bills look like the real thing. **2. pretended, simulated, feigned, affected, assumed, insincere** Nobody trusts him because his sincerity is often counterfeit. ◆ *noun* **fake, forgery, imitation, reproduction, phony, facsimile, substitute, copy, sham** This stock certificate looks real, but it is actually a counterfeit. ◈ **Antonyms:** *adjective* **1. authentic, genuine 2. sincere**

countermand *verb* **reverse, change, undo, contradict, cancel, recall** The officer countermanded the orders he had given his troops. ◈ **Antonyms: endorse, support**

counterpart *noun* **1. equal, equivalent, peer, parallel, analogue, complement** England's prime minister is roughly the counterpart of America's President. **2. match, twin, mate, companion, fellow, opposite number** I have one earring, but I can't find its counterpart.

country *noun* **1. nation, state, domain, kingdom, realm, homeland** Canada is the country that borders the United States to the north. **2. land, terrain, territory, region, area, province** California's vast central valley is good farming country. **3. countryside, rural area, hinterland, backcountry, wilds, outdoors** They sold their condominium and bought a house in the country.

couple *noun* **1. duo, pair, twosome, team, brace, span, yoke** Fourteen couples entered the dance contest. **2. few, some, several, set, bunch, group** I was hungry, so I ate a couple of bananas. ◆ *verb* **attach, connect, fasten, join, link, unite** I helped Dad couple the horse trailer to our pickup truck. ◈ **Antonyms:** *noun* **2. many, lots** ◆ *verb* **detach, separate**

courage *noun* **bravery, courageousness, fearlessness, gallantry, heroism, valor** The firefighter was commended for her great courage. ◈ **Antonyms: cowardice, fear**

courageous *adjective* **brave, fearless, gallant, heroic, valiant, intrepid** The courageous boy climbed a tree to rescue his neighbor's cat. ◈ **Antonyms: cowardly, fearful**

course *noun* **1. flow, march, movement, progress, progression, passage** In the course of a typical evening, I eat my dinner and do my homework. **2. direction, path, route, track, bearing, heading** The ocean liner changed course to avoid running into an iceberg. **3. plan, policy, procedure, approach, method, program** Your best course is to tell the truth. **4. class, lesson, subject, lecture, seminar** My mom is taking a writing course at the university. **5. chain, sequence, succession, series, order, progression** We studied the course of events that led up to the Civil War. ◆ *verb* **flow, run, stream, gush, surge, race** After the downpour, water coursed through the reservoir's spillway.

court *noun* **1. courtyard, atrium, cloister, enclosure, piazza, plaza** The court was planted with flowers and trees. **2. law court, bar, tribunal, bench, forum, judge** There are nine justices on the Supreme Court. **3. cortege, entourage, retinue, staff, suite, attendants** Queen Elizabeth I used to travel about the English countryside with her court. ◆ *verb* **woo, romance, date, pay court, seek, pursue, follow** I like to hear about the days when my dad and mom were courting.

courteous *adjective* **polite, civil, considerate, respectful, well-mannered, gracious** A courteous driver let Dad pull into the lane. ◈ **Antonyms: discourteous, rude**

courtesy *noun* **graciousness, politeness, respect, civility, courteousness, consideration** The salesperson treated her customer with courtesy. ◈ **Antonyms: rudeness, discourtesy**

cover *verb* **1. protect, shelter, shield, guard, defend, safeguard** The workers covered their ears before the explosion. **2. hide, conceal, blanket, coat, obscure, conceal, cloak** The first snow of the season covered the ground. **3. comprise, contain, embrace, include, occupy, consist of** The ranch covers more than 5,100 acres. **4. journey, pass over, travel, make, traverse, cross** The backpackers covered ten miles on their first day of hiking. **5. double, substitute, take over, stand in, fill in, relieve** The understudy covered for the sick actor. ◆ *noun* **1. lid, top, cap, stopper, seal, covering** Please put the cover on the pot. **2. shelter, refuge, protection, concealment, haven, asylum** The boat took cover in a harbor during the storm. ◈ **Antonyms:** *verb* **2. reveal, expose, uncover**

covert *adjective* **concealed, secret, hidden, clandestine, surreptitious, unknown** The government took covert action against the rebels. ◈ **Antonyms:** *adjective* **overt, open, candid**

covet *verb* crave, desire, want, wish for, long for, envy I think my dog covets my turkey sandwich. ➡ **Antonyms:** decline, renounce

covetous *adjective* envious, jealous, acquisitive, avaricious, greedy, rapacious I am covetous of the beautiful clothes I see in fashion magazines. ➡ **Antonyms:** generous, charitable, unselfish

cow *verb* frighten, scare, intimidate, menace, daunt, subdue My neighbor cowed the noisy children with his stern voice. ➡ **Antonyms:** encourage, support, hearten

cowardly *adjective* fearful, craven, timid, pusillanimous, recreant, timorous The Cowardly Lion in *The Wonderful Wizard of Oz* is my favorite character. ➡ **Antonyms:** brave, courageous

cozy *adjective* comfortable, comfy, snug, warm, safe, secure We felt cozy in front of the fireplace as it stormed outside. ➡ **Antonyms:** cold, uncomfortable

crack *verb* 1. snap, slap, smack, whack, bang, pop The cowboy cracked his whip. 2. break, fracture, splinter, split, rupture, shatter The severe cold last night cracked our windshield. 3. solve, decipher, decode, puzzle out, figure out, unscramble The spy cracked the code. ◆ *noun* 1. bang, blast, report, boom, clap, pop, explosion The crack of a rifle echoed through the canyon. 2. break, chink, crevice, gap, split, opening, fissure The boy peeked through a crack in the fence. 3. attempt, fling, go, shot, stab, try I think I'll take a crack at in-line skating. 4. witticism, joke, jest, quip, remark, gibe Even the teacher laughed when the boy made a funny crack. ◆ *adjective* expert, master, proficient, skilled, skillful, first-rate My uncle Bill is a crack marksman. ➡ **Antonyms:** *verb* 3. encode ◆ *adjective* inferior, second-rate, poor

cradle *noun* 1. baby bed, bassinet, basket, crib The baby sleeps in an antique cradle. 2. birthplace, origin, source, spring, fountain, wellspring Mesopotamia is often called the cradle of western civilization. ◆ *verb* hold, support, hug, embrace, cuddle, rock I cradled my baby brother until he went to sleep.

craft *noun* 1. ability, art, expertise, skill, talent, adeptness The embroidery on this scarf was done with great craft. 2. cunning, cleverness, craftiness, artifice, slyness, wiliness Many animals use craft in obtaining food. 3. handicraft, trade, art, occupation, profession, job, work, calling Violin-making is a difficult craft to learn. 4. boat, ship, vessel, watercraft, aircraft, airplane, plane, spacecraft Small craft were warned to stay in port during the storm. ◆ *verb* make, construct, create, fashion, build, fabricate, form The ancient Egyptians crafted flint knives of exquisite quality. ➡ **Antonyms:** *noun* 1. inability, incompetence

crafty *adjective* cunning, scheming, sly, wily, deceitful, artful, canny Genghis Khan was a crafty and fearless leader. ➡ **Antonyms:** honest, open, sincere

cram *verb* jam, load, pack, squeeze, stuff, force, compress I crammed all my T-shirts into one dresser drawer. ➡ **Antonyms:** empty, drain, clear

cramp *noun* contraction, convulsion, spasm, charley horse, twitch, crick I awoke during the night with a cramp in my leg. ◆ *verb* contract, convulse, seize, crick, tighten, stiffen I stretch before exercising so my muscles won't cramp.

cranky *adjective* cross, grouchy, grumpy, irritable, peevish, testy My little brother gets cranky if he misses his afternoon nap. ➡ **Antonyms:** cheerful, happy

crash *verb* 1. fall, topple, collapse, tumble, plunge, smash The huge pine tree crashed to the ground during the hurricane. 2. bump, collide, hit, smash, strike, wreck My radio-controlled car crashed into a tree. ◆ *noun* 1. bang, crack, slam, clatter, smash, racket, din I dropped my bowling ball, and it hit the floor with a loud crash. 2. accident, smashup, crackup, pileup, wreck, collision, impact The plane was destroyed in the crash. 3. collapse, ruin, failure, depression, breakdown, debacle An economic crash would cause many people to lose their jobs.

crass *adjective* crude, coarse, rude, indelicate, vulgar, boorish, churlish My mother scolded my brother for his crass behavior. ➡ **Antonyms:** refined, sensitive

crate *noun* box, carton, case, package, chest, container We packed the crate carefully for shipment overseas. ◆ *verb* pack, package, box, box up, encase, store Mom crated my old toys and put them in storage.

crave *verb* covet, desire, hunger for, long for, want, wish for, yearn for I am craving chocolate.

crawl *verb* creep, drag, inch, slither, plod, poke I watched a snail crawl across the patio. ◆ *noun* creep, snail's pace, plod, walk, trudge Traffic slowed to a crawl during rush hour.

crazy *adjective* 1. mentally ill, insane, mad, lunatic, demented, deranged, daft A crazy man stood on the street corner shouting at passersby. 2. absurd, dumb, foolish, silly, stupid, outrageous Putting ice cream on your pizza was a crazy thing to do. **3.** enthusiastic, excited, passionate, wild, ardent, fanatical I am crazy about rap music. ➻ **Antonyms: 1.** rational, sane **2.** sensible, practical **3.** apathetic, indifferent

creak *verb* squeak, screech, rasp, grate, squeal, groan The barn door creaked as I opened it. ◆ *noun* squeak, squeal, screech, rasp, groan The rocking chair makes a soft creak.

crease *noun* fold, wrinkle, rumple, line, pleat, crimp, pucker Dad ironed the creases out of his new shirt. ◆ *verb* fold, double, bend, pleat, crimp, crinkle, wrinkle A piece of paper tears in half more easily if you crease it first. ➻ **Antonyms:** *verb* smooth, flatten

create *verb* produce, establish, make, start, institute, originate The new factory is expected to create many jobs. ➻ **Antonyms:** destroy, demolish

creation *noun* **1.** making, development, establishment, formation, fabrication, origination, birth The creation of a seven-layer wedding cake takes many hours. **2.** product, achievement, work, masterpiece, conception, handiwork My latest creation is a self-portrait.

creative *adjective* ingenious, imaginative, inventive, innovative, resourceful, original, talented The creative teacher always has her class's attention. ➻ **Antonyms:** unimaginative, uninspired

creature *noun* **1.** animal, beast, critter, organism, entity, being, living being Unicorns are mythical creatures. **2.** person, soul, individual, human, human being My aunt is a lovely creature.

credence *noun* trust, belief, faith, credit, confidence, reliance I do not put much credence in fortune telling. ➻ **Antonyms:** doubt, disbelief, mistrust

credentials *noun* certificate, diploma, affidavit, reference, authorization, permit, license She has all the credentials to teach grade school.

credible *adjective* believable, plausible, likely, possible, tenable, convincing She had a credible excuse for missing the meeting. ➻ **Antonyms:** inconceivable, unbelievable, dubious

credit *noun* **1.** belief, confidence, trust, faith, reliance, credence Do you place any credit in astrology? **2.** acknowledgment, recognition, commendation, due, praise, acclaim I gave my sisters a lot of credit for the

wonderful party preparations. **3.** installment plan, loan, debt, trust My parents bought some new pieces of furniture on credit. ◆ *verb* **1.** believe, trust, accept, endorse, grant, acknowledge Do you credit his story? **2.** attribute, ascribe, accredit, assign, acknowledge, charge The invention of the telephone is credited to Alexander Graham Bell. ➻ **Antonyms:** *noun* **1.** doubt, mistrust ◆ *verb* **1.** doubt, mistrust, question

creditable *adjective* praiseworthy, commendable, respectable, laudable, meritorious, estimable, worthy Mom says I did a very creditable job with my first pie. ➻ **Antonyms:** disreputable, unworthy

credo *noun* creed, tenet, code, rule, philosophy, belief, doctrine Thomas A. Edison's credo was "There is no substitute for hard work."

credulous *adjective* gullible, naive, accepting, believing, susceptible, trusting My friend is so credulous that she will believe anything. ➻ **Antonyms:** incredulous, suspicious, wary

creed *noun* belief, doctrine, faith, principle, philosophy, dogma, credo Employers cannot discriminate on the basis of race, color, or creed.

creek *noun* brook, kill, stream, streamlet, run, branch Emilio and his brother are down at the creek trying to catch tadpoles.

creep *verb* crawl, slink, slip, sneak, steal, edge, inch The lion crept silently toward its prey.

crest *noun* **1.** topknot, comb, cockscomb, tuft, plume, crown My cockatiel raises its crest whenever it is alarmed. **2.** summit, top, peak, crown, zenith, culmination, height, pinnacle I climbed to the crest of the hill. ◆ *verb* peak, top, cap, crown, summit, surmount When we crested the ridge, we had a magnificent view of the valley below. ➻ **Antonyms:** *noun* **2.** base, bottom

crevice *noun* crack, fissure, chink, cleft, split, opening, slit I caught my high heel in a crevice in the sidewalk.

crew *noun* band, company, gang, group, team, staff, unit I joined the crew that was cleaning up the schoolyard.

crime *noun* **1.** offense, violation, felony, illegality, misdemeanor, infraction Shoplifting is a crime. **2.** outrage, sin, wrong, wrongdoing, iniquity, misdeed, offense It would be a crime to waste all this food.

criminal *adjective* **1. illegal, lawless, illegitimate, illicit, unlawful, felonious** Stealing a car is a criminal act. **2. shameful, disgraceful, wrong, wicked, immoral, sinful** I think it's criminal to waste water. ◆ *noun* **crook, felon, lawbreaker, malefactor, offender, outlaw, convict** Police are searching for the criminal who robbed the bank. ➦ **Antonyms:** *adjective* **1. lawful, legal 2. praiseworthy, right, just**

crimp *verb* **crease, crinkle, plait, flute, bend, wrinkle, pinch** I crimped the fabric to make a ruffle for the curtain. ◆ *noun* **fold, crease, pleat, flute, wrinkle, crinkle, wave** She used a curling iron to put crimps in her hair.

cringe *verb* **shrink back, draw back, flinch, blench, cower, recoil, shy** I cringed when I saw the snake.

cripple *verb* **disable, paralyze, knock out, immobilize, paralyze, damage, weaken, impair** A heavy snowstorm crippled the city's transportation system.

crisis *noun* **catastrophe, disaster, emergency, predicament, exigency, problem** A financial crisis ensued when the city government ran out of money.

critical *adjective* **1. disapproving, condemning, judgmental, censorious, captious, disparaging** My art teacher was critical of my efforts. **2. discerning, discriminating, judicious, fastidious, exact, precise** The wine taster has a very critical palate. **3. decisive, crucial, important, acute, urgent, pressing, vital** Negotiations have reached a critical stage. **4. dangerous, desperate, grave, serious, severe, risky, perilous** The accident victims were in critical condition. ➦ **Antonyms: 1. approving, complimentary 2. undiscriminating 3. unimportant, minor 4. safe, sound**

criticize *verb* **1. evaluate, judge, examine, appraise, review, analyze** How can you criticize that movie when you haven't seen it? **2. censure, fault, pan, blast, lambaste, denounce, condemn** It is common for people to criticize government policy. ➦ **Antonyms: 2. compliment, praise**

crook *noun* **1. staff, rod, pole, shaft, stick, cane, wand** The shepherd used his crook to control his flock. **2. bend, curve, hook, turn, fork, notch, angle** I live just past that crook in the road. **3. cheat, swindler, chiseler, criminal, thief, scoundrel, villain** That crook is trying to sell fake tickets to the Super Bowl. ◆ *verb* **bow, curve, turn, angle, bend, arc, hook** The river crooks around the hill and then meanders down the valley.

crop *noun* **harvest, yield, growth, production, fruits, produce** Farmers are expecting a good crop of rice this year.

◆ *verb* **clip, cut, prune, shear, trim, lop, mow** The barber cropped my hair too short.

cross *noun* **1. burden, affliction, load, trial, tribulation, adversity** Being the child of an alcoholic is a difficult cross to bear. **2. crossbreed, hybrid, mixture, blend, combination, mongrel** My dog is a cross between a Labrador and a golden retriever. ◆ *verb* **1. move across, transit, travel over, traverse, pass, navigate** An airplane can cross the United States in about five hours. **2. intersect, crisscross, join, meet, converge, connect** There is a gas station where those two streets cross. **3. thwart, obstruct, interfere with, frustrate, stymie, foil** The boss doesn't like his employees to cross him. **4. crossbreed, interbreed, blend, combine, join, mix** The boysenberry was developed by crossing blackberries with raspberries. ◆ *adjective* **angry, irritable, mad, annoyed, grouchy, grumpy** My dad was cross with me for leaving his tools outside. ➦ **Antonyms:** *verb* **3. support, assist** ◆ *adjective* **amiable, friendly, pleased**

crouch *verb* **squat, stoop, bend, kneel, hunker, hunch** I had to crouch to pass under the railing.

crowd *noun* **1. flock, horde, mob, multitude, swarm, throng** A crowd of people gathered to watch the parade. **2. clique, gang, bunch, circle, group, set, coterie** I've been hanging out with a new crowd for the past few months. ◆ *verb* **1. stuff, cram, pack, press, jam, squeeze, force** I can't crowd another piece of clothing into my closet. **2. cluster, flock, mob, throng, swarm, gather** Fans crowded around the hockey player to get his autograph. ➦ **Antonyms:** *verb* **2. disperse, scatter**

crown *noun* **1. diadem, coronet, tiara, chaplet, garland, headdress, wreath** The Iron Crown of Lombardy, made in A.D. 591, is perhaps the oldest in Europe. **2. monarchy, throne, kingdom, realm, monarch, sovereign, ruler** A representative of the Crown met with the visiting emissary. ◆ *verb* **1. enthrone, invest, install, empower, induct, anoint, sanction** Princess Elizabeth was crowned queen of the United Kingdom in June 1952. **2. cap, climax, consummate, culminate, top off, peak, fulfill** The honorary degree crowned the acclaimed poet's career. ➦ **Antonyms:** *verb* **1. depose, dethrone**

crucial *adjective* **critical, urgent, important, essential, acute, desperate** It is crucial that we submit the application by the deadline. ➦ **Antonyms: unimportant, insignificant**

crude *adjective* **1. raw, unrefined, unprocessed, coarse, simple, unfinished, original** Crude oil is shipped in tankers to refineries. **2. makeshift, rough, simplistic, primitive,**

rudimentary, basic My brother used old boards and packing crates to make a crude desk. **3. impolite, rude, boorish, churlish, crass, tasteless, uncivilized** Mother will not tolerate crude manners at the dinner table. ◈ **Antonyms: 2. fine, sophisticated 3. courteous, polite**

cruel *adjective* **brutal, mean, harsh, ruthless, unkind, savage** I believe that people should never be cruel to animals. ◈ **Antonyms: compassionate, kind**

cruise *verb* **navigate, sail, voyage, boat, travel, wander** We cruised out to Catalina Island in our neighbor's sailboat. ◆ *noun* **boat trip, sail, voyage, crossing, passage, jaunt, journey** Mom and Dad went on a cruise for their anniversary.

crumble *verb* **1. decay, disintegrate, collapse, break down, decompose, decline** The old building was starting to crumble. **2. break, crunch, crush, mash, pulverize, grind** I like to crumble crackers into my soup.

crumple *verb* **1. wrinkle, rumple, crease, crimp, crush, press, mash** Lucas crumpled his clothes when he packed his suitcase carelessly. **2. buckle, collapse, cave in, fall, topple, tumble** Our tent crumpled because we had not anchored it properly. ◈ **Antonyms: 1. smooth, iron**

crush *verb* **1. mash, squash, crumple, compress, flatten, pound** I always crush aluminum cans before recycling them. **2. squeeze, shove, push, jam, force, cram, wedge** I crushed the last sack of garbage into the can. **3. subdue, extinguish, quench, quash, defeat, quell, destroy** The dictator tried to crush all opposition. ◆ *noun* **1. crowd, pack, swarm, throng, mass, mob, press** After the concert, we made our way through the crush of people. **2. infatuation, passing fancy, puppy love, passion, fondness, liking** I have a crush on my sister's friend.

cry *verb* **1. shed tears, sob, weep, wail, bawl, blubber, keen** Many people cry at weddings. **2. call, shout, yell, bellow, scream, holler, exclaim** She cried out when she saw the speeding car. ◆ *noun* **1. exclamation, ejaculation, call, scream, shout, yell** The woman gave a cry of delight when she saw her long lost brother. **2. weeping, wailing, sobbing, bawling, tears, lamentation** The cries of the grieving family could be heard in the hospital hallway. **3. outcry, appeal, plea, call, clamor, protest, demand** We gave a cry of protest at being assigned homework over winter vacation.

crypt *noun* **vault, tomb, catacomb, sepulcher, grave, mausoleum** We visited the underground crypt of the castle.

cryptic *adjective* **mysterious, puzzling, enigmatic, mystifying, ambiguous, vague** The fortuneteller made some cryptic pronouncements about my future. ◈ **Antonyms: lucid, clear**

cuddle *verb* **nestle, snuggle, embrace, hug, nuzzle, clasp** My baby sister likes to cuddle with her teddy bear.

cue *noun* **signal, sign, prompt, word, warning, hint, reminder** I made my entrance on stage when I heard my cue.

culminate *verb* **climax, cap, top off, complete, consummate, end** A field day will culminate our school year. ◈ **Antonyms: begin, start**

culpable *adjective* **guilty, at fault, blameworthy, liable, responsible** The jury is debating whether or not the defendant is culpable. ◈ **Antonyms: innocent, blameless**

culprit *noun* **guilty party, wrongdoer, offender, criminal, lawbreaker, transgressor** Who's the culprit that ate my ice cream?

cultivate *verb* **1. grow, raise, farm, plant, till, breed, propagate** The French are famous for cultivating fine grapes. **2. foster, nourish, nurture, develop, improve, better** Reading can help to cultivate one's mind.

cultivation *noun* **1. farming, gardening, horticulture, husbandry, planting, plowing** This nursery specializes in the cultivation of tropical plants. **2. development, enhancement, furtherance, improvement, advancement, fostering, promotion** The cultivation of knowledge is valuable to future endeavors. **3. culture, refinement, sophistication, education, taste, manners** The speaker was a woman of wit and cultivation. ◈ **Antonyms: 2. degeneration, deterioration 3. boorishness, crassness**

culture *noun* **1. civilization, society, social order, customs** We are studying the culture of ancient Greece. **2. breeding, cultivation, refinement, urbanity, manners, taste** I admire my teacher because he is a man of culture. ◈ **Antonyms: 2. vulgarity, boorishness**

cumbersome *adjective* **bulky, awkward, unwieldy, unmanageable, ungainly** The cumbersome chair was difficult to move. ◈ **Antonyms: compact, manageable**

cunning *adjective* **1. clever, crafty, shrewd, ingenious, sly, tricky, artful** The cunning spy avoided capture. **2. charming, cute, appealing, dainty, sweet, quaint, petite** My friend has a cunning little statue of a bluebird. ◆ *noun* **1. craftiness, foxiness, slyness, shrewdness, guile, artifice** Sherlock Holmes was known for his skill and cunning. **2. cleverness, art, craft, skill, ability,**

expertise, dexterity Agatha Christie writes mystery novels with masterful cunning. ⏵ **Antonyms:** *adjective* 1. **honest, direct, straightforward** 2. **unappealing**

> ## Word Group
>
> A **cup** is a small open container, usually having a handle, from which to drink liquids. **Cup** is a general term with no true synonyms. Here are some common types of cups:
>
> A **beaker** is a drinking cup with a wide mouth. A small cup for serving strong black coffee is a **demitasse.** A **goblet** has a stem and a base. A **mug** is large and heavy and is typically used for hot drinks. A **noggin** is a small mug or cup. A beer mug is a **stein.** A **tankard** has a single handle and often a hinged cover.

curb *noun* **check, limit, limitation, restraint, restriction, constraint, control** The government is trying to put a curb on inflation. ◆ *verb* **restrict, restrain, check, control, hold in, rein in, inhibit, keep back, bridle** I am trying to curb my habit of interrupting. ⏵ **Antonyms:** *verb* **encourage, foster, advance**

curdle *verb* **congeal, coagulate, jell, solidify, set, clot** The milk curdled because it was heated too quickly. ⏵ **Antonyms: thin, dilute, weaken**

cure *noun* 1. **recovery, restoration, healing, recuperation, rehabilitation** My doctor expects me to realize a complete cure. 2. **remedy, curative, treatment, therapy, countermeasure, medicine** Medical researchers have yet to find a cure for the common cold. ◆ *verb* 1. **heal, remedy, help, improve, relieve, alleviate** These aspirin should cure your headache.

curious *adjective* 1. **inquiring, inquisitive, interested, questioning, investigative, concerned** The entire class was curious about our new teacher. 2. **peculiar, odd, remarkable, strange, unusual, weird** It is a curious fact that some catfish can walk on land. ⏵ **Antonyms:** 1. **indifferent, unconcerned** 2. **normal, usual, ordinary**

curl *verb* **twist, coil, wind, weave, spiral, twine, roll** The python curled itself around a tree branch. ◆ *noun* **coil, spiral, twist, roll, swirl, whorl, wave** We watched a curl of smoke rise from the campfire.

currency *noun* **cash, legal tender, money, coinage, lucre, specie** Before crossing the border, we exchanged our American dollars for Mexican currency.

current *adjective* 1. **latest, new, up-to-date, modern, contemporary, present-day** Kimberly bought the current issue of her favorite magazine. 2. **accepted, popular, prevailing, prevalent, predominant, common, general** Current theory holds that Earth was formed about 4.5 billion years ago. ◆ *noun* 1. **flow, draft, stream, course, tide, flux, flood** Many birds use air currents to glide across the sky. 2. **tendency, trend, direction, inclination, drift, tenor** The main current of public opinion is in favor of the President's policies. ⏵ **Antonyms:** *adjective* 1. **out-of-date, past** 2. **unpopular, uncommon**

curse *noun* 1. **oath, spell, jinx, charm, hex, appeal, prayer** The witch's curse changed the handsome prince into a frog. 2. **scourge, bane, affliction, burden, ill, woe, torment** Pollution and overcrowding are two curses of modern civilization. ◆ *verb* 1. **damn, cuss, swear at, revile, blast, condemn, denounce** The farmer cursed the tornado that had ruined his crops. 2. **afflict, burden, torment, torture, trouble, plague** The poor man seems to be cursed with bad luck.

cursory *adjective* **superficial, perfunctory, casual, random, haphazard, hasty** I took a cursory look at the book before buying it. ⏵ **Antonyms: thorough, painstaking, comprehensive**

curt *adjective* **abrupt, blunt, brusque, gruff, short, brief, terse** His answer was curt and to the point. ⏵ **Antonyms: courteous, verbose**

curtail *verb* **cut short, reduce, shorten, abbreviate, condense, truncate** We had to curtail our trip because of the storm. ⏵ **Antonyms: expand, extend, prolong**

curtain *noun* 1. **drape, drapery, valance, window dressing, hanging** Mom bought new curtains for the kitchen. 2. **cover, shield, screen, veil, cloak, mantle** The soldiers were hidden by a curtain of fog. ◆ *verb* **conceal, cover, hide, shade, screen, veil, block** We planted honeysuckle to curtain the chain link fence. ⏵ **Antonyms:** *verb* **uncover, expose, disclose**

curve *noun* **bend, turn, twist, bow, arch, arc, curvature** There are a lot of dangerous curves in this road. ◆ *verb* **bend, angle, turn, twist, wind, crook, coil** The trail curves around the base of that hill.

cushion *noun* 1. **bolster, pillow, pad, mat, padding, seat** Our couch needs new cushions. 2. **buffer, shield, protection, moderator, counterbalance** My parents set some money aside as a cushion against an emergency. ◆ *verb* **dampen, deaden, lessen, soften, suppress,**

absorb Our thick carpet cushioned the impact when I fell from the chair. ● **Antonyms:** *verb* amplify, increase

custodian *noun* caretaker, janitor, attendant, superintendent, guardian, keeper Our school custodian is well liked.

custody *noun* **1.** guardianship, care, charge, keeping, supervision, protection I was in my grandparents' custody while my parents were away. **2.** confinement, detention, jail, prison, imprisonment, incarceration Police have their prime suspect in custody.

custom *noun* **1.** rite, ritual, rule, tradition, practice, convention Many Jews observe the custom of fasting on the day of Yom Kippur. **2.** habit, routine, practice, procedure, wont, way It is my mother's custom to go for a two-mile walk every day.

customary *adjective* common, normal, routine, standard, traditional, usual It is customary to leave a tip when dining in a restaurant. ● **Antonyms:** rare, unusual

customer *noun* buyer, consumer, shopper, client, patron The store was swamped with customers during the big sale. ● **Antonyms:** merchant, vender, salesman

cut *verb* **1.** slice, carve, incise, slash, split, chop Please use this knife to cut the watermelon. **2.** clip, snip, trim, shear, shorten, crop, mow I get my hair cut every six weeks. **3.** chop down, fell, hew, topple, chop, harvest I helped Dad cut down the dead tree in our back yard. **4.** halt, interrupt, stop, end, quit, cease Dad cut the engine and let the car coast to a stop. **5.** decrease, lower, reduce, lessen, diminish, curtail, remove The candidate promised to cut taxes. **6.** abridge, edit, abbreviate, condense, shorten, reduce, trim My report was too long, so I cut it. **7.** offend, hurt, wound, affront, upset, pain, grieve Her harsh remark cut me deeply. ◆ *noun* **1.** laceration, gash, slash, slit, wound, incision The doctor said that my cut did not require stitches. **2.** cutback, decrease, reduction, slash, abatement, curtailment Cuts in the state budget mean no new highways will be built this year. **3.** percentage, share, slice, part, allotment, split, portion The business partners took equal cuts of the profits. **4.** insult, slight, offense, indignity, rebuff, dig, jibe I did not mean for that remark to be a cut at you. ● **Antonyms:** *verb* 4. begin, start 5. increase, amplify 6. lengthen, expand 7. compliment, praise ◆ *noun* 2. increase, expansion 4. compliment, praise

cute *adjective* adorable, attractive, charming, pretty, beautiful, sweet My baby niece looks cute in her Easter dress. ● **Antonyms:** ugly, unattractive

cycle *noun* chain, course, period, phase, sequence, series A caterpillar is just one stage in the life cycle of a butterfly or moth.

cynical *adjective* pessimistic, mocking, sarcastic, scornful, contemptuous, negative It is easy to be cynical about politics ● **Antonyms:** optimistic, positive

Dd

dab *verb* daub, pat, smear, swab, wipe, plaster, smudge Colin dabbed some grease on his bicycle chain. ◆ *noun* bit, drop, touch, speck, trace, mite, hint, jot I put on a dab of perfume.

dabble *verb* 1. splash, dip, sprinkle, slosh, wet, dampen We dabbled our feet in the fountain. 2. putter, tinker, play, trifle, dally, fiddle He likes to dabble with his chemistry set.

dainty *adjective* 1. delicate, fine, elegant, exquisite, pretty, fragile Those ballerina slippers look dainty but are actually sturdy. 2. choosy, finicky, fussy, particular, discriminating, exacting, fastidious My cousin is such a dainty eater that we never know what to fix for her. 3. delicious, delectable, tasty, appetizing, toothsome There was such a variety of dainty sweets at the bakery that I didn't know which to choose. ➡ **Antonyms:** 1. crude, gross

dam *noun* barrier, obstruction, hindrance, embankment, wall, levee, dike, weir The longest beaver dam on record is 2,296 feet in length. ◆ *verb* 1. bar, block, impede, obstruct, stop, confine My friends and I dammed the creek in order to form a swimming hole. 2. suppress, restrain, inhibit, repress, check I tried to dam my tears as I watched the sad movie. ➡ **Antonyms:** *verb* free, release

damage *noun* 1. destruction, harm, hurt, injury, impairment, wreckage A hailstorm did serious damage to our garden. 2. recompense, reparation, indemnity, reimbursement, expense The parents of the injured child sued for damages. ◆ *verb* harm, hurt, impair, injure, mar, blemish, spoil, ruin, disfigure The boat was damaged slightly in the storm. ➡ **Antonyms:** *verb* mend, repair

damp *adjective* moist, wet, clammy, dripping, soaked, soggy, sodden After soccer practice, my shirt was damp with perspiration. ◆ *noun* humidity, moistness, moisture, clamminess, wet The books in the basement of the old house were ruined by the damp. ➡ **Antonym:** *adjective* dry

dance *verb* frolic, gambol, leap, prance, skip, caper, cavort, romp, sway My dog dances with joy when I come home. ◆ *noun* ball, party, prom, social, hop Are you going to the dance next Saturday?

danger *noun* jeopardy, peril, risk, threat, hazard, endangerment The officer put her life in danger when she rescued the driver from the burning car. ➡ **Antonyms:** safety, security

dangerous *adjective* 1. hazardous, perilous, risky, unsafe, treacherous, precarious Riding a bicycle at night can be dangerous. 2. threatening, menacing, ominous, harmful, terrible, alarming A mother bear can be dangerous if you approach her cubs. ➡ **Antonyms:** 1. safe, secure 2. harmless

dangle *verb* hang, suspend, swing, sling, swish, dip, brandish I dangled a toy in front of my cat.

dank *adjective* clammy, damp, moist, wet, soggy, humid, sodden The caves at Carlsbad National Park are beautiful, but dank. ➡ **Antonyms:** dry, warm

dare *verb* 1. risk, venture, attempt, brave, gamble Only when I was done with my chores did I dare to ask my parents for a raise in my allowance. 2. challenge, defy, goad, provoke, taunt, confront My friends dared me to enter the haunted house. ◆ *noun* challenge, bet, provocation, taunt, ultimatum He accepted a dare to jump into the pool with his clothes on.

daring *adjective* bold, brave, courageous, gallant, intrepid, audacious, adventurous The warriors made a daring attack against the enemy. ◆ *noun* boldness, bravery, courage, nerve, valor, mettle The spy's mission required great skill and daring. ➡ **Antonyms:** *adjective* cowardly, timid ◆ *noun* cowardice, timidity

dark *adjective* 1. unlit, black, dim, murky, gloomy, shadowy I could barely see my way along the dark hall. 2. black, brown, dusky, tan, swarthy, charcoal, ebony Some Arctic animals have coats that are dark in summer and white in winter. 3. bleak, desolate, dismal, dreary, gloomy, dim, somber, mournful Our team's future looked dark when our goalie moved away. ◆ *noun* 1. blackness, darkness, gloom, murk I groped around in the dark to find a flashlight. 2. dusk, evening, night, nightfall, twilight I have to be home by dark. ➡ **Antonyms:** *adjective* 1. & 2. bright, light 3. cheerful ◆ *noun* 1. brightness, light 2. dawn, daytime

darling *noun* beloved, dear, precious, pet, sweetheart Grandma always calls me her darling. ◆ *adjective* 1. beloved, cherished, dear, precious, adored This is my darling dog, Charlemagne, who is named after the famous eighth-century ruler. 2. adorable, charming, cute, enchanting, sweet, Spencer bought his niece a darling little toy penguin.

dart *verb* 1. dash, race, rush, sprint, tear, bustle, scoot, scurry I caught a glimpse of a mouse as it darted away. 2. throw, shoot, cast, fling, launch, thrust She darted a quick look at the street sign. ◆ *noun* 1. bolt, arrow, shaft, missile, projectile, spear Some South American Indians hunt with poisoned darts. 2. dash, sprint, run, leap, jump, race We made a dart for shelter when it started to rain.

dash *verb* 1. bolt, hurry, race, rush, sprint, zip, dart, flash, fly, hustle, shoot, whiz The runner dashed across the finish line. 2. fling, hurl, knock, slam, smash, throw, cast, heave, pitch The gull dashed a clam against the rocks. 3. blast, frustrate, confound, thwart, foil, spoil, ruin, destroy, wreck Our hopes of winning the title were dashed when we lost the game. ◆ *noun* 1. bolt, dart, run, rush, sprint, leap The rabbit made a dash for safety when it saw the fox. 2. bit, drop, pinch, touch, trace, hint, taste, jot, smidgen, speck The soup tasted bland, so I added a dash of pepper. 3. verve, vigor, vim, vitality, energy, spirit, flair, panache, zest Mike's friends like his energy and dash. ◆ **Antonyms:** *verb* 3. support, aid, encourage

dashing *adjective* 1. brave, bold, daring, courageous, plucky, adventurous I like stories with a dashing hero. 2. showy, stylish, chic, fashionable, posh, smart, elegant, dapper What a dashing couple! ◆ **Antonyms:** 1. cowardly, timid 2. shabby

data *noun* information, facts, figures, statistics, evidence, details The scientist's data supported her theory.

date *noun* 1. day, hour, month, time, year, moment The date of the first manned space flight was April 12, 1961. 2. period, season, age, era, epoch, stage, phase, juncture These cave paintings are from an early date in human history. 3. appointment, engagement, meeting, rendezvous, tryst, commitment Dad made a date to go golfing next Saturday. ◆ *verb* determine, ascertain, fix, record, register, mark Fossils are important in helping to date the age of Earth.

daub *verb* smear, spread, cover, dab, smudge, brush My brother daubed paint on a piece of paper. ◆ *noun* dot, smear, blob, blotch, spot, smudge, stain You have a daub of mustard on your shirt.

daunt *verb* discourage, dishearten, consternate, dismay, shake, intimidate, faze The boxer was not daunted by the size of his opponent. ◆ **Antonyms:** encourage, hearten

dauntless *adjective* brave, courageous, fearless, valorous, intrepid, plucky, valiant Olympic athletes often demonstrate great skill and dauntless spirit. ◆ **Antonyms:** cowardly, fearful

dawdle *verb* linger, dally, dilly-dally, loiter, procrastinate, delay, tarry If you dawdle any longer, you won't make it to the library before it closes.

dawn *noun* 1. daybreak, sunrise, sunup, morning, daylight She has to get up before dawn to go to swim practice. 2. arrival, beginning, birth, commencement, origin, genesis, inception, onset The invention of the steam engine marked the dawn of the Industrial Age. ◆ *verb* 1. begin, start, commence, appear, arise, emerge A new stage in my life dawned when my family moved to New Zealand. 2. register, sink in, occur, strike, realize It suddenly dawned on me that I had forgotten my math book. ◆ **Antonyms:** *noun* 1. nightfall, sunset 2. end, finish ◆ *verb* 1. end, finish, close

day *noun* 1. daytime, daylight, light, sunshine, sunlight Owls sleep during the day. 2. age, epoch, era, period, time, generation, lifetime In my great-grandfather's day, people did not have TVs.

daze *verb* stun, stupefy, bemuse, benumb, bewilder, disorient, shock A blow to the head momentarily dazed the martial artist. ◆ *noun* muddle, trance, stupor, befuddlement, stupefaction, confusion I was in a daze after staying up late to work on my science project.

dazzle *verb* 1. blind, daze, bedazzle, disorient I was dazzled by bright sunlight after coming out of the movie theater. 2. amaze, impress, astonish, enchant, beguile, hypnotize, fascinate The magician dazzled us with his tricks. ◆ *noun* brightness, glare, gleam, blaze, brilliance, sparkle The dazzle of the sunlight on the snow was blinding.

dead *adjective* 1. deceased, expired, lifeless, perished, departed, gone, late I found a dead bug in the swimming pool. 2. motionless, stagnant, still, standing, unmoving, quiet, calm The sea was dead after the wind died down. 3. obsolete, outmoded, lost, vanished, extinct, inactive, archaic Some people say that good manners are dead. 4. spent, drained, finished, exhausted, inoperative, useless My flashlight won't work because the batteries are dead. 5. fatigued, weary, rundown, tired, exhausted, worn-out I enjoyed my vacation, but now I am dead from jet lag. 6. absolute, complete, entire, total, utter, plain, pure, unmitigated There was dead silence when our teacher announced a pop quiz. ◆ *noun* middle, heart, height, peak, depth, midst The temperature of Earth's surface is coolest in the dead of night. ◆ *adverb* 1. absolutely, completely, entirely, altogether, fully, utterly, perfectly My neighbor is dead certain that she has seen a UFO. 2. directly, exactly, precisely, right, straight, due, smack The lookout shouted that he saw another ship dead ahead.

⇒ **Antonyms:** *adjective* 1. alive, living 2. moving, dynamic 3. current 4. active, operating 5. fresh, rested 6. partial, incomplete

deadly *adjective* 1. fatal, lethal, mortal, deathly, destructive, harmful, malignant In the 14th century, a deadly plague killed almost half of the people in Europe. 2. death-like, cadaverous, deathly, ghastly, ghostly, spectral, wan The shock victim had a deadly appearance. 3. exact, sure, precise, accurate, effective, unerring, true The arrow flew through the air with deadly accuracy. ◆ *adverb* absolutely, extremely, utterly, very, totally, completely, fully The archer's aim is deadly accurate. ⇒ **Antonyms:** *adjective* 1. harmless, benign 2. healthy, ruddy 3. inaccurate

deal *verb* 1. concern, consider, involve, treat, handle, touch, relate Geology deals with the origin, composition, history, and structure of the planet Earth. 2. cope, manage, handle, function, practice, act, conduct I might need help dealing with this problem. 3. trade, sell, market, handle, peddle, retail, vend, barter My dad's store deals in both new and used books. 4. allot, distribute, administer, dispense, hand out, dole, ration Mom dealt out our weekly chore assignments. ◆ *noun* agreement, arrangement, bargain, contract, understanding, compact, pact I made a deal to trade my comic books for Seth's baseball cards. ⇒ **Antonyms:** *verb* 1. ignore, disregard

dear *adjective* 1. precious, loved, adored, esteemed, beloved, treasured, prized Our family photographs are very dear to us. 2. expensive, costly, priceless, high Those jade earrings weren't as dear as I'd expected. ◆ *noun* beloved, darling, love, precious, sweet, sweetheart I love you, my dear. ⇒ **Antonyms:** *adjective* 2. inexpensive, cheap

dearly *adverb* greatly, profoundly, much, tremendously, immensely, vastly, enormously Missing the review session cost me dearly. ⇒ **Antonyms:** little, somewhat

death *noun* 1. dying, passing, decease, demise, loss, expiration She was saddened by the death of her grandfather. 2. end, termination, finish, destruction, extermination, eradication, ruin My low grade in science was the death of my hopes to get on the honor roll. ⇒ **Antonyms:** 1. birth, life 2. beginning, inception

debacle *noun* disaster, collapse, downfall, breakdown, crash, ruin, catastrophe In 1998, Russian prime minister Boris Yeltsin fired his entire cabinet in response to the country's economic debacle.

debate *verb* deliberate, consider, mull, ponder, meditate, think, reflect The city council debated for several weeks before voting the new tax into law. ◆ *noun* discussion, argument, disagreement, dispute, altercation, quarrel The two men got into a heated debate over politics.

debris *noun* rubble, wreckage, fragments, pieces, rubbish, waste, trash After the storm the streets were filled with debris.

debt *noun* liability, obligation, arrears, debit, deficit, bill, claim, due If you lend me five dollars, I will pay my debt to you next week.

debunk *verb* discredit, expose, uncover, show up, criticize, ridicule I watched a TV program that debunked the myth of Atlantis.

decay *verb* 1. break down, decompose, rot, disintegrate, molder, spoil The fallen leaves decayed and became soil. 2. collapse, deteriorate, decline, degenerate, wane, ebb, crumble The house was gradually decaying into a pile of boards. ◆ *noun* collapse, dilapidation, ruin, decline, deterioration, disrepair, degeneration The old barn was in a state of decay.

deceit *noun* deception, trickery, duplicity, guile, fraud, treachery The gambler used deceit to win the card game. ⇒ **Antonyms:** honesty, sincerity

deceive *verb* fool, mislead, trick, bluff, dupe, delude, betray, cheat An opossum sometimes deceives its enemies by pretending to be dead.

decent *adjective* 1. appropriate, becoming, fit, proper, suitable, respectable, right, correct, seemly The decent thing to do is to apologize to your friend for missing her party. 2. considerate, generous, kind, nice, thoughtful, sympathetic It was decent of you to help him study for the test. 3. adequate, fair, passable, reasonable, satisfactory, acceptable, tolerable I can make decent cookies, but you bake a better pie.

deception *noun* 1. trickery, fraud, deceit, duplicity, guile, treachery The customer believed the car was in good condition because of the salesperson's deception. 2. trick, ruse, subterfuge, stratagem, deceit, artifice, ploy, maneuver, gimmick The Trojan horse is one of the most famous deceptions in history. ⇒ **Antonyms:** 1. honesty, sincerity

deceptive *adjective* deceitful, misleading, false, delusive, fraudulent, dishonest Certain laws protect consumers against deceptive advertising. ⇒ **Antonyms:** honest, truthful

decide *verb* **1. resolve, rule, decree, judge, adjudicate, arbitrate, umpire** The jury decided in favor of the defendant. **2. conclude, determine, resolve, settle, establish, clinch** I decided that one ride on the giant roller coaster was enough for me. **3. choose, determine, select, elect, pick, agree, figure, gather** I decided to buy an angelfish rather than a neon tetra for my aquarium.

decision *noun* **1. conclusion, determination, judgment, resolution, choice, selection** Sometimes I have a hard time making decisions. **2. verdict, finding, ruling, decree, outcome, opinion, result** The judges of the poetry contest will announce their decision next week.

decisive *adjective* **1. conclusive, definite, significant, crucial, definitive, unmistakable, convincing** The candidate defeated his opponent by a decisive margin. **2. determined, firm, resolute, resolved, positive, assured, certain** The decisive woman quickly picked out a movie to rent. ➡ **Antonyms: 1. inconclusive, dubious 2. hesitant, indecisive**

deck *verb* **dress, attire, clothe, adorn, array, festoon, decorate** We were decked out in our best clothes for the wedding.

declare *verb* **1. affirm, assert, say, state, swear, aver, avow, claim, maintain** She declared that she was telling the truth. **2. announce, decree, proclaim, pronounce, disclose, express, rule** The governor declared a state of emergency after the hurricane.

decline *verb* **1. refuse, reject, turn down, dismiss, spurn, eschew** She declined my invitation to go to a movie. **2. decrease, diminish, wane, deteriorate, fade, fail, flag, languish** The power of the Roman Empire began to decline in the second century A.D. due to plague and barbarian invasions. **3. descend, dip, drop, fall, pitch, sink, slope, bend** The hill declines gradually on one side. ◆ *noun* **decrease, reduction, slump, dip, downswing, drop, plunge** There has been a decline in the demand for typewriters since the introduction of the computer. ➡ **Antonyms:** *verb* **1. accept, consent 2. increase, improve 3. rise** ◆ *noun* **rise**

decompose *verb* **decay, break down, disintegrate, deteriorate, rot, spoil, go bad** Uranium 238 decomposes very slowly, as it has a half-life of 4.51 billion years.

decorate *verb* **1. adorn, ornament, trim, dress, embellish, garnish, beautify** She decorated the package with ribbon. **2. cite, recognize, honor, acknowledge, praise, pay tribute, laud, commend** The mayor will decorate outstanding citizens in a special ceremony.

decoration *noun* **1. ornament, embellishment, adornment, trim, garnish, trinket** Every year we buy a special decoration for our Christmas tree. **2. medal, badge, ribbon, citation, emblem, award** We found a Civil War decoration in an antique store to give to Dad for his collection.

decrease *verb* **diminish, lessen, lower, reduce, drop, wane, decline, shrink** Dad's doctor advised him to decrease the amount of fat in his diet. ◆ *noun* **decline, reduction, cut, slowdown, slash, abatement, drop** There was a decrease in umbrella sales during the drought. ➡ **Antonyms:** *verb* **increase, expand** ◆ *noun* **increase, growth**

decree *noun* **mandate, proclamation, command, order, edict, pronouncement, rule** The dictator issued a decree that made his birthday a national holiday. ◆ *verb* **mandate, proclaim, rule, command, order, prescribe, dictate** Our teacher decreed that there should be silence during the test.

dedicate *verb* **devote, commit, set apart, give, pledge, address, focus, apply, present, honor** This school is dedicated to the education of deaf children.

deduce *verb* **conclude, draw, gather, infer, derive, surmise, reason, ascertain** The literary character Sherlock Holmes is able to deduce information from obscure clues.

deduct *verb* **remove, subtract, take away, withdraw, eliminate, erase, cancel** My brother offered to deduct two dollars from what I owed him if I would clean his bike. ➡ **Antonym: add**

deed *noun* **1. act, action, exploit, feat, accomplishment, achievement, performance, undertaking** This movie is based on Sir Lancelot's heroic deeds. **2. title, contract, certificate, document, papers, record** Mom and Dad signed the deed to our new house. ◆ *verb* **cede, grant, sign over, convey, give, transfer, will** My grandfather deeded his farm to the state for use as a park.

deem *verb* **judge, consider, believe, think, suppose, hold, reckon, regard, see** Do you really deem it worthwhile to save all these catalogs?

deep *adjective* **1. low, cavernous, bottomless, yawning, abysmal** Arizona's Meteor Crater is approximately 650 feet deep. **2. great, intense, powerful, profound, strong, sincere, serious, heartfelt** I have a deep respect for those who generously give their time to help others. **3. absorbed, engrossed, occupied, involved, preoccupied, lost, immersed** I was deep in thought and didn't hear your question. **4. difficult, obscure, profound, mysterious, complex** He is reading an essay that discusses a deep philosophical theory. **5. rich, intense, vivid, strong, dark** Their living room is decorated in deep blues and golds. ⟿ **Antonyms: 1. shallow 2. light, shallow 4. superficial, simple 5. light, pale**

defeat *verb* **1. beat, overcome, conquer, vanquish, best, surmount, triumph, prevail** The United States achieved independence by defeating England in the American Revolution. **2. thwart, balk, check, foil, frustrate, stymie, stop, hinder** I was defeated in my efforts to start a recycling program at school. ◆ *noun* **1. loss, beating, downfall, rout, upset, thrashing** My football team has suffered three defeats this fall. **2. frustration, disappointment, failure, setback, reversal** She is not one to take defeat easily. ⟿ **Antonyms:** *noun* **1. triumph, victory 2. success**

defect *noun* **flaw, fault, imperfection, blemish, shortcoming, failing, drawback, weakness** This puppy is my favorite, although its curly tail is considered a defect. ◆ *verb* **desert, abandon, disavow, forsake, quit, leave, secede** The visiting athlete asked to defect to his host country. ⟿ **Antonyms:** *noun* **strength, forte, asset**

defective *adjective* **faulty, flawed, imperfect, broken, deficient, impaired, lacking** We returned our new TV because it was defective. ⟿ **Antonyms: perfect, adequate**

defend *verb* **1. guard, protect, safeguard, secure, shield, shelter, fortify** The commander called for reinforcements to help defend the fort. **2. maintain, support, sustain, uphold, champion, vindicate, corroborate** The scientist used facts and figures to defend his new theory. ⟿ **Antonyms: 1. attack, assail 2. subvert**

defense *noun* **1. guard, protection, safeguard, security, shield** The best defense against cavities is to brush your teeth regularly. **2. justification, vindication, support, reason, argument, case** I had to present a defense of the Second Amendment to the Constitution to the class.

defer[1] *verb* **delay, postpone, put off, wait, hold off, stall, table** I deferred making my decision about the party until I knew if my friends were going.

defer[2] *verb* **submit, demur, yield, bow, give in, capitulate, cede, acquiesce** I deferred to my mother's wish that I stay home to greet our guests.

deference *noun* **respect, courtesy, homage, honor, regard, esteem, consideration** It is common in many parts of the world to show deference by bowing. ⟿ **Antonyms: disrespect, rudeness**

defiance *noun* **disobedience, rebellion, obstinacy, contempt, resistance, opposition** When Joan refused to clean her room, she was punished for her defiance. ⟿ **Antonym: obedience**

deficiency *noun* **lack, scarcity, shortage, inadequacy, need, deficit, insufficiency** If you drink a lot of milk, you are unlikely to have a calcium deficiency. ⟿ **Antonyms: excess, surplus**

define *verb* **1. characterize, interpret, describe, explain, state, name** My dad defines happiness as a weekend fishing trip. **2. specify, outline, delineate, identify, clarify, establish, fix, detail** Can you define your reasons for wanting a part-time job?

definite *adjective* **certain, positive, sure, clear, distinct, precise, specific, unambiguous** Instead of saying "maybe," I wish you would answer with a definite "yes" or "no." ⟿ **Antonyms: uncertain, vague**

definitely *adverb* **absolutely, certainly, surely, positively, assuredly, undoubtedly, doubtless** I will definitely be ready at 7:30. ⟿ **Antonyms: perhaps, possibly, maybe**

definition *noun* **1. meaning, description, explanation, interpretation, sense, connotation, denotation, clarification** If you don't know what a word means, look up its definition in a dictionary. **2. clarity, distinctness, precision, focus, resolution, sharpness** His project is starting to gain definition after only a week of planning.

definitive *adjective* **1. final, conclusive, ultimate, definite, absolute, real** I will give you a definitive answer tomorrow. **2. authoritative, complete, standard, consummate, thorough, comprehensive** Dr. Edward O. Wilson won a Pulitzer Prize for his definitive book on ants.

deform *verb* **contort, disfigure, distort, twist, mar, misshape, damage, blemish** Is it true that you can deform your spine by slouching too much?

defy *verb* **1. disobey, oppose, disregard, withstand, flout, rebel, scorn** My little brother defied our parents by refusing to turn off the TV. **2. challenge, dare, brave, confront, face, summon, bid, invite** In the Bible, David is said to have defied Goliath in spite of great odds. ⟿ **Antonyms: 1. obey, cooperate**

degrade *verb* **disgrace, dishonor, shame, cheapen, lower, demean, abase, defile, corrupt** She refused to degrade herself by cheating. ⟿ **Antonyms: dignify, uplift, honor**

degree *noun* **1. class, grade, level, stage, step, peg, rung** In karate, a yellow belt is one degree above a white belt. **2. position, rank, class, status, station, standing, dignity** Only people of high degree may sit in the United Kingdom's House of Lords. **3. amount, extent, measure, range, scope, proportion, quantity** The gymnast's routine had a high degree of difficulty.

dejected *adjective* **depressed, gloomy, sad, unhappy, discouraged, down, downcast, blue, desolate, low** I felt dejected when I learned that my best friend was moving to another state. ➡ **Antonyms: cheerful, happy**

delay *verb* **1. defer, postpone, put off, stay, suspend, stall, wait** We had to delay the opening of our play because the sets were not ready. **2. detain, hold up, impede, hamper, hinder, obstruct, retard, slow** The bus was delayed by heavy traffic. **3. procrastinate, dawdle, linger, dally, loiter, tarry, lag, hesitate** I do not like to delay in returning my library books. ◆ *noun* **1. postponement, holdup, deferment, suspension, interruption, procrastination** What is the delay? **2. pause, lull, wait, lag, interlude, interval, hiatus, detainment** We learned that there would be a slight delay before takeoff. ➡ **Antonyms:** *verb* **2. expedite 3. hurry, rush**

delegate *noun* **agent, appointee, representative, deputy, envoy, emissary, ambassador** Our class elected Anthony to be a delegate to the student council. ◆ *verb* **1. appoint, assign, designate, name, commission, authorize, nominate** Our coach delegated me to play goalie for the first half of the game. **2. give, entrust, assign, relegate, commit, charge, trust** If you have too many tasks, you can delegate some of them to me.

delegation *noun* **1. appointment, assignment, designation, authorization, relegation** We were present at the delegation of the new ambassador. **2. representatives, commission, deputation, legation, mission, contingent** The President received the delegation from Brazil.

deliberate *adjective* **1. intentional, willful, purposeful, calculated, premeditated, planned, thoughtful** The man pretended to be joking, but he was actually making a deliberate insult. **2. slow, unhurried, measured, methodical, careful, cautious, leisurely** The sloth made deliberate progress from branch to branch. ◆ *verb* **1. reflect, think, consider, contemplate, ponder, meditate, muse, ruminate** It is often wise to deliberate before making a decision. **2. confer, debate, discuss, consult, parley, talk, reason** The jury deliberated for several days before reaching a verdict. ➡ **Antonyms:** *adjective* **1. spontaneous, impulsive 2. fast, hasty**

delicate *adjective* **1. dainty, exquisite, fine, elegant, precise, refined** The child in the painting has delicate features. **2. frail, weak, weakened, sickly, feeble, infirm, unsound, decrepit, puny** My sister's condition was delicate after her operation. **3. breakable, fragile, flimsy, brittle, weak, vulnerable** Eggs break easily because their shells are delicate. **4. demanding, difficult, tricky, ticklish, precarious, exacting, sensitive** Repairing a watch is often a delicate task. ➡ **Antonyms: 1. coarse, crude 2. hearty, robust 3. strong, sturdy 4. easy**

delicious *adjective* **appetizing, savory, tasty, delectable, scrumptious, luscious, toothsome** Those strawberries look delicious. ➡ **Antonyms: distasteful, unpalatable**

delight *noun* **gladness, happiness, joy, pleasure, rapture, gratification, elation, bliss** He was filled with delight when he saw his new in-line skates. ◆ *verb* **gladden, please, cheer, gratify, thrill, overjoy, enchant, amuse, excite** Nothing delights me more than playing basketball with my friends.

delightful *adjective* **charming, enjoyable, happy, pleasant, delectable, enchanting, pleasurable, lovely** They spent a delightful day at the beach. ➡ **Antonyms: awful, unpleasant, disagreeable**

delinquent *adjective* **1. remiss, neglectful, negligent, derelict, irresponsible, lax, careless** Our teacher says we should not be delinquent in practicing good study habits. **2. late, tardy, due, overdue, past due, in arrears, behind** Pay your traffic fine before it becomes delinquent. ◆ *noun* **lawbreaker, offender, miscreant, malefactor, perpetrator, wrongdoer, hoodlum** What percentage of teenagers are delinquents?

delirious *adjective* **1. incoherent, confused, hysterical, irrational, disturbed, deranged** Heatstroke caused the cyclist to become delirious. **2. ecstatic, excited, frantic, frenetic, frenzied, wild, crazed** The lottery winner was delirious with happiness. ➡ **Antonyms: 1. coherent, rational 2. calm, cool**

deliver *verb* **1. carry, bear, convey, transport, bring, distribute** Your pizza will be delivered to your door. **2. hand over, surrender, give, turn over, transfer, relinquish, cede, grant** My brother reluctantly delivered the dog to its rightful owner. **3. administer, deal, give, inflict, impart, cast, throw, strike** The prize-winning boxer delivered a knockout punch to his opponent. **4. communicate, present, proclaim, announce, express, say, speak, utter, voice** The new President will deliver his inaugural address tomorrow. ➡ **Antonyms: 2. keep, retain**

delivery *noun* **1. transfer, transmittal, transmission, shipment, distribution, conveyance** Max has a job making deliveries for an auto-parts warehouse. **2. presentation, performance, manner, execution, pronunciation, articulation, enunciation** My teacher complimented me on the delivery of my oral report.

delude *verb* **deceive, dupe, fool, mislead, take in, beguile, trick, hoax** My brother tried to delude me into thinking he had broken his arm.

deluge *noun* **flood, inundation, torrent, overflow, downpour, ocean, wave** The radio station received a deluge of phone calls from interested listeners. ◆ *verb* **inundate, overwhelm, flood, submerge, engulf, drown, swamp, immerse** The candidates deluged the public with campaign literature.

delusion *noun* **illusion, fantasy, misconception, fallacy, mistake, error, mirage** Your belief that your hamster understands you is just a delusion. ◈ **Antonyms: reality, fact**

demand *verb* **1. appeal for, insist on, claim, order, request, seek, importune** The workers demanded a raise in pay. **2. call for, need, require, necessitate, ask, beg, entail, involve** This problem demands our immediate attention. ◆ *noun* **1. appeal, call, command, order, request, bid, behest** The players tried to meet the coach's demand for better teamwork. **2. call, need, requirement, want, desire, interest, market** There is less demand for records and cassettes now that most people have CD players.

demeanor *noun* **deportment, bearing, manner, mien, presence, style, air, conduct** He had a friendly yet professional demeanor.

demented *adjective* **maniacal, insane, crazy, daft, lunatic, mad, unbalanced, irrational** The demented villain was my favorite character in the movie. ◈ **Antonyms: sane, rational**

demolish *verb* **destroy, ruin, wreck, level, tear down, raze, pulverize, smash, devastate, annihilate** A tornado demolished the trailer park.

demon *noun* **devil, evil spirit, fiend, beast, monster, ghoul, ogre** Kendra dressed up as a demon for Halloween.

demonstrate *verb* **1. exhibit, illustrate, show, reveal, describe, explain, teach, display** My teacher demonstrated the proper way to use a microscope. **2. prove, establish, authenticate, confirm, validate, verify, certify, support** The space cameras demonstrated that there were no visible signs of life on the asteroid. **3. march, protest, rally, parade, picket, strike** A group of students and teachers demonstrated against the building of a highway next to their school.

demonstration *noun* **1. presentation, display, show, exhibit, explanation, illustration** A salesperson gave us a demonstration of how the video camera worked. **2. proof, evidence, authentication, confirmation, verification, testimony, support** The writer's new book gives ample demonstration of her talent. **3. march, protest, rally, picket, meeting, sit-in, walkout, strike** We're holding a demonstration to protest the new dress code.

demure *adjective* **modest, reserved, shy, bashful, timid, retiring, coy, reticent** My cousin's demure manner hides a great love of practical jokes. ◈ **Antonyms: brazen, brash, bold**

den *noun* **1. lair, nest, burrow, hole, cave, shelter, covert, hideaway** A wolf's den is usually an underground burrow. **2. office, study, library, studio** Our house has three bedrooms and a den.

denote *verb* **designate, indicate, mean, point out, show, signify, connote, express, represent** A skull and crossbones on a sign usually denotes danger.

denounce *verb* **1. condemn, criticize, censure, deplore, attack, assail, vilify** My parents strongly denounce the use of illegal drugs. **2. expose, inform against, betray, implicate, incriminate, blame, accuse** The witness denounced her assailant. ◈ **Antonyms: 1. commend, praise**

dense *adjective* **1. thick, tight, solid, impenetrable, compact, crowded, packed, close, heavy, compressed** The rabbit ran into a dense thicket as I approached. **2. thick-headed, dull, stupid, obtuse, doltish, slow** My sister said that I was dense when I didn't get the hint to leave the room when her boyfriend came over. ◈ **Antonyms: 1. sparse, thin 2. quick, bright**

dent *noun* **nick, pit, indentation, depression, hollow, scrape, notch** The auto body shop fixed the dents in our car. ◆ *verb* **nick, pit, notch, indent, scrape, scratch, gouge** How did you dent this silver bowl?

deny *verb* **1. dispute, contradict, disagree, protest, gainsay, refute** The suspect denied that he had committed the crime. **2. disallow, forbid, refuse, reject, veto, turn down, withhold, oppose** My parents denied my request to stay out late. ◈ **Antonyms: 1. admit, confirm 2. allow, permit**

depart *verb* **1. go, leave, move, pull out, embark, exit, retire, withdraw, recede** My bus departs at 3:00. **2. deviate, vary, differ, diverge, stray, change, wander, veer** She departed from her usual routine by going to bed two hours early. ● **Antonyms: 1. arrive 2. adhere, remain**

department *noun* **area, branch, division, section, bureau, unit, office, quarter** I always head straight for the sports department whenever I go to the store.

departure *noun* **1. going, leaving, egress, exit, start, withdrawal, exodus** Our departure will be delayed because the airport has been closed by fog. **2. deviation, divergence, aberration, digression, variation, change, shift** Her role in the new comedy is a departure from the dramatic parts she usually plays. ● **Antonyms: 1. arrival 2. conformity**

depend *verb* **1. count on, rely, trust, believe, bank on** Mom depends on me to feed the pets. **2. hang, hinge, rest, be subject to, turn on, revolve** Whether or not I go to the movie depends on how much homework I get done.

dependable *adjective* **faithful, reliable, responsible, trustworthy, trusty, steadfast, solid, sound, true** A dependable friend is one who will be there in times of need. ● **Antonyms: undependable, unreliable**

depict *verb* **picture, portray, render, show, tell, detail, set forth, recount, chronicle, relate** This film depicts the life of George Washington.

deplete *verb* **drain, empty, exhaust, impoverish, sap, use up, reduce, consume** The long hike depleted our energy. ● **Antonyms: fill, replenish**

deplorable *adjective* **wretched, bad, lamentable, woeful, shameful, reprehensible, disgraceful, regrettable** My room was in a deplorable state while I was packing for camp. ● **Antonyms: good, decent**

deplore *verb* **1. disapprove, denounce, censure, condemn, reproach, abhor** My mother deplores the use of poor grammar. **2. regret, repent, rue, lament, mourn, grieve, bemoan** He deplored his embarrassing behavior at the dance. ● **Antonyms: 1. praise, commend 2. rejoice, exult**

deploy *verb* **position, distribute, arrange, array, order, organize, marshal** The general deployed his troops in preparation for battle.

depose *verb* **remove, oust, expel, throw out, dismiss, unseat, impeach, discharge** The club members voted to depose the treasurer for his mismanagement of funds. ● **Antonyms: install, empower**

deposit *verb* **1. place, put, set, leave, drop, accumulate, amass, lay, collect** The wind deposited a pile of leaves on our doorstep. **2. bank, lay away, entrust, consign, put away, store, stash, hoard** I deposited 50 dollars in my college savings account. ◆ *noun* **1. assets, cash, money, savings, stake, installment, security** The deposits in my savings account total 325 dollars. **2. residue, accumulation, dregs, lees, sediment, precipitate, alluvium** After Mount Saint Helens erupted, there were deposits of ash in our yard. ● **Antonyms: *verb* remove, withdraw**

depraved *adjective* **corrupt, perverted, degenerate, villainous, immoral, wicked, low, shameless, vile** People were shocked by the convict's depraved acts. ● **Antonyms: moral, virtuous, pure**

depravity *noun* **degradation, corruption, perversion, vice, wickedness, immorality, degeneracy** The depravity of the criminal shocked even the experienced detective. ● **Antonyms: morality, decency**

depress *verb* **1. discourage, dishearten, deject, sadden, oppress, dispirit, weigh down** Long spells of rainy weather always seem to depress me. **2. weaken, enervate, diminish, reduce, lessen, sap, cheapen, devalue** The Asian money crisis of the late 20th century depressed the United States stock market. ● **Antonyms: 1. cheer, gladden 2. increase, strengthen**

depression *noun* **1. dejection, despair, gloom, melancholy, sadness, despondency, unhappiness** The depression I felt when we moved ended once I made new friends. **2. cavity, dent, hole, hollow, basin, dip, pit, recess, indentation** Travis turned the rock over and found that the depression underneath was full of ants. **3. recession, slump, crash, downturn, decline** Many people lose their jobs during an economic depression. ● **Antonyms: 1. cheer, happiness 3. boom**

deprive *verb* **rob, strip, divest, deny, refuse, withhold, take away, remove** Don't let your worries deprive you of sleep.

depth *noun* **1. deepness, extent, measure, dimension, range, reach, size** The average depth of the ocean is 12,500 feet. **2. middle, bottom, heart, core, soul, center, bowels** My friend was in the depths of a serious depression until he went into therapy. **3. complexity, profundity, profoundness, intricacy, wisdom, insight** She writes novels of unusual depth. ● **Antonyms: 2. surface 3. superficiality**

deputy *noun* adjutant, aide, assistant, helper, lieutenant, delegate, representative, agent The chairperson sent a deputy on an overseas fact-finding tour.

derelict *adjective* 1. abandoned, deserted, forsaken, dilapidated, rundown, desolate The kids explored the derelict house. 2. neglectful, remiss, lax, negligent, careless, irresponsible, delinquent, slack My parents said that they would be derelict if they did not enforce my curfew.
➡ **Antonyms: 2. responsible, careful**

deride *verb* laugh at, scorn, ridicule, mock, scoff, jeer, taunt, sneer Please do not deride my fear of heights.

derision *noun* scorn, ridicule, mockery, laughter, sneering, disdain, contempt, disparagement His proposal was met with derision by the other members of the board.
➡ **Antonyms: respect, esteem**

derivation *noun* 1. derivative, product, byproduct, offshoot, outgrowth, spinoff, descendant Many recent products are derivations of items developed for exploring space. 2. origin, source, beginning, root, history, foundation, ancestry, etymology What is the derivation of that word?

derive *verb* 1. draw, gain, get, obtain, receive, take, extract, secure, enjoy Haley derives a lot of satisfaction from helping other people. 2. originate, issue, arise, come, emanate, rise, spring, stem, descend Many English words are derived from Latin roots.

descend *verb* 1. drop, fall, go down, move down, come down, plummet, plunge, tumble The parachute descended slowly to the ground. 2. decline, incline, dip, drop, sink, pitch, slope, slant The foothills descend to a wide desert. 3. come, issue, spring, derive, originate, arise, proceed, pass My friend Sawa is descended from a Miwok chieftain. 4. stoop, condescend, sink, decline, degenerate, deteriorate, lower I will not descend to making fun of others.
➡ **Antonyms: 1. ascend, climb 4. rise**

descendant *noun* heir, child, offspring, progeny, issue, scion, posterity, family Grandma says that she's proud to have me as a descendant. ➡ **Antonym: ancestor**

descent *noun* 1. drop, fall, collapse, plunge, tumble We stood on our balcony and watched the sun's descent toward the horizon. 2. slope, decline, declivity, drop, fall, pitch, incline, grade Rocks slid down the steep descent, barely missing the frightened climbers. 3. ancestry, heritage, lineage, origin, parentage, birth, blood, extraction, family, stock My friend Afshin is of Iranian descent.
➡ **Antonyms: 1. ascent, climb**

describe *verb* 1. recount, relate, report, tell, narrate, detail, explain Lori described her trip to Hawaii in vivid detail. 2. characterize, define, portray, picture, depict, render, represent, show Charles Dickens uses vivid details to describe the characters in his books.

description *noun* 1. depiction, portrayal, representation, expression, characterization, explanation I recognized the wombat at the zoo from its description in my encyclopedia. 2. account, report, statement, chronicle, history, narration, story Francis Parkman's description of the Oregon Trail was written in 1849. 3. variety, sort, kind, manner, order, type, breed, ilk, character, genre, class The buffet dinner featured desserts of every description.

desert[1] *noun* wasteland, waste, sand, barrens, badlands, wilderness The Mojave Desert was formed by volcanic eruptions and deposits from the Colorado River. ◆ *adjective* barren, uninhabited, desolate, deserted, bare, empty, vacant, arid The lifeboat finally came ashore on a desert island.

desert[2] *verb* abandon, forsake, give up, leave, quit, flee, vacate, defect The birds deserted their nest when they flew south for the winter. ➡ **Antonyms: remain, stay**

deserve *verb* earn, merit, rate, warrant, qualify, justify Patrick felt that he deserved a rest after cleaning out the garage.

design *verb* 1. conceive, create, devise, invent, plan, formulate, concoct, draft, outline, fashion Phil designed and built a model space station for his science project. 2. intend, mean, plan, project, propose, develop, destine This building was designed to be a residence, but it's been converted to a restaurant. ◆ *noun* 1. diagram, pattern, plan, blueprint, drawing, sketch, layout, outline This kit has a design and materials that let you build your own kite at home. 2. motif, pattern, arrangement, form, shape, configuration The brick sidewalk was laid in a herringbone design. 3. purpose, goal, intention, intent, aim, end, object, objective, scheme The landscape architect left in the big oak trees by design.

designate *verb* 1. indicate, mark, point out, show, specify, denote, signify, pinpoint, identify Brenda taped balloons to her front door to designate where her party was being held. 2. call, name, term, title, style, dub, label, nickname World War I was erroneously designated "the war to end all wars." 3. appoint, elect, name, select, pick, choose, assign, delegate Our teacher designated me to represent our class at the school assembly.

desirable *adjective* agreeable, attractive, good, pleasing, worthwhile, advantageous, choice, worthy, admirable Many people believe that small towns are desirable places to live. ➡ **Antonyms:** undesirable, disagreeable

desire *verb* 1. covet, crave, long for, want, wish, ache, yearn, hunger, fancy She desires a parakeet as a pet. 2. request, urge, ask, petition, importune, require, seek Will you do as I desire and bring me a candy bar from the grocery store? ◆ *noun* 1. craving, longing, want, wish, hunger, itch, yen, hope His desire is to someday be a race-car driver. 2. request, demand, requirement, petition, appeal, entreaty The workers made their desires known to the company president. ➡ **Antonyms:** *verb* 1. spurn, reject, dislike ◆ *noun* 1. aversion

desolate *adjective* 1. deserted, abandoned, uninhabited, lonely, lonesome, barren, empty We came upon the desolate farm during a drive in the country. 2. sad, dreary, forlorn, glum, somber, dismal, gloomy, bleak, hopeless I am going to be desolate without your company this summer. ◆ *verb* 1. raze, destroy, devastate, ravage, ruin, demolish, obliterate In 1988, forest fires desolated much of Yellowstone Park. 2. sadden, dismay, distress, depress, daunt, discourage Our neighbor's death desolated us. ➡ **Antonyms:** *adjective* 1. inhabited, populated 2. cheerful, happy ◆ *verb* 2. cheer, hearten

desolation *noun* 1. ruin, devastation, destruction, waste, wreckage, chaos, havoc The bombed city was a scene of total desolation. 2. emptiness, void, abandonment, loneliness, despair, distress, woe, sorrow, grief I felt great desolation when my cat ran away.

despair *noun* desperation, discouragement, dismay, distress, despondence, misery, depression We looked at each other in despair as we realized that we were lost. ➡ **Antonyms:** hope, optimism

desperado *noun* outlaw, bandit, brigand, criminal, convict, hoodlum, gangster, ruffian The desperado hid in a canyon in order to lose the sheriff's posse.

desperate *adjective* 1. hopeless, bleak, grim, despondent, forlorn, wretched, sad, dismal The criminal realized that his situation was desperate when he saw the SWAT team arrive. 2. bold, daring, rash, reckless, risky, dangerous, wild, frantic, impetuous, drastic For some pioneers, the trek west was a desperate attempt to start a new life. 3. intense, critical, urgent, compelling, acute, crucial, dire, serious, extreme The accident victim was in desperate need of medical care. ➡ **Antonyms:** 1. hopeful 2. cautious, careful

despicable *adjective* hateful, contemptible, abhorrent, detestable, loathsome, repugnant, odious, vile That actress is so good that she makes you believe she really is despicable. ➡ **Antonyms:** admirable, praiseworthy

despise *verb* dislike, detest, hate, loathe, scorn, disdain, abhor, revile, contemn I despise people who mistreat their pets. ➡ **Antonyms:** admire, respect

despondent *adjective* dejected, forlorn, hopeless, glum, depressed, melancholy, wretched I was despondent when I took stock of all the homework I had to do. ➡ **Antonyms:** cheerful, happy

despot *noun* tyrant, dictator, totalitarian, authoritarian, autocrat, oppressor Nero was a cruel Roman despot who fancied himself an actor and musician.

> ### Word Group
> A **dessert** is the last course of a meal, usually consisting of a sweet dish. **Dessert** is a general term with no true synonyms. Here are some common desserts from around the world:
>
> **Baklava** is a Mideastern dessert made of paper-thin layers of pastry, chopped nuts, and honey. A **cannoli** is an Italian pastry roll with a creamy filling. **Flan** is a Spanish custard topped with caramel syrup. **Halvah** is a Mideastern confection of sesame seeds and honey. **Litchi** is a nutlike fruit that is a popular Chinese dessert. **Spumoni** is a layered Italian ice cream dish. **Strudel** is a German pastry made of fruit or cheese rolled up in a thin sheet of dough.

destination *noun* stop, station, terminal, end, goal, objective, target, address This plane will make two stops before it reaches its final destination.

destiny *noun* fate, lot, fortune, predestination, kismet, karma, doom, providence He feels it is his destiny to be a writer.

destitute *adjective* 1. void, barren, devoid, empty, lacking, exhausted, deficient, without The Great Salt Lake is destitute of animal life except for brine shrimp and blue-green algae. 2. impoverished, poor, indigent, poverty-stricken, penniless, broke, penurious Horatio Alger wrote stories about boys who were destitute but achieved riches through hard work. ➡ **Antonyms:** 1. full, replete 2. rich, wealthy, affluent

destroy *verb* 1. annihilate, demolish, devastate, ruin, wreck, level, raze, pulverize, ravage In this movie, a giant lizard destroys most of downtown Tokyo. **2. eliminate, end, finish, undo, extinguish, erase, cancel, eradicate, terminate** The rain destroyed our plans to go boating. ➽ **Antonyms: 2. create, make**

destruction *noun* **1. devastation, havoc, ruin, wreckage, damage, waste, mayhem** The hurricane caused widespread destruction. **2. undoing, ruin, downfall, end, termination, breakup** Archaeologists have been unable to determine what led to the destruction of the Mayan Empire.

destructive *adjective* **1. harmful, injurious, damaging, ruinous, calamitous, devastating** We gave our puppy a chew toy as an outlet for his destructive urges. **2. damaging, negative, unfavorable, bad, detrimental, adverse, pernicious** It is destructive to children's emotional growth to constantly criticize them. ➽ **Antonyms: 2. constructive, positive**

detach *verb* **disconnect, remove, separate, unfasten, disengage, loosen, free, part** To get your bike into the trunk, you'll have to detach its front wheel. ➽ **Antonyms: attach, connect**

detail *noun* **1. element, feature, part, particular, point, factor, component, specific** His model of a steam locomotive is authentic in every detail. **2. technicality, minutia, particular, nicety, fine print, trivia** I like all the details involved in making a quilt. ◆ *verb* **1. describe, itemize, recite, relate, recount, specify, stipulate, list, enumerate** Her long letter detailed everything she did on her vacation. **2. appoint, charge, delegate, assign, name, select, allocate, send** The teacher detailed six of us to bring cookies to the class party.

detain *verb* **1. delay, hinder, impede, retard, slow, hold up, stall, set back, stop** We were detained by heavy traffic. **2. confine, keep, hold, restrain, arrest, imprison, incarcerate, lock up** Police officers detained the suspect for questioning. ➽ **Antonyms: 1. hasten, speed 2. free, release**

detect *verb* **discover, notice, reveal, uncover, see, discern, note, observe, find, perceive** An odor is added to natural gas to help people detect leaks. ➽ **Antonyms: miss, overlook**

deter *verb* **discourage, hinder, dissuade, divert, impede, daunt, check, inhibit** Car alarms are intended to deter thieves. ➽ **Antonym: encourage**

deteriorate *verb* **worsen, degenerate, decline, wane, ebb, sink, weaken, languish** My family's economic situation deteriorated when my dad was laid off from his job. ➽ **Antonyms: improve, strengthen**

determine *verb* **1. decide, resolve, settle, ordain, fix, establish, choose, arbitrate** The results of this field goal attempt will determine which team wins the game. **2. conclude, detect, discover, find out, learn, ascertain, infer, confirm** Investigators are trying to determine what caused the fire. **3. influence, affect, regulate, control, govern, define, shape, dictate** Time will determine how many of our errands we get done.

determined *adjective* **firm, intent, persistent, purposeful, steadfast, staunch, resolute, tenacious, obstinate** Only the most determined competitors will make it to the final round. ➽ **Antonyms: wavering, irresolute**

detest *verb* **despise, dislike, hate, loathe, abhor, abominate** I detest washing dishes. ➽ **Antonyms: like, love**

detour *noun* **alternate route, back road, bypass, byway, branch, diversion, substitute** We had to take a detour because the bridge was closed. ◆ *verb* **divert, deflect, turn aside, sidetrack, shift, bypass, circumvent, skirt** The police had to detour downtown traffic away from the burning building.

devastate *verb* **1. destroy, ravage, ruin, wreck, demolish, raze, lay waste, level** The eruption of Mount Vesuvius in A.D. 79 completely devastated the city of Pompeii. **2. disconcert, dismay, appall, shock, overwhelm, crush, shatter, desolate** I was devastated when I found out that I had missed the deadline to register for softball.

develop *verb* **1. expand, improve, strengthen, build up, advance, broaden, enlarge, cultivate** Reading is one of the best ways to develop your mind. **2. invent, fashion, originate, contrive, create, generate, produce** The scientist developed a new way to use lasers. **3. acquire, form, gain, pick up, establish, realize** I developed an interest in swimming last summer. **4. emerge, appear, arise, come about, occur, happen, begin, evolve** A friendship soon developed between the neighbors. ➽ **Antonyms: 1. stifle, impair 3. lose, forgo**

development *noun* **1. creation, production, advancement, evolution, growth, progress, rise, expansion** Medical researchers are always working on the development of more effective medicines. **2. event, happening, occurrence, incident, episode, news, circumstance, situation** It was an interesting development when two sets of twins enrolled in our class.

deviate *verb* **depart, stray, digress, diverge, swerve, veer, drift, vary, turn** The ants did not deviate from their path. ➽ **Antonyms: follow, remain, conform**

device *noun* **1. gadget, tool, apparatus, appliance, instrument, contraption, contrivance, utensil** Sometimes I think that the safety pin is the most practical device ever invented. **2. artifice, ruse, ploy, trick, plot, scheme, deception, gimmick, maneuver** A tantrum is often just a device for getting attention.

devil *noun* **1. Devil, Satan, Lucifer, Beelzebub, Mephistopheles, Belial, Prince of Darkness** In many religions, the devil is the archenemy of the Supreme Being. **2. demon, fiend, monster, ghoul, ogre, brute, scoundrel, villain** Many people believe that terrorists are inhuman devils. **3. rogue, imp, rascal, rapscallion, prankster, scamp, troublemaker** My brother acted like a little devil at his birthday party.

devious *adjective* **shifty, sneaky, underhand, deceitful, deceptive, dishonest, indirect** Tom Sawyer came up with a devious plan to get out of painting his aunt's fence. ➡ **Antonyms: straightforward, honest**

devise *verb* **concoct, contrive, create, design, fashion, invent, formulate, construct** My brother is trying to devise a system for getting his chores done more efficiently.

devote *verb* **1. commit, dedicate, pledge, focus, give, direct, concentrate** Dian Fossey devoted her life to studying and protecting the endangered mountain gorilla. **2. assign, allot, allocate, set aside, sanctify, dedicate** The hospital has devoted this room for use as a chapel.

devoted *adjective* **committed, dedicated, faithful, loyal, true, staunch, steadfast, constant, unwavering** They are devoted friends. ➡ **Antonyms: disloyal, unfaithful**

devotee *noun* **fan, disciple, enthusiast, fanatic, buff, lover, aficionado** I am a devotee of jazz.

devotion *noun* **1. commitment, dedication, attachment, faithfulness, affection, love, loyalty** The bride and groom exchanged rings as a sign of their devotion. **2. devoutness, piety, reverence, faith, holiness, spirituality** The monks pursued their way of life with great devotion. ➡ **Antonyms: 1. indifference, disloyalty 2. irreverence, impiety**

devour *verb* **1. consume, eat, dispatch, polish off, ingest, gobble, swallow, feast, bolt** He was so hungry that he devoured an entire pizza. **2. destroy, consume, waste, ravage, demolish, ruin, devastate** The Great Fire of 1871 devoured almost all of Chicago.

devout *adjective* **1. devoted, pious, religious, reverent, holy, faithful** Devout Muslims pray five times every day.

2. earnest, zealous, serious, sincere, genuine, ardent, fervent Sebastian is very devout in keeping to his workout schedule. ➡ **Antonyms: 1. irreverent, impious 2. insincere, halfhearted**

dexterity *noun* **agility, skill, adroitness, deftness, nimbleness, facility, quickness, grace** It takes dexterity to learn to type. ➡ **Antonyms: clumsiness, awkwardness**

dexterous *adjective* **skillful, adroit, deft, facile, handy, nimble, supple, agile** My sister is a dexterous potter. ➡ **Antonyms: awkward, clumsy**

diabolical *adjective* **satanic, devilish, fiendish, infernal, demonic, heinous, wicked, evil** The terrorist's plans were diabolical. ➡ **Antonyms: angelic, saintly, good**

diagram *noun* **design, drawing, outline, sketch, blueprint, illustration, layout, plan** This diagram shows the human digestive system. ◆ *verb* **draw, picture, portray, sketch, show, illustrate, chart, outline** The basketball coach used a chalkboard to diagram a zone defense.

dialect *noun* **tongue, vernacular, language, speech, idiom, lingo, argot, jargon, cant, patois** What dialect were they speaking?

dialogue *noun* **conversation, chat, discussion, speech, talk, discourse, colloquy** I loved the movie's dialogue because the actors sounded like my friends.

diary *noun* **journal, chronicle, log, album, register, record, notebook** I record my thoughts and feelings in my diary every night.

dice *verb* **cube, cut, chop, slice, hack, carve, mince** Please dice the potatoes for the casserole.

dictate *verb* **1. read, pronounce, say, speak, utter, verbalize, communicate** The lawyer dictated a letter to her secretary. **2. command, decree, direct, order, prescribe, impose, rule, fix, mandate, determine** The tyrant had so much power that he was able to dictate what the newspapers could print. ➡ **Antonyms: 2. follow, obey**

dictator *noun* **tyrant, despot, totalitarian, ruler, authoritarian, autocrat, oppressor** Joseph Stalin was dictator of the Soviet Union from 1929 until 1953.

die *verb* **1. expire, pass away, perish, decease, succumb, pass on** My African violet died because I forgot to water it. **2. want, long, pine, crave, yearn, desire, hunger, ache, wish** She is dying for an ice cream cone. **3. stop, fail, end,**

expire, give out, break down, run down, cease The battery in my watch finally died. **4. diminish, dwindle, ebb, fade, subside, wane, abate, weaken, disappear** The sound of the freight train's whistle gradually died away. ◆ **Antonyms: 1. exist, live 4. grow, increase**

diet *noun* **nourishment, sustenance, fare, food, provisions, meals, victuals** A healthy diet contains proteins, carbohydrates, fats, vitamins, and minerals. ◆ *verb* **reduce, fast, abstain, refrain** She was advised to exercise rather than diet.

differ *verb* **1. vary, disagree, deviate, diverge, contrast, alter** These cookies differ in the ingredients they have. **2. clash, conflict, contradict, disagree, oppose, disaccord, dissent** We all wanted to dine out, but we differed on which restaurant we should go to. ◆ **Antonyms: 1. coincide, match 2. agree, concur**

difference *noun* **1. distinction, dissimilarity, contrast, discrepancy, disparity, discrepancy** The biggest difference between whales and sharks is that whales are mammals and sharks are fish. **2. change, alteration, variation, transformation, modification, reform** What a difference that new skylight makes! **3. disagreement, dissension, dispute, quarrel, conflict, discord** Dylan and Curtis settled their differences and became friends again. ◆ **Antonyms: 1. similarity, resemblance 3. agreement, accord**

different *adjective* **1. dissimilar, unlike, contrasting, varied, disparate, divergent, incompatible** She and I have different opinions about when we should go home. **2. distinct, individual, separate, discrete, particular, specific** Mom and Dad are both teachers, but they work at different schools. **3. unusual, uncommon, unconventional, strange, distinctive, peculiar, unique, original** She likes to dress in a style that is very different. ◆ **Antonyms: 1. & 2. identical, same**

differentiate *verb* **1. distinguish, mark, set apart, individualize, separate, characterize** Do you know the characteristics that differentiate a rabbit from a hare? **2. discern, distinguish, sort out, discriminate, judge** I find it difficult to differentiate between the music of G.F. Handel and that of J.S. Bach.

difficult *adjective* **1. hard, strenuous, tough, arduous, demanding, taxing, laborious, burdensome** Moving the couch upstairs was a difficult job. **2. challenging, intricate, complicated, complex, puzzling, perplexing, baffling** The *New York Times* crossword puzzle can be difficult to solve. **3. obstinate, perverse, stubborn, ornery, willful, recalcitrant, intractable** When Jason refused to play by our rules, we told him to stop being so difficult. ◆ **Antonyms: 1. & 2. easy, simple 3. cooperative, accommodating**

difficulty *noun* **1. hardship, obstacle, problem, trouble, adversity, complication, trial** The Pilgrims who founded Plymouth Colony overcame many difficulties. **2. quandary, dilemma, predicament, quagmire, scrape, plight, jam, fix** I found myself in real difficulty when I lost my keys. **3. disagreement, dispute, altercation, quarrel, argument, clash, conflict, discord** My brother and I resolved our difficulty after realizing it was based on a miscommunication.

diffident *adjective* **timid, shy, bashful, demure, modest, timorous, self-effacing, hesitant** I am usually diffident when it comes to meeting new people. ◆ **Antonyms: bold, confident**

dig *verb* **1. excavate, burrow, bore, scoop, shovel, spade, tunnel** Workers dug a deep trench for the new water line. **2. delve, investigate, explore, probe, study, research, search, sift** Robert dug through an encyclopedia to find facts to use in his history report. **3. drive, force, stick, stab, jab, poke, thrust, prod** The frightened kitten dug its claws into my arm. ◆ *noun* **1. jab, nudge, poke, thrust, stab, punch** My brother gave me a dig in the ribs. **2. quip, crack, taunt, gibe, wisecrack, slight, insult, snub** I did not appreciate his dig about my haircut.

digest *verb* **1. absorb, assimilate, dissolve, take up, imbibe, eat** The Venus's-flytrap is an unusual plant that can trap and digest insects. **2. absorb, comprehend, understand, master, fathom, take in, grasp** I have to digest the information in this article for my English class. ◆ *noun* **abridgment, condensation, synopsis, summary, abstract, outline** I am reading a scientific digest to gather facts for my paper.

dignified *adjective* **formal, noble, proper, stately, majestic, distinguished, solemn, august** Coretta Scott King speaks with an authoritative and dignified tone in her speeches about civil rights. ◆ **Antonyms: undignified, informal**

dignity *noun* **1. formality, nobility, solemnity, stateliness, majesty, gravity** Judges typically preside over their courts with dignity. **2. respectability, honor, prestige, repute, status, rank, importance, worth** The secretary-general of the United Nations holds a position of great dignity. ◆ **Antonyms: 1. informality 2. insignificance, disrepute**

digress *verb* **stray, turn, depart, deviate, diverge, swerve, veer, wander** The speaker digressed from his topic to tell an amusing anecdote.

dilapidated *adjective* **rundown, ramshackle, tumbledown, rickety, decrepit, decaying, broken-down** Nobody lives in that dilapidated shack. ◆ **Antonyms: sturdy, solid**

dilate *verb* enlarge, expand, widen, broaden, distend, grow, spread The optometrist put some drops in my eyes to dilate my pupils. ⏵ **Antonyms:** contract, constrict

dilemma *noun* quandary, predicament, bind, plight, jam, fix, difficulty I have a dilemma because I received invitations for two parties on the same night.

dilettante *noun* dabbler, amateur, nonprofessional, tyro, beginner, novice Kate is a dilettante at oil painting. ⏵ **Antonyms:** master, expert, professional

diligent *adjective* industrious, studious, assiduous, persistent, conscientious, painstaking The best way to improve your grades is to become more diligent in your studying. ⏵ **Antonym:** lazy

dilute *verb* 1. cut, thin, water down, attenuate, adulterate, mix A can of condensed soup should be diluted with water before it is cooked. 2. weaken, diminish, temper, mitigate, moderate, lessen, reduce, diffuse Travel over land diluted the force of the hurricane. ⏵ **Antonyms:** 1. concentrate, thicken 2. strengthen, intensify

dim *adjective* 1. low, faint, soft, weak, dark, murky, shadowy Tim strained his eyes by reading in dim light. 2. dull, drab, flat, lackluster, faded, pale, muted The colors in the quilt have become dim with the passing of the years. 3. indistinct, blurry, hazy, vague, unclear, cloudy, indefinite, obscure On hazy days, Seattle residents can see only the dim outline of nearby Mount Rainier. 4. unfavorable, disapproving, discouraging, adverse, suspicious My parents took a dim view of my request to go to the all-night party. ◆ *verb* darken, lower, turn down, soften, subdue In a movie theater, lights are dimmed just before the film starts. ⏵ **Antonyms:** *adjective* 1. bright, brilliant 2. vivid, deep 3. clear, distinct 4. favorable, promising ◆ *verb* brighten, lighten

dimension *noun* 1. measurement, proportion, size, length, width, thickness We need to know the windows' dimensions so that we can buy curtains. 2. extent, magnitude, scope, range, scale, amplitude, reach Their vacation plans increased in dimension until they were planning a trip around the world.

diminish *verb* abate, decrease, ebb, lessen, lower, reduce, wane, dwindle, subside His enthusiasm for playing football diminished after he had been tackled a few times. ⏵ **Antonyms:** grow, increase

diminutive *adjective* small, tiny, dwarf, miniature, wee, little, minuscule, minute The diminutive dollhouse was a replica of a Victorian cottage. ⏵ **Antonyms:** large, big, huge

din *noun* clamor, noise, racket, tumult, uproar, hubbub, commotion The barking dogs made such a din that I could not sleep. ◆ *verb* instill, hammer, drum, drill The teacher repeated the instructions until they were dinned into our heads. ⏵ **Antonyms:** *noun* quiet, silence

dine *verb* eat, feast, feed, banquet, sup, consume, partake We decided to dine at a restaurant tonight.

dingy *adjective* dirty, grimy, soiled, discolored, tarnished, dusty, murky, drab Ivan couldn't see out of the dingy window. ⏵ **Antonyms:** bright, clean

dinner *noun* meal, supper, repast, banquet, fete, repast I am responsible for making dinner two nights a week.

Word Group

Dinosaurs were carnivorous or herbivorous reptiles that lived mostly on land many millions of years ago. **Dinosaur** is a general term with no true synonyms. Here are some common types of dinosaurs:

apatosaurus (also known as **brontosaurus**), **compsognathus**, **pterosaur**, **stegosaurus**, **triceratops**, **tyrannosaurus**, **velociraptor**

dip *verb* 1. dunk, immerse, duck, submerge, douse, rinse, soak I dipped my hand into the bathtub to check the water's temperature. 2. scoop, bail, ladle, spoon, dish We frantically dipped water out of the leaking rowboat. 3. descend, drop, sink, lower, plunge, plummet, fall The hawk dipped out of sight behind a grove of trees. ◆ *noun* 1. dunk, duck, plunge, swim, immersion, soak He suggested that we all take a dip in his pool to cool off. 2. downgrade, decline, descent, drop, slope, pitch, declivity, sag The driver slowed down when he saw a big dip in the road. ⏵ **Antonyms:** *verb* 3. ascend, rise

diploma *noun* certificate, certification, degree, credentials, recognition I received a diploma when I graduated from the eighth grade.

diplomat *noun* 1. ambassador, emissary, attaché, chargé d'affaires, envoy, minister, consul Diplomats from a dozen countries met to negotiate an international trade agreement. 2. moderator, arbitrator, negotiator, referee, conciliator, representative, go-between Mom called me a diplomat when I helped my younger brothers settle their quarrel.

dire *adjective* 1. dreadful, terrible, calamitous, appalling, scary, fearful, awful, ominous The TV announcer issued dire warnings about the approaching hurricane. **2. urgent, desperate, imperative, pressing, exigent, extreme, acute, critical** The family was in dire straits when their home burned down. ➨ **Antonyms: 1. favorable, pleasant 2. unimportant, trivial**

direct *verb* **1. supervise, administer, control, govern, manage, run, head, handle** A manager directs the activities of other employees. **2. bid, command, instruct, order, tell, charge, enjoin, demand** The police officer directed everyone to stand back. **3. aim, point, level, focus, address, zero in, train, head** In study hall, I directed my attention to my homework. **4. guide, lead, show, steer, shepherd, usher, conduct, escort** Could you direct me to the meeting? ◆ *adjective* **1. shortest, straight, straightforward, unswerving, through** The direct route to the coast is about an hour shorter than the scenic road. **2. frank, candid, forthright, honest, open, plain, straightforward, blunt** She was very direct about the amount of money she needed. **3. exact, precise, faithful, accurate, correct, true, literal, strict** This is the most direct translation of the Russian novel *The Master and Margarita.* ➨ **Antonyms:** *adjective* **1. roundabout, indirect 2. dishonest, devious 3. inexact, imprecise**

direction *noun* **1. guidance, leadership, management, supervision, administration, care, charge** Our school paper is under the direction of the new English teacher. **2. guideline, instruction, rule, directive, regulation, information** Follow the directions printed at the top of the page. **3. command, order, behest, bidding, decree, dictate, edict, mandate** I obeyed my parents' direction to put my bicycle in the garage. **4. course, path, route, track, way, tendency, trend** The wind blew in a northerly direction.

directive *noun* **order, decree, command, direction, injunction, mandate, dictate** The principal issued a directive regarding the school's detention policy.

directly *adverb* **1. right, straight, dead, direct, due, smack, square** Mandy's house is directly across the street from mine. **2. immediately, right, promptly, just, forthwith, shortly, soon** I have a doctor's appointment directly after school. ➨ **Antonyms: 1. indirectly 2. eventually, later**

director *noun* **1. leader, head, supervisor, manager, boss, overseer** My aunt is the director of a nursery school. **2. administrator, executive, officer, official, chairperson, chair** They serve as directors of an international corporation.

dirge *noun* **lament, hymn, requiem, threnody, song, chant** Frédéric Chopin composed the well-known dirge "The Funeral March."

dirt *noun* **1. earth, soil, loam, humus, ground, clay, land, sod** Myna raises earthworms in a bucket of dirt. **2. mud, muck, filth, grime, dust, slime, scum** I got a lot of dirt on my pants when I worked in the garage. **3. gossip, scandal, rumor, talk, slander** I like to read the tabloids because they always have the latest dirt.

dirty *adjective* **1. soiled, filthy, grimy, grubby, mucky, sullied, contaminated, polluted** My hands are dirty from weeding the flower bed. **2. obscene, bawdy, coarse, profane, smutty, vulgar** My brother and I made up dirty lyrics to the children's song. **3. unfair, foul, nasty, deceitful, mean, contemptible** The referee called a foul on the player for his dirty move on the field. **4. angry, disapproving, bitter, resentful, hostile, indignant, mean** Scott gave me a dirty look when I missed the basket. ◆ *verb* **soil, smudge, sully, mess, spot, stain, muddy, pollute** How did you dirty your shirt? ➨ **Antonyms:** *adjective* **1. clean 2. decent, moral 3. honest, fair 4. friendly, pleasant** ◆ *verb* **clean**

disabled *adjective* **1. inoperative, out of order, broken, broken-down, damaged** Our lawn mower is disabled because the cord is broken. **2. handicapped, impaired, crippled, incapacitated, infirm, lame, paralyzed, paraplegic, physically challenged** My brother spent his summer at a ranch for disabled children. ➨ **Antonyms: 1. working, functional 2. able-bodied, sound, healthy**

disadvantage *noun* **1. drawback, handicap, liability, problem, shortcoming, flaw** Flying is the fastest way to travel, but it has the disadvantage of being expensive. **2. detriment, harm, loss, disservice, damage, impairment, injury** Becoming famous too early in life can work to one's disadvantage. ➨ **Antonyms: 1. advantage, merit 2. improvement, advantage**

disagree *verb* **1. contradict, differ, oppose, diverge, vary, dissent, conflict** Henrietta and I always seem to disagree over which movie to rent. **2. dispute, quarrel, argue, bicker, fight, squabble, contest, debate, wrangle** Let's not disagree over such a small issue. ➨ **Antonyms: agree, concur**

disagreeable *adjective* **1. bad, offensive, repulsive, unpleasant, distasteful, repugnant, revolting** Rotten eggs have a disagreeable odor. **2. bad-tempered, cranky, surly, cross, grouchy, grumpy, irritable, cantankerous** She is so disagreeable because she didn't get much sleep last night. ➨ **Antonyms: 1. agreeable, pleasant 2. amiable, friendly**

disagreement *noun* **1. conflict, difference, opposition, dissension, disparity, discrepancy** These two books are in disagreement about who really discovered America.

2. altercation, argument, dispute, fight, quarrel, tiff, squabble, feud My parents had a big disagreement, but they worked it out. ↠ **Antonyms: 1. agreement, accord**

disappear *verb* **1. vanish, dissolve, evaporate, fade, vaporize, dematerialize, dissipate** The wizard disappeared in a puff of smoke. **2. die out, expire, perish, cease, end, depart** The woolly mammoth disappeared about ten thousand years ago. ↠ **Antonyms: appear, emerge**

disappoint *verb* **let down, discontent, dissatisfy, disillusion, frustrate, discourage, sadden** You will disappoint your brother if you don't take him to the park. ↠ **Antonyms: please, satisfy**

disappointment *noun* **1. disillusionment, displeasure, dissatisfaction, frustration, regret, discontent, discouragement** He hid his disappointment when his dad postponed their fishing trip. **2. letdown, dud, flop, disaster, failure, fiasco, lemon** The sequel to my favorite movie turned out to be a real disappointment. ↠ **Antonyms: 1. satisfaction, fulfillment 2. success**

disapprove *verb* **1. dislike, object to, condemn, frown on, criticize, denounce, deprecate** Michelle disapproves of littering. **2. reject, deny, refuse, turn down, disallow, veto, forbid** Our petition was disapproved by the city council. ↠ **Antonyms: 1. approve, praise 2. allow, authorize**

disaster *noun* **1. calamity, accident, catastrophe, cataclysm, tragedy, misfortune** One of the biggest natural disasters ever was the eruption of the Krakatoa volcano in 1883. **2. failure, debacle, fiasco, botch, bungle, flop, dud, mess** My first attempt to bake a cake was a disaster.

disbelief *noun* **doubt, skepticism, incredulity, mistrust, distrust, rejection** The sailor's tale of a giant sea serpent was met with disbelief. ↠ **Antonyms: belief, trust**

discard *verb* **dispose, dump, eliminate, throw out, chuck, scrap, abandon** We discarded a lot of old junk from the basement. ↠ **Antonyms: keep, save**

discern *verb* **1. detect, make out, glimpse, spot, note, see, behold, spy, perceive** From the mountaintop, it was possible to discern the ocean 25 miles away. **2. know, tell, ascertain, apprehend, understand, discriminate, distinguish** He could look at a horseshoe and discern which hoof of the horse it had been on. ↠ **Antonyms: 1. miss, overlook**

discerning *adjective* **perceptive, judicious, sensitive, discriminating, astute, sharp, intelligent** He is a discerning collector of antiques. ↠ **Antonym: undiscerning**

discharge *verb* **1. disembark, unload, offload, dump, disburden, send forth, remove** The flight from Houston will discharge its passengers at gate 17. **2. let go, dismiss, release, free, liberate, emancipate, drop, remove** The doctor discharged her patient from the hospital. **3. eject, emit, expel, gush, pour, issue, leak, ooze, drain** The broken fire hydrant discharged water all over the street. **4. perform, carry out, execute, exercise, fulfill, implement, do, achieve** He was commended for the way in which he discharged his duties as class secretary. ◆ *noun* **1. emission, ooze, excretion, flow, secretion, seepage, elimination** We could see a discharge from our car's leaking brake cylinder. **2. dismissal, release, expulsion, ejection, eviction, termination** The soldier received an honorable discharge. ↠ **Antonyms: *verb* 1. load, stow 2. hire, keep**

disciple *noun* **believer, devotee, follower, supporter, adherent, partisan, admirer, student** The religious leader had many disciples. ↠ **Antonyms: leader, master, teacher**

discipline *noun* **1. self-control, self-restraint, diligence, practice, preparation, training** It takes a lot of discipline to write a book. **2. correction, penalty, punishment, chastisement, reproof, reprimand** Mother's typical form of discipline is to send me to my room. **3. branch, area, field, subject, specialty, course, topic** Dad got his college degree in the discipline of chemistry. ◆ *verb* **1. coach, drill, educate, instruct, teach, train, tutor, school** The captain disciplined his crew until they were expert sailors. **2. chasten, correct, punish, penalize, chastise, reprimand, reprove, rebuke** It is not my place to discipline my brother.

disclose *verb* **1. reveal, expose, unveil, exhibit, display, uncover, bare** The runway model took off her bulky coat to disclose a lovely evening gown. **2. divulge, relate, report, impart, tell, betray, release, communicate, inform** The reporter refused to disclose the source of her information. ↠ **Antonyms: 1. conceal, hide 2. withhold**

discomfort *noun* **1. pain, suffering, malaise, distress, ache, anguish, misery** Headaches can cause a lot of discomfort. **2. irritation, annoyance, distress, inconvenience, trouble, bother** My mosquito bites are a source of minor discomfort. ↠ **Antonyms: 1. comfort 2. pleasure**

discontinue *verb* **cease, end, halt, stop, suspend, interrupt, break off, quit, terminate** I discontinued my subscription to the magazine. ↠ **Antonyms: begin, start, continue**

discord *noun* **1. conflict, disagreement, disharmony, dissension, confrontation, strife** The meeting ended in discord with everybody shouting at each other. **2. noise,**

clamor, din, racket, bedlam, dissonance, cacophony, uproar We could hear the discord of rush-hour traffic from our window. ◆ **Antonyms: 1. accord, agreement 2. quiet, peace**

discount *verb* **1. mark down, lower, reduce, subtract, deduct, take off, depreciate** These shoes are discounted well below their regular price. **2. disregard, dismiss, ignore, discredit, minimize, deprecate, slight** I would discount that Web site because its information is not always verified. ◆ *noun* **deduction, reduction, decrease, markdown, rebate, exemption** Senior citizens receive a discount at most movie theaters. ◆ **Antonyms:** *verb* **1. raise, increase 2. acknowledge, praise**

discourage *verb* **1. unnerve, daunt, dishearten, dispirit, intimidate, dismay, bother** The minor fall did not discourage the skater, and she continued to practice her jumps. **2. deter, dissuade, divert, restrain, prevent, hinder, oppose, warn** The city started an ad campaign to discourage young people from smoking. ◆ **Antonyms: 1. encourage, hearten 2. invite, urge**

discover *verb* **1. detect, find, locate, spot, see, view, behold, encounter, unearth** The Spanish explorer Juan Ponce de León hoped to discover the legendary Fountain of Youth. **2. ascertain, determine, find, learn, perceive, identify, recognize, realize** Did you ever discover where you put your tennis racket? ◆ **Antonyms: miss, overlook**

discovery *noun* **detection, disclosure, find, sighting, unearthing, identification** Marie Curie won a Nobel Prize in 1911 for her discovery of radium and polonium.

discreet *adjective* **prudent, diplomatic, tactful, sensitive, cautious, circumspect, considerate** It would be discreet to discuss the matter with him in private. ◆ **Antonyms: indiscreet, inconsiderate**

discretion *noun* **1. prudence, circumspection, caution, tact, diplomacy, thoughtfulness** The senator conducts himself with discretion when he is in public. **2. judgment, preference, pleasure, choice, option, wish, will, freedom** Deciding whether or not to attend the party was left to my discretion. ◆ **Antonyms: 1. indiscretion, folly**

discriminate *verb* **1. distinguish, differentiate, discern, separate, know, tell** Can you discriminate between rayon and polyester? **2. show bias, disfavor, segregate, victimize, disdain, criticize, judge** It is illegal for an employer to discriminate on the basis of race, creed, age, or gender in hiring or promoting employees.

discuss *verb* **speak, talk, consider, confer, debate, deliberate, review** Mom met with my teachers to discuss my progress at school.

discussion *noun* **conference, debate, dialogue, talk, conversation, colloquium, exchange** Our social studies class had a discussion about the documentary we had seen.

disdain *verb* **eschew, spurn, reject, ignore, despise, scorn, deride** He disdained the opportunity to cheat on the test. ◆ *noun* **scorn, contempt, disrespect, dislike, intolerance, indifference, haughtiness** The clerk lost an important sale because he treated the customer with disdain. ◆ **Antonyms:** *verb* **esteem, respect** ◆ *noun* **admiration, respect**

disease *noun* **ailment, illness, malady, sickness, affliction, disorder** Modern medicine can prevent many diseases.

disgrace *noun* **1. disrepute, ignominy, dishonor, humiliation, shame, disfavor** The politician had to resign in disgrace when the public learned that she had accepted a bribe. **2. embarrassment, scandal, stigma, blemish, stain, blot** I think it's a disgrace that there are so many homeless people in America. ◆ *verb* **dishonor, discredit, embarrass, humiliate, shame, tarnish, stain** The player's cheating disgraced his entire team. ◆ **Antonyms:** *noun* **1. honor, favor 2. credit** ◆ *verb* **honor**

disguise *verb* **1. costume, mask, cloak, masquerade, dress up, camouflage** He disguised himself as a pirate for Halloween. **2. cover, conceal, hide, obscure, pretend, fake, deceive, feign** Chester disguised his stumble by doing a few dance steps. ◆ *noun* **1. concealment, costume, mask, camouflage, dress, getup** The spy's disguise concealed her real identity. **2. act, pretense, pretext, deception, guise, sham, pose, screen, veil** His belligerent attitude was only a disguise to cover his hurt feelings. ◆ **Antonyms:** *verb* **2. reveal, uncover**

disgust *verb* **appall, nauseate, repel, revolt, sicken, offend, displease** My sister says that my messy room disgusts her. ◆ *noun* **aversion, nausea, queasiness, distaste, revulsion, repugnance, abhorrence** I was filled with disgust when I saw pictures of smokers' lungs in our health education class. ◆ **Antonyms:** *verb* **please, delight** ◆ *noun* **pleasure, delight**

dish *noun* **1. plate, china, tableware, platter, bowl, saucer, vessel** I have a set of dishes that belonged to my great-grandmother. **2. entrée, food, fare, recipe, course, serving, helping** That was a delicious dish you brought to the potluck. ◆ *verb* **serve, dispense, pour, ladle, scoop, spoon, dip** Will you please dish out the pudding?

dishearten *verb* **discourage, dispirit, dismay, daunt, disappoint, depress, faze** That huge pile of dirty dishes would be enough to dishearten anyone. ● **Antonyms: encourage, hearten**

dishonest *adjective* **deceitful, fraudulent, untruthful, lying, untrustworthy, false, unscrupulous, corrupt** A person who tells lies is dishonest. ● **Antonyms: honest, trustworthy**

dishonor *noun* **shame, discredit, disgrace, humiliation, insult, scandal, blemish** I do not want to do anything to bring dishonor to myself or my family. ◆ *verb* **disgrace, shame, debase, sully, discredit, insult, humiliate** The spirit of the Olympic games was dishonored in 1972 by the murder of 11 Israeli athletes. ● **Antonyms:** *noun* **honor, respect** ◆ *verb* **honor, credit**

disintegrate *verb* **break up, fall apart, crumble, fragment, shatter, splinter, separate** The meteor disintegrated when it entered Earth's atmosphere.

dislike *verb* **despise, detest, hate, loathe, resent, abhor, disapprove** I dislike people who are inconsiderate. ◆ *noun* **aversion, distaste, hatred, revulsion, antipathy, loathing, animosity** My cat and my dog have a mutual dislike. ● **Antonyms:** *verb* **like, love** ◆ *noun* **liking**

dismal *adjective* **1. bleak, dark, dreary, gloomy, depressing, glum, somber, drab** Rain clouds made the sky look dismal. **2. sad, melancholy, depressed, miserable, doleful, desolate, mournful** Eeyore, the donkey in *Winnie the Pooh*, has a dismal outlook on life. ● **Antonyms: 1. bright, cheerful 2. happy, gay**

dismay *verb* **1. alarm, daunt, distress, consternate, appall, horrify** The picnickers were dismayed to see the approaching storm. **2. dishearten, dispirit, discourage, upset, unsettle, unnerve** I was dismayed because I couldn't find anything to wear to the reception. ◆ *noun* **anxiety, apprehension, distress, consternation, concern, alarm, fear** I was filled with dismay when I realized I'd locked myself out of our apartment. ● **Antonyms:** *verb* **encourage, cheer** ◆ *noun* **confidence, assurance**

dismiss *verb* **1. discharge, drop, fire, terminate, release, oust, let go, lay off, retire** Because sales were slow, the company had to dismiss several employees. **2. excuse, release, let out, free, liberate, furlough** I was dismissed from gym class until my broken arm healed. **3. disregard, drop, give up, reject, spurn, dispel, repudiate, disdain** We dismissed the story as gossip. ● **Antonyms: 1. employ, hire 2. admit, hold 3. accept, credit**

disobedient *adjective* **defiant, rebellious, insubordinate, recalcitrant, stubborn, unruly, naughty** My disobedient sister refused to help out. ● **Antonyms: obedient, dutiful**

disobey *verb* **defy, flout, disregard, ignore, violate, transgress, rebel, resist, break** The driver disobeyed the speed limit and was fined. ● **Antonyms: heed, obey, comply**

disorder *noun* **1. chaos, confusion, disarray, disorganization, mess, jumble** The soldiers retreated in disorder when the enemy attacked. **2. disturbance, unrest, commotion, turmoil, uproar, pandemonium, anarchy** During natural disasters there is often civil disorder. **3. affliction, ailment, disease, illness, malady, sickness, infirmity** Asthma is a breathing disorder. ◆ *verb* **upset, muddle, mess, disarray, disarrange, disturb, unsettle** The wind disordered my hair. ● **Antonyms:** *noun* **1. & 2. organization, order** ◆ *verb* **organize, order**

disorderly *adjective* **1. cluttered, chaotic, jumbled, confused, unsystematic, untidy** Our hall closet is a disorderly jumble of hat, coats, boots, and umbrellas. **2. disruptive, unruly, rowdy, improper, recalcitrant, undisciplined, wild** Kevin had to stay after school because of his disorderly behavior in class. ● **Antonyms: 1. neat, tidy 2. orderly, civil**

disparage *verb* **belittle, ridicule, deprecate, discredit, discount, slight, criticize** Our neighbor disparages teenagers because he considers them to be loud and obnoxious. ● **Antonyms: praise, acclaim**

disparate *adjective* **unlike, different, dissimilar, divergent, diverse, various, contrasting** The two cousins have disparate personalities. ● **Antonyms: similar, like**

dispatch *verb* **1. send, ship, expedite, transmit, forward, route, assign** The customer service representative said my order had been dispatched yesterday. **2. kill, slay, destroy, finish off, exterminate, execute, assassinate** The hawk dispatched the field mouse in just a few moments. ◆ *noun* **1. quickness, celerity, speed, swiftness, haste, rapidity, alacrity** The radio station sent reporters to the scene of the disaster with great dispatch. **2. message, communiqué, report, bulletin, communication, missive, note, news** The dispatch from the embassy was delivered to the President.

dispel *verb* **banish, drive away, send away, dismiss, expel, remove, dissipate, scatter** The flight attendant helped to dispel my fear of flying.

dispense *verb* **administer, distribute, dole, ration, give, provide, supply, apportion** Every Monday, Dad dispenses our weekly allowances.

disperse *verb* disband, break up, dispel, diffuse, scatter, separate High winds caused the clouds to disperse. ➤ **Antonyms:** assemble, collect, gather

display *verb* 1. demonstrate, disclose, exhibit, reveal, show, manifest, present The firefighter displayed great courage by saving a child from the burning building. 2. flaunt, show off, brandish, parade, flourish, vaunt, advertise The peacock displayed its gorgeous tail. ◆ *noun* show, spectacle, demonstration, exhibit, exposition, presentation, panoply, ceremony Everyone enjoyed the New Year's fireworks display. ➤ **Antonyms:** *verb* conceal, hide

dispose *verb* 1. place, set, arrange, array, order, organize, distribute Please dispose this bouquet of flowers in a vase. 2. incline, ready, predispose, persuade, induce, motivate His story disposed me to believe him. 3. discard, dispense, dump, unload, scrap, throw away, throw out, jettison Mom disposes of our old newspapers by taking them to the recycling center.

disposition *noun* 1. mood, temperament, nature, attitude, temper, character, personality You always seem to have a cheerful disposition. 2. tendency, inclination, predilection, penchant, propensity, bent, leaning She has a disposition to argue minor points. 3. arrangement, distribution, layout, organization, lineup, grouping, placement The committee drew up a plan for the disposition of the tables at the banquet.

dispute *verb* 1. argue, clash, contend, debate, quarrel, squabble, fight, wrangle My brother and I disputed whose turn it was to wash the floors. 2. challenge, contest, doubt, oppose, question, contradict, resist Maria disputes my claim that I am stronger than she. ◆ *noun* argument, controversy, disagreement, quarrel, run-in, feud, fight, squabble The two countries found a peaceful solution to their dispute. ➤ **Antonyms:** *verb* 2. acknowledge, confirm ◆ *noun* accord, agreement

disregard *verb* ignore, neglect, overlook, slight, disdain, scorn, snub We disregarded the instructions for the board game and made up our own rules. ◆ *noun* neglect, indifference, inattention, disdain, disrespect, contempt, oversight She treated her old bicycle with disregard. ➤ **Antonyms:** *verb* heed, regard ◆ *noun* appreciation, consideration

disrespect *noun* irreverence, contempt, dishonor, rudeness, discourtesy, affront There is a code of etiquette to prevent disrespect to our country's flag. ➤ **Antonyms:** respect, regard, courtesy

disrupt *verb* disturb, interfere, muddle, upset, interrupt, mess up The fans disrupted the rock concert when they rushed onto the stage.

dissatisfaction *noun* discontent, disgruntlement, disappointment, regret, unhappiness, disapproval The pilots showed their dissatisfaction by going on strike. ➤ **Antonyms:** satisfaction, contentment

dissent *verb* contradict, disagree, differ, dispute, protest, vary, object, oppose Congress was unable to pass the bill because too many senators dissented. ◆ *noun* disagreement, dissension, opposition, difference, disaccord, discord, schism The jurors could not resolve their dissent and so could not reach a verdict. ➤ **Antonyms:** *verb* agree, concur ◆ *noun* agreement, consent

dissolve *verb* 1. liquefy, break down, break up, melt, mix, soften The directions on the medicine bottle said to dissolve two tablets in a glass of water. 2. end, terminate, conclude, finish, disband, dismiss, sever, annul The two men dissolved their business partnership when they sold the company. 3. dispel, fade, dwindle, vanish, disappear, disintegrate, melt The contestant's confidence dissolved once she began to lose. ➤ **Antonyms:** 1. congeal, solidify 2. start, begin 3. appear, form

distance *noun* interval, length, space, gap, span, stretch, expanse, range The shortest distance between two points is a straight line.

distant *adjective* 1. far, faraway, far-off, remote, removed, separate We could hear the distant thunder of the waterfall. 2. aloof, unfriendly, withdrawn, cool, reserved, reticent, detached, standoffish Our neighbor's cat was distant until it got to know us. ➤ **Antonyms:** 1. close, near 2. friendly, cordial

distasteful *adjective* unpleasant, disagreeable, disgusting, revolting, repugnant, offensive Elaine had the distasteful task of clearing spider webs out of the basement. ➤ **Antonyms:** pleasant, appealing

distend *verb* swell, expand, bulge, inflate, bloat, dilate, enlarge, balloon The balloon began to distend as I blew air into it. ➤ **Antonyms:** contract, shrink

distinct *adjective* 1. discrete, different, dissimilar, individual, separate, unique, singular I can easily tell Corey from his twin brother because they have such distinct personalities. 2. apparent, clear, definite, obvious, unmistakable, evident, manifest, visible A distinct aroma of baking bread filled the house. ➤ **Antonyms:** 1. identical, similar 2. vague

distinctive *adjective* unique, distinct, individual, singular, different, particular Thalia's perfume is very distinctive. ➡ **Antonyms:** typical, common, ordinary

distinguish *verb* 1. differentiate, discern, determine, know, tell, judge, separate It is important to learn to distinguish right from wrong. 2. identify, make out, perceive, recognize, tell, detect, note, observe, see I could not distinguish who was approaching through the fog. 3. honor, dignify, glorify, elevate, exalt, praise, celebrate John distinguished himself by winning a short story contest.

distort *verb* 1. bend, contort, deform, twist, warp, misshape, disfigure Don't leave video cassettes in the sun, because heat will distort them. 2. alter, change, misrepresent, misstate, pervert, stretch, fabricate Supermarket tabloids are famous for distorting the truth.

distract *verb* 1. divert, sidetrack, interrupt, interfere Close your door so the TV won't distract you from your studies. 2. unsettle, upset, agitate, bother, fluster, perturb, disturb, disquiet I was distracted all day when I learned that my favorite teacher was retiring.

distress *verb* disturb, trouble, upset, concern, worry, bother, perturb, pain I don't want to distress you, but the power will be off until tomorrow. ◆ *noun* 1. anguish, anxiety, concern, worry, uneasiness, care, grief, pain, sorrow His mischievousness is a constant source of distress to his parents. 2. difficulty, need, danger, peril, trouble, exigency, misfortune We pulled over to help a motorist in distress. ➡ **Antonyms:** *verb* relieve, console ◆ *noun* 1. comfort, solace

distribute *verb* 1. allot, deal, dole, ration, pass out, dispense, give That charity distributes food to needy families. 2. spread, disperse, scatter, diffuse, strew, disseminate Please distribute the icing evenly over the entire cake. 3. classify, categorize, class, grade, group, rank, sort, arrange The entries in the flower show were distributed according to variety.

district *noun* area, quarter, region, section, zone, neighborhood, locality, precinct, territory New York's financial district is located on Wall Street.

disturb *verb* 1. dislocate, displace, disorder, confuse, upset, move, shift I was careful not to disturb anything in the gift shop. 2. agitate, distress, disconcert, perturb, trouble, worry, unsettle, alarm My parents were disturbed when I stayed out too late. 3. annoy, bother, disrupt, distract, interrupt, aggravate, intrude, pester Please don't disturb me while I'm doing my homework. ➡ **Antonyms:** 1. organize, order 2. soothe, calm

disturbance *noun* 1. commotion, tumult, turmoil, uproar, riot, ruckus, stir, hubbub Andre's hamster created a disturbance when it got loose in our classroom. 2. distraction, interference, interruption, intrusion, disruption, bother, annoyance Dad loves his den because it's quiet and he can work without disturbance.

dive *verb* leap, jump, plunge, dip, sink, duck, dunk, drop, fall, plummet, descend The swimmers will dive into the pool at the start of the race. ◆ *noun* descent, plunge, nosedive, dip, drop, fall, slide The test pilot wanted to see how the new jet would perform in a steep dive.

diverge *verb* 1. branch, divide, fork, separate, split, spread, radiate The Platte River diverges from the Missouri River in southwestern Nebraska. 2. deviate, depart, swerve, veer, stray, digress, wander, drift She rarely diverges from her routine of jogging in the early morning.

diverse *adjective* different, distinct, disparate, variant, distinctive, assorted, miscellaneous, varied, eclectic One of the strengths of the United States is that its citizens have diverse backgrounds. ➡ **Antonyms:** identical, similar, same

divert *verb* 1. deflect, shift, sidetrack, turn aside, deviate, swing, change, alter Bad weather caused our Chicago flight to be diverted to Indianapolis. 2. amuse, entertain, occupy, distract, regale, engage, absorb The street musicians diverted us while we stood in line at the theater.

divide *verb* 1. cut, part, segment, separate, split, break, section, partition We divided the pizza into six equal pieces. 2. classify, categorize, class, arrange, sort, organize, group We divided the books according to whether they were nonfiction or fiction. 3. allot, apportion, deal, dole, ration, dispense, distribute, share We listed all the errands and then divided them among the three of us. ➡ **Antonyms:** 1. combine, join

divine *adjective* holy, religious, sacred, hallowed, consecrated, saintly, heavenly, godly, celestial The divine scripture of the Islamic religion is known as the Koran. ◆ *verb* predict, foretell, prophesy, augur, foresee, forecast, envision Tarot cards are a popular way to try to divine the future. ➡ **Antonyms:** *adjective* secular, profane

division *noun* 1. partition, parting, segmentation, separation, detachment, split The division of the year into 12 months began about 713 B.C. 2. department, section, segment, arm, branch, component, subdivision Mom works for the marketing division of her company. 3. divider, partition, wall, barrier, border, boundary Dad built a counter to serve as a division between our kitchen and dining room.

4. split, breach, disagreement, disunity, discord, dissent, conflict There is division in the club over who should be our next president. ⯈ **Antonyms: 4. unity, harmony**

divorce *noun* **breakup, separation, split, dissolution, rupture, severance** I was glad that my parents decided not to get a divorce. ◆ *verb* **break up, part, separate, split, divide, sever, dissolve, detach** The young couple divorced after only three months of marriage. ⯈ **Antonyms:** *noun* **union** ◆ *verb* **unite, join**

divulge *verb* **disclose, expose, reveal, tell, make known, unveil, confide, inform** My aunt divulged to me that she is going to have a baby. ⯈ **Antonyms: conceal, hide**

dizzy *adjective* **giddy, lightheaded, woozy, unsteady, faint, dazed, shaky** The carnival ride made me dizzy. ◆ *verb* **confuse, bewilder, addle, befuddle, confound, perplex, puzzle** The shopper was dizzied by all the choices in the huge electronics store.

do *verb* **1. accomplish, execute, perform, conduct, fulfill, carry out, undertake** Soldiers are expected to do whatever they're told. **2. compose, create, fashion, render, produce, make, design, concoct** My artist friend is doing a portrait of me. **3. bring, lead, cause, effect, give, perform, produce, generate** Complaining won't do you any good. **4. figure out, resolve, solve, work out, interpret, complete, finish** I like to do crossword puzzles. **5. answer, satisfy, serve, suffice, suit, avail, fit, pass** Those tennis shoes will do for the hike, though boots would be better. **6. fare, fend, make out, get along, manage** How are you doing with your drum lessons?

docile *adjective* **gentle, manageable, meek, tame, mild, obedient, submissive** I'm not going to get on that horse unless he's docile. ⯈ **Antonyms: unruly, wild**

dock *noun* **wharf, pier, quay, landing, berth, slip** I like to walk to the end of the dock and watch the boats. ◆ *verb* **anchor, berth, moor, land, tie up, hook up** We docked the boat and then went swimming.

doctor *noun* **physician, general practitioner, surgeon, medic, healer** Mom called the doctor because I had a persistent fever. ◆ *verb* **1. treat, medicate, administer to, mend, heal, cure** Most people doctor a cold by drinking lots of fluids and getting extra rest. **2. tamper, falsify, change, modify, alter, fabricate, fake** She tried to doctor her report card, but the changes were obvious.

doctrine *noun* **belief, creed, principle, dogma, tenet, teaching, credo, theory** I am studying the doctrine of my religion.

Word Group

A **document** is an official paper containing information or proof. **Document** is a general term with no true synonyms. Here are some related terms:

certificate, contract, credential, deed, license, memo, petition, record, testament, will

dodge *verb* **1. duck, move, sidestep, bob, weave, shift, swerve, veer** I dodged when my friend threw a water balloon at me. **2. evade, avoid, escape, elude, skirt, bypass, circumvent** The press secretary dodged all questions about the recent crisis. ◆ *noun* **artifice, deception, device, feint, ploy, ruse, subterfuge, trick** He faked mental illness as a dodge to avoid having to serve in the military. ⯈ **Antonyms:** *verb* **2. confront, face**

dogged *adjective* **persevering, tenacious, stubborn, obstinate, determined, headstrong** He made the honor roll as a result of dogged hard work. ⯈ **Antonyms: yielding, irresolute**

dogmatic *adjective* **opinionated, intolerant, fixed, arrogant, overbearing, imperious** Her approach is too dogmatic for me.

doleful *adjective* **mournful, rueful, sad, sorrowful, woeful, gloomy** My dog is doleful when I leave her home alone all day. ⯈ **Antonyms: happy, joyful, cheerful**

dolt *noun* **idiot, dunce, dummy, fool, simpleton, dimwit, imbecile, dullard** My sister begged me to not act like a dolt around her friends.

domain *noun* **1. realm, dominion, territory, estate, area, region, fiefdom, kingdom** The king extended his domain by invading and conquering two neighboring countries. **2. province, field, area, arena, bailiwick, sphere, specialty** The professor's domain was American literature.

domestic *adjective* **1. family, familial, home, household, private, residential** My parents rarely go out or travel because they're happiest in a domestic setting. **2. tame, domesticated, docile, obedient, submissive, trained** Horses, pigs, and cows are domestic animals. ⯈ **Antonyms: 2. untamed, wild**

domicile *noun* **home, house, abode, residence, lodging, dwelling, habitation, abode** The application form asked for the location of my domicile.

dominant *adjective* **commanding, controlling, ruling, predominant, leading, main, principal** The young wolf did not dare challenge the dominant member of the pack. ❧ **Antonyms: inferior, subordinate**

dominate *verb* **1. command, control, govern, lead, rule, domineer, direct** Among many animals, the strongest male dominates the group. **2. overshadow, tower above, tower over, dwarf, overlook, command** With its high tower, the church dominates the other buildings in the village.

dominion *noun* **1. control, power, sovereignty, jurisdiction, authority, command** In 1701, England's James I claimed dominion over Scotland. **2. realm, domain, land, territory, region, area, kingdom** There was rarely peace in the dominion.

donate *verb* **contribute, give, present, award, grant, bestow, pledge** Trevor donated half his allowance to his troop's fund-raising drive.

donation *noun* **contribution, gift, offering, present, grant, award, alms, bequest** That charity receives donations from all over the world.

done *adjective* **finished, complete, concluded, terminated, through, over, accomplished** I will be glad when exam week is done. ❧ **Antonyms: undone, incomplete**

donor *noun* **contributor, donator, giver, provider, supplier, benefactor** The Red Cross has issued a national appeal for blood donors.

doom *noun* **destruction, death, end, ruin, downfall, finish, fate** When the knight saw the fierce dragon, he thought that he was facing his doom. ◆ *verb* **condemn, fate, sentence, finish, ruin, destroy** News of the scandal doomed the senator's reelection campaign.

door *noun* **1. doorway, entrance, entry, gateway, threshold, portal** Someone came to our door selling magazine subscriptions. **2. means, approach, access, path, avenue, route, course, opening** A good education can be the door to success.

dormant *adjective* **inactive, quiescent, asleep, sleeping, inert, motionless, latent** Trees are usually dormant during the winter. ❧ **Antonyms: active, functioning, awake**

dosage *noun* **dose, amount, measure, portion, share, quantity, ration** Using the proper dosage of a medicine is very important.

dot *noun* **spot, dash, fleck, pinpoint, point, speck, circle, mark** Pointillism is an art form that creates colors and forms from tiny dots of paint. ◆ *verb* **spot, bespeckle, fleck, speck, speckle, sprinkle, dapple, stipple** The field was dotted with wildflowers.

dote *verb* **idolize, treasure, prize, worship, adore, pamper, spoil, indulge, love** My sister dotes on her new puppy.

double *adjective* **dual, paired, twin, duplex, twofold, duplicate** Dad installed double windows in our living room. ◆ *noun* **duplicate, twin, clone, copy, replica, facsimile** The new vase is a double of the one that got broken. ◆ *verb* **1. multiply, increase, enlarge, magnify, duplicate, redouble** The company doubled its output in just three years. **2. fold, double over, pleat, ply, crease** I doubled the blanket for extra warmth. **3. function, serve, act, work, substitute** She doubles as a waitress on the weekends. ❧ **Antonyms:** *adjective* **single, sole**

doubt *verb* **disbelieve, dispute, distrust, question, challenge, wonder, query** I doubt that ghosts actually exist. ◆ *noun* **misgiving, question, suspicion, uncertainty, skepticism, qualm, reservation** I have doubts about whether he's telling the truth. ❧ **Antonyms:** *verb* **trust, believe** ◆ *noun* **trust, belief**

doubtful *adjective* **1. dubious, questionable, uncertain, unclear, improbable, unlikely** It's doubtful that I'll be ready on time. **2. questionable, suspicious, suspect, shady, dubious, equivocal** That lawyer has a doubtful reputation. ❧ **Antonyms: 1. certain, sure**

dour *adjective* **gloomy, austere, bleak, grim, glum, harsh, forbidding, sullen, morose** Edgar Allan Poe is known for his dour poetry and short stories. ❧ **Antonyms: happy, cheerful, bright**

down *adverb* **downward, low, below, beneath, under** I fell down several times while I was learning to ski. ◆ *adjective* **1. depressed, sad, downcast, dejected, unhappy, low, despondent, melancholy, blue** He was feeling down after he failed his English test. **2. broken, inoperative, unserviceable, unusable, out, out of order** Two ski lifts were down, so lines were very long at the others. ◆ *preposition* **along, by, into, through** We walked down the block to the video store. ◆ *verb* **1. drop, fell, strike, hit, floor, beat, conquer** The fighter pilot downed two enemy aircraft. **2. drink, gulp, guzzle, swallow, imbibe, bolt, wolf, gobble** The player downed two bottles of water during the basketball game. ❧ **Antonyms:** *adjective* **1. happy, cheerful 2. functional, working**

downhearted *adjective* low, depressed, dejected, desolate, down, unhappy, melancholic I was downhearted when my favorite character in the soap opera was killed. ⏺ **Antonyms: happy, glad**

doze *verb* drowse, nap, sleep, slumber, snooze, nod off, catnap, rest My cat often dozes on the couch. ◆ *noun* nap, siesta, snooze, catnap, rest After a doze I was refreshed.

drab *adjective* colorless, dull, flat, dismal, dreary, somber, lackluster, lifeless She brightened the drab room with some new yellow curtains. ⏺ **Antonyms: bright, colorful**

draft *noun* 1. breeze, air, current, wind, waft, puff, flow If the draft is bothering you, please close the window. 2. sip, swallow, gulp, mouthful, drink, quantity, measure, portion I took another draft of my soda. 3. version, outline, sketch, rough, skeleton, plan The author spent an entire year writing the first draft of his novel. ◆ *verb* 1. conscript, induct, levy, call up, impress, muster, mobilize, recruit, enlist During World War I, German boys were drafted to serve in their country's army. 2. outline, plan, diagram, formulate, frame, sketch, plot, compose I drafted my report on note cards.

drag *verb* 1. draw, haul, pull, tow, trail, train, lug My tired little sister dragged her teddy bear behind her as she climbed the stairs. 2. crawl, creep, plod, trudge, poke, delay, linger, lag The weary hikers dragged into camp and collapsed in front of the fire. ⏺ **Antonyms: 1. push, shove 2. rush, speed**

drain *verb* 1. draw off, let out, tap, discharge, release, remove, flow, leak Dad drained the oil from the car. 2. consume, empty, exhaust, sap, use up, deplete, impoverish, decrease, diminish The long swim drained all my strength. ◆ *noun* 1. outlet, pipe, gutter, tube, sewer, channel, ditch, trench The sink drain is clogged. 2. strain, drag, sap, depletion, reduction, decrease The unexpected number of participants proved to be a drain on the camp's resources. ⏺ **Antonyms: *verb* replenish, fill**

drama *noun* 1. play, show, theatrical piece, pageant, melodrama, production Eugene O'Neill's dramas are considered among the most important in American theater. 2. dramatics, theatrics, histrionics, excitement, emotion, suspense, spectacle We enjoy the drama and pageantry of historical reenactments.

dramatic *adjective* exciting, sensational, spectacular, thrilling, suspenseful, emotional, vivid I was enthralled by the movie's dramatic high-speed chase scene. ⏺ **Antonyms: common, ordinary**

dramatize *verb* 1. perform, present, act, enact, put on, stage, show Our theater group is going to dramatize several of Aesop's fables. 2. exaggerate, embellish, intensify, amplify, overplay, overstate She tends to dramatize the events of her life. ⏺ **Antonyms: 2. understate, minimize**

drape *verb* wrap, swathe, cloak, cover, clothe, mantle, robe, hang Drape a blanket around yourself to keep warm.

drastic *adjective* extreme, radical, severe, powerful, strong, forceful, harsh, desperate Fasting is a drastic way to lose weight. ⏺ **Antonyms: moderate, mild**

draw *verb* 1. drag, pull, tow, tug, lug, lead, haul, convey Pioneers often used oxen to draw their covered wagons. 2. extract, remove, take, pull, withdraw Let's pick teams by drawing names from a hat. 3. attract, entice, lure, induce, elicit, evoke, summon The light of a lamp draws moths and other flying insects. 4. get, take, obtain, secure, procure, acquire, receive, gather Mom drew enough money from the bank to pay for my school supplies. 5. sketch, depict, etch, create, diagram, outline, trace, portray He drew a picture of a superhero. ◆ *noun* 1. attraction, lure, enticement, allure, appeal, inducement, pull The construction site was a draw for the kids in the neighborhood. 2. deadlock, stalemate, standoff, tie, dead heat If the score is still tied after overtime in professional hockey, the game is declared a draw. ⏺ **Antonyms: *verb* 1. push, shove 3. repel, repulse**

drawback *noun* disadvantage, problem, trouble, defect, difficulty, handicap, hindrance There are drawbacks to living in both the country and the city. ⏺ **Antonyms: advantage, benefit**

dread *verb* fear, be afraid, cower at, worry about I dreaded speaking in front of the class. ◆ *noun* apprehension, fear, fright, horror, terror, alarm, panic, trepidation Just thinking about rattlesnakes fills me with dread. ◆ *adjective* dreadful, terrible, awful, frightening, alarming, terrifying, scary Bubonic plague is a dread disease.

dreadful *adjective* 1. dread, frightful, dire, scary, frightening, terrible, ghastly A dreadful thunderstorm caused the power to go out for several hours. 2. shocking, distasteful, unpleasant, offensive, horrid, awful, bad We heard the dreadful news from our neighbor.

dream *noun* 1. reverie, daydream, fantasy, fancy, illusion, fiction His favorite dream as a child was of living in a treehouse. 2. ambition, aspiration, goal, hope, vision, ideal, desire, wish Her dream is to become an astronaut. ◆ *verb* daydream, muse, fantasize, conceive, imagine, suppose, think I never dreamed that I'd win the spelling bee.

dreary *adjective* **1. bleak, cheerless, dismal, gloomy, somber, dark, desolate** During the Industrial Revolution, many children spent long, dreary days working in factories and mills. **2. dull, boring, tedious, monotonous, uninteresting** The dreary lecture put me to sleep. ◆▶ **Antonyms: 1. bright, cheerful 2. exciting, lively**

drench *verb* **douse, saturate, soak, wet, souse, drown, inundate** A sudden downpour drenched me as I walked home from school.

dress *verb* **1. attire, clothe, outfit, garb, robe** I dressed my little sister warmly to go sledding. **2. adorn, trim, decorate, embellish, bedeck, ornament, array, festoon** We dressed up the gymnasium for our school dance. ◆ *noun* **1. apparel, attire, clothes, clothing, garment, raiment, garb** The dinner invitation stated that formal dress was required. **2. frock, gown, skirt, shift, jumper, pinafore** She bought a new dress to wear to her cousin's bat mitzvah.

drift *verb* **1. cruise, float, coast, sail, skim, slide, ride, waft, wash** The hot-air balloon drifted above our neighborhood. **2. wander, amble, mosey, stroll, meander, saunter, ramble** We drifted among the statues in the sculpture garden. **3. bank, accumulate, collect, amass, pile, stack** The wind caused snow to drift against our front door. ◆ *noun* **1. bank, dune, heap, hill, mass, mound, pile, stack** These drifts were formed by waves carrying sand onto the beach. **2. meaning, implication, gist, significance, sense, intention, import, essence** I didn't get the drift of the story until my friend explained it to me.

drill *noun* **exercise, practice, rehearsal, training, study, routine, regimen** Los Angeles schools hold regular earthquake drills. ◆ *verb* **1. bore, pierce, ream, tap, penetrate, puncture** The rancher drilled a well to procure water for his cattle. **2. coach, instruct, rehearse, teach, exercise, train, practice, work out** The teacher drilled the class on the states and their capitals.

drink *verb* **down, sip, swallow, gulp, guzzle, imbibe, quaff, swig** I drink a glass of orange juice every morning. ◆ *noun* **1. beverage, liquid, fluid, refreshment** His favorite drink is lemonade. **2. sip, swallow, draft, quaff, swill, taste, cup, glass** May I have a drink of water?

drip *verb* **dribble, drop, trickle, weep, leak, ooze, drizzle** I let the honey drip onto my cereal. ◆ *noun* **dribble, trickle, dripping, leak** The plumber fixed the drip in the faucet.

drive *verb* **1. herd, spur, run, move, guide, push, propel, press, conduct** Have you seen that movie about a pig who learns to drive sheep? **2. control, operate, run, steer, pilot,** wheel, ride Uncle Walter showed me how to drive his tractor. **3. motor, convey, transport, bus, chauffeur, taxi** Mom drove me to school today. **4. motivate, stimulate, compel, force, impel, coerce, require, push** The sprinter was driven by a desire to set a new world record. **5. hit, knock, pound, strike, propel, bat, belt, hammer** My dad can drive a golf ball almost 300 yards. ◆ *noun* **1. excursion, ride, journey, tour, trip, outing, spin, jaunt** My family enjoys taking weekend drives in the country. **2. campaign, crusade, movement, cause, effort, appeal** Our school sponsored a drive to collect money for new library books. **3. ambition, initiative, aggressiveness, hustle, energy, push, hustle** Wilma Rudolf showed great drive in overcoming childhood illnesses to become an Olympic medalist.

drivel *noun* **nonsense, balderdash, rubbish, poppycock, blather, babble** That talk show is nothing but drivel.

drone *verb* **drawl, intone, mumble, mutter, murmur, whisper, hum** As the speaker droned on, the audience became restless. ◆ *noun* **hum, burr, buzz, whir, whiz, thrumming, vibration, monotone** The drone of the ship's engines lulled me to sleep.

droop *verb* **1. bend, drop, hang, sag, dangle, sink, lower, slouch, flop** Heavy snow caused the tree branches to droop. **2. flag, weaken, fade, wither, wilt, ebb, diminish, languish, slump** The marathon runner's energy began to droop. ◆▶ **Antonyms: 1. stand, rise 2. revive, persist**

drop *noun* **1. bead, droplet, globule, glob, drip, dribble, trickle** Drops of sweat formed on my forehead in the hot sun. **2. trace, whiff, hint, smidgen, mite, particle, bit, dab, jot** Dad adds a drop of vanilla to the batter when he makes pancakes. **3. descent, fall, plunge, pitch, declivity, slope** It's a long drop from the top of the cliff to the valley below. **4. decline, decrease, dip, reduction, dive, slump, nosedive** There's been a drop in the price of wheat due to an abundant harvest. ◆ *verb* **1. drip, trickle, leak, dribble, drizzle, weep, sprinkle** Water dropped out of the leaky bucket. **2. descend, fall, plunge, sink, slump, dive, plummet, tumble** The temperature dropped more than 25 degrees last night. **3. cease, discontinue, end, stop, give up, abandon, relinquish** When Lisa joined a softball league, she had to drop her piano lessons. **4. eliminate, leave out, omit, exclude, remove, skip, release, let go, shed** We'll have to drop one of these dishes from the menu. ◆▶ **Antonyms:** *noun* **3. rise 4. increase, rise** ◆ *verb* **2. increase, rise 3. begin, continue 4. include**

drown *verb* **1. flood, inundate, submerge, immerse, drench, soak** The neighbors' sprinklers broke and drowned their lawn. **2. overpower, overwhelm, overcome, stifle, smother, muffle, mask** Applause drowned out the speaker's closing remarks.

drowsy *adjective* **sleepy, tired, groggy, somnolent, soporific, lethargic, listless** If you feel so drowsy, why don't you take a nap? ➽ **Antonyms: alert, awake**

drug *noun* **1. medication, medicine, pharmaceutical, physic, pill, remedy** Aspirin is one of the most commonly used drugs in the United States. **2. hallucinogen, narcotic, opiate, substance, depressant, stimulant** People who deal in illegal drugs run the risk of imprisonment. ◆ *verb* **sedate, tranquilize, dose, medicate, administer, treat** The veterinarian drugged the cow to make it easier to treat.

drum *noun* **barrel, keg, cask, tub, vat, hogshead, tun** They burn their trash in a 55-gallon drum. ◆ *verb* **1. rap, tap, thump, beat, tattoo, strum, thrum, pulsate, throb, reverberate, roar** I woke to the sound of a woodpecker drumming on a telephone pole. **2. drill, din, hammer, beat, drive, reiterate, instill** I am trying to drum French verbs into my head for the quiz tomorrow.

drunk *adjective* **drunken, intoxicated, inebriated, tipsy, sodden, besotted** Drunk drivers cause many serious accidents. ➽ **Antonym: sober**

dry *adjective* **1. waterless, arid, rainless, sere, parched, thirsty** Deserts can be hot or cold, but they are always dry. **2. boring, dreary, dull, monotonous, tedious, uninteresting, plain, bare** I thought his presentation was very dry. **3. droll, witty, wry, deadpan, subtle, understated, sly** We enjoy our teacher's dry wit. ◆ *verb* **dehydrate, dry out, parch, drain** We made raisins by drying grapes in the sun. ➽ **Antonyms:** *adjective* **1. moist, wet, damp 2. interesting, exciting** ◆ *verb* **moisten, soak**

dubious *adjective* **1. uncertain, doubtful, undecided, unclear, unsure, skeptical** I am dubious about whether I will enjoy this movie. **2. shady, suspicious, questionable, suspect, unreliable, undependable** That excuse sounds dubious to me. ➽ **Antonyms: 1. positive, certain 2. reliable, dependable**

duck *verb* **1. bend, crouch, drop, dip, dive, stoop, lower** The little girl ducked behind a bush during the hide-and-seek game. **2. avoid, dodge, elude, escape, evade, circumvent, sidestep, skirt** The politician ducked reporters by sneaking out the back door. ➽ **Antonyms: 1. rise 2. face, confront**

due *adjective* **1. appropriate, fit, fitting, proper, suitable, right, rightful, correct, just** Use due care when handling a sharp knife. **2. sufficient, adequate, ample, enough, plenty, abundant, satisfactory** The police had due cause to search the building. **3. anticipated, expected, scheduled,** slated, booked, coming Dad's plane is due at 3:00 this afternoon. ◆ *noun* **reward, recompense, compensation, payment, satisfaction, deserts** Albert Schweitzer received his due when he was awarded the Nobel Peace Prize in 1952. ◆ *adverb* **dead, direct, directly, exactly, right, straight** We drove due south through the desert. ➽ **Antonyms:** *adjective* **1. inappropriate, unsuitable 2. inadequate, insufficient**

dull *adjective* **1. blunt, unsharpened, edgeless** It's hard to cut fabric with dull scissors. **2. boring, monotonous, tedious, tiresome, uninteresting, vapid, humdrum** He walked out of the dull film. **3. mild, moderate, subdued, indistinct, feeble, softened, muted, faded** My pain lessened to a dull ache after I took the two aspirin. **4. dim, flat, drab, muddy, murky, lackluster** I like that dull shade of green. ◆ *verb* **blunt, dim, diminish, blur, fade, reduce, deaden, numb** Age has dulled our dog's hearing. ➽ **Antonyms:** *adjective* **1. sharp 2. exciting, interesting 3. intense, distinct 4. bright** ◆ *verb* **increase, sharpen**

dumb *adjective* **1. speechless, silent, mute, inarticulate, wordless, mum** I was dumb with surprise when my old friend suddenly appeared. **2. crazy, foolish, silly, senseless, thoughtless, stupid, unintelligent, thickheaded** I made a dumb mistake when I said that Thomas Jefferson was the first President of our country. ➽ **Antonyms: 1. articulate 2. bright, clever**

dummy *noun* **1. mannequin, manikin, doll, figure, puppet** The ventriloquist held the dummy on his lap. **2. fool, dunce, blockhead, dullard, dolt, numskull, simpleton, idiot** I felt like a dummy when I forgot my friend's name. **3. fake, simulation, imitation, likeness, counterfeit, copy** You can't open this drawer because it's a dummy. ◆ *adjective* **imitation, fake, phony, mock, counterfeit, sham, bogus** My sister made a dummy microphone and pretended that she was a rock star. ➽ **Antonyms:** *adjective* **real, genuine, authentic**

dump *verb* **drop, empty, deposit, pour, release, unload, upset, overturn** I was taking a nap on the beach when my sister dumped a bucket of water on me. ◆ *noun* **junkyard, rubbish heap, trash pile** Dad and I took a load of trash to the dump.

dunce *noun* **fool, dummy, blockhead, dullard, dolt, numskull, simpleton** I felt like a dunce when I misspelled half the words on the spelling test.

dupe *verb* **trick, deceive, fool, delude, mislead, bluff, hoax, swindle** My little brother tried to dupe our mother into thinking that he was sick.

duplicate *adjective* twin, matching, identical, like, similar, double Mom had duplicate keys made for the front door locks. ◆ *noun* copy, reproduction, double, facsimile, likeness, replica, imitation I made a duplicate of my book report in case something happened to the original. ◆ *verb* replicate, copy, imitate, repeat, reproduce, simulate, redo The scientist is duplicating her experiment to test her original results. ➜ **Antonyms:** *noun* original, master

duplicity *noun* deception, guile, artifice, deceit, deceitfulness, fraud, dishonesty, cunning My little sister looks as if she would be incapable of duplicity. ➜ **Antonyms:** honesty, candor

durable *adjective* enduring, lasting, long-lived, permanent, sound, strong, sturdy, tough Jan and I have a durable friendship that has lasted since the first grade. ➜ **Antonyms:** fragile, shoddy

duration *noun* course, period, span, term, time, stretch, life, lifetime, extent, interval I spent the duration of my summer vacation on a farm in Vermont.

dusk *noun* evening, nightfall, sundown, sunset, night, twilight The laser show will start at dusk.

duty *noun* 1. assignment, job, business, obligation, responsibility, task, chore It is my duty to walk the dog. 2. tariff, tax, fee, levy, assessment, impost, charge Mom had to pay a duty on pearls she bought abroad.

dwarf *verb* overshadow, tower above, tower over, dominate, predominate That new high-rise dwarfs the surrounding buildings.

dwell *verb* 1. abide, live, reside, stay, lodge, inhabit People have dwelled in cities for many thousands of years. 2. emphasize, focus, stress, linger, persist, elaborate, expound The naturalist dwelled on the importance of maintaining a diversity of species. 3. brood, fret, mope, worry, obsess, agonize, sulk Please do not dwell too much on the past.

dwelling *noun* house, residence, abode, home, domicile, habitation, lodgings, quarters Their dwelling was a picturesque stone cottage in the country.

dwindle *verb* decline, decrease, diminish, ebb, lessen, reduce, fade, abate The crowd began to dwindle as disappointed fans started leaving before the game was over. ➜ **Antonyms:** grow, increase

dye *noun* color, colorant, coloring, pigment, stain, tint This red dye is guaranteed not to fade. ◆ *verb* color, tint, shade, stain, tinge My art class dyed T-shirts as a project.

dynamic *adjective* energetic, forceful, lively, vigorous, active, strong, powerful, intense The dynamic performer had the whole audience singing along with her. ➜ **Antonyms:** weak, ineffectual

Ee

eager *adjective* avid, enthusiastic, keen, ardent, impatient, desirous, anxious, yearning I am eager for summer vacation to begin. ◈ **Antonyms:** indifferent, apathetic

early *adjective* **1.** beginning, first, initial, opening, starting, introductory, inaugural, primary My oldest brother is in his early twenties. **2.** primitive, ancient, prehistoric, archaic, primeval, primordial, original It is almost certain that early man originated in Africa. **3.** premature, untimely, hasty, precipitate, sudden, precocious, unseasonable The first snowfall came early this year. ◆ *adverb* before, beforehand, ahead, in advance, promptly, directly, shortly, prematurely She arrived early to help prepare for the party. ◈ **Antonyms:** *adjective* **1.** late, latter **2.** modern, recent **3.** tardy, delayed, late ◆ *adverb* late

earn *verb* **1.** get, make, obtain, gain, receive, acquire, collect, draw, reap I earn 20 dollars a week delivering newspapers. **2.** attain, gain, achieve, secure, win, deserve, rate, cause, produce She earned our admiration when her essay won first place. ◈ **Antonyms:** **1.** spend, waste **2.** lose, forfeit

earnest *adjective* sincere, determined, resolute, intent, serious, fervent, ardent I made an earnest apology. ◈ **Antonyms:** insincere, shallow, superficial

earth *noun* **1.** planet, world, globe, terrestrial sphere, orb, sphere Soviet astronaut Yuri Gagarin was the first person to orbit Earth. **2.** dirt, loam, soil, humus, ground, land, turf, topsoil, sod Most gardeners enjoy the smell of rich, moist earth. **3.** humanity, humankind, mankind, man, people, society, populace, citizens, human beings All of the earth celebrated the new millennium.

earthquake *noun* quake, tremor, temblor, shake, shock, jolt The largest recorded earthquake occurred in China in 1976.

ease *noun* **1.** comfort, contentment, leisure, relaxation, repose, rest, tranquility, idleness My cat lives a life of total ease. **2.** easiness, facility, effortlessness, readiness, aplomb, poise, composure, confidence She spoke with ease at the school assembly. ◆ *verb* **1.** lessen, lighten, relieve, soothe, allay, alleviate, diminish, mitigate, calm The nurse's friendly smile helped to ease my anxiety. **2.** maneuver, slide, slip, steer, squeeze, inch, insert, glide We eased the canoe into the water. **3.** loosen, slacken, relax, untighten, unbind, unlock, unchain I eased my belt after the big meal.

◈ **Antonyms:** *noun* **1.** toil **2.** awkwardness, clumsiness, difficulty ◆ *verb* **1.** aggravate, worsen **3.** tighten, bind

easy *adjective* **1.** plain, simple, uncomplicated, effortless, straightforward, uninvolved, basic, elementary I picked an easy pattern for my first sewing project. **2.** carefree, comfortable, cozy, pleasant, contented, peaceful, untroubled, serene My grandparents have been enjoying an easy life since they retired. **3.** casual, natural, easygoing, relaxed, informal, friendly, pleasant, gracious, open My friend has an easy manner. **4.** lenient, lax, tolerant, undemanding, merciful, gentle, moderate, indulgent Our coach was easy on us at the first two practices. ◆ *adverb* effortlessly, calmly, peacefully, serenely, casually, slowly, easily Now that I have my work done, I can rest easy. ◈ **Antonyms:** *adjective* **1.** difficult, hard **2.** uncomfortable, troubled **4.** harsh, strict

eat *verb* **1.** consume, devour, swallow, ingest, gulp, wolf, munch, feast, feed An adult elephant eats as much as 1,000 pounds of food every day. **2.** corrode, erode, wear, destroy, consume, dissolve, gnaw, rot The seawater has been slowly eating away the boat's old iron anchor. ◈ **Antonyms:** **1.** fast, starve

ebb *verb* **1.** flow back, recede, retreat, withdraw, retire, subside, go out, retract When the tide ebbed, I went looking for seashells. **2.** decline, decrease, diminish, lessen, reduce, flag, drop, slacken, abate The runner's strength began to ebb on the last lap. ◈ **Antonyms:** **1.** advance, rise **2.** grow, increase, flourish

eccentric *adjective* peculiar, odd, strange, weird, bizarre, unusual, queer, quirky My grandfather says he's entitled to be a little eccentric at his age. ◆ *noun* character, crackpot, crank, lunatic, misfit, nonconformist, freak, maverick The lady who raises goats in her front yard is considered an eccentric. ◈ **Antonyms:** *adjective* normal, ordinary, typical ◆ *noun* conformist

echo *noun* reflection, reverberation, resounding, answer, repetition, response, reply The quiet echo of voices could be heard throughout the museum. ◆ *verb* **1.** reverberate, rebound, reflect, ring, resound, resonate, vibrate The crowd's cheering echoed loudly in the gymnasium. **2.** imitate, copy, match, follow, parallel, mirror, duplicate, repeat, parrot The little girl echoed her mother's telephone conversation.

eclectic *adjective* diverse, broad, comprehensive, liberal, general, mixed, universal I have an eclectic taste in music.

eclipse *verb* 1. block, conceal, hide, obscure, shadow, darken, dim, erase When the moon passes between the sun and Earth, the sun is eclipsed. 2. exceed, outdo, surpass, excel, outshine, outstrip, transcend, top His drawing eclipsed the competition at the art contest.

economical *adjective* frugal, thrifty, prudent, saving, sparing, stingy, tight, cheap Shopping at sales is an economical habit. ✦ **Antonyms:** extravagant, wasteful

economy *noun* frugality, prudence, thrift, thriftiness, care, austerity, providence Our family practices economy so we can afford to travel overseas for our vacations. ✦ **Antonyms:** extravagance, wastefulness

ecstasy *noun* joy, exultation, delight, bliss, exhilaration, elation, rhapsody, euphoria We were filled with ecstasy when we won the lottery. ✦ **Antonyms:** gloom, misery, depression

ecstatic *adjective* thrilled, exultant, euphoric, rapturous, elated, delighted, overjoyed, glad, happy I was ecstatic when I got all A's on my report card. ✦ **Antonyms:** sad, depressed, miserable

edge *noun* 1. border, fringe, margin, rim, side, boundary, verge, limit, brink The lake has a sandy beach along its southern edge. 2. advantage, asset, benefit, head start, upper hand, vantage, lead, superiority Victoria's height gives her an edge when she plays basketball. ✦ *verb* 1. border, fringe, outline, trim, skirt, rim, hem, decorate Our neighbor edged her driveway with bricks. 2. sidle, ease, inch, slide, move, creep, slink, steal, sneak He edged away from the growling dog. ✦ **Antonyms:** *verb* 2. run, leap, rush

edit *verb* 1. correct, revise, rewrite, check, proofread, polish, condense, modify I have to edit the first draft of my book report. 2. compile, assemble, select, arrange, organize, supervise, order Our teacher edited an anthology of our class's short stories.

educate *verb* instruct, teach, edify, inform, tutor, enlighten, train, discipline, school A teacher's main job is to educate his or her students.

education *noun* instruction, learning, schooling, knowledge, training, scholarship, study Education can help you get an interesting job.

eerie *adjective* odd, strange, mysterious, ominous, weird, frightening, scary, unearthly, creepy We heard eerie noises coming from the old abandoned house. ✦ **Antonyms:** soothing, comforting

effect *noun* 1. consequence, end, outcome, result, conclusion, upshot, aftermath, development Tooth decay is one effect associated with eating too much sugar. 2. impact, impression, influence, meaning, significance, action, import, mark Improving my study habits had a good effect on my grades. ✦ *verb* accomplish, achieve, bring about, cause, make, create, initiate, produce, generate The development of electricity effected many changes in the way people live.

effective *adjective* 1. efficient, practical, productive, successful, capable, useful, valuable, worthwhile I try to make effective use of my study time. 2. operational, active, functioning, current, in effect, operative The new grading policy will be effective for the rest of the year. 3. strong, powerful, forceful, dynamic, impressive, successful, incisive, convincing He made an effective argument for raising the driving age to 18. ✦ **Antonyms:** 1. ineffective, inefficient 2. inactive, inoperative 3. weak, unconvincing

efficient *adjective* effective, practical, productive, competent, proficient, capable, able, apt When microchips were developed, computers became much more efficient. ✦ **Antonyms:** ineffective, inefficient

effort *noun* 1. exertion, labor, toil, work, strain, struggle, stress, energy, industry Painting the garage took more effort than we anticipated. 2. attempt, endeavor, try, trial, essay, venture, stab, crack My brother is making an effort to do better in school. 3. achievement, product, feat, production, accomplishment, attainment, deed, exploit My English teacher said that my latest essay is my best effort this year.

egocentric *adjective* self-centered, self-absorbed, self-involved, egomaniacal, egotistic, proud, arrogant The successful ballerina was egocentric. ✦ **Antonyms:** modest, humble

ejaculate *verb* exclaim, shout, cry, utter, proclaim, blurt, clamor, gush "Good heavens," she ejaculated, "you startled me!"

eject *verb* 1. discharge, disgorge, emit, spew, erupt, expel, throw out The geyser ejected a spray of hot water and steam. 2. oust, evict, expel, remove, force out, throw out, dismiss, banish The tenants were ejected for not paying their rent.

elaborate *adjective* complex, complicated, detailed, intricate, thorough, painstaking, careful, extravagant Edie's parents made elaborate preparations for her bat mitzvah. ◆ *verb* amplify, develop, expand, improve, enrich, enhance, add to, embellish My teacher asked me to elaborate on my brief answer. ➡ **Antonyms:** *adjective* plain, simple, basic ◆ *verb* condense, abbreviate

elastic *adjective* stretchable, flexible, pliable, yielding, resilient, supple, springy My gym shorts have an elastic waistband. ➡ **Antonyms:** hard, rigid

elated *adjective* overjoyed, jubilant, exhilarated, joyful, ecstatic, happy, glad, exultant I was elated to receive a mountain bike for my birthday. ➡ **Antonyms:** sad, depressed

elbow *verb* push, shove, shoulder, nudge, bump, jostle, hustle The man elbowed his way to the rail to watch the horserace.

elder *adjective* older, senior, prior, earlier, former, first-born, ancient My elder sister is in high school. ◆ *noun* senior, senior citizen, veteran, dignitary, ancient, ancestor, patriarch, matriarch I have found that my elders sometimes give good advice. ➡ **Antonym:** junior

elderly *adjective* aged, old, senior, advanced, mature, venerable, ancient Our elderly neighbor has been retired for 20 years. ➡ **Antonyms:** young, youthful

elect *verb* **1.** vote in, decide upon, determine, appoint, designate, name, nominate, ballot We elected our class officers today. **2.** choose, decide, pick, select, prefer I elected to go to the park rather than stay home.

electric *adjective* dynamic, exciting, thrilling, inspiring, stimulating, spirited, rousing It was an electric moment when our team won the state championship. ➡ **Antonyms:** boring, dull, ordinary

elegance *noun* refinement, sophistication, polish, luxury, grandeur, splendor, grace We stayed at a beautiful hotel that is famous for its elegance.

elegant *adjective* exquisite, fine, grand, majestic, graceful, rich, tasteful, refined Mom wore an elegant dress to the opera. ➡ **Antonyms:** coarse, crude, plain

element *noun* component, feature, ingredient, part, piece, factor, quality, property The basic elements of a successful movie include an interesting story and good acting.

elementary *adjective* basic, fundamental, beginning, introductory, primary, rudimentary, elemental We studied nouns and verbs as part of our class in elementary grammar. ➡ **Antonyms:** advanced, complex, higher

elevate *verb* **1.** lift, pick up, raise, hoist, boost, erect, upraise, uplift, heighten The nurse elevated the patient's leg. **2.** promote, advance, exalt, honor, enhance, strengthen, boost, further The professor was elevated to the position of department chair. ➡ **Antonyms:** 1. drop, lower 2. degrade, weaken

elevation *noun* **1.** height, altitude, lift, ascent, top, rise Mount Wilson in Colorado has an elevation of 14,246 feet. **2.** promotion, advancement, boost, raise, rise, improvement, magnification, glorification The loyal baron was rewarded with an elevation to viscount. ➡ **Antonyms:** 1. depth, valley 2. demotion

elfin *adjective* elfish, impish, playful, mischievous, prankish As a child actress, Shirley Temple enchanted audiences with her elfin smile.

eligible *adjective* qualified, authorized, fit, suitable, worthy, proper, acceptable, appropriate In the United States, citizens have to be 18 years old to be eligible to vote. ➡ **Antonyms:** ineligible, unqualified

eliminate *verb* drop, exclude, remove, purge, delete, erase, eradicate, banish It's a good idea to eliminate excess fat from your diet. ➡ **Antonyms:** include, obtain, add

elite *noun* best, choice, top, cream, flower, pick, aristocracy, gentry, nobility, elect The Oscar is an award made to the elite of the movie industry. ➡ **Antonyms:** worst, dregs

elongate *verb* lengthen, extend, stretch, distend, spread, draw out, enlarge The mirror in the fun house elongated my image. ➡ **Antonyms:** curtail, shorten, cut

elude *verb* avoid, dodge, duck, escape, evade, lose, flee, get around The quarterback eluded the other players and ran for a touchdown.

embarrass *verb* disconcert, fluster, humiliate, shame, abash, mortify, chagrin, upset, distress Mom has promised never to embarrass me by showing my baby pictures to my friends.

embarrassment *noun* **1.** chagrin, humiliation, shame, abashment, discomfort, mortification, uneasiness I felt great embarrassment when I spilled my glass of water in the restaurant. **2. trouble, vexation, bother, annoyance, distress, harassment, hindrance** My little sister can be an embarrassment to me when my friends are visiting. ◈ **Antonyms: 1. ease, composure**

emblem *noun* **badge, insignia, sign, symbol, token, crest, arms, mark, logo** Canada's official emblem is the maple leaf.

embrace *verb* **1. clasp, hug, hold, squeeze, snuggle, cuddle, grip** The couple embraced at the conclusion of their wedding ceremony. **2. accept, adopt, endorse, choose, welcome, receive, acknowledge, affirm, approve** By the fifth century A.D., most of the Roman world had embraced Christianity. **3. contain, cover, embody, have, include, comprise, comprehend, involve** The United Kingdom embraces four countries: England, Wales, Scotland, and Northern Ireland. ◆ *noun* **clasp, hug, squeeze, caress** Grandma gave us each a warm embrace. ◈ **Antonyms:** *verb* **2. spurn, reject, scorn 3. exclude, omit**

emerge *verb* **appear, come out, materialize, issue, show, arise, rise, loom** The sun emerged from behind a cloud. ◈ **Antonyms: disappear, hide**

emergency *noun* **crisis, extremity, accident, difficulty, predicament, trouble, danger** Where can I reach you in case of an emergency?

emigrate *verb* **move, migrate, relocate, remove, leave, go, immigrate** Her relatives emigrated from Japan.

eminent *adjective* **distinguished, famous, preeminent, prominent, top, renowned, notable, celebrated** Thomas Edison was an eminent scientist and inventor. ◈ **Antonyms: unknown, obscure**

emit *verb* **discharge, expel, give off, let off, issue, release, vent, radiate, shed** Plants take in carbon dioxide and emit oxygen.

emotion *noun* **feeling, sentiment, affection, passion, reaction, excitement** I am filled with emotion every time I watch the end of that movie.

Word Group

An **emperor** is a man who is the ruler of an empire. **Emperor** is a very specific term with no true synonyms. Here are some related words:

czar (also **tsar** or **tzar**), **kaiser, maharajah, mikado, pharaoh, rajah, sachem, shah, sultan**

emphasis *noun* **attention, stress, importance, significance, weight, accent, priority** Our gym teacher puts emphasis on developing our lung capacity.

emphasize *verb* **feature, highlight, stress, accent, accentuate, play up, underscore, underline** Our art teacher emphasizes creativity in his classroom.

employ *verb* **1. hire, engage, take on, enlist, retain, commission, contract** The new factory will employ 320 workers. **2. use, utilize, exercise, apply, manipulate, wield, ply, engage** Early computers employed bulky vacuum tubes instead of transistors and microchips. ◈ **Antonyms: 1. dismiss, fire, discharge**

employee *noun* **laborer, worker, assistant, helper, aide, hireling, staff member** My aunt's travel agency has five employees. ◈ **Antonyms: employer, boss**

employer *noun* **boss, hirer, owner, proprietor, manager, business, company, firm** Her employer gave her a promotion and a raise. ◈ **Antonyms: employee, worker**

Word Group

An **empress** is a woman who is the ruler of an empire. **Empress** is a very specific term with no true synonyms. Here are some related words:

czarina, Kaiserin, maharani, queen, rani, sultana

empty *adjective* **1. bare, unoccupied, vacant, blank, clear, void, barren** You can use this empty shelf for your shell collection. **2. idle, hollow, meaningless, ineffective, useless, insignificant, frivolous** My dog's growling is just an empty threat. ◆ *verb* **clean out, clear, drain, deplete, exhaust, evacuate, vacate** We had to empty the closet before we could paint it. ◈ **Antonyms:** *adjective* **1. full, stuffed 2. meaningful, significant** ◆ *verb* **fill, pack, stuff**

enchant *verb* **1. bewitch, charm, entrance, hypnotize, hex, spell, spellbind, mesmerize** In fairy stories, there is often a witch who enchants a prince or princess. **2. captivate, delight, entrance, fascinate, intrigue, beguile, enrapture, enthrall** The storyteller enchanted his audience with his tales of danger and romance. ◈ **Antonyms: 1. release, free 2. revolt, repel, repulse**

enclose *verb* **1. close in, envelop, hedge, hem, surround, circle, fence, shut in, bound** Our back porch is enclosed by screens. **2. add, include, insert, place, contain, hold, incorporate** Grandma and Grandpa enclosed a check with my birthday card.

encounter *noun* meeting, confrontation, face-off, brush, clash, run-in, skirmish Most of Lewis and Clark's encounters with Indians were peaceful. ◆ *verb* meet, face, confront, see, run into, chance upon, engage, experience Diane is the nicest person I've ever encountered.

encourage *verb* 1. inspire, motivate, persuade, urge, stimulate, induce, spur, impel My music teacher encouraged me to enter the state competition. 2. advance, foster, further, promote, help, favor, forward, assist Regular exercise encourages good health. ● **Antonyms:** 1. deter, discourage 2. hinder, retard, prevent

end *noun* 1. edge, extremity, limit, margin, border, boundary, terminus, tip, point This highway runs from one end of the continent to the other. 2. close, conclusion, ending, finale, finish, stop I read the entire book, from beginning to end, in one afternoon. 3. aim, goal, objective, purpose, intent, ambition, design, aspiration, object The movie's villain would stop at nothing to achieve his ends. ◆ *verb* close, complete, conclude, finish, halt, stop, cease, terminate, wind up, halt The game will end at 6 p.m., regardless of the score. ● **Antonyms:** *noun* 2. beginning, start ◆ *verb* begin, start, commence

endeavor *noun* attempt, effort, try, struggle, venture, undertaking, push He was successful in his endeavor to improve his grades. ◆ *verb* attempt, seek, strive, try, struggle, undertake, aspire, aim I believe that everyone should endeavor to be as good a person as possible.

endorse *verb* approve, back, champion, support, ratify, sustain, sanction, uphold The principal endorsed the teachers' request for a pay raise. ● **Antonyms:** disapprove, condemn

endure *verb* 1. continue, last, persist, remain, survive, abide, linger, prevail, live The Roman empire endured for hundreds of years. 2. bear, suffer, take, tolerate, withstand, undergo, sustain, support She endured the pain of having a tooth pulled without complaining. ● **Antonyms:** 1. perish, die, succumb 2. evade, avoid

enemy *noun* adversary, antagonist, foe, opponent, rival, competitor, nemesis The North and the South were enemies during the American Civil War. ● **Antonyms:** ally, friend, supporter

energetic *adjective* active, dynamic, lively, sprightly, spirited, vigorous, forceful, tireless She is an energetic soccer player. ● **Antonyms:** lazy, listless, languid

energy *noun* vigor, vitality, power, strength, verve, zip, vim, pep, drive, vivacity He is so full of energy that he has a hard time sitting still. ● **Antonyms:** inertia, listlessness

enforce *verb* administer, apply, impose, execute, invoke, accomplish, perform, support A team of lifeguards enforces the safety rules at our school's swimming pool. ● **Antonyms:** ignore, disregard

engage *verb* 1. employ, enlist, hire, take on, retain, reserve, commission, appoint, secure The couple engaged an architect to help remodel their home. 2. betroth, espouse, pledge, promise, agree, commit, contract, bind My brother and his girlfriend recently became engaged. 3. absorb, fascinate, interest, involve, occupy, engross, preoccupy, immerse, enthrall Grandpa and I were totally engaged by my new computer game and lost all track of time. 4. face, take on, assault, strike, meet, combat, assail, encounter The mother bear didn't hesitate to engage the mountain lion that threatened her cubs. ● **Antonyms:** 1. dismiss, fire, lay off

engagement *noun* 1. appointment, commitment, date, booking, obligation, promise, tryst My parents made a dinner engagement for Saturday night. 2. betrothal, troth, espousal, pledge, promise, vow, bond My cousin announced her engagement at a family dinner. 3. employment, job, position, situation, post, place, office, career My band recently got its first engagement. 4. battle, fight, skirmish, encounter, conflict, action, contest, struggle, fray Julius Caesar crossed the Rubicon in 49 B.C. and began the first engagement of the Roman civil war.

engrave *verb* carve, cut, etch, inscribe, chisel, print, imprint, scratch The jeweler engraved my name on my new silver bracelet.

enhance *verb* heighten, increase, intensify, strengthen, improve, better, reinforce Bodybuilders shave their bodies to enhance the appearance of their muscles. ● **Antonyms:** diminish, reduce, weaken

enjoy *verb* 1. delight in, like, love, relish, appreciate, admire, savor, revel I enjoy playing my guitar. 2. command, have, hold, own, possess, boast, retain, maintain, experience Despite our cat's age, he still enjoys good health. ● **Antonyms:** 1. dislike, hate, loathe

enjoyment *noun* 1. amusement, joy, pleasure, gratification, fun, entertainment, happiness, satisfaction I get more enjoyment from going to a live concert than from watching a band on TV. 2. privilege, benefit, right, use, advantage, blessing, ownership We had the enjoyment of my uncle's mountain cabin for the summer. ● **Antonyms: 1. displeasure, dissatisfaction 2. handicap, disadvantage**

enlarge *verb* **build up, expand, extend, increase, amplify, swell, magnify, develop** The city is planning to enlarge the airport by building two new runways. ● **Antonyms: reduce, shrink, decrease**

enlighten *verb* **educate, inform, instruct, teach, illuminate, apprise, school, acquaint** The movie enlightened us about peoples of the rain forest. ● **Antonyms: mystify, puzzle, confuse**

enlist *verb* **1. enroll, enter, join, sign up, volunteer, join up, register** My older sister enlisted in the United States Air Force. **2. engage, obtain, procure, recruit, secure, conscript, muster** I enlisted my friend's help in picking out a present for Mom. ● **Antonyms: 1. withdraw, resign 2. decline, refuse**

enormous *adjective* **gigantic, huge, immense, tremendous, vast, large, monstrous, gargantuan, colossal** Tyrannosaurus was an enormous dinosaur. ● **Antonyms: little, tiny, petite**

enough *adjective* **adequate, sufficient, ample, satisfactory, plenty, abundant, acceptable** I haven't yet saved enough money to buy a new softball glove. ◆ *adverb* **adequately, sufficiently, satisfactorily, acceptably, tolerably, reasonably** I can't wait until I am old enough to get a driver's license. ● **Antonyms:** *adjective* **inadequate, insufficient, scant**

enrage *verb* **anger, incense, infuriate, madden, provoke, aggravate, incite** The man was enraged when he found that his car had been stolen. ● **Antonyms: placate, soothe, pacify**

enrich *verb* **better, develop, enhance, improve, refine, elevate, supplement** A good education will enrich your mind. ● **Antonyms: degrade, weaken**

enroll *verb* **enlist, enter, join, register, sign up, matriculate, engage, admit, join up** I'm going to enroll in a tap-dancing class. ● **Antonyms: drop out, withdraw**

ensure *verb* **assure, confirm, establish, guarantee, insure, certify, warrant** Please ensure that your seat belt is properly fastened.

enter *verb* **1. come in, go in, approach, arrive, invade, penetrate** In Japan, it is customary to take off your shoes before entering someone's house. **2. enroll, join, register,**

begin, start, participate in, sign up, enlist I will be entering high school next year. **3. begin, embark, commence, start, launch, set out, take up, inaugurate** I am entering my teenage years. **4. insert, record, post, file, list, admit, note, register, inscribe** The teacher entered our test scores in her grade book. ● **Antonyms: 1. exit, leave 2. withdraw, leave 3. end, cease 4. erase, remove**

enterprise *noun* **1. endeavor, project, task, undertaking, venture, operation, adventure, stunt** Amundsen's 1911 journey to the South Pole by dogsled was a daring enterprise. **2. initiative, drive, gumption, ambition, determination, push, energy, vigor** The successful businesswoman has a lot of enterprise.

entertain *verb* **1. amuse, delight, divert, regale, interest, occupy, gratify, humor** With our TV broken, we had to find other ways to entertain ourselves. **2. host, house, treat, receive, welcome, lodge, board, chaperon** My family likes to entertain friends at dinner. **3. consider, think over, contemplate, ponder, study, deliberate, reflect, weigh** I am entertaining the idea of redecorating my bedroom. ● **Antonyms: 1. bore 3. reject, disregard**

entertainment *noun* **amusement, diversion, enjoyment, fun, pleasure, sport, pastime, recreation** My friend and I play video games for entertainment.

enthusiasm *noun* **eagerness, excitement, fire, passion, zeal, ardor, exuberance, fervor** The class showed great enthusiasm for a field trip to the aquarium. ● **Antonyms: apathy, indifference, detachment**

enthusiastic *adjective* **ardent, avid, fervent, eager, passionate, earnest, warm, exuberant** My dog always gives me an enthusiastic welcome when I get home. ● **Antonym: indifferent**

entire *adjective* **complete, full, total, whole, intact, perfect, unbroken, absolute** I'm so hungry that I could eat an entire pizza. ● **Antonyms: incomplete, partial**

entitle *verb* **1. call, designate, label, name, title, dub, term, christen** I read an article entitled "101 Ways to Give Your Dog a Bath Without Getting Yourself Wet." **2. allow, authorize, permit, qualify, empower, enable, license, warrant** In the United States, all children are entitled to an education. ● **Antonym: 2. disqualify**

entrance *noun* **1. appearance, entry, admission, approach, arrival, introduction, ingress** Everyone applauded when the conductor made his entrance. **2. access, entry,**

entryway, door, doorway, approach, gateway, portal There was a long line at the entrance to the stadium. ➻ **Antonyms:** 1. exit, departure 2. exit

entry *noun* 1. appearance, entrance, approach, arrival, admission, ingress Loud applause greeted the comedian when he made his entry. 2. entrance, entryway, door, doorway, opening, access, gate, threshold, lobby The treasure room had a secret entry. 3. posting, note, insertion, record, statement, memorandum, account, item I make sure to write an entry in my diary every night. 4. contestant, competitor, entrant, player, candidate Mom is an entry in the marathon. ➻ **Antonyms:** 1. exit, departure 2. exit

envelop *verb* cover, surround, wrap, enclose, blanket, cloak, shroud, clothe The silky cocoon completely enveloped the caterpillar. ➻ **Antonyms:** unwrap, expose

Word Group

An **envelope** is a flat, folded paper container, especially one used for mailing a letter. **Envelope** is a very specific term with no true synonyms. Here are some related words:

bag, casing, container, cover, jacket, mailer, pouch, receptacle, sheath, wrapper

envious *adjective* covetous, jealous, desirous, invidious, resentful, greedy, grudging I am envious of my friend's leather backpack.

environment *noun* atmosphere, conditions, setting, surroundings, locality, background, locale, scene Our school library provides a quiet environment for studying.

envy *noun* covetousness, jealousy, resentment, desire, spite, greed, malice I was filled with envy when my friend got a new puppy. ◆ *verb* begrudge, grudge, covet, desire, want, crave, hunger, long, yearn Everyone on the basketball team envies Walt's height.

episode *noun* 1. milestone, event, occurrence, happening, occasion, period, incident, affair, experience The summer I spent on my grandparents' farm was an important episode in my life. 2. installment, chapter, scene, passage, segment, part, section Next week's episode will reveal who committed the crime.

equal *adjective* even, identical, like, same, similar, alike, uniform, comparable, equivalent I dealt an equal number of cards to each player. ◆ *noun* equivalent, match, peer,

parallel, mate, twin, counterpart, fellow The undefeated boxer has yet to meet his equal in the ring. ◆ *verb* amount to, correspond to, match, constitute, compare, equate, balance Four quarters equal one dollar. ➻ **Antonyms:** *adjective* different, unequal

equip *verb* furnish, outfit, fit out, provide, supply, stock, array, provision The mountaineers equipped themselves with ropes and safety harnesses.

equipment *noun* apparatus, gear, supplies, material, paraphernalia, devices, things The local department store is having a sale on sports equipment.

equivalent *adjective* equal, even, identical, same, similar, alike, comparable, uniform, corresponding My brother and I are usually assigned equivalent amounts of housework. ◆ *noun* counterpart, equal, match, same, double, parallel, substitute, twin One cup is the equivalent of eight ounces. ➻ **Antonyms:** *adjective* different, unequal

era *noun* age, day, epoch, period, time, generation, cycle, date, term, stage The Victorian era is named after Queen Victoria.

erase *verb* remove, rub out, wipe out, cancel, clear, delete, expunge, eradicate, obliterate The teacher asked me to erase everything that was written on the blackboard.

erect *adjective* straight, upright, vertical, rigid, firm Erect posture is good for your back. ◆ *verb* build, construct, make, raise, put up, pitch, establish, assemble The farmer and his neighbors erected a new barn. ➻ **Antonyms:** *adjective* bent, horizontal ◆ *verb* demolish, destroy

erode *verb* wear, corrode, eat, gnaw, consume, wear, abrade, grind, crumble The water eroded the rocks into interesting shapes.

errand *noun* assignment, commission, mission, job, task, duty, undertaking My mother asked me to run an errand for her.

erratic *adjective* changeable, irregular, unpredictable, variable, volatile, unstable, strange, uncertain Spring weather is often erratic. ➻ **Antonyms:** normal, predictable, steady

error *noun* mistake, inaccuracy, blunder, fault, flaw, slip, oversight, miss I made only one error on my spelling test.

erupt *verb* break, burst, explode, blow up, gush, spout, spew, vent The audience erupted into laughter.

escape *verb* **1. break out, get away, run away, flee, run, fly, skip, bolt** The parakeet escaped from its cage. **2. avoid, dodge, elude, evade, skirt, shun, eschew, bypass, circumvent** I tried to escape having to do the dishes. **3. leak, seep, ooze, flow, stream, gush, emerge, emanate** Water escaped from an underground spring. ♦ *noun* **breakout, getaway, flight, departure, break, exodus, exit, retreat** The prisoners made their escape on a dark and stormy night. ➤ **Antonyms:** *verb* **1. capture, apprehend 2. meet, face 3. hold, contain**

escort *noun* **guard, cortege, retinue, entourage, attendant, companion, chaperon** The President's escort included more than a dozen bodyguards. ♦ *verb* **accompany, conduct, guide, lead, usher, chaperon, take, steer** The usher escorted us to our seats.

especially *adverb* **chiefly, mainly, particularly, primarily, very, expressly, principally** I like all desserts, but I am especially fond of carrot cake.

essay *noun* **composition, article, paper, theme, treatise, dissertation, exposition, thesis** Mickey is writing an essay about his favorite book.

essence *noun* **1. basis, core, heart, substance, quintessence, gist, kernel, crux, soul** The essence of Judaism is belief in a single God. **2. extract, distillation, concentrate, tincture, elixir, attar, juice** Turpentine is an essence of pine tar.

essential *adjective* **1. critical, important, necessary, vital, indispensable, requisite, crucial** Fire is essential to the germination of some seeds. **2. basic, fundamental, elemental, main, key, principal, cardinal, intrinsic** The essential ingredients of most cakes are milk, flour, eggs, and sugar. ♦ *noun* **necessity, basic, fundamental, rudiment, must, requirement, requisite** We are learning the essentials of English grammar. ➤ **Antonyms:** *adjective* **unimportant, unnecessary** ♦ *noun* **extra, option**

establish *verb* **1. install, situate, settle, fix, secure, seat, moor, lodge** I established a trellis and two climbing roses outside my bedroom window. **2. create, found, institute, start, set up, begin, inaugurate, open, build** Dad would like to establish his own business. **3. prove, confirm, verify, demonstrate, show, authenticate, corroborate, substantiate** Medical research has established that smoking can cause cancer.

establishment *noun* **1. creation, development, formation, start, founding, institution, inauguration** Our city is raising funds for the establishment of a community college. **2. business, company, enterprise, organization, foundation, firm, corporation, factory, outfit** He works for an establishment that sells and repairs vacuum cleaners.

esteem *verb* **1. admire, honor, respect, value, treasure, prize, praise, revere** Max Planck is esteemed for his theory of quantum physics. **2. judge, consider, believe, deem, view, reckon, hold, regard, think** She is esteemed a true expert in her field. ♦ *noun* **admiration, honor, regard, favor, respect, approval, deference, account** He is held in high esteem because he's honest and dependable. ➤ **Antonyms:** *verb* **1. scorn, disdain** ♦ *noun* **disrespect, contempt, ridicule**

estimate *verb* **calculate, evaluate, guess, judge, gauge, approximate, reckon, figure** I estimate that 1,500 people attended the demonstration. ♦ *noun* **appraisal, assessment, approximation, calculation, evaluation, guess, estimation** The mechanic gave Mom an estimate for the repairs.

eternal *adjective* **1. endless, everlasting, infinite, immortal, perpetual, permanent, enduring** I think that poem is about the eternal rhythm of the seasons. **2. incessant, continual, unending, constant, relentless, persistent, ceaseless** I can't take much more of his eternal complaining. ➤ **Antonyms: 1. brief, temporary, fleeting 2. rare, occasional**

etiquette *noun* **good manners, manners, propriety, decorum, courtesy, civility, politeness** I checked out a book on etiquette for teenagers. ➤ **Antonyms: rudeness, boorishness**

evacuate *verb* **abandon, depart, leave, vacate, desert, forsake, decamp, quit** Customers evacuated the store when the lights went out during the power failure. ➤ **Antonyms: enter, return**

evade *verb* **avoid, dodge, elude, escape, lose, duck, ditch, shun, circumvent** I evaded my little brother by going into my room. ➤ **Antonyms: face, meet, encounter**

evaluate *verb* **appraise, assess, judge, rate, value, weigh, reckon, gauge, estimate** I evaluated my wardrobe to see what new clothes I needed for school.

evaporate *verb* **disappear, dissipate, fade, vanish, vaporize, dissolve, dispel, pass** My boredom evaporated when my friend came over to visit. ➤ **Antonyms: appear, emerge**

even *adjective* **1. flat, horizontal, level, smooth, straight, flush, plumb, true** The putting green was very even. **2. constant, regular, steady, unchanging, uniform, unvarying,**

stable When you relax, your heart beats at an even rate. **3. equal, identical, same, similar, equivalent, balanced, matching** I put an even number of flowers in each vase. ◆ *adverb* **still, actually, indeed, just, exactly, precisely** I was encouraged to try even harder when my teacher told me how much I had improved. ◆ *verb* **tie, balance, equal, level, match, square, equalize, smooth** My home run evened the score. ● **Antonyms:** *adjective* **1. uneven, rough 2. irregular, variable 3. different**

evening *noun* **night, dusk, sundown, sunset, twilight, eventide, eve, nightfall** We waited until evening to take a walk so it would be cooler out. ● **Antonyms: dawn, morning, daylight**

event *noun* **1. circumstance, happening, incident, occasion, occurrence, episode, milestone** My confirmation was an important event in my life. **2. competition, contest, match, game, tournament, bout** I won three events at last week's swim meet.

ever *adverb* **always, forever, continuously, eternally, perpetually, constantly, unceasingly** Sleeping Beauty and the prince lived happily ever after. ● **Antonym: never**

everlasting *adjective* **ceaseless, endless, enduring, eternal, perpetual, unending, permanent, infinite** There seems to be an everlasting supply of candy every Halloween. ● **Antonyms: temporary, passing**

every *adjective* **each, all, any, each one, every one** Every student received a textbook. ● **Antonym: none**

everyday *adjective* **regular, usual, customary, habitual, familiar, daily, ordinary, routine** Eating dinner out is not an everyday occurrence for our family. ● **Antonyms: infrequent, rare, occasional**

evidence *noun* **proof, facts, documentation, indication, information, grounds, confirmation** There wasn't enough evidence to convict the defendant so she was released.

evident *adjective* **apparent, certain, clear, obvious, plain, visible, patent, manifest, distinct** It is evident that my cell phone battery needs to be recharged. ● **Antonyms: doubtful, uncertain, unclear**

evil *adjective* **bad, immoral, wicked, hateful, villainous, vile, foul, nefarious** I read a story about an evil wizard. ◆ *noun* **sin, wickedness, crime, harm, vice, misery, woe, misfortune, sorrow** It is said that the love of money is the root of all evil. ● **Antonyms:** *adjective* **good, moral, honorable** ◆ *noun* **goodness, virtue**

evolve *verb* **derive, develop, emerge, unfold, grow, result** Darwin's theory posits that present-day plants and animals evolved from earlier forms.

exact *adjective* **1. precise, accurate, correct, right, true, definite, specific** Are you sure those were her exact words? **2. careful, painstaking, strict, methodical, systematic, meticulous, rigorous** It is important to be exact when performing a scientific experiment. ◆ *verb* **demand, require, claim, extract, compel, wrench, wrest, wring** The coach exacts our attention at each practice. ● **Antonyms:** *adjective* **1. approximate, inexact 2. sloppy, careless**

exactly *adverb* **absolutely, completely, just, precisely, specifically, truly, totally** I know exactly what I want to wear on the first day of school. ● **Antonyms: approximately, nearly**

exaggerate *verb* **overstate, expand, inflate, magnify, stretch, embroider, embellish** He exaggerated when he said that he had a million comic books. ● **Antonyms: minimize, understate**

examination *noun* **1. check, checkup, inspection, review, survey, perusal, probe, analysis, study** My doctor gave me a thorough examination. **2. exam, test, quiz, midterm, final, catechism** Our teacher said that our examination would consist of true-false questions.

examine *verb* **1. check, inspect, investigate, study, analyze, probe, scan, test** The jeweler examined the diamond. **2. interrogate, query, question, quiz, ask, inquire, grill, pump** The police examined the suspect to see if she had an alibi.

example *noun* **1. sample, specimen, case, instance, illustration, representation** This bracelet is a fine example of Navajo jewelry. **2. model, ideal, standard, paragon, paradigm, pattern, prototype** You will get the problem right if you follow this example. **3. warning, lesson, caution, precedent, notification** Let that be an example to you!

exasperate *verb* **aggravate, annoy, bother, irritate, infuriate, irk, anger, provoke** Sometimes my little brother exasperates me.

excavate *verb* **dig up, uncover, unearth, mine, tunnel, quarry, scoop, shovel** Archaeologists excavated King Tutankhamen's tomb in 1922.

exceed *verb* **beat, better, outdo, pass, surpass, top, excel, transcend, best** My performance at the track meet exceeded my expectations.

excel *verb* dominate, prevail, exceed, outdo, surpass, outshine, top, transcend, best A triathlon requires an athlete to excel in three sports—running, swimming, and bicycling.

excellence *noun* superiority, fineness, distinction, merit, quality, eminence, greatness, perfection I received an award for scholastic excellence. ◈ **Antonyms:** inferiority, inadequacy, deficiency

excellent *adjective* fine, great, outstanding, first-rate, splendid, superb, superior, terrific, remarkable This is an excellent day for a picnic. ◈ **Antonyms:** inferior, poor, mediocre

except *preposition* excluding, other than, barring, excepting, besides, but, save I have been in all 50 states except Alaska and Maine. ◆ *verb* exempt, excuse, exclude, eliminate, omit, bar, keep out, reject Members of the track team are excepted from the requirement to take a gym class. ◈ **Antonyms:** *preposition* including ◆ *verb* include, count

exceptional *adjective* 1. unique, peculiar, uncommon, rare, unusual, odd, strange, unnatural The exceptional ram had four horns. 2. outstanding, superior, extraordinary, magnificent, wonderful, terrific, great, noteworthy Five students were honored for exceptional academic ability. ◈ **Antonyms:** 1. ordinary, usual, common 2. mediocre, average

excess *noun* surplus, overflow, overload, oversupply, fullness, profusion, glut, plethora We gave our neighbors the excess from our vegetable garden. ◆ *adjective* excessive, extra, spare, surplus, residual, superfluous Dad trimmed the excess fat off the steaks before he cooked them. ◈ **Antonyms:** *noun* shortage, lack, scarcity

excessive *adjective* exorbitant, inordinate, undue, unreasonable, extravagant, immoderate, overabundant I think I have an excessive amount of homework. ◈ **Antonyms:** insufficient, scant, skimpy

exchange *verb* trade, swap, switch, change, substitute, alternate, replace My friend and I exchanged telephone numbers. ◆ *noun* interchange, switch, trade, substitution, barter, swap, shift, transposition Our economy is based on the exchange of money for goods.

excite *verb* 1. arouse, rouse, stimulate, stir, animate, inflame, energize The home run excited the team's fans. 2. elicit, pique, evoke, waken, awaken, stimulate, whet, spur The magazine article excited my interest in space flight. ◈ **Antonyms:** 1. calm 2. appease, allay, deaden

exciting *adjective* inspiring, rousing, sensational, stimulating, thrilling, dramatic, breathtaking It was an exciting moment when Neil Armstrong first set foot on the moon. ◈ **Antonyms:** boring, dull, unexciting

exclaim *verb* shout, yell, call, cry, ejaculate, bellow, blurt out, howl "Stop!" I exclaimed, as my little brother started to run into the street.

exclude *verb* 1. prohibit, forbid, ban, bar, keep out, disallow, refuse, shut out People with serious medical conditions are excluded from riding on roller coasters. 2. reject, rule out, leave out, count out, eliminate, omit, pass over, except The doctor excluded the possibility of cancer in his diagnosis. ◈ **Antonyms:** 1. invite, welcome 2. consider, include

excursion *noun* jaunt, journey, outing, tour, trip, junket, drive, voyage We took an excursion to Coney Island during the summer.

excuse *verb* 1. disregard, forgive, overlook, pardon, tolerate, condone, ignore Please excuse my messy room. 2. release, relieve, dismiss, discharge, free, exempt, absolve, let off I was excused from school because I had a doctor's appointment. ◆ *noun* explanation, rationalization, reason, argument, alibi, defense, apology The teacher accepted my excuse for being tardy. ◈ **Antonyms:** *verb* 1. censure, criticize

execute *verb* 1. carry out, dispense, administer, administrate, discharge, enforce, fulfill, implement The mayor's policies were executed by his staff. 2. perform, accomplish, do, act, complete, create, render, pull off, achieve I am learning how to execute a single axle in my ice skating class. 3. put to death, kill, murder, slay, dispatch, assassinate, lynch The traitor was executed by a firing squad.

executive *noun* officer, official, leader, administrator, director, manager, superintendent The company's executives meet once a week. ◆ *adjective* directorial, managerial, supervisory, administrative, official, managing My dad has an executive position at the local branch of the telephone company.

exempt *verb* excuse, free, release, relieve, dismiss, clear, let off, dispense, discharge The government exempts most charities from the requirement to pay taxes. ◆ *adjective* free, excused, spared, clear, released, relieved, immune, pardoned Food is exempt from a sales tax in most states. ◈ **Antonyms:** *verb* oblige ◆ *adjective* responsible, accountable

exercise *noun* **1. application, employment, operation, implementation, execution, usage, utilization** The best way to stay on a diet is through the exercise of self-control. **2. workout, training, conditioning, drill, regimen, exertion, activity** Yoga is an excellent form of exercise. **3. problem, task, lesson, study, homework, assignment, training, practice** We were assigned the even-numbered exercises in chapter 10. ◆ *verb* **1. use, apply, employ, utilize, wield, exploit, implement, practice** My parents told me to exercise my own judgment in choosing my school electives **2. work out, train, condition, practice, drill, discipline, develop, prepare** My grandparents exercise by walking two miles every day.

exert *verb* **apply, exercise, use, utilize, put out, expend, employ, discharge** Dad had to exert a lot of willpower in order to stop smoking.

exhaust *verb* **1. fatigue, wear out, weary, debilitate, tire, weaken, enervate, drain** The long workout exhausted me. **2. expend, spend, consume, finish, use up, deplete, dissipate, drain** The campers nearly exhausted their water supply before they found another source.

exhaustion *noun* **fatigue, tiredness, weariness, weakness, debility, enervation, prostration** We were in a state of exhaustion by the end of the game.

exhibit *verb* **display, present, show, demonstrate, reveal, expose, parade** He exhibited his Alpine goats at the county fair. ◆ *noun* **display, exhibition, presentation, show, exposition, demonstration, fair, performance** Her watercolors were put on exhibit in the school lobby. **Antonyms:** *verb* **hide, conceal**

exhilarate *verb* **energize, invigorate, stimulate, animate, elate, uplift, excite, cheer, enliven** The cold winter air exhilarated the skiers. **Antonyms: depress, deject, discourage**

exile *noun* **1. banishment, expulsion, deportation, expatriation, ostracism** The fallen dictator was forced into exile. **2. émigré, refugee, expatriate, deportee, outcast, pariah, fugitive** The Puritans were exiles in Holland before sailing to the New World. ◆ *verb* **banish, deport, expel, expatriate, oust, remove, eject, cast out** In the past, England exiled criminals to Australia. **Antonyms:** *verb* **welcome, accept**

exist *verb* **1. live, survive, continue, endure, persist, last, subsist, stay** A fish cannot exist out of water. **2. happen, occur, persist, take place, arise, reside, dwell, prevail** Social problems exist in every part of the world. **Antonyms: 1. die, perish**

existence *noun* **1. life, survival, subsistence, being, living, animation, continuance** A koala bear's existence is dependent on a few species of eucalyptus trees. **2. actuality, fact, occurrence, presence, reality, substance, materiality** Some people believe in the existence of ghosts.

exit *noun* **1. door, doorway, opening, outlet, egress, vent, gate** School buses have emergency exits in the back. **2. departure, escape, retreat, withdrawal, exodus, evacuation, egress** When a skunk came in the front door, we all made a hasty exit out the back door. ◆ *verb* **depart, go out, leave, retreat, withdraw, move out, retire, escape** A flight attendant told the passengers to exit from the rear of the plane. **Antonyms:** *noun* **entrance** ◆ *verb* **enter**

expand *verb* **1. swell, distend, enlarge, grow, increase, extend, dilate, puff up** A balloon expands when you blow air into it. **2. develop, elaborate, amplify, elucidate, embellish, draw out, augment** The speaker expanded on his topic to answer a question from the audience. **3. unfold, open, unfurl, fan out, wax, spread, stretch, unroll** We watched as the bud of the evening primrose expanded into a flower. **Antonyms: 1. contract, shrink 3. fold, furl, close**

expect *verb* **1. anticipate, count on, depend on, look for, foresee, envisage, await** The weather forecaster said that we could expect rain. **2. require, demand, insist, want, wish, hope for, call for, intend** Our teacher expects us to be on time. **3. presume, suppose, assume, imagine, guess, reckon, trust, think** I expect that we will go to my grandparents' for Thanksgiving.

expedition *noun* **1. journey, trip, excursion, trek, tour, voyage, safari, mission, junket** I would like to go on an expedition to photograph wild animals. **2. company, group, party, team, troop, squadron, crew, explorers** Roald Amundsen led the first expedition to reach the South Pole. **3. promptness, dispatch, alacrity, quickness, haste, rapidity, speed, swiftness** This project is important and must be completed with expedition. **Antonyms: 3. slowness, tardiness**

expel *verb* **eject, evict, throw out, remove, banish, discharge, dismiss, ostracize, exile** The noisy patrons were expelled from the restaurant. **Antonyms: admit, accept, invite**

expense *noun* **1. sacrifice, loss, toll, cost, price, risk, harm, detriment** The company's profit was earned at its competitors' expense. **2. expenditure, disbursement, outlay, cost, price, charge, payment** I am learning how to keep track of my personal expenses. **Antonyms: 1. gain, reward 2. income, profit**

expensive *adjective* costly, high-priced, overpriced, exorbitant, steep, extravagant, dear I like this dress, but it is too expensive. ✦ **Antonyms:** cheap, inexpensive, economical

experience *noun* 1. background, training, knowledge, practice, know-how, wisdom, education My father has a lot of experience as a carpenter. 2. adventure, event, incident, happening, episode, occurrence, affair, ordeal Rafting down the river was an exciting experience. ✦ *verb* encounter, have, meet with, see, undergo, go through, sustain, bear, suffer Did you experience any difficulty in finding your way here?

experiment *noun* test, trial, experimentation, demonstration, investigation, check Our class did an experiment that showed how electricity is generated. ✦ *verb* test, try, analyze, investigate, assess, examine, research, probe I like to experiment with different recipes.

experimental *adjective* test, trial, developmental, new, provisional, unproved, rough A test pilot is someone who flies experimental aircraft.

expert *noun* authority, specialist, master, professional, critic, connoisseur, ace, adept That archaeologist is an expert on prehistoric stone tools. ✦ *adjective* adept, proficient, skilled, able, master, skillful, adroit, professional I would like to be an expert scuba diver. ✦ **Antonyms:** *noun* amateur, novice ✦ *adjective* unskilled, inept

expire *verb* 1. lapse, end, finish, stop, terminate, cease, run out, conclude My magazine subscription will expire in two months. 2. die, pass away, decease, perish, succumb, depart, demise The invalid expired after a long illness. 3. exhale, breathe out, blow, puff, pant It was so cold that we could see our breath each time we expired. ✦ **Antonyms:** 1. begin, start 2. live 3. inhale

explain *verb* 1. describe, clarify, define, interpret, explicate, demonstrate, illuminate Our teacher explained the difference between a frog and a toad. 2. account for, justify, excuse, rationalize, vindicate, support, defend Please explain why you are so late.

explode *verb* 1. burst, blast, discharge, erupt, fulminate, detonate, go off, blow up The firecracker exploded with a loud bang. 2. invalidate, refute, disprove, debunk, discredit, repudiate, puncture, burst Galileo exploded the idea that Earth is the center of the solar system.

exploit *noun* achievement, adventure, deed, feat, stunt, accomplishment, escapade, act Davy Crockett's exploits have been written about in many books. ✦ *verb* 1. utilize, employ, apply, exercise, implement, use, work, milk He exploited every opportunity to make money. 2. control, manipulate, maneuver, abuse, misuse, finesse, deceive The politician had exploited the media to get press coverage.

explore *verb* 1. look into, examine, investigate, probe, research, scrutinize, delve My Boy Scout troop is exploring ways to raise some money. 2. scout, reconnoiter, search, survey, travel, traverse, penetrate, tour Sir Henry Stanley explored much of central Africa in the late 1800s.

explosion *noun* 1. blast, burst, detonation, discharge, fulmination, report, bang, boom The explosion could be heard for miles. 2. outburst, spurt, eruption, outbreak, increase, intensification, acceleration There has been an explosion of interest in the Internet in recent years.

expose *verb* 1. subject, lay open, submit, jeopardize, endanger, imperil, hazard The cyclists were exposed to bad weather. 2. reveal, bare, uncover, unveil, show, display, exhibit, unmask The archaeologists removed a layer of dirt to expose the ancient burial chamber. 3. disclose, divulge, reveal, tell, air, let out, give away, broadcast A newspaper article exposed the drug-smuggling operation. ✦ **Antonyms:** conceal, hide, veil

express *verb* 1. declare, state, voice, utter, tell, assert, verbalize, vocalize, speak Everybody expressed a preference for tacos. 2. reveal, show, communicate, divulge, disclose, exhibit, manifest Her smile expressed her happiness. ✦ *adjective* 1. definite, distinct, particular, set, specific, precise, explicit This room was built for the express purpose of storing historical documents. 2. nonstop, high-speed, fast, quick, rapid, speedy, swift, direct We took the express train. ✦ **Antonyms:** *adjective* 1. unclear, vague 2. slow, sluggish

expression *noun* 1. communication, language, articulation, utterance, verbalization, wording He is good at written expression. 2. countenance, visage, mien, appearance, look, air, aspect I knew by her expression that she was in a good mood. 3. eloquence, fluency, facility, emotion, style, delivery, execution James Earl Jones, the actor, is noted for wonderful expression in his speaking voice. 4. saying, phrase, remark, statement, declaration, maxim, adage, axiom Maya's favorite expression is: "Bloom where you are planted."

exquisite *adjective* 1. beautiful, delicate, elegant, fine, lovely, dainty, charming, precious Her silver and amber necklace is exquisite. 2. perceptive, astute, discriminating, consummate, perfect, flawless, incomparable, meticulous My uncle's taste in antique furniture is exquisite. **3. intense, keen, acute, extreme, poignant, delightful, thrilling** It was an exquisite pleasure to see our old friends after so many years.

extend *verb* **1. expand, lengthen, open, stretch out, increase, elongate, enlarge** This ladder can be extended to a length of 12 feet. **2. go, reach, run, stretch, carry, spread, unfold, unroll** The ocean extends farther than the eye can see. **3. offer, present, give, proffer, submit, volunteer, tender, grant** I extended them an invitation to my party. **4. prolong, lengthen, draw out, protract, continue, delay, postpone** We had so much fun that we extended our visit. ➡ **Antonyms: 1. contract, shorten**

extensive *adjective* **widespread, extended, broad, great, huge, vast, considerable, enormous** Did the earthquake cause extensive damage? ➡ **Antonyms: limited, restricted**

exterior *adjective* **external, outer, outside, outdoor, outward, out, outlying** Many castles have exterior walls that are separate from the central stronghold. ◆ *noun* **1. outside, surface, façade, cover, coating, face, shell** The exterior of our house is made of brick. **2. demeanor, deportment, manner, bearing, appearance, air, attitude, disposition, mien** The teacher's calm exterior was helpful in quieting the noisy children. ➡ **Antonyms:** *adjective* **interior, inner, internal** ◆ *noun* **1. interior**

exterminate *verb* **eliminate, destroy, kill, eradicate, annihilate, extinguish, remove, wipe out** We had to exterminate a colony of termites that were damaging our house.

external *adjective* **exterior, outer, outside, outward, out, surface** All insects have six legs and an external skeleton. ➡ **Antonym: internal**

extinct *adjective* **nonexistent, defunct, vanished, inactive, dead, deceased, lifeless** Dinosaurs became extinct about 65 million years ago.

extinguish *verb* **1. put out, quench, smother, douse, suffocate, snuff out** We used both water and dirt to extinguish our campfire. **2. abolish, destroy, eliminate, end, erase, annihilate, kill, quash, eradicate** Last night's defeat extinguished our hopes of winning the championship. ➡ **Antonyms: 1. ignite, light**

extra *adjective* **additional, spare, surplus, reserve, excess, supplemental, more, new** I have a flashlight and

extra batteries in my bedroom. ◆ *adverb* **exceptionally, extremely, especially, very, greatly, highly, most** I made the chili with extra-lean ground beef. ◆ *noun* **accessory, addition, supplement, bonus, attachment, appendage, adjunct** Our new car came with many extras.

extract *verb* **1. draw out, pull, remove, withdraw, take, pry, pluck** Saffron is the most expensive spice in the world because it has to be extracted by hand. **2. derive, obtain, gather, reap, collect, glean, cull, garner** I extracted a lot of information from this book for my report. ◆ *noun* **1. excerpt, passage, selection, fragment, quotation, citation** I read an extract from *Alice's Adventures in Wonderland* for my oral reading assignment. **2. concentrate, essence, elixir, juice, oil, distillation, infusion, spirits** A teaspoon of vanilla extract can flavor a whole batch of cookies. ➡ **Antonyms:** *verb* **1. insert, embed**

extraordinary *adjective* **exceptional, remarkable, unusual, magnificent, rare, incredible, phenomenal, outstanding** Hercules was a mythological hero known for his extraordinary strength. ➡ **Antonyms: normal, usual, ordinary**

extravagant *adjective* **1. lavish, excessive, exorbitant, spendthrift, profligate, wasteful, imprudent** Buying three new coats would definitely be extravagant. **2. extreme, immoderate, excessive, unreasonable, inordinate** No one was willing to hire the actor because his fees were too extravagant. ➡ **Antonyms: 1. economical, thrifty 2. modest**

extreme *adjective* **1. farthest, remotest, outermost, outmost, utmost, supreme, last** Pluto is located at the extreme edge of our solar system. **2. excessive, intense, severe, immoderate, unusual, exorbitant, drastic, great** California's Death Valley is known for its extreme heat. **3. radical, revolutionary, extremist, fanatical, outrageous, unreasonable, advanced** Many now accepted scientific theories were considered at first to be extreme. ◆ *noun* **end, extremity, limit, degree, length, height, depth, boundary** My emotions sometimes shift from one extreme to the other.

eye *verb* **observe, scrutinize, study, scan, watch, regard, survey, contemplate** She eyed the flowers thoughtfully before arranging them.

eyesight *noun* **1. seeing, sight, vision, perception, eye** A rabbit's large, round eyes give it keen eyesight. **2. view, seeing, viewing, sight, perspective, gaze** I waved at my friend as soon she came into eyesight.

Ff

fable *noun* **1. parable, story, tale, allegory, legend, myth, fairy tale, romance** Fables often teach a moral lesson. **2. lie, falsehood, fantasy, fiction, fabrication, fib, tall tale** She told us a fable about finding a valuable diamond ring.

fabric *noun* **1. cloth, material, textile, dry goods, fiber, stuff** I sewed squares of fabric together to make a quilt. **2. structure, framework, texture, construction, configuration, organization, substance** Institutions form the basic fabric of society.

fabricate *verb* **1. build, make, manufacture, assemble, construct, produce, fashion, shape** He is fabricating a racecar. **2. invent, contrive, concoct, make up, counterfeit, hatch, devise** They fabricated a story to explain their absence. ➤ **Antonyms: 1. destroy, demolish, raze**

fabulous *adjective* **1. extraordinary, amazing, astonishing, fantastic, incredible, unbelievable** Harry Houdini is famous for his fabulous escapes. **2. legendary, mythical, mythic, fabled, storied, fictitious, unreal, imaginary** Early explorers searched for fabulous cities filled with treasure. **3. wonderful, pleasing, great, superb, divine, marvelous, super, terrific** I had a fabulous time at your party. ➤ **Antonyms: 1. believable 2. actual, real, historical 3. ordinary, common**

façade *noun* **pose, veneer, affectation, semblance, guise, show, face, front** His façade of friendliness is helpful in his job.

face *noun* **1. expression, look, visage, appearance, countenance** I could tell by her face that she was not happy. **2. front, surface, exterior, obverse, facet, top, façade** The climbers went up the cliff's face. **3. appearance, look, surface, nature, sight, aspect, cast, visage** Strip miners have changed the face of the countryside. **4. semblance, display, guise, show, disguise, mask, pretense, front** I lost the match but put on a face of good sportsmanship. ◆ *verb* **1. front, look, point, overlook, look on, turn, border** Traditional Navajo homes face east. **2. brave, challenge, confront, meet, encounter, defy, realize, recognize** Police officers sometimes have to face danger in the line of duty. **3. cover, surface, coat, side, dress, trim, clad, sheathe** Our house is faced with brick on two sides. ➤ **Antonyms: *noun* 2. back, reverse ◆ *verb* 2. avoid, evade**

facet *noun* **aspect, feature, specific, phase, angle, particular, part, respect** I like many facets of camping.

facile *adjective* **1. quick, adroit, dexterous, clever, proficient, skillful, effortless, deft** The audience enjoyed the comedian's facile wit. **2. careless, superficial, slick, shallow, cursory, hasty, glib, light** The speaker's facile presentation overlooked many important points. ➤ **Antonyms: 1. awkward, clumsy 2. thorough, painstaking**

facilitate *verb* **ease, simplify, expedite, accelerate, lighten, aid, assist, foster** An accountant can facilitate the process of paying taxes. ➤ **Antonyms: hamper, hinder, complicate**

facility *noun* **1. ease, effortlessness, easiness, ability, aptitude, skill, talent, dexterity** He performs magic tricks with great facility. **2. aid, appliance, equipment, resource, convenience, tool, amenity, comfort** Our apartment building has laundry facilities in the basement. ➤ **Antonyms: 1. clumsiness, difficulty, awkwardness**

facsimile *noun* **copy, duplicate, reproduction, likeness, replica, twin, reprint, image** We have a facsimile of the Declaration of Independence on display in our classroom. ➤ **Antonym: original**

fact *noun* **1. actuality, certainty, reality, truth, verity, certitude, truism** It is a fact that an insect has six legs. **2. data, information, knowledge, detail, particular, specific, evidence** I used an encyclopedia to look up facts for my science report. **3. event, occurrence, circumstance, deed, episode, affair, phenomenon** We found out after the fact that we had been cheated.

faction *noun* **coalition, bloc, combination, cartel, party, ring, group, side** One faction within Congress is trying to block the new legislation.

factor *noun* **circumstance, consideration, component, part, aspect, detail, particular, fact** Age is a factor that is considered when movies are assigned ratings.

factory *noun* **plant, shop, workshop, company, works, mill, firm, foundry** That factory across town makes cars and trucks.

factual *adjective* **accurate, correct, exact, real, true, valid, authentic, genuine** The book gave a factual account of President Teddy Roosevelt's life. ➤ **Antonyms: false, incorrect, speculative**

faculty *noun* **1. power, capacity, capability, endowment, function, potential** Hearing-impaired individuals have difficulty developing the faculty of speech. **2. skill, ability, knack, talent, gift, aptitude, flair, genius** She has a faculty for storytelling. **3. professors, teachers, lecturers, instructors, educators, scholars, staff** My grandfather is one of the faculty at Lehigh University.

fad *noun* **craze, fancy, fashion, style, trend, mania, vogue, mode** Pet rocks were a fad in the 1970s.

fade *verb* **1. dim, dull, pale, whiten, age, blanch, wash out, bleach** Sunlight caused our living room curtains to fade. **2. wither, wilt, decline, die, diminish, lessen, wane, weaken** The thunder began to fade away as the storm passed. **3. vanish, disappear, end, cease, expire, dissolve, evaporate** Her interest in horses faded as she grew older. ➧ **Antonyms: 1. brighten 2. increase, grow 3. appear, materialize**

fail *verb* **1. fall short, fall through, flop, miss, lose, blunder, fizzle, slip** The pole vaulter failed on his first attempt to clear the bar. **2. decline, diminish, dwindle, lessen, wane, weaken, sink, die** My dog is getting old, and his hearing is beginning to fail. **3. neglect, disregard, overlook, omit, avoid, ignore, default** My friend failed to show up for our meeting. **4. abandon, forsake, disappoint, neglect, forget, desert, let down** His companions failed him at the crucial part of the climb. ➧ **Antonyms: 1. succeed, triumph, win 2. flourish, thrive**

failure *noun* **1. lack of success, defeat, miss, breakdown, outage** My failure to win today's race does not discourage me. **2. omission, dereliction, negligence, default, nonobservance, lapse** Failure to maintain a car's brakes can result in a serious accident. **3. bankruptcy, insolvency, delinquency, default, crash, ruin, collapse** The company averted failure by securing a bank loan. **4. fiasco, bust, dud, flop, disappointment, mess, ruin, washout** My first cake was a failure, but my second was a success. ➧ **Antonym: success**

faint *adjective* **1. dim, indistinct, fuzzy, hazy, shadowy, unclear, vague** The flashlight's faint beam indicated that the batteries were almost dead. **2. weak, slight, feeble, low, soft, muted, frail, little** The mother cat heard the kitten's faint cry. **3. dizzy, giddy, lightheaded, delirious, woozy, torpid, lethargic, sick** I felt faint after climbing ten flights of stairs. **4. timid, cowardly, frightened, faint-hearted, fearful** Some sports are not for those who have faint hearts. ◆ *verb* **black out, pass out, swoon, collapse, drop, succumb, keel over** The man fainted when he heard that he had won a million dollars. ➧ **Antonyms:** *adjective* **1. & 2. clear, strong 3. steady, healthy 4. brave, courageous, bold**

fair¹ *adjective* **1. just, honest, impartial, objective, unbiased, equitable, nonpartisan, evenhanded** Our teacher tries to be fair in grading her students. **2. attractive, beautiful, lovely, pretty, charming, enchanting, handsome, exquisite** Welcome to our fair city. **3. light, pale, white, creamy, milky, blonde, snowy, ivory** She has a strikingly fair complexion. **4. clear, cloudless, sunny, fine, mild, clement, bright, pleasant** The forecast is for fair weather this weekend. **5. decent, average, adequate, moderate, satisfactory, good, reasonable, respectable** There's a fair chance that Dad will be home early tonight. ➧ **Antonyms: 1. biased, unfair 2. ugly, unattractive 3. dark 4. cloudy, stormy 5. poor**

fair² *noun* **1. carnival, festival, celebration, fete, gala, spectacle, pageant** The city holds a street fair twice a year. **2. market, bazaar, exposition, exhibit, show, display** I entered a cake in the county fair.

faith *noun* **1. confidence, dependence, reliance, belief, credence, trust, hope, conviction** Before the playoff game, our coach told the team that she had faith in us. **2. belief, creed, doctrine, religion, principle, denomination, persuasion, principle** In the United States, people of all faiths are allowed to worship freely. ➧ **Antonyms: 1. doubt, mistrust**

faithful *adjective* **1. dutiful, devoted, loyal, reliable, steadfast, trustworthy, true, staunch** My dog is my faithful companion. **2. accurate, exact, authentic, close, strict, true, precise, correct** The movie *To Kill a Mockingbird* is a faithful adaptation of the book. ➧ **Antonyms: 1. disloyal, unfaithful 2. inaccurate, imprecise**

fake *adjective* **imitation, phony, sham, counterfeit, false, bogus, mock, simulated** My winter coat is lined with fake fur. ◆ *verb* **imitate, feign, pretend, simulate, sham, counterfeit, affect, assume** I sometimes fake a foreign accent to amuse my friends. ◆ *noun* **1. faker, charlatan, impostor, cheat, deceiver, quack, fraud, pretender** The man who claimed to be a famous historian turned out to be a fake. **2. counterfeit, imitation, forgery, sham, phony, hoax, copy, reproduction** Only an expert can tell that this diamond is a fake. ➧ **Antonyms:** *adjective* **authentic, genuine, real**

fall *verb* **1. drop, pitch, plunge, topple, tumble, crash, descend, plummet** I bumped into the lamp and it fell to the floor. **2. hang down, droop, drop, cascade, descend, decline, dip, sink** The king's robe fell from his shoulders in graceful folds. **3. decrease, diminish, ebb, lessen, lower, reduce, abate, subside** John's voice fell to a whisper when he told me his secret. **4. surrender, submit, succumb, yield, capitulate, resign, drop, give in** Rome fell to barbarians in the year A.D. 476. **5. arrive, come, happen, occur, take place, transpire, come about, chance** My birthday falls on a Tuesday this year. ◆ *noun* **1. drop, plunge, spill, tumble, descent, plummet, dive, nosedive** The climber's safety rope stopped her fall. **2. waterfall, cascade, cataract, rapids, torrent, fountain, flood** We could hear the sound of the falls as we approached. **3. downfall, overthrow, defeat, collapse, surrender, capture, rout, conquest** Democracy was restored after the dictator's fall from power. **4. lapse, disgrace, downfall, slip, degradation, humiliation, ruin, corruption** The actor's fall did not affect his popularity for very long. ➨ **Antonyms:** *verb* **1. climb, rise 3. grow, increase 4. resist, withstand** ◆ *noun* **1. rise, ascent**

fallacy *noun* **error, untruth, falsehood, mistake, misconception, delusion, illusion, deception** The controversial theory was shown to be full of fallacies. ➨ **Antonyms: truth, verity**

false *adjective* **1. inaccurate, incorrect, untrue, erroneous, wrong, mistaken, untruthful** The dishonest witness gave false testimony. **2. disloyal, faithless, unfaithful, dishonest, deceitful, traitorous, false-hearted** Brutus was a false friend to Julius Caesar. **3. fake, artificial, imitation, phony, bogus, counterfeit, fraudulent, sham** George Washington's false teeth were made of wood. ➨ **Antonyms: 1. correct, right, true 2. loyal, faithful 3. real, genuine, authentic**

falter *verb* **1. hesitate, vacillate, dither, pause, waver, wobble, dillydally** As I fell down for the fourth time, my enthusiasm for learning to ski began to falter. **2. stutter, stammer, halt, mumble, sputter, splutter** I faltered during my speech when I forgot my next point. **3. stumble, reel, weave, wobble, stagger, lurch, shuffle, flounder** Our footsteps faltered when we stepped off the boat.

fame *noun* **renown, celebrity, glory, honor, esteem, prominence, popularity, distinction** Charles Lindbergh won fame as the first person to fly solo across the Atlantic Ocean. ➨ **Antonyms: obscurity, dishonor**

familiar *adjective* **1. common, everyday, frequent, regular, routine, well-known, ordinary** Swings and jungle gyms are familiar sights at playgrounds. **2. acquainted, aware, experienced, informed, knowledgeable, cognizant, conversant** Are you familiar with the song "Happy Birthday to You"? **3. close, friendly, intimate, sociable, amicable, cordial, neighborly, affable** I am on familiar terms with most of the other students in my grade. **4. presumptuous, forward, rude, impudent, disrespectful, pushy, bold, nervy** I did not like the salesman's familiar manner. ➨ **Antonyms: 1. unusual, extraordinary 2. ignorant, uninformed 3. formal, distant 4. shy, retiring**

family *noun* **1. kin, relations, relatives, kinsmen, kith and kin, kinfolk** On Rosh Hashanah, my family goes to temple to pray together. **2. bloodline, lineage, house, clan, stock, ancestry, breed, tribe** Queen Elizabeth I was the last monarch from the Tudor family. **3. class, division, group, order, kind, classification, category, set** The violin and cello belong to the family of stringed instruments.

famine *noun* **hunger, starvation, scarcity, want, lack, destitution** The United Nations sent food to the countries that were experiencing famine. ➨ **Antonyms: abundance, feast, bounty**

famous *adjective* **renowned, well-known, celebrated, illustrious, popular, prominent, notable, eminent** Abraham Lincoln was one of the most famous of United States Presidents. ➨ **Antonyms: obscure, unknown**

fan[1] *verb* **1. cool, refresh, aerate, ventilate, blow, stir, air-condition** I fanned myself with a magazine. **2. inflame, provoke, stir up, excite, agitate, arouse, kindle, whip up** Propaganda is used to fan public opinion. **3. open up, open out, unfurl, unfold, spread out, unroll, expand** I fanned the cards in my hand. ➨ **Antonyms: 2. smother, calm 3. fold, close**

fan[2] *noun* **admirer, follower, devotee, enthusiast, aficionado, partisan, lover** Fans mobbed the rock star as he left the dressing room.

fanatic *noun* **zealot, extremist, maniac, enthusiast, militant, radical, revolutionary** The religious fanatic was willing to die for his beliefs.

fancy *noun* **1. imagination, creativity, inspiration, fantasy, vision, dream, ingenuity, conception** *Alice's Adventures in Wonderland* was a creation of Lewis Carroll's fancy. **2. impulse, whim, whimsy, caprice, notion, urge, desire, idea** I had a sudden fancy to go for a walk in the rain. **3. liking, fondness, love, desire, longing, craving, relish, yearning** I took a fancy to the baby rabbit the moment I saw it. ◆ *adjective* **1. decorative, elaborate, elegant, gaudy, ornate, showy, embellished** She bought some fancy stationery for writing thank-you notes. **2. complex, intricate, elaborate, involved, difficult, knotty, convoluted** The necklace was made up of fancy knots. **3. fine, choice, exceptional, superior, first-rate, quality, first-class, exclusive** We ate at a fancy restaurant last night. ◆ *verb* **1. imagine, see, picture, conceive, envision, think, visualize, fantasize** Can you fancy her becoming a top athlete? **2. enjoy, relish, like, love, crave, prefer, favor** Would you fancy pasta for dinner tonight? **3. guess, surmise, reckon, speculate, presume, conjecture, believe,**

assume I fancy that he is too shy to go to the school dance. ➡ **Antonyms:** *adjective* **1. plain, unadorned 2. simple, easy 3. inferior, mediocre**

fantastic *adjective* **1. imaginary, imaginative, fanciful, fabulous, fictional, whimsical** Jules Verne's fantastic stories were unbelievable a century ago. **2. bizarre, odd, strange, weird, unbelievable, outlandish, wild, crazy** The wind on the Monterey Peninsula has twisted the trees into fantastic shapes. **3. outstanding, marvelous, remarkable, superb, terrific, wonderful, great, sensational** She has more than two hundred CDs in her fantastic collection of rock music. ➡ **Antonyms: 1. real 2. believable 3. common, ordinary**

fantasy *noun* **daydream, dream, vision, reverie, fancy, imagination, whimsy** I have a fantasy in which I am the first astronaut to go to Jupiter.

far *adverb* **considerably, much, significantly, decidedly, notably, quite, extremely** The book was far more interesting than I expected. ◆ *adjective* **1. distant, faraway, remote, removed, far-flung, far-off** Dinosaurs lived in the far past. **2. extensive, long, extended, lengthy, considerable, great** We have a far distance to go before we reach our destination. ➡ **Antonyms:** *adverb* **less** ◆ *adjective* **1. close, near 2. short, brief**

fare *verb* **do, get along, get by, manage, fend, thrive, succeed, make out, shift** Mom says that she is faring well at her new job. ◆ *noun* **1. fee, price, toll, charge, token, cost, ticket, passage** I paid my fare as I boarded the bus. **2. food, victuals, provisions, rations, meals, edibles, table, menu** The fare at the truck stop buffet was delicious.

farm *noun* **homestead, plantation, ranch, spread, acreage, pasture, land, field** My uncle grows soybeans on his farm. ◆ *verb* **cultivate, grow, plant, till, harvest, plow, sow, raise** People first began to farm crops more than 10,000 years ago.

fascinate *verb* **captivate, charm, enchant, entrance, intrigue, engross, enthrall, beguile** The astronaut fascinated us with tales of his adventures in outer space. ➡ **Antonyms: bore, repel**

fashion *noun* **1. trend, style, vogue, convention, fad, custom, craze, rage** At my school, the current fashion is to wear your baseball cap backwards. **2. mode, manner, method, style, way, system, form, order** Hold the chopsticks in this fashion. ◆ *verb* **build, construct, fabricate, form, make, shape, model, create** I used papier-mâché to fashion a five-foot-tall giraffe.

fast *adjective* **1. fleet, quick, rapid, speedy, swift, hurried, expeditious, hasty** The cheetah is the fastest animal on land. **2. firm, fixed, secure, strong, tight, sure, fastened, tenacious** Whenever I go on a carnival ride, I keep a fast grip on the safety bar. **3. faithful, loyal, steadfast, true, staunch, constant, resolute, steady** Alicia and Erica have been fast friends for years. **4. wild, immoral, reckless, loose, careless, wanton, intemperate, libertine** That group is too fast for me. ◆ *adverb* **1. quick, quickly, rapidly, speedily, swiftly, hastily, fleetly** I like to walk fast. **2. firmly, hard, securely, soundly, tightly, tight, solidly, deeply** The gum was stuck fast to the bottom of my shoe. ➡ **Antonyms:** *adjective* **1. slow 2. insecure, loose 3. disloyal, unfaithful 4. respectable** ◆ *adverb* **1. slow, slowly**

fasten *verb* **attach, bind, connect, fix, secure, join, affix, anchor** Make sure the shelf is securely fastened to the wall. ➡ **Antonyms: free, loosen, release**

fat *noun* **grease, oil, lard, tallow, suet** French fries contain a lot of fat. ◆ *adjective* **1. heavy, obese, overweight, plump, stout, corpulent, rotund, pudgy** Dad started exercising because he thought that he was getting fat. **2. big, ample, generous, plentiful, lavish, rich, lucrative, lush** Gary received a fat reward for returning the money. ➡ **Antonyms:** *adjective* **1. slender, thin 2. meager**

fatal *adjective* **1. deadly, lethal, mortal, terminal, incurable, poisonous, killing** Black widow spider bites are almost never fatal. **2. calamitous, disastrous, ruinous, destructive, catastrophic, cataclysmic, damaging** The flood was fatal to the crops. **3. critical, crucial, determining, fateful, momentous, decisive, final, important** I reached the fatal moment when I had to make my decision. ➡ **Antonyms: 1. harmless 2. beneficial, constructive 3. unimportant, minor**

fate *noun* **1. destiny, luck, fortune, providence, predestination, lot, portion** Mom says that fate smiled on her the day she met Dad. **2. result, outcome, end, future, upshot, effect, consequence, destination** The fate of the President's peace initiative is uncertain.

father *noun* **1. dad, daddy, papa, pop, sire, parent, forefather, ancestor, progenitor** My father and I went to a ball game together. **2. founder, creator, inventor, architect, designer, originator, maker, author** Charles Babbage is considered to be the father of the computer. ◆ *verb* **found, originate, create, begin, make, produce, establish, sire, parent** The United States was fathered by men who believed the American colonies should be independent.

fathom *verb* **understand, comprehend, apprehend, interpret, divine, grasp, perceive, see, read, follow** Scientists are just beginning to fathom many of the functions of the brain.

fatigue *noun* **exhaustion, tiredness, weariness, languor, lethargy, listlessness** His fatigue was caused by staying up past midnight. ◆ *verb* **drain, exhaust, tire, wear out, weary, enervate, debilitate, tucker** The long walk across town fatigued me. ◈ **Antonyms:** *noun* **energy, vigor** ◆ *verb* **energize, refresh**

fault *noun* **1. defect, flaw, imperfection, shortcoming, bug, error, mistake, blemish** My computer isn't working right because there's a fault in its programming. **2. blame, guilt, responsibility, onus, offense, culpability, error, lapse** It's my fault that the dishes aren't done yet. ◆ *verb* **criticize, censure, blame, reprove, accuse, impugn, reprehend, challenge** You can't fault his enthusiasm for the project. ◈ **Antonyms:** *noun* **1. strength 2. credit** ◆ *verb* **praise**

faultless *adjective* **perfect, flawless, ideal, impeccable, exemplary, consummate** My music teacher praised me for my faultless performance at the recital. ◈ **Antonyms: flawed, defective, imperfect**

favor *noun* **1. courtesy, good deed, good turn, kindness, service, indulgence** My brother did me a favor by helping me study for my history test. **2. acceptance, approval, approbation, respect, esteem, admiration, support** The politician worked hard to win the voters' favor. **3. partiality, bias, preference, favoritism, inclination, predilection, leaning** A good referee does not show favor to either team. **4. behalf, interest, advantage, avail, benefit, assistance, service, good** The bad weather worked to the soldiers' favor by concealing their movements. ◆ *verb* **1. accommodate, oblige, gratify, indulge, reward, please, honor** The pianist favored her audience with two encores. **2. like, prefer, support, approve, commend, accept, praise, endorse** Which of the two proposals do you favor? **3. aid, promote, help, assist, support, sustain, further, abet** The south side of the hill favors the growth of peach and apricot trees. **4. resemble, take after, look like, mirror, match,**

approximate Mom says that I favor my grandfather. ◈ **Antonyms:** *noun* **1. injury, harm 2. disapproval, ill will 4. loss, disadvantage** ◆ *verb* **2. disapprove, dislike 3. thwart, impair**

favorable *adjective* **1. advantageous, beneficial, beneficent, good, helpful, propitious** The upgrade on my computer is a favorable improvement. **2. pleasing, good, agreeable, pleasant, pleasurable, satisfying, promising, welcome** My new teacher made a favorable impression on me right away. **3. approving, good, excellent, great, wonderful, splendid, positive, nice** Martha received a favorable grade on her report. ◈ **Antonyms: bad, unfavorable**

favorite *noun* **preference, first choice, choice, predilection, pick, pet, darling, fancy** Licorice-flavored jelly beans are my favorites. ◆ *adjective* **favored, preferred, well-liked, special, prized, pet, popular, darling** One of my favorite books is *The Wind in the Willows.*

fawn *verb* **toady, kowtow, grovel, flatter, court, pander, cringe** We tried not to fawn over the movie star when we met him.

fear *noun* **anxiety, dread, fright, panic, terror, alarm, concern, apprehension** I experienced a brief moment of fear when the lights went out. ◆ *verb* **be afraid of, be scared of, dread, cower, flinch, quail, tremble** My daredevil friend seemingly fears nothing.

fearful *adjective* **1. afraid, apprehensive, frightened, scared, anxious, timid, nervous, panicky** I was fearful of losing my way in the dark. **2. horrifying, appalling, dreadful, ghastly, horrible, shocking, terrible, awful** The accident scene was a fearful sight. ◈ **Antonyms: 1. brave, courageous, bold 2. pleasant, encouraging**

fearless *adjective* **intrepid, daring, bold, brave, courageous, valiant, heroic, unafraid** The fearless mouse plucked a thorn from the lion's paw. ◈ **Antonyms: cowardly, fearful**

feast *noun* **banquet, dinner, meal, repast, spread, feed, gala, festival** My family has a special feast to celebrate Kwanzaa. ◆ *verb* **banquet, dine, feed, indulge, devour, eat, regale, gorge** We feast on roast turkey every Thanksgiving.

feat *noun* **act, deed, exploit, stunt, achievement, trick, accomplishment, coup** The magician performed a remarkable feat when he made the child disappear.

feature *noun* **1. attribute, characteristic, quality, trait, mark, property, detail** Our new refrigerator has some fancy features our old one lacked. **2. article, piece, report, story, column, comment, item, lead** I read an interesting feature about wolves in the newspaper. ◆ *verb* **emphasize, highlight, stress, star, headline, accent, accentuate, spotlight** The concert will feature folk songs from around the world.

fee *noun* **charge, toll, payment, price, cost, wage, compensation, remuneration** Dad had to pay a fee to park our car at the fairground.

feeble *adjective* **1. weak, fragile, frail, sickly, ailing, decrepit, puny, delicate** I felt feeble while suffering from the flu. **2. inadequate, ineffective, flimsy, vapid, lame, tenuous, paltry, dim, faint** I made a feeble attempt to apologize. ➡ **Antonyms: 1. strong, vigorous, healthy 2. forceful, effective**

feed *verb* **nourish, serve, maintain, satisfy, sustain, nurture, fuel, live, subsist** There's enough lasagna here to feed ten people. ◆ *noun* **fodder, food, forage, provisions, silage, chow, fare, victuals** The farmer used some of his corn crop as feed for his cattle.

feel *verb* **1. finger, handle, touch, palpate, manipulate, rub, stroke, press, ply** The doctor felt my arm gently to see if it was broken. **2. detect, notice, perceive, sense, discern, apprehend, intuit** You look like you feel a headache coming on. **3. grope, fumble, poke, reach, probe, search, hunt** I felt alongside the door for the light switch. **4. believe, think, deem, consider, hold, presume, judge, suppose, surmise** I feel that my parents are usually fair. **5. sympathize, empathize, understand, pity, commiserate, condole, ache, suffer** I really felt for my friend when she lost her pet kitten. ◆ *noun* **feeling, texture, touch, sensation, sense, nature, character, consistency** She loves the feel of her hamster's fur.

feeling *noun* **1. sensation, awareness, perception, feel, touch, sense, sensitivity** I had no feeling in my foot when it went to sleep. **2. emotion, mood, sense, sentiment, attitude, reaction, excitement, affect** Eric had a feeling of pride when his article was printed in the school paper. **3. belief, idea, notion, opinion, thought, judgment, conviction, impression, suspicion, intuition** I have a feeling that it's going to rain today.

feign *verb* **pretend, fake, simulate, sham, imitate, act, counterfeit, affect** Sometimes I feign being sick so that I can stay home from school.

felicity *noun* **bliss, happiness, delight, rapture, elation, ecstasy, cheer, joy** My sister's wedding was an occasion of great felicity. ➡ **Antonyms: sorrow, misery**

Word Group

A **feline** is an animal belonging to the cat family. **Feline** is a general term with no true synonyms. Many **felines** are very well known, such as the leopard, lion, and tiger. Here are some other felines:

A **bobcat** is a North American wildcat with reddish-brown fur. **Catamounts, cougars,** and **pumas** are mountain lions. A **cheetah** is a long-legged, swift-running wildcat of Africa and southwest Asia. A **jaguar** is a large tropical American wildcat having spotted fur. A **lynx** is a North American wildcat that has a short tail and tufted ears. An **ocelot** is a wildcat of Mexico, Central America, and South America. A **panther** is a black unspotted leopard. A **serval** is a long-legged wildcat of Africa.

---

fell¹ *verb* **chop down, cut down, down, drop, level, hew, raze, flatten, knock down** I helped Dad fell the dead tree in the back yard. ➡ **Antonyms: raise, grow**

fell² *adjective* **fierce, cruel, ruthless, violent, savage, vicious, merciless, sinister** I like stories in which the fell plans of the villain are foiled. ➡ **Antonyms: gentle, tame, kind**

fellow *noun* **1. man, boy, guy, lad, chap, person, individual** That fellow over there is waiting to use the telephone. **2. comrade, associate, colleague, confederate, companion, equal, mate, peer** The politician had lunch with his fellows.

felon *noun* **criminal, lawbreaker, convict, malefactor, offender, culprit, outlaw** The felon was instructed to report to his parole officer on a regular basis.

female *noun* **girl, lady, woman, gal, she, madam, matron** We didn't realize that our turtle was a female until she laid some eggs. ➡ **Antonyms:** *noun* **male, man, he**

feminine *adjective* **womanly, ladylike, matronly, effeminate, female** The actress was famous for her feminine charm. ➡ **Antonyms: masculine, manly**

fence *noun* **barrier, boards, pickets, posts, rails, wall, barricade** Our landlord installed a fence to enclose the back yard. ◆ *verb* **wall, shut in, encircle, surround, bound, corral, cage, pen** We fenced our garden to protect it from rabbits.

fend *verb* **1. repulse, parry, ward off, beat off, resist, repel, rebuff, oppose, defend** The wrestler fended off his opponent's attempts to pin him to the mat. **2. get along,**

get by, provide, manage, cope, survive, shift, subsist, support The striped tenrec is able to fend for itself when it is only six days old. ❖ **Antonyms: 1. submit, succumb**

ferocious *adjective* **1. brutal, cruel, fierce, savage, vicious, wild, rapacious, fiendish** Judging by their teeth, velociraptors must have been ferocious dinosaurs. **2. extreme, intense, harsh, severe, strong, powerful, violent, drastic** The winter storms have been ferocious this year. ❖ **Antonyms: 1. gentle, tame 2. moderate, mild**

ferret *verb* **uncover, discover, reveal, disclose, find, dig up, probe, ascertain** Scientists are trying to ferret out the information encoded in DNA. ❖ **Antonyms: hide, cover, bury**

fertile *adjective* **1. fruitful, fecund, productive, plentiful, bountiful, rich, prolific, abundant** The farmland in Illinois is very fertile. **2. creative, inventive, active, prolific, imaginative, ingenious, resourceful** The artist Toulouse-Lautrec had a fertile imagination. ❖ **Antonyms: 1. sterile, barren 2. inactive, feeble**

fervent *adjective* **ardent, zealous, enthusiastic, intense, keen, fervid, vehement** He is a fervent supporter of animal rights. ❖ **Antonyms: dispassionate, apathetic, detached**

fervor *noun* **ardor, excitement, enthusiasm, zeal, passion, drive, gusto, fire** The cast of the school musical brought great fervor to their performance. ❖ **Antonyms: apathy, ennui, boredom**

festival *noun* **celebration, jubilee, fair, fete, fiesta, gala, carnival, revels** Gilroy, California, is famous for its Garlic Festival.

festive *adjective* **joyous, merry, gay, convivial, playful, jolly, jubilant, happy, cheerful** The holiday shoppers were in a festive mood. ❖ **Antonyms: gloomy, sad**

festivity *noun* **celebration, merrymaking, rejoicing, mirth, revelry, joyfulness, glee, fun** We entered into the happy spirit of the Christmas festivity.

fetch *verb* **go for, retrieve, bring, carry, transport, tote, deliver, bear** When Mary plays with her dog, she throws a ball for him to fetch.

fetish *noun* **1. charm, amulet, talisman, image, idol, totem, scarab** My grandmother gave me a fetish that has been in our family for many years. **2. obsession, mania, fixation, preoccupation, propensity, penchant, desire** Some people have a fetish for washing their hands many times during the day.

feud *noun* **disagreement, dispute, quarrel, conflict, fight, schism, breach, vendetta** The cousins didn't speak to each other because of a family feud. ◆ *verb* **quarrel, fight, duel, bicker, contest, squabble, contend, dispute** She is a peaceable person who doesn't like to feud with anyone. ❖ **Antonyms:** *noun* **peace, harmony** ◆ *verb* **agree, cooperate**

fever *noun* **frenzy, turmoil, unrest, fervor, ferment, passion, enthusiasm, excitement** There was a fever of activity in the anthill when it became flooded. ❖ **Antonyms: calm, serenity, tranquillity**

few *adjective* **not many, scant, limited, meager, skimpy, rare, scarce, scanty** Few people went to the museum's new exhibit. ❖ **Antonyms: ample, many, sufficient**

fiasco *noun* **debacle, failure, bust, washout, flop, dud, disaster, catastrophe** I had so many gutter balls that my first attempt at bowling was a fiasco. ❖ **Antonyms: success, triumph, hit**

fib *noun* **falsehood, lie, untruth, story, tale, deceit, fabrication, deception** I told a fib when I said that I knew a famous rock star. ◆ *verb* **falsify, lie, misrepresent, fabricate, distort, embroider, invent** I don't think people should fib about their age. ❖ **Antonyms:** *noun* **truth, fact**

fiber *noun* **1. strand, filament, line, string, thread, tendril, web, hair** Data can be transmitted through very fine fibers made of glass. **2. character, structure, makeup, nature, spirit, substance, temperament, disposition** Having a sense of what is right is part of a person's moral fiber.

fickle *adjective* **changeable, inconstant, erratic, mercurial, unpredictable, variable, unstable** The weather has been fickle this spring. ❖ **Antonyms: constant, dependable**

fiction *noun* **concoction, fantasy, invention, fable, story, tale, fib, lie** I couldn't tell if his story was fact or fiction. ❖ **Antonyms: fact, reality**

fiddle *verb* **tinker, dabble, toy, tamper, fool, mess, putter, play** I like to fiddle with cars and engines.

fidelity *noun* **1. loyalty, faithfulness, devotion, allegiance, constancy, fealty** Patriots are people who have great fidelity to their nation. **2. accuracy, precision, exactitude, exactness, realism, correctness, veracity** His model ships replicate the originals with remarkable fidelity. ❖ **Antonyms: 1. treachery, infidelity 2. inaccuracy**

fidget *verb* squirm, wriggle, writhe, wiggle, twitch, stir, twiddle, fuss My 7-year-old brother fidgets when he sits in a chair.

field *noun* 1. lot, ground, meadow, pasture, plot, tract, acreage, area We play baseball in the vacant field near my house. 2. athletic field, arena, court, stadium, track, green, turf, course, theater Our soccer coach made us run up and down the field. 3. area, realm, domain, subject, specialty, province, circle, world Dr. Seuss was a leading author in the field of children's literature. 4. profession, business, occupation, vocation, line, trade, employment What field is your father in? 5. range, scope, expanse, reach, sweep, spectrum, extent My new eyeglasses have increased my field of vision.

fierce *adjective* 1. dangerous, ferocious, savage, vicious, cruel, brutal Mother bears can be very fierce when their cubs are threatened. 2. extreme, high, powerful, strong, violent, heavy, intense, intensive Antarctica's fierce winds have been clocked at more than 200 miles per hour. 3. ardent, fervent, passionate, zealous, avid, impassioned, enthusiastic Patrick Henry, a fierce American patriot, said, "Give me liberty or give me death!" ➜ **Antonyms: 1.** docile, tame, meek **2.** moderate, mild, gentle **3.** indifferent, cool

fiery *adjective* 1. blazing, burning, flaming, smoldering, alight, afire, ablaze A fiery meteor blazed a bright trail through the night sky. 2. tempestuous, wild, impassioned, high-spirited, ardent, fervid, fervent I was enthralled by the fiery flamenco music. ➜ **Antonyms: 2.** mild, tame

fight *verb* 1. battle, combat, struggle, war, contend, brawl, duel, feud, clash Americans fought against each other in the Civil War. 2. argue, bicker, dispute, quarrel, squabble, tiff, spat, wrangle Let's not fight over what TV show to watch. ◆ *noun* 1. clash, conflict, battle, combat, brawl, scuffle, duel, skirmish The sounds of a cat fight woke me last night. 2. disagreement, dispute, feud, quarrel, squabble, fuss, altercation, argument My sister and I had a fight over whose turn it was to use the computer. 3. pluck, grit, mettle, spirit, toughness, combativeness, pugnacity The patient's fight helped her pull through.

figment *noun* fabrication, concoction, improvisation, creation, invention, fantasy That story sounds like a figment of someone's imagination. ➜ **Antonyms:** truth, certainty

figure *noun* 1. digit, number, numeral, ordinal He can add up a long list of figures in his head. 2. contour, form, outline, shape, silhouette, configuration, structure I could see two figures walking in the distance. 3. dignitary, leader, personality, notable, person, personage, celebrity The secretary-general of the United Nations is an important world figure. 4. illustration, diagram, drawing, sketch, representation, outline, image I studied the figure in the botany book that delineated the parts of the blossom. ◆ *verb* 1. calculate, compute, reckon, estimate, solve, assess, measure, evaluate I helped Mom figure out how much we should tip the waiter. 2. guess, think, believe, suppose, feel, reason, infer, consider, presume I figure I'll give my sister a new mystery novel for her birthday.

filch *verb* pilfer, steal, snatch, thieve, purloin, lift, swipe, rob I filched a cookie from the cookie jar.

file *noun* 1. record, documents, information, dossier, folder, portfolio, data Doctors keep medical files on all of their patients. 2. column, line, row, string, queue, rank, parade, chain I saw a long file of ants heading toward our picnic basket. ◆ *verb* 1. arrange, classify, organize, sort, order, assort, group, array Catalog cards are filed in alphabetical order. 2. enter, register, submit, record, document, apply, seek, claim He filed a claim with his insurance company. 3. march, parade, troop, walk, move, promenade, step, proceed During fire drills, we have to file out of the building in an orderly manner.

fill *verb* 1. load, pack, stock, jam, stuff, cram, crowd, heap, pile I filled my suitcase with clothes and books. 2. plug, close, seal, stop up, block, choke, congest The dentist filled my cavity. 3. occupy, function, perform, serve, execute, fulfill, answer, meet, satisfy Faisal volunteered to fill the office of student-council chair until someone could be elected. ➜ **Antonyms: 1.** empty, remove **2.** open

film *noun* 1. coating, layer, coat, sheet, veneer, scum, membrane, skin There was a film of ice on the windshield this morning. 2. movie, cinema, picture, moving picture, motion picture, show I enjoy foreign films most of all.

filter *noun* screen, strainer, sieve, purifier, cleaner, sifter Dad installed a filter to purify our drinking water. ◆ *verb* 1. clear, cleanse, purify, screen, strain, filtrate, refine, percolate When firefighters enter smoke-filled buildings, they wear masks to filter their air. 2. flow, ooze, seep, trickle, drain, dribble, drip, sift, escape Sunlight filtered through the leaves and branches.

filthy *adjective* 1. dirty, grimy, muddy, soiled, messy, unclean, stained, grubby My friends and I were filthy after we played football in the mud. 2. indecent, obscene, lewd, gross, smutty, pornographic, vulgar, nasty, foul Some people consider the photographs of Robert Mapplethorpe to be filthy; others consider them to be art. ➜ **Antonyms: 1.** clean, washed **2.** decent, pure, virtuous

final *adjective* **1. closing, concluding, ending, finishing, last, end, terminal, ultimate** I missed the final part of the movie because I fell asleep. **2. conclusive, decisive, definitive, definite, authoritative, irrevocable, determinate** Decisions made by referees or umpires are final. ◆ **Antonyms: 1. beginning, first 2. inconclusive**

finale *noun* **climax, close, conclusion, end, finish, finis, consummation** The concert's grand finale included stirring music and lots of fireworks. ◆ **Antonyms: beginning, opening**

finance *noun* **economics, business, investment, commerce, money, capital** My mother became interested in finance when she inherited some money. ◆ *verb* **capitalize, fund, subsidize, stake, back, endow, aid, sponsor** I pledged a contribution to help finance a community senior citizens' center.

find *verb* **1. come upon, chance on, detect, locate, spot, recover, retrieve** I found a beautiful conch shell at the beach. **2. determine, learn, perceive, see, ascertain, notice, discover, observe** Have you found the answer to my riddle yet? **3. gain, get, obtain, acquire, attain, earn, win, achieve** I finally found the courage to ask her for a date. ◆ *noun* **discovery, acquisition, catch, bonanza, windfall, serendipity** That rare baseball card was a real find. ◆ **Antonyms:** *verb* **1. lose, misplace**

fine[1] *adjective* **1. excellent, good, splendid, superb, superior, terrific, choice, first-class** It's a fine day for a picnic. **2. little, minute, small, tiny, diminutive, miniature, light, thin** I used a magnifying glass to read the fine print in my dictionary. **3. keen, sharp, acute, edged, honed, cutting, serrated** The carving knife had a fine edge. **4. refined, elegant, exquisite, polished, choice, delicate, refined** Her fine manners are an example to us all. **5. healthy, well, hale, hearty, vigorous, wholesome, fit, sound** I am feeling fine! ◆ *adverb* **excellently, nicely, splendidly, well, superbly, magnificently** She is getting along fine at summer camp. ◆ **Antonyms:** *adjective* **1. inferior, mediocre 2. large, thick 3. blunt, dull 4. crude, rough, rude 5. sick, weak** ◆ *adverb* **badly, poorly**

fine[2] *noun* **fee, penalty, settlement, damages, punishment, forfeit, reparation** I had to pay a fine for my overdue library books. ◆ *verb* **levy, tax, exact, extort, penalize, charge, punish** How much did the judge fine you?

finesse *noun* **skill, tact, diplomacy, delicacy, circumspection, discretion, subtlety, consideration** The teacher handled the delicate situation with finesse. ◆ *verb* **manipulate, maneuver, finagle, wangle, angle, operate, play,**

beguile The billiards player finessed the ball in one of the corner pockets. ◆ **Antonyms:** *noun* **clumsiness, stupidity, ineptitude**

finger *verb* **touch, handle, feel, caress, stroke, palpate, squeeze, thumb** I fingered the soft fur of my kitten.

finish *verb* **1. accomplish, complete, conclude, end, wind up, wrap up, finalize, achieve** I finished my chores in no time at all. **2. consume, exhaust, drain, expend, empty, use up, dispatch, devour** The drive to Springfield finished the gas in our tank. ◆ *noun* **1. close, completion, conclusion, end, ending, wind-up, finale, stop** I missed the start of the race, but I saw the finish. **2. surface, texture, veneer, coat, coating, exterior, polish, feel** My mother's antique desk has a beautiful hand-rubbed finish. ◆ **Antonyms:** *verb* **1. begin, start** ◆ *noun* **1. beginning, opening, start**

fire *noun* **1. blaze, conflagration, burning, combustion, flame, flare, glow, heat** We learned about forest fire prevention on our camping trip. **2. intensity, ardor, zeal, fervor, spirit, passion, energy, enthusiasm** We had a lot of fire at the beginning of the project. **3. gunfire, firing, shooting, shelling, bombing, bombardment** The soldiers were exposed to enemy fire. ◆ *verb* **1. ignite, kindle, light, spark, set afire, enkindle** Dad fired up our wood-burning stove. **2. shoot, discharge, fire off, detonate, blast, bombard, shell** We fire our guns at empty cans to practice target shooting. **3. arouse, animate, inspire, stimulate, rouse, galvanize, stir** Watching the Olympics fired my interest in ice skating. **4. discharge, dismiss, drop, let go, release, cashier, lay off, terminate** The man was fired because he was late to work too many times. ◆ **Antonyms:** *noun* **2. boredom, apathy** ◆ *verb* **1. douse, extinguish 3. dampen, quell, calm**

Word Group

A **firework** is an explosive device set off to create bright lights and loud noises for amusement. **Firework** is a general term with no true synonyms. Here are some specific types of fireworks:

A **firecracker** is a small explosive charge in a heavy paper casing, exploded to make noise. A **pinwheel** forms a rotating wheel of colored flames. A **Roman candle** is a cylindrical firework that emits balls of fire and a shower of sparks. A **serpent** writhes while burning. A **skyrocket** ascends high into the air, where it explodes in a brilliant cascade of flares and starlike sparks. A **torpedo** is small and explodes when thrown against a hard surface.

firm[1] *adjective* 1. hard, rigid, solid, stiff, compact, dense, unyielding, sturdy I like to sleep on a firm mattress. 2. certain, definite, steadfast, steady, unwavering, constant, resolute, staunch He is firm in his beliefs. 3. fast, secure, steady, strong, sure, tight, sound, stable Keep a firm grip on the rope.

firm[2] *noun* business, company, corporation, enterprise, establishment, concern, organization More than a dozen lawyers work for that law firm.

first *noun* outset, beginning, start, onset, inception, commencement, original The sky was overcast at first, but then the sun came out. ◆ *adjective* 1. earliest, initial, original, pioneer, prime, premier, previous, preceding, front Amelia Earhart was the first woman to fly across the Atlantic Ocean. 2. highest, main, chief, principal, preeminent, supreme, foremost, greatest My first priority is getting my homework handed in on time. ◆ *adverb* ahead, before, in front, initially, firstly, at first, originally Who wants to go first?

fiscal *adjective* financial, economic, monetary, pecuniary, budgetary, commercial The company accountant finished the monthly fiscal report.

fish *verb* angle, wheedle, finagle, solicit, ask for, hint, seek, look for I fished for an invitation to her party.

fit[1] *verb* 1. suit, befit, conform, accord, belong, correspond, match Your clothes fit the occasion perfectly. 2. equip, furnish, rig, outfit, provide, supply, fix, clothe We're having our living room fitted with new carpeting. ◆ *adjective* 1. appropriate, correct, proper, right, suitable, apt, fitting, becoming Alex is quite fit for his new position in the company. 2. hale, robust, healthy, sound, strong, well, hardy, toned, muscular I exercise regularly to stay fit. ● **Antonyms:** *adjective* 1. improper, unsuitable 2. sick, weak

fit[2] *noun* attack, spell, seizure, convulsion, spasm, paroxysm, frenzy, stroke I took some cough drops to control my coughing fit.

fitting *adjective* appropriate, fit, suitable, seemly, becoming, correct, proper, right It is fitting to show respect for our elders. ● **Antonyms:** inappropriate, improper

fix *verb* 1. anchor, install, secure, attach, moor, set, fasten, bind, cement The fence posts are fixed in concrete. 2. arrange, conclude, determine, establish, settle, specify, designate I fixed a time for my next dentist appointment.

3. mend, repair, correct, patch, remedy, renew, revamp, overhaul Mom fixed our toaster. ◆ *noun* jam, plight, predicament, difficulty, trouble, mess, quandary, corner I was in a fix when I couldn't find my homework.

fixture *noun* apparatus, appliance, equipment, fittings, installation, attachment We installed new lighting fixtures in our kitchen.

fizzle *verb* 1. fizz, bubble, gurgle, sizzle, sputter, hiss, pop, crackle Soda fizzles when you pour it into a glass. 2. fail, collapse, wane, fade, decline, fold, misfire, die Our cleanup campaign fizzled when everyone lost interest. ● **Antonym:** 2. succeed

flabbergast *verb* astound, astonish, confound, boggle, dumbfound, surprise, bewilder His lack of preparation for the voyage flabbergasted us all.

flag[1] *noun* banner, ensign, pennant, standard, colors, emblem, jack, streamer A pirate's flag usually has a white skull and crossbones on a black background. ◆ *verb* hail, signal, gesture, motion, wave, salute, beckon When we ran out of gas, we flagged a passing car for assistance.

flag[2] *verb* weaken, fade, decline, abate, languish, fail, wilt, deteriorate The runner's stamina began to flag toward the end of the race. ● **Antonyms:** recover, strengthen

flair *noun* talent, aptitude, knack, ability, instinct, gift, faculty, feel She has a flair for writing poetry.

flake *noun* chip, shaving, paring, fleck, scale, layer, leaf, wafer I usually have corn flakes for breakfast. ◆ *verb* peel, chip, scale, fall, strip, shed, slice Paint is flaking off the old house.

flamboyant *adjective* flashy, elaborate, ornate, vivid, loud, dazzling, showy, ostentatious The entertainer was famous for his flamboyant costumes. ● **Antonyms:** plain, dull

flame *noun* 1. blaze, flare, glow, fire, light, spark, gleam, flicker Moths are attracted to a candle's flame. 2. sweetheart, love, honey, heartthrob, darling, truelove, girlfriend, boyfriend She is his new flame. ◆ *verb* burn, blaze, combust, kindle, fire, flare, ignite, spark, light The charcoal flamed when I held a match to the lighter fluid.

flank *noun* side, hip, thigh, loin, ham, haunch, quarter The cattle were branded on their flanks. ◆ *verb* line, edge, border, fringe, skirt, surround, abut The boulevard was flanked by rows of palm trees.

flap *verb* flutter, wave, beat, fly, swing, slap, flitter, flop The flag was flapping in the wind.

flare *verb* erupt, blow, explode, burst, shoot, burn, blaze, flame Tempers flared during the argument.

flash *verb* 1. blaze, flame, flare, gleam, glimmer, shimmer, shine, spark Lightning flashed on the horizon. 2. dash, fly, hasten, hurry, race, rush, speed, streak, dart Race cars flashed by the grandstand. ◆ *noun* 1. blaze, burst, flare, gleam, glimmer, shimmer, twinkle, glow The fireworks exploded with colorful flashes and a lot of noise. 2. jiffy, instant, moment, second, wink, breath, trice I'll be back in a flash.

flashy *adjective* showy, flamboyant, gaudy, garish, cheap, chintzy, vulgar, tawdry The jewelry was flashy and poorly made. ➡ **Antonyms:** tasteful, plain

flat *adjective* 1. horizontal, level, even, smooth, flush, uniform, regular, straight He sanded the tabletop until it was perfectly flat. 2. bland, flavorless, tasteless, dull, vapid, insipid, weak, stale If the sauce tastes flat, add a little salt. 3. complete, absolute, unequivocal, positive, decisive, downright, utter The senator issued a flat denial of the charges made against him. 4. constant, firm, fixed, set, uniform, permanent, steady The restaurant charges a flat rate for delivery. ➡ **Antonyms:** 1. rough, uneven 2. tasty, flavorful 3. vague, ambiguous 4. changing, variable

flatter *verb* compliment, praise, charm, gratify, please, glorify, butter up, humor He definitely knows how to flatter people. ➡ **Antonyms:** insult, criticize

flattery *noun* praise, adulation, blarney, compliments, applause, acclaim, cajolery Do you really think that I sing as well as the soloist, or is that just flattery? ➡ **Antonyms:** criticism, slight

flavor *noun* 1. taste, relish, savor, tang, zest, flavoring, smack This salad dressing has great flavor. 2. quality, characteristic, essence, nature, property, spirit, aura Her books have the same flavor as those by Agatha Christie. ◆ *verb* season, spice, salt, infuse, tinge, color, instill, leaven, lace He flavors his chili with pepper and barbecue sauce.

flaw *noun* blemish, defect, fault, imperfection, shortcoming, deformity, scar, bug This suit is inexpensive because it has a flaw. ◆ *verb* blemish, mar, injure, tarnish, damage, harm, hurt, impair Her skating performance was flawed by a fall.

fleck *noun* speck, bit, dot, speckle, mite, jot, dash, spot, pinpoint, flake I have a fleck of dirt in my eye. ◆ *verb* sprinkle, speckle, spot, dust, dapple, bespeckle, pepper, freckle I flecked the top of the cake with powdered sugar.

flee *verb* depart, escape, leave, run away, get away, scamper, scoot, retreat, fly We watched the deer flee over the hill. ➡ **Antonyms:** remain, stay

fleet *adjective* fast, quick, rapid, speedy, swift, expeditious, spry, agile, nimble Pony-express riders were so fleet they traveled from Missouri to California in less than ten days. ➡ **Antonyms:** slow, plodding

fleeting *adjective* brief, momentary, transient, ephemeral, flitting, temporary, passing, short-lived I had a fleeting desire to take flying lessons. ➡ **Antonyms:** lasting, permanent

flexible *adjective* 1. bendable, pliable, elastic, springy, pliant, supple, ductile, malleable My fishing pole is made of flexible plastic. 2. adaptable, adjustable, changeable, variable, versatile, manageable She has flexible working hours. ➡ **Antonyms:** 1. rigid, stiff 2. fixed, set

flicker *verb* blink, flash, twinkle, wink, glimmer, shimmer, glisten, gleam Hundreds of lightning bugs flickered in the darkness. ◆ *noun* flash, flare, blink, glimmer, spark, twinkle, wink, ray There was a flicker of lightning in the stormy sky.

flight[1] *noun* 1. flying, gliding, soaring, winging, aviation Ostriches, emus, and a few other birds are incapable of flight. 2. formation, squadron, wing, flock, swarm, group, migration We watched in awe as a flight of jets passed overhead.

flight[2] *noun* escape, break, breakout, getaway, bolt, exit, departure, release Moses led the Israelites during their flight from Egypt.

flimsy *adjective* 1. fragile, frail, thin, weak, feeble, delicate, insubstantial Tissue paper is too flimsy for making paper airplanes. 2. unbelievable, unconvincing, implausible, improbable, feeble, poor, inadequate I made up a flimsy excuse. ➡ **Antonyms:** 1. strong, sturdy 2. convincing, believable

flinch *verb* start, cringe, draw back, shrink, blanch, recoil, cower, wince I flinched when the nurse stuck a needle in my arm.

fling *verb* heave, hurl, pitch, throw, toss, cast, sling, chuck The angry toddler flung his toy across the room. ◆ *noun*

1. cast, heave, pitch, throw, toss, lob, shot, chuck, serve In our game of horseshoes, Grandpa got a ringer on his first fling. **2. spree, binge, splurge, rampage, party, lark, revel** We decided we needed a fling after working so hard. **3. try, crack, stab, go, whirl, attempt, effort, gamble** I gave snowboarding a fling last winter.

flip *verb* **turn, turn over, flick, toss, throw, fling, pitch, cast** We flipped a coin to decide who should go first.

flippant *adjective* **irreverent, impertinent, impudent, cheeky, sassy, disrespectful, rude** I laughed at his flippant remark.

flirt *verb* **tease, banter, dally, tantalize, toy, trifle, play, beguile** Those two like to flirt with one another, but they are just friends.

float *verb* **drift, glide, sail, skim, ride, wash, waft, swim** The model boat floated all the way across the pond. ➡ **Antonym: sink**

flock *noun* **herd, group, pack, swarm, throng, mass, drove, brood** A shepherd watches over a flock of sheep. ◆ *verb* **collect, crowd, gather, press, swarm, throng, congregate, assemble** The young campers flocked around their counselor.

flog *verb* **whip, lash, beat, thrash, paddle, strike, spank, cane** It was common to flog a criminal in earlier times.

flood *noun* **deluge, inundation, overflow, stream, tide, torrent, downpour, cascade** A flood of light filled the room. ◆ *verb* **inundate, deluge, overflow, drown, submerge, immerse, engulf** Spring rains flooded the low-lying farmland.

floor *noun* **1. bed, bottom, ground, base, flooring, foundation, footing, seat** Stalagmites are mineral deposits that form on cave floors. **2. level, story, deck, tier, flat, flight, stage, mezzanine** The gym is on the first floor of our school building. ◆ *verb* **1. drop, fell, flatten, knock down, level, beat, ground, prostrate** The boxer floored his opponent with a single punch. **2. stun, stagger, boggle, dumbfound, overwhelm, perplex, confuse, baffle** I am floored by your news.

flop *verb* **tumble, drop, plop, plunk, plump, sag, slouch, wilt** I flopped on my bed after my tiring day at school. ◆ *noun* **failure, bomb, dud, fiasco, disaster, debacle, bust, washout, fizzle** We agreed with the critics that the movie was a flop. ➡ **Antonyms:** *noun* **success, hit, smash**

flotsam *noun* **wreckage, debris, cargo, trash, scraps, junk** The survivors clung to bits of flotsam after their boat sank.

flounder *verb* **struggle, stumble, blunder, wallow, thrash, shuffle, stagger, lurch** We floundered through the ocean surf.

flourish *verb* **1. burgeon, bloom, blossom, grow, thrive, increase, prosper, wax** The roses flourished after I fertilized them. **2. wave, brandish, display, swing, sweep, flutter, wield, exhibit** My sister flourished her diploma with pride. ◆ *noun* **embellishment, adornment, ornamentation, decoration, garnish, display** She signed her name with a flourish.

flout *verb* **scorn, spurn, disregard, taunt, ridicule, defy, break, disobey** It is not wise to flout school regulations.

flow *verb* **1. discharge, empty, issue, pour, gush, run, stream, surge** The Mississippi River flows into the Gulf of Mexico. **2. hang, drape, fall, swing, dangle, droop, roll, glide** Her gown flowed gracefully from shoulder to ankle. ◆ *noun* **current, stream, tide, flood, rush, surge, sweep, wave** There was a steady flow of traffic on the busy highway.

flower *noun* **bloom, blossom, bud, floret, posy, cluster** I received a bouquet of flowers last Valentine's Day. ◆ *verb* **bloom, blossom, bud, flourish, thrive, ripen, mature, peak, sprout** Cherry trees flower in the springtime.

fluctuate *verb* **oscillate, change, vary, waver, undulate, wobble, flicker, flutter** The temperature can fluctuate rapidly at this time of year. ➡ **Antonyms: stabilize, settle**

fluent *adjective* **articulate, eloquent, glib, loquacious, talkative, vocal, expressive** He is fluent in two languages.

fluid *noun* **liquid, drink, broth, juice, solution, water, beverage** I drank a lot of fluids when I was sick. ◆ *adjective* **1. liquid, flowing, runny, watery, moist, wet, running, liquefied** Freshly mixed concrete is fluid. **2. changeable, flexible, indefinite, adaptable, unsettled, variable, uncertain** Our vacations plans are fluid. ➡ **Antonyms:** *adjective* **1. solid, dry 2. settled, fixed, set**

flush *verb* **1. blush, color, glow, redden, crimson, flame, burn** He flushed when I told him how nice he looked. **2. rinse, wash, hose, drown, flood, drench, deluge, clean** I used a garden hose to flush out the rain gutters. ◆ *noun* **blush, color, glow, redness, rosiness, pink, ruddiness, bloom** Her face had a healthy flush after basketball practice. ◆ *adjective* **1. overflowing, full, replete, plentiful,**

abundant, rich, lavish, copious The wedding reception was flush with refreshments. **2. even, level, flat, smooth, straight, true, square** The carpenter fitted the door so it was flush with the jamb.

fly *verb* **1. take flight, glide, sail, soar, wing, flap, flitter, flutter, swoop** Pterodactyls were reptiles that could fly. **2. bolt, dash, hasten, hurry, run, rush, zoom, shoot** My cat flew to the kitchen when he heard me opening his can of food.

foam *noun* **froth, suds, lather, bubbles, spume, fizz, spray, head** I waited for the foam on the soda to disappear. ◆ *verb* **bubble, froth, fizz, lather, effervesce, spume, boil, ferment** The bubble bath foamed in the tub.

focus *noun* **center, core, heart, hub, seat, locus, target, spotlight, point** She was the focus of attention at her graduation party. ◆ *verb* **center, concentrate, devote, direct, fix, give, aim, apply, turn** He focused his attention on the computer screen.

foe *noun* **adversary, antagonist, enemy, opponent, rival, competitor, nemesis** The two members of Parliament were political foes. ◆ **Antonyms: ally, friend**

fog *noun* **1. haze, mist, cloud, vapor, whiteout, veil, smog, murk** We did not set sail until the fog lifted. **2. daze, stupor, trance, confusion, disorientation, bewilderment, muddle** I was in a fog when I first woke up. ◆ *verb* **1. blur, cloud, mist, blanket, blear, obscure, becloud, bedim** Steam from the kettle fogged our kitchen windows. **2. daze, muddle, confuse, perplex, bewilder, blind, addle, stupefy** A lack of communication fogged the issue.

foggy *adjective* **1. cloudy, hazy, misty, murky, dim, bleary, smoggy, dark** The airport had to be closed because the day was so foggy. **2. vague, dim, fuzzy, indistinct, unclear, confused, uncertain, hazy** I have only a foggy recollection of my dream. ◆ **Antonyms: 1. clear, sunny, bright 2. accurate, lucid**

foil[1] *verb* **check, defeat, frustrate, hinder, thwart, stymie, outwit, prevent** The security guard foiled our attempt to slip in the back door of the theater. ◆ **Antonyms: aid, support**

foil[2] *noun* **balance, complement, antithesis, counterpart, contrast** This dark vase is a good foil for these bright flowers.

fold *verb* **1. crease, pleat, bend, double over, furrow, ply, plait, wrinkle** I folded the note and put it into my pocket.

2. enfold, envelop, clasp, hug, gather, tuck, embrace, wrap My grandfather folded me in his arms for a big hug. **3. fail, close, go under, collapse, bust, crash, break, succumb, capitulate** The company folded after only six months in operation. ◆ *noun* **crease, pleat, wrinkle, furrow, crimp, crinkle, rumple, pucker, ridge** I ironed the folds out of my shirt. ◆ **Antonyms:** *verb* **1. open, unfold, flatten 3. continue, flourish**

folklore *noun* **legend, lore, fable, story, myth, mythology, tradition, custom** I am very interested in Chinese folklore.

follow *verb* **1. come after, go after, succeed, replace, supercede, supplant, displace** February follows January. **2. trail, track, dog, shadow, stalk, hunt, pursue, hound** The detective followed the suspect. **3. abide by, heed, obey, observe, mind, attend, comply, conform** Everyone followed the rules during our softball game. **4. catch, get, comprehend, grasp, understand, see, perceive, fathom** I wasn't able to follow what you were saying. ◆ **Antonyms: 1. lead, precede 3. disobey, ignore 4. misunderstand**

following *adjective* **next, subsequent, coming, succeeding, ensuing** We arrived in Paris and visited the Eiffel Tower on the following day. ◆ *noun* **audience, public, fans, followers, entourage, patrons, supporters** That popular radio psychologist has a large following. ◆ **Antonym:** *adjective* **preceding**

folly *noun* **foolishness, nonsense, silliness, lunacy, imprudence, stupidity, craziness, madness** It was folly to come out in this weather without a coat. ◆ **Antonyms: wisdom, prudence, sanity**

fond *adjective* **affectionate, loving, warm, devoted, close, adoring** Jake gave a fond greeting to his old friend. ◆ **Antonyms: cool, distant**

food *noun* **edibles, victuals, fare, foodstuff, nourishment, provisions, rations, sustenance** Grandmother served us more food than we could possibly eat.

fool *noun* **dummy, idiot, moron, simpleton, imbecile, nincompoop, blockhead, nitwit** A fool and his money are soon parted. ◆ *verb* **1. trick, bluff, deceive, mislead, dupe, delude, con, gull, hoax** My friend fooled me into thinking that today was our big test. **2. jest, joke, tease, pretend, feign, kid, play** I was only fooling when I said that I hate ice cream. **3. fiddle, mess, monkey, toy, trifle, tinker, meddle, tamper** Please don't fool with the TV controls.

foolhardy *adjective* **bold, rash, reckless, impetuous, daring, heedless, ill-considered** It was foolhardy of him to go swimming so soon after eating. ● **Antonyms: cautious, wise, circumspect**

foolish *adjective* **dumb, silly, stupid, crazy, senseless, unwise, idiotic, harebrained** I felt foolish when I realized I had my shirt on inside-out. ● **Antonyms: sensible, wise, intelligent**

foot *noun* **base, bottom, foundation, pedestal, floor, footing, heel, ground** There's a lake near the foot of the mountain. ● **Antonyms: head, top**

forage *verb* **search, scrounge, hunt, comb, rummage, scour, ransack** The hungry animals foraged for food.

forbear *verb* **refrain, resist, abstain, hold off, withhold, eschew, shun, forgo, avoid** Please forbear from rushing to open your Christmas presents.

forbearance *noun* **patience, tolerance, restraint, understanding, self-control, resignation** It takes great forbearance to be a good parent. ● **Antonyms: intolerance, impatience**

forbid *verb* **ban, bar, disallow, prevent, prohibit, proscribe, stop, outlaw** The rules forbid swimming unless a lifeguard is present. ● **Antonyms: allow, permit**

force *noun* **1. energy, might, power, strength, vigor, potency, pressure, violence** The wind blew with so much force that it knocked down our power lines. **2. corps, body, crew, gang, group, team, unit, army** A force of at least 100 volunteers helped search for the lost child. ◆ *verb* **1. coerce, compel, make, obligate, oblige, require, necessitate, demand** Bad weather forced us to cancel soccer practice. **2. pry, drive, press, push, thrust, burst, wrench, break, blast** The window was stuck tight, and I had to force it open. ● **Antonyms: *noun* 1. weakness, feebleness**

forceful *adjective* **dynamic, effective, powerful, strong, vigorous, potent, mighty, compelling** The governor drew large crowds because she was such a forceful speaker. ● **Antonyms: weak, powerless**

fore *adjective* **front, foremost, first, forward, anterior, former** The fore part of a ship is known as its bow. ● **Antonyms: last, posterior, rear**

foreboding *noun* **anxiety, dread, fear, apprehension, premonition, omen, misgiving** My feelings of foreboding about the trip were justified.

forecast *verb* **call for, foretell, predict, project, prophesy, foresee, anticipate, envisage** The weather bureau is forecasting freezing rain for tomorrow. ◆ *noun* **outlook, projection, prediction, prophecy, prognosis, divination, anticipation** The economic forecast is for lower prices and higher wages.

foreign *adjective* **1. alien, exotic, distant, faraway, remote, unfamiliar, strange** He is from a foreign land. **2. extraneous, aberrant, odd, abnormal, uncharacteristic, unusual, unnatural** The test was invalid because there was foreign material in the sample. ● **Antonyms: 1. native, indigenous 2. characteristic, typical**

foreigner *noun* **alien, outsider, stranger, newcomer, immigrant, émigré** I felt like a foreigner when I moved to the big city. ● **Antonyms: native, citizen**

foresight *noun* **forethought, farsightedness, discretion, prudence, caution, anticipation, good sense** I had the foresight to bring extra money with me. ● **Antonyms: hindsight, retrospect**

forest *noun* **timber, timberland, woods, woodland, grove, thicket, copse** Forests provide food and shelter for many animals.

foretell *verb* **forecast, foresee, predict, project, tell, augur, divine, prophesy** Do you believe that some people can foretell the future?

forever *adverb* **always, eternally, perpetually, constantly, continuously, evermore, endlessly** I wish summer vacation would last forever. ● **Antonym: temporarily**

forfeit *verb* **drop, lose, sacrifice, surrender, yield, pay, renounce, waive** The customer had to forfeit his deposit when he canceled his order. ● **Antonyms: keep, retain**

forge[1] *verb* **1. create, fashion, form, make, mold, shape, design, produce** He forged a unique chair out of horseshoes. **2. copy, counterfeit, fake, falsify, feign, duplicate, imitate** The expert discovered that the painting had been forged.

forge[2] *verb* **drive, plunge, slog, plod, advance, progress, push, lunge** The pioneers forged on despite many hardships.

forgery *noun* **fake, imitation, counterfeit, phony, sham, copy, fraud, hoax** The 20-dollar bill was an obvious forgery.

forget *verb* **fail to remember, disregard, neglect, overlook, ignore** Don't forget to bring your membership card when you go to the museum. → **Antonyms: recollect, remember**

forgive *verb* **excuse, pardon, condone, acquit, clear, exonerate, absolve** Please forgive me for interrupting you. → **Antonyms: blame, condemn**

forgo *verb* **do without, give up, surrender, relinquish, sacrifice, waive, yield** I hate to forgo pizza on Friday nights. → **Antonyms: keep, retain**

fork *noun* **branch, arm, leg, offshoot, division, tributary, extension, section** When the trail branched, we took the left-hand fork. ◆ *verb* **divide, split, part, branch, diverge, angle, branch off** The river forks here.

forlorn *adjective* **lonely, lonesome, despondent, abandoned, deserted, forsaken, pitiful, desolate** I could not resist taking the forlorn puppy home with me.

form *noun* **1. design, figure, outline, pattern, shape, appearance, cast, configuration** I made a cake in the form of a snowman. **2. kind, sort, style, type, variety, system, way, mode** Television is a popular form of entertainment. **3. document, paper, application, questionnaire, sheet, chart** The catalog came with a form for placing orders. **4. behavior, etiquette, conduct, decorum, formality, rule, custom, ceremony** After a game, it is good form to shake hands with members of the opposing team. ◆ *verb* **1. create, fashion, make, shape, produce, carve, configure, delineate** The city council voted to form a new school district. **2. appear, develop, grow, materialize, emerge, arise, show up, acquire** Mold has formed on this old loaf of bread.

formal *adjective* **1. official, proper, conventional, regular, established, orthodox, systematic** My grandfather did not have a formal education. **2. ceremonious, ceremonial, ritual, ritualistic, solemn, stiff, grand** The Japanese tea ceremony is a formal occasion. → **Antonyms: 1. irregular, unconventional 2. informal**

formation *noun* **1. development, creation, evolution, genesis, establishment, generation, production** We were involved in the formation of the school's literary magazine. **2. arrangement, design, configuration, layout, pattern, order, figure, structure** I saw a cloud formation that looked like a horse.

former *adjective* **previous, prior, earlier, past, preceding, late, old, bygone** Our former teacher was promoted to principal. → **Antonym: current**

formidable *adjective* **1. fearful, frightful, terrifying, horrible, dreadful, terrible, awful, intimidating** Goliath was a formidable opponent. **2. difficult, rough, tough, overwhelming, onerous, strenuous, arduous, challenging** Reading *War and Peace* was a formidable challenge. → **Antonyms: 2. easy, simple**

formula *noun* **method, plan, system, rule, recipe, equation, principle, outline** Do you know what the formula is for making toothpaste?

forsake *verb* **abandon, desert, disown, leave, quit, forswear, renounce, spurn, reject** I love my country, and I will never forsake it.

fort *noun* **fortification, fortress, stockade, stronghold, blockhouse, citadel, garrison, keep** In the Old West, forts were usually made of logs.

forth *adverb* **forward, on, onward, out, outward, ahead, first, along, away** The cavalry soldiers rode forth to meet the enemy.

forthright *adjective* **direct, straightforward, honest, open, candid, plain, sincere** He gave a forthright answer to my very direct question. → **Antonyms: devious, misleading**

fortify *verb* **1. barricade, wall, fence, entrench, guard, defend, man, arm** It was once common to fortify a village by building a wall around it. **2. brace, gird, steel, strengthen, ready, prepare, energize, boost** I fortified myself with a good breakfast. → **Antonyms: 2. weaken, sap**

fortitude *noun* **courage, mettle, pluck, spirit, grit, spunk, heart, bravery** She suffered the painful medical tests with great fortitude. → **Antonyms: cowardice, timidity**

fortress *noun* **fort, citadel, stronghold, bastion, fortification, rampart, blockhouse** The typical fortress had massive stone walls.

fortunate *adjective* **blessed, favored, lucky, happy, charmed, good** I feel very fortunate that my best friend lives next door. → **Antonyms: unfortunate, unlucky**

fortune *noun* **1. treasure, riches, wealth, property, resources, capital, estate** He made a fortune on some shrewd real estate transactions. **2. chance, destiny, fate, luck, lot, providence, karma** Fortune was with us when we found a parking space.

forward *adjective* **1. fore, front, advance, head, leading, foremost** Our seats are in the plane's forward cabin. **2.**

presumptuous, bold, brash, impertinent, impudent, rude, audacious It was forward of them to crowd into line ahead of us. ♦ *adverb* forth, ahead, before, onward, outward, out, along, fore Please step forward when your name is called. ♦ *verb* 1. deliver, dispatch, send, ship, transmit, route, freight, post Mom asked the principal to forward my records to my new school. 2. promote, advance, further, champion, assist, spread, hasten The actor appeared on TV to forward his favorite cause. ➡ **Antonyms:** *adjective* 1. back, rear 2. timid, shy ♦ *adverb* backward ♦ *verb* 2. hinder, impede, block

foster *verb* 1. nurture, tend, nourish, mother, raise, nurse, rear The hen fostered the baby ducks as well as her own chicks. 2. promote, support, advance, further, champion, encourage, back, uphold Good teachers foster a love for learning in their students. ➡ **Antonyms:** 2. hamper, frustrate

foul *adjective* 1. disgusting, nasty, offensive, repulsive, revolting, putrid, rank, rotten, vile Spoiled milk has a foul odor. 2. vulgar, offensive, indecent, lewd, profane, filthy, raunchy, coarse Our school has a rule against the use of foul language. 3. inclement, unfavorable, bad, blustery, rainy, stormy, tempestuous, wet We had to reschedule our trip to the beach because of foul weather. ♦ *verb* contaminate, pollute, dirty, soil, taint, befoul, sully, tarnish, stain Automobile emissions foul the air. ➡ **Antonyms:** *adjective* 1. pure, sweet 2. decent, polite 3. clear, fair ♦ *verb* clean, purify

found *verb* create, establish, institute, originate, start, set up, inaugurate, begin My friends and I decided to found a computer club.

foundation *noun* 1. basis, rudiments, root, basics, base, groundwork, cornerstone Reading, writing, and arithmetic are the traditional foundations of a good education. 2. base, bottom, bed, foot, footing, support, underpinning, framework The foundation of our house is made of concrete blocks. 3. charity, endowment, institute, society, association, trusteeship, establishment I sent a contribution to the Foundation for Public Broadcasting.

fountain *noun* 1. fount, spout, geyser, spring, stream, well, spray I took a drink from the water fountain. 2. origin, source, beginning, wellspring, root, fountainhead, birthplace Schools are often called fountains of knowledge.

fraction *noun* part, piece, portion, section, share, bit, fragment, division Only a small fraction of the class was unable to go on the field trip. ➡ **Antonyms:** whole, entirety, totality

fracture *noun* break, crack, rupture, separation, split, fissure, breach, rent, rift Our first-aid instructor showed us how to splint a fracture. ♦ *verb* break, crack, shatter, split, splinter, chip, fragment, fissure, burst The bone had fractured in two places.

fragile *adjective* breakable, brittle, delicate, feeble, frail, weak, flimsy Fragile items should be packed carefully for mailing. ➡ **Antonyms:** strong, sturdy

fragment *noun* bit, chip, part, piece, scrap, portion, shred, sliver The archaeologist found a fragment of ancient pottery. ♦ *verb* break, split, divide, splinter, smash, crumble, disintegrate, burst The top of the mountain was fragmented by the volcano's eruption. ➡ **Antonyms:** *noun* whole, total ♦ *verb* unite, combine, merge

fragrance *noun* scent, smell, odor, aroma, perfume, sweetness, bouquet I enjoy the fragrance of carnations and chrysanthemums. ➡ **Antonyms:** stench, stink

frail *adjective* 1. feeble, infirm, sickly, weak, delicate, puny, slight, unsound Teddy Roosevelt, the 26th President of the United States, was frail as a child. 2. delicate, brittle, flimsy, fragile, dainty, crumbly, crisp, insubstantial Flowers that have been dried and pressed are very frail. ➡ **Antonyms:** 1. healthy, robust 2. strong, sturdy

frame *verb* 1. draft, draw up, fashion, shape, fabricate, devise, build, construct Thomas Jefferson framed most of the Declaration of Independence. 2. mount, border, enclose, hem, rim, fringe, set off I framed my eighth-grade diploma. ♦ *noun* 1. framework, framing, shell, mount, mounting, skeleton, structure, body My new bicycle has a steel frame. 2. body, build, form, physique, anatomy, figure, construction He has a small, wiry frame.

frank *adjective* straightforward, honest, candid, aboveboard, direct, blunt, open, plainspoken She gave me a frank answer to my question. ➡ **Antonyms:** guarded, ambiguous, sly

frantic *adjective* desperate, frenzied, agitated, distressed, excited, wild, distraught, panicky The robin became frantic when it saw a hawk circling over its nest. ➡ **Antonyms:** calm, composed

fraud *noun* 1. deceit, deception, trickery, swindle, swindling, fraudulence, duplicity Advertisers who make false claims about their products are guilty of fraud. 2. fake, impostor, phony, pretender, swindler, charlatan, crook,

rogue, liar The character in *The Adventures of Huckleberry Finn* who claims to be a king is a fraud. ● **Antonyms: 1. integrity, honesty**

fray[1] *noun* **scuffle, brawl, fracas, skirmish, fight, melee, rumble, commotion** The fans of the rival teams got into a fray after the game.

fray[2] *verb* **shred, unravel, tear, frazzle, disintegrate, tatter, rip, wear** The cuffs on my shirt are beginning to fray.

freak *noun* **rarity, anomaly, abnormality, aberration, irregularity, curiosity, oddity, mutation** Chinook winds are freaks of nature, bringing extremely warm weather in the middle of winter.

free *adjective* **1. independent, liberated, unconfined, unrestrained, self-governing, autonomous** The judge told the prisoner that he was now a free man. **2. complimentary, costless, gratis, gratuitous** If you rent two movies, the third one is free. **3. clear, empty, void, rid, devoid, unoccupied, open, vacant** We went swimming in an area that was free of boats. **4. liberal, lavish, generous, handsome, big, bounteous, unstinting** They are free with their hospitality during the holiday season. ◆ *verb* **1. let go, liberate, release, set free, emancipate, parole, deliver,** We freed the snake that got caught in our garden netting. **2. relieve, excuse, exempt, discharge, spare, let off, clear, unload** I was freed from doing any more chores for the day.

freedom *noun* **1. independence, liberty, emancipation, exemption, immunity, autonomy, sovereignty** Harry S. Truman said that the Bill of Rights guarantees freedom to every American. **2. frankness, openness, license, spontaneity, ease, informality, boldness, brazenness** People often write in journals or diaries in order to express themselves with freedom. ● **Antonyms: 1. slavery, bondage 2. restraint, caution**

freeze *verb* **1. ice over, ice up, chill, frost, nip, harden, congeal, solidify** The river freezes in winter. **2. halt, stand still, stop, stay, hold up, arrest, check, suspend** The deer froze when it saw the car's headlights. ● **Antonyms: 1. thaw, warm 2. move**

freight *noun* **goods, cargo, merchandise, wares, shipment, load, pack, burden, haul** The variety of freight coming through the port was astounding. ◆ *verb* **load, lade, encumber, burden, saddle, tax, weigh down, hamper** The plane was so heavily freighted that it barely cleared the runway. ● **Antonyms:** *verb* **remove, unload**

frenzy *noun* **furor, turmoil, agitation, excitement, fury, rage, passion, fever, craze** I was in a frenzy trying to finish my project on time.

frequent *adjective* **constant, numerous, repeated, regular, routine, usual, habitual, continual** I made frequent trips to the library to do research for my report. ◆ *verb* **haunt, hang around, return to, visit, dwell, occupy, stay** My brother frequents the coffeehouse near his college. ● **Antonyms:** *adjective* **infrequent, rare**

frequently *adverb* **commonly, repeatedly, regularly, often, customarily, habitually, usually** I frequently go swimming on the weekend. ● **Antonyms: rarely, infrequently**

fresh *adjective* **1. novel, original, innovative, inventive, unfamiliar, current, new, recent** The magazine editor was known for her fresh ideas. **2. another, new, different, additional, added, further, other, extra** Our house needs a fresh coat of paint. **3. clean, pure, immaculate, healthy, invigorating, refreshing, bracing, vital** I opened a window to let fresh air into the room. **4. bold, impertinent, sassy, brazen, flippant, presumptuous, insolent** Don't talk in that fresh way to me! ● **Antonyms: 1. old, stale 2. original, old 3. impure, polluted 4. polite, civil**

fret *verb* **vex, worry, disturb, agitate, irritate, annoy, bother, irk** I fret over the idea of getting a bad grade. ● **Antonyms: soothe, calm**

friction *noun* **1. abrasion, grinding, rubbing, scraping, resistance** If your shoe rubs against your foot, the friction can produce a blister. **2. antagonism, conflict, disagreement, discord, tension, animosity, dispute, hostility** The dispute over property lines caused friction between the two neighbors. ● **Antonym: 2. cooperation**

friend *noun* **chum, buddy, companion, comrade, pal, acquaintance, confidant, mate** She and I have been best friends for years. ● **Antonyms: enemy, foe, adversary**

friendship *noun* **companionship, comradeship, fellowship, intimacy, attachment, amity, love** Your friendship is important to me.

fright *noun* **alarm, apprehension, dread, fear, panic, terror, shock, horror** The loud crash outside our door filled me with fright.

frighten *verb* **alarm, intimidate, scare, terrify, startle, shock, petrify, unnerve, spook** Flying in an airplane frightens me. ● **Antonyms: soothe, calm, reassure**

frigid *adjective* **1. chill, cold, freezing, icy, polar, wintry, bitter, frosty** A frigid wind blew over the Arctic tundra. **2. aloof, formal, stiff, distant, cool, chilly, unfriendly, reserved** Her voice grew frigid when she realized the caller was a telephone solicitor. ⇒ **Antonyms: 1. hot, warm 2. cordial, friendly**

fringe *noun* **1. outskirts, periphery, border, edge, rim, margin, boundary, brink** The people on the fringes of the crowd couldn't hear the speaker. **2. trimming, edging, ruffle, flounce, tassel, rickrack, ruff** I bought lace to use as a fringe on my bedroom curtains. ⇒ **Antonyms: 1. center, middle**

frolic *noun* **merriment, gaiety, romp, picnic, party, jamboree, fete, spree** My brother says there's more to college life than fun and frolic. ◆ *verb* **play, romp, prance, cavort, frisk, leap, sport, caper, gambol** The kittens often frolic with each other.

front *noun* **1. beginning, head, lead, start, fore, forepart, vanguard, point, bow** Locomotives are usually at the front of a train. **2. appearance, behavior, deportment, manner, bearing, persona, air, show** He kept up a confident front despite his insecurities. ◆ *adjective* **beginning, first, initial, fore, foremost, lead, leading, head, frontal** I like to sit in the front row of the classroom. ◆ *verb* **face, look on, look upon, overlook, border** Our house fronts a pond. ⇒ **Antonyms: noun 1. back, rear 2. essence, nature** ◆ *adjective* **last, back**

frontier *noun* **1. border, borderland, borderline, boundary, march, limit, edge** The frontier between the United States and Canada is not fortified. **2. backwoods, hinterland, outpost, bush, outback, outskirts, backwater** My ancestors helped to settle a town on the Arizona frontier.

frosting *noun* **icing, topping, glaze, meringue, whipped cream** I think the best part of a cupcake is the frosting.

frosty *adjective* **1. icy, frigid, wintry, gelid, freezing, hoary, nippy, frozen** It was very frosty last night. **2. unfriendly, aloof, distant, formal, icy, imperious, cold-hearted, chilly** His manner grew frosty after I asked to borrow money from him. ⇒ **Antonyms: 1. warm, balmy 2. friendly, informal**

frown *verb* **1. scowl, grimace, glower, sulk, lower, pout** I frowned at the clock when I saw the time. **2. object, disapprove, discourage, censor, restrict, disfavor, deprecate** My parents frown on my sister's or my arriving home late. ◆ *noun* **scowl, grimace, glower, black look,**

pout, glare, lower The clown painted a frown on his face. ⇒ **Antonyms: verb 1. smile 2. approve, encourage, favor**

frugal *adjective* **thrifty, saving, stingy, prudent, tight, economical, sparing** The city government encourages us to be frugal in using water. ⇒ **Antonyms: extravagant, liberal**

> ### Word Group
> A **fruit** is the ripened part of a flowering plant that contains the seeds. **Fruit** is a general term with no true synonyms. Common **fruits** include apples, bananas, berries, grapes, melons, oranges, peaches, and pears. Here are some other common foods that you may not have realized were also fruits:
>
> **avocado, bell pepper, cucumber, eggplant, olive, pumpkin, squash, tomato, zucchini**

fruitful *adjective* **beneficial, rewarding, valuable, gratifying, profitable, productive** The typing class I took this summer has proven to be very fruitful. ⇒ **Antonyms: fruitless, useless**

frustrate *verb* **1. cancel, defeat, foil, prevent, thwart, stymie, impede, hamper, check** The falling snow frustrated my efforts to keep the driveway clear. **2. discourage, disappoint, upset, baffle, depress, dispirit, fluster** My inability to advance to a higher level is beginning to frustrate me. ⇒ **Antonyms: 1. foster, forward, promote 2. encourage, cheer**

fuel *noun* **encouragement, nourishment, incitement, food, provocation, propellant** I used my teacher's praise as fuel to keep working hard in the class. ◆ *verb* **fire, energize, stoke, ignite, kindle, activate, incite, stimulate** Our coach's pep talk fueled our determination to do well in the game. ⇒ **Antonyms: noun damper, hindrance** ◆ *verb* **dampen, extinguish, starve**

fugitive *noun* **escapee, runaway, outlaw, criminal, refugee, outcast, deserter** Police finally caught the fugitive who had escaped from prison.

fulfill *verb* **1. accomplish, achieve, realize, attain, finish, effect, carry out** My aunt has fulfilled her dream of owning her own bookstore. **2. answer, fill, finish, meet, satisfy, perform, observe, discharge** I have fulfilled all of the requirements to get my next Scouting badge.

fulfillment *noun* **satisfaction, achievement, culmination, realization, completion, consummation** I had a sense of fulfillment when I made the honor roll.

full *adjective* **1. filled, loaded, packed, stuffed, jammed, crowded, brimful, replete** I couldn't find a seat because the bus was full. **2. complete, comprehensive, entire, thorough, whole, perfect, intact** You need a full deck of cards to play gin rummy. ◆ *adverb* **completely, entirely, wholly, thoroughly, totally, perfectly, absolutely** The ship turned full about. ➡ **Antonyms:** *adjective* **1. empty, void 2. incomplete, partial** ◆ *adverb* **partially**

fumble *verb* **blunder, grope, feel, flounder, stumble, muddle, bungle** I fumbled around in the dark to find a flashlight.

fume *noun* **gas, vapor, smoke, smog, exhaust, pollution, odor** I can smell the fumes from the gasoline. ◆ *verb* **rant, rage, seethe, boil, chafe, bristle, flare up, storm** My father fumed when he could not get a refund on his unused airplane ticket.

fun *noun* **amusement, enjoyment, entertainment, pleasure, mirth, romping, merriment** Did you have fun at the party? ➡ **Antonyms: boredom, tedium**

function *noun* **1. duty, role, job, task, business, purpose, operation, office** One function of a judge is to preside over trials. **2. affair, ceremony, meeting, ritual, celebration, occasion, gala, fete, reception** The President has to attend many political functions. ◆ *verb* **act, perform, serve, work, operate, run, behave, do, move** My knife can also function as a screwdriver.

fund *noun* **account, holding, reserve, stock, supply, store, reservoir, trust** My mother makes monthly contributions to her retirement fund. ◆ *verb* **back, subsidize, finance, capitalize, stake, support, endow, bankroll** We are looking for someone to fund our project.

fundamental *adjective* **basic, essential, key, major, primary, necessary, indispensable, vital** Addition is a fundamental part of mathematics. ◆ *noun* **basic, essential, foundation, principle, rule, rudiments, element** I learned the fundamentals of making jam from a cookbook. ➡ **Antonyms:** *adjective* **minor, superficial**

funnel *verb* **channel, pass, conduct, convey, siphon, sift, filter, pipe** I funneled water from a large container into a smaller one.

funny *adjective* **1. amusing, comical, hilarious, humorous, laughable, droll, absurd, witty** She told us a funny story. **2. curious, odd, peculiar, strange, unusual, weird, bizarre, mysterious** There is a funny smell coming from the refrigerator. ➡ **Antonyms: 1. humorless 2. normal, usual**

furious *adjective* **1. angry, enraged, irate, mad, wrathful, rabid, fuming, incensed** The furious bear stood on its hind legs and roared. **2. fierce, strong, turbulent, violent, wild, intense, mighty, high, heavy** The furious gale knocked down many trees. ➡ **Antonyms: 2. mild, calm, weak**

furnish *verb* **1. equip, fit, outfit, appoint, decorate, array, stock, provide** Dad furnished his office with bookshelves and a desk. **2. give, provide, supply, deliver, present, grant, bestow, dispense** My uncle furnished the tools that I needed to repair my bike.

Word Group

Furniture is a general term for the movable articles, such as chairs, tables, or appliances, that make a room fit for living or working. **Furniture** is a general term with no true synonyms. Here are some common types of furniture:

An **armoire** is a large, often ornate cabinet or wardrobe. A **buffet** is a large piece of furniture with drawers and cupboards for storing china, silverware, and table linens. A **chesterfield** is a large, overstuffed sofa with rounded armrests. A **davenport** is a large sofa that converts into a bed. A **hassock** is a thick cushion used as a footstool. An **ottoman** is a sofa that has no arms or back. A **secretary** is a desk with a small bookcase on top. A **wardrobe** is a cabinet for holding clothes.

furrow *noun* **ditch, trench, rut, channel, groove, gutter, crease, wrinkle** We walked along the furrows in the corn field.

furry *adjective* **fuzzy, fleecy, downy, hairy, woolly, shaggy, soft** I like the furry texture of this blanket.

further *adjective* **added, additional, extra, more, new, other, another, fresh** The news report carried further details on the coach's retirement. ◆ *adverb* **additionally, more, longer, yet, also, moreover, furthermore, still** I'll have to study the problem further before I can give you my opinion. ◆ *verb* **advance, forward, promote, aid, assist, support, encourage, facilitate** My parents have helped to further my interest in music. ➡ **Antonyms:** *verb* **hinder, retard**

furtive *adjective* **stealthy, secretive, sneaky, skulking, cautious, underhanded, sly** The shoplifter looked around in a furtive manner. ➡ **Antonyms: open, direct, overt**

fury *noun* **1. anger, ire, rage, wrath, madness, furor, indignation, vehemence** I was filled with fury when the umpire made a bad call. **2. ferocity, intensity, severity, violence, turbulence, might, energy** The storm raged with awesome fury.

fuse *verb* melt, blend, combine, merge, mix, alloy, amalgamate, join, unite Bronze is made by fusing copper and tin. ◆ **Antonyms: separate, divide, split**

fuss *noun* 1. bother, bustle, commotion, disturbance, stir, ado, flutter, twitter My parents made a fuss over me when I won a prize at the science fair. 2. protest, complaint, objection, challenge, quarrel, dispute, contention, tiff The angry customer raised a fuss when he was shortchanged. ◆ *verb* fret, worry, bustle, fidget, complain, chafe, wail The whole family fussed over the baby when she had a cold.

futile *adjective* pointless, hopeless, useless, vain, worthless, fruitless, ineffective, unsuccessful It is futile to try to get him to change his mind about the trip. ◆ **Antonyms: worthwhile, successful**

future *adjective* approaching, coming, forthcoming, prospective, later, next, eventual, imminent My friends and I like to plan out our future activities. ◆ **Antonyms: past, previous**

fuzzy *adjective* 1. downy, velvety, hairy, woolly, fluffy, fleecy, furry, soft This angora sweater is so warm and fuzzy. 2. blurry, unclear, hazy, indistinct, bleary, faint, obscure, dim, indefinite, foggy, misty, vague I have only a fuzzy memory of the accident. ◆ **Antonyms: 2. clear, sharp, distinct**

Gg

gadget *noun* **contraption, contrivance, apparatus, appliance, device, implement, tool** We have a gadget that automatically peels apples.

gag *noun* **1. muzzle, restraint, check, shackle, fetter, curb** There was a gag on the discussion of slavery in Congress in the 1830s. **2. joke, jest, quip, witticism, wisecrack, hoax, ruse, trick** He used hair coloring on his dog as a gag. ♦ *verb* **choke, be nauseated, retch, vomit, heave, throw up, sicken** I gagged at the smell of the skunk.

gain *verb* **1. acquire, come by, get, pick up, procure, secure, win** I gained experience working in the library last summer. **2. build up, develop, increase, acquire, advance** The outdoor adventure group gained knowledge with each new task it met. **3. reach, arrive, accomplish, achieve, attain, realize, make, approach** We gained the top of the cliff and could see the ocean below. ♦ *noun* **1. advance, addition, improvement, increase, advancement, acquisition, attainment** The quarterback carried the ball for a gain of 15 yards. **2. earnings, profit, return, benefit, yield, proceed, revenue** My mother checked the paper to see if her stocks had made any gains. ● **Antonyms:** *verb* **1. lose, forfeit 2. lose** ♦ *noun* **loss**

gait *noun* **walk, stride, step, tread, pace, motion, movement** The model walked down the runway with a fluid gait.

gale *noun* **1. wind, windstorm, squall, storm, tempest, blow, gust, breeze** The gale blew with such fury that many boats almost capsized. **2. outburst, eruption, burst, surge, outbreak, explosion, uproar, roar** The class erupted in a gale of laughter.

gallant *adjective* **1. brave, courageous, daring, heroic, valiant, bold, valorous** Firefighters made a gallant attempt to save the burning building. **2. chivalrous, courtly, gracious, courteous, polite, attentive, gentlemanly** He opened the door for her in a gallant gesture. ● **Antonyms: 1. cowardly, craven 2. impolite, discourteous**

gallery *noun* **1. passage, passageway, hall, hallway, loggia, arcade, corridor, aisle** We passed through the gallery from the garage to the house. **2. audience, spectators, onlookers, crowd, public, house, listeners** The gallery voiced its disapproval of the speaker. **3. art gallery, show room, salon, exhibition hall, museum** We went to an art exhibit at the gallery near us.

gallop *noun* **canter, jog, run, trot, lope, sprint** Adrienne exercised her horse by taking it for a gallop. ♦ *verb* **1. canter, run, trot, jog, lope, sprint** The horse galloped across the finish line. **2. fly, race, rush, speed, zoom, dash, hurry, hasten** The summer is galloping by. ● **Antonyms:** *verb* **2. crawl, creep**

galvanize *verb* **spur, prod, prompt, stimulate, motivate, inspire, arouse, excite, stir** I was galvanized into action when I saw how late it was.

gamble *verb* **bet, wager, chance, risk, stake, venture, put, speculate, hazard** I gambled a dollar on my favorite football team. ♦ *noun* **chance, risk, bet, wager, speculation, hazard, stake, venture** We took a gamble with the weather when we went boating on a cloudy day.

game *noun* **1. amusement, entertainment, recreation, pastime, diversion, activity, fun, sport** My favorite game is charades. **2. competition, contest, match, meet, tournament, tourney, event, encounter** The Super Bowl is the most important game of the football season. ♦ *adjective* **1. courageous, plucky, intrepid, resolute, bold, brave, valiant, valorous** The losing team made a game effort. **2. ready, willing, able, agreeable, prepared, disposed, inclined, interested** He is game for any outdoor adventure. ● **Antonyms:** *adjective* **1. timid, cautious 2. unwilling, disinclined**

gang *noun* **1. band, pack, ring, mob, party, company, outfit, crew** Jesse James led a famous gang of outlaws. **2. set, circle, crowd, group, bunch, clique, coterie** I have had the same gang of friends since grade school. ♦ *verb* **gather, group, band, ring, mob, circle, unite, join** We ganged around the coach to hear his instructions. ● **Antonyms:** *verb* **scatter, disperse**

gap *noun* **1. opening, space, break, crack, hole, breach, crevice, fissure** My rabbit has a gap between its two front teeth. **2. interruption, pause, interval, interim, void, break, separation** There was a gap in the concert when the microphone broke. **3. difference, divergence, disagreement, discrepancy, disparity, incongruity, inconsistency, imbalance** There was a gap in the defendant's testimony.

gape *verb* **1. stare, gawk, gaze, ogle, eye, peer, goggle, look** We gaped at the jewelry in the shop window. **2. open, gap, yawn, part, split, separate, cleave, spread, divide** The baby bird's beak gaped as its mother approached the nest.

garb *noun* **clothes, clothing, garments, apparel, dress, attire, outfit, costume** She likes to wear casual garb to school. ◆ *verb* **clothe, attire, dress, outfit, apparel, array, clad, deck** We garbed ourselves in rain gear to go for a walk along the stormy beach.

garbage *noun* **refuse, rubbish, trash, waste, junk, litter, debris, scraps, offal** Whose turn is it to take the garbage out?

garble *verb* **mix up, distort, confuse, muddle, jumble, warp, twist** My sister garbled the phone number when she took the message. ◈ **Antonyms: clarify, clear up**

Word Group

A **garden** is either a piece of land used for growing plants or a public place ornamented with flowers, shrubs, and the like. **Garden** is a general term with no true synonyms. Here are some common types of gardens:

botanical garden, flower garden, herb garden, nursery, orchard, rock garden, tea garden, vegetable garden, vineyard

---

garland *noun* **wreath, crown, chaplet, coronet, lei, chain, festoon** The bride wore a garland of flowers in her hair. ◆ *verb* **festoon, decorate, trim, crown, circle, ring, encircle, wreathe** I like to garland the doorways with fir boughs at Christmas.

garment *noun* **apparel, attire, clothes, clothing, dress, raiment, outfit, garb** Mom took a class in how to make baby garments.

garner *verb* **gather, collect, harvest, reap, glean, amass, accumulate, store** We garnered enough wild blackberries to make a pie.

garnish *verb* **adorn, decorate, embellish, ornament, trim, dress up, festoon** I garnished the salad with chopped herbs. ◆ *noun* **ornamentation, decoration, embellishment, adornment, trim** The dessert had a garnish of whipped cream and chopped nuts.

garrison *noun* **1. fort, post, fortress, fortification, stronghold, citadel, presidio** We visited the frontier garrison in Vancouver, Washington. **2. detachment, unit, guard, brigade, regiment, squadron, troops, soldiers** The entire garrison was transferred to another military base. ◆ *verb* **station, position, assign to, man, bivouac, camp** My brother was garrisoned in Oklahoma when he first joined the army.

gas *noun* **gaseous mixture, vapor, fume, miasma, smoke, steam** Did you know that the sun is made up mostly of hydrogen gas?

gasp *verb* **gulp, pant, huff, puff, wheeze, blow, heave, snort** He gasped for air after swimming the pool's length underwater. ◆ *noun* **gulp, pant, puff, wheeze, blow, huff, heave, snort** I was breathing in short gasps by the time I ran up the fourth flight of stairs.

gate *noun* **door, doorway, entrance, entry, gateway, entranceway, entryway, portal** I closed the gate so that the dog wouldn't get out.

gather *verb* **1. accumulate, assemble, cluster, collect, group, convene, congregate, get together** Pigeons gathered around the woman who was tossing out bread crumbs. **2. harvest, pick, pluck, garner, glean, reap, cull** We gathered wildflowers for a bouquet. **3. conclude, infer, deduce, draw, understand, assume, judge, surmise** I gather that you are not in favor of term limits for members of Congress. ◈ **Antonyms: 1. disperse, scatter**

gathering *noun* **assembly, meeting, conclave, rally, party, company, crowd, group** We have a family gathering each Thanksgiving.

gaudy *adjective* **loud, showy, garish, glaring, tawdry, flashy, ostentatious, vulgar** She has a weakness for gaudy shoes. ◈ **Antonyms: subtle, quiet, tasteful**

gauge *noun* **test, criterion, yardstick, mark, measure, standard, meter, benchmark** How we survive a month of travel together will be a gauge of our friendship. ◆ *verb* **calculate, compute, measure, estimate, figure, determine, judge, assess, rate** It is difficult to gauge the speed of the wind without the right equipment.

gaunt *adjective* **1. bony, lean, skinny, thin, haggard, emaciated, lank, scrawny, slim** Many wild animals become gaunt during winter due to a scarcity of food. **2. bleak, desolate, stark, grim, forbidding, harsh, barren, forsaken** The empty landscape seemed gaunt and forbidding as the night fell. ◈ **Antonyms: 1. fat, obese 2. lush, luxurious**

gay *adjective* **1. cheerful, happy, jolly, merry, mirthful, jovial, lighthearted, blithe** Everyone was in a gay mood at the Halloween party. **2. lively, colorful, rich, vivid, brilliant, sparkling, showy, bright** The actors at the Elizabethan pageant wore gay costumes. ◈ **Antonyms: 1. unhappy, joyless 2. dull, drab**

gaze *verb* look, stare, eye, gape, ogle, peer, observe, scrutinize I gazed at the stars for a long time. ◆ *noun* stare, look, eye, scrutiny, glance The teacher's gaze fell on me.

gear *noun* apparatus, equipment, outfit, stuff, things, tackle, accouterments, paraphernalia If you want to play tennis during our vacation, don't forget to bring your gear. ◆ *verb* 1. adapt, adjust, suit, fit, tailor, conform, accommodate, match A good teacher gears her lesson plans to her class. 2. equip, fit out, outfit, furnish, rig, prepare, organize, ready We geared up to go bicycle riding.

gem *noun* 1. gemstone, jewel, precious stone, semi-precious stone, stone The king's crown was covered with diamonds and other gems. 2. marvel, masterpiece, masterwork, prize, treasure, wonder, pearl He has some real gems in his baseball card collection.

general *adjective* 1. common, communal, universal, whole, total, public, collective The museum is open to the general public. 2. prevalent, broad, overall, widespread, popular, all-around, comprehensive, extensive There was general satisfaction with the plan. 3. normal, routine, usual, typical, ordinary, regular, habitual As a general rule, you should save your work often while working on a computer. 4. vague, loose, inexact, imprecise, indefinite, generalized, approximate We had only a general idea of when the concert would begin. ➡ **Antonyms: 1.** individual **2.** limited, restricted **3.** uncommon, unusual **4.** exact, precise

generally *adverb* 1. normally, routinely, typically, usually, often, habitually, regularly, ordinarily I generally have cereal and fruit for breakfast. 2. broadly, commonly, popularly, widely, publicly, universally It is not generally known that Russia is only 36 miles away from Alaska. ➡ **Antonyms: 1.** rarely, seldom

generate *verb* create, make, produce, develop, form, originate, effect, cause A fire generates both heat and light. ➡ **Antonyms:** end, stifle, extinguish

generous *adjective* 1. considerate, kind, thoughtful, unselfish, gracious, magnanimous I appreciate your generous offer to give me a ride home. 2. large, abundant, ample, big, bountiful, copious, plentiful, substantial My mother served me a generous helping of mashed potatoes. ➡ **Antonyms: 1.** selfish, stingy **2.** scanty, meager, small

genial *adjective* cheerful, friendly, good-humored, affable, congenial, pleasant, sociable, cordial My friends say I am a genial person. ➡ **Antonyms:** unfriendly, unpleasant

genius *noun* 1. brilliance, creativity, intelligence, inspiration, imagination, originality Mozart's operas are widely considered to be works of genius. 2. talent, ability, gift, knack, flair, faculty, aptitude, instinct, bent Our mechanic has a genius for fixing cars. 3. expert, master, wizard, ace, prodigy, whiz, virtuoso, maestro My sister is a real genius with computers. ➡ **Antonyms: 1. & 2.** ineptitude

genre *noun* type, class, classification, style, kind, sort, variety, category I enjoy reading books in many different genres.

gentle *adjective* 1. considerate, kindly, thoughtful, tender, compassionate It is important to be gentle with small animals. 2. light, low, mild, moderate, slight, soft, balmy, temperate A gentle breeze made the evening cool and pleasant. 3. docile, tame, meek, manageable, tractable, compliant, domesticated Our dog is very gentle when she plays with us. ➡ **Antonyms: 1.** inconsiderate, cruel **2.** strong, harsh **3.** wild, fierce

genuine *adjective* 1. actual, authentic, real, true, bona fide, legitimate, pure, original My dad has a genuine Model T Ford. 2. sincere, honest, heartfelt, natural, frank, candid, plain, unaffected His behavior is always genuine. ➡ **Antonyms: 1.** fake, artificial **2.** insincere

Word Group

Geology is the science that studies the origin, composition, history, and structure of the earth. Geology is a general term with no true synonyms. Here are some of the branches of geology:

Geodesy is the study of the size and shape of the earth. Geophysics is the application of physics to the study of the earth and its environment. Mineralogy is the study of minerals. Oceanography is the scientific study of oceans. Paleontology is the study of fossils and ancient forms of life. Seismology is the study of earthquakes and other movements of the earth's crust.

gesture *noun* 1. motion, movement, sign, signal, gesticulation Police officers use hand and arm gestures to direct traffic. 2. symbol, indication, sign, token, expression, demonstration We bought a present for our director as a gesture of our appreciation. ◆ *verb* motion, sign, signal, gesticulate, indicate, wave, flag Mom gestured for us to be quiet as we entered the baby's room.

get *verb* 1. receive, come by, acquire, obtain, procure, secure, attain I got a stereo for my birthday. 2. earn, win, make, reap, achieve, merit, gain, realize How much did you get for mowing the lawn? **3. fetch, go for, go after, pick up, catch, capture, seize** Please get some peanut butter when you go to the store. **4. catch, contract, develop, take, sicken, have, fall, succumb** How did you get the measles? **5. become, grow, turn, develop, come, wax, effect** It's getting cold outside. **6. convince, influence, persuade, urge, induce, coax, sway, cause** I'll get my parents to let you stay over tonight. **7. catch, comprehend, grasp, understand, apprehend, follow, see** I didn't get the joke at first. **8. arrive, reach, show up, approach, come, draw near, turn up** When will the bus get here? ● **Antonyms: 1. & 2. lose 5. stay, remain 6. dissuade 7. misunderstand 8. leave, depart**

ghastly *adjective* **1. terrifying, dreadful, gruesome, hideous, horrible, grisly, frightful** The ghastly monster was half human and half bug. **2. pale, wan, pallid, ashen, cadaverous, deathly, ghostly, spectral** The actor used stage makeup to give himself a ghastly appearance. **3. bad, unpleasant, awful, appalling, terrible, disagreeable, sorry, disgusting** Ryan had a ghastly day at school. ● **Antonyms: 2. ruddy, healthy 3. pleasant, agreeable**

ghost *noun* **1. apparition, phantom, phantasm, specter, spirit, spook, wraith** The house was supposedly haunted by two ghosts. **2. trace, bit, hint, shadow, tinge, dash, suggestion, whiff** There was a ghost of perfume in the air.

giant *noun* **behemoth, titan, colossus, leviathan, gargantuan, Goliath** Beethoven was a musical giant. ● *adjective* **gigantic, colossal, enormous, huge, immense, jumbo, mammoth, monstrous** Some people claim that they have seen a giant sea serpent. ● **Antonyms:** *noun* **dwarf, pygmy** ● *adjective* **tiny, little**

gibberish *noun* **nonsense, drivel, rubbish, prattle, babble, jabber, mumbo jumbo** Any language can sound like gibberish until we learn to speak it.

giddy *adjective* **1. dizzy, lightheaded, reeling, woozy, faint, unsteady** I felt giddy after the roller coaster ride. **2. frivolous, silly, scatterbrained, flighty, foolish, capricious, whimsical** Playing games all morning put everyone in a giddy mood. ● **Antonyms: 1. steady 2. serious, sober**

gift *noun* **1. contribution, donation, present, offering, presentation, gratuity, grant** The man gave a gift of 1,500 dollars to his favorite charity. **2. aptitude, faculty, knack, talent, ability, flair, genius, instinct** My sister has a gift for making people laugh.

gifted *adjective* **talented, accomplished, capable, expert, skillful, qualified, clever, master** My aunt is a very gifted photographer. ● **Antonym: unskilled**

gigantic *adjective* **colossal, enormous, giant, huge, immense, mammoth, stupendous, vast** Redwoods are gigantic trees that can grow to be over 350 feet high. ● **Antonyms: tiny, small, miniature**

giggle *verb* **laugh, titter, cackle, chuckle, snicker, snigger, chortle** The girls giggled when they met their favorite TV star. ● *noun* **laugh, laughter, cackle, chuckle, snicker, snigger, titter, chortle** Giggles filled the room when someone cracked a joke during the test.

gild *verb* **embellish, color, exaggerate, twist, slant, gloss over, sugarcoat, whitewash** My brother gilded his adventures at camp.

gingerly *adverb* **cautiously, carefully, warily, prudently, timidly, hesitantly** I walked gingerly down the icy steps. ● **Antonyms: boldly, rashly**

girdle *noun* **belt, loop, band, sash, ring, band, circle, hem** The garden was ornamented with a girdle of roses. ● *verb* **circle, belt, band, ring, encircle, hem, surround, enclose** The valley was girdled by mountains.

girl *noun* **young lady, miss, lass, colleen, maiden, maid, damsel, daughter** There are two girls and two boys in my family.

give *verb* **1. present, contribute, donate, hand out, bestow, provide, supply** My brother gave me his old baseball glove. **2. hand, pass, deliver, hand over, let have, transfer, turn over, convey** Please give me a glass of water. **3. pay, expend, lay out, tender, disburse, sell, compensate, trade** How much did you give for your new bicycle? **4. allow, grant, permit, let have, offer, accord, provide, supply** My teacher gave me an extra day to complete my homework. **5. allot, assign, allocate, apportion, appoint, measure out, mete out** We were given our seating assignments on the first day of class. **6. have, hold, stage, do, perform, execute, conduct, direct** Let's give a party to surprise Mom on her birthday. **7. produce, yield, bear, make, generate, furnish, issue, put forth** This walnut tree gives a good crop every year. **8. yield, concede, relinquish, surrender, cede, part with, retreat** I gave up the argument when my brother made me laugh. ● *noun* **bounce, spring, elasticity, flexibility, resilience, pliability, plasticity** A trampoline has lots of give.

glad *adjective* **1. happy, cheerful, lighthearted, joyful, merry, gay, gratified** Receiving presents on my birthday made me glad. **2. pleased, willing, delighted, happy, amenable, inclined, disposed, ready** I would be glad to help you with your art project. ● **Antonyms: 1. unhappy, sad, gloomy 2. unwilling, hesitant**

glamorous *adjective* exciting, fascinating, enchanting, alluring, dazzling, attractive, charming Directing movies sounds like a glamorous career. ➡ **Antonyms:** unexciting, dull

glance *verb* 1. look, peek, peep, glimpse, peer, scan I glanced into the oven to see if the brownies were done. 2. reflect, ricochet, bounce, graze, careen, skim, skip, brush, rebound Sunlight glanced off the windows. ◆ *noun* look, peek, peep, glimpse, squint, scan From a glance at the test, I could see it would be easy.

glare *verb* 1. glower, scowl, stare, frown, gaze, lower I glared at the students who were talking loudly in the library. 2. blaze, flash, shine, dazzle, glisten, sparkle, flare, beat down Sunlight glared off the snow and ice. ◆ *noun* 1. scowl, glower, stare, frown, gaze, lower My cat gave me a glare when I served him the wrong food. 2. blaze, glow, light, shine, brilliance, dazzle, incandescence, luminosity The glare from the rocket's engines could be seen for miles.

glaring *adjective* 1. blinding, bright, brilliant, dazzling, glowing, blazing, harsh, strong The glaring sunlight made my eyes water. 2. loud, flashy, garish, gaudy, tawdry, vivid, showy, lurid I found some glaring curtains to use in our school play. 3. conspicuous, evident, blatant, noticeable, obvious, flagrant, gross, arrant Sam made a glaring error on his spelling test. ➡ **Antonyms:** 1. & 2. soft, subdued 3. inconspicuous, imperceptible

glaze *noun* coating, finish, covering, veneer, patina, polish, gloss, sheen I put a crackle glaze on my dresser to make it look like an antique.

gleam *noun* 1. flash, flicker, glimmer, twinkle, glow, glint, ray, beam We saw the gleam of a distant campfire. 2. trace, hint, suggestion, inkling, glimpse, bit, speck, spark At first it was just a gleam of an idea. ◆ *verb* glisten, sparkle, glow, shine, twinkle, glitter, flash, radiate She polished the silver tea set until it gleamed.

glean *verb* gather, garner, collect, cull, pick up, accumulate, extract, harvest I gleaned some facts for my report from the video.

glee *noun* delight, gladness, happiness, joy, merriment, mirth, gaiety, exultation My little sister cried out with glee when she saw the kitten. ➡ **Antonyms:** sadness, sorrow, misery

gleeful *adjective* happy, elated, glad, merry, joyous, exultant, blissful, gay We were gleeful when the teacher let us out fifteen minutes early. ➡ **Antonyms:** sad, gloomy, miserable

glen *noun* valley, dell, dale, vale, hollow, glade We spent a pleasant day beneath the shady trees in the mountain glen.

glib *adjective* facile, slick, smooth-tongued, smooth, ready, easy, insincere I told my parents a glib story about why I was late, but they didn't fall for it. ➡ **Antonyms:** sincere, hesitant, reticent

glide *verb* coast, sail, soar, flow, slide, slip, drift, pass Seagulls glided through the sky above the docks.

glimmer *noun* 1. flash, flicker, gleam, glow, twinkle, glint, spark, shimmer The embers gave off glimmers of reddish light. 2. hint, suggestion, gleam, indication, intimation, trace, speck, bit I don't have a glimmer of what you are trying to tell me. ◆ *verb* shimmer, gleam, flicker, sparkle, twinkle, shine, glow, glitter Stars glimmered in the night sky.

glimpse *noun* peek, peep, glance, look, squint, sight, view He had a glimpse of the cardinal before it flew away. ◆ *verb* make out, spy, see, catch, detect, discern, spot, peek at I barely glimpsed the mayor in the crowd.

glisten *verb* sparkle, glitter, shimmer, glimmer, flash, twinkle, gleam, glint The sequins on the woman's dress glistened as she walked.

glitter *noun* 1. brilliance, sparkle, light, shine, shimmer, flash, glint, twinkle The glitter of the sun on the water looked like diamonds. 2. showiness, glamour, splendor, magnificence, grandeur, pomp, pageantry I was awed by the glitter of Las Vegas. ◆ *verb* glisten, shine, sparkle, flash, twinkle, flicker, shimmer The city glitters at night with lights and traffic.

gloat *verb* exult, boast, brag, crow, vaunt, revel, bask, delight He didn't gloat over winning the race.

globe *noun* 1. ball, sphere, orb, spheroid Our kitchen light is covered by a glass globe. 2. earth, planet, world My grandparents' travels have taken them all over the globe.

gloom *noun* 1. dark, darkness, dimness, murk, murkiness, blackness, shadow, shade We couldn't see very far in the gloom of the long tunnel. 2. dejection, glumness, sadness, unhappiness, depression, despondence, melancholy, despair I was filled with gloom when I thought of my friend moving away. ➡ **Antonyms:** 1. brightness, light 2. happiness, joy

gloomy *adjective* 1. bleak, dark, dismal, dreary, somber, black, glum, murky The castle was cold and gloomy.

2. dejected, glum, sad, unhappy, depressed, sullen, moody, morose He has been in a gloomy mood ever since his team lost in the playoffs. ➡ **Antonyms: 1. light, bright 2. happy, cheerful**

glorious *adjective* **gorgeous, magnificent, marvelous, splendid, superb, resplendent, wonderful, majestic** The Grand Canyon is one of the most glorious sights I have ever seen.

glory *noun* **1. honor, praise, prestige, fame, renown, distinction, celebrity** The ice skater's masterful performance brought her glory. **2. grandeur, magnificence, splendor, majesty, greatness, brilliance, beauty** The sun rose in a blaze of glory. ♦ *verb* **rejoice, exult, delight, revel, bask, gloat, boast, vaunt** We gloried in the beautiful sunset. ➡ **Antonyms:** *noun* **1. dishonor, disgrace 2. ugliness**

glow *verb* **1. shine, beam, gleam, glimmer, radiate, shimmer** My alarm clock has a dial that glows in the dark. **2. redden, blush, color, flush, tingle, bloom** Our faces glowed after the long walk. ♦ *noun* **gleam, glimmer, light, radiance, glare, shine, brightness, shimmer** The room was lit by the glow of candles.

glower *verb* **stare, glare, lower, scowl, frown, look** My little brother glowered at me when I said that he couldn't go with me. ♦ *noun* **stare, glare, lower, scowl, frown, black look, look** The man's glower was intimidating. ➡ **Antonyms: smile, grin**

glue *noun* **adhesive, cement, mucilage, paste, rubber cement, gum, epoxy** I used glue to repair my model airplane. ♦ *verb* **paste, stick, cement, fasten, affix, fix, seal, gum** She glued pictures of her family into her scrapbook.

glum *adjective* **sad, dejected, gloomy, morose, sullen, unhappy, low, down** I was glum when I did not receive an invitation to the party. ➡ **Antonyms: happy, cheerful**

glut *verb* **gorge, satiate, sate, stuff, cram, fill, overeat, feast** We glutted ourselves at the buffet dinner. ♦ *noun* **oversupply, excess, overage, surplus, overflow, plenitude, surfeit, abundance** A glut of houses for sale caused prices to drop. ➡ **Antonyms:** *noun* **scarcity, shortage**

gnarled *adjective* **misshapen, twisted, lumpy, knobby, bent, crooked, warped, contorted** That gnarled tree has been exposed to constant wind. ➡ **Antonyms: smooth, straight**

gnaw *verb* **1. chew, nibble, bite, eat, munch, chomp, gnash, masticate** Our dog gnawed on Dad's shoes. **2. erode,**

corrode, wear, wear away, eat, eat away, consume, devour Rain and wind have gnawed caves in the sandstone cliff. **3. trouble, distress, worry, torment, bother, annoy, irritate** I try not to let my problems gnaw at me.

go *verb* **1. head, move, journey, proceed, progress, travel, advance, voyage** Where is your family going on vacation? **2. depart, leave, exit, retire, withdraw, remove, set out, set off** I have to go now. **3. function, operate, work, run, perform, move, act, thrive** My dad's old car is not going very well these days. **4. fit, match, suit, agree, belong, conform, harmonize, blend** Does this tie go with my shirt? **5. lead, extend, head, reach, run, carry, stretch** Where does this road go? **6. pass, slip away, elapse, lapse, expire, disappear, vanish, evaporate** The summer went by too fast. **7. turn out, fare, transpire, occur, happen, result** How did things go at school today? **8. fail, weaken, give, decline, degenerate, wear out, collapse, fade** Mom says that the washing machine is starting to go. ♦ *noun* **1. attempt, effort, try, endeavor, stab, crack, fling, shot** Let's give it a go! **2. energy, vitality, pep, zip, vigor, vim, drive** My dog has more go than I do. ➡ **Antonyms:** *verb* **1. stay, remain 2. arrive, come** ♦ *noun* **2. laziness, lethargy**

goad *noun* **stimulus, prod, incentive, inducement, motivation, provocation, trigger** Money is often the goad that motivates people to get a job. ♦ *verb* **prod, prompt, stimulate, inspire, motivate, move, spur, drive** We each need to discover what it is that goads us to do our best. ➡ **Antonyms:** *verb* **deter, restrain**

goal *noun* **ambition, aim, objective, end, purpose, target, design, intent** My goal is to read five books this summer.

gobble *verb* **bolt, gulp, wolf, devour, eat, stuff, guzzle, swill** It's not polite to gobble your food.

good *adjective* **1. enjoyable, fine, nice, excellent, great, satisfying** We saw a good movie yesterday. **2. advantageous, beneficial, favorable, helpful, proper, suitable** A good diet includes fruits and vegetables. **3. able, capable, competent, skilled, skillful, efficient, talented** She is a good teacher. **4. serviceable, intact, sound, unbroken, usable** My bicycle is old but still good. **5. genuine, real, authentic, bona fide, actual, valid, legitimate** I know this is a good 20-dollar bill, not a counterfeit one. **6. honorable, moral, honest, righteous, upright, virtuous** I try to be a good person. **7. obedient, well-behaved, dutiful, proper, well-mannered** I give my dog a treat when she is good. **8. loyal, devoted, dependable, reliable, trustworthy** He is a good employee. **9. substantial, ample, great, large, considerable, sizable** We have a good amount of time left to finish the project. **10. full, complete, thorough, solid** I gave my room a good cleaning. ◆ *noun* **1. advantage, benefit, interest, welfare, profit, success** Our coach urges us to play for the good of the team. **2. merchandise, commodities, wares, stock, inventory** The shipping clerk packed the goods. **3. belongings, effects, property, possessions, things, gear, stuff** The moving van picked up our household goods. ◈ **Antonyms:** *adjective* **1. bad, poor, inferior 2. disadvantageous, improper 3. incompetent, unskilled 4. broken, damaged 5. fake, phony 6. immoral, dishonorable 7. mischievous, naughty 8. disloyal, undependable 9. small, insubstantial 10. partial, incomplete** ◆ *noun* **1. detriment, disadvantage**

gore *verb* **pierce, stab, impale, spear, puncture, gouge, stick** Even a good matador is at risk of being gored by a bull.

gorge *noun* **canyon, chasm, gulch, ravine, defile** A river runs through the gorge. ◆ *verb* **satiate, glut, sate, cram, fill, stuff, engorge, overeat** We gorged ourselves with cake and ice cream at my birthday party.

gorgeous *adjective* **beautiful, glorious, magnificent, splendid, superb, lovely, pretty, resplendent** It was such a gorgeous day that we decided to go to the beach. ◈ **Antonyms: ugly, unattractive**

gossip *noun* **1. hearsay, rumor, scandal, slander, tattle, prattle, talk** I read some gossip about my favorite actor. **2. gossiper, tattler, tattletale, busybody, chatterbox, snoop, meddler** We tease her about being a gossip, but we all listen to her. ◆ *verb* **chatter, chitchat, jabber, talk, tattle, prattle, blab, whisper** We gossiped about last night's party.

gouge *noun* **groove, scratch, gash, furrow, cut, channel, notch, hole** There was a gouge in one corner of the dining table. ◆ *verb* **scoop, cut, hollow, groove, chisel, incise, dig, scratch** I gouged out the center of the watermelon and filled it with strawberries.

govern *verb* **1. direct, lead, manage, run, control, rule, administer, head, reign** Elections determine who will govern the country. **2. determine, influence, control, regulate, decide, establish, fix** The number of questions on the test will govern the amount of time I will need to finish. **3. control, restrain, discipline, tame, check, curb, master, subdue** It is important to learn to govern one's temper. ◈ **Antonyms: 1. follow, submit**

government *noun* **1. control, direction, management, rule, command, guidance, regulation** The federal bureaucracy is responsible for the day-to-day government of the nation. **2. state, administration, regime, rule, ministry, bureaucracy** Monarchies and republics are two different forms of national government.

gown *noun* **dress, formal dress, frock, garment, nightgown, robe, habit** Mom still has her wedding gown.

grab *verb* **1. clutch, grasp, seize, snatch, catch, pluck, take, clasp** I grabbed my little brother's hand before he stepped off the curb. **2. capture, seize, commandeer, confiscate, appropriate, usurp** The rebels were able to grab power and overthrow the government. ◆ *noun* **lunge, snatch, clutch, grasp, pass, catch, grip** The bear made a grab for the salmon. ◈ **Antonyms:** *verb* **1. release, let go 2. yield, surrender**

grace *noun* **1. ease, elegance, gracefulness, suppleness, refinement, polish, charm** The figure skater performed with remarkable grace. **2. decency, manners, politeness, kindness, tact, etiquette, charity** He had the grace to apologize for his careless behavior. **3. reprieve, respite, delay, stay, immunity, exemption, clemency** Our teacher gave us three days' grace to get our reports finished. ◆ *verb* **1. honor, favor, dignify, ennoble, distinguish, enrich** The president of the school board graced our graduation ceremony with his presence. **2. adorn, decorate, beautify, enhance, ornament, trim** The bank lobby had several paintings gracing its walls. ◈ **Antonym:** *noun* **2. impertinence**

graceful *adjective* **easy, effortless, flowing, fluid, smooth, refined, agile, elegant** Her dive was so graceful that she hardly made a splash. ◈ **Antonyms: awkward, clumsy**

gracious *adjective* **cordial, courteous, hospitable, kind, affable, amiable, polite, warm** They are always such gracious hosts at their annual holiday party. ◈ **Antonyms: rude, unfriendly**

grade *noun* **1. category, degree, level, rank, stage, class, kind, type** Sandpaper comes in different grades of coarseness. **2. incline, pitch, slant, slope, rise, gradient, inclination, tilt** I walked my bicycle up the steep grade. **3. mark, score, evaluation, rating** He got the best grade on yesterday's test. ◆ *verb* **1. categorize, classify, order, rank, sort, group, class** Lumber is graded according to its quality. **2. mark, score, evaluate, rate, correct** Our teacher grades our papers in red ink. **3. flatten, level, smooth, bulldoze, even** Before construction can begin, the lot will have to be graded.

gradual *adjective* **moderate, slow, steady, even, regular, piecemeal, easy, continual** The mountaineers made gradual progress up the steep slope. ◈ **Antonyms: sudden, abrupt**

graduate *verb* 1. advance, complete, finish, pass Both of my parents graduated from college. 2. mark off, calibrate, grade, scale, arrange, divide, measure This measuring cup has been graduated in ounces. ➡ **Antonyms: 1. flunk, fail, drop out**

grain *noun* 1. particle, granule, piece, pellet, seed, kernel I got a grain of sand in my eye. 2. bit, drop, fragment, iota, mite, scrap, shred, speck There is not a grain of evidence to support that theory. 3. pattern, direction, weave, texture, surface, character, nap, fiber It is important to sand wood in the direction of the grain.

grand *adjective* 1. luxurious, magnificent, majestic, stately, grandiose, imposing, elegant, large The dance will be held in the palace's grand ballroom. 2. excellent, great, splendid, superb, wonderful, terrific, fabulous, fine We had a grand time on our trip to Washington, D.C. 3. highest, principal, main, chief, supreme, head, leading, foremost My science experiment won the grand prize. 4. noble, dignified, lofty, exalted, high, venerable, august The country was founded on grand principles. ➡ **Antonyms: 1. modest, small 2. poor, mediocre 3. secondary, minor**

grandeur *noun* magnificence, grandness, greatness, majesty, splendor, resplendence, glory We admired the grandeur of the Lincoln Memorial. ➡ **Antonyms: insignificance, unimportance**

grandiose *adjective* 1. grand, magnificent, majestic, noble, impressive, imposing, gigantic The plans for the party became more grandiose as time went on. 2. pompous, pretentious, self-important, flamboyant, extravagant, ostentatious The mayor's speech was grandiose, but everyone enjoyed it. ➡ **Antonyms: 1. insignificant, paltry 2. modest, humble**

grant *verb* 1. accord, allow, award, give, permit, authorize, confer, bestow The genie of the lamp granted Aladdin three wishes. 2. acknowledge, admit, agree, concede, confess, avow, consent I'll grant that you're a faster runner than I am. ◆ *noun* contribution, donation, gift, allotment, award, bestowal, present, offering Our school received a grant to buy computers for all the classrooms. ➡ **Antonyms:** *verb* **1. withhold, refuse 2. deny, refute**

graphic *adjective* 1. visual, visible, photographic, pictorial, illustrative, representational Our teacher frequently uses videos, slides, and other graphic aids. 2. vivid, explicit, realistic, clear, distinct, detailed, particular, precise The professor gave graphic examples of the consequences of hypothermia. ➡ **Antonyms: 2. unrealistic, vague**

grapple *verb* wrestle, contend, face, confront, struggle, contest, combat, fight We grappled with the problem for several days before arriving at a solution.

grasp *verb* 1. clasp, clutch, grab, grip, seize, clench, snatch, catch We all grasped the rope tightly and pulled to win the tug-of-war. 2. comprehend, perceive, see, understand, know, apprehend, follow, get Do you grasp the meaning of this poem? ◆ *noun* 1. clasp, clutch, grip, clench, hold, embrace, possession The garter snake wriggled out of my grasp. 2. comprehension, perception, understanding, apprehension, awareness, insight, knowledge His grasp of American history is impressive. ➡ **Antonyms:** *verb* **1. release, let go 2. misunderstand**

grateful *adjective* appreciative, thankful, gratified, pleased, indebted, beholden Mom was grateful that I helped cook dinner. ➡ **Antonym: unappreciative**

gratification *noun* satisfaction, fulfillment, pleasure, delight, enjoyment, comfort, solace I could see the gratification on my parents' face when I showed them my report card. ➡ **Antonym: disappointment**

gratify *verb* 1. cheer, delight, gladden, please, comfort, tickle The librarian said that it gratified him to see me so interested in reading. 2. indulge, satisfy, fulfill, appease, content, cater to, humor, pamper I gratified my craving for sweets with a bowl of ice cream. ➡ **Antonyms: 1. disappoint 2. control, check, curb**

gratitude *noun* appreciation, gratefulness, thankfulness, thanks, acknowledgment, recognition The director expressed her gratitude when she won an Oscar.

grave[1] *noun* burial place, crypt, tomb, vault, sepulcher, mausoleum, catacomb This pioneer cemetery contains the graves of several Civil War veterans.

grave[2] *adjective* 1. serious, severe, significant, momentous, important, critical, consequential In our school, cheating is a grave offense. 2. sober, solemn, serious, somber, earnest, thoughtful, quiet The reporter described the car accident in a grave tone of voice. ➡ **Antonyms: 1. trivial, minor 2. flippant, frivolous**

gravity *noun* 1. gravitation, gravitational attraction, attraction, force, pull Gravity is one of the four fundamental forces of nature. 2. seriousness, importance, momentousness, significance, magnitude, consequence Our teacher emphasized the gravity of taking responsibility for our actions. ➡ **Antonyms: 2. insignificance, unimportance**

graze[1] *verb* **browse, crop, eat, feed, forage, pasture** Sheep were grazing in the fields.

graze[2] *verb* **brush, swipe, touch, glance off, skim, flick, rub** I just grazed the edge of the curb with my bicycle tire.

grease *noun* **1. drippings, fat, lard, tallow, suet** Some people fry their eggs in bacon grease. **2. oil, lubricating oil, petroleum, lubricant** Mom was covered with grease after working on her jeep. ◆ *verb* **lubricate, oil** I greased the hinges of the squeaky door.

great *adjective* **1. big, enormous, huge, large, vast, tremendous, colossal, massive** Elephants are known for their great size. **2. important, outstanding, remarkable, significant, consequential, momentous, major** Many people think Franklin D. Roosevelt was a great President. **3. prominent, distinguished, notable, noted, illustrious, famous, eminent, renowned** We were excited that the great writer was signing autographs. **4. excellent, superior, first-rate, fantastic, fabulous, marvelous, splendid, terrific** I think it is great that you get to go to Europe. ◆ **Antonyms: 1. small, little 2. & 3. unimportant, insignificant 4. bad, awful, terrible**

greed *noun* **avarice, covetousness, cupidity, craving, desire, hunger, longing, yearning** Trick-or-treating brings out my greed for candy.

greedy *adjective* **acquisitive, avaricious, covetous, grasping, hungry, avid, rapacious** The greedy investor wanted to earn a million dollars right away.

green *noun* **common, lawn, yard, sward, park, grass, grassland** There is a beautiful green in the center of our housing development. ◆ *adjective* **1. unripe, immature, undeveloped, developing, unseasoned, young, juvenile** I like green tomatoes that have been pickled. **2. inexperienced, new, unsophisticated, naive, raw, inexpert, unskilled, amateur** The green recruit had never been in combat before. ◆ **Antonyms: adjective 1. mature, ripe 2. experienced, expert**

greet *verb* **1. hail, salute, meet, welcome, address, accost** I greeted her with a wave of my hand. **2. receive, meet, acknowledge, embrace, encounter, take, react, accept** She greeted the news with aplomb.

grief *noun* **heartache, heartbreak, sadness, sorrow, despair, distress, anguish, misery** Grief is a natural response to the death of a loved one.

grieve *verb* **1. aggrieve, distress, pain, wound, hurt, sadden, depress, deject** It grieved me that I did not get to see her before she moved. **2. lament, mourn, sorrow, suffer, cry, weep, wail, keen, sob** Everyone at the funeral grieved for the friend they had lost. ◆ **Antonyms: 1. console, comfort, gladden**

grill *verb* **1. barbecue, fry, cook, broil, roast, sauté** We grilled hamburgers at the party. **2. interrogate, question, cross-examine, pump, quiz, query, interview** I grilled my sister about college life.

grim *adjective* **1. rigid, relentless, stubborn, unrelenting, resolute, firm** The rescue team worked with grim determination. **2. forbidding, hard, harsh, severe, stern, dour, austere, somber** The judge had a grim look on his face. **3. dismal, gloomy, bleak, dreary, ominous, murky, dim** It was a cold, wet, and grim day. **4. ghastly, sinister, grisly, gruesome, hideous, horrible, horrid, lurid** The bullet holes in the building's walls were grim reminders of the recent unrest. ◆ **Antonyms: 1. yielding 2. amiable, benign 3. bright, cheerful 4. pleasant, pleasing**

grimace *noun* **scowl, sneer, smirk, glower, lower, frown, pout, expression** The gargoyle had a horrible grimace on its face. ◆ *verb* **scowl, sneer, smirk, pout, mug, glower, lower, frown** The sight of the needle for my polio shot made me grimace.

grime *noun* **dirt, filth, dust, mire, mud, soil, soot, muck** The garage windows were covered with grime.

grimy *adjective* **dirty, filthy, grubby, soiled, messy, unclean, black, dingy** I was all grimy after helping Dad work on the car. ◆ **Antonyms: clean, immaculate**

grin *verb* **beam, smile, simper, smirk** My little sister grinned happily when I offered her a piggyback ride. ◆ *noun* **smile, beam, simper, smirk** I could tell from his grin that he was happy.

grind *verb* **1. mill, pulverize, pound, crumble, crush, powder, mash, beat** Millstones were once used to grind grain into flour. **2. abrade, file, rub, polish, sharpen, smooth, whet, rasp** Early peoples made stone axes by grinding the ax head against a sandstone slab. **3. trample, crush, beat down, subdue, oppress, tyrannize, harass** The peasants' spirits were ground down by heavy taxation and unfair laws. ◆ *noun* **routine, rut, treadmill, tedium, drudgery, task, chore, travail** She would like to quit the daily grind and retire in Hawaii.

grip *noun* **1. clasp, grasp, hold, clutch, clench, seizure** My tennis instructor taught me to keep a firm grip on the racket. **2. understanding, comprehension, mastery,**

apprehension, perception, awareness It is important to have a firm grip on the fundamentals of any sport that you play. ◆ *verb* **1. clasp, clutch, grasp, hold, grab, clench, seize** The baseball player gripped his bat. **2. enthrall, fascinate, mesmerize, rivet, spellbind, transfix, arrest, hold** The exciting book gripped me for hours. ● **Antonyms:** *verb* **1. release, let go 2. bore**

gripe *verb* **complain, grumble, whine, grouch, grump, grouse, protest, carp** We griped so much about dinner that Mom threw it in the garbage. ◆ *noun* **complaint, grievance, protest, objection, grumble, criticism** I wrote to our state representative because I had a gripe.

grisly *adjective* **repugnant, gruesome, hideous, horrible, grim, ghastly, macabre, lurid** The horror movie was really grisly. ● **Antonyms: pleasant, nice, agreeable**

grit *noun* **1. dirt, dust, sand, debris, gravel, stone, particle** The wind blew a piece of grit into my eye. **2. spirit, courage, determination, pluck, fortitude, spunk, mettle, backbone** I admire people who show grit when faced with a challenge. ◆ *verb* **clamp, clench, gnash, grate, grind, scrape, rub** I grit my teeth whenever I get a shot. ● **Antonyms:** *noun* **2. timidity, cowardice**

groan *verb* **moan, sigh, whimper, whine, complain, gripe, grumble** She groaned when she looked at her homework. ◆ *noun* **cry, moan, sigh, sob, murmur, whimper, whine** The traveler gave a groan of relief when he set down his heavy suitcase.

groom *verb* **1. tend, brush, clean, comb, curry, tidy up, neaten, spruce** She grooms her horse after every ride. **2. train, prepare, prime, educate, coach, tutor, develop** My father says he is grooming me to be a plumber like him.

groove *noun* **channel, slot, cut, furrow, rut, hollow, score** My school desk has a groove for holding pencils.

grope *verb* **feel, fumble, poke, probe, flounder, fish, explore, search** I groped for the light switch in the dark room.

gross *adjective* **1. total, complete, whole, all, entire, aggregate** We made a gross profit of over one hundred dollars at our bake sale. **2. flagrant, glaring, obvious, plain, arrant, blatant, outrageous** The tabloid article contained nothing but gross lies. **3. vulgar, coarse, rude, tasteless, crass, crude, uncouth, obscene** I did not like his gross behavior at the party. **4. disgusting, offensive, repulsive, revolting, nauseating, repellent** The smell from the garbage can was gross. ◆ *noun* **aggregate, total, whole, sum, all,**

entirety Mom calculated the gross from our yard sale to be almost 350 dollars. ◆ *verb* **earn, receive, realize, draw, make, bring in, clear, yield** How much did the movie gross during its first week of release? ● **Antonyms:** *adjective* **2. minor, trivial 3. decent, clean 4. pleasant, agreeable**

grotesque *adjective* **bizarre, strange, unnatural, freakish, fantastic, odd, weird, ugly** The mythical Cerberus was a grotesque dog that had three heads. ● **Antonyms: ordinary, normal**

grouchy *adjective* **peevish, bad-tempered, cranky, cross, grumpy, irritable, surly, cantankerous** My little brother becomes grouchy if he doesn't take a nap. ● **Antonyms: good-humored, cheerful, amiable**

ground *noun* **1. land, dirt, earth, terra firma, surface, soil** I was glad to be back on the ground after our bumpy flight. **2. field, lot, property, terrain, yard, area, estate** Our band uses the football field as a parade ground. **3. basis, cause, evidence, reason, motive, call, justification, necessity, excuse** The lawyer believed there were sufficient grounds for taking the case to court. **4. subject, topic, area, range, sphere, arena, territory, realm** We covered new ground in our English class discussion today. ◆ *verb* **1. instruct, teach, educate, train, coach, tutor, prepare, drill** Our science teacher is grounding us in the scientific method. **2. base, establish, found, build, fix, rest, set, institute** The French Revolution was grounded on the principles of liberty, equality, and fraternity.

group *noun* **1. bunch, cluster, crowd, gang, party, body, set, company** A group of students gathered on the playground. **2. category, class, classification, branch, division, section, grade, set** Vegetables form one of the basic food groups. ◆ *verb* **1. arrange, classify, organize, sort, separate, place, distribute, divide** The clothes were grouped by size. **2. assemble, gather, cluster, muster, collect, congregate, convene, get together** My friends and I grouped together after lunch to visit until the bell rang. ● **Antonyms:** *verb* **2. scatter, disperse**

grove *noun* **stand, thicket, copse, forest, woods, woodland, orchard** There's a grove of oak trees in the field behind the school.

grow *verb* **1. mature, ripen, age, develop, mellow** Tomatoes turn red as they grow. **2. flourish, live, thrive, exist, arise, issue, sprout, prosper** Weeds can grow almost anywhere. **3. enlarge, expand, increase, swell, develop, amplify, mount, soar** The population in our town is growing rapidly. **4. cultivate, plant, produce, raise, breed, propagate, farm, sow** Aztec farmers grew corn, tomatoes, and chilies. **5. become, come to be, get, turn** It grows light just before dawn. ● **Antonyms: 3. decrease, shrink**

growl *noun* **snarl, bark, bellow, grunt, roar, rumble** We heard a low growl in the dark. ◆ *verb* **snarl, bark, bellow, grunt, roar, boom, rumble** Did you know that raccoons and opossums can growl?

growth *noun* **1. accumulation, buildup, proliferation, collection, mass, crop** There was a thick growth of weeds around the abandoned house. **2. development, expansion, increase, advance, progress, hike, rise** The mayor was pleased by the rapid growth of business in the town. **3. lump, excrescence, tumor, bump, swelling, cyst, wart, mole** I went to a dermatologist to have a growth removed. ● **Antonyms: 2. decline, decrease**

grub *verb* **dig, uproot, pull up, unearth, extract, clear, excavate, shovel** The early settlers grubbed out rocks and tree roots in order to plant grain. ◆ *noun* **larva, maggot, worm, caterpillar** The fisherman used a grub as bait.

grubby *adjective* **dirty, grimy, soiled, filthy, unclean, black, messy, sloppy** Barb was grubby after working in the garden. ● **Antonyms: neat, clean, tidy**

grudge *noun* **resentment, hard feelings, ill will, rancor, malice, spite, bitterness, animosity** Anthony doesn't stay mad long, and he never holds a grudge.

gruesome *adjective* **ghastly, grim, horrendous, hideous, horrible, shocking, terrible, awful** There was a gruesome accident on the highway last night. ● **Antonyms: pleasing, pleasant**

gruff *adjective* **1. abrupt, curt, harsh, stern, brusque, impolite, rude, short** He spoke to her in a gruff manner. **2. hoarse, husky, croaky, cracked, guttural, rough, low, deep** My voice was gruff because my throat was dry. ● **Antonyms: 1. polite, friendly 2. smooth, clear**

grumble *verb* **1. complain, gripe, grouse, grouch, whine, moan, mutter, carp** My brother grumbles when he has to empty the trash. **2. rumble, boom, roll, thunder, roar, growl** Lightning flashed and thunder grumbled in the distance. ◆ *noun* **1. complaint, protest, gripe, whine, moan, mutter** Mom didn't want to hear my grumbles any longer and sent me to my room. **2. rumble, boom, roll, thunder, roar, growl** We heard the grumble of a far-off avalanche.

grumpy *adjective* **surly, peevish, bad-tempered, cantankerous, cranky, cross, grouchy, irritable** The player was grumpy because he had to sit out the first half of the game. ● **Antonyms: good-humored, amiable, cheerful**

guarantee *noun* **assurance, promise, pledge, warranty, insurance, guaranty, bond** There are no guarantees when it comes to predicting the weather. ◆ *verb* **guaranty, assure, ensure, certify, warrant, secure, pledge, promise** The victory guarantees that our team will be in the state finals.

guard *verb* **defend, protect, safeguard, shield, preserve, watch over, watch** One of the missions of the Secret Service is to guard the President. ◆ *noun* **1. sentinel, sentry, watchman, protector, caretaker** This bank is protected by an armed guard. **2. supervision, security, control, protection, watch, vigilance** Police kept the two prisoners under guard. **3. protector, defense, safeguard, shield, screen, buffer, pad** Baseball catchers should wear shin guards.

guarded *adjective* **cautious, restrained, circumspect, wary, discreet, careful, reticent** I was guarded in my response. ● **Antonyms: careless, reckless**

guardian *noun* **protector, defender, custodian, keeper, caretaker, warden, guard** Some people believe that angels serve as our guardians.

guess *verb* **1. estimate, judge, reckon, calculate, speculate, divine** Can you guess how many marbles are in this jar? **2. assume, suppose, surmise, believe, think, presume, conjecture, infer** I guess she's not coming to school today. ◆ *noun* **conjecture, speculation, assumption, surmise, supposition, estimate, belief, opinion** It's my guess that we'll have a mild winter this year.

guest *noun* **1. company, visitor, caller, visitant, friend** We have guests coming for dinner tonight. **2. customer, patron, lodger, tenant, renter, boarder, roomer, client** This hotel can accommodate more than 250 guests.

guide *noun* **leader, escort, scout, conductor, shepherd, usher, director, pilot** A park ranger was our guide for the nature hike. ◆ *verb* **1. conduct, escort, lead, direct, usher, shepherd, show, accompany** Our teacher guided us through the museum. **2. steer, pilot, maneuver, jockey, navigate, direct, handle, control** I guided my mountain bike carefully down the trail.

guile *noun* **cunning, deceit, deception, duplicity, artifice, trickery, fraud, dishonesty** Many of the Roman emperors used guile to obtain the throne. ● **Antonyms: honesty, candor**

guilt *noun* 1. blame, fault, culpability, responsibility, wrongdoing, guiltiness, offense The jury ruled that the defendant was free of guilt. 2. remorse, shame, regret, contrition, repentance, rue, sorrow, penitence I felt a sense of guilt at not being able to do what she asked. ⏺ **Antonym:** 1. innocence

guilty *adjective* 1. at fault, blameworthy, blamable, culpable, responsible, wrong The suspect claimed that she was not guilty. 2. contrite, regretful, remorseful, repentant, sorry, rueful, penitent I felt guilty when I forgot my friend's birthday. ⏺ **Antonyms:** 1. innocent, blameless

> ### Word Group
>
> A **guitar** is a stringed musical instrument having a long neck and a large sound box. **Guitar** is a specific term with no true synonyms. Here are some related stringed instruments:
>
> A **banjo** has a narrow neck and a circular body that is covered with skin on one side. A **dulcimer** has three or four strings stretched over a sound box. A **lute** has a body shaped like a pear sliced lengthwise. A **mandolin** has a body shaped like a pear and has four pairs of strings. A **saz** is a long-necked stringed instrument, popular throughout the Middle East. A **sitar** is a stringed instrument of India that is made of gourds and has up to twenty strings. A **ukulele** is a small Hawaiian guitar with four strings.

gulf *noun* 1. bay, inlet, lagoon, sound, estuary, cove, firth, fjord The explorers mapped the newly discovered gulf. 2. difference, disparity, gap, separation, split, space, distance, chasm There's a big gulf between the richest and the poorest members of our society.

gullible *adjective* credulous, believing, trustful, trusting, naive, unsuspecting, innocent When I was younger, I was gullible enough to believe the moon was made of cheese. ⏺ **Antonyms:** cynical, skeptical

gully *noun* channel, ditch, ravine, trench, watercourse, gulch The downpour etched gullies in the hillside.

gulp *verb* bolt, gobble, wolf, guzzle, swallow, down, swill, devour My dog gulped down my ice cream cone when I offered him a taste. ◆ *noun* mouthful, swallow, swig I was so thirsty that I drank a glass of water in big gulps.

guru *noun* spiritual leader, teacher, mentor, leader, guide, master, sage, swami He is the current guru of pop psychology.

gush *verb* 1. flow, pour, run, rush, stream, surge, spout, spurt Water gushed from the broken fire hydrant. 2. carry on, rave, rant, prattle, babble, blabber, jabber, prate My aunt gushed about her trip to Europe. ◆ *noun* outflow, outpour, spate, spurt, stream, jet, spout, flow, squirt Her gush of words overwhelmed me.

gust *noun* blast, blow, breeze, draft, wind, puff, rush, burst A gust of wind knocked a branch off the old tree.

gusto *noun* zest, enthusiasm, zeal, eagerness, delight, relish, pleasure He entered into our plans with gusto. ⏺ **Antonyms:** loathing, reluctance, hesitation

gutter *noun* ditch, drain, channel, pipe, trough, groove, sewer, culvert Our street doesn't have gutters.

guttural *adjective* husky, throaty, hoarse, rasping, rough, deep, low, gruff He spoke in such a guttural voice that I could hardly understand him. ⏺ **Antonyms:** high, clear

guy *noun* fellow, person, chap, bloke, boy, lad, man, gentleman Your brother is a great guy.

guzzle *verb* gulp, swill, swig, imbibe, quaff, tipple, drink We guzzled iced tea during the hot afternoon.

gyrate *verb* spin, twirl, turn, circle, rotate, whirl, wheel, pirouette It was fun to watch the dancers gyrate.

Hh

habit *noun* **custom, practice, routine, tendency, pattern, trait, mode** I am in the habit of doing my homework before dinner.

habitual *adjective* **customary, normal, regular, routine, usual, standard, common, accustomed** Everyone in my family has a habitual place at the dinner table. ➡️ **Antonyms: rare, unusual**

hack *verb* **chop, slash, whack, cut, slice, hew, cleave, gash** I hacked at the weeds with a garden hoe.

haggard *adjective* **worn, exhausted, gaunt, weary, tired, spent, wan, drawn** The refugees looked haggard after their journey. ➡️ **Antonyms: robust, energetic**

hail *verb* **1. greet, salute, welcome, address, receive, accost, meet, recognize** My friend hailed me when we met on the way to school. **2. flag, signal, summon, wave down, shout at, call to, motion** Dad hailed a passing driver when our car broke down.

hale *adjective* **robust, healthy, sound, strong, fit, vigorous, hearty, well, strapping** The farmer and his sons were hale men. ➡️ **Antonyms: sickly, feeble, ailing**

hall *noun* **1. corridor, hallway, passageway, passage, gallery, arcade** She said to meet her in the hall after class. **2. entryway, lobby, foyer, vestibule, entrance, antechamber, waiting room** There was a suit of armor displayed in the large hall. **3. auditorium, building, lyceum, chamber, room, theater, arena, amphitheater** University classes are sometimes taught in huge lecture halls.

hallowed *adjective* **consecrated, dedicated, holy, sacred, blessed, divine, sanctified** Cemeteries, battlefields, and religious sites are considered to be hallowed ground. ➡️ **Antonym: profane**

hallucination *noun* **delusion, illusion, dream, fantasy, vision, mirage, phantasm** Some drugs can cause hallucinations.

halt *noun* **break, pause, recess, rest, stop, lapse, delay** Conversation came to a halt when the principal entered the room. ◆ *verb* **stop, cease, discontinue, pause, rest, hold, quit, wait, check** The soldiers halted after having marched several miles. ➡️ **Antonyms:** *noun* **beginning, start** ◆ *verb* **begin, start**

hammer *verb* **1. beat, pound, strike, smash, tap, thump, batter, bang, whack** The blacksmith hammered the horseshoe into shape. **2. persevere, persist, continue, keep on, work, try, endeavor** I hammered away at my math homework.

hamper *verb* **impede, hinder, obstruct, restrict, frustrate, inhibit, prevent, thwart** The rain hampered our efforts to light a campfire. ➡️ **Antonyms: assist, help**

hand *noun* **1. aid, assistance, assist, help, support, relief, succor** We gave Mom a hand with washing the windows. **2. assistant, employee, helper, laborer, worker, aide, associate** The rancher hired extra hands to help with the roundup. **3. part, role, share, responsibility, portion, function, job** Everyone on the team had a hand in winning the game. **4. keeping, care, charge, custody, jurisdiction, possession, ownership** I know my pet will be in good hands while I am on vacation. ◆ *verb* **give, pass, convey, deliver, transfer, turn over, hand over, present** I handed a copy of the assignment to my friend.

handicap *noun* **disadvantage, drawback, hindrance, disability, impediment, defect, obstacle** We tried to arrive early, but the snow proved a handicap. ◆ *verb* **burden, hamper, hinder, impede, restrain, encumber, limit, frustrate** I was handicapped by a broken arm. ➡️ **Antonyms:** *noun* **advantage, asset** ◆ *verb* **assist, help**

handle *verb* **1. hold, touch, feel, grasp, grip, fondle, finger, manipulate** I handled the delicate crystal bowl with care. **2. command, control, direct, manage, supervise, maneuver, steer, administer** She handles her horse extremely well. ◆ *noun* **arm, grip, handgrip, shaft, stem, haft, hilt, crank, stock** This shovel has a wooden handle.

handsome *adjective* **1. attractive, beautiful, gorgeous, pleasing, comely, lovely, pretty, good-looking** This suit is made of a handsome woolen fabric. **2. generous, liberal, bounteous, lavish, large, ample, tidy, considerable** The buyer submitted a handsome offer for our house. ➡️ **Antonyms: 1. plain, unattractive 2. small, paltry, meager**

handy *adjective* **1. proficient, skilled, skillful, adroit, deft, expert, adept, dexterous** He is handy with carpentry tools. **2. accessible, available, close, nearby, close by, adjacent, at hand, ready** It is smart to keep a flashlight handy. **3. convenient, efficient, helpful, practical, useful, functional, beneficial, advantageous** An almanac is a handy reference book. ➡ **Antonyms: 1. awkward, clumsy 2. unavailable 3. useless**

hang *verb* **1. dangle, suspend, swing, hover, fix, sag, droop, sling, attach** The swing hangs from a tree limb. **2. lynch, string up, gibbet, execute** In the Old West, outlaws were often hanged. **3. depend, await, hinge, turn, rest, base, stand** Her decision to start her own business hangs on her securing a loan.

haphazard *adjective* **careless, chance, indiscriminate, random, unplanned, arbitrary, aimless** The videos were put back on the shelves in haphazard order. ➡ **Antonyms: organized, deliberate**

happen *verb* **arise, develop, occur, take place, chance, pass, materialize, befall** What happened in school when I was absent?

happiness *noun* **bliss, cheer, delight, gladness, joy, pleasure, contentment, elation, felicity** Drawing in my sketchbook always fills me with happiness. ➡ **Antonyms: misery, unhappiness, despair**

happy *adjective* **1. delighted, glad, pleased, thrilled, joyful, joyous, overjoyed, cheerful, tickled** I'm happy to make your acquaintance. **2. lucky, fortunate, opportune, favorable, auspicious, timely, providential** It was a happy day when he picked the right numbers to win the lottery. ➡ **Antonyms: 1. sad, unhappy 2. unfortunate, unlucky**

harass *verb* **annoy, bother, disturb, pester, trouble, irritate, torment, vex, plague** Ants and flies frequently harass picnickers.

harbor *noun* **1. port, bay, cove, inlet, gulf** Two tugboats guided the ocean liner into the harbor. **2. refuge, sanctuary, asylum, haven, retreat, cover, protection, shelter** I took harbor in the old barn during the sudden rainstorm. ◆ *verb* **1. shelter, house, shield, lodge, guard, put up, safeguard, hide, conceal** We harbored the stray dog until we could locate its owner. **2. bear, entertain, hold, foster, cherish, nurse, indulge, maintain** I think he is harboring a grudge.

hard *adjective* **1. firm, rigid, solid, stiff, compact, incompressible, stony** That bed is too hard to be comfortable. **2. forceful, heavy, powerful, severe, strong, serious, terrible, hefty** I arrived home just before a hard rain began to fall.

3. difficult, laborious, rough, tough, arduous, formidable, troublesome, fatiguing We had a hard time driving up the icy mountain road. **4. harsh, severe, stern, strict, stringent, exacting, pitiless, unsympathetic** Her experiences have made her hard. **5. definite, real, true, unchangeable, positive, absolute, indisputable, concrete** It is a hard truth that we all must die someday. ◆ *adverb* **1. diligently, earnestly, intently, industriously, painstakingly, determinedly** I worked hard to memorize all the state capitals. **2. forcefully, heavily, powerfully, strongly, vigorously, roughly, sharply** You have to pull hard on that drawer, for it sticks. ➡ **Antonyms:** *adjective* **1. flexible, soft 2. mild, weak 3. easy, simple 4. lenient, indulgent** ◆ *adverb* **1. easily, lazily 2. gently, weakly**

hardly *adverb* **barely, just, scarcely, only, not quite, faintly, somewhat** This subway car rattles so loudly that I can hardly hear you.

hardship *noun* **adversity, difficulty, trouble, danger, misfortune, trial, rigor** The Pilgrims experienced many hardships during their first winter in America.

hardy *adjective* **fit, robust, strong, sturdy, tough, healthy, hale, brawny, hearty** The hardy tree survived the hurricane. ➡ **Antonyms: feeble, weak**

hark *verb* **listen, hearken, hear, pay attention, attend, heed** Please hark to what I am saying. ➡ **Antonyms: ignore, disregard**

harm *noun* **1. injury, hurt, damage, misfortune, loss, impairment, detriment** Automobile seat belts help protect passengers from harm. **2. wrong, sin, sinfulness, wickedness, immorality, evil, iniquity, vice** The convict claimed to feel remorse for the harm he had done. ◆ *verb* **injure, hurt, damage, mar, wound, impair, abuse, destroy** My dog won't harm you. ➡ **Antonyms:** *noun* **1. benefit, good 2. goodness** ◆ *verb* **heal, cure, help**

harmful *adjective* **damaging, injurious, bad, detrimental, deleterious, hurtful, unhealthy** Exposure to too much sunlight is harmful. ➡ **Antonyms: harmless, safe**

harmless *adjective* **safe, innocuous, benign, good, innocent, inoffensive, nontoxic** Some berries are poisonous, but many others are harmless. ➡ **Antonyms: dangerous, harmful**

harmonize *verb* **agree, correspond, match, coordinate, blend, conform, concur** My political views don't harmonize with his. ➡ **Antonyms: clash, disagree, contradict**

harmony *noun* **1. balance, order, symmetry, correspondence, proportion, conformance** The new park did not disrupt the harmony of its natural setting. **2. accord, agreement, concord, concurrence, unity, rapport, friendship, sympathy** Our committee members worked in harmony. ● **Antonyms: 1. imbalance 2. conflict, disagreement**

harness *verb* **1. yoke, hitch, couple, connect, bridle, fetter, leash, rig** I harnessed my dog to my little sister's wagon. **2. control, direct, exploit, utilize, employ, channel** The power of the Columbia River has been harnessed to provide electricity.

harsh *adjective* **1. raucous, grating, hoarse, jarring, strident, gruff, rasping, coarse** A blue jay has a harsh cry. **2. bitter, brutal, cruel, hard, rough, severe, stark, grim, bleak, nasty** Winter last year was especially harsh, with record cold temperatures and snowfall. ● **Antonyms: 1. pleasant, melodious 2. easy, gentle**

harvest *noun* **crop, yield, produce, product, fruit, result, consequence, reward** The corn harvest in Illinois was abundant this year. ◆ *verb* **reap, collect, garner, gather, glean, pick, cut, mow** Winter wheat is harvested in the spring or early summer.

haste *noun* **hustle, quickness, rapidity, speed, hurry, rush, swiftness, urgency** Trying to make up time for having overslept, I dressed with great haste. ● **Antonyms: slowness, delay**

hasten *verb* **hurry, race, run, rush, dash, hustle, speed, scurry, sprint** I hastened to answer the phone. ● **Antonyms: delay, slow**

hasty *adjective* **fast, hurried, quick, rapid, speedy, swift, sudden, abrupt** We made a hasty retreat when we saw the bull. ● **Antonyms: leisurely, slow**

Word Group

A **hat** is a covering for the head, especially one with a crown and brim. **Hat** is a general term with no true synonyms. Here are some common types of hats:

beret, bonnet, bowler, cap, cowboy hat, derby, fedora, fez, kepi, Panama hat, sombrero, top hat

---

hatch *verb* **concoct, create, devise, invent, make up, plot, contrive, formulate** My friends and I hatched a plan to give a surprise party for Ian.

hate *verb* **despise, detest, dislike, loathe, abhor, disdain, abominate, scorn** I hate dusting the furniture. ◆ *noun* **hatred, animosity, dislike, abhorrence, hostility, loathing, antagonism** Her eyes were filled with hate. ● **Antonyms:** *verb* **like, love, adore** ◆ *noun* **liking, fondness, love**

hateful *adjective* **nasty, obnoxious, odious, offensive, awful, heinous, spiteful** I am sorry for the hateful things I said to you. ● **Antonyms: pleasant, likable**

hatred *noun* **abhorrence, aversion, loathing, detestation, revulsion, animosity, hostility, hate** My hatred of lima beans increases every time I eat them. ● **Antonyms: liking, love**

haughty *adjective* **arrogant, conceited, proud, vain, high-and-mighty, insolent, egotistical** Do you feel sorry for the haughty queen in *Snow White*? ● **Antonyms: humble, modest**

haul *verb* **1. drag, draw, pull, tow, tug, tote, lug, cart** It took four men to haul the piano up a flight of stairs. **2. carry, convey, move, transport, truck, tow, take, deliver** Dad hired a truck to haul our furniture to our new house. ◆ *noun* **catch, take, yield, booty, cargo, load, spoils, freight** The boat sailed back to port carrying a large haul of fish.

haunt *verb* **1. frequent, hang around, habituate, visit, inhabit, dwell in, possess** Being a bookworm, I haunt our neighborhood library. **2. obsess, torment, trouble, worry, vex, weigh on, madden, plague** The memory of my first piano recital still haunts me.

have *verb* **1. own, possess, hold, keep, maintain, retain, bear** I have a hamster, a guinea pig, and a cockatiel. **2. comprise, contain, embrace, include, involve, embody, encompass** A week has seven days. **3. accept, receive, take, acquire, get, obtain, procure, secure** Will you have another piece of cake? **4. encounter, experience, endure, know, meet, see, enjoy, undergo** Did you have a good day at the beach? **5. need, must, ought, should, compel, oblige, require, necessitate** I have to go home right after school today.

haven *noun* **asylum, refuge, retreat, sanctuary, shelter, hideaway, harbor** My room is my haven.

havoc *noun* **destruction, devastation, chaos, ruin, disorder, mayhem, wreckage** Flooding has caused havoc throughout the county. ● **Antonyms: peace, order**

hazard *noun* **danger, peril, risk, threat, jeopardy, uncertainty, chance, accident** Getting kicked and stepped on are a couple of the hazards of working with horses. ◆ *verb* **dare, venture, risk, gamble, attempt, chance, wager, stake** I don't know the answer, but I could hazard a guess.

hazardous *adjective* **dangerous, perilous, risky, unsafe, uncertain, chancy** Playing with matches is hazardous. ◗ **Antonyms: safe, secure, reliable**

hazy *adjective* **1. cloudy, foggy, misty, overcast, smoky, murky, filmy, smoggy** The sky was hazy when I got up this morning. **2. dim, faint, indistinct, uncertain, vague, fuzzy, indefinite, unclear** I have only a hazy recollection of my early childhood. ◗ **Antonyms: 1. clear, cloudless 2. distinct, precise, exact**

head *noun* **1. brain, mind, intelligence, intellect, wits, perception, wisdom** You have to use your head to solve a crossword puzzle. **2. aptitude, instinct, talent, ability, gift, knack, capacity, flair, genius** He has a head for knowing what to do in emergencies. **3. boss, chief, director, leader, manager, superintendent, ruler, commander** She is the head of her company's sales department. **4. beginning, front, start, vanguard, forefront, origin, source** A high-school band marched at the head of the parade. **5. apex, turning point, climax, crisis, acme, culmination, top** The difficulties between them came to a head on the third day of the trip. ◆ *adjective* **chief, leading, main, principal, top, first, supreme, foremost** The head counselor gave us a tour of the camp. ◆ *verb* **1. aim, direct, guide, steer, turn, point, lead, conduct** We headed our sailboat into the wind. **2. direct, lead, govern, manage, run, administer, supervise, rule** Michael will head this year's student council. ◗ **Antonyms:** *noun* **4. end** ◆ *adjective* **secondary, minor**

heal *verb* **mend, recover, restore, cure, remedy, repair, recuperate, treat** The doctor said that my broken arm will heal within six weeks. ◗ **Antonyms: wound, injure, harm**

health *noun* **haleness, well-being, healthiness, vitality, soundness, hardiness, vigor, strength** Yoga can often help maintain good health. ◗ **Antonyms: illness, sickness**

healthy *adjective* **1. fit, hale, sound, well, hearty, all right, vigorous, strong** I was sick last week, but I'm healthy now. **2. healthful, beneficial, helpful, nourishing, wholesome, sustaining, desirable** Vegetables and fruits are important parts of a healthy diet. **3. great, sizable, generous, large, huge, enormous, big, considerable** Our school received a healthy donation for the new computer lab. ◗ **Antonyms: 1. ill, sick 2. unhealthy, unhelpful 3. small, stingy**

heap *noun* **mass, mound, pile, stack, hill, deposit, collection, accumulation** We raked the leaves into a big heap.

◆ *verb* **lump, mound, pile, stack, bank, load, amass, dump** I heaped the laundry next to the washing machine.

hear *verb* **1. attend to, heed, listen to, hearken, hark, catch, regard** The captain called for the crew's attention by saying, "Now hear this." **2. understand, gather, find out, learn, discover, ascertain, perceive** I hear there is going to be a special art exhibit next month. ◗ **Antonyms: 1. ignore, disregard**

heart *noun* **1. soul, nature, emotion, feeling, sentiment, sympathy, understanding, humanity** She has a good heart and is considerate of others. **2. courage, mettle, nerve, pluck, spirit, guts, fortitude, bravery** Our football team has a lot of heart. **3. center, core, middle, nucleus, essence, gist, root** We went for a hike through the heart of the forest. ◗ **Antonyms: 2. timidity, fear 3. outside, outskirts**

hearty *adjective* **1. friendly, cheerful, genial, cordial, enthusiastic, warm, sincere** We received a hearty welcome. **2. healthy, vigorous, well, active, hale, hardy, robust, strong** She is still hearty despite her advancing years. ◗ **Antonyms: 1. cool, aloof, reserved 2. weak, frail, feeble**

heat *noun* **hotness, warmth, temperature, warmness, fever, fieriness** That fire is putting out a lot of heat. ◆ *verb* **make hot, warm, warm up, fire, cook, bake, kindle, reheat** I'll get out the bowls while you heat the soup. ◗ **Antonyms:** *noun* **cold, coolness** ◆ *verb* **chill, cool**

heave *verb* **1. hoist, lift, pick up, raise, boost, heft, elevate, drag** It took two men to heave the anchor aboard. **2. fling, hurl, pitch, cast, throw, toss, chuck, sling** We heaved a big rock into the pond just to see the splash. **3. vomit, throw up, spew, spit up, disgorge, gag, puke, retch** Our cat heaved up the remains of a mouse.

heaven *noun* **bliss, ecstasy, joy, paradise, rapture, nirvana, happiness** She was in heaven when she got to meet her favorite author. ◗ **Antonyms: agony, torment**

heavenly *adjective* **lovely, blissful, delightful, marvelous, pleasing, wonderful** Those roses have a heavenly scent. ◗ **Antonyms: awful, terrible**

heavy *adjective* **1. massive, weighty, big, bulky, huge, large, ponderous, cumbersome** He helped us move the heavy sofa. **2. abundant, ample, excessive, plentiful, voluminous, intense, substantial, copious** There will be no school today because of the heavy snow. **3. gloomy, sad, depressed, sorrowful, dismal, melancholy, grieving**

The tragic news left us with heavy hearts. **4. grave, serious, solemn, ponderous, somber, momentous, severe** Global warming, pollution, world hunger, and endangered species are heavy subjects. **5. demanding, difficult, hard, laborious, tough, arduous, grueling, taxing** Digging a deep ditch is heavy work. ◆ **Antonym: light**

hectic *adjective* **frantic, chaotic, turbulent, confused, frenzied, feverish, wild, furious** Shopping can be hectic during the holidays. ◆ **Antonyms: placid, calm**

hedge *noun* **hedgerow, bushes, shrubbery, thicket, screen, boundary, windbreak** A tall hedge marks the bounds of our property. ◆ *verb* **edge, enclose, ring, surround, fence, hem, girdle, border** My garden is hedged with roses.

heed *verb* **follow, mind, obey, observe, regard, attend, listen to, consider** Everyone is expected to heed traffic laws. ◆ *noun* **notice, attention, consideration, regard, care, note, caution** She didn't give any heed to the sign that said "No Trespassing." ◆ **Antonyms:** *verb* **disregard, ignore** ◆ *noun* **neglect, inattention**

height *noun* **1. elevation, highness, tallness, altitude, loftiness, extent** The height of the Empire State building is 1,250 feet. **2. climax, crest, peak, top, zenith, pinnacle, summit, culmination, acme** At the height of the baseball season, there are games almost every day. ◆ **Antonyms: 1. depth 2. bottom, nadir**

heinous *adjective* **abominable, horrifying, atrocious, evil, wicked, monstrous, outrageous, shocking** He was given a sentence of life in prison for his heinous crimes. ◆ **Antonyms: good, decent**

hell *noun* **misery, agony, anguish, torment, trial, ordeal, nightmare, torture** The movie portrayed the hell of battle very realistically. ◆ **Antonyms: heaven, bliss, joy**

help *verb* **1. aid, assist, benefit, serve, support, contribute, pitch in, abet** She helps her parents run their doughnut shop. **2. ease, improve, relieve, cure, heal, allay, remedy, restore** I drank a cup of peppermint tea to help my upset stomach. ◆ *noun* **1. aid, assistance, support, hand, succor, collaboration, cooperation** Dad asked for my help in painting the porch. **2. employee, hand, helper, laborer, assistant, worker, colleague, attendant** The company hired new help. ◆ **Antonyms:** *verb* **1. hinder, impede 2. aggravate, worsen**

helpful *adjective* **beneficial, handy, useful, valuable, practical, good, productive, constructive** My friend gave me some helpful advice. ◆ **Antonyms: useless, worthless**

helpless *adjective* **defenseless, unprotected, dependent, vulnerable, incapable, powerless, feeble** Baby kittens are helpless for the first eight weeks after birth. ◆ **Antonyms: strong, independent**

hem *noun* **edge, border, boundary, lip, verge, fringe, flounce** The curtains had a hem of antique lace. ◆ *verb* **edge, envelop, bound, circle, rim, ring, fence, encircle, frame** We hemmed the yard with shrubs and flowers.

herald *noun* **portent, precursor, harbinger, omen, sign, signal, forerunner, messenger** The early snow was a herald of winter. ◆ *verb* **usher in, foretell, announce, introduce, proclaim, prophesy, forecast** The dropping of the atom bomb in August 1945 heralded the end of World War II.

Word Group

An **herb** is any of various often aromatic plants used in medicine or as seasoning. **Herb** is a general term with no true synonyms. Here are some **herbs** that are commonly used as food seasonings:

basil, coriander, dill, fennel, marjoram, mint, oregano, parsley, rosemary, sage, tarragon, thyme

herd *noun* **drove, group, horde, pack, throng, mass, multitude** My grandmother has a herd of dairy cows. ◆ *verb* **drive, guide, lead, round up, run, collect, gather, assemble** The collies herded the sheep into the barn.

heritage *noun* **tradition, legacy, inheritance, endowment, ancestry** Every family has a heritage of traditions and customs.

hero *noun* **champion, idol, inspiration, role model, heroine, ideal, star** Some of my heroes are real people, and some are figures from stories and legends.

heroic *adjective* **bold, brave, courageous, fearless, gallant, valiant, principled, grand** Sir Lancelot was one of the heroic knights in King Arthur's court. ◆ **Antonyms: cowardly, fearful**

hesitant *adjective* **reluctant, doubtful, indecisive, uncertain, tentative, unsure, halting** I was hesitant to go in the baby's room while she was sleeping. ◆ **Antonyms: certain, decisive, confident**

hesitate *verb* **delay, falter, waver, vacillate, pause, wait, balk, hedge** We hesitated a moment before entering the carnival's haunted house.

hew *verb* split, hack, cut, chisel, fell, chop down, drop, ax The lumberjack hewed the tree into logs.

hide *verb* conceal, cover up, mask, screen, veil, cloak, camouflage, shroud My uncle wears a wig to hide his bald spot. ● **Antonyms:** reveal, uncover

hideous *adjective* revolting, disgusting, ghastly, gruesome, horrible, repulsive, ugly, appalling I bought a hideous mask to wear to the Halloween party. ● **Antonyms:** attractive, pleasing

high *adjective* **1.** tall, lofty, towering, soaring, raised, big, large Mount Everest is 29,028 feet high. **2.** excessive, extreme, fierce, furious, heavy, strong, great, stiff A hurricane's high winds can do considerable damage. **3.** piercing, sharp, shrill, treble, piping, penetrating, high-pitched My dog whistle has a high pitch. **4.** chief, eminent, leading, important, prominent, significant, ruling, grand She holds a high diplomatic post in Europe. **5.** happy, cheerful, joyful, exhilarated, excited, exuberant, bouncy I was in high spirits when I heard I had been selected to join the marching band. ◆ *noun* maximum, peak, top, zenith, acme, culmination, crown, summit Test scores in our school reached an all-time high last year. ● **Antonyms:** *adjective* **1.** low, short, little **2.** weak **3.** deep, bass **4.** unimportant, insignificant **5.** low, sad, depressed ◆ *noun* low, depression

highway *noun* expressway, freeway, interstate, turnpike, road, thoroughfare, thruway Will this highway take us to Indianapolis?

hike *verb* **1.** march, trek, walk, ramble, stroll, travel, traipse, tramp The backpackers hiked 17 miles on the first day of their trip. **2.** boost, raise, increase, jump, lift, hitch The store owner had hiked up the price of the popular toy. ◆ *noun* **1.** ramble, stroll, trek, walk, trip, journey, excursion, walkabout I enjoy taking hikes through the hills behind our house. **2.** increase, raise, boost, jump, advance, rise Bad weather caused a hike in the price of fresh fruits and vegetables.

hill *noun* knoll, mound, rise, elevation, hilltop, prominence, ascent, hummock He rode his bike to the top of the hill. ● **Antonyms:** valley, hollow, dell

hinder *verb* delay, impede, hamper, obstruct, slow down, stall, hold back, block Heavy snow hindered the flow of traffic. ● **Antonyms:** aid, assist, help

hinge *verb* depend, rest, hang, revolve, turn, pivot, stand Whether the drought will end hinges on the amount of rain we get in the next few months.

hint *noun* **1.** cue, clue, sign, suggestion, tip, pointer, lead, indication She guessed the riddle without any hints. **2.** trace, tinge, touch, pinch, iota, dash, breath, suspicion There is a hint of garlic in the salad dressing. ◆ *verb* imply, indicate, insinuate, suggest, mention, intimate, infer I hinted that I would like in-line skates for my birthday.

hire *verb* **1.** employ, engage, retain, take on, enlist, appoint, authorize, draft I wish I could hire someone to clean my room. **2.** charter, lease, rent, let, procure, sublease, commission, secure We hired a houseboat on Lake Shasta for our vacation. ● **Antonyms: 1.** dismiss, fire, release

history *noun* **1.** chronicle, account, record, narration, annals, journal, report The explorer wrote a history of his travels. **2.** antiquity, past, yore, background, yesterday, yesteryear, old days I like to read about teenagers in history.

hit *verb* **1.** beat, club, hammer, knock, pound, strike, smack, swat I hit the clay it with my fist to flatten it. **2.** collide, knock, smash, bump, crash, jostle, scrape The car skidded on the ice and hit a tree. **3.** achieve, attain, catch, gain, reach, accomplish, secure, take I hit my stride as I rounded third base and ran toward home plate. **4.** affect, impress, move, touch, overwhelm, upset, stir, perturb The news of my grandfather's illness hit me hard. ◆ *noun* **1.** blow, impact, shot, strike, knock, slap, whop, bang My arrow scored a direct hit on the bull's-eye. **2.** sensation, smash, success, triumph, achievement, winner, favorite His article for the school paper was a big hit. ● **Antonyms:** *noun* **2.** flop, failure, miss

hitch *verb* yoke, harness, tether, attach, fasten, join, tie The farmer hitched the oxen to the cart. ◆ *noun* difficulty, mishap, problem, snag, delay, catch, hindrance, impediment Our trip to the mountains went off without a hitch. ● **Antonyms:** *verb* detach, release

hoard *noun* stock, stockpile, store, supply, treasure, cache, inventory, reserve The dragon kept a watchful eye on its hoard of gold coins. ◆ *verb* lay away, stockpile, store, accumulate, gather, amass, save Squirrels hoard nuts for the winter. ● **Antonyms:** *verb* scatter, disperse, waste

hoarse *adjective* harsh, rough, scratchy, gruff, husky, grating, jarring A hoarse voice is a common symptom of a sore throat. ● **Antonyms:** clear, smooth

hoary *adjective* age-old, old, olden, ancient, antiquated, archaic, venerable "Haste makes waste" is a hoary saying.

hoax *noun* joke, prank, trick, stunt, deception, fraud, lie, scam My dad always thinks of a funny hoax to pull on

April Fools' Day. ◆ *verb* **trick, deceive, mislead, hoodwink, fool, swindle, con, cheat** I tried to hoax my mom into letting me stay home from school.

hobble *verb* **1. limp, stumble, shuffle, stagger, dodder, falter, totter** The tired runner hobbled to the finish line. **2. restrict, hinder, impede, cripple, chain, curb, fetter** Lack of money hobbled the family's efforts to buy a new home.

hobby *noun* **pastime, diversion, pursuit, recreation, fun, leisure, amusement** Her hobby is collecting stamps.

hoist *verb* **haul, lift, raise, run up, boost, elevate, erect, upraise** I was chosen to hoist the flag this morning. ◆ **Antonyms: drop, lower**

hold *verb* **1. clasp, clutch, grasp, grip, squeeze, clench, embrace, hug** I held the bat with both hands. **2. control, restrain, curb, prevent, stop, inhibit, keep back, withhold** Please hold your applause until the play is over. **3. accommodate, contain, take, include, comprise, seat, carry, have** This carton holds a dozen eggs. **4. bear, support, take, shoulder, bolster, brace, sustain, uphold** The porch swing will hold the weight of two people. **5. conduct, give, have, stage, direct, run, carry on, convene** We are planning to hold a garage sale next Saturday. **6. continue, endure, last, persist, remain, stay, hold out, keep** I hope this good weather will hold for a few more days. **7. believe, assume, consider, maintain, presume, esteem, deem, reckon** I hold that art, music, and athletics are good for people of all ages. ◆ *noun* **1. clasp, clutch, grasp, grip, clench, clamp, embrace, purchase** I kept a firm hold on the ladder. **2. control, sway, influence, power, authority, dominion, mastery** The charismatic speaker had a firm hold over his audience.

hole *noun* **1. breach, gap, opening, slit, slot, aperture, rent, rupture** The dog got out of the yard through a hole in the fence. **2. cavity, crater, depression, hollow, pit, gorge, dip, cave** I helped Dad dig holes for the rhododendron bushes. **3. fault, defect, error, omission, loophole, fallacy, flaw, shortcoming** There was a hole in her theory.

holiday *noun* **1. celebration, festival, jubilee, holy day, fete, fiesta, revel** The Fourth of July is a holiday in the United States. **2. break, leave, recess, vacation, respite, furlough** I visited my cousins during the summer holiday.

hollow *adjective* **1. empty, unfilled, vacant, void** Birds can fly because most of their bones are hollow. **2. meaningless, insincere, vain, artificial, idle, pointless, worthless** His apology was hollow. ◆ *noun* **cavity, hole, pocket, crater, depression, basin, indentation, dent** I found a raccoon den in the hollow of a tree. ◆ *verb* **scoop, dig, excavate,**

shovel, remove, channel, pit We hollowed out the pumpkin to carve a jack-o'-lantern. ◆ **Antonyms:** *adjective* **1. solid, full 2. sincere, significant**

holocaust *noun* **disaster, catastrophe, destruction, annihilation, inferno** The huge fire amounted to a holocaust, so many lives were lost.

holy *adjective* **divine, religious, sacred, revered, pious, blessed, sacrosanct, hallowed** The Koran is the holy book of Islam. ◆ **Antonyms: secular, profane**

homage *noun* **honor, respect, reverence, deference, devotion, admiration, veneration, tribute** It is common to show homage to Nobel Prize winners.

home *noun* **1. abode, domicile, house, residence, dwelling, habitation, lodging** A new home is being built in our neighborhood. **2. birthplace, hometown, homeland, fatherland, motherland, neighborhood** Nampa, Idaho, is my home. **3. asylum, hospital, institution, shelter, orphanage, hospice** Our elderly neighbor just moved to a nursing home.

homely *adjective* **1. ugly, unattractive, unlovely, uncomely, repulsive, disgusting, plain** I think vultures are homely. **2. simple, plain, ordinary, everyday, informal, rustic, natural** We live a homely life when we go to our mountain cabin. ◆ **Antonym: 2. sophisticated**

honest *adjective* **honorable, trustworthy, upright, upstanding, truthful, true, good** An honest person would return a lost wallet to its rightful owner. ◆ **Antonyms: dishonest, deceitful**

honesty *noun* **integrity, truthfulness, honor, trustworthiness, candor, rectitude, principle** Honesty and kindness are two important virtues.

honor *noun* **1. acclaim, award, distinction, laurels, praise, tribute, accolade** The straight-A student graduated with honors. **2. honesty, integrity, virtue, dignity, morality, principles, nobleness** A sense of honor makes us want to do the right thing. ◆ *verb* **1. celebrate, eulogize, exalt, glorify, acclaim, commend, praise, recognize** This memorial honors the men and women who died in the Vietnam War. **2. admire, esteem, respect, revere, venerate, worship, value, regard** We honor those who speak the truth and act with integrity. ◆ **Antonyms:** *noun* **1. disgrace, shame 2. duplicity, treachery** ◆ *verb* **2. despise, disdain**

hoodlum *noun* **gangster, thug, hooligan, ruffian, tough, rowdy, criminal, mobster** The police arrested the hoodlums responsible for the vandalism.

hook *noun* hanger, holder, catch, clasp, fastener, peg, stud, barb, claw We have coat hooks in our classroom. ◆ *verb* catch, fasten, latch, secure, hitch, clasp, clip, lock, attach Please hook the screen door so it will stay closed.

hoop *noun* ring, band, strap, circle, circlet, loop, belt, girdle The barrel staves were held together with iron hoops.

hoot *verb* jeer, mock, boo, hiss, scoff, deride, shout, clamor The fans hooted when the player missed the basket. ◈ **Antonyms:** hail, applaud, cheer

hop *verb* bounce, bound, jump, leap, skip, spring, trip, prance A rabbit hopped across the golf course. ◆ *noun* bounce, bound, jump, leap, skip, spring, step The robin moved across the lawn in short hops.

hope *verb* wish, look forward to, desire, aspire, pray, anticipate, expect, want I hope to go to the beach during vacation. ◆ *noun* desire, dream, longing, wish, expectation, ambition, expectancy, aspiration My hope is to win next week's tennis tournament.

hopeful *adjective* 1. confident, expectant, optimistic, anticipatory, sanguine My aunt is hopeful that she will find a good job. 2. encouraging, favorable, good, promising, auspicious, bright The doctor said that signs for a full recovery were hopeful. ◈ **Antonyms:** 2. hopeless, unfavorable

hopeless *adjective* 1. despairing, disconsolate, despondent, abject, dejected, sad, forlorn I feel hopeless about my chances of making the honor roll this semester. 2. bad, desperate, futile, impossible, unfavorable, poor, lost, pointless We were in a hopeless situation when we were behind by 50 points at halftime. ◈ **Antonyms:** 1. hopeful, optimistic 2. favorable, promising

horde *noun* crowd, herd, mob, pack, swarm, throng, multitude, crush There was a horde of people at the street fair.

horizon *noun* limit, perspective, range, scope, reach, grasp, sphere, extent Reading has expanded my horizons.

horizontal *adjective* level, flat, plane, smooth, straight, even, flush, regular A dining table has a large, horizontal top. ◈ **Antonyms:** vertical, uneven

horrible *adjective* awful, dreadful, frightful, ghastly, grim, horrid, terrible, hideous Fog caused a horrible accident on the freeway. ◈ **Antonyms:** delightful, wonderful

horrid *adjective* ghastly, grim, gruesome, grisly, hideous, horrible, revolting, repugnant The mythological Gorgon is a horrid creature with writhing snakes for hair. ◈ **Antonyms:** pleasant, pleasing

horrify *verb* shock, repel, alarm, appall, dismay, sicken, outrage, disgust It horrified me to learn how many people are homeless. ◈ **Antonyms:** please, delight, soothe

horror *noun* alarm, dread, fear, fright, panic, terror, repugnance, abhorrence I had a feeling of horror when my dog ran in front of a car.

hospitality *noun* cordiality, geniality, warmth, friendliness, sociability, generosity, welcome We appreciated their generous hospitality.

host[1] *noun* hostess, receptionist, attendant, entertainer, emcee, presenter, chaperon I am going to be one of the hosts at our school's open house. ◆ *verb* have, accommodate, treat, receive, present, welcome, entertain It was our turn to host the meeting. ◈ **Antonym:** *noun* guest

host[2] *noun* multitude, swarm, drove, crowd, legion, mob, throng A host of reporters surrounded the candidates.

hostile *adjective* antagonistic, belligerent, aggressive, bellicose, combative, militant, malicious, unfriendly A hostile force had the soldiers surrounded. ◈ **Antonyms:** friendly, peaceful

hot *adjective* 1. scorching, searing, sizzling, sweltering, torrid, burning, blistering, roasting On hot summer days, I cool off by going swimming. 2. sharp, spicy, zesty, acrid, biting, peppery, piquant, pungent He likes hot sauce on his hamburgers. 3. angry, fiery, intense, passionate, ardent, violent, raging, stormy Sarah has a very hot temper. 4. new, fresh, current, recent, latest, up-to-date, brand-new I heard some hot news at school today. ◈ **Antonyms:** 1. cold, freezing 2. bland, mild 3. calm 4. old, stale

Word Group

A **hotel** is a place that provides lodging and often meals for paying guests. **Hotel** is a general term with no true synonyms. Here are some different kinds of hotels:

bed-and-breakfast, hospice, hostel, inn, lodge, motel, motor inn, resort

hound *noun* dog, hunting dog, pointer, retriever, setter, mutt, mongrel The hounds caught the fox's scent. ◆ *verb* badger, bother, harass, nag, pester, prod, plague, harry Sometimes I hound my mom to let me stay up late.

house *noun* **1. abode, dwelling, home, residence, habitation, lodging, domicile** My family lives in a house that has three bedrooms. **2. place, building, hall, structure, auditorium, shelter** Temples, mosques, churches, and synagogues are houses of worship. **3. business, company, outfit, firm, partnership, corporation, organization, shop** She submitted her novel to a publishing house. **4. assembly, congress, legislature, parliament, council, legislative body** The House of Representatives submitted a bill of impeachment to the Senate. ◆ *verb* **lodge, put up, shelter, board, dwell, reside, quarter, billet** The horses are housed in the barn.

hovel *noun* **shack, shanty, hut, dump, hole, shed, cabin** The destitute man lived in a hovel.

hover *verb* **1. hang, drift, float, flutter, fly, flit, dance, flitter** The butterfly hovered over a flower. **2. hang around, linger, loiter, remain, tarry, haunt, wait, idle** We hovered near the kitchen, hoping for a snack. ➡ **Antonyms: 1. fall, drop 2. depart, leave, go**

however *adverb* **nevertheless, still, yet, though, nonetheless, anyhow** My library book is not due until next week; however, I plan to return it today.

howl *verb* **bay, wail, yowl, bawl, bellow, cry, scream, keen** Wolves howl at night to keep in touch with other members of their pack. ◆ *noun* **cry, scream, wail, yell, yowl, shout, shriek, groan, moan** I let out a howl of pain when I stubbed my toe.

hub *noun* **center, seat, headquarters, core, middle, focus, nub, nucleus** Kansas City, Missouri, is a transportation hub.

huddle *noun* **knot, bunch, clump, cluster, mass, group, ball, pack** The team gathered in a huddle and gave a cheer. ◆ *verb* **bunch, cluster, crowd, flock, gather, cram, press, nestle** Sheep huddle together for warmth. ➡ **Antonyms:** *verb* **disperse, separate**

hue *noun* **color, shade, tint, tone, complexion, cast, tinge, dye** I would like that coat in a darker hue.

hug *verb* **clasp, embrace, hold, squeeze, cuddle, nestle, enfold, press** Grandmother always hugs me because she's so happy to see me. ◆ *noun* **clasp, embrace, squeeze, clinch, grip, caress, press** My dad gave me a big hug when he returned from his trip.

huge *adjective* **big, enormous, gigantic, immense, large, massive, tremendous, great, colossal** Although many dinosaurs were huge, some were as small as chickens. ➡ **Antonyms: little, small, tiny**

hum *verb* **buzz, burr, drone, whir, vibrate, murmur, thrum, purr** My radio hums when it's not tuned to a station. ◆ *noun* **buzz, burr, drone, whir, vibration, murmur, thrum, purr** I heard the distant hum of a large generator.

human *noun* **person, individual, human being, soul, body, mortal, man, woman** All humans have a need for affection, acceptance, and achievement.

humane *adjective* **compassionate, kind, merciful, tender, good, charitable, benevolent, sympathetic** It is important to be humane to your pets. ➡ **Antonyms: cruel, mean**

humble *adjective* **1. modest, unassuming, unpretentious, reserved, shy, bashful, meek** Because he was humble, he was even more popular. **2. common, lowly, mean, obscure, poor, simple, rough, plebeian** My grandfather is proud of his humble background. ◆ *verb* **humiliate, shame, chasten, degrade, demean, abash, crush, mortify** The vain tennis player was humbled by his defeat. ➡ **Antonyms:** *adjective* **1. proud, vain 2. elegant, high**

humid *adjective* **damp, moist, muggy, steamy, clammy, soggy, misty, sultry** The bathroom was humid after I took a shower. ➡ **Antonyms: arid, dry**

humiliate *verb* **disgrace, embarrass, shame, dishonor, mortify, humble, degrade** I was humiliated when I forgot my lines during the school play.

humor *noun* **1. comedy, wit, wittiness, jocosity, funniness, kidding, amusement, jest** A good sense of humor makes life more enjoyable. **2. disposition, mood, temper, bent, frame of mind, nature, spirits** I was in a good humor when I won the chess tournament. ◆ *verb* **cater to, indulge, pamper, spoil, coddle, baby, gratify** I humor my parakeets by whistling to them.

humorous *adjective* **amusing, comic, comical, funny, witty, jocose, zany, droll** He told a humorous story that made us laugh. ➡ **Antonyms: serious, grave, sad**

hump *noun* **bulge, bump, lump, mound, swelling, knob, rise, swell** A dromedary camel has one hump on its back, and a Bactrian camel has two.

hunch *noun* **feeling, idea, impression, notion, suspicion, premonition, instinct** I had a hunch that we would have a quiz today.

hunger *noun* **1. lack of food, hungriness, starvation, malnutrition, famine, destitution** The stray kitten was weak from hunger. **2. desire, craving, appetite, longing, wish, itch, thirst, yearning** I have an insatiable hunger for knowledge. ◆ *verb* **crave, desire, long, want, yearn, thirst, itch, hanker** Most people hunger for praise and recognition.

hungry *adjective* **1. famished, ravenous, starved, starving, voracious, undernourished** I was hungry after the canoe trip. **2. avid, avaricious, greedy, covetous, needful, yearning, keen, desirous** I am always hungry for a new book by my favorite author. ➤ **Antonyms: 1. sated, full 2. indifferent, averse**

hunk *noun* **chunk, piece, wad, lump, slab, slice, wedge, clump** I pulled a hunk of bread from the loaf.

hunt *verb* **1. chase, pursue, stalk, track, trail, kill, shoot, snare** He hunts wild animals with a camera. **2. look, search, seek, cast about, quest, track down, rummage, forage** I hunted for my missing house key. ◆ *noun* **quest, search, pursuit, hunting, chase, probe, investigation** *The Treasure of the Sierra Madre* is a movie about a hunt for gold.

hurdle *noun* **barrier, obstacle, obstruction, problem, impediment, snag, difficulty, hindrance** Getting the President's signature is the last hurdle a bill faces before it becomes law. ◆ *verb* **jump, leap, spring, vault, bound, clear, surmount, negotiate** In a steeplechase, horses have to hurdle hedges, walls, and streams.

hurl *verb* **fling, heave, hurtle, launch, pitch, throw, toss, lob, cast** The pitcher hurled three strikes in a row.

hurried *adjective* **hasty, rushed, swift, fast, speedy, quick, rapid, short** His speech was hurried because he was so excited. ➤ **Antonyms: slow, deliberate**

hurry *verb* **dash, hasten, fly, race, run, rush, speed, scamper, hustle** I grabbed my jacket as I hurried out of the house. ◆ *noun* **rush, hustle, haste, dispatch, quickness, speed, swiftness, celerity** I was in a hurry to get home before dark. ➤ **Antonyms:** *verb* **dawdle, delay** ◆ *noun* **slowness, dawdling**

hurt *verb* **1. wound, injure, damage, harm, cripple, maim, ruin, impair** This bad weather is hurting the local tourist trade. **2. distress, offend, aggrieve, upset, insult, abuse, vex, wrong, victimize** Your thoughtless remark hurt me. **3. ache, smart, pain, suffer, throb, ail, burn, twinge** My arms hurt from the push-ups I did yesterday. ◆ *noun* **anguish, distress, torment, woe, agony, torture, misery, pain, harm** He was unaware of the hurt his thoughtless remark caused. ➤ **Antonyms:** *verb* **1. heal, aid, help 2. calm, console**

hurtle *verb* **rush, dash, fly, race, speed, shoot, plunge, charge, lunge** Trucks hurtled past us on the freeway.

husband *noun* **spouse, mate, partner, helpmate, consort, groom** Mom says that Dad is the best husband in the world. ◆ *verb* **conserve, save, preserve, treasure, guard, spare, reserve, store** Diabetics in some countries must husband their insulin, as supplies are scarce. ➤ **Antonyms:** *verb* **waste, squander**

hush *verb* **quiet, shush, shut up, silence, muffle, stifle, soothe, mute** The teacher hushed us and told us to listen to the speaker. ◆ *noun* **silence, quietness, quiet, stillness, calm, peace, still, tranquillity** There was a hush in the neighborhood after the snowfall.

husky[1] *adjective* **gruff, hoarse, scratchy, harsh, rasping, deep** We could hear the husky cries of the crows. ➤ **Antonyms: clear, sweet, melodious**

husky[2] *adjective* **burly, big, brawny, stocky, muscular, robust, hefty, strapping** My brothers are all quite husky. ➤ **Antonyms: puny, frail, weak**

hustle *verb* **1. jostle, push, shove, poke, elbow, shoulder, knock, joggle** Security guards hustled the unruly customer out of the store. **2. hasten, hurry, race, run, sprint, rush, speed, bustle** The basketball players hustled up and down the court. ◆ *noun* **1. bustle, activity, stir, fuss, excitement, flurry, speed, quickness** I enjoy the hustle of the holiday season. **2. energy, drive, ambition, push, motivation, initiative, zeal, enterprise** He has enough hustle for two people! ➤ **Antonyms:** *verb* **2. dawdle, dally** ◆ *noun* **1. calmness, peace, tranquillity**

hut *noun* **shack, shanty, shed, shelter, cabin, cottage, lean-to, hovel** Some ski resorts have warming huts.

hypnotize *verb* **mesmerize, spellbind, entrance, captivate, transfix, fascinate, bewitch** I was hypnotized by the colorful floats in the parade.

hysteria *noun* **frenzy, agitation, panic, delirium, madness, excitement, hysterics** There was hysteria when it was discovered that the disease had a 90-percent fatality rate.

hysterical *adjective* **1. frantic, frenzied, panic-stricken, upset, distraught, emotional, excited** Some people become hysterical when they see snakes or spiders. **2. hilarious, uproarious, funny, comical, absurd, farcical, ridiculous, laughable** We thought that the comedian's comments were hysterical. ➤ **Antonyms: 1. calm, composed 2. sad, serious, somber**

I i

icy *adjective* **1. wintry, frozen, freezing, chilly, cold, frigid, glacial, frosty** We took a walk through the icy woods. **2. unfriendly, aloof, distant, remote, cold, chilly, forbidding, cold-hearted** Her icy manner changed when I spoke to her. ● **Antonyms: 1. warm, hot 2. friendly, cordial**

idea *noun* **1. belief, concept, notion, opinion, thought, plan, sense, view** Everyone had a different idea about where we should hold our family reunion. **2. point, purpose, objective, function, aim, reason, rationale, intention** The idea of the concert is to have fun and to raise money.

ideal *noun* **1. aim, goal, aspiration, hope, wish, dream** Balancing the needs of the individual with those of society is a worthy ideal. **2. epitome, paragon, paradigm, model, pattern, standard, example** Her courtesy was the ideal of good manners. ◆ *adjective* **excellent, fitting, perfect, satisfactory, suitable, optimal, flawless, supreme** This pond is ideal for a bird refuge. ● **Antonyms:** *adjective* **flawed, imperfect**

identical *adjective* **equal, exact, like, matching, same, corresponding, twin, duplicate** My sister and I have identical computers. ● **Antonyms: different, distinct**

identify *verb* **1. distinguish, know, recognize, place, pinpoint, specify, determine, name** I was easily able to identify my dog at the animal shelter. **2. sympathize, empathize, understand, relate, associate, respond** I can identify with someone who has lost a friend.

identity *noun* **individuality, character, self, personality, identification, selfhood, individualism** It is important for an individual to develop a personal identity.

ideology *noun* **belief, doctrine, creed, credo, principles, theory, dogma, philosophy** Every religion has its own ideology.

idiot *noun* **dummy, fool, blockhead, nitwit, moron, imbecile, dunce, simpleton** I felt like an idiot when I arrived at the beach and found I had forgotten my swimsuit. ● **Antonyms: genius, mastermind**

idle *adjective* **1. inactive, still, unused, inert, stationary, unemployed, inoperative** The town's snowplow stood idle until January. **2. lazy, indolent, shiftless, slothful, sluggardly, listless** I enjoyed being idle during spring vacation.

3. empty, hollow, useless, vacant, worthless, irrelevant, trivial, frivolous We passed the time in idle chatter while we waited for our bus. ◆ *verb* **dawdle, fiddle, while, waste, fritter, loaf, lounge, laze** We idled away the day by playing computer games. ● **Antonyms:** *adjective* **1. employed, busy 2. active, energetic 3. meaningful, significant** ◆ *verb* **toil, work**

idol *noun* **1. deity, god, goddess, image, statue, effigy, icon, fetish** The archaeologist found a gold idol in the ruins of the temple. **2. hero, heroine, celebrity, star, notable, favorite, darling, superstar** My idol is a famous talk show host.

idolize *verb* **adore, revere, honor, venerate, admire, love, worship, glorify** Many people idolize celebrities. ● **Antonyms: disdain, despise, scorn**

ignite *verb* **kindle, light, fire, catch fire, burn, explode** Dry leaves ignite easily.

ignorant *adjective* **1. illiterate, uneducated, unschooled, unlearned, untaught, unenlightened** I do not want to be ignorant. **2. oblivious, unaware, uninformed, unfamiliar, unknowing, unacquainted, innocent, naive** Many pioneers were ignorant of the dangers that they would have to face. ● **Antonyms: 1. schooled, educated 2. aware, informed**

ignore *verb* **disregard, overlook, forget, neglect, snub, skip, slight, avoid** I tried to ignore the sound of the barking dog. ● **Antonyms: heed, notice**

ill *adjective* **1. ailing, sick, unhealthy, unwell, sickly, down, laid up, queasy** I felt ill and went to bed early. **2. adverse, bad, evil, harmful, unfavorable, deleterious, injurious, hostile** It's an old belief that spilling salt will bring ill fortune. ◆ *noun* **affliction, ailment, evil, misery, misfortune, trouble, illness, bane** Poverty, hunger, and disease are some of the ills of society. ● **Antonyms:** *adjective* **1. healthy, well 2. good, helpful**

illegal *adjective* **illicit, criminal, prohibited, unlawful, wrongful, illegitimate, taboo, lawless** Vandalism is illegal. ● **Antonyms: lawful, legal**

illness *noun* **affliction, ailment, disease, malady, sickness, disorder, infirmity, malaise** His illness caused him to miss two days of school. ● **Antonym: health**

illogical *noun* unreasonable, senseless, irrational, preposterous, absurd, groundless, inconsistent I have an illogical fear of dogs. ➤ **Antonyms:** logical, reasonable, valid

illuminate *verb* 1. light, lighten, light up, brighten, spotlight, highlight Floodlights illuminated the football field. 2. clarify, clear up, elucidate, educate, explain, enlighten, illustrate, interpret The TV special illuminated the roots of the crisis. ➤ **Antonyms:** 1. darken, dim 2. confuse, obscure

illumination *noun* light, lighting, brightness, luminescence, radiance, glow, gleam This lamp provides enough illumination for me to read. ➤ **Antonym:** darkness

illusion *noun* 1. impression, appearance, mirage, apparition, image, hallucination The ventriloquist gave the illusion that the puppet was actually talking. 2. falsehood, fantasy, misconception, mistake, fallacy, error, delusion, deception The concept that public education is free is an illusion. ➤ **Antonyms:** 1. reality 2. truth, fact

illustrate *verb* 1. clarify, demonstrate, explain, clear up, show, illuminate, exemplify The teacher illustrated her point by giving several examples. 2. draw, paint, picture, sketch, adorn, decorate, ornament, portray I would like to write and illustrate children's books.

illustration *noun* 1. picture, drawing, sketch, diagram, chart, depiction, image The illustration showed the orbit of the moon around Earth. 2. demonstration, example, representative, sample, specimen, instance, case, proof Our science teacher presented an illustration of Boyle's law.

illustrious *adjective* famous, celebrated, prominent, distinguished, famed, renowned, prestigious She comes from an illustrious family. ➤ **Antonyms:** obscure, lowly

image *noun* 1. likeness, picture, portrait, reflection, resemblance, form, representation, drawing A one-dollar bill bears the image of George Washington. 2. notion, concept, vision, impression, conception, perception, idea, thought My image of a TV studio proved to be accurate.

imaginary *adjective* fictional, nonexistent, unreal, fanciful, fabulous, legendary, mythological, hypothetical Dragons and unicorns are imaginary creatures. ➤ **Antonyms:** actual, real

imagination *noun* 1. fancy, fantasy, whimsy, mind, notion, thought The ghost was probably just a figment of my imagination. 2. resourcefulness, creativity, inspiration, originality, ingenuity, vision My teacher said that my story shows imagination.

imagine *verb* 1. conceive, fancy, fantasize, picture, visualize, envision, figure I can imagine how you felt when you got a perfect score on the test. 2. assume, guess, presume, suppose, suspect, think, surmise, hypothesize I imagine you'll want to know all the details about the party.

imbecile *noun* fool, nitwit, idiot, dolt, simpleton, moron, blockhead, dunce I was so nervous that I acted like an imbecile. ➤ **Antonyms:** genius, prodigy

imbecilic *adjective* stupid, foolish, dumb, idiotic, silly, preposterous, ludicrous, absurd, insane That was an imbecilic thing to do! ➤ **Antonyms:** smart, intelligent

imitate *verb* copy, duplicate, mimic, repeat, reproduce, ape, parrot, replicate Comedians often imitate the mannerisms of famous people.

imitation *noun* copy, duplicate, likeness, replica, reproduction, counterfeit, simulation This statue is an imitation of an Egyptian artifact. ◆ *adjective* fake, artificial, simulated, false, copied, mock, synthetic Imitation fur coats are becoming increasingly popular. ➤ **Antonyms:** *noun* original ◆ *adjective* authentic, genuine

immaculate *adjective* 1. clean, spotless, unsoiled, spick-and-span, stainless, neat, tidy I cleaned my room until it was immaculate. 2. pure, perfect, flawless, faultless, impeccable, unsullied, unblemished My attendance record is immaculate. ➤ **Antonyms:** 1. dirty, filthy 2. imperfect, flawed

immature *adjective* childish, juvenile, foolish, sophomoric, infantile, puerile, young It was immature of me to hang up on him. ➤ **Antonyms:** mature, adult, sophisticated

immediate *adjective* 1. instant, prompt, instantaneous, speedy, sudden, swift, timely, punctual This medicine is guaranteed to give immediate relief. 2. close, near, direct, firsthand, adjacent, next, contiguous, nearby, primary Only the immediate family will be invited to my wedding. ➤ **Antonyms:** 1. delayed, slow 2. distant, remote

immediately *adverb* at once, instantly, now, promptly, right away, forthwith, straightaway, directly We need to leave immediately or we'll be late. ➤ **Antonyms:** eventually, later

immense *adjective* colossal, enormous, gigantic, huge, large, vast, mammoth, massive, tremendous

The Mayas built immense stone pyramids in Central America. ● **Antonyms: little, small, tiny**

immerse *verb* **1. dip, douse, dunk, submerge, steep, bathe, drench, souse** A fox will immerse itself in water to get rid of fleas. **2. absorb, consume, engross, preoccupy, involve, engage, interest, occupy** I was so immersed in my computer game that I lost track of the time.

immigrate *verb* **migrate, move, relocate, colonize, settle, transfer, arrive** My family immigrated to Canada from Vietnam. ● **Antonyms: emigrate, depart, leave**

imminent *adjective* **close, near, immediate, impending, likely, looming, momentary, inevitable** Defeat seemed imminent, but we won the game at the last moment. ● **Antonyms: distant, remote**

immobile *adjective* **motionless, stationary, still, rigid, unmoving, frozen, steady, fixed** The baby quail were immobile until their mother gave them the signal to move. ● **Antonyms: mobile, movable**

immoral *adjective* **bad, evil, sinful, wicked, wrong, unscrupulous, corrupt, unethical** Most people would agree that cheating is immoral. ● **Antonyms: good, moral**

immortal *adjective* **1. eternal, everlasting, undying, ceaseless, endless, abiding, perpetual** According to ancient Greek religion, Zeus was the king of the immortal gods. **2. classic, timeless, famous, celebrated, illustrious, renowned, eminent, epic** Wolfgang Amadeus Mozart's music is immortal. ● **Antonyms: 1. mortal, temporary 2. obscure**

immune *adjective* **resistant, unsusceptible, impervious, invulnerable, exempt, free, safe** Some people are immune to poison ivy. ● **Antonyms: vulnerable, susceptible**

immunity *noun* **insusceptibility, exemption, clearance, amnesty, protection, resistance, release** The witness was granted immunity from prosecution. ● **Antonyms: vulnerability, susceptibility**

imp *noun* **1. brat, troublemaker, prankster, rascal, rogue, urchin, scamp** My little cousin is an unruly imp. **2. devil, demon, elf, gnome, pixie, sprite, hobgoblin, fiend** *The Screwtape Letters* is the story of an imp and his apprentice.

impact *noun* **1. collision, crash, strike, blow, contact, shock, bump, smash** This crater was formed by the impact of a meteor. **2. effect, impression, influence, meaning, force, significance, consequence** That book had a strong impact on my life.

impair *verb* **decrease, hinder, reduce, damage, harm, hurt, injure, cripple** Clipping a bird's wing feathers impairs its ability to fly. ● **Antonyms: better, improve**

impart *verb* **1. give, bestow, confer, present, grant, offer, furnish, yield** The corporation imparted a large sum of money to charity. **2. communicate, disclose, reveal, relate, tell, divulge, convey, announce** The scientist imparted the results of his experiments to the press.

impartial *adjective* **fair, unprejudiced, just, neutral, objective, unbiased, evenhanded, equitable** A good referee is able to make impartial decisions. ● **Antonyms: biased, unfair**

impatient *adjective* **1. anxious, avid, eager, keen, restless, ardent, bursting** I am impatient for school to start this fall. **2. annoyed, exasperated, irritated, intolerant, testy, short-tempered, irritable** The impatient driver kept honking her horn. ● **Antonyms: 1. patient 2. calm, cool, composed**

impeach *verb* **indict, charge, arraign, accuse, discredit, denounce, censure, blame** The President of the United States can be impeached only before Congress.

impede *verb* **slow, delay, hamper, obstruct, hinder, block, frustrate, hold back** Traffic was impeded by a bad accident. ● **Antonyms: aid, further, help**

impediment *noun* **hindrance, barrier, obstruction, bar, handicap, obstacle, snag** She found her lack of a high school diploma to be an impediment to getting a job. ● **Antonyms: support, benefit, help**

impel *verb* **drive, move, prod, prompt, goad, spur, incite, push, induce** Lack of money impelled him to seek a job. ● **Antonyms: restrain, discourage**

imperative *adjective* **essential, necessary, mandatory, urgent, crucial, important, critical, dire** It is imperative to get accident victims to the hospital as quickly as possible. ● **Antonyms: optional, unnecessary**

imperfect *adjective* **defective, deficient, faulty, flawed, incomplete, unfinished, inferior** Imperfect vision can usually be corrected with eyeglasses. ● **Antonyms: flawless, perfect**

imperious *adjective* **authoritarian, overbearing, domineering, dictatorial, arrogant, haughty, bossy** The manager's imperious manner often irritates his subordinates. ● **Antonyms: humble, submissive**

impertinent *adjective* insolent, rude, offensive, bold, impudent, disrespectful, brash I apologized for being impertinent to my mother. ➤ **Antonyms:** civil, respectful, courteous

impetuous *adjective* impulsive, rash, ill-considered, reckless, spontaneous, hasty, foolhardy I made an impetuous choice and took home a video that I didn't like. ➤ **Antonyms:** cautious, prudent

impetus *noun* stimulus, spur, incentive, stimulant, force, motivation, impulse, push The assassination of Archduke Ferdinand was the impetus for World War I.

implement *noun* device, instrument, tool, utensil, object, gadget, appliance, contraption Pencils and pens are writing implements. ◆ *verb* effect, execute, carry out, realize, accomplish, achieve, fulfill, perform The police chief began to implement a neighborhood watch program.

implicate *verb* incriminate, accuse, blame, charge, involve, impute, embroil The evidence implicated two suspects.

implicit *adjective* 1. implied, inferred, understood, unspoken, tacit, unsaid It was implicit that we would be home by 10 p.m. 2. absolute, unconditional, undoubting, unreserved, wholehearted, firm, full It was an implicit condition that payments on the loan be made by the first of the month. ➤ **Antonyms:** 1. spoken, explicit 2. conditional, partial

implore *verb* entreat, beg, beseech, importune, urge, plead, appeal, supplicate I implore you to reconsider your decision.

imply *verb* hint, indicate, suggest, allude, mean, import, insinuate, signify His expression implied that he disagreed with what I said.

impolite *adjective* discourteous, disrespectful, inconsiderate, rude, uncivil, crude, unmannerly It is impolite to talk with your mouth full. ➤ **Antonyms:** courteous, polite, mannerly

import *noun* 1. importance, significance, consequence, weight, concern, moment, worth The effects of pollution have great import for each of us. 2. idea, point, meaning, sense, purport, thrust, implication, drift What was the import of his speech?

importance *noun* significance, import, weight, consequence, gravity, moment, concern The development of aspirin in the early 20th century was of great importance.

important *adjective* 1. critical, consequential, meaningful, serious, significant, valuable, major, vital I have an important meeting after school today. 2. distinguished, eminent, influential, prominent, powerful, notable, illustrious The most important guests were seated at the head table. ➤ **Antonyms:** insignificant, unimportant

impose *verb* 1. decree, dictate, put, lay down, ordain, exact, assess, levy, prescribe The library imposed restrictions on the use of multimedia equipment. 2. intrude, trespass, bother, inconvenience, trouble, encroach, presume, abuse I'd love to stay for dinner, if I wouldn't be imposing on you.

impossible *adjective* 1. unattainable, impractical, futile, hopeless, inconceivable, unreal, unworkable It's impossible to be in two places at one time. 2. intolerable, insufferable, unbearable, difficult, unruly, stubborn, contrary Sometimes his behavior is impossible. ➤ **Antonyms:** 1. possible, conceivable 2. tolerable, easy

impostor *noun* fake, fraud, phony, pretender, charlatan, impersonator, humbug The man claimed to be a movie star, but he was an impostor.

impotent *adjective* helpless, powerless, ineffectual, incapable, frail, weak, feeble The rebel troops were impotent when their leader was jailed. ➤ **Antonyms:** powerful, potent, strong

impress *verb* 1. affect, influence, move, touch, strike, stir, reach, interest Seeing the rings of Saturn through a telescope really impressed me. 2. stamp, press, imprint, mark, shape, mold, indent, engrave, etch The design was impressed into a sheet of copper.

impression *noun* 1. effect, impact, influence, appearance, image, feeling, sensation The new coach made a good impression at our first practice. 2. feeling, hunch, idea, notion, opinion, theory, view, inkling I have the impression that you're ready to go now. 3. imprint, indentation, outline, mark, stamp, trace, cast, figure This rock contains the fossilized impression of a leaf. 4. parody, imitation, impersonation, portrayal, mimicry, copy, takeoff He did an impression of a famous movie star.

impressive *adjective* affecting, moving, stirring, awesome, remarkable, striking The Grand Canyon is an impressive sight. ➤ **Antonyms:** ordinary, unimpressive

imprint *verb* 1. mark, stamp, engrave, press, etch, impress I have some stationery with my name imprinted on each sheet. **2. ingrain, instill, establish, stick, settle, fix** I tried to imprint the information in my memory. ◆ *noun* **impression, indentation, print, mark, dent, stamp, seal** The detective looked for the imprint of the suspect's shoes.

imprison *verb* **jail, incarcerate, immure, lock up, cage, confine, detain, retain** The criminal was imprisoned for many years. ● **Antonyms: free, release**

impromptu *adjective* **spontaneous, improvised, unrehearsed, extemporaneous, ad-lib, snap, offhand** We had an impromptu picnic. ● **Antonyms: planned, rehearsed**

improper *adjective* **inappropriate, incorrect, unbecoming, unbefitting, unsuitable, unfit, wrong** Sweat pants are improper attire at a formal wedding. ● **Antonyms: fitting, proper, right**

improve *verb* **1. better, perfect, polish, refine, enhance, help, benefit, upgrade** My visit to Quebec this summer improved my French. **2. get better, convalesce, recover, recuperate, mend, rally, gain** The patient is improving daily. ● **Antonyms: 1. impair, worsen 2. weaken, deteriorate**

improvement *noun* **enhancement, advance, progress, enrichment, betterment, upgrade, development** The garden showed an improvement with the new fertilizer.

improvise *verb* **concoct, contrive, devise, make up, invent, originate, compose, ad-lib** I improvised a bookshelf out of boards and bricks.

impudent *adjective* **bold, shameless, disrespectful, insolent, rude, presumptuous, audacious, brazen** The impudent fan interrupted the actor's dinner to ask for an autograph. ● **Antonyms: respectful, courteous**

impulse *noun* **urge, whim, caprice, fancy, notion, wish, itch, desire** I had an impulse to go to a movie.

impulsive *adjective* **impetuous, spontaneous, rash, unplanned, hasty, reckless, imprudent, unconsidered** I soon regretted my impulsive behavior. ● **Antonyms: deliberate, planned, considered**

impure *adjective* **1. dirty, polluted, filthy, unclean, contaminated, sullied, foul** We had our drinking water tested to find out if it is impure. **2. immoral, wicked, corrupt, bad, immodest, indecent, obscene, lewd** Parents try to protect their children from impure influences. ● **Antonyms: 1. pure, clean 2. moral, decent, wholesome**

in *adjective* **fashionable, popular, current, in vogue, chic, modish, smart, trendy** Fashion colors are usually in for only a few years.

inaccurate *adjective* **false, incorrect, mistaken, wrong, erroneous, faulty, inexact, imprecise** The tabloid article was full of inaccurate information. ● **Antonyms: accurate, correct, right**

inactive *adjective* **dormant, quiescent, idle, immobile, inert, stationary, retired, inoperative** Many animals are inactive during the winter. ● **Antonyms: active, busy, energetic**

inane *adjective* **foolish, stupid, senseless, silly, absurd, vacuous, mindless, banal** I made an inane comment about the weather. ● **Antonyms: significant, meaningful, profound**

inappropriate *adjective* **improper, unfit, unsuitable, incorrect, unseemly, wrong, unbefitting** The dress code specifies clothing that is inappropriate to wear to school. ● **Antonyms: appropriate, proper, fitting**

inaugurate *verb* **1. induct, install, invest, instate, commission, ordain** The new President will be inaugurated next month. **2. begin, commence, initiate, start, introduce, institute, launch, open** Postal service was inaugurated in the United States in 1710. ● **Antonyms: 1. remove 2. end, conclude, finish**

inauguration *noun* **1. inaugural, investiture, induction, installation, initiation, ordination, crowning** We attended the governor's inauguration. **2. commencement, debut, beginning, opening, premiere, launch, inception, introduction** The inauguration of the new magazine was a success.

incapable *adjective* **unable, helpless, ineffective, powerless, unskilled, unsuited, unfit** Whales are incapable of breathing under water. ● **Antonyms: able, capable**

incense[1] *verb* **anger, enrage, infuriate, madden, irritate, provoke, exasperate** It incenses me when someone cuts in front of me in a line. ● **Antonyms: calm, soothe**

incense[2] *noun* **fragrance, aroma, odor, perfume, scent, essence, frankincense, myrrh** Do you like the smell of this incense?

incentive *noun* **inducement, encouragement, motivation, prod, spur, stimulus, bait** The magazine offered a large discount as an incentive to new subscribers. ● **Antonyms: curb, deterrent**

incessant *adjective* **continuous, constant, ceaseless, persistent, unending, relentless, eternal** The wind was nearly incessant during last night's storm. ➤ **Antonyms: occasional, intermittent**

incident *noun* **affair, event, experience, happening, occurrence, circumstance, act, episode** She didn't remember the funny incident until I reminded her. ◆ *adjective* **related, connected, associated, accompanying, dependent, linked, contingent** Hamstring injuries are incident to long-distance running.

incisive *adjective* **perceptive, sharp, clear, penetrating, keen, direct, sensitive** He made an incisive speech regarding the current political situation. ➤ **Antonyms: vague, unclear**

incite *verb* **provoke, encourage, instigate, stimulate, prod, goad, urge, induce** High taxes incited English noblemen to force the Magna Carta on King John. ➤ **Antonyms: deter, restrain, dissuade**

incline *verb* **1. lean, slant, slope, tilt, tip, list, cant, veer** The Leaning Tower of Pisa inclines more than 14 feet to one side. **2. dispose, predispose, sway, tend, favor, prefer, gravitate, lean** Your cough inclines me to believe that you might be getting a cold. ◆ *noun* **grade, rise, slope, ramp, gradient, tilt, slant, inclination** We walked up the incline to the stadium bleachers.

inclined *adjective* **likely, apt, prone, liable, disposed, willing, given, partial** I am inclined to follow your suggestion. ➤ **Antonyms: disinclined, unlikely**

include *verb* **contain, cover, involve, embody, incorporate, encompass, embrace, have** The price of the meal includes fries and a medium drink. ➤ **Antonyms: exclude, omit**

incoherent *adjective* **unintelligible, illogical, confused, jumbled, irrational, unclear, rambling** The accident victim gave an incoherent report to the police officer. ➤ **Antonyms: coherent, plain, clear**

income *noun* **revenue, earnings, pay, salary, royalty, wage** My sister's after-school job is her main source of income.

incompetent *adjective* **inefficient, unskilled, inadequate, incapable, unable, unfit, inept, unqualified** The incompetent worker lost his job. ➤ **Antonyms: competent, efficient**

incomplete *adjective* **deficient, fragmentary, partial, unfinished, wanting, lacking, rough** My collection of French coins is incomplete. ➤ **Antonyms: complete, finished**

inconvenience *noun* **annoyance, bother, difficulty, trouble, drawback, complication, nuisance, vexation** It was an inconvenience to have lost the TV's remote control. ◆ *verb* **trouble, disrupt, put out, discomfit, annoy, bother, disturb, upset** Would it inconvenience you to give me a ride home?

inconvenient *adjective* **bothersome, troublesome, annoying, awkward, untimely, difficult, cumbersome** My favorite TV show comes on at an inconvenient time. ➤ **Antonyms: convenient, helpful**

incorrect *adjective* **1. false, inaccurate, mistaken, wrong, untrue, erroneous, faulty, inexact** The incorrect answers are circled with red ink. **2. improper, unfit, inappropriate, unbecoming, unseemly, unsuitable, unfitting** It is considered incorrect to interrupt when someone else is speaking. ➤ **Antonyms: 1. correct, right, true 2. proper, fitting**

incorrigible *adjective* **bad, ineradicable, unmanageable, hardened, incurable, inveterate, uncorrectable** I have the incorrigible habit of reading the end of a book first. ➤ **Antonyms: correctable, good**

increase *verb* **augment, enlarge, expand, grow, multiply, swell, advance, intensify** Regular practice will increase our chances of winning. ◆ *noun* **advance, expansion, gain, growth, raise, rise, upsurge, boost** The world is experiencing a population increase of almost 90 million people per year. ➤ **Antonyms:** *verb* **decrease, lessen** ◆ *noun* **decrease, drop**

incredible *adjective* **1. inconceivable, unbelievable, improbable, implausible, doubtful, absurd, ridiculous** Your excuse about aliens stealing your homework is incredible. **2. amazing, astonishing, extraordinary, fantastic, fabulous, astounding, phenomenal** The hurricane struck land with incredible fury. ➤ **Antonyms: 1. believable 2. ordinary, common**

incredulous *adjective* **disbelieving, doubtful, skeptical, dubious, distrustful, unbelieving, suspicious** Mom was incredulous when I told her that my teacher thinks I am shy. ➤ **Antonym: accepting**

increment *noun* **increase, advance, boost, hike, jump, raise, rise, gain** Some people think that the increment in government spending will result in higher taxes.

indeed *adverb* **certainly, definitely, positively, really, truly, genuinely, absolutely, undeniably** You are indeed my best friend.

indefinite *adjective* **open, uncertain, undecided, vague, doubtful, unknown, unsettled, loose** My plans for the weekend are still indefinite. ◈ **Antonyms: certain, definite**

independence *noun* **freedom, liberty, autonomy, self-rule, sovereignty, self-government, self-reliance** Traveling by myself gives me a feeling of independence. ◈ **Antonyms: dependence, subjugation**

independent *adjective* **1. free, liberated, sovereign, self-governing, autonomous, uncontrolled** The United States became an independent nation on September 3, 1783. **2. self-reliant, self-sufficient, self-supporting, individualistic, self-contained, self-confident** My sister feels very independent now that she has her own apartment. ◈ **Antonyms: dependent, subject**

index *noun* **sign, indication, symptom, manifestation, indicator, clue, mark** My friend says that one index of an impending earthquake is an increase in the number of missing pets.

indicate *verb* **1. designate, mark, point out, signify, denote, specify, illustrate** I put a big "X" on the map to indicate my destination. **2. read, register, record, mark, show, suggest, reveal, disclose** The thermometer indicates that the temperature is dropping.

indict *verb* **arraign, charge, accuse, prosecute, incriminate, cite, summon** He was indicted on charges of perjury.

indifferent *adjective* **1. apathetic, unconcerned, uninterested, uninvolved, detached, impassive, nonchalant** How could anyone be indifferent to the suffering of others? **2. impartial, objective, neutral, equitable, unbiased, unprejudiced, fair** A judge should be indifferent when presiding over a trial. ◈ **Antonyms: 1. concerned, involved 2. partial, biased**

indignant *adjective* **irate, angry, mad, furious, irked, irritated, resentful, exasperated** I was indignant when I was not invited to attend the party. ◈ **Antonyms: calm, composed**

indirect *adjective* **1. circuitous, roundabout, oblique, long, rambling, winding, meandering** I wasn't in a hurry, so I took an indirect route home. **2. ambiguous, evasive, vague, sneaky, devious, shifty, underhand** The politician gave an indirect answer to the journalist's probing question. **3. secondary, incidental, circumstantial, subordinate, distant, tangential** Your argument has only an indirect bearing on the subject. ◈ **Antonyms: 1. direct, straight 2. clear, explicit 3. primary, direct**

indiscriminate *adjective* **1. uncritical, casual, undiscriminating, unselective, careless, aimless, promiscuous** His indiscriminate spending left him heavily in debt. **2. random, confused, haphazard, hit-or-miss, unplanned, unsystematic, miscellaneous** I'm trying to organize the indiscriminate piles of belongings in my bedroom. ◈ **Antonyms: 1. selective, strict 2. orderly, systematic**

indispensable *adjective* **essential, necessary, key, crucial, fundamental, required, vital, basic** I think that sunshine is an indispensable ingredient for a good vacation. ◈ **Antonyms: unnecessary, superfluous**

indistinct *adjective* **unclear, hazy, dim, faint, indefinite, imperceptible, weak, vague** The stereo system's poor speakers made the music indistinct. ◈ **Antonyms: distinct, clear**

individual *adjective* **1. lone, separate, single, sole, solitary, discrete, different** This store allows you to buy candy in bulk or by the individual piece. **2. characteristic, personal, private, distinctive, idiosyncratic, particular, singular** Which movies we enjoy is a matter of individual taste. ◆ *noun* **being, human, human being, person, creature, soul, man, woman** Sherry is a thoughtful and methodic individual.

induce *verb* **persuade, influence, encourage, prompt, urge, influence, spur, trigger** Is there anything that would induce you to change your mind? ◈ **Antonyms: hinder, dissuade, prevent**

indulge *verb* **1. baby, pamper, spoil, overindulge, coddle, humor, cater to** The doting parents indulged their child. **2. appease, gratify, satisfy, content, fulfill, accommodate, favor** I indulged my craving for ice cream with a strawberry sundae.

indulgent *adjective* **permissive, tolerant, lenient, easygoing, obliging, kind, gentle, giving** My grandmother is indulgent toward her grandchildren. ◈ **Antonyms: strict, stern**

industrious *adjective* **active, busy, diligent, energetic, productive, hardworking, tireless** Beavers are considered to be industrious animals. ◈ **Antonyms: lazy, idle, slothful**

industry *noun* **1. business, commerce, trade, manufacturing, production** The American automobile industry is centered in Detroit. **2. diligence, industriousness, exertion, perseverance, labor, effort, application** The classroom was quiet as the students worked with industry. ◈ **Antonyms: 2. laziness, sloth, idleness**

inept *adjective* **1. awkward, clumsy, unskilled, incompetent, graceless, bumbling, bungling** My first attempts at skiing were inept. **2. inappropriate, unsuitable, unfit, improper, unbecoming, unbefitting, unseemly** His inept behavior was excused because of his sincere regret. ➤ **Antonyms: 1. graceful, competent, adroit 2. proper, suitable**

inert *adjective* **immobile, motionless, still, unmoving, stationary, inactive, paralyzed** An opossum will sometimes lie inert to make its enemies think that it is dead. ➤ **Antonyms: active, moving**

inevitable *adjective* **certain, inescapable, sure, unavoidable, destined, doomed, fated** It was inevitable that my little brother would want a jacket like mine. ➤ **Antonyms: avoidable, uncertain**

inexpensive *adjective* **cheap, low-cost, low-priced, economical, reasonable, budget, thrifty** An animal shelter is an inexpensive place to get a pet. ➤ **Antonyms: costly, expensive**

inexperienced *adjective* **green, new, raw, untried, unskilled, untrained, unpracticed, inexpert** Our junior varsity teams are composed mostly of inexperienced players. ➤ **Antonyms: experienced, trained, knowledgeable**

infamous *adjective* **notorious, disreputable, scandalous, disgraceful, villainous, ignoble, shameful** Jesse James was an infamous outlaw. ➤ **Antonyms: honorable, noble**

infant *noun* **baby, newborn, toddler, tot, babe, suckling, nursling, neonate, bambino** The infant slept peacefully in its crib.

infect *verb* **afflict, sicken, contaminate, blight, taint, spread to, pollute** If you have the flu, you should be careful not to infect anyone else.

infectious *adjective* **contagious, communicable, transmissible, catching, spreading, transferable** Vaccines are helpful in preventing the spread of many infectious diseases.

infer *verb* **conclude, deduct, gather, presume, understand, deduce, glean, surmise** I infer from your smile that you did well on the test.

inference *noun* **conclusion, deduction, judgment, supposition, presumption, assumption** The inference made by the newspaper reporter was correct.

inferior *adjective* **1. lesser, lower, secondary, subordinate, under, smaller, low** Silver is inferior in value to gold. **2. mediocre, poor, substandard, bad, low-grade, deficient, shabby** This radio is inexpensive because it is of inferior quality. ➤ **Antonyms: 1. superior, higher 2. superior, excellent**

infinite *adjective* **boundless, endless, limitless, unlimited, immense, incalculable, vast** The number of stars in the night sky is seemingly infinite. ➤ **Antonyms: limited, finite**

inflate *verb* **1. blow up, dilate, distend, expand, swell, stretch, spread** He can inflate a balloon with just one breath. **2. exaggerate, magnify, overstate, enlarge, aggrandize, amplify** The candidate inflated his qualifications when filling out the job application. ➤ **Antonyms: 1. collapse, deflate**

inflict *verb* **impose, wreak, administer, foist, visit, work, exact, subject** The hailstones inflicted great damage on the fruit crop.

influence *noun* **effect, impact, impression, power, sway, control, importance, dominance** The school librarian has had a lot of influence on my choice of books. ◆ *verb* **effect, change, shape, affect, alter, move, sway, impress** TV has greatly influenced the way Americans get their news.

influential *adjective* **important, consequential, significant, powerful, forceful, potent, compelling** The Internet is very influential in the lives of many people. ➤ **Antonyms: unimportant, powerless**

inform *verb* **advise, notify, tell, relate, report, enlighten, apprise, explain** I called my parents to inform them that I was at a friend's house.

informal *adjective* **casual, easygoing, simple, relaxed, spontaneous, unceremonious, unofficial** We had an informal dinner party at my house. ➤ **Antonyms: formal, stiff**

information *noun* **data, facts, knowledge, lore, intelligence, wisdom, instruction, material** I need to find information about Venus and Mars for my science report.

infrequent *adjective* **isolated, rare, sporadic, uncommon, unusual, occasional, odd, irregular** Total solar eclipses are infrequent events. ➤ **Antonyms: common, frequent, regular**

infuriate *verb* **anger, enrage, incense, madden, provoke, exasperate, rile** You really infuriate me when you skip class. ➤ **Antonyms: calm, soothe**

infuse *verb* **instill, implant, imbue, impart, suffuse, pervade** The coach gave a speech that infused us with new enthusiasm.

ingenious *adjective* **clever, brilliant, inventive, creative, resourceful, original, imaginative** She came up with an ingenious solution to her problem. ● **Antonyms: clumsy, unimaginative**

ingenuous *adjective* **innocent, simple, unaffected, naive, honest, candid, natural, unsophisticated** The little boy's ingenuous question made us all smile. ● **Antonyms: wily, sophisticated**

ingredient *noun* **component, constituent, element, factor, part, item, piece** Milk and ice cream are the main ingredients of a milk shake.

inhabit *verb* **occupy, abide, dwell, live, reside, settle, tenant** I was unhappy to discover that a mouse inhabits my closet.

inherent *adjective* **innate, basic, natural, elemental, intrinsic, characteristic, inborn** The ability for language is inherent in human beings.

inheritance *noun* **heritage, legacy, estate, bequest, endowment, bestowal, gift, heirloom** I received a gold ring as part of my inheritance from my grandmother.

inhibit *verb* **restrain, prevent, curb, check, discourage, frustrate, hinder, constrain** His lack of enthusiasm for the movie inhibited my enjoyment. ● **Antonyms: allow, permit, encourage**

initial *adjective* **beginning, earliest, first, original, early, primary, introductory** My initial opinion of her changed when I got to know her better. ● **Antonyms: final, last**

initiate *verb* **1. begin, commence, start, establish, introduce, launch, enter, create** Our history teacher initiated the discussion by asking us questions. **2. induct, install, admit, receive, invest, instate, inaugurate** He recited the Scout oath when he was initiated into the Boy Scouts. ◆ *noun* **neophyte, apprentice, novice, beginner, recruit, learner, freshman, newcomer** She was an initiate in a religious order.

initiative *noun* **enterprise, drive, enthusiasm, energy, push, ambition, hustle** His initiative is one of the qualities that makes him a good leader.

injure *verb* **1. harm, hurt, wound, traumatize, pain, bruise, mutilate, cripple** How did you injure yourself? **2.** damage, blemish, mar, impair, flaw, undermine, worsen, weaken The bad publicity injured his good name. ● **Antonyms: 2. improve, strengthen**

injury *noun* **wound, harm, hurt, trauma, damage, disfigurement, affliction** I received only a minor injury when I fell off my bike.

injustice *noun* **unfairness, inequity, wrong, crime, offense, outrage, injury** Sending an innocent person to prison is a terrible injustice. ● **Antonyms: justice, fairness, right**

inn *noun* **hostel, hotel, lodge, motel, resort, bed-and-breakfast, tavern, restaurant** We stayed in a quaint little inn while vacationing in New England.

innate *adjective* **inborn, native, inherited, natural, congenital, inherent, elemental** Most children have an innate sense of rhythm. ● **Antonyms: learned, acquired**

inner *adjective* **inside, interior, internal, inward, central, nuclear** The inner bark of a willow tree is edible. ● **Antonyms: exterior, outer**

innocent *adjective* **1. blameless, guiltless, not guilty, faultless, impeccable, clean, legal, lawful** According to the law, a person is innocent until proven guilty. **2. naive, simple, unsophisticated, artless, unworldly, honest, childlike, youthful** The innocent boy trusted everyone he encountered. **3. harmless, innocuous, inoffensive, safe, benign, inoffensive** Our math teacher was the target of several innocent pranks on April Fool's Day. ● **Antonyms: 1. guilty, sinful 2. wily, worldly 3. harmful, injurious**

innovation *noun* **change, variation, shift, novelty, invention, modernism** Automobile manufacturers make design innovations every year.

innumerable *adjective* **infinite, many, countless, untold, incalculable, myriad** We have innumerable opportunities to perform acts of kindness. ● **Antonyms: finite, few**

inordinate *adjective* **excessive, extreme, exorbitant, unreasonable, unnecessary, undue, overabundant, unwarranted** It took an inordinate amount of time to get home from the airport because of the heavy traffic. ● **Antonyms: reasonable, due, moderate**

inquire *verb* **ask, query, question, interview, investigate, look into, examine, explore** My parents inquired about the house that was for sale.

inquiry *noun* **1. query, question, request, interrogative, interview, questionnaire** I e-mailed an inquiry to the company's Web site. **2. study, inquest, examination, investigation, probe, research, scrutiny, inspection, analysis** There was an inquiry into the causes of juvenile delinquency.

inquisitive *adjective* **curious, inquiring, questioning, searching, investigative, nosy, snoopy** It's easy to think of questions when you have an inquisitive mind. ➡ **Antonyms: indifferent, incurious**

insane *adjective* **1. mentally ill, crazy, mad, deranged, psychotic, demented, maniacal** Doctors determined that the man was legally insane. **2. dumb, foolish, ridiculous, senseless, silly, stupid, idiotic, mad, impractical** I think that you are insane to go out in this horrible weather. ➡ **Antonyms: 1. rational, sane 2. wise, reasonable**

insatiable *adjective* **voracious, ravenous, gluttonous, endless, unquenchable, greedy, infinite** I have an insatiable curiosity about famous people. ➡ **Antonym: limited**

inscribe *verb* **1. engrave, carve, etch, chisel, cut, impress, imprint, stamp** The mason inscribed the names of the town's veterans on a memorial tablet. **2. write, print, sign, endorse, autograph, record, set down, write down** I inscribed a message on the inside cover of the book.

inscription *noun* **imprint, engraving, lettering, writing, dedication, impression, mark** My parents have inscriptions on the inside of their wedding rings.

Word Group

An **insect** is a small animal that in the adult stage has six legs, a body with three main divisions, and usually two pairs of wings. **Insect** is a general term with no true synonyms. Here are some common types of insects:

ant, bee, beetle, butterfly, chigger, cicada, cockroach, dragonfly, flea, fly, gnat, grasshopper, hornet, katydid, locust, louse, mantis, moth, termite, wasp, weevil

---

insecure *adjective* **1. uncertain, unsure, hesitant, apprehensive, worried, vulnerable, anxious** I felt a little insecure the first day at my new school. **2. shaky, unstable, unsteady, weak, wobbly, precarious, tottering, dangerous** Get a different chair to stand on—that one is too insecure. ➡ **Antonyms: 1. certain, sure, confident 2. secure, stable**

insert *verb* **place, put, enter, introduce, set, implant** I inserted the letter into the envelope. ➡ **Antonyms: remove, withdraw**

inside *noun* **interior, center, core, middle, recess, heart, nucleus, belly** The inside of the jewelry box is lined with red velvet. ◆ *adjective* **1. inner, interior, central, internal, inward, innermost** He uses the inside lane when he runs laps on the school track. **2. secret, classified, restricted, confidential, private, exclusive** That is inside information. ➡ **Antonyms:** *noun* **exterior, outside** ◆ *adjective* **1. external, outer 2. public**

insignia *noun* **badge, crest, emblem, mark, symbol, regalia, label, decoration** A three-leaf clover is the official insignia of the Girl Scouts of America.

insignificant *adjective* **trivial, meaningless, unimportant, inconsequential, petty, little, slight** The teacher said that my mistake was too insignificant to worry about. ➡ **Antonyms: important, significant**

insincere *adjective* **artificial, phony, pretended, affected, dishonest, deceitful, false, fake** Did you think her apology sounded insincere? ➡ **Antonyms: honest, sincere**

insinuate *verb* **hint, suggest, imply, intimate, indicate, allude, refer, signify** I did not mean to insinuate that you were rude.

insipid *adjective* **1. bland, flat, tasteless, stale, mild, unsavory, flavorless** This soda tastes insipid because it is flat. **2. boring, dull, unexciting, uninteresting, dry, drab, vapid, unimaginative** The insipid TV show bored me. ➡ **Antonyms: 1. savory, flavorful 2. interesting, lively**

insist *verb* **demand, require, stress, assert, urge, press, request** The teacher insisted that homework assignments be turned in on time.

insolent *adjective* **impudent, rude, disrespectful, bold, presumptuous, insulting, discourteous, impertinent** Don't be insolent to your parents. ➡ **Antonyms: respectful, courteous**

inspect *verb* **check, examine, investigate, scrutinize, study, survey, search, look over** Schools are inspected regularly by fire department officials.

inspection *noun* **check, checkup, examination, survey, scrutiny, review, investigation, inquiry** Commercial airplanes undergo regular safety inspections.

inspiration *noun* **1. encouragement, incentive, motivation, stimulation, animation, lift, uplift** The coach's speech at halftime gave inspiration to his players. **2. idea, thought, revelation, vision, brainstorm, creativity, flash** Some inventors say that their best inspirations have come from dreams.

inspire *verb* **encourage, motivate, prompt, stimulate, stir, hearten, spur, trigger** Her success at debating inspired her to consider a career in law. ● **Antonyms: deter, discourage**

install *verb* **1. place, position, put in, set up, locate, situate, station, plant** I installed a new game on my computer. **2. instate, induct, initiate, inaugurate, invest, seat, ordain, establish** Our new student council president will be installed next week. ● **Antonyms: 1. remove, disconnect 2. oust, divest**

instance *noun* **case, example, occasion, situation, time, sample, illustration, occurrence** I can't think of an instance when I was late for school.

instant *noun* **minute, moment, second, flash, jiffy, blink, breath, trice, twinkle** I'll be with you in an instant. ◆ *adjective* **instantaneous, immediate, prompt, quick, swift, direct, rapid, fast** Our school play was an instant success. ● **Antonyms:** *adjective* **slow, delayed**

instantly *adverb* **at once, immediately, right away, quickly, now, straightaway, instantaneously** I recognized my friend instantly despite her new haircut. ● **Antonyms: eventually, later**

instead *adverb* **in place of, rather than, alternatively, in lieu of, preferably** We started off for the movies but decided to go bowling instead.

instigate *verb* **provoke, urge, incite, prompt, stimulate, spur, foment** The Boston Tea Party was instigated by Sam Adams.

instinct *noun* **1. impulse, urge, tendency, leaning, drive, bent, feeling** Animals are born with certain basic instincts. **2. talent, gift, aptitude, flair, head, genius, knack, faculty, ability** He has a natural instinct for making people feel at ease.

instinctive *adjective* **instinctual, reflexive, automatic, intuitive, innate, inherent, inborn, involuntary** The pecking response is instinctive in most birds. ● **Antonyms: learned, acquired**

institute *verb* **begin, establish, found, organize, originate, start, initiate, introduce** The city government instituted a new recycling program. ◆ *noun* **academy, institution, school, foundation, union, society, guild, conservatory** I want to study at an art institute after I graduate from high school. ● **Antonyms:** *verb* **cease, stop, end**

institution *noun* **1. custom, practice, convention, rite, ritual, pattern** Going out for pizza on Friday night is one of our family's institutions. **2. academy, institute, establishment, foundation, organization, school, asylum** Colleges and universities are institutions of higher education.

instruct *verb* **1. coach, educate, school, teach, train, tutor, inform, guide** My skydiving coach instructed me in the proper use of a parachute. **2. charge, command, direct, order, tell, bid, prescribe, enjoin** My parents instructed me to be home by 10 p.m.

instruction *noun* **1. education, schooling, teaching, training, tutoring, lessons, guidance, coaching** I would like instruction on how to play a guitar. **2. command, demand, mandate, order, direction, ruling, directive, injunction** The captain expected his men to follow his instructions.

instrument *noun* **1. device, implement, mechanism, tool, utensil, appliance, equipment, machine** A barometer is an instrument for measuring atmospheric pressure. **2. means, agent, agency, channel, medium, vehicle, mechanism, force** The news media has been an instrument of change in American society.

insubordinate *adjective* **disobedient, rebellious, unruly, defiant, mutinous, insolent, contrary** The insubordinate student was suspended from school. ● **Antonyms: obedient, submissive**

insult *verb* **affront, offend, pique, humiliate, scorn, snub, outrage, ridicule** My disparaging comment about cats insulted her. ◆ *noun* **affront, offense, slight, outrage, scorn, snub, taunt, indignity** I'm sorry if I offended you, but I meant no insult. ● **Antonyms: compliment, praise**

integrate *verb* **incorporate, include, combine, unify, mix, merge, synthesize, fuse** Our English class will integrate elements of history when we study the Elizabethan period. ● **Antonyms: separate, fragment, divide**

integrity *noun* **1. honesty, honor, virtue, character, principle, uprightness, purity, decency** It takes integrity to always do the right thing. **2. completeness, wholeness, totality, intactness, unity, cohesion, oneness** The inspector tested the integrity of the unit before shipping it to the customer. ● **Antonyms: 1. dishonesty, dishonor 2. division, segregation**

intellectual *adjective* **1. cerebral, sophisticated, thoughtful, highbrow, literate, learned, scholarly** The library subscribes to several intellectual magazines. **2. intelligent, smart, bright, brilliant, knowledgeable, brainy, rational** She is one of the most intellectual people I have ever met. ◆ *noun* **mind, thinker, brain, intellect, genius, sage, scholar, academician** Albert Einstein was one of the greatest intellectuals of the 20th century.

intelligence *noun* **1. brains, intellect, mind, brainpower, mentality, perception, comprehension, understanding** It is important to develop your intelligence. **2. information, news, data, facts, knowledge, message, tidings** The media gathered intelligence regarding the oil spill.

intelligent *adjective* **alert, bright, brilliant, clever, smart, wise, quick, astute, sharp** My parents admitted I had made an intelligent choice in deciding to study music. ⏵ **Antonyms: stupid, unintelligent**

intend *verb* **aim, expect, mean, plan, propose, design, plot** What do you intend to do this summer?

intense *adjective* **1. extreme, great, strong, fierce, furious, violent, powerful, forceful** Antarctica is known for its intense cold. **2. deep, profound, fervent, passionate, ardent, keen, strong** I have an intense love for my family. ⏵ **Antonyms: 1. feeble, weak 2. casual, cool, indifferent**

intensity *noun* **energy, ferocity, fury, power, strength, violence, severity** The forest fire burned for days with great intensity. ⏵ **Antonym: weakness**

intent *noun* **ambition, aim, goal, intention, objective, purpose, inclination, design** It is my intent to go to college someday. ◆ *adjective* **1. intense, absorbed, attentive, deep, preoccupied, determined, earnest, heedful** He had an intent look on his face as he worked on the problem. **2. set, resolute, determined, bent, decided, fixed, firm, insistent** I am intent on making the high honor roll. ⏵ **Antonyms: adjective 1. distracted 2. indifferent**

intention *noun* **purpose, plan, design, goal, target, aim, ambition, intent, objective** It is my intention to submit a story to the contest.

intentional *adjective* **deliberate, intended, planned, premeditated, purposeful, willed, calculated** Doctors take an oath in which they promise never to do any intentional harm to their patients. ⏵ **Antonyms: accidental, unintentional**

intercept *verb* **cut off, head off, block, interrupt, catch, seize, stop, deflect** Two fighter planes were sent to intercept the enemy aircraft.

interest *noun* **1. attention, curiosity, care, concern, notice, absorption, regard, inquisitiveness** I watched the work on the construction site with interest. **2. activity, hobby, pastime, pursuit, recreation, avocation** My interests include reading books and playing soccer. **3. advantage, benefit, good, profit, welfare, gain** It is in your interest to turn your homework in on time. **4. claim, stake, portion, share, right, part, piece, investment** My stepfather inherited a small interest in a copper mine. ◆ *verb* **intrigue, absorb, attract, engage, fascinate, hold, occupy, delight** Everything about airplanes interests me. ⏵ **Antonyms: noun 1. apathy, boredom 3. disadvantage** ◆ *verb* **bore, weary**

interesting *adjective* **absorbing, appealing, entertaining, fascinating, exciting, amusing, enthralling** He told us an interesting story about swimming with dolphins. ⏵ **Antonyms: boring, dull**

interfere *verb* **interrupt, intervene, meddle, butt in, disturb, hinder, tamper, obstruct** I didn't interfere with my friends' private conversation.

interior *noun* **1. inside, center, core, heart, middle, lining, belly** Our new car has a tan leather interior. **2. inland, midland, hinterland, heartland, backcountry, backwoods, bush** Most of Australia's interior is very hot and dry. ◆ *adjective* **inside, inner, internal, inmost, innermost, inward, indoor** The science teacher took a telephone apart to show us the interior structure. ⏵ **Antonyms: noun 1. exterior, outside** ◆ *adjective* **outer, exterior, external**

intermediate *adjective* **halfway, middle, midway, central, medium, transitional, intermediary** A cocoon is the intermediate stage between a caterpillar and a butterfly.

intermission *noun* **break, pause, recess, rest, stop, interlude, respite, time-out, breather** There will be a brief intermission halfway through the play.

intermittent *adjective* **periodic, sporadic, recurring, irregular, discontinuous, interrupted, occasional** The beacon sent out intermittent flashes of light. ⏵ **Antonyms: steady, continuous**

internal *adjective* **inner, inside, interior, hidden, inward, inmost, innermost** The internal workings of a clock are complicated. ⏵ **Antonyms: exterior, external**

international *adjective* global, world, worldwide, universal, intercontinental, cosmopolitan, foreign The first international conference on environmental pollution was held in 1972. ➡ **Antonyms: domestic, national**

interpret *verb* define, explain, understand, clarify, decipher, decode, solve, translate I read a book about how to interpret dreams.

interrogate *verb* question, examine, cross-examine, quiz, query, investigate, grill, pump The detective will interrogate all the suspects in the robbery.

interrupt *verb* 1. break into, cease, stop, halt, interfere, suspend The alarm clock interrupted my dream. 2. disturb, intervene, intrude, cut, break, barge in I didn't mean to interrupt your conversation. ➡ **Antonyms: 1. continue, resume**

interval *noun* period, gap, space, spell, interlude, break, pause, rest We had a welcome interval of warm weather in February.

intervene *verb* intercede, mediate, negotiate, settle, arbitrate, interfere, interrupt Mom intervened when my brother and I were arguing.

interview *noun* conference, consultation, meeting, discussion, talk, dialogue, communication Our teacher is scheduling interviews with all of our parents. ◆ *verb* examine, interrogate, question, talk to, quiz, consult, converse I interviewed a police officer for my report on law enforcement.

intimate[1] *adjective* 1. near, close, dear, personal, bosom, familiar, thick, fast Only intimate family members were invited to the wedding. 2. private, personal, secret, confidential, innermost, deep I keep a journal of my intimate thoughts. ◆ *noun* friend, comrade, confidante, chum, crony, companion, mate, pal She and I have been intimates ever since we met in second grade. ➡ **Antonyms: *adjective* 1. distant, remote 2. public ◆ *noun* stranger**

intimate[2] *verb* hint, imply, insinuate, suggest, allude Why did you intimate that I don't like him?

intimidate *verb* frighten, threaten, scare, menace, unnerve, ruffle, cow, bully The kitten arched its back and hissed in order to intimidate our dog.

intolerant *adjective* biased, close-minded, narrow-minded, prejudiced, bigoted I try not to be intolerant when I meet people whose beliefs are different from my own. ➡ **Antonyms: tolerant, understanding**

intrepid *adjective* brave, bold, fearless, courageous, daring, audacious, gallant, valiant I admire the astronauts for being so intrepid. ➡ **Antonyms: fearful, cowardly, timid**

intricate *adjective* complex, complicated, detailed, elaborate, involved, fancy A computer program has many intricate parts that must work together. ➡ **Antonyms: plain, simple**

intrigue *noun* scheme, machination, ruse, deal, trick, conspiracy, stratagem, plot I like books and movies that have lots of intrigue. ◆ *verb* 1. plot, scheme, connive, conspire, maneuver, devise, plan Iago intrigues to discredit Desdemona in Shakespeare's play *Othello*. 2. charm, enthrall, excite, fascinate, interest, enchant, entertain, attract Many people are intrigued by the possibility of life on other planets. ➡ **Antonyms: *verb* 2. bore, repel, repulse**

introduce *verb* 1. announce, present, acquaint, proclaim, herald, familiarize I introduced myself to our new neighbor. 2. launch, originate, put forth, inaugurate, begin, establish, start, embark Fashion designers introduce their new collections twice a year. 3. bring up, preface, usher in, broach, raise, precede, lead The radio announcer introduced a commercial at the station break. 4. bring in, insert, inject, add, interject, interpose, put in, enter In 1876, tumbleweed was accidentally introduced to America from a shipment of Russian flax seed.

introductory *adjective* first, basic, preliminary, initial, preparatory, rudimentary, starting The speaker made a few introductory comments. ➡ **Antonyms: final, concluding**

intrude *verb* trespass, interrupt, invade, encroach, infringe, meddle, interfere, disturb He burst through the door without knocking and intruded on our conversation.

intuition *noun* instinct, hunch, feeling, sense, insight, perception, impression, suspicion My intuition tells me that tomorrow is going to be a great day.

inundate *verb* overwhelm, deluge, flood, overrun, immerse, submerge, overflow, swamp Our farm was inundated during the flood.

invade *verb* 1. assail, assault, attack, raid, strike, foray, storm, pillage Germany invaded many countries during World War II. 2. occupy, overrun, usurp, enter, penetrate, permeate, infest, trespass My cat and her kittens have temporarily invaded my closet.

invaluable *adjective* precious, priceless, valuable, expensive, matchless, dear, indispensable Reading and writing are invaluable skills. ➡ **Antonyms: worthless, useless**

invariable *adjective* unchanging, constant, unvarying, uniform, regular, changeless, consistent, dependable The professor had an invariable routine. ▪ **Antonyms:** changing, variable

invasion *noun* assault, attack, raid, aggression, offensive, incursion, trespass, foray The Great Wall of China was built to protect the country from invasion.

invent *verb* **1.** contrive, create, devise, develop, originate, fashion, conceive Alexander Graham Bell invented the telephone in 1876. **2.** fabricate, counterfeit, concoct, make up, lie, fib, falsify, pretend My sister invented a story about seeing a UFO.

invention *noun* **1.** creation, development, discovery, design, concoction, improvisation Thomas Edison is credited with the invention of the first practical light bulb. **2.** fabrication, lie, falsehood, fib, story, fiction, distortion, fantasy, untruth The newspaper story was pure invention. ▪ **Antonyms:** 2. truth, reality

inventory *noun* **1.** catalog, file, list, record, register, summary, roster, schedule, table The teacher made an inventory of all classroom supplies. **2.** reserve, stock, stockpile, store, supply, reservoir, backlog The department store had a sale to reduce its inventory.

invest *verb* **1.** allot, devote, apportion, give, contribute, spend, entrust I invest my money in penny stocks. **2.** endow, empower, authorize, enable, sanction, entitle, permit, license A minister is invested with the authority to marry people.

investigate *verb* look into, probe, analyze, examine, inspect, study, survey, research Will you investigate that strange noise?

invisible *adjective* imperceptible, unobservable, unnoticeable, concealed, hidden, veiled, screened The green parakeet was almost invisible against the tree leaves. ▪ **Antonyms:** visible, perceptible, obvious

invite *verb* ask, bid, request, summon, beckon, tempt, encourage, persuade, welcome I invited two of my friends to spend the night at my house.

involuntary *adjective* automatic, reflexive, unwilled, instinctive, impulsive, spontaneous, unintentional Breathing and digestion are involuntary actions. ▪ **Antonyms:** voluntary, intentional

involve *verb* **1.** call for, contain, have, include, require, entail, comprise, incorporate His job involves a great deal of traveling. **2.** draw in, mix up, embroil, entangle, tangle, implicate, concern I try not to get involved in other people's private affairs. **3.** absorb, engage, immerse, occupy, engross, preoccupy, take in Her story so involved us that we didn't hear the phone ring.

irate *adjective* angry, enraged, angered, furious, fuming, mad, incensed, wrathful, infuriated I was irate when I found that the puppy had chewed on one of my shoes. ▪ **Antonyms:** calm, pleasant, tranquil

irk *verb* annoy, bother, irritate, vex, nettle, rile, upset, trouble, aggravate It irked me that no one noticed I had painted the porch steps. ▪ **Antonyms:** please, soothe, calm

irrational *adjective* unreasonable, illogical, senseless, unsound, absurd, foolish, nonsensical I have an irrational fear of small spaces. ▪ **Antonyms:** rational, sensible, logical

irregular *adjective* **1.** abnormal, unusual, atypical, strange, uncommon, deviant, unnatural His morning routine of consuming chocolate cake and cola is highly irregular. **2.** uneven, variable, unsteady, changeable, fluctuating, erratic The patient had an irregular heartbeat. **3.** uneven, unequal, asymmetrical, jagged, bumpy, crooked, rough These patio stones have irregular shapes. ▪ **Antonyms:** 1. normal, typical 2. even, regular 3. smooth, symmetrical

irrelevant *adjective* unrelated, immaterial, inapplicable, extraneous, impertinent, incidental That argument is irrelevant to the discussion. ▪ **Antonyms:** relevant, pertinent

irritate *verb* **1.** annoy, bother, disturb, exasperate, provoke, nettle, vex, gall That noisy car alarm irritates me. **2.** aggravate, inflame, hurt, worsen, chafe, fester, exacerbate, abrade You'll irritate that mosquito bite if you continue to scratch it. ▪ **Antonyms:** 1. calm, comfort 2. relieve, soothe

Word Group

An **island** is a body of land, especially one smaller than a continent, entirely surrounded by water. **Island** is a specific term with no true synonyms. Here are some related words:

An **archipelago** is a large group of islands. An **atoll** is a coral island or a string of coral islands and reefs enclosing a lagoon. A **holm** is an island in a river. An **isle**, a **cay**, and an **islet** are very small islands. A **key** is a low-lying island or reef along a coast, especially in the Gulf of Mexico. A **shoal** is a shallow place beneath water, sometimes exposed at low tide. A **skerry** is a small rocky reef or island.

isolate *verb* quarantine, segregate, separate, set apart, seclude, sequester, cut off, insulate The hospital is required to isolate patients with contagious diseases.

issue *noun* 1. edition, copy, publication, printing, volume, number, installment, version The new magazine's first issue will be published next month. 2. matter, problem, question, subject, topic, controversy, point Health care is an issue that affects everyone. 3. offspring, progeny, children, young, family, descendants, line, heirs, seed He willed everything to his nephews and nieces because he had no legal issue of his own. ◆ *verb* 1. emit, emerge, ooze, flow, proceed, spurt, spring, well Natural gas issued from the well. 2. publish, print, release, circulate, bring out, put forth, put out The publisher issued two dozen books last year. 3. deliver, dispense, distribute, give out, allot, apportion, send Music stands were issued to the orchestra members. ◆ **Antonyms:** *noun* 3. parents, sire, ancestor

itch *noun* craving, desire, yearning, hunger, appetite, want, yen, longing I have an itch to go out for pizza. ◆ *verb* crave, desire, yearn, want, hanker, long They itched to go on a long cruise.

item *noun* 1. article, object, thing, commodity, ware, product, element, particular I made a list of the items that I need for my trip. 2. account, article, entry, feature, report, story, piece, bit, dispatch Did you read the item in the paper about our school concert?

itemize *verb* detail, document, list, record, catalog, specify, enumerate, inventory This receipt itemizes everything that we bought.

itinerary *noun* schedule, plan, agenda, path, course, proposal, account The travel agent gave me the itinerary for my trip to South America.

J j

jab *verb* **thrust, plunge, stab, poke, push, pierce, punch, dig, prod** He jabbed his fork into the baked potato to see if it was done. ◆ *noun* **blow, punch, strike, hit, poke, thrust, dig, nudge** The boxer threw a series of quick jabs at his opponent.

jabber *verb* **chatter, babble, prattle, run on, rattle on, blather, prate** The students jabbered while they waited for the assembly to begin. ◆ *noun* **babble, prattle, gibberish, nonsense, chatter, blather, prate, blabber** A baby's jabber is the beginning of learning a language.

jacket *noun* 1. **coat, parka, mackinaw, windbreaker, tunic, blazer** He took a warm jacket with him to the football game. 2. **cover, wrapper, envelope, folder, case, sheath, container** Martin keeps his older comic books in protective plastic jackets.

jagged *adjective* **ragged, serrated, uneven, pointed, notched, rough, craggy** She cut her finger on a jagged piece of glass. ➤ **Antonyms: even, smooth**

jail *noun* **jailhouse, prison, pen, penitentiary, house of correction, brig, lockup** The sheriff kept the outlaws in jail. ◆ *verb* **imprison, lock up, confine, detain, incarcerate, intern** The police have arrested and jailed two suspects. ➤ **Antonyms:** *verb* **release, parole**

jam *verb* 1. **cram, pack, stuff, squeeze, wedge, load, push, shove, crowd, press** My sister tried to jam more books into her backpack. 2. **block, clog, plug, obstruct, stop, halt, stall** The sink drain is jammed with carrot peelings. ◆ *noun* 1. **blockage, obstruction, barrier, block, obstacle, congestion, gridlock** A traffic jam made us late for our flight. 2. **predicament, dilemma, quandary, plight, mess, trouble, fix, bind** The tourists were in a real jam when their money was stolen.

jar¹ *noun* **bottle, jug, vase, container, vessel, beaker** Dad keeps his loose change in a jar on his desk.

jar² *verb* 1. **jangle, grate, irritate, upset, agitate, shock, rankle** The sound of chalk scraping on a blackboard jars my nerves. 2. **rock, jolt, rattle, shake, vibrate, jiggle, jog, jounce** The earthquake jarred our house but didn't cause any damage. ◆ *noun* **jolt, bounce, bump, jounce, thud, thump, shock** I felt a jar as the car drove over a large pothole. ➤ **Antonyms:** *verb* 1. **calm, soothe**

jargon *noun* **terminology, vocabulary, language, idiom, lingo, cant, parlance** The magazine article about comets was full of scientific jargon.

jaunty *adjective* 1. **carefree, lighthearted, lively, spirited, vivacious, buoyant** The happy boy had a jaunty walk. 2. **debonair, dapper, neat, natty, dashing, smart** I like your jaunty new hat. ➤ **Antonyms: staid, sedate**

jealous *adjective* 1. **resentful, insecure, threatened, possessive, anxious** Sometimes I feel jealous when my parents pay attention to my brother. 2. **envious, covetous, desirous, grudging, begrudging** Who wouldn't be jealous of your new computer?

jealousy *noun* **envy, covetousness, resentment, spite, grudge** The man was filled with jealousy when his neighbor won the lottery.

jeer *verb* **ridicule, taunt, insult, heckle, mock, deride, sneer** I thought the comedian was very funny, but some people in the audience jeered him. ◆ *noun* **ridicule, derision, mockery, gibe, insult, taunt, sneer** The umpire's call was received with jeers from the fans.

jeopardy *noun* **danger, peril, risk, threat, trouble, vulnerability** The ship's crew members placed their lives in jeopardy to protect the passengers. ➤ **Antonym: safety**

jerk *verb* **pull, yank, wrench, snap, twist, tug, wrest, grab** Amy's dog jerked the leash out of her hand and ran off. ◆ *noun* **bump, jolt, lurch, snap, bounce, jounce, pull, tug, yank** The roller coaster started with a jerk.

jest *noun* **joke, hoax, prank, trick, gag, witticism, gibe, quip** I hope you were making a jest when you said that dinner would be three hours late. ◆ *verb* **joke, kid, tease, fool, spoof, clown, fool, gibe** Grandpa was jesting when he said that mice are the best bait for catfish.

jet *noun* **spray, fountain, gush, spurt, squirt, spout, stream, rush** An erupting geyser shoots a jet of steam and water high into the air. ◆ *verb* **gush, spray, spurt, squirt, surge, flow, pour, stream** Water jetted from the broken fire hydrant.

jettison *verb* **eject, expel, dump, discharge, throw overboard, dispose, discard** The airplane jettisoned excess fuel in preparation for an emergency landing.

jewel *noun* **1. gem, gemstone, precious stone, ornament, bangle, bauble, trinket** Sapphires are my favorite jewels. **2. treasure, marvel, wonder, paragon, rarity, prize, gem** The Taj Mahal is a jewel of architectural design.

> **Word Group**
>
> A piece of **jewelry** is an ornament that is worn as decoration on the body. **Jewelry** is a general term with no true synonyms. Here are some different kinds of jewelry:
>
> **anklet, bracelet, brooch, cameo, cuff link, diadem, earring, locket, necklace, pendant, ring, solitaire, stickpin, tiara**

jibe *verb* **agree, correspond, match, concur, square, tally, check** Does the suspect's alibi jibe with the witness's statement? ◆ **Antonyms: contradict, differ, disagree**

jiffy *noun* **instant, moment, minute, second, flash, trice, twinkling** Lunch will be ready in a jiffy.

jingle *verb* **chime, ring, tinkle, jangle, clink, ding** The bell on the shop door jingled as I entered. ◆ *noun* **chime, ring, tinkle, jangle, ding, clink** I enjoy listening to the jingle of our wind chimes.

jittery *adjective* **nervous, agitated, fidgety, jumpy, restless, skittish, anxious** Drinking too much coffee makes Harmon jittery. ◆ **Antonyms: calm, serene**

job *noun* **1. chore, task, duty, assignment, obligation, responsibility, role, function** My sister's job is to clear the table. **2. position, situation, employment, work, occupation, career, place** Mom recently got a job as a computer programmer.

jockey *verb* **maneuver, navigate, steer, move, pilot, deploy** We jockeyed our way through the crowd at the fair.

jog *verb* **1. stir, prompt, stimulate, activate, nudge, jar, prod** Your library book jogged my memory about the report that we have due next week. **2. run, trot, lope, sprint, race, dash** I jogged around the track. ◆ *noun* **run, sprint, trot, dash, race, lope** I like to go for a jog first thing in the morning.

join *verb* **1. link, connect, attach, fasten, couple, yoke, tie, splice, bind** A special coupling mechanism joins railroad cars. **2. ally, unite, combine, merge, band, associate, affiliate, consolidate** Two Scout troops joined together to paint the playground equipment. **3. sign up, enroll,** participate, enter, enlist My mom has decided to join an indoor soccer league. ◆ **Antonyms: 1. & 2. separate, divide 3. leave, resign**

joint *noun* **link, connection, seam, union, coupling, junction, intersection** The maintenance crew checked the joints in the train track. ◆ *adjective* **mutual, shared, communal, combined, common, collective, united** Mom and Dad have a joint bank account. ◆ **Antonyms: *adjective* separate, individual**

joke *noun* **1. gag, witticism, jest, anecdote, story, yarn, quip, wisecrack** I forgot the punch line to the joke I was telling. **2. trick, prank, shenanigan, antic, caper, mischief, lark** Many people play jokes on April Fool's day. ◆ *verb* **fool, jest, kid, tease, josh, wisecrack** I was joking when I said that I wanted a peanut butter pizza.

jolly *adjective* **cheerful, gay, happy, jovial, merry, blithe, lighthearted, convivial** Our jolly neighbor is always smiling and laughing. ◆ **Antonyms: gloomy, sad**

jolt *verb* **bounce, jar, jerk, shake, jostle, knock, throw, bump, lurch** We were jolted out of our seats when the bus went over a speed bump too quickly. ◆ *noun* **1. bump, bounce, jar, lurch, shake, jerk, impact** The plane landed with a small jolt. **2. shock, surprise, start, blow, revelation, bombshell** I got a big jolt when I looked at my new haircut.

jostle *verb* **bump, crowd, push, shove, press, collide, elbow** The pigs jostled each other on their way to the feeding trough.

jot *noun* **bit, iota, whit, smidgen, mite, modicum, shred, speck, dot** I couldn't remember a jot of what I had studied. ◆ *verb* **write, note, record, scribble, list, put, register** He jotted down the message on a notepad by the phone.

journal *noun* **1. diary, log, chronicle, record, memoir, notebook** She kept a journal during her vacation. **2. magazine, periodical, publication, review, bulletin, newspaper** I read an article about ancient Rome in a history journal.

journalist *noun* **reporter, correspondent, writer, columnist, newsperson, editor** A journalist interviewed the mayor for a newspaper article.

journey *noun* **expedition, trip, trek, excursion, tour, voyage, jaunt, odyssey** Marco Polo's famous journey to China lasted 24 years. ◆ *verb* **tour, travel, trek, ramble, roam, voyage, wander, go** My parents journeyed through South America on their honeymoon.

jovial *adjective* **jolly, cheerful, merry, mirthful, gleeful, jocund** A jovial clown greeted everyone who entered the circus tent. ➤ **Antonyms: melancholy, sad**

joy *noun* **delight, happiness, pleasure, glee, ecstacy, bliss, cheer, enjoyment** Charles was filled with joy when he won first place in the statewide science fair. ➤ **Antonyms: sadness, sorrow, grief**

joyful *adjective* **glad, happy, joyous, merry, festive, cheerful, pleasing, jubilant** This year Thanksgiving was especially joyful because our whole family was together. ➤ **Antonyms: sad, unhappy**

jubilant *adjective* **ecstatic, exultant, thrilled, overjoyed, elated, triumphant** The prospector was jubilant when he discovered a rich vein of gold. ➤ **Antonym: disappointed**

jubilee *noun* **celebration, festival, fete, gala, festivity, party, revelry** Our town has an annual jubilee that includes a chili cook-off.

judge *verb* **1. assess, evaluate, appraise, review, calculate, estimate, gauge, rate** One way to judge the quality of a garment is to examine its seams. **2. decide, determine, settle, decree, adjudge, arbitrate, try** The defendant's guilt or innocence will be judged in a court of law. ◆ *noun* **1. justice, magistrate, justice of the peace, jurist** My new family and I were very happy when the judge finalized my adoption. **2. evaluator, reviewer, critic, referee, umpire, arbitrator, moderator** I was one of the judges for our school art contest.

judgment *noun* **1. common sense, discretion, prudence, sense, wisdom, discernment** I am glad to have parents who respect my judgment. **2. opinion, view, notion, assessment, estimate, appraisal, evaluation** In my judgment, Baltimore has the best aquarium in the country. **3. conclusion, decision, finding, ruling, verdict, opinion, determination** The judgment of a court is always based on existing laws as well as the evidence presented.

jug *noun* **bottle, jar, container, flask, crock, pitcher, vessel, ewer** We bought a jug of maple syrup while vacationing in Vermont.

juggle *verb* **manipulate, shuffle, alter, modify, tamper, maneuver,** Mom had to juggle her schedule in order to take me to the dentist.

jumble *verb* **disarrange, disorganize, muddle, confuse, scramble, mess up** I jumbled the clothes in my closet while searching for my favorite sweater. ◆ *noun* **clutter, mess,** hodgepodge, muddle, tangle, disarray, confusion My brother left a jumble of his dirty clothes on the floor. ➤ **Antonyms: *verb* order, organize**

jumbo *adjective* **colossal, enormous, gigantic, huge, immense, mammoth, massive** I ordered a jumbo plate of French fries. ➤ **Antonyms: small, tiny**

jump *verb* **1. leap, spring, vault, bound, hop, hurdle, bounce** Our dog jumped off the chair when we came home. **2. start, flinch, recoil, jerk, wince, blench, bolt** I jumped when the wind slammed the door. **3. increase, advanced, surge, gain, skyrocket** My grades jumped when my friends and I formed a study group. ◆ *noun* **1. leap, spring, bound, hop, vault, bounce, skip** He cleared the pole on his first jump. **2. increase, hike, advance, gain, rise, boost** When my father was promoted, he got a big jump in salary. ➤ **Antonyms: *verb* 3. lower, decrease ◆ *noun* 2. decrease, reduction**

junction *noun* **convergence, intersection, confluence, juncture, joining, union, connection** St. Louis is located at the junction of the Mississippi and Missouri rivers.

jungle *noun* **rain forest, tropical forest, primeval forest, bush, undergrowth** Jungles are humid because they receive a lot of rain.

junior *adjective* **1. adolescent, juvenile, youthful, younger** He entered the junior division of the surfing tournament. **2. new, recent, minor, secondary, subordinate, lesser, lower, under** She is a junior member of the club, but one of the most active.

junk *noun* **debris, rubbish, trash, garbage, litter, scrap, refuse, waste** We threw away large amounts of junk when we cleaned out the garage. ◆ *verb* **discard, throw away, throw out, dump, dispose of, scrap** My parents have threatened to junk the TV set if my grades do not improve.

jurisdiction *noun* **authority, control, command, rule, prerogative, dominion, power** The FBI has jurisdiction over kidnapping investigations.

just *adjective* **1. fair, impartial, objective, unbiased, sound, valid** This judge is known for making just decisions. **2. merited, appropriate, deserved, fitting, apt, proper, suitable** The Oscar was a just reward for the actor's brilliant performance. ◆ *adverb* **1. exactly, entirely, precisely, completely, perfectly, absolutely, thoroughly** Mom says that I look just like my grandfather. **2. recently, now, presently, newly, lately** The concert had only just started when we arrived at the park. **3. barely, hardly, scarcely, merely, only, simply** You'll just have time to get to the store before it closes. ● **Antonyms:** *adjective* **1. biased, unfair 2. inappropriate, unfit**

justice *noun* **1. fairness, justness, lawfulness, due process, integrity, honesty** The innocent man must be released if justice is to be achieved. **2. judge, magistrate, justice of the peace, jurist** Everyone stood up when the justice entered the courtroom. ● **Antonym: 1. injustice**

justification *noun* **basis, foundation, reason, cause, grounds, argument** The original justification for summer vacation was the need for children to help bring in the harvest.

justify *verb* **confirm, verify, vindicate, validate, sustain, uphold, support** Ed justified my trust by returning my book.

jut *verb* **stick out, bulge, project, extend, protrude, overhang** The woman's packages jutted into the aisle of the bus.

juvenile *adjective* **1. young, youthful, developing, undeveloped, adolescent, infant, green** Juvenile elephants stay with their mothers for up to ten years. **2. immature, childish, babyish, infantile, puerile, unsophisticated, callow** Putting a frog in your sister's bed was a juvenile prank. ◆ *noun* **child, minor, youngster, youth, boy, girl, teenager, infant** Juveniles under the age of 18 may not sign a legal contract. ● **Antonym: adult**

keen *adjective* **1. sharp, fine, honed, edged, cutting, pointed, penetrating, piercing** Scalpels have very keen edges. **2. acute, sensitive, marked, fine, alert, strong, probing, penetrating** Bears have a keen sense of smell. **3. astute, perceptive, shrewd, intelligent, smart, clever, bright, alert** Carl Jung had many keen insights into human nature. **4. eager, enthusiastic, excited, avid, ardent, fervent, zealous, hot** I wasn't too keen on the idea of going to a movie by myself. ◆ **Antonyms: 1. dull, blunt 4. reluctant, apathetic, indifferent**

keep *verb* **1. retain, have, own, possess, hold, maintain, acquire** Mom said that I could keep the lizard I found. **2. save, preserve, husband, amass, store, hold, hold back** We keep our vegetable peelings for the compost heap. **3. store, place, maintain, stock, cache, put, deposit, stack** I keep my socks in the top drawer of my dresser. **4. persist, continue, persevere, maintain, remain, carry on, endure** I keep trying to run a mile in less than eight minutes. **5. observe, celebrate, honor, maintain, commemorate, hold to** It is traditional for Muslims to keep Ramadan by fasting from sunup to sundown. **6. fulfill, honor, respect, carry out, adhere to, observe, abide by, follow, obey** Matthew kept his promise to send me a postcard from New York. **7. prevent, stop, hinder, impede, detain, delay, restrain, retard, hold back** A rainstorm kept us from going sailing. ◆ *noun* **1. living, livelihood, support, upkeep, maintenance, room and board, subsistence** The nanny earned her keep by caring for three small children. **2. donjon, tower, citadel, stronghold, castle, fortress, fort, fortification** A castle's keep was considered the last defense against attackers.

keeper *noun* **1. attendant, custodian, overseer, guard, warden, guardian** We asked the lodge keeper for directions to the boathouse. **2. curator, caretaker, manager, superintendent, trustee** The lion keeper from the zoo spoke to our science class.

keg *noun* **barrel, cask, drum, tub, container, tank, tun, hogshead** Carpenters used to buy their nails by the keg.

kettle *noun* **pot, pan, teakettle, saucepan, Dutch oven, caldron, vat, vessel** I boiled water in the kettle to make some hot chocolate.

key *noun* **1. solution, answer, explanation, clue, guide, secret, resolution** The key to solving a riddle is to listen carefully to its exact wording. **2. means, path, route, way, formula, ticket, passport, blueprint** Hard work is frequently the key to success. ◆ *adjective* **crucial, vital, indispensable, central, leading, fundamental, essential, important, major, main** Your contributions were a key factor in making our school carnival a success. ◆ *verb* **adapt, adjust, gear, suit, fit, direct, steer, shape, accommodate, reconcile** The candidate keyed his speech to the audience of farm workers. ◆ **Antonyms:** *adjective* **minor, insignicant, unnecessary**

kick *verb* **boot, punt, drop-kick, hit, knock, strike, tap, slam, smash** Dennis kicked the football between the goal posts. ◆ *noun* **blow, hit, poke, nudge, knock, stroke, bang, bump** The rider gave her horse a gentle kick in the ribs to get it moving.

kid *noun* **child, youngster, boy, girl, juvenile, youth, adolescent, teenager, baby** Some of the neighborhood kids got together for a game of hide-and-seek. ◆ *verb* **tease, taunt, josh, rib, banter, jest, joke, fool, ridicule, heckle** I like to kid my sister about her boyfriend. ◆ **Antonyms:** *noun* **adult, grownup**

kidnap *verb* **abduct, carry off, capture, seize, shanghai, snatch, waylay, hijack, skyjack, steal** The revolutionaries kidnapped the governor.

kill *verb* **1. slay, exterminate, annihilate, assassinate, execute, murder, slaughter, eradicate** I don't like to kill spiders because they eat flies. **2. destroy, demolish, eliminate, end, extinguish, finish, ruin, wipe out, squash, thwart** The athlete's injury has killed her chances of winning the competition. **3. torment, torture, hurt, irritate, chafe, distress, pain** These new braces are really killing my teeth. ◆ *noun* **prey, victim, quarry, game** The lioness stood guard over her kill. ◆ **Antonyms:** *verb* **2. encourage, create**

kin *noun* **family, kindred, kinfolk, relations, relatives, blood, clan, lineage, tribe, stock, connection** I have kin in Pakistan.

kind¹ *adjective* **compassionate, kindly, goodhearted, helpful, altruistic, good, benevolent, considerate, friendly, generous, humane** A kind woman helped me pick up the books that I had dropped. ◆ **Antonyms: mean, unkind**

kind² *noun* **sort, type, variety, breed, category, class, manner, nature, genus, strain, ilk** The red panda and the giant panda are the only two kinds of pandas.

kindle *verb* **1. ignite, light, fire, fuel, burn** I used a match and some crumpled newspaper to kindle the campfire. **2. arouse, inspire, stir, stimulate, awaken, induce, excite, animate, whet** A friend kindled my interest in origami. ➡ **Antonyms: 1. extinguish, quench, smother 2. stifle, dampen, discourage**

kindly *adjective* **helpful, kind, good, goodhearted, sympathetic, genial, friendly, kindhearted, generous** My grandmother gave me kindly advice about getting along with my sister. ♦ *adverb* **helpfully, generously, thoughtfully, benevolently, compassionately, graciously** My older brother kindly offered to help me with my geometry homework. ➡ **Antonyms:** *adjective* **unsympathetic, hostile, inconsiderate**

kindness *noun* **compassion, benevolence, consideration, decency, goodwill, sympathy, tenderness, grace, humanity** I believe that all people should be treated with kindness. ➡ **Antonym: cruelty**

king *noun* **monarch, sovereign, majesty, ruler, liege, potentate, regent, prince, lord** Henry VIII was the king of England from 1509 to 1547.

kingdom *noun* **monarchy, principality, dominion, empire, country, nation, territory, province, domain, realm, sphere** Saudi Arabia is a kingdom that was founded in 1932.

kink *noun* **1. curl, twist, bend, coil, knot, tangle, crimp** The garden hose had a kink in it that impeded the flow of water. **2. cramp, spasm, knot, pain, pang, stiffness, twinge, crick** The man got a kink in his back from lifting the heavy box. **3. complication, hitch, flaw, defect, rough spot, difficulty, impediment** The rain put a kink in our plan to picnic in the park.

kit *noun* **outfit, tools, gear, equipment, utensils, implements, bag, collection, supplies** We carry an emergency kit in our car.

knack *noun* **talent, skill, aptitude, flair, gift, ability, facility, capacity** My dad has a real knack for making delicious pancakes.

knave *noun* **rogue, scoundrel, swindler, charlatan, shyster, villain, rascal** The knave tricked the woman into giving him money.

knead *verb* **manipulate, work, mix, blend, fold, stretch, press, squeeze, roll** We kneaded the dough until it became smooth and elastic.

kneel *verb* **stoop, bend, rest, bow, curtsy, genuflect** I knelt down to pet the kittens.

> **Word Group**
>
> A **knife** is a sharp instrument used for cutting and piercing. **Knife** is a general term with no true synonyms. Here are some specific types of knives:
>
> A **bowie knife** has a single-edged blade and is named after James Bowie (1799–1836). A **lancet** is a surgical knife with a short, pointed, double-edged blade. A **machete** has a heavy, broad blade and is used as a tool. A **pocketknife** is small and has a blade or blades that fold into the handle. A **Swiss army knife** is a pocketknife with multiple blades and tools (screwdriver, can opener, tweezers, etc.).

knit *verb* **1. bind, join, unite, link, connect, ally, attach, draw together** Yearly reunions have helped knit my family together. **2. mend, heal, grow together, repair, attach, join, unite, connect** The doctor said that the broken bone in my arm should knit in about six weeks.

knob *noun* **1. bump, lump, hump, mass, bulb, bulge, protrusion** I have a knob on my forehead where I was hit by a baseball. **2. handle, handhold, hold, grip, lever, latch, dial** Our kitchen cabinets have wooden knobs on them.

knock *verb* **1. strike, hit, pound, beat, bash, smash, smite, wallop, thump, tap** Otters open mussels and other mollusks by knocking them against rocks. **2. criticize, disparage, belittle, deprecate, lambaste, condemn, denounce, censure** I used to knock professional wrestling, but now I am a fan. ♦ *noun* **rap, tap, bang, pounding, thump, blow, hit** I heard a knock at the door and went to see who was there.

knoll *noun* **hillock, hummock, mound, hill, dune, butte, elevation, rise** We picnicked on a small knoll in the park.

knot *noun* **1. bow, hitch, loop, tie, braid, splice** I tied a double knot in the laces of my soccer shoes. **2. snarl, tangle, snag, gnarl, kink, whorl** He carefully combed the knots from the fur of his Persian cat. **3. cluster, bunch, crowd, clump, group, batch, band, swarm, bevy** A knot of people gathered at the bus stop.

know *verb* **1. realize, perceive, discern, ascertain, appreciate, sense** I know that you will do your best to finish the report on time. **2. understand, comprehend, apprehend, perceive, grasp, fathom, recall** Do you know how to snowboard? **3. identify, recognize, discern, distinguish, tell, differentiate, perceive, notice** I know every instrument in an orchestra.

knowledge *noun* **understanding, comprehension, cognizance, awareness, recognition, consciousness, erudition, expertise, facts, data, ideas** Our algebra teacher tested our knowledge of quadratic equations. **⇒ Antonym: ignorance**

knowledgeable *adjective* **well-informed, educated, familiar, expert, experienced, acquainted, up-to-date, enlightened** Ray is knowledgeable about old cars and trucks. **⇒ Antonyms: ignorant, uninformed, unaware**

kowtow *verb* **1. kneel, bow, genuflect, bend, stoop, worship** The temple priest kowtowed in front of the altar. **2. grovel, fawn, bootlick, toady, soft-soap, pander** The sniveling servant kowtowed to his menacing master.

kudos *noun* **praise, honor, acclamation, accolade, acclaim, plaudit, applause, glory, credit** The straight-A students received kudos at the awards assembly.

L1

label *noun* **sign, tag, sticker, marker, ticket, brand, mark, trademark, name** I read the label on the cereal box to find out the nutritional information. ◆ *verb* **identify, designate, name, mark, tag, ticket, classify, describe, brand** Nadia labeled each leaf that she collected for her science project.

labor *noun* **1. work, effort, exertion, toil, drudgery, travail, struggle** It took years of labor to dig the Panama Canal. **2. task, undertaking, assignment, chore, job, endeavor, employment, exercise** In the fairy tale "Rumpelstiltskin," the princess has to perform three labors in order to marry the prince. **3. workers, employees, help, laborers, workmen, workwomen, hands** The company is a success because it uses highly skilled labor. ◆ *verb* **work, toil, strain, strive, struggle, drudge, slave, sweat** The highway crew labored all week to repair the road. ⏺ **Antonyms:** *noun* **1. idleness, inactivity, rest** ◆ *verb* **rest, relax**

labyrinth *noun* **maze, complex, web, network, morass, puzzle, tangle** The hallways at my new school seemed like a labyrinth at first.

lace *noun* **shoelace, shoestring, lacing, cord, string, thread, rope, tie** I tie my laces in a double knot when I play soccer. ◆ *verb* **1. tie, strap, bind, secure, fasten, lash, thread, close** I laced my boots tightly to go hiking. **2. weave, twist, twine, interlace, intertwine, interweave, plait, braid** Mom laced the climbing rose through the trellis.

lacerate *verb* **rip, tear, cut, slash, gash, slice, wound, hurt, injure** I lacerated my knee when I fell off my bike.

laceration *noun* **cut, tear, gash, slash, wound, injury, rip** It took five stitches to close the laceration on the boy's arm.

lack *noun* **shortage, absence, deficiency, scarcity, dearth, paucity, want** Few plants grow in the desert due to the lack of rainfall. ◆ *verb* **need, require, miss, want, be without** Our town lacks the money to renovate the library. ⏺ **Antonyms:** *noun* **abundance, surplus** ◆ *verb* **have**

lackluster *adjective* **dull, lifeless, drab, flat, prosaic, vapid, bland, uninspired** The band director criticized us for our lackluster rehearsal. ⏺ **Antonyms: vivid, lively, exciting**

lad *noun* **boy, young man, youngster, youth, adolescent, teenager, kid** My grandfather tells me stories about his adventures as a lad.

laden *adjective* **burdened, loaded, weighed down, heavy, encumbered, full, oppressed** The holiday shoppers were laden with packages. ⏺ **Antonyms: unencumbered, free**

lady *noun* **woman, gentlewoman, noblewoman, matron, dame, female** The lady who lives next door let us use her telescope to view the comet.

lag *verb* **1. straggle, trail, dawdle, linger, plod, loiter, tarry, dally** I lagged behind my friends on our walk home. **2. slacken, diminish, decrease, abate, flag, wane, ebb, slow down, falter** The team's spirit lagged when they lost their third game in a row. ◆ *noun* **break, gap, pause, delay, interruption, hesitation, interval, interlude** There was a lag in the conversation when the waiter came to take our order. ⏺ **Antonyms:** *verb* **2. increase, grow**

lair *noun* **den, burrow, refuge, nest, retreat, sanctuary, hole** A wolf's lair is commonly a hole dug in the ground.

lake *noun* **pond, pool, reservoir, loch, lagoon** Carcy caught three bass at the lake.

lame *adjective* **1. disabled, crippled, handicapped, infirm, game, sore, stiff, painful** My dog limps because he is lame in his left front leg. **2. unsatisfactory, poor, unconvincing, weak, feeble, flimsy, inadequate, ineffective** My brother gave me a lame excuse for being late to pick me up. ⏺ **Antonyms: 1. able-bodied 2. convincing, satisfactory**

lament *verb* **mourn, grieve, weep, sorrow, suffer, deplore, regret** The nation lamented when President John F. Kennedy was assassinated. ◆ *noun* **lamentation, moaning, wailing, sobs, crying, grieving, mourning** I could not contain my tears and laments when my cat was hit by a car.

lamentable *adjective* **regrettable, deplorable, sad, woeful, grievous, wretched, miserable, awful** The stray dog was in lamentable condition. ⏺ **Antonyms: fortunate, happy**

lance *noun* **spear, javelin, harpoon, pike, halberd, gaff** The horse soldiers were armed with swords and lances. ◆ *verb* **pierce, puncture, incise, slit, prick, cut, open** I lanced my blister with a needle.

land *noun* **1. ground, soil, earth, terrain, dirt, loam, turf** This is good land for growing soybeans. **2. region, country, nation, state, homeland, realm, territory** America has been called "the land of opportunity." **3. property, real estate, acreage, acres, grounds** My grandmother owns land in Idaho. ◆ *verb* **1. alight, set down, touch down, arrive, disembark** Astronauts first landed on the moon on July 20, 1969. **2. get, secure, win, gain, obtain, catch, procure** My sister just landed the lead role in the school play. ◆ **Antonyms:** *verb* **1. embark, take off 2. lose, relinquish**

lane *noun* **1. avenue, road, street, drive, roadway, byway, thoroughfare** I live on a country lane that is lined with maple trees. **2. path, route, way, passageway, track, trail** After the *Titanic* disaster, Atlantic shipping lanes were moved south in order to avoid icebergs.

language *noun* **1. dialect, speech, tongue, vernacular, patois** My best friend can speak two languages. **2. communication, expression, signals, representation, symbols** American Indians used sign language to communicate with colonists. **3. terminology, vocabulary, words, jargon, lingo, cant, parlance** Every profession has its own specialized language.

languid *adjective* **weak, listless, lethargic, weary, enervated, torpid, slow** I felt languid in the hot weather. ◆ **Antonyms: active, energetic, strong**

languish *verb* **decline, deteriorate, fade, flag, wane, weaken, wither, ebb, diminish** My interest in music camp languished when I learned my friend couldn't go. ◆ **Antonyms: thrive, prosper, flourish**

lanky *adjective* **gangling, rangy, spindly, scrawny, gaunt, lean, thin** Abraham Lincoln was tall and lanky.

lapse *verb* **1. slip, fall, slide, sink, fade, drop, subside, collapse** The tired baby cried a while before lapsing into sleep. **2. end, expire, run out, terminate, cease, stop, quit, die** My gym membership lapses next month. ◆ *noun* **1. failure, slip, blunder, error, mistake, slip-up, omission** I had a memory lapse and couldn't think of my classmate's name. **2. interval, gap, interruption, pause, lull, break, hiatus** Kamilah returned to her ballet lessons after a lapse of three months.

larceny *noun* **theft, thievery, pilferage, stealing, robbery, burglary, looting** The shoplifter was convicted of larceny.

large *adjective* **big, enormous, giant, great, huge, immense, vast, sizable, colossal, substantial** A large crowd attended the free concert. ◆ **Antonyms: little, small, tiny**

largess *noun* **generosity, charity, munificence, gifts, presents, contributions, donations** The guest of honor was acknowledged for his largess at the charity banquet.

lark *noun* **escapade, fling, spree, romp, gambol, prank, adventure, frolic, joke** Adrian expects that the weekend at the lake will be quite a lark.

lash[1] *noun* **stroke, blow, hit, rap, smack, whip, slash, swipe, cut** The lash of the cowboy's whip got the cattle moving. ◆ *verb* **1. whip, switch, wave, flick, whisk, toss, swish, swing** A strong wind lashed the trees back and forth. **2. dash, beat, hit, strike, smite, buffet, pummel, drum, pound, hammer, flail, thrash** Waves lashed the shore during the storm.

lash[2] *verb* **fasten, secure, bind, leash, strap, tie, rope, truss, fix** I lashed my jacket to my backpack. ◆ **Antonyms: release, untie**

lass *noun* **girl, young woman, maid, maiden, young lady** The lass married a young man from a neighboring village.

last[1] *adjective* **1. final, closing, concluding, ending, finishing, terminal, ultimate, hindmost** The last concert of the season featured a harp solo. **2. latest, most recent, newest, previous, current, latter** What is the name of the last movie you saw? ◆ *adverb* **finally, lastly, ultimately, after, behind** Pumpkin pie was served last at our Thanksgiving dinner. ◆ **Antonyms:** *adjective* **1. first, initial 2. earliest, original**

last[2] *verb* **continue, go on, endure, persist, remain, stay, abide, persevere** Do you know how long this warm spell is supposed to last? ◆ **Antonyms: fail, end, stop**

lasting *adjective* **enduring, abiding, continuing, permanent, persistent, durable** My mother and her college roommate have a lasting friendship. ◆ **Antonyms: temporary, short-lived**

latch *noun* **catch, hook, bar, bolt, clamp, lock, snap, fastening** The latch on the screen door is broken. ◆ *verb* **fasten, secure, bar, bolt, close, lock, shut, hook** Please latch the gate when you leave. ◆ **Antonyms:** *verb* **open, unlatch**

late *adjective* **1. delayed, belated, slow, overdue, tardy, behindhand** I got a late start but managed to finish my homework before bedtime. **2. recent, current, new, last, fresh, modern, up-to-date** Have you read that author's latest book? **3. dead, deceased, departed, perished, expired, defunct, extinct** I live in a house that was built by my late grandfather. ◆ *adverb* **behind, belatedly, tardily, slow, behindhand** She arrived at the party an hour late. ◆ **Antonym: early**

lately *adverb* **recently, of late, currently, heretofore, now, previously** The weather has been humid lately.

later *adjective* ensuing, subsequent, following, succeeding, after The club members decided to discuss the bake sale at a later meeting. ● **Antonyms:** earlier, prior

latter *adjective* end, final, last, terminal, concluding, closing, later Where I live, it usually gets cold by the latter part of October. ● **Antonyms:** beginning, first

laudable *adjective* praiseworthy, admirable, estimable, commendable, meritorious, exemplary Planning to attend college shows laudable ambition.

laugh *verb* chuckle, giggle, snicker, chortle, titter, snigger, cackle, guffaw Everyone laughed when Bernie told his favorite joke. ◆ *noun* chuckle, giggle, laughter, snicker, snigger, chortle, cackle, guffaw, titter The comedian got a lot of laughs from the audience.

laughable *adjective* amusing, comical, funny, humorous, droll, ludicrous, silly, ridiculous, absurd I thought the kitten's antics were laughable. ● **Antonyms:** solemn, serious

launch *verb* **1.** send off, fire, propel, shoot, rocket, blast off, drive The Soviet Union launched the world's first satellite on October 4, 1957. **2.** begin, commence, initiate, open, originate, start, inaugurate, introduce, undertake I helped my friend launch his campaign for class president. ● **Antonyms: 2.** end, finish, stop

launder *verb* wash, clean, cleanse, scrub, soap, lave My new sweater has to be laundered in cold water.

laurels *noun* accolades, kudos, honor, praise, glory, commendation, fame, renown The young author won many laurels for her first book.

lavish *adjective* abundant, extravagant, generous, profuse, bountiful, plentiful, copious, luxurious The cruise ship was famous for its lavish meals. ◆ *verb* bestow, expend, heap, pour, rain, shower, squander Carrie lavishes a lot of care and attention on her birds. ● **Antonyms:** *adjective* sparing, meager

law *noun* **1.** ordinance, regulation, rule, statute, decree, mandate, order If you break a traffic law, you usually have to pay a fine. **2.** principle, theory, axiom, postulate, theorem, rule, standard Isaac Newton formulated the law of gravity in the 17th century.

lawful *adjective* **1.** legal, allowable, permissible, allowed, permitted, sanctioned Some cities have blue laws that specify activities that are not lawful on Sunday. **2.** legal, authorized, legitimate, rightful, valid, proper, just,

established The stolen car was returned to its lawful owner. ● **Antonyms: 1.** illegal, unlawful **2.** illegitimate

lawyer *noun* attorney, attorney at law, counsel, counselor, jurist, advocate People in the United States have the right to be represented by a lawyer.

lax *adjective* **1.** negligent, remiss, neglectful, derelict, indifferent, lenient My piano teacher forbids me to be lax in my practicing. **2.** loose, slack, droopy, weak, limp, dangling, relaxed The sails on the boat became lax when the wind died. ● **Antonyms: 1.** strict, stringent **2.** taut, rigid

lay *verb* **1.** leave, place, put, set, deposit, rest, position, locate, settle, situate Our cat laid a mouse at my mom's feet. **2.** produce, bear, deposit, bring forth, drop, spawn The platypus is the only mammal that lays eggs. **3.** present, offer, proffer, submit, put forth, cite, advance, propose At the student council meeting, the vice-president laid out her plans for the fundraiser.

layer *noun* coat, coating, cover, covering, blanket, film, sheet The chocolate cake had a thick layer of vanilla icing. ◆ *verb* spread, cover, coat, put on, lay down, laminate, sheathe To make the hatbox, first I layered the cardboard with glue. ● **Antonyms:** *verb* remove, take off

lazy *adjective* idle, listless, slothful, sluggish, indolent, shiftless, lethargic, slow, inactive I am feeling lazy today and probably won't do much. ● **Antonyms:** active, busy

leach *verb* extract, remove, wash out, draw, extricate, dissolve, take Water leaches minerals from the soil.

lead *verb* **1.** conduct, direct, escort, guide, steer, show, pilot, usher A search dog led rescuers to the lost child. **2.** go, run, reach, stretch, extend, proceed This path leads straight to the beach. **3.** command, direct, govern, manage, supervise, head General Robert E. Lee led the Confederate army during the American Civil War. **4.** influence, persuade, motivate, convince, induce, cause, dispose A good salesperson can lead a customer to buy any product. ◆ *noun* **1.** advantage, edge, front, head start, advance, preeminence Carlos had the lead as the wrestlers began the last match. **2.** precedent, example, model, pattern, standard, direction I followed my friend's lead and signed up for voice lessons. **3.** evidence, clue, indication, trace, hint, tip, cue The police officers searched for leads in order to solve the case.

leader *noun* chief, director, head, ruler, supervisor, commander, superior, guide, boss I'm the leader of the committee that plans our school dances. ● **Antonyms:** follower, subordinate

league *noun* **association, alliance, group, organization, union** President Woodrow Wilson was instrumental in forming the League of Nations in 1920.

leak *verb* **1. drip, flow, ooze, seep, spill, trickle, dribble, exude** Oil slowly leaked from the car's engine. **2. disclose, release, reveal, tell, divulge, confide, let out** Someone on the governor's staff has been leaking secrets to the press. ◆ *noun* **1. hole, crack, opening, break, chink, puncture, crevice, fissure, breech** They finally fixed the leak in our gymnasium's roof. **2. disclosure, revelation, declaration, divulgence, exposure, publication** The leak of FBI information made dealing with the terrorist more difficult. ● **Antonyms:** *verb* **2. conceal, hide** ◆ *noun* **2. cover-up, concealment**

lean[1] *verb* **1. incline, slant, slope, tilt, tip, cant, list, lurch** The telephone pole leaned dangerously after the terrible storm. **2. depend, rely, trust, rest, believe, bet, count, bank** He is someone you can lean on in an emergency.

lean[2] *adjective* **1. slender, slim, svelte, thin, skinny, angular, gaunt, spare** The athlete was lean and muscular. **2. meager, sparse, scant, scanty, deficient, inadequate, tight** Times were lean during the Great Depression of the 1930s. ● **Antonyms: 1. fat, plump 2. bountiful, abundant**

leaning *noun* **tendency, preference, inclination, predilection, predisposition, propensity, proclivity, penchant, bias** He has a leaning toward bright colors for decorating. ● **Antonyms: dislike, aversion**

leap *verb* **spring, bound, hop, jump, skip, bounce, vault, hurdle** A kangaroo can leap more than 25 feet in a single bound. ◆ *noun* **spring, jump, bound, hop, skip, bounce, vault, hurdle** The deer made a graceful leap over the fallen tree.

learn *verb* **1. study, pick up, get, gather, understand, grasp, master, memorize, review** I am learning how to use a computer. **2. find out, discover, detect, determine, realize, ascertain, discern, uncover, perceive** Doctors hope to learn how to cure the mysterious disease.

lease *noun* **rental agreement, contract, arrangement, deal, sublet** My parents signed a one-year lease for our new apartment. ◆ *verb* **rent, hire, charter, engage, employ, sublease, sublet, commission, let** Mom decided to lease a new car instead of buying one.

leash *noun* **cord, rein, rope, strap, tether, restraint, chain, bit, bridle, harness** Kristin put a leash on her pet iguana and took it for a walk around her front yard. ◆ *verb* **restrain, chain, hold, rein, tie up, tether, fetter, hobble, curb, check, harness** You will have to leash your dog to walk her through the park. ● **Antonyms:** *verb* **release, let go**

least *adjective* **slightest, smallest, tiniest, lowest, minimal, minimum, fewest** Of all my pets, my hamster requires the least amount of food. ● **Antonym: most**

> ### Word Group
>
> **Leather** is a material made by cleaning and tanning the skin or hide of an animal. **Leather** is a general term with no true synonyms. Here are some specific types of leather:
>
> **buckskin, buff, chamois, cordovan, cowhide, morocco, patent leather, suede**

leave[1] *verb* **1. depart, exit, go, set out, start, take off, get away, run** I have to leave by 7:00 in order to catch the school bus. **2. quit, resign, relinquish, renounce, terminate, abandon, desert, forsake, retire** My older brother plans to leave his job and return to college. **3. keep, maintain, retain, sustain, render, hold, allow** Please leave the door unlocked for me. **4. entrust, assign, consign, give, allot, release, cede, relinquish, yield, surrender** You can leave that job to me. **5. will, endow, give, bequeath, deed, transfer, hand down, turn over** The millionaire left his entire fortune to charity. ● **Antonyms: 1. arrive, come 2. join, stay**

leave[2] *noun* **1. permission, consent, approval, authorization, sanction, allowance, license** The farmer gave us leave to pick apples from the trees in his field. **2. furlough, holiday, liberty, vacation, absence** The soldier came home on leave. ● **Antonyms: 1. refusal, denial, prohibition**

lecture *noun* **1. talk, lesson, address, speech, discourse, chat, oration** The forest ranger gave a lecture on bird identification. **2. scolding, chiding, reprimand, reproof, sermon, harangue, castigation, reproach** My mother gave me a lecture because I left the refrigerator door open. ◆ *verb* **1. address, speak, talk, teach, discourse, expound, preach, orate, recite** A police officer lectured our class on the dangers of using drugs and alcohol. **2. scold, rebuke, reproof, admonish, reprimand, berate, chide, remonstrate, reproach** Please don't lecture me any more about being late to dinner.

ledge *noun* **shelf, projection, edge, rim, overhang, sill, bench, mantle, step** Eagles often build their nests on small, rocky ledges.

leg *noun* **1. appendage, limb, member, extremity, shank, stump** I have long legs. **2. column, post, upright, stake, support, brace, prop** The table wobbles because one leg is shorter than the others. **3. stage, lap, part, segment, stretch, section, portion, length, phase** I drove the final leg of our trip home.

legacy *noun* **1. bequest, inheritance, estate, gift, endowment, patrimony** My grandfather left a legacy to my mother and her brothers. **2. heritage, tradition, vestige, remnant, product, result** The primary legacy of the American Civil War is that the United States remained one nation.

legal *adjective* **lawful, legitimate, allowable, permissible, authorized, statutory, valid, sanctioned, decreed, prescribed** The legal voting age in the United States is 18. ⏺ **Antonyms: illegal, unlawful**

legend *noun* **1. fable, folklore, myth, mythology, story, tale, lore, tradition, fiction, saga, epic** According to legend, Robin Hood robbed from the rich in order to give to the poor. **2. inscription, key, caption, imprint, lettering, motto, code, device, slogan, title** The legend on the map is in very small lettering.

legendary *adjective* **1. fabled, storied, mythical, mythological, fictional, proverbial, traditional, epic, heroic, fabulous** El Dorado was a legendary city whose streets were said to be paved with gold. **2. well-known, famous, renowned, acclaimed, celebrated, illustrious, immortal, great** The actor Boris Karloff is legendary for his portrayal of Frankenstein. ⏺ **Antonyms: 1. historical, factual 2. unknown**

legible *adjective* **readable, clear, distinct, understandable, plain, neat, decipherable, comprehensible** I am practicing my penmanship to make my handwriting more legible. ⏺ **Antonyms: illegible, unclear**

legion *noun* **1. army, company, corps, division, force, troop, host, brigade** A legion of cavalry guarded the army's left flank. **2. crowd, throng, mass, mob, multitude, flock, horde, drove** The singer has a legion of fans who attend all of his concerts.

legitimate *adjective* **1. lawful, legal, rightful, true, statutory, just, official, sanctioned** Only a legitimate heir could claim the fortune. **2. valid, genuine, real, justifiable, authentic, reasonable, proper, correct, acceptable, sound** He had a legitimate reason for not attending school on Tuesday. ⏺ **Antonyms: 1. illegitimate, illegal 2. spurious, false**

Word Group

A **legume** is a plant with pods that contain a large number of seeds. **Legume** is a general term with no true synonyms. Here are some common legumes:

alfalfa, bean, carob, clover, lentil, pea, peanut, soybean

leisure *noun* **recreation, relaxation, rest, ease, repose, free time, spare time, respite, liberty** The busy doctor had very little time for leisure. ⏺ **Antonyms: labor, work**

lend *verb* **loan, provide, give, extend, furnish, supply, confer, bestow, grant, entrust** Will you lend me your bicycle for the afternoon? ⏺ **Antonym: borrow**

length *noun* **1. distance, measure, size, magnitude, measurement, extent, reach, space** *Tyrannosaurus rex* had teeth that were up to seven inches in length. **2. duration, span, term, stretch, continuance, interval, period** Summer vacation is usually about three months in length. **3. segment, piece, portion, section, unit, part, quantity, amount** The driver used a length of rope to tie down the cargo.

lengthen *verb* **elongate, extend, stretch, expand, increase, prolong, protract, draw out** Pulling on a piece of taffy will lengthen it. ⏺ **Antonyms: shorten, decrease, curtail, contract**

lenient *adjective* **tolerant, indulgent, mild, kind, compassionate, merciful, generous, easy** My father was lenient the first time I arrived home late from the movies. ⏺ **Antonyms: harsh, strict**

less *adjective* **reduced, shortened, fewer, lower, smaller, slighter, diminished, limited** I have less time to play now that school has started. ⏺ **Antonyms: more, greater**

lessen *verb* **decrease, diminish, lower, reduce, shrink, abate, allay, alleviate, assuage, ease, mitigate, relieve** This medicine should lessen the pain of your headache. ⏺ **Antonyms: expand, increase**

lesson *noun* **1. instruction, class, education, schooling, teaching, exercise, assignment, session, drill** My brother is taking driving lessons. **2. moral, warning, admonition, caution, model, guide, notice, precept, example** I learned a lesson when my report was graded lower for being late.

let *verb* **1. allow, authorize, permit, grant, consent, agree to, sanction, endorse, tolerate** My parents let me stay up late on weekend nights. **2. rent, lease, hire, charter, sublease, sublet** The marina lets boats by the hour or the day. ⇒ **Antonyms: 1. forbid, prevent**

lethal *adjective* **deadly, fatal, deathly, mortal, destructive, dangerous** Rabies is a dangerous, lethal disease. ⇒ **Antonyms: harmless, innocuous**

lethargic *adjective* **sluggish, torpid, languid, languorous, listless, slothful, slow, apathetic, enervated** The zoo animals were lethargic in the summer heat. ⇒ **Antonyms: active, energetic**

lethargy *noun* **apathy, indifference, laziness, indolence, lassitude, sluggishness, listlessness, torpor** Lethargy kept me from cleaning my messy room. ⇒ **Antonyms: vitality, vigor**

letter *noun* **1. character, sign, symbol, figure, mark, expression** The last letter in the English alphabet is *Z*. **2. note, message, missive, epistle, communiqué, memo, dispatch, correspondence, line, communication** I wrote my parents a letter every day while I was away at camp. ◆ *verb* **write, inscribe, spell out, initial, sign, print, engrave** Please letter our school motto on this poster.

level *noun* **1. grade, stage, standard, step, position, rank, point, standing** My younger brother reads at a high-school level. **2. height, altitude, elevation, stage, stratum, plane, depth** During the flood, the waters reached a level that was 30 feet above normal. ◆ *adjective* **1. flat, horizontal, smooth, straight, plane** We don't have any level ground for playing soccer. **2. steady, stable, constant, consistent, unchanging, regular, unvarying, uniform** I kept my voice level, even though I was very nervous. **3. even, equal, flush, parallel, matched, equivalent, comparable, aligned** The top of my little sister's head is level with my shoulder. ◆ *verb* **1. flatten, smooth, even, plane, straighten, grade** A park employee used a rake to level the sand in the children's play area. **2. demolish, destroy, knock down, tear down, raze, wreck, dismantle, pull down, topple** Construction workers leveled the old building in order to clear the site. **3. aim, point, direct, train, turn, focus, head, set** He carefully leveled the dart at the bullseye. ⇒ **Antonyms:** *adjective* **1. sloping, uneven 2. irregular, erratic 3. unequal** ◆ *verb* **2. erect, raise**

liable *adjective* **1. obligated, responsible, accountable, answerable, amenable** If you lose a library book, you might be held liable for its replacement cost. **2. subject, prone, likely, apt, inclined, open, probable, susceptible, vulnerable** You're liable to get wet if you don't take your umbrella. ⇒ **Antonyms: 1. exempt, unaccountable 2. unlikely**

liaison *noun* **contact, intermediary, agent, go-between, mediator, middleman, medium** A lobbyist is often a liaison between business and government officials.

liar *noun* **fibber, falsifier, prevaricator, perjurer, equivocator, fabricator, storyteller** You can believe what Toni says because she's not a liar.

liberal *adjective* **1. unsparing, unstinting, openhanded, magnanimous, free, lavish** My stepfather is liberal with his help and advice when I ask for it. **2. abundant, plentiful, generous, copious, profuse, full, big, ample** This sapling needs liberal amounts of water to help it grow. **3. approximate, figurative, general, loose, rough, relative, lax, casual, broad** My friend gave a liberal account of our adventures at camp. **4. broad-minded, open-minded, progressive, tolerant, unbiased, impartial, humanistic, lenient** My parents have liberal ideas about raising children. ⇒ **Antonyms:** *adjective* **1. stingy 2. skimpy, inadequate 3. exact, precise 4. biased, narrow**

liberate *verb* **set free, release, free, emancipate, loose, deliver, discharge** Paris was liberated from German occupation on August 25, 1944. ⇒ **Antonyms: subjugate, capture, confine**

liberty *noun* **1. freedom, emancipation, liberation, release, delivery** I gave the injured bird its liberty after its wing had healed. **2. freedom, independence, sovereignty, autonomy, self-government, self-rule** Mexico won its liberty from Spain in 1821. **3. privilege, right, franchise, authorization, authority, sanction, permission, license** Freedom of speech is one of the liberties guaranteed by the Bill of Rights. ⇒ **Antonyms: 1. slavery, bondage 2. dependence, subjection 3. restraint, prohibition, ban**

license *noun* **1. authorization, permission, allowance, approval, leave, sanction, right, freedom, liberty** Do you have license to stay out late on the weekend? **2. permit, certificate, warrant, form, pass, credential, paper** My older sister and her fiancé just got their marriage license. ◆ *verb* **certify, accredit, authorize, approve, validate, document, qualify, commission, allow, permit** Teachers must be licensed by the state. ⇒ **Antonyms:** *noun* **1. prohibition, denial** ◆ *verb* **prohibit, forbid**

lick *verb* **lap, flick, touch, wash, lap against, dart, flicker** The cat licked her kittens to clean them. ◆ *noun* **1. bit, speck, touch, dab, hint, dash, suggestion, trace** I gave the sauce another lick of salt. **2. blow, hit, stroke, swat, clout, sock, pound, slug** The boxer got in a last lick at his opponent just as the round ended. ⇒ **Antonyms:** *noun* **1. mass, heap**

lid *noun* **cover, top, cap, stopper, hood, cork, plug** I used a screwdriver to pry the lid off the can of paint.

lie¹ *verb* **1. lie down, recline, stretch out, sprawl, lounge, loll, retire** Brian likes to lie on the couch and watch TV. **2. rest, sit, exist, reside, extend, abide, range, occupy, dwell** The lake lies just beyond that grove of trees.

lie² *noun* **falsehood, fib, untruth, falsity, canard, prevarication, misrepresentation, story, tale, fabrication** No one has known her to deliberately tell a lie. ◆ *verb* **fib, falsify, deceive, distort, mislead, prevaricate, equivocate, invent** Sometimes I am tempted to lie about how old I am. ➤ **Antonyms:** *noun* **fact, truth**

life *noun* **1. existence, sentience, being, organism, creature, living being, animal** Many people wonder if there is life on other planets. **2. lifetime, existence, life span, term, duration, time, career, days** I've been outside the United States only once in my life. **3. person, human, human being, individual, mortal, soul, body** Luckily, no lives were lost when the ship sank. **4. liveliness, spirit, vigor, vitality, energy, animation, bounce, dash, verve, vim, zip, zest** My puppy is so full of life that he can never sit still. ➤ **Antonym: 1. death**

lift *verb* **1. pick up, hoist, heft, raise, elevate, boost, heave** This crate is too heavy for me to lift by myself. **2. ascend, climb, rise, take off, soar, arise, mount** Airplanes have to gain sufficient speed before they can lift into the air. **3. improve, uplift, animate, buoy, elate, exhilarate, inspire, exalt, enhance** The movie lifted our spirits. **4. repeal, rescind, suspend, discontinue, terminate, revoke, cancel, end, stop** The national prohibition on alcohol began in 1919 and was lifted in 1933. **5. disappear, disperse, dissipate, scatter, vanish, withdraw, fade, fade away** The fog lifted at noon. ◆ *noun* **1. boost, hoist, heave, assist, hand, rise** My little sister couldn't reach the water fountain, so I gave her a lift. **2. thrill, elation, euphoria, exaltation, exhilaration, inspiration, encouragement, boost** I got a lift from hearing Beethoven's Third Symphony.

light¹ *noun* **1. illumination, brightness, glow, gleam, radiance, shine, brilliance, luminescence, glare, luminosity** The river looked silver in the light of the moon. **2. daylight, dawn, daybreak, day, sunlight, sunrise, sunshine** I got up at first light to go birding with my grandparents. **3. awareness, knowledge, understanding, information, clarification, insight, enlightenment** The speaker shed additional light on my knowledge of nuclear fission. **4. aspect, regard, slant, attitude, angle, side, respect, viewpoint, direction, facet** I saw things in a different light after hearing Meg's side of the story. ◆ *verb* **1. ignite, kindle,**

set afire, burn, fire, spark Gabriel lit the campfire while I got the marshmallows. **2. light up, illuminate, brighten, illumine, lighten, shine** Will one lamp be enough to light the entire room? ◆ *adjective* **1. bright, brilliant, sunny, radiant, luminous, illuminated** My bedroom is very light when I open the curtains. **2. pale, whitish, bleached, pallid, colorless, fair, blonde, white** When I made a picture of the view, I painted the sky a light blue. ➤ **Antonyms:** *noun* **1. dark, darkness** ◆ *verb* **1. extinguish, put out 2. darken** ◆ *adjective* **1. dark, dim**

light² *adjective* **1. lightweight, underweight, weightless, not heavy, scant, slight, sparse** When we go hiking I carry only a light pack. **2. slight, insignificant, small, little, faint, gentle, mild, moderate, weak, modest** Yesterday's light rain barely wet the ground. **3. carefree, lighthearted, cheerful, happy, blithe, merry, gay, jolly** I was in a light mood at lunch. **4. nimble, agile, graceful, limber, spry, lithe, light-footed, lissome** The acrobats were light on their feet as they did their routine. **5. easy, simple, undemanding, manageable, effortless, moderate** Our teacher gave us a light homework assignment on the first day after break. ◆ *verb* **land, alight, set down, settle, touch down, descend, perch** The blue jay swooped down to light on a low branch. ➤ **Antonyms:** *adjective* **1. heavy, hefty 2. full, strong 3. serious, grave 4. clumsy 5. hard, difficult**

lighten¹ *verb* **brighten, light up, gleam, shine, illuminate, illumine, clear up** The sky began to lighten just before the sun appeared. ➤ **Antonyms: darken, dim**

lighten² *verb* **1. empty, lessen, unload, unburden, cut down** I lightened the heavy box by removing some of the contents. **2. ease, lessen, relieve, reduce, diminish, decrease, allay, mitigate, alleviate** Her sorrow was lightened by the comfort of her many friends. **3. gladden, cheer, enliven, hearten, lift, revive, buoy, encourage, inspire, elate** Let's go to a funny movie to lighten our mood. ➤ **Antonyms: 1. load, weight 2. increase, intensify 3. sadden**

like¹ *verb* **1. enjoy, love, relish, savor, cherish, adore, fancy, appreciate, esteem, admire** I like playing ball after school. **2. care for, desire, want, choose, prefer, crave, wish, please, elect, ask** I would like a piece of apple pie. ➤ **Antonyms: 1. dislike, hate**

like² *preposition* **similar to, identical to, same as, comparable to, equivalent to, analogous to** Your computer is like mine except for the mouse. ◆ *adjective* **similar, equivalent, comparable, identical, matching, alike, analogous, corresponding, parallel, same** We got five inches of snow yesterday and a like amount today. ➤ **Antonyms:** *adjective* **different, unlike**

likely *adjective* **1. apt, expected, inclined, liable, prone, probable, disposed** The storm is likely to hit tomorrow morning. **2. plausible, conceivable, reasonable, tenable, believable, rational** It is not likely that space travel will be commonplace very soon. **3. suitable, appropriate, acceptable, reasonable, prospective, possible** I found a likely spot to hang the new painting. ♦ *adverb* **probably, doubtless, no doubt, undoubtedly, presumably, seemingly** I'll likely be late, so don't wait for me. ➡ **Antonyms:** *adjective* **1. improbable, unlikely 2. implausible 3. dubious**

likeness *noun* **1. similarity, resemblance, correspondence, agreement, comparison** There is often a strong likeness between parents and children. **2. representation, portrait, depiction, image, replica, reproduction, copy, picture, duplicate, facsimile** The artist at the craft fair sketched a good likeness of my friend. ➡ **Antonyms: 1. difference, disparity**

limb *noun* **1. extremity, appendage, arm, leg, member, extension, wing** It is important to stretch your limbs before and after vigorous exercise. **2. branch, bough, stem, sprig, twig, shoot, spray** I sawed off the broken limb of the pine tree.

limber *adjective* **flexible, supple, agile, nimble, elastic, pliant, pliable, malleable, lithe, loose** The dancer was very limber. ➡ **Antonyms: stiff, inflexible**

limit *noun* **1. border, boundary, bounds, edge, confines, margin, perimeter, area, extent, zone** We have trained our dog not to go beyond the limits of our yard. **2. limitation, maximum, restriction, quota, ceiling, top, end, ration, cap** There is a limit on how many fish you may catch at this lake. ♦ *verb* **restrict, confine, set, fix, check, restrain, circumscribe** The coach decided to limit the basketball team to ten players.

limp *verb* **hobble, shuffle, stagger, stumble, totter, dodder, halt, flounder** I limped around for two days after I sprained my ankle. ♦ *noun* **hobble, lameness, shuffle, stagger, waddle** After the motorcycle accident, he walked with a limp for several months. ♦ *adjective* **droopy, floppy, flaccid, loose, slack, soft, weak, flabby** Flowers get limp if you don't water them. ➡ **Antonyms:** *adjective* **firm, stiff**

limpid *adjective* **clear, translucent, crystalline, transparent, pellucid, lucid, see-through** The children looked at their reflection in the limpid water of the pool. ➡ **Antonym: opaque**

line *noun* **1. band, stripe, strip, bar, mark, streak, belt, ribbon** White lines were painted on the blacktop to indicate parking places. **2. wrinkle, crease, groove, furrow, crinkle, striation** My grandmother has many lines on her face. **3. border, boundary, edge, limit, margin, threshold, frontier** This fence sits right on our property line. **4. row, rank, file, column, queue, string, tier, train, procession** The marching band walked in straight lines. **5. note, card, postcard, word, letter, message** Please drop me a line while you're on vacation. **6. cable, wire, cord, rope, strand, string, filament, thread** Our telephone doesn't work because the lines are down. **7. ancestry, lineage, genealogy, origin, stock, heredity, roots, blood, bloodline** I can trace my family line back to the 16th century. **8. variety, range, assortment, brand, kind, make, type** This store carries a full line of cameras and video equipment. **9. trade, occupation, business, vocation, career, profession, pursuit** What line is your father in? ♦ *verb* **assemble, align, queue, organize, order, file** We lined up in two rows to go to the assembly.

linger *verb* **1. stay, remain, dally, wait, loiter, tarry, pause, delay** I lingered after school to talk to my favorite teacher. **2. continue, persist, last, remain, endure, hang on, persevere, survive, abide** Humidity lingered in the air after the thunderstorms ended. ➡ **Antonyms: 1. hurry, hasten 2. end, cease**

link *noun* **association, connection, relationship, bond, tie, correlation, interdependence, relation, attachment** Detectives found no apparent links between the two robberies. ♦ *verb* **connect, join, unite, attach, combine, fasten, couple, marry, unify, bind** The Brooklyn Bridge links Brooklyn with Manhattan Island. ➡ **Antonyms:** *verb* **disconnect, separate**

lip *noun* **brim, rim, border, edge, margin, verge, flange, flare** The lip of a cup is usually smooth and rounded.

liquid *noun* **fluid, solution, drink, beverage, water, juice, liquor** Water, oil, and milk are all liquids. ♦ *adjective* **fluid, flowing, liquefied, runny, wet, aqueous, watery, viscous, molten** Some rockets use liquid oxygen as part of their fuel. ➡ **Antonym: solid**

list[1] *noun* **listing, record, catalog, file, inventory, register, roll, index** I made a list of the CDs that I want to buy. ♦ *verb* **itemize, record, register, write down, enumerate, catalog, file, numerate, set down, tabulate** Our English teacher asked us to list all of the books that we read over the summer.

list[2] *noun* **tilt, lean, inclination, cant, slant, slope, tip** The Leaning Tower of Pisa has a list of approximately 17.5 feet. ♦ *verb* **tilt, lean, cant, tip, heel, incline, slant, slope** The boat listed sharply when the wind changed.

listen *verb* pay attention, heed, attend, hark, hearken, mind, hear We listened closely to the instructions on how to make an origami crane. ⏺ **Antonyms:** disregard, ignore

listless *adjective* lethargic, sluggish, flagging, languid, languorous, limp, spiritless, torpid, enervated Our neighbor's potbelly pig was listless in the late afternoon heat. ⏺ **Antonyms:** lively, energetic, vigorous

literal *adjective* verbatim, word-for-word, exact, precise, factual, faithful, strict, true, correct My French teacher asked us for a literal translation of the poem.

literally *adverb* really, actually, truly, precisely, indeed, utterly, closely, strictly Our front door was literally blocked by a snowdrift.

literate *adjective* educated, enlightened, informed, knowledgeable, learned, lettered, schooled, versed He is literate in the fields of mathematics and economics. ⏺ **Antonyms:** illiterate, uninformed

litter *noun* 1. debris, refuse, rubbish, trash, garbage, waste, junk, clutter My Girl Scout troop volunteered to pick up litter along the lakeshore. 2. brood, young, offspring, issue, progeny Our cat had a litter of five kittens. ◆ *verb* clutter, mess up, cover, scatter, strew, heap, pile, disorder Our living room was littered with wrapping paper after my birthday party.

little *adjective* 1. small, tiny, diminutive, minuscule, wee, minute, bantam, petite, miniature A Chihuahua is a very little dog. 2. brief, limited, short, scant, slight, meager I have only a little time left before my report is due. 3. young, younger, small, smaller, immature My little sister is eight years younger than I. 4. inconsequential, insignificant, trifling, minor, negligible, paltry, trivial, unimportant My mother reassured me that the broken dish was of little importance. ◆ *adverb* slightly, somewhat, barely, hardly, scarcely, not much I am getting a little tired of leftovers. ◆ *noun* bit, portion, fragment, touch, dab, particle, pittance, speck, crumb, hint Colin reads a little of his library book every night. ⏺ **Antonyms:** *adjective* 1. big, large 2. long, much 3. old, older 4. important, significant

live[1] *verb* 1. exist, survive, thrive, endure, function, subsist, last, persist, be, breathe, continue Human beings need food, water, and air to live. 2. reside, dwell, stay, abide, domicile, inhabit, occupy, lodge, room Kathleen and her family live in a three-bedroom house. 3. experience, undergo, encounter, sustain, have, lead, pass, pursue, conduct He likes to live life to its fullest. ⏺ **Antonyms:** 1. die, expire

live[2] *adjective* 1. alive, living, existing, animate, existent, breathing, conscious Yogurt is made by adding live bacteria to milk. 2. burning, red-hot, hot, flaming, glowing, fiery, alight, afire, ablaze, aflame We roasted our potatoes in the live coals of our campfire. 3. active, energetic, animated, lively, spirited, dynamic, vigorous, busy, brisk The speaker had a live and enthusiastic manner. ⏺ **Antonyms:** 1. dead, lifeless 3. dull, vapid

lively *adjective* spirited, vigorous, active, sprightly, fast, zippy, energetic, brisk, dynamic The lively music made me want to dance. ⏺ **Antonyms:** lifeless, inactive, slow

livid *adjective* 1. discolored, black-and-blue, black, purple, bruised, contused I have a livid bruise on my leg where I bumped into the corner of my desk. 2. angry, furious, infuriated, enraged, incensed, indignant, outraged, wrathful, mad, irate My parents were livid when my older brother came home two hours late. ⏺ **Antonyms:** 3. calm, content

living *adjective* 1. existing, live, animate, alive, conscious, breathing, existent I believe that all living creatures should be treated with respect. 2. active, current, operative, extant, enduring, surviving, continuing, persisting, remaining English is a living language. ◆ *noun* 1. existence, life, being, lifestyle, existing I love city living. 2. livelihood, income, keep, maintenance, subsistence, career, occupation, profession, job, work, employment Aunt Joy makes her living as a writer. ⏺ **Antonyms:** *adjective* 1. dead, deceased 2. extinct, inactive

Word Group

A **lizard** is a reptile that has a scaly body, a tapering tail, and usually four legs. **Lizard** is a specific term with no true synonyms. Here are some common lizards:

A **chameleon** can rapidly change its color to blend in with its surroundings. A **gecko** is a tropical lizard with adhesive toe tips that allow it to climb walls. The **Gila monster** is a poisonous lizard of the southwest United States and northern Mexico. An **iguana** is a large tropical American lizard with a ridge of spines along its back.

load *noun* 1. burden, weight, cargo, freight, shipment, lading, consignment Camels can carry heavy loads for long distances without needing water. 2. care, worry, burden, trouble, anxiety, pressure, encumbrance That secret has been a great load to carry. ◆ *verb* 1. fill, pack, stuff, heap, pile, lade, weight, stack, cram We'll be ready to leave on vacation as soon as we finish loading the car. 2. weigh down, burden, oppress, encumber, saddle, overwhelm, afflict,

trouble Sometimes I feel as if I am loaded with too many responsibilities. ➤**Antonyms:** *verb* **1. unload, unpack 2. relieve, unburden**

loaf¹ *noun* **block, brick, slab, chunk, cube, cake, lump, mass** I put the loaf of bread in the refrigerator.

loaf² *verb* **lounge, relax, rest, laze, lie, loll, vegetate, idle, loiter, dally** I plan to loaf around the house for the first few days of summer vacation. ➤**Antonyms: toil, work**

loan *noun* **advance, credit, accommodation, allowance, extension** I asked my sister for a loan so that I could go to the movies. ◆ *verb* **lend, advance, allow, provide, entrust, credit, stake** Will you loan me your soccer ball? ➤**Antonyms:** *verb* **borrow, return**

loathe *verb* **detest, despise, hate, abhor, abominate, dislike, scorn, disdain, shun** I don't mind most chores, but I loathe cleaning out the basement. ➤**Antonyms: like, love**

loathsome *adjective* **abhorrent, disgusting, hideous, revolting, nasty, abominable, despicable, foul, repugnant, vile, wretched, detestable** The movie was about some loathsome creatures that came out of the swamp at night. ➤**Antonyms: appealing, pleasant**

lobby *noun* **1. entry, lounge, waiting room, foyer, entrance hall, hall, gallery** The hotel's lobby was filled with sofas and easy chairs. **2. pressure group, special-interest group, group, coterie, party** My uncle is a member of the farm lobby. ◆ *verb* **pressure, urge, push, pitch, promote, persuade, campaign for, press, solicit** My brother and I lobbied our parents to let us stay up and watch TV.

local *adjective* **community, neighborhood, close, near, nearby, regional, adjacent, neighboring, district** I get most of my reading material from the local library. ◆ *noun* **resident, native, inhabitant, citizen, denizen** We asked a local how to get to the museum. ➤**Antonyms:** *adjective* **distant, foreign** ◆ *noun* **foreigner, stranger**

locale *noun* **location, place, site, scene, setting, area, locality, surroundings, environs, vicinity, district** It was very exciting when our neighborhood was used as a movie locale.

locate *verb* **1. find, detect, discover, spot, pinpoint, discern, track down, uncover** Moles use their sense of smell and touch to locate food. **2. place, situate, position, put, set, install, establish, base, site, station** This looks like a good place to locate our lemonade stand.

location *noun* **site, place, locality, locale, area, district, position, spot, locus, setting** Our school will be moving to a new location next year.

lock¹ *noun* **fastening, catch, clasp, hook, latch, padlock, bolt** Dad changed the broken lock on our garage door today. ◆ *verb* **1. secure, latch, fasten, bolt, bar, clamp, padlock** Did you lock the car door? **2. confine, restrict, jail, immure, imprison, incarcerate, cage, detain** The inmates were locked in their cells. **3. join, link, connect, fasten, grasp, hold, clasp, seize, clinch** The plastic blocks are designed to lock together. ➤**Antonyms:** *verb* **1. unlock 2. free, release 3. disconnect**

lock² *noun* **strand, curl, tress, tuft, ringlet, piece** My mother has a lock of my hair in her jewelry box.

lodge *noun* **1. inn, hotel, chalet, resort, cabin, cottage, shelter** It was pleasant to be in the warm lodge after skiing all day. **2. den, lair, home, abode, dwelling, burrow, tunnel, habitation** Beavers build lodges of trees and branches. ◆ *verb* **1. house, shelter, harbor, quarter, billet, put up, accommodate** During World War II, many children from London were lodged with families in the countryside. **2. reside, stay, live, dwell, domicile, abide, room, bunk** My cousin plans to lodge in hostels on his bike trip through Europe. **3. catch, stick, snag, wedge, entrench, fix, implant** My kite is lodged in the branches of that tree. **4. file, enter, record, register, submit, tender, present, propose, proffer, offer** The angry tenant lodged a complaint with the housing agency.

lofty *adjective* **towering, high, tall, sky-high, airy, soaring, aerial, elevated** The mountain's lofty summit was hidden by clouds. ➤**Antonyms: low, short**

log *noun* **1. stick, wood, lumber, timber, beam, trunk, block, chunk** We gathered logs for the fire. **2. record, journal, diary, logbook, register, chronicle, notebook** My mother keeps a gardening log.

logic *noun* **reasoning, thinking, analysis, reason, induction, deduction, judgment, thought** I was able to solve the word puzzle by using logic.

logical *adjective* **intelligent, reasonable, sensible, sound, practical, wise, rational, obvious** It is logical to eat when you are hungry. ➤**Antonyms: illogical, irrational**

loiter *verb* **dawdle, idle, linger, tarry, dally, delay, loaf, pause, procrastinate, lag** We could not loiter over dinner because we had to get to the play. ➤**Antonyms: hasten, hurry**

lone *adjective* **sole, solitary, single, individual, unaccompanied, separate, unique, only, alone, lonely** A lone pear tree grew in the middle of the field.

lonely *adjective* **1. friendless, reclusive, lone, lonesome, single, solitary, alone, outcast** In the novel *Silas Marner*, the hero is a lonely and bitter miser until a child named Eppie comes into his life. **2. desolate, forlorn, isolated, barren, secluded, deserted, uninhabited, remote** Some people think that the desert is a lonely place.

long[1] *adjective* **1. extended, extensive, lengthy, great, large, elongate, elongated, considerable** California has a very long coastline. **2. lengthy, sustained, prolonged, protracted, overlong, unending** We spent a long time going over the answers to the math test. ● **Antonyms: 1. short, little 2. brief, short**

long[2] *verb* **desire, want, wish, yearn, crave, covet, hanker, pine, ache, hunger, thirst** My grandmother longs to visit her childhood home in Italy. ● **Antonyms: spurn, disdain**

longing *noun* **desire, craving, yearning, wish, yen, hunger, thirst, fancy, appetite, itch** We had a longing for hamburgers and French fries. ● **Antonyms: aversion, reluctance, antipathy**

look *verb* **1. gaze, stare, glance, observe, see, view, watch, ogle, peek, scan, behold, regard** We sat on a bench in the park and looked at the people walking by. **2. appear, seem, resemble, show, exhibit, manifest** Do you think this shirt looks wrinkled? **3. search, hunt, seek, explore, quest, survey, scour, scout, probe, investigate** I'll help you look for your missing book. ◆ *noun* **1. glance, peek, peep, view, gaze, glimpse** I took a look out the window to see if my ride had come. **2. expression, appearance, manner, countenance, bearing, aspect, mien, visage** The father of the sick boy wore a worried look.

loom *verb* **1. appear, arise, emerge, materialize, show, take shape** Storm clouds loomed on the horizon. **2. threaten, portend, impend, brew, menace, hover, overshadow, bode** Trouble loomed when my sister brought home a second cat in two weeks. ● **Antonyms: 1. disappear, recede**

loop *noun* **coil, noose, ring, circle, knot, spiral, eye, whorl** The cowboy slipped a loop of rope over the bull's horns. ◆ *verb* **encircle, circle, wind, twist, coil, turn, bend, spiral, curl, ring, tie** The climber anchored her rope by looping it around a tree.

loose *adjective* **1. untied, unfastened, detached, unsecured, unattached, unbound, unconnected** The boat came loose and floated down the stream. **2. unconfined, unrestrained, at large, at liberty, free** Dad called the police about a big dog that was loose in our neighborhood. **3. baggy, slack, flowing, hanging, sagging, drooping, dangling** Daniel likes to wear loose clothing when he plays tennis. **4. indefinite, general, rough, inexact, vague, imprecise, broad, free** The mechanic could give only a loose estimate of repair costs without seeing the car. ◆ *verb* **1. set free, release, free, liberate, let go, discharge, emancipate, dismiss** The prisoners of war were loosed when the victorious army captured the town. **2. unfasten, unloosen, loosen, unloose, untie, undo, unwrap, disengage, unbind, unclasp** I loosed my hair from the rubber band. ● **Antonyms:** *adjective* **1. bound, tied 2. confined, restrained 3. tight 4. precise, exact** ◆ *verb* **1. capture, imprison 2. fasten, tie, bind**

loosen *verb* **1. loose, unloosen, unloose, untie, undo, unfasten, free, release, disengage, unbind, unclasp** My necktie was too tight, so I loosened it. **2. relax, ease, soften, let up, slacken, weaken, decrease, moderate, temper** The federal government loosened import restrictions. ● **Antonyms: 1. tie, tighten 2. stiffen**

loot *noun* **booty, plunder, spoils, haul, pillage, prize** The robbers hid their loot in a cave. ◆ *verb* **plunder, pillage, raid, ransack, sack, burglarize, thieve, rob, steal, take** The pirates looted the town and took the valuables back to their ships.

lope *verb* **gallop, sprint, run, jog, trot, stride, canter** The herd of horses loped across the prairie. ◆ *noun* **trot, run, jog, canter, gallop, stride, sprint** The dog ran down the beach going at a fast lope.

lord *noun* **ruler, master, king, sovereign, monarch, aristocrat, overlord, noble** In medieval times, the lord of the castle was responsible for the safety of the surrounding villages.

lose *verb* **1. mislay, misplace, miss, drop** Damon is always losing his house key. **2. be defeated, succumb, forfeit, fail, surrender, yield, capitulate, fall** Our team won the first two games of the tournament, but we lost in the semifinals. **3. spend, expend, waste, squander, miss, forget, ignore, give up, relinquish, exhaust** If you don't join the club now, you will lose your only chance. ● **Antonyms: 1. find, locate 2. win 3. get, gain**

loss *noun* **1. reduction, shrinkage, removal, depletion, deficit, disappearance, erosion** Dad has been exercising, and he is pleased with his weight loss. **2. defeat, failure, upset, overturn, downfall, forfeiture** My sister took the loss of the volleyball championship very hard. **3. ruin,**

destruction, annihilation, devastation, wreck, crash Early frosts caused the loss of this year's orange crop. **4. misfortune, setback, impairment, calamity, damage, injury, disappointment, suffering, trouble** It was a great loss for our school when two of the best teachers moved away. ● **Antonyms: 1. gain, acquisition 2. win 4. advantage**

lost *adjective* **1. missing, mislaid, misplaced, vanished, absent, gone, stray** I found my lost sweater under the bed. **2. wasted, squandered, misapplied, exhausted, depleted, dissipated, misused** Lost time can never be recovered. **3. past, obsolete, dead, defunct, extinct, passé, forgotten, bygone** The days of the horse and carriage are lost forever. **4. ruined, destroyed, demolished, devastated, wrecked, obliterated, annihilated** The politician soon realized that his campaign for reelection was a lost cause. **5. involved, preoccupied, absorbed, occupied, spellbound, entranced, engrossed, rapt** I didn't hear you come in because I was lost in thought. ● **Antonyms: 1. found, recovered 2. saved 3. current, contemporary**

lot *noun* **1. profusion, great deal, abundance, quantity, pile, loads, mass, mountain, wealth, heap** Hannah received a lot of presents for her birthday this year. **2. batch, consignment, bunch, collection, set, group, cluster, body, assortment** The store will be receiving a new lot of furniture tomorrow. **3. plot, tract, parcel, land, property, field, acreage** My parents are planning to buy the vacant lot next to our house. **4. fate, destiny, fortune, luck, kismet, predestination, chance, accident, providence** It was his lot in life to work hard. ● **Antonyms: 1. few, little**

loud *adjective* **1. noisy, deafening, blaring, earsplitting, booming, thunderous, roaring, resounding** The band was so loud that my friends and I could hardly hear each other speak. **2. bright, gaudy, flashy, showy, garish, colorful, ostentatious, tawdry, tasteless** Jan bought a loud T-shirt that has orange lettering on a dark purple background. ● **Antonym: 1. quiet, silent 2. subdued, sedate**

lounge *verb* **relax, repose, recline, idle, laze, loaf, loiter, loll, vegetate, languish** I like to lounge in the shade of a tree when it is hot. ◆ *noun* **lobby, waiting room, foyer, reception room, antechamber, vestibule, sitting room** We waited in the lounge of the hotel until our friends arrived.

lousy *adjective* **miserable, bad, awful, terrible, rotten, inferior, poor, worthless, base, shoddy** We had a lousy time at the dance. ● **Antonyms: superior, good, fine**

lout *noun* **oaf, ox, gawk, hulk, lump, boor, churl, ape, bumpkin, lummox, clod, dullard** I volunteered to play the part of a lout in the school play.

love *noun* **1. affection, fondness, tenderness, warmth, devotion, adoration, attachment, sentiment** I have much love for my family. **2. predilection, penchant, partiality, inclination, weakness, delight, enjoyment, relish, desire, longing** Robert has always had a love for reading. **3. beloved, darling, dear, honey, precious, sweet, sweetheart, truelove, dearest, lover** You are my only love. ◆ *verb* **1. adore, cherish, treasure, worship, idolize, admire, hold dear, prize, esteem** My old cat is grumpy sometimes, but I love him anyway. **2. enjoy, like, delight in, fancy, relish, savor, appreciate** I love going to the movies with my friends. ● **Antonyms:** *noun* **1. hatred, dislike 2. aversion** ◆ *verb* **hate, dislike**

lovely *adjective* **1. beautiful, attractive, pretty, good-looking, endearing, adorable, comely, fair, handsome** That is a lovely dress you're wearing. **2. pleasing, enjoyable, delightful, gratifying, satisfying, pleasurable, pleasant, agreeable** We had a lovely time at the vicar's tea. ● **Antonyms: 1. plain, ugly 2. unpleasant, disagreeable**

loving *adjective* **affectionate, caring, devoted, warm, tender, kind, adoring, doting, fond** We have a warm and loving family. ● **Antonyms: unloving, cold**

low *adjective* **1. short, little, small, squat, stubby, flat** The horse easily jumped over the low fence. **2. inferior, bad, inadequate, poor, unsatisfactory, mediocre, deficient, shabby, substandard, moderate** This job has excellent benefits, but the pay is low. **3. soft, hushed, quiet, subdued, low-pitched, low-key, muted, muffled, stifled** The two friends spoke to each other in low tones when they were in the museum. **4. scant, meager, scarce, insufficient, limited, lean, short, down** Our supply of milk is low. **5. mean, vile, nasty, detestable, abhorrent, abominable, base, immoral, contemptible, despicable, rotten, wretched** That was a low thing to say to me! **6. sad, dejected, depressed, melancholic, downcast, gloomy, unhappy, downhearted, blue** I have been feeling low ever since my best friend moved away. ● **Antonyms: 1. high, tall 2. good, satisfactory 3. loud 4. abundant, plentiful 5. commendable, praiseworthy 6. cheerful, happy**

lower *adjective* **inferior, subordinate, lesser, low, minor, secondary, junior, subsidiary** She took a lower position in order to work for the company she preferred. ◆ *verb* **1. let down, bring down, drop, move down, descend, take down** The stage crew lowered the curtain after the final act. **2. reduce, drop, cut, slash, decrease, diminish, lessen, pare** The teacher will lower our grades if our reports are late. **3. degrade, abase, disgrace, dishonor, debase, shame, demean, sink, stoop, humble** He would not lower himself to lie about the incident. ➻ **Antonyms:** *adjective* **higher, superior** ◆ *verb* **1. raise, lift 2. increase, enlarge**

loyal *adjective* **dependable, devoted, faithful, steadfast, true, trustworthy, constant, staunch, fast, firm, reliable, dutiful** A loyal friend will stand by you even when you have troubles. ➻ **Antonyms: disloyal, unfaithful**

loyalty *noun* **allegiance, faithfulness, devotion, fealty, fidelity, constancy, reliability, dedication, dependability** The king knew he could count on the loyalty of his knights. ➻ **Antonyms: disloyalty, treachery**

lucid *adjective* **1. clear, understandable, comprehensible, intelligible, unambiguous, rational, reasonable** I recommend this lucid account of Queen Boadicea's revolt against the Romans in first-century Britain. **2. transparent, clear, limpid, see-through, crystal clear, pellucid, crystalline, sheer** The lake's water was so lucid that we could see the bottom. ➻ **Antonyms: 1. unclear, confusing 2. opaque**

luck *noun* **1. chance, fate, fortune, providence, hazard, accident, destiny, fortuity, serendipity, kismet** I prefer games of skill over games of luck. **2. good fortune, success, good luck, luckiness, advantage, prosperity, fulfillment** Finding a four-leaf clover is said to bring luck. ➻ **Antonyms: 2. misfortune, bad luck**

lucky *adjective* **fortunate, successful, good, auspicious, favorable, happy, providential, fortuitous, opportune** I made a lucky guess on the quiz and chose the right answer. ➻ **Antonyms: unfortunate, unlucky**

ludicrous *adjective* **ridiculous, comic, comical, silly, absurd, preposterous, farcical, laughable, crazy** I dressed up in a ludicrous costume for the Halloween party. ➻ **Antonyms: sensible, serious**

lug *verb* **carry, haul, tote, bear, drag, tow, transport, pull, heave** I lugged the heavy groceries up two flights of stairs.

luggage *noun* **baggage, bags, suitcases, valises, belongings, gear, trunks, boxes, effects** A porter helped us carry our luggage to the train.

lull *verb* **calm, soothe, quiet, settle, pacify, allay, becalm, still, tranquilize** The soft music lulled me to sleep. ◆ *noun* **break, lapse, pause, intermission, respite, interlude, hiatus, delay, suspension** The rain started up again after a brief lull. ➻ **Antonyms:** *verb* **agitate, excite, arouse**

lumber¹ *noun* **boards, planks, wood, beams, timber** There is a pile of old lumber in our backyard.

lumber² *verb* **clump, stump, waddle, trudge, plod, stamp, shamble, shuffle, trundle, slog** The circus elephants lumbered into the tent.

luminous *adjective* **shining, gleaming, shimmering, glowing, bright, brilliant, effulgent, incandescent, radiant** The streetlights were luminous in the early evening rain.

lump *noun* **1. clump, chunk, clod, hunk, mass, piece, wad, gob, wedge, cake** Grandfather uses a hoe to break up the lumps of dirt in his garden. **2. bump, swelling, knot, bulge, hump, nub, protuberance, protrusion** The bee sting raised a big lump on my arm. ◆ *verb* **consolidate, group, heap, combine, pool, collect, assemble, amass, join, gather** I lumped all the dark clothing in a pile before doing the laundry. ➻ **Antonyms:** *verb* **scatter, disperse, separate**

lunatic *noun* **madman, maniac, crank, loon, eccentric, crackpot, psychopath, crazy** Because of their attempts to build a flying machine, the Wright brothers were considered by many to be lunatics. ◆ *adjective* **1. insane, mad, crazy, demented, deranged, mentally ill, daft, psychotic, unbalanced, irrational** People once believed that looking at the moon too long would cause lunatic behavior. **2. foolish, absurd, harebrained, idiotic, preposterous, silly, nonsensical, stupid, inane, illogical** Jumping into the lake with all your clothes on was a lunatic thing to do. ➻ **Antonyms:** *adjective* **1. sane, rational 2. logical, sensible**

lunge *noun* **charge, dive, pounce, rush, spring, leap, jump, thrust, attack** When I dangled a toy mouse in front of my kitten, she made a lunge for it. ◆ *verb* **charge, dive, jump, leap, spring, dash, pounce, thrust, bound** Susan lunged forward to catch the lamp before it hit the floor.

lurch *verb* **1. stagger, stumble, reel, weave, wobble, teeter, totter, falter, careen** The exhausted marathon runner lurched across the finish line. **2. roll, pitch, yaw, sway, toss, swing, tilt, list, heel, cant, keel** The ship lurched from side to side in the heavy seas.

lure *noun* **attraction, draw, invitation, temptation, bait, allurement, enticement, magnet, decoy, snare** The lure of adventure makes some people want to travel and see new places. ◆ *verb* **attract, tempt, draw, pull, invite, allure, entice, hook, seduce, charm, bait, induce** We were lured into the bakery by the wonderful smells. ➻ **Antonyms:** *verb* **repel, repulse**

lurk *verb* **lie in wait, hide, wait, hide out, creep, skulk, prowl** The cat lurked beside the chipmunk hole.

lush *adjective* **1. abundant, dense, luxuriant, rich, sumptuous, thick, heavy, teeming, overgrown, riotous** We saw deer browsing on the lush grass of a mountain meadow. **2. extravagant, lavish, luxurious, opulent, plush, posh, elegant, ornate, grand** The limousine had a lush interior. ❧ **Antonyms: 1. sparse, barren 2. plain, simple**

lust *noun* **desire, craving, appetite, hunger, itch, longing, thirst, eagerness, voracity** The painter Vincent Van Gogh is said to have had a great lust for life.

luster *noun* **1. sheen, gloss, brightness, brilliance, glow, radiance, shine, burnish, polish** We admired the luster of the marble statues in the museum. **2. glory, splendor, fame, prestige, renown, repute, honor, distinction** Winning a Nobel Prize added luster to the scientist's distinguished career.

luxurious *adjective* **sumptuous, elegant, magnificent, splendid, expensive, rich, lavish, lush, posh** The princess wore a luxurious gown to the grand ball. ❧ **Antonyms: poor, shabby**

luxury *noun* **1. extravagance, frill, indulgence, rarity, delight, enjoyment, pleasure, treat** Dining at an expensive restaurant is a rare luxury for us. **2. affluence, comfort, extravagance, splendor, elegance, opulence, grandeur, richness, riches, wealth** The wealthy movie star's home had every conceivable luxury. ❧ **Antonyms: 2. poverty, austerity**

Mm

macabre *adjective* **gruesome, grisly, ghastly, grim, hideous, horrible, spooky, frightening** The horror movie was too macabre for me. ➨ **Antonym: pleasant**

machine *noun* **1. appliance, device, mechanism, engine, motor, machinery, instrument, tool** I asked Mom if I could use her sewing machine. **2. robot, automaton, drone, puppet, marionette, drudge, slave** The man was so tired that he went through his day like a machine. **3. organization, establishment, system, administration, bureaucracy, party, movement, agency** The legal machine went to work to get the legislation passed.

machinery *noun* **1. equipment, mechanism, device, apparatus, instrument, motor, engine, tool** The technician oils the machinery regularly. **2. system, organization, structure, means, agency, process, vehicle** The federal bureaucracy constitutes the machinery that keeps the government functioning.

mad *adjective* **1. angry, furious, incensed, indignant, upset, wrathful, exasperated, resentful** I was mad when my sister borrowed my skateboard without asking. **2. crazy, insane, demented, lunatic, unbalanced, psychotic, deranged, berserk** This movie is about a mad scientist who believes he has invented a time machine. **3. absurd, foolish, rash, silly, harebrained, idiotic, reckless, senseless** It was a mad idea to try to swim so far on a full stomach. **4. ardent, enthusiastic, excited, fanatic, zealous, fanatical, avid, impassioned** The audience erupted into mad cheering when the rock star appeared on stage. **5. confused, frantic, frenzied, wild, frenetic, violent, turbulent** There was a mad scramble for the baseball that was hit into the crowd. ➨ **Antonyms: 2. rational, sane 3. sensible, reasonable 4. & 5. calm, cool**

magazine *noun* **journal, periodical, publication, newsletter, serial, paper, gazette, digest** I subscribe to four magazines about gardening.

magic *noun* **1. witchcraft, wizardry, sorcery, enchantment, voodoo** The witches performed their magic in the forest late at night. **2. charm, allure, enchantment, lure, appeal, fascination, spell, magnetism** We enjoyed the magic of the beautiful desert sunset. ◆ *adjective* **magical, charming, enchanting, fascinating, bewitching, spellbinding, hypnotic, entrancing** The meteor shower against the dark sky made it seem a magic night.

magician *noun* **entertainer, enchanter, wizard, witch, sorcerer, conjurer, prestidigitator** The magician pulled a rabbit out of his hat.

magnetic *adjective* **appealing, captivating, charming, fascinating, alluring, charismatic, dynamic, entrancing** The actor was known for his magnetic personality. ➨ **Antonyms: repulsive, offensive, repellent**

magnificent *adjective* **beautiful, fantastic, glorious, grand, splendid, wonderful, stately, impressive** A peacock looks magnificent when it spreads its tail feathers. ➨ **Antonyms: ordinary, plain**

magnify *verb* **1. enlarge, expand, swell, amplify, boost, augment, heighten, extend** When Grandpa reads the newspaper, he wears glasses that magnify the print. **2. exaggerate, inflate, enhance, overstate, overrate, embroider, dramatize, embellish** She magnifies everything that happens to her. ➨ **Antonyms: 1. diminish, reduce 2. minimize, underrate**

magnitude *noun* **degree, extent, measure, proportion, size, importance, weight, significance** The sun is a star of average magnitude.

maiden *noun* **girl, mademoiselle, damsel, maid, lass, miss, gal, young lady** I have a Bavarian maiden's costume. ◆ *adjective* **first, initial, original, pioneer, inaugural, earliest, introductory** The *Titanic* sank on its maiden voyage. ➨ **Antonyms:** *adjective* **final, last**

mail *noun* **cards, letters, packages, messages, postcards, parcels, post** More mail is delivered during the Christmas season than at any other time of the year. ◆ *verb* **post, send, dispatch, forward, ship, transmit, drop, express** Please mail this letter for me.

maim *verb* **disable, cripple, mutilate, lame, dismember, wound, injure, hurt** The fox was maimed by the trap in which it was caught.

main *adjective* **chief, head, leading, major, primary, principal, foremost, dominant, paramount** This is the main road leading into town. ◆ *noun* **pipe, line, tube, duct, conduit, sewer, drain** The water company turned off the main that leads to our house. ➨ **Antonyms:** *adjective* **minor, secondary**

mainly *adverb* chiefly, generally, mostly, primarily, usually, predominantly, largely I like to read mainly science fiction novels. ➻ **Antonyms: secondarily, slightly**

maintain *verb* 1. keep, preserve, retain, sustain, extend, continue, prolong, perpetuate I have a yearly physical examination to help maintain my health. 2. care for, look after, service, condition, fix, repair, manage, mend My brother and I help maintain the yard. 3. finance, support, pay for, provide for, sustain, nourish, supply My parents maintain my sister at college. 4. affirm, assert, claim, declare, insist, state, say, profess, contend The defendant maintained that he was innocent. ➻ **Antonyms: 1. terminate, discontinue 2. & 3. neglect, abandon 4. deny, refute**

majestic *adjective* grand, impressive, magnificent, splendid, stately, regal, imposing, noble Redwoods are majestic trees that can grow to be more than 300 feet tall. ➻ **Antonyms: ordinary, modest, humble**

majesty *noun* stateliness, splendor, grandeur, magnificence, pomp, dignity, greatness, glory The royal wedding was conducted with great majesty. ➻ **Antonyms: meanness, shabbiness**

major *adjective* chief, first, foremost, leading, main, primary, superior, uppermost My major focus this year has been to improve my math grade. ➻ **Antonyms: minor, lesser**

majority *noun* 1. bulk, mass, predominance, preponderance, major part, main body, plurality The majority of students in my class walk to school. 2. adulthood, maturity, manhood, womanhood, prime, seniority, legal age We celebrated when my brother reached the age of majority. ➻ **Antonyms: 1. minority, few 2. immaturity, childhood**

make *verb* 1. create, fashion, produce, build, form, manufacture, assemble, forge, construct My grandmother made me a quilt for my birthday. 2. establish, enact, formulate, draft, draw up, prepare, decree A legislature is empowered to make laws. 3. cause, compel, force, bring, bring about, effect, induce, drive Peeling onions always makes my eyes water. 4. reach, attain, arrive, get to, come to, catch, meet Did you make it to school on time? 5. acquire, earn, gain, get, obtain, receive, accumulate, reap I make enough money mowing lawns to buy my own clothes and school supplies. 6. comprise, constitute, form, add up to, amount to, come to, equal, total, embody Four quarts make one gallon. ◆ *noun* 1. style, cut, form, shape, structure, frame, construction, makeup I like the make of your suit. 2. brand, kind, model, style, variety, name, trademark, type Dad bought a new car that was the same make as his old one.

malady *noun* disease, illness, ailment, sickness, disorder, infirmity, disability, complaint She has a chronic malady that requires daily medication.

male *adjective* masculine, manly, mannish, manful, manlike, virile, paternal He played the male lead in the school play. ◆ *noun* he, boy, man, guy, fellow, lad, gentleman, chap Our new dog is a male. ➻ **Antonyms: *adjective* feminine ◆ *noun* female, she, woman**

malice *noun* ill will, malevolence, hostility, hatred, vengeance, spite, rancor Lincoln said, "With malice toward none, with charity for all" in a speech just one month before he was assassinated. ➻ **Antonyms: good will, kindness**

malignant *adjective* 1. malicious, spiteful, evil, vile, vengeful, bitter, hostile, resentful The man had angry and malignant thoughts about the thief who stole his bicycle. 2. deadly, pernicious, cancerous, mortal, fatal, pestilent, lethal We were relieved and thankful when the tumor was found not to be malignant. ➻ **Antonyms: 1. friendly, beneficial 2. benign, harmless**

Word Group

A **mammal** is any of various warm-blooded animals that have a backbone, hair or fur, and, in the females, mammary glands that produce milk. **Mammal** is a specific term with no true synonyms. Here are some notable mammals:

The **African elephant** is the largest mammal living on land. **Bats** are the only mammals that can fly. The **blue whale** is the largest of all the mammals. The **echidna** and the **platypus** are the only mammals that lay eggs. **Human beings** are the mammals with the longest potential lifespan. The **shrew** is both the shortest-lived mammal and the smallest mammal.

mammoth *adjective* colossal, enormous, gigantic, huge, immense, large, gargantuan, massive Sending astronauts to the moon was a mammoth undertaking. ➻ **Antonyms: little, small, tiny**

man *noun* 1. fellow, gentleman, gent, guy, male, chap, lad A kind man helped us fix our flat tire. 2. humanity, humankind, mankind, human beings, Homo sapiens, people, humans Nicotine is said to be the most addictive substance known to man. ◆ *verb* staff, attend, inhabit, occupy, cover, work, operate, people All hands were ordered to man their battle stations.

manage *verb* **1. administer, control, direct, run, supervise, head, guide, govern** My aunt manages a flower shop. **2. succeed, contrive, arrange, accomplish, achieve, perform, fulfill** I managed to get my homework done before it was time for dinner. **3. survive, cope, fare, fend, do, get along, carry on, provide** Will you be able to manage without my help?

management *noun* **1. control, direction, leadership, supervision, administration, superintendence, guidance** The restaurant reopened under new management. **2. authorities, executives, administration, board, cabinet, regime, directorate** The management issued new directives regarding vacation time.

manager *noun* **head, supervisor, boss, administrator, director, leader, chief, superintendent, overseer** I spoke to the store's manager when I applied for a job. ⬧ **Antonyms: employee, worker**

maneuver *noun* **1. move, movement, turn, operation, mission, exercise, action** During halftime, the marching band executed a series of complicated maneuvers. **2. ploy, stratagem, tactic, feint, dodge, trick, ruse, step, artifice, gambit** The company's maneuver to corner the market was thwarted by its competitors. ◆ *verb* **1. guide, navigate, pilot, steer, jockey, move, handle, drive** The pilot carefully maneuvered his river boat past a dangerous sandbar. **2. plan, scheme, plot, trick, manipulate, connive, angle, finesse** My friends and I maneuvered to be on the same team in gym class.

mangy *adjective* **shabby, threadbare, ragged, frayed, scruffy, tattered, shoddy, rundown** The carpet in the old house was mangy.

mania *noun* **fixation, craze, obsession, passion, enthusiasm, infatuation, madness, rage** He has a mania for old science fiction movies.

manifest *adjective* **clear, apparent, obvious, evident, plain, distinct, conspicuous, patent** It was manifest to me from page one that the history test was difficult. ◆ *verb* **reveal, show, display, exhibit, indicate, demonstrate, evidence, signify** His behavior clearly manifested his desire to leave the party early. ⬧ **Antonyms:** *adjective* **hidden, vague** ◆ *verb* **hide, conceal**

manipulate *verb* **1. operate, control, guide, maneuver, handle, wield, employ, use** He learned to manipulate the controls of the forklift. **2. influence, finesse, beguile, negotiate, trick, steer, jockey, exploit** I tried to manipulate my mother into letting me stay home from school.

manner *noun* **1. way, method, practice, procedure, process, mode, fashion, custom** The manner in which broken bones are treated has changed over the years. **2. demeanor, behavior, conduct, air, cast, bearing, comportment, mien** Her manner was kind and gracious. **3. kind, sort, variety, class, category, nature, type, order, brand** What manner of weather does this region usually have this time of year?

Word Group

A **mansion** is a large, stately house. **Mansion** is a general term with no true synonyms. Here are some related words:

chateau, estate, hacienda, hall, manor, manse, palace, plantation, villa

---

mantle *noun* **1. cloak, cape, shawl, poncho, robe, wrap, mantilla, tunic, coat** Little Red Riding Hood wore a red mantle to her grandmother's house. **2. covering, coating, blanket, curtain, veil, canopy, envelope, cover, pall** The ground was covered with a mantle of snow after the blizzard. ◆ *verb* **cover, cloak, conceal, shroud, screen, obscure, veil, envelop, blanket** Fog mantled the skyline until the afternoon.

manual *noun* **guide, guidebook, handbook, text, textbook, directory, primer, workbook** I read the instruction manual before programming the VCR.

manufacture *verb* **assemble, build, construct, make, produce, create, fabricate, fashion** Our class toured a factory that manufactures boxes.

many *adjective* **abundant, numerous, countless, plentiful, several, manifold, myriad, uncounted** There are many books on astronomy in our school library. ◆ *noun* **lots, numbers, scores, multitude, throng, mass, host, flock** Many of our relatives were able to attend the family reunion. ⬧ **Antonym: few**

map *noun* **chart, representation, diagram, drawing, graph, sketch, design** We used a map of the city to find the art museum. ◆ *verb* **chart, plot, lay out, diagram, draw, sketch, outline, blueprint** Astronomers use images received from spacecraft to map the planet Mars.

mar *verb* **1. deface, damage, blemish, disfigure, spot, mark, stain, scar** An ink stain marred the surface of the antique writing table. **2. spoil, ruin, wreck, botch, disrupt, upset, hurt, impair, harm** We didn't let the rain mar our enjoyment of the picnic.

march *verb* **1. parade, hike, stride, trek, walk, strut, file, promenade** My Scout troop will march in this year's Memorial Day parade. **2. progress, advance, proceed, pass, move, journey, course** Summer vacation marched steadily to a close. ◆ *noun* **1. parade, procession, walk, hike, trek, tramp, demonstration** Some local environmentalists are planning a protest march. **2. progress, progression, advance, headway, development, furtherance** The forward march of medicine has resulted in many new treatments for cancer.

margin *noun* **1. border, edge, fringe, boundary, rim, hem, side, periphery** I left a one-inch margin on all sides of each page. **2. leeway, room, latitude, elbowroom, extra amount, surplus, allowance** We had a margin of one hour before our flight's departure. **3. interval, clearance, gap, separation, range, scope, space** He won the class election by a narrow margin.

mark *noun* **1. spot, stain, print, blemish, impression, imprint, indent, stamp** The wet glass left a mark on the table. **2. token, sign, symbol, indication, note, measure, evidence** The senators stood up as a mark of respect when the chief justice entered. **3. target, goal, objective, aim, end, ambition, destination, object** I tried to hit the tree with a snowball, but I missed my mark. **4. grade, rating, score, evaluation, standing, percentage, result** I earned a better mark on this test than I did on the last one. ◆ *verb* **1. blemish, mar, spot, stain, scar, nick, splotch, score** Be careful not to mark the freshly waxed floor. **2. designate, identify, indicate, point out, show, reveal, distinguish, label** Flags were used to mark the corners of the playing field. **3. heed, notice, mind, observe, see, note, regard, attend, remark** Please mark where I step. **4. grade, rate, score, correct, evaluate, assess, appraise, judge** The student teacher marked our papers.

market *noun* **1. grocery, store, supermarket, marketplace, shop, mart, general store** Could you get me a candy bar when you go to the market? **2. call, demand, need, business, commerce, trade, traffic, dealings** There is a very large market for health foods in this city. ◆ *verb* **sell, offer, peddle, vend, trade, barter, retail, merchandise** These television sets are marketed worldwide.

marriage *noun* **1. matrimony, wedlock, wedding, nuptials, espousal, match** The man and woman were joined in marriage. **2. union, combination, joining, linking, connection, junction** Water ballet is a marriage of swimming and dance.

marrow *noun* **essence, pith, heart, soul, core, kernel, substance, quintessence** The marrow of the problem is

that we do not have enough time to finish the project without employing more people.

marry *verb* **wed, espouse, mate, join, unite, match, couple, pledge** My aunt is planning to marry her fiancé next June.

marsh *noun* **swamp, bog, wetland, swampland, fen, slough, everglade, marshland, quagmire** The marsh on our farm serves as a bird sanctuary.

marshal *noun* **law officer, law enforcement officer, peace officer, sheriff, constable** Wyatt Earp was a famous federal marshal back in the 1880s. ◆ *verb* **arrange, array, order, organize, assemble, gather, group, rally** The colonel marshaled his troops for inspection.

martyr *verb* **put to death, kill, slay, torture, torment, persecute, harass, punish** Saint Stephen was the first Christian to be martyred.

marvel *noun* **wonder, astonishment, phenomenon, curiosity, miracle, sensation, spectacle, mystery** Egypt's ancient marvels include the Sphinx and the Great Pyramid at Giza. ◆ *verb* **wonder, admire, gape, gaze, stare, goggle, be amazed** Visitors to the Grand Canyon marvel at its great length and depth.

marvelous *adjective* **1. miraculous, unbelievable, astounding, amazing, extraordinary, phenomenal, preternatural** Treatment with the new drug achieved marvelous results. **2. excellent, superior, remarkable, glorious, splendid, wonderful, superb, exceptional** He had a marvelous opportunity to be an exchange student to Finland for his junior year. ➤ **Antonyms: 1. natural, normal 2. commonplace, ordinary**

mash *verb* **crush, squash, pound, pulverize, smash, press, squish** Mash the garlic before you add it to the pesto.

mask *noun* **disguise, masquerade, guise, camouflage, cloak, cover, veil** My friend wore a gorilla mask to the costume party. ◆ *verb* **conceal, cover, disguise, hide, camouflage, veil, screen, obscure** Whenever I have to eat fish, I mask its flavor by adding lemon. ➤ **Antonyms: *verb* expose, uncover**

mass *noun* **1. pile, heap, hill, mound, drift, clump, mound, block, hunk** The snowplow left a mass of snow and ice in front of our house. **2. profusion, abundance, wealth, lot, quantity, multitude, crowd, horde, flock** A mass of people showed up for the store's grand opening sale. **3. majority, best part, preponderance, plurality, bulk,**

main body The mass of people are law-abiding citizens. **4. bulk, size, volume, extent, magnitude, weight, amplitude, dimension** The mass of a blue whale is almost incalculably greater than that of a goldfish. ◆ *verb* **accumulate, assemble, cluster, collect, gather, consolidate, congregate, amass** I knew that a storm was coming when I saw dark clouds massing on the horizon. ➧ **Antonyms:** *verb* **disperse, scatter**

massacre *noun* **killing, slaughter, slaying, decimation, mass murder, carnage, butchery** Many people are outraged by the massacre of baby seals. ◆ *verb* **kill, slaughter, slay, murder, annihilate, exterminate, decimate, wipe out, butcher** African elephants are being massacred for their ivory.

massage *noun* **rubdown, back rub, rub, manipulation, stroking, kneading** The doctor prescribed massages as part of the athlete's physical therapy. ◆ *verb* **knead, rub, stroke, manipulate, rub down, squeeze** I massaged my neck to ease the stiffness.

massive *adjective* **1. bulky, hefty, heavy, solid, heavyweight, ponderous, unwieldy** *Apatosaurus* was a massive dinosaur that weighed over 30 tons. **2. enormous, gigantic, huge, immense, mammoth, towering, large, monumental** Mount Rushmore is famous for its massive portraits of four United States Presidents. **3. impressive, imposing, substantial, great, grand, tremendous** I was amazed at the massive bass voice that came out of such a small man. ➧ **Antonyms: 1. lightweight 2. little, small, tiny 3. modest**

master *noun* **1. leader, head, director, ruler, superior, chief, governor, boss, lord** Caesar was the master of the Roman Empire. **2. expert, genius, professional, wizard, ace, maestro, authority, mastermind** The chef is a master at creating new dishes. ◆ *adjective* **1. chief, main, primary, principal, major, foremost, supreme** The mayor's office drew up a master plan for the city's future development. **2. masterful, expert, professional, skilled, proficient, experienced, competent, adept** The antique dresser was made by a master craftsperson. ◆ *verb* **1. command, dominate, quell, subjugate, subdue, defeat, bridle, tame** My uncle has the training to master wild horses. **2. learn, acquire, understand, pick up, comprehend, grasp, get** My little brother has yet to master the art of riding a bicycle. ➧ **Antonyms:** *noun* **1. subordinate, follower 2. amateur, beginner** ◆ *adjective* **1. secondary, auxiliary 2. incompetent, unskilled**

match *noun* **1. complement, companion, counterpart, mate, supplement, balance, parallel** His striped tie is a good match for his white shirt. **2. double, duplicate, equal,** **equivalent, analogue, fellow, twin** We need a match for the bedroom wallpaper so we can fix a tear. **3. competition, contest, game, meet, tournament, encounter, bout, tourney** I played well, but not well enough to win our tennis match. ◆ *verb* **1. agree with, correspond to, duplicate, resemble, harmonize, accord, fit** Do you think that this paint matches the color of our curtains? **2. compare with, equal, rival, compete with, approach, measure up** No one on their team can match our quarterback.

matchless *adjective* **incomparable, unmatched, unrivaled, peerless, excellent, supreme, unsurpassed, first-rate** Rudolf Nureyev was a matchless ballet dancer known for his spectacular technical virtuosity. ➧ **Antonyms: mediocre, second-rate**

mate *noun* **1. counterpart, companion, match, duplicate, double, twin, fellow** I have one earring, but I can't find its mate. **2. spouse, partner, companion, match, consort, husband, wife, bride, groom** A swan stays with its mate for life. **3. partner, comrade, friend, buddy, fellow, confederate, pal, chum** I went camping with my mates. ◆ *verb* **couple, pair off, cohabit, join, unite, marry, wed, espouse** Wolves mate for life.

material *noun* **1. component, element, ingredient, substance, matter, stuff, constituent** Wood is a common building material. **2. cloth, fabric, textile, dry goods, yard goods, goods** I picked out the material for my new dress. ◆ *adjective* **1. concrete, physical, solid, real, corporeal, substantial, tangible, palpable** Anything that you can see or touch is a part of the material world. **2. important, relevant, significant, germane, apropos, pertinent, crucial, salient** She was a material witness in the criminal case. ➧ **Antonyms:** *adjective* **1. unreal 2. unimportant, immaterial**

matter *noun* **1. material, substance, stuff, components, elements, constituents** A space that has no matter is known as a vacuum. **2. theme, topic, point, subject, issue, argument, content, text, thesis** The Treaty of Ghent did not deal with matters of boundary disputes following the War of 1812. **3. affair, business, concern, transaction, proceeding, thing, situation** Mom went to the bank this morning to take care of some financial matters. **4. difficulty, problem, trouble, predicament, worry, bother, distress, annoyance** What is the matter with the car? ◆ *verb* **be important, concern, weigh, count, affect, influence, import, signify, mean** It matters to me that you remember my birthday every year.

mature *adjective* **1. adult, full-grown, grown, developed, older, ready, ripe, big** A mature elephant can weigh as much as five tons. **2. experienced, grown-up, wise, practiced, capable, responsible, stable, sensible, sophisticated** My parents feel that I am mature enough to baby-sit my younger brothers. ◆ *verb* **1. develop, evolve, grow, age, ripen, progress, flower, blossom, mellow** Most trees mature very slowly. **2. fall due, accrue, be payable, finish, conclude, complete, arrive** The savings bonds will mature in time for me to go to college. ➡ **Antonyms:** *adjective* **1. immature, young 2. inexperienced, undeveloped**

maturity *noun* **adulthood, completion, development, majority, manhood, womanhood** Hamsters reach maturity at 11 weeks.

maxim *noun* **proverb, saying, adage, motto, truism, moral, platitude** It is a maxim that the early bird catches the worm.

maximum *noun* **limit, peak, top, ceiling, zenith, climax, most, limitation** This elevator is designed to carry a maximum of 12 people. ◆ *adjective* **greatest, supreme, top, ultimate, biggest, largest, paramount, best** A Boeing 747 jetliner has a maximum speed of more than 550 nautical miles per hour. ➡ **Antonyms:** *noun* **minimum, least** ◆ *adjective* **lowest, smallest**

maybe *adverb* **conceivably, perhaps, possibly, perchance, feasibly** Maybe my mom will let me go to the movie. ➡ **Antonyms: certainly, surely**

mayhem *noun* **confusion, disorder, chaos, anarchy, pandemonium, violence, damage** There was mayhem in the city after the earthquake.

maze *noun* **1. network, labyrinth, complex, tangle, web** Carlsbad Caverns is a complex maze of interconnecting tunnels and chambers. **2. muddle, morass, jungle, confusion, mess, disorder** Negotiating the maze of bureaucratic red tape takes patience and persistence.

meadow *noun* **lea, pasture, field, grassland, green, sward, prairie** There is a wildflower meadow on my grandmother's ranch.

meager *adjective* **inadequate, poor, scant, scanty, small, sparse, paltry, deficient** The coyote was thin because his food supply had been meager all winter long. ➡ **Antonyms: large, plentiful**

meal *noun* **banquet, feast, dinner, supper, repast, breakfast, lunch, snack** Our family enjoys a large meal when we celebrate Thanksgiving.

mean[1] *verb* **1. denote, indicate, signify, designate, imply, convey, suggest** A red traffic light means that drivers are supposed to stop. **2. aim, expect, intend, plan, propose, want, wish, anticipate, contemplate** What do you mean to do about that stray dog you brought home? **3. portend, indicate, signify, denote, imply, foreshadow, foretell, presage, suggest** Some people think that if the groundhog does not see his shadow on February 2, it means there will be an early spring.

mean[2] *adjective* **1. cruel, malicious, hateful, malevolent, nasty, spiteful, rude, unkind, hostile** The mean man screamed at us to get out of his way. **2. miserly, stingy, close, tight, ungenerous, selfish, greedy, penny-pinching** Ebenezer Scrooge was too mean to give Bob Cratchit a raise. **3. inferior, low-grade, poor, second-rate, mediocre, common, shabby, substandard** These boots are of mean quality. ➡ **Antonyms: 1. kind, nice 2. generous, unselfish 3. superior, select**

mean[3] *noun* **1. center, median, medium, middle, average, balance, norm, par** The golden mean is the ethical midpoint between two unethical extremes. **2. agent, agency, mechanism, instrument, force, device, tool, way** An airplane is the fastest means of travel available today. **3. assets, resources, capital, wealth, fortune, wherewithal, income** I don't have the means to buy a new modem for my computer right now. ◆ *adjective* **average, median, central, intermediate, middle, midway, medium** The mean score on our last quiz was 75.

meaning *noun* **1. message, import, spirit, content, significance, sense, drift, gist** I read the story twice, but I still don't understand its meaning. **2. purpose, goal, object, point, aim, intent, idea, end, design** After he got a good job, his life took on new meaning.

measure *noun* **1. amount, portion, share, allowance, quota, lot, ration, volume, unit** The recipe calls for equal measures of flour and sugar. **2. extent, degree, magnitude, proportion, amplitude, scope, reach, depth** The full measure of the damage from the hurricane has not been learned. **3. gauge, rule, scale, standard, test, benchmark, yardstick, criterion** The amount of money you make should not be the only measure of your success. **4. limit, bounds, constraint, restraint, borders, boundaries** My happiness is beyond measure. **5. action, procedure, step, course, move, maneuver, means, tactic** The government took temporary measures to control the import of automobiles. **6. bill, act, legislation, resolution, law, statute, enactment** The representative introduced a new measure in the legislature. ◆ *verb* **1. calculate, compute, figure, count, gauge, rule, size, estimate** We measured our garage to see if it would hold a pickup truck. **2. compare, evaluate, judge, contrast, assess, appraise, balance, rank, rate** We measured the convenience of having an air conditioner against the cost before buying one.

mechanical *adjective* **automatic, perfunctory, reflexive, unconscious, unthinking, dull, routine** My little brother has told me his favorite joke so many times that my laugh has become mechanical.

mechanism *noun* **apparatus, device, instrument, machine, tool, agent, medium** Our VCR has a mechanism that automatically rewinds and ejects the tapes.

medal *noun* **medallion, award, badge, decoration, ribbon, laurel, citation** During the 1972 Olympics, swimmer Mark Spitz won seven gold medals.

meddle *verb* **interfere, intervene, fool, mess, tamper, intrude, butt in** It's not polite to meddle in other people's affairs.

meddlesome *adjective* **interfering, intrusive, prying, bothersome, impertinent, officious, pushy** Our neighbor accused me of being meddlesome. ➡ **Antonyms: reserved, indifferent**

mediate *verb* **settle, moderate, negotiate, referee, arbitrate, umpire** The two parties agreed to have an arbitrator mediate the issue.

medicine *noun* **drug, medication, prescription, cure, remedy, dose, physic** The doctor gave me some medicine for my sore throat.

mediocre *adjective* **ordinary, undistinguished, average, commonplace, medium, fair, unexceptional** I love to play the guitar, but I am a mediocre performer. ➡ **Antonyms: superior, outstanding, exceptional**

meditate *verb* **contemplate, ponder, reflect, consider, think, deliberate, muse, ruminate** I meditated a long time before making my decision.

medium *noun* **1. mean, compromise, median, average, middle, balance, norm, par** My height is a happy medium between too short and too tall. **2. atmosphere, environment, setting, surroundings, circumstances, milieu, ambiance** Moist soil in a dark room is the perfect medium for growing mushrooms. **3. agency, agent, instrument, means, tool, vehicle, mechanism, channel** Gold was commonly used as a medium of exchange before paper money was introduced. ◆ *adjective* **average, intermediate,**

middle, median, moderate, normal, standard These shirts come in small, medium, and large sizes.

medley *noun* **mixture, variety, arrangement, assortment, jumble, hodgepodge, potpourri, mishmash** The band played a medley of old rock 'n' roll tunes.

meek *adjective* **1. humble, modest, gentle, shy, deferential, patient, mild, agreeable** She does not have a meek personality. **2. submissive, obedient, compliant, passive, timid, tame, docile, weak** His meek behavior pleased the judge. ➡ **Antonyms: 1. proud, bold 2. rebellious**

meet *verb* **1. get together, rendezvous, encounter, come upon, contact, greet, run into** Let's meet at that new restaurant. **2. come together, cross, intersect, connect, join, link, converge, touch** A new truck stop was built at the spot where the two highways meet. **3. fill, fulfill, satisfy, equal, match, reach, comply** My brother received a letter saying that he meets all the university's admission requirements. **4. take on, pay, settle, discharge, cover, answer, heed** He can meet the obligation of a car payment. **5. assemble, congregate, convene, collect, gather, muster, rally** The chess club meets once a week. ◆ *noun* **competition, contest, match, tournament, event, tourney, meeting** I will be competing in next week's swim meet. ➡ **Antonyms: *verb* 1. evade, miss 2. separate, diverge, part 3. fall short, fail 4. default, renege 5. disperse, scatter**

meeting *noun* **1. assembly, conference, gathering, affair, session, congress, council, convention** The meeting will begin as soon as everyone gets here. **2. junction, intersection, confluence, convergence, union, connection, joining** There is a meeting of the Missouri and Mississippi rivers near Saint Louis, Missouri.

melancholy *noun* **dejection, depression, gloom, sadness, unhappiness, woe, sorrow, wistfulness** A feeling of melancholy came over me as I listened to the sad song. ◆ *adjective* **1. sad, glum, depressed, downcast, blue, melancholic, unhappy, low-spirited** I get melancholy during the winter. **2. depressing, saddening, disheartening, dismal, tragic, woeful, dire, gloomy** She told us her melancholy story. ➡ **Antonyms: *noun* joy, happiness ◆ *adjective* 1. cheerful, happy 2. encouraging, cheering**

melee *noun* **fight, brawl, fracas, row, riot, ruckus** There was a melee among the fans after the hockey game.

mellow *adjective* **1. ripe, soft, sweet, juicy, rich, flavorful, aged, seasoned** The mellow taste of pears is delicious. **2. soft, pleasant, soothing, smooth, relaxed, easygoing,**

mild, gentle The mother sang a mellow tune to lull her baby to sleep. **3. mature, wise, tolerant, gentle, understanding, compassionate** My grandmother is a very mellow woman. ◆ *verb* **mature, age, develop, grow, ripen, evolve, season, soften** The unruly youth mellowed as he grew older. ➡ **Antonyms:** *adjective* **1. green, sour 2. harsh, sharp, strident 3. childish, intolerant**

melody *noun* **harmony, tune, music, refrain, song, air, aria, strain, theme** I was awakened by the pleasing melody of a robin singing outside my window.

melt *verb* **1. thaw, dissolve, liquefy, evaporate, fuse, disintegrate, run** My snowman began to melt as soon as the sun came out. **2. fade, disappear, disperse, vanish, dissipate, dwindle, scatter, dispel** The crowd melted away after the police arrived. **3. soften, touch, warm, mollify, pacify, appease, relax, relent** The roly-poly puppy melted my heart. ➡ **Antonyms: 1. harden, solidify, freeze 2. gather, converge 3. toughen, harden**

member *noun* **associate, participant, constituent, initiate, fellow, enrollee, colleague** She is our science club's newest member.

memento *noun* **souvenir, keepsake, reminder, token, relic, remembrance, gift** I bought a cup as a memento of my trip to Niagara Falls.

memorable *adjective* **important, noteworthy, remarkable, unforgettable, extraordinary, historic, momentous** One's high-school graduation is a memorable event. ➡ **Antonyms: insignificant, unimportant**

memorial *noun* **monument, shrine, remembrance, tribute, cairn, statue, plaque, obelisk** This memorial honors the Americans who died in the Vietnam War. ◆ *adjective* **commemorative, testimonial, retrospective** The city will hold a memorial service for police officers who died in the line of duty.

memory *noun* **1. reminiscence, thought, recollection, remembrance, retention** The earliest memory I have is of my father reading me a story. **2. remembrance, homage, honor, tribute, respect, reminder, celebration** A ceremony was held in memory of the university's founder.

menace *noun* **danger, hazard, peril, threat, risk, jeopardy, troublemaker, pest** Our cat is a menace to any bird that enters our yard. ◆ *verb* **endanger, imperil, threaten, scare, intimidate, jeopardize, terrorize, frighten** The shepherd protected his sheep from the wolf that menaced them. ➡ **Antonyms:** *noun* **blessing, boon** ◆ *verb* **help, safeguard**

mend *verb* **1. fix, patch, repair, restore, overhaul, recondition, renovate, revamp** The crew mended the ship's torn sails. **2. reform, correct, improve, rectify, amend, ameliorate, better, right** You need to mend your ways. **3. heal, cure, recover, improve, recuperate, restore, knit, get well** The doctor said that my broken hand would mend in about six weeks.

mental *adjective* **1. intellectual, cerebral, thinking, rational, reasoning, thoughtful, scholarly** I like the mental challenge of solving crossword puzzles. **2. insane, mentally ill, psychiatric, irrational, mad, psychotic, disturbed, lunatic, unbalanced** This institution is for mental patients. ➡ **Antonyms: 1. unthinking, brainless 2. sane, normal, rational**

mention *verb* **disclose, remark, say, tell, divulge, declare, state, allude, infer** She mentioned that she would be away next weekend. ◆ *noun* **comment, note, notice, reference, statement, observation, acknowledgment, remark** Last night's thunderstorm received only a brief mention on the morning news.

mentor *noun* **advisor, teacher, guide, tutor, guru, master, counselor, sponsor** My math teacher is also the mentor for our chess club.

menu *noun* **index, inventory, register, file, table, list, catalog, schedule** Andre scanned the list of programs on his computer's menu.

merchandise *noun* **goods, products, stock, wares, articles, things, commodities** All merchandise on sale is marked with a red tag. ◆ *verb* **1. sell, trade, peddle, vend, exchange, wholesale, retail, buy, handle** He plans to merchandise tools at the swap meet. **2. market, promote, advertise, distribute, push, publicize, show, tout** Our group came up with a clever way to merchandise the coupon booklets.

merchant *noun* **retailer, shopkeeper, storekeeper, dealer, trader, vendor** Several merchants in our neighborhood have advertised sales for next week.

merciful *adjective* **compassionate, kind, humane, sympathetic, charitable, clement, lenient** The merciful nurse gave me medicine when I was in pain. ➡ **Antonyms: cruel, merciless, pitiless**

mercurial *adjective* **1. clever, shrewd, quick, eloquent, lively, sharp, ingenious** He has a mercurial mind that responds quickly to every situation. **2. changeable, variable, unstable, erratic, fickle, volatile, temperamental,**

unpredictable The weather is so mercurial lately that it has been hard to make plans. ➡ **Antonyms: 1.** slow, stodgy **2.** stable, predictable, constant

mercy *noun* **1.** charity, clemency, compassion, kindness, pity, sympathy, benevolence I showed mercy to the spider by putting it outside. **2.** blessing, boon, benefit, windfall, godsend, grace, relief, favor It was a mercy that our house escaped the floodwaters. ➡ **Antonyms: 1.** cruelty **2.** curse, scourge

mere *adjective* insignificant, paltry, negligible, plain, simple, scant, minor, little I was lucky to have received a mere scrape on the knee when I fell off my bicycle.

merge *verb* combine, come together, join, meet, link, unite, blend, mingle, mix I know of a good fishing spot where two creeks merge. ➡ **Antonyms:** divide, split

merit *noun* value, virtue, worth, benefit, quality, excellence, ability, achievement The teacher said that my story idea has real merit. ◆ *verb* deserve, justify, rate, earn, gain, get, incur, warrant Your idea merits further consideration.

merry *adjective* cheerful, gay, jolly, jovial, happy, mirthful, lighthearted, blithe Everyone at the party was in a merry mood. ➡ **Antonyms:** gloomy, unhappy, sober

mess *noun* **1.** pile, stack, heap, hill, mass, mound, accumulation, jumble There's a mess of dirty clothes on my bedroom floor. **2.** clutter, litter, disorganization, eyesore, disorder, disarray, shambles I am cleaning up the mess I left in the kitchen. **3.** muddle, mix-up, difficulty, predicament, quandary, plight, fix I got myself into a mess by spending more than I could afford. ◆ *verb* **1.** disarrange, disorder, dishevel, muss, tangle, clutter, dirty, litter The wind messed up my hair. **2.** ruin, spoil, bungle, muddle, botch, muff I messed up my chance to go to the mall today. ➡ **Antonyms:** *noun* **2.** order, tidiness ◆ *verb* **1.** tidy, clean

message *noun* **1.** notice, report, statement, communication, note, word I left a message on her answering machine. **2.** point, lesson, moral, theme, sense, purport, gist, significance When Dad talked to me, I got the message that I shouldn't get home late.

messenger *noun* courier, carrier, delivery person, envoy, runner, emissary Paul Revere is one of history's most famous messengers.

messy *adjective* **1.** cluttered, dirty, disorganized, untidy, sloppy, unkempt, disheveled, mussy I finally cleaned and organized my messy room. **2.** difficult, unpleasant, complicated, muddled, confused, tricky, uncomfortable I found myself in a messy situation when I tore a jacket I had borrowed from a friend. ➡ **Antonyms: 1.** neat, tidy **2.** easy, comfortable, pleasant

metamorphosis *noun* change, transformation, mutation, conversion, shift, transfiguration, permutation The pollywog we caught has gone through metamorphosis and become a frog.

meter *noun* beat, rhythm, cadence, measure, stress, swing, pattern The conductor tapped out the meter with his baton.

method *noun* **1.** manner, mode, style, system, technique, way, process, fashion I prefer air travel to other methods of long distance transportation. **2.** order, system, orderliness, regularity, structure, design, organization, plan I couldn't see the method in his actions.

metropolis *noun* city, metropolitan area, municipality, town, capital Having experienced both, my aunt says she prefers country living to life in a metropolis.

metropolitan *adjective* urban, cosmopolitan, municipal, suburban, populated My family enjoys the opportunities that living in a metropolitan area has to offer. ➡ **Antonyms:** rural, rustic

middle *adjective* center, central, inner, inside, intermediate, medial, mean, halfway He held up three straws, and I picked the middle one. ◆ *noun* center, core, heart, inside, midpoint, marrow, kernel, midst These candies have soft middles.

middleman *noun* intermediary, go-between, agent, broker, representative, liaison The book distributor serves as a middleman between the publisher and our library.

midst *noun* center, bosom, middle, core, eye, thick, interior, inside There were weeds in the midst of the flower bed. ➡ **Antonyms:** edge, periphery

might *noun* power, force, strength, potency, brawn, muscle, energy, capability The United States threw its might behind the Allied cause during World War II. ➡ **Antonyms:** frailty, weakness, infirmity

mighty *adjective* **1.** powerful, strong, potent, forceful, burly, brawny, stout, sturdy Crocodiles have mighty jaws for crushing their prey. **2.** great, huge, vast, enormous, stupendous, gigantic, colossal, tremendous The mighty Mississippi River flows from Minnesota to the Gulf of Mexico. ➡ **Antonyms: 1. frail, weak 2. small, slight, paltry**

migrate *verb* **immigrate, journey, move, travel, wander, emigrate, trek, rove, voyage** The American West was settled in part by pioneers who migrated there from the East.

mild *adjective* **1. gentle, kind, easygoing, amiable, tenderhearted, mellow, soft** My dad gave me a mild reprimand for leaving the milk on the counter. **2. moderate, temperate, balmy, clement, warm, summery, pleasant** We enjoyed the mild spring weather. ➡ **Antonyms: harsh, severe**

milestone *noun* **turning point, high point, landmark, achievement, breakthrough, event, issue** I consider my 13th birthday a milestone.

milieu *noun* **environment, surroundings, world, setting, scene, place, locale, ambiance** Sue loves research, and the science lab is her milieu.

militant *adjective* **aggressive, combative, warlike, bellicose, belligerent, hostile, truculent, pugnacious** The militant nation received an admonishment from the secretary general of the United Nations. ➡ **Antonyms: peaceful, passive**

military *adjective* **armed, martial, militaristic, soldierly, warlike, bellicose, militant** The United States maintains a large military force. ◆ *noun* **army, armed forces, armed services, navy, air force, militia, guard, reserves** The military has bases scattered throughout the United States.

mill *noun* **factory, shop, works, foundry, plant, yard** My dad works in a lumber mill. ◆ *verb* **1. grind, crush, pulverize, granulate, pound, powder, grate, press** It is possible to mill grain at home. **2. swarm, teem, stir, move, churn, shift** The crowd milled around while waiting for the gates to open.

mimic *verb* **copy, echo, imitate, repeat, mock, ape, parrot, parody, reproduce** My parrot mimics a lot of what he hears. ◆ *noun* **impressionist, impersonator, imitator, mime, copycat** This comedian is also an excellent mimic.

mince *verb* **1. chop, dice, cut up, cut, hash, hack, cleave, slash** I minced onion to add to the meat loaf. **2. qualify, soften, diminish, lessen, mitigate, moderate** Just say what you mean without mincing your words.

mind *noun* **1. brain, intellect, head, intelligence, thinking, reasoning, perception, mentality** A good education helps to develop a person's mind. **2. opinion, view, judgment, outlook, conviction, position, belief** She changed her mind after she did more research on the issue. **3. desire, inclination, tendency, notion, leaning, fancy, urge, liking** I have a mind to buy new hiking boots. **4. sanity, wits, senses, lucidity, lucidness, rationality, faculties** If I have to write another 20-page report, I think I will lose my mind. ◆ *verb* **1. heed, listen to, obey, follow, comply, defer to, respect, observe** Mom and Dad told my little sister to mind me while they were gone. **2. attend to, care for, look after, tend, watch, guard, protect, supervise** Who is going to mind the dog while we're away? **3. care, object, disapprove, dislike, resent, deplore, take offense** Do you mind if I borrow your sweater?

mine *noun* **1. excavation, pit, quarry, hole, shaft, tunnel, crater** My grandfather once worked in a silver mine in Idaho. **2. supply, source, store, fountain, well, treasury, bonanza, wellspring** She is a mine of information about the early history of our town. ◆ *verb* **excavate, dig up, quarry, extract, tunnel, shovel, scoop out** Gold, silver, and other minerals are mined in Nevada.

mingle *verb* **1. blend, combine, join, merge, mix, unite, compound, intermingle, marry** When I saw the bear in the distance, my fear was mingled with awe. **2. socialize, associate, hobnob, fraternize, mix, consort, network** We mingled with everyone at the company picnic. ➡ **Antonyms: 1. divide, separate 2. retire, withdraw**

miniature *adjective* **little, minute, small, tiny, wee, mini, minuscule, dwarf, model** I have a collection of miniature cars. ➡ **Antonyms: big, large**

minimum *adjective* **least, lowest, slightest, littlest, smallest, merest, tiniest, minimal** The minimum speed at which this airplane can be flown is 70 miles per hour. ➡ **Antonyms: greatest, most**

minister *noun* **1. clergyman, cleric, parson, preacher, reverend, priest, ecclesiastic, padre, chaplain** My grandfather was a Unitarian minister. **2. secretary, administrator, executive, consul, envoy, ambassador, legate** Ministers of agriculture from throughout the world held an international conference. ◆ *verb* **care for, aid, comfort, attend, serve, assist, nurse, help, tend** The nurse ministered to the accident victims.

minor *adjective* **insignificant, petty, slight, small, trivial, unimportant, low, trifling, inconsequential, negligible** There was a minor problem when we found the museum closed. ◆ *noun* **adolescent, juvenile, youngster, youth, child, teenager, junior, infant** Minors cannot vote in state or federal elections. ➻ **Antonyms:** *adjective* **significant, major** ◆ *noun* **adult, grownup**

minstrel *noun* **troubadour, bard, musician, singer, entertainer, poet** In the Middle Ages, wandering minstrels traveled from castle to castle.

minus *noun* **drawback, disadvantage, handicap, detriment, defect, deficiency, weakness** It is definitely a minus that the electricity is off. ➻ **Antonyms: advantage, bonus, asset**

minute[1] *noun* **instant, jiffy, moment, second, trice, twinkling, shake, flash** I'll be with you in just a minute.

minute[2] *adjective* **1. little, small, tiny, wee, microscopic, diminutive, miniature, infinitesimal** The bug was so minute that I almost couldn't see it. **2. insignificant, unimportant, piddling, negligible, immaterial, trivial, trifling** My brother's minute problem was quickly resolved. **3. full, detailed, exhaustive, close, careful, thorough, particular** We subjected the results of our experiment to minute scrutiny. ➻ **Antonyms: 1. huge, large 2. significant, important 3. casual, careless**

miracle *noun* **marvel, wonder, phenomenon, rarity, oddity** It was a miracle that no one was injured in the car wreck.

miraculous *adjective* **amazing, astonishing, extraordinary, incredible, marvelous, remarkable, awesome** The gravely ill man made a miraculous recovery. ➻ **Antonyms: normal, ordinary**

mirage *noun* **illusion, fata morgana, vision, delusion, hallucination, phantasm** Seeing nonexistent water on a road is the most common type of mirage.

mire *noun* **1. bog, fen, marsh, swamp, marshland, morass, quagmire, wetland** We went out to the mire to see if the frogs had emerged yet this spring. **2. mud, slush, muck, ooze, slime, sludge, slop** My boot came off in the mire. ◆ *verb* **ensnare, entangle, trap, embroil, delay, detain, slow, retard** Our application to build a house was mired in the bureaucratic process.

mirth *noun* **gaiety, merriment, joy, glee, delight, joviality, festivity, fun, levity** Our family gathering was filled with happiness and mirth. ➻ **Antonyms: sadness, misery**

miscellaneous *adjective* **assorted, diverse, mixed, varied, various, sundry, mingled, motley** Their shed contains a lot of miscellaneous junk. ➻ **Antonyms: similar, homogeneous**

mischief *noun* **1. mischievousness, misbehavior, misconduct, tomfoolery, rascality, deviltry** I wonder what mischief my little brother is up to now? **2. damage, injury, harm, hurt, detriment, trouble, destruction, vandalism** The mischief done by the pranksters was expensive to repair.

mischievous *adjective* **1. bad, misbehaving, naughty, troublesome, annoying, playful, impish** The mischievous puppy chewed up my new gloves. **2. ill, damaging, injurious, deleterious, dangerous, harmful, hazardous** The mischievous wind did a lot of damage to the trees and roofs in our neighborhood. ➻ **Antonyms: 1. good, well-behaved 2. favorable, benevolent, benign**

miser *noun* **penny pincher, skinflint, Scrooge, niggard, hoarder** I don't consider myself a miser just because I like to save my money. ➻ **Antonyms: philanthropist, wastrel, spendthrift**

miserable *adjective* **1. dejected, desolate, gloomy, sad, unhappy, wretched, woeful** My sister felt miserable when she couldn't find her favorite earrings. **2. awful, bad, lousy, inferior, poor, rotten, unsatisfactory, cheap** I had miserable luck the last time I played chess with my computer. ➻ **Antonyms: 1. cheerful, happy 2. good, superior**

misery *noun* **1. pain, anguish, suffering, woe, distress, grief, agony, torment** Arthritis is a condition that causes much misery to its sufferers. **2. poverty, penury, adversity, need, trial, tribulation, hardship, misfortune** The homeless man lived in misery. ➻ **Antonyms: 1. well-being 2. wealth, prosperity**

misfortune *noun* **1. bad luck, ill fortune, trouble, ill luck, adversity, misery, sorrow** We had the misfortune to get a flat tire just as we set out on our trip. **2. blow, catastrophe, disaster, tragedy, trouble, setback, calamity, loss** The loss of our best player was a great misfortune for our volleyball team. ➻ **Antonyms: 1. good luck, fortune 2. blessing, advantage**

misgiving *noun* **qualm, reservation, anxiety, concern, doubt, fear, worry, hesitation, apprehension** He has no misgivings about doing a backward dive off the high board.

mishap *noun* **accident, mischance, misfortune, slip, misadventure, setback, disaster** I had a mishap with the hose while I was watering the plants. ➻ **Antonyms: luck, success, fortune**

mislead *verb* **deceive, fool, trick, dupe, hoodwink, delude, betray, gull** The advertisement misled people into thinking that the exercise machine would be easy to use.

misplace *verb* lose, mislay, forget, miss, displace, drop I occasionally misplace my eyeglasses. ➡ **Antonyms:** find, locate

miss *verb* 1. forget, neglect, overlook, skip, drop, let go, fail, omit, waste He fell asleep on the subway and missed his stop. 2. long for, yearn for, crave, desire, want, pine for, need I missed my family while I was away at summer camp. 3. avoid, dodge, escape, evade, lose, bypass, skip, leave out We'll miss the lunch-hour rush if we go to the restaurant early. ➡ **Antonyms: 1.** catch, get **3.** make, meet

missile *noun* 1. projectile, arrow, bolt, lance, dart, shaft, harpoon, spear, javelin The catapult was an early type of artillery that hurled stones, spears, and other missiles. 2. rocket, guided missile, ballistic missile, torpedo The fighter plane was armed with air-to-air missiles.

mission *noun* 1. assignment, job, objective, task, responsibility, goal, aim, undertaking The spy's mission was to gather information about the enemy. 2. commission, delegation, task force, embassy, deputation, legation, representative The United Nations sent a peacekeeping mission to help stop the war.

mist *noun* cloud, fog, haze, drizzle, vapor, steam, film, smog A heavy mist hung in the air just before sunrise. ◆ *verb* cloud, fog, steam, blur, becloud, befog, drizzle, sprinkle, rain The bathroom mirror mists up whenever anyone takes a hot shower.

mistake *noun* error, blunder, fault, inaccuracy, lapse, slip, slip-up, miscalculation I made only one mistake on my spelling test. ◆ *verb* confuse, mix up, confound, blunder, misinterpret, misconceive, slip up, err I mistook her for her twin sister.

mistaken *adjective* false, faulty, inaccurate, incorrect, wrong, untrue, fallacious, erroneous People once had the mistaken belief that Earth was flat. ➡ **Antonyms:** accurate, correct

mistreat *verb* abuse, harm, hurt, injure, damage, mishandle, maltreat, misuse, wrong Kind people don't mistreat their pets.

misty *adjective* cloudy, foggy, hazy, dewy, faint, vague We were not able to see the lunar eclipse because the evening was misty. ➡ **Antonyms:** clear, distinct

misunderstand *verb* confuse, misinterpret, misjudge, mistake, misread, confound, misconstrue I had trouble finding your house because I misunderstood the directions. ➡ **Antonyms:** comprehend, understand

misunderstanding *noun* 1. misconception, mix-up, confusion, error, mistake, blunder There was a misunderstanding about the time of our meeting. 2. quarrel, disagreement, argument, fight, conflict, squabble, breach, spat My sister and I resolved our misunderstanding. ➡ **Antonyms: 1.** understanding, comprehension **2.** agreement, harmony

misuse *noun* abuse, misapplication, mishandling, perversion, mistreatment, maltreatment, corruption The misuse of power can have disastrous consequences. ◆ *verb* abuse, mishandle, maltreat, corrupt, pervert, misapply, exploit Do not misuse the pencil sharpener by sharpening crayons in it.

mix *verb* 1. blend, combine, merge, scramble, mingle, stir, alloy, synthesize Cement is mixed with gravel and water to make concrete. 2. socialize, mingle, associate, fraternize, consort, hang out, hobnob I like to mix with a variety of people. 3. disorder, disorganize, disturb, disrupt, mess up, muddle, confuse, jumble I have just alphabetized my books—please don't mix them up. ◆ *noun* assortment, variety, combination, jumble, mixture, hodgepodge, potpourri There was an interesting mix of food at our potluck supper. ➡ **Antonyms:** *verb* **1.** divide, separate **2.** withdraw, retreat **3.** order, organize

mixture *noun* blend, combination, compound, mix, hodgepodge, medley, jumble, assortment My favorite drink is a mixture of cold tea and fruit juice.

moan *noun* howl, wail, yowl, groan, sob, whimper, murmur, whine, bay I heard an eerie moan that turned out to be the wind. ◆ *verb* wail, howl, groan, yowl, cry, sigh, sob, keen, whimper, bay Every Halloween, my brother walks around the house moaning like a ghost.

mob *noun* crowd, horde, mass, pack, swarm, throng, group, crush, multitude There was a mob of people at the shopping mall on the day before Christmas. ◆ *verb* crowd, press, swarm, throng, jostle, flock, surround Dozens of shouting reporters mobbed the politician.

mobile *adjective* movable, moving, portable, transportable, traveling, nomadic Volunteers set up a mobile kitchen to feed the homeless. ➡ **Antonyms:** immobile, stationary

mobilize *verb* assemble, marshal, muster, rally, prepare, ready, organize, summon The Red Cross mobilized its workers for disaster relief. ➡ **Antonyms:** disband, dismiss

mock *verb* laugh at, insult, jeer, ridicule, taunt, tease, scorn, scoff, deride Many people mocked the early automobiles. ◆ *adjective* artificial, fake, imitation, simulated, false, feigned, phony, sham The film crew built a mock spaceship for the science-fiction movie. ➡ **Antonyms:** *verb* compliment, praise ◆ *adjective* authentic, real

mode *noun* 1. fashion, manner, method, style, system, way, form, procedure, technique Steamboats and stagecoaches are two old-fashioned modes of transportation. 2. style, trend, fad, craze, fashion, vogue, furor, rage, chic, tone, thing The modes in clothing can change a lot from year to year.

model *noun* 1. miniature, replica, copy, duplicate, imitation, facsimile, figure I like to build models of military airplanes. 2. design, kind, style, type, variety, version, make, form We traded in our old car for a newer model. 3. example, ideal, pattern, standard, archetype, paradigm, paragon, hero My dancing teacher serves as a model of patience and persistence. ◆ *verb* design, fashion, make, shape, form, mold, copy, imitate, create The courthouse was modeled after an ancient Greek temple. ◆ *adjective* ideal, perfect, representative, standard, typical, admirable, exemplary He believes that being active in community affairs is part of being a model citizen.

moderate *adjective* 1. modest, reasonable, conservative, average, medium, ordinary, typical I like to shop at this store because they have good merchandise at moderate prices. 2. acceptable, adequate, decent, fair, common, passable, satisfactory, sufficient, mediocre This cellular phone is of only moderate quality. 3. mild, temperate, balmy, pleasant, calm The temperatures at this time of year are moderate. ◆ *verb* 1. restrain, tame, tone down, lessen, reduce, abate, temper My uncle has to moderate his eating habits for health reasons. 2. preside, chair, mediate, arbitrate, referee, umpire, regulate, control I was chosen to moderate a panel discussion on sex and dating. ➡ **Antonyms:** *adjective* 1. excessive, extreme 2. remarkable, extraordinary 3. stormy, extreme

modern *adjective* contemporary, current, new, present, recent, fresh, late, latter-day, modern-day, up-to-date High-rise office buildings are a modern form of architecture. ➡ **Antonyms:** ancient, old

modest *adjective* 1. humble, quiet, reserved, shy, demure, self-effacing, diffident The research scientist was modest about his discoveries. 2. limited, moderate, reasonable, average, small, middling, mediocre, medium My grandparents live on a modest income now that they have retired. ➡ **Antonyms:** 1. arrogant 2. excessive, large

modify *verb* adjust, alter, change, vary, reorganize, transform, adapt, moderate We modified our vacation plans to take advantage of the early snowfall.

moist *adjective* damp, wet, soggy, humid, dewy, dank, watery He used a moist rag to clean the dirt off his bicycle. ➡ **Antonyms:** dry, parched, arid

moisten *verb* dampen, wet, sprinkle, rinse, wash, spray Moisten the sponge before you wipe the counter. ➡ **Antonym:** dry

moisture *noun* dampness, wetness, water, fluid, liquid, humidity, drizzle, mist, dew Try to keep your books dry, for moisture will harm them. ➡ **Antonym:** dryness

mold[1] *noun* 1. form, cast, die, pattern, stamp, outline, shape, frame Candles are made by pouring hot wax into a mold. 2. type, character, description, stripe, temperament, nature, sort, bent, ilk He is of an independent mold. ◆ *verb* 1. fashion, form, shape, build, forge, make, model, sculpt, contour I molded small lumps of clay into beads. 2. influence, affect, guide, teach, indoctrinate, transform, control Parents are responsible for molding the characters of their children.

mold[2] *noun* blight, fungus, mildew, rot There's mold on this loaf of bread.

moment *noun* 1. instant, minute, second, flash, jiffy, wink, breath, twinkling, trice The doctor will be with you in just a moment. 2. hour, point, juncture, stage, period, time, spell, interval, season The end of a millennium is an important moment in time. 3. significance, importance, weight, consequence, note, value, import The first national radio broadcast was of great moment.

momentary *adjective* fleeting, temporary, transitory, short, brief, transient, ephemeral, short-lived He felt only momentary pain from the injection. ➡ **Antonyms:** lasting, permanent, prolonged

momentous *adjective* important, historic, major, significant, serious, crucial, weighty, memorable, fateful The lunar landing on July 20, 1969, was truly momentous. ➡ **Antonyms:** insignificant, unimportant

momentum *noun* impetus, energy, force, power, propulsion, thrust The bicyclist gained momentum as he coasted down the hill. ➡ **Antonyms:** rest, inactivity

monarch *noun* queen, ruler, sovereign, king, majesty Queen Elizabeth I was England's monarch from 1558 to 1603.

money *noun* **cash, currency, funds, revenue, lucre, specie, capital** I intend to save all the money that I earn until I have enough for an electric guitar.

monitor *noun* **overseer, director, guide, supervisor, watchdog, authority, auditor** Our school selects older students to be hallway monitors. ◆ *verb* **check, observe, watch, supervise, survey, audit, follow, control** Doctors monitored the seriously ill patient closely.

monopoly *noun* **sole possession, corner, ownership, control, syndicate, cartel, trust, consortium** The government has laws against a business gaining a monopoly of an industry.

monotonous *adjective* **boring, dull, tedious, tiresome, dreary, routine, uninteresting, wearisome** We found the long transcontinental flight monotonous. ● **Antonyms: exciting, interesting**

monotony *noun* **sameness, repetition, repetitiveness, boredom, tedium, humdrum, ennui** The monotony of the sound of the ship's engines lulled me to sleep. ● **Antonyms: variety, excitement, interest**

monster *noun* **1. giant, behemoth, mammoth, titan, leviathan, Goliath, colossus** The largest pumpkin on record was a monster that weighed over six hundred pounds. **2. beast, creature, brute, demon, fiend, freak, ogre, mutant, ghoul** My favorite movie monster is a giant lizard that destroys Tokyo.

monstrous *adjective* **1. frightening, gruesome, hideous, horrible, terrifying, shocking, dreadful** According to folklore, ogres are monstrous creatures that eat human beings. **2. colossal, enormous, gigantic, huge, immense, mammoth, jumbo, massive, tremendous** The sailboat was almost capsized by a monstrous wave. ● **Antonyms: 2. small, little, tiny**

monument *noun* **1. memorial, commemoration, remembrance, shrine, testament, tribute, reminder, witness** This statue is a monument to the pioneers who founded our town. **2. masterpiece, masterwork, classic, landmark, accomplishment, legacy, treasure** New York's Chrysler Building is a monument of the art deco movement.

mood *noun* **frame of mind, spirits, temper, temperament, disposition, humor, vein** I am usually in a cheerful mood.

moody *adjective* **1. temperamental, mercurial, erratic, volatile, capricious, changeable, flighty** The moody man was happy one moment and sad the next. **2. gloomy, sulky,** melancholy, sullen, morose, sad, doleful, surly She prefers to be by herself when she is feeling moody. ● **Antonyms: 1. stable, calm, balanced 2. cheerful, happy**

moor *verb* **fasten, fix, lash, secure, tie, anchor, tether, bind, rope** The crew moored their ship to the dock. ● **Antonyms: release, untie**

mop *verb* **swab, sponge, wipe, clean, scrub, wash, brush, rub** Please mop up the spilled milk.

mope *verb* **brood, pout, sulk, languish, worry, grieve, whine, fret** I moped all afternoon when my package didn't arrive in the mail.

moral *adjective* **good, honest, honorable, upright, virtuous, just, principled, scrupulous, ethical** A moral person does not cheat or steal. ◆ *noun* **lesson, meaning, message, teaching, proverb, ethic, dictum, rule** A fable is a story that has a moral. ● **Antonyms:** *adjective* **immoral, unethical, dishonorable**

morale *noun* **spirit, mood, attitude, self-esteem, resolve, disposition, confidence, esprit** Morale at our school has improved under our new principal.

morbid *adjective* **1. diseased, malignant, infected, pathological, decaying, contaminated, festering, infectious** The doctor said that the wound, if not cared for, would become morbid. **2. gloomy, gruesome, macabre, unwholesome, grisly, sick, dark, hideous** Psychologists say that it is normal to have morbid thoughts sometimes. ● **Antonyms: 1. healthy, sound 2. wholesome**

more *adjective* **additional, extra, added, further, new, other, fresh, another** Do you need more time to finish? ◆ *noun* **extra, addition, another, increase, supplement, refill, surplus, replenishment** When we ran out of bagels, I went to the bakery to get more. ◆ *adverb* **additionally, further, beyond, still, too, yet, longer, also** Our coach said that we will have to practice more.

moreover *adverb* **additionally, furthermore, besides, further, still, yet, too, also, likewise** Moreover, we are required to include a bibliography with our report.

morning *noun* **sunup, dawn, sunrise, daybreak, morn, forenoon** Saturday morning is my favorite time of the week. ● **Antonyms: sunset, evening**

moron *noun* **idiot, half-wit, imbecile, dolt, ninny, dunce, dullard, dummy, blockhead** We acted like morons when we were at the mall.

morsel *noun* **bite, crumb, mouthful, tidbit, taste, bit, dollop, scrap** When we were finished with the cake, there wasn't a morsel left.

mortal *adjective* **1. human, perishable, earthly, impermanent, transient, vulnerable** We are all mortal beings, and none of us will live forever. **2. deadly, fatal, lethal, terminal, deathly, killing, murderous** A lion delivers a mortal wound by biting its prey on the back of the neck. **3. unrelenting, implacable, bitter, murderous, merciless, ruthless** A shrew is a snake's mortal enemy. **4. extreme, dire, desperate, grave, deep, intense, terrible, urgent** We were in mortal danger during the hurricane. ◆ *noun* **human, human being, person, man, woman, body, soul, individual** In Greek mythology, Hercules was a mortal who possessed godlike strength. ➡ **Antonyms:** *adjective* **1. immortal 2. harmless, safe 3. lenient**

most *adjective* **greater, greatest, larger, largest, maximum, top, better, best** The person who can lift the most weight will win the medal. ◆ *noun* **almost all, nearly all, best part, majority, maximum, peak, bulk** I spend most of my allowance on CDs. ◆ *adverb* **exceedingly, extremely, exceptionally, quite, very, remarkably, greatly, highly** The magician's performance was most impressive. ➡ **Antonyms:** *adjective* **least, lowest**

mostly *adverb* **chiefly, largely, mainly, primarily, principally, generally, overall, predominantly** I read mostly adventure stories.

mother *noun* **mom, mama, ma, mommy, mamma, mummy, female parent** I love my mother. ◆ *verb* **nurture, foster, nurse, nourish, protect, sustain, watch, care for** I mothered the injured hummingbird until it could fly again.

motion *noun* **1. movement, flux, locomotion, progress, action, activity, move, stir** Because sharks are very heavy, they have to remain in constant motion or they will sink. **2. proposal, recommendation, suggestion, measure, proposition, submission, plan** I made a motion that the meeting be adjourned. ◆ *verb* **beckon, gesture, indicate, signal, wave, gesticulate, flag, nod, direct** My aunt motioned for me to sit down beside her.

motivate *verb* **stimulate, inspire, induce, propel, stir, provoke, prompt, persuade** The graduation speaker motivated us to set goals for our lives. ➡ **Antonyms: discourage, dissuade**

motive *noun* **motivation, incentive, objective, aim, purpose, reason, rationale, stimulus, inducement** My motive for doing extra credit is to get a better grade.

motley *adjective* **assorted, mixed, varied, heterogeneous, diverse, disparate** There was a motley assortment of winter clothing in the hall closet. ➡ **Antonyms: uniform, homogeneous**

motor *noun* **engine, power plant, power source, machine, mechanism, appliance, generator** My model airplane has a miniature, battery-powered motor. ◆ *adjective* **mobile, moving, traveling, mechanized, motorized, vehicular** My grandparents are traveling through Alaska in their motor home.

motto *noun* **expression, saying, slogan, principle, rule, maxim, proverb, adage, cry** The Boy Scout motto is "Be Prepared."

mound *noun* **heap, hill, mass, pile, stack, mountain, dune, hillock, knoll, hummock** Some species of ants form huge mounds of soil when they dig their nests.

mount *verb* **1. climb, ascend, rise, go up, clamber up, scale** I mounted the ladder to hang a picture. **2. install, place, position, affix, fit, exhibit, frame, show** Dad mounted a pair of antique snowshoes above our fireplace. **3. build, grow, increase, rise, heighten, soar, swell, multiply** Excitement mounted as the swimmers neared the finish line. ➡ **Antonyms: 1. descend, go down 2. remove, dismount 3. decrease, lower**

mountain *noun* **1. peak, summit, hill, mound, crag, mesa, dome, mount** We camped at the base of a majestic, snow-capped mountain. **2. heap, mass, pile, stack, abundance, accumulation, ton, slew** We have a mountain of trash that we need to take to the dump.

mourn *verb* **grieve, sorrow, lament, suffer, cry, keen, sob, wail, weep, pine** It is natural to mourn when someone we care about dies.

mouth *noun* **opening, entrance, portal, door, aperture, gateway, outlet, access** We paused at the mouth of the cave before deciding to explore it. ◆ *verb* **speak, say, voice, pronounce, utter, spout, orate, repeat** The actor mouthed his lines without paying attention.

move *verb* **1. carry, convey, shift, change, transport, budge, dislodge, stir** I moved my chair closer to the TV. **2. relocate, transfer, depart, leave, travel, migrate, remove** My uncle recently moved from Maryland to Iowa. **3. advance, progress, go forward, press on, get along, proceed, start, act** The police officer motioned the traffic to move. **4. propose, advocate, urge, submit, put forth, recommend, request** I move that we have a party to raise money. **5. cause, influence, inspire, motivate, persuade, stimulate, convince, prompt** What moved you to join the karate club? **6. affect, disturb, touch, impress, stir, excite, rouse, provoke, agitate** I was deeply moved by the book's tragic love story. ◆ *noun* **1. motion, movement, action, maneuver, step, turn** The police officer ordered the suspect not to make a move. **2. step, tactic, maneuver, procedure, measure, deed, act, artifice** In a surprising move, the president of the company announced his resignation.

movement *noun* **1. motion, stirring, action, activity, move, shift, stir, operation** A sudden movement in the bushes caught my attention. **2. campaign, crusade, drive, push, cause, group, faction, coalition** There is a movement in our neighborhood to start a community garden. **3. tendency, trend, drift, leaning, inclination, swing, flow, current** Our market survey revealed a movement towards smaller and more powerful computers.

movie *noun* **film, motion picture, cinema, feature, picture, show** My favorite movie will soon be available on video.

moving *adjective* **1. mobile, changing, shifting, movable, traveling, transportable** The baby gave rapt attention to the moving figures on the mobile over his crib. **2. affecting, stirring, touching, poignant, heart-rending, emotional, inspiring, provoking** I think *Black Beauty* is a moving story. ● **Antonyms: 1. stationary, still 2. unaffecting, uninspiring**

mow *verb* **clip, cut, trim, crop, shear, hack, shorten, scythe** The grass is too wet to mow right now.

much *adjective* **abundant, considerable, great, plentiful, ample, profuse** Your visit has brought us much joy. ◆ *noun* **lot, great deal, loads, abundance, plenty, profusion, wealth** Much had been done to rebuild the area since the hurricane passed through last fall. ◆ *adverb* **1. exceedingly, greatly, highly, very, considerably, exceptionally** We are much taken with the idea of living abroad for a year. **2. quite, about, almost, approximately, nearly, roughly, rather, somewhat** Frozen yogurt tastes much like ice cream. ● **Antonyms:** *adjective* **little, scarce** ◆ *noun* **little**

muck *noun* **slime, mire, mud, ooze, slop, dirt, filth, sludge, slush** We wiped off the muck that was splashed on us from the passing car.

mud *noun* **1. mire, muck, slime, dirt, ooze, slop, filth, earth** I took off my boots to avoid tracking mud into the house. **2. accusation, slander, libel, dirt, defamation, mudslinging, vilification** The candidates threw a lot of mud during the campaign.

muffle *verb* **1. wrap, swathe, cover, envelop, veil, enfold, swaddle, conceal, protect** I muffled my throat with a scarf to keep warm. **2. dampen, silence, soften, stifle, suppress, gag, hush, quiet** I put my hand over my mouth to muffle my giggles. ● **Antonyms: 1. unwrap, reveal 2. amplify**

muggy *adjective* **humid, sticky, damp, moist, steamy, soggy, sultry, clammy** I never feel like doing much on hot, muggy days. ● **Antonyms: dry, arid**

multiply *verb* **grow, increase, mount, swell, burgeon, proliferate, mushroom, expand** The difficulties of the climb multiplied as the mountaineers got close to the summit. ● **Antonyms: decrease, diminish**

multitude *noun* **crowd, host, legion, horde, throng, mob, army, drove** A multitude of tourists boarded the ferry to cross the English Channel.

mumble *verb* **murmur, mutter, whisper, stammer, stutter** It's hard for me to understand you when you mumble. ◆ *noun* **murmur, whisper, mutter, undertone, stammer, stutter** Please stop speaking in a mumble.

munch *verb* **chew, snack, gnaw, grind, champ, chomp, crunch, bite, eat** I like to munch on carrots and celery.

municipal *adjective* **public, civic, community, city, metropolitan, town, urban** Our town has both a municipal swimming pool and a library.

municipality *noun* **city, town, metropolis, burg, village, township, district, borough** Our municipality is governed by a mayor and a city council.

murder *noun* **homicide, killing, slaying, assassination, massacre, manslaughter, bloodshed** The suspect has been charged with attempted murder. ◆ *verb* **assassinate, kill, slay, massacre, slaughter, annihilate, finish off, liquidate** President Abraham Lincoln was murdered by John Wilkes Booth on April 14, 1865.

murmur *noun* **drone, rumble, purr, hum, whisper, undertone, swish, purl, sigh** The murmur of the wind through the pine trees is very soothing. ◆ *verb* **sigh, rustle, burble, purr, buzz, drone, ripple, trickle** I can hear the sea as it murmurs in the distance.

muscle *noun* **1. strength, brawn, prowess, might, fitness, endurance, vigor, stamina** It takes a lot of muscle to lift 250 pounds. **2. power, authority, influence, force, clout, potency, weight, impact** Only the governor has the muscle to push the program through the legislature. ◆ *verb* **elbow, push, jostle, ram, shove, shoulder, squeeze, poke** We muscled our way through the crowd.

muse *verb* **consider, ponder, meditate, mull, think, reflect, deliberate, contemplate** I mused all afternoon on whether I should try to get a part-time job.

> ### Word Group
>
> **Music** is a pleasing or meaningful combination of sounds. **Music** is a general term with no true synonyms. Here are some common types of music:
>
> big band, bluegrass, blues, calypso, classical, country, disco, folk, gospel, heavy metal, hip-hop, jazz, New Age, pop, rap, reggae, rock, salsa, soul, swing

musical *adjective* **melodious, harmonious, sweet, lyrical, mellow, tuneful, symphonic, trilling, warbling** The canary is prized for its musical song. ◆ **Antonyms: harsh, shrill, discordant**

muss *verb* **mess up, disorder, rumple, disturb, dishevel, jumble, tangle, muddle** Please don't muss my hair. ◆ **Antonyms: tidy, straighten, smooth**

must *verb* **have to, have got to, need to, ought to, should, be necessary** Our book reports must be turned in next Wednesday. ◆ *noun* **necessity, requirement, essential, imperative, fundamental, duty, need, prerequisite** Having water to drink is a must for human beings.

muster *verb* **1. assemble, mobilize, round up, rally, marshal, convene, organize, group** The general mustered his troops. **2. gather, summon, invoke, call forth, send for, draw on, elicit** I had to muster all my resolve in order to finish the triathlon. ◆ *noun* **roundup, assembly, meeting, gathering, convocation, convention** The calves are branded during the muster in the fall.

musty *adjective* **1. moldy, funky, foul, rancid, rank, rotten, stale** These books smell musty after having been stored in the basement. **2. overused, old-fashioned, trite, hackneyed, dull, obsolete, worn-out, antiquated** You have musty ideas for someone so young. ◆ **Antonyms: 1. fresh, sweet 2. new, original**

mutation *noun* **change, metamorphosis, alteration, transformation, permutation, shift, modification, variation** The movie is about a man who goes through a mutation and becomes a fly.

mute *adjective* **silent, inarticulate, dumb, voiceless, mum, tongue-tied, quiet, speechless, wordless, reserved** I was mute during class discussion because I had not done the assigned reading. ◆ *verb* **muffle, soften, dampen, deaden, stifle, tone down, reduce, silence, quiet, lower** I muted the volume of the radio when the telephone rang. ◆ **Antonyms:** *adjective* **talkative, garrulous** ◆ *verb* **amplify, intensify, raise**

mutilate *verb* **1. dismember, maim, disfigure, cripple, mangle, lame, amputate** In horror movies, the villains frequently mutilate their victims. **2. ruin, damage, spoil, mar, destroy, impair, demolish, butcher, wreck** I mutilated my hair by trying to cut it myself. ◆ **Antonyms: 2. repair, improve**

mutiny *noun* **rebellion, revolt, uprising, insurrection, takeover, revolution, insurgence** The mutiny on HMS *Bounty* in 1789 is one of the most famous in history. ◆ *verb* **rebel, revolt, rise up, resist, riot, disobey, defy** The sailors mutinied and took charge of the ship.

mutter *verb* **1. mumble, murmur, whisper, jabber, gibber, splutter, stutter** I could hear her muttering to herself. **2. complain, grumble, carp, gripe, grouch, grouse, deplore, criticize** We muttered about the lack of time we had to prepare for the test.

mutual *adjective* **common, joint, shared, communal, similar, equivalent, reciprocal** My best friend and I have a mutual love of dancing.

muzzle *verb* **gag, quiet, suppress, restrain, throttle, stifle, censor, curb** The dictator muzzled the press. ◆ **Antonyms: free, loose**

myriad *adjective* **numerous, many, legion, countless, multitudinous, innumerable, limitless** Her myriad interests bring her into contact with people from diverse backgrounds. ◆ **Antonym: few**

mysterious *adjective* **1. secretive, furtive, secret, concealed, hidden, veiled, dark, covert** Many people think that mysterious experiments take place in Area 51. **2. strange, puzzling, weird, inexplicable, uncanny, baffling, enigmatic, inscrutable** We became somewhat apprehensive when we heard a mysterious sound. ◆ **Antonyms: 1. open, revealed 2. obvious, clear**

mystery *noun* **question, puzzle, riddle, enigma, secret, problem, perplexity, conundrum** Why so many ships have been lost in the Devil's Triangle remains a mystery. ◆ **Antonyms: solution, answer**

mystical *adjective* mystic, spiritual, transcendental, metaphysical, occult, magical, supernatural, visionary His mystical beliefs stress the importance of insight and intuition.

mystify *verb* baffle, bewilder, confuse, perplex, puzzle, confound, stump, elude Easter Island's huge statues continue to mystify archaeologists. ◆ **Antonyms:** clarify, illuminate, explain

myth *noun* **1.** folk tale, legend, story, fable, lore, saga There are myths from many cultures describing how the world was made. **2.** fantasy, fiction, figment, invention, untruth, nonsense, superstition, absurdity Most people think that flying saucers are a myth.

mythical *adjective* fictitious, imaginary, legendary, unreal, fabled, fanciful, mythological, fabulous Shangri-La is a mythical paradise where people never grow old. ◆ **Antonyms:** actual, real

mythology *noun* folklore, myth, legend, lore, tradition, belief, tales, story In Greek mythology, Poseidon was god of the sea.

Nn

nab *verb* **arrest, apprehend, capture, seize, catch, collar, snatch, grab** The police nabbed the rioters as they were looting the store. ⟐ **Antonyms: release, liberate**

nag *verb* **carp at, pick on, hound, pester, scold, complain, torment, badger** My parents don't nag me as long as I get my chores done on time. ⟐ *noun* **complainer, scold, tormentor, pest, nuisance, shrew, vixen** Sometimes my sister is a nag.

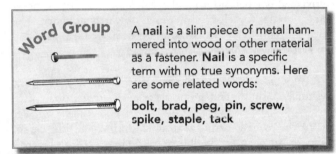

Word Group A **nail** is a slim piece of metal hammered into wood or other material as a fastener. **Nail** is a specific term with no true synonyms. Here are some related words:

bolt, brad, peg, pin, screw, spike, staple, tack

naive *adjective* **simple, unsophisticated, artless, trusting, childlike, guileless, innocent, ingenuous** It is naive to believe that we can maintain good health without proper nutrition and exercise. ⟐ **Antonym: sophisticated**

naked *adjective* **1. bare, nude, unclad, unclothed, exposed, undressed, stripped** My little brother ran naked through the house after his bath. **2. unaided, unassisted, unadorned, natural, plain, simple, open, direct** Bacteria are too small to be seen by the naked eye. ⟐ **Antonyms: 1. clothed, dressed**

name *noun* **1. appellation, designation, title, label, term, nickname, tag, epithet** The name of the tallest mountain in the world is Mount Everest. **2. reputation, repute, character, distinction, fame, eminence, esteem** My brother wants to go to a college that has a good name. **3. celebrity, star, superstar, notable, personality, luminary** The Academy Awards ceremony always has a famous name as the emcee. ⟐ *verb* **1. call, designate, title, label, term, dub, christen, nickname, baptize** I named my dog Guy Fawkes. **2. identify, itemize, list, mention, specify, cite, indicate, enumerate** Can you name all 50 states? **3. set, fix, specify, announce, designate, choose, pick, denote, make** We named the date for the next meeting of our club. **4. nominate, appoint, delegate, elect, select, ordain, authorize** We have to name someone to represent us on the student council.

nap[1] *noun* **catnap, doze, rest, siesta, snooze, sleep, slumber** My grandmother takes afternoon naps. ⟐ *verb* **catnap, doze, drowse, snooze, sleep, slumber, nod off** Our turtle is napping in the sun.

nap[2] *noun* **fuzz, pile, shag, flocking, woof, bristle, fluff** The nap on velvet is soft and smooth.

narcotic *noun* **opiate, sedative, soporific, anesthetic, painkiller, drug** Doctors sometimes prescribe narcotics for patients who are in great pain.

narrate *verb* **describe, recite, recount, relate, report, tell, chronicle, detail** Our class listened intently as the wild animal photographer narrated her adventures.

narrative *noun* **history, account, chronicle, report, story, tale, yarn, saga, description** I wrote a narrative of my grandmother's life.

narrow *adjective* **1. confining, cramped, snug, tight, slender, thin, close, constricted** The cavers inched their way along the narrow passage. **2. scant, meager, paltry, spare, limited, poor** Our library is small and has a narrow selection of books on tape. **3. narrow-minded, rigid, petty, bigoted, intolerant, prejudiced, biased** He has a narrow outlook on that issue. **4. close, small, little, tiny, slim, fine, thin, tenuous, precarious** The horse won the race by a narrow margin. ⟐ *verb* **contract, taper, reduce, tighten, diminish, constrict, shrink** The road narrows as it goes through the tunnel. ⟐ **Antonyms:** *adjective* **1. & 2. broad, wide 3. liberal, tolerant 4. big, extensive** ⟐ *verb* **widen**

nasty *adjective* **1. filthy, dirty, unclean, foul, vile, awful, bad, atrocious, offensive** A nasty smell came from the container of leftovers. **2. indecent, smutty, sordid, obscene, ribald, immodest, lewd** My parents do not condone nasty language. **3. malicious, spiteful, cruel, evil, hateful, mean, vicious, wicked** The movie audience cheered when the nasty villain was defeated. **4. dangerous, harmful, injurious, painful, serious, severe, terrible, dreadful** The skier took a nasty fall. ⟐ **Antonyms: 1. clean, pure, fresh 2. decent, virtuous 3. honorable, good 4. safe, minor**

nation *noun* **1. country, state, domain, land, realm, republic, commonwealth** Canada and Mexico are the two nations that border the continental United States. **2. people,**

race, tribe, stock, line, population, society About six thousand members of the Hopi nation live in Arizona.

native *adjective* 1. innate, natural, hereditary, inherited, congenital, inborn All humans have certain native abilities. 2. indigenous, endemic, aboriginal, original, domestic, local Giant pandas are native to China. ◆ *noun* citizen, inhabitant, resident, local, dweller, national, countryman, countrywoman We are both natives of South Dakota. ➡ **Antonyms:** *adjective* 1. learned 2. foreign ◆ *noun* foreigner, stranger

natural *adjective* 1. organic, pure, raw, unrefined, plain, unprocessed, unadulterated Honey is a natural sweetener. 2. native, wild, lifelike, realistic, untamed, normal, regular, typical The San Diego Zoo is famous for displaying animals in their natural surroundings. 3. instinctive, inherent, innate, hereditary, inborn, genetic, intrinsic Lions and tigers have a natural tendency to chase anything that runs away from them. 4. unaffected, straightforward, open, unsophisticated, sincere, true, real Small children act in a natural manner. ➡ **Antonyms:** 1. artificial, cultured 2. unnatural 3. learned 4. insincere, sophisticated

naturally *adverb* 1. normally, genuinely, regularly, routinely, typically, inherently, spontaneously I tried to speak naturally even though I was nervous. 2. logically, obviously, of course, certainly, surely, clearly, plainly Naturally we'll be having turkey for Thanksgiving dinner.

nature *noun* 1. environment, outdoors, world, creation, universe, countryside, cosmos I learn more about nature every time I take a walk in the woods. 2. kind, sort, type, stripe, variety, stamp, brand, mold, ilk I am here on business of a personal nature. 3. character, disposition, essence, personality, quality, spirit, makeup, temper I get along with people who have gentle natures.

naughty *adjective* 1. bad, disobedient, ill-behaved, mischievous, unruly, headstrong, troublesome My little sister was being naughty when she threw her food onto the floor. 2. bad, indecent, dirty, vulgar, improper, immodest, unbecoming, unbefitting My little brother got into trouble for saying a naughty word. ➡ **Antonyms:** 1. obedient, good 2. clean, decent, proper

nausea *noun* upset stomach, indigestion, sickness, queasiness, biliousness, qualm, vomiting My nausea was caused by riding the roller coaster right after I had eaten.

nautical *adjective* marine, maritime, naval, shipping, boating, sailing, seagoing, navigational "Forecastle" is a nautical term that refers to the forward part of a ship's deck.

navigate *verb* guide, pilot, steer, direct, maneuver, voyage, run, head, lead Early sailors navigated by using the stars as a guide.

navy *noun* armada, fleet, naval forces, flotilla, task force, ships England's navy gained control of the seas by defeating the Spanish in 1588.

near *adverb* 1. nearly, almost, about I was near exhausted by the long climb. 2. close, nearby, nigh, hard Winter drew near and the days began to be shorter and colder. ◆ *adjective* 1. close, adjacent, immediate, nearby, adjoining, next, contiguous Our nearest neighbor lives two miles away. 2. close, immediate, related, intimate, connected The orphaned boy had no near relatives. ◆ *verb* approach, draw near, come to, close on, move toward, advance The freight train blew its whistle as it neared the station. ➡ **Antonyms:** *adjective* distant, far

nearly *adverb* about, almost, approximately, roughly, virtually, nigh, near I am nearly as tall as my mom.

neat *adjective* 1. orderly, organized, precise, tidy, clean, spruce, trim, smart, well-groomed He stacked his baseball cards in neat piles. 2. skillful, adroit, deft, clever, expert, nimble, dexterous Her dance movements are neat. ➡ **Antonyms:** 1. sloppy, disorderly 2. clumsy, inept, awkward

nebulous *adjective* vague, unclear, indefinite, hazy, indistinct, cloudy, ambiguous Grace's plans for the future are still nebulous. ➡ **Antonyms:** clear, distinct, definite

necessary *adjective* 1. essential, important, needed, required, requisite, indispensable My art teacher furnished all of the necessary supplies for making masks. 2. required, compulsory, imperative, mandatory, obligatory, inevitable, unavoidable, certain It is necessary to pay taxes on earned income. ➡ **Antonyms:** optional, unnecessary

necessity *noun* 1. essential, need, requirement, fundamental, basic, prerequisite, must Water is a necessity for all life on Earth. 2. call, cause, grounds, occasion, reason, demand, imperative, exigency There was great necessity to hurry, as we had to catch the last train into town.

need *noun* 1. essential, necessity, want, requirement, exigency, desire, fundamental Pioneer families had to provide for most of their own needs. 2. necessity, obligation, call, demand, imperative, responsibility, commitment My father commented that there was no need to tie up the telephone all evening. 3. poverty, misfortune, neediness, penury, indigence, destitution, impoverishment

My family was in need until my dad got a new job. ◆ *verb* **require, want, lack, demand, desire, crave, covet, miss** We need two more players for our team. ● **Antonyms:** *verb* **have, possess**

needle *verb* **tease, taunt, heckle, hector, annoy, badger, goad, provoke** My brother needles me about my height.

needless *adjective* **pointless, useless, unnecessary, redundant, nonessential, dispensable, superfluous** It is needless to ask me again because I have made up my mind. ● **Antonyms: essential, necessary**

needy *adjective* **destitute, impoverished, penniless, poor, poverty-stricken, indigent, broke, bankrupt** Every Thanksgiving, our school holds a drive to collect food for needy families. ● **Antonyms: rich, wealthy**

nefarious *adjective* **evil, wicked, bad, sinful, heinous, villainous, infamous, abominable, vile** His nefarious plan was discovered just in time to prevent a catastrophe. ● **Antonyms: good, virtuous, noble**

negative *adjective* **adverse, bad, pessimistic, unfavorable, unsatisfactory, unenthusiastic, contrary** The movie received many negative reviews. ● **Antonyms: positive, good**

neglect *verb* **fail, omit, disregard, ignore, overlook, skip, forget, slight** The man's phone was disconnected because he neglected to pay the bill. ◆ *noun* **disregard, inattention, oversight, negligence, dereliction, forgetfulness, slight** The dilapidated old barn has suffered from years of neglect. ● **Antonyms:** *verb* **regard, attend** ◆ *noun* **attention, care**

negligent *adjective* **careless, inattentive, remiss, irresponsible, lax, neglectful, slack, derelict** The negligent driver got a ticket for running a red light. ● **Antonyms: attentive, careful**

negligible *adjective* **insignificant, slight, minor, modest, minute, inconsiderable, small, trifling, trivial** The errors made during our concert were negligible. ● **Antonyms: considerable, large**

negotiate *verb* **1. arrange, conclude, fix, set, settle, resolve, decide** The details of the agreement have been negotiated. **2. cross, traverse, pass, clear, surmount, travel, move** The Khyber Pass on the border of Pakistan and Afghanistan is difficult to negotiate. **3. confer, discuss, parley, bargain, talk, speak, debate, haggle, dicker** The players and team owners have agreed to negotiate.

neighborhood *noun* **area, community, district, locality, block, street, quarter, region, precinct, territory** We have lived in the same neighborhood for ten years.

nerve *noun* **1. boldness, bravery, courage, daring, grit, mettle, spirit, pluck, fortitude** It took a lot of nerve to ski down that steep hill. **2. audacity, impudence, insolence, chutzpah, brashness, effrontery, disrespect** The clerk showed a lot of nerve when he talked back to his boss. ● **Antonyms: 1. cowardice, timidity 2. respect, courtesy**

nervous *adjective* **anxious, distressed, fearful, tense, uneasy, upset, edgy, skittish** Big dogs make me nervous. ● **Antonyms: calm, relaxed**

nest *noun* **retreat, refuge, shelter, sanctuary, hideaway, den, hangout, home** My bedroom is a welcome nest after a hard day at school.

nestle *verb* **cuddle, snuggle, huddle, nuzzle, settle, embrace, clasp, hug, squeeze** My little sister nestled in my arms as I read her a story.

net[1] *noun* **netting, mesh, screen, web, webbing, network, seine** On my serve, I hit the tennis ball into the net. ◆ *verb* **capture, catch, get, snare, trap, bag, grab, secure, take** Dad netted several trout on his last fishing trip.

net[2] *noun* **yield, gain, profit, proceeds, earnings, returns, winnings** We calculated the net from our book sale. ◆ *verb* **earn, clear, gain, reap, bring in, make, realize, win, profit** I hope to net enough money from the garage sale to buy a snowboard.

nettle *verb* **annoy, provoke, harass, upset, irritate, vex, bother, irk** Don't nettle the bees!

neutral *adjective* **1. nonpartisan, detached, impartial, indifferent, unbiased, uninvolved, uncommitted** Switzerland was neutral during both world wars. **2. bland, colorless, drab, flat, achromatic, toneless, pale, weak** The cafeteria is painted a neutral color. ● **Antonyms: 1. aligned, partial 2. colorful**

nevertheless *adverb* **anyway, nonetheless, regardless, however, still, yet, anyhow, all the same** I didn't feel very well this morning, but I went to school nevertheless.

new *adjective* **1. brand-new, fresh, unused, current, modern, recent, up-to-date, newfangled** Everyone in the family wants to use our new camcorder. **2. different, fresh, strange, unfamiliar, unknown, unheard-of** There are many new students in my class this year. **3. additional, further,**

more, added, other, supplementary, another, extra Medical researchers have recently made new gains in cancer prevention. 4. novel, original, unique, unusual, untried, distinct, different, creative I have an idea for a new way to recycle soda bottles. ◆ Antonyms: 1. old, used 2. familiar 4. common, unoriginal

newly *adverb* just, freshly, lately, recently, fresh, of late, anew, afresh I love my newly redecorated bedroom.

news *noun* information, report, story, intelligence, tidings, data, bulletin, knowledge Have you heard the news about the movie that is going to be made in our town?

newspaper *noun* gazette, journal, paper, daily, tabloid, weekly, review Our local newspaper is published just once a week.

next *adjective* 1. coming, following, subsequent, ensuing, succeeding, successive I ordered a book on Tuesday, and it arrived the next week. 2. adjacent, adjoining, contiguous, nearest, closest, immediate My best friend lives on the next block. ◆ *adverb* hereafter, later, subsequently, after, afterward, since, thereafter I've seen this movie before, but I don't recall what happens next. ◆ Antonyms: *adjective* 1. preceding, previous 2. distant, farthest

nibble *verb* chew, gnaw, munch, bite, nip, peck, nosh, crop, eat My rabbit nibbled on the carrot that I gave him. ◆ *noun* bite, taste, bit, morsel, peck, snack, tidbit, crumb I took a nibble of the cheesecake.

nice *adjective* 1. agreeable, delightful, enjoyable, good, pleasant, pleasing, enchanting, wonderful To me, no flower smells as nice as a rose. 2. decent, kind, polite, thoughtful, courteous, proper, considerate, cordial It was nice of you to share your umbrella with me. 3. skilled, precise, accurate, exacting, meticulous, subtle, delicate, fine She does nice work repairing antique furniture. 4. polished, refined, cultured, respectable, becoming, correct, cultivated His manners are not as nice as they could be. ◆ Antonyms: 1. terrible, unpleasant 2. mean, unkind 3. crude, coarse 4. rough

niche *noun* recess, alcove, nook, hollow, cavity, crevice, opening, place I like to keep a vase of fresh flowers in the niche in the living room wall.

nick *noun* chip, cut, dent, notch, scar, scratch, mark, mar, gash The antique table was in good condition except for a few nicks on its legs. ◆ *verb* cut, scratch, injure, chip, dent, mar, notch, scar, score Dad nicked himself while shaving this morning.

nigh *adverb* almost, nearly, near, practically, about, approximately, close to It is nigh time for me to go to play rehearsal.

night *noun* nighttime, evening, nightfall, sundown, bedtime, eventide, twilight I like to see the fireflies come out at night. ◆ Antonyms: day, daytime

nil *noun* nothing, not anything, zero, naught, null, aught, cipher Our efforts to get him to go to the party amounted to nil.

nimble *adjective* 1. agile, deft, adroit, dexterous, spry, lively, swift, sprightly You have to have nimble fingers to play the guitar. 2. clever, smart, alert, bright, quick, quick-witted, facile, prompt The quiz show contestant had a nimble mind. ◆ Antonyms: 1. awkward, clumsy 2. dull, slow

nip[1] *verb* 1. bite, snap at, snatch at, clip, squeeze, tweak, pinch My dog got overexcited and nipped me as we played together. 2. thwart, stop, check, cut, curtail, prevent, frustrate, destroy, discourage Dad nipped our plan to jump off the roof into a pile of leaves. ◆ Antonyms: 2. encourage, promote

nip[2] *noun* drop, swallow, mouthful, taste, sip, shot, dram, swig He took a nip of brandy.

noble *adjective* 1. aristocratic, highborn, royal, upperclass, titled, blue-blooded, elite, wellborn The prince was required to marry a woman who was of noble birth. 2. honorable, generous, virtuous, chivalrous, admirable, magnanimous, excellent Helping people learn to read is a noble cause. 3. grand, imposing, magnificent, majestic, stately, dignified, splendid, august, impressive The Sierra Nevada is a chain of noble mountains. ◆ *noun* aristocrat, lady, lord, nobleman, noblewoman, patrician, peer, blue blood, royalty Many nobles attended the queen's coronation. ◆ Antonyms: *adjective* 2. self-serving, base, mean 3. unimpressive ◆ *noun* commoner

noise *noun* clamor, din, racket, sound, tumult, uproar, hubbub, pandemonium The noise from the barking dogs woke me. ◆ Antonyms: quiet, silence

noisy *adjective* loud, blaring, clamorous, deafening, resounding, rackety, earsplitting Our old lawnmower is very noisy. ◆ Antonyms: quiet, silent, noiseless

nomad *noun* wanderer, roamer, migrant, pilgrim, rover, wayfarer, gypsy, tramp Nomads are considered an intermediate group between hunter-gatherers and farmers.

nominate *verb* **appoint, choose, designate, name, propose, select, commission, assign** We nominated three candidates for the office of class president.

nonchalant *adjective* **calm, cool, collected, carefree, even-tempered, casual, easygoing, detached** The actor's nonchalant style is much admired by his fans. ● **Antonyms: anxious, agitated**

nonsense *noun* **absurdity, craziness, foolishness, silliness, stupidity, balderdash, poppycock, drivel** We made up a funny story that was pure nonsense. ● **Antonyms: fact, reason, sense**

nook *noun* **recess, alcove, niche, corner, cubbyhole, bay, inglenook, place** Our kitchen has a breakfast nook.

normal *adjective* **average, ordinary, regular, standard, typical, usual, habitual, common, conventional** The river returned to its normal level one week after the flood. ● **Antonyms: abnormal, unusual**

nostalgia *noun* **yearning, longing, homesickness, sentimentality, wistfulness, pining** This author writes about the early 20th century with nostalgia.

notable *adjective* **eminent, great, important, memorable, noteworthy, striking, famous, remarkable** The signing of the Declaration of Independence was a notable event in American history. ● **Antonyms: ordinary, unimportant**

notch *noun* **groove, indentation, nick, chip, cut, cleft, dent, serration** An arrow has a notch on its end to allow it to get a good grip on the bowstring. ◆ *verb* **chip, cut, nick, chop, scratch, scallop, gash, chisel** We notched the logs so that they would fit together snugly.

note *noun* **1. notation, comment, observation, remark, record, memorandum, commentary** The teacher made notes in the margin of my book report. **2. card, letter, message, communication, memo, dispatch, epistle, missive** I sent my friend a note thanking her for my birthday present. **3. notice, regard, heed, observation, mark, awareness, cognizance** I took note of my friend's melancholy mood. **4. hint, indication, suggestion, trace, evidence, sign, manifestation, bit** There was a note of sadness in her voice when she told us that she was moving away. ◆ *verb* **1. notice, observe, mark, mind, perceive, regard, see, catch** Please note that your appointment is for 3:00. **2. record, inscribe, log, register, enter, chronicle, jot down** The teacher notes our attendance in a record book. **3. point out, emphasize, highlight, spotlight, stress, mention, report, remark** Mom noted that it was important for us to get home early.

noteworthy *adjective* **notable, significant, important, prominent, outstanding, noted, exceptional, impressive** It is noteworthy that this project was done by a 12-year-old. ● **Antonyms: unimportant, insignificant**

nothing *noun* **naught, zero, nil, not anything, none, cipher, aught** The final score was ten to nothing.

notice *noun* **1. attention, consideration, heed, regard, observation, note, remark** I was happy when my work received favorable notice. **2. announcement, bulletin, statement, notification, directive, instruction** Mom received a notice to report for jury duty next month. **3. warning, forewarning, caution, notification, communication, information, declaration** We gave the landlord a month's notice before moving. ◆ *verb* **note, observe, see, spot, perceive, recognize, heed, espy, discern** Did you notice the flock of chickadees in the yard?

noticeable *adjective* **conspicuous, evident, distinct, obvious, significant, visible, patent, marked** She made noticeable progress in math this quarter.

notify *verb* **advise, alert, inform, tell, instruct, apprise** We notified the post office that we were going on vacation.

notion *noun* **1. belief, idea, opinion, thought, impression, conviction, assumption** Some people have the notion that extraterrestrial beings visited Earth in the ancient past. **2. whim, fancy, inclination, impulse, penchant, intention, conceit, caprice** I have a notion to buy an ice cream cone.

notorious *adjective* **infamous, scandalous, ignominious, disreputable, famous, well-known** Edward Teach, known also as Blackbeard, was a notorious pirate.

nourish *verb* **feed, maintain, supply, support, sustain, nurture, provide, promote** Your blood nourishes your body by carrying oxygen and nutrients to every living cell.

nourishment *noun* **feed, food, sustenance, nutrition, provisions, nutriment, diet, victuals** All baby animals need nourishment to grow.

novel *adjective* **fresh, new, original, innovative, unique, different, unusual, unorthodox** Someone came up with a novel idea for turning old automobile tires into pavement. ● **Antonyms: common, familiar, usual**

novelty *noun* **1. freshness, newness, originality, strangeness, uniqueness, surprise, unfamiliarity** Some people lose interest in new undertakings once the novelty wears off. **2. trinket, gadget, bauble, gimcrack, gewgaw,**

trifle, curiosity, souvenir, oddity I bought a teddy bear and other novelties at the carnival.

novice *noun* beginner, trainee, neophyte, pupil, greenhorn, newcomer, learner, apprentice When it comes to fishing, I am a novice. ⏺ **Antonyms: veteran, master**

now *adverb* at once, directly, immediately, instantly, right away, presently, in a minute, straightaway, currently If I don't leave now, I'll be late for school. ⏺ **Antonyms: eventually, later**

noxious *adjective* harmful, deadly, injurious, toxic, malignant, dangerous, poisonous Noxious fumes spewed from the smokestack. ⏺ **Antonyms: beneficial, healthy**

nuance *noun* shade, hint, tinge, trace, shadow, touch, suggestion, variation He thought her voice held a nuance of smugness.

nucleus *noun* center, core, focus, heart, kernel, seed, nub, pith This year's team will be formed around a nucleus of returning players.

nude *adjective* naked, bare, unclothed, stripped, uncovered, undressed, bald, stark, raw Some of Michelangelo's greatest works are of the nude human body. ⏺ **Antonyms: clothed, dressed**

nudge *verb* push, shove, prod, press, propel, jab, jog, poke, elbow Tugboats nudged the ocean liner away from the pier. ◆ *noun* jab, poke, prod, push, tap, jog, touch, shove, jolt She gave me a nudge with her elbow.

nuisance *noun* aggravation, annoyance, bother, irritation, pest, pain, torment, vexation Our neighbor's barking dog is a real nuisance. ⏺ **Antonym: delight**

numb *adjective* 1. unfeeling, asleep, dead, deadened, insensible, insensate, frozen My ears were numb from walking in the cold wind without a hat. 2. apathetic, indifferent, unfeeling, detached, disinterested, unresponsive, dazed The refugees were numb from despair. ◆ *verb* blunt, deaden, dull, freeze, paralyze, desensitize, benumb, stun Before extracting my tooth, the dentist gave me a shot to help numb the pain.

number *noun* 1. numeral, character, digit, figure, sign, symbol, integer, unit When we went to the bakery, we had to take a number and wait our turn. 2. amount, quantity, sum, total, aggregate, count, whole, collection Five is the maximum number of players that a basketball team can have on the court at one time. 3. company, crowd, multitude,

group, horde, bunch, throng, flock A large number of guests attended my sister's wedding. ◆ *verb* 1. total, amount, reach, add up, tally, count, enumerate, compute, reckon The attendance at the pep rally numbered in the hundreds. 2. include, encompass, contain, comprise, figure, constitute, amount We are numbered among those who attended the Mardi Gras in Louisiana.

numeral *noun* digit, number, character, figure, sign, symbol, cipher, integer Our car's license plate is a combination of letters and numerals.

numerous *adjective* abundant, many, plentiful, profuse, infinite, myriad, multitudinous On a clear night, the stars are too numerous to be counted. ⏺ **Antonym: few**

nurse *noun* caregiver, aide, attendant, guardian, orderly, nursemaid, medic Several wonderful nurses took care of me when I was in the hospital. ◆ *verb* 1. aid, help, minister to, tend, treat, care for, doctor, medicate, treat I found an injured owl and nursed it back to health. 2. harbor, bear, foster, cherish, succor, nourish, nurture, humor, cultivate He nurses an ambition to be a rock star.

nurture *noun* upbringing, training, breeding, rearing, development, education, preparation Psychologists continue to debate which is more important, nature or nurture. ◆ *verb* 1. nurse, nourish, feed, protect, doctor, sustain, strengthen, bolster I nurtured the dying plant back to health. 2. cultivate, foster, develop, nourish, teach, train, rear, educate My music teacher nurtures a love of music in her students.

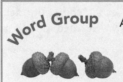

Word Group

A **nut** is a fruit having a hard shell and one seed. **Nut** is a general term with no true synonyms. Here are some common types of nuts:

acorn, Brazil, butternut, chestnut, filbert, hickory, macadamia, pecan, walnut

nutrition *noun* diet, food, nourishment, nutriment, sustenance, victuals, provisions Good nutrition is essential to a healthy and active life.

nutritious *adjective* healthful, healthy, nourishing, wholesome, beneficial, nutritional, strengthening Fresh fruits and vegetables are nutritious foods.

nuzzle *verb* rub, cuddle, nestle, press, snuggle, touch, nudge The kitten nuzzled against his mother.

Oo

oath *noun* **1.** pledge, vow, affirmation, declaration, promise, statement The knights of the Round Table took an oath of loyalty to King Arthur. **2.** expletive, profanity, curse, blasphemy, malediction, obscenity, cuss The angry man uttered an oath.

obedient *adjective* dutiful, loyal, submissive, faithful, conscientious, docile, respectful, compliant The obedient dog followed the whistled commands of his master. ● **Antonyms:** disobedient, rebellious, stubborn

obese *adjective* fat, heavy, overweight, plump, stout, tubby, portly, corpulent, rotund The vet told us that our cat is obese and must go on a diet. ● **Antonyms:** slender, thin, skinny

obey *verb* abide by, carry out, follow, fulfill, heed, mind, observe, respect, comply Soldiers are expected to obey the orders given by an officer. ● **Antonyms:** defy, disobey

object *noun* **1.** article, item, thing, device, commodity, gadget, something This antique store has many unusual objects for sale. **2.** focus, subject, target, mark, receiver, recipient, quarry, victim I was the object of much attention when my poster won a national art contest. **3.** aim, end, goal, objective, purpose, idea, intention, motive, design The object of chess is to checkmate your opponent's king. ◆ *verb* challenge, dispute, protest, argue, oppose, dissent, denounce, disapprove The ballplayer objected to the umpire's decision. ● **Antonyms:** *verb* agree, approve

objection *noun* challenge, protest, complaint, opposition, question, dispute, argument, disagreement No one had an objection to adjourning the meeting early. ● **Antonyms:** agreement, approval

objective *adjective* **1.** concrete, corporeal, physical, tangible, material, substantial, real, actual We live in an objective world. **2.** fair, impartial, just, unbiased, impersonal, detached, unprejudiced, equitable The referee was careful to be objective when she made her calls. ◆ *noun* aim, goal, point, object, purpose, intention, target, design, end Our objective in clearing this vacant lot is to start a neighborhood garden. ● **Antonyms:** *adjective* **1.** mental, intellectual **2.** biased, prejudiced

obligation *noun* **1.** commitment, duty, requirement, responsibility, burden, charge Police officers have an obligation to uphold the law. **2.** debt, liability, promise, agreement, contract, bond He has incurred several financial obligations.

oblige *verb* **1.** compel, force, make, obligate, require, impel, bind, constrain Now that I have joined the band, I am obliged to attend practice every day. **2.** accommodate, aid, serve, support, favor, benefit, gratify, indulge My friend's mother obliged me by giving me a ride home. ● **Antonyms:** **1.** liberate, release, free **2.** inconvenience

oblique *adjective* indirect, evasive, allusive, sly, vague, devious, obscure, roundabout She was very oblique in asking for help with her homework. ● **Antonyms:** direct, candid, straightforward

obliterate *verb* **1.** destroy, raze, pulverize, ruin, annihilate, wipe out, extinguish, eradicate The city of Dresden, Germany, was almost obliterated by Allied bombing during World War II. **2.** cover, hide, veil, obscure, cloak, conceal, screen, mask The smoke from the forest fire obliterated the sun. ● **Antonyms:** **2.** expose, reveal

oblivious *adjective* unaware, ignorant, unknowing, unmindful, unconscious, heedless, inattentive I was concentrating so hard on my homework that I was oblivious of the conversation around me. ● **Antonyms:** aware, mindful

obnoxious *adjective* unpleasant, offensive, disgusting, foul, repugnant, revolting, odious, hateful I think that some plants have an obnoxious smell. ● **Antonyms:** pleasant, agreeable

obscure *adjective* **1.** indistinct, dim, fuzzy, hazy, faint, dark, murky The path through the woods is very obscure because of the dense underbrush. **2.** hidden, unclear, vague, cryptic, ambiguous, enigmatic, puzzling, uncertain The meaning of this poem is very obscure. **3.** unknown, insignificant, minor, unimportant, unsung, nameless, inconsequential The actress isn't a big star because all of her roles have been in obscure movies. ◆ *verb* block, conceal, cover, screen, veil, shield, hide, obstruct, mask In a solar eclipse, the moon obscures the sun. ● **Antonyms:** *adjective* **1.** distinct, bright **2.** clear, obvious **3.** famous ◆ *verb* reveal, expose

observation *noun* **1.** examination, inspection, observance, notice, heed, regard, scrutiny, watch Scientists have made careful observations of the communication patterns of whales. **2. comment, remark, statement, view, opinion, assertion, idea, judgment** Will Rogers was famous for his folksy observations about people and life.

observe *verb* **1. notice, see, spot, witness, espy, discern, glimpse, watch** Mom called the fire department when she observed smoke coming from our neighbor's garage. **2. say, remark, mention, state, announce, note, comment, declare** Our teacher observed that we were one of the best classes she had ever had. **3. abide by, comply with, follow, heed, keep, obey, respect, mind** The referee told both boxers to observe the rules at all times. **4. celebrate, honor, sanctify, keep, consecrate, commemorate, solemnize** My family observes the holy days of our religion. **Antonyms: 1. overlook, ignore 3. disregard, flout 4. dishonor, forget**

obsession *noun* **fixation, mania, preoccupation, fascination, infatuation, compulsion, delusion** My grandmother has developed an obsession with the stock market.

obsolete *adjective* **obsolescent, superseded, outmoded, passé, dated, out-of-date, old-fashioned** That software is obsolete. **Antonyms: current, modern, new**

obstacle *noun* **impediment, hurdle, barricade, barrier, block, snag, hindrance, obstruction** An icy ridge was the last obstacle between the climbers and the mountain's summit. **Antonyms: aid, help, support**

obstinate *adjective* **headstrong, stubborn, uncontrollable, unruly, recalcitrant, obdurate, ornery** The obstinate mule refused to budge. **Antonyms: obedient, submissive**

obstruct *verb* **1. bar, block, close, stop, choke, barricade, clog, dam** Our rain gutter overflowed because leaves were obstructing it. **2. impede, hinder, halt, thwart, frustrate, stall, delay, retard, restrict** Several senators engaged in a filibuster to obstruct the passage of the legislation. **3. hide, veil, screen, shield, curtain, obscure, conceal, cut off** Clouds obstructed our view of the moon. **Antonyms: 1. clear, open 2. help, promote, aid 3. expose, reveal**

obstruction *noun* **barrier, obstacle, bar, block, check, impediment, hindrance, stoppage** The fallen tree was an obstruction to traffic. **Antonyms: aid, assistance**

obtain *verb* **acquire, attain, gain, get, earn, secure, win, procure, gather** You have to be 16 years old before you can obtain a driver's license. **Antonyms: lose, relinquish**

obvious *adjective* **apparent, clear, distinct, plain, unmistakable, manifest, evident, conspicuous** It was obvious that our female cat was pregnant. **Antonyms: hidden, unclear**

occasion *noun* **1. event, incident, happening, time, occurrence, episode, experience, milestone** My grandparents' 50th anniversary was an important occasion for the entire family. **2. chance, opportunity, opening, break, time, possibility, instance, excuse** I haven't had many occasions to play tennis this summer. **3. reason, cause, call, grounds, justification, necessity, basis, warrant** What was the occasion for changing the time of the workshop? *verb* **cause, effect, elicit, prompt, lead to, induce, make, inspire, generate** The leaking sink occasioned us to call the plumber.

occasional *adjective* **infrequent, irregular, odd, rare, random, sporadic, intermittent, uncommon** The weather has been fine except for an occasional afternoon shower. **Antonyms: frequent, regular**

occupant *noun* **inhabitant, resident, renter, tenant, dweller, occupier, lodger, lessee** The former occupants of our apartment left it very clean.

occupation *noun* **1. business, career, job, profession, work, vocation, craft, employment** My father's occupation is teaching school. **2. control, possession, rule, subjugation, ownership, tenancy, takeover, seizure** China was under Japanese occupation during World War II.

occupy *verb* **1. dwell in, inhabit, live in, reside in, lodge, room, tenant** My uncle and aunt have occupied the same house for more than 25 years. **2. control, possess, hold, subjugate, capture, conquer, seize, invade** During the War of 1812, British troops briefly occupied Washington, D.C. **3. employ, engage, fill, use, busy, utilize, involve** My schoolwork occupies a lot of my time.

occur *verb* **develop, happen, result, take place, come about, transpire, emerge, materialize** Thunder occurs when the heat from a flash of lightning expands the surrounding air.

occurrence *noun* **development, event, experience, circumstance, incident, occasion, happening** The local airport is very busy, and flight delays are a common occurrence.

ocean *noun* **sea, high seas, main, deep, water, brine** It took Columbus more than two months to cross the Atlantic Ocean.

odd *adjective* **1. curious, peculiar, strange, unusual, weird, bizarre, funny, eccentric** My cousin has the odd habit of looking up at the ceiling when he's thinking of what to say next. **2. lone, single, unmatched, extra, leftover, surplus, sole** I have several odd socks that are missing their mates. **3. random, miscellaneous, various, chance, irregular, occasional, sporadic** My brother earns extra money by doing odd jobs at the hardware store after school. ➻ **Antonyms: 1. normal, ordinary 2. matched 3. regular, steady**

oddity *noun* **rarity, abnormality, curiosity, freak, monstrosity, peculiarity** A snake with two heads is an oddity.

odious *adjective* **abhorrent, hateful, repugnant, foul, horrible, disgusting, repulsive, offensive, abominable** The anonymous letter was full of odious statements. ➻ **Antonyms: delightful, charming, pleasant**

odor *noun* **aroma, scent, smell, fragrance, stench, stink, reek, bouquet** Garlic has a distinctive, strong odor and flavor.

odyssey *noun* **journey, quest, expedition, trip, pilgrimage, crusade, adventure, voyage** Marco Polo's odyssey to China lasted more than 15 years.

off *adverb* **away, far, far off, far away, afar, ahead, apart** The hill lies about a mile off. ◆ *adjective* **1. remote, distant, unlikely, slight, slim, minor, improbable** I went to the store on the off chance that they might have caramel popcorn. **2. bad, unsatisfactory, poor, substandard, down, sluggish, slow, disappointing** I had an off day yesterday. **3. incorrect, erroneous, inaccurate, wrong, false, mistaken, fallacious** I was given partial credit on the test question because my answer was only slightly off. ➻ **Antonyms:** *adjective* **1. likely 2. good, superior 3. correct, accurate**

offend *verb* **anger, annoy, displease, insult, irritate, vex, nettle, provoke, gall, affront** My friend was offended when I forgot to meet her as planned. ➻ **Antonyms: flatter, please**

offense *noun* **1. crime, misdeed, infraction, violation, vice, misdemeanor, felony** Jaywalking is only a minor offense. **2. affront, disrespect, insult, rudeness, indignity, indignation, outrage, resentment** I meant no offense when I said that you look different today. **3. offensive, charge, attack, assault, aggression, strike, onrush** The best defense is a good offense. ➻ **Antonyms: 1. innocence 2. compliment, praise 3. defense**

offensive *adjective* **1. atrocious, disgusting, foul, bad, nasty, revolting, unpleasant, disagreeable, repugnant** Sulfur hot springs have an offensive odor similar to that of rotten eggs. **2. discourteous, disrespectful, insulting, rude, impertinent, unmannerly, insolent** My friend is so

tactful that she can point out a person's faults without being offensive. **3. aggressive, attacking, hostile, invading, belligerent, warlike, bellicose** Artillery is commonly used as an offensive weapon. ◆ *noun* **assault, attack, aggression, charge, strike, offense, onslaught** The generals hoped that their big offensive would end the war. ➻ **Antonyms:** *adjective* **1. agreeable, pleasant 2. courteous, polite 3. defensive, peaceful** ◆ *noun* **defense, retreat**

offer *verb* **1. afford, furnish, present, provide, supply, give, impart** Our city offers a wide variety of cultural activities. **2. propose, suggest, advance, submit, present, propound, pose** My dad offered me some good advice regarding my summer plans. **3. volunteer, proffer, extend, grant, donate, tender, lend, bestow** Karen offered to help clean up after the party. ◆ *noun* **proposal, proposition, suggestion, invitation, overture, tender, bid** I gladly accepted my brother's offer to let me have his old baseball glove. ➻ **Antonyms:** *verb* **withdraw, refuse, deny**

office *noun* **1. headquarters, room, shop, workplace, department, suite, center, agency** The principal will be back in her office this afternoon. **2. position, post, job, role, situation, task, slot, commission, appointment** Aaron is running for the office of class president.

official *adjective* **authorized, formal, legitimate, proper, sanctioned, accredited, approved, licensed** An ambassador is an official representative from one country to another. ◆ *noun* **executive, leader, administrator, director, officer, functionary, manager, supervisor** The President is the highest elected official in the United States. ➻ **Antonyms:** *adjective* **unauthorized, unofficial**

often *adverb* **commonly, frequently, regularly, generally, usually, oft, habitually, oftentimes** I like to play hockey as often as I can. ➻ **Antonyms: never, rarely, seldom**

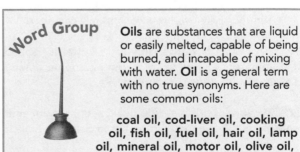

Word Group

Oils are substances that are liquid or easily melted, capable of being burned, and incapable of mixing with water. **Oil** is a general term with no true synonyms. Here are some common oils:

coal oil, cod-liver oil, cooking oil, fish oil, fuel oil, hair oil, lamp oil, mineral oil, motor oil, olive oil, petroleum, vegetable oil, whale oil

old *adjective* **1. aged, elderly, mature, advanced, senior, hoary, venerable** Social security was created to benefit old people after they retire. **2. antique, ancient, old-fashioned,**

outdated, obsolete, vintage, antiquated, obsolescent, out-of-date This old car was made in the 1930s. **3. run-down, used, worn, worn-out, shabby, decrepit, dilapidated, timeworn** These shoes are so old that they're starting to fall apart. **4. former, past, previous, late, onetime, erstwhile, sometime** I like to return to my old neighborhood to visit with my friends there. **5. enduring, lasting, lifelong, long-standing, permanent, traditional, dear, firm** Mom was thrilled to see all of her old friends at her high school reunion. ➡ **Antonyms: 1. young, immature 2. modern, up-to-date 3. unused, fresh 4. current 5. new, recent**

omen *noun* **indication, sign, token, prediction, portent, prophecy, harbinger, herald** Some people think that finding a four-leaf clover is an omen of good luck.

ominous *adjective* **threatening, sinister, menacing, inauspicious, foreboding, unfavorable, unlucky** A rise in prices is often an ominous warning of economic inflation. ➡ **Antonyms: favorable, auspicious, encouraging**

omit *verb* **drop, eliminate, exclude, forget, neglect, skip, miss, disregard, ignore** I want to hear everything that happened at the party, so please don't omit any details. ➡ **Antonyms: add, include**

once *adverb* **at one time, formerly, previously, already, before, earlier, heretofore** Dinosaurs were once the largest creatures living on Earth.

ongoing *adjective* **continuous, continuing, constant, nonstop, endless, relentless, unbroken, uninterrupted** There is an ongoing effort to save endangered species from extinction. ➡ **Antonyms: sporadic, concluding**

only *adjective* **lone, single, sole, solitary, one, singular** He is the only student who earned a perfect score on the math test. ◆ *adverb* **just, merely, solely, exclusively, uniquely, purely, simply** I have two brothers, but only one sister.

onward *adverb* **onwards, forward, forwards, ahead, forth, along, on** We had no choice but to continue onward. ➡ **Antonyms: backward, rearward, aft**

ooze¹ *verb* **drain, dribble, drip, leak, seep, trickle, emit, discharge, exude** Sap oozed from the tree's broken branch.

ooze² *noun* **slush, slop, slime, mud, silt, sludge, muck, mire, alluvium** The melting snow cause the ground to turn to ooze.

opaque *adjective* **1. impenetrable, impervious, dark, black, cloudy, murky, muddy, smoky** The statuette was molded from opaque black glass. **2. abstruse, obscure, incomprehensible, unintelligible, vague, cryptic, difficult, unfathomable** The scientist's examples were too opaque for me to understand. ➡ **Antonyms: 1. clear, transparent 2. lucid, comprehensible, intelligible**

open *adjective* **1. ajar, unclosed, unfastened, unlocked, accessible, unblocked** Somebody left the window open, and our parakeet got out. **2. bare, clear, empty, vacant, free, unoccupied, deserted, wide, spacious** My friends and I like to play baseball in the open field behind my house. **3. uncapped, uncovered, unsealed, exposed, unprotected** Please use the bottle of ketchup that is already open. **4. accessible, available, obtainable, allowable, free, public** This contest is open only to students between the ages of 12 and 16. **5. undecided, indefinite, uncertain, unresolved, unsure, vague, unsettled** My weekend plans are still open. **6. responsive, receptive, amenable, vulnerable, susceptible, liable, prone** The teacher was open to my project idea. **7. objective, unbiased, disinterested, nonpartisan, fair, impartial, impersonal** It is important to keep an open mind. ◆ *verb* **1. unfasten, untie, unwrap, free, release, unclose, unstop, unlock** My nephew eagerly opened his birthday presents. **2. begin, commence, initiate, start, inaugurate, kick off, launch, institute** School opens on the day after Labor Day. ➡ **Antonyms:** *adjective* **1. closed, shut 2. cluttered, full 3. covered, sealed 4. inaccessible, restricted 5. definite, certain 7. prejudiced, biased, unfair** ◆ *verb* **1. wrap, close, shut 2. end, stop, conclude**

opening *noun* **1. hole, gap, breach, orifice, chasm, break, rift, chink, space** I watched activity on the construction site through an opening in the fence. **2. start, beginning, commencement, onset, origination, inception, dawn, launch** There were several local celebrities at the opening of the new civic auditorium. **3. opportunity, chance, possibility, occasion, shot, break** The rabbit saw its opening and shot past us.

operate *verb* **1. function, perform, run, work, go, behave, run** Our VCR isn't operating properly. **2. drive, handle, run, manage, use, manipulate, work** The farmer taught his son and daughter how to operate a tractor.

operation *noun* **1. action, functioning, performance, working, running, behavior** This new factory has computers that control the operation of all its machinery. **2. use, employment, utilization, application, play, usage, exercise** This old steam locomotive is no longer in operation. **3. maneuver, campaign, action, assault, offensive, attack, expedition** The commander in chief is in charge of all military operations.

opinion *noun* belief, conviction, idea, judgment, view, estimation, assessment, evaluation In my opinion, *The View from Saturday* is one of the best books ever written.

opponent *noun* adversary, challenger, contender, competitor, rival, enemy, foe, opposition Alice defeated two opponents to become our class president. ⇒ **Antonyms:** ally, partner

opportunity *noun* chance, occasion, moment, time, situation, opening I haven't had an opportunity to fly my new kite yet.

oppose *verb* disagree with, disapprove of, object to, contest, challenge, defy, protest, resist, deny, fight I wonder if my parents would oppose my desire to dye my hair green. ⇒ **Antonyms:** defend, support

opposite *adjective* 1. facing, opposing, other, reverse, inverse, converse The football teams lined up on opposite sides of the field. 2. conflicting, contradictory, contrary, different, counter, antithetical, diametrical "Up" and "down" have opposite meanings. ◆ *noun* reverse, antithesis, contrary, converse, obverse, counter She said the opposite of how she felt. ⇒ **Antonyms:** *adjective* identical, same, similar

opposition *noun* 1. resistance, disagreement, disapproval, objection, defiance, hostility, animosity Albert Einstein once said, "Great spirits have always encountered violent opposition from mediocre minds." 2. competition, adversary, enemy, opponent, foe, antagonist, rival, competitor We took a moment to size up the opposition before the game began. ⇒ **Antonyms:** 1. support, cooperation 2. ally, supporter

oppress *verb* 1. subjugate, overpower, tyrannize, persecute, abuse, trample, harass, crush History is filled with examples of one group trying to oppress another. 2. vex, worry, trouble, deject, depress, dishearten, burden, overwhelm Sometimes thinking about the future oppresses me. ⇒ **Antonyms:** 1. liberate, free 2. relieve, encourage, cheer

oppressive *adjective* 1. harsh, severe, brutal, unjust, cruel, tyrannical, despotic, repressive Our congressional representative pledged to fight oppressive taxes. 2. depressing, worrisome, burdensome, difficult, trying, discouraging, uncomfortable He felt an oppressive sense of regret. ⇒ **Antonyms:** 1. gentle, lenient 2. cheering, encouraging, heartening

opt *verb* choose, decide, elect, pick, select, single out, prefer Which of the movies did you finally opt to see? ⇒ **Antonyms:** reject, exclude

optimistic *adjective* confident, hopeful, positive, upbeat, sanguine, trusting, cheerful The drama teacher was optimistic that the school play would be a success. ⇒ **Antonyms:** pessimistic, gloomy

optimum *adjective* best, optimal, peak, highest, greatest, select The athlete trained to be in optimum condition for the Olympics. ⇒ **Antonyms:** lowest, worst, inferior

option *noun* 1. choice, alternative, selection, possibility, preference, opportunity, recourse In the United States there are many options for higher education. 2. privilege, franchise, right, discretion, decision, volition The employee exercised her option to buy stock in the company.

optional *adjective* not required, elective, voluntary, discretionary, possible, permissible, unforced The math quiz contained an optional problem that could be completed for extra credit. ⇒ **Antonyms:** compulsory, mandatory, required

opulence *noun* luxury, wealth, riches, richness, affluence, prosperity, abundance, plenty The opulence of the Hearst Castle is beautiful and impressive. ⇒ **Antonyms:** poverty, need, scarcity

opus *noun* work, masterpiece, composition, creation, invention, production, piece *Brandenburg Concerto #1* is an opus by J.S. Bach.

oracle *noun* 1. prophet, seer, psychic, clairvoyant, sage, sibyl, soothsayer, augur, fortuneteller Ancient Greeks used to travel to Delphi to consult the oracle. 2. answer, prediction, prophesy, revelation, vision, divination Throughout history people have used many different methods, such as astrology, tarot cards, and the *I Ching* to obtain oracles.

oral *adjective* spoken, verbal, vocal, voiced, verbalized, uttered, articulated I have to give an oral report about my favorite author.

oration *noun* speech, address, talk, discourse, lecture, sermon, homily, monologue Winston Churchill was famous for his skill in delivering orations.

orator *noun* speaker, speechmaker, lecturer, rhetorician, talker, preacher Franklin D. Roosevelt was a great orator.

orbit *noun* 1. revolution, rotation, circuit, round, tour, course, path, trajectory Russia's *Sputnik I* was the first artificial satellite to be placed in orbit around Earth. 2. domain, realm, province, compass, sphere, range, terrain, arena

We discussed China's orbit of influence. ◆ *verb* **circle, revolve around, circumnavigate** Earth orbits the sun once every year.

ordain *verb* **1. invest, authorize, consecrate, appoint, commission, name, delegate** Our rabbi was ordained just last year. **2. order, decree, dictate, rule, command, prescribe, legislate** My parents ordained that I be home by midnight.

ordeal *noun* **trial, tribulation, trouble, test, difficulty, experience, hardship, distress** The shipwrecked sailors said that the worst part of their ordeal was going without water. ➤ **Antonyms: delight, joy, pleasure**

order *noun* **1. condition, form, shape, trim, state, fettle, kilter, repair** The pilot checked her plane to ensure that all the equipment was in working order. **2. sequence, arrangement, classification, organization, pattern, system, categorization** I put my books in alphabetical order by author. **3. calm, control, discipline, peace, quiet, silence, decorum, tranquillity** The teacher had trouble restoring order after the fire drill. **4. command, directive, instruction, dictate, mandate, demand, direction** The soldier received an order to report to his commanding officer. **5. society, brotherhood, sisterhood, fraternity, fellowship, association, organization, lodge** My aunt belongs to a religious order. **6. class, grade, category, classification, set, division, kind, type, sort** There are five orders of architectural columns: Doric, Ionic, Corinthian, Tuscan, and Composite. ◆ *verb* **1. command, direct, instruct, tell, bid, compel, force, require, rule** Firefighters ordered everyone to leave the building at once. **2. ask for, request, requisition, buy, purchase, reserve, hire, engage** We ordered a large pizza with extra cheese. **3. organize, systematize, catalog, classify, categorize, group, array, rank** I order my homework according to the date the assignments are due. ➤ **Antonyms:** *noun* **3. chaos, anarchy 4. plea, request** ◆ *verb* **3. scramble, disarrange**

orderly *adjective* **1. methodical, neat, organized, regular, shipshape, spruce, trim, tidy** The band marched in an orderly line. **2. calm, disciplined, peaceful, quiet, well-behaved, civil, law-abiding, well-mannered** The fans remained orderly even though the concert did not start on time. ➤ **Antonyms: 1. disorderly, sloppy 2. unruly, lawless**

ordinarily *adverb* **generally, normally, regularly, usually, habitually, customarily, routinely** Dad is on vacation this week, but ordinarily he would be at work now. ➤ **Antonyms: occasionally, rarely**

ordinary *adjective* **1. common, normal, regular, standard, usual, typical, general, routine** On an ordinary day,

school begins at 8 a.m. **2. average, modest, plain, simple, commonplace, run-of-the-mill, mediocre** We were surprised to see the famous actress dressed in ordinary clothes. ➤ **Antonyms: 1. unusual, odd 2. exceptional, extraordinary, noteworthy**

organism *noun* **living thing, being, creature, animal, plant, body, entity, cell, microorganism** Bacteria are very small, one-celled organisms.

organization *noun* **1. planning, establishment, arrangement, organizing, coordination, foundation, start-up** The entire sixth-grade class helped with the organization of this year's school picnic. **2. order, structure, form, design, methodology, formulation, planning** My teacher said that my history report showed good organization. **3. association, group, society, club, party, guild, institute, federation, league** I joined an organization that rescues injured wildlife.

organize *verb* **1. arrange, categorize, classify, group, order, sort, coordinate, systematize** I need to organize the photos that I have taken over the past year. **2. create, start, develop, establish, form, found, institute, constitute** Our class organized a tree-planting campaign to celebrate Arbor Day. ➤ **Antonyms: 1. disorder, mess up 2. disband, end**

orient *verb* **orientate, familiarize, acclimatize, adjust, reconcile, conform, fit** The purpose of the assembly was to help orient us to junior high.

origin *noun* **1. beginning, source, start, root, fountain, inception, basis, cause** The explorers traveled up the river to find its point of origin. **2. ancestry, parentage, descent, lineage, extraction, genealogy, derivation** My family is of Hispanic origin. ➤ **Antonyms: 1. end, finish**

original *adjective* **1. first, initial, primary, beginning, early, basic, fundamental, elementary** Our car still has its original coat of paint. **2. fresh, imaginative, new, novel, unique, creative, inventive, innovative** The idea for your story should be original, not copied from something you've read. **3. actual, authentic, genuine, real, true, bona fide, good, legitimate** My grandfather owns an original Model-T Ford. ◆ *noun* **archetype, prototype, model, forerunner, paradigm, master, standard** Many types of airplanes have been developed, but the Wright brothers' flying machine is the original. ➤ **Antonyms:** *adjective* **1. final, last 2. old, ordinary 3. duplicate** ◆ *noun* **copy, reproduction**

originate *verb* **1. create, concoct, pioneer, invent, make, introduce, launch** The modern paperback was originated in 1935 when Sir Allen Lane published the first

Penguin book. **2. start, rise, begin, arise, commence, sprout, flow, emerge, issue** The use of paper money originated in China almost one thousand years ago. ◆ **Antonyms: 2. conclude, end, stop**

ornament *noun* **decoration, trimming, accessory, adornment, garnish, embellishment, bauble, trinket** Mom bought a box of new ornaments for our Christmas tree. ◆ *verb* **festoon, decorate, embellish, garnish, trim, bedeck, adorn** Gothic cathedrals were typically ornamented with arches, pinnacles, and gargoyles.

orthodox *adjective* **traditional, customary, approved, usual, conventional, recognized, sanctioned, accepted** Members of the Jewish Hasidic sect adhere to orthodox beliefs and practices. ◆ **Antonyms: unorthodox, unusual, unconventional**

ostentatious *adjective* **pretentious, flashy, showy, flamboyant, garish, gaudy** Movie theaters used to be decorated in an ostentatious style. ◆ **Antonyms: modest, plain, simple**

ostracize *verb* **reject, snub, shun, isolate, exclude, banish, expel, oust, exile** In *The Scarlet Letter*, Hester Prynne was ostracized for immoral behavior. ◆ **Antonyms: include, welcome, embrace**

other *adjective* **1. alternate, different, disparate, unlike, distinct, contrasting, divergent** Does this shirt come in any other colors? **2. additional, extra, added, supplementary, auxiliary, spare, more, further** Did you check to see if we have any other spoons? ◆ **Antonyms: 1. like, similar, same**

ought *verb* **had best, should, have, must, need** As long as I'm at the pet store, I ought to buy some food and litter for my cat.

oust *verb* **banish, eject, expel, evict, remove, depose, fire, throw out, dismiss** The city council voted to oust the corrupt mayor. ◆ **Antonyms: admit, install**

out *adverb* **outdoors, outside, out-of-doors, abroad, outward** My little brother and his friends went out to play. ◆ *adjective* **passé, out-dated, outmoded, dead, gone, done, finished, over** Bell-bottoms were popular in the 1970s, but they were out in the 1980s. ◆ *noun* **escape, excuse, alibi, dodge, explanation, loophole, defense, justification** I need an out for not going to the party.

outbreak *noun* **epidemic, outburst, eruption, uprising, explosion, paroxysm, storm, surge** Measles vaccinations can help prevent outbreaks of the disease.

outburst *noun* **burst, eruption, gush, outbreak, flood, torrent, fit, flare-up** There was a sudden outburst of applause in the middle of the mayor's speech.

outcast *noun* **exile, pariah, fugitive, outlaw, vagabond, castaway, refugee** Buddha said, "Not by birth does one become an outcast; by deeds one becomes an outcast."

outcome *noun* **conclusion, end, result, consequence, upshot, fruit, issue, aftermath** I couldn't wait to hear about the outcome of the game.

outcry *noun* **clamor, hullabaloo, uproar, tumult, exclamation, demonstration, protest, complaint** There was an outcry among the students and parents when cuts in the athletic program were proposed.

outdo *verb* **beat, better, exceed, surpass, top, excel, transcend, eclipse** I am determined to outdo my previous personal record for the long jump.

outer *adjective* **exterior, external, outside, outward, peripheral, outlying, outermost** Crabs, lobsters, and clams all have hard outer shells for protection. ◆ **Antonyms: inner, inside**

outfit *noun* **1. clothing, dress, garb, equipment, gear, getup, rig, costume** For safety's sake, a hunter's outfit should include a brightly colored vest and cap. **2. detachment, company, squad, troop, group, detail, troupe, team, crew** My grandfather served in an infantry outfit during the Korean War. ◆ *verb* **accouter, equip, furnish, provide, provision, supply, clothe, rig, fit out** They went shopping to outfit themselves for their week-long rafting trip.

outgrowth *noun* **1. shoots, sprouts, bud, branch, node, bulge, projection, swelling** I am happy that the forsythia I planted last year has such heavy outgrowth this spring. **2. result, effect, byproduct, offshoot, spinoff, derivative, consequence, development** The Internet is the outgrowth of a United States federally funded research program that was begun in 1973.

outing *noun* **excursion, jaunt, junket, trip, expedition, tour, vacation, holiday** Our Explorer troop is taking an outing to Annapolis.

outlandish *adjective* **unconventional, strange, bizarre, weird, peculiar, eccentric, odd, outrageous** My mother said that I could wear outlandish clothes if I wished as long as I stayed on the honor roll. ◆ **Antonyms: usual, ordinary, commonplace**

outlaw *noun* **bandit, criminal, crook, robber, highwayman, gangster, desperado, felon** Billy the Kid was a notorious outlaw of the Old West. ◆ *verb* **abolish, ban, banish, forbid, prohibit, proscribe, bar, disallow, suppress** The Eighteenth Amendment to the United States Constitution outlawed alcoholic beverages. ⏺ **Antonyms:** *verb* **allow, legalize, permit**

outlet *noun* **1. opening, gateway, passage, passageway, exit, portal** Russia's Lake Baikal has only one outlet. **2. release, vent, escape, relief, safety valve, channel, avenue, means** Tyler took up painting as an outlet for his creative energy. **3. store, shop, emporium, department store, market, boutique, mall** A big sporting goods chain is opening an outlet in our town.

outline *noun* **1. contour, profile, silhouette, form, shape, map, drawing, blueprint** I have to draw an outline of the United States for tomorrow's geography lesson. **2. draft, sketch, summary, brief, synopsis, digest, plan** Giving a speech is easier if you have an outline to follow. ◆ *verb* **1. delineate, draw, sketch, diagram, trace, draft, limn, silhouette** Police used white chalk to outline the corpse. **2. summarize, digest, abstract, compress, sum up, recapitulate, abridge** The author outlined the plot of his new novel.

outlook *noun* **1. point of view, attitude, perspective, view, viewpoint, stance, standpoint** A positive outlook on life can help you get through a bad day. **2. forecast, prediction, projection, prognosis, chance, future, prospect** Experts say that the economic outlook for the next few years is quite good. **3. vista, view, panorama, scene, lookout, sight, spectacle, prospect** We climbed the mountain and enjoyed the outlook over the valley.

output *noun* **production, productivity, turnout, volume, harvest, crop, yield** The companies that make exercise equipment have recently been increasing their output.

outrage *noun* **1. atrocity, monstrosity, evil, crime, offense, sin, barbarity, wrong** Slavery is an outrage that has existed throughout human history. **2. offense, insult, affront, slight, indignity, disrespect, contempt, slap, blow** His remark was an outrage to my feelings. **3. anger, fury, indignation, resentment, wrath, vexation** The principal expressed outrage when she learned that her school's budget was to be cut. ◆ *verb* **anger, incense, offend, affront, insult, shock, provoke, vex** Many people were outraged when they saw the polluted beach. ⏺ **Antonyms:** *noun* **1. blessing, boon 2. compliment 3. contentment** ◆ *verb* **calm, soothe**

outrageous *adjective* **1. awful, despicable, disgraceful, offensive, scandalous, shameful, shocking, atrocious** The movie star said that the scandal was based on an outrageous lie. **2. excessive, immoderate, preposterous, inordinate, extravagant, ridiculous, extreme** Her hairstyle is outrageous, but I kind of like it. ⏺ **Antonyms: 1. fair, just 2. reasonable, moderate, conservative**

outside *noun* **exterior, surface, face, front, façade, skin, coating, sheath** We painted the outside of the old shed. ◆ *adjective* **1. exterior, external, outer, outward, outermost, outlying** These caramels have an outside layer of chocolate. **2. strange, alien, unfamiliar, foreign, exotic, extraneous, different, new** Some countries are very conservative and do not want any outside influences. **3. extreme, uppermost, maximum, highest, greatest, biggest** The outside price that we can pay for a new computer is 2,300 dollars. **4. slight, remote, small, slender, faint, negligible, slim, unlikely, distant** There is an outside chance that I will be able to go on the choir's tour to Canada. ⏺ **Antonyms:** *noun* **inside, interior, center** ◆ *adjective* **1. inner 2. known, familiar 3. minimal, lowest 4. likely, certain**

outstanding *adjective* **1. preeminent, prominent, distinguished, principal, main, eminent, noteworthy** My school gives an annual award to the outstanding student in each grade. **2. exceptional, superior, excellent, extraordinary, magnificent, remarkable, great** My teacher said I did an outstanding job on my science project. **3. due, owed, owing, payable, unpaid, unsettled, receivable, remaining** My aunt says she has only 500 dollars outstanding on her college loans. ⏺ **Antonyms: 1. undistinguished 2. average, ordinary 3. paid, settled**

outward *adjective* **exterior, external, outside, apparent, perceptible, visible, superficial** His outward appearance was one of calm and self-control. ⏺ **Antonyms: inward, interior, inside**

outwit *verb* **outsmart, fool, foil, outfox, dupe, baffle, confuse, thwart, outmaneuver** The roadrunner always managed to outwit the coyote in the cartoons.

over *preposition* **higher than, above, across, beyond, past, to, through** The batter hit the ball over the outfield fence. ⏺ **Antonyms: below, under**

overcast *adjective* **cloudy, dark, gray, hazy, murky, gloomy, dim, sunless** The sky was overcast all day long, but it never rained. ⏺ **Antonyms: clear, sunny**

overcome *verb* **master, surmount, subdue, subjugate, beat, conquer, defeat, quell, vanquish** Jeremy worked hard to overcome his shyness. ⏺ **Antonyms: submit, yield**

overdue *adjective* **1. past due, late, delinquent, outstanding** I need to pay this bill before it becomes overdue. **2. behind, late, tardy, behindhand, belated, slow** The bus is overdue. ❖ **Antonyms: 1. paid, settled 2. early, punctual**

overflow *verb* **cascade, flood, pour, spill, deluge, inundate** When I accidentally left the bathtub faucet on, water overflowed onto the floor. ◆ *noun* **surplus, excess, glut, overstock, oversupply, overage, plethora, deluge** When a large order was canceled, the company was left with an overflow of goods.

overhaul *verb* **rebuild, recondition, fix up, repair, service, mend, renovate** My dad bought an old jeep for us to overhaul. ◆ *noun* **renovation, repair, checkup, servicing, reconditioning, examination** Mechanics completed the overhaul of the plane's jet engines.

overlook *verb* **1. tower over, command, dominate, overshadow, look over, scan, survey** Frazier Mountain overlooks our community. **2. miss, neglect, skip, forget, omit, slight, pass over** I overlooked two misspelled words when I proofread my report. **3. ignore, disregard, forgive, condone, excuse, pardon, accept** I am grateful that my mother often overlooks my bad moods. ❖ **Antonyms: 2. notice, remember 3. censure, criticize**

overrule *verb* **disallow, reject, repeal, revoke, veto, override, nullify, countermand, rescind** The Supreme Court has the power to overrule decisions made by lower courts. ❖ **Antonyms: approve, sustain**

oversee *verb* **supervise, direct, manage, superintend, regulate, administer, command, watch** He was hired to oversee the work crew.

oversight *noun* **lapse, slip, omission, blunder, error, mistake, fault, neglect** Due to an oversight, we forgot to take a stove on our camping trip. ❖ **Antonyms: care, attention**

overt *adjective* **open, manifest, apparent, evident, plain, patent, obvious, clear, visible** The untamed cat finally started to make overt gestures of wanting to be petted. ❖ **Antonyms: hidden, secret**

overtake *verb* **catch, catch up, overhaul, pass, beat, outdo, outrun, outstrip** The motorboat easily overtook our rowboat.

overthrow *verb* **bring down, oust, remove, topple, depose, overturn, subvert, defeat** The people rose up to overthrow the oppressive dictator. ◆ *noun* **downfall, ouster, removal, dethronement, collapse, defeat, upset, coup** A few of Hitler's generals plotted his overthrow. ❖ **Antonyms: *verb* install, preserve, maintain ◆ *noun* preservation, defense**

overture *noun* **offer, proposal, approach, proposition, advance, bid, opening, invitation** I was glad that I had accepted his overtures of friendship.

overturn *verb* **1. capsize, roll, knock over, turn over, topple, upend, upset** A kayak is a type of canoe that can be easily righted if it overturns. **2. bring down, topple, remove, overpower, overthrow, depose, unseat, vanquish** The government in power was overturned by popular vote. ❖ **Antonyms: 1. right 2. seat, install, preserve**

overweight *adjective* **fat, heavy, obese, plump, stout, pudgy, chunky, corpulent, portly** Exercise is the single best way to avoid becoming overweight. ❖ **Antonyms: slender, thin**

overwhelm *verb* **1. engulf, drown, swamp, deluge, submerge, flood, inundate, overflow** A tsunami overwhelmed Java and Sumatra in 1883, drowning thirty thousand people. **2. beat, defeat, overpower, crush, overcome, destroy, shatter, conquer** The attacking army quickly overwhelmed the small band of defenders. **3. devastate, demoralize, stun, disturb, confuse, confound, stagger** The sad news overwhelmed me. ❖ **Antonyms: 2. capitulate, surrender 3. encourage, lift, cheer**

own *adjective* **personal, private, individual, particular, exclusive, intimate** Please bring your own towel to the swimming party. ◆ *verb* **1. have, possess, hold, keep, retain, maintain, boast, enjoy** I own more than a hundred books. **2. acknowledge, admit, allow, grant, concede, profess, disclose, confess** She owned that she did not like to ride the roller coaster. ❖ **Antonyms: *verb* 2. deny, disclaim, refute**

Pp

pace *noun* **1. step, stride, gait, footstep, tread, shuffle, walk** The recruits took a pace forward and were sworn into military service. **2. rate, speed, velocity, tempo, clip, momentum, swiftness, rapidity** He can run at a faster pace than I can. ◆ *verb* **step, stride, tread, walk, traverse, march** The lion paced back and forth in its cage.

pacify *verb* **calm, quiet, appease, relax, mollify, placate, allay, soothe** I pacified my little niece by rocking her. ➡ **Antonyms: agitate, alarm, aggravate**

pack *noun* **1. packet, package, bundle, carton, container, parcel, trunk, bag** Please get me a pack of gum when you go to the store. **2. band, bunch, group, gang, herd, mob, body, swarm, flock, party** We could hear a pack of coyotes howling in the distance. **3. lot, load, mass, profusion, wealth, abundance, much, heap** I got into a pack of trouble when I skipped school for a day and lied to my parents. ◆ *verb* **1. fill, load, stuff, cram, crowd, squeeze, jam, press, force** I tried to pack too many clothes into my suitcase. **2. package, wrap, wrap up, enwrap, bundle, encase, truss, bind** I packed her books and mailed them to her.

package *noun* **box, carton, parcel, bundle, container, pack, case, packet** The mail carrier left a package on our front porch. ◆ *verb* **pack, wrap, wrap up, enwrap, encase, bundle, enclose, contain** I packaged the cup decorated with pansies and sent it to my sister.

pact *noun* **accord, concord, agreement, alliance, treaty, bargain, deal, covenant, contract** The two nations signed a pact to help defend each other.

pad¹ *noun* **1. cushion, mat, mattress, pillow, bolster, bedding, pallet** We used a blanket and a foam pad to make a bed for our dog. **2. notepad, tablet, notebook, memo pad, writing tablet, ledger** Each student received two pencils and a pad of paper. ◆ *verb* **1. protect, pack, cushion, secure, safeguard, line, stuff, cover** I padded the cup for my sister with crumpled newspapers when I packed it for shipping. **2. protract, embellish, expand, enlarge, amplify, augment, exaggerate** The reporter padded her story with extra background information.

pad² *verb* **walk, patter, tiptoe, stroll, traipse, pussyfoot, tramp, creep, sneak** I padded through the house in my bare feet.

paddle *noun* **oar, sweep, scull, blade** The life raft came equipped with two paddles. ◆ *verb* **1. row, scull, cruise, navigate, sail, punt, run, pull** My brother and I can paddle our boat across the lake in less than half an hour. **2. beat, flog, spank, thrash, batter, lambaste, wallop, drub, whip** Were you ever paddled when you were a child?

page¹ *noun* **1. leaf, sheet, paper** I tore a page from my notebook to write a list. **2. stage, time, phase, period, point, chapter, episode, event, occasion** The decade of the 1920s was an interesting page in United States history.

page² *noun* **attendant, servant, messenger, squire, lackey, flunky** The senator asked his page to run an errand. ◆ *verb* **call, summon, send for, bid, ask, invite, order** The principal paged a student over the school intercom.

pageant *noun* **play, show, performance, drama, spectacle, ceremony, celebration, procession** I will be playing a Pilgrim in this year's Thanksgiving pageant.

pail *noun* **bucket, can, container, vessel, receptacle, dipper, hod, scuttle** I use a plastic pail to carry water to my flower garden.

pain *noun* **1. ache, hurt, soreness, pang, discomfort, smart, twinge, sting, stitch** I felt surprisingly little pain when I broke my arm. **2. distress, anxiety, woe, heartache, grief, sorrow, misery, anguish** My family went through a lot of pain when my dad was laid off. **3. trouble, care, effort, difficulty, labor, toil, exertion, strain, stress** I went to great pains to make my report as complete as possible. **4. nuisance, pest, bother, annoyance, aggravation, headache, vexation, irritation** Sometimes my older brother is a pain. ◆ *verb* **1. hurt, ache, sting, smart, throb, ail, twinge, wound, injure** My sprained thumb pains me. **2. distress, trouble, vex, grieve, disquiet, bother, sadden, worry** It pains me to see you so unhappy. ➡ **Antonyms: *noun* 1. comfort, relief 2. happiness, satisfaction 4. joy, pleasure ◆ *verb* 2. please, gladden, delight**

painstaking *adjective* **careful, meticulous, thorough, diligent, scrupulous, conscientious, assiduous, fastidious** The copyeditor did a painstaking job. ➡ **Antonyms: careless, sloppy, negligent**

paint *noun* **color, coloring, pigment, dye, oils, stain, tint, varnish** Mom told me to put two coats of green paint on our old picnic table. ◆ *verb* **1. color, tint, dye, shade,**

stain, cover, decorate, smear, brush, daub The clown painted his face red and white. **2.** describe, relate, portray, depict, tell, recount, represent, picture The travel lecturer painted a fascinating portrait of the Far East.

painting *noun* picture, portrait, canvas, drawing, oil, sketch, art, artwork One of the world's most famous paintings is the *Mona Lisa* by Leonardo da Vinci.

pair *noun* couple, twosome, duo, team, unit, match, set, brace, combination I think you and I would make a good pair. ◆ *verb* match, match up, couple, join, mate, team, combine, unite The wrestling coach paired his students according to their weight.

pal *noun* buddy, chum, companion, comrade, friend, mate, crony, associate, confidant George and I have been pals for years.

palace *noun* royal residence, castle, manor, mansion, villa, chateau, hacienda, hall The queen lived in a magnificent palace.

pale *adjective* faint, light, dim, colorless, whitish, pallid, wan, ashen, livid Her dress is a pale shade of green. ◆ *verb* blanch, whiten, lose color, bleach, fade, dim, dull His face paled when he realized the danger that he was in. ◈ **Antonyms:** *adjective* bright, vivid

pallor *noun* paleness, whiteness, pastiness, colorlessness, bloodlessness I could tell the accident victim was going into shock by the sudden pallor of her face. ◈ **Antonyms:** flush, ruddiness

palpable *adjective* **1.** tangible, physical, corporeal, material, concrete, solid Each beat of his heart became a palpable force as his anxiety increased. **2.** obvious, perceivable, noticeable, distinct, clear, apparent, conspicuous, plain The musical *West Side Story* was a palpable success from its opening night. ◈ **Antonyms: 1.** intangible, spiritual **2.** obscure, unnoticeable

paltry *adjective* **1.** trivial, petty, trifling, piddling, small, negligible, meager, insignificant, picayune They had a paltry argument that was soon forgotten. **2.** lowly, contemptible, rotten, lousy, miserable, wretched, vile, despicable In old-fashioned melodramas, the villain always behaves in a paltry manner. ◈ **Antonyms: 1.** important, significant **2.** honorable, worthy

pamper *verb* baby, cater to, coddle, indulge, spoil, humor, gratify, please My aunt pampers her cat by feeding it fresh tuna and chicken.

pamphlet *noun* booklet, brochure, leaflet, manual, book, text, tract, folder My new bicycle came with a pamphlet on safety tips.

pan *noun* frying pan, saucepan, skillet, pot, vessel, container When I wash dishes, I do the pans last. ◆ *verb* **1.** wash, rinse, sift, sieve, search, scan, move, separate The prospector panned a lot of dirt before he found his first nugget of gold. **2.** criticize, attack, castigate, roast, flay, condemn, denounce, fault The critics panned the new adventure movie, but I enjoyed it. ◈ **Antonyms:** *verb* **2.** praise, approve

pandemonium *noun* chaos, uproar, hullabaloo, tumult, bedlam, clamor, turbulence, din There was pandemonium when the winner of the presidential nomination was announced at the political convention. ◈ **Antonyms:** peace, order, calm

panel *noun* committee, assembly, board, commission, group, jury, tribunal, forum The talk show featured a panel of teachers who discussed how the quality of public education might be improved.

pang *noun* ache, pain, throe, smart, twinge, stab, soreness, discomfort, irritation I get hunger pangs if I go too long without eating.

panic *noun* alarm, dread, fear, fright, terror, hysteria, frenzy, horror, distress I felt a sudden panic when I thought the car was going to go off the road. ◆ *verb* alarm, frighten, scare, terrify, terrorize, unnerve, shock, startle The horse galloped away after a rattlesnake panicked it.

panorama *noun* scene, vista, perspective, prospect, tableau, picture, scenery, diorama John Constable was famous for painting panoramas of the English countryside.

pant *verb* **1.** gasp, huff, puff, wheeze, blow, breathe, respire On hot days, my dog lies in the shade and pants with his tongue hanging out. **2.** yearn, long, wish, crave, hunger, ache, pine, want, thirst, desire I am panting for a chance to attend this year's Scout jamboree. ◆ *noun* gasp, huff, puff, gulp, wheeze, snort, inhalation, exhalation, breath The old steam engine gave several pants, then started to move along the track.

paper *noun* **1.** stationery, writing paper, notepaper, letterhead, parchment, sheet, page I need a piece of paper to write a letter to Grandmother. **2.** legal form, certificate, document, contract, deed, permit, affidavit, record Mom and Dad had to sign a bunch of papers when they bought our new house. **3.** gazette, newspaper, journal, periodical, tabloid, chronicle, daily, weekly Our local paper is called the *Daily Enterprise*. **4.** composition, essay, report, theme, treatise, article, study, dissertation, thesis I have to select a President and write a paper about his life.

parade *noun* **1.** march, procession, cavalcade, motorcade, caravan, promenade, cortege, review Our school band will march in this year's Fourth of July parade. **2.** display, spectacle, array, show, exposition, pomp, panoply, exhibition The parade of talent during the opening ceremonies was enthralling. ◆ *verb* **1.** file, march, step, stride, stroll, walk, promenade The graduating students paraded across the stage to pick up their diplomas. **2.** vaunt, show off, exhibit, display, flaunt, brandish, strut, prance She paraded her new coat in front of her friends.

paradise *noun* heaven, utopia, promised land, delight, ecstasy, glory, bliss, rapture Many people think that Hawaii is a tropical paradise. ➬ **Antonyms:** misery, hell, desolation

paradox *noun* contradiction, incongruity, inconsistency, puzzle, enigma, mystery, riddle, conundrum Dickens's *A Tale of Two Cities* opens with a famous paradox: "It was the best of times, it was the worst of times. . . ."

paragon *noun* model, example, ideal, paradigm, nonpareil, symbol, prototype, pattern Abraham "Honest Abe" Lincoln was a paragon of many virtues.

parallel *adjective* **1.** side by side, collateral, abreast, aligned, alongside, even, equidistant The rails of a railroad track are parallel to each other. **2.** alike, corresponding, equivalent, like, similar, analogous, duplicate, matching The two scientists are conducting parallel experiments to see if they get the same results. ◆ *noun* **1.** twin, counterpart, equivalent, match, double, duplicate, analogue Her movie role was the parallel of her part in the stage play. **2.** comparison, likeness, resemblance, similarity, analogy, correspondence, parallelism There are some obvious parallels between the two bank robberies. ◆ *verb* compare, correspond, equal, match, resemble, duplicate, copy The subjects covered in home schooling parallel what is taught in public schools. ➬ **Antonyms:** *adjective* **2.** different, dissimilar ◆ *noun* **2.** difference ◆ *verb* differ, diverge

paralyze *verb* cripple, disable, immobilize, knock out, incapacitate, numb, stun, halt A massive power failure paralyzed the entire West Coast.

paramount *adjective* primary, supreme, foremost, utmost, principal, leading, capital, premier My parents have told me that getting an education is of paramount importance. ➬ **Antonyms:** least, secondary, smallest

paranoid *adjective* fearful, suspicious, apprehensive, distrustful, wary, paranoiac, psychotic She is so paranoid that she thinks she is being followed everywhere she goes.

parcel *noun* **1.** box, carton, package, bundle, container, pack, packet The post office delivers millions of parcels every year. **2.** lot, plot, tract, section, field, patch, property, acreage My grandparents have several parcels of land. **3.** collection, assortment, group, bunch, multitude, mass, batch I looked through the parcel of books at the library sale and found several to buy. ◆ *verb* portion out, allocate, distribute, dispense, dole out, assign, ration, disperse I helped Mom parcel out sandwiches and lemonade to my friends.

parch *verb* dehydrate, dry out, burn, roast, scorch, wither, blister, sear, bake The long drought has parched all the cornfields. ➬ **Antonyms:** wet, water, moisten

pardon *verb* excuse, forgive, absolve, overlook, condone, acquit, exonerate, remit Please pardon my barging in like this. ◆ *noun* forgiveness, mercy, acquittal, amnesty, exoneration, excuse, release, remission I beg your pardon, but I didn't mean to bump into you. ➬ **Antonyms:** *verb* accuse, charge, condemn

pare *verb* **1.** peel, skin, strip, cut, scale, shave I pared several cups of apples for a pie. **2.** cut down, cut back, trim, prune, shear, slash, lower, reduce, decrease The firm had to pare its prices in order to remain competitive. ➬ **Antonyms:** **2.** increase, inflate

parent *noun* father, mother, begetter, progenitor, sire, ancestor, forefather, foremother I live with only one parent.

pariah *noun* outcast, untouchable, castaway, leper, undesirable, exile, outlaw Victims of leprosy used to be pariahs of society.

parish *noun* congregation, flock, parishioners, churchgoers, laity, brethren, church The entire parish attended the memorial service.

park *noun* **1.** common, square, field, green, grounds, playground, lawn, picnic ground My friends and I like to play softball in the park. **2.** reserve, sanctuary, preserve, reservation, refuge, haven, shelter There is a big game park near San Diego where the animals roam free. ◆ *verb* leave, place, position, put, store, station, stand, deposit Mom parked the car around the corner from the train station.

parlor *noun* sitting room, salon, drawing room, living room, reception room, lounge The old farmhouse had a small front parlor.

parody *noun* burlesque, caricature, imitation, lampoon, takeoff, satire, travesty, farce We did a parody of a popular TV show for our school talent contest. ◆ *verb* imitate, spoof, lampoon, burlesque, mimic, satirize, mock, caricature The comedian parodied famous people as part of his act.

parrot *verb* repeat, imitate, ape, echo, copy, mimic, mirror, quote I heard my little sister parrot my mother's style of answering the telephone.

part *noun* 1. passage, section, segment, element, piece, portion, division Some parts of the book were better than others. 2. measure, portion, ration, share, split, allotment, allocation, lot The inheritance was divided into equal parts. 3. role, share, duty, function, responsibility, task, job, work, business Everyone did their part to help clean up the classroom. ◆ *verb* 1. divide, open, separate, split, section, segment, cleave Please part the curtains so we can get some light in here. 2. go, depart, leave, quit, exit, part company, break up, withdraw I was sad when I had to part from my friends. ● **Antonyms:** *noun* 1. & 2. all, whole ◆ *verb* 1. connect, join 2. stay, linger, remain

partial *adjective* 1. incomplete, limited, part, fragmentary, fractional, unfinished, halfway, imperfect I got only partial credit for my report because I didn't submit a bibliography. 2. biased, one-sided, prejudiced, unfair, unjust, sectarian, factional, partisan A good referee is not partial. ● **Antonyms:** 1. complete, total 2. fair, impartial

participate *verb* join in, take part, partake, contribute, cooperate, share, engage Everybody participated in the sing-along.

particle *noun* bit, fragment, grain, piece, speck, trace, iota, jot, scrap, morsel The dog ate every last particle of food in his dish.

particular *adjective* 1. precise, specific, exact, singular, single, discrete, individual, separate, distinct There is a particular quote that I plan to include in my oral report. 2. close, detailed, special, thorough, full, painstaking, meticulous Whenever I get ready to go out, I pay particular attention to my hair. 3. choosy, fussy, picky, dainty, careful, finicky, selective, fastidious She's very particular about what she eats. ◆ *noun* detail, fact, factor, point, specific, item, circumstance, feature, instance Please tell me all the particulars about your trip to Mexico.

partition *noun* 1. barrier, divider, screen, wall, panel, fence, curtain Some libraries have partitions between the desks so that patrons can study in privacy. 2. division, split, separation, severance, cleavage, disunion, parting The partition of Korea into two separate countries took place in 1945. ◆ *verb* divide, section, separate, split, break up, segment, subdivide, fence, wall Dad partitioned off part of the garage to make a workshop for himself.

partly *adverb* partially, partway, slightly, somewhat, halfway, part Please leave the window partly open until the room cools off. ● **Antonyms:** completely, totally

partner *noun* 1. associate, colleague, affiliate, cohort, confederate, ally, fellow My dad and my uncle are business partners. 2. friend, companion, comrade, amigo, chum, buddy, pal, crony Mom has several golf partners. 3. spouse, mate, helpmate, consort, wife, husband When a couple marries, they promise to be partners for life.

partnership *noun* alliance, association, business, company, affiliation, combination, club My two aunts have formed a business partnership.

party *noun* 1. celebration, festivity, get-together, social, fete, gala, affair, function We're going to give our parents a surprise party for their anniversary. 2. group, company, bunch, set, band, crowd, gang, crew Dad asked the waiter to seat our entire party at one table. 3. coalition, league, alliance, faction, cabal, bloc, sect, interest Which political party do you support? 4. participant, player, actor, principal, side, member, person, individual The two parties in the lawsuit reached a settlement out of court.

pass *verb* 1. go, journey, move, proceed, progress, fare, travel, wend A fire engine passed by about ten minutes ago. 2. accomplish, achieve, complete, fulfill, satisfy, finish, answer, qualify My older sister just passed all the requirements to get her driver's license. 3. go away, cease, depart, end, expire, lapse, die, disappear, evaporate If you take these aspirin, your pain should soon pass. 4. ignore, disregard, neglect, skip, omit, eschew, miss, overlook I passed on watching TV last night and did some reading instead. 5. surpass, beat, excel, better, best, transcend, outstrip, surmount, top I was pleased when I passed my own best record. 6. give, convey, deliver, hand, hand over, transfer, transmit, present, send Please pass me the butter. 7. spend, occupy, consume, fill, wile away, expend, put in I passed the evening sorting out my drawers and closet. 8. adopt, approve, enact, confirm, ratify, sanction, authorize, certify The state legislature passed a bill requiring bicyclists to wear helmets. 9. discharge, drain, issue, flow, pour, release, empty, expel I cleaned the leaves out of the gutter so the water could pass freely. ◆ *noun* 1. saddle, cut, notch, gap, divide, opening, passage, ridge The trail climbs steadily to a narrow pass. 2. ticket, voucher, admission, permit, authorization, permission, warrant I have two free passes to attend a movie tonight. **3. toss, throw, cast, fling, lob, pitch, delivery, transfer** The quarterback threw a long pass. **4. predicament, pinch, jam, crisis, plight, exigency, state, emergency** The house has been neglected, and the need for repairs has come to an extreme pass. ⬧**Antonyms:** *verb* **2. fail, flunk 3. begin, start, commence 4. observe, attend 5. lag, fall behind**

passage *noun* **1. course, flow, movement, passing, progression, change, shift, transition** I hope I will grow taller with the passage of time. **2. corridor, passageway, path, walkway, way, hall, hallway, route, arcade** There is an underground passage that connects these two buildings. **3. enactment, passing, ratification, approval, resolution, legislation, establishment** The lobbyist worked hard to ensure passage of the bill. **4. selection, excerpt, part, portion, section, segment, extract, quotation** Our teacher read us a passage from her favorite book.

passenger *noun* **rider, traveler, fare, commuter, tourist, wayfarer** A Boeing 747 can carry more than four hundred passengers.

passion *noun* **1. emotion, enthusiasm, ardor, fervor, feeling, fire, intensity, zeal** He spoke with passion about his homeland. **2. love, desire, craze, obsession, mania, fancy, fascination, infatuation** She has a passion for collecting antique dolls. ⬧**Antonyms: 1. indifference, apathy**

passionate *adjective* **emotional, forceful, heated, intense, impassioned, moving, fervent, poignant** The charity's spokesperson made a passionate plea for donations. ⬧**Antonyms: apathetic, indifferent**

passive *adjective* **acquiescent, submissive, unassertive, docile, compliant, deferential, yielding** According to one longevity test, being laid-back and passive can take years off your life. ⬧**Antonyms: assertive, aggressive**

past *adjective* **1. gone, dead, over, finished, ended, expired, defunct, forgotten** The day of the steam engine is long past. **2. bygone, ancient, archaic, old, olden, old-time, historic, immemorial** The resort town has cultivated an air of years past. **3. just over, preceding, previous, prior, earlier, foregoing, recent** I've been pretty busy for the past few days. **4. former, old, late, erstwhile, previous, one-time, once, sometime** A past president of our club will be speaking tonight. ◆ *noun* **1. former times, previous times, yesterday, yesteryear, yore, bygone days, ancient times, antiquity** In the past, people did not live as long as they do now. **2. background, history, heritage, life story, life, experiences, circumstances** The senator has a distinguished

past. ◆ *preposition* **after, beyond, behind, over, across, through** To get to the municipal swimming pool, turn left just past the library.

Word Group

Pasta refers to dough that has been formed into shapes and is often dried for later use. **Pasta** is a general term with no true synonyms. Here are some common types of pasta:

cannelloni, fettuccine, lasagna, linguine, macaroni, manicotti, mostaccioli, ravioli, rigatoni, spaghetti, tortellini, vermicelli, ziti

paste *noun* **adhesive, glue, mucilage, cement, fixative, binder, plaster, gum** We used paste to hang the new wallpaper in our living room. ◆ *verb* **glue, cement, stick, attach, fasten, fuse, gum, bind** Chris pasted some new photographs into his scrapbook.

pastime *noun* **diversion, entertainment, amusement, hobby, recreation, sport, distraction, relaxation** Baseball is one of America's most popular pastimes.

pasture *noun* **field, meadow, grassland, pastureland, sward, greensward, lea** We saw some cows and horses grazing in the same pasture.

pasty *adjective* **pale, livid, pallid, chalky, white, ashen, sallow, wan, gray, waxen** She had a pasty complexion after being ill for so long. ⬧**Antonyms: rosy, ruddy, florid**

pat[1] *verb* **1. tap, pet, stroke, caress, touch** I patted my dog on the head when he brought me my slippers. **2. flatten, shape, form, mold, press, knead, hit, tap, slap** I patted the bread dough smooth. ◆ *noun* **1. slap, tap, hit, rap, strike, stroke, caress** My friend gave me a pat on the back. **2. dab, cake, lump, portion, piece, daub, square** The waitress gave me a pat of butter for my toast.

pat[2] *adjective* **1. trite, glib, facile, smooth, simplistic, banal, familiar, thoughtless** He dismissed her question with a pat answer. **2. suitable, fitting, apt, perfect, apropos, neat, felicitous, appropriate** The grounds crew came up with a pat solution to the litter problem. ⬧**Antonyms: 1. sincere, thoughtful 2. imperfect, unsuitable**

patch *noun* **1. overlay, cover, plug, square, tab, sheet, slab, layer, panel** The carpenter put a patch over the hole in the roof. **2. plot, lot, ground, tract, field, land, area, clearing, parcel** Our town has set aside a patch of land for community gardens. **3. area, space, spot, stretch, section, strip, piece** There were some patches of ice on our driveway this morning. ◆ *verb* **cover, mend, fix, repair, restore, recondition, revamp, reconstruct** I patched the hole in my blue jeans.

patent *noun* **license, registration, permit, grant, charter, franchise, copyright** A patent protects an inventor's rights. ◆ *adjective* **obvious, plain, distinct, manifest, conspicuous, blatant, express, clear, unmistakable** The company's new product has been a patent success.

path *noun* **pathway, trail, walk, walkway, course, route, way, road, lane** This path goes all the way around the lake.

pathetic *adjective* **forlorn, heartbreaking, moving, sad, pitiful, sorry, woeful, piteous, wretched** The lost puppy looked so pathetic that I decided to take him home.

patience *noun* **calmness, restraint, self-control, composure, serenity, tolerance, understanding, forbearance** When the concert didn't start on time, the audience waited with admirable patience. ➧ **Antonyms: impatience, intolerance**

patient *adjective* **1. calm, tolerant, understanding, lenient, compassionate, sympathetic** She is a popular baby sitter in part because she is very patient with young children. **2. persevering, persistent, steadfast, enduring, dogged, diligent, determined** His patient efforts at loading the new software on his computer paid off. ➧ **Antonyms: 1. impatient, intolerant 2. impatient, hasty, impulsive**

patriotic *adjective* **devoted, faithful, loyal, true** We know that our neighbor is a patriotic citizen because he flies the American flag every day.

patrol *verb* **police, inspect, watch, guard, protect, safeguard, defend, cruise** The security officers patrolled the university's building and grounds. ◆ *noun* **scout, sentinel, guard, lookout, watch, vanguard, escort** The captain sent a patrol out ahead of the rest of the troops.

patron *noun* **1. benefactor, sponsor, champion, backer, supporter, contributor, philanthropist** She is a music patron who provides scholarships for promising young musicians. **2. client, customer, regular, habitué, visitor, shopper, buyer, purchaser** The barber shop has dozens of regular patrons.

patronize *verb* **1. frequent, shop at, visit, support, back, assist, help, fund** We patronize that supermarket because they make donations to our school. **2. talk down to, condescend, humor, humiliate, scorn, snub, indulge** Please don't patronize me!

patter[1] *verb* **1. rap, pelt, beat, drum, pat, hit, strike** The rain pattered against the window. **2. tiptoe, scurry, scuttle, scamper, pad, move, walk** My little brother and sister pattered through the house in their pajamas. ◆ *noun* **pitter-patter, pat, tapping, drumming, rapping, tap, tattoo, beat** We could hear the patter of a squirrel running across the roof.

patter[2] *noun* **chatter, chitchat, prattle, babble, jabber, blabber, talk, gibberish** The radio announcer had a witty line of patter.

pattern *noun* **1. arrangement, design, motif, figure, form, shape, scheme, composition** The shadows of the trees make a pretty pattern on the snow. **2. diagram, plan, model, guide, template, blueprint, sketch, drawing** Making a dress is easier if you have a pattern to follow. **3. system, method, order, organization, theme, orderliness, plan** Researchers have discovered a pattern in the way the disease is spread. ◆ *verb* **model, design, fashion, form, build, structure** The architect patterned the museum building after a medieval castle.

pause *verb* **discontinue, break, rest, delay, hesitate, cease, stop, wait, quit** The speaker paused for a moment to glance at his notes. ◆ *noun* **break, interruption, lull, delay, halt, intermission, gap, rest, stop** There was a brief pause in our conversation. ➧ **Antonyms: *verb* continue, persevere**

pave *verb* **coat, cover, surface, top, layer, tar, cement, asphalt** We had our driveway paved with asphalt.

pavilion *noun* **tent, awning, canopy, kiosk, shelter, booth, gazebo** He put up a pavilion at the swap meet.

paw *noun* **pad, foot, forepaw, forefoot, sole, hoof, hand** I took the thorn out of my dog's paw. ◆ *verb* **scratch, rub, scrape, claw, scuff, brush, tear, maul** The bull pawed the ground.

pawn[1] *verb* **pledge, deposit, offer, post, place, risk, gamble, mortgage** The man pawned his favorite camera for money to pay the rent.

pawn[2] *noun* **puppet, tool, instrument, dupe, stooge, victim, cat's-paw** The young princes were pawns in their uncle's bid for the throne.

pay *verb* **1. compensate, give, recompense, remunerate, reimburse, repay** My brother paid me 15 dollars to mow the lawn for him. **2. spend, give, disburse, expend, lay out, render, remit, offer** I paid 30 dollars for this watch. **3. pay off, discharge, settle, satisfy, clear, square, honor, meet** He paid all his debts in full. **4. yield, return, draw, earn,**

gain, gross, net, realize, produce My savings account pays two percent interest. **5. benefit, profit, avail, reward, serve, help, aid, assist, advance** It pays to be studious. ◆ *noun* **compensation, salary, wage, earnings, stipend, remuneration, income, fee** My sister took the baby-sitting job because the pay was very good.

peace *noun* **1. accord, harmony, amity, friendship, neutrality, armistice, truce** There has always been peace between the United States and Canada. **2. calm, peacefulness, quiet, serenity, tranquillity, quietude, relaxation, rest** Dad loves the sense of peace that he finds on his fishing trips. ◆ **Antonyms: 1. conflict, war 2. chaos, turmoil**

peaceful *adjective* **1. nonviolent, peaceable, pacific, pacifistic, friendly, amicable, neutral** Switzerland is a peaceful country that hasn't been at war since 1848. **2. calm, quiet, serene, tranquil, placid, restful, halcyon, still, untroubled** The little village lay in the middle of a peaceful valley. ◆ **Antonyms: 1. hostile, violent 2. noisy, troubled, restless**

peak *noun* **1. summit, crest, crown, tip, top, roof, height, pinnacle** The mountain's peak was covered with snow. **2. apex, climax, height, top, zenith, limit, maximum, acme, culmination** The actress would appear to be at the peak of her career. ◆ *verb* **crest, climax, culminate, crown, top out, consummate, cap** My interest in the book peaked about halfway through. ◆ **Antonyms: *noun* 1. bottom, base, foot 2. nadir, low point** ◆ *verb* **abate, diminish**

peal *noun* **1. knell, chime, ring, ringing, tolling, clang, reverberation, clangor, clamor** I paused to listen to the peal of the church bells. **2. clap, boom, rumble, roar, crack, crash, blast, roll, noise, sound** I was startled by the sudden peal of thunder. ◆ *verb* **ring, chime, knell, toll, strike, roll, rumble, thunder, roar, resound** The wind chimes pealed musically in the back yard.

peasant *noun* **farmer, sharecropper, tenant, laborer, rustic, yeoman, peon, fellah** My ancestors were peasants in Europe.

pebble *noun* **stone, rock, gravel, shingle** I stopped to take a pebble out of my shoe.

peck[1] *verb* **pick, poke, rap, tap, jab, knock, pound, hit, beat** The bird pecked at the tree bark to find insects. ◆ *noun* **rap, tap, hit, jab, stroke, poke, flick, knock** The sound of the bird's peck on the window woke me up.

peck[2] *noun* **world, wealth, ton, bunch, heap, load, slew, gobs, abundance** He was in a peck of trouble.

peculiar *adjective* **1. curious, odd, strange, queer, funny, eccentric, weird, bizarre, unusual** Our next-door neighbors have some very peculiar habits. **2. unique, distinctive, characteristic, singular, specific, particular, individual** The duck-billed platypus has a peculiar mouth that looks like a bird's beak. ◆ **Antonyms: common, ordinary**

peddle *verb* **hawk, vend, sell, market, barter, trade, merchandise, retail** Vendors were peddling caps, pennants, and other souvenirs at the baseball stadium.

pedestrian *noun* **walker, hiker, stroller, ambler, passer-by** The sidewalk was crowded with pedestrians. ◆ *adjective* **commonplace, prosaic, ordinary, dull, lackluster, boring, uninspired, mundane, tedious** The music critic claimed that the orchestra had given a pedestrian performance. ◆ **Antonyms: *adjective* unique, extraordinary, imaginative**

peek *verb* **glance, glimpse, look, peep, peer, snoop, spy** I peeked into the closet to see if Mom had hidden my presents there. ◆ *noun* **glance, glimpse, look, peep, gander, view** I was tempted to take a peek at my sister's diary.

peel *noun* **skin, rind, cover, layer, bark** I put the apple peels in the compost. ◆ *verb* **pare, strip, skin, cut, shave, scale, flake** I peeled a banana.

peep *noun* **chirp, cheep, chirrup, piping, twitter, trill, squeak, tweet, warble** The chicks made little peeps when I scattered grain for them. ◆ *verb* **chirp, cheep, chirrup, twitter, squeak, trill, warble, sing, pipe** The baby quail peeped as their mother called to them.

peer[1] *verb* **gaze, look, stare, search, examine, scan, observe, watch** I peered into the stream to see if I could see any fish.

peer[2] *noun* **equal, fellow, mate, colleague, associate, teammate** The young doctor had gained the respect of his peers.

peevish *adjective* **irritable, ill-tempered, querulous, cantankerous, cranky, cross, grouchy, crabby** I woke up feeling peevish, but my mood soon changed. ◆ **Antonyms: genial, amiable, agreeable**

peg *noun* **1. knob, pin, spike, dowel, spur, hook, stud, stake, button** I bought a rack with pegs on which to hang hats and coats. **2. rung, step, level, degree, mark, notch, grade, position, stage** Her promotion put her up another peg on the company ladder. ◆ *verb* **fasten, pin, tack, nail, attach, secure, affix, clasp** I pegged the towels to the clothesline.

pellet *noun* ball, sphere, bead, blob, stone, globule, pearl Mom put fertilizer pellets around the base of each tree in our yard.

pelt[1] *noun* coat, hide, skin, fur, hair, fell, fleece During the 19th century, many people wore hats made from beaver pelts.

pelt[2] *verb* batter, beat, hammer, hit, pummel, strike, buffet, knock, whack We listened to the hail as it pelted the roof.

pen[1] *noun* ballpoint pen, fountain pen, quill, nib, marker People usually sign important documents with a pen. ◆ *verb* write, scribble, scrawl, draft, compose, jot down, inscribe I penned a note to my friend and taped it on her locker.

pen[2] *noun* enclosure, cage, coop, corral, sty, stall, pound The farmer keeps his pigs in one large pen. ◆ *verb* confine, corral, enclose, cage, coop, shut in, restrain, imprison We penned the geese for the night.

penalize *verb* punish, discipline, correct, castigate, chastise, fine, sentence The professor penalizes students who turn papers in late by giving them lower grades. ➡ **Antonym:** reward

penalty *noun* punishment, discipline, retribution, fine, correction, castigation, payment, price The penalty for disrupting class is staying after school. ➡ **Antonyms:** reward, prize

pending *adjective* 1. unfinished, undecided, unsettled, unresolved, undetermined, incomplete The meeting agenda included a listing of pending business that has yet to be resolved. 2. forthcoming, impending, upcoming, imminent, looming, approaching, near An announcement from the President's press secretary is pending. ➡ **Antonyms:** 1. complete, resolved

penetrate *verb* 1. pierce, pass through, puncture, enter, perforate, impale An arrow can penetrate several inches of wood. 2. permeate, pervade, suffuse, spread, saturate, impregnate, infuse The smell of the smoldering fire penetrated throughout the house. 3. understand, perceive, comprehend, fathom, discern, unravel, decipher, catch Physicist Stephen Hawking was the first to penetrate several mysteries of the universe.

penitentiary *noun* pen, prison, jail, house of correction, reformatory, stockade, brig The felon was sentenced to ten years in the penitentiary.

pennant *noun* banner, flag, standard, streamer, ensign, jack, colors, bunting I have a collection of college pennants.

penniless *adjective* impoverished, destitute, poor, broke, indigent, poverty-stricken, impecunious, bankrupt Sometimes people who are penniless are arrested for vagrancy. ➡ **Antonyms:** wealthy, affluent, rich

pension *noun* allowance, allotment, benefit, support, payment, premium, annuity, social security Grandfather receives a monthly pension.

pensive *adjective* 1. thoughtful, reflective, meditative, contemplative, preoccupied, thinking, speculative She was in a pensive mood. 2. sad, wistful, melancholy, solemn, somber, grave, sorrowful, mournful Sometimes I feel pensive when I think of growing up and leaving home. ➡ **Antonyms:** 2. happy, cheerful

people *noun* 1. human beings, humans, individuals, persons, mortals, souls, folks More than three hundred people attended our school play. 2. citizens, citizenry, populace, public, community, inhabitants, population, society The people voted in favor of the new recycling law. 3. relatives, family, ancestors, kin, kinfolk, kinsmen, kinswomen, clan Most of my people came from Africa. ◆ *verb* populate, inhabit, occupy, settle Bedouins are among the few who people the Sahara Desert.

perceive *verb* 1. discover, note, notice, observe, see, recognize, glimpse, spot, tell Can you perceive the differences between the twin sisters? 2. apprehend, comprehend, grasp, know, realize, understand, fathom, discern The teacher quickly perceived that some students had not understood her directions. ➡ **Antonyms:** 1. ignore, overlook 2. misunderstand, miss

percentage *noun* fraction, part, percent, proportion, share, ratio, piece, allotment A large percentage of the voters are opposed to the new taxes.

perceptive *adjective* insightful, astute, alert, sensitive, incisive, keen, shrewd, intuitive, perspicacious Jane Austen is considered to have been a perceptive observer of society. ➡ **Antonyms:** insensitive, obtuse

perch *noun* seat, vantage point, spot, position, location, roost, nest, aerie I had a good perch from which to watch the parade. ◆ *verb* roost, settle, rest, sit, squat, alight, land, balance, poise The flock of blackbirds perched in the cattails for the night.

perennial *adjective* enduring, perpetual, lasting, abiding, permanent, persistent, timeless, continuous Forgetting my house keys is a perennial fault of mine. ➡ **Antonyms:** fleeting, temporary

perfect *adjective* **1. complete, whole, intact, full, entire, consummate, good** I have a perfect understanding of the situation. **2. accurate, correct, exact, precise, right, strict, faithful, true** My model space station is perfect in every detail. **3. faultless, flawless, impeccable, sound, unbroken, unimpaired, good** My aunt can speak perfect Russian. **4. ideal, excellent, superlative, fine, good, peerless, supreme, superb** This is a perfect day for a picnic. **5. complete, thorough, utter, absolute, pure, sheer, outright, total** Stop acting like a perfect fool! ◆ *verb* **develop, polish, refine, hone, smooth, complete, evolve, accomplish** The gymnast perfected his technique by practicing several hours every day. ➤ **Antonyms:** *adjective* **1. imperfect, deficient 2. inexact, inaccurate 3. faulty, flawed 4. poor, mediocre 5. partial**

perform *verb* **1. accomplish, complete, do, effect, achieve, execute, conclude, dispatch** The surgeon performed two operations in one day. **2. fulfill, heed, satisfy, carry out, realize, discharge, observe, keep** He performed the required steps as outlined in the instruction manual. **3. dramatize, enact, give, present, put on, stage, produce, exhibit** Our class will perform Shakespeare's *Romeo and Juliet*. **4. function, operate, work, behave, run, go, manage, serve** Our new car performs better than we expected. **5. act, play, portray, characterize, impersonate, represent, depict** I will perform the role of Juliet in our class play.

performance *noun* **1. operation, functioning, effectiveness, efficiency, working, behavior, action** I bought a new hard drive to improve my computer's performance. **2. play, show, spectacle, production, presentation, pageant, recital, revue** My aunt and uncle attended a performance of Agatha Christie's play *The Mousetrap* while they were in London. **3. accomplishment, realization, discharge, execution, conduct, fulfillment** The mayor saluted the firefighters for their outstanding performance of their duties.

perfume *noun* **fragrance, scent, cologne, aroma, bouquet, odor, smell, redolence** The saleswoman gave me a sample of a new perfume.

perhaps *adverb* **conceivably, maybe, possibly, perchance, imaginably, reasonably** Perhaps we'll be able to get together tomorrow night. ➤ **Antonyms: certainly, surely**

peril *noun* **danger, hazard, risk, threat, jeopardy, menace, pitfall, exposure** The astronauts on the flight of *Apollo 13* faced severe peril on their mission. ➤ **Antonyms: safety, security**

period *noun* **interval, phase, season, span, term, time, cycle, stage, course, spell** We have been experiencing a period of rainy weather.

periodic *adjective* **cyclic, recurrent, intermittent, sporadic, occasional, regular, routine, repeated** Victims of malaria have periodic bouts of fever.

periodical *noun* **magazine, journal, publication, paper, bulletin, newsletter** My family subscribes to a number of periodicals.

perish *verb* **die, expire, pass away, succumb, decease, depart, drop, disappear** Many animals perished in the forest fire. ➤ **Antonyms: survive, thrive**

permanent *adjective* **durable, enduring, lasting, long-lasting, old, constant, abiding, persistent** I have a permanent scar on my arm. ➤ **Antonyms: temporary, fleeting, impermanent**

permit *verb* **1. allow, authorize, warrant, sanction, tolerate, approve, consent, endorse** My school does not permit smoking on campus. **2. allow, admit, oblige, be favorable, let, empower, enable, grant** If the weather permits, we can go swimming. ◆ *noun* **license, authorization, permission, sanction, pass, approval, warrant** My brother's learner's permit allows him to drive a car if a licensed adult is present. ➤ **Antonyms:** *verb* **forbid, prohibit**

perpetrate *verb* **commit, do, perform, execute, effect, carry out, pull off** Did they find out who perpetrated the robbery?

perpetrator *noun* **offender, wrongdoer, transgressor, lawbreaker, outlaw, malefactor, suspect** The police arrested the perpetrator yesterday.

perpetual *adjective* **1. endless, eternal, enduring, unending, everlasting, permanent, infinite** No one has ever built a machine capable of perpetual motion. **2. continual, ceaseless, incessant, constant, uninterrupted, persistent, relentless, interminable** That dog's perpetual barking is starting to annoy me. ➤ **Antonyms: 1. transient, temporary 2. interrupted, inconstant**

perplex *verb* **baffle, bewilder, confuse, mystify, puzzle, stump, dumbfound, confound** The cat's strange behavior perplexed its owner. ➤ **Antonyms: enlighten, clarify**

persecute *verb* **harass, oppress, punish, torment, abuse, wrong, victimize, molest** Throughout history many religious groups have been persecuted for their beliefs. ➤ **Antonyms: support, uphold**

persevere *verb* **persist, carry on, keep on, continue, endure, maintain** He persevered in his efforts to learn the challenging piano piece for his recital. ● **Antonyms: give up, waver, vacillate**

persist *verb* **1. persevere, carry on, strive, struggle, insist** The early suffragists persisted in their campaign to gain women the right to vote. **2. continue, endure, go on, last, remain, linger, abide, stay** The hailstorm persisted long enough to damage most of the crops. ● **Antonyms: 1. waver, falter 2. end, vanish, disappear**

persistent *adjective* **1. determined, firm, insistent, persevering, stubborn, dogged, resolute, tenacious** The persistent salesman would not take "no" for an answer. **2. chronic, constant, continual, lasting, lingering, long-lived, perennial, permanent** He went to the doctor because he had a persistent cough. ● **Antonyms: 1. irresolute, vacillating 2. short-lived, temporary**

person *noun* **human, human being, individual, man, woman, soul, mortal, earthling** The claim that Robert Peary was the first person to reach the North Pole is disputed.

personal *adjective* **1. private, intimate, individual, own, particular, special, exclusive** I keep my personal thoughts in a diary. **2. bodily, physical, corporeal, corporal, material, tangible** Personal cleanliness is an important attribute. ● **Antonyms: 1. common, public 2. spiritual**

personality *noun* **1. character, disposition, nature, temperament, makeup, complexion, identity** My twin brothers may look alike, but they have very different personalities. **2. charm, charisma, allure, magnetism, glamour, attractiveness** The actor succeeded more on personality than talent. **3. celebrity, notable, personage, star, dignitary, luminary, superstar, hero** The TV weatherman is a local personality. ● **Antonyms: 3. nobody, has-been**

perspective *noun* **1. view, vista, prospect, panorama, scene, outlook, lookout** Ansel Adams, the photographer, chose outdoor perspectives for his photographs. **2. viewpoint, standpoint, position, attitude, angle, orientation, belief** From my perspective, the problem doesn't look so big. **3. context, proportion, relation, relativity, reference, balance** To put the size of a blue whale into perspective: a full-grown one can weigh as much as two thousand men.

perspire *verb* **sweat, lather, excrete, drip, pour, exude, swelter** I was perspiring heavily after I finished the mile run.

persuade *verb* **coax, convince, get, influence, sway, talk into, urge, cajole, entice** I'm trying to persuade my parents to let me go on the overnight camping trip. ● **Antonyms: dissuade, deter, discourage**

pertain *verb* **apply, bear on, concern, relate, touch, connect, refer, regard** The judge would only allow testimony that pertained to the case.

pertinent *adjective* **applicable, relevant, related, germane, fitting, suitable, apropos** Our teacher cautioned us to include only pertinent information in our reports. ● **Antonyms: irrelevant, extraneous, impertinent**

pessimistic *adjective* **dark, dismal, cynical, gloomy, glum, sullen, hopeless, despairing** The movie we saw takes a pessimistic view of human nature. ● **Antonyms: hopeful, optimistic**

pest *noun* **annoyance, bother, irritation, nuisance, pain, trouble, headache, aggravation** My little brother is a big pest when he won't leave me alone.

pester *verb* **annoy, bother, disturb, harass, irritate, torment, trouble, vex** Please don't pester me while I'm trying to do my homework.

pestilence *noun* **disease, plague, epidemic, pandemic, infestation, infection, scourge, outbreak, malignancy** Smallpox is a pestilence that has been eliminated through aggressive vaccination programs.

pet *noun* **darling, dear, favorite, love, treasure, beloved, precious** My little nephew is my pet. ◆ *adjective* **cherished, favored, favorite, preferred, special, precious, choice** Dad's pet project is the canoe that he's been working on for years. ◆ *verb* **caress, fondle, stroke, cuddle, pat, rub** My cat purrs when I pet her.

petition *noun* **appeal, plea, proposal, request, application, suit, solicitation** Hundreds of parents signed a petition asking the city to hire more teachers. ◆ *verb* **appeal to, apply to, ask, call upon, entreat, request, sue, beg, supplicate** The scientists petitioned the government for more money to support their research.

petrify *verb* **1. dry, harden, set, solidify, fossilize, calcify** Under the right conditions, wood will petrify into stone. **2. frighten, horrify, paralyze, scare, terrify, shock, stun** That scene in the horror movie petrified me. ● **Antonyms: 1. melt, liquefy, soften 2. soothe, delight**

petty *adjective* **1. insignificant, minor, small, little, trifling, trivial, unimportant, inconsequential** My friend doesn't let petty problems bother her. **2. mean, intolerant, narrow-minded, small-minded, spiteful, selfish, malicious** Gossip is spread by petty people. ● **Antonyms: 1. important, significant 2. tolerant**

petulant *adjective* **crabby, cross, grumpy, irritable, peevish, sullen, grouchy, ugly** The baby was in a petulant mood. ◆ **Antonyms: cheerful, pleasant, agreeable**

phantom *noun* **ghost, spirit, wraith, apparition, specter, phantasm, spook, shade** A phantom was believed to haunt the opera house.

phase *noun* **1. period, stage, state, step, level, condition** A tadpole is one phase in the life cycle of a frog. **2. aspect, part, feature, facet, angle, viewpoint, side, position** I am to report on one phase of the current political crisis.

phenomenal *adjective* **extraordinary, outstanding, remarkable, stupendous, prodigious, marvelous, fantastic** In Rabelais's *Gargantua and Pantagruel*, the two giants had phenomenal appetites for food and drink. ◆ **Antonyms: common, routine, average**

phenomenon *noun* **1. occurrence, fact, reality, happening, event, actuality, occasion, circumstance, thing** Fire is a natural phenomenon. **2. marvel, sensation, wonder, miracle, rarity, prodigy, spectacle, curiosity** My grandmother says that every baby is a phenomenon.

philosophy *noun* **1. knowledge, learning, wisdom, thought, theory, principles, ideas, metaphysics** The ancient Greeks believed that philosophy should guide human conduct. **2. ideology, doctrine, dogma, rationale, tenet, outlook, belief, value** My personal philosophy is based on the principle that everyone deserves respect.

phobia *noun* **fear, terror, horror, dread, loathing, aversion, dislike, apprehension** I have a phobia of snakes. ◆ **Antonyms: love, attraction**

phony *adjective* **artificial, counterfeit, fake, false, pretend, spurious, fraudulent, bogus** The actor's phony American accent didn't fool anyone. ◆ *noun* **charlatan, fake, fraud, impostor, pretender, sham, hoax, imitation, forgery** The woman claimed to be a fortuneteller, but she turned out to be a phony. ◆ **Antonyms:** *adjective* **authentic, genuine, real**

photograph *noun* **picture, photo, snapshot, image, portrait, still, slide, print** Grandma has dozens of family photographs on display in her home.

phrase *noun* **expression, motto, saying, slogan, clause, tag, byword, catchword** The word "good-bye" is derived from the phrase "God be with you." ◆ *verb* **couch, express, formulate, present, put, state, word, term, style** Perhaps your question will be easier to answer if you phrase it differently.

physical *adjective* **1. bodily, fleshly, corporal, corporeal, vital, somatic** Athletes exercise regularly to maintain their physical fitness. **2. concrete, material, solid, substantial, actual, real, tangible, palpable, sensible** Anything that you can touch is a physical object. ◆ **Antonyms: 1. mental, spiritual 2. intangible**

physician *noun* **doctor, medical doctor, healer, intern, medical examiner, medical practitioner** If your cold doesn't go away soon, you should see a physician.

pick *verb* **1. choose, decide on, elect, select, single out, settle on, mark, name** I was picked to be the captain of our soccer team. **2. collect, gather, harvest, garner, reap, pluck, get, cull** I helped our next-door neighbor pick raspberries in his garden. **3. open, break open, jimmy, crack, pry, force, lever** The road service had to pick the car door lock when Mom shut the keys and the dog inside. **4. nag, carp, criticize, bully, goad, cavil, bait, badger** I wish that you would quit picking on me! ◆ *noun* **1. choice, preference, selection, election, option, fancy, alternative** You can take your pick of any piece of candy here. **2. best, prize, gem, cream, elite, choice, pride, flower, top** This puppy is the pick of the litter.

picket *noun* **1. stake, pale, peg, pin, post, stanchion, rod, rail, spike** The surveyor put wooden pickets in the ground to mark the corners of the property. **2. guard, sentry, sentinel, lookout, watch, scout, patrol, spotter** Pickets were posted 50 yards in front of the army's main encampment. ◆ *verb* **1. tether, tie, secure, enclose, corral, fence, shut in, restrict, restrain** We picketed the horses for the night. **2. blockade, besiege, demonstrate, protest, strike, boycott, walk out** Striking employees picketed the company's headquarters.

picture *noun* **1. sketch, illustration, drawing, painting, portrait, portrayal, depiction** I would like to draw a picture of you. **2. photo, photograph, snapshot, image, still, print, slide** My friend showed me her vacation pictures. **3. likeness, duplicate, double, copy, image, facsimile, reproduction** My grandfather says I am the picture of my mother when she was my age. **4. film, motion picture, movie, cinema, feature, show, picture show** My favorite movie won an Oscar for best picture. **5. example, epitome, embodiment, personification, ideal, paragon, model, archetype** We cleaned our house until it was the picture of cleanliness. ◆ *verb* **1. draw, illustrate, sketch, paint, represent, depict, portray, render** In religious paintings, the Virgin Mary is commonly pictured holding the baby Jesus. **2. conceive, imagine, envision, visualize, see, think, vision, fancy** I'm trying to picture what my room will look like with new curtains and wallpaper.

piece *noun* **1. part, portion, section, segment, share, unit, division, measure, chunk** I cut the cake into eight pieces. **2. work, creation, masterpiece, production, opus, composition, treatment, painting, song** That piece by Chopin is one of my favorites. **3. specimen, sample, example, article, thing, entity, instance, case** This piece of rock is from the Mount Saint Helens volcanic eruption. **4. token, chip, counter, tile, checker, disk, figure, chessman** I put the last piece on the card and cried, "Bingo!" ◆ *verb* **connect, assemble, join, fix, patch, repair, restore, mend, unite** Dad took it apart, but he could not piece the lawn mower back together.

pier *noun* **1. dock, wharf, quay, landing** Several gift shops and a seafood restaurant are located on the pier. **2. column, buttress, brace, pillar, support, upright, post** There are massive concrete piers supporting the bridge.

pierce *verb* **prick, puncture, penetrate, stab, stick, impale, cut, drill, bore** I hardly felt it when the nurse pierced my skin with a needle.

pile¹ *noun* **1. heap, lump, mass, mound, stack, hill, accumulation, collection** I changed in a hurry and left my dirty clothes in a pile on the floor. **2. great deal, abundance, wealth, world, profusion, quantity, plenty, much** The person who designed this computer program made a pile of money. ◆ *verb* **heap, lump, mass, mound, stack, collect, jam, crowd, amass, accumulate** I piled the leaves into a big heap. ⇒ **Antonyms:** *noun* **2. little, nothing** ◆ *verb* **scatter, disperse**

pile² *noun* **post, column, timber, foundation, support, stake, upright, stanchion** The piles underneath the pier were coated with creosote to keep them from rotting in the water.

pile³ *noun* **nap, fuzz, fleece, fluff, shag, plush** The baby likes to pick at the pile on her blanket.

pilfer *verb* **filch, steal, take, lift, swipe, snatch, rob, thieve, purloin** The shoplifter pilfered a candy bar.

pilgrim *noun* **traveler, seeker, wayfarer, journeyer** John Bunyan's *Pilgrim's Progress* is an allegory about a spiritual journey.

pilgrimage *noun* **journey, quest, mission, expedition, voyage, trip, trek** Muslims are encouraged to make at least one pilgrimage to the holy city of Mecca.

pill *noun* **capsule, tablet, lozenge, dose, medication, medicine, remedy** I take a vitamin pill every morning.

pillar *noun* **1. column, post, pilaster, pier, shaft, support, prop** Our courthouse has two big pillars on either side of the door. **2. mainstay, support, rock, leader, personage, notable, champion** She is one of the pillars of our small community.

pilot *noun* **1. aviator, airman, flyer, captain, commander** Small aircraft usually require only one pilot. **2. helmsman, steersman, navigator, boatman, conductor, director, guide** As the ship neared land, a licensed pilot came on board to guide it into port. ◆ *verb* **fly, operate, guide, navigate, steer, maneuver, conduct, direct, lead** I'd love to be able to pilot an airplane.

pin *noun* **1. skewer, peg, screw, bolt, bar, fastener, support, prong, dowel** I have a pin in the bone of my leg. **2. brooch, clasp, clip, ornament, stickpin, tiepin, decoration, medal** She wore a silver and turquoise pin that was shaped like a little dolphin. ◆ *verb* **1. attach, fasten, fix, secure, stick, staple, bolt, nail, join** I have pinned lots of buttons to my denim jacket. **2. hold, press, restrain, clasp, immobilize, pinion, fix, hold fast** The wrestler pinned his opponent to the mat, winning the match.

pinch *verb* **compress, nip, squeeze, crush, tweak, cramp, contract, bind** I accidentally pinched my hand in the front door. ◆ *noun* **1. nip, tweak, squeeze, press, crush** My friend gave me a playful pinch on the arm. **2. bit, dash, speck, trace, little, dab, jot, mite, taste** I added a pinch of salt to my bowl of chili. **3. crisis, emergency, predicament, difficulty, trouble, strait, plight, clutch** This umbrella isn't very good, but it will do in a pinch. ⇒ **Antonyms:** *noun* **2. bunch, lot**

pine *verb* **1. ache, yearn, desire, crave, covet, hanker, hunger, thirst, wish** I pined for the beautiful necklace that I saw at the Renaissance Faire. **2. languish, wither, grieve, mourn, weaken, waste away, decline, flag** When one of my dogs died, the other one pined.

pinnacle *noun* **1. steeple, belfry, turret, spire, campanile, bell tower, tower** Some shingles blew off the church pinnacle during the last storm. **2. peak, acme, zenith, climax, summit, crown, meridian, apex** Is it true that most scientists and musicians attain the pinnacle of their success before they reach the age of 35? ⇒ **Antonyms: 2. nadir, bottom**

pioneer *noun* **1. settler, homesteader, colonist, explorer, frontiersman, pathfinder, homesteader, trailblazer** During the 1840s, at least ten thousand pioneers made the difficult journey to America's West. **2. creator, developer, forerunner, founder, originator, innovator, builder** The

Wright brothers were among the pioneers of aviation. ◆ *adjective* **early, earliest, first, original, maiden, primary, initial, lead** Pioneer efforts in road construction were made by John Loudon McAdam and Thomas Tilford. ◆ *verb* **originate, invent, develop, found, create, inaugurate, launch, explore** Nicholas Tesla pioneered several applications of high-voltage electricity. ➻ **Antonyms:** *noun* 2. **follower, imitator** ◆ *adjective* **later, successive** ◆ *verb* **copy, imitate**

pious *adjective* 1. **devout, religious, reverential, holy, saintly, godly, devotional, righteous** The pious man attended church every day. 2. **self-righteous, sanctimonious, holier-than-thou, hypocritical, virtuous, unctuous, insincere** She acts so pious that it displeases others around her. ➻ **Antonyms:** 1. **sacrilegious, profane**

pipe *noun* **main, line, pipeline, tube, vent, conduit, duct, hose, canal, spout** Our water pipes froze last winter. ◆ *verb* 1. **transport, transmit, convey, carry, channel, guide, funnel, supply** The ancient Romans piped water to their cities via aqueducts. 2. **sing, chirp, tweet, whistle, trill, warble, twitter, toot, sound** Our canary began piping when it heard the music on the radio.

pirate *noun* **buccaneer, privateer, corsair, freebooter, marauder, plunderer** Pirates typically attacked lightly armed merchant ships. ◆ *verb* **plagiarize, steal, lift, borrow, appropriate, copy, reproduce, crib** The judge ruled that the musician had pirated the melody of his hit song.

pistol *noun* **handgun, automatic, side arm, revolver, firearm, gun, small arm** Police officers are usually armed with pistols.

pit[1] *noun* **hole, cavity, excavation, depression, hollow, basin, crater** The city turned the abandoned gravel pit into a fishing pond. ◆ *verb* 1. **mark, scar, gouge, dent, hollow, nick, notch, dig** Rust has pitted our car's bumper. 2. **match, oppose, set against, counter, play off, counterbalance, counterpoise** In wrestling matches, people of about the same weight are pitted against each other.

pit[2] *noun* **kernel, seed, stone, pip, core, nut** An avocado pit is much larger than a cherry pit.

pitch *verb* 1. **throw, toss, cast, fling, heave, hurl, send, put, launch** I pitched a stone far out into the lake. 2. **erect, put up, raise, set up, establish, place, plant, locate** We pitched our tent in the lee of the hill. 3. **plunge, topple, tumble, dive, drop, fall, wobble, stagger, slump** The soldier pitched forward in a dead faint. 4. **heave, rock, roll, toss, lift, tilt, lurch, seesaw** Waves pitched our rowboat back and forth. ◆ *noun* 1. **toss, throw, cast, delivery, fling, hurl, chuck, lob, heave** The batter hit a home run on the first pitch. 2. **degree, level, point, height, depth, peak, intensity** The mood of the crowd reached a high pitch of excitement as the band began to play. 3. **angle, grade, incline, slant, slope, tilt, cant, dip, list, rake** The roof of a Swiss chalet has a steep pitch so that snow will slide off it easily. 4. **rise, fall, rocking, lurching, bobbing, undulation, dip, plunge** The boat made a sudden pitch when it was hit by a big wave. 5. **advertisement, advertising, promotion, spiel, buildup, publicity** The TV ad used humor in a pitch for its product.

piteous *adjective* **pathetic, heartbreaking, distressing, pitiful, touching, poignant, rueful, sad** We heard the piteous cry of the lost kitten. ➻ **Antonyms: heartwarming, cheering, joyful**

pitiful *adjective* 1. **pathetic, piteous, forlorn, lamentable, touching, heartbreaking, sad, sorrowful** The injured bird looked pitiful, but we were able to nurse it back to health. 2. **contemptible, abominable, despicable, dreadful, abject, paltry, sorry** That was a pitiful thing to do. ➻ **Antonyms:** 1. **fortunate, happy** 2. **respectable**

pity *noun* 1. **compassion, mercy, sympathy, charity, humanity, empathy, clemency** Many people donated clothes and money out of pity for the hurricane victims. 2. **shame, crime, disgrace, misfortune, regret, sorrow, sadness, catastrophe** It's a pity that you won't be able to join us. ◆ *verb* **feel sorry, have mercy, commiserate, sympathize** I pity the earthquake victims.

pivot *noun* **axis, hinge, swivel, fulcrum, focus, hub, center, axle** The quarterback has become the pivot on which our offense depends. ◆ *verb* **revolve, rotate, swing, swivel, turn, veer, shift** The outcome of the election may pivot on the candidates' final debate.

placate *verb* **calm, soothe, appease, mollify, pacify, quiet, assuage, conciliate** I tried to placate my little sister when we ran out of her favorite cookies. ➻ **Antonyms: vex, nettle, anger**

place *noun* 1. **area, location, point, position, site, spot, plot, space, section** This is a good place to plant the rosebush. 2. **district, locale, locality, region, vicinity, city, town, suburb** It is my uncle's opinion that Wellfleet, Massachusetts, is a great place to live. 3. **abode, dwelling, home, house, residence, domicile, quarters, lodgings** Mom invited some friends over to our place for dinner. 4. **position, post, rank, situation, station, niche, status, grade** George Washington occupies a place of honor in our country's history. **5. duty, role, concern, affair, charge, function, responsibility, privilege, right** It is every citizen's place to vote. **6. job, position, post, berth, appointment, office, employment** My aunt got a place at a firm near her home. ◆ *verb* **1. locate, position, put, set, situate, arrange, deposit, install, park** Please place a chair at each end of the table. **2. appoint, assign, install, establish, commission, settle, nominate** He was placed at the head of the auditing committee. **3. rank, order, array, catalog, range, group, arrange, organize, sequence** I placed the books in alphabetical order. **4. identify, recognize, remember, associate, classify, connect, know** I know I've seen that boy before, but I just can't place him. **5. put, pin on, affix, fix, fasten, assign, set, give, attach** The defendant placed the blame on someone else.

placid *adjective* **still, calm, peaceful, quiet, serene, tranquil, undisturbed, pacific** The lake is placid and smooth whenever the wind dies down. ➤ **Antonyms: agitated, turbulent**

plague *noun* **1. epidemic, pestilence, outbreak, disease, illness, infection, sickness** A deadly plague hit Europe in the mid-14th century. **2. affliction, burden, curse, hardship, problem, trouble, blight, bane, scourge** Poverty and crime are two plagues that society is trying to overcome. ◆ *verb* **afflict, burden, curse, torment, trouble, annoy, bother, pester, distress** The patient was plagued by a cough that lasted all winter.

plain *adjective* **1. apparent, clear, distinct, evident, obvious, unmistakable, patent** You have made your meaning perfectly plain. **2. average, common, ordinary, routine, simple, standard, commonplace, everyday** We use our plain dishes unless we have company. **3. homely, ugly, unattractive, unlovely, uncomely, drab** A baby parrot is plain, even downright ugly! **4. modest, simple, unassuming, unpretentious, frugal** He lives a very plain lifestyle. **5. absolute, frank, honest, sincere, straightforward, blunt, candid, forthright** Please tell me the plain truth. ◆ *noun* **prairie, grassland, steppe, flatland, field, plateau, meadow** Enormous herds of buffalo once roamed the American plains. ➤ **Antonyms:** *adjective* **1. indistinct, vague 2. extraordinary, uncommon 3. beautiful, pretty, attractive 4. fancy, adorned 5. deceptive, evasive**

plan *noun* **1. aim, goal, intent, intention, idea, scheme, strategy, program, method** My brother's plan is to go to college after he graduates from high school. **2. diagram, drawing, outline, blueprint, sketch, layout, design, map** We looked at the plans for our new house. ◆ *verb* **1. arrange, design, devise, organize, contrive, invent, concoct, formulate** Everyone in the class helped to plan the field trip.

2. intend, mean, aim, propose, contemplate, project, foresee, envisage I plan to have a good during my summer vacation.

plane *noun* **1. level, degree, grade, stage** Ancient Greek civilization reached a very high plane of development. **2. aircraft, airplane, airliner, jet, turboprop, ship, hydroplane** Hundreds of planes land at Los Angeles International Airport every day.

> ### Word Group
>
> A **planet** is a celestial body that is larger than an asteroid and that moves in an orbit around a star. **Planet** is a specific term with no true synonyms. Here are some types of planets:
>
> An **inferior planet** has an orbit that is closer to the sun than is Earth's (Mercury, Venus). The **Jovian planets** are the four large, outer planets (Jupiter, Saturn, Uranus, Neptune). A **minor planet** is an asteroid. A **planetoid** is an asteroid. A **superior planet** has an orbit that is farther away from the sun than is Earth's (Mars, Jupiter, Saturn, Uranus, Neptune, Pluto).

plant *noun* **1. bush, grass, herb, shrub, tree, vegetable** We have lots of different plants in our garden. **2. factory, mill, shop, works, facility, foundry, yard, forge** My father works at an automobile plant. ◆ *verb* **1. seed, sow, bury, set, start, root, place, scatter, grow, raise** Winter wheat is planted in the fall. **2. implant, instill, establish, set, install, introduce, fix, found** The book I'm reading planted several new ideas in my mind.

plastic *adjective* **pliable, malleable, flexible, soft, pliant, ductile, elastic, changeable** I was able to change the shape of my vase because the clay was still plastic. ➤ **Antonyms: rigid, hard, stiff**

plate *noun* **1. sheet, panel, scale, layer, lamina, coat** Steel plates were used in the heavy vault doors. **2. platter, serving dish, dish, saucer, china, dinnerware** My father passed the plate of food to me. ◆ *verb* **laminate, gild, coat, electroplate, cover, layer, overlay, face** The goblet was plated with gold.

plateau *noun* **tableland, mesa, upland, plain, flat, steppe, savanna** The Sahara Desert has mountain ranges, rocky plateaus, gravelly plains, and sandy wastes.

platform *noun* **1. dais, rostrum, podium, pulpit, stage, scaffold, scaffolding** The speaker glanced at his notes as he approached the platform. **2. program, policy, agenda,**

plank, plan, principle, promise, goal The mayor ran for reelection on a platform of lower taxes and more support for the schools.

plausible *adjective* believable, credible, creditable, convincing, persuasive, likely, true, reasonable She gave a plausible explanation for being late. ➧ **Antonyms:** unlikely, unbelievable, improbable

play *verb* 1. disport, sport, recreate, frolic, romp I was able to play with my friends the whole afternoon. 2. compete, participate, take part, contend, vie, join in, undertake Everyone on the team played in yesterday's soccer game. 3. fool, tease, joke, jest, toy, trifle, flirt, dally, monkey She is playing with you. 4. act, perform, portray, represent, impersonate, do, depict, render Trish is going to play Snow White in the Childrens Theater's next production. 5. run, show, present, put on, exhibit, air, display, broadcast I want to see the movie that is playing at the local cinema. ◆ *noun* 1. drama, performance, show, production, theatrical, melodrama, pageant Every student will have a role in the class play. 2. amusement, diversion, entertainment, fun, pleasure, recreation, sport, game If you get your chores done in the morning, there will be time for play in the afternoon. 3. actions, conduct, behavior, comportment, deportment, method, manner The police think that foul play may be involved. 4. action, use, application, operation, exercise, motion, utilization, employment I had to bring all my powers of concentration into play.

player *noun* 1. participant, competitor, contestant, contender, opponent, adversary, member A baseball team may have only nine players on the field at one time. 2. performer, actor, actress, thespian, trouper, entertainer The program listed the cast of players.

playful *adjective* energetic, frisky, frolicsome, mischievous, sportive, impish, lively, sprightly My kitten is in a playful mood. ➧ **Antonyms:** serious, solemn

plea *noun* 1. appeal, request, entreaty, cry, prayer, supplication, solicitation The Red Cross made a plea for the donation of warm clothing. 2. claim, suit, petition, excuse, pretext, alibi, apology The defendant entered a plea of "not guilty."

plead *verb* appeal, ask, beg, entreat, implore, press, supplicate, sue, request My little sister pleaded for a puppy of her very own.

pleasant *adjective* agreeable, delightful, enjoyable, nice, pleasing, pleasurable, refreshing, mild I like spring because the days are so warm and pleasant. ➧ **Antonyms:** disagreeable, unpleasant

please *verb* 1. delight, gladden, gratify, satisfy, overjoy, charm, warm, captivate My parents were pleased when I won a prize in the science fair. 2. choose, desire, like, prefer, want, will, wish, elect, opt My grandparents gave me 25 dollars to buy whatever I please for my birthday. ➧ **Antonyms:** 1. displease, offend

pleasure *noun* 1. cheer, enjoyment, delight, gladness, happiness, joy, satisfaction, relish My little brother smiled with pleasure when I read his favorite book to him. 2. gratification, amusement, fun, merriment, diversion, play, recreation A hedonist is someone who devotes his or her life to the pursuit of pleasure. 3. choice, will, desire, wish, bent, inclination, preference, selection It is my pleasure to treat you to a movie for your birthday. ➧ **Antonyms:** 1. unhappiness, sadness 2. work, toil 3. duty, obligation

plebeian *adjective* base, vulgar, coarse, crude, common, lowly, banal, unrefined He has plebeian tastes in art. ◆ *noun* commoner, peasant, proletarian, masses, public, bourgeois The plebeians were the ordinary citizens of ancient Rome. ➧ **Antonyms:** *adjective* refined, cultured ◆ *noun* aristocrat, noble

pledge *noun* 1. agreement, commitment, promise, oath, vow, avowal, word, covenant, compact My parents made a pledge to contribute money to the national trail system. 2. deposit, guaranty, security, collateral, earnest, token, stake, bail, surety She left some jewelry at the pawnshop as a pledge for the money she borrowed. ◆ *verb* 1. affirm, promise, swear, vow, assert, guarantee, vouch In our Scout meetings, we pledge allegiance to the flag of the United States of America. 2. pawn, deposit, mortgage, contract, bind, gamble, stake, hazard He pledged his guitar for the loan.

plentiful *adjective* abundant, copious, ample, generous, substantial, bounteous, lavish, profuse There is a plentiful supply of food for the deer this year. ➧ **Antonyms:** scarce, sparse

plenty *noun* 1. abundance, lots, much, quantity, wealth, plenitude, profusion, enough We have plenty of food for tomorrow's picnic. 2. abundance, prosperity, wealth, luxury, riches, affluence, opulence The discovery of oil in Oklahoma provided many people with plenty. ➧ **Antonyms:** 1. scarcity, shortage 2. poverty, lack

pliant *adjective* 1. flexible, supple, malleable, ductile, pliable, elastic, plastic The flap on our cat's pet door is made of a pliant material. **2. compliant, docile, tractable, manageable, submissive, obedient, adaptable, willing** Mom said I used to be much more pliant when I was younger. ► **Antonyms: 1. stiff, rigid 2. stubborn, headstrong, obstinate**

plight *noun* **difficulty, jam, predicament, dilemma, fix, quandary, trouble, peril** I am very concerned about the plight of the wild horses and burros.

plod *verb* **1. trudge, drag, tramp, tread, walk, slog, lumber, waddle, shuffle** We plodded steadily up the steps of the Washington Monument. **2. toil, grind, drudge, moil, labor, slave, plug, grub, sweat** I plodded through several hours' worth of boring homework.

plot *noun* **1. patch, lot, parcel, tract, field, area, ground, land, acreage** Grandpa has a small plot of land that he uses for a vegetable garden. **2. story, story line, narrative, theme, scenario, design, structure** This book has an exciting plot. **3. conspiracy, intrigue, plan, scheme, design, collusion, machination** There was a plot to overthrow the cruel dictator. ◆ *verb* **1. map, draw, graph, mark, outline, diagram, chart, sketch** We plotted our course on a map. **2. conspire, intrigue, plan, scheme, contrive, connive, collude, maneuver** The bandits were plotting to rob a bank.

plow *verb* **1. furrow, harrow, till, turn over, hoe, dig, cultivate, farm** Farmers usually plow their fields in the spring. **2. push, press, shove, forge, drive, cut, plunge, advance, progress** The speeding car ran off the road and plowed through a fence.

plug *noun* **1. stopper, cork, cap, closure, bung, stop, fitting, filling** Pull the plug to let the water drain out of the sink. **2. pitch, promotion, advertisement, publicity, mention, buildup, blurb** The newscaster slipped in a plug for his new book. ◆ *verb* **1. block, close, fill, seal, stop, stuff, stopper, occlude, cap, cover** I plugged the leak in the pipe with a piece of bubble gum. **2. promote, advertise, publicize, ballyhoo, advocate, endorse, mention** The owner of the used car lot plugged his cars on TV. **3. persist, grind, persevere, drudge, work, plod, toil, moil, labor** We plugged away until we were completely finished. ► **Antonyms: verb 1. open, unplug 2. criticize, pan 3. quit, discontinue**

plummet *verb* **fall, drop, dive, plunge, descend, nose-dive, tumble, sink** The skydivers plummeted toward the ground in free fall before opening their parachutes.

plump[1] *adjective* **fat, stout, chubby, fleshy, full, obese, rotund, pudgy, corpulent** Grandma bought a nice plump turkey for our Thanksgiving dinner. ► **Antonyms: skinny, slender, thin**

plump[2] *verb* **plop, plunk, collapse, tumble, sink, drop, slump, fall** I plumped down in a chair.

plunder *verb* **loot, pillage, sack, ransack, raid, rob, steal, maraud** Back about a thousand years ago, Vikings plundered Europe's coastal villages. ◆ *noun* **1. rapine, pillage, robbery, looting, sack, sacking, depredation** The plunder of the village left the survivors in desperate circumstances. **2. booty, loot, pillage, spoils, prize, winnings** The Vikings divided their plunder into equal shares.

plunge *verb* **1. thrust, stab, stick, jam, drive, force, push, press, dig, run** He plunged a wooden stake into the vampire's heart. **2. dive, jump, leap, hop, dip, immerse, submerge, dunk, splash** I ran down the path and plunged into the lake. **3. drop, fall, tumble, descend, topple, pitch, plummet, nose-dive, spill** The climber would have plunged 50 feet if her rope hadn't caught her. **4. lunge, rush, hurtle, lurch, dash, spring, start, spurt** I plunged after my dog when he headed for the road. ◆ *noun* **1. drop, fall, nosedive, descent, plummet, decline, downturn** It was warm earlier, but then the temperature took a sudden plunge. **2. dip, duck, dunk, swim, immersion, dive, jump, leap** Dad enjoys taking a plunge in our pool after work. ► **Antonyms: verb 3. rise, ascend** ◆ *noun* **1. rise, ascent**

plus *adjective* **added, additional, extra, auxiliary, supplemental, further, spare** I enjoyed being an extra for the TV commercial, thus getting paid was a plus benefit. ◆ *noun* **advantage, benefit, asset, bonus, perk, gain, boon, addition** It was a plus when our teacher let us leave as soon as we finished our work. ► **Antonyms: noun liability, drawback**

ply[1] *noun* **layer, thickness, sheet, slice, lamina, leaf, plate, sheath, stratum** This panel has several plies of wood glued together.

ply[2] *verb* **1. handle, use, wield, employ, utilize, manipulate, operate, work** I watched the man skillfully ply his chisel. **2. engage in, carry on, perform, practice, pursue, follow, undertake, exercise** She plies her trade in a shop in an industrial park. **3. sail, traverse, run, navigate, cruise, travel, cross, journey** This ferry plies the route from Seattle to Juneau.

pocket *noun* **1. center, concentration, cluster, gathering, area, zone, spot** The rebellion was quickly put down, except for a few isolated pockets of resistance. **2. cavity, chamber, hole, hollow, depression, pit, compartment** The miner found a pocket of gold. ◆ *adjective* **compact, concise, little, portable, small, diminutive, miniature** My pocket encyclopedia is a handy reference book. ◆ *verb* **filch, steal, pilfer, purloin, lift, take, swipe, snatch, appropriate** Someone pocketed the tip that was left on the table for the waiter.

Word Group

A **poem** is a vivid and imaginative verbal composition. **Poem** is a general term with no true synonyms. Here are some common types of poems:

A **ballad** tells a story in stanzas and is often meant to be sung. A **cinquain** is a poem or stanza having 5 lines. An **epic** is a long poem about the deeds of heroic characters. A **haiku** is a Japanese poem with 3 lines and a total of 17 syllables. An **idyll** is a short poem describing country life. A **limerick** is a humorous 5-line poem. A **lyric poem** expresses personal feelings and thoughts. An **ode** is a lyric poem written in exalted style. A **prose poem** is a work of prose that contains poetic characteristics such as vivid imagery and concentrated expression. A **sonnet** is a 14-line poem with a rhyme scheme.

point *noun* **1. end, tip, top, head, peak, prong, spike, spire, apex, tine** Your pencil will write better if you sharpen its point. **2. cape, headland, promontory, peninsula, spit, tongue** A lighthouse sits out on the end of this point. **3. speck, dot, period, pinpoint, dash, spot, tick, mark, tittle** I made a point on the map to indicate our destination. **4. locality, location, area, place, position, site, spot, locus, station** There are many points of interest in Yellowstone National Park. **5. instant, moment, period, time, juncture, stage, date** At this point in the school year, the first report card is given out. **6. meaning, essence, gist, theme, subject, import, purport, case** The point of his speech was easy to grasp. **7. idea, purpose, reason, aim, end, objective, value, design, object** There doesn't seem to be much point in watering the lawn on a rainy day. **8. detail, fact, item, matter, particular, specific, subject, article, topic** The mayor's speech covered many important points. ◆ *verb* **1. aim, direct, cast, level, head, set, train, turn, steer, guide** You have to point the remote control straight at the TV. **2. indicate, show, mention, name, refer to, touch on, designate** The tour guide pointed out many interesting sights.

poise *verb* **balance, perch, hang, hover, suspend, steady, float** I poised for a moment on the edge of the diving board before jumping. ◆ *noun* **1. balance, stability, equilibrium, steadiness, equipoise, bearing, mien** The dancer's poise and rapid footwork were exciting to watch. **2. assurance, composure, confidence, self-control, equanimity, calmness, serenity** It's not easy to maintain your poise while speaking in front of a large group.

poison *noun* **toxin, bane, malignancy, cancer, venom, plague, rot** An exterminator sprayed ant poison around the outside of the building. ◆ *verb* **1. kill, destroy, wipe out, exterminate, annihilate, eliminate, eradicate** The soldier poisoned the rats that were in his bunker. **2. infect, pollute, contaminate, defile, weaken, impair, ruin, corrupt** Jealousy poisoned their friendship. ➡ **Antonyms:** *noun* **cure, remedy** ◆ *verb* **2. improve, strengthen**

poisonous *adjective* **dangerous, toxic, deadly, fatal, lethal, baneful, deleterious, pernicious** Most insecticides are poisonous to humans. ➡ **Antonyms: healthy, harmless, beneficial**

poke *verb* **1. jab, nudge, prod, touch, jostle, jog, press, stab, bump, hit** I gently poked the lizard to see if it was alive. **2. stick, thrust, push, shove, protrude, project, raise, extend** The gopher poked its head out of its hole. **3. pry, meddle, interfere, snoop, tamper, peek, dig, probe** I get annoyed when my little brother pokes into my things. **4. dawdle, lag, loiter, linger, dilly-dally, delay, putter, idle, drag, tarry** I poked along on my way home from school. ◆ *noun* **hit, jab, prod, punch, thrust, dig, thump, push, shove** My friend gave me a playful poke in the ribs.

pole *noun* **staff, stave, shaft, rod, bar, stake, stick, beam, mast** We staked our string bean plants with eight-foot poles.

police *noun* **authorities, the law, police force, police officers, patrolmen, patrolwomen, policemen, policewomen** The police are looking for the men who robbed that bank. ◆ *verb* **1. patrol, defend, guard, protect, watch, oversee, regulate, supervise** We need more officers to police our neighborhood. **2. tidy, clean, clear, spruce up, clean up, neaten, straighten** We were assigned to police the football field.

policy *noun* **code, guideline, procedure, rule, custom, practice, program, method** According to school policy, students may not smoke on campus.

polish *verb* **1. burnish, buff, shine, brighten, furbish, clean, rub, wax, gloss** Grandmother polished her silverware before the big family dinner. **2. improve, perfect, refine, touch up, enhance, smooth, finish** The President's aides had been polishing his inauguration speech for weeks. ◆ *noun* **1. burnish, gloss, glow, luster, shine, sparkle, glaze, sheen** I buffed my shoes until they had a beautiful polish. **2. elegance, grace, refinement, class, style, finesse, cultivation, breeding** The actor worked hard to give polish to his performance.

polite *adjective* **civil, considerate, courteous, respectful, well-mannered, gracious, thoughtful** A polite person treats everyone with respect. ➡ **Antonyms: discourteous, impolite, rude**

poll *noun* **survey, census, sampling, canvass, vote, tally, register** The latest poll shows that the senator is likely to be reelected. ◆ *verb* **interview, question, survey, sample, canvass, examine, interrogate** One hundred students were polled about their summer vacation plans.

pollute *verb* **1. contaminate, foul, dirty, poison, infect, soil, stain, tarnish, befoul** The exhaust from cars and trucks pollutes the air. **2. corrupt, defile, profane, dishonor, debase, violate, pervert, desecrate** Drug dealers help pollute other people's lives. ➡ **Antonyms: 1. purify, clean 2. honor, redeem**

pomp *noun* **show, display, flourish, pageantry, splendor, magnificence, formality, ceremony** The state occasion was conducted with pomp and ceremony.

pompous *adjective* **grandiose, self-important, arrogant, egotistic, bombastic, pretentious, haughty** We tease Dad when he starts sounding pompous. ➡ **Antonyms: simple, modest**

pond *noun* **pool, lake, fishpond, millpond, tarn, water hole** I like to go rowing on the pond.

ponder *verb* **consider, contemplate, deliberate, reflect, study, think, muse, brood, mull** Let's ponder the situation a while longer before we decide what to do.

pool[1] *noun* **pond, lake, puddle, lagoon, swimming hole, reservoir, spring** There's a swimming pool in this creek.

pool[2] *noun* **group, body, collection, supply** He was chosen from a pool of workers and assigned a special project. ◆ *verb* **merge, unite, join, combine, consolidate, share, league, associate** My friends and I pooled our money to buy refreshments after the movie.

poor *adjective* **1. destitute, impoverished, needy, penniless, poverty-stricken, bankrupt, indigent** This shelter provides free meals for people who are too poor to buy their own food. **2. bad, deficient, inadequate, inferior, unsatisfactory, worthless, shoddy** You can't get a good crop out of poor soil. **3. pathetic, pitiful, unfortunate, unlucky, wretched, sad, abject, unhappy, pitiable** That poor cat was abandoned by its owners. ➡ **Antonyms: 1. rich, wealthy 2. excellent, good 3. fortunate, lucky**

pop *verb* **1. bang, explode, burst, erupt, snap, crack, detonate, blast** The soda can popped open when I dropped it. **2. spring, dart, leap, break, jump, rush, run** The ground squirrel popped out of its burrow. **3. thrust, shove, put, poke, plunge, toss, throw, stick** I popped the clothes into

the washing machine and turned it on. ◆ *noun* **bang, crack, report, boom, explosion, snap, detonation, discharge** The firecracker went off with a loud pop.

popular *adjective* **1. widespread, general, public, universal, prevalent** Due to popular demand, the circus will stay in town for another week. **2. favored, favorite, preferred, well-liked, leading, well-known, respected, famous** Soccer is a popular sport in most parts of the world. ➡ **Antonyms: 1. restricted, private 2. disliked, unpopular**

popularity *noun* **celebrity, fame, renown, acceptance, acclaim, favor, support, esteem, approval** That singer is currently enjoying great popularity. ➡ **Antonyms: disfavor, unpopularity**

population *noun* **citizenry, populace, inhabitants, residents, folk, natives, people, public** The little village has a population of almost two hundred people.

pore[1] *verb* **scrutinize, read, study, examine, peruse, review, search** I pored over the book about classic cars. ➡ **Antonyms: skim, skip**

pore[2] *noun* **opening, aperture, orifice, hole, vent, gap, stoma** Transpiration takes place through the pores on the surfaces of leaves.

port *noun* **harbor, wharf, dock, pier, landing, anchorage, seaport, haven** The ship sailed into port.

portable *adjective* **movable, transportable, transferable, manageable, compact, light, lightweight, convenient** Laptop computers are small enough to be easily portable. ➡ **Antonyms: fixed, stationary**

porter *noun* **doorman, attendant, bellhop, bellboy, redcap, baggage carrier, conductor, doorkeeper** The porter opened the door to the limousine.

portion *noun* **fraction, part, percentage, share, piece, section, segment, slice** I save a portion of my weekly allowance. ◆ *verb* **deal out, dispense, distribute, divide, disperse, allocate, share, allot** We portioned out the snacks so that everyone got an equal share. ➡ **Antonym: *noun* whole**

portrait *noun* **1. painting, picture, drawing, likeness, image, photograph, snapshot** Sir Joshua Reynolds painted portraits of most of the famous people of the second half of the 18th century. **2. description, account, profile, portrayal, representation, depiction, vignette** This book gives a short portrait of each of the signers of the Declaration of Independence.

portray *verb* 1. characterize, depict, describe, show, represent, illustrate, picture, render History books usually portray Thomas Jefferson as an effective and honest President. 2. act, perform, play, impersonate, imitate, pose as, ape, mimic I am going to portray an elderly woman in our school play.

pose *verb* 1. model, sit, posture, stand, position, arrange Once a year, we get dressed up and pose for a family portrait. 2. impersonate, masquerade, pass for, pretend to be, act, simulate The man posed as a reporter to get into the sold-out concert. 3. advance, present, propose, raise, state, suggest, extend, submit, tender He posed a suggestion to buy more shares of Harley-Davidson. ◆ *noun* 1. position, attitude, posture, stance, aspect, cast, bearing The dancers held their poses until the curtain came down. 2. pretense, façade, masquerade, affectation, deception, act, show His bravado was just a pose to impress us.

position *noun* 1. place, spot, area, location, site, station, scene, locus, locale The parade will start as soon as all of the floats are in their proper positions. 2. stance, posture, pose, attitude, arrangement, orientation My back is sore from sitting in the same position too long. 3. condition, situation, state, circumstance, status, footing, capacity, place I'm not in a position to ask my sister for a favor, because she's still mad at me. 4. belief, conviction, feeling, opinion, stand, view, judgment, standpoint The President stated his position on the new tax bill. 5. post, appointment, job, office, employment, duty, berth, role, slot In 1933, Frances Perkins became the first woman to hold a cabinet position in the United States government. ◆ *verb* arrange, array, place, locate, install, set, site, situate, spot, put The general positioned his troops for battle.

positive *adjective* 1. favorable, good, optimistic, constructive, helpful, useful, practical, beneficial Our teacher always has something positive to say about our work. 2. conclusive, decisive, clear, clear-cut, precise, specific, unequivocal During the police lineup, the witness made a positive identification. 3. certain, confident, convinced, definite, sure, assured, satisfied I'm positive that I have seen this movie before. ⏺ **Antonyms: 1. bad, negative 2. & 3. doubtful, uncertain**

possess *verb* 1. have, hold, own, carry, boast, command, control, retain, enjoy, bear Our local library possesses more books than I can ever hope to read. 2. obsess, consume, control, dominate, preoccupy, fixate, bewitch He is possessed by his desire to be famous.

possession *noun* 1. custody, ownership, title, proprietorship, occupancy, control, hold We will be able to take possession of our new condominium any day now. 2. belonging, asset, effect, property, resource, good, chattel, furnishing, equipment My most valuable possession is a quilt that my great-grandmother made. 3. colony, dependency, territory, province, dominion, protectorate, holding Greenland is a possession of Denmark.

possibility *noun* chance, likelihood, probability, odds, prospect, eventuality There is a good possibility that we will get out of school early today.

possible *adjective* conceivable, potential, workable, feasible, viable, probable, likely Together we worked out a possible solution to the problem. ⏺ **Antonyms: impossible, unlikely**

possibly *adverb* perhaps, conceivably, feasibly, maybe, perchance, probably Could you possibly stop by on your way home from school?

post[1] *noun* picket, pole, pale, stake, column, pillar, prop, rail, stud The fence posts were spaced ten feet apart. ◆ *verb* fasten, place, put, set, attach, install, display, publicize, announce Room assignments will be posted on the bulletin board.

post[2] *noun* 1. base, camp, garrison, station, fort, headquarters, encampment The soldiers returned to their post after the maneuvers. 2. appointment, assignment, office, position, duty, job, billet, place Dad knows someone who was just appointed to an important post in the state department. ◆ *verb* place, position, situate, station, establish, install, fix, locate, assign A guard was posted outside the jewelry store.

post[3] *verb* 1. mail, dispatch, ship, send, transmit, convey, forward Could you post this letter for me? 2. inform, apprise, advise, brief, notify, enlighten, report, tell, acquaint I'm interested in hearing about how you're doing, so please keep me posted.

postpone *verb* delay, defer, put off, hold off, suspend, stay, shelve, waive, table The weather caused me to postpone planting my garden.

posture *noun* 1. carriage, bearing, stance, attitude, pose, position, shape, set Good posture helps to keep your spine straight and strong. 2. stand, stance, view, standpoint, viewpoint, outlook, belief, opinion The senator took a conservative posture on the issue. ◆ *verb* pose, show off, display, affect, masquerade, pretend, feign, act My little sister postured proudly in Mom's dress and high heels.

potent *adjective* **1. powerful, strong, vigorous, mighty, formidable, tough, invincible, omnipotent** The United States' army is a potent fighting force. **2. effective, convincing, persuasive, influential, forceful, compelling, cogent, authoritative** Your argument was so potent that it changed my mind. ⏵**Antonyms: 1. weak, feeble 2. ineffective, unconvincing**

potential *adjective* **likely, possible, probable, promising, conceivable, latent, plausible** I had a potential buyer for my bike, but she changed her mind. ◆ *noun* **potentiality, aptitude, possibility, capability, capacity, ability, talent, power** She has lots of potential as an athlete. ⏵**Antonyms:** *adjective* **actual, real**

Word Group

Pottery refers to objects made from moist clay and then hardened by heat. **Pottery** is a general term with no true synonyms. Here are some types of pottery:

bone china, china, crackleware, delft, earthenware, ironstone, lusterware, majolica, porcelain, raku, stoneware, terra cotta

pouch *noun* **bag, satchel, sack, poke, carryall, handbag, pocket, container, receptacle** The courier filled the pouch with important documents.

pounce *verb* **jump, leap, spring, strike, swoop, ambush, attack, dive, fall** The cat pounced on the unsuspecting mouse. ◆ *noun* **spring, leap, jump, hop, swoop, strike, pass, attack** The lion caught his prey in a single pounce.

pound[1] *verb* **1. beat, hammer, pummel, hit, strike, thump, wallop, whack, buffet** The impatient man pounded on the door of the elevator. **2. crush, powder, pulverize, grind, crumble, pulp, mill, smash** I pounded the pill into fragments and put it into a bowl of milk for my cat. **3. tromp, tramp, stomp, clomp, march, walk, trudge, plod** The football players pounded down the field. **4. throb, pulse, pulsate, beat, palpitate, drum** My heart pounded with fright.

pound[2] *noun* **kennel, shelter, pen, enclosure, sty, fold, coop, paddock, corral** My family adopted a puppy from the pound.

pour *verb* **1. cascade, spill, flow, stream, sluice, splash, drop, drain, decant** After the heavy rains, water poured over the top of the dam. **2. surge, gush, rush, run, swarm, stream, throng, teem, stampede** Students poured from the

building after the bell rang. **3. rain, shower, precipitate, deluge, flood** It's pouring out, so be sure that you take your umbrella.

poverty *noun* **1. destitution, neediness, pennilessness, need, want, privation, penury, impoverishment, indigence** The actor endured years of poverty before he finally started to get good roles. **2. lack, dearth, deficiency, scarcity, shortage, insufficiency, paucity, skimpiness, deficit** I felt a poverty of imagination as I faced my writing assignment. ⏵**Antonyms: 1. wealth, prosperity, affluence 2. abundance, sufficiency**

powder *noun* **dust, flour, grit, meal, sand, talc, crumb, grain, seed** The chalk turned to powder when I stepped on it. ◆ *verb* **1. mill, pulverize, grind, granulate, pound, smash, crush, crumble** Confectioners' sugar is made from regular sugar that has been powdered. **2. scatter, sprinkle, spread, spray, dust, strew, cover** I powdered the flower bed with a mixture of sand and wildflower seed.

power *noun* **1. ability, capability, capacity, faculty, endowment, gift, talent, flair** James Earl Jones, the actor, has the power to enthrall audiences with his magnificent voice. **2. strength, brawn, muscle, might, vim, vigor, potency, energy, force** Superman has the power to leap tall buildings with a single bound. **3. authority, command, control, rule, sway, dominion, mastery, sovereignty** The election will decide which political party will be in power. ◆ *verb* **activate, energize, operate, run, supply, propel, vitalize, drive** My model car is powered by batteries.

powerful *adjective* **1. mighty, strong, sturdy, robust, stalwart, brawny, stout, potent** Paul Bunyan is the mythical and powerful lumberjack of the Northwest. **2. effective, forceful, persuasive, influential, compelling, convincing, irresistible** The speaker presented a powerful argument to support his ideas. ⏵**Antonyms: 1. feeble, weak, frail 2. unconvincing, flimsy**

practical *adjective* **1. experienced, skilled, accomplished, proficient, qualified, able, veteran** The practical businessman knows how to get things done quickly and efficiently. **2. helpful, sensible, sound, useful, worthwhile, efficient, handy, functional** Your suggestion that I fix my glasses with a paper clip was very practical. ⏵**Antonyms: 1. inexperienced, unqualified 2. impractical, useless**

practice *verb* **1. drill, rehearse, train, prepare, exercise, discipline, study, work out** The marching band will practice once more before next Saturday's performance. **2. apply, employ, perform, use, do, follow, observe, pursue, undertake** I practice good oral hygiene by flossing and brushing every day. ◆ *noun* **1. custom, habit, routine, tradition, rule, way, wont, convention, policy** It is our practice to have dinner at 6 p.m. every day. **2. preparation, rehearsal, training, drill, exercise, discipline, repetition, study** It takes a lot of practice to become a good violinist. **3. action, execution, operation, performance, use, application, play, usage** The school will soon put its new grading procedures into practice.

pragmatic *adjective* **practical, sensible, expedient, logical, realistic, objective, hard, sober** The rescue workers made a pragmatic decision to amputate the victim's leg in order to save her life. ➡ **Antonyms: impractical, theoretical**

prairie *noun* **plain, flatland, steppe, grassland, range, veldt** The prairies of Canada are very beautiful.

praise *noun* **acclaim, commendation, compliment, recognition, approval, kudos, tribute, applause** She received a lot of praise for her outstanding science project. ◆ *verb* **acclaim, commend, compliment, congratulate, honor, approve, extol** The conductor praised the orchestra for having played so well. ➡ **Antonyms:** *noun* **criticism, disapproval** ◆ *verb* **criticize, disapprove**

prank *noun* **trick, shenanigan, joke, caper, antic, lark, escapade, mischief** I hid my brother's bicycle as a prank.

pray *verb* **appeal, beg, entreat, implore, plead, supplicate, ask, request** The farmer prayed for rain.

preach *verb* **1. sermonize, evangelize, moralize, proclaim, prophesy, lecture, talk** At the revival, the minister preached about fire and brimstone. **2. teach, exhort, advise, advocate, counsel, urge, admonish, caution** Our principal sometimes preaches about the dangers of using illegal drugs.

precarious *adjective* **1. hazardous, dangerous, unsafe, perilous, treacherous, insecure, risky, unstable** We were in a precarious situation, with one wheel of the truck over the cliff. **2. uncertain, iffy, questionable, doubtful, dubious, unpredictable, unreliable** The school's economic situation is precarious. ➡ **Antonyms: 1. safe 2. certain, reliable, predictable**

precaution *noun* **safeguard, safety measure, caution, care, prevention, defense, provision** If you take a few simple precautions, rock climbing actually can be quite safe. ➡ **Antonyms: risk, chance**

precede *verb* **come before, go before, usher in, lead, introduce, preexist, preface, head** High winds and dark clouds preceded the thunderstorm. ➡ **Antonyms: follow, succeed**

precious *adjective* **1. costly, expensive, valuable, invaluable, priceless, rare, dear, worthy** Diamonds and emeralds are precious stones. **2. dear, beloved, adored, cherished, darling, loved, pet, prized** My little brother is precious to me. ◆ *noun* **love, dear, darling, pet, beloved, honey, sweet, sweetheart** "Come here, my precious," said the evil witch. ➡ **Antonyms:** *adjective* **1. cheap, worthless 2. unloved, unvalued, rejected**

precipice *noun* **cliff, bluff, height, crag, face, escarpment, palisades** We stood at the top of the precipice of the Grand Canyon and looked at the Colorado River far below.

precise *adjective* **1. exact, specific, explicit, literal, accurate, correct, definite, true** What were her precise words? **2. proper, prim, strait-laced, rigid, strict, meticulous, fastidious, genteel** His manner of eating is very precise. ➡ **Antonyms: 1. approximate, vague 2. easygoing, relaxed**

precision *noun* **attention, care, carefulness, meticulousness, correctness, exactness, accuracy, preciseness** The jeweler worked with great precision as he repaired the watch. ➡ **Antonyms: inaccuracy, vagueness**

precocious *adjective* **advanced, progressive, bright, intelligent, smart, clever, gifted, mature** Mom said that I was a precocious child. ➡ **Antonyms: immature, slow**

predatory *adjective* **rapacious, ravenous, greedy, larcenous, carnivorous, aggressive** A lion is a predatory animal.

predicament *noun* **crisis, fix, jam, difficulty, trouble, mess, quandary, corner, spot** The man was in a predicament when he accidentally locked his keys in his car.

predict *verb* **forecast, foresee, foretell, prophesy, project, presage, divine, tell** The fortuneteller looked at her tarot cards and began to predict the future for me.

predominant *adjective* **dominant, prevailing, prevalent, primary, principal, superior, ruling, chief** Blue is the predominant color in this painting. ➡ **Antonyms: subordinate, inferior**

preen *verb* **dress, groom, primp, spruce up, plume, clean, smooth** The bird preened its feathers by running each one through its beak.

preface *noun* **foreword, introduction, prologue, preamble, preliminary, beginning** The book's preface included a discussion of what had led the author to undertake the work. ◆ *verb* **introduce, begin, launch, commence, start, initiate,**

open, precede The speaker prefaced his speech with a joke. ➧ **Antonyms:** *noun* **epilogue, conclusion** ◆ *verb* **close, end, conclude,**

prefer *verb* **favor, like, choose, elect, pick, select, fancy, wish, want** Which would you prefer, frozen yogurt or ice cream? ➧ **Antonyms: dislike, scorn, reject**

preference *noun* **1. predilection, proclivity, favoritism, partiality, fondness, appetite, relish, weakness** He has a preference for action movies. **2. choice, desire, pick, option, selection, fancy, liking, inclination** My preference is to go to a movie rather than to stay home and watch TV.

pregnant *adjective* **1. with child, expecting, expectant, gravid** My Sunday school teacher is pregnant with her second child. **2. meaningful, significant, telling, suggestive, indicative, weighty, important** There was a pregnant pause in the middle of his sentence. **3. full, replete, teeming, brimming, fraught, charged, rich, fertile, fecund** The atmosphere just before the holidays was pregnant with excitement and anticipation. ➧ **Antonyms: 2. pointless, meaningless 3. arid, barren, sterile**

prejudice *noun* **bias, one-sidedness, partiality, intolerance, bigotry, unfairness, preconception** Children are born without prejudice. ◆ *verb* **bias, influence, sway, turn against, slant, predispose, incline, warp** I found that my dislike of one of the actors prejudiced me against the whole movie. ➧ **Antonyms:** *noun* **objectivity, fairness, detachment**

preliminary *adjective* **beginning, introductory, opening, preparatory, prefatory, starting, initial** The speaker made a few preliminary remarks before addressing his main topic. ◆ *noun* **opening, introduction, preamble, prelude, start, initiation, preparation** The committee skipped the usual preliminaries and got right down to business. ➧ **Antonyms:** *adjective* **concluding, ending, final** ◆ *noun* **conclusion, end**

premature *adjective* **early, untimely, beforehand, sudden, ill-timed, rash, impulsive, hasty** The runner was disqualified for making a premature start. ➧ **Antonyms: late, tardy**

premise *noun* **1. supposition, proposition, hypothesis, assumption, postulate, theory, presumption** She is writing a story based on the premise that we are not alone in the universe. **2. grounds, property, site, vicinity, area, spot, locality, environs** They are building a miniature golf course on those premises.

preoccupied *adjective* **engrossed, absorbed, distracted, rapt, intent, busy, involved, absent-minded** I found him preoccupied with organizing his CD collection.

preoccupy *verb* **engage, interest, engross, absorb, consume, fascinate, immerse, arrest** The challenging jigsaw puzzle preoccupied us for the entire afternoon.

prepare *verb* **fix, make, ready, develop, arrange, form, organize, plan** I prepared everything for the luncheon well ahead of time.

prescribe *verb* **recommend, advise, order, impose, direct, decree, institute, dictate** Mom prescribed a warm bath and bed for me when I told her that I wasn't feeling well.

presence *noun* **1. appearance, existence, occurrence, attendance, being, emergence, development** The presence of smoke usually means that there is a fire. **2. company, vicinity, midst, nearness, proximity, propinquity** There are some things that my parents won't discuss in my presence. **3. style, poise, self-assurance, aplomb, bearing, air, manner, comportment** Although the singer is young, he has quite a presence. **4. spirit, force, energy, influence** I could feel a friendly presence in the room after my grandmother died.

present[1] *noun* **now, this moment, this instant, here and now, today** There is a saying that "There is no time like the present." ◆ *adjective* **1. contemporary, current, existing, existent, present-day, immediate, recent, modern** Mom wants to quit her present job and find a better one. **2. at hand, attending, here, near, nearby, there, available, about** The meeting will start as soon as everyone is present. ➧ **Antonyms:** *adjective* **2. absent, missing**

present[2] *verb* **1. introduce, make known, acquaint** I presented my parents to my teacher at the school open house. **2. hand out, award, confer, give, donate, grant, offer, bestow** The field hockey coach will now present the trophy for Best Athlete. **3. extend, proffer, offer, furnish, produce, display, exhibit, show** The lawyer presented evidence that proved the innocence of his client. ◆ *noun* **gift, presentation, donation, grant, offering, favor, handout** I got this camera as a birthday present.

preserve *verb* **1. save, defend, guard, protect, safeguard, secure, shield, ward** Everyone should help to preserve our natural resources. **2. maintain, uphold, keep, perpetuate, sustain, continue, conserve** Diplomats worked hard to preserve the fragile truce. **3. conserve, put up, can, pickle, salt, cure, freeze, dehydrate** We preserve enough fruits and vegetables from our garden to give us a good supply for the winter. ◆ *noun* **1. spread, conserve, jam, jelly, marmalade, compote** I like to put raspberry preserves on my toast. **2. refuge, reservation, reserve, sanctuary, park, retreat, asylum, haven** Our class is taking a field trip to a wildlife preserve.

preside *verb* officiate, oversee, head, direct, chair, lead, moderate, administer The vice-president will preside over the meeting when the president is absent.

press *verb* 1. depress, push, shove, ram, compress, crush, squeeze, bear, mash Press this button to start the elevator. 2. iron, flatten, smooth, steam, straighten My dad presses his shirts for the week each Sunday. 3. clasp, hold, squeeze, grip, hug, cuddle, embrace, huddle, nestle I pressed my little sister to me in a big hug. 4. beg, entreat, urge, plead, importune, implore, exhort, persuade My friend pressed me to stay for dinner. 5. crowd, jam, congregate, gather, swarm, throng, cluster, herd, mill Fans pressed around the star hoping to get her autograph. 6. pressure, demand, insist, prod, order, require, command The boss pressed him for a decision. ◆ *noun* 1. media, TV, newspapers, radio, reporters, journalists The President refused to grant interviews to the press. 2. crowd, crush, flock, horde, mob, mass, throng, swarm With the approach of quitting time, the press of people increased on the city sidewalks.

pressure *noun* 1. weight, force, heaviness, burden, load, stress, strain, mass The shelf sagged under the pressure of the heavy books. 2. compression, constriction, tension, squeeze, pinch A paramedic applied pressure to the wound to stop the bleeding. 3. strain, stress, duress, tension, obligation, urgency, anxiety, distress I was under a lot of pressure to get my book report done on time. ◆ *verb* force, coerce, compel, make, influence, persuade, coax, oblige I pressured my mother to change her mind and let me go to the movie with my friends.

prestige *noun* distinction, importance, influence, status, honor, prominence, eminence, respect Justice of the Supreme Court is a position of great prestige in the United States judiciary.

presume *verb* 1. assume, believe, guess, imagine, suppose, surmise, think, conclude, trust I stopped by my friend's house because I presumed that he would be home. 2. dare, hazard, venture, chance, risk, undertake, impose, infringe, intrude No one in the family presumes to enter my room without knocking.

pretend *verb* 1. fake, feign, simulate, sham, affect, bluff, pose, act, assume I pretended to be asleep so that my little brother wouldn't bother me. 2. fantasize, imagine, make believe, masquerade, play-act, suppose, fancy My friends and I sometimes pretend that we are famous athletes. 3. lie, claim, allege, profess, purport, deceive He pretended that he had been at the library when he had really been at the billiard parlor.

pretense *noun* 1. show, pose, façade, mask, front, disguise, charade, cover The grouse ruffled its feathers and made a pretense of being larger and fiercer than it really was. 2. excuse, pretext, claim, ruse, wile, bluff, dodge, feint, tactic She used the pretense that she had to baby-sit. 3. sham, make-believe, act, acting, disguise, masquerade, mimicry, imitation Her friendliness was all pretense; we knew we couldn't trust her. ● **Antonyms: 3. truth, honesty, candor**

pretentious *adjective* 1. pompous, boastful, snobbish, self-important, haughty, arrogant, insincere The woman became pretentious after she inherited money. 2. showy, ornate, elaborate, fancy, grandiose, flamboyant, ostentatious, extravagant The Victorian era is characterized by a pretentious decorating style. ● **Antonyms: 1. humble, modest 2. simple, plain, austere**

pretext *noun* pretense, excuse, reason, device, ploy, ruse, bluff, subterfuge I used the pretext of having a lot of homework as an excuse to leave early.

pretty *adjective* 1. attractive, beautiful, lovely, good-looking, fetching, cute, comely, fair My little sister looks very pretty in her new holiday dress. 2. clever, adroit, deft, sharp, smart, ingenious, shrewd, imaginative He pulled off a pretty business deal. 3. bad, terrible, horrible, awful, ghastly, dire, unpleasant, appalling The situation has come to a pretty pass. 4. large, huge, great, big, fat, generous, immense, sizable He made a pretty profit on the transaction. ◆ *adverb* fairly, quite, rather, somewhat, very, reasonably, moderately It's pretty cold out for a late spring day. ● **Antonyms:** *adjective* 1. plain, ugly, unattractive 2. clumsy, unimaginative 3. good, pleasant 4. small, paltry, little

prevail *verb* 1. triumph, surmount, win out, overcome, conquer, succeed, dominate The stranded mountaineers prevailed over the harsh elements. 2. abound, flourish, overflow, exist, predominate, swarm, thrive Good feeling and laughter prevail at our family gatherings. 3. talk into, convince, persuade, induce, sway, influence, bring My brother prevailed upon me to take him with me to the mall. ● **Antonyms: 1. lose, fail**

prevalent *adjective* widespread, common, pervasive, predominant, commonplace, popular Public education is prevalent in the United States. ● **Antonyms: rare, unusual, uncommon**

prevent *verb* avert, forestall, preclude, stave off, halt, stop, avoid, obstruct, inhibit Only you can prevent forest fires. ● **Antonyms: allow, permit**

previous *adjective* **earlier, former, past, prior, advance, preceding, antecedent** Only people with previous experience should apply for this job. ● **Antonyms: following, later**

prey *noun* **quarry, chase, catch, game, target, victim, kill, casualty** The tiger pounced upon its prey. ◆ *verb* **1. eat, feed on, consume, live on, hunt, stalk, pursue, attack, catch** Spiders prey on flies and other small insects. **2. exploit, manipulate, use, cheat, swindle, fleece, defraud, rob** The salesman preyed on his customers' fears in order to sell his product.

price *noun* **1. cost, expense, value, worth, amount, charge, fee, payment, expenditure** The price of fresh vegetables varies from season to season. **2. sacrifice, loss, penalty, consequence, toll, cost, fine, dues** The man rescued his son, but it was at the price of his own life. ◆ *verb* **appraise, assess, estimate, evaluate, value, rate, fix, assay** The merchant priced the diamond ring at 3,400 dollars.

priceless *adjective* **1. invaluable, precious, valuable, costly, expensive, dear, worthy, inestimable** The museum has several works of art that are rare and priceless. **2. amusing, droll, funny, hilarious, witty, absurd, rich, wonderful, splendid** Your story about the dumb criminal is priceless! ● **Antonyms: 1. worthless, cheap, common 2. dull, trite**

prick *noun* **pinhole, puncture, hole, nick, cut, stab, wound, perforation** I put a bandage over the prick I received from the rose thorn. ◆ *verb* **puncture, poke, pierce, jab, perforate, impale, stab, lance** The nurse pricked my finger with a needle to get a blood sample.

pride *noun* **1. self-esteem, self-respect, self-regard, self-worth, dignity, honor, ego** The author's pride was hurt when she failed to win the writing contest. **2. fulfillment, satisfaction, delight, enjoyment, pleasure, happiness, gratification, joy** Dad takes great pride in his ability to fix things around the house. **3. treasure, jewel, glory, pick, flower, best, cream, choice, trophy** The model of the *Graf Spee* is the pride of his collection. **4. arrogance, conceit, self-importance, vanity, egotism, haughtiness** The man would not apologize for making a mistake because he had too much pride. ● **Antonyms: 1. self-loathing 4. humility, modesty**

prim *adjective* **precise, proper, fussy, prissy, prudish, puritanical, formal, stiff** I would describe her as quiet rather than prim. ● **Antonyms: easygoing, casual, relaxed**

primary *adjective* **1. chief, foremost, leading, main, prime, principal, top, paramount** My primary interests are reading

books, listening to music, and playing soccer. **2. beginning, first, initial, original, earliest, pioneer, elementary, rudimentary** The project is still in its primary stage of development. **3. basic, fundamental, underlying, elemental, essential, direct, immediate** The primary reason I am taking this dance class is to be with my friends. ● **Antonyms: 1. minor, secondary 2. last, later 3. indirect, subordinate**

Word Group

A **primate** is a mammal that has a highly developed brain and hands that have thumbs. **Primate** is a general term with no true synonyms. Here are some common primates:

ape, baboon, capuchin, chimpanzee, gibbon, gorilla, human being, lemur, mandrill, marmoset, monkey, orangutan

prime *adjective* **1. superior, optimal, top, excellent, prize, select, first-rate, first-class, choice** We had prime seats for the opera. **2. chief, leading, primary, principal, main, top, leading, first, preeminent** She is the prime suspect in the case. ◆ *noun* **heyday, bloom, flower, peak, zenith, height, acme, pinnacle, maturity** The movie star is still beautiful, although she is past her prime. ◆ *verb* **prepare, ready, groom, coach, school, train, inform, fit, fix** I primed my little brother for his math test. ● **Antonyms:** *adjective* **1. inferior, second-rate 2. least, secondary** ◆ *noun* **decline, wane**

primitive *adjective* **1. primary, basic, elemental, essential, elementary, fundamental, underlying** The desire to make music is a primitive impulse. **2. ancient, early, prehistoric, old, primeval, primordial, archaic, antediluvian** Archaeologists have found primitive stone tools that are more than 2.5 million years old. **3. simple, crude, rough, raw, rude, unsophisticated, rustic, plain, unpolished** We learned how to build a primitive shelter in our survival class. ● **Antonyms: 2. new, modern 3. fancy, elaborate**

principal *adjective* **foremost, key, leading, main, major, primary, top, dominant** Farmers in Idaho grow a lot of wheat, but the state's principal crop is potatoes. ◆ *noun* **administrator, director, head, chief, leader, ruler, dean, master, superior** The principal of our school was once a teacher herself. ● **Antonyms:** *adjective* **minor, secondary**

principle *noun* **1. assumption, proposition, doctrine, precept, tenet, belief, truth** The United States is founded on the principle that all people are created equal. **2. character, honesty, integrity, morality, virtue, honor, ethics, scruples** A person of high principle is not likely to lie, steal, or cheat. **3. theory, fundamental, basis, axiom, rule, law, standard, maxim, rationale** The Goudreau Mathematics Museum offers the opportunity to have fun while gaining understanding of mathematical principles.

print *noun* **1. impression, imprint, mark, stamp, indentation, impress, seal** My dog left a paw print in the wet cement. **2. letters, printing, type, text, typescript, font, typeface, writing** There are many people who prefer to read books and magazines with large print. **3. engraving, etching, illustration, reproduction, lithograph, photograph** These prints have been signed and numbered by the artist. ◆ *verb* **1. imprint, engrave, letter, mark, stamp, impress, emboss, set** The business owner had new stationery printed when his telephone area code was changed. **2. issue, publish, release, bring out, reissue, reprint, disseminate, run off** The publisher printed 10,000 copies of the new cookbook.

prior *adjective* **earlier, former, past, preceding, previous, antecedent, beforehand** The beginner's class is for people who do not have prior experience using this software. ➡ **Antonyms: following, later**

prison *noun* **jail, penitentiary, pen, brig, dungeon, stockade, keep, reformatory** The thief was caught and sent to prison.

pristine *adjective* **pure, original, uncorrupted, untouched, virgin, uncontaminated, immaculate, unspoiled** The blanket of newly fallen snow was pristine and unmarked. ➡ **Antonyms: contaminated, polluted**

privacy *noun* **solitude, seclusion, isolation, aloneness, retreat, withdrawal, retirement** Everyone needs some privacy in his or her daily life.

private *adjective* **1. out-of-the-way, secluded, isolated, remote, separate, apart, inaccessible** The mountain cabin was very private. **2. individual, personal, own, intimate, solitary, withdrawn, lonely, singular** I like to have private time to write in my journal everyday. **3. not public, restricted, reserved, exclusive, special, independent, autonomous** We can't play here because this is private property. **4. confidential, hidden, secret, classified, clandestine, undercover, top-secret, covert** My best friend and I have a private meeting place that no one else knows about. ➡ **Antonyms: 1. accessible, close 3. public, community 4. known, exposed**

privilege *noun* **advantage, benefit, right, prerogative, freedom, liberty, allowance, permission** The company's top executives enjoy certain privileges that are not available to other employees.

prize *noun* **1. award, premium, reward, trophy, winnings, recognition, laurels, honor** The prize for first place was a scholarship for 1,500 dollars. **2. gem, pearl, jewel, treasure, choice, pick, flower, top, elite** This arrowhead is the prize of my collection. ◆ *adjective* **acclaimed, champion, top, winning, cherished, valued, valuable, best, prime** The rancher's prize bull won a blue ribbon at the county fair. ◆ *verb* **cherish, esteem, treasure, value, admire, appreciate, regard, like** Lawrence has one coin in his collection that he prizes above all the others.

probable *adjective* **apparent, likely, presumable, possible, reasonable, seeming, plausible** Investigators are trying to determine the fire's probable cause. ➡ **Antonyms: improbable, unlikely**

probe *noun* **examination, investigation, inquiry, research, study, search, analysis, exploration** The police probe revealed that several people were involved in the crime. ◆ *verb* **examine, inspect, investigate, search, explore, study, scrutinize, delve** The dentist probed inside my mouth to see if I had any problems with my teeth.

problem *noun* **1. question, mystery, puzzle, riddle, conundrum, enigma, issue, topic** Dad helped me solve the difficult math problem. **2. complication, difficulty, trouble, fault, flaw, imperfection, shortcoming** It took us a few days to work all of the problems out of our new computer system. ◆ *adjective* **unruly, difficult, stubborn, unmanageable, perverse, intractable, refractory** The instructor has a reputation for being able to train even problem dogs. ➡ **Antonyms:** *noun* **1. solution, answer** ◆ *adjective* **manageable, compliant**

procedure *noun* **method, process, technique, course, routine, strategy, approach, sequence** This booklet explains the procedure for programming our new VCR.

proceed *verb* **advance, continue, move on, progress, go on, start, fare, travel** We proceeded cautiously along the icy sidewalk. ➡ **Antonyms: halt, stop**

process *noun* **method, procedure, system, technique, way, routine, mode, operation** In 1856, Henry Bessemer developed a new process for making steel from cast iron. ◆ *verb* **deal with, handle, treat, prepare, ready, regulate, transform, organize** Modern computers process information very quickly.

procession *noun* **parade, cavalcade, caravan, train, review, line, column, queue, file** Jazz funeral processions evolved from the days of slavery.

proclaim *verb* announce, declare, herald, report, state, call, profess, reveal The judge proclaimed John to be the winner of the spelling bee.

procrastinate *verb* stall, delay, hesitate, put off, prolong, lag, dawdle, shilly-shally Some people procrastinate because they are afraid they can't do a perfect job. ➡ **Antonyms:** hasten, hurry

procure *verb* acquire, gain, get, obtain, secure, buy, win, appropriate The coin collector finally managed to procure the 1898 Morgan silver dollar that he had desired.

prod *verb* **1.** jab, jog, nudge, poke, dig, push, shove, spur, whip When the mule refused to budge, its owner prodded it with a stick. **2.** prompt, urge, encourage, inspire, motivate, goad, drive, impel, nag No one has to prod me to do my homework. ◆ *noun* incentive, encouragement, motivation, impetus, goad, push, spur, stimulant That my favorite TV show would be on in an hour was a prod to get my homework done.

prodigal *adjective* **1.** wasteful, profligate, spendthrift, immoderate, wanton, reckless, extravagant The prodigal man spent all his money and ended up penniless. **2.** lavish, abundant, profuse, copious, bountiful, generous, plentiful, ample Her prodigal praise made me self-conscious. ◆ *noun* wastrel, spender, spendthrift, squanderer, profligate, waster The prodigal went through his inheritance very quickly. ➡ **Antonyms:** *adjective* **1.** thrifty, economical **2.** meager, spare ◆ *noun* miser, penny pincher

prodigious *adjective* **1.** huge, great, enormous, immense, mammoth, gargantuan, colossal, tremendous, vast Whales and elephants are of prodigious size. **2.** extraordinary, fantastic, fabulous, astounding, spectacular, marvelous, wonderful, surprising Jared is a craftsperson of prodigious skill. ➡ **Antonyms: 1.** small, puny **2.** ordinary, common

prodigy *noun* genius, talent, wizard, wonder, phenomenon, marvel, miracle A musical prodigy, Julie Andrews had an incredible four-octave vocal range by the time she was 8.

produce *verb* **1.** give, furnish, provide, supply, yield, generate, develop, bear This well produces more than 150 barrels of oil every day. **2.** create, compose, author, write, paint, draw, draft, accomplish Wolfgang Amadeus Mozart produced three of his greatest symphonies in a three-month period in 1788. **3.** assemble, build, construct, create, make, manufacture, fabricate, fashion Dad works at a factory that produces microwave ovens. **4.** cause, initiate, engender, beget, originate, achieve,

accomplish, effect His joke produced a lot of laughter. **5.** bring forth, bring out, display, exhibit, present, show, materialize The magician reached into his top hat and produced a rabbit. ◆ *noun* agricultural products, fruits, vegetables, greens Our local supermarket carries a wide selection of fresh produce.

product *noun* **1.** commodity, goods, merchandise, ware, article, item This store carries TVs, stereos, and other electronic products. **2.** outcome, result, issue, effect, consequence, upshot, offshoot, yield Her politeness is the product of a good upbringing.

production *noun* **1.** manufacture, fabrication, making, creation, construction, assembly, building Hundreds of people are involved in the production of a single commercial jetliner. **2.** drama, play, show, performance, presentation, film, movie, motion picture The playwright's latest production will be appearing off-Broadway.

profess *verb* affirm, announce, declare, proclaim, state, confirm, assert, avow The engaged couple professed their love for each other.

profession *noun* **1.** calling, career, field, occupation, vocation, job, business, craft, trade, employment Medicine is a profession that requires years of specialized education and training. **2.** affirmation, announcement, declaration, pledge, statement, assertion, asseveration, avowal The jury did not believe the defendant's profession of innocence.

professor *noun* faculty member, educator, instructor, lecturer, teacher She is a professor at the state university.

proficient *adjective* adept, skillful, competent, able, capable, qualified, skilled, expert, masterful I am learning to be more proficient in taking care of my dirt bike. ➡ **Antonyms:** unskilled, incompetent

profile *noun* **1.** side view, portrait, contour, outline, silhouette, form, likeness Abraham Lincoln's profile appears on United States pennies. **2.** biography, life story, history, chronicle, record, characterization, sketch, portrait I am reading a profile of President John F. Kennedy.

profit *noun* **1.** advantage, benefit, use, value, good, avail, utility, boon, blessing The time you spend in school now will be of profit to you in the future. **2.** earnings, return, income, revenue, gain, yield Profits for computer manufacturers are expected to grow this year. ◆ *verb* benefit, gain, capitalize, reap, earn, advance A lot of companies will profit from the President's plan to lower corporate taxes.

profound *adjective* **1. thoughtful, wise, deep, intellectual, intelligent, knowledgeable, scholarly, philosophical** The historian's book presented some profound insights into the effects of war. **2. deep, intense, extreme, great, strong, thorough, total, complete, utter** I have profound admiration for people who risk their lives to rescue others from danger. ◈ **Antonyms: 1. thoughtless, shallow 2. partial, slight, incomplete**

profuse *adjective* **1. abundant, plentiful, copious, bounteous, riotous, lush, ample, rich** When we saw the profuse display of flowers at the farmer's market, we could not resist buying some. **2. extravagant, generous, abundant, excessive, lavish, liberal, prodigal** Their profuse thanks for our hospitality overwhelmed us. ◈ **Antonyms: 1. scarce, sparse 2. miserly, stingy**

program *noun* **1. agenda, calendar, docket, bulletin, index, lineup, list, prospectus** We were handed a program as we entered the exposition. **2. broadcast, show, performance, presentation, production, series** My favorite TV program airs at 7 p.m. tonight. **3. plan, policy, procedure, course, project, line, system, scheme, strategy** Our school just started a program to help students learn how to use computers. ◆ *verb* **schedule, book, slate, docket, bill, list, plan, arrange, organize** The popular talk show is programmed several weeks in advance.

progress *noun* **improvement, betterment, headway, advancement, development, progression, growth** My music teacher assures me that I am making good progress on the clarinet. ◆ *verb* **1. advance, go forward, get along, proceed, develop, grow, move, continue** Work on the school's new gymnasium progressed at a steady pace. **2. improve, advance, grow, better, gain** We progressed in our ability to speak French until we could even read a story. ◈ **Antonyms:** *noun* **relapse, decline** ◆ *verb* **1. stop, stall 2. decline, degenerate**

prohibit *verb* **ban, disallow, forbid, outlaw, proscribe, prevent, restrict, inhibit** Parking is prohibited on this street. ◈ **Antonyms: allow, permit**

project *noun* **enterprise, task, undertaking, venture, plan, scheme, job, pursuit** Dad's latest project is to build an outdoor barbecue. ◆ *verb* **1. extend, jut, protrude, stick out, stand out, bulge, overhang, arch** The rocky promontory projected several hundred feet into the water. **2. shoot, throw, hurl, hurtle, expel, eject, cast, fling, launch, loose** The cork from the champagne bottle was projected at least 20 feet. **3. calculate, estimate, compute, reckon, predict, forecast, guess, approximate** Our school's budget is projected to be over one million dollars next year. **4. plan,**

intend, propose, contemplate, design, devise, contrive, invent My parents are projecting to put an addition on our house in the near future.

proliferate *verb* **multiply, increase, burgeon, spread, abound, propagate, breed** Rumors that the governor would not run for office again proliferated.

prolong *verb* **draw out, extend, lengthen, protract, stretch out, sustain, continue** We decided to prolong our visit for two more days. ◈ **Antonyms: curtail, shorten**

prominent *adjective* **1. noticeable, conspicuous, visible, evident, striking, eye-catching, obvious, unmistakable** The bank's four-story building was the most prominent structure in the entire downtown area. **2. distinguished, eminent, important, notable, famous, illustrious, noteworthy, celebrated** The mayor invited several prominent citizens to lunch to discuss the city's future. ◈ **Antonyms: 1. inconspicuous 2. unimportant, unknown**

promise *noun* **1. pledge, vow, word, assurance, commitment, covenant, oath** People trust Stephanie because she always keeps her promises. **2. possibility, prospect, hope, potential, likelihood, ability, talent, aptitude** The rookie baseball player shows a lot of promise. ◆ *verb* **1. pledge, swear, vow, agree, assure, guarantee, vouch, plight** You may borrow my bicycle if you promise to return it tomorrow. **2. indicate, foretell, augur, suggest, hint, bode, imply, portend** The clearing skies promise better weather ahead.

promote *verb* **1. advance, elevate, move up, raise, upgrade, jump, graduate** The store promoted two sales clerks to management positions. **2. aid, assist, encourage, foster, further, support, stimulate, boost, help** Proper eating habits promote good health. **3. advocate, urge, support, champion, back, sponsor, endorse, recommend** The movie star promoted the saving of old growth timber in the Northwest. **4. advertise, publicize, popularize, talk up, ballyhoo, tout, push, sell** The author promoted her latest book with a multicity tour. ◈ **Antonyms: 1. demote, downgrade 2. hinder, impede 3. criticize, condemn**

promotion *noun* **1. advancement, advance, raise, elevation, jump, rise, upgrade** The receptionist is hoping to receive a promotion soon. **2. encouragement, furtherance, stimulation, cultivation, development, improvement, support, hype** One of our principal's goals is the promotion of extracurricular activities. **3. pitch, advertisement, advertising, buildup, publicity, endorsement, ballyhoo** We received coupons in the mail as a promotion for the new toothpaste. ◈ **Antonyms: 1. demotion 2. impediment, discouragement, hindrance**

prompt *adjective* immediate, instant, quick, rapid, swift, punctual, timely, speedy Fast food restaurants try to give prompt service to all customers. ◆ *verb* **1.** cause, inspire, motivate, prod, stimulate, spur, move, incite My curiosity prompted me skip to the last page of the mystery. **2.** remind, advise, urge, suggest, cue, jog, hint, nudge, push Mom prompted me to write a thank-you note to my grandmother. ◆ *noun* reminder, cue, hint, prod, spur, stimulus, suggestion, help The stage manager did not have to give me a prompt for my entrance. ➡ **Antonyms:** *adjective* slow, tardy ◆ *verb* **1.** deter, discourage

promptly *adverb* quickly, swiftly, immediately, directly, rapidly, speedily, at once, hastily I promptly paid back the money that I had borrowed from my friend. ➡ **Antonyms:** slowly, lazily

prone *adjective* **1.** face down, flat, horizontal, reclining, prostrate, recumbent, level Everyone lay in a prone position, waiting for the coach's command to start doing pushups. **2.** apt, given, inclined, liable, likely, subject, partial, disposed, bent, tending My friends tease me because I am prone to talk too much. ➡ **Antonyms: 1.** vertical, upright, standing **2.** reluctant, unlikely

pronounce *verb* **1.** articulate, enunciate, utter, vocalize, sound, say, speak I was embarrassed when I didn't pronounce his name correctly. **2.** announce, declare, decree, proclaim, state, assert, rule, opine The judge pronounced a verdict of "not guilty."

pronounced *adjective* clear, distinct, evident, noticeable, obvious, plain, strong, conspicuous The tourist spoke English with a pronounced accent. ➡ **Antonyms:** inconspicuous, subtle

proof *noun* authentication, certification, evidence, verification, confirmation, corroboration, documentation I had to show proof of my citizenship to get a passport.

prop *noun* support, buttress, brace, truss, shore, stay, reinforcement I used bricks as a prop for the side of the trellis that was broken. ◆ *verb* support, bolster, shore, hold up, buttress, reinforce, truss, sustain We propped our shed's sagging roof with a two-by-four.

propel *verb* drive, move, run, impel, mobilize, launch, push, thrust My little brother has a toy airplane that is propelled by a rubber band.

proper *adjective* **1.** appropriate, correct, right, suitable, apt, fitting, meet, applicable If you wear the proper clothing, you can stay warm and dry on stormy days. **2.** accepted, correct, standard, usual, traditional, conventional, orthodox The proper way to hold eating utensils varies from country to country. **3.** becoming, mannerly, decent, respectable, polite, courteous, seemly Her proper manners helped her make a good impression. **4.** own, individual, specific, distinctive, particular, private, special Please return your books to their proper places. ➡ **Antonyms: 1.** wrong, inappropriate **2.** unorthodox **3.** rude, impolite

property *noun* **1.** assets, belongings, effects, goods, possessions, things, stuff My personal property includes all of my clothes, books, and sports equipment, and my computer. **2.** land, real estate, realty, acreage, estate, plot, tract, grounds My grandparents bought property out in the country. **3.** attribute, characteristic, feature, quality, trait, peculiarity, mark, ingredient Heat and light are properties of fire.

prophecy *noun* foretelling, prediction, forecast, vision, divination, revelation, oracle, fortunetelling A wise old woman made a prophecy that the king's reign would be long and prosperous.

prophesy *verb* foresee, foretell, predict, forecast, warn, augur, forewarn, presage, portend One scientist has prophesied that an asteroid will strike Earth within the next 20 years.

prophet *noun* oracle, soothsayer, seer, fortuneteller, augur, clairvoyant, sibyl, diviner Nostradamus was a famous 16th-century prophet whose prophecies are still being studied today.

proportion *noun* **1.** ratio, distribution, fraction, measure, percent, relationship, part, share The proportion of milk to ice cream in a milk shake is usually about two to one. **2.** balance, symmetry, harmony, perspective, relation, correspondence, agreement Picasso was a famous artist who frequently rendered people's features out of proportion. **3.** size, dimensions, magnitude, measurement, degree, extent, volume, expanse Though some dinosaurs were small, many grew to massive proportions.

proposal *noun* **1.** invitation, offer, proposition, request, appeal, bid, overture, proffer I've decided to accept his proposal and go skiing next weekend. **2.** idea, plan, recommendation, scheme, suggestion, program, project, design The city council is studying the mayor's proposal to hire more police officers.

propose *verb* **1.** present, offer, submit, introduce, recommend, suggest, tender, advance I proposed the idea that we order a pizza for dinner tonight. **2.** aim, expect, intend, mean, plan, contemplate, aspire, hope, design My older brother proposes to go to college after he graduates from high school.

proprietor *noun* owner, holder, possessor, master, mistress, landlord, landlady, manager My uncle is the proprietor of a flower shop.

prosaic *adjective* unimaginative, ordinary, dull, humdrum, commonplace, pedestrian, tedious, routine, banal We often think our everyday routine is prosaic, but to someone else it may seem interesting. ➨ **Antonyms:** imaginative, exciting

prosecute *verb* 1. try, bring suit, litigate, sue The district attorney intends to prosecute this case to the fullest extent of the law. 2. pursue, carry on, wage, execute, stick to, continue, persist, sustain The country was determined to prosecute the war until the enemy surrendered.

prospect *noun* 1. chance, expectation, hope, possibility, likelihood, probability I am excited by the prospect of getting my own computer. 2. view, vista, scene, sight, panorama, scenery, landscape, outlook Many artists have painted that particular prospect. ◆ *verb* explore, go after, look, probe, search, seek, dig, survey In 1849 thousands of people journeyed to California and prospected for gold.

prosper *verb* boom, flourish, thrive, progress, gain, increase, succeed, advance The town prospered when an automobile factory was built nearby. ➨ **Antonyms:** decline, fail

prosperity *noun* success, affluence, comfort, wealth, ease, luxury, fortune, riches With two books on the best-seller lists, the author had achieved prosperity. ➨ **Antonyms:** poverty, want, destitution

prosperous *adjective* well-off, successful, thriving, prospering, wealthy, flourishing, rich, comfortable After many years of hard work, the couple was now prosperous. ➨ **Antonyms:** failing, unsuccessful

protect *verb* defend, guard, safeguard, preserve, save, shield, secure, cover The United States Secret Service protects the life and safety of the President.

protection *noun* 1. safety, security, defense, safekeeping, preservation, support When my little sister gets scared, she runs to Mom for protection. 2. shield, barrier, screen, buffer, harbor, shelter, refuge, sanctuary We planted a row of Russian olive trees as a protection against the wind.

protest *verb* 1. argue against, challenge, object, remonstrate, inveigh, oppose, demonstrate, disapprove Our coach quietly protested the umpire's decision. 2. affirm, declare, contend, insist, state, pronounce, maintain, allege I protested that I wasn't tired. ◆ *noun* challenge, objection, remonstrance, complaint, opposition, dissent, resistance Protests have been made by people who are opposed to the new power plant. ➨ **Antonyms:** *verb* 1. approve, endorse 2. deny, refute ◆ *noun* agreement, approval

prototype *noun* model, master, archetype, example, pattern, original, standard, paradigm The company machine shop produces the prototypes designed by the engineering department. ➨ **Antonyms:** copy, reproduction

protrude *verb* bulge, stick out, swell, balloon, jut, belly, project, overhang Our cat's belly protruded as she reached the end of her pregnancy.

proud *adjective* 1. pleased with, satisfied with, delighted, glad, happy, honored, contented Mom said that she was proud of me for working so hard on my studies. 2. arrogant, conceited, haughty, self-important, vain, smug, superior, prideful Although the athlete has achieved fame, he is not too proud to associate with his old friends. 3. majestic, stately, magnificent, great, noble, grand, venerable, glorious The once proud ship now lay at the bottom of the sea. ➨ **Antonyms:** 1. ashamed, displeased 2. humble, modest

prove ◆ *verb* demonstrate, establish, show, verify, certify, confirm, validate, authenticate, uphold My birth certificate proves that I am 14 years old. ➨ **Antonyms:** disprove, refute, contradict

proverb *noun* adage, saying, motto, credo, maxim, byword, saw, axiom "The early bird gets the worm" is a proverb that late sleepers may not appreciate.

provide *verb* 1. contribute, furnish, supply, deliver, give, submit, present, offer My parents are providing the dessert for our church's potluck dinner tonight. 2. stipulate, state, specify, require, designate, indicate, prescribe A book contract typically provides a deadline for completion of the book. ➨ **Antonym:** 1. withhold

province *noun* 1. territory, state, dominion, district, domain, region, county, area Quebec is the largest province in Canada. 2. sphere, arena, department, bailiwick, field, realm, scope, capacity Diagnosing what was wrong with my cat was out of my province, so I took her to a vet.

provincial *adjective* unsophisticated, narrow-minded, parochial, backward, insular, intolerant, unsophisticated, hidebound He has a provincial mind.

provision *noun* 1. food, groceries, comestibles, supplies, edibles, victuals, provender We bought extra provisions when a blizzard was forecast. 2. arrangements, preparations, plans, measures, steps, precautions Mom and Dad have made provisions for our care should something happen to them. 3. stipulation, qualification, proviso, reservation, condition, terms, limitation I can go to the mall on the provision that I buy a pair of shoes for school.

provocative *adjective* provoking, aggravating, vexing, annoying, challenging, irritating, exciting I did not respond to his provocative statement.

provoke *verb* 1. aggravate, anger, annoy, bother, disturb, irritate, vex, rile, outrage Our dog is usually gentle, but he growls at people who provoke him. 2. instigate, cause, incite, trigger, produce, start, prompt, stimulate, induce That bully is always trying to provoke a fight. ⚫ **Antonyms:** 1. calm, soothe 2. prevent, stop

prowess *noun* 1. skill, ability, dexterity, adroitness, deftness, facility, mastery, command He has great prowess in hunting with a bow and arrow. 2. bravery, courage, daring, fearlessness, boldness, mettle, valor, heroism The sailor was awarded a medal for his prowess during the battle. ⚫ **Antonyms:** 1. incompetence, ineptness 2. cowardice, fear, timidity

prowl *verb* slink, skulk, sneak, stalk, steal, creep, roam, cruise, tiptoe A raccoon was prowling around our garbage cans last night.

prudent *adjective* 1. careful, cautious, circumspect, chary, wary, sensible, thoughtful, wise Prudent pilots always check their airplanes before they take off. 2. frugal, economical, provident, thrifty, saving, sparing, temperate My mother is a prudent shopper and saves money regularly. ⚫ **Antonyms:** 1. careless, foolish, reckless 2. liberal, wasteful

prune *verb* 1. cut back, clip, trim, snip, thin, crop, lop, chop In January we prune our rosebushes and fruit trees. 2. edit, reduce, condense, abbreviate, abridge, shorten, cut, pare, trim The newspaper reporter pruned her story to fit the space available. ⚫ **Antonyms:** 2. lengthen, expand

pry[1] *verb* poke, snoop, meddle, intrude, interfere, investigate, nose around My friend said she didn't want to talk about why she was upset, so I didn't pry.

pry[2] *verb* lever, lift, force, raise, work, break, move, open, jimmy I pried the lid off the paint can with a screwdriver.

public *adjective* 1. civic, civil, communal, community, state, governmental I feel very fortunate to live in a town that has a good public library. 2. common, general, popular, universal, widespread, open, known, overt That information has been public knowledge for quite some time. ◆ *noun* citizens, citizenry, community, people, populace, masses, population The university museum is open to the public. ⚫ **Antonyms:** *adjective* 1. private, personal 2. secret, covert

publicity *noun* 1. advertising, advertisement, ballyhoo, hype, promotion, buildup, pitch, propaganda After the barrage of publicity before it was released, the movie itself was a letdown. 2. notice, attention, interest, exposure, review, notoriety, fame, celebrity We received a lot of publicity when we started a shelter for homeless animals.

publicize *verb* promote, advertise, ballyhoo, broadcast, announce, spread, spotlight My mother's agency publicizes the activities of a national basketball team. ⚫ **Antonyms:** conceal, hide, suppress

publish *verb* bring out, issue, put out, release, pen, write, author, print, circulate I've read every book that author has published.

puff *noun* 1. gust, draft, waft, blow, breath, whiff, blast A puff of wind blew out the candle. 2. draw, pull, drag, inhalation, exhalation, pant The man took another puff on his cigar. ◆ *verb* 1. pant, wheeze, gasp, heave, huff, breathe, gulp I was puffing as I rode my bike up the steep hill. 2. smoke, draw, pull on, suck, blow, inhale, exhale, emit, discharge The author likes to puff on his pipe as he works. 3. swell, dilate, distend, expand, stretch, bloat, inflate The hot-air balloon began to puff up as the pilot used a fan to fill it. ⚫ **Antonyms:** *verb* 3. deflate, shrink

pull *verb* 1. tow, haul, drag, draw, lug, tug Dad's pickup truck can pull a horse trailer. 2. draw out, extract, remove, take out, pluck, yank, wrest, uproot The dentist said that she would have to pull my bad tooth. 3. drive, move, go, steer, maneuver, manipulate, arrive, depart A truck pulled up to the loading dock. 4. rip, shred, tear, rend, break, divide, separate The wrestler pulled a phone book apart with his bare hands. 5. sprain, strain, injure, tear, wrench, stretch, twist, dislocate I pulled my intercostal muscles when I tried to lift a heavy box. 6. attract, draw, entice, lure, get, obtain, pick up, secure, reach The new movie pulled in a large crowd. ◆ *noun* jerk, tug, wrench, yank, drag, draw, pluck, twitch The fisherman hooked a fish by giving the line a quick pull. ➡ **Antonyms:** *verb* **1.** push, shove **2.** insert, return **6.** repulse, repel

pulsate *verb* beat, throb, pulse, vibrate, drum, flutter, palpitate, pound The stereo began to pulsate when I cranked up the volume.

pulse *noun* beat, throb, rhythm, stroke, vibration, pounding, drumbeat, thump The dancers at the powwow moved to the steady pulse of the drums. ◆ *verb* beat, throb, vibrate, drum, pulsate, pound, palpitate The whole ship began to pulse when the engines were put on full throttle.

punch[1] *verb* drill, bore, poke, perforate, prick, pierce, cut, stab, stamp The machinist punched holes in the metal sheet.

punch[2] *verb* hit, jab, knock, strike, wallop, smack, cuff, clout, pummel, box The boxer tried to punch his opponent in the jaw. ◆ *noun* **1.** blow, hit, jab, smack, wallop, swat, slug, clout, box The punch missed because the other boxer ducked. **2.** impact, effect, wallop, vigor, drive, energy, vim, vitality, verve The new ad has a lot of punch and is very effective.

punctual *adjective* on time, prompt, timely, early, quick, immediate, instant I was punctual for my appointment with the doctor. ➡ **Antonyms:** late, tardy

puncture *verb* **1.** penetrate, perforate, pierce, prick, cut, stick, lance, drill, spear A piece of glass punctured my bicycle tire. **2.** deflate, explode, ruin, humble, dishearten, disillusion, discourage The loss punctured our dream of winning the championship. ◆ *noun* hole, perforation, prick, break, cut, opening, slit, leak Fortunately I had a repair kit, and I was able to patch the puncture in my bike tire.

pungent *adjective* **1.** tangy, sharp, piquant, aromatic, spicy, zesty, keen, flavorful I like the pungent smell of curry sauce. **2.** caustic, biting, sharp, cutting, acerbic, vitriolic, stinging His remark had been pungent, but accurate. ➡ **Antonyms: 1.** bland, mild **2.** kind, sweet

punish *verb* **1.** discipline, penalize, admonish, correct, chasten, castigate, sentence I try to avoid doing anything that my parents will punish me for. **2.** abuse, harm, injure, hurt, maltreat, batter, thrash, torture It is important to avoid punishing your body with extremes of diet.

punishment *noun* **1.** discipline, consequence, penalty, correction, sentence, retribution, castigation, payment The usual punishment for misbehaving in class is detention

after school. **2.** abuse, mistreatment, maltreatment, hurt, damage, injury, harm My old bicycle has taken a lot of punishment.

pupil *noun* student, learner, scholar, schoolboy, schoolgirl, trainee, disciple, follower There are 20 pupils in my science class. ➡ **Antonyms:** teacher, instructor

puppet *noun* **1.** dummy, marionette, doll, figurine, toy, hand puppet, manikin *Pinocchio* is the story of a wooden puppet that wants to become a real boy. **2.** pawn, dupe, tool, instrument, servant, slave, agent, mouthpiece The ruler was merely a puppet of the country's powerful prime minister.

purchase *verb* pay for, buy, acquire, get, obtain, procure, secure, achieve I am saving my money so I can purchase a snowboard. ◆ *noun* **1.** acquisition, buy, possession, property, procurement When my sister got home from the mall, she showed me her purchases. **2.** foothold, toehold, footing, grip, grasp, hold, handhold The climber carefully gained a secure purchase on the small ledge.

pure *adjective* **1.** genuine, real, undiluted, unmixed, plain, simple, unadulterated, straight My new necklace is made of pure gold. **2.** absolute, complete, sheer, total, thorough, utter, downright, perfect Grandpa thinks that the whole idea of UFO abductions is pure nonsense. **3.** clean, innocent, good, decent, sinless, moral, sincere, honest His motives in helping his elderly neighbor were pure. **4.** chaste, virgin, virginal, virtuous, immaculate, modest, undefiled, angelic The nun took a vow to lead a pure life. **5.** theoretical, abstract, speculative, hypothetical, ideal, visionary, fundamental This author has published articles on both pure and applied mathematics. ➡ **Antonyms: 1.** impure **3.** dishonest, immoral **4.** unchaste **5.** applied, practical

purify *verb* **1.** clean, cleanse, decontaminate, sterilize, filter The filter Dad installed on the furnace helps purify the air in our house. **2.** cleanse, purge, hallow, sanctify, ennoble, absolve The young man was purified by ritual and ceremony before he set out on his vision quest. ➡ **Antonyms: 1.** contaminate, pollute **2.** debase, degrade

purpose *noun* **1.** aim, end, intent, intention, goal, objective, point, meaning, design The purpose of my visit is to ask you a favor. **2.** resolve, determination, persistence, resoluteness, steadfastness, will, willpower It takes a sense of purpose to complete one's education.

purse *noun* **1.** pocketbook, handbag, bag, pouch, sack, tote, carryall, wallet Mom keeps her wallet and checkbook in her purse. **2. prize, stake, winnings, award, proceeds, receipts, reward** The purse for the Breeder's Cup horse race was 250 thousand dollars. ◆ *verb* **pucker, wrinkle, contract, compress, pinch, gather, bunch, fold** She pursed her lips as she thought about the idea.

pursue *verb* **1. chase, run after, go after, follow, hunt, track, trail, shadow, stalk** A police officer pursued the thief on foot. **2. strive for, work for, lead, live, undertake, seek, aspire, follow** My older sister is pursuing her dream of becoming a veterinarian. **3. court, woo, pay court to, attract, entice, lure, charm, date** A male bird will often pursue the female with a special song or display of feathers. **4. haunt, beset, torment, plague, hound, harass, pester** The demons of worry and doubt pursued him, despite his success.

pursuit *noun* **1. chase, hot pursuit, hunt, quest, search** A rabbit dashed across the yard with two dogs in pursuit. **2. activity, hobby, pastime, recreation, occupation, vocation, business, job** Fishing is Dad's favorite leisure pursuit.

push *verb* **1. press, poke, shove, jam, ram, nudge, force, move, thrust** Push this button to turn on the VCR. **2. encourage, pressure, prod, prompt, urge, coerce, incite, motivate** The mayor is pushing the city council to adopt new parking regulations. ◆ *noun* **1. shove, thrust, butt, jolt,** nudge, poke, prod The door won't open unless you give it a hard push. **2. attack, assault, offensive, foray, sortie, advance, incursion, invasion, drive** The allies coordinated forces to make a strong push into enemy territory.

put *verb* **1. place, set, deposit, lay, position, situate, park, plunk, settle** Please put the dishes in the cupboard as soon as I have dried them. **2. impose, levy, assess, assign, set, fix, make, require** The county government put a tax on all residential property. **3. submit, offer, present, propose, pose, suggest, tender, bring up** The developer put his plan for the housing tract to the city council. **4. express, formulate, phrase, say, state, word, articulate, translate** It wasn't what he said, it was the way he put it that made me angry.

putrid *adjective* **rotten, stinking, foul-smelling, rancid, foul, fetid, rank, decomposed** We tried to stop our dog before he rolled on the putrid carcass.

puzzle *verb* **1. baffle, bewilder, confuse, mystify, perplex, confound, foil, flummox** The man's unusual symptoms puzzled his doctor. **2. ponder, think, mull, brood, wonder, contemplate, meditate, study** They puzzled over the missing man's whereabouts. ◆ *noun* **mystery, riddle, problem, question, conundrum, enigma, difficulty, perplexity** Scientists are closer to solving the puzzle of the sudden extinction of the dinosaurs.

Qq

quack *noun* **charlatan, fraud, fake, humbug, impostor, pretender, mountebank** In earlier times, quacks often peddled cure-all elixirs. ◆ *adjective* **fake, fraudulent, phony, pseudo, sham, bum, counterfeit, false** The traveling peddler was selling quack medicines. ➧ **Antonyms:** *adjective* **genuine, real, honest**

quail *verb* **cower, cringe, recoil, flinch, shudder, shrink, tremble** I quailed at the thought of my parents' reaction to my report card.

quaint *adjective* **1. old-fashioned, picturesque, charming, cute, enchanting, captivating, antique** The quaint cottage had stone walls and a slate roof. **2. unusual, bizarre, eccentric, fantastic, odd, queer, outlandish, peculiar, strange** There are many quaint species in the insect world. ➧ **Antonyms: 1. modern, new 2. common, normal**

quake *verb* **1. shake, vibrate, rock, pulsate, wobble, fluctuate, move** The washing machine began to quake when the load became off balanced. **2. shiver, tremble, quaver, quiver, shake, shudder, convulse** I started quaking with cold once the rain soaked through my jacket. ◆ *noun* **1. shiver, tremble, shudder, shake, quiver, twitch** The speaker was so nervous that there was a quake in his voice. **2. earthquake, temblor, tremor, shake, shock, aftershock** The small quake woke up a few people, but it didn't do any damage.

qualification *noun* **1. capability, ability, capacity, competence, experience, skill, aptitude, certification** What are your qualifications for this job? **2. prerequisite, requirement, condition, restriction, provision, proviso, stipulation, term** One of the qualifications for getting a driver's license is passing a written test. **3. exception, limitation, reservation, modification, objection, hesitancy, doubt, uncertainty** I can say without qualification that she is the kindest person I've ever met.

qualify ◆ *verb* **1. authorize, enable, entitle, license, sanction, permit, empower** A teaching credential qualifies a person to be a teacher. **2. soften, temper, mitigate, moderate, modify, assuage, limit, narrow** I qualified my objection to the plan. ➧ **Antonyms: 1. invalidate, disqualify 2. aggravate, intensify**

quality *noun* **1. attribute, characteristic, feature, trait, property, nature, essence, aspect** One of the qualities of a gas is that it spreads by diffusion and will fill a container of any size. **2. excellence, superiority, merit, value, worth, status, stature, caliber** This brand of stereo equipment is known for its high quality.

qualm *noun* **1. faintness, sickness, nausea, queasiness, giddiness, vertigo** I felt a qualm in my stomach when the boat began to roll and pitch. **2. scruple, misgiving, compunction, reservation, uneasiness, hesitation, doubt, reluctance** We were quite shocked to hear he had no qualms about not returning the briefcase he had found. ➧ **Antonyms: 2. confidence, comfort, security**

quandary *noun* **dilemma, difficulty, predicament, strait, mire, pinch, fix, bind** I was in a quandary over which electives to choose for next year.

quantity *noun* **1. amount, measure, portion, volume, mass, total, aggregate, sum** My family consumes a large quantity of milk every week. **2. bulk, abundance, mass, profusion, volume, magnitude, amplitude, greatness** Our family finds it more economical to buy paper goods in quantity.

quarantine *noun* **isolation, segregation, confinement, separation, privacy** Patients who have infectious diseases must sometimes be placed in quarantine. ◆ *verb* **isolate, segregate, sequester, confine, detain, separate, set apart** When I took my dog to England, he had to be quarantined for six months.

quarrel *noun* **argument, dispute, fight, squabble, disagreement, altercation, brawl, spat** The two brothers had a quarrel over who should wash the dishes. ◆ *verb* **1. argue, bicker, dispute, fight, squabble, disagree, wrangle, clash** Let's not quarrel over who gets to sit in the easy chair. **2. cavil, disapprove, object, complain, decry, quibble, nitpick, disagree** I cannot quarrel with her reasons for wanting to stay home. ➧ **Antonyms:** *noun* **agreement, accord** ◆ *verb* **1. agree, concur 2. approve, support**

quarry[1] *noun* **prey, game, victim, quest, prize, aim, objective, goal** I enjoy paint ball because in it you are both the quarry and the hunter.

quarry[2] *noun* **pit, excavation, mine, abyss, chasm, crater, cavity, hole** The abandoned rock quarry was filled with water. ◆ *verb* **excavate, extract, dig out, unearth, mine, scoop, burrow, gouge** The megaliths at Stonehenge were quarried in Wales.

quarter *noun* **1. area, district, neighborhood, region, zone, locale, precinct, section** New Orleans is known for its picturesque French Quarter. **2. abode, accommodations, dwelling, lodging, residence, barracks, chambers, rooms** Military bases usually have separate quarters for officers and enlisted men. ◆ *verb* **1. divide, slice, cut, cleave, cut up, dismember** He quartered the apple. **2. billet, lodge, house, install, put up, station, accommodate, harbor, shelter** Soldiers were sometimes quartered in the homes of private citizens.

quaver *verb* **quake, quiver, tremble, shake, vibrate, wobble, waver, falter** My voice quavered from nervousness as I read my story to the class. ◆ *noun* **tremor, trembling, quiver, throb, vibration, trill, shaking, shiver** We could hear the quaver in her voice as she read her story.

queen *noun* **1. monarch, sovereign, ruler, empress, princess, czarina** Victoria was Great Britain's queen from 1837 to 1901. **2. belle, star, flower, goddess, best, choice, pick, select, elect** Doug Kershaw sings a song about Jolie Blon, the Queen of the Bayou.

queer *adjective* **1. odd, peculiar, strange, weird, unusual, curious, funny, bizarre** The clown wore a queer hat that looked like a flower pot. **2. sick, ill, queasy, dizzy, faint, light-headed, uneasy, woozy** I felt queer after eating too many greasy onion rings. ➧ **Antonyms: 1. conventional, normal**

quell *verb* **1. crush, put down, squelch, quench, extinguish, quash, suppress, subdue** The police swiftly quelled the disturbance. **2. allay, calm, quiet, still, pacify, alleviate, assuage, ease** I quelled the baby's crying by rocking her. ➧ **Antonyms: 1. incite, arouse, encourage**

quench *verb* **1. douse, extinguish, put out, smother, snuff out, suppress, stifle** The campers quenched their fire with a bucketful of water. **2. slake, satisfy, fulfill, allay, appease, gratify, relieve** I quenched my thirst with a long drink of water. ➧ **Antonyms: 1. light, kindle 2. whet, aggravate**

query *noun* **inquiry, question, concern, doubt, reservation, demand, interrogative** The salesclerk answered all my queries. ◆ *verb* **ask, examine, inquire, interrogate, question, quiz, grill, cross-examine** When I arrived home late, my parents queried me about where I had been.

quest *noun* **exploration, expedition, journey, adventure, search, pursuit, pilgrimage, mission** English explorer David Livingstone went on a quest in Africa in the mid-19th century.

question *noun* **1. inquiry, query, interrogative** The teacher asked if anybody had questions about the assignment. **2. issue, matter, point, problem, subject, topic, proposition, motion** The meeting dealt with the question of whether or not a new freeway was needed. **3. doubt, uncertainty, confusion, suspicion, misgiving, objection, dispute, qualm** Without any question, you are my best friend. ◆ *verb* **1. interrogate, interview, query, examine, quiz, grill, pump, ask** The police questioned two witnesses to the robbery. **2. challenge, distrust, doubt, dispute, mistrust, oppose, refute** I never question my coach's judgment. ➧ **Antonyms:** *noun* **1. answer, response 3. certainty, conviction** ◆ *verb* **1. answer, reply 2. trust, accept**

questionable *adjective* **uncertain, dubious, debatable, doubtful, disputable, equivocal, suspicious** Whether I can save enough money for a new bike by spring is questionable. ➧ **Antonyms: certain, sure**

quibble *verb* **criticize, object, complain, nitpick, fault, quarrel** She quibbled over my seasoning of the soup. ◆ *noun* **criticism, objection, protest, complaint, dissidence, disagreement, dispute** The quibble about the order of business during the club meeting was resolved quickly.

quick *adjective* **1. fast, hasty, rapid, speedy, immediate, prompt, brief, short** I made a quick stop at the drug store. **2. bright, alert, perceptive, keen, smart, sharp, clever, intelligent** The quick little girl solved the tough riddle. ➧ **Antonyms: 1. slow, gradual, long 2. dull, stupid**

quicken *verb* **1. accelerate, speed up, step up, hasten, hurry, hustle, rush** I quickened my pace when I realized I was late. **2. excite, stimulate, stir, arouse, kindle, inspire, fire, enliven** My interest in astronomy was quickened by a TV documentary. ➧ **Antonyms: 1. slow 2. deaden, impede**

quiet *adjective* **1. noiseless, silent, soundless, hushed, inaudible, mute, muffled, low** Our new air conditioner is very quiet. **2. calm, peaceful, restful, serene, tranquil, untroubled, placid, still** I am looking forward to a quiet evening at home. **3. unobtrusive, subdued, conservative, restrained, plain, simple, unpretentious, tasteful** He has a very quiet manner. ◆ *noun* **hush, quietness, silence, stillness, calm, tranquillity, serenity, peacefulness** The hikers enjoyed the quiet of the deep woods. ◆ *verb* **calm, settle, shut up, silence, still, lull, hush, shush** If we don't quiet down, we might wake the baby. ➧ **Antonyms:** *adjective* **1. loud, noisy 2. disturbed, restless 3. conspicuous, loud** ◆ *noun* **disturbance, noise**

> ### Word Group
>
> A **quilt** is a bed covering made of two layers of cloth with a layer of batting in between. **Quilt** is a specific term with no true synonyms. Here are some other types of bed coverings:
>
> **afghan, bedspread, blanket, comforter, counterpane, coverlet, crazy quilt, duvet, mantle, patchwork quilt**

quirk *noun* **1. mannerism, trait, habit, affectation, idiosyncrasy, peculiarity, oddity** Twisting my ring when I am nervous is one of my quirks. **2. twist, turn, vagary, caprice, trick, freak** By a quirk of fate, Angkor Wat was rediscovered in 1858 by a butterfly collector.

quit *verb* **1. abandon, depart, give up, leave, desert, forsake, relinquish, renounce** Our neighbors decided to quit the city and move to the country. **2. cease, give up, discontinue, stop, end, halt, terminate, desist** My uncle quit smoking one year ago today. ● **Antonyms: 1. remain, stay 2. begin, start, continue**

quite *adverb* **1. completely, entirely, thoroughly, totally, fully, really, precisely, perfectly** These two puzzle pieces don't quite fit together. **2. extremely, rather, really, somewhat, very, considerably, much, well** It's quite warm in this classroom. ● **Antonyms: barely, hardly, scarcely**

quiver *verb* **quaver, shiver, tremble, quake, shake, vibrate, shudder** My dog quivers with anticipation whenever she hears the word *walk*. ◆ *noun* **shiver, tremble, shudder, tic, tremor, twitch, spasm, convulsion** Quivers of excitement ran through me when I was announced the winner.

quiz *verb* **question, examine, test, query, ask, interrogate, pump, grill** Our teacher will quiz us tomorrow on our spelling words. ◆ *noun* **exam, examination, test, inquisition, inquiry, questioning** We will be having a math quiz today.

quota *noun* **allotment, allowance, ration, share, allocation, quantity, maximum** There is a quota on the number of cars that can be imported into this country.

quotation *noun* **1. quote, citation, excerpt, passage, selection, extract, reference** My report included numerous quotations. **2. bid, estimate, assessment, appraisal, price, charge, cost, rate** We received a quotation from two stores for the installation of new carpeting.

quote *verb* **1. cite, refer to, allude to, extract, mention, reference, paraphrase, parrot** The congressman quoted the Constitution of the United States in his speech. **2. bid, offer, state, estimate, guess, approximate, assess, appraise** The salesman quoted us a price that did not include delivery.

Rr

race *noun* **competition, contest, event, tournament, meet, run, relay, match, rivalry** Joe won second place in the annual Three Falls bike race. ◆ *verb* **dash, hurry, run, rush, speed, sprint, hasten, scramble, scamper, dart, shoot, bolt** My little brother raced to the car to make sure that he got the front seat.

rack *noun* **holder, stand, frame, shelf, counter, ledge, hanger** I selected a paperback book from the rack. ◆ *verb* **torture, afflict, torment, harass, distress, harrow, punish** The accident victim was racked with pain. ➡ **Antonyms:** *verb* **comfort, soothe**

racket *noun* **1. commotion, noise, uproar, din, clamor, clatter, hubbub, tumult** The racket from the party could be heard a block away. **2. fraud, swindle, graft, extortion, scheme, crime, conspiracy** The police arrested the perpetrators of the racket. ➡ **Antonyms: 1. quiet, silence**

radiant *adjective* **1. bright, brilliant, gleaming, shining, sparkling, glowing, incandescent, luminous, dazzling** It was a radiant morning without a cloud in the sky. **2. beaming, blissful, happy, joyful, elated, ecstatic, glowing, gay** My parents look radiant in their wedding picture. ➡ **Antonyms: 1. dull, gloomy 2. sad, unhappy**

radiate *verb* **1. shine, glow, gleam, beam, illuminate, diffuse, emit, flow** The light from the oil lamp radiated throughout the living room. **2. exude, project, show, demonstrate, evince, emanate, issue, exhibit** The dogs radiated confidence as they gathered the sheep into a flock.

radical *adjective* **extreme, fanatical, revolutionary, iconoclastic, lawless, rabid, militant, zealous** Radical environmentalists have occupied the tops of old-growth timber to save it from being cut down. ◆ *noun* **extremist, fanatic, revolutionary, rebel, freethinker, leftist, militant, liberal, insurgent, anarchist** The early American patriots were considered radicals by those who supported the British monarchy. ➡ **Antonyms:** *adjective* **moderate, conservative**

rag *noun* **scrap, cloth, dish rag, tatter, remnant, piece, shred, fragment, bit** I used a flannel rag to wipe the dirt off my bicycle.

rage *noun* **1. frenzy, fury, tantrum, fit, temper, passion, furor, rampage** My little brother flew into a rage when he couldn't find his favorite blanket. **2. craze, fad, mania, trend, vogue, mode, fashion, style** Saddle shoes were all the rage in the 1950s. ◆ *verb* **rant, storm, scream, yell, roar, blaze, flare, explode, rave** An angry customer raged at the store manager. ➡ **Antonyms:** *noun* **1. calm, coolness, serenity** ◆ *verb* **appease, mollify, soothe**

ragged *adjective* **1. frayed, tattered, worn-out, shabby, dilapidated, torn, threadbare** The old blanket was ragged from much use. **2. jagged, uneven, rough, unfinished, abrasive, frayed, harsh** I tore my skirt on a ragged piece of metal.

raid *noun* **assault, attack, offensive, strike, foray, invasion, roundup, incursion** The police prepared for the raid by putting on bulletproof vests. ◆ *verb* **assault, attack, invade, storm, pillage, plunder, ravage, ransack, loot** Between the 9th and 11th centuries A.D., Viking warriors raided European coastal villages.

rail[1] *noun* **railing, banister, handrail, guard, bar** We leaned over the rail of the balcony to look at the view.

rail[2] *verb* **fume, rant, criticize, abuse, complain, berate, castigate** The political candidates railed at one another.

Word Group

A **railroad** is a road built of parallel steel rails and used by trains and other wheeled vehicles. **Railroad** is a general term with no true synonyms. Here are some types of railroads:

cog railway, el, electric railway, monorail, narrow-gauge railroad, streetcar line, subway, tramline, trolley, underground

rain *noun* **precipitation, rainfall, shower, drizzle, downpour, cloudburst, mist, torrent, deluge** Rain was coming down, but the sun was still shining. ◆ *verb* **pour, shower, heap, lavish, sprinkle, spatter, deluge, deposit** The guests rained rose petals on the bride and groom.

raise *verb* **1. elevate, haul up, hoist, lift, pull up, pick up, rear** Guards raised the castle's drawbridge. **2. erect, build, fabricate, construct, frame, establish, mount** The construction crew raised the walls of the warehouse. **3. improve, upgrade, boost, increase, enhance, advance,**

amplify, heighten I studied hard to raise my test scores. **4. bring up, produce, rear, cultivate, grow, nurse, foster, breed** When I grow up I want to raise a large family. **5. put forward, propose, suggest, advance, bring up, broach, introduce** The committee chairman raised several ideas for recruiting new members. **6. provoke, awaken, stir, excite, spur, kindle, rouse, stimulate, motivate** Our science teacher raises our interest with intriguing experiments. **7. accumulate, collect, gather, get, amass, obtain, acquire, solicit** Our Girl Scout troop raises money by selling cookies. ◆ *noun* **increase, boost, advance, promotion, addition, supplement, gain, augmentation** Mom told us she had been given a raise in salary.

rake¹ *verb* **1. scrape, collect, gather, mass, scratch, graze** Mom and I planted the tulip bulbs and raked soil over them. **2. search, comb, hunt, ransack, sweep, rummage, scan, scour, examine** I raked the house looking for my math homework. **3. pepper, bombard, strafe, barrage, fire up, blitz** The soldiers raked the building with gunfire. ➡ **Antonyms: 1. scatter, strew**

rake² *noun* **libertine, seducer, swinger, chaser, rogue, rascal, lecher** The unexpurgated *Memoirs* of Casanova, a famous 18th-century rake, were not published until 1960.

rake³ *noun* **cant, list, incline, heel, tilt, slant, tip, lean** The rake of that barn makes it look very picturesque.

rally *verb* **1. assemble, collect, gather, marshal, muster, mobilize, call, summon, convene, converge** The commander rallied his troops around him. **2. get better, improve, recover, revive, perk up, pull through, rebound, rejuvenate** My friend rallied quickly after having her appendix removed. ◆ *noun* **1. assembly, gathering, get-together, meeting, convention, congregation, convocation, muster** Do you know if there will be a pep rally before the big game? **2. recovery, rebound, revival, recuperation, improvement, renewal, restoration, convalescence** We hope to see a rally in the stock market soon. ➡ **Antonyms:** *verb* **1. disband, scatter 2. fail, worsen** ◆ *noun* **2. collapse, decline**

ram *verb* **1. hit, bump, strike, slam, smash, batter, crash, butt, hammer, beat, pound** I wasn't watching where I was going and rammed the person in front of me. **2. jam, force, cram, shove, thrust, stuff, wedge, press** He rammed the piece of wood into the stove and shut the door.

ramble *verb* **1. amble, roam, saunter, stroll, wander, trek, drift, rove, cruise, stray** Max and his friends like to ramble around the neighborhood. **2. zigzag, twist, wind, snake, meander, bend, curve** The creek rambles through miles of farmland before flowing into the river. **3. babble, chatter, rattle on, speak, talk, drone, gab** The old man rambled on about his days as a gold prospector. ◆ *noun* **hike, saunter, stroll, walk, jaunt, trek, excursion, traipse, tour** My dog and I went for a ramble in the woods.

ramp *noun* **incline, slope, access, grade, ascent, rise, gradient, bank** Most public buildings have a ramp for handicapped access.

rampart *noun* **bastion, barrier, blockade, bulwark, wall, fortification, stronghold, barricade, palisade** The soldiers positioned themselves behind the rampart and fired on the enemy.

rancid *adjective* **spoiled, putrid, noxious, curdled, soured, moldy, off, fetid, rotten** Butter can become rancid if exposed to heat for too long a time. ➡ **Antonyms: fresh, sweet, pure**

random *adjective* **chance, arbitrary, haphazard, variable, unorganized, unplanned, accidental, irregular** The books were in random order on the shelf. ➡ **Antonyms: deliberate, intentional, planned**

range *noun* **1. scope, extent, sphere, bounds, limits, reach, stretch, field, domain** Mom feels that her new job is well within her range of ability. **2. array, assortment, selection, variety, collection, gamut, field, order, series** I considered a wide range of colors before making my choice. **3. extent, amplitude, radius, span, orbit, compass, stretch, latitude** The physiotherapist checked the range of motion in my arms and legs. **4. grasslands, pasture, plains, territory, meadow, pastureland, lea, space** This ranch contains more than 850 acres of open range. **5. band, chain, line, row, series, group, ridge, tier, sierra** You can see many farms and a range of hills from my bedroom window.

rank¹ *noun* **1. level, position, status, eminence, grade, class, station, echelon** An international meeting was called for leaders of the highest rank. **2. row, line, column, file, group, series, range, queue, string, tier** He is in that rank of soldiers over there. ◆ *verb* **1. align, arrange, line up, array, dispose, locate, position, settle, sort** I ranked my CDs on the shelf in the order in which I wanted to listen to them. **2. classify, categorize, organize, class, judge, evaluate, value, estimate** The teams were ranked according to their win-loss records. **3. rate, stand, come first, count, place, measure, weigh, outrank** A new computer ranks high on my wish list.

rank² *adjective* **1. abundant, luxurious, dense, overabundant, rampant, lavish, overgrown, wild** The old shed was covered with a rank growth of wild blackberries. **2. bad, foul, offensive, pungent, rotten, gross, putrid, noxious, fetid, revolting** Skunks have a rank smell. **3. complete, absolute, total, utter, downright, sheer, outright, thorough, glaring** His statements are rank exaggerations. ⏺ **Antonyms: 1. sparse, scanty, scraggly 2. pleasant, sweet**

ransack *verb* **1. search, scour, comb, rifle, rummage, rake, probe, examine** I ransacked the house trying to find my homework. **2. rob, pillage, plunder, raid, ravage, spoil, sack, loot, thieve** The enemy soldiers ransacked the village.

rap[1] *verb* **1. bang, hit, knock, strike, tap, whack, slap** I rapped at his door and called my brother to supper. **2. criticize, blame, censure, castigate, attack, blast, denounce, scold, reprimand** The citizens' group rapped the nuclear agency's safety report on radiation levels. ◆ *noun* **blow, knock, cuff, tap, conk, whack, pat, swat** I gave the jar lid a light rap to loosen it.

rap[2] *verb* **converse, talk, speak, chatter, babble, commune, parley, chat** My friends and I stood and rapped for half an hour after the game.

rapid *adjective* **fast, quick, speedy, swift, brisk, hasty, hurried, rushing, prompt, fleet** The jet made a rapid climb at takeoff. ⏺ **Antonyms: gradual, slow**

rapport *noun* **relationship, compatibility, understanding, camaraderie, accord, harmony, concord, agreement, sympathy** My English teacher has a great rapport with his students. ⏺ **Antonyms: antagonism, uneasiness, distance**

rapture *noun* **bliss, delight, happiness, joy, ecstasy, exultation, elation, enchantment** Melissa was filled with rapture when she finally got tickets to the rock concert. ⏺ **Antonyms: misery, sorrow**

rare *adjective* **1. scarce, uncommon, unusual, unique, singular, valuable, precious** Dwight's hobby is collecting rare coins. **2. excellent, superb, choice, fine, admirable, exquisite, peerless, great, superior** We had a rare time this evening. ⏺ **Antonyms: 1. common, ordinary 2. inferior, mediocre**

rarely *adverb* **infrequently, not often, seldom, hardly, occasionally, scarcely, uncommonly** It rarely rains in the desert. ⏺ **Antonyms: often, frequently, regularly**

rascal *noun* **prankster, trickster, jokester, scalawag, scamp, imp, mischief-maker, scoundrel, villain, knave**

In Native American myth, the coyote is usually a mischievous rascal.

rash[1] *adjective* **reckless, thoughtless, heedless, foolhardy, careless, hasty, impetuous, impulsive, audacious** It was rash of me to raise my hand when I didn't know the answer. ⏺ **Antonyms: careful, thoughtful**

rash[2] *noun* **eruption, outbreak, plague, flood, wave, spate, epidemic, succession, series** There was a serious rash of cases of yellow fever in 1855 in Norfolk, Virginia.

raspy *adjective* **husky, rasping, rough, gruff, scratchy, grating, harsh** The blues singer had a raspy baritone voice.

rate *noun* **1. pace, speed, velocity, tempo, time, flow, clip** The roller coaster was going at a breakneck rate as it went into the last turn. **2. percentage, ratio, fraction, proportion, quota, amount, scale, comparison** They have a mortgage rate of 7¼ percent. **3. fee, charge, cost, price, amount, assessment, tariff, toll** This motel offers low rates. ◆ *verb* **appraise, evaluate, grade, judge, rank, gauge, measure, classify, assess** We were asked to rate our favorite TV shows for a class assignment.

rather *adverb* **1. more willingly, sooner, as soon, much sooner, in preference, preferably** I'd rather go to the arboretum tomorrow than today. **2. somewhat, fairly, moderately, slightly, comparatively, tolerably, pretty, sort of** It seems rather cool today. ⏺ **Antonyms: 2. highly, very, extremely**

ratify *verb* **affirm, approve, authorize, confirm, sanction, validate, certify, endorse** The factory workers ratified the pact to end the strike. ⏺ **Antonyms: veto, invalidate, disapprove**

ratio *noun* **proportion, percentage, correspondence, fraction, relationship, share** The ratio of boys to girls on our softball team is two to one.

ration *noun* **allotment, allowance, provision, quota, share, dole, portion, distribution, helping** A daily ration of water and a tent are provided to competitors in the two-week-long Marathon of Sand. ◆ *verb* **allot, distribute, dispense, deal, dole, mete, budget, parcel out** We rationed out our Halloween candy so that it would last the week.

rational *adjective* **logical, prudent, reasonable, sane, sensible, sound, wise, sage, advisable** When you have had a sore throat for several days, the rational thing to do is to see a doctor. ⏺ **Antonyms: irrational, rash**

rationale *noun* reason, basis, grounds, principle, reasoning, logic, justification, explanation, theory The excuse that everyone else is doing it is not a sound rationale for committing a wrong action.

rattle *verb* **1.** jangle, jingle, shake, clatter, clang, clink, bang I rattled a tambourine to amuse my baby sister. **2.** chatter, jabber, run on, babble, gush, gibber, yak She rattled on about her new video game. **3.** fluster, confuse, disturb, disconcert, muddle, upset, unnerve The near-accident so rattled him that he missed his exit off the highway. ◆ *noun* banging, clang, clanging, clank, clatter, racket, noise, din, hubbub I heard a rattle coming from the car's transmission.

ravage *verb* destroy, damage, desolate, ruin, wreck, devastate, shatter The forests of northern Canada are periodically ravaged by fire. ➡ **Antonyms:** build, construct, repair

rave *verb* **1.** rant, rail, fume, roar, harangue, rage, babble, prattle, gibber, jabber The man raved about all the forms he had to fill out for the government agency. **2.** gush, rhapsodize, praise, extol, glorify, eulogize, bubble My friends raved about the food at the new restaurant. ◆ *noun* praise, tribute, accolade, eulogy, kudos, applause, acclaim Did you read the raves in the newspaper for the mayor's new program? ◆ *adjective* enthusiastic, favorable, good, positive, commendatory, affirmative The new TV series is receiving rave reviews. ➡ **Antonyms:** *verb* **2.** disparage, criticize ◆ *noun* condemnation, criticism ◆ *adjective* poor, critical, unfavorable

ravenous *adjective* **1.** hungry, starving, starved, famished, voracious, empty The ravenous wild pigs came into our yard to eat the dog food that we left for them. **2.** greedy, avid, grasping, predatory, insatiable, rapacious, eager Because Hitler was ravenous for power and land, he invaded neighboring countries. ➡ **Antonyms: 1.** full, sated

ravine *noun* gorge, canyon, chasm, gap, flume, crevasse We stood on the edge of the ravine and looked at the river below.

raw *adjective* **1.** uncooked, unprepared, fresh, natural, rare, unripe Pies can be made from either cooked or raw fruits. **2.** inexperienced, unskilled, untrained, green, new, unprepared, ignorant The coach transformed the raw players into a skilled team. **3.** painful, sensitive, sore, irritated, tender, inflamed, open, uncovered My feelings were raw after the scolding I received. **4.** chilly, harsh, bitter, cold, numbing, wet, biting, chill, bleak The cold, raw weather made me glad to be inside by the fire.

➡ **Antonyms: 1.** cooked, prepared **2.** experienced, trained **4.** mild, balmy, sunny

ray *noun* **1.** beam, flash, gleam, shaft, streak, glimmer, glint, flicker The moon's bright rays shone through my bedroom window. **2.** trace, hint, breath, suspicion, speck, glimmer, touch, bit, scintilla, indication My mother has a ray of suspicion as to who took the last of the cookies.

reach *verb* **1.** stretch, extend, go, run, span, spread, sprawl, unfold, continue Interstate 40 reaches across the entire United States. **2.** get, grab, grasp, touch, seize, clutch, take, hand Can you reach that box on the top shelf? **3.** achieve, attain, make, realize, accomplish, arrive at, gain I reached my goal of reading ten books over the summer. **4.** contact, find, get hold of, approach, touch, get to, communicate with Pamela tried to reach you to say that she would be late. ◆ *noun* grasp, range, touch, expanse, span, stretch, compass, sweep, length The goat poked his head through the fence and ate all the grass within reach.

react *verb* respond, reply, reciprocate, answer, counter, acknowledge, return She reacted with a smile when she heard the good news.

reaction *noun* **1.** response, answer, reply, result, acknowledgment, effect, reciprocation I got a positive reaction to my suggestion. **2.** backlash, result, consequence, effect, repercussion, recoil, counteraction, opposition A giant "sunquake" was generated as a reaction to shock waves from a solar flare on July 9, 1996.

read *verb* **1.** peruse, study, review, look at, skim, cover, scan, view, glance at We had to read two chapters in our history book for homework last night. **2.** understand, comprehend, interpret, apprehend, construe, translate, decipher I am learning to read topographical maps in our orienteering class. **3.** detect, perceive, glimpse, observe, note, discern, notice, spot I clearly read a note of alarm in his expression. **4.** register, indicate, show, display, reflect, record, exhibit, signify The odometer read 14,061 miles. **5.** learn, discover, find out, uncover, gather, deduce, infer, ascertain What did you read in last night's assignment?

ready *adjective* **1.** prepared, set, arranged, organized, fixed, furnished, equipped, qualified I was ready for school early today. **2.** inclined, willing, disposed, agreeable, predisposed, prone, apt, likely, happy I am ready to do whatever the rest of you want to do. **3.** quick, alert, bright, perceptive, clever, eager, attentive, fit, skillful, deft, astute Our new dog has a ready intelligence. **4.** available, accessible, handy, free, prepared, willing, waiting, at hand, set I am ready whenever you are. ◆ *verb* prepare, equip, fix, arrange, make, prime, fit, outfit, develop, adapt, complete The ground crew readied the plane for takeoff.

real *adjective* **1.** actual, concrete, objective, true, solid, veritable, unquestionable, tangible I have a real opportunity to go to Alaska this summer. **2.** authentic, genuine, legitimate, actual, bona fide, verifiable, good The necklace my parents gave me for graduation is made of real gold. **3.** sincere, honest, unaffected, natural, unpretentious, intrinsic, heartfelt, serious He is a real friend. ➨ **Antonyms: 1.** imaginary, nonexistent **2.** fake, imitation **3.** pretended, insincere

reality *noun* actuality, fact, certainty, existence, truth, verity, phenomenon, deed Our family's dream of owning a house is about to become a reality. ➨ **Antonyms:** illusion, dream, myth

realize *verb* **1.** comprehend, grasp, perceive, recognize, understand, discern, apprehend, fathom I suddenly realized that the surprise party was for me. **2.** accomplish, achieve, attain, complete, gain, reach, execute, carry out, actualize I realized my goal of learning to program my computer by reading books and taking a class. **3.** obtain, gain, earn, net, clear, win, make, acquire, effect, profit We realized a profit of 300 dollars from our rummage sale. ➨ **Antonyms: 1.** misunderstand, miss **3.** lose, give up

really *adverb* truly, genuinely, certainly, honestly, especially, particularly, unquestionably, truthfully, positively, indeed I really enjoy going to the beach.

realm *noun* **1.** kingdom, empire, country, domain, dominion, land, principality, state, polity, monarchy, duchy Recently, the queen traveled on a good will tour to all parts of her realm. **2.** field, world, sphere, province, department, area, arena, turf, orbit Admiral Grace Hopper was eminent in the realm of computer languages.

reap *verb* **1.** cut, garner, glean, harvest, gather, pluck, cull, mow, strip A truck farmer we know reaps his vegetable crop by hand. **2.** earn, acquire, obtain, secure, win, gain, realize, receive, draw The company reaped its first profit this year. ➨ **Antonyms: 1.** plant, grow **2.** lose, waste, forfeit

rear[1] *noun* back, end, rear end, posterior, tail, tail end, heel, stern My uncle put me on the rear of his motorcycle and took me for a ride. ◆ *adjective* back, rearmost, hind, aft, last, rearward, stern, hindmost My brother and I usually sit in the rear seat of Mom's van.

rear[2] *verb* **1.** bring up, care for, nurture, raise, develop, foster, educate, nurse Grandmother reared four children on her own after Grandfather died. **2.** build, erect, construct, fabricate, set up, raise, make, loft, lift They reared that new office building very quickly. **3.** raise, rise, lift, soar, tower, spring up, elevate, upraise, loom The bear reared up on his hind legs when he smelled something strange. ➨ **Antonyms: 2.** level, raze, demolish **3.** drop, lower

reason *noun* **1.** excuse, explanation, justification, basis, rationale, motive, apology, cause I hope that he had a good reason for missing soccer practice. **2.** logic, rationality, wisdom, comprehension, judgment, cognition, intellect, sense Scientists are conducting experiments to see whether or not animals possess powers of reason. ◆ *verb* **1.** solve, figure, deduce, work, reckon, understand, calculate I reasoned out the math problem without assistance. **2.** talk with, discuss, confer, debate, argue, convince, persuade, dissuade, influence No one could reason with the hijacker.

reasonable *adjective* **1.** logical, rational, sensible, practical, intelligent, wise, sane, believable When I asked for a 100-dollar allowance, my dad told me to be reasonable. **2.** moderate, acceptable, fair, suitable, just, honest, inexpensive, average This store has good quality clothing at reasonable prices. ➨ **Antonyms: 1.** impractical, unreasonable **2.** extreme, immoderate, excessive

reassure *verb* comfort, assure, soothe, bolster, hearten, encourage, calm, sustain, cheer, inspire We were reassured by our parents' provisions for an emergency or disaster. ➨ **Antonyms:** discourage, dishearten

rebel *verb* revolt, mutiny, resist, riot, strike, challenge, defy, criticize The workers rebelled against their low wages by going on strike. ◆ *noun* revolutionary, mutineer, dissenter, traitor, anarchist, separatist, freedom fighter Guy Fawkes was an English rebel who tried to blow up Parliament in 1605. ➨ **Antonyms:** *verb* comply, obey ◆ *noun* loyalist, conformist

rebellion *noun* revolt, revolution, mutiny, uprising, insurgence, upheaval, coup, disobedience, defiance The American Revolution was a rebellion against British control. ➨ **Antonyms:** obedience, submission

rebuff *noun* rejection, brushoff, snub, slight, refusal, rebuke, defeat, denial, repulse, discouragement, opposition It is difficult emotionally to receive a rebuff. ◆ *verb* reject, refuse, snub, discourage, check, repulse, resist, oppose, repel My cat rebuffed my invitation to come inside. ➨ **Antonyms:** *noun* encouragement, support ◆ *verb* encourage, accept, support

rebuke *verb* chastise, reprimand, chide, scold, upbraid, admonish, reproach, censure, castigate, criticize My mother rebuked us for creating such a mess in the living room. ◆ *noun* criticism, reprimand, admonishment, censure, reproof, chastisement, disapproval, blame, castigation The newspaper editorial was a rebuke of the government's escalation of military action. ➡ **Antonyms:** *verb* approve, praise, compliment ◆ *noun* approval, applause

recall *verb* 1. remember, think of, recollect, cite, summon up, evoke, place, recapture I can't recall the name of that restaurant that I liked so much. 2. call back, withdraw, repeal, revoke, cancel, rescind, retract The company had to recall a toy with a faulty part. ◆ *noun* 1. cancellation, retraction, annulment, repeal, withdrawal, nullification, denial The congressman lost his position when voters approved a recall. 2. memory, recollection, remembrance, retention, reminiscence Jennifer has such excellent recall that she can name all of last year's Grammy winners. ➡ **Antonyms:** *verb* 1. forget ◆ *noun* 2. forgetfulness, amnesia

recede *verb* 1. ebb, retreat, subside, leave, regress, retire, withdraw, drain, depart, retract I like to explore the pools that are left behind as the tide recedes. 2. dwindle, diminish, fade, decrease, abate, shrink, wane, decline, disappear We listened as the sound of the train's whistle receded in the distance. ➡ **Antonyms:** 1. advance, proceed 2. increase, loom

receipt *noun* 1. delivery, receiving, reception, acquisition, arrival, possession The shipping clerk took receipt of the parts. 2. proceeds, gain, profit, net, money, return, earnings, income, revenue The week's receipts for the top ten movies are published each Monday. 3. ticket, stub, sales slip, acknowledgment, voucher, release We will need our receipt in order to return this shirt.

receive *verb* 1. get, acquire, gain, obtain, attain, win, collect, accept, gather, procure Each team member will receive a trophy. 2. learn, hear, glean, perceive, understand, apprehend, ascertain, encounter In our math class we receive interesting information about the history of mathematics. 3. support, shoulder, stay, sustain, uphold, bear The load-bearing walls of a building receive the weight of the roof. 4. experience, undergo, encounter, sustain, endure, suffer, meet with, take He received a minor injury in the accident. 5. greet, welcome, entertain, admit, shelter, accommodate, invite They received us warmly.

recent *adjective* new, current, contemporary, brand-new, fresh, modern, latest, now, novel I went to the bookstore to find my favorite author's most recent book. ➡ **Antonyms:** old, dated, former

reception *noun* 1. greeting, welcome, response, treatment, salutation, recognition, encounter, acceptance We received a warm reception from everyone at the family reunion. 2. affair, function, occasion, gathering, party, social, fete A reception for the new club members will be held next Friday night.

recess *noun* 1. break, interlude, interim, rest, halt, pause, stop, respite, lull, intermission, interval Our lunch recess is 45 minutes long. 2. alcove, nook, slot, niche, cubbyhole, corner, hollow, cranny, cleft, indentation I put a vase of flowers in the wall recess. ◆ *verb* adjourn, break, pause, stop, quit, discontinue, suspend, rest, postpone At our school, classes recess for the day at 3:30 p.m. ➡ **Antonyms:** *verb* persist, continue

recipe *noun* formula, directions, prescription, ingredients, method, program, technique, plan Mom has an old-fashioned recipe for cough syrup made of lemon juice and honey.

recital *noun* 1. description, narration, telling, report, account, recitation, particulars, statement We listened to the recital of their trip to the Holy Land with great interest. 2. performance, concert, show, musicale, presentation, festival, entertainment, production My cousin played a solo for clarinet in a music recital.

recite *verb* 1. narrate, quote, repeat, speak, deliver, perform, render, declaim My little sister can recite her favorite poem from memory. 2. report, detail, itemize, enumerate, particularize, recount, tell, impart I called my mom at work, and she asked me to recite my homework assignments.

reckless *adjective* careless, heedless, irresponsible, rash, thoughtless, imprudent, wild, foolhardy, impulsive The hockey player's reckless actions earned him a penalty. ➡ **Antonyms:** careful, responsible, thoughtful

reckon *verb* 1. compute, calculate, figure, total, count, tally, number The waiter reckoned our bill. 2. consider, regard, judge, esteem, rate, rank, assess, deem I reckon him to be one of my closest friends. 3. guess, estimate, suppose, think, figure, imagine, surmise, fancy, expect, presume How many jelly beans do you reckon are in the jar? 4. anticipate, expect, bank on, count on, hope for, trust, plan, depend I didn't reckon on having to clean my room before I could go to the movie.

reckoning *noun* count, calculation, tally, approximation, determination, appraisal, evaluation, account, settlement The teacher made a reckoning of how many students were going on the field trip.

reclaim *verb* retrieve, regain, recoup, recover, redeem, rescue, salvage, restore, reform, recycle Charles II reclaimed the English throne in 1660 after the fall of the Protectorate. ● **Antonyms: discard, abandon, waste**

recline *verb* lie down, lounge, rest, stretch out, repose, relax, loll, sprawl, lean I reclined in Grandpa's lounge chair and promptly fell asleep. ● **Antonyms: stand, get up**

recognize *verb* **1.** distinguish, identify, discern, make out, place, tell, know, spot, sight Sam can recognize many kinds of birds on sight **2.** remember, recollect, place, recall, retain, revive I recognized our old neighborhood when we drove through that part of the city. **3.** acknowledge, endorse, support, salute, approve, honor, greet, accept The master of ceremonies recognized all the people who had worked to make the occasion possible.

recollect *verb* recall, remember, think of, summon, evoke, place, retain, revive She told me her phone number, but I can't recollect it right now. ● **Antonyms: forget, overlook**

recommend *verb* **1.** praise, commend, endorse, promote, acclaim, extol, celebrate My friend recommended this book to me, and I am really enjoying it. **2.** advocate, advise, suggest, prescribe, counsel, urge, exhort, support My gym teacher recommends regular exercise for good health. ● **Antonyms: 1. disapprove, condemn 2. discourage**

recommendation *noun* **1.** advice, guidance, counsel, suggestion, direction, prompting, urging I followed the doctor's recommendation in taking care of my broken arm. **2.** commendation, endorsement, testimonial, praise, promotion, approval, support, blessing I asked my teacher for a letter of recommendation. ● **Antonyms: 1. warning, objection 2. criticism, disapproval**

reconcile *verb* **1.** conciliate, make up, reunite, disarm, settle The brother and sister soon reconciled after their argument. **2.** resign, submit, accept, accommodate, yield, bear, accede, brook I reconciled myself to staying home. **3.** adjust, square, resolve, settle, rectify, adapt, arrange, arbitrate, intercede, mediate The bookkeeper reconciled the company accounts. ● **Antonyms: 1. anger, antagonize 2. object, resist**

record *verb* **1.** chronicle, document, note, write down, enter, list, transcribe, report, post The secretary records the minutes of our club meetings. **2.** register, indicate, show, designate, read, denote, display, reflect, say The Web site counter recorded the number of visitors. ◆ *noun* **1.** account, chronicle, log, journal, register, report, diary, recording I am keeping a daily record of the weather as part of my science project. **2.** résumé, file, dossier, portfolio, account, history, background, case He has an excellent school record. **3.** mark, time, achievement, performance, deed, maximum, minimum, ceiling The swimmer is hoping to beat his own record.

recount *verb* relate, describe, recall, depict, narrate, tell, retell, report, communicate, recite I like to hear my mother recount the days when she was a little girl.

recourse *noun* alternative, option, choice, resort, resource, support, remedy, help I have no recourse but to take the class over.

recover *verb* **1.** find, get back, regain, recoup, retrieve, reclaim, redeem, recapture I was happy when I recovered the book that I thought was lost. **2.** recoup, compensate, requite, balance, offset, repay, recompense We recovered the cost of advertising when we sold our car. **3.** get better, improve, rally, revive, heal, mend, rejuvenate, survive You certainly recovered quickly from your cold. ● **Antonyms: 3. worsen, succumb, debilitate**

recovery *noun* **1.** recuperation, convalescence, healing, comeback, revival, improvement, restitution, restoration We were pleased to hear that he made a full recovery from his illness. **2.** retrieval, reclamation, regaining, salvaging, retaking, recapture, redemption *Ship of Gold in the Deep Blue Sea* tells the exciting story of the recovery of a sunken ship filled with treasure.

recreation *noun* pastime, sport, relaxation, diversion, amusement, fun, play, hobby, entertainment Mountain biking is my favorite form of outdoor recreation.

recruit *verb* draft, enlist, assemble, gather, muster, rally, round up, enroll, induct Our church is recruiting people to help with the craft fair. ◆ *noun* trainee, novice, beginner, fledgling, initiate, newcomer, conscript, inductee, draftee My older brother is a Marine recruit.

rectify *verb* correct, improve, fix, redress, amend, repair, remedy, adjust, square I am trying to rectify my low grade by doing work for extra credit.

recuperate *verb* **1. recover, rally, convalesce, improve, strengthen, heal, get well, mend, survive** He recuperated fully from his surgery. **2. recoup, regain, retrieve, repossess, recapture, reclaim** My uncle recuperated his earlier losses in the stock market. ⏺ **Antonyms: 1. weaken, sicken, succumb**

recur *verb* **repeat, persist, reappear, come back, reoccur, return, resume, continue** The need for more space in the schools was an issue that kept recurring as the town's population continued to grow.

redeem *verb* **1. reclaim, recover, recoup, repossess, regain, buy back, ransom** The man redeemed his ring from the pawn shop. **2. liberate, emancipate, loose, rescue, set free, ransom, deliver** The soldiers redeemed the prisoners of war from the camp. **3. neutralize, offset, compensate, rehabilitate, rescue, counterbalance, defray, redress** He redeemed his earlier behavior by apologizing.

reduce *verb* **1. curtail, cut, decrease, diminish, lessen, restrict, abridge, slash, prune, dilute, abate** Through hard practice, our team has reduced the number of mistakes we make. **2. demolish, level, raze, flatten, destroy, ruin, crush, waste, wreck, devastate, ravage** Many homes and public buildings were reduced to rubble in bombing raids during World War II. **3. demote, downgrade, lower, humble, abase, debase, devalue, break** The police officer was reduced in rank for his misuse of the computer files. ⏺ **Antonyms: 1. increase, amplify 3. promote, elevate, upgrade**

redundant *adjective* **1. verbose, repetitious, tautological, wordy, repetitive, padded, rambling, long-winded** The magazine article was redundant. **2. excess, superfluous, unnecessary, extra, additional, surplus, spare** In restructuring and economizing, the company laid off its redundant workers. ⏺ **Antonyms: 1. concise, terse 2. essential, necessary**

> ## Word Group
>
> A **reef** is a strip of rock or corral that rises to or close to the surface of a body of water. **Reef** is a specific term with no true synonyms. Here are some related terms:
>
> **atoll, bank, bar, barrier reef, cay, coral reef, key, sandbank, sandbar, shallow, shelf, shoal**

reel¹ *noun* **spool, bobbin, frame, wheel, cylinder** My fishing rod needs a new reel.

reel² *verb* **lurch, roll, spin, stagger, sway, weave, wobble, totter** I was reeling when I got off the carnival ride.

refer *verb* **1. direct, send, recommend, turn over, transfer, consign, introduce, aim, point** The doctor referred her patient to a specialist. **2. pertain, concern, relate, apply, connect, encompass, bear upon, regard** This book refers to the subject of my essay. **3. cite, mention, point out, touch on, allude, speak of, credit, notice** My art teacher referred to an artist who has a special exhibit at the museum. **4. consult, go, look at, resort, turn, use, apply** We referred to the answers in the back of the book to check our work.

referee *noun* **official, judge, umpire, negotiator, intermediary, arbitrator, arbiter** We had a good referee for our volleyball game. ◆ *verb* **umpire, judge, officiate, rule, mediate, arbitrate, decide, determine, moderate, settle** Volunteers referee the games in our soccer league.

refine *verb* **1. process, purify, clean, filter, strain, rarefy, prepare** Sugar was first refined in 700 B.C. **2. perfect, polish, develop, cultivate, smooth, better, hone, finish** Through hours of practice, I have refined my solo for the recital. ⏺ **Antonyms: 1. pollute, contaminate 2. downgrade, coarsen**

reflect *verb* **1. cast back, return, send back, mirror, ricochet, echo, image, repeat, reproduce, rebound** The windowpane reflected the light from my candle. **2. indicate, manifest, signify, show, evince, bespeak, imply, register, demonstrate** His speech reflected thorough research on the topic. **3. consider, contemplate, deliberate, ponder, think, reason, study, ruminate, meditate** I reflected long and hard before deciding to drop French and study Spanish. ⏺ **Antonyms: 1. absorb 2. conceal, cover, mask**

reflex *noun* **response, instinct, impulse, reaction** It is a natural reflex to want to yawn if you see someone else do it.

reform *verb* **change, correct, improve, reorganize, alter, remedy, revise, better, amend** Both presidential candidates would reform the educational system. ◆ *noun* **change, revision, reformation, correction, improvement, progress, betterment, amendment** The decade of the 1960s was one of significant social reform in the United States. ⏺ **Antonyms:** *verb* **ignore, worsen** ◆ *noun* **deterioration, regression**

refrain¹ *verb* **abstain, forgo, forbear, avoid, renounce, refuse, quit, resist, eschew** I refrained from turning my stereo up while my parents had company. ⏺ **Antonyms: indulge, yield**

refrain² *noun* **chorus, theme, melody, strain, motif, tune, song, chant** I hummed the refrain to the song.

refresh *verb* **1. freshen, renew, revive, restore, invigorate, rejuvenate, revitalize, strengthen, energize** The bicyclists refreshed themselves with a rest and a snack. **2. jog, stimulate, prompt, kindle, activate, rekindle, spur, prod** She refreshed her memory before the test by rereading her English notes. ⏵ **Antonyms: 1. drain, exhaust, tire**

refreshment *noun* **1. renewal, revival, recreation, invigoration, revitalization, rejuvenation, restoration** Summer vacation offers a wonderful opportunity for refreshment. **2. snack, treat, drink, food, nourishment, repast, meal, appetizer, bite** We bought refreshments before the movie.

refrigerate *verb* **chill, cool, ice, freeze, preserve** Mayonnaise must be refrigerated after the jar is opened.

refuge *noun* **preserve, sanctuary, haven, retreat, oasis, shelter, cover, protection, security, preservation** Our class took a tour of a wildlife refuge.

refugee *noun* **émigré, displaced person, pilgrim, exile, outcast, fugitive, runaway, evacuee** Many Americans have ancestors who came to this country as political or religious refugees.

refund *verb* **return, repay, reimburse, give back, pay back, restore, adjust** The store will refund your money if you are not satisfied. ◆ *noun* **repayment, restitution, reimbursement, adjustment, settlement, compensation, satisfaction** The clerk said that the refund would be mailed to us.

refuse¹ *verb* **decline, reject, turn down, spurn, resist, balk, evade, veto, forbid** Grandma didn't refuse me when I offered to help her with the crossword puzzle. ⏵ **Antonyms: consent, allow, accept**

refuse² *noun* **garbage, rubbish, trash, waste, litter, junk, debris, sweepings** The refuse from cleaning up our yard filled several trash cans.

refute *verb* **challenge, counter, discredit, deny, negate, rebut, disprove, gainsay, contradict** The skeptical scientist refuted the idea of an invasion by aliens from outer space. ⏵ **Antonyms: agree, corroborate, uphold**

regal *adjective* **royal, majestic, noble, magnificent, splendid, stately, august, kingly, queenly** I think a ship sailing on the ocean is a regal sight.

regard *verb* **1. observe, scrutinize, view, eye, scan, watch, notice, mark** The art dealer thoughtfully regarded the painting before making an offer to buy it. **2. consider, think, believe, rate, judge, estimate, deem, hold, see, reckon, fancy** I regard that lawn furniture to be both useful and attractive. **3. concern, relate, bear upon, refer, apply, involve, pertain, appertain** This decision regards my application for summer school. ◆ *noun* **1. attention, consideration, heed, thought, notice, contemplation, mind, care** Please give more regard to the advice that I give you. **2. respect, appreciation, esteem, admiration, honor, affection, favor, warmth, homage** We have great regard for the firefighters who saved our home. **3. good wishes, compliments, respects, best wishes, salutations, greetings** I signed the letter with my best regards. **4. point, matter, particular, concern, detail, feature, item, aspect** Where do you stand on that regard? ⏵ **Antonyms:** *noun* **1. inattention, neglect 2. disrespect, contempt, scorn**

regime *noun* **government, dynasty, administration, reign, rule, command, leadership** Kabuki theater, which integrates song, dance, and drama, originated under the Tokugawa regime in Japan.

regiment *verb* **systematize, standardize, mechanize, organize, methodize, regulate, order** The company regimented its manufacturing procedures.

region *noun* **1. locale, area, zone, district, territory, environs, section, province, country, space** Tropical regions receive a lot of rainfall. **2. area, field, sphere, domain, realm, arena, province, scene, bailiwick** I became interested when the discussion entered the region of psychic experiences.

register *noun* **1. log, logbook, record, guest book, journal, list, roll, slate, diary** The museum has a register for visitors to sign. **2. counter, recorder, dial, indicator, gauge, calculator, meter** The electronic register indicated that 1,500 people had visited the Web site. **3. duct, vent, heat vent, grill, outlet** The repairman cleaned out the school registers. **4. range, scale, scope, command, sweep, reach, limits, extent, compass** Not until the late 15th century did interest in the bass register of the human singing voice develop. ◆ *verb* **1. display, reveal, show, manifest, express, indicate, exhibit, signify, disclose** I could see happiness register on my mom's face when my dad brought her flowers. **2. enroll, sign up, schedule, check in, enlist, subscribe, enter, join** My brother has registered to take a class at the community college. **3. dawn on, sink in, get through, impress, affect, reach** It finally registered with me that I was late for school.

regress *verb* revert, backslide, decline, deteriorate, worsen, recede, go back, reverse, retrogress The team regressed during the second half of the season. ◈ **Antonyms:** progress, proceed, advance

regret *verb* be sorry, feel sorry, bemoan, rue, lament, grieve, mourn, apologize We regret that we will not be able to attend your New Year's Eve celebration. ◆ *noun* remorse, sorrow, qualms, misgivings, dissatisfaction, woe, guilt, bitterness, disappointment I have no regrets that I stayed home this evening.

regular *adjective* **1.** usual, customary, normal, routine, standard, fixed, set, established, common School will not start at the regular time because of the snowstorm. **2.** recurring, recurrent, periodic, steady, consistent, frequent, cyclic, habitual My mom is careful to have the car's motor oil changed at regular intervals. **3.** likable, nice, friendly, amiable, good, pleasant, kindly, genial, approachable He is a regular guy. **4.** complete, thorough, absolute, total, sheer, unmitigated, thoroughgoing, acknowledged, perfect I think that picture of the UFO is a regular hoax! ◈ **Antonyms: 1.** uncommon, unusual **2.** infrequent, variable **3.** formal, aloof **4.** partial

regulate *verb* **1.** monitor, supervise, manage, oversee, control, administer, direct, police The veterinarian told me to regulate my cat's diet carefully. **2.** adjust, calibrate, modify, reset, balance, moderate, fix, straighten, modulate, equalize I regulated the furnace thermostat.

regulation *noun* **1.** supervision, control, management, organization, government, guidance The Department of Transportation is charged with the regulation of interstate commerce. **2.** rule, law, statute, requirement, dictate, decree, principle, order Several new regulations were put into effect by the agency.

rehearse *verb* drill, practice, review, study, run through, recite, learn, polish, prepare The cast of the school play rehearsed after school every day this week.

reign *noun* administration, regime, rule, sovereignty, government, dominion, sway, dominance The British Empire reached its peak during the reign of Queen Victoria. ◆ *verb* govern, rule, command, lead, manage, guide, dominate, administer, head, control Queen Victoria reigned from 1837 to 1901.

reinforce *verb* bolster, buttress, fortify, brace, support, strengthen, toughen, secure, enhance, augment The beavers reinforced their dam with additional twigs and branches.

reject *verb* **1.** dismiss, veto, refuse, spurn, turn down, drop, rebuff, deny, decline The city council rejected the proposal to build a new courthouse. **2.** repudiate, discard, throw out, dump, scrap, jettison, abandon, expel, repel The club rejected the committee's controversial proposal. ◆ *noun* discard, scrap, refuse, mistake, error, outcast, exile, castaway We gathered up the rejects from our cooking class and put them in the garbage. ◈ **Antonyms:** *verb* accept, approve

rejoice *verb* celebrate, exult, glory, delight, revel, pleasure, be happy, brighten The whole family rejoiced when my cousin recovered from her serious illness. ◈ **Antonyms:** grieve, mourn

relapse *verb* **1.** lapse, regress, fall back, revert, deteriorate, backslide, retrogress My dog relapsed into his old behavior when he had missed two obedience training classes. **2.** sicken, weaken, degenerate, deteriorate, fail, decline, fade, worsen, sink The patient had been improving, but then he relapsed. ◆ *noun* deterioration, decline, sinking, regression, failure, fall, return, lapse My python is suffering a relapse in his fight against inclusion body disease.

relate *verb* **1.** describe, recount, tell, communicate, disclose, detail, impart, summarize, recite The author's latest book relates his experiences in Africa. **2.** apply, bear on, concern, pertain, refer, correlate, link, connect The teacher showed a video that relates to the subject we've been studying.

relation *noun* **1.** relationship, association, connection, link, similarity, affiliation, bond, tie, regard Many movies about the Old West have almost no relation to the way things really were. **2.** family member, kin, relative, in-law, blood, kinsman, clan, folk, people, tribe I met some of my distant relations at my great-grandmother's birthday party. **3.** account, narration, report, description, recital, communication, recounting Did you hear the announcer's relation of the incidents leading up to the oil spill?

relative *adjective* **1.** related, pertinent, germane, relevant, analogous, correlated, connected, affiliated I found the movie *Those Magnificent Men in Their Flying Machines* relative to my interest in early aviation. **2.** comparative, comparable, approximate, near, respective, proportionate, conditional, contingent After the fight with my brother, I enjoyed the relative peace of being at school. ◆ *noun* family member, kin, kinfolk, relation, in-law, blood, kinsman, kinswoman My friends and relatives attended my graduation.

relax *verb* 1. loosen, slacken, free, release, unfasten, soften, calm, unbind The sails relaxed as the wind died down. 2. ease, lessen, reduce, diminish, modify, waive, moderate, mitigate The recreation department recently relaxed the regulations regarding admission of guests to the town pool. 3. rest, unwind, recreate, lounge, loaf, laze Dad likes to relax after work by puttering in his shop. ● **Antonyms: 1. tense, bind 2. increase, tighten 3. toil, labor, work**

release *verb* 1. discharge, free, let go, liberate, emancipate, parole, loose, surrender The prisoner was released on parole. 2. extricate, disengage, detach, unloose, loose, unbind, untie, unchain I released the snake that was caught in the garden netting. 3. issue, publish, distribute, put out, present, circulate, communicate The publisher plans to release several new books this spring. ◆ *noun* 1. liberation, emancipation, delivery, discharge, freedom, liberty, exoneration, dispensation I read about the release of several Mexican gray wolves in the forests of eastern Arizona. 2. publication, circulation, distribution, proclamation, notice, announcement I am looking forward to the release of the new science fiction movie.

relent *verb* accede, yield, acquiesce, capitulate, relax, soften, weaken, give in, submit My parents finally relented and allowed me to spend the night at my friend's house. ● **Antonyms: withstand, toughen**

relentless *adjective* 1. merciless, cruel, ruthless, harsh, pitiless, unyielding, uncompromising, inhuman, strict Joseph Stalin was a relentless dictator who was known for putting down all opposition. 2. steady, tenacious, persistent, continuous, unflagging, stubborn, dogged, incessant, nonstop That group is known for its relentless pursuit of reform of campaign finance laws. ● **Antonyms: 1. lenient, compassionate 2. intermittent, occasional**

relevant *adjective* applicable, pertinent, related, connected, germane, significant, fitting, appropriate I looked in the encyclopedia for information relevant to my report. ● **Antonyms: irrelevant, unrelated**

reliable *adjective* dependable, capable, responsible, competent, conscientious, trustworthy, stable, steadfast I need a reliable person to help me organize the talent show. ● **Antonyms: undependable, unreliable**

relic *noun* artifact, keepsake, souvenir, memento, curio, heirloom, reminder, remembrance My grandfather collects medals and other relics from World War II.

relief *noun* 1. comfort, cure, ease, release, remedy, alleviation, balm, easement This medicine provides immediate relief for an upset stomach. 2. aid, assistance, help, support, comfort, consolation, succor, charity, welfare The Red Cross sent relief to the hurricane victims. 3. rest, break, respite, pause, recess, interlude, intermission, suspension, vacation I expect this weekend will provide a welcome relief from the pressures of school. ● **Antonyms: 1. discomfort, aggravation**

relieve *verb* 1. alleviate, comfort, soothe, ease, help, mitigate, subdue These lozenges should relieve your sore throat. 2. replace, spell, discharge, free, release, excuse, spare, substitute The desk clerk had to stay on duty until someone could relieve him. 3. aid, comfort, assist, support, treat, refresh, succor, improve The new bridge should help relieve traffic congestion through the city. ● **Antonyms: 1. aggravate 3. burden, oppress**

religion *noun* 1. theology, creed, faith, denomination, belief, devotion, worship, orthodoxy Christianity, Islam, and Judaism are three of the world's major religions. 2. cause, principle, commitment, enthusiasm, love, interest, passion, life Preserving endangered species is a religion with her.

religious *adjective* 1. devout, pious, spiritual, reverent, holy, devoted, godly, orthodox, saintly A religious man, he prays several times every day. 2. faithful, staunch, zealous, conscientious, meticulous, scrupulous, strict, exact, fastidious He is religious in his adherence to his exercise routine. ● **Antonyms: 1. agnostic, atheistic 2. casual, careless**

relinquish *verb* give up, surrender, let go, renounce, yield, abandon, abdicate I relinquished the remote control to my mom. ● **Antonyms: keep, hold, retain**

relish *noun* 1. enthusiasm, zest, delight, fondness, love, liking, appetite, taste She has a great relish for surfing. 2. spice, excitement, gusto, tang, zip, zest, flavor, pleasure, enjoyment Challenging yourself to do something new adds relish to life. ◆ *verb* appreciate, treasure, value, like, enjoy, love, savor, cherish I relished the opportunity to go to a dude ranch. ● **Antonyms: *noun* 1. dislike, distaste, hatred 2. boredom, dullness ◆ *verb* dislike, abhor, avoid**

reluctant *adjective* averse, hesitant, opposed, resistant, unwilling, disinclined, loath, shy The horse was reluctant to jump the wide ditch. ● **Antonyms: eager, enthusiastic**

rely *verb* count, depend, trust, expect, swear by, bank, believe I'm relying on you to bring the beverages to our cookout. ● **Antonyms: distrust, question, disbelieve**

remain *verb* stay, endure, exist, last, linger, persist, continue, abide Beavers can remain underwater for up to 15 minutes. ● **Antonyms:** leave, go, depart

remark *verb* 1. comment, mention, declare, state, assert, express, utter Our teacher remarked that the snowy weather might cause school to be canceled. 2. notice, observe, note, perceive, mark, sense, register, detect Many people have remarked that I am getting tall. ◆ *noun* 1. comment, observation, statement, expression, mention, utterance, saying, commentary My friend cheered me up with her remark about our plans for the coming weekend. 2. notice, acknowledgment, awareness, thought, attention, look, perception, detection Mom said that my new outfit definitely was worthy of remark. ● **Antonyms:** *verb* 2. overlook, ignore ◆ *noun* 2. inattention, disregard

remarkable *adjective* 1. impressive, outstanding, exceptional, significant, phenomenal, glorious, noteworthy, striking Modern computers can process information at remarkable speeds. 2. extraordinary, unique, rare, unexpected, odd, strange, uncommon, surprising We saw a remarkable sight in the sky last night. ● **Antonyms:** ordinary, everyday, routine

remedy *noun* 1. cure, therapy, treatment, antidote, medicine, relief, medication, corrective The best remedy for a cold is to drink lots of fluids and get plenty of rest. 2. solution, correction, resolution, help, betterment, countermeasure, answer The committee investigated possible remedies to the problem of overcrowding in the schools. ◆ *verb* 1. cure, relieve, medicate, treat, heal, soothe, doctor I remedied the pain in my shoulder with an ice pack. 2. correct, set right, improve, rectify, redress, repair, fix, adjust, better We need to remedy the poor lighting in the kitchen. ● **Antonyms:** *verb* 1. sicken 2. damage, worsen

remember *verb* 1. recall, recollect, know, call to mind, retain, think of, review Do you remember who played the vampire in that movie? 2. recognize, reward, tip, note, appreciate We remembered our waiter with a generous tip. ● **Antonyms:** 1. forget 2. neglect, overlook

remind *verb* prompt, inform, notify, advise, warn, caution, tell, cue, jog Please remind me when it's time to leave for my music lesson.

reminisce *verb* recall, reflect, recollect, remember, look back, hark back, ponder, muse My friends and I reminisced about our kindergarten days.

remnant *noun* 1. scrap, piece, fragment, shred, bit, leftover, strip, remains I am saving fabric remnants to make

a quilt. 2. vestige, trace, relic, residue, evocation, token, remainder, balance There was only a remnant of my family left after the war.

remorse *noun* regret, contrition, sorrow, ruefulness, self-reproach, guilt, shame, anguish I felt remorse over the mean things I said to my sister. ● **Antonyms:** satisfaction, pride

remote *adjective* 1. distant, faraway, far-off, isolated, removed, secluded, inaccessible, outlying The explorers were shipwrecked on a remote island. 2. ancient, prehistoric, primitive, forgotten, unremembered, immemorial, antediluvian Human beings learned the benefits of fire sometime in our remote past. 3. faint, slight, slim, unlikely, improbable, slender, negligible, poor, small There is only a remote possibility that we will get another dog. 4. irrelevant, obscure, pointless, extraneous, unrelated, separate, strange, alien When I was in junior high, college and career choices still seemed remote to me. ● **Antonyms:** 1. close, near, nearby 2. recent, current 3. likely, probable 4. relevant, pertinent

removal *noun* 1. evacuation, extraction, withdrawal, elimination, uprooting, erasure, deletion The city made arrangements for the removal of the debris from the vacant lot. 2. expulsion, ejection, eviction, ousting, dismissal, firing, termination, unseating The sheriff supervised the removal of the delinquent tenants. ● **Antonym:** installation

remove *verb* 1. move, uproot, clear, transplant, shift, relocate, take away, transfer, reposition The landscapers removed the old shrubs and replaced them with rosebushes. 2. eliminate, extract, eradicate, clean, cleanse, purge, get rid of, detach You can remove candle wax from cloth with a paper bag and a hot iron. 3. dismiss, displace, unseat, eject, wrest, depose, oust, disqualify, fire In the recent election several incumbents were removed from office. ● **Antonyms:** 1. leave 2. leave, attach 3. hire, enthrone, install

renaissance *noun* revival, renewal, revitalization, rejuvenation, reawakening, rebirth, resurrection There has been a renaissance of interest in poetry.

rend *verb* tear, pull, break, split, divide, rip, sunder Religious or political intolerance can rend a country apart. ● **Antonyms:** join, mend

render *verb* 1. make, cause to become, leave The accident rendered him paralyzed for six months. 2. do, perform, give, provide, administer, contribute, tender, deliver, furnish The stranger rendered us a great service when our car broke down. **3. surrender, relinquish, renounce, yield, hand over, tender, turn over** The general forced the losing army to render its weapons to the victors. **4. hand down, pronounce, deliver, announce, give** The judge will render his decision soon. **5. present, show, picture, depict, represent, portray, express, outline, describe, tell** The architect has rendered the proposed community center in a series of drawings. ● **Antonyms: 2. & 3. withhold, keep, retain**

rendezvous *noun* **meeting, get-together, appointment, tryst, assignation, engagement, encounter, date** We set up a rendezvous for 2:00. ◆ *verb* **meet, gather, assemble, collect, converge, convene, muster** Let's rendezvous in front of the theater before the movie starts.

renew *verb* **1. renovate, recondition, repair, fix up, rejuvenate, refurbish, restore, improve** Dad renewed the kitchen cabinets. **2. rekindle, reestablish, resume, continue, recommence, revitalize, restart, reaffirm** We renewed our friendship after my friend and his family returned from a year in England. **3. update, extend, restart, maintain, retain, prolong, continue, sustain, perpetuate** I need to renew my library card. **4. replenish, restock, refill, reload, refresh, replace, reorder** I want to renew my supply of pistachio nuts. ● **Antonyms: 2. & 3. cancel, lapse, drop 4. empty, deplete**

renounce *verb* **abdicate, relinquish, abandon, surrender, forfeit, sacrifice, quit** King Edward VIII renounced the throne of England in 1936. ● **Antonyms: maintain, keep, accept**

renown *noun* **distinction, fame, popularity, prestige, reputation, celebrity, acclaim, note, eminence** Steven Spielberg is a movie director of great renown. ● **Antonyms: obscurity, disgrace, infamy**

rent¹ *noun* **rental, fee, payment, cost, dues, price, lease, hire, tariff** My parents are pleased with our new apartment because the monthly rent is reasonable. ◆ *verb* **charter, contract, hire, lease, sublet, borrow, lend, loan, engage** My family rented a sailboat for the weekend.

rent² *noun* **1. tear, rip, split, cut, cleft, damage, leak** I need to fix the rent in my skirt. **2. schism, fissure, fracture, rift, break, split, divide, estrangement** Henry VIII's refusal to acknowledge the authority of the pope caused a rent between England and Rome.

repair¹ *verb* **1. fix, mend, patch, rebuild, restore, overhaul, renew, refurbish** I repaired my model airplane's broken wing. **2. remedy, rectify, compensate, correct,** redress, square, set right He tried to repair the situation by writing a check to cover the damages. ◆ *noun* **fixing, servicing, adjustment, conditioning, restoration, mending, patching, refurbishment, renovation** Our washing machine is in need of repair. ● **Antonyms:** *verb* **1. damage, break 2. aggravate, worsen**

repair² *verb* **withdraw, retire, go, adjourn, remove, move, leave** I repaired to a quiet church to meditate for a while.

reparation *noun* **compensation, restitution, payment, reimbursement, amends, atonement, redress, retribution** He wrote a check in reparation for the damages.

repeal *verb* **revoke, reverse, rescind, retract, lift, abolish, nullify, withdraw, cancel** The state legislature repealed the unpopular law. ◆ *noun* **revocation, retraction, recall, withdrawal, abolition, cancellation, annulment** Our representative had strongly supported the repeal of the unpopular law. ● **Antonyms:** *verb* **confirm, install** ◆ *noun* **installation, confirmation**

repeat *verb* **1. restate, reiterate, retell, say again, recite, emphasize, reaffirm, redo** The teacher repeated her instructions to make sure that everyone understood them. **2. relate, impart, divulge, quote, recount, report, communicate, blab** She repeated the good news she had heard about one of our friends. **3. duplicate, reproduce, imitate, mimic, copy, echo** The band was asked to repeat their successful performance. ◆ *noun* **repetition, duplication, reiteration, copy, reprise, rerun, replay** The sequel to the bestseller seemed no more than a repeat of the original.

repel *verb* **1. repulse, fend off, rout, chase away, ward off, drive away, hold off, foil, oppose** A porcupine's quills help it to repel attackers. **2. refuse, reject, rebuff, decline, snub, spurn, disdain** My little brother repelled my offer of help. **3. repulse, disgust, appall, horrify, offend, revolt, sicken, nauseate** The last scene in the movie really repelled me. ● **Antonyms: 1. attract, draw 2. encourage, approve 3. please, delight**

repent *verb* **regret, lament, rue, deplore, reform, bewail, apologize, atone** I repented my greediness when I got an upset stomach.

replace *verb* **1. supersede, displace, depose, supplant, succeed, follow, spell, relieve** The computer is replacing the typewriter. **2. change, exchange, substitute, restock, alter, restore, return, reload** I need to replace the batteries in my flashlight.

replenish *verb* restore, replace, refill, refresh, restock, reload, renew, provision I need to replenish my supply of pencils. ⇒ **Antonyms: drain, empty, deplete**

replica *noun* copy, facsimile, model, likeness, reproduction, imitation, duplicate, clone My dad's hobby is collecting replicas of antique cars and trucks. ⇒ **Antonyms: original, master**

reply *verb* respond, answer, acknowledge, react, return, retort, rejoin Everyone who replies to the survey will receive a free gift. ◆ *noun* answer, response, acknowledgment, reaction, feedback, confirmation, return, rejoinder I received a reply to my e-mail inquiry. ⇒ **Antonyms:** *verb* ask, question ◆ *noun* inquiry, question

report *noun* 1. essay, composition, theme, account, article, narrative, summary, statement, description I have to write a report about one of the planets for my science class. 2. rumor, gossip, scoop, talk, scandal, tidbit, hearsay, news Did you hear the latest report about what happened at the city council meeting? 3. reputation, standing, repute, character, caliber, note, rank, fame, status He is a man of good report. ◆ *verb* 1. describe, disclose, relate, state, tell, advise, recite, narrate, record The army scout returned to headquarters and reported what he had seen. 2. publish, broadcast, announce, publicize, circulate, disclose, put out, spread The Warren Commission reported their findings concerning the Kennedy assassination. 3 check in, go to, show up, appear, arrive, reach, come, proceed to, be present You should report to the principal's office for your classroom assignment. ⇒ **Antonyms:** *verb* 1. & 2. conceal, withhold

repose *noun* 1. rest, sleep, slumber, respite, nap, doze, relaxation, ease I had a good night's repose. 2. serenity, composure, placidity, quiet, calm, tranquillity, peacefulness, stillness The lake waters went from quiet repose to violent agitation when the storm hit. ◆ *verb* rest, relax, settle, stretch, recline, lie, slumber, sleep The cat and dog reposed in front of the fireplace for an afternoon nap. ⇒ **Antonyms:** *noun* activity, excitement ◆ *verb* work, bustle, toil

represent *verb* 1. symbolize, characterize, signify, mean, indicate, express, portray, illustrate, depict The stars on the American flag represent the 50 states. 2. exemplify, epitomize, embody, demonstrate, characterize, personify, typify The TV program *Mister Roger's Neighborhood* represents outstanding broadcasting for young children. 3. act for, serve, speak for, stand for I will be representing our school at Girls' State.

representative *noun* 1. example, instance, sample, illustration, type, personification, model This painting, with its clear colors and simple forms, is a good representative of the artistic style of Georgia O'Keeffe. 2. delegate, emissary, ambassador, deputy, agent, legislator, surrogate In 1917 Jeannette Rankin became the first woman to be elected as a representative to Congress. ◆ *adjective* 1. characteristic, typical, indicative, descriptive, illustrative, emblematic, symbolic Those hills are representative of the geography of this area. 2. democratic, elected, elective, republican The United States has a representative form of government.

repress *verb* 1. check, curb, restrain, inhibit, stifle, hold back, mask I repressed my desire to give an angry answer. 2. suppress, crush, quell, subjugate, subdue, put down, quash, censor Free speech is often repressed in a dictatorship. ⇒ **Antonyms: 1. express, release 2. encourage, permit**

reprieve *verb* relieve, release, suspend, remit, pardon, stay Mom came home early and reprieved me from baby-sitting. ◆ *noun* suspension, stay, respite, pause, relief, delay, deferment, pardon There was a reprieve in the exchange of gunfire on Christmas Day of 1914, during World War I.

reprimand *verb* rebuke, censure, reprove, admonish, scold, castigate, reproach, chastise We were reprimanded for being too noisy in the hall at school. ◆ *noun* admonishment, rebuke, chastisement, reproof, scolding, censure, denunciation, castigation I received a reprimand for turning my homework in late. ⇒ **Antonyms:** *verb* praise, approve, compliment ◆ *noun* commendation, approval

reproach *verb* admonish, rebuke, reprimand, chastise, criticize, upbraid, scold, blame The band director reproached us for our unruly behavior. ◆ *noun* 1. criticism, censure, disapproval, blame, scolding, reproof, rebuke, accusation, denunciation The new appellate court judge is considered to be impartial and beyond reproach. 2. disgrace, shame, infamy, dishonor, humiliation, discredit, embarrassment Slavery is a reproach to any society. ⇒ **Antonyms:** *verb* praise, approve, commend ◆ *noun* 1. approval, praise 2. honor, glory

reproduce *verb* 1. copy, duplicate, photocopy, mirror, match, redo, repeat, echo I thought the cartoon so funny that I reproduced it to give to my friend. 2. breed, spawn, procreate, multiply, beget, generate The Madagascar hissing cockroach reproduces every 60 to 70 days, bearing 20 to 40 babies that are each the size of a watermelon seed.

Word Group A **reptile** is a cold-blooded animal that has a backbone, is covered by scales or horny plates, and breathes with lungs. **Reptile** is a specific scientific term with no true synonyms. Here are some common reptiles:

alligator, caiman, crocodile, lizard, snake, tortoise, tuatara, turtle

repulse *verb* **1. repel, drive back, check, resist, withstand, fight off, thwart** General George Meade's Union troops repulsed the Confederates at Cold Harbor. **2. refuse, decline, rebuff, repel, snub, reject, shun, spurn** My little brother repulsed my offer of help. ◆ *noun* **rejection, snub, rebuff, spurning, refusal, shunning, denial, cold shoulder** The envoy received a repulse from the country's president. ◈ **Antonyms:** *verb* **1. submit, yield 2. welcome, encourage** ◆ *noun* **acceptance, welcome**

repulsive *adjective* **revolting, repugnant, disgusting, offensive, hideous, nauseating, distasteful** Do you think violet-fuchsia hair would look repulsive on me? ◈ **Antonyms: pleasant, attractive**

reputation *noun* **name, status, position, standing, stature, esteem, fame, renown** This restaurant has a good reputation because the food is always excellent.

request *verb* **appeal, ask for, seek, apply for, solicit, petition, beg, plead** I requested permission to leave school early because I had a doctor's appointment. ◆ *noun* **wish, desire, prayer, supplication, appeal, call, plea, petition, summons** This foundation fulfills the special requests of children with life-threatening illnesses.

require *verb* **1. need, want, desire, call for, crave, miss, covet** What is it that you require? **2. direct, command, demand, compel, oblige, order, enjoin, instruct, cause** A law requires bicyclists under the age of 18 to wear a helmet.

requisite *adjective* **required, mandatory, prerequisite, necessary, compulsory, needed, obligatory, essential** She has the requisite experience for that job. ◆ *noun* **requirement, precondition, prerequisite, essential, necessity, fundamental, must, demand, mandate** Graduation from high school is a requisite for admission to college. ◈ **Antonyms:** *adjective* **unnecessary, superfluous**

rescue *verb* **free, release, liberate, help, save, deliver, recover, ransom, salvage** Mom rescued the baby quail that was trapped in the flower pot. ◆ *noun* **aid, assistance, relief,**

help, recovery, deliverance, liberation, salvation, release My brother came to the rescue when I got my hand stuck in a pickle jar.

research *noun* **study, investigation, inquiry, analysis, experimentation, probe, inspection** I went to the library to do the research for my physics paper. ◆ *verb* **explore, investigate, study, analyze, examine, test, scrutinize** I am researching the sources of air pollution for my science project.

resemblance *noun* **closeness, likeness, similarity, comparison, sameness, kinship, correspondence, analogy** Many people say that I bear a remarkable resemblance to my aunt. ◈ **Antonyms: difference, distinction**

resemble *verb* **look like, favor, take after, approximate, echo, parallel, match, correspond, mirror** My brother and I resemble one another.

resentful *adjective* **hurt, offended, bitter, angry, upset, wounded, indignant, outraged, riled, spiteful** I felt quite resentful when my friend forgot it was my birthday. ◈ **Antonyms: forgiving, tolerant**

resentment *noun* **anger, bitterness, indignation, animosity, annoyance, hostility, ill will, outrage, rancor** I felt a lot of resentment when my friend took credit for my idea. ◈ **Antonyms: goodwill, forgiveness, understanding**

reservation *noun* **1. doubt, hesitancy, misgiving, uncertainty, reluctance, qualification, objection** I had some reservations about riding my dirt bike down the rocky hill. **2. territory, settlement, retreat, reserve, colony, encampment, preserve, sanctuary** We went camping on the Apache Reservation in the White Mountains of Arizona. **3. booking, accommodation, arrangement, appointment, engagement, date** We have a reservation for two nights at the Grand Hotel.

reserve *verb* **1. book, engage, schedule, secure, register, retain, contract, prearrange** Dad reserved a train compartment for our trip. **2. conserve, save, hold, keep, preserve, earmark, cache, store** The runner reserved some of her strength for the final lap. ◆ *noun* **1. stock, stockpile, store, supply, cache, reservoir, hoard** We have an emergency reserve of food and water stored in our basement. **2. aloofness, coolness, restraint, detachment, self-control, self-restraint, reluctance, diffidence** The man's apparent reserve was really shyness. ◈ **Antonyms:** *verb* **2. discard** ◆ *noun* **2. involvement, warmth**

reservoir *noun* **1. lake, pool, pond, millpond, spring, basin, well, cistern, fount, tank** We went fishing at the reservoir. **2. supply, stockpile, reserve, store, stock, hoard, cache** The explorers kept an emergency reservoir of food and water at their base camp.

reside *verb* **abide, dwell, live, inhabit, stay, occupy, encamp, lodge, remain, room** My uncle's family resides in a small town in Nebraska.

residence *noun* **abode, dwelling, habitation, home, household, house, apartment, address, domicile** The President's official residence is the White House in Washington, D.C.

resident *noun* **citizen, dweller, inhabitant, native, settler, occupant, householder, local** My grandmother is a long-time resident of Milwaukee.

residue *noun* **remainder, remains, scraps, remnant, dregs, leavings, rest, leftover, balance** This company tests for residue of pesticides in soil, water, plants, and animals.

resign *verb* **1. reconcile, yield, surrender, submit, adapt, acclimate, give in** I resigned myself to not making the all-star team. **2. forsake, give up, leave, quit, abdicate, surrender, withdraw, step down, depart** Richard Nixon is the only President ever to have resigned from the office. ➡ **Antonyms: 1. battle, oppose, fight 2. keep, maintain**

resignation *noun* **1. departure, retirement, notice, renunciation, abdication, abandonment, withdrawal** The press secretary announced her resignation. **2. submission, surrender, passivity, acceptance, patience, endurance, fortitude** There was a tone of resignation in her voice as she agreed to reschedule her vacation. ➡ **Antonyms: 1. retention 2. opposition, protest, resistance**

resist *verb* **refuse, reject, forgo, fight, withstand, battle, thwart, oppose, counter, defy** I can't resist his offer of half-price tickets to the final game of the basketball championship. ➡ **Antonyms: yield, submit, surrender**

resistance *noun* **defiance, opposition, protest, rebellion, struggle, refusal, mutiny, insubordination** Our dog puts up a lot of resistance when we bathe him. ➡ **Antonyms: compliance, cooperation, surrender**

resolute *adjective* **steadfast, diligent, determined, persistent, unwavering, earnest, intrepid, steady, firm** The resolute student finished her homework before going out with her friends. ➡ **Antonyms: wavering, irresolute**

resolution *noun* **1. determination, resolve, steadfastness, tenacity, perseverance, courage, fortitude, spirit**

We faced the chore of cleaning up after the party with resolution. **2. pledge, promise, vow, resolve, goal, aim, purpose, ambition, intention** I made only two New Year's resolutions. **3. solution, explanation, answer, upshot, conclusion, determination, analysis, windup** I enjoyed that movie because its resolution of the hero's problem was clever and original. ➡ **Antonyms: 1. uncertainty, fickleness**

resolve *verb* **1. decide, determine, mean, propose, plan, undertake, intend, desire** He resolved to study harder for his next test. **2. clear up, fix, settle, solve, answer, unravel, straighten, explain** Our family holds regular meetings to resolve our problems. ◆ *noun* **1. firmness, purpose, resoluteness, willpower, courage, boldness, steadfastness** The firemen entered the burning building with great resolve. **2. decision, resolution, plan, conclusion, vow, commitment, objective** The committee concluded their meeting with the resolve to meet again in two weeks.

resort *verb* **refer, turn, apply, employ, go, use, utilize, make use of** I thought I knew how to load my computer game but finally had to resort to the instruction manual. ◆ *noun* **1. tourist spot, destination, hideaway, haunt, retreat, refuge, haven** Cancún, Mexico, is a popular tourist resort. **2. alternative, choice, hope, option, possibility, resource, recourse** If we can't get plane or train tickets, we can take the bus as a last resort.

resource *noun* **1. aid, help, source, support, reserve, recourse, assistance** A thesaurus is an excellent resource for anyone who wants to expand his or her vocabulary. **2. asset, capital, cash, funds, money, wealth, revenue, collateral** We don't have the resources to buy a new house at this time. **3. capacity, strength, ability, capability, talent, initiative, wherewithal, expertise** The runner drew on his inner resources to make a final burst for the finish line.

resourceful *adjective* **imaginative, clever, creative, capable, cunning, able, shrewd, ingenious** People can become surprisingly resourceful when it is necessary. ➡ **Antonyms: incompetent, incapable**

respect *verb* **1. esteem, honor, revere, regard, value, admire, cherish, prize** The youth of Sparta were taught to respect strength, courage, simplicity, and harmony. **2. heed, obey, follow, adhere to, observe, uphold, note, appreciate** It is important to respect the safety instructions given by our bus driver. ◆ *noun* **1. admiration, esteem, regard, approval, honor, homage, worship, veneration, praise, reverence** Lycurgus, founder of Sparta, won the respect of his people because of his leadership, wisdom, and public spirit. **2. best wishes, greetings, salutations, compliments, regards, remembrances** Please give my respects to your mother. **3. aspect, feature, particular, regard, detail, sense, angle, facet** We enjoyed our Caribbean cruise in every respect. ➡ **Antonyms:** *verb* **1. ridicule, scorn 2. ignore, disregard** ◆ *noun* **1. contempt, disdain**

respectful *adjective* **civil, considerate, courteous, mannerly, polite, gracious, obedient, reverent** Our team maintained a respectful silence during the singing of the national anthem. ➡ **Antonyms: rude, disrespectful**

respite *noun* **break, recess, lull, relief, interlude, breather, reprieve, stay** I offered to baby-sit for my cousin in order to give my aunt and uncle a respite.

respond *verb* **answer, reply, acknowledge, return, notice, counter, react** I sent an e-mail to my cousin in West Virginia, but she hasn't responded yet. ➡ **Antonyms: ignore, neglect, disregard**

response *noun* **acknowledgment, answer, reaction, reply, retort, feedback, return** I knocked on the door, but got no response.

responsibility *noun* **1. dependability, reliability, trustworthiness, honesty, faithfulness, loyalty, stability** My mom wants me to develop a sense of responsibility. **2. charge, chore, duty, function, job, obligation, task, burden, trust** It is my responsibility to load the dishwasher this week.

responsible *adjective* **1. liable, answerable, accountable, amenable, obligated, subject** The chief engineer is responsible for signing off on any design changes in company products. **2. dependable, reliable, trustworthy, accountable, honest, capable, sensible, moral** We must elect a responsible person for class treasurer. ➡ **Antonyms: 2. irresponsible, unreliable**

rest[1] *noun* **1. break, halt, intermission, pause, recess, breather, interlude, holiday** We sat on a bench in the mall to take a rest from shopping. **2. relaxation, sleep, slumber, nap, snooze, doze, refreshment, peace** You should get plenty of rest before the game tomorrow. **3. halt, stop, standstill, surcease, pause** The grocery cart rolled across the parking lot and came to a rest against a wall. **4. prop, base, foundation, pillar, support, stand** This block of wood can serve as a rest for the flower pot. ◆ *verb* **1. sleep, nap, doze, snooze, drowse, relax, unwind, lounge** My mother likes to rest on Sunday afternoons. **2. lay, lean, place, position, prop, set, stand, deposit** The worker rested his shovel against a tree. **3. depend, rely, hinge, turn, hang** Whether or not we go on vacation rests on my dad's being able to get the time off work.

rest[2] *noun* **balance, excess, leftover, remainder, extra, remains, surplus, remnant** We ate half of the pizza and took the rest home for tomorrow's lunch.

restless *adjective* **agitated, fidgety, jumpy, nervous, uneasy, fitful, fretful, edgy, unsettled** The restless tiger paced back and forth in its cage. ➡ **Antonyms: peaceful, calm, relaxed**

restore *verb* **1. reestablish, reinstate, reinstall, return, resuscitate, recoup** The electric company restored our service after the storm. **2. recondition, renew, renovate, revive, refurbish, recover, reclaim, patch** This wax should help restore the table's original finish.

restrain *verb* **stop, check, control, curb, hamper, hold, curtail, handicap** I have to use a leash to restrain my dog from jumping up on people. ➡ **Antonyms: encourage, spur, urge**

restrict *verb* **limit, contain, confine, narrow, check, moderate, constrict** The couple decided to restrict their guest list to 75 people.

restriction *noun* **check, condition, limitation, constraint, regulation, boundary** Our town has placed restrictions on where it is permissible to go skateboarding.

result *verb* **1. arise, develop, emerge, follow, stem, originate, evolve, ensue** His good grades resulted from his improved study habits. **2. bring about, cause, effect, induce, trigger** High speed chases can result in serious accidents involving innocent people. ◆ *noun* **consequence, effect, outcome, product, verdict, outgrowth, upshot, fruit** One result of the election is that the country now has a number of new senators.

resume *verb* **begin again, go on, continue, proceed, reopen, recommence** The meeting will resume after a one-hour lunch break. ➡ **Antonyms: discontinue, halt, stop**

retain *verb* **1. hold, keep, maintain, preserve, save, contain, reserve** A thick layer of blubber helps whales retain heat even in arctic waters. **2. remember, recollect, recall, memorize, know, keep** I use word association tricks to help me retain people's names. **3. hire, engage, lease, contract, employ, commission** My parents retained a lawyer to help probate my grandfather's will. ➡ **Antonym: 1. lose, give up 2. forget, ignore**

retire *verb* **1. leave, resign, depart, exit, vacate, abdicate, withdraw, step down** Next month, Grandfather is going to retire from his job as a civil engineer. **2. fall back,**

retreat, flee, decamp, evacuate, pull out The troops retired after being repulsed by the enemy. ➡ **Antonyms: 1. stay on, continue 2. advance, stand**

retort *verb* **reply, retaliate, respond, rebut, rejoin, answer, counter** My sister retorted that the situation was just as much my fault as hers. ◆ *noun* **reply, comeback, rejoinder, rebuttal, answer, repartee** My brother's witty retort made me laugh.

retreat *noun* **1. fallback, withdrawal, departure, escape, flight, retirement, getaway, evacuation** The army made an orderly retreat. **2. asylum, haven, refuge, sanctuary, shelter, harbor** The doctor's private office is her retreat from the pressures of her job. ◆ *verb* **fall back, disengage, withdraw, depart, escape, flee, retire** The army was forced to retreat when the enemy attacked. ➡ **Antonyms:** *noun* **1. charge** ◆ *verb* **engage, advance**

retrieve *verb* **fetch, get back, reclaim, recover, regain, repossess** Dad retrieved his hat after the wind blew it away.

return *verb* **1. go back, come back, reappear, revisit, repair, rebound** The Scouts returned to camp after their hike. **2. give back, hand back, restore, replace, reinstall, reinstate, repay** I will return your book as soon as I finish reading it. **3. respond, answer, reply, rejoin, retort, rebut** When I asked Marie when she would be ready, she returned that she didn't know. ◆ *noun* **1. homecoming, reappearance, arrival, entrance, rebound** Our cat's sudden return delighted me because I had thought that he was lost. **2. earnings, gain, income, profit, revenue, yield** My mom was pleased with the return on her investment. ➡ **Antonyms:** *verb* **1. leave, depart 3. question, ask** ◆ *noun* **1. departure 2. loss, cost**

reveal *verb* **disclose, expose, give away, tell, bare, unveil, show** Please don't reveal how the movie ends. ➡ **Antonyms: conceal, hide**

revel *verb* **1. rejoice, delight, enjoy, indulge, bask, love, luxuriate, savor, relish** I revel in sleeping late on Saturday mornings. **2. make merry, party, celebrate, frolic, carouse, caper, romp, feast** My sister and her classmates reveled all night after their graduation. ◆ *noun* **party, spree, fete, celebration, festivity, revelry, gala, jamboree** Our club sponsors a Mardi Gras revel each year.

revelation *noun* **news, disclosure, announcement, telling, exposé, admission, divulgence, surprise** The revelation of this latest government scandal should certainly come as no surprise.

revenge *verb* **avenge, get even, pay back, repay, counterattack, retaliate** Hamlet was urged to revenge his father's murder, but he bungled the job. ◆ *noun* **vengeance, vindication, retaliation, repayment, satisfaction, compensation, counterattack** "Revenge is a dish best served cold" is a common saying.

revenue *noun* **income, profit, net, yield, gain, earnings** The company accountant keeps track of revenue received.

revere *verb* **esteem, venerate, honor, adore, exalt, idolize, worship, admire, respect** The guru's followers all revere him. ➡ **Antonyms: scorn, disparage**

reverence *noun* **worship, awe, admiration, regard, praise, love, homage, esteem, fealty** The paintings of Georgia O'Keeffe inspire a feeling of reverence in me. ➡ **Antonyms: scorn, contempt**

reverse *adjective* **back, converse, counter, opposite, contrasting, mirror** The song that I would like to hear is on the reverse side of this tape. ◆ *noun* **1. contrary, counter, converse, opposite, antithesis, contradiction** I thought that you were older than me, but it turns out that the reverse is true. **2. reversal, setback, hardship, misfortune, adversity, upset, mishap, bad luck, trial** Many families experienced economic reverses during the Great Depression of the 1930s. ◆ *verb* **counter, override, overturn, alter, annul, abolish, retract, overrule, invalidate** A higher court has the power to reverse a lower court's ruling. ➡ **Antonyms:** *verb* **keep, maintain, uphold**

revert *verb* **return, go back, relapse, lapse, backslide, retrogress, regress, repeat** He reverted to his old habits as soon as he moved back home.

review *verb* **1. reexamine, look over, reconsider, think over, remember, recapitulate, examine, study** We start each lesson by reviewing what we learned the day before. **2. criticize, evaluate, judge, assess, analyze, scrutinize, weigh, discuss** Our journalism assignment is to review a book for the school paper. ◆ *noun* **criticism, evaluation, notice, analysis, assessment, report, commentary, judgment** The movie received favorable reviews.

revile *verb* **denounce, abuse, scold, castigate, curse, malign, vilify, rebuke** My sister reviled me loudly for scaring her. ➡ **Antonyms: praise, acclaim, commend**

revise *verb* **1. edit, polish, correct, perfect, clean up, tighten, tune** My mom helped me revise my English essay. **2. alter, amend, change, modify, reconsider, revamp,**

overhaul, redo, vary The pilots' strike forced us to revise our vacation plans.

revive *verb* refresh, renew, restore, revitalize, rejuvenate, enliven I was very tired, but a short nap revived me.

revoke *verb* cancel, annul, invalidate, nullify, recall, repeal, abolish, void, erase If a driver has too many tickets, his or her license can be revoked.

revolt *verb* 1. rebel, rise up, mutiny, protest, riot, strike, boycott, oppose In 1789, the people of France revolted against the nobility who ruled the country. 2. disgust, repel, horrify, sicken, shock, nauseate, appall Gory movies revolt me. ♦ *noun* rebellion, revolution, uprising, mutiny, insurrection, sedition, coup, takeover Patrick Henry was one of the leaders of the American colonies' revolt against Great Britain. ➡ **Antonyms:** *verb* 1. follow, obey 2. attract, please

revolution *noun* 1. circle, cycle, rotation, spin, turn, round, circuit, lap The second hand of a clock makes one full revolution every minute. 2. rebellion, revolt, uprising, insurrection, coup, mutiny, overthrow The Russian Revolution of 1917 created the world's first Communist state. 3. change, upheaval, transformation, metamorphosis, shift, sea change The answering machine, fax machine, and Internet e-mail have brought about a revolution in the way we communicate.

revolve *verb* circle, orbit, spin, turn, reel, rotate, wheel, twirl Earth revolves around the sun at a rate of 18.5 miles per second.

reward *noun* award, bounty, compensation, payment, prize, recompense We offered a reward for the return of our lost cat. ♦ *verb* award, compensate, repay, acknowledge, honor, requite, remunerate The student's hard work was rewarded when he got an excellent grade on the test. ➡ **Antonyms:** *noun* penalty, punishment ♦ *verb* penalize, punish

rhythm *noun* beat, pulse, throb, measure, cadence, meter, tempo, pattern The doctor listened to the rhythm of my heartbeat.

rich *adjective* 1. prosperous, wealthy, affluent, well-off, well-to-do, successful, fortunate, comfortable, moneyed Whoever owns that yacht must be very rich. 2. luxurious, opulent, lavish, lush, profuse, splendid, elegant, superb, extravagant, expensive The antique shawl is covered with rich embroidery. 3. bountiful, fertile, productive, plentiful, prolific, lush, generous, profuse, fruitful The Midwest

region of the United States is known for its rich farmland. 4. sweet, heavy, creamy, flavorful, indigestible, succulent, buttery Cheesecake is a rich dessert. 5. full, mellow, sonorous, resonant, expressive, rotund, dulcet The radio announcer has a rich bass voice. 6. warm, deep, intense, dark, vibrant, strong, lustrous The judge's chambers are decorated in rich colors. ➡ **Antonyms:** 1. poor, penniless 2. simple, drab, plain 3. barren, unfertile 4. bland, light 6. cool, pale

riches *noun* wealth, abundance, fortune, capital, assets, plenty, treasure, property Whoever wins the lottery will receive vast riches.

rid *verb* purge, free, clear, eliminate, remove, exterminate, divest, expel, relieve, liberate Dad hired an exterminator to rid our house of termites.

riddle[1] *verb* 1. perforate, pierce, puncture, prick, punch, pelt, pepper, fire, pit, bore The marksman riddled the target with bullets. 2. permeate, corrupt, damage, spoil, infiltrate The old tractor was riddled with rust.

riddle[2] *noun* mystery, enigma, secret, problem, puzzle, question, brainteaser, knot, conundrum In many adventure stories, the hero has to solve a riddle before continuing on his journey.

ride *verb* drive, handle, control, manage, pilot, steer, move My dad is teaching me how to ride a dirt bike. ♦ *noun* drive, jaunt, spin, excursion, journey, trip, tour, commute Mom suggested that we go for a ride in the country.

ridge *noun* 1. crest, spine, backbone, rise, strip, elevation We climbed up the hill and walked along the ridge. 2. fold, wrinkle, crease, furrow, crimp There was a ridge in my shirt from the hanger.

ridicule *noun* mockery, scorn, scoffing, disdain, contempt, sarcasm, sneering, teasing, taunting The inventor's apparatus was met with ridicule until he gave a demonstration. ♦ *verb* insult, jeer, laugh at, mock, sneer, taunt, tease, roast, belittle The politician ridiculed his opponent during a press conference. ➡ **Antonyms:** praise, respect, honor

ridiculous *adjective* absurd, droll, silly, comical, foolish, funny, laughable, crazy My dad has a ridiculous tie that lights up like a Christmas tree. ➡ **Antonyms:** sensible, serious

rifle *verb* ransack, burglarize, pillage, rob, plunder, loot The purse snatcher rifled the contents of the woman's handbag.

rift *noun* **1. fissure, split, opening, fault, gap, crevice, chink, crack, break, cranny** Erosion had caused the rift in the rock to widen considerably over time. **2. alienation, separation, breach, schism, clash, disagreement, misunderstanding** A misunderstanding caused a rift between the two friends.

rig *verb* **1. equip, outfit, supply, fit, provide, furnish, provision, attire** We rigged our boat for a fishing trip. **2. manipulate, arrange, fix, falsify, engineer, sway, doctor, maneuver** The loser in the election claimed that it had been rigged.

right *adjective* **1. honorable, ethical, honest, moral, virtuous, fair, good, just, noble, proper, responsible** You did the right thing in turning in the wallet to the police. **2. accurate, correct, faultless, exact, perfect, true, valid, precise** All of my answers on the test were right. **3. fitting, proper, appropriate, seemly, suitable, becoming, ideal, preferable** I could have gotten the job done sooner if I'd had the right tools. **4. healthy, sound, sane, balanced, rational, normal, wholesome, solid, reasonable** The defendant was proved to be in his right mind. ◆ *noun* **1. morality, virtue, propriety, goodness, honor, integrity, justice, truth, honesty** Parents are responsible for teaching their children the difference between right and wrong. **2. freedom, liberty, privilege, prerogative, permission, license** When a suspect is arrested, he or she has the right to remain silent. ◆ *adverb* **1. properly, correctly, suitably, fittingly, appropriately, becomingly, adequately, satisfactorily** Everything turned out right. **2. exactly, just, precisely, directly** Please leave the package right there. **3. immediately, instantly, at once, promptly, quickly, without delay, straight** I need you to help me right after you're done with your homework. ◆ *verb* **1. restore, straighten, fix, adjust, position, order, square, normalize** I righted the cup after it tipped over. **2. remedy, correct, solve, redress, vindicate, rectify, amend, reform** We considered the situation righted when we received a check from the insurance company. ◈ **Antonyms:** *adjective* **1. wrong, unethical, immoral 2. inaccurate, incorrect** ◆ *noun* **1. wrong** ◆ *verb* **1. upset, upend**

rigid *adjective* **1. inflexible, solid, stiff, inelastic, firm, hard, immovable, taut, unbending, wooden** The frozen fish were very rigid. **2. harsh, severe, strict, hard, stern, tough, stringent, unrelenting, set, stubborn** Do you think that no discipline is better than rigid discipline? ◈ **Antonyms: 1. flexible, pliable 2. lenient, tolerant**

rigorous *adjective* **1. demanding, exacting, challenging, severe, harsh, trying, tough** New military recruits are put through rigorous training. **2. precise, strict, meticulous,** exact, accurate, scrupulous, full, correct, punctilious Medical drugs that are released for public use are put through rigorous testing. ◈ **Antonyms: 1. easy, soft 2. inexact, sloppy**

rim *noun* **brim, brink, edge, lip, border, ledge, hem, perimeter, margin, side, verge** We stood on the rim of Bryce Canyon and admired the magnificent view.

ring[1] *noun* **1. circle, band, hoop, wheel, coil, link, belt, loop** The Scouts sat in a ring around their campfire. **2. group, bunch, gang, cabal, circuit, clique, syndicate, cartel, league** All members of the international drug ring were arrested. ◆ *verb* **circle, encompass, hem, hedge, loop, surround, wreathe, girdle, enclose** We ringed the garden patch with stones.

ring[2] *verb* **jingle, trill, jangle, sound, chime, peal, toll, tinkle** Did you hear the phone ring? ◆ *noun* **1. chime, peal, toll, clang, knell, ringing, sound, tinkle, call** Every Sunday morning I listen for the ring of church bells. **2. appearance, feeling, mark, tenor, character, quality, aura, tone, flavor** His story has the ring of truth.

rinse *verb* **clean, launder, bathe, cleanse, wash, wet, dip, flush** I rinsed my hair after I shampooed it. ◆ *noun* **shower, wash, washing, cleaning, soak, laundering, bath** I gave the car a rinse after washing it.

riot *noun* **disturbance, protest, unrest, disorder, uprising, violence, fracas, turmoil, tumult, trouble** Many windows were broken during the riot. ◆ *verb* **rebel, revolt, protest, rally, rage, fight, resist** During the 1960s, some college students rioted against the Vietnam War.

rip *verb* **tear, cut, slash, slit, split, run, shred, gash, rent** I ripped my jeans on a barbed wire fence. ◆ *noun* **hole, tear, split, slit, cut, gash, run, rent** The rip in your shirt is too ragged to mend.

ripe *adjective* **1. mature, ready, developed, full-grown, plump, adult, seasoned** Pick only the ripe strawberries. **2. ready, fit, set, primed, disposed, in position, available, prepared** Financial reports say that this company is ripe for takeover by another company. ◈ **Antonyms: 1. green, raw, unripe**

ripen *verb* **develop, mature, age, mellow, season, grow, advance, progress** We let the tomatoes ripen on the vine.

ripple *verb* **undulate, wave, sway, move, flow, splash** The wheat rippled in the breeze. ◆ *noun* **wave, wavelet,**

undulation, swell, flutter, ruffle, corrugation, wrinkle Ripples formed on the water when I threw a stone into the pond.

rise *verb* **1. arise, ascend, climb, soar, go up** The sun rises in the east and sets in the west. **2. arise, stand, stand up, spring up, get up, raise** Will everyone please rise? **3. arise, awaken, waken, wake up, get up, rouse, stir** I usually rise at 7:00 in the morning. **4. expand, grow, increase, swell, billow, burgeon, crest** The river rose and overflowed its banks. **5. advance, climb, progress, get ahead, succeed, proceed** The new employee rose swiftly to a management position. **6. rebel, revolt, mutiny, resist, defy, strike, riot, disobey** Every group that is downtrodden will eventually rise up against its oppressors. ◆ *noun* **increase, jump, surge, gain, boost, upswing, growth** There was a rise in donations after the appeal on TV. ◈ **Antonyms:** *verb* **1. sink, set, drop 2. sit, recline 4. fall, shrink, wane 6. obey, comply** ◆ *noun* **decline, drop**

risk *noun* **chance, gamble, bet, wager, pitfall, threat, danger, hazard, jeopardy, peril** The photographer took a risk by standing in an open field during the lightning storm. ◆ *verb* **bet, chance, gamble, wager, venture, speculate, hazard, jeopardize, dare, endanger, imperil** Our grandmother risks two dollars every week on lottery tickets. ◈ **Antonyms:** *noun* **safety, security**

rite *noun* **ceremony, ritual, sacrament, celebration, formality, observance, service** Baptism is one of the rites of many religions.

ritual *noun* **1. ceremony, rite, observance, service, communion, formality, ordinance** Each religion has its own particular rituals. **2. habit, routine, practice, schedule, program, convention, way, custom, tradition, formula** Going for a morning walk is one of his rituals.

rival *noun* **competitor, adversary, contestant, contender, opponent, challenger, antagonist, foe, enemy** The two friends are rivals for the lead in the class play. ◆ *verb* **approach, equal, match, challenge, compare, meet, touch, compete, vie** She rivals you in both musical and scholastic ability. ◈ **Antonyms:** *noun* **ally, friend**

rivalry *noun* **competition, conflict, opposition, struggle, antagonism, strife** Our school has a strong rivalry with the school across town. ◈ **Antonyms: cooperation, alliance, collaboration**

river *noun* **stream, flow, gush, surge, torrent, current, flood, rush** A river of oil poured out of the broken tank.

road *noun* **route, street, avenue, boulevard, lane, freeway, highway, trail, thruway, byway, concourse** Our town is building a road that will lead directly from the shopping mall to the highway.

roam *verb* **wander, rove, amble, travel, journey, drift, meander, ramble, range, stray, jaunt, stroll, traipse, gallivant** The sheep roamed over a wide area in the countryside.

roar *verb* **1. bellow, shout, yell, bawl, howl, scream, shriek, hoot** The drill master roared at his troops. **2. thunder, rumble, blast, boom, shriek, reverberate, crash** The jet roared through the sky above us. **3. laugh, guffaw, whoop, howl, scream, hoot** The audience roared at the comedian's routine. ◆ *noun* **1. growl, howl, bellow, cry, bawl, bay, holler, yell, yowl, yelp, wail** The gazelles stampeded when they heard the lion's roar. **2. blast, boom, rumble, bang, thunder, crack, clamor, clap** There was a roar when the plane passed overhead.

rob *verb* **1. burglarize, hold up, stick up, pilfer, steal, swipe** The police caught the people who robbed a liquor store last week. **2. deprive, wrest, usurp, cheat, swindle, fleece, appropriate** The other team's touchdown robbed us of our victory.

robe *noun* **housecoat, kimono, smock, toga, mantle** I took a bath, put on a robe, and settled down to watch my favorite TV program. ◆ *verb* **cloak, cover, drape, adorn, clothe, garb, dress** The fields and woods were robed in snow.

robust *adjective* **healthy, strong, sturdy, vigorous, hearty, hale, stout, stalwart, strapping** I feel more robust during the summer than I do during the winter. ◈ **Antonyms: delicate, weak, unhealthy**

rock[1] *noun* **1. stone, boulder, cobblestone, pebble, gravel** The cabin's fireplace is made out of big, flat rocks. **2. bulwark, pillar, support, tower of strength, mainstay, foundation** The police chief was a rock during the disturbance.

rock[2] *verb* **1. heave, pitch, roll, toss, jar, shake, swing, oscillate, wobble, sway** Waves rocked the boat. **2. shock, stun, upset, agitate, disturb, unnerve, disconcert** I was rocked by the news.

rod *noun* **1. pole, bar, stick, dowel, shaft, stave, baton, staff** Mom replaced the curtain rods. **2. lash, whip, switch, cane** "Spare the rod and spoil the child" is an old saying.

Word Group

A **rodent** is a mammal that has large front teeth used for gnawing. **Rodent** is a specific scientific term with no true synonyms. Here are some common rodents:

beaver, capybara, chipmunk, gerbil, gopher, groundhog, ground squirrel, guinea pig, hamster, lemming, marmot, mouse, muskrat, porcupine, rat, squirrel, vole, woodchuck

rogue *noun* scoundrel, villain, cur, knave, wretch, fraud, scalawag, swindler, trickster He dressed as a Renaissance rogue.

role *noun* **1.** character, part, bit, portrayal What role did you get in the school play? **2.** function, duty, position, purpose, obligation, place, work, post, job, task What role do you have at the store?

roll *verb* **1.** pitch, throw, toss, flip, tumble, revolve, rotate, whirl I rolled the dice and took my turn in the game. **2.** move, flow, glide, proceed, advance, sail, pass, file, slide, slip The floats in the parade rolled slowly by us. **3.** rock, sway, pitch, swing, lurch, waver, reel, yaw, undulate, stagger The fishing boat rolled from side to side. **4.** wind, twist, wrap, coil, curl, turn, loop, furl, knot I rolled the leftover wrapping paper back onto the tube. **5.** flatten, spread, level, press, smooth, even I rolled out the dough for the cookies. ♦ *noun* **1.** spool, reel, cylinder, bobbin, scroll, wheel We used a roll of twine to tie up the vines. **2.** sway, pitch, lurch, waver, reel, saunter, swing Our cockatiel had a roll in his step as he walked across the floor. **3.** attendance, lineup, list, register, schedule, roster, catalogue, tally, index The coach calls roll at the start of every practice. **4.** bread, bun, croissant, biscuit, pastry, scone, bagel We bought fresh rolls at the bakery. **5.** rumble, thunder, boom, clap, peal, growl, drone We could hear the roll of thunder in the distance.

romance *noun* **1.** affair, courtship, love, relationship, passion, flirtation, infatuation Mom and Dad's romance began when a friend introduced them. **2.** ballad, narrative, love story, novel, legend, fantasy, fiction, lyric, fairy tale *Tristan and Isolde* is a medieval romance. **3.** adventure, excitement, glamour, fascination, charm, mystery, intrigue, color Some people think that jet planes and superhighways have taken the romance out of travel.

romantic *adjective* **1.** ardent, emotional, amorous, tender, loving, devoted, affectionate, adoring, passion-

ate, fond Sara Teasdale won the Pulitzer Prize in 1918 for her book of romantic poems, *Love Songs*. **2.** exciting, mysterious, colorful, glamorous, adventurous, mythical, legendary I think Alexandria would be a romantic city to visit. **3.** idealistic, sentimental, fanciful, optimistic, dreamy, improbable, imaginative, utopian She has romantic ideas about starting an animal shelter. ♦ *noun* idealist, sentimentalist, visionary, dreamer, adventurer, enthusiast, optimist My mom says I am a romantic. ➡ **Antonyms:** *adjective* **1.** unromantic, cold-hearted **2.** dull, commonplace **3.** realistic, practical ♦ *noun* pragmatist, realist

romp *verb* frolic, caper, cavort, play, rollick, gambol, frisk, sport, skip, hop, jump, prance We watched the puppies romp in the pet store window. ♦ *noun* frolic, escapade, lark, caper, horseplay, hop, play I took my turtle for a romp in the park, but he just sat there looking at me.

room *noun* **1.** territory, space, scope, expanse, area, latitude, leeway, elbowroom On the frontier there was plenty of room for people to start a new life. **2.** chamber, apartment, suite, area, space, compartment, lodging, den, cell I am glad that I have my own room.

roost *verb* perch, land, settle, alight, camp, nest, bunk, dwell, berth, park Our parakeet likes to roost on my head.

root[1] *noun* **1.** taproot, bulb, tuber, shoot, rootstock Carrots are edible roots. **2.** beginning, origin, source, base, fountainhead, germ, inception My family has its roots in Central America. **3.** core, heart, essence, cause, bottom, foundation, nucleus, base We're trying to get to the root of the problem.

root[2] *verb* **1.** fix, establish, anchor, ground, moor, entrench, set, plant We rooted the posts for the grape arbor firmly in the ground. **2.** rummage, dig, poke, burrow, search, forage, hunt, delve, grub My little brother rooted in his toy box for his baseball glove.

root[3] *verb* cheer, support, encourage, applaud, back, promote, boost We rooted for the Denver Broncos in the Super Bowl.

rot *verb* decay, spoil, decompose, turn, go bad, crumble, degenerate The overripe bananas had begun to rot. ♦ *noun* **1.** blight, fungus, mildew, mold, decay, spoilage Mom was upset when she found some rot on her rosebushes. **2.** nonsense, drivel, foolishness, silliness, poppycock, rubbish, trash, jabber, babble Don't talk rot!

rotate *verb* **1. revolve, spin, turn, twirl, whirl, swivel, wind, crank** Rotate this knob to focus the binoculars. **2. alternate, interchange, take turns, switch, exchange, change, revolve, shift, vary** We rotate chores in our family.

rotten *adjective* **1. decayed, decomposed, rancid, rank, moldy, putrid** We threw the rotten food away. **2. dishonest, immoral, corrupt, crooked, untrustworthy, deceitful, treacherous, degenerate** The manager discovered that the rotten accounting clerk was embezzling money. **3. awful, bad, terrible, horrible, nasty, miserable, unlucky, rough** That was a rotten thing to have happen to you. ⭐**Antonyms: 1. fresh, pure 2. honest, reliable 3. good, pleasant**

rough *adjective* **1. uneven, irregular, broken, bumpy, rugged, craggy, jagged** We hiked over the rough terrain. **2. violent, fierce, stormy, tempestuous, choppy, wild, turbulent, agitated** We had difficulty getting the boat to shore because of the rough weather. **3. taxing, demanding, difficult, hard, tough, strenuous, laborious** Mom was tired because she had a rough day at work. **4. impolite, boorish, uncivil, crass, unrefined, crude, rude, raw, uncultivated** His manners are rough. **5. preliminary, crude, incomplete, unfinished, imprecise, general, basic, quick, unpolished** The artist made a rough sketch before she started painting. ⭐**Antonyms: 1. smooth, flat, level 2. calm, placid, still 3. easy, light 4. refined, gracious 5. precise, final**

round *adjective* **1. circular, curved, spherical, globular, rotund** My watch has a round face. **2. arched, curved, rounded, bowed, looped** My school desk has round corners. **3. resonant, sonorous, full, rich, smooth, mellifluous, vibrant** The choir has a pleasing, round tone. ◆ *noun* **1. cycle, series, string, run, succession, sequence, chain** There was a round of parties for the newly engaged couple. **2. beat, circuit, route, turn, loop, tour, watch, course** The museum guard walked his round. ◆ *verb* **1. curve, smooth, loop, crook, form, arch** I rounded the corners of the board. **2. circle, turn, spin, go around, travel, pivot, rotate, roll** The cyclists were going very fast when they rounded the bend. ⭐**Antonyms: *adjective* 1. & 2. angular, square 3. harsh, hoarse, gruff**

rouse *verb* **1. awaken, wake, wake up, arouse, summon, call** My mother roused me in time to get ready for school. **2. animate, excite, move, exhilarate, agitate, galvanize, spur** Music has the ability to rouse the emotions. ⭐**Antonyms: 2. calm, pacify**

rout *noun* **defeat, disaster, overthrow, conquest, upset, beating, drubbing, licking** The game ended in a complete rout. ◆ *verb* **crush, beat, conquer, defeat, overcome,** overwhelm, repulse, vanquish, trounce The guerilla soldiers routed the government forces.

route *noun* **1. road, avenue, lane, roadway, drive, boulevard, street** We live on a rural route. **2. course, path, way, itinerary, passage** Wendy planned the route for our trip. **3. way, means, medium, agency, instrument, course, procedure** Mistakes in procedures have often been the route to new discoveries. ◆ *verb* **send, convey, ship, direct, dispatch, forward, transfer, steer** My overseas package was routed through San Francisco.

routine *noun* **procedure, custom, habit, pattern, practice, formula, program** Making my bed is the first step of my morning routine. ◆ *adjective* **1. customary, familiar, normal, regular, standard, usual, accepted, accustomed, habitual** We followed routine procedure during the fire drill. **2. typical, everyday, ordinary, predictable, dull, unexceptional, tedious, boring** Today has been a routine day. ⭐**Antonyms: *adjective* unusual, exceptional**

rove *verb* **wander, roam, ramble, travel, traipse, range, stray, meander, gad, tramp** My dream is to rove around the country in search of adventure.

row[1] *noun* **line, string, column, queue, file, sequence, chain** My parents planted a row of lilac bushes along the back of our property.

row[2] *verb* **paddle, scull, sail, scud, oar, pull, drag, navigate** Every summer I get to row a boat on Lake McCall.

row[3] *noun* **quarrel, argument, fight, spat, squabble, dispute, hassle, disagreement, brawl, tiff, fracas, ruckus** My brother and I got into a row over whose turn it was to use the car.

royal *adjective* **1. imperial, regal, sovereign, noble, aristocratic, highborn** The royal family appeared on the palace balcony. **2. grand, magnificent, lavish, splendid, majestic, stately, dignified, grandiose** The troops received a royal sendoff. ⭐**Antonyms: 1. common 2. modest, plain**

rub *verb* **knead, massage, stroke, press, finger, manipulate** I rubbed my temples to help myself relax. ◆ *noun* **kneading, massage, rubdown, manipulation, brushing, scouring, scrubbing** Will you give me a back rub, please?

rubbish *noun* **1. garbage, junk, litter, refuse, trash, waste, debris, rubble** We threw away a lot of rubbish when we cleaned out the garage. **2. nonsense, rot, inanity, silliness, blather, gibberish, idiocy, foolishness** I thought the infomercial was full of rubbish.

ruddy *adjective* blushing, rosy, red, flushed, glowing, pink, florid, healthy, blooming My face was ruddy after I went for a jog in the park.

rude *adjective* **1.** discourteous, disrespectful, impolite, inconsiderate, ill-bred, boorish Please forgive me, I didn't mean to be rude. **2.** rustic, crude, makeshift, primitive, rough, simple, unrefined, rough-hewn, rugged, coarse The sheepherder built a rude shelter out of stones and brush. **3.** sudden, jarring, harsh, abrupt, unpleasant, violent, stormy, sharp I had a rude awakening when I realized it was already a new month. ➧ **Antonyms: 1.** considerate, courteous, polite **2.** finished, sound **3.** gradual, gentle

ruffian *noun* brute, rowdy, bully, villain, hooligan, roughneck, gangster, thug There were ruffians and outlaws as well as honest citizens on the early frontier.

ruffle *noun* trouble, mix-up, confusion, upset, irregularity, disturbance, commotion, agitation There was a slight ruffle in our plans when the taxi arrived late. ◆ *verb* **1.** mess up, disturb, disorder, rumple, dishevel, muss, jumble The wind ruffled my hair. **2.** upset, fluster, confuse, unsettle, irritate, aggravate, provoke, perturb, excite It embarrassed and ruffled me to have the teacher mispronounce my name. ➧ **Antonyms:** *verb* **1.** settle, smooth **2.** calm, compose

rugged *adjective* **1.** rough, uneven, harsh, rocky, craggy, bumpy, ridged, hilly, mountainous, jagged It is easy to get lost in such rugged terrain. **2.** solid, sturdy, hardy, healthy, robust, husky, stalwart, brawny, durable The cowboys were rugged after being on the trail for months. **3.** difficult, tough, rigorous, trying, demanding, arduous, taxing That was a rugged math test! ➧ **Antonyms: 1.** flat, level **2.** weak, delicate **3.** easy, effortless

ruin *noun* **1.** collapse, bankruptcy, catastrophe, destruction, decay, crash, havoc, demolition The new company is facing financial ruin. **2.** downfall, undoing, bane, disintegration, havoc, affliction, overthrow, failure, curse, nemesis If I'm not careful, candy will be the ruin of my teeth. **3.** debris, rubble, wreckage, relic, remains, shell, remnant, wreck We explored the ruins of an old silver mine. ◆ *verb* demolish, destroy, wreck, mangle, decimate, annihilate, spoil The puppy ruined my leather belt by chewing on it. ➧ **Antonyms:** *noun* **1.** success **2.** blessing, boon

rule *noun* **1.** dominion, reign, administration, government, power, sovereignty, authority, command Robin Hood is said to have lived during the rule of King Richard the Lion-Hearted. **2.** guideline, regulation, law, order, principle, dictum, ordinance, edict The lifeguard at the swimming pool enforces the safety rules. **3.** routine, way, practice, method, procedure, course, pattern, habit It is the rule at our house to ask to be excused when we are finished eating. ◆ *verb* **1.** govern, reign, administer, head, command, control, lead, manage Empress Catherine the Great ruled Russia from 1762 until 1796. **2.** dominate, influence, move, sway, prompt, decide His head ruled his heart in that situation. **3.** decide, determine, judge, resolve, adjudge, find, conclude, decree The referee ruled that the player had committed a foul.

ruler *noun* sovereign, monarch, king, queen, czar, commander, leader, dictator, administrator Louis XVI was ruler of France when the French Revolution began.

rumble *verb* growl, grumble, roll, roar, boom, resound, thunder, sound My stomach rumbled because I was hungry. ◆ *noun* boom, roar, roll, thunder, clap, reverberation, crash, growl We could hear the rumble of distant thunder.

rummage *verb* search, ransack, comb, forage, poke, scour, seek, hunt, explore I rummaged through the house for my binder.

rumor *noun* gossip, hearsay, talk, report, news, story, innuendo, tale, whisper There is a rumor that you will get the lead in the musical. ◆ *verb* report, say, suggest, chatter, gossip, whisper, circulate, intimate It is rumored that there will be early dismissal next Friday.

run *verb* **1.** dash, hasten, hurry, hustle, race, rush, scurry, scoot, fly We must run to the post office before it closes. **2.** escape, flee, abscond, leave, steal away, clear out, decamp, retreat Let's run away to the beach. **3.** roam, rove, wander, meander, drift, gad, walk, stray, traipse, stroll, cruise, range I unsaddled my horse and put it in the corral to run. **4.** campaign, compete, contend, contest, stand, oppose, stump, challenge The senator is going to run for office again. **5.** drive, function, go, operate, perform, work, handle A car runs better after a tune-up. **6.** flow, gush, rush, surge, pour, spill, roll, course The fireman opened the hydrant and let the water run into the street. **7.** extend, spread, reach, stretch, continue, cover, range, proceed, go Interstate 10 runs from Los Angeles, California, to Jacksonville, Florida. **8.** control, direct, maintain, manage, supervise, administer, govern, regulate, lead My parents run a doughnut shop. ◆ *noun* **1.** dash, jog, sprint, trot, scurry, gallop, race We went for a run around the block. **2.** trip, visit, outing, ride, drive, tour, excursion, spin, journey I need to make a run to the store **3.** streak, stretch, string, spell, round, course, cycle, sequence I've been having a run of good luck.

rupture *noun* **1. break, crack, fracture, gap, hole, split, fissure, breach** Our basement was flooded because of a rupture in our hot water tank. **2. breach, schism, split, rent, rift, estrangement, fissure, quarrel** There was a rupture in the community over the proposal for a new freeway. ◆ *verb* **break, burst, explode, split, crack, fracture, tear** The water balloon ruptured when I filled it too full. ➡ **Antonyms:** *noun* **2. understanding, cooperation**

rural *adjective* **country, provincial, agricultural, farm, simple, rustic, pastoral** My family comes from a rural town in Minnesota. ➡ **Antonyms: urban, sophisticated**

ruse *noun* **trick, deception, gambit, deceit, artifice, fraud, hoax** The fraudulent company operated under the ruse of being a collection agency.

rush *verb* **1. dash, hasten, hurry, hustle, fly, race, run, dart, tear, sprint** I rushed over to my friend's house as soon as she got home from vacation. **2. attack, charge, blitz, storm, raid, beset, assail** Soldiers rushed the enemy stronghold. ◆ *noun* **1. hurry, scramble, race, run, sprint, bustle, flurry** We were in a rush to finish our holiday shopping. **2. attack, charge, blitz, raid, surge, onslaught, assault** The soldiers made a rush at the enemy.

rust *noun* **corrosion, oxidation, rot, blight, decay** Dad sandblasted rust off the cast iron frying pan. ◆ *verb* **corrode, oxidize, decay, crumble, weaken, deteriorate** The old metal milk can rusted over years of being in the weather.

rustic *adjective* **1. rural, country, pastoral, agrarian, agricultural, provincial, bucolic** The rustic area of Tuscany is very picturesque. **2. plain, unsophisticated, unpolished, crude, simple, homespun, rough** My grandparents' vacation cottage is furnished in a rustic style. ◆ *noun* **peasant, farmer, countryman, countrywoman, provincial, hillbilly, yokel** The exasperated rustics rose up against their Roman masters.

rustle *verb* **flutter, sigh, crackle, whir, swish, shuffle, whisk, whisper, swoosh** The leaves rustled in the wind. ◆*noun* **rustling, whisper, sound, noise, stir, swish, ripple, crackle** We could hear the rustle of the leaves in the wind.

rusty *adjective* **1. oxidized, corroded, rusted, decayed, rotten** The old milk can was rusty. **2. unpolished, inept, unpracticed, diminished, impaired, stale, weak, feeble, slow** Dad's golf game is rusty because he hasn't played in a long time. ➡ **Antonyms: 2. polished, impeccable**

rut *noun* **track, ditch, channel, groove, furrow, gutter, score** The tractor left big ruts in the muddy road. ◆ *verb* **furrow, groove, score, mark, track** Heavy rains rutted the hillside.

ruthless *adjective* **brutal, cruel, harsh, heartless, merciless, severe, pitiless, callous, vicious, unforgiving** The ruthless general was known for treating his enemies harshly. ➡ **Antonyms: compassionate, kind, merciful**

Ss

sabotage *noun* **destruction, demolition, disruption, impairment, subversion, undermining, overthrow** Acts of sabotage are common during wartime. ◆ *verb* **destroy, wreck, disable, damage, cripple, subvert, undermine, disrupt** The soldiers sabotaged the railroad bridge.

sack[1] *noun* **bag, pack, pouch, satchel, knapsack, handbag** We bought a sack of potatoes at the grocery store. ◆ *verb* **bag, pack, package, load, put in, fill, stuff** The clerk sacked our groceries for us.

sack[2] *verb* **pillage, plunder, ransack, loot, despoil, attack, raid, rob, ravage** The Vikings sacked many villages over a period of about 300 years. ◆ *noun* **pillage, looting, plundering, robbing, burning, destruction, raid, waste, ravage** The sack of Rome by the Vandals occurred in A.D. 455.

sacred *adjective* **divine, holy, religious, saintly, spiritual, blessed, dedicated, hallowed** Jerusalem is a sacred city to Christians, Jews, and Muslims. ❖ **Antonyms: profane, secular**

sacrifice *noun* **1. offering, gift, homage, victim, killing, slaughter, immolation** The ancient Greeks made offerings to their gods with the sacrifice of sheep and other animals. **2. concession, forfeit, relinquishment, loss, surrender, renunciation** Our family has had to make sacrifices in order to put my brother through college. ◆ *verb* **1. kill, slay, slaughter, butcher, victimize, immolate** The ancient Aztecs frequently sacrificed human victims. **2. give up, let go, lose, offer, surrender, yield, waive, forfeit, forgo** In chess, it is often necessary to sacrifice pieces in order to win the game.

sad *adjective* **1. dejected, depressed, desolate, gloomy, melancholy, unhappy, downcast, morose** I was sad when I could not go skiing with my friends. **2. deplorable, pitiful, regrettable, grievous, lamentable, sorry, unfortunate, dire** I think it is very sad that the rain forests are being cut down. ❖ **Antonyms: 1. glad, joyful, happy 2. good, fortunate**

sadden *verb* **depress, deject, oppress, dispirit, dishearten, sorrow, grieve** My friend's serious illness saddens me. ❖ **Antonyms: please, delight**

saddle *noun* **riding saddle, seat, perch, pad, howdah, sidesaddle** The cowboy put a saddle on his horse. ◆ *verb* **burden, load, tax, weigh down, charge, impose, inflict,**

encumber I was saddled with my brother's chores when he went away to camp. ❖ **Antonyms:** *verb* **free, relieve**

safe *adjective* **1. protected, secure, defended, guarded, snug, immune, impregnable** The rabbit felt safe and comfortable in its burrow. **2. prudent, reliable, sound, sure, clear, certain, dependable, secure** I think you made a safe choice. **3. unhurt, unharmed, uninjured, unscathed, sound, whole, intact, alive** The driver and his passengers were safe after the accident. ❖ **Antonyms: 1. exposed 2. risky, unreliable 3. injured, hurt**

safeguard *noun* **protection, shield, defense, guard, screen, security, buffer** The school installed a fence around the schoolyard as a safeguard. ◆ *verb* **protect, defend, guard, preserve, secure, shield, ward, fortify** Helmets help safeguard bicyclists from serious head injuries. ❖ **Antonyms:** *noun* **peril, hazard, danger** ◆ *verb* **endanger, jeopardize**

sag *verb* **dip, droop, drop, sink, slump, bend, give, bow, flop, wilt** The clothesline sagged when we hung up our wet beach towels.

saga *noun* **legend, story, chronicle, narrative, epic, tale, myth, history, romance** The Norse sagas were written between the 7th and 14th centuries.

sage *noun* **scholar, intellectual, pundit, philosopher, authority, highbrow, guru** Albert Einstein was considered a mathematical sage. ◆ *adjective* **wise, sound, prudent, sagacious, sensible, profound, astute, intelligent** You have always given me sage advice. ❖ **Antonyms:** *noun* **fool, idiot** ◆ *adjective* **silly, foolish**

sail *noun* **boat trip, cruise, voyage, excursion, passage, run, crossing** We decided to go on a sail across the bay. ◆ *verb* **1. cruise, voyage, cross, set sail, boat, put to sea, embark** It took us two hours to sail across the lake. **2. navigate, pilot, captain, guide, steer, run, govern, control** My father is teaching me how to sail a boat. **3. drift, float, fly, glide, soar, skim, sweep, coast, wing** We watched as the hawk sailed on the thermal winds.

saintly *adjective* **virtuous, benevolent, kindly, charitable, holy, divine, pious, angelic** Dr. Tom Dooley, in a compassionate and saintly action, established medical clinics to care for refugees in Southeast Asia. ❖ **Antonyms: malicious, immoral**

sake *noun* **1. purpose, motive, reason, objective, cause, aim, end, principle** I agreed to go to the beach for the sake of keeping my friends happy. **2. benefit, good, interest, gain, behalf, advantage, welfare, well-being** The research to find a cure for cancer has been done for the sake of humanity. ➡ **Antonyms: 2. detriment, disadvantage**

salary *noun* **compensation, earnings, remuneration, pay, wage, fee, income, stipend** The store owner raised her employee's salary.

sale *noun* **1. exchange, marketing, purchase, selling, transfer, auction, trade** Our neighbor hopes that the sale of his house will go smoothly. **2. bargain, deal, discount, markdown, closeout, cut, special, reduction** We plan to take advantage of the big holiday sale.

sally *verb* **rush, surge, leap, spring, erupt, attack, issue, pour** My friends and I sallied across the auditorium to find seats before the game. ◆ *noun* **1. attack, raid, sortie, rush, foray, excursion, expedition, jaunt** The guerrilla soldiers planned a sally on the approaching government troops. **2. retort, witticism, banter, quip, jibe, joke, wisecrack** I laughed at my brother's sally.

saloon *noun* **bar, tavern, pub, barroom, bistro, cocktail lounge, lounge, club** The old saloon had swinging doors at its entrance.

salty *adjective* **colorful, witty, pungent, risqué, earthy, humorous, coarse, racy** He told a salty story that made us all laugh.

salute *verb* **1. greet, hail, welcome, recognize, address, bow, receive, accost** I saluted my friend with a friendly wave. **2. praise, honor, congratulate, compliment, laud, commend, extol, applaud** The company manager saluted the employees for their increased productivity. ➡ **Antonyms: 2. rebuke, criticize**

salvation *noun* **deliverance, preservation, redemption, delivery, liberation, escape, rescue, salvage** These waterproof boots were my salvation when it started raining during our hike. ➡ **Antonyms: doom, downfall**

same *adjective* **alike, identical, matching, duplicate, equal, similar, related, like** My sister and I have the same color eyes. ➡ **Antonyms: different, unlike**

sample *noun* **example, specimen, model, representative, case, illustration, instance, taste** This is a sample of one of the kinds of cookies I can bake. ◆ *verb* **experience,** taste, test, try, partake, inspect, examine, judge The clerk asked if we would like to sample the new ice cream flavor.

sanction *noun* **1. approval, authorization, confirmation, endorsement, support, assent, consent** Our teacher gave us her sanction to read the play in class. **2. penalty, punishment, injunction, boycott, embargo, fine** Economic sanctions were imposed on the nation for allowing copyright infringements. ◆ *verb* **authorize, approve, confirm, allow, ratify, certify, support, encourage** Our school sanctions student participation in community activities. ➡ **Antonyms:** *noun* **1. disapproval, objection** ◆ *verb* **disapprove, denounce**

sanctuary *noun* **1. temple, shrine, church, sanctum, holy place, mosque** The Grotto in Portland, Oregon, is a beautiful, naturally formed Catholic sanctuary. **2. asylum, haven, protection, refuge, safety, shelter, cover, retreat** The refugees found sanctuary at the embassy. **3. preserve, reserve, park, reservation, shelter, conservation area, refuge** I took part in the annual bird count at a nearby bird sanctuary.

sane *adjective* **prudent, rational, reasonable, sensible, sound, wise, judicious, sober** I need some sane advice about the problems I am having with my stepsister. ➡ **Antonyms: foolish, insane**

sanity *noun* **mental health, reason, common sense, judgment, lucidity, saneness, mind, sense** I thought my grandfather would question my sanity when I went bungee jumping, but he wanted to go along. ➡ **Antonyms: insanity, madness**

sap[1] *noun* **fluid, liquid, juice, elixir, extract, milk** Maple syrup is made from the sap of the sugar maple tree.

sap[2] *verb* **deplete, exhaust, drain, weaken, enervate, debilitate, undo, undermine** The hot and muggy weather sapped my energy. ➡ **Antonyms: strengthen, fortify, restore**

sarcastic *adjective* **derisive, insulting, jeering, mocking, scornful, sneering, taunting, caustic** The politician made a sarcastic remark about her opponent's campaign promise. ➡ **Antonyms: complimentary, flattering**

sash *noun* **belt, band, ribbon, scarf, tie, cummerbund, waistband** I put on my karate uniform and tied the yellow sash around my waist.

sate *verb* **satisfy, satiate, slake, gratify, content, surfeit, glut, gorge** I sated my thirst with a tall glass of iced tea.

satire *noun* lampoon, parody, burlesque, mockery, irony, ridicule, sarcasm, humor *Gulliver's Travels* is a satire written in 1726 by Jonathan Swift.

satisfaction *noun* 1. contentment, fulfillment, gratification, pleasure, happiness, pride, enjoyment Renata felt immense satisfaction when she completed her art project. 2. reparation, recompense, compensation, restitution, reimbursement, settlement, amends The traffic judge allows first-time offenders to make satisfaction by performing community service. ➻ **Antonyms: 1. displeasure, discontent**

satisfactory *adjective* acceptable, adequate, all right, sufficient, competent, decent, suitable, fair The teacher said that the rough draft of my report was satisfactory. ➻ **Antonyms: unacceptable, unsatisfactory**

satisfy *verb* 1. appease, content, fulfill, gratify, pacify, please, indulge, satiate The bowl of soup satisfied my need for something warm and filling. 2. assure, convince, persuade, reassure, sway, answer, meet, suffice The suspect's alibi satisfied the police that he was innocent. 3. pay, discharge, settle, compensate, clear, repay, remunerate, reward The insurance company satisfied the accident victim's claim.

saturate *verb* douse, drench, soak, fill, sop, wet, souse, permeate, pervade Mom saturated our houseplants with water before we left for the week. ➻ **Antonyms: dehydrate, dry, evaporate**

saunter *verb* stroll, amble, sashay, mosey, traipse, walk, ramble, meander I sauntered to home base after the batter hit a home run. ◆ *noun* walk, stroll, ramble, amble, hike, promenade, jaunt We went for a saunter after our big meal.

savage *adjective* 1. wild, untamed, rugged, rough, uncivilized, primitive, barbaric, natural The North and South Poles are savage areas where preparation is the key to survival. 2. brutal, cruel, ferocious, fierce, ruthless, vicious, murderous, fell, furious The hungry shark made a savage attack on its prey. ➻ **Antonyms: 1. tame, civilized 2. mild, gentle**

save *verb* 1. rescue, deliver, help, aid, assist, recover, free, liberate Many people worked together to save the birds that had been caught in an oil spill. 2. conserve, preserve, spare, husband, maintain, sustain, protect, safeguard Turning off the tap while brushing your teeth saves water. 3. keep, store, lay away, stockpile, accumulate, amass, cache, stash I'm saving coupons until I have enough for a free set of headphones. ➻ **Antonyms: 1. endanger, risk 2. exhaust, waste**

savior *noun* rescuer, liberator, protector, redeemer, champion, benefactor, lifesaver, angel Anyone who rescues someone in danger is a savior.

savor *noun* 1. taste, flavor, tang, smell, fragrance, aroma, scent, odor This barbecue sauce has the savor of hickory. 2. attribute, property, trait, characteristic, quality, feature, suggestion This new series has the savor of a TV show from the 1970s. ◆ *verb* relish, enjoy, appreciate, cherish, revel, smell, taste, experience I savored the first day of vacation by sleeping late.

savory *adjective* 1. delicious, appetizing, scrumptious, tasty, toothsome, flavorful, delectable She made a savory appetizer to take to the party. 2. proper, decent, respectable, reputable, moral, honorable, righteous, good His reputation is not savory. ➻ **Antonyms: 1. bland, tasteless 2. disreputable, unsavory**

say *verb* 1. articulate, enunciate, pronounce, recite, state, utter, remark, tell, declare Can you say "The frog flopped" ten times in a row? 2. suppose, assume, think, hold, maintain, assert, contend, claim I think it's going to rain today—what do you say? ◆ *noun* voice, vote, chance, opinion, turn, comment, opportunity, suffrage All the club members had a say in the decision.

saying *noun* adage, expression, motto, proverb, byword, aphorism, maxim, saw "There's no use crying over spilt milk" is a common saying.

scale[1] *noun* lamina, layer, veneer, coat, film, crust, scab, flake, chip The inside of this teakettle has a scale of mineral deposits.

scale[2] *noun* 1. calibration, measure, gauge, degrees, graduation, gradation This yardstick has scales for both inches and centimeters. 2. system, range, register, ladder, hierarchy, chart, progression, ranking The pay scale for government workers is public information. ◆ *verb* 1. climb, ascend, rise, mount, go up, surmount, clamber She scaled the climbing wall with ease. 2. prorate, adjust, regulate, calibrate, gauge, balance, compute, measure My Internet provider scales subscription rates to the number of hours used. ➻ **Antonyms: *verb* 1. descend, go down**

scamper *verb* run, scurry, dash, scuttle, scoot, sprint, dart, rush, hurry We scampered into the nearest store to get out of the rain. ➻ **Antonyms: lag, dawdle**

scan *verb* look, search, survey, examine, check, study, scour, inspect We scanned the night sky in hopes of seeing shooting stars.

scandal *noun* disgrace, dishonor, embarrassment, outrage, shame, slander, offense The mayor's dishonesty is a public scandal.

scant *adjective* little, meager, scanty, skimpy, sparse, insufficient, inadequate, poor I paid scant attention to the boring TV show. ● **Antonyms:** abundant, sufficient

scanty *adjective* meager, insufficient, skimpy, deficient, inadequate, poor, stingy, sparse I ate a scanty meal because I was in such a hurry to get to school. ● **Antonyms:** ample, copious, plentiful

scar *noun* blemish, cicatrix, keloid, mark, injury, wound, pockmark, pit My cousin has a scar from when she had her appendix removed. ◆ *verb* blemish, damage, deface, mark, disfigure, injure, wound, brand The trees had been scarred by the forest fire.

scarce *adjective* 1. insufficient, inadequate, deficient, wanting, short, shy We have scarce information about other galaxies. 2. rare, infrequent, uncommon, unusual, sparse, sporadic, occasional, scanty Water is scarce in the desert. ● **Antonyms:** 1. sufficient, adequate 2. common, frequent, usual

scarcely *adverb* barely, hardly, just, only, scarce, merely I had scarcely hung up the phone when it rang again.

scare *verb* alarm, frighten, shock, startle, terrify, terrorize, intimidate I had a bad dream that really scared me. ◆ *noun* alarm, fright, shock, start, startle, surprise, horror, panic You gave me quite a scare when you came in without knocking. ● **Antonyms:** *verb* soothe, calm, reassure ◆ *noun* reassurance

scary *adjective* frightening, alarming, frightful, fearful, fearsome, dreadful, ghastly I do not like scary movies.

scatter *verb* 1. strew, spread, distribute, sprinkle, sow, disseminate, shower, throw We scatter sand on our front steps when they get icy. 2. disperse, dispel, separate, disband, break up, dissipate, diffuse All the friends I made at camp scattered when summer was over. ● **Antonyms:** collect, gather, assemble

scenario *noun* 1. plot, story, story line, synopsis, summary, screenplay The director briefly gave the scenario of the play. 2. situation, circumstance, state of affairs, condition Even in the worst-case scenario, our plan should still work.

scene *noun* 1. view, sight, panorama, outlook, vista, prospect, vision, spectacle The snow-covered mountains made a beautiful scene. 2. locale, location, setting, site, area, place, spot, stage The police quickly arrived at the scene of the crime. 3. act, episode, segment, chapter, part, section, bit, spot, piece The murderer was revealed in the last scene of the play. 4. to-do, display, commotion, fuss, exhibition The 2-year-old child created an embarrassing scene in the supermarket.

scenery *noun* 1. view, vista, panorama, outlook, scene, terrain, landscape, spectacle We paused on our hike to admire the scenery. 2. backdrop, stage, set, setting, background I enjoyed working on the scenery for our school play.

scenic *adjective* picturesque, beautiful, pretty, spectacular, striking, breathtaking Our train route through the mountains was very scenic. ● **Antonyms:** ordinary, unattractive

scent *noun* 1. aroma, fragrance, odor, smell, bouquet, incense, savor, essence I like the scent of gardenias. 2. spoor, track, trail, trace, sign The dog followed the quail until he lost their scent. ◆ *verb* 1. nose out, smell, sniff, whiff, detect, perceive, sense, identify, recognize The dog was trained to scent the presence of drugs. 2. perfume, sweeten, imbue, deodorize The lilies scented the evening air.

schedule *noun* calendar, lineup, program, timetable, docket, list, register, table The coach gave each player a copy of this year's game schedule. ◆ *verb* arrange, book, slate, program, reserve, plan, prepare, assign Mom scheduled a dentist appointment for me.

scheme *noun* 1. plan, program, system, outline, design, project, scenario, procedure Diet schemes that promise quick results usually don't work. 2. plot, strategy, intrigue, conspiracy, machination, contrivance, gimmick My friends tease me about my schemes to get rich. ◆ *verb* conspire, contrive, intrigue, plan, plot, concoct, collude, machinate The con artist schemed to cheat people out of their money.

scholar *noun* 1. intellectual, sage, pundit, professor, savant, philosopher, authority Many scholars use university libraries to do their research. 2. pupil, learner, student, disciple, apprentice, schoolgirl, schoolboy I intend to be a scholar all my life.

school *noun* educational institution, academy, institute, university, college, seminary Otis Institute is a nationally known art school. ◆ *verb* teach, train, educate, instruct, coach, tutor, drill, discipline, prepare Peter is schooled in the art of self-defense.

science *noun* **1. scholarship, education, learning, erudition, instruction, knowledge** My dream is to pursue a career in medical science. **2. art, system, method, technique, discipline, craft, skill, expertise** There is a science to playing billiards.

scoff *verb* **jeer, laugh, sneer, gibe, mock, deride, ridicule** The prosecuting attorney scoffed at the defendant's alibi. ◆**Antonyms: praise, commend, extol**

scold *verb* **admonish, criticize, chastise, rebuke, berate, reproach, chide, reprimand** Dad scolded me for not closing the front door. ◆ *noun* **nag, faultfinder, criticizer, complainer, shrew, virago, harpy, vixen** Do you think that Lady Macbeth was a scold? ◆**Antonyms:** *verb* **compliment, praise**

scoop *noun* **1. trowel, spoon, ladle, dipper, shovel, spade, bucket, bail** I used a scoop to put fertilizer on my shrubs. **2. news, information, intelligence, exposé, revelation, story, gossip** The reporter was promoted for getting the scoop on the embezzlement story at city hall. ◆ *verb* **1. dig, shovel, excavate, hollow, gouge, burrow, mine, spade** I helped Mom scoop out a hole for her new rosebush. **2. bail, dip, ladle, spoon, lade** I scooped cat food out of the sack.

scope *noun* **1. extent, range, reach, spread, realm, sphere, amplitude, capacity** The scope of my teacher's knowledge is impressive. **2. room, opportunity, elbowroom, freedom, space, liberty, latitude** The western frontier gave many people the scope to start a new life.

scorch *verb* **char, singe, sear, blacken, burn, roast, toast, parch, wither** The iron was too hot, and I scorched my silk shirt.

score *noun* **1. total, tally, count, record, reckoning, amount, outcome** What was the final score? **2. mark, grade, point, percentage, result, standing** I got a score of 95 on my spelling quiz. **3. debt, wrong, grievance, grudge, injustice, obligation, hurt, bill** The angry man vowed to even the score against his enemies. **4. group, host, multitude, throng, lot, mass, army, crowd, legion, swarm** Scores of people attended the rally. **5. composition, arrangement, music, orchestration, chart, transcript** The conductor handed out the score for the concerto. ◆ *verb* **1. achieve, attain, earn, gain, make, win, count, tally, total, post** The team scored three more goals during the last quarter. **2. evaluate, grade, judge, mark, rank, rate** The teacher scored our tests. **3. mark, scar, cut, nick, groove, slash, gash, scratch** The gardener scored a branch and planted it in sand so new roots would form.

scorn *noun* **contempt, disdain, mockery, ridicule, derision, taunt, jeer** Gilbert Blythe endured the scorn of Anne Shirley until the very end of *Anne of Green Gables*. ◆ *verb* **spurn, despise, deride, refuse, reject, mock, detest, flout** He scorned to ride his bicycle to school. ◆**Antonyms:** *noun* **esteem, respect, admiration** ◆ *verb* **value, admire**

scoundrel *noun* **rascal, rogue, villain, cad, blackguard, swindler, crook, thief** The scoundrel was caught and punished for his crimes.

scour[1] *verb* **polish, rub, scrub, cleanse, wash, brush, scrape** We scoured the dirty floor until it gleamed.

scour[2] *verb* **search, comb, ransack, rummage, scrutinize, probe, seek, hunt** I scoured the beach for sand dollars.

scourge *noun* **1. curse, plague, affliction, evil, bane, woe, ill, calamity** Attila the Hun was called the "scourge of God" because of the devastation he caused the Roman Empire. **2. switch, whip, lash, thong, strap, cat-o'-nine-tails** We saw an old scourge hanging up on the wall in the museum. ◆ *verb* **1. devastate, plague, curse, torment, afflict, ravage, smite** The deadly disease scourged much of the country. **2. flog, whip, flagellate, lash, smite, thrash, beat, flail, hit** People have been scourged as punishment throughout history.

scout *noun* **advance guard, guide, lookout, escort, spy, vanguard, watchman** Kit Carson was a famous frontier scout. ◆ *verb* **probe, reconnoiter, explore, search, inspect, survey, scrutinize, investigate** A father quail always scouts an area for danger before letting his chicks come out to eat.

scramble *verb* **1. climb, scuttle, crawl, clamber, jostle, scrabble, worm** We scrambled over the rocks at the base of the mountain. **2. hasten, hurry, hustle, race, rush, run, scurry, strive, struggle** Everybody scrambled to put their papers away when the bell rang. **3. disorder, jumble, mess up, mix, shuffle, confuse, disorganize, muddle** I like to solve word puzzles in which all the letters have been scrambled. ◆ *noun* **mess, mix-up, muddle, struggle, tumble, tussle, skirmish, race, rush** There was a scramble in the end zone when the player dropped the ball. ◆**Antonyms:** *verb* **2. dawdle 3. arrange, order**

scrap[1] *noun* **bit, fragment, part, piece, portion, shred, segment, morsel** I am saving scraps of cloth to make a quilt. ◆ *verb* **abandon, discard, dispose of, dump, junk, throw away, reject, jettison** The navy plans to scrap this old battleship. ◆**Antonyms:** *verb* **keep, repair, salvage**

scrap[2] *verb* **fight, brawl, argue, wrangle, quarrel, row, battle, contend** My brother and I scrap over who really owns our cat. ◆ *noun* **fight, quarrel, fracas, melee, scuffle, tiff, row, squabble** There was a scrap between the two cats over the dead mouse.

scrape *verb* **1. clean off, remove, rub off, scour, scrub, peel, smooth** Dad scraped the ice from the windshield of his car. **2. scratch, scuff, skin, abrade, rasp, hurt, injure, damage** I wear pads when I go roller-skating so that I won't scrape my knees. **3. amass, produce, gather, acquire, glean, accumulate, get, secure** I scraped together enough money to go to the movie with my friends. ◆ *noun* **1. mark, scratch, scuff, abrasion, gash, gouge, damage, injury** My brother's car has a scrape on the right front fender. **2. difficulty, dilemma, predicament, strait, jam, plight, trouble, fix** I had to think fast to get out of the scrape I was in.

scratch *verb* **1. graze, score, cut, lacerate, gash, prick, incise, scar** I scratched myself while picking blackberries. **2. rub, scrape, abrade, grate, rasp, chafe** Bears like to scratch their backs against trees. **3. erase, strike, delete, cross off, expunge, cancel, obliterate** When she said she couldn't come, I scratched her name from the list of attendees. ◆ *noun* **gash, mark, scrape, scuff, score, furrow, nick, damage, injury** This wax should cover the scratch on the table. ➧ **Antonyms:** *verb* **3. add, include**

scrawny *adjective* **thin, bony, skinny, gaunt, lean, scraggy, spare, underweight, lanky** Our dog looked scrawny after we shaved him for the summer.

scream *verb* **cry out, screech, shout, shriek, yell, bellow, roar, howl, wail** Everybody screamed as the roller coaster rushed around the bend. ◆ *noun* **1. cry, howl, screech, shout, shriek, yell, wail, outcry** We heard lots of screams coming from the carnival's haunted house. **2. sensation, hit, success, character, winner, laugh** We thought the actor was a scream.

screech *noun* **cry, scream, shriek, squawk, squeal, wail, yip, yap** The blue jay's screech woke me up. ◆ *verb* **cry out, scream, shriek, squawk, squeal, shrill, wail** I screeched when I opened the drawer and saw the mouse.

screen *noun* **1. cover, protection, shade, shelter, shield, veil, curtain** This elm tree acts as a screen to keep the sun off our porch. **2. mesh, netting, net, screening, lattice** Our tent has a small screen that serves as a window. ◆ *verb* **1. cloak, conceal, hide, obscure, veil, shroud, protect, shelter, guard** The dark night screened the attacking army. **2. sift, filter, winnow, sieve, strain, separate, divide, cull** I screened through the mail looking for the phone bill.

3. examine, process, scan, evaluate, select, grade, gauge, eliminate Many companies screen employees for drug use.

screw *noun* **fastener, pin, bolt, rod, nail** My bookshelves are held together with wood screws. ◆ *verb* **1. tighten, turn, twist, rotate, attach, fasten, wind** I screwed the cap onto the toothpaste tube. **2. twist, contort, distort, pucker, wrinkle, contract, rumple, deform** He screwed up his face in disgust when I suggested we get anchovies on our pizza.

scribble *verb* **draw, scrawl, write, jot, mark, doodle, scratch** My little brother scribbled on his bedroom wall with crayons. ◆ *noun* **drawing, scrawl, writing, handwriting, jotting, doodle, mark** Mother washed the scribbles off the wall with soap and water.

script *noun* **1. handwriting, longhand, calligraphy, penmanship, writing, cursive** Sometimes I print and sometimes I use script. **2. book, manuscript, screenplay, scenario, libretto, dialogue** Everybody in the play has to have a copy of the script.

scrub *verb* **cleanse, scour, wash, swab, sponge, polish, rub** I scrubbed the kitchen counters after doing the dishes. ◆ *noun* **cleaning, cleansing, washing, polish, rub, scrubbing, scouring** I gave the tub a good scrub.

scrupulous *adjective* **1. careful, painstaking, critical, meticulous, exact, fastidious, precise** The lawyers paid scrupulous attention to the details of the case. **2. honest, ethical, conscientious, moral, righteous, upright, just, honorable** He was scrupulous about dividing the profits from the neighborhood garage sale. ➧ **Antonyms: 1. sloppy, negligent, careless 2. dishonest, immoral**

scrutinize *verb* **observe, examine, analyze, scan, probe, search, inspect, investigate** The botanist scrutinized the tiny wildflower before taking a photograph. ➧ **Antonyms: ignore, overlook, neglect**

scrutiny *noun* **surveillance, observation, examination, study, research, inspection, perusal** The chipmunk was unaware of my scrutiny.

scuffle *verb* **fight, brawl, scrap, skirmish, tussle, grapple, wrestle** The boys scuffled playfully in the hall. ◆ *noun* **struggle, tussle, fracas, fray, brawl, ruckus, commotion** A scuffle broke out in the locker room.

sculpture *noun* **statue, figure, bust, carving, figurine, cast, statuette, statuary, relief** There is a sculpture of Robert E. Lee and his horse, Traveler, in Charlottesville, Virginia.

scuttle[1] *verb* abandon, discard, give up, forgo, scrap, sink We scuttled our plans for a weekend in the country.

scuttle[2] *verb* scamper, scurry, scramble, hurry, run, hasten, speed, rush We watched the crabs scuttle across the beach.

sea *noun* 1. ocean, main, deep, brine, water, lake, surf, swell, breaker I like to go swimming in the sea. 2. expanse, extent, multitude, mass, flood, torrent, abundance, profusion I found a sea of information on the Internet.

seal *noun* emblem, insignia, mark, sign, stamp, badge, brand, signet, impression Legal documents often have an official seal on them. ◆ *verb* 1. bind, close, fasten, secure, shut, stop, glue, lock, bar I sealed the carton with packing tape. 2. validate, confirm, ratify, establish, authenticate, certify, determine We sealed our pact with a handshake. ➡ **Antonyms:** *verb* 1. open, unseal, unfasten

seam *noun* line, ridge, groove, crack, layer, stratum, junction, joint, bond, union We could see a seam of calcium carbonate in the hillside. ◆ *verb* wrinkle, mark, furrow, line, groove, incise, ridge, scar, stitch The old man's face was seamed with wrinkles. ➡ **Antonyms:** *verb* smooth, flatten

sear *verb* 1. scorch, burn, char, singe, cauterize, brand, sizzle, toast Dad seared the steaks on the barbecue. 2. shrivel, dry, parch, dehydrate, desiccate, wither, fade, blight The heat of the summer sun seared the grass.

search *verb* explore, hunt, look, seek, probe, investigate, forage, ransack I like to search for arrowheads. ◆ *noun* exploration, hunt, check, probe, investigation, pursuit, inquiry, quest The rescue team began a search for the missing boy.

season *noun* period, time, occasion, spell, term, era, epoch, stage, tenure A lot of people decorate their homes during the holiday season. ◆ *verb* 1. flavor, spice, enhance, enliven, zest, pep up Mom uses curry powder to season her baked chicken. 2. age, cure, dry, ripen, mature, treat, condition, temper, prepare The salmon was seasoned in a smoker. 3. toughen, harden, discipline, steel, acclimate, inure The troops were seasoned by months of campaigning and battle.

seat *noun* locus, site, center, location, base, headquarters, post, heart, cradle, hub The seat of the United States government is in Washington, D.C. ◆ *verb* place, perch, plant, deposit, install, settle, establish, roost, sit Dad seated the fence posts in concrete.

second[1] *noun* instant, minute, moment, jiffy, twinkling, wink, trice, flash I will be with you in a second.

second[2] *adjective* next, additional, secondary, subsequent, subordinate, lesser, lower We were instructed to list our second choice as well as our first. ◆ *verb* endorse, support, approve, further, assist, back, promote, encourage No one would second the unpopular motion he proposed.

secret *adjective* 1. confidential, private, unknown, clandestine, classified, undisclosed, personal, covert I have a secret password to access my e-mail account. 2. secluded, isolated, unfrequented, private, hidden, concealed The billionaire bought an island to use as a secret hideaway. 3. mysterious, occult, mystical, esoteric, mystic, enigmatic, strange During the Middle Ages, alchemy was considered secret knowledge. ◆ *noun* 1. confidential information, restricted information, confidence, intrigue, intimacy Don't you dare tell anyone my secret! 2. mystery, puzzle, enigma, conundrum, riddle, problem, question There are secrets regarding the Egyptian pyramids that still need to be answered. ➡ **Antonyms:** *adjective* 1. revealed, open 2. public

secrete[1] *verb* produce, excrete, discharge, exude, sweat, emit, give off Pine trees secrete a resin that can be used for a variety of purposes.

secrete[2] *verb* hide, conceal, bury, cache, stow, stash, squirrel, horde We watched the blue jays secrete sunflower seeds around the yard. ➡ **Antonyms:** reveal, show, uncover

sect *noun* religious order, denomination, faction, clique, group, cult, school, camp The Sikhs are a sect that fuses Hindu and Muslim beliefs.

section *noun* part, piece, portion, segment, division, unit, subdivision, member I like to read the sports section of the newspaper. ◆ *verb* cut, divide, separate, slice, split, sever, part, partition, segment I sectioned the pie into six pieces. ➡ **Antonyms:** *noun* all, whole ◆ *verb* join, merge, unite

secure *adjective* 1. safe, defended, protected, sheltered, guarded, invulnerable, immune Having my dog with me when I take a walk makes me feel secure. 2. firm, fast, reliable, stable, solid, fixed, sure, strong, sound We checked to make sure that the lock on our storage unit was secure. 3. assured, certain, guaranteed, stable, steady, sure, definite, positive My dad has a secure position with his company. ◆ *verb* 1. defend, guard, protect, safeguard, shelter, shield, preserve, ward The alarm system will help secure the office against intruders. 2. anchor, attach, bind,

chain, fasten, tie, fix, moor, set, lash I used a chain and lock to secure my bicycle to a fence post. **3. acquire, gain, get, obtain, procure, attain, win, earn, reap** We were able to secure good seats for the baseball game.

sedate *adjective* **dignified, serious, calm, composed, steady, serene, earnest, solemn** My grandmother is the most sedate person I know. ◆ **Antonyms: restless, nervous**

sedative *adjective* **soothing, calming, hypnotic, comforting, soporific, narcotic, relaxing** Steven Halpern's music has a sedative effect on me. ◆ *noun* **drug, barbiturate, medication, pain-killer, sleeping pill, tranquilizer, depressant** The nurse gave the preoperative patient a sedative to help control his anxiety. ◆ **Antonyms:** *adjective* **stimulating, agitating**

sedentary *adjective* **inactive, unmoving, motionless, sluggish, torpid, stationary, still, lazy** It is important to balance sedentary activities with exercise.

see *verb* **1. behold, glimpse, notice, observe, spot, view, watch, witness, survey** You can see the ocean from here. **2. comprehend, understand, grasp, perceive, realize, appreciate, imagine** I can see why you're upset. **3. visualize, foresee, envision, conceive, imagine, picture, foretell** Martin Luther King Jr. spoke of the vision that he could see for America. **4. ascertain, determine, discover, find out, learn, detect, discern** Call your mom to see if you can spend the night. **5. date, court, romance, woo, go out, take out** I like the boy that my sister is seeing. **6. escort, attend, accompany, guide, conduct, direct, show, usher, shepherd** We waited for the usher to see us to our seats.

seed *noun* **source, beginning, basis, foundation, start, origin, kernel, nucleus** My mom works for a think tank that provides the seed for the government's political strategy.

seek *verb* **1. go after, hunt, look, pursue, search, want, desire, quest** Birds seek safe places for nesting sites. **2. attempt, try, endeavor, aim, undertake, essay, strive, aspire** We sought to reassure her.

seem *verb* **appear, look, resemble, sound, suggest, pretend** That girl over there seems to be waving at you.

seep *verb* **drain, dribble, drip, leak, ooze, trickle, leach, exude, soak** Oil seeped from the car's engine onto the driveway.

seethe *verb* **1. churn, foam, froth, boil, bubble, brew, steam, fizz, ferment** We watched the ocean seethe through the narrow opening in the rocks. **2. bristle, boil over, fume, rage, burn, flare, smolder, simmer** His rude remark made me seethe.

segment *noun* **part, piece, portion, section, slice, bit, division, subdivision** I gave my friend several segments of my orange. ◆ *verb* **divide, separate, part, dissever, break up, section, partition** I segmented the apple into four parts.

segregate *verb* **cut off, separate, isolate, insulate, sequester, seclude, exclude** The police segregated the demonstrators from the speaker's supporters. ◆ **Antonyms: integrate, desegregate**

seize *verb* **1. clutch, grab, grasp, grip, clench, snag, pluck, catch, embrace** I seized my little sister to keep her from running into the street. **2. understand, comprehend, perceive, get, apprehend, grasp, realize** He seized the concept of negative numbers immediately. **3. capture, take, abduct, kidnap, nab, apprehend, snatch, arrest** Some people claim to have been seized by aliens. **4. commandeer, appropriate, usurp, take, confiscate, impound, hijack, expropriate** My brother seized my bike when he found that his had a flat tire. ◆ **Antonyms: 3. & 4. release, set free, liberate**

seldom *adverb* **hardly ever, infrequently, not often, rarely, occasionally, scarcely, little** I seldom forget to brush my teeth before I go to bed. ◆ **Antonyms: commonly, always, frequently**

select *verb* **choose, decide on, elect, name, pick, settle on, opt for** Our teacher is letting us select our own report topics. ◆ *adjective* **exclusive, choice, special, rare, first-class, superior, fine, elect** My friend goes to a select high school for students who are gifted in the arts. ◆ **Antonyms:** *adjective* **common, ordinary**

selection *noun* **1. choice, pick, preference, election, option, favorite, winner** My cousin was the judges' selection for rodeo queen. **2. assortment, range, variety, array, medley, collection, stock, mixture** The stationery store has a large selection of birthday cards.

self-conscious *adjective* **bashful, modest, shy, nervous, embarrassed, insecure, uneasy, unsure** I felt very self-conscious when I had to give an oral report in front of the whole class. ◆ **Antonyms: bold, confident**

selfish *adjective* **greedy, self-centered, stingy, ungenerous, inconsiderate, egotistical, self-serving** I was selfish and took the last piece of pie. ◆ **Antonyms: generous, unselfish**

sell *verb* **1. deal in, market, peddle, trade, retail, carry, handle, offer, merchandise** This bookstore sells both new and used books. **2. surrender, give away, deliver, provide, betray, exchange** The POW refused to sell information for better food. ➨ **Antonyms: 1. buy, purchase**

send *verb* **1. mail, post, dispatch, forward, transmit, ship, transfer, route** I sent a picture of my family to my pen pal. **2. direct, refer, point, show, guide, lead, transfer, conduct, turn over** I was sent to the reference librarian because the clerk couldn't answer my question. **3. emit, give off, project, emanate, radiate, give forth, discharge** His facial expression sends the message that he is angry. ➨ **Antonyms: 1. get, receive**

senior *adjective* **1. older, oldest, first-born, elderly, elder, old, aged, advanced** In some societies, the senior son is the one who inherits all property. **2. chief, higher, leading, major, superior, top, major, ranking** My aunt is a senior buyer at an aerospace firm. ◆ *noun* **1. elder, ancient, matriarch, patriarch, senior citizen, oldster, old-timer, veteran** In most societies it is common to seek out and respect the opinions of the seniors. **2. better, superior, elder, master, chief, boss, supervisor, leader** The army lieutenant was constantly trying to impress his seniors. ➨ **Antonyms:** *adjective* **1. junior, younger 2. inferior, lower** ◆ *noun* **2. inferior, subordinate**

sensation *noun* **1. feeling, perception, impression, sense, sentiment, response, reaction** Déjà vu is the sensation of having already experienced something before. **2. stir, commotion, uproar, furor, scandal, excitement, surprise, wonder** The new swing band caused a sensation at their opening concert.

sensational *adjective* **1. shocking, lurid, dramatic, scandalous, melodramatic, vulgar, histrionic, startling** I like to read the sensational magazines at the hairdresser's while I get my hair cut. **2. extraordinary, outstanding, spectacular, superb, terrific, wonderful, fabulous** The special effects in that movie were absolutely sensational. ➨ **Antonyms: boring, dull, ordinary**

sense *noun* **1. faculty, function, capability, capacity, power, ability, aptitude** An Alsatian dog has a sense of smell that is about one million times stronger than a human's. **2. sensation, feeling, perception, realization, impression, suspicion, apprehension** Sometimes I have the sense that my grandmother's spirit is close to me. **3. understanding, appreciation, consciousness, awareness, receptivity, responsiveness, discernment** John Muir had a sense of the great beauty of California's Sierra Nevada. **4. common sense, judgment, wisdom, prudence, logic, intelligence,** reason, rationality Her good sense was welcome in our discussion. **5. meaning, import, message, significance, intent, connotation, value** Many English words have more than one sense. ◆ *verb* **detect, feel, perceive, recognize, see, think, apprehend, notice, discern** I sense that you are anxious to leave.

sensible *adjective* **intelligent, logical, prudent, reasonable, thoughtful, wise, sharp, sound** It is sensible to warm up before you exercise. ➨ **Antonyms: foolish, senseless, stupid**

sensitive *adjective* **1. perceptive, receptive, conscious, aware, sympathetic, understanding, feeling** A teacher needs to be sensitive to the needs of his or her students. **2. emotional, temperamental, touchy, testy, huffy, indignant, impatient, petulant** Sometimes I get very sensitive when I am criticized. **3. delicate, touchy, ticklish, tricky, discreet, tactful, difficult** Sex education is a sensitive subject for many people. ➨ **Antonyms: 1. indifferent, insensitive 2. indifferent, unemotional**

sentence *noun* **1. verdict, ruling, judgment, decision, decree, determination, edict, dictum** The judge will announce her sentence as soon as she has had a chance to review the evidence. **2. penalty, punishment, chastisement, condemnation, term, time, fine** The young man got off with a light sentence. ◆ *verb* **condemn, doom, convict, punish, penalize, fine, judge, jail** She was sentenced to 30 days in jail for shoplifting. ➨ **Antonyms:** *verb* **exonerate, pardon**

sentiment *noun* **1. opinion, belief, attitude, position, disposition, view, mind, leaning** The reporter took a poll on the sentiment of viewers regarding violence on TV. **2. feeling, emotion, affection, sentimentality, tenderness, passion, romance** Don't let your sentiments get in the way of doing the right thing.

sentry *noun* **guard, sentinel, lookout, picket, watch, ward, protector** The sentry will not admit cars that do not have proper identification.

separate *verb* **1. divide, part, split, detach, sever, cleave, tear, cut, sunder** To make vanilla pudding, you should separate the egg whites from the yolks. **2. isolate, segregate, sort, classify, class, categorize, group, order** I separated my library books from my school books. **3. distinguish, discern, differentiate, discriminate, know, tell** It is sometimes difficult to separate fact from fiction. **4. break up, divorce, part, leave, disunite, split up, part company** The married couple decided to separate. ◆ *adjective* **different, distinct, discrete, unique, particular, single,**

lone, individual, independent Put the light and dark laundry into separate piles. ➡ **Antonyms:** *verb* **1. & 2. blend, mix, join** ◆ *adjective* **same, similar**

sequence *noun* **1. order, arrangement, succession, organization, placement, distribution, spacing** The custodian checked the sequence of numbers before he set the alarm. **2. series, course, round, chain, procession, string, array, cycle, set** We are studying the sequence of events that led to the American Revolution.

serene *adjective* **1. placid, tranquil, cool, peaceful, untroubled, composed, calm, relaxed, easygoing** Carl has a serene personality. **2. unclouded, clear, fair, cloudless, idyllic, quiet, pleasant** We have been enjoying serene weather. ➡ **Antonyms: 1. agitated, disturbed 2. stormy, cloudy**

serial *adjective* **consecutive, sequential, continual, successive, succeeding, following, progressive** When car engines are manufactured, they are stamped with identification numbers in serial order.

series *noun* **course, cycle, run, sequence, set, succession, order, chain, string** The science channel is airing a series of shows on African wildlife.

serious *adjective* **1. grave, grim, sober, solemn, somber, sad, pensive, thoughtful** You look serious today—is there something wrong? **2. earnest, sincere, intent, decided, definite, resolute, determined, bound** Are you serious about not going to the party? **3. heavy, important, momentous, significant, weighty, profound, considerable** My friends and I often discuss serious topics. **4. alarming, bad, critical, dangerous, difficult, tough** Drug abuse is a serious problem. ➡ **Antonyms: 1. happy 2. indefinite, undecided 3. & 4. minor, trivial**

sermon *noun* **address, lecture, speech, talk, discourse, lesson, instruction, advice** The principal gave us a sermon on the value of a good education.

servant *noun* **domestic, retainer, attendant, helper, server, minion, drudge, employee** My great-grandmother was a servant in a wealthy household when she was young.

serve *verb* **1. aid, assist, attend, help, support, wait on, minister to, oblige, accommodate** The salesclerk was very polite when she served us. **2. deliver, give, offer, pass, provide, supply, provision, distribute** We served each guest a piece of cake. **3. act, function, labor, perform, toil, work, behave, enlist** Dad serves as a volunteer firefighter. **4. honor, revere, respect, venerate, obey, follow, heed,**

submit to The soldiers pledged to serve their country. **5. act, answer, operate, fulfill, suffice, do, satisfy, suit** Our spare bedroom serves as a storage area.

service *noun* **1. agency, bureau, department, office, branch, facility, arm, division** Some college students work for the Forest Service during the summer. **2. armed forces, military, air force, army, Marine Corps, navy, duty, active duty** My uncle is home on leave from the service for one week. **3. aid, assistance, attendance, help, support, attention, ministration** The sick man needed the services of a doctor. **4. maintenance, repair, overhaul, upkeep, servicing, installation, labor** We took our car in for routine service. ◆ *verb* **fix, repair, adjust, maintain, restore, readjust, tune up, inspect** We had our refrigerator serviced by a repairman.

servile *adjective* **slavish, submissive, groveling, humble, obsequious, meek, subservient, abject** In Dickens's novel *David Copperfield*, Uriah Heep is a servile clerk who tries to curry favor with his superiors. ➡ **Antonyms: proud, powerful**

session *noun* **meeting, gathering, assembly, conference, congress, council, huddle, discussion** The legislature met in a special session this week.

set¹ *verb* **1. lay, place, put, locate, rest, stick, position, situate** Please set the groceries on the counter. **2. fasten, lodge, cement, plant, mount, settle, anchor, install** I set the broken pieces of the plate with a special glue. **3. adjust, regulate, arrange, fix, order, prepare, coordinate, tune** I set my alarm to go off at 7 a.m. **4. establish, appoint, designate, allocate, schedule, delegate, arrange** We set a time at which to meet at the restaurant. **5. congeal, dry, harden, solidify, stiffen, thicken, clot, coagulate, firm** This glue will set in 15 minutes. **6. fall, lower, sink, wane, disappear, vanish, fade, ebb, die, recede** The moon rises in the east and sets in the west. **7. depart, embark, begin, commence, start, start out, undertake** The cruise ship set off on its voyage. ◆ *adjective* **1. established, fixed, customary, definite, habitual, regular, specific** I walk a set route to school everyday. **2. obstinate, stubborn, rigid, adamant, inflexible, unyielding, determined** He is set in his way of doing things. ➡ **Antonyms:** *verb* **2. unfasten, dislodge 6. rise 7. arrive, end** ◆ *adjective* **1. irregular, variable 2. flexible, adaptable**

set² *noun* **1. assortment, batch, collection, array, lot, bundle, pack, kit** Dad bought a set of metric wrenches to fix our car. **2. circle, coterie, crowd, clique, bunch, group, gang, band, party** I have made a new set of friends since transferring to this school.

settle *verb* **1. locate, move to, dwell, inhabit, live, reside, abide, colonize, establish** Many European immigrants settled in New York City in the 1880s. **2. calm, relieve, pacify, quiet, soothe, relax, lull, allay, still, sedate** This herbal tea will help settle your upset stomach. **3. alight, lower, set down, descend, drop, sink, rest, perch** The huge flock of crows settled in the trees for the night. **4. agree, arrange, choose, decide, fix, set, conclude, determine, find** We finally settled on a menu for our party. **5. reconcile, resolve, smooth over, negotiate, clear up, rectify** We were able to settle our dispute quickly.

sever *verb* **1. divide, separate, cut, rend, split, cleave, segment** The Spanish civil war in the 1930s severed the country. **2. dissociate, dissolve, divorce, abandon, break off, cease, terminate, quit** The dissidents severed themselves from the army and established a guerrilla group. ➡ **Antonyms: unite, join, combine**

several *adjective* **some, various, numerous, certain, divers, quite a few** The actor Tommy Lee Jones has been in several of my favorite movies.

severe *adjective* **1. harsh, strict, tough, hard, rigid, stern, demanding, exacting** At our school there is a severe penalty for cheating. **2. grim, austere, bleak, dour, stark, grave, serious, stern, earnest** I hope that this winter won't be as severe as the last one. **3. plain, spare, unadorned, austere, restrained, minimal, bare** I like the severe lines of this coat. **4. difficult, trying, arduous, oppressive, intense, rigorous, formidable** The refugees went through severe difficulties before reaching the United States. ➡ **Antonyms: 1. lenient, light 2. friendly, compassionate 3. baroque, fancy 4. easy, frivolous**

shabby *adjective* **1. worn-out, frayed, threadbare, tattered, scruffy, seedy, decrepit, rundown** My favorite pair of jeans is quite shabby. **2. despicable, mean, lousy, low, wretched, shameful, unkind, dishonorable** That was a shabby way to treat a good customer. ➡ **Antonyms: 1. new, pristine 2. admirable, kind**

shack *noun* **hut, shanty, shed, cabin, shelter, hovel, lean-to, cottage** We found an abandoned shack in the woods.

shade *noun* **1. shadow, umbra, darkness, gloom, murk, shadiness, cover, screen** My dog likes to lie in the shade of our big oak tree. **2. color, hue, tint, tone, tinge, cast, gradation, stain** The sunset turned the clouds different shades of pink and orange. ◆ *verb* **screen, shadow, shield, cover, veil, curtain, darken, protect** The honeysuckle shaded the gazebo in our back yard.

shadow *noun* **1. reflection, silhouette, umbra, penumbra, image, outline** Your shadow is shortest at noon. **2. darkness, dimness, gloom, murk, shade, dusk, twilight, murkiness** I can see my brother hiding in the shadows. **3. cloud, blot, stain, stigma, curse, blight, pall** The scandal cast a shadow on his good name. **4. hint, suspicion, breath, suggestion, touch, vestige, trace, intimation** There was a shadow of sadness in her voice. ◆ *verb* **follow, trail, hound, pursue, dog, watch, track, spy on** In the comedy *The Secret World of Henry Orient*, two teenage girls shadow their idol. ➡ **Antonyms:** *noun* **2. light, sunlight**

shady *adjective* **1. shaded, shadowy, dark, dim, dusky, murky, sheltered** Let's find a shady spot for our picnic. **2. questionable, suspect, disreputable, suspicious, illicit, dubious, dishonest, crooked** The scheme to sell land turned out to be shady. ➡ **Antonyms: 1. sunny, bright 2. honest, upright**

shaft *noun* **1. ray, beam, stream, streak, gleam, flash, flare, patch** A shaft of sunlight filtered through the leaves. **2. handle, shank, hilt, pole, rod, stem, trunk, staff, stick, column** The shaft of a spear is longer than that of an arrow. **3. tunnel, passage, passageway, tube, channel, hole, pit, chimney, conduit** The mine's main shaft was lined with large timbers.

shaggy *adjective* **hairy, fuzzy, woolly, rough, bushy, ruffled, disheveled, rumpled** Our Old English sheepdog has a shaggy coat. ➡ **Antonyms: smooth, sleek**

shake *verb* **1. jiggle, rattle, joggle, jog, waggle, jounce, wiggle, bounce, wag** She shook her tambourine in time to the music. **2. tremble, vibrate, rock, quake, churn, quiver, convulse, shudder** I watched the field of corn shake in the wind. **3. diminish, discourage, weaken, undermine, impair, reduce, unsettle** No one can shake my determination to join the rodeo when I grow up. **4. disturb, agitate, upset, appall, shock, horrify, consternate, unnerve, daunt** It shook me when the veterinarian said my dog might have cancer. ◆ *noun* **shaking, jar, jiggle, jolt, vibration, jog, jounce, bounce, twitch** I gave my sweater a shake to get the dog hair off.

shame *noun* **1. disgrace, embarrassment, humiliation, regret, sorrow, remorse, contrition, chagrin** The student was filled with shame when she was caught cheating. **2. pity, disappointment, misfortune, crime, scandal, sorrow, sadness** It is a shame that your injury kept you from playing in the last game of the season. ◆ *verb* **disgrace, dishonor, humiliate, discredit, embarrass, mortify, stain, degrade** The spy shamed his country by selling secrets to the enemy. ➡ **Antonyms:** *noun* **1. honor, pride** ◆ *verb* **honor**

shape *noun* 1. configuration, figure, form, outline, pattern, contour, profile, semblance We made Christmas cookies in the shape of snowmen, wreaths, and stars. 2. condition, health, state, trim, order, fitness, form, fettle My cat is still in good shape even though he's 17 years old. ◆ *verb* 1. fashion, form, mold, sculpt, model, contour, design, make Mom shaped the bread dough into a loaf. 2. define, determine, build, mold, influence, pattern, develop We are shaped by our environment as well as our genetic heritage.

share *noun* division, part, percentage, piece, portion, segment, fraction, lot, quota Each employee got a share of the profits. ◆ *verb* distribute, divide, split, partition, deal out, parcel, slice, ration The three friends shared their lunches.

sharp *adjective* 1. keen, sharp-edged, acute, sharpened, pointed, pointy, honed, edged Piranhas have teeth that are as sharp as a razor. 2. abrupt, rapid, steep, sudden, clear, distinct, blatant, striking The temperature took a sharp drop last night. 3. alert, bright, clever, intelligent, quick, smart, canny, shrewd It takes a sharp mind to complete this crossword puzzle. 4. cold, cutting, biting, stinging, nippy, fierce, keen, smart The wind was sharp, but we decided to go for a walk anyway. 5. caustic, bitter, harsh, severe, nasty, barbed, acerbic, trenchant The entire cast was upset over the director's sharp criticism of their rehearsal. 6. zesty, tangy, piquant, pungent, spicy, tart, lemony, vinegary, sour I like the taste of sharp cheese. 7. stylish, fashionable, dapper, dashing, spruce, debonair, chic, smart He has always been a sharp dresser. ◆ *adverb* exactly, precisely, promptly, punctually, accurately, just, right The train to Seattle will leave at 8 p.m. sharp. ➡ **Antonyms:** *adjective* 1. blunt, dull 2. gradual, slow 3. dull, slow 4. mild 6. bland 7. shabby, sloppy

sharpen *verb* make sharp, edge, hone, whet, file, grind, strop This saw needs to be sharpened. ➡ **Antonyms:** blunt, dull

shatter *verb* 1. break, burst, shiver, fragment, smash, disintegrate, splinter, crumble The car's windshield shattered in the accident. 2. demolish, destroy, finish, ruin, spoil, undo, topple, blast, devastate Last night's loss shattered our dream of winning the championship. ➡ **Antonyms:** 2. strengthen, fortify

shave *verb* 1. crop, shear, clip, trim, snip, barber, shorten, cut The athlete shaved his head in order to be more aerodynamic. 2. graze, brush, skim, touch, scrape, sideswipe, glance, sweep The crop-dusting plane shaved a treetop.

shear *verb* shave, trim, fleece, clip, cut, prune, pare, crop, mow, scythe Sheep are sheared at least once a year.

sheath *noun* wrapper, covering, jacket, casing, skin, container, case, receptacle Sausage is stuffed into an edible sheath.

shed[1] *verb* 1. cast off, drop, molt, discard, slough, remove, peel, scrap, eliminate I watched our pet snake shed its skin. 2. cast, emit, give, project, throw, radiate, release, spread, broadcast The sun sheds little warmth on cold winter days. 3. pour, discharge, spill, rain, drip, dribble, trickle, stream, cry The clouds shed a mixture of rain and snow. ➡ **Antonyms:** keep, retain

shed[2] *noun* hut, lean-to, shack, shanty, outbuilding, shelter, barn We keep the lawnmower in the tool shed.

sheer *adjective* 1. see-through, thin, translucent, transparent, gossamer, diaphanous, clear The sheer lace curtains let a lot of light into the room. 2. absolute, complete, pure, thorough, total, utter, downright, consummate My brother told me a story that was sheer nonsense. 3. abrupt, perpendicular, steep, vertical, precipitous, plumb The climbers scaled the cliff's sheer face. ➡ **Antonyms:** 1. coarse, thick 2. incomplete, partial 3. gradual

sheet *noun* layer, coating, covering, blanket, film, lamina, expanse, surface The streets were covered with a sheet of ice.

shell *noun* 1. carapace, covering, case, capsule, exterior, pod, shuck, husk The turtle withdrew its head into its shell. 2. frame, skeleton, framework, façade, exterior, hull, mold, chassis Only the building's shell was left standing after the earthquake. 3. casing, cartridge, bullet, shot, ammunition, projectile, bomb We found empty shotgun shells at the shooting range. ◆ *verb* 1. shuck, hull, husk, peel, strip, crack, open, remove We shelled the entire bowl of walnuts. 2. fire on, shoot at, bombard, rake, cannonade, bomb, strafe, besiege The American Civil War began on April 12, 1861, when Confederate artillery shelled Fort Sumter.

shelter *noun* 1. cover, protection, safety, security, refuge, haven, preservation The birds sought shelter when it began to rain. 2. asylum, haven, home, refuge, sanctuary, hospital, hospice, retreat Our veterinarian also runs a shelter for homeless cats and dogs. ◆ *verb* shield, cover, protect, screen, safeguard, preserve, harbor, house The man sheltered the accident victim from the rain with a blanket.

shepherd *verb* herd, guide, lead, steer, usher, conduct, guard, tend, supervise Our teacher shepherded us to the auditorium.

shield *noun* **cover, guard, safeguard, screen, protection, defense, bulwark** A power saw has a shield that is designed to protect the user from injury. ◆ *verb* **cover, guard, protect, screen, shelter, defend, safeguard, house** I used a newspaper to shield my head from the hot sun. ➧ **Antonyms:** *verb* **expose, uncover**

shift *verb* **1. move, maneuver, relocate, transfer, reposition, transplant, carry, transport** I shifted my book bag from one shoulder to the other. **2. alter, change, switch, vary, swerve, veer, reverse, turn, swing** The wind had shifted direction during the night. ◆ *noun* **1. alteration, change, changeover, move, switch, transfer, turnabout, reversal** I haven't gotten used to the shift from standard to daylight-saving time yet. **2. assignment, duty, tour, watch, period, stint, stretch, time** The night shift begins at midnight.

shimmer *verb* **flash, glimmer, glisten, glitter, sparkle, twinkle, glow, shine, gleam** The lights from the cruise ship shimmered on the dark water.

shine *verb* **1. beam, flash, glare, gleam, glow, blaze, radiate, flicker** Please shine the flashlight over here. **2. flourish, flower, excel, lead, star, outclass, eclipse, surpass, stand out** My sister shines in her math class. **3. buff, polish, burnish, gloss, furbish, rub, wax, glaze, scour** I need to shine my shoes. ◆ *noun* **luster, sheen, polish, gloss, burnish, gleam, glow, sparkle, radiance** My brother buffed his car until it had a bright shine.

ship *noun* **boat, vessel, watercraft, freighter, trawler, tanker, ocean liner, steamer** There were more than a dozen large ships in the harbor. ◆ *verb* **deliver, dispatch, forward, send, transport, move, convey, carry, mail** How much will it cost to ship this package overnight to New Orleans?

shirk *verb* **avoid, neglect, duck, dodge, shun, elude, sidestep** I tried to shirk cleaning my room. ➧ **Antonyms: confront, face**

shiver *verb* **shake, tremble, quake, quiver, shudder, vibrate, quail, pulsate** The skiers shivered from the cold as they waited for the ski lift. ◆ *noun* **shake, shudder, jitter, tremble, quake, quiver, thrill, twitch** The eerie story gave us the shivers.

shock *noun* **1. concussion, blast, jar, jolt, blow, impact, collision, crash, smash** When the atomic bomb was first tested, the shock caused nearby buildings to collapse. **2. blow, jolt, surprise, start, upset, trauma, distress, scare, bombshell** It was a shock to the family when

my aunt lost her job. ◆ *verb* **appall, dismay, stagger, startle, stun, surprise, offend, horrify, shake** Dad was shocked when he saw last month's phone bill.

Word Group

Shoes are outer coverings for the human foot. **Shoe** is a general term with no true synonyms. Here are some common types of shoes:

athletic shoe, brogan, brogue, clod-hopper, clog, flats, gym shoe, high heels, Loafers, mule, oxford, patent leather, pumps, running shoe, sabot, sandal, tennis shoe, wingtip, work shoe

shoot *verb* **1. gun down, pick off, blast, shell, rake, hit, kill, wound** The police officers threatened to shoot the suspect if he didn't stop. **2. discharge, loose, fire, launch, let fly, propel, hurl, project** I shot an arrow into the air. **3. bolt, dart, dash, flash, rocket, run, rush, hurry, scoot** A rabbit shot out of the sagebrush when we rode by on our dirt bikes. ◆ *noun* **bud, sprout, runner, stem, sucker, tendril, growth, twig, branch** The daffodils sent up new shoots through the spring snow.

shop *noun* **store, boutique, department store, outlet, market, showroom, emporium, stand** This mall has over a hundred different shops. ◆ *verb* **browse, go shopping, look, seek, buy, purchase, procure, window-shop** My friend and I like to shop for clothes together.

shore[1] *noun* **beach, coast, seacoast, seaside, seashore, waterfront, strand, seaboard** My brothers and I built a sandcastle at the shore.

shore[2] *verb* **prop, brace, buttress, support, reinforce, strengthen, bolster** We shored up the sagging fence. ➧ **Antonyms: weaken, topple, tumble**

short *adjective* **1. diminutive, little, slight, small, tiny, wee, low, petite, compact** My little sister is too short to ride this roller coaster. **2. brief, concise, terse, succinct, laconic, hurried, fast, swift** Our teacher gave us a short talk about the importance of being on time. **3. shy, under, deficient, inadequate, lacking, insufficient, scarce, meager** Our profits from the fundraiser were a little short of our goal. **4. curt, abrupt, rude, brusque, gruff, testy, uncivil, discourteous, impatient** I gave him a short answer because I was impatient to leave. ◆ *adverb* **abruptly, instantly, suddenly, quickly, unexpectedly, immediately** The hikers stopped short when they came to the edge of a cliff. ➧ **Antonyms:** *adjective* **1. long, tall 2. lengthy, long 3. ample, sufficient 4. polite, civil** ◆ *adverb* **gradually, slowly**

shortage *noun* deficit, lack, scarcity, shortfall, paucity, dearth, insufficiency, deficiency There are so many players on my soccer team that we have a shortage of game jerseys. ➤ **Antonyms:** excess, surplus

shortcoming *noun* drawback, fault, flaw, imperfection, defect, weakness, inadequacy, failing My friend's forgetfulness is her only real shortcoming. ➤ **Antonyms:** strength, virtue

shorten *verb* decrease, reduce, trim, abridge, abbreviate, condense, cut, contract I shortened the straps on my overalls. ➤ **Antonyms:** extend, increase, lengthen

shortly *adverb* soon, promptly, anon, directly, quickly, immediately, forthwith, momentarily The plane will leave shortly. ➤ **Antonyms:** later, eventually

shot *noun* 1. discharge, report, blast, gunshot, gunfire, shooting We heard a rifle shot off in the distance. 2. try, attempt, chance, effort, stab, turn, whirl, crack, fling I would like to have a shot at being a movie extra. 3. ball, slug, bullets, buckshot, shells, cartridges, ammunition He made a new batch of shot for his muzzleloading rifle.

shoulder *noun* edge, margin, rim, side, bank, ledge, shelf, verge Dad pulled onto the shoulder of the road to check his map. ◆ *verb* 1. assume, take on, accept, carry, bear, endure, undertake, sustain My older sister shouldered the responsibility for me when our mother died. 2. push, force, jostle, elbow, press, thrust, shove, ram We shouldered our way through the underbrush.

shout *noun* call, cry, scream, yell, howl, roar, whoop, bellow, exclamation When I heard my friend's shout, I went outside to see what he wanted. ◆ *verb* bellow, cry out, scream, yell, howl, roar, holler, bawl I had to shout in order to be heard over the blaring music. ➤ **Antonyms:** mumble, whisper

shove *verb* move, push, nudge, press, thrust, impel, drive, propel, shoulder We shoved our desks into a circle. ◆ *noun* nudge, push, thrust, boost, prod, propulsion, bump I gave my model boat a shove, and it floated across the pool.

shovel *verb* scoop, spoon, ladle, lade, spade, bail, remove, dig, excavate Will you shovel the ashes from the fireplace?

show *verb* 1. display, exhibit, present, expose, unveil, reveal, uncover, bare The scientist showed us a fossil and told us how it was formed. 2. indicate, reveal, designate, express, register, read, record, mark A speedometer shows how fast a vehicle is moving. 3. conduct, direct, escort, guide, lead, steer, usher, accompany, shepherd A docent showed us through President Nixon's boyhood home. 4. teach, instruct, inform, demonstrate, explain, tell, describe My friend showed me how to use his camcorder. ◆ *noun* 1. display, exhibition, exhibit, exposition, demonstration, pageant, fair We entered our border collie in the local dog show. 2. act, pretense, appearance, illusion, semblance, guise, pose, façade I gave a show of calmness in order to reassure my little brother. 3. performance, production, program, drama, entertainment, spectacle, pageant, carnival The school talent show was a big success. ➤ **Antonyms:** *verb* 1. cover, screen, hide

shower *noun* 1. rain, drizzle, sprinkle, downpour, cloudburst, flurry Scattered showers are forecast for tomorrow. 2. deluge, surge, torrent, flood, inundation, profusion, plethora, wealth There was a shower of petals from our cherry tree. ◆ *verb* 1. sprinkle, splash, spray, spatter, rain, spit, pour, drizzle My dog showered me with water when he shook himself. 2. lavish, flood, deluge, inundate, overwhelm, heap, bombard I was showered with gifts on my birthday.

shred *noun* 1. piece, scrap, strip, tatter, bit, fragment, ribbon, band, particle We tore the newspapers into shreds for our papier-mâché project. 2. bit, iota, jot, ounce, whit, dab, mite, grain, smidgen, speck He didn't have a single shred of evidence to support his accusation. ◆ *verb* cut up, rip up, tear up, grate, slice, dice, slit, shave, sliver I shredded some cabbage for the coleslaw.

shrewd *adjective* clever, intelligent, keen, sharp, smart, wise, cunning, astute, canny I made a shrewd guess and got the answer right. ➤ **Antonyms:** foolish, stupid

shriek *noun* cry, scream, screech, shout, squeal, yell, yelp, holler I let out a shriek when I saw the snake. ◆ *verb* cry out, scream, screech, shout, squeal, yell, squawk, wail, holler Lots of people began shrieking when the rock band came onstage.

shrill *adjective* piercing, high, high-pitched, earsplitting, deafening, sharp, treble, piping The factory whistle let out a shrill blast. ➤ **Antonyms:** low, bass, gentle

shrine *noun* memorial, sanctuary, tomb, grave, mausoleum, altar, temple We made a pilgrimage to the shrine of Santiago de Compostela in Spain.

shrink *verb* 1. constrict, shrivel, contract, compact, compress, reduce, dwindle, wither Many plastics shrink when they are heated. **2. retreat, withdraw, cower, cringe, recoil, draw back, flinch, quail** The child shrank back from the barking dog. ➤ **Antonyms: 1. expand, increase 2. confront, face**

shrivel *verb* **dry up, wilt, wither, fade, droop, flag, shrink, wrinkle, dehydrate** The rose petals shriveled after they fell to the ground.

shroud *noun* **cover, screen, cloak, veil, sheet, covering, mantle, blanket, jacket** The stone cottage was covered with a shroud of ivy. ◆ *verb* **conceal, screen, cloak, hide, block, cover** Fog shrouded our view of the ocean. ➤ **Antonyms:** *verb* **reveal, expose, unveil**

shrubbery *noun* **shrubs, bushes, brush, underbrush, undergrowth, hedge, hedgerow, thicket, greenery** The tall shrubbery with its bright red berries provided food for the birds during the winter.

shudder *verb* **quake, quiver, shake, shiver, tremble, convulse, twitch** We all shuddered as we listened to the scary ghost story. ◆ *noun* **convulsion, quiver, shiver, tremble, tremor, twitch, jerk, spasm** I gave a shudder when I saw the spider.

shuffle *verb* **1. hobble, limp, drag, scuff, shamble** The injured player shuffled off the field. **2. jumble, mix up, scramble, disorder, rearrange, confuse, intermix, interchange** The teacher shuffled the papers on his desk. ◆ *noun* **hobble, limp, toddle, shamble** I walked with a shuffle when I twisted my ankle. ➤ **Antonyms:** *verb* **2. arrange, order, organize**

shun *verb* **avoid, duck, dodge, evade, elude, eschew, ignore, snub, scorn** Our cat shuns the neighbor's dog.

shut *verb* **1. close, fasten, secure, latch, lock, seal, catch, bolt, slam** Please shut the window. **2. cage, confine, coop up, enclose, pen, imprison, corral, impound** I shut the horses in the corral. ➤ **Antonyms: 1. open, unlock 2. free, release**

shy *adjective* **1. bashful, meek, modest, reserved, timid, coy, sheepish, retiring** The teacher's praise made me feel shy. **2. cautious, watchful, wary, distrustful, chary, fearful, nervous, skittish** Our new kitten is shy around big cats. **3. deficient, lacking, missing, short, under, wanting, inadequate, insufficient** Our soccer team is shy one player. ◆ *verb* **cringe, flinch, quail, blench, jerk, recoil, shrink, start, jump** The horse shied when Ivy reached out to pet it. ➤ **Antonyms:** *adjective* **1. bold, confident 2. trustful, fearless 3. over**

sick *adjective* **1. ill, sickly, unhealthy, unwell, nauseated, queasy, down, weak** The greasy onion rings made me sick. **2. morbid, unwholesome, grisly, macabre, sadistic, gross, bad, immoral** The violence in the movie was very sick. **3. weary, tired, fed up, displeased, revolted, bored, disgusted, jaded** I am sick of his constant complaining. ➤ **Antonyms: 1. healthy, well 2. wholesome, good**

sickening *adjective* **revolting, disgusting, foul, repulsive, noxious, offensive, nauseating, loathsome** Where is that sickening smell coming from? ➤ **Antonyms: healthful, invigorating**

sickness *noun* **illness, indisposition, debility, infirmity, affliction, disease, disorder, malady** Mom took care of me during my sickness. ➤ **Antonyms: health, vitality, vigor**

side *noun* **1. face, surface, hand, part, plane, flank, top, bottom** I turned the letter over and read what was on the other side. **2. edge, end, border, boundary, margin, rim, perimeter, bound** The teams lined up on opposite sides of the field. **3. squad, team, group, party, faction, staff, unit, crew, sect** Which side do you think will win the game? **4. aspect, facet, angle, position, version, view, viewpoint, opinion** The judge listened to both sides before she made up her mind. ◆ *adjective* **secondary, incidental, accessory, auxiliary, minor, subordinate, subsidiary** When we visited Rome, we took a side trip to Siena. ➤ **Antonyms:** *adjective* **primary, principal, main**

sift *verb* **1. filter, strain, winnow, sieve, screen, separate, sort, pan** The cook sifted the flour into the cake batter. **2. look, probe, examine, scrutinize, search, study, evaluate, inspect** The archaeologists carefully sifted through the ruins of the ancient city.

sigh *verb* **1. moan, groan, murmur, whistle, whisper, whine, gasp, hiss** I sighed when I looked at my long list of homework assignments. **2. pine, long for, crave, thirst, hunger, mourn, ache, yearn** The pioneer woman sighed for her comfortable home back east. ◆ *noun* **moan, groan, murmur, whisper, whine, sob, hiss** I gave a sigh of relief when all my homework was finally done.

sight *noun* **1. eyesight, seeing, vision, eye, perception, ken** A hawk's sight is very keen. **2. view, glance, glimpse, look, regard, perspective, scrutiny, gaze** I lost sight of the hot-air balloon as it floated over the ridge. **3. scene, view, spectacle, display, vista, panorama, outlook, picture, image** Our magnolia tree is a beautiful sight when it is in full bloom. **4. fright, mess, eyesore, monstrosity, disaster, spectacle, curiosity** I looked a sight after being caught in the sudden rainstorm. ◆ *verb* **behold,**

glimpse, observe, perceive, see, spot, view, identify, look The soldiers sighted an enemy plane approaching.

sign *noun* **1.** expression, gesture, mark, signal, symbol, token, indication The teacher raised her hand as a sign for the class to be quiet. **2.** announcement, bulletin, notice, poster, billboard, placard, signboard The sign said that the store was open. **3.** evidence, hint, indication, trace, clue, manifestation, symptom The space probe will look for signs of life on Mars. **4.** herald, harbinger, warning, forewarning, forerunner, omen, portent The season's first robins are a sign of spring. ◆ *verb* **1.** endorse, inscribe, autograph, initial, countersign, subscribe, undersign We all signed our teacher's birthday card. **2.** gesture, wave, flag, signal, beckon, motion, indicate The flagman signed for us to move forward.

signal *noun* cue, sign, indication, gesture, beacon, mark, indicator, warning The firing of a gun is the signal for the race to begin. ◆ *adjective* extraordinary, notable, distinguished, outstanding, striking, remarkable, illustrious, memorable She was given a plaque commemorating her signal achievement. ◆ *verb* wave, motion, gesture, flag, beckon, sign, indicate, nod, wink I signaled to my brother to follow me. ● **Antonyms:** *adjective* ordinary, unremarkable

significance *noun* **1.** consequence, importance, meaning, weight, value, relevance, influence This test is of great significance to my grade. **2.** meaning, sense, idea, point, gist, drift, purport, message, import What is the significance of that pink ribbon you're wearing?

significant *adjective* **1.** meaningful, suggestive, expressive, pregnant, informative, deep, telling My friend gave me a significant glance. **2.** big, consequential, historic, important, monumental, notable, crucial, meaningful My family's move to the country was a significant event in my life. ● **Antonyms: 1.** meaningless, ambiguous **2.** insignificant, unimportant

signify *verb* **1.** mean, represent, suggest, indicate, import, insinuate, portend, connote Those dark clouds signify that it will rain soon. **2.** express, communicate, announce, reveal, say, declare, convey, tell He signified that the workshop would be over soon.

silence *noun* **1.** hush, quiet, quietness, stillness, calm, peace, lull, still, quietude There was silence in the house when everybody was off to either school or work. **2.** speechlessness, dumbness, muteness, reticence, reserve, taciturnity I interpret your silence to mean that you disagree with me. ◆ *verb* **1.** hush, shush, still, calm, quiet, soothe, shut up, deaden The mother silenced her crying baby by rocking it gently. **2.** censor, quell, crush, subdue, muzzle, stifle, suppress, muffle An open and free society does not silence its press. ● **Antonyms:** *noun* **1.** noise, sound **2.** talkativeness, conversation ◆ *verb* **1.** rouse, agitate **2.** support, encourage

silent *adjective* **1.** noiseless, quiet, soundless, still, hushed, calm, peaceful I enjoy the desert because the nights are clear and silent. **2.** mute, speechless, voiceless, dumb, mum, inarticulate, uncommunicative I was silent in the presence of such magnificent natural beauty. **3.** implied, undeclared, unexpressed, unsaid, unspoken, tacit, understood, wordless My brother and I have a silent agreement not to tell on each other. ● **Antonyms: 1.** loud, noisy **2.** talkative, garrulous, vocal **3.** declared, spoken

silly *adjective* **1.** stupid, foolish, dumb, witless, brainless, senseless, thoughtless It was silly to forget my grocery list. **2.** playful, flighty, comical, crazy, frivolous, ridiculous, clownish, immature We were in a silly mood and ordered dessert for breakfast. ● **Antonyms: 1.** intelligent, wise, sensible **2.** mature, serious

similar *adjective* close, comparable, equivalent, like, identical, corresponding, matching My friends and I have similar tastes in clothes and movies. ● **Antonyms:** different, dissimilar

simmer *verb* cook, heat, warm, stew, boil, bubble, seethe The spaghetti sauce has to simmer for another hour.

simple *adjective* **1.** easy, effortless, uncomplicated, basic, elementary, straightforward, manageable I finished the simple homework assignment in 20 minutes. **2.** plain, modest, unadorned, spare, bare, commonplace, ordinary We ate a simple meal of bread, fruit, and cheese. **3.** artless, innocent, naive, natural, open, guileless, unpretentious, sincere She has a simple manner that is pleasing to others. **4.** idiotic, moronic, stupid, dense, silly, slow, slow-witted, simple-minded I was so embarrassed that I gave a simple answer. **5.** humble, lowly, mean, poor, low, modest Many famous people come from simple backgrounds. ● **Antonyms: 1.** complicated, difficult, hard **2.** fancy, ornate **3.** artful, deceitful **4.** intelligent, sharp **5.** wealthy

simplify *verb* cut down, facilitate, make easy, reduce, shorten, streamline, abridge Using a microwave oven has helped to simplify our cooking.

simulate *verb* **1.** imitate, mimic, copy, duplicate, replicate, reproduce, ape I have a computer game that simulates being in the cockpit of an airplane. **2. fake, feign, counterfeit, fabricate, pretend, affect, assume, act, pose** Dogs will sometimes simulate an injury in order to get attention.

simultaneous *adjective* **synchronous, concurrent, coinciding, coexistent, contemporary, attendant** I listened to the simultaneous radio and TV broadcast.

sin *noun* **evil, misdeed, offense, trespass, violation, wrong, vice, wickedness, crime** Many religions consider lying and stealing to be sins. ◆ *verb* **err, trespass, stray, transgress, offend, fall, lapse, misbehave** He sinned by not returning the wallet to its rightful owner. ● **Antonyms:** *noun* **virtue, good deed**

sincere *adjective* **earnest, genuine, heartfelt, honest, real, true, trustworthy** My brother's apology seemed to be sincere. ● **Antonyms: fake, false, insincere**

Word Group

To **sing** is to utter words or sounds in musical tones. **Sing** is a general terms with no true synonyms. Here are some different ways in which to sing:

carol, chant, chirrup, croon, drone, hum, intone, serenade, trill, vocalize, warble, yodel

single *adjective* **1. alone, solitary, lone, solo, companionless, unaccompanied, lonesome** I saw a single wolf out hunting for food. **2. individual, sole, separate, only, discrete, one, particular, singular** She ordered a single scoop of ice cream. **3. unmarried, unwed, unattached, spouseless, maiden, footloose** I have two uncles who are single. ● **Antonyms: 1. accompanied, attended 3. wed, married**

singular *adjective* **individual, unique, separate, rare, uncommon, particular, unmatched** He has a singular way of speaking. ● **Antonyms: common, typical**

sinister *adjective* **threatening, evil, menacing, nasty, malevolent, ominous, dire, baleful, malign** I like to read mystery novels that have sinister settings. ● **Antonyms: benevolent, benign**

sink *verb* **1. go down, go under, submerge, founder, submerse, settle** We rowed for shore when our boat began to sink. **2. descend, dip, fall, lower, plunge, decline, set, collapse** The pavement began to sink because of a large cavity beneath the road. **3. worsen, deteriorate, decline, degenerate, disintegrate, die, fade, dwindle**

The country's economic situation continued to sink. **4. bore, drill, dig, ram, plunge, plant, drive, penetrate, thrust** The farmer sank the well to a depth of 220 feet. ◆ *noun* **basin, washbasin, washbowl, washstand, lavatory, bowl** Daniel washed the vegetables in the kitchen sink. ● **Antonyms:** *verb* **2. rise, ascend 3. improve, better**

sip *verb* **swallow, drink, imbibe, quaff, sup** We slowly sipped our iced tea and enjoyed our visit. ◆ *noun* **drink, swallow, draft, sup, pull, nip, drop, dram** I took a sip of water.

sit *verb* **1. be seated, sit down, settle, perch, roost, squat** You may sit wherever you like. **2. be located, be situated, lie, occupy, reside, stand, rest** The farm sits on 90 acres of rich farmland. **3. meet, convene, congregate, assemble, gather, deliberate** The assizes court sits periodically in the counties of England.

site *noun* **area, location, place, position, spot, point, setting, locale** We picked a level site on which to set up the tent.

situate *verb* **place, set, position, install, locate, plant, post, establish** We decided to situate the vegetable garden in the sunniest place in the yard.

situation *noun* **1. placement, position, location, place, site, spot, locale** The lookout tower has an excellent situation on top of the mountain. **2. circumstances, status, place, condition, position, state, predicament** I am in a fortunate financial situation at present. **3. job, appointment, position, office, employment, profession, post** She checked the newspaper listings for available situations.

size *noun* **1. dimension, extent, measurement, proportions, volume, area, mass** A stegosaurus had a brain that was about the size of a walnut. **2. enormity, vastness, magnitude, amplitude, scope, extent, dimensions** He was concerned when he realized the true size of the problem.

skeleton *noun* **1. bones, remains, carcass, body, corpse, cadaver** I once found the skeleton of a sheep. **2. framework, frame, shell, structure, support, scaffolding, chassis** After the German airship *Hindenburg* burned in 1937, only its skeleton remained.

skeptic *noun* **doubter, nonbeliever, unbeliever, cynic, rationalist, questioner, freethinker** Carl Sagan, the astronomer and cosmologist, was a skeptic. ● **Antonyms: believer, adherent, follower**

sketch *noun* **1. drawing, picture, illustration, portrait, diagram, cartoon, likeness, figure** I made a pencil sketch of the blooming cherry tree. **2. outline, note, brief, summary,**

abstract, synopsis, draft, composition I wrote a rough sketch of my English essay and handed it in to my teacher. **3. vignette, skit, act, scene, play, story, burlesque, satire, lampoon** I enjoyed the comedy sketches on the TV program. ◆ *verb* **depict, draw, portray, diagram, outline, trace, draft, represent** In art class, we sketch both people and objects.

skid *verb* **slip, slide, glide, skim, coast, skate, skitter** The car skidded on a patch of ice.

skill *noun* **1. adroitness, dexterity, skillfulness, facility, competence, proficiency, artistry** I admire her skill in working with such small beads. **2. art, craft, technique, methods, trade, principles, strategy** Our Scout leader is teaching us some outdoor survival skills. **3. talent, aptitude, ability, capability, knack, flair, faculty, prowess** I have developed my typing skills.

skillful *adjective* **adept, capable, competent, expert, good, masterful, skilled, proficient, adroit** The cellist's skillful performance was a great pleasure to experience. ◗ **Antonyms: clumsy, incapable, unskilled**

skim *verb* **1. scrape, ladle, spoon, scoop, sweep** I used a spoon to skim the cream from the top of my glass of whole milk. **2. glide, coast, sail, float, skate, scud, skid, skitter, fly, shoot** We watched the skaters skim across the ice. **3. browse, glance, scan, leaf through, thumb through, read** I skimmed through the history book and highlighted the main ideas. ◗ **Antonyms: 3. scrutinize, peruse**

skin *noun* **1. hide, pelt, coat, fur, epidermis, integument, membrane, slough** Beavers were almost exterminated because of the fad for hats made of their skins. **2. peel, rind, husk, hull, shell, crust, veneer, covering, sheath** The skins of some fruits, such as apples, pears, and apricots, are edible. ◆ *verb* **peel, strip, pare, scrape, shuck, flay, husk, scale, uncover** I skinned the bark from the willow branch.

skinny *adjective* **gaunt, lean, slender, slim, thin, bony, scrawny, lanky, spare** My grandmother is always feeding me because she thinks that I'm too skinny. ◗ **Antonyms: fat, plump, stout**

skip *verb* **1. bounce, bound, gambol, hop, jump, leap, spring, frisk, prance** I was so happy that I skipped all the way home from school. **2. skim, ricochet, skitter, skid, glance, graze, carom, scoot, flip** I threw a stone, and it skipped across the water. **3. bolt, sprint, flee, fly, get away, run away, split, escape** I skipped out of the house before my little sister could ask to go with me. **4. leave out, omit,**

drop, overlook, ignore, disregard, neglect, cut, miss The movie version skipped my favorite part that was in the book. ◆ *noun* **bounce, spring, bound, hop, leap, jump, caper, prance** The little girl walked down the street with a skip in her step. ◗ **Antonyms:** *verb* **3. lag, stay, remain 4. include, contain**

skirmish *noun* **dispute, scuffle, tussle, battle, fight, conflict, clash, argument** There was a brief skirmish in the hall after school, but the principal broke it up. ◆ *verb* **fight, clash, scuffle, tussle, struggle, contend, scrap, combat** My brother and I skirmish over our favorite spot on the sofa.

skirt *noun* **1. miniskirt, dirndl, kilt, frock** My school uniform consists of a blue sweater and a plaid skirt. **2. border, edge, fringe, margin, rim, limit, verge, periphery, outskirts** The skirt of the king's coronation robe was trimmed with ermine. ◆ *verb* **1. border, flank, fringe, edge, hem, rim, bound, surround** Woods skirt our school on the north side. **2. bypass, go around, circumvent, detour, avoid, dodge, evade, duck** This freeway skirts the city to avoid the downtown traffic. ◗ **Antonyms:** *verb* **2. embrace, confront, meet**

skulk *verb* **sneak, steal, pussyfoot, slink, prowl, creep, slip, lurk** The cat skulked down the alley.

sky *noun* **atmosphere, firmament, heavens, air, blue, celestial sphere** The sky looks especially blue in October.

slab *noun* **panel, block, chunk, hunk, board, plank, slice, plate, bar** The pastry chef uses a large slab of marble on which to roll out dough.

slack *adjective* **1. limp, loose, relaxed, flexible, soft, flaccid, pliant, flabby** My muscles felt slack after a few minutes in the hot tub. **2. down, off, slow, sluggish, idle, dormant, quiet** During the winter, business is slack at the tourist resort. **3. careless, negligent, heedless, lax, remiss, neglectful, derelict, delinquent** He is a good salesperson, but he is slack in keeping track of his expenses. ◆ *noun* **give, play, excess, stretch, leeway, room, latitude, looseness** The slack in the line caused the clothes to sag. ◗ **Antonyms:** *adjective* **1. rigid, tense, tight 2. active, busy 3. strict, attentive** ◆ *noun* **tightness, tension**

slacken *verb* **1. moderate, reduce, lessen, ease off, slow, delay, retard, brake** The yellow light led the driver to slacken her speed. **2. relax, loosen, subside, weaken, relent, let up, release, free, abate** The pressure at school started to slacken a bit as summer vacation neared. ◗ **Antonyms: 1. hasten, quicken 2. tighten, increase**

slam *verb* bang, dash, smack, smash, crash, close, shut, clap, push *A gust of wind slammed the door shut.* ◆ *noun* bang, crash, smack, smash, whack, wham, blow *I dropped a book, and it hit the floor with a slam.*

slander *noun* libel, defamation, aspersion, calumny, scandal, lie, deprecation *The movie star sued the tabloid for slander.* ◆ *verb* deprecate, defame, malign, revile, disparage, vilify, smear, slur *The political opponents slandered each other throughout the campaign.* ➡ **Antonyms:** *noun* praise, eulogy, applause ◆ *verb* praise, laud, extol

slant *verb* **1.** incline, lean, pitch, slope, tilt, tip, list, skew, cant, rake *The telephone pole slants to one side ever since someone backed into it.* **2.** bias, skew, color, distort, angle, prejudice, twist, warp *That reporter tends to slant the news toward a liberal perspective.* ◆ *noun* **1.** incline, pitch, slope, tilt, list, cant, rake, grade, rise *There is a slant in the ceiling of my attic bedroom.* **2.** bias, standpoint, opinion, attitude, outlook, view, angle, leaning *There was a conservative slant to the magazine article.*

slap *noun* **1.** blow, clap, hit, smack, swat, wallop, pat, whack, thwack *The prospector gave his mule a slap on the rump to get it to move.* **2.** insult, rebuff, reprimand, rebuke, criticism, snub, injury *His remark was a slap to my dignity.* ◆ *verb* hit, smack, strike, swat, wallop, pat, spank, paddle *My baby niece slaps the water when she takes a bath.*

slash *verb* **1.** cut, hack, chop, slice, carve, gash, sever, cleave *The explorers slashed at the thick undergrowth with their machetes.* **2.** decrease, drop, lower, mark down, pare, reduce, diminish, prune *After the holidays, stores usually slash prices on leftover Christmas decorations.* ◆ *noun* **1.** cut, gash, incision, slice, slit, rip, split, tear, cleft *The doctor stitched up the slash on my hand.* **2.** cut, decrease, drop, markdown, reduction, lowering *The store's latest price slash has attracted lots of new customers.* ➡ **Antonyms:** *verb* **2.** increase, raise

slate *noun* ballot, ticket, roster, roll, list, lineup, register, catalog *The slate of candidates was selected at the political convention.* ◆ *verb* program, schedule, set, fix, plan, book, arrange, designate *Our club outing is slated for next Saturday.*

slaughter *noun* massacre, murder, butchery, annihilation, bloodshed, carnage, genocide, pogrom *A coyote was responsible for the slaughter of the sheep.* ◆ *verb* massacre, kill, slay, exterminate, murder, annihilate, decimate, butcher *A dog got into the chicken house and slaughtered our chickens.*

slave *noun* **1.** helot, vassal, serf, bondservant, bondman, bondwoman *Ancient Rome once had almost 21 million slaves at a time when the free population was less than 7 million.* **2.** drudge, hack, workhorse, menial, servant, peon, laborer, worker *My uncle says he is just a slave at his office.* ◆ *verb* toil, drudge, work, labor, travail, sweat, grind, plod, moil *I slaved to get my homework done in time to go to the football game.*

slavery *noun* enslavement, bondage, captivity, serfdom, subjugation, vassalage, indenture *The Thirteenth Amendment abolished slavery in the United States.*

slay *verb* kill, exterminate, slaughter, assassinate, execute, murder, dispatch, butcher *This movie is about a knight who slays dragons.*

sleek *adjective* gleaming, glossy, lustrous, shiny, silky, smooth, silken, satiny *The seal's fur was sleek and smooth when it came out of the water.* ➡ **Antonyms:** coarse, dull, rough

sleep *noun* slumber, nap, rest, snooze, siesta, hibernation, repose, catnap *We spend about one third of our lives in sleep.* ◆ *verb* slumber, doze, drowse, nap, rest, snooze, hibernate *I like to sleep late on Saturday mornings.*

sleepy *adjective* **1.** tired, drowsy, somnolent, soporific, weary, exhausted, nodding *My busy day outdoors had made me sleepy.* **2.** quiet, dull, inactive, lazy, languid, sluggish, indolent, torpid *I spent a sleepy evening relaxing at home.* ➡ **Antonyms: 1.** alert, wakeful **2.** active, energetic, lively

slender *adjective* **1.** bony, lean, skinny, slim, spare, thin, lanky, willowy *Deer have slender legs.* **2.** remote, slight, slim, faint, outside, negligible, meager, tenuous, poor *There is a slender chance that I may be able to join you for the weekend.* ➡ **Antonyms: 1.** stout, thick **2.** strong, considerable, good

slice *noun* **1.** slab, chunk, piece, wedge, portion, section, segment, rasher *Our toaster can hold four slices of bread at a time.* **2.** share, percentage, cut, lot, allotment, part, allowance, quota *A slice of the company's profits is donated to charity.* ◆ *verb* carve, cut, split, divide, section, segment, separate, sunder *She sliced her birthday cake and served it to her guests.*

slick *adjective* **1.** slippery, smooth, waxy, glassy, oily, greasy, soapy, icy *The ice on the sidewalk is very slick.* **2.** adroit, skillful, deft, facile, dexterous, nimble, handy, clever *The juggler gave a slick performance.* **3.** shrewd, crafty, cagey, wily, smart, artful, canny, sophisticated The slick promoter was able to get many people to sign up for his service. ➥ **Antonyms: 1. coarse, rough 2. clumsy, awkward 3. naive, innocent**

slide *verb* **1. coast, glide, skid, skim, shoot, glissade, slip, drift, skitter** The hockey puck slid across the ice. **2. creep, slink, slip, ease, skulk, sneak, lurk, steal, pussyfoot** A fox slid into the chicken house unnoticed. **3. fall, drop, dip, plummet, slump, decline, sag, tumble** The stock market slid to a new low. ◆ *noun* **avalanche, landslide, mudslide, rockslide** The road was closed because it was blocked by a slide.

slight *adjective* **1. faint, insignificant, minor, small, trivial, unimportant, paltry, negligible** There is only a slight difference between these two colors. **2. skinny, slender, slim, thin, gaunt, delicate, frail, petite, spare** My older brother is so slight that he can fit into my clothes. ◆ *verb* **1. snub, spurn, affront, insult, offend, disdain, reject, scorn** I didn't mean to slight her, but I forgot to return her call. **2. neglect, shirk, disregard, ignore, forget, skip** I slighted my homework over the weekend. ◆ *noun* **affront, insult, snub, offense, slur, cut, rebuff, indignity** She forgave him the slight when he apologized. ➥ **Antonyms:** *adjective* **1. considerable, great 2. large, solid** ◆ *verb* **1. acclaim, praise 2. attend, heed** ◆ *noun* **compliment, praise, tribute**

slim *adjective* **1. lean, slender, thin, skinny, slight, spare, narrow, twiggy** I feel slim since I began exercising. **2. faint, negligible, scant, remote, outside, slight, modest, poor, tenuous** There is a slim chance that I will get my homework done in time. ◆ *verb* **reduce, trim, trim down, narrow, taper, diet** I definitely have slimmed down since I began exercising regularly. ➥ **Antonyms:** *adjective* **1. fat, thick 2. substantial, great** ◆ *verb* **fatten, swell**

slime *noun* **ooze, muck, goo, mud, mire, gunk, sludge, slop** Slugs and snails leave a trail of slime behind them.

sling *verb* **cast, fling, heave, hurl, pitch, throw, toss, chuck, catapult** How far can you sling a rock?

slip[1] *verb* **1. glide, move, pass, slide, steal, slither, slink, creep, prowl** The wolf slipped silently through the trees. **2. slide, stumble, trip, fall, tumble, skid** I slipped on the icy steps. **3. err, blunder, miscalculate, misjudge, fluff, slip up, trip up** I slipped and called my teacher "Mom." **4. decline, decrease, lapse, sink, vanish, drop, fall, sag** My attention began to slip as I grew tired. ◆ *noun* **1. fall, trip, tumble, stumble, skid, slide, plunge, drop** I've been careful walking on ice ever since I took a nasty slip. **2. blunder,**

slip-up, oversight, error, lapse, mistake, goof, misstep Calling my teacher by the wrong name was just a minor slip.

slip[2] *noun* **certificate, note, page, paper, sheet, document, tag, ticket** Mom signed my permission slip so that I could go on the field trip.

slippery *adjective* **1. smooth, slick, soapy, icy, greasy, glassy, oily** I dropped the piece of slippery soap. **2. tricky, deceitful, crafty, wily, elusive, evasive, duplicitous, untrustworthy** The salesman was slippery and did not tell us everything we needed to know. ➥ **Antonyms: 1. coarse, dry, rough 2. straightforward, trustworthy**

slit *noun* **aperture, hole, opening, slot, cut, split, slash, fissure, cleft** Castle walls commonly had slits through which archers could shoot at enemy soldiers. ◆ *verb* **cut, slash, slice, split, carve, rip, sunder, cleave, sever** The clerk slit the cardboard box open.

slither *verb* **writhe, wiggle, slip, glide, slide, snake, slink, twist, undulate** The kitten slithered out of my arms.

slogan *noun* **motto, saying, expression, phrase, jingle, catchword, byword, watchword** The company printed its slogan on all of its stationery.

slope *verb* **angle, incline, slant, lean, list, tip, tilt, pitch, cant** The park slopes down to the river. ◆ *noun* **1. inclination, slant, pitch, cant, gradient, lean, list, tilt, tip** The slope of this roof is very steep. **2. descent, grade, hill, downgrade, upgrade, incline, rise, ramp, bank** In the winter, we go sledding on a slope near our house.

sloppy *adjective* **1. disorderly, messy, slovenly, untidy, frowzy, unkempt, disheveled** He is a sloppy dresser. **2. careless, slapdash, slipshod, poor, substandard, remiss, second-rate** His lack of interest in the experiment resulted in sloppy work. ➥ **Antonyms: 1. neat, orderly, tidy 2. careful, meticulous**

sloth *noun* **laziness, languor, inertia, indolence, idleness, sluggishness, lethargy** I couldn't get going and was a model of sloth the entire weekend. ➥ **Antonyms: industry, exertion**

slouch *verb* **slump, hunch, bend, droop, stoop, loll, wilt, flop** Don't slouch when you sit up to the dinner table. ◆ *noun* **slump, stoop, droop, sag, hunch, crouch** She walks with a slouch.

slow *adjective* **1. gradual, moderate, plodding, sluggish, unhurried, slow-going, leisurely** The tortoise made slow progress across the sand. **2. stagnant, slack, soft, down, off, dormant, static, sluggish, inactive** Business was slow after the holidays. **3. obtuse, dense, thick, dumb, unintelligent, dim-witted, dull, simple** I felt slow because I didn't understand the joke. **4. unexciting, dull, uninteresting, boring, tedious, ponderous, tiresome** The book got off to a slow start. ◆ *verb* **decrease, moderate, reduce, slacken, brake, check, choke, rein in** The rider slowed her horse's pace from a trot to a walk. ◈ **Antonyms:** *adjective* **1. fast, rapid 2. active 3. intelligent, bright, smart 4. interesting, exciting** ◆ *verb* **accelerate**

sluggish *adjective* **lethargic, listless, slow, idle, inactive, lazy, torpid, languid** Reptiles are sluggish in cold weather. ◈ **Antonyms: active, frisky, lively**

slumber *verb* **sleep, doze, drowse, nap, snooze, rest** My cat likes to slumber on the windowsill. ◆ *noun* **sleep, snooze, doze, nap, rest, dormancy, coma** I fell into a deep slumber that lasted all night long.

slump *verb* **1. slouch, lean, droop, bend, sink, hunch, loll, hump** The sleeping man slumped forward in his chair. **2. deteriorate, plummet, plunge, sink, crash, dive, drop, collapse** Demand for the company's product slumped. ◆ *noun* **decline, dive, plunge, dip, drop, downturn, recession** A slump in the market caused the company to cancel its plans for expansion.

sly *adjective* **1. clever, crafty, cunning, shrewd, sneaky, tricky, wily, foxy** He managed to accomplish his goal in such a sly way that no one was offended. **2. furtive, sneaky, secretive, surreptitious, veiled, covert, evasive, artful** Debbie gave us a sly hint that her birthday was coming up. ◈ **Antonyms: 1. innocent, naive 2. direct, open, straightforward**

smack[1] *verb* **hit, slam, slap, strike, swat, punch, cuff, whack, buffet** I smacked the mosquito that had landed on my arm. ◆ *noun* **blow, hit, slam, thump, slap, strike, swat, tap, plunk, whack** The carpenter gave the nail a hard smack with his hammer.

smack[2] *verb* **suggest, smell, taste, indicate, reveal, embody, evince, manifest** That remark smacks of regret.

small *adjective* **1. little, miniature, puny, tiny, wee, minute, petite, diminutive** *Compsognathus* was a small dinosaur no bigger than a chicken. **2. limited, meager, scant, scanty, slight, paltry, insufficient, inadequate** There is only a small amount of feed left in the bird feeder. **3. insignificant, minor, petty, trifling, trivial, unimportant, negligible** I have a small part in the school play.

4. narrow, narrow-minded, petty, mean, bigoted, intolerant, illiberal Some of her opinions are surprisingly small. ◈ **Antonyms: 1. big, large 2. adequate, sufficient 3. major, significant 4. tolerant, broad-minded**

smart *adjective* **1. bright, brilliant, intelligent, quick, sharp, clever, keen** My friend is so smart that she can do long division in her head. **2. flippant, impertinent, cheeky, rude, impudent, sassy, nervy, saucy** He gave a smart answer that made us all laugh. **3. quick, fast, energetic, brisk, spry, lively, active, nimble** The horse kept up a smart pace. **4. fashionable, elegant, spruce, chic, trim, dapper, debonair, natty, stylish** He makes sure he looks smart before going to work. ◆ *verb* **ache, hurt, sting, throb, burn, itch, prickle, bite** Does that bee sting still smart? ◈ **Antonyms:** *adjective* **1. dumb, stupid 2. polite, civil 3. slow, weak 4. shabby, dowdy**

smash *verb* **1. break, crush, disintegrate, pulverize, pound, mash, shatter** I stepped on one of my brother's toy cars and smashed it. **2. slam, crash, bash, strike, hit, knock, collide, pound** One car smashed into another on the freeway. **3. annihilate, destroy, ruin, defeat, wreck, decimate, trash, demolish** Our offensive drive smashed the other team's defense. ◆ *noun* **1. blow, crash, clash, slam, bang, shock, impact** We heard the smash of breaking glass as the ball came through the window. **2. success, sensation, triumph, winner, hit, wow** Our school musical was a smash.

smear *verb* **1. apply, daub, layer, spread, coat, cover, rub, streak, smudge** I smeared sunscreen on my face and hands. **2. defame, sully, slander, slur, denigrate, vilify, taint, tarnish, blacken** The magazine article smeared a famous TV star. ◆ *noun* **blot, blotch, smudge, spot, stain, streak, smirch, splotch** There is a smear of jam on your cheek.

smell *verb* **1. scent, sniff, whiff, snuff, nose, sense, detect, perceive** We could smell bread baking in the oven. **2. stink, reek, smell bad, smell awful** Rotten eggs really smell. ◆ *noun* **1. aroma, fragrance, scent, whiff, perfume, bouquet** I love the smell of lilacs in the springtime. **2. stink, stench, reek, odor, fetidness, malodorousness** There was a strong smell coming from the garbage can.

smile *noun* **grin, simper, smirk** My Aunt Miriam has a lovely smile. ◆ *verb* **beam, shine, favor, encourage, aid, support, assist, grin** Fortune seems to be smiling on you. ◈ **Antonym: frown**

smirk *verb* **grin, simper, sneer, leer, smile, grimace** He just smirked at me when I said I could beat him at tennis. ◆ *noun* **grin, simper, sneer, leer, smile, grimace** Her self-satisfied smirk irritated me.

smooth *adjective* **1. even, flat, level, plane, straight, regular, flush, unbroken** Pool tables have smooth playing surfaces. **2. tranquil, calm, untroubled, peaceful, serene, gentle** The surface of the lake becomes smooth when the wind dies down. **3. flattering, ingratiating, diplomatic, glib, facile, urbane, suave** He talked in a smooth manner. **4. easy, effortless, simple, orderly, uneventful, graceful, untroubled** The veteran pilot brought the plane in for a smooth landing. ◆ *verb* **1. even, flatten, level, straighten, press, iron, plane** Please smooth the tablecloth before you set out the dishes. **2. calm, mollify, alleviate, tranquilize, soothe, assuage, appease, mitigate** She smoothed the committee's ruffled feelings with her calm words. ●**Antonyms:** *adjective* **1. rough, uneven 2. agitated 3. awkward 4. difficult, hard** ◆ *verb* **2. agitate, irritate, provoke**

smother *verb* **1. extinguish, snuff, stifle, suffocate, choke, strangle, asphyxiate** Small kitchen fires can be smothered with flour or a frying pan lid. **2. muffle, suppress, repress, hide, conceal, mask, disguise, veil** I tried to smother my giggles when my little sister said something funny in church.

smudge *verb* **blur, mess up, rub, smear, soil, spot, stain, dirty, blot** I smudged the lines of my pencil drawing to give it a soft look. ◆ *noun* **blot, blotch, smear, spot, stain, streak, smirch, mark** I wiped the dirt smudge off my face.

smug *adjective* **cocky, conceited, pompous, superior, self-satisfied, self-important, self-righteous** He deserved to win, but his smug attitude is irritating. ●**Antonyms: modest, sheepish, self-effacing**

snack *noun* **bite, morsel, refreshment, light meal, lunch, meal, repast** Let's stop and get a snack before we go home. ◆ *verb* **nibble, munch, feed, eat, consume, dine** We snacked on popcorn while watching the movie.

snag *noun* **1. projection, stump, knob, protuberance, overhang, knot, knurl** I caught my fishing line on a snag in the middle of the creek. **2. obstacle, hindrance, impediment, difficulty, barrier, block, drawback, catch** We ran into a snag when we tried to schedule our holiday party. ◆ *verb* **catch, hook, rip, tear, rend, grab, fasten** I snagged my shirt on a barbed-wire fence.

snake *noun* **1. serpent, reptile, viper, constrictor, asp, adder** The snake wriggled through the grass. **2. traitor, serpent, evildoer, double-crosser, turncoat, rascal, knave** The spy was a snake who betrayed his partner and sold secrets to the enemy.

snap *verb* **1. break, crack, fracture, splinter, split, crackle, pop** The twig snapped when I stepped on it. **2. break down, collapse, sunder, give way, fail, disintegrate, fracture** Mom's temper snapped, and she sent us all to our rooms. **3. snatch, strike, lunge, grasp, seize, catch, nip, bite, gnash, eat** My parrot snapped at the lettuce leaf that I put in its cage. ◆ *noun* **1. crack, crackle, pop, click, clack, bark, bang, explosion** We could hear the snap of the logs as they started to burn. **2. clasp, catch, fastener, clip** Dan's Western shirt has mother-of-pearl snaps. ◆ *adjective* **abrupt, hasty, quick, sudden, spontaneous, impromptu, offhand** I try to avoid making snap decisions.

snare *noun* **trap, net, noose, ruse, trick, subterfuge, deception** The false message was a snare for the enemy troops. ◆ *verb* **ensnare, capture, catch, trap, seize, entrap** In our outdoor survival class, we learned how to snare small animals.

snarl[1] *verb* **growl, grumble, bark, snap, thunder, bluster, rumble** Sometimes my grandfather snarls when he is not feeling well. ◆ *noun* **growl, bark, snap, rumble, grumble, bluster, threat** The sudden snarl of the big dog frightened me.

snarl[2] *noun* **1. tangle, maze, labyrinth, web, jungle, ravel, knot, kink** The countryside was a snarl of cow paths, animal trails, and narrow dirt roads. **2. confusion, mess, muddle, morass, chaos, complication, predicament** The accident created a huge traffic snarl. ◆ *verb* **tangle, complicate, confuse, scramble, mess up, muddle, disorder** The pilots' strike snarled air traffic all across the nation.

snatch *verb* **grab, pluck, seize, snap, take, catch, nip, wrest, clutch** I snatched an apple from the bowl as I ran out the door. ◆ *noun* **1. grab, clutch, grasp, catch, seizure, pounce, reach, lunge** The basketball player made a successful snatch for the ball. **2. bit, fragment, part, piece, portion, segment, snippet, spell** The woman caught brief snatches of the TV news as she made dinner.

sneak *verb* **1. crawl, creep, slink, slither, skulk, lurk, prowl, slip, glide** The cat sneaked up on a bird that had come to our feeder. **2. slip, smuggle, spirit, steal, run** Mom will sneak Dad's birthday presents into the house while we distract him. ◆ *noun* **weasel, rogue, rascal, scoundrel, knave, coward** I trusted her, but she turned out to be a sneak.

sneer *noun* **grimace, grin, smirk, leer, scoff** I did not like the sneer on her face. ◆ *verb* **scoff, snicker, jeer, mock, taunt, deride, belittle, scorn** He sneered when I told him about my bargain.

snide *adjective* sarcastic, disparaging, cruel, nasty, mean, malicious, hateful, scornful I don't like to listen to snide remarks. ➡ **Antonyms:** friendly, complimentary, sincere

snip *verb* clip, cut, trim, remove, pare, prune, shear, lop, nip I snipped some pictures out of the magazine.

Word Group

Snow refers to crystals of ice that form in the atmosphere and fall to earth. **Snow** is a general term with no true synonyms. English has more than two dozen words for snow in various forms. Here are some of them:

Corn snow is snow that has melted and refrozen into granular pellets. **Firn** is granular, partially consolidated snow on a glacier. **Graupel** is snow in the form of pellets that break apart when they hit the ground. **Hail** is precipitation in the form of pellets of hard snow and ice. **Powder** is light, dry snow. **Sastruga** are wavelike ridges of snow formed by the wind. **Slush** is partially melted snow or ice.

---

snub *verb* avoid, ignore, shun, spurn, rebuff, insult, offend, slight, disdain My cat snubbed me for days after I left him alone for the weekend. ◆ *noun* insult, offense, slight, spurn, rebuff, discourtesy, cut It was an unintentional snub when I forgot to respond to my friend's party invitation.

snug *adjective* 1. comfortable, cozy, safe, secure, sheltered, private, homey The cabin was warm and snug during the storm. 2. confining, small, tight, skintight, cramped, close, compact, narrow I gave my favorite coat to my sister because it is too snug for me. ➡ **Antonyms:** 1. uncomfortable, exposed 2. loose

snuggle *verb* cuddle, curl up, nestle, nuzzle, embrace, hug, caress, enfold I like to snuggle inside with a blanket and a book when it snows.

soak *verb* 1. immerse, steep, marinate, sop, drench, wet, saturate, souse, wash These beans have to soak in water overnight. 2. absorb, sop up, take up, dry, mop, imbue, take in, drink I soaked up the spilled milk with a towel.

soar *verb* 1. coast, float, fly, glide, sail, wing, hover, lift A hot-air balloon soared high above us. 2. climb, increase, lift, mount, multiply, rise, ascend, grow The company's profits soared as their product became popular. ➡ **Antonyms:** 2. fall, descend

sob *verb* bawl, cry, wail, weep, blubber, whimper, yowl, lament, keen The baby sobbed because it was tired. ◆ *noun* sobbing, crying, weeping, blubbering, bawling, wail, whimper, yowl, tears There were sobs from the audience during the sad movie.

sober *adjective* 1. grave, grim, sad, serious, solemn, somber, mournful We were all in a sober mood after we heard the bad news. 2. dignified, proper, staid, prim, quiet, correct, sedate, serious He has a sober personality but a good sense of humor. 3. reasonable, practical, pragmatic, objective, realistic, matter-of-fact The lawyer gave us sober advice as to how to proceed in the matter. ➡ **Antonyms:** 1. lighthearted, carefree 2. frivolous, undignified 3. subjective, unrealistic

sociable *adjective* gregarious, cordial, friendly, genial, neighborly, social, hospitable, affable, social Our sociable neighbor is always coming over for a visit. ➡ **Antonyms:** unfriendly, unsociable

social *adjective* 1. communal, societal, community, collective, public, group, popular The quality of public education is an important social issue. 2. amiable, cordial, friendly, outgoing, sociable, neighborly, convivial Mom says my wide range of friends shows that I am a social person. ➡ **Antonyms:** 1. individual 2. unfriendly, cold

society *noun* 1. civilization, community, humanity, people, public, commonwealth, folk The criminal was sent to prison because he was a threat to society. 2. association, club, group, organization, order, league, union, alliance, federation My cousin and I joined a bird-watching society. 3. gentry, gentility, aristocracy, elite, upper class, nobility, plutocracy I like to read stories about high society in Regency England. 4. fellowship, comradeship, company, companionship, amity, friendship, intimacy I am lucky to have the society of many good friends.

sodden *adjective* drenched, saturated, soaked, dripping, wet, soggy, soppy I was sodden from being caught in the rain on my way home from school. ➡ **Antonyms:** dry, dehydrated

soft *adjective* 1. mushy, pulpy, spongy, fleshy, squishy, squashy, yielding These apples have gotten too soft to eat. 2. delicate, fine, fluffy, smooth, satiny, silky, velvety, downy My pet guinea pig has soft fur. 3. hushed, low, mellow, quiet, subdued, gentle, mild Dad uses a soft voice when he's reading my little brother to sleep. 4. mild, gentle, light, faint, slight, fair, balmy, clement We enjoyed the soft breeze coming off the ocean. 5. sympathetic, affectionate, tender, compassionate, tenderhearted, sensitive, kind

Mom says that my grandfather didn't always have a soft heart. **6. lenient, permissive, liberal, indulgent, forgiving, lax, tolerant** I wish my parents had softer rules. ⬦ **Antonyms: 1. firm, hard 2. rough, stiff 3. harsh, loud 4. inclement 5. hardhearted, insensitive 6. strict**

soggy *adjective* **sodden, saturated, soaked, sopping, wet, dripping, drenched** The cardboard box was soggy after having been left outside in the rain. ⬦ **Antonyms: dry, hard**

soil[1] *noun* **dirt, earth, humus, loam, ground, clay, dust, topsoil, land** We mixed fertilizer with the soil when we planted our garden.

soil[2] *verb* **1. dirty, muddy, smear, smudge, stain, foul, splotch, begrime** We soiled our soccer uniforms when we played on the muddy field. **2. tarnish, disgrace, discredit, contaminate, corrupt, sully, damage, blacken, taint** Cheating on a test can soil your reputation. ⬦ **Antonyms: 1. clean, wash 2. honor, glorify**

solace *noun* **comfort, peace, relief, condolence, consolation, encouragement, support, help** My father offered me solace, and I felt better. ◆ *verb* **comfort, calm, console, cheer, ease, alleviate, soothe** I tried to solace my friend when she was upset. ⬦ **Antonyms:** *noun* **burden, anxiety, worry** ◆ *verb* **depress, sadden**

soldier *noun* **1. combatant, fighter, infantryman, warrior, serviceman, servicewoman, recruit** There were hundreds of soldiers involved in the battle. **2. follower, activist, campaigner, adherent, loyalist, warhorse, partisan** We were soldiers in the campaign to save waterways for migratory birds.

sole *adjective* **lone, one, only, single, solitary, exclusive, unique, particular** My sole excuse for being late was that my alarm clock didn't go off.

solemn *adjective* **1. grave, grim, serious, sober, somber, gloomy, funereal, earnest** Everybody at the funeral had solemn expressions on their faces. **2. majestic, impressive, sobering, grand, momentous, ceremonious** The inauguration of the President of the United States is a solemn occasion. ⬦ **Antonyms: 1. happy, jolly 2. frivolous**

solicit *verb* **beg, ask, entreat, appeal, importune, supplicate, sue, beseech, plead** The telephone caller was soliciting for donations to a charitable cause.

solid *adjective* **1. substantial, dense, firm, compact, hard, strong, sturdy, durable, rugged** The building may

be old, but it has solid walls. **2. complete, entire, whole, pure, real, genuine, unmixed** Some of the candies were made of solid chocolate, while others had cream fillings. **3. continual, constant, continuous, unbroken, uninterrupted, steady, undivided** There was a solid line of traffic all the way to the airport. **4. dependable, secure, sound, stable, steady, steadfast, stalwart, reliable** My best friend and I have a solid friendship. ⬦ **Antonyms: 1. flimsy 2. hollow, impure 3. broken, interrupted 4. unsteady, shaky**

solitary *adjective* **1. lone, lonely, alone, individual, solo, single, companionless** We passed a solitary runner beside the canal. **2. secluded, remote, lonely, desolate, isolated, uninhabited** The desert is a solitary place. ⬦ **Antonyms: 1. social, accompanied 2. busy, popular**

solution *noun* **1. mixture, blend, compound, brew, infusion, emulsion** We cleaned the carpet with a special solution designed to remove stains. **2. answer, explanation, key, interpretation, result, revelation, determination, clarification** Lawrence guessed the solution to my riddle.

solve *verb* **answer, figure out, resolve, work out, explain, analyze, unravel, decipher** I finally solved the tough math problem.

somber *adjective* **dismal, grim, melancholy, sad, sober, solemn, gloomy, joyless** We were in a somber mood after hearing about the accident.

some *adjective* **a few, several, various, divers, numerous, sundry** I had some grapes with my lunch.

sometimes *adverb* **at times, now and then, occasionally, periodically, sporadically, irregularly, intermittently** I usually walk to school, but sometimes I ride my bike. ⬦ **Antonyms: always, never**

song *noun* **ballad, hymn, ditty, chant, melody, tune, anthem, carol, lilt, lullaby** We sang songs around the campfire.

soon *adverb* **before long, directly, promptly, quickly, rapidly, shortly, anon, presently** If we don't get there soon, they might be sold out.

soothe *verb* **1. quiet, calm, settle, tranquilize, lull, relax, solace, console, pacify** When my dog is upset, I soothe him by scratching behind his ears. **2. ease, relax, relieve, allay, mitigate, mollify, reduce, assuage** The long, hot bath soothed the stiffness in my tired muscles. ⬦ **Antonyms: 1. irritate, upset 2. exacerbate, aggravate**

sophisticated *adjective* **1. worldly, experienced, cosmopolitan, worldly-wise, knowledgeable, seasoned, urbane** My uncle is a sophisticated world traveler who speaks several languages. **2. complex, elaborate, intricate, involved, complicated, advanced** I had trouble learning the sophisticated computer program. ➡ **Antonyms: 1. naive, inexperienced 2. simple, easy, obvious**

sore *adjective* **1. aching, hurting, painful, sensitive, tender, achy** My sprained wrist is still sore. **2. great, serious, desperate, extreme, critical, grave, profound, urgent** Our class has a sore need for additional textbooks. **3. angry, offended, mad, upset, affronted, hurt, indignant, miffed** I am sore at not being included. ◆ *noun* **hurt, inflammation, injury, wound, infection, ulcer** I got sores on my feet from my new shoes.

sorrow *noun* **1. anguish, distress, grief, heartache, sadness, unhappiness, despair** Elephants feel great sorrow when one of their herd dies or is injured. **2. misfortune, trouble, loss, tribulation, adversity, calamity, setback, shock** It was a time of sorrow when our apartment house burned down. ◆ *verb* **grieve, despair, mourn, lament, weep, brood, cry, agonize, sob** The whole town sorrowed when one of their police officers died in the line of duty. ➡ **Antonyms:** *noun* **1. gladness, happiness 2. blessing, benefit, boon**

sorry *adjective* **1. apologetic, contrite, regretful, sad, sorrowful, penitent, repentant, remorseful** I am sorry that I forgot your birthday. **2. inferior, pitiful, poor, disappointing, worthless, ridiculous, petty, cheap** The double chocolate cupcakes I made turned out to be a sorry mess. **3. grievous, sad, distressing, wretched, bad, terrible, miserable, depressing** War is a sorry business. ➡ **Antonyms: 1. pleased 2. decent, fine 3. good, pleasant**

sort *noun* **1. kind, manner, type, variety, brand, style, category, classification** We tried all sorts of different foods at the state fair. **2. character, nature, quality, description, strain, breed, disposition, stripe** What sort is he? ◆ *verb* **arrange, categorize, classify, group, organize, order, separate, grade** We sorted the items for our community rummage sale.

soul *noun* **1. spirit, psyche, vital force, life force** Most religions teach that the soul lives on after death. **2. person, individual, human, mortal, man, woman, creature, being, body** He is known as a generous soul. **3. center, core, heart, basis, root, essence, quintessence, foundation** From the day she became librarian, she was the soul of our town library.

sound[1] *noun* **1. noise, clamor, din, racket, tone, ringing, reverberation, loudness** Do you hear that strange sound? **2. import, implication, meaning, drift, tone, tenor, impression, effect** From the sound of your report, I gather you enjoyed the book ◆ *verb* **1. chime, peal, ring, toll, resound, boom** The cook sounded the dinner bell. **2. appear, look, look like, seem, feel, sound like, strike one as** It sounds as if you had a good day at school.

sound[2] *adjective* **1. solid, strong, sturdy, undamaged, firm, intact, good, whole** The old barn is still sound. **2. healthy, fit, hale, hearty, well, hardy, robust, wholesome** The doctor told me that I have a sound constitution. **3. secure, reliable, stable, solid, safe, sure, solvent, trustworthy** The company has a sound financial base. **4. good, logical, prudent, reasonable, sensible, wise, levelheaded, intelligent** My older sister gave me some sound advice about school. **5. thorough, complete, thoroughgoing, vigorous, strenuous, severe, utter** The boxer gave his opponent a sound thrashing. **6. deep, unbroken, intense, profound, undisturbed** I felt better after getting a night of sound sleep. ➡ **Antonyms: 1. damaged, defective 2. unhealthy, ailing 3. unreliable, shaky 4. senseless, silly 5. partial, ineffectual 6. restless, broken**

sour *adjective* **1. acidic, bitter, tangy, tart, sharp, acrid, lemony, piquant** The sour candy made my mouth water. **2. spoiled, rancid, bad, curdled, fermented, harsh, unpleasant** Sour milk has a disgusting smell. **3. cross, peevish, bad-tempered, crabby, grouchy, surly, irritable** I was in a sour mood. ◆ *verb* **curdle, go bad, spoil, ferment, acidify, turn** Milk will sour if it is not refrigerated. ➡ **Antonyms:** *adjective* **1. mild, sweet 2. fresh**

source *noun* **1. beginning, head, origin, start, wellspring, headwaters, fount** The Colorado River has its source in the Rocky Mountains. **2. resource, reference, authority, basis, fountain, supply, reserve, reservoir** An encyclopedia is a good source for facts about many things and places.

souvenir *noun* **memento, keepsake, gift, reminder, token, trophy, relic** My friend brought me a souvenir from his trip to South Carolina.

sovereign *noun* **monarch, emperor, king, queen, tsar, ruler, majesty** The United States has never had a sovereign. ◆ *adjective* **1. free, independent, self-governing, autonomous, self-ruling** Mozambique became a sovereign nation in 1975. **2. absolute, imperial, supreme, governing** The emperor exercised his sovereign power when he declared a national holiday.

space *noun* **1. gap, opening, separation, break, crack, hole, chasm, fissure** I'm wearing braces to close the spaces between my teeth. **2. area, expanse, room, distance, volume, extent, range, width** Our new piano takes up a lot of space in the living room. **3. period, duration, time, season, stretch, term, spell, while** I am going skiing in the space between Christmas and New Year's. ◆ *verb* **arrange, array, place, set, separate, order, organize, range** The trees had been spaced far enough apart to give them room to grow.

span *noun* **duration, interval, length, period, range, term, breadth, extent, scope** A sequoia tree's life span can be several thousand years. ◆ *verb* **bridge, cover, cross, stretch over, traverse, arch, reach** The fallen telephone pole spanned the width of the road.

spar *verb* **banter, bandy, debate, match wits, wrangle, haggle, bicker, squabble** The two comedians sparred with each other, trading witticisms.

spare *verb* **1. save, exempt, reprieve, pardon, rescue, liberate, let off, acquit** We spared the mouse's life by using a no-kill trap. **2. part with, donate, let go, give, lend, afford, grant, yield, surrender** Can you spare a few sheets of paper? ◆ *adjective* **1. additional, extra, reserve, substitute, surplus, superfluous, excess** We have a spare bedroom for overnight guests. **2. meager, sparse, skimpy, frugal, scanty, minimal, stingy, poor** I ate a spare meal before the race. **3. gaunt, lean, skinny, slender, slim, thin, rangy, scrawny** Greyhound dogs have a spare build. ◆ *noun* **substitute, replacement, alternate, duplicate, extra, leftover** You may use this flashlight because I have a spare. ➡ **Antonyms:** *verb* **1. condemn, doom** ◆ *adjective* **2. abundant, plentiful 3. large, stocky, plump**

spark *noun* **1. flash, flare, ray, burst, pulse, glimmer, gleam, shimmer** The car battery shot off sparks of electricity when I attached the cable to it. **2. seed, embryo, force, impulse, stimulus, inspiration, spur, incitement** The spark of curiosity has led to many experiments and important discoveries. ◆ *verb* **activate, stimulate, incite, provoke, generate, fire, cause, inspire** The home run sparked a rally that led to extra innings.

sparkle *verb* **gleam, glitter, twinkle, flash, glimmer, shimmer, scintillate, dazzle** The new-fallen snow sparkled in the moonlight. ◆ *noun* **1. gleam, glitter, twinkle, flash, flicker, glimmer, shine, scintillation** The diamond earrings gave off sparkles of light. **2. radiance, glow, brilliance, liveliness, vivacity, animation, life** Your eyes are full of sparkle.

spasm *noun* **contraction, twitch, tic, cramp, convulsion, seizure, fit, knot** A muscle spasm can be painful.

spasmodic *adjective* **fitful, periodic, intermittent, irregular, occasional, erratic, changeable** Our family has reunions on a spasmodic basis. ➡ **Antonyms: regular, continuous**

speak *verb* **1. declare, express, say, state, tell, utter, voice, vocalize** The witness swore that he spoke the truth. **2. talk, chat, converse, communicate, chatter, discourse, rap** We were just speaking about you, and suddenly here you are. **3. lecture, address, orate, preach, sermonize, declaim, descant, expound** We heard a physics professor from the university speak about chaos theory.

spear *noun* **lance, javelin, pike, trident, assegai, harpoon, spike** Roman soldiers frequently carried spears into battle. ◆ *verb* **jab, stab, stick, impale, gore, thrust, pierce, lance, harpoon** He speared a piece of chicken with his fork.

special *adjective* **1. exceptional, rare, extraordinary, remarkable, unique, different, peculiar** The appearance of a white buffalo calf is of special importance to some groups of Native Americans. **2. particular, specific, unique, definite, express, distinctive, individual** Crystals are of special importance to radio and related fields. ➡ **Antonyms: common, ordinary**

specialty *noun* **forte, specialization, feature, strength, accomplishment, strong point, skill, talent** My brother's cooking specialty is popcorn.

species *noun* **category, classification, kind, sort, type, variety, breed, description** There are about 750 thousand known species of insects.

specific *adjective* **clear, definite, exact, explicit, particular, precise, express, clear-cut** The teacher gave us specific directions for the science project. ➡ **Antonyms: general, ambiguous, vague**

specify *verb* **designate, indicate, state, particularize, name, cite, stipulate, list** I specified my first and second choices.

specimen *noun* **example, sample, model, representative, type, piece, exhibit** He has several dozen specimens in his rock collection.

speck *noun* **bit, grain, particle, fleck, mote, speckle, spot, dot, drop** The wind blew a speck of dirt into my eye.

spectacle *noun* **1. display, exhibition, performance, presentation, show, sight, scene, event** The laser light show was a fascinating spectacle. **2. laughingstock, fool, jackass, dupe, joke, butt, target** Quit making a spectacle of yourself.

spectacular *adjective* **impressive, magnificent, remarkable, sensational, marvelous, breathtaking, dramatic** On New Year's Eve we watched a spectacular display of fireworks. ➡ **Antonyms: ordinary, unimpressive**

spectator *noun* **observer, onlooker, watcher, witness, beholder, bystander, playgoer, fan** The spectators at the wrestling match were very enthusiastic.

spectrum *noun* **range, distribution, spread, sweep, extent, scope** The cafeteria has a wide spectrum of choices for the entree.

speculate *verb* **1. ponder, contemplate, meditate, reflect, think, cogitate, wonder** The philosopher speculated on the meaning of life. **2. conjecture, guess, surmise, suppose, infer, hypothesize, theorize** I'm only speculating, but I think he will come to your party.

speech *noun* **1. speaking, talk, talking, dialect, language, vocalization, utterance** Parrots can be trained to imitate human speech. **2. address, lecture, talk, oration, discourse, sermon, eulogy** The mayor gave a speech at the annual Fourth of July picnic.

speed *noun* **pace, rate, velocity, clip, tempo, haste, quickness, swiftness, rapidity** The cheetah can run at a speed of about 60 miles per hour. ◆ *verb* **race, rush, fly, shoot, whiz, zoom, dart, sprint, hasten** The black horse sped past the others to win the race. ➡ **Antonyms:** *noun* **slowness** ◆ *verb* **halt, slow**

spell[1] *verb* **signify, indicate, mean, imply, connote, suggest, promise, augur, herald** Does all this uncertain weather spell anything significant?

spell[2] *noun* **1. charm, enchantment, magic spell, incantation, invocation, abracadabra, hex, curse** The main characters in this book cast a spell to turn a dog into a horse. **2. enchantment, fascination, bewitchment, charm, trance, magic, hypnotism, allure** We fell under the spell of the beautiful tropical beach.

spell[3] *noun* **1. interval, period, span, stretch, time, bout, stint, interlude** The sunshine was most welcome after the long spell of rainy weather. **2. attack, fit, seizure, spasm, stroke, paroxysm** I had a spell of homesickness when I was at camp. ◆ *verb* **relieve, cover, pinch-hit, substitute, release, take over, free** We spelled one another at the refreshment stand.

spend *verb* **1. expend, disburse, dispense, bestow, give, lay out, pay out** How much money did you spend on your new skateboard? **2. fill, occupy, pass, put in, consume, squander, waste** He spends a lot of his time exploring web sites on the Internet. **3. exhaust, drain, consume, deplete, empty, dissipate, scatter, finish** She was careful not to spend all her energy at the beginning of the marathon. ➡ **Antonyms: 1. earn, acquire 2. & 3. save, conserve**

sphere *noun* **1. ball, globe, spheroid, bubble, bulb, globule** Earth is a sphere that is slightly flattened at its poles. **2. area, domain, realm, field, bailiwick, territory, scope, reach** During the 19th century, England's sphere of influence included India and parts of Africa.

spice *noun* **1. flavoring, seasoning, condiment, herb, relish** Ginger is a spice that is commonly used in Chinese cooking. **2. zest, zip, excitement, gusto, stimulation, life, energy, piquancy** The band added a lot of spice to our party. ◆ *verb* **flavor, season, enhance, enliven, accent, dramatize, pep up** I spiced the hot apple cider with cinnamon, nutmeg, and clove.

spicy *adjective* **1. pungent, flavorful, piquant, tangy, zesty, fragrant, sharp, fiery** I like spicy foods. **2. scandalous, vulgar, racy, risqué, sensational, provocative, suggestive** Supermarket tabloids thrive on spicy gossip. ➡ **Antonyms: 1. bland, tasteless 2. proper, polite**

Word Group A **spider** is a small animal that has eight legs and a body divided into two parts. **Spider** is a specific term with no true synonyms. Here are some common American spiders:

black widow, brown recluse, camel, crab, funnel-web, garden, jumping, orb weaver, sea, sun, tarantula, trap-door, water, wolf

spike *noun* **point, prong, barb, spine, projection, picket, peg, stake, nail** The wrought iron fence had ornamental spikes along the top rail. ◆ *verb* **pierce, prick, spear, stick, lance, impale, skewer, spit, nail, pin** He spiked the marshmallow with a long, sharp stick.

spill *verb* **1. flow, pour, run, slop, splash, overflow, spray** Root beer spilled all over when I dropped my glass. **2. divulge, tell, reveal, disclose, expose, blab, tattle, leak** I was mortified that she had spilled my secret to Karen. ◆ *noun* **fall, dive, plunge, tumble, nosedive, flop, drop, accident** I took a spill when I went skateboarding yesterday.

spin *verb* **1. narrate, recount, relate, tell, report, recite, repeat, render** I like to hear my grandmother spin tales about her childhood. **2. revolve, rotate, turn, twirl, whirl, swirl, wheel, gyrate, reel** I like amusement park rides that really spin you around. ◆ *noun* **1. revolution, rotation, turn, twirl, whirl, gyration, swirl, twist** He gave the bicycle wheel a spin to see if it was in balance. **2. drive, jaunt, ride, excursion, run, whirl, outing** My parents took our new car for a spin around the neighborhood.

spine *noun* **barb, spike, point, projection, prong, horn, spur, bristle, thorn, quill** The stegosaurus had diamond-shaped plates on its back and four long spines at the end of its tail.

spirit *noun* **1. soul, consciousness, essence, life force, vital force, psyche** Most religions teach that the spirit lives within the body. **2. bravery, courage, fortitude, gallantry, valor, mettle, nerve, pluck** The early pioneers are known for their daring spirit. **3. mood, temperament, disposition, humor, temper, attitude, tenor, tone** He is in good spirits today. **4. energy, enthusiasm, pep, vigor, vim, verve, vivacity, zip** The cheerleaders shouted with lots of spirit. **5. ghost, phantom, spook, specter, wraith, shadow, shade, angel** People say that this house is haunted by several spirits. **6. meaning, intent, sense, gist, purpose, essence, significance, aim** A judge considers the spirit as well as the letter of the law when making a decision. ◆ *verb* **carry off, kidnap, make off with, smuggle, sneak, steal, snatch** We spirited him away for a surprise birthday party.

spirited *adjective* **lively, vivacious, dynamic, animated, high-spirited, vivacious, frisky, feisty** Our history class's discussion was spirited today. ⇒ **Antonyms: timid, fearful, sluggish**

spiritual *adjective* **1. mystical, metaphysical, intuitive, philosophical, psychic, immaterial** I enjoy reflecting on spiritual ideas. **2. pious, religious, holy, sacred, divine, godly, ecclesiastical** The monk leads a spiritual life. ⇒ **Antonyms: 1. corporeal, earthly 2. secular, mundane, worldly**

spite *noun* **animosity, ill will, malice, nastiness, resentment, malevolence, hostility** She made that mean remark out of spite. ◆ *verb* **annoy, irritate, needle, nettle, vex, provoke, upset, aggravate** He withheld the information just to spite her. ⇒ **Antonyms: *noun* good will, benevolence** ◆ *verb* **please**

splash *verb* **dash, splatter, spatter, plash, sprinkle, spray, slosh, slop, strew** I splashed cold water on my face to cool off. ◆ *noun* **1. spatter, splatter, plash, sprinkle, spray,** **dash, bit, shower** There were splashes of paint on the artist's shirt. **2. stir, impact, impression, sensation, commotion** The new animated movie made a big splash.

splendid *adjective* **beautiful, impressive, glorious, magnificent, remarkable, wonderful, grand, terrific** The peacock's tail looked splendid in the sun. ⇒ **Antonyms: plain, ordinary**

splendor *noun* **beauty, brilliance, glory, magnificence, majesty, grandeur, greatness, impressiveness** We were impressed by the splendor of the Great Smoky Mountains.

splinter *noun* **sliver, shiver, flake, shaving, fragment, chip, bit, shard** I got a splinter in my foot from the rough board. ◆ *verb* **shatter, break, shiver, split, fragment, smash, disintegrate** The glass jar splintered when it hit the floor.

split *verb* **1. cleave, sever, cut, slice, slit, crack, rupture, rift, break** I split the watermelon in two with a big knife. **2. disunite, disband, diverge, part, break up, disperse, divorce, segregate** At Farewell Bend, Oregon, a company of pioneers split into two groups and took different routes. **3. divide, distribute, separate, share, apportion, dispense** We agreed to split the work so that we could get it done faster. ◆ *noun* **1. rip, slash, tear, slit, gash, break, crack, separation, fissure** There is a split in the seam of my blue jeans. **2. schism, rift, breach, rupture, dissension, division, feud, difference** There was a split in the ham radio club, and many members left. ⇒ **Antonyms: *verb* 1. & 2. join, unite** ◆ *noun* **2. agreement, unity, solidarity**

spoil *verb* **1. foul up, mess up, ruin, upset, wreck, mar, botch** The sudden rainstorm spoiled our day at the beach. **2. baby, cater to, coddle, pamper, indulge, overindulge, humor** The woman spoiled her cats by feeding them fresh fish. **3. decay, decompose, go bad, rot, putrefy, taint, turn, curdle, sour** I threw the fruit away because it had spoiled. ◆ *noun* **loot, booty, pillage, plunder, prizes, pickings, goods, take** Vikings raided the village and took away all the spoils they could carry. ⇒ **Antonyms: *verb* 1. better, improve 2. discipline 3. keep, preserve**

sponsor *noun* **backer, contributor, promoter, supporter, benefactor, patron, champion, booster** Dad's company is one of the sponsors of our roller hockey team. ◆ *verb* **back, finance, promote, support, patronize, fund, champion** That bakery sponsors an annual pie-eating contest.

spontaneous *adjective* **ad-lib, improvised, impromptu, extemporaneous, impulsive, informal, unplanned** Our teacher set aside her lesson plan and gave us a spontaneous talk. ⇒ **Antonyms: deliberate, planned**

sporadic *adjective* irregular, infrequent, spasmodic, intermittent, periodic, occasional, rare, fitful Sporadic lightning flashes lit up the night sky. ➡ **Antonyms:** regular, frequent, continuous

sport *noun* athletics, competition, contest, game, recreation, play, exercise My dad played sports in high school and college. ◆ *verb* **1.** play, romp, frolic, cavort, gambol, caper, frisk, revel I like to sport with my dog after school. **2.** wear, display, brandish, flourish, exhibit, show, flash, flaunt He sported his new team jacket proudly.

spot *noun* **1.** blotch, dot, fleck, mark, patch, speck, blot, stain, dapple, mottle Dalmatians have black spots on white fur. **2.** area, location, place, point, position, site, region, locality This looks like a good spot to look for arrowheads. **3.** predicament, dilemma, fix, jam, quandary, plight, trouble, mess, scrape I was in a spot when I lost my note cards for my presentation. **4.** blemish, stain, flaw, defect, stigma, taint, discredit, fault The incident is a spot on his otherwise perfect record. ◆ *verb* **1.** dot, fleck, mark, spatter, splatter, sprinkle, stain, stud, blot The leaves of our rosebushes are spotted with fungus. **2.** glimpse, observe, see, spy, detect, perceive, distinguish, identify The boaters were thrilled when they spotted the migrating whales.

spouse *noun* mate, partner, wife, husband, helpmate, consort, companion The man looked at his spouse and smiled.

spout *verb* **1.** gush, flow, spray, squirt, spurt, spew, stream, issue, discharge The broken pipe spouted water under the house. **2.** ramble, rant, bluster, pontificate, orate, boast, sermonize, chatter He spouted on about the superiority of his new computer.

sprawl *verb* loll, spread, lounge, drape, recline, stretch I sprawled across my bed to read my magazine.

spray *noun* mist, shower, sprinkle, drizzle, squirt, jet, spout, spurt, squirt There are birds bathing in the spray from our sprinkler. ◆ *verb* shower, spurt, squirt, splash, spout, sprinkle, shoot Firefighters sprayed water on the burning building.

spread *verb* **1.** expand, extend, open up, stretch out, unfold, unfurl, outstretch The pigeons spread their wings and flew away. **2.** open, separate, part, divide, splay, pry open, split, cleave The veterinarian spread the dog's jaws to look at its teeth. **3.** layer, put, smear, overlay, blanket, coat, cover, apply I spread cream cheese on my bagel. **4.** scatter, strew, disperse, distribute, diffuse, spread out,

radiate I helped spread the grass seed for our new lawn. **5.** circulate, disseminate, communicate, transmit, repeat, broadcast, air We need to spread the word about our fundraiser next month. ◆ *noun* **1.** advance, development, expansion, growth, increase, enlargement, extension This ointment can stop the spread of your rash. **2.** breadth, expanse, extent, reach, range, size, stretch, sweep, scope The wandering albatross's wings have a spread of 12 feet. **3.** bedspread, coverlet, blanket, cover, quilt, bedcover My aunt made me a quilted spread for my bed. **4.** feast, banquet, dinner, table, repast, buffet, meal, board The sumptuous spread was admired by all of the guests. ➡ **Antonyms:** *verb* **1.** contract, fold **2.** close, shut **4.** gather, assemble **5.** suppress, hush

spree *noun* binge, fling, rampage, splurge, bash, caper, celebration, party We went on a shopping spree just before school started.

spring *verb* **1.** bounce, bound, hurdle, jump, leap, hop, skip, vault, dart Our dog sprang to the door to greet Mom when he heard her come home. **2.** appear, arise, emerge, grow, rise, sprout, crop up, issue, mushroom Flowers sprang up overnight in the desert after the heavy rainfall. ◆ *noun* **1.** elasticity, bounce, flexibility, give, resilience, suppleness, pliability Our trampoline has lots of spring. **2.** jump, vault, bound, leap, bounce, hop, skip, lunge The kangaroo covered ten feet in a single spring. **3.** fountain, fountainhead, wellspring, water hole, hot spring, stream, brook, well We discovered a natural spring on the old ranch.

sprinkle *verb* **1.** scatter, shake, dust, spread, dribble, trickle, shower, strew I sprinkled salt on my popcorn. **2.** drizzle, rain, shower, spit, precipitate, mist It sprinkled lightly during the football game. ◆ *noun* **1.** bit, dash, touch, trace, dribble, trickle, pinch, drop I put a sprinkle of sugar on top of the cookies. **2.** drizzle, rain, rainfall, shower, precipitation, mist This afternoon's sprinkle barely wet the pavement.

sprint *verb* run, dash, race, scurry, rush, scoot, bolt, whisk, whiz I sprinted across the street when the light changed.

sprout *verb* arise, bud, come up, germinate, grow, bloom, flower, blossom Everything that we planted in the garden is beginning to sprout. ◆ *noun* seedling, shoot, bud, runner, stem, sprig We grew alfalfa sprouts in a jar.

spruce *adjective* well-groomed, dapper, natty, chic, clean, neat, tidy, trim, smart He always looks very spruce. ◆ *verb* clean, tidy, freshen, neaten, straighten, groom, wash, fix, slick We spruced up our house before we put it on the market. ➤ **Antonyms:** *adjective* **sloppy, untidy, slovenly**

spry *adjective* **active, nimble, lively, sprightly, agile, quick, vigorous, energetic** My grandfather is still very spry. ➤ **Antonyms: sluggish, inactive, lethargic**

spur *noun* **stimulus, incentive, goad, motive, impetus, provocation, prod, stimulant** His good example served as a spur to get me busy. ◆ *verb* **encourage, goad, motivate, move, prompt, stimulate, urge, incite** The coach's pep talk spurred us to win the game. ➤ **Antonyms:** *noun* **deterrent, discouragement** ◆ *verb* **deter, discourage, hinder**

spurn *verb* **reject, snub, scorn, dismiss, repel, rebuff, slight, decline, disdain** She spurned my overtures of friendship. ➤ **Antonyms: accept, welcome, embrace**

spurt *noun* **1. jet, spout, spray, squirt, fountain, gush, stream, geyser** Some geysers send spurts of water hundreds of feet high. **2. blast, burst, outbreak, flurry, eruption, surge, fit, outpouring** He reacted with a spurt of angry words. ◆ *verb* **1. gush, jet, spout, stream, squirt, spray, shoot, spew, erupt** The crowd gathered as Old Faithful started to spurt. **2. burst, sprint, dart, dash, tear, speed, rush, spring** A rabbit spurted from the bushes and raced across the road.

sputter *verb* **1. splutter, crackle, clatter, spit, rattle, pop** Our car's engine sputters on cold mornings. **2. stammer, stutter, splutter, blurt, babble, jabber, gibber** I felt ill at ease and sputtered an inane remark.

spy *noun* **operative, secret agent, undercover agent, agent, informer, scout** The spy stole some secret government documents. ◆ *verb* **1. scout out, eavesdrop, peep, pry, scout, snoop, watch, stalk** The secret agent had been spying on the enemy for months. **2. detect, glimpse, notice, observe, see, spot, discover, perceive** I spied my friend in the crowded cafeteria.

squabble *verb* **argue, bicker, dispute, fight, quarrel, feud, conflict, clash** My sister and I squabbled over who would get to wear Mom's charm bracelet. ◆ *noun* **argument, disagreement, dispute, fight, quarrel, feud, difference, tiff** The two friends quickly resolved their squabble. ➤ **Antonyms:** *verb* **agree, concur** ◆ *noun* **agreement, peace**

squad *noun* **detail, force, group, outfit, unit, company, platoon, team, task force** A squad of soldiers was sent to guard the embassy.

squalid *adjective* **1. dirty, filthy, foul, grubby, dilapidated, untidy, slummy, grimy** Mom says my room is squalid and that I need to clean it immediately. **2. sordid, repulsive, vile, low, base, ignoble, despicable, contemptible** Thomas Huxley said that it is futile to expect a hungry and squalid population to be anything but violent and gross. ➤ **Antonyms: 1. tidy, clean 2. decent, noble, honorable**

squall[1] *noun* **cry, squawk, wail, scream, yell, bawl, shriek** The baby pig let out a loud squall when I caught it. ◆ *verb* **cry, scream, squawk, wail, bawl, shriek** The baby is squalling because he's hungry.

squall[2] *noun* **gale, storm, tempest, windstorm, flurry, hurricane** We got caught in a squall on our fishing trip.

squander *verb* **waste, fritter away, dissipate, misspend, exhaust, misuse, deplete** I squandered all my allowance on a ticket to a concert by my favorite rock band. ➤ **Antonyms: save, conserve**

square *noun* **1. box, cube, rectangle, quadrangle, block** Graph paper is marked into many small squares. **2. common, green, park, plaza, quad, quadrangle, piazza** We gathered in the square to hear the band concert. ◆ *adjective* **1. foursquare, rectangular, rectilinear, boxy, equilateral** Our kitchen table is square. **2. honest, direct, genuine, decent, straightforward** He gave a square answer to my question. ◆ *verb* **1. agree, correspond, accord, check, tally, match, fit, jibe** That article squares with what I heard on TV. **2. settle, resolve, reconcile, mend, rectify, conciliate, mediate, heal** The two friends talked and squared their differences. ➤ **Antonyms:** *adjective* **2. dishonest, evasive** ◆ *verb* **1. disagree, contradict**

squash *verb* **1. crush, mash, smash, press, squeeze, flatten, compress** I squashed the bananas to make banana bread. **2. quash, squelch, put down, repress, crush, quell, extinguish, trample** The dictatorial government squashed all opposition.

squat *verb* **crouch, hunker, hunch** My father squatted down to tie his shoe. ◆ *adjective* **chunky, heavyset, stocky, thickset, stout, stumpy, pudgy** Winnie-the-Pooh is a squat little bear. ➤ **Antonyms:** *adjective* **willowy, slender**

squawk *verb* **1. screech, scream, shriek, hoot, cry, squeal, howl** We could hear the gulls squawk as they fought over the garbage. **2. complain, gripe, protest, grumble, object, demur, challenge** We squawked when the teacher gave us extra pages to read. ◆ *noun* **shriek, screech, squeal, croak, whoop, cry, hoot, caterwaul, yelp** The squawk of the radio alarm woke me up.

squeak *verb* creak, screech, squeal, tweet, peep, cheep, rasp The chair squeaked when he sat down. ◆ *noun* squeal, cry, screech, peep, chirp, creak, cheep We heard mouse squeaks coming from behind the wall.

squeal *verb* scream, screech, shriek, yell, wail, cry We squealed loudly during our pillow fight at the slumber party. ◆ *noun* scream, screech, shriek, yell, wail, cry, bawl My little sister let out a squeal when she stubbed her toe.

squeamish *adjective* **1.** delicate, queasy, nauseous, sickly, dizzy, upset I can't eat greasy food because I have a squeamish stomach. **2.** priggish, proper, prim, modest, prudish, fastidious, delicate He is so squeamish that he won't watch an R-rated movie.

squeeze *verb* **1.** force, wring, press, extract, wrest, express, compress I squeezed the water from the sponge. **2.** embrace, hug, cuddle, clasp, clutch, press I squeezed my baby sister to me. **3.** crowd, cram, stuff, jam, force, wedge, crush, press We were barely able to squeeze the Thanksgiving leftovers into the refrigerator. ◆ *noun* embrace, hug, clasp, clutch, grasp, grip, press Dad put his arm around my shoulder and gave me a quick squeeze.

squirm *verb* twist, wiggle, wriggle, writhe, worm, turn The garter snake squirmed out of my grasp.

squirrel *verb* stockpile, store, hoard, stash, cache, stow, save, hide We squirreled away a month's worth of food.

squirt *verb* discharge, eject, expel, jet, spray, spurt, gush An octopus typically squirts a cloud of ink when it is frightened. ◆ *noun* jet, spray, spurt, stream, gush, splash, spout A squirt of juice from the grapefruit hit me in the eye.

stab *verb* jab, prick, stick, plunge, puncture, thrust, ram, run, sink, lance The zoo's veterinarian stabbed a big needle through the elephant's thick skin. ◆ *noun* **1.** jab, plunge, thrust, lunge, pass, swipe, poke I made a stab at the meatball with a toothpick. **2.** try, attempt, go, shot, essay, pass, trial, crack I made another stab at learning chess.

stable[1] *adjective* **1.** firm, fixed, immovable, secure, steady, solid, fast, stationary I positioned the ladder so that it was stable. **2.** steadfast, staunch, unswerving, persistent, stalwart, reliable, resolute She has a stable character. ➡ **Antonyms: 1.** shaky, unsteady **2.** irresolute, hesitant

stable[2] *noun* barn, shed, shelter, corral, pen, stall, paddock My friends have a small stable for their horse. ◆ *verb* house, quarter, keep, lodge, board, pen I stable my horse at a local farm.

stack *noun* **1.** pile, mound, heap, mass, batch, bundle, sheaf We have stacks of old magazines in the basement. **2.** funnel, smokestack, chimney, flue, vent, pipe Smoke poured out of the ship's stack as it left port. ◆ *verb* pile, heap, mound, bank, assemble, group, arrange, load I helped my neighbor stack a cord of firewood.

staff *noun* **1.** crook, rod, stave, cane, pole, walking stick, wand, baton, stick The shepherd used his staff to herd his sheep. **2.** assistants, employees, help, personnel, crew, team, cadre, retinue The senator's staff did the research for his proposed bill.

stage *noun* **1.** platform, rostrum, dais, scaffolding, scaffold, podium, pulpit I was in charge of putting the props on the stage before the play began. **2.** spot, setting, site, location, scene, place, theater Gettysburg was the stage for one of the greatest battles of the Civil War. **3.** level, phase, period, point, step, degree, grade, rung The new housing project is in its final stage of development. ◆ *verb* act, dramatize, perform, present, produce, put on, give, direct My sisters and I like to stage plays for our friends.

stagger *verb* **1.** lurch, stumble, sway, weave, wobble, reel, totter, teeter She whirled around and around until she staggered from dizziness. **2.** amaze, astonish, astound, overwhelm, startle, dumbfound, flabbergast, stupefy The man was staggered by the news that he had won the lottery.

stagnant *adjective* **1.** contaminated, dirty, filthy, foul, stale, still, motionless, standing I changed the stagnant water in my vase of flowers. **2.** inactive, dormant, dead, sluggish, dull, static, inert, lifeless, slow The tourist business is stagnant during the off-season. ➡ **Antonyms: 1.** clean, fresh, moving **2.** lively, busy

stain *verb* **1.** dirty, discolor, smear, smudge, soil, blot, blemish, smirch The leaky ballpoint pen stained my fingers. **2.** dishonor, sully, defile, besmirch, tarnish, disgrace, taint, discredit The scandal stained his good name. ◆ *noun* **1.** blemish, blot, blotch, spot, smear, smudge, daub, smirch I hope this paint stain on my shirt will come out. **2.** taint, fault, dishonor, stigma, onus, disgrace, discredit, blemish The soldier's cowardice was a stain on his military record. ➡ **Antonyms:** *verb* **1.** clean **2.** redeem, honor ◆ *noun* **2.** credit, glory, honor

stake *noun* **1.** picket, pole, post, stick, peg, pin, spike, rod, bar We tied the tomato plant to a stake. **2.** bet, wager, ante, jackpot, prize, reward, purse My mom put a stake of two dollars on the horse race. **3.** share, interest, claim, investment, risk, involvement Each member of the group has a stake in the success of our project. ◆ *verb* **1.** mark, mark off, outline, define, limit, demarcate, delineate We staked out the borders for our new flower garden. **2. gamble, risk, wager, bet, venture, chance, put, hazard, ante** Dad staked a dollar on the football game. **3. back, sponsor, finance, fund, subsidize, capitalize, support** My grandparents staked my dad when he started his company.

stale *adjective* **1. dry, hard, moldy, old, spoiled, rotten, rancid, wilted, flat** We fed the stale bread to the ducks. **2. clichéd, banal, hackneyed, worn, trite, tired, overused, common, vapid** Our teacher encourages us to avoid stale writing in our weekly essays. **3. listless, lethargic, weak, sluggish, lazy, rusty, stiff** We felt stale after being cooped up so long because of the snow. ➡ **Antonyms: 1. fresh, new 2. original, creative, novel 3. dynamic, vigorous**

stalk[1] *noun* **stem, leafstalk, pedicel, petiole, cane, reed, shaft** We gathered stalks from the corn field to make our Halloween decorations.

stalk[2] *verb* **1. march, stamp, stomp, stride, swagger, strut, parade** The angry customer stalked out of the store. **2. follow, hunt, pursue, shadow, track, trail, chase** The lion stalked its prey with great patience.

stall *noun* **1. enclosure, compartment, pen, stable, cell** It's your turn to clean out the horse's stall. **2. booth, stand, counter, table, store, shop, kiosk** We set up a stall at the swap meet to sell our comic books. ◆ *verb* **die, halt, quit, stop, cease, arrest, check** Our car's engine stalled at the stoplight. ➡ **Antonyms:** *verb* **continue, start**

stalwart *adjective* **1. strong, robust, powerful, brawny, mighty, stout, hale, strapping** My father and his brothers are all stalwart men. **2. brave, resolute, valiant, gallant, courageous, valorous, intrepid, bold** The stalwart Scottish Highlanders lost more than a thousand men in the battle of Culloden Moor. ➡ **Antonyms: 1. puny, weak 2. cowardly, timid**

stamina *noun* **endurance, staying power, strength, perseverance, hardiness, fortitude** I have lots of stamina, but not much speed. ➡ **Antonyms: weakness, frailty**

stammer *verb* **stutter, sputter, falter, stumble, splutter** I stammer sometimes when I get excited.

stamp *verb* **1. step, trample, tread, crush, mash, squash, plod, stomp** I stamped the aluminum can flat before putting it in the recycling bin. **2. eradicate, extinguish, annihilate, kill, smother, erase, destroy, suppress** The government stamped out all opposition. **3. label, mark, imprint, print, seal, impress, inscribe, engrave, fix** She stamped the package with her return address. **4. reveal, identify, classify, type, brand, characterize, mark, tag** Salvador Dali's unique style stamps him as a surrealist painter. ◆ *noun* **emblem, label, mark, seal, symbol, design, impression, sign** The clerk put the bank's stamp on the document.

stampede *noun* **charge, dash, flight, race, rush, onslaught** There was a stampede to the creek when the thirsty cattle smelled the water. ◆ *verb* **bolt, flee, take flight, panic, rush, dash, run** The buffalo stampeded when they sensed danger.

stand *verb* **1. arise, get up, rise, stand erect, stand upright** We all stood up when the national anthem began. **2. be located, be situated, rest, sit, persist, remain, exist** The Eiffel Tower stands in Paris, France. **3. apply, exist, last, persist, hold, obtain, endure, remain, continue** I tried to change Mom's mind, but she said that her decision still stands. **4. support, defend, uphold, champion, endorse, advocate, back** I stand by my earlier decision. **5. abide, bear, endure, handle, take, tolerate, stomach, withstand** How can you stand to live without a TV set? ◆ *noun* **1. booth, stall, store, shop, kiosk, counter, tent, pushcart** We bought oranges at the fruit stand. **2. rack, support, counter, table, pedestal, frame, platform, prop** I use a stand to hold my music when I practice my clarinet. **3. attitude, position, viewpoint, stance, standpoint, policy, opinion, belief** Grandfather tends to take a conservative stand on political issues. ➡ **Antonyms:** *verb* **1. lie, recline, sit 4. renounce, repudiate**

standard *noun* **1. banner, ensign, flag, pennant, colors, insignia, streamer, jack** He carried the school standard in the parade. **2. requirement, criterion, measure, guideline, ideal, principle, example, pattern** Our teacher sets high standards for us. ◆ *adjective* **customary, normal, ordinary, regular, typical, usual, familiar** A standard baseball team has nine players. ➡ **Antonyms:** *adjective* **atypical, unusual**

stanza *noun* **verse, stave, strophe, part, section, segment, portion, paragraph** She recited all three stanzas of her favorite poem.

staple *noun* **1. basics, essentials, commodity, resource, raw material** Most families keep staples such as salt, sugar, and flour in their kitchen. **2. feature, fundamental, characteristic, component, hallmark, earmark, attribute** His monthly column is a staple of the magazine. ◆ *adjective* **basic, essential, principal, main, prime, chief, predominant, primary, major** Rice is a staple food throughout much of the world. ➡ **Antonyms:** *adjective* **minor, secondary, subordinate**

star *noun* **1. lead, principal, leading lady, leading man, hero, heroine, protagonist** My best friend was the star of our school play. **2. celebrity, superstar, name, notable, luminary, starlet, idol** The teenager became a star overnight after appearing in the hit movie. ◆ *adjective* **prominent, important, major, outstanding, eminent, illustrious, famous** She is a star ice skater. ◆ *verb* **feature, showcase, spotlight, headline, introduce, present, promote** This opera stars two of my favorite singers. ◈ **Antonyms:** *adjective* **obscure, unknown**

stare *verb* **gape, gawk, gaze, look, glare, ogle, goggle, peer, watch** My dog stares at me whenever I am eating something. ◆ *noun* **glare, look, gape, gaze, glower, inspection, regard** The librarian gave us a disapproving stare when we talked too loud.

stark *adjective* **1. bare, barren, unadorned, austere, plain, simple, bleak, dour** Quaker meeting houses are traditionally stark in design. **2. utter, complete, total, outright, sheer, pure, absolute, thorough, perfect** That rumor you heard is stark nonsense! **3. harsh, grim, severe, cruel, ruthless, extreme, stiff, hard, difficult** I thought that the punishment was too stark for the crime. ◆ *adverb* **utterly, totally, completely, entirely, altogether, wholly, quite** I caught my little brother before he ran outside stark naked. ◈ **Antonyms:** *adjective* **1. fancy, adorned 2. partial, incomplete 3. easy, mild**

start *verb* **1. depart, embark, get going, leave, set out, go, take off, move** We'll need to start early if we want to get back before dark. **2. begin, commence, initiate, open, kick off, activate, undertake, launch** I start my day by feeding the fish in my aquarium. **3. jerk, flinch, jump, wince, recoil, twitch, cringe, shy, shrink** I started at the sudden loud noise. **4. create, establish, found, institute, launch, inaugurate, originate, organize** Henry Ford started the Ford Motor Company in 1903. ◆ *noun* **1. beginning, commencement, onset, opening, initiation, outset, kickoff, inauguration** I am looking forward to the start of the holiday season. **2. flinch, cringe, wince, jerk, spasm, bolt, recoil, jump** He gave a start of surprise when his name was called. **3. opening, opportunity, chance, advantage, lead, head start, edge, drop** He got his start by acting in school plays. ◈ **Antonyms:** *verb* **2. & 4. end, finish, stop** ◆ *noun* **1. ending, finish**

startle *verb* **surprise, alarm, shock, frighten, scare, jolt, unnerve, stun, unsettle** You startled me, because I hadn't heard you come home. ◈ **Antonyms: reassure, settle**

starve *verb* **1. underfeed, undernourish, fast, waste away, perish, die, wither** "Feed a cold and starve a fever" is an old saying. **2. hunger, thirst, yearn, pine, long, want, suffer, languish** The unhappy child is starving for attention. ◈ **Antonyms: 1. overfeed, glut**

state *noun* **1. condition, situation, position, circumstance, status, stage, phase, mode** Our house was in a state of confusion while we were having the kitchen remodeled. **2. mood, attitude, temper, humor, disposition, frame** Mom and Dad are in a good state this evening. **3. country, nation, dominion, land, republic, commonwealth, polity, government** The state of Israel was founded in 1948. ◆ *verb* **announce, declare, express, proclaim, say, speak, recite, report, articulate** The witness stated her name for the record.

stately *adjective* **august, dignified, grand, majestic, noble, regal, solemn, impressive, elegant** The presidential inauguration is a stately occasion. ◈ **Antonyms: ordinary, common**

statement *noun* **1. announcement, bulletin, declaration, proclamation, speech, remark, comment** The congressman's aide read a statement to the press. **2. invoice, bill, tally, account, reckoning, tab, balance, sheet** My dad's plumbing company sends statements out to its customers once a month.

station *noun* **1. position, post, location, place, locus, seat, area** There is a nurses' station on each floor of the hospital. **2. headquarters, station house, base, center, office, precinct, complex** We went down to the police station to turn in the purse that we had found. **3. depot, terminal, stop, whistle stop, terminus, spot** The bus station is on Main Street. **4. rank, status, class, degree, level, position, standing, rating** Many Americans do not think it is polite to discuss a person's social or economic station. ◆ *verb* **assign, post, place, position, locate, situate, install, appoint, set** He was stationed at the information booth during the school carnival.

stationary *adjective* **fixed, immobile, motionless, unmoving, steady, still, stock-still** Mom likes to read while she rides her stationary bike. ◈ **Antonyms: changing, moving**

stationery *noun* **notepaper, letter paper, writing paper, bond paper, letterhead, parchment, pad** I wrote my grandmother a letter on a piece of my favorite stationery.

statue *noun* **sculpture, image, figure, figurine, bust, likeness, bronze, effigy, idol** The statue of Abraham Lincoln at his memorial in Washington, D.C., was sculpted by Daniel Chester French in 1922.

stature *noun* **prestige, reputation, distinction, level, status, esteem** Dr. Albert Schweitzer attained great stature as a doctor, a musician, and a humanitarian.

status *noun* **1. rank, standing, grade, place, position, station, situation** The status of a bank president is higher than that of a teller. **2. prestige, eminence, worth, merit, prominence, stature, distinction** Occupations that require education, skill, or talent tend to have greater status than those that don't.

statute *noun* **rule, law, act, ordinance, regulation, decree, edict, bylaw, prescript** I think that for every new statute that is passed an old one should be taken off the books.

staunch *adjective* **1. firm, steadfast, constant, faithful, fast, true, loyal, resolute, stalwart** We have been staunch friends for years. **2. strong, solid, sturdy, stout, substantial, tough, rugged, sound** The staunch little boat has weathered many storms. ➧ **Antonyms: 1. unfaithful, fickle 2. weak, frail**

stay *verb* **1. linger, remain, wait, tarry, loiter, bide, pause, dally** We stayed in the movie theater until everyone else had left. **2. abide, dwell, live, lodge, reside, sojourn, room, visit** I'm going to stay with my cousin in Florida over spring vacation. **3. go on, keep, stick, remain, endure, persist, continue, persevere** He has decided not to stay with his present job. ◆ *noun* **1. stopover, visit, holiday, stop, sojourn, vacation** I'm looking forward to our stay in London. **2. postponement, deferment, reprieve, break, respite, delay, hiatus** The judge announced a stay in the trial proceedings.

steady *adjective* **1. stable, firm, solid, sound, strong, secure, fixed, immovable** Is that old ladder steady enough to hold my weight? **2. constant, continuous, even, regular, uniform, persistent, determined** The ferry made steady progress toward the island. **3. self-composed, composed, levelheaded, cool, calm, equable, even, controlled** She is steady and reliable in difficult situations. **4. determined, steadfast, resolute, persistent, unwavering, firm, decided** I am steady in my decision to take classes at the junior college this summer. ◆ *verb* **stabilize, balance, brace, hold, secure, support, immobilize** Please help steady the canoe while I get in. ➧ **Antonyms:** *adjective* **1. shaky, unstable 2. irregular, unreliable 3. jittery, nervous 4. wavering, vacillating**

steal *verb* **1. pilfer, rob, snatch, thieve, loot, plunder, lift, swipe, purloin, embezzle** Magpies often steal shiny objects and take them back to their nests. **2. creep, slide,** slip, sneak, tiptoe, prowl, skulk, slink, pussyfoot** I didn't hear my little brother steal into the room.

stealth *noun* **furtiveness, slyness, secrecy, stealthiness, covertness, sneakiness, subterfuge** Early medical experiments often had to be carried out with great stealth. ➧ **Antonyms: openness, candidness**

stealthy *adjective* **quiet, secretive, cautious, furtive, slinky, sneaky, sneaking, clandestine** The cat made a stealthy move toward the bird. ➧ **Antonyms: open, overt, direct**

steam *noun* **1. condensation, mist, vapor, fog, moisture, gas, exhalation, fume** Steam from the shower fogged up the bathroom mirror. **2. power, energy, drive, vigor, strength, vim, vitality, potency, might, pep** We had lots of steam left after the game. ◆ *verb* **1. cruise, navigate, ply, run, sail, voyage, travel** During the 1800s, riverboats steamed up and down the Mississippi River. **2. cook, heat, simmer, warm** We steamed the broccoli just until it was tender.

steep¹ *adjective* **1. perpendicular, sheer, vertical, sharp, abrupt, precipitous** The walls of the Grand Canyon are steep cliffs. **2. excessive, exorbitant, high, dear, inflated, stiff, immoderate, undue, expensive** I paid a steep price for those jeans. ➧ **Antonyms: 1. level, flat 2. moderate, inexpensive, cheap**

steep² *verb* **1. soak, brew, infuse, saturate, souse, douse, drench, marinate** The tea leaves have to steep in water that has boiled. **2. immerse, bury, plunge, submerge, involve, absorb, occupy, engage** I steeped myself in the life of Laura Ingalls Wilder after reading all her books.

steer *verb* **1. maneuver, pilot, navigate, guide, jockey, operate, sail** I can steer my bicycle with no hands. **2. lead, manage, supervise, govern, oversee, head, run, control, direct** He was appointed to steer the nominating committee.

stem¹ *noun* **1. trunk, shoot, stalk, cane, spear, petiole, pedicel, stock, leafstalk** The stems of giant bamboo plants can grow several feet a day. **2. shank, rod, spindle, shaft, pin, peg, axis, base, support** I pulled out the stem on my watch to set the time. ◆ *verb* **originate, spring, rise, ensue, issue, derive, arise, proceed, result** Many scientists believe that humanity stems from a single ancestor.

stem² *verb* **stop, check, arrest, slow, stay, obstruct, restrain, dam, quell, stanch** He stemmed the flow of blood by pressing on the wound with a pressure bandage. ➧ **Antonyms: hasten, encourage**

stench *noun* stink, odor, reek, fetor, smell, malodor, redolence The stench of the skunk outside my window woke me up. ➽ **Antonyms:** fragrance, perfume

step *noun* 1. footstep, pace, stride, tread, move, walk I took a step forward when the coach called my name. 2. footfall, footstep, tread, tromp, stomp I heard my mother's step as she came into the house. 3. footprint, track, trail, spoor, mark, trace, vestige, print, impression The search and rescue team followed the steps left by the boy. 4. gait, stride, swagger, strut, shamble, walk, shuffle He walked with a confident step. 5. measure, move, tactic, maneuver, procedure, act, action, deed, method Installing a smoke alarm is an important step in fire safety. 6. grade, rank, level, rung, peg, degree, position, point, notch My aunt was promoted up a step at work. ◆ *verb* walk, advance, shuffle, stride, tread, tramp, stroll, move, march He stepped up to the ticket window.

stereotype *noun* cliché, characterization, categorization, image, banality, formula, mold, convention It is unfortunate when a person is judged according to a stereotype rather than individual merit. ◆ *verb* pigeonhole, categorize, define, identify, describe, characterize Sometimes people stereotype others from unfamiliar cultures.

sterilize *verb* 1. sanitize, disinfect, clean, cleanse, decontaminate, purify, pasteurize Mom sterilized the needle by holding it in a flame. 2. neuter, alter, spay, castrate, fix, geld, change Our dog was sterilized when she was 5 months old. ➽ **Antonyms:** 1. infect, contaminate

stern[1] *adjective* 1. grave, grim, hard, harsh, severe, sharp, strict, tough, pitiless I received a stern look when I slammed the door. 2. firm, unyielding, uncompromising, resolute, steadfast, determined The army met with stern resistance. ➽ **Antonyms:** 1. gentle, kind, lenient 2. hesitant, wavering

stern[2] *noun* back, end, rear, tail, heel, posterior We stood at the stern of the boat to watch the dolphins. ➽ **Antonyms:** bow, front, head

stew *verb* 1. cook, heat, simmer, boil, fricassee Dad stewed a ham hock in order to flavor the bean soup. 2. worry, fret, brood, mope, agonize I stewed about my bad grade on the French test. ◆ *noun* dither, fluster, flutter, sweat, fuss, agitation, turmoil, tumult, upset She was in a stew when she lost her homework.

stick *noun* 1. twig, branch, stem, switch, limb, shoot, stalk I wrote my name in the sand with a stick. 2. staff, cane, crook, pole, shaft, stave, rod, stake, bar My father

has had his walking stick ever since he was a teenager. 3. backwoods, backcountry, outback, hinterland, countryside, woodland, wilds I live in a small mountain town in the sticks. ◆ *verb* 1. jab, stab, pierce, poke, puncture, prick, spear, impale, perforate I stuck holes in the potato so that it wouldn't explode in the microwave. 2. attach, fasten, glue, nail, paste, pin, tape, fix, affix, tack, cement My brother stuck up posters all over his bedroom walls. 3. put, thrust, push, place, stuff, insert, deposit, set, install, lay I stuck my coat and boots in my locker and ran to class. 4. mire, stall, detain, delay, hamper, inhibit, impede, immobilize, obstruct The accident in the tunnel stuck up traffic back to the airport. 5. burden, charge, encumber, incriminate, foist, inflict My sister stuck me with a larger share of the chores. 6. extend, project, poke, protrude, put, jut My dog likes to stick his head out the window when we take him for a ride in the car. ➽ **Antonyms:** *verb* 2. detach, unfasten 3. withdraw, remove 4. hasten, expedite 5. relieve, free, clear

sticky *adjective* 1. gluey, gummy, adhesive, tacky The sap of a pine tree is very sticky. 2. clammy, humid, muggy, sultry, damp, moist, wet, sweaty, steamy The cooling rain was a relief after the hot and sticky weather. 3. difficult, uncomfortable, complicated, tricky, delicate, awkward, thorny We tried to resolve the sticky situation as best we could. ➽ **Antonyms:** 1. slippery, slick 2. arid, dry 3. easy, comfortable

stiff *adjective* 1. inflexible, rigid, unbending, solid, unyielding, hard, taut, tight Coat hangers are made from stiff wire. 2. formal, stilted, starchy, forced, wooden, prim, uneasy, unnatural He had a very stiff manner. 3. rigorous, intense, keen, exacting, difficult, hard, tough, formidable Competition was stiff at the football playoffs. 4. firm, resolute, determined, unflinching, steadfast, steady, unwavering, tenacious His resolve was stiff in the face of opposition. 5. harsh, severe, tough, strict, stern, stringent, cruel, drastic, merciless There are stiff penalties for the possession of illegal drugs. ➽ **Antonyms:** 1. flexible 2. relaxed, easy 3. weak, soft, easy 4. irresolute, wavering 5. easy

stifle *verb* 1. control, hold back, restrain, muffle, stop, suppress, stem, squelch I tried to stifle my laughter as I read the funny book in the library. 2. choke, smother, suffocate, asphyxiate, strangle We felt the heat would stifle us.

still *adjective* 1. hushed, noiseless, quiet, soundless, silent The students were still as their teacher read to them. 2. calm, motionless, placid, undisturbed, tranquil, serene, pacific, peaceful The lake was still after the storm. ◆ *noun* hush, quiet, quietness, silence, stillness, tranquillity, quietude, calm The still of the night was broken by an owl's screech. ◆ *adverb* nevertheless, nonetheless, however, yet My hair is getting long, but I'm still letting it grow. ➨ **Antonyms:** *adjective* 1. loud, noisy 2. turbulent ◆ *noun* commotion, noise

stilted *adjective* formal, wooden, stiff, stuffy, starchy, unnatural He has a stilted manner in spite of his efforts to be relaxed. ➨ **Antonyms:** natural, spontaneous

stimulate *verb* arouse, awaken, excite, quicken, spur, provoke, animate, spark Going to the air show stimulated my desire to become a pilot. ➨ **Antonyms:** deaden, dull, kill

sting *verb* 1. bite, burn, smart, pierce, penetrate, stab, prick The cold wind stung my cheeks. 2. hurt, wound, injure, grieve, vex, distress, trouble, incense, madden, provoke The low grade I got on my history essay really stung me. ◆ *noun* wound, bite, prick, ache, pain, pang, stab, stitch, twinge What do you recommend as an antidote for a bee sting? ➨ **Antonyms:** *verb* 2. soothe, calm, assuage

stingy *adjective* 1. cheap, miserly, sparing, ungenerous, tight, greedy, tightfisted, niggardly My brother is really stingy with his candy. 2. scanty, meager, thin, lean, inadequate, scrimpy, insufficient, paltry There was a stingy amount of food at the party. ➨ **Antonyms:** generous, lavish

stink *verb* smell bad, smell, reek, offend The dead fish on the beach are beginning to stink. ◆ *noun* bad smell, foul odor, stench, fetor, reek, smell There is quite a stink coming from the garbage can.

stir *verb* 1. agitate, beat, blend, churn, mix, whip, whisk, mingle, combine I stirred the cake batter until it was smooth. 2. rustle, move, flutter, quiver, shift, budge A towhee stirred in the shrubbery. 3. awaken, waken, bestir, animate, energize, inspire, kindle Some movies really stir my imagination. 4. incite, provoke, prod, stoke, inflame, goad, spur, instigate He stirred dissension in the group with his challenging remark. ◆ *noun* 1. movement, rustle, sough, motion, move, activity I heard a stir in the bushes. 2. commotion, disturbance, tumult, turmoil, uproar, fury, ferment, to-do Mom's long-lost brother caused quite a stir when he showed up at our front door. ➨ **Antonyms:** *verb* 3. & 4. calm, suppress, stifle

stock *noun* 1. hoard, reserve, store, supply, pile, accumulation, fund, reservoir, cache We keep a stock of canned foods for emergency use. 2. inventory, selection, line, assortment, array, merchandise, goods, commodities This store has a large stock of camping gear. 3. livestock, animals, herd, beasts, creatures, cattle, cows The stock were branded before being turned loose on the range. 4. ancestry, blood, descent, line, lineage, parentage, clan, kindred, family Dad likes to say that he comes from sturdy farming stock. ◆ *verb* 1. fill, furnish, provide, supply, provision, load, store We stocked our refrigerator with fresh fruits and vegetables. 2. carry, handle, sell, vend, merchandise, retail, offer, keep I'm looking for a store that stocks birdseed. ◆ *adjective* commonplace, hackneyed, banal, worn, routine, ordinary, typical, usual He played a stock character in the movie. ➨ **Antonyms:** *verb* 1. deplete, expend ◆ *adjective* new, original, fresh

stockade *noun* 1. barricade, bulwark, fence, palisade, fortification, barrier, obstacle The rebels built a stockade across the road. 2. guardhouse, jail, prison, pen, penitentiary, brig, dungeon, keep The soldier was put in the stockade for being absent without leave.

stocky *adjective* heavyset, solid, stout, sturdy, thick, thickset I'm built just like my uncle—short and stocky. ➨ **Antonyms:** skinny, slender

stomach *noun* 1. belly, tummy, gut, abdomen, midriff, solar plexus My stomach is growling because I am hungry. 2. hunger, taste, appetite, relish, thirst, craving I have a stomach for pizza. 3. desire, inclination, fancy, leaning, mind, propensity, disposition I don't have the stomach for arguing with him about it. ◆ *verb* bear, tolerate, endure, stand, brook, take, abide, suffer, countenance I can't stomach people who complain all the time. ➨ **Antonyms:** *noun* 2. distaste 3. disinclination, aversion

stone *noun* 1. rock, cobble, pebble, boulder, cobblestone, gravel I helped Dad collect stones to build a wall. 2. gem, gemstone, jewel, precious stone, semiprecious stone The stone in my ring is an opal. 3. pit, kernel, nut, seed, center, nucleus Apricots are an edible fruit with a large stone.

stoop¹ *verb* 1. bend, sag, crouch, duck, bow, slouch She stooped down to pick up the pencil that I dropped. 2. resort, sink, deign, succumb, descend, lower, fall, condescend I would never stoop to cheating. ◆ *noun* slouch, bend, bow, droop, sag, slump, bad posture Mom always corrects my posture so that I don't develop a stoop.

stoop² *noun* doorstep, porch, step, staircase, entranceway There is a pot of flowers on the stoop.

stop *verb* **1. bar, block, check, prevent, restrain, intercept, impede, thwart** The manager stopped us from entering the pool hall because we weren't 18 years old. **2. cease, discontinue, halt, pause, quit, suspend, desist, refrain** I had to stop running because I got a bad cramp in my leg. **3. plug, close, choke, cork, caulk, fill, stanch, seal, occlude, congest** She stopped the oil leak by tightening the drain cap. **4. sojourn, lodge, dwell, stop over, visit, tarry, abide, rest** We stopped at a motel for the night. ◆ *noun* **1. halt, standstill, stoppage, pause, end, finish, arrest, cessation** At a flashing red light, drivers have to come to a full stop. **2. visit, stay, sojourn, layover, rest, pause, stopover, break, respite** Our stop in Rhode Island was very enjoyable. ➡ **Antonyms:** *verb* **1. assist, encourage 2. begin, continue, start 3. unplug, open** ◆ *noun* **1. start, commencement**

store *noun* **1. shop, boutique, emporium, outlet, department store, market, establishment, retailer** I bought Mom's present at a stationery store. **2. accumulation, hoard, inventory, reserve, stock, supply, cache, reservoir** We keep a store of candles for use when the power goes out. **3. abundance, wealth, plethora, volume, profusion, host, quantity, fund** She has a rich store of words in her vocabulary. ◆ *verb* **hoard, stockpile, stash, cache, put away, stock, collect, save, keep** Squirrels store nuts in the fall so they'll have food in the winter. ➡ **Antonyms:** *noun* **3. lack, dearth, poverty**

storm *noun* **1. downpour, tempest, gale, hurricane, blizzard, tornado, squall, cloudburst, torrent** The storm was accompanied by lots of thunder and lightning. **2. disturbance, upheaval, ruckus, hubbub, commotion, stir, agitation, furor** There was quite a storm at our house when my sister said she wanted to quit school. **3. outburst, outbreak, deluge, flood, shower, hail, salvo, barrage, volley** There was a storm of protest against the unjust law. **4. rush, attack, onslaught, assault, charge, strike, offensive, invasion** Attackers took the castle by storm. ◆ *verb* **1. bluster, blow, hail, pour, rain, snow, sleet, gust** It stormed all night, but in the morning the air was fresh and clear. **2. stomp, stamp, tear, rush, rampage, rage, rant, rave, fume** He stormed out of the meeting in a fit of anger. **3. assail, assault, attack, beset, charge, raid, rush, besiege, strike** In the Gallipoli campaign of 1915, Allied troops stormed the beaches but were beaten back. ➡ **Antonyms:** *noun* **2. calm, peace, tranquillity**

story[1] *noun* **1. account, anecdote, narrative, report, description, version, chronicle, history** My grandmother told me the story about how she met my grandfather. **2. tale, yarn, fable, fiction, legend, narrative, short story, plot, sketch** I like to read ghost stories. **3. lie, falsehood,** fabrication, fib, untruth, falsity, fiction, excuse My little brother told a big story about how he got all wet on the way home from school.

story[2] *noun* **floor, level, tier, layer, flat** The Empire State Building in New York City is 102 stories tall.

stout *adjective* **1. bold, brave, stalwart, courageous, dauntless, valiant, resolute, intrepid** Pioneer women must have had stout hearts to withstand such difficulties as they did. **2. brawny, burly, heavyset, husky, thickset, stocky, sturdy, muscular** Saint Bernards are big, stout dogs. **3. overweight, fat, heavy, plump, corpulent, obese** I hugged my stout basset hound. ➡ **Antonyms: 1. cowardly, fearful 2. weak, puny 3. lean, slender, thin**

stow *verb* **load, pack, deposit, stuff, jam, put, place, arrange, store, cache** We stowed our athletic gear in the back of the van.

straggle *verb* **fall behind, dawdle, lag, linger, ramble, stray, wander** I straggled so far behind my parents at the mall that I almost lost track of them.

straight *adjective* **1. erect, upright, in line, perpendicular, vertical, even, rectilinear, plumb** My dance instructor told me to keep my back straight. **2. direct, frank, honest, candid, true, truthful, forthright, straightforward** I gave my mom a straight answer when she asked where I had been. **3. uninterrupted, consecutive, solid, unbroken, successive, nonstop, constant, ceaseless** I read the whole book in three straight days. ◆ *adverb* **at once, directly, right, immediately, instantly, forthwith, straightaway** When I got home from school, I went straight to the refrigerator for a snack. ➡ **Antonyms:** *adjective* **1. bent, curved 2. false, untruthful**

strain[1] *verb* **1. draw, stretch, tighten, pull, tense, distend, extend** The holidays really can strain the family budget. **2. labor, strive, struggle, toil, moil, work, exert, sweat, overexert** I had to strain to hear my friend's whisper. **3. pull, sprain, wrench, twist, overextend, injure, hurt, impair** I strained my calf muscles by carrying such a heavy load on the hike. **4. filter, sieve, sift, winnow, screen** My grandmother strained the milk to separate out the cream. ◆ *noun* **pressure, tension, stress, force, pull, draw, weight, burden** The clothesline broke from the strain of too much weight.

strain[2] *noun* **1. breed, line, stock, lineage, family, extraction, race** My grandmother has a strain of dairy cows famous for producing milk. **2. streak, vein, characteristic, tendency, inclination, disposition, trace** He has a generous strain in his nature. **3. tone, style, air, manner, tenor, cast, accent, theme, substance** I like stories with a romantic strain.

strait *noun* **predicament, difficulty, plight, distress, fix, emergency, dilemma, mess** Many people were in dire straits after the flood.

strand[1] *verb* **maroon, leave behind, leave, abandon, desert, forsake** Robinson Crusoe was stranded on a desert island.

strand[2] *noun* **filament, fiber, thread, yarn, string, cord, rope, tress** I used three strands of thread to embroider my pillowcase.

strange *adjective* **1. unknown, unfamiliar, new, unusual, novel, foreign, exotic, alien** I like to try strange new foods. **2. bizarre, eccentric, peculiar, odd, weird, curious, queer, outlandish, fantastic** We have a strange cat that likes to take baths. ➤ **Antonyms: 1. familiar, usual 2. normal, ordinary**

stranger *noun* **newcomer, outsider, foreigner, visitor, immigrant, alien, émigré** Strangers have moved into the house down the street. ➤ **Antonyms: acquaintance, friend, resident**

strangle *verb* **1. choke, suffocate, throttle, asphyxiate, smother, hang, garrote** I loosened my tie because it was almost strangling me. **2. suppress, stifle, muffle, repress, squelch, quell, stop, restrain, subdue** My brother strangled what he was going to say when I looked at him with a frown. ➤ **Antonyms: 2. help, promote, encourage**

strap *noun* **band, lash, strip, thong, cord, string, ribbon, leash** My sandals have two straps in front and one in back. ◆ *verb* **lash, tie, truss, bind, attach, fasten, secure, tether** Dad strapped our luggage to the roof of the car. ➤ **Antonyms:** *verb* **unfasten, untie**

strategy *noun* **method, plan, procedure, scheme, system, tactic, program, design** My strategy for getting good grades is to pay attention at school and do my homework.

stray *verb* **1. drift, wander, meander, ramble, roam, range, rove, straggle** My mind strayed during the boring movie. **2. depart, deviate, digress, diverge, swerve, veer, shift** The speaker strayed from her topic. ◆ *adjective* **1. abandoned, homeless, lost, vagrant, misplaced, wandering, derelict** We adopted the stray dog because it was so friendly. **2. random, erratic, chance, separate, lone, occasional, scattered** A stray bullet injured a bystander.

streak *noun* **1. band, line, stripe, bar, strip, ribbon, vein** The golden-mantled ground squirrel has two streaks down its back. **2. trace, hint, touch, dash, vein, trait, tendency, characteristic** She has a streak of shyness. **3. interval, run, period, spell, stretch, bout, course, chain, string** I've had a streak of good luck lately. ◆ *verb* **1. band, stripe, mark, smear, smudge, stain** The sky was streaked with red at dawn. **2. dash, flash, race, rush, sprint, zoom, hurtle, tear, fly, dart, whiz** The runner streaked across the finish line. ➤ **Antonyms:** *verb* **2. creep, crawl**

stream *noun* **1. brook, creek, rill, kill, rivulet, streamlet, river, feeder, tributary** This little stream dries up in the summer. **2. gush, jet, spurt, flow, current, torrent, burst, deluge, flood** Dad sprayed a stream of water on his vegetable garden. ◆ *verb* **course, flow, gush, pour, run, rush, spill, flood, cascade, surge** I was laughing so hard that tears streamed down my face.

street *noun* **avenue, boulevard, drive, lane, road, route, roadway, highway, alley** My best friend and I live on the same street.

strength *noun* **1. brawn, might, power, force, muscle, stamina, hardiness, sinew** My brother has been working out with weights to increase his strength. **2. potency, efficacy, effectiveness, intensity, punch, bite, concentration** These vitamin tablets are double the strength of the ones I used to take. **3. courage, fortitude, pluck, willpower, tenacity, determination, persistence** I am proud of my sister for having the strength to cope with spina bifida. ➤ **Antonyms: 1. weakness, frailty 3. timidity, cowardice**

strengthen *verb* **brace, buttress, fortify, reinforce, toughen, harden, restore, support** Workers strengthened the old bridge by adding new beams. ➤ **Antonyms: weaken, soften**

strenuous *adjective* **active, brisk, dynamic, energetic, vigorous, hard, tough, rigorous, arduous** Our coach puts us through a strenuous practice every afternoon. ➤ **Antonyms: easy, mild, effortless**

stress *noun* **1. emphasis, importance, significance, value, weight, consideration, accent** My family puts a lot of stress on getting a college education. **2. anxiety, strain, distress, tension, worry, pressure, nervousness, dread** Some people experience stress when they go to a dentist. ◆ *verb* **1. emphasize, accent, feature, highlight, accentuate, affirm, assert** My teacher stresses the importance of creativity. **2. strain, pressure, burden, afflict, traumatize, fret, upset, disturb** The loss of her job stressed her. ➤ **Antonyms:** *verb* **1. minimize, belittle 2. soothe, help**

stretch *verb* **1. draw out, expand, elongate, lengthen, pull, widen, distend, protract** I stretched the neck of my T-shirt when I pulled it on over my hat and sunglasses. **2. extend, reach, spread, open up, run, unfold** This lake stretches farther than the eye can see. **3. strain, bend, break, warp, distort, change, alter, modify, overtax** We stretched the rules so that more of us could play at one time. ◆ *noun* **1. elasticity, flexibility, spring, resiliency, plasticity, give, ductility** There is a lot of stretch in this rope. **2. span, expanse, extent, length, reach, distance, course, space, measure** We drove down a stretch of dirt road to get to the pond. **3. period, term, time, spell, stint, span, interval, season, duration** There was a long stretch of history when human beings were hunter-gatherers. ◆ **Antonyms:** *verb* **1. contract, compress**

stricken *adjective* **damaged, spoiled, ruined, injured, crippled, hurt, impaired** The farmer's crop was stricken by a horde of grasshoppers.

strict *adjective* **1. complete, absolute, full, exact, precise, meticulous, particular, careful** I paid strict attention to what the police officer was saying. **2. rigorous, exacting, stringent, firm, rigid, unyielding** Our school has a strict policy against the use of illegal drugs. ◆ **Antonyms: 1. careless, negligent 2. lax, lenient**

stride *verb* **walk, pace, tread, step, march** I watched the winner stride up to the podium to receive her award. ◆ *noun* **walk, step, footstep, tread, pace, march** He walked along with a confident stride.

strident *adjective* **shrill, harsh, grating, screeching, jarring, hoarse, rasping, raucous** Crows and blue jays have strident calls. ◆ **Antonyms: gentle, soothing**

strife *noun* **conflict, struggle, discord, friction, confrontation, hostility, war, warfare** There has been periodic strife between the two countries for several centuries. ◆ **Antonyms: harmony, peace, concord**

strike *verb* **1. hit, knock, slam, smack, pound, punch, whack, wallop, tap** The tennis ball struck my opponent on the shoulder. **2. attack, assault, charge, raid, storm, advance, invade, besiege** The patrol struck the enemy outpost at midnight. **3. impress, affect, touch, move, appear, seem, occur to** My cousin's joke didn't strike me as being very funny. **4. come upon, discover, find, detect, locate, uncover, unearth** The drill rig struck oil at last. **5. make, reach, conclude, agree, settle, ratify, confirm, effect** My brother and I struck a deal that gave each of us what we wanted most. **6. walk out, go on strike, picket, protest, quit, resist** The coal miners are planning to strike for better working conditions. ◆ *noun* **1. stroke, blow, hit, knock, punch, smack, rap, clout, stab, slam** The old oak tree was destroyed by a lightning strike. **2. raid, attack, assault, onslaught, offensive, invasion, bombardment** The air strikes are intended to destroy the bridge.

striking *adjective* **bold, conspicuous, eye-catching, prominent, arresting, remarkable, outstanding** That house is painted in a striking combination of colors. ◆ **Antonyms: neutral, bland**

string *noun* **1. cord, twine, thread, ribbon, band, line, rope, strand, fiber, filament** I tied the package with a piece of string. **2. series, chain, row, line, run, bunch, sequence, set, succession** The director has had a long string of box office successes. **3. condition, provision, stipulation, qualification, term, reservation, proviso, specification** I wondered what strings were attached to such a good bargain.

stringent *adjective* **rigorous, severe, demanding, hard, exacting, strict, stiff, tough** The requirements for entering a United States military academy are stringent. ◆ **Antonyms: lax, lenient**

strip[1] *verb* **1. disrobe, unclothe, undress, bare, divest, uncover** I stripped in order to take a shower. **2. remove, take away, take off, peel, skin, flake, pare, shave, denude** We stripped paint from the desk we had bought at the yard sale. **3. rob, plunder, loot, ransack, sack, pillage, ravage, rifle, despoil** The gang of highwaymen stripped the passengers in the coach of all their valuables.

strip[2] *noun* **band, ribbon, swatch, bar, belt, shred, piece, swath, stripe** I showed my little sister how to weave place mats out of strips of construction paper.

stripe *noun* **1. band, bar, line, streak, strip, striation, vein, belt** A zebra has black and white stripes. **2. sort, kind, type, variety, breed, species, manner, nature, order, lot** My uncle is a man of a different stripe.

strive *verb* **try, attempt, seek, struggle, strain, aim, endeavor, labor, vie** Our youth group is striving to raise more money for charity this year than we did last year.

stroke[1] *noun* **1. blow, hit, smack, strike, knock, tap, whack, swat** I drove the golf ball well down the fairway on my first stroke. **2. event, feat, occurrence, happenstance, accomplishment, achievement, accident, coincidence** Getting home before the snow started was a stroke of good luck.

stroke[2] *verb* **pet, rub, brush, smooth, caress, pat, touch, fondle** Julia likes to stroke her pet rabbit's fur.

stroll *verb* **amble, hike, ramble, roam, saunter, walk, wander, meander, mosey** I like to stroll through the woods behind my house. ◆ *noun* **hike, ramble, walk, saunter, excursion, promenade, turn** My friend and I took a stroll around the neighborhood.

strong *adjective* **1. brawny, mighty, muscular, powerful, hale, hearty, robust, stout** Elephants are strong enough to carry big logs in their trunks. **2. strong-minded, resolute, firm, staunch, unyielding, determined, courageous** He was strong enough to stand up for his beliefs in the face of ridicule. **3. firm, secure, solid, stout, sturdy, substantial, stable, sound, sure** This tree limb is not strong enough to bear my weight. **4. intense, deep, ardent, fervent, impassioned, profound, unshakable** Her feelings of patriotism are very strong. **5. fierce, furious, heavy, high, violent, forceful, vigorous, energetic** Strong winds knocked over a tree in our front yard. **6. persuasive, effective, cogent, compelling, moving, convincing** My friend presented a strong argument for my trying out for the water polo team. **7. concentrated, potent, intense, powerful** The seasoning in this salsa is very strong. ➡ **Antonyms: 1. weak, frail 2. wavering, indecisive 3. flimsy, delicate 4. shallow 5. mild, moderate 6. weak, ineffective 7. weak, mild**

structure *noun* **1. arrangement, form, organization, pattern, design, shape, anatomy, constitution** The human brain has a complex structure. **2. building, construction, edifice, establishment, house, shed, shelter** The ranch has a house, a barn, and several smaller structures. ◆ *verb* **arrange, organize, compose, configure, form, pattern, shape, design** I structured my report along the lines that my teacher had suggested.

struggle *verb* **1. strain, strive, work, labor, grind, drudge, toil, moil** I struggled all afternoon to get the weeds out of the garden. **2. fight, battle, combat, duel, vie, contend, compete, contest, wrestle** Oliver Cromwell's army struggled against the forces of King Charles at Naseby in 1645. ◆ *noun* **1. effort, endeavor, strain, trouble, exertion, stress, labor, striving** It was a struggle to get the big chair into the small car. **2. combat, battle, fight, war, strife, contest, competition, rivalry, duel** After a struggle with King Charles and the Royalists, Oliver Cromwell was appointed Lord Protector of England.

strut *verb* **swagger, sashay, parade, flounce, prance, mince, sweep** The children laughed as they watched the rooster strut around the chicken yard.

stubborn *adjective* **determined, headstrong, obstinate, uncooperative, tenacious, intractable, willful** The stubborn camel refused to budge. ➡ **Antonyms: cooperative, docile**

student *noun* **learner, pupil, scholar, schoolboy, schoolgirl, collegian, undergraduate** The students bought a birthday present for their teacher.

studious *adjective* **1. bookish, scholarly, learned, educated, literate, academic, intellectual** He has been a studious person since he first learned to read. **2. careful, thorough, diligent, attentive, earnest, assiduous, painstaking, rigorous** The pupils made a studious effort to memorize the periodic table of the elements. ➡ **Antonyms: 1. illiterate, uneducated 2. careless, negligent**

study *noun* **1. education, schooling, learning, training, scholarship, instruction, lessons** It took him months of hard study to learn computer programming. **2. analysis, examination, investigation, observation, inquiry, survey** Our class made a thorough study of the events that led up to World War II. **3. report, survey, review, overview, treatise, thesis, paper, dissertation** I read a study about the effect of global warming on weather patterns. **4. den, library, office, studio, workroom, reading room** We turned the spare bedroom into a study. ◆ *verb* **1. review, go over, read, learn, research, master, peruse, reflect** I have to study my notes for tomorrow's history quiz. **2. examine, scrutinize, consider, survey, deliberate, observe, contemplate** We need to study the requirements before we make a decision.

stuff *noun* **1. material, matter, substance, soul, essence, basis, heart, core, pith** I think that fun, adventure, work, and study are the stuff of life. **2. articles, goods, things, items, gear, effects, possessions, belongings** Here's a list of the stuff that we need for the trip. ◆ *verb* **1. cram, crowd, fill, jam, load, pack, charge, squeeze, heap** The piñata was stuffed with candy. **2. fill, sate, satiate, glut, gorge, surfeit, overeat, engorge** I stuffed myself with macaroni and cheese.

stuffy *adjective* **1. airless, close, stifling, suffocating** I opened the windows to air out my stuffy room. **2. blocked, clogged, congested, filled, stopped-up, plugged** My sinuses are stuffy because I have allergies. **3. dull, boring, tiresome, formal, staid, stodgy, strait-laced** Sometimes I think my parents are stuffy. ➡ **Antonyms: 1. airy, fresh 2. open, unblocked 3. natural, informal**

stumble *verb* **1. trip, stagger, lurch, reel** I stumbled over my brother's toy train. **2. blunder, err, muff, bungle, botch,**

slip, fumble, boggle At the first rehearsal, I stumbled through my lines of the play. **3. chance on, happen on, encounter, find, run across, run into, discover** I stumbled across an old friend while I was at the library.

stump *verb* **baffle, bewilder, mystify, puzzle, thwart, frustrate, stymie, confound** The homework question stumped me, so I asked Mom for help.

stun *verb* **1. daze, stagger, stupefy, paralyze, deaden, benumb, numb** I was stunned when I hit my head getting out of the car. **2. shock, amaze, astonish, overwhelm, startle, surprise, awe, flabbergast** I was stunned to hear that my calf had won first place at the state fair.

stunning *adjective* **1. beautiful, lovely, attractive, striking, pretty, gorgeous, handsome, good-looking** The actress wore a stunning dress to the awards ceremony. **2. impressive, astonishing, dazzling, marvelous, remarkable, sensational, spectacular, astounding** The concert pianist thrilled the audience with her stunning performance. ➡ **Antonyms: 1. plain, drab 2. dull, unremarkable**

stunt[1] *verb* **check, curb, curtail, impede, limit, restrict, slow** Doctors warn that poor nutrition can stunt a young person's growth.

stunt[2] *noun* **feat, trick, act, deed, exploit, achievement, performance, maneuver** My cat's best stunt is to roll over when he wants me to feed him.

stupid *adjective* **1. unintelligent, dumb, silly, idiotic, foolish, brainless, simple-minded, vacuous** I made a stupid mistake on the spelling quiz. **2. dumb, rash, reckless, foolhardy, irresponsible, senseless, pointless** It is stupid to race across the railroad tracks in front of a train. ➡ **Antonyms: 1. bright, clever, intelligent 2. sensible, prudent, wise**

stupor *noun* **daze, trance, fog, muddle** I was in a stupor when I first woke up after my nap.

sturdy *adjective* **1. strong, muscular, brawny, sinewy, burly, athletic, robust, hale, hardy** The mountaineer has sturdy legs. **2. strong, tough, rugged, firm, durable, solid, substantial, secure, sound** We tied our rowboat to the dock with a sturdy rope. ➡ **Antonyms: 1. weak, frail, feeble 2. flimsy, fragile**

stutter *verb* **stammer, falter, stumble, hesitate** My friend often stutters when she feels shy. ◆ *noun* **stammer, stammering, stuttering** I am going to a speech therapist to correct my stutter.

style *noun* **1. arrangement, design, pattern, shape, configuration, form, type, treatment** That haircut is a great style for you. **2. kind, sort, type, variety, manner, mode, brand, category** What style of car does your dad drive? **3. luxury, wealth, affluence, comfort, pomp, extravagance, elegance** The TV program's format is to visit famous people who live in style. **4. vogue, fashion, fad, craze, trend, custom, taste, mode** Long skirts are back in style.

stylish *adjective* **fashionable, modish, dapper, spruce, elegant, chic, natty, smart** Edward VII was famous for being a stylish dresser. ➡ **Antonyms: unfashionable, old-fashioned**

suave *adjective* **smooth, urbane, charming, glib, facile, refined, polished, elegant** I enjoyed listening to his suave conversation. ➡ **Antonyms: vulgar, boorish**

subdue *verb* **1. conquer, vanquish, defeat, overcome, crush, whip, thrash, drub, subjugate** Genghis Khan subdued many enemies in intertribal wars. **2. check, control, reduce, suppress, curb, calm, ease** The medicine subdued my coughing. **3. tone down, soften, muffle, mute, quiet, moderate, modulate** We subdued our laughter when we saw people looking at us. ➡ **Antonyms: 1. lose, surrender 2. irritate, provoke 3. amplify, increase**

subject *adjective* **1. subordinate, dependent, subservient, answerable, captive, obedient** We are all subject to the laws of society. **2. prone, susceptible, disposed, inclined, liable, open, exposed, vulnerable** I am subject to allergies. ◆ *noun* **1. follower, citizen, liege, vassal, national, inhabitant** She claimed to be one of the queen's loyal subjects. **2. subject matter, theme, topic, issue, point, text, question, proposition** The teacher told us to pick a report subject by the end of the week. **3. class, course, topic, field, discipline, study, lesson, branch** My favorite subject is geography. ◆ *verb* **expose, put through, undergo, endure, suffer, experience, submit** During the medical exam, I was subjected to a CAT scan. ➡ **Antonyms: *adjective* 2. exempt, immune ◆ *verb* spare, exempt**

sublime *adjective* **majestic, grandiose, inspiring, superb, marvelous, grand, glorious, moving, wonderful** We listened to a performance of Beethoven's sublime Ninth Symphony. ➡ **Antonyms: ordinary, poor**

submerge *verb* **1. dip, douse, duck, immerse, plunge, soak, sink, submerse** The tired hiker submerged her feet in the cold mountain stream. **2. deluge, drown, inundate, engulf, flood, swamp, overwhelm, drench** The heavy rains caused the river to overflow its banks and submerge the downtown streets.

submit *verb* **1.** defer, give in, surrender, yield, comply, acquiesce, capitulate, cede The pilots refused to submit to the demand that they be inoculated for anthrax. **2.** hand in, turn in, offer, present, proffer, propose, tender, suggest, advance We submitted our test papers to the teacher at the end of class. ● **Antonyms: 1.** resist, withstand

subordinate *adjective* junior, auxiliary, inferior, lower, minor, secondary, ancillary The company's president accepts suggestions from subordinate employees. ◆ *noun* aide, assistant, employee, servant, slave, lackey, underling, attendant It makes me angry when my older brother acts like I'm his subordinate. ● **Antonyms:** superior, senior

subsequent *adjective* following, later, succeeding, consequent, future, next, ensuing The misunderstanding and subsequent bad feelings were quickly resolved. ● **Antonyms:** earlier, previous

subside *verb* **1.** go down, sink, lower, fall, settle, decline, sag, droop, slump The water gradually subsided after the flood. **2.** abate, decrease, diminish, dwindle, ebb, lessen, wane, ease up When the storm subsided, we went outside to go for a walk. ● **Antonyms: 1.** rise, climb, ascend **2.** grow, increase

substance *noun* **1.** element, ingredient, material, matter, stuff, constituent, item Flour is the main substance in most cakes. **2.** essence, depth, meaning, import, significance, content, value, worth, merit The comic book was fun to read, but it didn't have much substance. **3.** wealth, affluence, riches, money, means, resources, property, possessions She is a woman of substance.

substantial *adjective* **1.** solid, sturdy, strong, stable, sound, rugged, durable, stout We have a substantial dining table made of oak. **2.** ample, considerable, generous, great, large, significant, sizable, copious Dad got a substantial raise. ● **Antonyms: 1.** flimsy, frail, fragile **2.** small, little

substitute *noun* alternate, alternative, replacement, stand-in, surrogate, equivalent Mom often uses honey as a substitute for sugar when she bakes. ◆ *verb* change, exchange, replace, swap, switch, trade, alternate, interchange The coach substituted players every quarter to let everyone get some experience.

subtle *adjective* **1.** elusive, slight, understated, light, delicate, indirect, gentle The changes are subtle, but spring is definitely coming. **2.** keen, discerning, discriminating, sensitive, perceptive, acute, sharp, critical The lawyer has a subtle understanding of the complexities of the case. **3.** clever, skillful, ingenious, dexterous, agile, adroit, deft, cunning, shrewd The teacher's subtle control of his eager, excited students was impressive. ● **Antonyms: 1.** obvious, blunt **2.** dense, obtuse **3.** inept, awkward

subtract *verb* deduct, remove, take off, withdraw, decrease, diminish, discount The clerk subtracted the value of our coupons from our grocery bill. ● **Antonym:** add

succeed *verb* **1.** follow, ensue, come after, replace, supersede, relieve, inherit The election will determine who will succeed the current president. **2.** be successful, thrive, flourish, prosper, win, gain, conquer, accomplish Her bookstore has succeeded beyond all her expectations. ● **Antonyms: 1.** precede, introduce **2.** fail, founder

success *noun* **1.** triumph, victory, achievement, accomplishment, attainment, sensation, satisfaction Our school's fund-raising drive was a big success. **2.** eminence, prestige, fame, prosperity, status, wealth, fortune, luck John D. Rockefeller achieved great success in his lifetime. ● **Antonyms: 1.** disaster, failure **2.** disgrace, poverty

successful *adjective* **1.** effective, efficient, favorable, efficacious, productive, winning, fruitful My parents helped me to develop successful study habits. **2.** accomplished, famous, notable, prominent, well-known, prosperous, rich, wealthy Her dream is to be a successful engineer. ● **Antonym:** unsuccessful

succession *noun* **1.** order, sequence, course, progression, run, series, line, string I read the seven books of the Chronicles of Narnia in succession. **2.** accession, ascension, assumption, attainment, inheritance, elevation Henry IV won succession to the English throne by forcing Richard II to abdicate.

succinct *adjective* concise, short, brief, laconic, terse, compact, abbreviated, lean Lincoln's Gettysburg Address was a succinct and deeply moving speech. ● **Antonyms:** verbose, long

succumb *verb* **1.** yield, submit, capitulate, bow, buckle, surrender, accede, acquiesce I succumbed to my desire for a cheeseburger and fries. **2.** die, perish, decease, expire, depart, pass away, pass on He made a brave fight against his cancer, but he finally succumbed. ● **Antonyms: 1.** resist, withstand **2.** live, survive

sudden *adjective* **1.** unforeseen, unexpected, unanticipated, unpredictable, surprising, astonishing The sudden appearance of my friend was very welcome. **2.** abrupt, instant, quick, rapid, hasty, prompt, immediate The driver had to make a sudden stop in order to avoid hitting the squirrel. ➡ **Antonyms: 1. expected, foreseen 2. slow, gradual**

sue *verb* **appeal, entreat, ask, beseech, plead, solicit, beg, implore, supplicate** The defeated army sued for peace.

suffer *verb* **1. feel pain, ache, hurt, languish, agonize, ail, grieve, mourn** Many people suffer from migraine headaches. **2. accept, bear, endure, experience, sustain, undergo, stand, tolerate** Mom said that I'll have to suffer the consequences if I don't study for my math test.

suffering *noun* **1. anguish, distress, misery, agony, woe, torment, ordeal, sorrow** Suffering can be mental as well as physical. **2. pain, hurt, ache, aching, stab, sting, pang** The nurse gave the patient an injection to help ease his suffering. ➡ **Antonyms: 1. comfort, peace**

suffice *verb* **do, answer, satisfy, fulfill, serve, content, meet, suit** Dad said that my efforts to clean the garage would suffice.

sufficient *adjective* **adequate, enough, abundant, ample, satisfactory, liberal, decent** Do we have sufficient time to stop at the video store? ➡ **Antonyms: inadequate, insufficient**

suffocate *verb* **asphyxiate, choke, smother, stifle, gag, throttle** Dense smoke can suffocate a person.

suggest *verb* **1. offer, propose, put forward, recommend, advise, counsel, urge, advocate** My teacher suggested a report topic that he thought I might like. **2. hint, imply, intimate, signify, insinuate, denote, indicate, evoke** His tone suggested that he was in a hurry.

suggestion *noun* **1. proposal, proposition, recommendation, advice, counsel, idea, thought** I like your suggestion that we go bowling after dinner. **2. trace, touch, hint, shade, dash, dab, tinge, taste, intimation** He puts just a suggestion of marjoram in his scrambled eggs.

suit *noun* **1. outfit, ensemble, apparel, clothes, clothing, attire, garments** I have a new suit for my brother's wedding. **2. lawsuit, case, charge, action, proceeding, litigation** The store filed suit against the shoplifter. ◆ *verb* **1. fill, fit, accommodate, meet, do, serve, suffice, answer** Does this backpack suit your needs? **2. agree with, please, satisfy, content, delight, fit, gratify, become** My new room suits me better than my old one. ➡ **Antonyms: *verb* 2. displease, dissatisfy**

suitable *adjective* **acceptable, appropriate, apt, fit, good, proper, right, satisfactory** Mom bought a new dress that was suitable for more than one type of occasion. ➡ **Antonyms: inappropriate, unsuitable**

sulky *adjective* **moody, withdrawn, temperamental, sullen, morose, glum, grouchy, grumpy** I admit that I am sometimes sulky. ➡ **Antonyms: cheerful, merry, lively**

sullen *adjective* **glum, moody, morose, sulky, surly, angry, bitter, cross, resentful** My brother gets sullen when he thinks nothing is going his way. ➡ **Antonyms: happy, cheerful**

sultry *adjective* **humid, hot, stifling, close, stuffy, sticky, muggy, sweltering** On sultry days I like to find a cool place and read. ➡ **Antonyms: cool, breezy, brisk**

sum *noun* **1. amount, gross, grand total, sum total, total, value, aggregate, tally, number** Ticket sales for the charity raffle came to a larger sum than we had expected. **2. summary, summation, essence, heart, gist, core, rundown, recapitulation** The sum of his argument was that he wanted a raise. ◆ *verb* **add, calculate, compute, figure, total** Dad summed up the expenses from his business trip.

summary *noun* **digest, outline, review, rundown, survey, synopsis, summation, abstract** We had to read a book and turn in a summary of its contents. ◆ *adjective* **quick, swift, prompt, speedy, peremptory, immediate, hasty, instant** Hanging on the spot was a form of summary justice practiced in the Old West. ➡ **Antonyms: *adjective* slow, deliberate**

summit *noun* **1. peak, top, tip, pinnacle, crest, cap, roof, crown, height, vertex** There was snow on the mountain's summit until the middle of the summer. **2. apex, zenith, climax, acme, apogee, culmination, meridian** The actress enjoyed great fame and popularity at the summit of her career. ➡ **Antonyms: 1. base, bottom 2. nadir**

summon *verb* **1. convene, convoke, gather, rally, assemble, muster, collect** The President summoned his cabinet members for a special briefing. **2. call, page, send for, bid, ask, invite, order, command, invoke** The doctor was summoned to the hospital.

sundry *adjective* **various, miscellaneous, assorted, manifold, divers, myriad, numerous** Skiing is one of my sundry interests.

sunrise *noun* **sunup, dawn, daybreak, daylight, morning, dawning** Our rooster always crows at sunrise. ➡ **Antonyms: dusk, sunset, twilight**

sunset *noun* sundown, nightfall, twilight, evening, eventide The planet Venus will be visible just after sunset. ● **Antonyms:** dawn, daybreak, sunrise

super *adjective* excellent, outstanding, great, superior, prime, superb, extraordinary, terrific You did a super job! ● **Antonyms:** mediocre, average

superb *adjective* **1.** excellent, fine, splendid, superior, terrific, marvelous, exquisite, wonderful The actress received an award for her superb performance as a police chief. **2.** magnificent, majestic, grand, impressive, imposing, elegant, grandiose, stately New Mexico has some of the most superb scenery in the United States. ● **Antonyms: 1.** awful, bad, poor **2.** ordinary, plain

superficial *adjective* **1.** surface, skin-deep, external, exterior, outside, outer A scratch is a superficial wound. **2.** shallow, frivolous, trivial, uncritical, silly, mindless, glib, trite The movie was fun, but superficial. ● **Antonyms: 1.** internal, interior **2.** serious, profound

superintendent *noun* **1.** supervisor, foreman, foreperson, forewoman, overseer, leader, boss, chief, director My dad is a construction superintendent. **2.** janitor, custodian, caretaker, super, keeper, warden, guardian The superintendent made sure that the building was secure.

superior *adjective* **1.** excellent, exceptional, first-rate, first-class, premium, top, fine, prime This store carries furniture of superior quality. **2.** arrogant, haughty, insolent, proud, disdainful, conceited, snobbish, lofty, stuck-up We were annoyed by her superior attitude. ◆ *noun* senior, boss, chief, head, manager, supervisor, commander, director In the army, a captain is a lieutenant's immediate superior. ● **Antonyms:** *adjective* **1.** inferior, poor **2.** modest, humble ◆ *noun* subordinate, underling

supernatural *adjective* preternatural, unnatural, unearthly, metaphysical, transcendental, spiritual, occult, mystic The lights and colors of the aurora borealis can seem supernatural. ● **Antonyms:** natural, earthly

superstition *noun* old wives tale, notion, lore, fable, myth, fear George Bernard Shaw said that "fear is the main source of superstition."

supervise *verb* administer, direct, govern, manage, run, head, oversee, superintend My friend and I supervised the bake sale.

supervisor *noun* foreman, forewoman, foreperson, overseer, manager, boss, chief, director The factory has a supervisor in charge of each shift. ● **Antonyms:** employee, subordinate

supple *adjective* **1.** flexible, ductile, malleable, pliable, pliant, elastic, resilient My cowboy boots are made of supple leather. **2.** flexible, agile, limber, lithe, lissome, willowy, nimble, graceful My mother and I do yoga in order to stay supple. ● **Antonyms:** stiff, inflexible

supplement *noun* addition, complement, extra, accessory, addendum, adjunct, appendix The teacher gave us a magazine article as a supplement to our textbook. ◆ *verb* add to, fill out, augment, extend, increase, complement, complete I supplement my allowance with the money that I make recycling soda cans.

supply *verb* equip, furnish, provide, outfit, present, contribute, give, stock Our team sponsor supplied us with basketball jerseys. ◆ *noun* inventory, stock, store, hoard, reserve, quantity, allocation, fund The convenience store gets a fresh supply of doughnuts every morning.

support *verb* **1.** bear, brace, hold up, prop, reinforce, buttress, bolster, sustain The cabin has a big beam that supports the roof. **2.** substantiate, corroborate, uphold, authenticate, verify, document, testify I read several books that supported my position. **3.** back, endorse, foster, promote, aid, assist, help, encourage, advocate My parents have always supported my interest in music. ◆ *noun* **1.** backing, encouragement, aid, assistance, help, relief, succor My friends have given me lot of support. **2.** brace, buttress, pillar, post, prop, frame, backbone, bulwark, stay, shoring In the 12th century, the flying buttress was developed as a support for the walls of Gothic cathedrals.

suppose *verb* assume, believe, expect, guess, imagine, think, reckon, presume Do you suppose it will snow tonight?

suppress *verb* **1.** subdue, crush, quash, put down, squelch, stop, end, repress Four students were killed when the Ohio National Guard suppressed a riot at Kent State University on May 4, 1970. **2.** withhold, censor, ban, inhibit, muzzle, block, gag, muffle, control The editor of the newspaper decided to suppress the story. ● **Antonyms: 1.** encourage, inflame **2.** release, expose

supreme *adjective* top, topmost, foremost, head, highest, primary, principal, chief, ultimate The United States President is the supreme commander of the nation's military forces. ● **Antonyms:** lowest, secondary

sure *adjective* **1. certain, definite, positive, convinced, satisfied, confident** I am sure that I can finish my chores before noon. **2. certain, unavoidable, inevitable, inescapable, undeniable, guaranteed, assured** It is sure that we will attend Dad's company picnic. **3. secure, steady, firm, stable, fixed, solid, strong, fast, sturdy** Mountain goats are known for their sure footing. **4. dependable, reliable, trustworthy, sound, infallible, unfailing, sure-fire** Mom is confident that her investment is a sure thing. ➡ **Antonyms: 1. uncertain, unsure 2. avoidable 3. unsteady, insecure 4. unreliable, undependable**

surface *noun* **exterior, outside, top, cover, face, façade, skin, veneer** A pore is a tiny opening in the surface of the skin. ◆ *verb* **1. cover, pave, top, coat, overlay, spread, blacktop, asphalt** Ancient Roman roads were surfaced with stone. **2. emerge, appear, materialize, rise, arise, show up, crop up** Let's wait and see what surfaces from our inquiries.

surge *verb* **swell, rise, flow, gush, pour, rush, flood, stream, run** With the heavy rains, water surged over the banks of the river. ◆ *noun* **1. swell, wave, billow, gush, flood, heave, roller, torrent, current** There was a surge of water when we jumped into the swimming pool together. **2. increase, hike, rise, climb, jump, explosion, leap** The surge of requests for information overloaded the company's phone system. ➡ **Antonyms:** *noun* **2. plunge, decline, crash**

surly *adjective* **gruff, sullen, ill-humored, insolent, rude, brusque, discourteous, nasty** My brother gave me a surly look when I teased him about his terrible new haircut. ➡ **Antonyms: courteous, civil**

surmise *verb* **conclude, conjecture, guess, infer, speculate, suppose, theorize, presume** I surmised the result of the experiment correctly. ◆ *noun* **opinion, idea, guess, conjecture, presumption, inference, theory, assessment** What is your surmise as to which team will win the World Series?

surmount *verb* **overcome, defeat, conquer, vanquish, master, triumph over, prevail against** John Milton, the great epic English poet, surmounted many personal difficulties, including blindness.

surpass *verb* **better, eclipse, exceed, outdo, pass, top, beat, outshine, transcend** The cheetah surpasses all other land animals in speed.

surplus *adjective* **extra, leftover, spare, remaining, superfluous, residual, excess** We give away our surplus vegetables. ◆ *noun* **excess, overstock, oversupply, glut, plethora, reserve, extra** There is a surplus in the national budget. ➡ **Antonyms:** *noun* **shortage, lack**

surprise *verb* **amaze, astonish, awe, astound, shock, startle, stun, daze, flabbergast** When I saw them up close, I was surprised by how big the redwoods really are. ◆ *noun* **amazement, astonishment, awe, shock, bewilderment, wonder, incredulity** Imagine Mom's surprise when I cleaned my room without being told.

surrender *verb* **1. give up, capitulate, yield, submit, quit, succumb, collapse, topple** The troops surrendered after being surrounded by the enemy. **2. abandon, cede, relinquish, abdicate, renounce, resign, waive** She refused to surrender her rights to the inheritance. ◆ *noun* **capitulation, submission, concession, yielding, resignation, compliance, abandonment** Displaying a white flag to the enemy is the traditional sign of surrender. ➡ **Antonyms:** *verb* **1. resist, withstand 2. keep, retain**

surround *verb* **circle, encircle, envelop, ring, enclose, bound, girdle, beset** The actor was surrounded by reporters after he won an Oscar.

survey *verb* **1. inspect, observe, scan, view, watch, look over, reconnoiter** The general surveyed the battlefield as he planned his attack. **2. scrutinize, inspect, examine, study, search, peruse, contemplate** Darryl surveyed the literature that was available on the subject. ◆ *noun* **poll, study, review, investigation, search, inquiry, analysis, probe** The latest survey shows that support for the President has grown.

survive *verb* **exist, live, persist, thrive, endure, last, continue, prevail, abide** Polar bears can survive in extremely cold climates. ➡ **Antonyms: die, perish, succumb**

susceptible *adjective* **vulnerable, prone, open, subject, liable, responsive, disposed, given** He is not susceptible to flattery.

suspect *verb* **1. think, believe, assume, imagine, feel, surmise, presume, reckon** I suspect that I will overestimate how much time I have to get ready. **2. doubt, distrust, mistrust, disbelieve, question, challenge, query** I suspect her motives in offering to help me. ◆ *noun* **accused, defendant, prisoner, captive, internee, culprit** The police have two suspects in custody. ◆ *adjective* **suspicious, doubtful, dubious, problematic, questionable, uncertain, shady** His "evidence" of the existence of the Loch Ness monster is highly suspect. ➡ **Antonyms:** *verb* **1. know 2. believe, trust** ◆ *adjective* **certain, reliable**

suspend *verb* **1. bar, exclude, ban, banish, dismiss, evict, eject, exile** The student was suspended from school for a week. **2. break off, defer, delay, discontinue, interrupt, postpone, adjourn, quit** The baseball game had to be suspended because of rain. **3. dangle, hang, sling, swing, attach, fasten, connect** Dad suspended his hammock between two trees.

suspense *noun* **uncertainty, doubt, anticipation, tension, stress, nervousness, excitement** The mystery novel kept me in suspense.

suspension *noun* **1. interruption, pause, intermission, abeyance, break, disruption, halt** The cable company announced a brief suspension of service while they replaced their old equipment. **2. dismissal, expulsion, removal, ejection, banishment, separation, discharge** The rowdy student received a two-week suspension.

suspicion *noun* **1. belief, feeling, guess, hunch, idea, inkling, notion, impression** I have a suspicion that my little brother is the one who left a rubber snake in my bed. **2. distrust, doubt, mistrust, question, skepticism, wariness, misgiving** When we discovered that the hamburger meat was missing, our suspicions fell on the dog. ➡ **Antonyms: 2. trust, confidence, faith**

sustain *verb* **1. maintain, keep up, preserve, continue, carry on, retain, uphold** I hope to sustain my efforts to keep my room neat. **2. nourish, feed, nurture, foster, nurse, support, supply, furnish** In the winter many birds sustain themselves on the feed that people provide. **3. endure, experience, suffer, tolerate, bear, stand, withstand, brave** I am inspired by stories of people who sustain great hardship and yet achieve success. **4. corroborate, confirm, prove, verify, uphold, affirm, validate** She sustained my story.

swagger *verb* **strut, stride, sashay, saunter, flounce, parade** The members of the winning team swaggered off the field. ➡ **Antonyms: slink, creep**

swallow *verb* **1. ingest, bolt, consume, devour, down, take, gulp, guzzle** She can swallow a vitamin pill without taking any water. **2. tolerate, endure, take, suffer, withstand, stomach, abide, accept** I'm not going to swallow any more of your insults. **3. repress, stifle, hold back, withhold, choke, suppress, restrain** I swallowed my feelings at the time, but wrote about them later in my journal. ◆ *noun* **drink, gulp, mouthful, sip, taste, nip, bit** I tried a swallow of coffee, but I didn't like it.

swamp *noun* **bog, marsh, marshland, mire, morass, swampland, wetland, fen, 'everglade** Alligators live in Florida's swamps. ◆ *verb* **1. engulf, flood, inundate, deluge,**

immerse, submerge, sink, drown, drench A huge wave swamped the boat. **2. overwhelm, flood, burden, beset, besiege, overload, overtax, strain** Cards, packages, and letters swamp the postal system during the holidays.

swap *verb* **trade, exchange, barter, switch, substitute, change** I swapped my sandwich for my friend's bagel.

swarm *noun* **crowd, horde, host, mass, multitude, throng, group, flock, mob** A swarm of fans ran onto the field as the game ended. ◆ *verb* **congregate, crowd, flock, mass, throng, teem, cluster** At the school dance, most of the students swarmed around the refreshment table. ➡ **Antonyms:** *verb* **disperse, scatter**

swarthy *adjective* **dark, brunette, dusky, brown, black, tan** My favorite movie star has black hair and a swarthy complexion. ➡ **Antonyms: light, pale, fair**

swat *verb* **smack, whack, slap, hit, knock, clout, smite, strike, wallop** I tried to swat the fly with a newspaper. ◆ *noun* **slap, blow, smack, strike, hit, lick, crack, whack, strike, slug** I got that pesky fly with my second swat.

sway *verb* **1. move, ripple, wave, swing, wobble, bend, shake** The flowers swayed in the evening breeze. **2. dispose, influence, incline, predispose, persuade, induce, move, prompt** The talk show host swayed his listeners to take action to save the ancient ruins. ◆ *noun* **power, influence, leverage, weight, authority, control, mastery, force** That magazine has great sway over its readers.

swear *verb* **pledge, state, testify, vow, affirm, assert, promise, vouch, guarantee** Immigrants have to swear an oath of loyalty to become citizens of the United States.

sweep *verb* **1. brush, dust, whisk, wipe, clean, tidy, clear, gather** I swept the kitchen floor. **2. remove, convey, carry, wash away, overwhelm, destroy, demolish** Floodwaters swept the bridge downstream. **3. glide, scud, sail, float, skim, fly, march, scurry, swoop** I watched the clouds sweep across the sky. ◆ *noun* **1. pass, stroke, swoop, thrust, motion, movement, swing** I cleaned off the cookie crumbs with one sweep of my hand. **2. expanse, stretch, reach, span, range, spread, length, distance** I love the sweep of the Canadian prairies.

sweet *adjective* **1. sugary, sweetened, rich, saccharine, honeyed** I don't eat sweet cereals anymore. **2. pleasing, delightful, agreeable, enjoyable, gratifying, pleasant, delectable** The flowers smell sweet this evening. **3. considerate, courteous, friendly, gracious, kind, nice, charming, adorable** It was sweet of him to send you a birthday card. ➹ **Antonyms: 1.** bitter, sour **2.** unpleasant, offensive **3.** inconsiderate, selfish

swell *verb* **1.** bulge, puff, balloon, expand, grow, rise, enlarge, thicken, fatten My finger swelled where the bee had stung me. **2.** build, intensify, amplify, mount, throb, heighten, rise, surge, heave The music began to swell as the conductor indicated a crescendo. ◆ *noun* **1.** increase, expansion, upturn, growth, jump, escalation, rise The swell in orders came from our increase in advertising. **2.** wave, roller, billow, ripple, surge The ocean swells gently rocked our boat. ◆ *adjective* great, fantastic, wonderful, superb, marvelous, fabulous, splendid, excellent I had a swell time at your party. ➹ **Antonyms:** *verb* **1.** shrink, contract **2.** ebb, wane ◆ *noun* **1.** reduction, drop ◆ *adjective* rotten, miserable

sweltering *adjective* hot, humid, torrid, scorching, blistering, burning, stifling, sultry It is hard to do anything active on a sweltering day like this. ➹ **Antonyms:** cool, dry

swerve *verb* turn aside, veer, sheer, dodge, cut, move, shift, detour, deviate The driver swerved in order to avoid hitting the pothole.

swift *adjective* fast, fleet, quick, rapid, speedy, hasty, brisk, flying He is our swiftest runner. ➹ **Antonyms:** slow, sluggish

swindle *verb* defraud, cheat, deceive, fool, trick, dupe, finagle, rook, bilk The dishonest jeweler tried to swindle people by selling them fake diamonds. ◆ *noun* deception, fraud, hoax, racket, trick, cheat, theft After the swindle was discovered, the people responsible were sent to jail.

swing *verb* **1.** dangle, hang, suspend, sway, oscillate, seesaw, move We watched the monkeys swing from a branch. **2.** circle, curve, swerve, turn, twist, shift, veer, pivot, rotate, wheel The boomerang swung around and came back to me. ◆ *noun* stroke, swat, blow, hit, strike, thrust, poke, slice, jab The golfer took a swing at the ball.

swirl *verb* spin, twirl, twist, whirl, rotate, eddy, churn The dancer's skirts swirled around her as she moved.

switch *noun* **1.** stick, branch, twig, cane, shoot, stalk, rod, pole He improvised a fishing pole from a long switch and a piece of string. **2.** alteration, change, shift, modification, exchange, substitution, swap, trade We made a last-minute switch in our vacation plans. ◆ *verb* **1.** waggle, wag, whip, wave, swish, whisk, swing, lash The angry cat switched its tail back and forth. **2.** change, exchange, swap, trade, shift, substitute, interchange My sister and I sometimes switch rooms for the night.

swoop *verb* sweep, dive, plummet, descend, plunge, drop, fall, pounce The owl swooped down to catch a mouse.

> ### Word Group
>
> A **sword** is a hand weapon that has a long blade set in a handle, or hilt. **Sword** is a general term with no true synonyms. Here are some common types of swords:
>
> A **broadsword** has a broad blade, used for cutting rather than thrusting. A **claymore** is a large broadsword formerly used by Scottish Highlanders. A **cutlass** has a curved, single-edged blade. An **épée** is a fencing sword with a fluted blade. A **falchion** is a short sword used in medieval times. A **foil** is long and thin and used in fencing. A **gladius** is the short sword used by Roman legionnaires. A **rapier** is a light sword with a sharp point, used for thrusting. A **saber** is a cavalry sword with a single-edged, curved blade. A **scimitar** is a curved, single-edged Asian sword.

symbol *noun* emblem, mark, sign, token, badge, character, indication, image The dove and the olive branch are both symbols of peace.

sympathize *verb* commiserate, feel, pity, grieve, ache, condole, comfort, understand I sympathized with my friend when she told me about her dad's accident.

sympathy *noun* **1.** commiseration, empathy, comfort, compassion, condolence, support, concern My friends gave me lots of sympathy when I had my appendix removed. **2.** accord, agreement, concurrence, harmony, consent, approval, favor I am in sympathy with Mothers Against Drunk Driving. ➹ **Antonyms: 1.** indifference

symptom *noun* indication, sign, warning, evidence, feature, mark His fever was a symptom of the flu.

synopsis *noun* summary, outline, digest, sketch, brief, abstract, condensation This magazine gives a good synopsis of the movie.

synthetic *adjective* artificial, manmade, manufactured, unnatural, imitation, fake, phony Plastic is a synthetic material made from petroleum.

system *noun* **1.** set, unit, arrangement, combination, complex, entity, structure My parents just bought a new stereo system. **2.** method, order, pattern, plan, procedure, way, principle, rule, scheme In 1876, Melvil Dewey developed a system for shelving library books that is still in use today.

Tt

tab[1] *noun* **flap, tongue, strip, string, pull, projection, lip, tag, label** I opened the padded envelope by pulling its tab.

tab[2] *noun* **bill, check, invoice, statement, account, price, charge, rate, cost** We looked at the tab and figured out the tip.

table *noun* **1. dining table, dinner table, bar, counter, stand, buffet, desk** Please put the silverware on the table. **2. meal, food, fare, repast, feast, board, victuals, spread** That restaurant sets a delicious table. **3. plateau, mesa, steppe, upland, tableland** Many mountains have summits that are high, flat tables. **4. chart, list, appendix, graph, register, agenda, catalog, column** My encyclopedia has a table of facts about the planets in our solar system. ◆ *verb* **postpone, defer, shelve, delay, stay, suspend, hold off, wait** We tabled discussion of the issue until the next meeting.

tablet *noun* **1. pad, notepad, notebook, writing pad, sketchbook, memo pad, book** I keep a tablet of writing paper by my bed. **2. capsule, pill, medication, medicine, lozenge, wafer, pellet, dose** When I have a headache, I usually take two aspirin tablets.

tabulate *verb* **classify, arrange, rank, group, order, list, categorize, index, figure** The committee tabulated the responses to their questionnaire. ➡ **Antonyms: jumble, mix, confuse**

tack *noun* **1. thumbtack, pin, brad, nail, pushpin, staple** I used a tack to put up my new calendar. **2. approach, direction, strategy, tactic, course, plan, way, line** I decided to try a different tack to get Mom to let me go to the dance. ◆ *verb* **1. attach, fasten, nail, secure, pin, stick, staple, mount, affix** I tacked a poster of my favorite singer to my closet door. **2. swerve, shift, turn, veer, sheer, zigzag, change, switch** The sailboat tacked into the wind. ➡ **Antonyms:** *verb* **1. detach, remove**

tackle *noun* **equipment, gear, apparatus, material, trappings, goods, implements, rig** We gathered our fishing tackle and headed to our favorite lake. ◆ *verb* **1. undertake, attempt, endeavor, try, essay, accept, begin, take on** I know that you will succeed at whatever you tackle. **2. pounce on, grab, seize, stop, capture, catch, block, attack** The receiver was tackled just as he crossed the 20-yard line. ➡ **Antonyms:** *verb* **1. avoid, evade**

tact *noun* **tactfulness, diplomacy, consideration, thoughtfulness, courtesy, politeness, discretion, sensitivity** It takes tact to be able to tell a person about his or her faults without giving offense. ➡ **Antonyms: tactlessness, insensitivity**

tactful *adjective* **diplomatic, thoughtful, delicate, discreet, sensitive, polite, courteous, considerate** It was tactful of you to leave the room when I received the phone call. ➡ **Antonyms: tactless, thoughtless**

tactic *noun* **stratagem, scheme, device, move, ploy, maneuver, plan, strategy** He used flattery as a tactic to get what he wanted.

tag *noun* **label, sticker, marker, ticket, slip, tab, card, stub** All items with red tags are on sale. ◆ *verb* **1. label, mark, ticket, designate, identify, name, title, check** The porter tagged each piece of baggage to show its destination. **2. follow, tail, trail, accompany, chase, pursue, dog, hound** My little brother tags along whenever I go outside to play with my friends.

tail *noun* **back, end, rear, tip, extremity, rump, backside, extremity, posterior** The airplane's identification number was painted on its tail. ◆ *verb* **follow, trail, pursue, stalk, track, hound, shadow, dog, chase** A police detective tailed the suspect from the airport to her apartment.

tailor *verb* **adjust, alter, style, mold, fit, change, modify, cut, shape** Mom tailored Dad's old jacket so that it would fit me.

taint *verb* **spoil, putrefy, rot, decay, contaminate, dirty, ruin, adulterate, corrupt** Sitting out too long has tainted these egg salad sandwiches. ◆ *noun* **stain, spot, blemish, stigma, onus, flaw, contamination, corruption, pollution** The taint of his expulsion for cheating will be with him for a long time.

take *verb* **1. capture, seize, gain, get, win, confiscate, secure, appropriate** The soldiers were instructed to take the enemy camp. **2. catch, hook, snare, ensnare, trap, entrap, kill, hunt** We throw back whatever fish we take because we believe in "catch-and-release." **3. charm, captivate, enchant, entertain, bewitch, please, delight** I was taken with the beautiful photography in this magazine. **4. ingest, swallow, consume, devour, drink, eat, imbibe, inhale**

Take this medicine twice a day. **5. abide, endure, suffer, tolerate, withstand, accept, brave, undergo** I'm not sure if I can take another day of this rainy weather. **6. have, receive, accept, select, choose, draw, get, buy, hold** I'll take this book on anthropology. **7. call for, involve, entail, need, require, demand, want, necessitate, use** This assignment should take about one hour to complete. **8. bear, bring, carry, fetch, convey, haul, move, transport** Jacob takes his lunch to school every day. **9. interpret, understand, comprehend, grasp, assume, perceive, sense, regard** Did you take her comment to mean the same thing I did? **10. heed, accept, obey, observe, respect, adopt, follow, comply, embrace** I took my teacher's advice and narrowed my report topic. **11. deduct, remove, subtract, withdraw, eliminate, discount, knock off** If you had 18 quarters and took away 2, how many dollars would you have? ◆ *noun* **net, profit, gross, receipts, revenue, share, yield, proceeds** What was the take from the arts and crafts festival?

tale *noun* **1. anecdote, story, yarn, narrative, fable, romance, myth, legend, saga** The old sailor had many tales to tell about his days at sea. **2. lie, falsehood, fib, untruth, fabrication, fiction, tall tale, canard** My little sister tells tales that she swears are true.

talent *noun* **ability, aptitude, skill, gift, genius, faculty, bent, flair** Melissa has a talent for expressing her thoughts in an original way.

talk *verb* **1. speak, verbalize, vocalize, articulate, enunciate, utter, pronounce, say, voice** Most children learn to talk at approximately 2 years of age. **2. chat, converse, speak, chatter, communicate, discuss, confer, parley** My friends and I can talk on the phone for hours. **3. persuade, influence, convince, sway, induce, motivate, coax, cajole** I talked my friend into going shopping with me. **4. inform, disclose, reveal, broadcast, divulge, air, intimate, betray, leak** The criminal was caught because his accomplice talked. ◆ *noun* **1. conference, consultation, conversation, discussion, chat, meeting, dialogue, visit** My parents had a talk with my teacher about my progress in school. **2. address, lecture, speech, presentation, sermon, discourse, homily, oration** A firefighter gave our class a talk about fire safety. **3. hearsay, gossip, rumor, speculation, chatter, chat, tidings, report, news** The actor's lewd behavior has caused a lot of talk.

tall *adjective* **1. high, lofty, big, lengthy, long, towering, soaring, giant, elevated** The tallest building in the world is the Sears Tower in Chicago. **2. exaggerated, imaginative, fanciful, boastful, fantastic, implausible, unbelievable, absurd** I like the tall tales about Pecos Bill and Paul Bunyan. ◆ **Antonyms: 1. low, short 2. believable, plausible**

tally *noun* **score, amount, total, summation, sum, reckoning, count, computation** She looked at the tally of her bowling game and groaned. ◆ *verb* **1. add up, count, enumerate, total, reckon, number, record** We tallied the votes for our class officers election. **2. match, agree, jibe, fit, coincide, correspond, conform, accord, parallel** His version of the accident tallies with yours. ◆ **Antonyms:** *verb* **2. disagree, clash, contradict**

tame *adjective* **1. tamed, domesticated, broken, obedient, housebroken, domestic, tractable** Our parakeet is so tame that he will sit on my finger. **2. docile, gentle, meek, pliable, submissive, controllable, compliant, timid** To ensure a tame Germany after World War I, the world powers imposed many penalties and sanctions. **3. dull, boring, uninteresting, bland, humdrum, spiritless, tepid, prosaic, commonplace** For an action movie, it was very tame. ◆ *verb* **break, bust, domesticate, master, discipline, subdue, train, gentle, housebreak** It's not easy to catch and tame a wild horse. ◆ **Antonyms:** *adjective* **1. wild, untamed 2. willful, stubborn 3. interesting, exciting**

tamper *verb* **1. fool, meddle, mess, tinker, fiddle, interfere, pry, alter, damage** Dad told us not to tamper with his new fax machine. **2. fix, influence, bribe, corrupt, sway, manipulate, buy, rig, coerce** The prosecution had tried to tamper with the jury.

tang *noun* **1. flavor, savor, taste, zest, sharpness, punch, spice, nip, zip** Some cheeses are aged to give them more tang. **2. hint, suggestion, trace, bit, dab, touch, smack, tinge** There is a tang of salt in sea air.

tangible *adjective* **real, concrete, substantial, solid, objective, actual, palpable, touchable, physical** The gun found at the scene of the crime was tangible evidence. ◆ **Antonyms: intangible, imaginary**

tangle *verb* **1. kink, knot, snarl, twist, disorder, mess, scramble, dishevel** The wind tangled Rebecca's long hair. **2. fight, wrangle, tiff, contend, spat, quarrel, argue, dispute** We tangled over whose turn it was to empty the cat box. ◆ *noun* **kink, knot, snarl, twist, maze, mess, muddle, web, jungle** Rebecca combed the tangles out of her hair.

tank *noun* **vessel, receptacle, container, vat, basin, reservoir, cask, tub, cistern, well** At our summer cabin, we have a huge tank for collecting rainwater.

tantalize *verb* **tease, provoke, tempt, bait, captivate, entice, fascinate, torment** Mom likes to tantalize us by giving us clues about our birthday presents. ◆ **Antonyms: appease, satisfy**

tantrum *noun* **blowup, fit, temper tantrum, outburst, rage, scene, rampage, storm, huff** When I was little, I used to have huge tantrums when I didn't get what I wanted.

tap[1] *verb* **drum, rap, hit, knock, pat, strike, thump, beat, bob** Our teacher taps his pencil on his desk when he's thinking. ◆ *noun* **knock, rap, hit, pat, slap, strike, thump, smack, stroke, blow** Did you hear a tap on the door?

tap[2] *noun* **faucet, spigot, spout, valve, cock, petcock, nozzle** We need to fix that dripping tap. ◆ *verb* **drain, draw, siphon, bleed, milk, pump, drill, bore, pierce, spike** We tapped the maple trees in February this year to harvest sap for syrup.

tape *noun* **band, ribbon, strap, strip, braid, rope, cord, roll** The lead runner broke the tape that was stretched across the finish line. ◆ *verb* **fasten, secure, stick, bind, seal, tie, wrap, bandage** I taped basketball posters all over my wall. ➽ **Antonyms:** *verb* **remove, unfasten**

taper *verb* **diminish, fade, wane, ebb, abate, subside, decline, dwindle, decrease** The conversation tapered off. ➽ **Antonyms: increase, grow**

tardy *adjective* **1. late, overdue, detained, delayed, belated, behind, behindhand** I have been tardy two times this year. **2. slow, sluggish, laggard, reluctant, slack, leisurely, slow-going** He was tardy in sharing his opinion with the rest of us. ➽ **Antonyms: 1. punctual 2. prompt, fast**

target *noun* **1. goal, mark, objective, aim, end, object, intention, point, dream** We have set a target of 1,000 dollars for our fund-raising drive. **2. butt, victim, mark, sitting duck, prey, quarry, scapegoat** I was the target of my friends' teasing when I came to school with a fake tattoo.

tariff *noun* **duty, impost, levy, tax, assessment, fee, charge, rate** The government froze tariffs on textiles for a period of five years.

tarnish *verb* **1. corrode, oxidize, discolor, darken, dim, dull, stain** Copper turns green when it tarnishes. **2. defile, sully, discredit, blemish, besmirch, blot, stain, taint, soil** The name of Benedict Arnold was tarnished when he attempted to deliver West Point into the hands of the British. ◆ *noun* **corrosion, oxidation, discoloration, dullness, rust, blemish, stain, taint** The tarnish on the silver pitcher obscured the detail of its engraving. ➽ **Antonyms:** *verb* **1. shine, polish 2. honor, praise** ◆ *noun* **shine, luster**

tarry *verb* **linger, remain, dawdle, dally, stay, delay, bide, wait** I tarried after school to talk to my friends. ➽ **Antonyms: rush, hasten**

tart[1] *adjective* **1. acid, bitter, sour, sharp, tangy, astringent, vinegary, piquant, pungent** Lemons are very tart. **2. biting, sharp, bitter, unkind, caustic, cutting, scathing, harsh** I made a tart remark to my sister because I was feeling cranky. ➽ **Antonyms: 1. sugary, sweet 2. gentle, kind, friendly**

tart[2] *noun* **fruit tart, pastry, pie, tartlet, turnover** My English grandmother makes raspberry tarts every Christmas.

task *noun* **assignment, chore, duty, job, obligation, responsibility, mission, business** The Greek hero Hercules was assigned 12 tasks by the oracle of Apollo.

taste *verb* **1. sample, test, try, partake of, eat, relish, savor, criticize, chew** Please taste this soup and tell me if it needs more salt. **2. experience, know, undergo, encounter, feel, meet, see, sense, perceive** Last weekend I tasted the pleasures of sailing. ◆ *noun* **1. flavor, savor, tang, relish, zest, essence, aroma, smack, aftertaste** I love foods that have a spicy taste. **2. bit, bite, morsel, nibble, sample, sip, swallow, mouthful, slice, piece** May I have a taste of your apple pie? **3. liking, preference, leaning, bent, penchant, appreciation, fondness, fashion, style** I like your taste in music. **4. judgment, discernment, perception, discrimination, discretion, propriety, tastefulness** Jacqueline Kennedy was known as a woman of wonderful taste. ➽ **Antonyms:** *noun* **3. distaste, hatred 4. impropriety, tastelessness**

tasteless *adjective* **1. bland, flat, flavorless, unsavory, insipid, plain, mild, weak** The spaghetti sauce was rather tasteless, so Mom added some herbs and spices. **2. indelicate, vulgar, coarse, crass, rude, crude, boorish, unbecoming** That was a tasteless joke. ➽ **Antonyms: 1. flavorful, spicy 2. polite, civil**

taunt *verb* **insult, mock, provoke, sneer, ridicule, tease, bother, torment** My brother taunted me about my bad haircut. ◆ *noun* **jeer, insult, sneer, gibe, scoff, dig, barb, teasing, derision, ridicule, sarcasm** I ignored his taunts. ➽ **Antonyms:** *verb* **flatter, compliment** ◆ *noun* **praise, compliment**

taut *adjective* **1. stretched, tight, firm, rigid, stiff, tense, drawn, hard** Please hold the measuring tape taut. **2. strained, tense, jittery, nervous, stressed, uneasy, anxious, fidgety** Her nerves were taut from working so many hours. ➽ **Antonyms: 1. loose, slack 2. relaxed**

tavern *noun* **pub, bar, saloon, barroom, cabaret, night-club, bistro, inn** Dad met his friends at the tavern for a drink.

tawny *adjective* **golden, brownish, dusky, beige, light brown, sandy** My dog has tawny fur.

tax *noun* **1. assessment, levy, charge, duty, tariff, toll, custom, impost, cost** We have to pay a sales tax on almost everything we buy. **2. burden, load, strain, pressure, hardship, weight, demand, responsibility** The large number of students put a tax on the school's resources. ◆ *verb* **1. assess, levy, charge, exact, impose, encumber, tithe** The county government taxes property owners. **2. drain, exhaust, sap, weaken, burden, strain, overwork, weary, tire** The long hike taxed my strength.

taxi *noun* **cab, taxicab, hack, hired car, limousine** Dad called a taxi to take us to the airport.

teach *verb* **educate, inform, instruct, train, tutor, coach, drill, enlighten, school** My brother is teaching me how to play his new computer game. ◆ **Antonyms: learn, study**

teacher *noun* **schoolteacher, educator, instructor, professor, schoolmaster, schoolmistress, mentor** My parents met all my teachers at our school's open house last week. ◆ **Antonyms: student, pupil, learner**

team *noun* **1. group, unit, band, company, crew, force, squad, bunch, body** A team of investigators probed the accident site. **2. pair, couple, yoke, span, tandem, duo, twosome, brace, set** The wagon was pulled by a team of horses. ◆ *verb* **ally, combine, couple, join, pair, unite, mate, unify, cooperate** The three authors teamed up to write a book. ◆ **Antonyms:** *verb* **divide, separate**

tear[1] *verb* **1. pull, rip, shred, split, cut, slice, tatter, rend, mangle** My gerbils tore apart a piece of cardboard for nesting material. **2. injure, wound, harm, hurt, gash, lacerate, rupture, mutilate** I take my earrings out when I play sports so that I don't tear my earlobes. **3. charge, fly, race, rush, speed, bolt, dash, hurry, gallop, run, zoom** A group of boys came tearing down the street on their bicycles. ◆ *noun* **rip, split, gash, rent, slit, cut, gap, hole, crack** My jeans have a tear in the knee.

tear[2] *noun* **teardrop, drop, moisture, water, fluid** I laughed so hard I had tears in my eyes.

tease *verb* **annoy, bother, harass, irritate, pester, vex, torment, plague, taunt** The dog growled at the boys who were teasing him. ◆ *noun* **gibe, taunt, ridicule, heckling,** **dig, barb, persecution** Our teases were meant in jest. ◆ **Antonyms:** *verb* **soothe, pacify** ◆ *noun* **compliment, praise**

technique *noun* **1. method, procedure, system, way, formula, manner, approach, course** Making your own flash cards is a great study technique. **2. form, skill, style, craftsmanship, facility, expertise, proficiency, art** The guitarist practiced hard to improve her technique.

tedious *adjective* **boring, dull, tiresome, uninteresting, wearisome, dreary, monotonous, laborious** I find chopping vegetables for a large salad to be a tedious task. ◆ **Antonyms: exciting, interesting, stimulating**

teem *verb* **swarm, abound, gush, overflow, bustle, brim, crawl, bristle, crowd** The stadium teemed with fans.

telescope *verb* **compress, condense, shorten, abridge, shrink, lessen, cut, curtail** I telescoped my lengthy report down to only three pages. ◆ **Antonyms: extend, amplify, lengthen**

televise *verb* **air, broadcast, telecast, show, transmit, relay, announce, publish** I hope that today's Dodgers game will be televised.

tell *verb* **1. narrate, recite, relate, recount, describe, report, chronicle, depict** Please tell me a story. **2. indicate, show, inform, identify, acquaint, apprise, advise, educate** A watch tells the time. **3. say, speak, state, utter, voice, talk, verbalize, communicate, express** My friend always tells the truth. **4. disclose, divulge, expose, give away, reveal, betray, leak, tattle, spill** I promised my friend that I wouldn't tell her secret to anyone. **5. differentiate, know, distinguish, determine, discover, ascertain, discern, recognize** Can you tell a ripe watermelon from an unripe one? **6. bid, command, direct, order, demand, require, oblige, charge, instruct** Mom told me to clean up my room.

telling *adjective* **striking, substantial, powerful, effective, significant, considerable, decisive, good** Seeing a tutor has had a telling effect on my geometry grade. ◆ **Antonyms: minor, negligible, trivial**

temper *verb* **1. moderate, mitigate, soften, tone down, subdue, modify, adjust, attune** The aerobics instructor tempers her routine according to the class needs. **2. anneal, harden, set, dry, bake, strengthen, stiffen, toughen** We tempered our clay sculptures in a kiln. ◆ *noun* **1. nature, disposition, mood, spirit, temperament, makeup, complexion** Our dog has a very sweet temper. **2. calmness, composure, poise, tranquillity, coolness, serenity, calm,**

balance Several drivers lost their tempers during the traffic jam. **3. anger, fury, rage, wrath, irritation, agitation, passion, fit, tantrum** When I am upset, I count to ten to control my temper. ⏵ **Antonyms:** *verb* **1. intensify, increase 2. soften, weaken**

temperament *noun* **disposition, nature, humor, make-up, spirit, personality, soul, mood, complexion** She has an easygoing temperament.

temperate *adjective* **1. levelheaded, sensible, sober, restrained, reasonable, prudent, judicious** The judge was a temperate person. **2. clement, balmy, warm, pleasant, mild, moderate, agreeable, gentle, sunny** Southern California is known for its temperate climate. ⏵ **Antonyms: 1. unrestrained, immoderate 2. harsh, cold**

tempest *noun* **storm, commotion, tumult, uproar, disturbance, outbreak, upheaval, chaos, furor** There was a tempest over the high gas prices. ⏵ **Antonyms: calm, peace, quiet**

temporary *adjective* **short-term, short-lived, interim, transitional, brief, momentary, passing, fleeting** My sister is looking for a temporary job this summer. ⏵ **Antonyms: lasting, long-lived, permanent**

tempt *verb* **1. attract, invite, lure, entice, coax, draw, seduce, solicit** The bakery tempted potential customers with free samples. **2. goad, provoke, bait, arouse, incite, prick, dare, court, try** Walking along the edge of a high roof is tempting fate. ⏵ **Antonyms: 1. discourage, dissuade**

temptation *noun* **attraction, lure, bait, draw, pull, enticement, magnet, snare, seduction** Chocolate is a temptation that many people find difficult to resist.

tenacious *adjective* **firm, unyielding, persistent, dogged, resolute, relentless, obstinate, stubborn** Thomas Edison was tenacious in his pursuit of the light bulb. ⏵ **Antonyms: wavering, flexible**

tenant *noun* **lodger, renter, lessee, inhabitant, occupant, resident, dweller, roomer** My parents have found a tenant for their rental house.

tend[1] *verb* **be apt, be likely, incline, lean, slant, favor, verge, trend, gravitate** New Mexico's climate tends to be hot and dry.

tend[2] *verb* **attend, care, look after, see to, watch, guard, protect, minister, shepherd** I tend my horse after school. ⏵ **Antonyms: ignore, neglect, shirk**

tendency *noun* **disposition, inclination, propensity, penchant, bias, bent, leaning, trend** I have a tendency to stay up late on weekends. ⏵ **Antonyms: disinclination, aversion**

tender[1] *adjective* **1. delicate, soft, fragile, frail, weak, flimsy, dainty, supple** Broccoli becomes tender when it is steamed. **2. young, vulnerable, inexperienced, immature, childish, green, juvenile, impressionable** Alexander Pope was an established poet by the tender age of 17. **3. painful, sensitive, sore, uncomfortable, aching, throbbing, inflamed, raw, swollen** I sprained my ankle last week, and it's still tender. **4. caring, gentle, loving, compassionate, kindhearted, warm, sympathetic, sweet, thoughtful** The mother cat was very tender with her newborn kittens. ⏵ **Antonyms: 1. tough, hard 2. mature, old 4. harsh, merciless, uncaring**

tender[2] *noun* **bid, offer, suggestion, proposal, presentation, proposition, advance** Their tender for the book contract was rejected by the author. ◆ *verb* **offer, suggest, present, submit, propose, advance, propound** I tendered my opinion on the marketing strategy for the new product.

tense *adjective* **1. rigid, stiff, strained, stretched, taut, tight, drawn, inflexible** When a cat is frightened, its whole body becomes tense. **2. anxious, apprehensive, nervous, restless, uneasy, edgy, jittery, fidgety** The actor was tense on the opening night of his first play. ◆ *verb* **flex, brace, tighten, stiffen, strain, pull, draw, stretch** I tensed my muscles as I prepared to jump. ⏵ **Antonyms:** *adjective* **1. limp, slack 2. calm, relaxed** ◆ *verb* **relax, loosen**

tension *noun* **1. tautness, pull, rigidity, force, pressure, traction, stiffness** There is a lot of tension on the surface of a drum. **2. worry, anxiety, apprehension, stress, strain, restlessness, dread, uneasiness** I experience a great deal of tension when I have to take a test. ⏵ **Antonyms: 1. slack 2. calm, tranquillity, relaxation**

Word Group

A **tent** is a portable shelter stretched over a supporting framework of poles. **Tent** is a general term with no true synonyms. Here are some types of tents from all over the world:

A-frame tent, beit al-sha'r, dome tent, marquee, pavilion, pup tent, tepee, tupik, yurt

tentative *adjective* **1. conditional, provisional, unconfirmed, indefinite, dependent, contingent, undecided** My report topic is still tentative. **2. timid, hesitant, uncertain,**

insecure, anxious, shaky, wavering, shy, faltering The foal took its tentative first steps shortly after being born. ❧ **Antonyms: 1. confirmed, resolved 2. confident, assured**

tepid *adjective* lukewarm, temperate, warm, moderate, mild, cool My tea has become tepid. ❧ **Antonyms: hot, boiling**

term *noun* **1. duration, interval, period, time, span, stretch, tenure, spell, reign, administration** Our mayor was elected for a term of four years. **2. expression, word, locution, name, phrase, appellation, designation, terminology** That dictionary defines more than one thousand computer terms. **3. condition, provision, qualification, requirement, proviso, clause, requisite, reservation** One of the terms of the loan was that it had to be paid off in two years. **4. standing, relations, circumstance, status, footing, state, connection, association** We are on friendly terms with our neighbors. ◆ *verb* **name, call, designate, title, specify, style, label, dub, define, tag** George Washington has been termed the father of our country.

terminal *adjective* **1. deadly, fatal, mortal, incurable, lethal** He died of a terminal illness. **2. ultimate, maximum, final, last, closing, concluding, ending** A falling object quickly reaches its terminal velocity. ◆ *noun* **depot, station, stop, destination, terminus** We arrived at the terminal just in time to catch our bus. ❧ **Antonyms:** *adjective* **1. curable 2. beginning, initial**

terminate *verb* stop, finish, end, culminate, conclude, cease, discontinue, abort, complete I try to terminate one sewing project before beginning another. ❧ **Antonyms: begin, open, inaugurate**

terrain *noun* landscape, country, territory, topography, environment, surroundings, area, ground, turf Much of Ireland's terrain is rolling and green.

terrible *adjective* **1. dreadful, appalling, dire, scary, alarming, distressing, terrifying, horrifying, frightening** The terrible news caused her to faint. **2. intense, severe, formidable, overwhelming, powerful, strong, extreme** The terrible storm caused a lot of damage. **3. disagreeable, offensive, intolerable, insufferable, revolting, repulsive, unpleasant** Rotten meat has a terrible smell. **4. awful, bad, dreadful, horrible, poor, rotten, atrocious, inferior** I'm usually pretty good at tennis, but my game was terrible today. ❧ **Antonyms: 1. comforting, soothing 2. mild, gentle 3. pleasant, agreeable 4. good, superior**

terrific *adjective* **1. awesome, astounding, extraordinary, amazing, incredible, intense, terrible, powerful** The hurricane had terrific winds of more than 95 miles per hour. **2. great, magnificent, marvelous, splendid, superb, wonderful, remarkable, fine, stupendous** I had a terrific time at your party. ❧ **Antonyms: 1. moderate 2. poor**

terrify *verb* alarm, frighten, panic, petrify, scare, terrorize, shock, intimidate Thunder and lightning terrify my dog. ❧ **Antonyms: soothe, lull, calm**

territory *noun* **1. area, region, district, locality, terrain, locale, expanse, zone, land** A grizzly bear roams over a territory of about 100 square miles. **2. domain, realm, province, state, nation, dominion, commonwealth** The United States purchased the Louisiana Territory in 1803.

terror *noun* alarm, dread, fear, fright, horror, panic The rabbit froze in terror when it saw a hawk circling overhead.

terse *adjective* concise, brief, short, condensed, abrupt, curt, pithy, laconic, precise I gave a terse answer to the question. ❧ **Antonyms: wordy, verbose, vague**

test *noun* **1. probe, study, analysis, trial, tryout, diagnosis, inspection, check, assessment** Ivan Pavlov conducted tests of conditioned reflexes using a dog, a bell, and a food reinforcer. **2. exam, examination, quiz, midterm, final, questionnaire, catechism** We are having a history test tomorrow. ◆ *verb* **analyze, check, examine, investigate, assess, grade, question, verify** Cities routinely test their water to make sure that it is safe to drink.

testify *verb* affirm, assert, avow, attest, profess, claim, confirm, declare, swear Two witnesses testified that they saw the defendant at the crime scene.

testimony *noun* **1. declaration, statement, assertion, claim, affidavit, deposition, avowal, admission** The jury listened carefully as the witness gave her testimony. **2. verification, proof, evidence, demonstration, witness, affirmation, corroboration, indication** Her smile was testimony of her happiness.

testy *adjective* irritable, touchy, crabby, cranky, peevish, snappy, impatient, petulant, grumpy He is often testy in the morning. ❧ **Antonyms: kindly, patient, affable**

tether *noun* leash, rope, cord, chain, fetter, shackle, restraint The cowboy used a tether to keep his horse from wandering away. ◆ *verb* tie, leash, fasten, bind, chain, moor, shackle, restrain, secure We tether our parrot to its perch. ❧ **Antonyms:** *verb* loose, untie, release

text *noun* **1. words, writing, lines, contents, passage, document, matter** My dictionary contains 840 pages of text. **2. theme, topic, argument, point, subject, thesis, focus, issue** The text that Martin Luther King Jr. spoke to in his most famous speech was civil rights. **3. book, schoolbook, textbook, primer, manual, reference, workbook, reader** I have to read a chapter in my history text.

textile *noun* **cloth, fabric, material, fiber, thread, yarn, goods, filament** Rayon was the first synthetic textile to be developed.

texture *noun* **feel, consistency, grain, makeup, character, composition, structure** Sandpaper has a rough texture.

thankful *adjective* **appreciative, grateful, content, glad, pleased, happy, relieved** We were thankful to be inside all warm and snug while the blizzard raged outside. ➤ **Antonyms: thankless, ungrateful**

thankless *adjective* **1. ungrateful, unappreciative, unthankful, ungracious, thoughtless, inconsiderate, rude** The thankless guest left without saying goodbye. **2. unacknowledged, unappreciated, useless, fruitless, unrewarding, uninviting, distasteful** Doing the dishes is often a thankless chore. ➤ **Antonyms: 1. grateful, thankful 2. appreciated, rewarding**

thaw *verb* **1. defrost, warm, warm up, soften, dissolve, melt, liquefy** Take the steaks out of the freezer so they can thaw. **2. melt, moderate, temper, relax, unwind, relent, mellow, yield, loosen** Her aloofness was thawed by the child's friendly smile. ◆ *noun* **melting, thawing, spring, warm weather** Tulips and daffodils bloom after the first thaw in the spring. ➤ **Antonyms:** *verb* **1. freeze 2. stiffen** ◆ *noun* **freeze, frost**

Word Group

The term **theater** refers to dramatic literature or its performance. **Theater** is a general term with no true synonyms. Here are some common types of dramatic performances:

A **comedy** has a funny story with humorous characters and a happy ending. **Drama** tells a story in prose or verse. **Improvisation** refers to an improvised dramatic skit. **Kabuki** refers to traditional Japanese drama with rich costumes and conventional gestures. A **musical** contains song and dance numbers. **No** refers to classical Japanese drama with music and dance performed in a highly stylized manner. A **tragedy** is a serious play that ends with great misfortune.

theft *noun* **larceny, stealing, burglary, robbery, looting, pilfering, pinching, lifting** The man reported the theft of his car to the police.

theme *noun* **1. point, premise, subject, subject matter, topic, text, thought, argument** The theme of the mayor's speech was the need for budgetary support of law enforcement efforts. **2. article, composition, essay, paper, report, thesis, manuscript, statement** Our English teacher had us write a theme about what we did on summer vacation. **3. melody, refrain, motif, tune, song, strain, air, theme song** I keep humming the theme from that musical.

theory *noun* **1. proposition, concept, thesis, idea, postulate, principle, law, explanation, philosophy** There are many different theories about how the universe may have originated. **2. hypothesis, assumption, supposition, guess, conjecture, speculation, intuition, suspicion, opinion** The detective had a theory as to who committed the crime.

therapy *noun* **treatment, remedy, corrective, regimen, rehabilitation, cure, care, medicine** A soak with epsom salts is a good therapy for aching muscles.

therefore *adverb* **accordingly, as a result, consequently, hence, so, thus, ergo, wherefore** Monique did an independent research project and therefore did not have to take the final exam.

thick *adjective* **1. broad, deep, wide, fat, big, bulky, large, thickset, solid, compact** A castle's walls are usually quite thick. **2. stiff, firm, viscid, viscous, gelatinous, glutinous, dense, solid, syrupy** Honey gets thick when it is cold. **3. crowded, dense, packed, tight, impenetrable, lush, luxuriant, profuse** We couldn't see very far into the thick forest. **4. noticeable, pronounced, strong, deep, heavy, conspicuous, great** He speaks with a thick accent. **5. close, devoted, friendly, familiar, chummy, intimate, inseparable** My cousin and I are thick friends. ➤ **Antonyms: 1. thin, narrow 2. runny, liquid 3. bare, sparse 4. slight, small**

thicket *noun* **brush, underbrush, shrubbery, bushes, covert, copse, grove** A rabbit bounded out of the thicket.

thief *noun* **burglar, robber, stealer, criminal, crook, bandit, highwayman** The police are looking for the thief who broke into our neighbor's house.

thin *adjective* **1. fine, delicate, gossamer, flimsy, translucent, filmy, gauzy, fragile** The thin paper tore easily. **2. lean, skinny, slender, slim, lanky, gaunt, slight, spare, scrawny** The distance runner was thin but strong. **3. rare,**

scarce, sparse, meager, scant, scanty, skimpy, spare Grandpa's hair is getting thin on top. **4.** dilute, runny, watered-down, watery, weak, light, diffuse Thin paint is easier to apply than thick paint. **5.** flimsy, weak, lame, poor, implausible, insufficient, inadequate, sketchy, superficial He gave a thin excuse for being late. ♦ *verb* decrease, disperse, diminish, reduce, dilute, water down, weaken, attenuate The crowd began to thin before the game was over. ➤**Antonyms:** *adjective* **1.** thick, heavy **2.** fat, heavy **3.** thick, abundant **4.** viscous, syrupy **5.** believable, plausible ♦ *verb* increase, thicken

thing *noun* **1.** article, item, object, contraption, gadget, stuff, device, entity I saw some really neat things at the museum. **2.** act, action, deed, feat, accomplishment, job, task, transaction, obligation Mom said that I did the right thing when I turned in the wallet to the lost and found. **3.** belongings, goods, personal effects, possessions, gear, property, effects, stuff Dad told me to pick up my things and take them to my room. **4.** affair, circumstance, happening, event, condition, matter, business, concern How are things at school? **5.** fad, craze, fashion, vogue, style, obsession, mania, notion Saddle shoes and bobby socks were quite the thing in the 1950s.

think *verb* **1.** consider, contemplate, deliberate, ponder, meditate, mull, muse Charles had to think for a few moments before he could solve the riddle. **2.** assume, believe, conclude, guess, presume, suppose, judge, reckon, deem My friend and I look so much alike that people often think we are related. **3.** recall, remember, reminisce, reflect, recollect, bethink, revive, retain I haven't thought of that in years!

thirsty *adjective* **1.** parched, dry, dehydrated, arid, bone-dry, waterless This heat makes me thirsty. **2.** eager, keen, avid, anxious, greedy, impatient, inclined, craving I am thirsty to learn about Native American customs.

thorough *adjective* **1.** complete, exhaustive, extensive, full, total, entire, thoroughgoing, meticulous, careful I gave my horse a thorough brushing. **2.** utter, absolute, sheer, downright, unqualified, perfect, pure, entire, consummate, outright That is thorough nonsense. ➤**Antonyms: 1.** partial, careless **2.** imperfect, qualified

thought *noun* **1.** belief, concept, idea, notion, opinion, view, conviction, perception, judgment What are your thoughts on this subject? **2.** consideration, contemplation, deliberation, reflection, meditation, study, attention I have given your suggestion a lot of thought. **3.** intention, purpose, goal, intent, plan, aim, object, expectation, aspiration, hope My thought was to surprise you.

thoughtful *adjective* **1.** contemplative, meditative, reflective, thinking, pensive, introspective, rapt I get very quiet when I am in a thoughtful mood. **2.** careful, attentive, prudent, cautious, circumspect, heedful, wary Sarah gave a thoughtful answer to my question. **3.** caring, considerate, kind, kindly, courteous, polite, civil, tactful, solicitous It was very thoughtful of you to send me a get-well card. ➤**Antonyms: 1.** shallow **2.** heedless, rash **3.** inconsiderate, thoughtless

thrash *verb* **1.** flog, whip, scourge, beat, strike, lash, strap, flail, pommel, thresh The mutinous sailor was thrashed at the captain's orders. **2.** beat, crush, defeat, overwhelm, trounce, whip, vanquish, drub Our softball team thrashed our opponents by a score of 7 to 0. **3.** writhe, jerk, flail, squirm, toss, thresh, twist, tumble, flounder The fish thrashed about on the deck of the boat.

thread *noun* **1.** filament, strand, fiber, yarn, cord, line, twine, string, wire There's a thread hanging from your sweater. **2.** theme, topic, drift, gist, tenor, subject, course, matter, thesis, train I have lost the thread of this conversation. ♦ *verb* wend, wind, meander, twist, zigzag, snake, weave, ramble, inch We threaded our way through the woods.

threat *noun* **1.** warning, caution, notice, notification, promise, intimidation, admonition The teacher carried out her threat to send the rude students to the principal's office. **2.** omen, portent, indication, forewarning, intimation, premonition, signal, sign Those clouds hold a threat of rain. **3.** danger, hazard, menace, peril, risk, jeopardy, endangerment, trouble, distress A spokesperson said that the forest fire does not pose a threat to any homes.

threaten *verb* **1.** intimidate, menace, bully, terrorize, cow, browbeat, harass, pressure The belligerent country threatened its neighbor by moving troops to the border. **2.** put at risk, endanger, jeopardize, imperil, hazard, menace, risk This year's harvest is being threatened by drought.

threshold *noun* **1.** doorsill, doorstep, entryway, sill, entranceway, portal, gateway, doorway, entrance My cat was sitting on the threshold waiting to be let in. **2.** brink, edge, point, verge, borderline, beginning, gate, dawn, start Teenagers stand at the threshold of adulthood. ➤**Antonyms: 2.** termination, conclusion

thrift *noun* frugality, economy, thriftiness, prudence, husbandry, saving, conservation, management I practice thrift with the money I earn from baby-sitting. ➤**Antonyms:** waste, extravagance

thrifty *adjective* **economical, frugal, prudent, saving, chary, provident, sparing, careful** A thrifty shopper tries to buy things on sale. ➤ **Antonyms: extravagant, wasteful**

thrill *verb* **delight, excite, please, tickle, electrify, stimulate, enchant, stir, charge** Getting a perfect score on the math test thrilled me. ◆ *noun* **1. tingle, tremor, tremble, quiver, shake, shiver, shudder, quake** A thrill ran through the audience when the curtain went up. **2. excitement, joy, pleasure, sensation, adventure, stimulation, fun** I can still recall the thrill of my first motorcycle ride.

thrive *verb* **flourish, prosper, succeed, grow, progress, bloom, develop, boom, shine** Dad is pleased that his new business has begun to thrive. ➤ **Antonyms: die, fail, wane**

throb *verb* **pulsate, pulse, beat, pound, thump, flutter, tremble, vibrate, quaver** After running the race, I could feel my pulse throb. ◆ *noun* **beat, pulse, tremor, vibration, pulsation, reverberation, palpitation** The crew could feel the throb of the engines as the tugboat began to move.

throng *noun* **crowd, flock, horde, mass, mob, multitude, swarm, bunch, army** A throng of fans waited all night to buy tickets to the concert. ◆ *verb* **crowd, flock, mob, press, swarm, jam, assemble, gather, congregate** After the game, the fans thronged around the players. ➤ **Antonyms:** *verb* **disperse, scatter, separate**

through *preposition* **around, in, among, between, into, past, throughout, within** We took a drive through the countryside. ◆ *adverb* **completely, thoroughly, entirely, totally, utterly, fully, over, throughout** I read the book through. ◆ *adjective* **1. direct, nonstop, uninterrupted, straight, express, constant, regular** We got a through flight from Boston to Los Angeles. **2. done, finished, completed, ended, over, concluded, terminated, past** Are you through with your homework yet?

throw *verb* **1. pitch, toss, cast, fling, heave, hurl, sling, lob, chuck, hurtle** I threw the boomerang correctly on my first try. **2. project, send forth, emit, expel, throw off, eject, radiate, issue, release** My flashlight can throw a beam 150 feet. **3. confuse, baffle, mix up, confound, bewilder, perplex, dumbfound, stump** The false clues threw the detective. ◆ *noun* **pitch, toss, cast, delivery, fling, hurl, lob, sling, heave, shot** The pitcher's first throw was high and wide.

thrust *verb* **1. force, jam, push, ram, shove, drive, plunge, propel, press** David thrust his hands into his pockets to keep them warm. **2. inject, interpose, insert, impose, interrupt, intervene, intrude** He thrust his comments into our conversation. **3. plunge, jab, poke, stab, pierce, stick, puncture, spear, skewer** I thrust a toothpick into the cheese cube. ◆ *noun* **1. lunge, stab, plunge, drive, push, shove, advance, jab, charge, blow** In fencing, competitors use their swords to block their opponents' thrusts. **2. power, force, energy, momentum, drive, boost, propulsion** I want a car that has a lot of thrust in the engine. **3. essence, theme, gist, drift, meaning, import, sense, substance, significance** The thrust of the article was the importance of recycling.

thump *noun* **thud, thwack, bang, thunk, clunk, knock, clump, throb, pulse** The chair fell over with a thump. ◆ *verb* **hit, beat, pound, strike, whack, slam, thud, rap, smack** Rabbits sometimes thump the ground with their hind legs.

thunder *noun* **roar, rumble, blast, boom, peal, crash, explosion, clap, crack** The thunder of the race cars was deafening. ◆ *verb* **1. boom, reverberate, roar, blast, drum, rumble, resound, crack, explode** Music thundered from my brother's room. **2. bellow, shout, yell, bark, holler, fulminate, snarl, threaten** The angry drivers thundered at each other.

thus *adverb* **accordingly, as a result, consequently, hence, therefore, ergo, so** I overslept, and thus I was late to school.

thwart *verb* **defeat, foil, frustrate, hinder, obstruct, prevent, stop, stump, check** I thwarted my dog's attempt to eat the cat's food. ➤ **Antonyms: assist, help, support**

tick *noun* **1. beat, click, clack, tap, pulse, sound, ticktock** The tick of the metronome helps me when I practice my piano music. **2. checkmark, line, cross, stroke, dot, blaze, notch, nick, scratch, indication** I put a tick mark next to the items on the list that we had gathered. ◆ *verb* **click, clack, thump, beat, tap, oscillate, vibrate, swing, pulsate** The grandfather clock ticked quietly.

ticket *noun* **1. admission, pass, coupon, permit, slip, card, token, voucher, stub** Dad has two free tickets for tonight's concert. **2. label, tag, sticker, marker, slip, tab, docket** According to the ticket, this shirt costs 32 dollars. **3. ballot, list, slate, roster, roll, catalog, register** There are several candidates on the Green Party ticket. ◆ *verb* **label, tag, sticker, mark, brand, docket, earmark, characterize, identify** The clerk ticketed the items for the sale.

tickle *verb* **1. stroke, touch, brush, caress, pet, fondle, cuddle, scratch** My little sister always squirms and giggles when I tickle her feet. **2. amuse, delight, entertain, captivate, please, fascinate, gladden, regale, cheer** The children's performance tickled the entire audience.

tidy *adjective* **1. neat, orderly, organized, clean, uncluttered, trim, spruce, shipshape, groomed** I like to keep my room tidy. **2. considerable, respectable, sizable, large, substantial, ample, generous, handsome, goodly** I have a tidy sum saved for college. ◆ *verb* **neaten, organize, straighten, arrange, clean, spruce, pick up, groom, police** We tidied the kitchen when we were done making brownies. ➡ **Antonyms:** *adjective* **1. messy, untidy 2. small, paltry** ◆ *verb* **mess up**

tie *verb* **1. attach, bind, fasten, secure, connect, join, knot, band, tether** Dad tied a tarp over our stack of firewood. **2. deadlock, balance, equal, even, draw, match, meet, parallel** That last touchdown tied the score. **3. unite, connect, affiliate, associate, link, bind, team, ally, league** My cousin and I are tied by family. ◆ *noun* **1. cinch, fastener, fastening, cord, line, ribbon, rope, string, band** Do you have a tie for this garbage bag? **2. bond, attachment, connection, link, relationship, allegiance, kinship, commitment, affiliation** There is a strong tie between my uncle and my dad. **3. deadlock, draw, standoff, stalemate, equality, dead heat, even game** The hockey game ended in a tie. ➡ **Antonyms:** *verb* **1. detach, untie 3. separate**

tier *noun* **layer, level, step, rank, row, story, stratum, echelon, course** The wedding cake had three tiers.

tight *adjective* **1. secure, immovable, impenetrable, strong, snug, fixed, set, fast, sealed** It took a lot of time to undo the tight knot. **2. stretched, taut, tense, strained, pulled, rigid, stiff, firm** The guitar strings are too tight. **3. full, packed, demanding, busy, active, heavy, hectic, involved** My schedule is tight during basketball season. **4. close, compact, compressed, crowded, packed, thick, dense, clustered** The military jets were flying in a tight formation. **5. little, small, snug, close, formfitting, skintight, narrow, constrictive** I've been growing so quickly that some of my clothes are now too tight for me. **6. frugal, sparing, cheap, close, miserly, stingy, tightfisted, ungenerous, mean** My parents had to be tight with their money when they were college students. **7. scarce, scanty, skimpy, deficient, inadequate, insufficient, rare, dear** Money is tight for many people after the holidays. ◆ *adverb* **firmly, securely, tightly, closely, solidly, hard, close** Hold the rope tight. ➡ **Antonyms:** *adjective* **1. loose, insecure 2. slack, flexible 3. empty, open 4. loose, open 5. big, roomy, ample 6. generous, liberal 7. abundant, plentiful** ◆ *adverb* **loosely, insecurely**

tighten *verb* **contract, tense, clench, stiffen, narrow, pinch, constrict, fix, secure** I tightened my grip on my little brother's hand as we stepped off the curb. ➡ **Antonyms: loosen, relax, slacken**

till[1] *verb* **plow, cultivate, harrow, furrow, prepare, hoe, turn** Farmers once tilled their fields with horse-drawn plows.

till[2] *preposition* **until, before, prior to, up to** We can't leave till the meeting is over.

till[3] *noun* **register, cash drawer, cash box, safe, vault, tray, box, treasury** The money in the till has to be counted every night.

tilt *verb* **1. lean, tip, incline, slant, dip, slope, list, yaw, pitch** I tilted my head in order to hear my friend as she whispered in my ear. **2. combat, fight, battle, contest, joust, duel, contend, skirmish, clash** The muckrakers of the early 20th century tilted against corruption by writing exposés. ◆ *noun* **1. angle, lean, slant, slope, list, pitch, incline, cant, rake** This table has a noticeable tilt. **2. debate, argument, altercation, squabble, combat, battle, contest, encounter, fray** My brother and I got into a tilt over who could make the most baskets in a row.

timber *noun* **1. trees, woods, woodland, timberland, forest, copse, grove, thicket, bush** The northern part of the state has vast areas of dense timber. **2. lumber, wood, board, logs, plank, lath, rafter, cross beam, puncheon** Our house is built of timber and brick.

time *noun* **1. interval, space, span, spell, stretch, term, while, duration, stint, turn** It seems like a long time until summer vacation. **2. meter, tempo, measure, rhythm, beat, cadence, pulse** The ice skater moved to the time of the music. **3. chance, moment, occasion, opening, opportunity, juncture, place, point, shot** Now would be a good time to ask Mom if we can to go to a movie. **4. age, period, era, day, epoch, season, heyday, lifetime, culture** I like to read about the life and times of King Arthur. ◆ *verb* **schedule, adjust, synchronize, set, regulate, measure, pace, plan** Our lawn sprinklers are timed to go on at regular intervals.

timid *adjective* **shy, bashful, afraid, cautious, fearful, timorous, apprehensive, hesitant, cowardly** When my little brother is feeling timid, he hides behind Dad's legs. ➡ **Antonyms: bold, confident, fearless**

tinge *verb* **shade, tint, color, dye, season, stain, tincture** My new contact lenses are tinged with green. ◆ *noun* **trace, touch, shade, dash, bit, suspicion, smack, pinch, hint** There is a tinge of autumn in the air.

tingle *verb* **sting, bite, prickle, ring, quiver** The fierce wind made my ears tingle. ◆ *noun* **sting, prickle, thrill, throb, shiver, quiver, itch, chill** I felt a tingle of nervousness just before I went on stage.

tinker *verb* **putter, fiddle, play, dabble, trifle, meddle, experiment** I tinkered with the settings for the colors on my computer screen.

tinkle *verb* **ring, jangle, jingle, clink, ping, ting, chime, ding, sound** The pennies tinkled when they fell to the floor. ◆ *noun* **chime, jingle, peal, clink, chink, ting** I like the tinkle of wind chimes.

tint *noun* **hue, shade, tinge, tone, color, dye, stain, pigmentation, wash** Emerald and jade are two common tints of green. ◆ *verb* **color, dye, shade, stain, imbue, tone, frost, tinge, wash, rinse** I tinted my hair a darker shade of brown.

tiny *adjective* **diminutive, little, miniature, minute, small, wee, midget, microscopic, minuscule** A Chihuahua is a tiny dog. ➡ **Antonyms: big, huge, large**

tip[1] *noun* **peak, point, top, end, extremity, tiptop, crown, apex, head** Only the tip of an iceberg shows above water.

tip[2] *verb* **1. knock over, overturn, upset, capsize, topple, upend, dump, tilt, overthrow, pitch** I accidentally tipped over my glass of milk. **2. lean, tilt, list, angle, bend, heel, cant, slant, pitch** The sunflower began to tip from the weight of its head.

tip[3] *noun* **1. gratuity, bonus, reward, perk, perquisite** Dad left a generous tip for the waiter. **2. pointer, suggestion, clue, hint, advice, admonition, information, warning** The police officer gave us several tips on bicycle safety. ◆ *verb* **caution, forewarn, advise, tip off, clue, suggest, inform, tell** The weather man tipped us that there was a chance of rain.

tire *verb* **exhaust, fatigue, weary, drain, weaken, wear out, enervate, debilitate, sap** The long bike ride tired me. ➡ **Antonyms: invigorate, refresh, revive**

tired *adjective* **1. exhausted, fatigued, weary, bushed, drooping, worn-out, spent, drained, sleepy, drowsy** The tired workers took a break and rested. **2. bored, irked, exasperated, fed up, sick of, impatient, bothered** I am tired of your constant complaining. **3. hackneyed, trite, clichéd, overworked, stereotypical, stale, unoriginal, overused, commonplace** The writer brought new life to the tired plot. ➡ **Antonyms: 1. energetic, fresh 3. original, new**

tiresome *adjective* **boring, irritating, tedious, irksome, exasperating, monotonous, arduous, wearisome, vexing** People who complain constantly are tiresome.

titanic *adjective* **huge, giant, tremendous, colossal, gigantic, monster, immense, mighty** An English mastiff is a titanic dog. ➡ **Antonyms: small, puny**

title *noun* **1. name, designation, heading, appellation, brand, handle, term** What is the title of that book you are reading? **2. claim, deed, ownership, possession, right, interest, privilege, tenure, entitlement** There is some question as to who really has title to the mansion. **3. championship, crown, honors, laurels, cup, emblem, ribbon, medal** The boxer who wins this bout will hold the world title. ◆ *verb* **call, designate, name, label, entitle, term, christen, dub, baptize** I don't know what to title my report.

together *adverb* **collectively, concurrently, jointly, en masse, mutually, simultaneously, closely, unanimously, all together** If we work together, we can finish faster. ➡ **Antonyms: separately, alone, individually**

toil *verb* **labor, slave, work, strain, strive, struggle, moil, grub, drudge** The farm workers toiled in the field from dawn to dusk. ◆ *noun* **drudgery, exertion, labor, work, effort, struggle, moil, industry, application, sweat** The coal miner finally retired after many years of toil. ➡ **Antonyms: verb relax, loll ◆ noun ease, leisure**

token *noun* **1. expression, mark, sign, symbol, badge, indication, proof, manifestation, evidence** The couple exchanged rings as a token of their love for each other. **2. keepsake, souvenir, remembrance, memento, trophy, reminder, relic** This barrette is a token of my trip to Ensenada. ◆ *adjective* **nominal, minimal, small, partial, superficial, surface, symbolic, hollow, slight** She displayed only token happiness when her rival was cast in the lead role. ➡ **Antonyms: adjective genuine, wholehearted, serious**

tolerance *noun* **1. open-mindedness, respect, good will, patience, understanding, compassion, leniency, mercy** Tolerance between nations is vital for world peace. **2. endurance, resilience, resistance, stamina, strength, steadfastness, hardiness** The skydiver has a high tolerance for cold and fear. ➡ **Antonyms: 1. bigotry, prejudice, bias**

tolerate *verb* **1. allow, permit, stand for, indulge, condone, approve, authorize, concede, sanction** Our teacher does not tolerate any boisterous behavior in her classroom. **2. endure, bear, take, withstand, abide, stomach, brook, suffer, swallow, undergo** I can tolerate hot weather better than cold weather. ➡ **Antonyms: 1. ban, forbid, prohibit**

toll[1] *noun* **charge, fee, price, cost, expense, tariff, tax, fare, levy, impost** Drivers have to pay a toll to use this expressway.

toll[2] *verb* peal, ring, chime, knell, sound, strike, bong, clang, signal In colonial days, bells were tolled to gather people together.

tomb *noun* burial chamber, crypt, grave, sepulcher, vault, catacomb, mausoleum, monument The Taj Mahal in India is a grand tomb that was built for an emperor's wife.

ton *noun* load, mass, lot, pile, great deal, profusion, abundance, glut, avalanche I have a ton of homework to do.

tone *noun* 1. note, pitch, sound, noise, harmonic, intonation, overtone, resonance, timbre I like the tone of the cello. 2. hue, shade, tinge, tint, color, cast, value, coloring Our new drapes have three tones of blue in them. 3. firmness, fitness, resiliency, elasticity, strength, health, vigor My grandmother does yoga to maintain her muscle tone. 4. mood, spirit, attitude, feel, tenor, overtone, quality, note, manner From the tone of my friend's voice, I could tell that she was glad to see me.

tongue *noun* dialect, language, speech, talk, voice, vernacular, cant, lingo, discourse, idiom My friend Tuyen's native tongue is Vietnamese.

too *adverb* 1. also, as well, likewise, additionally, besides, furthermore, plus, more When I asked for a hot dog, my brother said that he wanted one too. 2. very, excessively, extremely, overly, unduly, inordinately, greatly This shirt is too small for me.

tool *noun* 1. implement, instrument, apparatus, device, utensil, machine, appliance, equipment, gadget A hammer is one tool that every carpenter possesses. 2. means, agent, mechanism, vehicle, weapon, avenue, agency, apparatus A person's vote is his or her tool for effecting change in government. 3. puppet, pawn, stooge, dupe, victim, fool, idiot, accomplice, messenger He used his coworkers as tools for his own success.

top *noun* 1. crest, peak, summit, tip, crown, head, zenith, apex, point, roof The top of Mount Everest is 29,028 feet above sea level. 2. cap, lid, cover, stopper, covering, cork, ceiling, canopy I can't find the top to the tube of toothpaste. ◆ *adjective* best, greatest, highest, topmost, chief, leading, main, supreme, elite She is the top student in our class. ◆ *verb* 1. garnish, dress, cover, tip, crown, cap, finish, clothe, cloak The caterer topped the wedding cake with fresh flowers. 2. scale, climb, mount, ascend, go up, gain We topped the hill and set up our picnic. 3. better, beat, exceed, surpass, best, outdo, outstrip, outshine That joke tops the one you told yesterday. ➡ **Antonyms:** *noun* 1. base, bottom ◆ *adjective* lowest, worst

topic *noun* subject, theme, point, issue, matter, text, question, business, thesis The weather is a common topic of conversation.

topple *verb* knock over, fell, demolish, destroy, overturn, upset, collapse, overthrow, unseat Last night's strong wind toppled the old oak tree in our front yard.

torch *noun* flare, fire, flame, lamp, light, beacon, signal, flashlight At the start of the Olympic games, a torch is used to light the Olympic flame.

torment *noun* 1. agony, anguish, distress, misery, suffering, torture, woe, curse, affliction The families of drug addicts suffer great torment. 2. pain, trouble, irritation, vexation, harassment, provocation, bother, nuisance, annoyance A toothache can be a source of torment. ◆ *verb* 1. torture, plague, afflict, hurt, pain, rack, crucify, abuse Starvation tormented the settlers at Jamestown. 2. annoy, bother, pester, trouble, irritate, bedevil, nettle, worry, nag A thick cloud of mosquitoes tormented the campers. ➡ **Antonyms:** *noun* joy, pleasure, delight ◆ *verb* soothe, please

torrent *noun* 1. river, cataract, rapid, flood, spate, gush, deluge, stream, cascade Heavy rain turned the creek into a rushing torrent. 2. outpouring, burst, gushing, deluge, barrage, rush, flow, avalanche, tide My dad received a torrent of get-well cards after he had heart surgery.

torture *noun* suffering, tribulation, torment, misery, anguish, agony, persecution, punishment, cruelty Many refugees experience the torture of hardship and deprivation. ◆ *verb* torment, maim, mutilate, afflict, injure, harrow, hurt, persecute, punish The prisoner was tortured in the dungeon.

toss *verb* 1. cast, fling, heave, hurl, pitch, sling, throw, dump, chuck I tossed my coat on the bed. 2. twist, turn, roll, stir, thrash, squirm, flounder, heave Last night I tossed and turned all night long. ◆ *noun* throw, cast, fling, shake, flourish, pitch, heave, chuck, lob Many games start with a toss of the dice.

total *noun* sum, aggregate, tally, quantity, amount, figure, whole, gross, result We collected a total of 241 cans during our food drive. ◆ *adjective* full, whole, entire, absolute, complete, comprehensive, overall, outright, thorough, utter The total cost of the party was less than 50 dollars. ◆ *verb* add, calculate, compute, figure, sum up, reckon, yield, reach, amount When we totaled the scores for the game, I found that I had won by ten points. ➡ **Antonyms:** *adjective* incomplete, partial

tote *verb* haul, carry, move, lug, convey, drag, transport, deliver I toted the groceries into the house for my mother.

totter *verb* stumble, stagger, careen, weave, wobble, reel, sway, tremble, teeter, dodder The injured player tottered off the field.

touch *verb* 1. feel, finger, handle, manipulate, palpate, stroke, tap, rub, disturb Please don't touch my model airplane before the paint dries. 2. contact, meet, press, reach, adjoin, abut, verge on, neighbor, join Let's move the couch so that it doesn't touch the wall. 3. affect, move, stir, impress, influence, strike, melt, soften, thrill Your thoughtfulness touched me deeply. 4. eat, taste, drink, ingest, partake, consume, savor, take, imbibe You barely touched your dinner. 5. tinge, color, tint, frost, brush, wash, dye, stain Her brown hair is touched with blond from being outdoors. ♦ *noun* 1. contact, feel, brush, caress, pressure, sensation, tap, impact, rub I looked up when I felt the touch of someone's hand. 2. bit, dash, hint, tinge, trace, suggestion, drop, taste, intimation Mom added a touch of garlic to the spaghetti sauce. 3. flair, skill, facility, ability, knack, technique, aptitude, deftness, finesse You have a good touch for cooking.

touching *adjective* poignant, moving, affecting, stirring, sad, heartrending, distressing *All Quiet on the Western Front* by Erich Maria Remarque is a touching book set in World War I.

touchy *adjective* 1. oversensitive, thin-skinned, testy, grumpy, irritable, petulant, cranky, temperamental Sometimes I am touchy about being asked personal questions. 2. delicate, sensitive, ticklish, tricky, uncertain, critical, hazardous, dangerous, explosive The negotiations were at a touchy stage. ➡ **Antonyms:** 1. nonchalant, cheerful 2. safe, stable

tough *adjective* 1. durable, rugged, strong, sturdy, hardy, dense, resilient, firm, stout Leather is a tough material. 2. demanding, difficult, hard, rough, intricate, baffling, strenuous, laborious, troubling I spent a long time trying to solve the tough math problem. 3. strict, resolute, unyielding, fixed, uncompromising, intractable, immutable, decided, stern My teacher has a tough policy on handing assignments in on time. ➡ **Antonyms:** 1. delicate, fragile 2. easy, simple 3. flexible, lenient

tour *noun* 1. excursion, outing, trip, expedition, journey, voyage, junket, jaunt, visit If we take this tour, we will be able to see the Tower of London. 2. assignment, stint, hitch, shift, circuit, period, term, round, turn When my uncle joined the Marines, his first tour of duty was in Spain.

♦ *verb* travel through, visit, explore, see, rove, traverse, roam, cruise, sightsee My sister toured Europe last summer.

tourist *noun* sightseer, traveler, visitor, wayfarer, vagabond, globetrotter, day-tripper Tourists from all over the world come to Anaheim to visit Disneyland.

tournament *noun* competition, contest, match, meet, tourney, open, game, series, duel This chess tournament is open to players of all ages.

tow *verb* draw, pull, tug, drag, haul, push, propel, lug, ferry Tugboats towed the ocean liner into port. ♦ *noun* haul, pull, towing, drag, draw, push, pull We called for a tow when we had car trouble.

tower *noun* belfry, spire, steeple, campanile, minaret, turret, monument, obelisk, skyscraper, pylon Our church has a bell tower. ♦ *verb* loom, rear, rise, soar, dominate, overlook, surmount, surpass, top A huge pine tree towers over our house.

town *noun* community, municipality, settlement, city, village, hamlet, metropolis, burg, borough, township Dad grew up in a small town in the Midwest.

toxic *adjective* deadly, pernicious, lethal, poisonous, injurious, harmful, unhealthy, virulent, septic, baneful Toxic chemicals have to be handled carefully. ➡ **Antonyms:** harmless, healthful, medicinal

toy *noun* plaything, amusement, gadget, novelty, trifle, trinket, gewgaw, bauble, knickknack When I was younger, my favorite toy was a yellow dump truck. ♦ *verb* play, trifle, putter, tease, tinker, flirt, sport, fool, fiddle I toyed with my dinner because I wasn't hungry.

trace *noun* 1. remains, evidence, indication, sign, mark, proof, spoor, trail, vestige, remnant The hikers found traces of an old mining camp. 2. dash, hint, inkling, suggestion, tinge, touch, shade, dab, pinch There is a trace of cumin in this soup. ♦ *verb* 1. seek, find, track, discover, trail, unearth, hunt, pursue, follow The FBI traces missing people. 2. delineate, draw, sketch, diagram, copy, outline, reproduce, duplicate I traced an outline of North America for my geography class.

track *noun* 1. footprint, print, mark, sign, trace, trail, spoor, indication, imprint We found some raccoon tracks down by the creek. 2. path, trail, pathway, route, way, course, footpath, road, orbit There's a rough track through those hills. ♦ *verb* 1. follow, hunt, pursue, trail, search, seek, stalk, shadow, chase The wildlife photographer tracked a bear and her cubs through the forest. **2. bring, carry, drag, trail, bear, convey, lug, transport** I took off my sandals so that I wouldn't track sand into the house. **3. follow, record, monitor, log, register, observe, note, list** I tracked noontime temperatures for a month for my earth science project.

tract[1] *noun* **lot, parcel, plot, section, area, district, region, site, belt, expanse** This tract of land is going to be used for a housing development.

tract[2] *noun* **pamphlet, leaflet, brochure, booklet, treatise, article, sermon, critique** The man was handing out tracts to people who walked by.

trade *noun* **1. business, commerce, exchange, traffic, dealing, enterprise, industry** The United States engages in trade with most of the countries in the world. **2. exchange, swap, switch, substitution, interchange, deal, barter** Do you think that my baseball glove would be a fair trade for your tennis racket? **3. customers, clientele, patrons, following, patronage, shoppers, public** Our neighborhood diner has a steady breakfast trade. **4. craft, occupation, field, work, profession, vocation, business, pursuit, game, line** Workers in the plumbing trade have to serve an apprenticeship. ◆ *verb* **1. exchange, swap, switch, change, interchange, substitute** My brother and I sometimes trade chores. **2. deal, handle, traffic, sell, retail, merchandise, peddle, shop, buy, barter** That store trades in antique furniture.

tradition *noun* **1. mythology, legend, lore, folklore, superstition, saga, epic, story** According to ancient Greek tradition, a hero is someone who is half god and half human. **2. custom, habit, practice, ritual, convention, standard, institution, ethic, law** It is our family tradition to celebrate Passover at my grandparents' house.

traditional *adjective* **conventional, customary, habitual, normal, routine, usual, regular, familiar, ritual** My aunt and her fiancé decided to have a traditional wedding. ➡ **Antonyms: unusual, unconventional**

traffic *noun* **commerce, market, trade, business, trading, buying, marketing, selling, barter** The government is trying to suppress the traffic in illegal drugs. ◆ *verb* **deal, trade, barter, buy, market, sell, retail, handle** It is rumored that this repair shop traffics in stolen cars.

tragedy *noun* **catastrophe, disaster, calamity, misfortune, accident, mishap, woe, heartache** The sinking of *Titanic* was one of the worst maritime tragedies of the 20th century. ➡ **Antonyms: fortune, blessing, boon**

tragic *adjective* **dreadful, unfortunate, disastrous, ruinous, catastrophic, miserable, sorrowful, unhappy, sad** The nuclear disaster at Chernobyl was a tragic event. ➡ **Antonyms: fortunate, happy**

trail *verb* **1. drag, draw, pull, tow, haul, lug, train, trawl, dangle** Dan trailed a shoelace in front of his kitten for her to play with. **2. pursue, search for, seek, track, hunt, trace, chase, shadow, dog** The shepherd and his dog trailed the lost sheep. **3. follow, come after, lag behind, straggle, tail, traipse, trudge** The ducklings trailed behind their mother. ◆ *noun* **1. footpath, path, route, track, course, way, road, byway, bridle path** This trail leads to the pond. **2. trace, track, mark, scent, sign, footprints, spoor, wake** The wolf followed a rabbit's trail. ➡ **Antonyms: *verb* 3. go before, lead**

train *noun* **1. caravan, convoy, cavalcade, procession, column, line, queue** In the Old West, mule trains were used to transport military supplies. **2. retinue, entourage, cortege, staff, escort, court, suite, retainers, attendants, followers, guard** The queen and her train entered the throne room. **3. series, string, succession, sequence, set, run, chain, course** In his journal, the Civil War soldier recorded the train of events that led to his meeting Abraham Lincoln. ◆ *verb* **teach, coach, drill, educate, instruct, tutor, groom, prime, school** My sister trained her dog to roll over.

trait *noun* **attribute, characteristic, feature, property, quality, earmark, quirk, peculiarity, habit** Honesty and kindness are two of my friend Petra's best traits.

traitor *noun* **betrayer, double-crosser, spy, informer, turncoat, mutineer, deserter, snitch, quisling, tattletale** A traitor sold secret plans to the enemy. ➡ **Antonyms: patriot, loyalist**

trajectory *noun* **orbit, course, flight path, track, route, line, path, curve** We followed the trajectory of the arrow as it arced up and over to find its mark in the bull's-eye.

tramp *verb* **1. walk, roam, rove, ramble, trek, hike, slog, plod, trudge** We tramped through the woods carrying all our camping gear on our backs. **2. trample, crush, flatten, press, tread, stamp, stomp, clomp, squash** The deer had tramped down the grass where it slept. ◆ *noun* **1. footfall, tread, footstep, stomp, stamp, thud, clomp, pound** I heard the tramp of feet in the hall above us. **2. walk, hike, ramble, excursion, march, trek, jaunt, tour** We went for a tramp along the hill overlooking the harbor. **3. hobo, vagabond, drifter, vagrant, wayfarer, wanderer, derelict, panhandler, beggar** Several tramps were riding on the freight train.

trample *verb* **1. crush, flatten, squash, stamp, tramp, pound, tromp, squish, stump, press** Our dog trampled our newly planted pansies. **2. hurt, injure, bruise, harm, scorn, disdain, disregard, slight** What you said trampled my feelings.

trance *noun* **daze, dream, reverie, spell, stupor, abstraction, unconsciousness, rapture, ecstasy** The oracle of Delphi was reputed to go into a trance and then utter prophecies.

tranquil *adjective* **1. peaceful, quiet, restful, serene, calm, soothing, halcyon, relaxed** We enjoyed our tranquil weekend at the lake. **2. sedate, even-tempered, self-possessed, reasonable, easygoing, sober, collected, cool, dispassionate** Julianne has a tranquil personality. ◆ **Antonyms: 1. busy, restless 2. agitated, disturbed**

transcend *verb* **surpass, outdo, exceed, outstrip, overshadow, go beyond, top, overstep, eclipse** My birthday party transcended all my expectations.

transcribe *verb* **copy, duplicate, reprint, reproduce, transliterate, replicate, render, interpret** My classmate transcribed her notes for me.

transfer *verb* **convey, move, shift, change, send, ship, transport, dispatch, pass** I transferred information to my computer's hard drive from a floppy disk. ◆ *noun* **relocation, reassignment, transferal, change, move, shift, relegation, transmittal, removal** My uncle got a transfer from Pennsylvania to Oregon. ◆ **Antonyms:** *verb* **keep, retain**

transform *verb* **transfigure, alter, change, convert, turn, modify, metamorphose, translate, remake** Cinderella's fairy godmother transformed a pumpkin into a carriage.

transient *adjective* **1. transitory, brief, momentary, fleeting, passing, short-lived, ephemeral, temporary, impermanent** The East Coast is known for its transient thunder showers on summer afternoons. **2. nomadic, migratory, footloose, transitional, uprooted, vagrant, migrating, unsettled** Many people became transient in the 1930s because jobs were hard to find. ◆ *noun* **vagabond, nomad, wayfarer, wanderer, bum, tramp, derelict, hobo** The transient went to the soup kitchen to get a warm meal. ◆ **Antonyms:** *adjective* **1. lasting, enduring, permanent 2. settled, resident**

transition *noun* **metamorphosis, shift, transformation, alteration, change, modification, passage, conversion, progress** My science project was a photographic chronicling of a caterpillar's transition to a butterfly.

translate *verb* **change, convert, reword, decode, render, transform, explain, paraphrase** Dad received a letter in Italian that he translated into English.

transmission *noun* **1. transfer, transference, passage, passing, delivery, carrying, conveyance, sending, shipment** Regular washing of the hands helps to prevent the transmission of germs. **2. broadcast, signal, message, communication, report, dispatch, note** We can receive transmissions from radio stations that are more than two hundred miles away.

transmit *verb* **convey, pass, relay, send, transfer, deliver, disperse, broadcast, conduct, carry** Fax machines transmit written messages over telephone lines.

transparent *adjective* **1. clear, see-through, translucent, lucid, pellucid, gauzy, sheer, diaphanous, glassy** Jellies and jams usually come in transparent jars. **2. apparent, evident, plain, obvious, visible, unmistakable, blatant, patent, glaring** My little sister's desire to go with us was transparent. ◆ **Antonyms: 1. opaque 2. concealed, hidden**

transpire *verb* **happen, occur, ensue, befall, develop, chance, come about, result, arise** No matter what transpires, we will always be friends.

transport *verb* **1. carry, convey, move, shift, take, transfer, ferry, bear, haul** We can't transport all this luggage in our little car. **2. enrapture, delight, captivate, excite, spellbind, entrance, enchant, thrill** My little sister was transported by all the Christmas lights on our block. ◆ *noun* **conveyance, shipment, shipping, transfer, transportation, carriage, hauling, transit** Trucks, trains, and airplanes are used for the transport of freight.

transportation *noun* **conveyance, transport, transit, dispatch, shipment, transference, portage** My neighbor's favorite form of transportation is a motorcycle.

transpose *verb* **reverse, interchange, switch, shift, alter, invert, change, swap, exchange** I got a wrong number when I accidentally transposed the last two digits as I dialed.

trap *noun* **1. snare, deadfall, pitfall, booby trap, hook, net** A gopher was caught in the trap we had laid. **2. trick, stratagem, deception, hoax, feint, ruse, wile, ploy** Undercover officers pretended to buy stolen goods as a trap to catch a ring of thieves. ◆ *verb* **ensnare, capture, catch, net, seize, snare, hook, ambush, snag, trick** Many people prefer to trap mice alive rather than poison them.

trash *noun* **1. garbage, refuse, rubbish, waste, debris, junk, offal, residue, leavings, dregs** It's your turn to take out the trash. **2. nonsense, prattle, drivel, gibberish, hogwash, foolishness, twaddle, rot, balderdash** Most of the articles in tabloid newspapers are trash.

trauma *noun* **ordeal, shock, jolt, blow, upheaval, damage, wound, upset, injury** The trauma of my sister's death has affected our entire community.

travail *noun* **1. toil, hardship, drudgery, discomfort, exertion, effort, burden, difficulty, struggle** The serfs of the Middle Ages lived lives of travail. **2. anguish, suffering, unhappiness, misery, distress, heartache, pain, torment, agony, tribulation** Adolescence can be a time of travail. ♦ *verb* **work, toil, labor, strain, grub, moil, sweat, drudge, strive, struggle** We travailed in the garden all day long.

travel *verb* **1. journey, roam, tour, wander, trek, cruise, voyage, ramble** Many people travel through Europe by bicycle. **2. pass, go, move, proceed, progress, spread, advance, circulate** Light can travel through a vacuum. ♦ *noun* **excursion, journey, tour, trek, trip, voyage, drive, passage, movement** We enjoyed our travels through Italy.

traverse *verb* **1. travel, pass, transit, negotiate, navigate, journey, range, travel, walk** We traversed the narrow, rocky path to the lake. **2. bridge, cross, span, cover** A fallen tree traversed the creek.

tray *noun* **platter, trencher, salver, plate, receptacle** We set out a tray of appetizers.

treacherous *adjective* **1. disloyal, traitorous, treasonous, unfaithful, perfidious, duplicitous, sly, deceitful** A treacherous guard assassinated Indira Gandhi, then prime minister of India, in 1984. **2. dangerous, hazardous, perilous, risky, unsafe, precarious, unsound, shaky, difficult, slippery** Sailing can be treacherous if the wind is too strong. ➡ **Antonyms: 1. faithful, loyal 2. safe**

tread *verb* **1. walk, step, march, hike, amble, trudge, stride, rove, range** I trod quietly past my parents' bedroom door. **2. trample, crush, stamp, stomp, tramp, squash, press, flatten** "Don't tread on me" was an early American motto. ♦ *noun* **footfall, footstep, step, stride, pace, gait, tramp, march** You can hear the tread of the people in the apartment above us.

treason *noun* **disloyalty, treachery, betrayal, conspiracy, deceit, sedition, insubordination, mutiny** Benedict Arnold committed an act of treason during the American Revolution. ➡ **Antonyms: loyalty, patriotism**

treasure *noun* **1. fortune, riches, wealth, gold, money, valuables, hoard, treasure-trove, store** Deep-sea divers have found sunken ships that have been full of treasure. **2. dear, darling, angel, beloved, prize, gem, jewel, paragon, find** My parents think I'm a treasure. ♦ *verb* **cherish, prize, value, adore, esteem, love, revere, venerate, appreciate** My mother treasures the rocking chair that she received from her grandmother. ➡ **Antonyms:** *verb* **disregard, scorn**

treat *verb* **1. deal with, handle, address, consider, regard, manage, use, employ, welcome** The saleslady treated us with courtesy. **2. explain, tackle, interpret, discuss, discourse, evaluate, approach, consider, study, weigh** This chapter in my math book treats compound fractions. **3. host, pay for, give, entertain, provide, take out, indulge, escort, regale** My tennis coach treated me to lunch. **4. relieve, care for, medicate, nurse, minister, cure, heal, dress, dose** I treated my poison ivy with calamine lotion. ♦ *noun* **delight, enjoyment, pleasure, joy, gratification, celebration, luxury, indulgence, bonus** Our Friday night treat is pizza and a movie.

treatment *noun* **1. care, handling, approach, management, reception, mode, way, method** We appreciated the friendly treatment we received from the store manager. **2. cure, remedy, therapy, prescription, healing, medication, rehabilitation, diet, operation** Laughter is a great treatment for the blues.

treaty *noun* **compact, pact, agreement, covenant, accord, arrangement, bargain, deal** Representatives from six nations were present at the signing of the peace treaty.

Word Group

A **tree** is a usually tall woody plant having a single main stem or trunk. **Tree** is a specific term with no true synonyms. Here are some common types of trees:

alder, beech, cedar, cork, dogwood, eucalyptus, fir, grapefruit, hemlock, ironwood, juniper, kumquat, locust, mahogany, nutmeg, oak, pine, quince, redwood, spruce, tamarack, upas, willow, yew

trek *verb* **1. hike, plod, tramp, slog, walk, trudge, march, toil, lumber** The soldiers trekked through the swamp. **2. journey, hike, travel, roam, tour, wander, rove, range, traipse** My parents trekked across Ireland on their honeymoon. ♦ *noun* **trip, journey, excursion, tour, hike, pilgrimage, voyage, odyssey, junket** My aunt is planning a trek through Nepal.

tremble *verb* shake, shiver, shudder, quake, quiver, twitch The campers trembled with cold until they got their fire going. ◆ *noun* quiver, flutter, ripple, quaver, sway, vibration, waver, movement, oscillation We could see the tremble of the leaves in the wind.

tremendous *adjective* 1. enormous, gigantic, huge, immense, large, giant, mammoth, mountainous, massive A tremendous wave capsized the boat. 2. marvelous, wonderful, superb, fabulous, excellent, stunning, amazing, great, exceptional I had a tremendous time at your party. ⬧ **Antonyms:** 1. little, small, tiny 2. mediocre, rotten, lousy

tremor *noun* quake, shake, shock, earthquake, temblor, tremble, vibration, spasm, quaver We felt little tremors for several days after the earthquake.

trench *noun* ditch, furrow, trough, channel, gully, depression, rut, hollow, excavation Workers dug a trench to lay the water pipe.

trend *noun* 1. tendency, direction, movement, progression, inclination, orientation, flow, current, course The current trend in home entertainment is toward wide-screen TVs. 2. vogue, fashion, choice, fad, rage, look, craze, furor, mode, style That haircut is the trend right now. ◆ *verb* tend, veer, incline, drift, run, bend, lean, swing, head The road trends northward.

trespass *verb* invade, encroach, intrude, violate, infringe, penetrate, impinge, crash My neighbor doesn't want anybody to trespass on his property. ◆ *noun* 1. transgression, infraction, violation, offense, crime, error, misconduct, sin, wrong His interruption of our conversation was a trespass of good manners. 2. invasion, intrusion, infringement, incursion, violation, breach, inroad, aggression, encroachment The Great Wall of China was built to protect the country from trespass.

trial *noun* 1. hearing, inquiry, proceeding, case, suit, court, court martial The trial will start as soon as a jury has been selected. 2. check, test, tryout, analysis, examination, experiment, probe, dry run, scrutiny The new airplane will be put through a series of trials to see how it performs. 3. adversity, affliction, hardship, ordeal, trouble, grief, sorrow, tribulation, vexation For early pioneers, the westward trek was a time of both trial and adventure.

tribe *noun* clan, group, family, stock, kin, kindred, house, dynasty, lineage There are more than five hundred Native American tribes in the United States today.

tribunal *noun* court, law court, bar, bench, judiciary, judges, adjudicators, arbitrators The case was presented before the tribunal.

tribute *noun* 1. homage, honor, recognition, praise, memorial, acknowledgment, award, testimonial, eulogy This statue is a tribute to the man who founded our town. 2. assessment, levy, payment, tax, offering, bribe, dues, impost, exaction Ancient Rome collected tribute from conquered nations. ⬧ **Antonyms:** 1. disdain, dishonor, condemnation

trick *noun* 1. deceit, deception, ruse, subterfuge, device, pretense, stratagem, ploy, tactic An opossum uses the trick of playing dead as a defense against predators. 2. gag, prank, jest, joke, mischief, lark, antic, monkey business My friends play tricks on each other on April Fools' Day. 3. skill, knack, technique, art, talent, facility, gift, finesse, expertise I don't think I'll ever learn the trick of making flaky pie crusts. ◆ *verb* trap, deceive, cheat, mislead, fool, swindle, gull, bamboozle I tricked my brother into thinking he was late by setting his clock ahead.

trickery *noun* deception, fraud, pretense, craftiness, wile, cunning, subterfuge, artifice, lies The gambler used trickery to win the poker game. ⬧ **Antonyms:** honesty, fairness, truth

trickle *verb* dribble, ooze, flow, leak, seep, exude, issue, run, percolate The audience began to trickle out of the auditorium before the concert was over. ◆ *noun* dribble, crawl, creep, drop, drip, seepage, drizzle, runnel, rivulet This creek slows to a trickle during the summer. ⬧ **Antonyms:** *verb* surge, gush ◆ *noun* flood, cascade

trifle *noun* 1. novelty, trinket, knickknack, plaything, toy, bagatelle, bauble, curio We bought balloons and other trifles to hand out as party favors. 2. little, piece, morsel, bit, fraction, touch, crumb, pinch, drop May I try a trifle of your dessert? ◆ *verb* fidget, fool, toy, play, putter, fiddle, dabble, monkey I trifled with the papers on my desk while I waited for the computer to boot up.

trim *verb* 1. prune, clip, crop, cut, nip, snip, pare, lop, whittle, shorten We trimmed the rosebushes and covered them with straw for the winter. 2. adorn, decorate, edge, embroider, ornament, embellish, array, deck, emblazon Mom and I trimmed my dress with lace. ◆ *noun* 1. condition, order, repair, shape, fettle, kilter, form, readiness, commission My uncle's boat is always in good trim. 2. edge, border, fringe, edging, piping, garnish, frill, decoration, adornment The trim on our house is blue. 3. clipping, cutting, cropping, shortening, shearing, pruning, paring We gave our front hedge a trim this spring. ◆ *adjective* **1. spruce, tidy, smart, neat, clean, uncluttered, orderly, shipshape** I like to keep my room trim. **2. fit, lean, slender, slim, svelte, sleek, compact, streamlined, graceful** Mom and Dad looked trim after their vacation at a health spa.

trip *noun* **1. excursion, journey, vacation, outing, jaunt, voyage, pilgrimage, cruise, flight** We made a trip to Mexico to visit our relatives. **2. mistake, blunder, lapse, error, oversight, miscalculation, faux pas** It was a trip of the tongue to introduce my friend by the wrong name. ◆ *verb* **1. stumble, fall, tumble, flounder, slip, sprawl, lurch, pitch, topple** Our puppy sometimes trips over its own feet. **2. leap, dance, prance, spring, cavort, caper, flit, frisk, canter** The ballerina tripped gracefully across the stage. ➶ **Antonyms:** *verb* **2. plod, lumber, shuffle**

trite *adjective* **overused, commonplace, banal, unimaginative, hackneyed, stale, tired, stereotyped, stock** The ending of the movie was disappointingly trite. ➶ **Antonyms: original, new, imaginative**

triumph *verb* **1. prevail, succeed, win, master, best, overpower, rout, outdo** We rejoiced when our team finally triumphed over our greatest rival. **2. rejoice, celebrate, exult, delight, boast, crow** The players triumphed for days after their great victory. ◆ *noun* **1. accomplishment, achievement, success, attainment, feat, coup, victory, win, conquest** I experienced a feeling of triumph when I finally finished the quilt. **2. masterpiece, paragon, model, archetype, example, ideal, jewel, apotheosis** The Pyramids of Egypt are a triumph of engineering and craftsmanship. **3. exultation, jubilation, celebration, rejoicing, joy, reveling, pride** The runner gave a shout of triumph as he crossed the finish line. ➶ **Antonyms:** *verb* **1. succumb, lose 2. mourn, regret** ◆ *noun* **1. defeat, failure 3. shame, humiliation**

triumphant *adjective* **1. joyful, triumphal, glorious, exultant, happy, jubilant, celebratory, proud** The soldiers received a triumphant welcome home. **2. victorious, successful, conquering, winning, triumphal, ascendant, masterful, dominant** The British were triumphant against Napoleon at the Battle of Waterloo.

trivial *adjective* **insignificant, petty, slight, trifling, unimportant, small, immaterial, minute, meaningless** The music students played their recital pieces with only a few trivial mistakes. ➶ **Antonyms: important, significant**

troop *noun* **1. group, unit, band, company, squad, corps, bunch, gang, assemblage** Our Boy Scout troop will be going to next summer's jamboree. **2. soldiers, troopers, infantry, cavalry, army, military, militia, corps** American troops liberated Paris from German occupation in 1944. ◆ *verb* **file, march, parade, step, stride, advance, go, proceed, traipse** The crowd cheered as the football team trooped into the stadium.

trophy *noun* **1. award, prize, citation, honor, medal, blue ribbon, crown, laurels, wreath** Our school awards a trophy to the winner of the spelling bee each year. **2. memento, keepsake, reminder, memorial, souvenir, remembrance, token, relic** My sister has kept her corsage as a trophy of her junior prom.

tropical *adjective* **tropic, equatorial, hot, humid, torrid, sultry, steamy, muggy, lush** Florida has a tropical climate. ➶ **Antonyms: cold, dry**

trot *noun* **jog, run, dash, run, sprint, pace, gait** She came into the house at a trot when she heard the phone ringing. ◆ *verb* **1. hurry, rush, hasten, jog, run, scamper, bustle, scoot, hie** I trotted down the hall to get to my classroom before the bell rang. **2. display, show, exhibit, bring out, demonstrate, proffer, flaunt** My brother is always trotting out a picture of his girlfriend. ➶ **Antonyms:** *noun* **walk, crawl** ◆ *verb* **1. creep, dawdle 2. hide**

trouble *noun* **1. fix, jam, predicament, dilemma, difficulty, problem, squeeze, mess, inconvenience** We will be in trouble if we don't get to school on time. **2. bother, inconvenience, effort, vexation, annoyance, worry, grief, pain, discomfort** It won't be any trouble for me to get your tickets for you. **3. effort, care, exertion, work, fuss, labor, concern, toil, bother** We went to a lot of trouble in picking out our new car. **4. disorder, complaint, malady, affliction, disease, disability, ailment, illness, upset** I have stomach trouble if I drink milk. ◆ *verb* **1. distress, disturb, upset, worry, concern, agitate, annoy, afflict, torment** What is troubling you? **2. inconvenience, bother, burden, distract, intrude, impose, hinder** Would it trouble you to help me study for my history test? ➶ **Antonyms:** *noun* **2. pleasure, joy** ◆ *verb* **1. soothe, please, appease**

troublemaker *noun* **mischief-maker, delinquent, agitator, instigator, incendiary, rascal, rogue, knave, rebel** The troublemaker ended up in juvenile hall.

trough *noun* **receptacle, gutter, trench, ditch, gully, depression, furrow** Rain had filled the cows' water trough.

truant *noun* **delinquent, absentee, runaway, fugitive, idler, drifter, deserter, slacker, layabout** The truant was always ditching school.

truce *noun* **armistice, cease-fire, peace, halt, respite, lull, stop, delay, moratorium** The fighting will end when the truce takes effect at midnight.

trudge *verb* **plod, slog, toil, lumber, hike, tramp, trek, drag, march** The tired Scouts trudged back to their camp. ➡ **Antonyms: skip, prance**

true *adjective* **1. accurate, correct, factual, right, valid, exact, literal, reliable, sure, strict** The witness swore that everything she said was true. **2. dependable, faithful, loyal, reliable, steadfast, trustworthy, constant, devoted, sincere** My dog is a true companion who always wants to be with me. **3. lawful, legal, legitimate, rightful, just, official, proper, licit, authorized, sanctioned** I call it my car, but my parents are the true owners. **4. authentic, genuine, real, actual, bona fide, undoubted, pure, original, positive** Do you know if this book is a true first edition? ◆ *adverb* **truly, honestly, truthfully, accurately, frankly, straightforwardly, sincerely, candidly, genuinely** To speak true, I have to say I prefer the other sweater on you. ➡ **Antonyms:** *adjective* **1. false, incorrect 2. disloyal 3. illegal 4. artificial, phony** ◆ *adverb* **falsely, dishonestly**

trunk *noun* **footlocker, locker, chest, container, box, bin, basket, hamper, case** Mom stores our winter clothes in trunks.

trust *noun* **1. confidence, conviction, faith, reliance, belief, dependence, stock, credence, sureness** I value the trust that my friends have in me. **2. care, custody, charge, guardianship, keeping, protection, responsibility, safekeeping** Carrie left her hamster in my trust while she was away on vacation. **3. monopoly, cartel, conglomerate, corporation, syndicate, combine, pool** The telephone company trust was broken up by the government. ◆ *verb* **1. rely on, swear by, bank on, believe, depend, bet, gamble, accept** Self-confident people trust their instincts. **2. assume, believe, presume, suppose, expect, hope, reckon, anticipate** I trust that you will keep my secret. ➡ **Antonyms:** *noun* **1. doubt, suspicion** ◆ *verb* **1. mistrust, question**

trustworthy *adjective* **dependable, reliable, responsible, loyal, scrupulous, steadfast, ethical, upright, honorable** My friend is trustworthy and will pay back the money that I loaned him. ➡ **Antonyms: unreliable, untrustworthy**

truth *noun* **1. fact, actuality, reality, truthfulness, verity, authenticity, correctness** The truth is that I did eat the last piece of lemon pie. **2. sincerity, integrity, honesty, loyalty, faithfulness, candor, openness, frankness** He is a man of truth. ➡ **Antonyms: 1. falsehood, untruth 2. dishonesty, insincerity, deceit**

try *verb* **1. aim, attempt, endeavor, seek, struggle, strive, essay, aspire, work** I always try to get my homework done before dinner. **2. sample, taste, test, check, examine, inspect, analyze, evaluate, investigate** Would you like to try one of the cookies I made? **3. consider, hear, judge, adjudicate, arbitrate, decide, deliberate, referee** The Supreme Court tries important cases that are referred to it by lower courts. **4. tax, burden, stress, upset, inconvenience, plague, afflict, rack, trouble** The dog's barking is trying my patience. ◆ *noun* **attempt, effort, endeavor, trial, turn, test, experiment, opportunity** Our lawnmower usually doesn't start on the first try.

trying *adjective* **demanding, difficult, hard, troublesome, distressing, irritating, vexing, rough, tough** My parents had a trying time when my brother and I both were sick. ➡ **Antonyms: easy, simple**

tryout *noun* **test, audition, evaluation, chance, trial, experiment, demonstration, inspection, check** I'm waiting for the results of the cheerleading tryouts.

tub *noun* **vat, cask, bucket, keg, vessel, bathtub, washtub, basin, sink** There is a tub of flowers outside our front door.

tube *noun* **hose, pipe, conduit, duct, cylinder, canal, tunnel, passage** The tube of the vacuum cleaner was clogged with cat hair.

tuck *verb* **fold, pleat, gather, stitch, pinch, tighten, press, stuff** The seamstress tucked and pinned the pleats of the dress.

tuft *noun* **clump, cluster, knot, bunch, sheaf, tussock, plume, shock, ruff** During the hot weather, my dog leaves tufts of fur everywhere.

tug *verb* **pull, draw, strain, jerk, drag, haul, heave, wrench, yank** I tugged on the door to the shed, but it was swollen shut. ◆ *noun* **jerk, pull, yank, heave, tow, wrench, hitch, lug, haul** Give this rope a tug to ring the bell.

tumble *verb* **1. roll, somersault, stumble, trip, flip, spill, cascade, toss, bounce** The children tumbled over one another to get to the candy from the piñata. **2. drop, fall, topple, plummet, plunge, pitch, slip, descend, sink** The lamp tumbled to the floor when I bumped the table. ◆ *noun* **fall, spill, trip, dive, drop, plunge, slip, skid** My sister took a lot of tumbles while she was learning to walk.

tumor *noun* growth, swelling, nodule, cyst, lump, bump, polyp, sarcoma, cancer, malignancy The tumor was diagnosed as benign.

tumult *noun* uproar, confusion, chaos, bedlam, furor, commotion, agitation, excitement, pandemonium, melee There was tumult on the softball field when somebody's dog ran away with the ball. ◈ **Antonyms:** peace, tranquillity, order

tune *noun* 1. air, melody, refrain, song, ditty, chorus, jingle, theme, strain That tune keeps running through my head. 2. agreement, harmony, unison, affinity, accord, concurrence, concord, conformity, sympathy My sister and I are often in tune. ◆ *verb* harmonize, adjust, modulate, calibrate, regulate, set, align, coordinate Milo tuned my guitar for me.

tunnel *noun* underground passage, underpass, passageway, subway, corridor, shaft, tube, mine, burrow The longest railway tunnel in the world is in Japan. ◆ *verb* burrow, dig, excavate, mine, furrow, penetrate, scoop out Gophers are tunneling through our back yard.

turbulent *adjective* 1. agitated, tempestuous, stormy, moiling, rough, foaming, swirling, boiling, raging The seas were turbulent during the storm. 2. rebellious, riotous, unruly, lawless, restless, violent, disorderly, unsettled, mutinous The French Revolution was a turbulent time. ◈ **Antonyms:** calm, placid, still

turmoil *noun* chaos, uproar, commotion, confusion, pandemonium, tumult, excitement, bedlam, unrest The ants were in turmoil when their nest was disturbed. ◈ **Antonyms:** order, peace, quiet

turn *verb* 1. rotate, swivel, spin, twirl, whirl, pivot, gyrate, wheel, roll Turn the faucet to the left to get hot water. 2. sprain, twist, wrench, hurt, strain, injure, tear, pull I turned my ankle playing soccer. 3. go, move, shift, swerve, wheel, veer, swing, detour, divert, face We have to turn right at the corner of Almond Street to get to my aunt's house. 4. become, change, transform, convert, modify, metamorphose, alter, recast, reconstruct I read my little sister a story about an ugly duckling that turns into a beautiful swan. 5. change, alter, shift, reverse, sidetrack, digress, redirect, deflect, return He turned his attention back to his math homework. 6. spoil, go bad, sour, deteriorate, decay, ferment, putrefy, curdle, molder After sitting out on the counter for several hours, the milk had turned. 7. resort to, use, run, address, repair, apply, go, appeal Where do we turn now? ◆ *noun* 1. revolution, rotation, loop, pirouette, gyration, whirl,

wheel, twirl, twist The couple took a turn around the dance floor. 2. bend, curve, arc, corner, hairpin, dogleg, zigzag, twist, angle The path takes a turn to the left just before the pond. 3. chance, opportunity, time, stint, spell, attempt, round, move, moment Whose turn is it to bat? 4. change, shift, switch, alteration, modification, deviation, detour The weather has taken a turn for the better. 5. deed, act, action, gesture, service, effort, step, response We did our elderly neighbor a kind turn by shoveling the snow from his walk.

turret *noun* tower, watchtower, lookout, steeple, belfry, campanile, minaret, observatory, spire The guard stood watch in the castle turret.

tussle *verb* scuffle, fight, brawl, scrap, spar, contest, vie, wrestle, battle The puppies tussled over the old sock. ◆ *noun* fight, scrap, fracas, skirmish, scuffle, brawl, melee, altercation, contest Two students were suspended after they got into a tussle in the school lobby.

tutor *noun* instructor, teacher, coach, mentor, trainer, educator, guide, master, guru My school has volunteer tutors in every classroom. ◆ *verb* educate, instruct, teach, coach, inform, train, explain, drill, guide My uncle tutors me in math.

twilight *noun* 1. dusk, nightfall, sundown, sunset, evening, gloaming, eventide Deer come out to feed just after dawn and just before twilight. 2. decline, ebb, end, finale, last, fall, collapse, wane, slump The twilight of the Roman Empire was marked by decadence and corruption. ◈ **Antonyms:** 1. dawn, daybreak, sunrise 2. prime, rise

twine *verb* coil, twist, wrap, loop, entwine, spiral, thread, knot, braid, tangle The vine twined around the trellis. ◆ *noun* string, yarn, cord, rope, thread, cable, hemp The package was bound with twine.

twinkle *verb* flash, flicker, gleam, glimmer, glitter, sparkle, shine, glint, scintillate The sequins on Mom's dress twinkle in the light. ◆ *noun* 1. flash, glimmer, flicker, glimmering, sparkle, spark, glint, flare I saw the twinkle of fish scales as the trout leapt out of the water. 2. moment, jiffy, instant, minute, second, blink, trice, flash I'll call you back in a twinkle.

twirl *verb* whirl, rotate, spin, swirl, wheel, pivot, gyrate, pirouette, turn The drum majorette twirled her baton and then threw it into the air.

twist *verb* 1. coil, curl, roll, wind, wrap, weave, braid, plait, wreathe The cowboy twisted his rope into a coil. 2.

sprain, turn, wrench, injure, hurt, strain, bruise, dislocate, crick How did you twist your ankle? **3.** alter, change, distort, misrepresent, contort, warp, confuse, misquote, misstate, garble Some authors twist the facts in order to make their books more interesting. **4.** meander, loop, circle, spiral, snake, wind, corkscrew, wander, arc, veer The highway twists around the city. **5.** squirm, fidget, wriggle, writhe, twitch, joggle, wiggle, jump, shudder I kept twisting in my chair because I was impatient to leave. ◆ *noun* **1.** angle, bend, curve, turn, zigzag, spiral, dogleg, loop This road is full of twists and turns. **2.** slant, alteration, change, variation, treatment, development, trick A pun makes us laugh by putting an unexpected twist on a word's meaning.

twitch *verb* jerk, quiver, shiver, quaver, wiggle, shake, tremble, throb The cat's whiskers twitched when he saw a mouse. ◆ *noun* spasm, paroxysm, tic, shake, tremor, throb, fit, convulsion, blink My leg gave a twitch when the doctor tested my reflexes.

tycoon *noun* millionaire, industrialist, financier, magnate, capitalist, baron, entrepreneur, mogul, executive Cornelius Vanderbilt was a tycoon who made a fortune in steamships and railroads.

type *noun* **1.** category, genre, kind, sort, class, variety, nature, ilk, stamp, genus, strain, breed Our library has all types of books. **2.** example, embodiment, epitome, essence, specimen, model, prototype, archetype, standard Unfortunately, she's the perfect type of an obnoxious relative. **3.** typeface, printing, characters, typography, print, font, design The type on the wedding invitation was ornate. ◆ *verb* classify, categorize, class, organize, rate, rank, sort, peg, pigeonhole She types the rocks in her collection by their mineral composition.

typical *adjective* average, normal, ordinary, standard, usual, regular, representative, conventional, characteristic The typical American household has at least one TV set.
● **Antonyms:** unusual, atypical, abnormal

tyranny *noun* oppression, repression, suppression, domination, subjugation, dictatorship, fascism, absolutism, totalitarianism The government's tyranny ended when the dictator was overthrown and a democratic leader was elected. ● **Antonym:** freedom

tyrant *noun* dictator, oppressor, despot, autocrat, totalitarian, authoritarian, ruler, fascist, overlord The tyrant was overthrown by the people he had long oppressed.

Uu

ubiquitous *adjective* **omnipresent, pervasive, widespread, prevalent, universal** Computers will someday be as ubiquitous as the telephone is now.

ugly *adjective* **1. bad-looking, homely, unattractive, unsightly, plain, hideous, unlovely** We entered our iguana in the ugly pet contest. **2. disgusting, repulsive, atrocious, foul, nasty, disagreeable, unpleasant, vile** There was an ugly smell coming from the town dump. **3. cantankerous, cranky, cross, disagreeable, grouchy, grumpy, irritable, surly** The coach was in an ugly mood after the team's unsatisfactory practice. ● **Antonyms: 1. beautiful, pretty 2. agreeable, pleasant 3. friendly, nice**

ulterior *adjective* **concealed, hidden, covert, buried, secret, private, undisclosed, unrevealed** The congressman had ulterior motives for supporting the controversial bill. ● **Antonyms: overt, open, plain**

ultimate *adjective* **1. concluding, end, final, last, terminal, eventual, extreme** The plane will make two stops before reaching its ultimate destination. **2. greatest, top, highest, supreme, topmost, utmost, uttermost, paramount, preeminent** The Nobel Prize for Literature is the ultimate literary award. ◆ *noun* **maximum, top, utmost, uttermost, height, peak, apex, summit, culmination** I think that digital video disks are the ultimate in home video systems. ● **Antonyms:** *adjective* **1. beginning, first 2. least, lowest**

umpire *noun* **arbiter, arbitrator, judge, referee, mediator, moderator, negotiator** We need an umpire for next week's baseball game. ◆ *verb* **arbitrate, judge, referee, rule, decide, determine, mediate, moderate** The President sent a special envoy to umpire the trade dispute.

unable *adjective* **not able, incapable, unfit, unqualified, incompetent, inadequate, powerless, helpless** Baby birds are unable to fly until they grow feathers. ● **Antonyms: able, capable**

unabridged *adjective* **complete, uncut, full-length, uncensored, intact, whole, entire** The unabridged edition of Tolstoy's *War and Peace* is more than one thousand pages long. ● **Antonyms: abridged, condensed**

unanimous *adjective* **undivided, unified, united, likeminded, harmonious, common, solid, universal** We reached a unanimous decision only after many hours of reviewing our options. ● **Antonyms: differing, divided**

unaware *adjective* **not aware, ignorant, uninformed, unknowing, oblivious, blind, heedless** She is usually unaware of how much time she spends on the telephone. ● **Antonyms: aware, conscious, informed**

unbecoming *adjective* **1. unattractive, inelegant, tasteless, unsightly, ugly, homely, unlovely** I find orange to be a most unbecoming color on me. **2. unbefitting, improper, unsuitable, inappropriate, unseemly, offensive, indecent** The colonel was reprimanded for conduct unbecoming an officer. ● **Antonyms: 1. attractive, pretty 2. proper, suitable**

unbelievable *adjective* **incredible, dubious, absurd, implausible, improbable, questionable, unconvincing** The sailor told an unbelievable story about seeing a mermaid. ● **Antonyms: believable, convincing**

unbiased *adjective* **impartial, objective, fair, fair-minded, neutral, equitable, unprejudiced** The judge instructed the jurors to be unbiased in their deliberations. ● **Antonyms: biased, bigoted**

uncanny *adjective* **1. eerie, mysterious, unearthly, unnatural, supernatural, strange, unusual, weird** There was an uncanny silence in the old house. **2. remarkable, incredible, exceptional, fantastic, unbelievable, extraordinary, preternatural, unusual** The Gypsy could predict the future with uncanny accuracy. ● **Antonyms: 1. normal, natural 2. common, ordinary**

uncertain *adjective* **1. questionable, ambiguous, unclear, indefinite, dubious, doubtful, vague** With the slowdown in the economy, the new company faces an uncertain future. **2. not certain, undecided, undetermined, unresolved, unsure, ambivalent, indecisive** My plans for the weekend are still uncertain. **3. capricious, changeable, erratic, unpredictable, unsettled, variable, unstable, unsteady** Uncertain weather forced us to postpone our sailing trip. ● **Antonyms: 1. & 2. certain, definite 3. predictable, steady**

uncomfortable *adjective* **1. ill-at-ease, embarrassed, nervous, self-conscious, uneasy, upset, awkward** I'm uncomfortable when I must speak in front of a large group.

2. **comfortless, hard, rough, irritating, painful, cramped, disagreeable** This old couch is lumpy and uncomfortable. ➡ **Antonyms: 1. relaxed, composed 2. comfortable**

uncommon *adjective* **1. rare, scarce, unique, unusual, infrequent, unfamiliar, occasional, sporadic** I spotted a bird in our yard that is uncommon in this area. **2. wonderful, remarkable, exceptional, extraordinary, magnificent, striking, impressive, outstanding** The ballerina danced with uncommon beauty and grace. ➡ **Antonyms: 1. familiar, frequent 2. common, ordinary**

unconcerned *adjective* **1. apathetic, indifferent, uninterested, careless, heedless, unmindful, forgetful** He seems to be unconcerned about his appearance. **2. aloof, detached, disinterested, uninvolved, nonchalant, untroubled, distant, unfeeling** The defendant had an unconcerned expression as she listened to the charges being filed against her. ➡ **Antonyms: 1. concerned, interested 2. involved, worried**

unconditional *adjective* **absolute, unqualified, complete, entire, utter, unlimited, unrestricted** General Ulysses S. Grant typically demanded an unconditional surrender from his defeated foes. ➡ **Antonyms: conditional, qualified**

unconscious *adjective* **1. knocked out, out cold, senseless, stunned, comatose, insensate** The man was unconscious for several minutes after falling and hitting his head. **2. heedless, ignorant, oblivious, unaware, unknowing, unmindful, innocent** I was unconscious of the fact that my friend was bored and wanted to go home. ➡ **Antonyms: conscious, aware**

uncouth *adjective* **crude, rude, crass, coarse, gross, churlish, unrefined, vulgar** We were offended by his uncouth remarks. ➡ **Antonyms: polite, courteous**

uncover *verb* **1. open, expose, unwrap, bare, strip, denude, disrobe, undress** I uncovered the casserole so that it could brown on top. **2. reveal, expose, disclose, unveil** The news story uncovered new facts about the corruption scandal at city hall. ➡ **Antonyms: 1. wrap, cover 2. hide, conceal**

undecided *adjective* **1. open, indefinite, uncertain, vague, tentative, undetermined, unresolved** Our summer vacation plans are still undecided. **2. unsure, indecisive, uncertain, uncommitted, ambivalent, irresolute, hesitant** My sister is undecided about which colleges she wants to apply to. ➡ **Antonyms: 1. certain, definite 2. certain, decided**

under *preposition* **1. below, beneath, underneath, neath, covered by** I found my house key under a stack of papers. **2. less than, lower than, smaller than, inferior to, short of, shy of** Anyone under the age of 17 may not attend this movie. **3. according to, subject to, controlled by, dependent upon, following** Under the rules of basketball, a team can have only five players on the court at one time. ➡ **Antonyms: 1. & 2. above, over**

undercover *adjective* **secret, clandestine, covert, hush-hush, surreptitious, hidden, concealed** FBI agents are conducting an undercover investigation. ➡ **Antonyms: open, aboveboard**

undergo *verb* **1. encounter, experience, go through, have, meet with, feel** Babies undergo many changes during the first year of their lives. **2. endure, suffer, weather, brave, bear, withstand, stand** The Pilgrims underwent many hardships during their first years in America. ➡ **Antonyms: avoid, miss**

underground *adjective* **1. belowground, subterranean, buried, covered, sunken** Wolves typically live in underground dens. **2. secret, covert, clandestine, concealed, hidden, surreptitious, undercover** The Underground Railroad helped many slaves escape. ➡ **Antonyms: 1. aboveground, surface 2. open, known**

undermine *verb* **sabotage, subvert, weaken, impair, erode, cripple, foil, thwart** Management undermined the workers' attempts to form a labor union. ➡ **Antonyms: strengthen, support**

underneath *adverb* **below, beneath, under, down, downward, lower** The leaf was green above and silver underneath. ◆ *preposition* **beneath, under, below, neath** I wore a wool sweater underneath my jacket. ➡ **Antonyms: above, over**

understand *verb* **1. comprehend, get, grasp, master, follow, know, realize, recognize** The teacher took great care to ensure that everyone understood the homework assignment. **2. sympathize with, appreciate, accept, acknowledge, apprehend** I understand your not wanting to go alone. **3. infer, believe, conclude, deduce, gather, hear, perceive, presume** I understand that the meeting might be postponed.

understanding *noun* **1. comprehension, grasp, grip, hold, knowledge, perception, apprehension** My understanding of quantum theory is limited. **2. interpretation, judgment, opinion, view, viewpoint, belief, notion, idea** My understanding of our agreement is different from yours.

3. agreement, arrangement, bargain, compromise, deal, pact, accord, compact War was averted when the two countries reached an understanding. **4. sensitivity, discernment, compassion, sympathy, empathy, kindness, insight** I like to confide in my friend because she has so much understanding. ◆ *adjective* **compassionate, sympathetic, kind, sensitive, tender, feeling, tolerant** I told my troubles to an understanding friend. ➤ **Antonyms:** *adjective* **insensitive, unsympathetic**

undertake *verb* **assume, attempt, tackle, take on, begin, start, incur, shoulder** Cleaning out the basement was a chore that no one wanted to undertake. ➤ **Antonyms: avoid, drop, discontinue**

undertaking *noun* **task, job, enterprise, assignment, venture, endeavor, project, business** Building a space station is a particularly difficult undertaking.

> ## Word Group
>
> The **underworld** is the region of the dead in Greek and Roman mythology. **Underworld** is a specific term with no true synonyms. Here are some related words:
>
> **Hades, hell, inferno, limbo, netherworld, perdition, purgatory**

undo *verb* **1. erase, neutralize, cancel, defeat, annul, wipe out, reverse, nullify** I regret what I did, but I cannot undo my actions. **2. free, open, loosen, unfasten, unravel, untie, disengage, unclasp** Mom had to undo the seams of the dress she was altering. **3. ruin, destroy, end, demolish, spoil, smash, torpedo, shatter, sink** Our hopes of getting to the state finals were undone when we lost the big game. ➤ **Antonyms: 1. do, uphold 2. close, fasten, tie 3. foster, encourage**

undoubtedly *adverb* **without doubt, doubtless, absolutely, certainly, positively, indubitably, unquestionably** You're undoubtedly right that college tuition costs will continue to rise.

uneasy *adjective* **1. anxious, apprehensive, nervous, worried, troubled, concerned, upset** I felt a little uneasy about diving off the high board. **2. awkward, embarrassed, uncomfortable, constrained, unpleasant, shy** There was an uneasy pause in our conversation. ➤ **Antonyms: easy, comfortable**

unemployed *adjective* **jobless, out-of-work, inactive, idle, unoccupied** The state government has a bureau that

helps unemployed workers find jobs. ➤ **Antonyms: busy, employed, working**

unequal *adjective* **1. different, dissimilar, uneven, unlike, irregular, unbalanced** This chair wobbles because the legs are of unequal length. **2. lopsided, unfair, unjust, inequitable, one-sided, partial, biased** It turned out to be an unequal contest because our players were much more experienced than theirs. ➤ **Antonyms: 1. equal, even, similar 2. fair, just**

uneven *adjective* **1. lopsided, mismatched, one-sided, unbalanced, unequal, different, unlike** The volleyball game was uneven because one team had much taller players. **2. varying, erratic, inconsistent, spotty, variable, changeable, unsteady** Several reviewers said that the author's writing was uneven. **3. bumpy, irregular, rough, rugged, ragged, jagged, crooked** We had difficulty walking across the uneven ground. ➤ **Antonyms: 1. equal, even 2. uniform, constant 3. level, smooth, straight**

unexceptional *adjective* **average, common, ordinary, plain, routine, unremarkable, standard, mediocre** I was surprised that the orchestra gave such an unexceptional performance. ➤ **Antonyms: remarkable, outstanding, exceptional**

unexpected *adjective* **unanticipated, unforeseen, abrupt, fortuitous, chance, sudden, surprising** She was delighted when she received an unexpected present. ➤ **Antonyms: anticipated, expected**

unfair *adjective* **one-sided, unjust, inequitable, uneven, unequal, biased, prejudiced** Wrestlers are matched up according to their weight so that no one has an unfair advantage. ➤ **Antonyms: fair, just**

unfaithful *adjective* **disloyal, false, untrue, traitorous, treacherous, false-hearted, perfidious** The woman divorced her unfaithful husband. ➤ **Antonyms: faithful, true, loyal**

unfamiliar *adjective* **1. inexperienced, unacquainted, ignorant, unaware, uninformed, oblivious, innocent** Many people are unfamiliar with the sign language used by hearing-impaired individuals. **2. strange, unknown, new, different, original, uncommon, fresh, unusual** The explorers moved slowly across the unfamiliar terrain. ➤ **Antonyms: 1. familiar, knowledgeable 2. familiar, common**

unfit *adjective* **1. unsuitable, inappropriate, ill-suited, improper, unsuited, unbecoming** The health department deemed water from the town well to be unfit for human consumption. **2. unqualified, incompetent, incapable, inept, inadequate, unequal, unsuited** He lacked relevant experience or training and was unfit for the position we had open. **3. unhealthy, weak, frail, sick, sickly, infirm, feeble, poorly, unwell** This cold has left me feeling unfit for anything but sleep. ➡ **Antonyms: 1. fit, suitable 2. competent, qualified 3. healthy, robust**

unfortunate *adjective* **1. unlucky, unhappy, ill-starred, disastrous, hapless, unfavorable, adverse, bad, poor** An unfortunate accident put him in the hospital. **2. inappropriate, regrettable, ill-chosen, inopportune, awkward, unbecoming** Her unfortunate slip gave away our plans for a surprise party. ➡ **Antonyms: 1. fortunate, lucky 2. opportune, appropriate**

unfriendly *adjective* **aloof, cold, cool, distant, unsociable, haughty, inimical, hostile** Our cat is usually unfriendly toward strangers. ➡ **Antonyms: friendly, warm**

unhappy *adjective* **1. depressed, dejected, downcast, gloomy, sad, sorrowful, low, melancholy** I cheered Mom up when she was feeling unhappy. **2. unlucky, unfortunate, hapless, ill-fated, unfavorable, inappropriate, inept** The long series of misunderstandings came to an unhappy conclusion. ➡ **Antonyms: 1. cheerful, happy 2. lucky, fortunate**

unhealthy *adjective* **1. ill, sick, sickly, unwell, ailing, infirm, frail, weak, poorly** My plant looks unhealthy because it hasn't been getting enough water. **2. negative, bad, corrupt, corruptive, undesirable, perverse, rotten** Kids who use drugs are an unhealthy influence on their peers. **3. dangerous, harmful, risky, unhealthful, unwholesome, detrimental, unsafe** People used to think that it was unhealthy to have fresh air in the bedroom at night. ➡ **Antonyms: 1. healthy, well 2. beneficial, good 3. healthful, wholesome**

uniform *adjective* **1. constant, even, regular, steady, unchanging, consistent, same** A good refrigerator keeps everything at a uniform temperature. **2. comparable, equal, identical, like, corresponding, equivalent, similar, alike** Most bricks in this wall are of uniform size. ◆ *noun* **outfit, attire, costume, livery, dress, garb, habit, regalia** My stepdad still has his old air force uniform. ➡ **Antonyms:** *adjective* **1. uneven, variable 2. unequal, dissimilar**

unify *verb* **unite, combine, connect, consolidate, join, link, merge, couple** In 1990 East and West Germany unified to form one nation. ➡ **Antonyms: divide, separate**

union *noun* **1. combination, consolidation, joining, marriage, merger, unification, unity** The United Arab Emirates is a country that was formed in 1971 by the union of seven sheikdoms. **2. guild, alliance, association, league, coalition, organization, society** Dad is a member of the labor union for his trade. ➡ **Antonyms: 1. division, separation**

unique *adjective* **1. different, distinctive, individual, separate, singular, particular** Nature has endowed every snowflake with a unique shape. **2. incomparable, unmatched, unrivaled, peerless, remarkable, unusual, exceptional** We had a unique opportunity to tour the museum's back rooms. ➡ **Antonyms: common, ordinary**

unison *noun* **agreement, harmony, accord, concord, unity, unanimity, consonance** Several nations acted in unison to end the world crisis. ➡ **Antonyms: dissonance, disagreement**

unit *noun* **1. component, element, item, part, piece, section, segment, portion** Our car needs a new heating unit. **2. outfit, detachment, force, squad, corps, crew, team, body, gang** Dad's old army unit is having a reunion. **3. quantity, unit of measure, amount, interval, increment** Seconds, minutes, and hours are units used to measure time.

unite *verb* **1. consolidate, combine, join, link, merge, unify, confederate, connect** Chief Tecumseh's dream was to unite all North American tribes into one Indian nation. **2. join, band together, associate, cooperate, ally, league** Local citizens are uniting to oppose gang violence. ➡ **Antonyms: 1. divide, separate 2. disband, part**

unity *noun* **1. completeness, wholeness, oneness, integrity, identity, singularity, union** President Lincoln worked to preserve the unity of the United States. **2. accord, harmony, agreement, concord, rapport, consensus, solidarity** In a rare show of unity, Congress passed the bill with no opposition. ➡ **Antonyms: 1. division, separation 2. disunity, discord, disagreement**

universal *adjective* **1. global, international, worldwide, planetary, cosmic, cosmopolitan, catholic** Esperanto was developed as a universal language. **2. boundless, broad, general, unlimited, widespread, common, ubiquitous, total** Books become classics if they have universal appeal. ➡ **Antonyms: 1. parochial 2. limited, restricted**

unkempt *adjective* **disheveled, messy, sloppy, slovenly, untidy, neglected** The hunter had an unkempt appearance after spending a week in the woods. ➡ **Antonyms: neat, tidy, well-groomed**

unkind *adjective* cruel, harsh, inconsiderate, mean, thoughtless, insensitive, callous She apologized for having made an unkind remark about her friend's appearance. ✒ **Antonyms:** considerate, kind, thoughtful

unknown *adjective* anonymous, nameless, unidentified, unrecognized, obscure Arlington National Cemetery contains the Tomb of the Unknown Soldier.

unlawful *adjective* illegal, illicit, outlawed, wrongful, illegitimate, lawless, prohibited It is unlawful to steal someone else's property. ✒ **Antonyms:** legal, lawful

unlike *adjective* different, dissimilar, disparate, divergent, distinct, opposite, separate Though a whale and a mouse are both mammals, they are completely unlike in most respects. ✒ **Antonyms:** identical, like, similar

unlikely *adjective* doubtful, questionable, improbable, unexpected, inconceivable, unbelievable When I saw the clear sky, I knew that rain was unlikely. ✒ **Antonyms:** certain, likely, probable

unlucky *adjective* luckless, unfortunate, hapless, ill-fated, ill-starred, unhappy, untoward The unlucky gambler lost all of his money during three hours at the casino. ✒ **Antonyms:** fortunate, lucky

unnatural *adjective* 1. abnormal, unusual, supernatural, bizarre, curious, eerie, peculiar, strange, weird We saw an unnatural light coming from the abandoned research building. 2. artificial, affected, contrived, feigned, insincere, phony, fake, stiff Her laughter sounded unnatural. ✒ **Antonyms:** natural, normal

unnecessary *adjective* needless, unrequired, nonessential, unneeded, uncalled-for, excessive Police officers are cautioned against using unnecessary force.

unpack *verb* empty, unload, clear, offload, disburden, dump When I got to camp, the first thing I did was unpack my suitcase. ✒ **Antonyms:** fill, pack

unpaid *adjective* 1. due, payable, owed, owing, outstanding, unsettled, receivable He plans to settle his unpaid bills after payday. 2. uncompensated, unsalaried, volunteer, voluntary, free, gratuitous Unpaid volunteers help the library's staff on weekends.

unpleasant *adjective* bad, disagreeable, offensive, repulsive, repugnant, objectionable, nasty Do you find the odor of the mud flats at low tide as unpleasant as I do? ✒ **Antonyms:** agreeable, pleasant, good

unpopular *adjective* disliked, unwanted, unwelcome, undesirable, unacceptable, friendless The unpopular representative was unsuccessful in his bid to get reelected. ✒ **Antonyms:** liked, popular

unreal *adjective* imaginary, imagined, nonexistent, fanciful, hypothetical, illusory, visionary Unicorns and mermaids are unreal creatures. ✒ **Antonyms:** real, actual

unreasonable *adjective* 1. absurd, foolish, illogical, irrational, senseless, silly, preposterous, ridiculous Mom said that I was being unreasonable when I insisted on staying up all night. 2. immoderate, excessive, exorbitant, extreme, outrageous, inordinate, extravagant Marcus spends an unreasonable amount of time combing his hair. ✒ **Antonyms:** 1. logical, reasonable 2. fair, moderate

unreliable *adjective* questionable, uncertain, undependable, untrustworthy, dubious, unsure, flimsy The newspaper didn't print the story because the information came from an unreliable source. ✒ **Antonyms:** reliable, dependable

unrest *noun* agitation, disorder, disturbance, trouble, turmoil, turbulence, distress Periods of political unrest can occur when people are unhappy with their leaders. ✒ **Antonyms:** calm, peace, quiet

unruly *adjective* disorderly, uncontrollable, unmanageable, fractious, wild, disobedient, refractory, intractable More police were called in to help control the unruly mob. ✒ **Antonyms:** docile, obedient

unsafe *adjective* dangerous, hazardous, treacherous, perilous, risky, precarious, unreliable All this snow has made the roads unsafe for travel. ✒ **Antonyms:** safe, reliable

unsatisfactory *adjective* inadequate, insufficient, unacceptable, bad, poor, unfavorable, inferior He lost his job because his work was unsatisfactory.

unsavory *adjective* 1. insipid, flat, bland, tasteless, flavorless, unappetizing, disagreeable The sailors lived on an unsavory diet of gruel and hardtack. 2. disreputable, scandalous, infamous, shady, notorious, bad, repellent, repugnant With a long criminal history, the gangster had an unsavory reputation. ✒ **Antonyms:** 1. savory, appetizing 2. good, upright

unskilled *adjective* inexperienced, unprofessional, untrained, unqualified, untalented, inexpert, amateur Unskilled workers usually make less money than those with special training. ✒ **Antonyms:** skilled, professional

unstable *adjective* **1. changeable, variable, erratic, unsettled, uncertain, unpredictable, shifting** We yearned for a clear, sunny day after four days of unstable weather. **2. unsteady, rickety, unsound, shaky, wobbly, precarious, tottering, weak** This shelf is too unstable to hold those heavy books. **3. temperamental, irrational, volatile, mercurial, unbalanced, excitable, hysterical** The unstable man was advised to seek counseling. ⏺ **Antonyms: 1. stable, unchanging 2. steady, firm 3. stable, level-headed**

unsteady *adjective* **1. shaky, unstable, wobbly, insecure, rickety, tottering, precarious, infirm** The books had been stacked carelessly in a tall, unsteady pile. **2. wavering, uneven, erratic, inconsistent, irregular, unreliable, changeable** I was so nervous that my voice was unsteady. ⏺ **Antonyms: 1. firm, stable 2. steady, regular**

unsuccessful *adjective* **futile, vain, useless, fruitless, ineffectual, unproductive** The mountaineer's attempt to reach the summit was unsuccessful. ⏺ **Antonyms: victorious, successful**

untie *verb* **loosen, unbind, undo, unfasten, unclasp, disengage, detach, disconnect** We untied our mooring rope and paddled our canoe out into the river.

unused *adjective* **1. new, pristine, untouched, untried, fresh, original, firsthand** Mom found an unused toaster oven at a garage sale. **2. unaccustomed, unfamiliar, inexperienced** I am unused to getting up early in the morning. ⏺ **Antonyms: 1. old, used 2. accustomed**

unusual *adjective* **exceptional, extraordinary, rare, strange, bizarre, uncommon, freakish, unique** In a highly unusual occurrence, a blizzard hit Nebraska in July 1816. ⏺ **Antonyms: common, ordinary, usual**

unwieldy *adjective* **cumbersome, awkward, unhandy, unmanageable, clumsy, bulky, heavy, inconvenient** I found the heavy, wooden bat too unwieldy and used an aluminum one instead. ⏺ **Antonyms: handy, convenient**

up *adverb* **above, overhead, upward, skyward, aloft, higher** I looked up just in time to see an eagle soaring overhead. ◆ *adjective* **cheerful, elated, excited, optimistic, upbeat, joyful, happy** Our spirits definitely were up after we won the game. ◆ *verb* **raise, increase, boost, hike, jack, inflate, amplify** The store upped its prices on everything that was in popular demand. ⏺ **Antonyms:** *adverb* **below, down** ◆ *adjective* **down, sad** ◆ *verb* **lower, reduce**

upbeat *adjective* **optimistic, sanguine, positive, cheerful, hopeful, favorable, promising** With all committees

reporting a profit, our monthly meeting ended on an upbeat note. ⏺ **Antonyms: negative, pessimistic**

upbraid *verb* **admonish, criticize, chastise, castigate, reproach, rebuke, chide** The soldier was upbraided for not fulfilling his duties. ⏺ **Antonyms: praise, compliment**

upheaval *noun* **disturbance, change, unrest, turmoil, cataclysm, disruption, revolution** Russia underwent great political upheaval in the years between the revolution of 1917 and the formation of the Soviet Union in 1922.

uphill *adjective* **1. rising, ascending, climbing, upward, steep** We were tired after completing the uphill portion of the trail. **2. difficult, arduous, tough, hard, laborious, strenuous, wearisome** The patient is facing a long, uphill battle before he recovers fully. ⏺ **Antonyms: 1. downhill 2. easy, simple**

uphold *verb* **maintain, support, sustain, defend, preserve, protect, champion, advocate** Police officers take an oath in which they promise to uphold the law.

upkeep *noun* **maintenance, repair, support, overhead, preservation** Dad has been spending a lot of money on the upkeep of his old car.

upper *adjective* **1. higher, superior, better, eminent, outstanding, greater** Only people from the upper third of the class made the honor roll. **2. higher, top, topmost, uppermost, high, overhead, upward, above** There is still snow on the mountain's upper slopes.

upright *adjective* **1. vertical, erect, plumb, raised, perpendicular, standing** Please place your seat in the upright position before takeoff. **2. good, honest, honorable, moral, ethical, trustworthy, virtuous, incorruptible** The upright politician was admired and trusted by his constituents. ⏺ **Antonyms: 1. horizontal, prone 2. corrupt, dishonest**

uproar *noun* **clamor, commotion, disturbance, noise, tumult, turmoil, pandemonium** There was such an uproar from the audience that I couldn't hear the band.

upset *verb* **1. capsize, overturn, turn over, tip over, knock over, topple** We tried to rearrange our gear and accidentally upset our canoe. **2. disorganize, disrupt, jumble, mess up, muddle, unsettle, cancel, change** The unexpected arrival of company upset our dinner plans. **3. agitate, distress, disturb, perturb, trouble, annoy, bother, fluster, distract** The news that our teacher was leaving upset everyone in the class. **4. overthrow, overcome, defeat, beat, vanquish, rout, thrash, crush** The challenger upset his opponent in a surprise victory. ◆ *adjective* **1. overturned, upside-down, upturned, capsized, inverted, upturned, toppled** The road was blocked by an upset truck. **2. distressed, disturbed, troubled, annoyed, bothered, perturbed** Mary was upset when she lost her necklace.

urban *adjective* **city, metropolitan, municipal, civic, cosmopolitan** When the Industrial Revolution began, many people moved to urban areas to find work. ➡ **Antonym: rural**

urchin *noun* **waif, gamin, brat, hooligan, ragamuffin, juvenile delinquent, child** Dickens's *Oliver Twist* is a novel about the plight of street urchins in Victorian England.

urge *verb* **1. drive, force, goad, press, prod, push, spur, impel** When the cattle refused to cross the river, a cowboy urged them on. **2. entreat, exhort, implore, insist, beg, encourage, persuade, plead, advocate** The sick man's friends urged him to see a doctor. ◆ *noun* **impulse, desire, drive, longing, wish, yearning, hunger, thirst** I had a sudden urge to run outside and play in the rain.

urgent *adjective* **critical, crucial, essential, important, pressing, imperative** The charity spokesperson said that there was an urgent need for donations. ➡ **Antonyms: minor, trivial, unimportant**

usage *noun* **handling, operation, treatment, use, application, play, employment** My bicycle is still in good shape despite years of hard usage.

use *verb* **1. employ, make use of, utilize, wield, manipulate, handle, operate** I used a knife to open my birthday cards. **2. apply, exercise, practice, employ, implement, exert, exploit** Use caution when crossing a busy street. **3. consume, expend, drain, take, exhaust, eat up, finish, spend** Our refrigerator is an old model that uses a lot of electricity. ◆ *noun* **1. operation, service, action, duty, employment, handling, play, work** We will have to wait because the elevator is in use right now. **2. application, function, utilization, usage, utility, practice, purpose** A computer has many practical uses. **3. usefulness, advantage, benefit, avail, account, profit, value** There's no use calling her because she's not home now.

used *adjective* **secondhand, cast-off, old, worn, worn-out, out-of-date** I know a terrific store that sells used books at very low prices. ➡ **Antonym: new**

useful *adjective* **beneficial, handy, helpful, practical, valuable, functional, convenient** An electric saw is a useful tool for people who do carpentry. ➡ **Antonym: useless**

useless *adjective* **1. unserviceable, worthless, unusable, inoperative, unworkable, futile, vain** A flashlight without batteries is useless. **2. inefficient, incompetent, inept, hopeless, ineffective** The new employee was useless until he learned the proper procedures. ➡ **Antonyms: 1. useful, 2. efficient, effective**

usher *noun* **attendant, escort, guide, conductor, pilot, shepherd, guard, leader** An usher showed us to our seats at the theater. ◆ *verb* **1. conduct, escort, guide, lead, direct, show, shepherd, steer, pilot** The waiter ushered us to our table. **2. introduce, inaugurate, launch, precede, preface, herald, announce** The microprocessor ushered in a new era of home computing.

usual *adjective* **accustomed, customary, habitual, normal, regular, routine, common, ordinary** I took my usual seat near the front of the classroom. ➡ **Antonyms: rare, unusual**

usually *adverb* **customarily, regularly, typically, normally, frequently, generally, commonly** We usually have a cooked breakfast of pancakes or eggs on Sunday mornings. ➡ **Antonyms: rarely, infrequently**

usurp *verb* **preempt, arrogate, assume, take, appropriate, commandeer, grab** Mary Queen of Scots was executed for trying to usurp the English throne from Elizabeth I.

utensil *noun* **implement, instrument, tool, apparatus, device, gadget** Forks and spoons are utensils for eating.

utilize *verb* **make use of, apply, use, implement, employ, handle, exploit** The first automobile to utilize a gasoline-powered engine was developed in the 1880s.

utmost *adjective* **greatest, maximum, highest, most, extreme, absolute, supreme, top** National security is a matter of the utmost importance. ◆ *noun* **maximum, top, best, most, ultimate, acme, zenith, peak** The author did his utmost to get the book done on time.

utter[1] *verb* **pronounce, say, speak, state, articulate, enunciate, voice, vocalize** The witch uttered a spell, and the prince was turned into a frog.

utter[2] *adjective* **absolute, complete, entire, thorough, total, all-out, perfect, outright** When the electricity went out, the house was plunged into utter darkness.

utterly *adverb* **completely, totally, thoroughly, entirely, absolutely, fully, altogether** After helping our friends move into their new house, we were utterly exhausted.

Vv

vacant *adjective* **1. empty, uninhabited, unoccupied, abandoned, deserted, bare, available, open** Someone finally moved into the house that has been vacant for a year. **2. blank, hollow, uncomprehending, senseless, vacuous, inane, foolish, dull, stupid** The survivors of the disaster had vacant looks on their faces. ➡ **Antonyms: 1. full, occupied 2. alert, thoughtful**

vacate *verb* **leave, depart, give up, clean out, clear, evacuate, abandon, surrender, withdraw** When our lease is up, we are going to vacate this apartment and find another one. ➡ **Antonyms: occupy, possess**

vacation *noun* **break, holiday, recess, furlough, leave, rest, respite, sabbatical** I hope to visit my grandparents during my summer vacation.

vacillate *verb* **waver, dither, hesitate, pause, shilly-shally, sway, swing, halt, wobble, falter, oscillate** Stephanie has a job offer, but she is vacillating over whether or not to accept it.

vacuum *noun* **void, emptiness, absence, gap, free space, empty space, nothingness, vacuity, hole** Sound waves cannot travel through a vacuum. ◆ *verb* **clean, clear, suction, brush, dust, tidy** As one of my weekly chores, I vacuum the carpet in my bedroom.

vague *adjective* **1. ambiguous, muddled, unclear, cryptic, incomprehensible, befuddled, garbled, imprecise** The instructions for this homework assignment are vague. **2. dim, faint, blurry, fuzzy, indefinite, indistinct, hazy, cloudy, blurred** The lookout saw the vague outline of a ship approaching through the fog. **3. indefinite, mysterious, elusive, unfixed, random, casual, unspecific, doubtful, inconclusive** I have a vague feeling that I've forgotten something important. ➡ **Antonyms: 1. comprehensible, clear 2. clear, well-defined 3. specific, certain, definite**

vain *adjective* **1. futile, ineffective, unsuccessful, useless, worthless, unprofitable, senseless, fruitless, hopeless** We made a vain attempt to get to the post office before it closed. **2. arrogant, conceited, haughty, proud, smug, egotistic, narcissistic, foppish, dandified, pompous** The vain man assumed that everyone agreed with him. ➡ **Antonyms: 1. effective, successful 2. humble, modest**

valiant *adjective* **brave, courageous, fearless, gallant, heroic, valorous, bold, chivalrous, unafraid** The valiant bystander succeeded in rescuing several passengers from the airplane that crashed in the river. ➡ **Antonyms: cowardly, fearful**

valid *adjective* **1. good, sound, acceptable, suitable, convincing, logical, true, effective, compelling** I had a valid excuse for being late to school. **2. lawful, legal, legitimate, authentic, genuine, real, official, original, unexpired** You must have a valid driver's license in order to legally operate a motor vehicle. ➡ **Antonyms: 1. unconvincing, unacceptable, false 2. invalid, unofficial, illegal**

validate *verb* **1. authorize, stamp, endorse, certify, legalize, ratify, sanction, affirm, authenticate** The clerk validated my gift certificate. **2. corroborate, substantiate, support, prove, verify, confirm, bear out, affirm, back** New evidence has validated the prosecution's case. ➡ **Antonyms: 1. cancel, annul, invalidate 2. contradict, disprove**

valley *noun* **vale, dale, dell, glen, basin, hollow, gorge, bowl, lowland** The peaceful valley was nestled between two mountain ranges.

valuable *adjective* **1. costly, expensive, high-priced, precious, priceless, dear** The antique chair is very valuable. **2. beneficial, helpful, important, useful, worthwhile, worthy, esteemed, advantageous, fruitful** My sister's summer job gave her valuable experience. ◆ *noun* **possession, antique, collectible, heirloom, commodity, treasure, asset** My parents store their valuables in a safety deposit box. ➡ **Antonyms:** *adjective* **1. cheap, inexpensive 2. unimportant, worthless**

value *noun* **1. merit, sense, worth, usefulness, importance, significance, utility, benefit, substance** My parents' advice usually has a lot of practical value. **2. cost, price, appraisal, amount, market, price, quotation, equivalent** The value of our house has gone up since we bought it. **3. standard, principle, ethic, guide, belief, purpose, precept, goal, tenet** Many people's values are rooted in their religion. ◆ *verb* **1. appraise, assess, estimate, evaluate, price, measure, reckon, judge, determine** A jeweler valued the emerald ring at 550 dollars. **2. appreciate, cherish, esteem, prize, respect, treasure, love, regard** I really value your friendship. ➡ **Antonyms:** *verb* **2. disdain, spurn**

van *noun* **car, truck, caravan, wagon, lorry, trailer, camper** A van is considered a family vehicle.

vandal *noun* hooligan, delinquent, wrecker, saboteur, destroyer, pillager, marauder, savage, barbarian Vandals painted obscenities on the street sign.

vanish *verb* disappear, evaporate, go away, dissolve, fade, sink, perish, exit, dematerialize Many ships are said to have vanished in the Bermuda Triangle. ▸ **Antonyms:** appear, materialize

vanity *noun* 1. arrogance, conceit, pride, smugness, self-admiration, narcissism, hauteur His friends describe him as a humble man of little vanity. 2. fruitlessness, folly, futility, uselessness, pointlessness, hollowness Trying to hold back the tides is pure vanity. ▸ **Antonyms:** 1. modesty, humility

vanquish *verb* 1. defeat, beat, quell, overwhelm, best, crush, rout, subjugate, trample Union troops vanquished the Confederate army at the battle of Gettysburg in 1863. 2. overcome, eliminate, eradicate, master, transcend, surmount, control, suppress With the help of a speech therapist, she vanquished her lisp.

vantage *noun* 1. advantage, superiority, authority, purchase, dominance, footing, leadership Her height does give her a vantage on the basketball court. 2. view, vista, lookout, position, perspective, outlook, angle, standpoint From this vantage I can see the whole town.

vapor *noun* fog, mist, haze, smog, smoke, steam, fumes, gas, moisture High-flying jet aircraft leave visible trails of water vapor.

variable *adjective* changeable, erratic, shifting, fitful, unstable, unsteady, fickle, capricious, volatile This is not a good day for sailing, because the winds are quite variable. ◆ *noun* factor, condition, circumstance, possibility, unknown, happenstance There are many variables that could affect the outcome of this experiment. ▸ **Antonyms:** *adjective* constant, unchanging

variety *noun* 1. change, diversity, variation, difference, nonconformity, diversification, dissimilarity For the sake of variety, let's have something other than pepperoni on our pizza tonight. 2. array, assortment, collection, mixture, selection, potpourri, hodgepodge, medley Fishermen usually carry a wide variety of hooks and lures. 3. kind, sort, type, brand, category, grade, ilk, strain, description There are several thousand varieties of apples grown around the world.

various *adjective* 1. assorted, different, diverse, varied, dissimilar, heterogeneous, unlike, divergent This skirt is available in various colors and styles. 2. several, numerous, some, innumerable, few, countless, manifold, sundry Various students in my class bring their lunch to school. ▸ **Antonyms:** 1. alike, similar, identical

vary *verb* change, shift, differ, fluctuate, alter, mutate, modify, switch Fashions vary from season to season.

vast *adjective* huge, enormous, extensive, colossal, immense, endless, measureless, monumental, monstrous The Sahara Desert occupies a vast part of the African continent. ▸ **Antonyms:** limited, small, tiny

vault[1] *noun* 1. strong room, safe, storeroom, strong box, repository, depository Bank vaults usually have massive steel doors. 2. grave, tomb, crypt, sepulcher, burial chamber, mausoleum, catacomb, cavern Several English monarchs have been entombed in the vault at Westminster Abbey.

vault[2] *verb* hurdle, jump, leap, spring, bound, hop, leapfrog, clear I vaulted over our neighbors' fence in my dash to catch the school bus. ◆ *noun* leap, spring, jump, bound, hop, hurdle The gymnast's exceptional vault over the horse moved her into first place.

veer *verb* swerve, dodge, turn, deviate, depart, pivot, tack, swivel, change The driver veered aside sharply to avoid hitting the pothole.

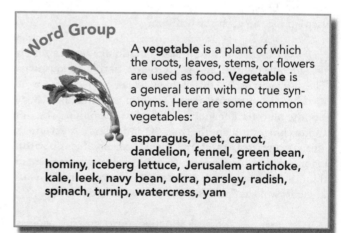

Word Group

A **vegetable** is a plant of which the roots, leaves, stems, or flowers are used as food. **Vegetable** is a general term with no true synonyms. Here are some common vegetables:

asparagus, beet, carrot, dandelion, fennel, green bean, hominy, iceberg lettuce, Jerusalem artichoke, kale, leek, navy bean, okra, parsley, radish, spinach, turnip, watercress, yam

vegetation *noun* flora, plant life, plants, shrubbery, greenery, verdure, foliage, leaves, grass, weeds Hawaii is famous for its lush vegetation.

vehement *adjective* fervent, passionate, zealous, forceful, ardent, heated, fierce, opinionated, furious Many people have vehement opinions when it comes to politics. ▸ **Antonyms:** apathetic, indifferent

vehicle *noun* means, medium, device, agent, mechanism, agency, tool, instrument, apparatus Exercise is a vehicle to good health.

veil *noun* curtain, cloak, cover, mask, screen, shroud, mantle, covering, façade The mountaintop was hidden behind a veil of clouds. ◆ *verb* cloak, conceal, cover, hide, mask, screen, shroud, obscure, envelope In the spy movie I watched last night, the heroine veiled her face to keep her identity a secret. ➽ **Antonyms:** *verb* expose, reveal, show

vein *noun* **1.** deposit, lode, streak, line, seam, layer, stripe, rib, stratum The prospector found a rich vein of gold. **2.** tone, manner, spirit, style, mood, turn, attitude, tenor, course, disposition She spoke in a serious vein.

velocity *noun* rate, speed, quickness, rapidity, swiftness, pace Sound waves travel at a velocity of approximately 740 miles per hour.

vendor *noun* peddler, dealer, merchant, salesperson, supplier, seller, trader, wholesaler We bought some fruit from a vendor on the corner.

venerable *adjective* revered, respected, august, estimable, illustrious, worthy, noble, venerated, admired The Dalai Lama, leader of Tibetan Buddhists, is a venerable personage. ➽ **Antonyms:** infamous, unknown, unworthy

vengeance *noun* punishment, revenge, retaliation, retribution, reprisal, counterattack, wrath, fury England's King Henry VIII had his wife Anne Boleyn beheaded in an act of vengeance. ➽ **Antonyms:** mercy, forgiveness, forbearance

venom *noun* **1.** poison, toxin, bane Black widow spiders produce a venom that is harmful to humans. **2.** malice, spite, rancor, hatred, ill-will, maliciousness, bitterness, anger, spitefulness The rejected suitor was filled with venom. ➽ **Antonyms: 1.** antidote, antitoxin **2.** love, goodwill, kindness

vent *noun* **1.** expression, outlet, airing, articulation, utterance, voice, disclosure, proclamation Writing stories is a good vent for my creativity. **2.** opening, outlet, hole, aperture, passage, flue, drain, duct, spout Our clothes dryer is connected to a vent that releases the heat outside the house. ◆ *verb* **1.** express, air, communicate, verbalize, utter, reveal, let out, declare, divulge I felt better once I had vented my feelings. **2.** discharge, spout, release, pour, drip, exude, gush, escape Yellowstone National Park has over three thousand geysers and hot springs that vent steam and hot water. ➽ **Antonyms:** *noun* **2.** obstruction, closure, stoppage ◆ *verb* **1.** suppress, repress **2.** block, stop, obstruct

venture *noun* endeavor, undertaking, chance, gamble, risk, enterprise, feat, essay Columbus's expeditions to the New World were risky ventures. ◆ *verb* **1.** gamble, wager, risk, chance, dare, jeopardize She ventured three dollars on her favorite horse. **2.** tender, submit, hazard, put forward, offer, proffer, volunteer, attempt May I venture a suggestion as to how to proceed?

verbal *adjective* **1.** oral, spoken, unwritten, stated, voiced, declared, expressed The two women made a verbal agreement to go into business together. **2.** verbatim, exact, literal, precise, word-for-word, faithful, accurate He gave me a verbal report of the message my friend had sent. ➽ **Antonyms: 1.** written, documented **2.** inexact, vague, inaccurate

verdict *noun* **1.** conclusion, decision, finding, judgment, ruling, consensus, adjudication, decree The jury's verdict was that the defendant was not guilty. **2.** opinion, reaction, conclusion, judgment, assertion, diagnosis, evaluation, estimation, sentiment It's my verdict that *Roll of Thunder, Hear My Cry* is a wonderful book.

verge *noun* edge, perimeter, extremity, boundary, fringe, brink, rim, border, lip There is a track around the verge of the park. ◆ *verb* approach, near, border, gravitate, tend, converge, touch, join Their happiness verged on bliss.

verify *verb* **1.** confirm, prove, support, authenticate, establish, witness, guarantee, validate, substantiate The evidence verifies his alibi. **2.** analyze, test, determine, examine, probe, estimate, sound, judge My science class verified the digestive property of saliva in an experiment in which we spat into test tubes holding grated potato. ➽ **Antonyms: 1.** disprove, refute

versatile *adjective* **1.** talented, multifaceted, clever, adaptable, gifted, accomplished, adroit, ingenious, able The versatile hockey player was good at both defense and offense. **2.** handy, all-purpose, functional, flexible, useful, practical, adjustable, convertible A hammer is a versatile tool. ➽ **Antonyms: 1.** specialized, limited **2.** impractical, useless

version *noun* account, description, report, statement, story, viewpoint, understanding, interpretation, chronicle, tale Each boy gave his own version of how the fight started.

vertical *adjective* upright, perpendicular, standing, plumb, steep, up-and-down A referee's shirt has vertical stripes. ▶ **Antonyms: horizontal, level**

very *adverb* 1. exceedingly, extremely, especially, greatly, immensely, awfully, terribly, highly, profoundly, deeply My brother was very angry when I lost his watch. 2. truly, absolutely, actually, unquestionably, really, obviously, veritably I think that's the very best option. ♦ *adjective* 1. exact, precise, specific, identical, same, appropriate, fitting, wanted, applicable, desired That's the very present I wanted. 2. sheer, mere, simple, pure, bare, plain, whole, total The very idea of going away to outdoor school is exciting.

vessel *noun* 1. container, receptacle, bottle, cup, jar, pitcher, pot, basin, cask This old earthenware vessel was used for storing wine. 2. boat, craft, ship, liner, freighter, tanker, yacht, barge Oceangoing vessels are usually quite large.

veteran *noun* professional, authority, master, expert, specialist, old hand, old-timer, virtuoso, adept, pro Our new police chief is a veteran with 20 years' experience in law enforcement. ▶ **Antonyms: beginner, greenhorn, apprentice**

veto *noun* denial, disapproval, rejection, ban, cancellation, prohibition, restraint, disallowance The President's veto kept the bill from becoming law. ♦ *verb* disapprove, reject, turn down, void, block, stop, bar, ban, disallow State governors can veto bills passed by their legislatures. ▶ **Antonyms: *noun* approval ♦ *verb* approve, endorse, ratify**

vex *verb* annoy, bother, irritate, pester, irk, distress, grate, trouble, aggravate Not being able to find an overdue library book is vexing. ▶ **Antonyms: soothe, calm, please**

vexation *noun* irritation, bother, trouble, affliction, distress, worry, harassment, annoyance I enjoyed my trip to Peru, but the language barrier was a source of vexation. ▶ **Antonyms: pleasure, comfort, blessing**

viable *adjective* 1. living, alive, growing, vital, developing, sprouting, thriving This old rosebush is still viable. 2. possible, feasible, doable, practical, workable, promising, useful, reasonable That sounds like a viable alternative. ▶ **Antonyms: 1. dead 2. unworkable, futile**

vibrant *adjective* vigorous, lively, vital, strong, energetic, vivacious, animated, dynamic, spirited She has a vibrant personality. ▶ **Antonyms: sluggish, listless, boring**

vibrate *verb* 1. quake, quiver, shake, tremble, waver, oscillate, fluctuate, swing The old window vibrated under the strong winds. 2. resonate, sound, peal, ring, reverberate, resound, echo, quaver, clang When you strike a tuning fork, it vibrates for several moments.

vibration *noun* quiver, shake, throb, tremor, tremble, quake, pulse, oscillation I can feel vibrations inside the car whenever the engine is started.

vice *noun* 1. evil, corruption, wantonness, wickedness, depravity, immorality, debauchery, indecency, offense The criminal led a life of vice. 2. foible, weakness, lapse, defect, flaw, shortcoming, frailty, imperfection Procrastination is my main vice. ▶ **Antonyms: 1. virtue, morality 2. strength, asset**

vicinity *noun* area, locality, neighborhood, region, surroundings, bounds, environs, precincts There are many stores and restaurants in this vicinity.

vicious *adjective* 1. atrocious, bad, evil, immoral, terrible, wicked, vile, depraved, shocking The dictator had committed many vicious crimes. 2. cruel, hateful, hurtful, malicious, mean, spiteful, cutting, hostile, slanderous, vindictive The vicious taunt made me cry. 3. dangerous, ferocious, fierce, savage, violent, wild, aggressive, bloodthirsty, brutal The mongoose is a vicious predator of poisonous snakes. ▶ **Antonyms: 1. noble, virtuous 2. complimentary, kindly 3. tame, playful**

victim *noun* 1. casualty, wounded, injured, fatality, sufferer, invalid Paramedics rushed the accident victim to a hospital. 2. dupe, quarry, prey, lamb, target, butt, gull, mark, scapegoat, innocent Sometimes I am the victim of my older sister's practical jokes.

victorious *adjective* successful, triumphant, winning, champion, conquering, undefeated, jubilant, exultant The victorious candidate thanked everyone who had helped her get elected. ▶ **Antonyms: defeated, losing**

victory *noun* success, triumph, conquest, win, supremacy, mastery, superiority, control Joan of Arc was only 17 when she led the French army to victory at the Battle of Orléans. ▶ **Antonyms: defeat, loss**

vie *verb* contend, compete, wrestle, strive, challenge, tussle, grapple, dispute The boxers vied for the title of world champion. ▶ **Antonyms: cooperate, negotiate**

view *noun* 1. glimpse, glance, look, peek, sight, gaze, survey, examination, observation Dad lifted my little sister up so that she could get a better view of the parade. **2. belief, conviction, feeling, opinion, position, thought, judgment, verdict, theory** What are your views on TV and movie rating systems? **3. outlook, panorama, scene, scenery, spectacle, vision, vista, landscape, sight** We paused during our hike to admire the view. **4. purpose, aim, intention, ambition, target, prospect, hope, goal** I did my homework Friday night with the view of having the weekend free. ◆ *verb* **1. see, watch, look at, behold, observe, witness, eye, perceive, discern** We can view the solar eclipse only indirectly, through a special apparatus. **2. examine, inspect, scrutinize, explore, survey, study, analyze, scan, reconnoiter** The scientist viewed the microbes through a microscope. **3. regard, consider, think, judge, deem, believe, review, contemplate, react** My parents view my interest in reading with approval.

viewpoint *noun* **standpoint, angle, perspective, opinion, attitude, position, slant, sentiment** Consider it from my viewpoint.

vigilant *adjective* **alert, watchful, wary, heedful, cautious, observant, careful, attentive, aware** The gardener was vigilant for signs of pest damage. ➽ **Antonyms: unaware, careless**

vigor *noun* **1. might, strength, sturdiness, fitness, stamina, muscle, hardiness, power** My mom is going to aerobics class to improve her vigor. **2. enthusiasm, intensity, spirit, gusto, zeal, verve, passion, fire, vim, pep** The candidate spoke with great vigor. ➽ **Antonyms: 1. weakness, feebleness 2. indifference, apathy**

vigorous *adjective* **active, brisk, dynamic, energetic, lively, strenuous, spirited, hearty, intense** Vigorous exercise gives me an appetite. ➽ **Antonyms: inactive, lethargic**

vile *adjective* **1. terrible, rotten, unpleasant, hateful, disgusting, awful, lousy, revolting, bad** I think blue cheese smells vile. **2. evil, wicked, sinful, ignoble, corrupt, villainous, base, depraved, immoral, heinous** Genocide is a vile crime. ➽ **Antonyms: 1. pleasant, good 2. moral, honorable, noble**

village *noun* **hamlet, community, settlement, town, municipality, burg, one-horse town** One village we stayed in when we visited Italy had just one store, two churches, and fewer than a hundred homes.

villain *noun* **criminal, rascal, rogue, scoundrel, knave, fiend, swindler, cad, brute** In old-time Westerns, the good guys wear white and the villains wear black. ➽ **Antonyms: hero, gentleman**

vindicate *verb* **1. clear, exonerate, free, absolve, discharge, excuse, acquit, pardon** New evidence has vindicated the condemned man. **2. defend, justify, champion, support, maintain, advocate, shield, corroborate** My mom and dad vindicated my decision to quit gymnastics. ➽ **Antonyms: 1. accuse, blame, charge 2. oppose, contradict**

> ## Word Group
>
> A **vine** is a plant having a stem that climbs or clings to something for support. **Vine** is a general term with no true synonyms. Here are some common vines:
>
> **bittersweet, clematis, grape, honeysuckle, hop, ivy, jasmine, liana, morning glory, wisteria**

violate *verb* **1. break, defy, disobey, disregard, ignore, resist, shirk, overlook** Police officers give tickets to drivers who violate traffic laws. **2. desecrate, dishonor, mock, defile, offend, profane, blaspheme, revile, scorn** Wearing shoes into a temple violates Buddhist custom. **3. interrupt, interfere, encroach, disturb, usurp, impinge, invade, impose** I hung a sign saying "Do Not Disturb" on my door so that no one would violate my privacy. ➽ **Antonyms: 1. obey, observe 2. respect, honor**

violence *noun* **1. brutality, savagery, assault, attack, destructiveness, madness, rampage, terrorism** The movie depicted fist fights, car wrecks, and other forms of violence. **2. force, fury, intensity, power, severity, strength, magnitude, turbulence** The mud slide moved with such violence that it snapped trees in two. ➽ **Antonyms: 1. tenderness, humanity 2. gentleness, mildness**

violent *adjective* **1. savage, berserk, bloodthirsty, mad, murderous, vicious, homicidal, cruel** The violent murder has upset the whole town. **2. burning, fiery, passionate, excitable, impetuous, inflamed, uncontrollable, wild** He is able to control his violent temper by counting to ten. **3. fierce, forceful, furious, intense, powerful, strong, extreme, mighty** In 1988, Hurricane Gilbert's violent winds were clocked at 175 miles per hour. ➽ **Antonyms: 1. sane 2. cool, calm 3. moderate, mild**

virgin *adjective* **pristine, unspoiled, unused, fresh, new, pure, untouched** Alaska has vast tracts of virgin wilderness that very few people have ever seen.

virtual *adjective* **practical, tacit, implicit, effective, essential, fundamental, understood, implied, assumed** My mother's best friend has been a virtual aunt to me all my life. ➽ **Antonyms: explicit, actual**

virtually *adverb* nearly, essentially, practically, effectively, fundamentally, basically, principally I am virtually done with my report.

virtue *noun* 1. decency, goodness, honor, integrity, morality, honesty, rectitude, nobility, uprightness People respect our fire chief because he is a man of great virtue. 2. innocence, purity, modesty, decency, chastity, virginity, virtuousness Unicorns are symbols of virtue. 3. plus, benefit, advantage, merit, blessing, gift, strength, boon, value Traveling by plane has the virtue of speed.
➡ Antonyms: 1. wickedness, vice 3. disadvantage, curse

virulent *adjective* 1. pernicious, toxic, noxious, deadly, poisonous, unwholesome, harmful, destructive He died of a virulent strain of pneumonia. 2. bitter, hostile, malicious, hateful, antagonistic, vindictive, spiteful, malevolent The controversial book received many virulent reviews.
➡ Antonyms: 1. harmless, nontoxic 2. kind, friendly

visible *adjective* 1. noticeable, observable, seeable, viewable, visual, distinct, perceivable, perceptible There are billions of stars, but fewer than six thousand are visible to the naked eye. 2. apparent, clear, distinct, evident, plain, obvious, conspicuous, manifest, marked The doctor said that her patient was making visible improvement.
➡ Antonyms: invisible, hidden

vision *noun* 1. eyesight, sight, seeing, perceiving, optics, view, eye, faculty Hawks have extremely keen vision. 2. farsightedness, foresight, imagination, perception, wisdom, discernment, sense, prescience Benjamin Franklin was a man of great vision. 3. dream, idea, notion, fancy, fantasy, plan, reverie, ideal, concept, conception Martin Luther King Jr. is famous for his vision of all races living together in harmony. 4. apparition, ghost, phantom, specter, hallucination, wraith, delusion, phenomenon The elderly lady claims to have seen a vision of her deceased husband. 5. picture, sight, spectacle, study, image, dream, beauty, dazzler, stunner The field of tulips was a vision of springtime. ➡ Antonyms: 1. blindness 2. hindsight

visit *verb* 1. see, stay at, stay with, drop by, sojourn, tour, call on, journey, travel Next year I will visit my grandparents in Vermont. 2. haunt, assail, afflict, bother, smite, assault, touch, affect, befall Misfortune has visited all the owners of the Hope Diamond. ◆ *noun* stay, visitation, call, stopover, vacation, get-together, sojourn, weekend, meeting My cousin will be coming for a visit sometime this summer.

visitor *noun* caller, company, guest, tourist, traveler, houseguest, sightseer, vacationer We're expecting visitors for the holidays.

vista *noun* view, prospect, outlook, landscape, scene, seascape, panorama, perspective I like the vista from the roof of my apartment building.

visual *adjective* visible, manifest, apparent, plain, discernible, observable, perceivable, seeable, viewable The footprints in the snow were visual proof that a fox had been checking out the chicken coop.

vital *adjective* 1. living, alive, animate, viable, biological, live, existing, breathing, quick There are vital bacterial cultures in yogurt. 2. essential, critical, crucial, important, necessary, meaningful, required, needed, elementary Our drama teacher reminded us that everyone's cooperation is vital in making the play a success. 3. lively, vivacious, spirited, animated, energetic, exuberant, peppy, active, vigorous The puppy was his usual vital self when he woke up from his nap.

vivacious *adjective* lively, cheerful, animated, sparkling, irrepressible, happy, bouncy, chipper, pert, high-spirited The vivacious actress charmed the audience. ➡ Antonyms: listless, dull

vivid *adjective* 1. bright, brilliant, colorful, loud, rich, deep, luminous, garish I painted my dresser a vivid shade of yellow. 2. acute, clear, intense, keen, sharp, strong, powerful, graphic, striking, unforgettable He still has vivid memories of his first piano recital. ➡ Antonyms: 1. drab, dull 2. hazy, unclear

vocal *adjective* 1. oral, spoken, uttered, voiced, verbal, verbalized, intoned Parrots, cockatiels, and parakeets don't really speak—they just make vocal imitations of sounds that they have heard. 2. outspoken, candid, blunt, open, forthright, noisy, expressive, clamorous, direct There have been many vocal protests against the new landfill. ➡ Antonyms: 1. unspoken, unvoiced 2. quiet, reserved

vocation *noun* 1. profession, career, employment, business, livelihood, job, trade, work, specialty, field Teaching is my mother's vocation. 2. calling, pursuit, cause, devotion, forte, aptitude, dedication, life's work The missionary's vocation took him to several very remote places.

voice *noun* 1. speech, articulation, verbalization, vocalization, intonation, expression, tone, utterance, modulation When I answered the telephone, I immediately recognized my best friend's voice. 2. part, role, say, share, choice, opinion, vote, suffrage, participation In a true democracy, all citizens have a voice in running their government.

◆ *verb* **1. communicate, express, proclaim, declare, vent, say, air, divulge, tell** I voiced my concerns about the assignment to my teacher. **2. pronounce, enunciate, utter, speak, vocalize, articulate, verbalize** It was hard for me to voice *l, r,* and *th* sounds when I was first learning English.

void *adjective* **1. vacant, blank, unoccupied, unfilled, empty, hollow, devoid, barren, destitute** I think we found the only void parking spot in the whole lot. **2. invalid, nonviable, inoperative, useless, powerless, null, dead, annulled, canceled** This old lottery ticket is void. ◆ *noun* **vacuum, nothingness, emptiness, blank, chasm, hole, pit, abyss, oblivion** Sound waves cannot travel through a void. ◆ *verb* **1. empty, drain, evacuate, eject, discharge, purge, exhaust, cleanse** We had to void the car radiator of its old coolant and flush the system. **2. cancel, revoke, annul, nullify, rescind, veto, negate, undo** The contract was voided when a new one was drawn up. ➡ **Antonyms:** *adjective* **1. full, occupied 2. valid, operative** ◆ *verb* **1. fill, replenish 2. uphold**

volatile *adjective* **mercurial, inconstant, fickle, changeable, unstable, erratic, moody, capricious, flighty** He has a volatile temper. ➡ **Antonyms: constant, stable**

volition *noun* **will, free will, choosing, selection, choice, determination, decision, discretion, preference, option** I cleaned my room of my own volition.

volley *noun* **salvo, barrage, burst, shower, discharge, bombardment, fusillade, hail, rain** The soldiers fired a volley of bullets at the enemy position.

volume *noun* **1. book, edition, publication, paperback, folio, tome, album, treatise, hardcover** I have read many volumes of poetry by American authors. **2. capacity, amount, extent, measure, quantity, size, bulk, mass** This plastic milk jug has a volume of one gallon. **3. loudness, sound, intensity, power, degree, sonority, strength** Could you please turn down the volume on the TV?

voluntary *adjective* **freewill, optional, unforced, willing, spontaneous, volunteer, chosen, deliberate** The voluntary donations that visitors make help the museum pay for new exhibits. ➡ **Antonyms: forced, involuntary**

volunteer *adjective* **voluntary, unpaid, nonprofessional, unsalaried, uncompensated** My dad and older brother are volunteer firefighters. ◆ *verb* **contribute, donate, give, offer, provide, propose, suggest, present, supply, bestow** We volunteered our time to help with the community cleanup of the arroyo.

vote *noun* **ballot, election, choice, preference, ticket, selection, poll** The vote for class president was close this year. ◆ *verb* **ballot, choose, elect, select, designate, pick** Our town voted to buy more land for conservation purposes.

vouch *verb* **confirm, guarantee, endorse, certify, warrant, underwrite, corroborate, substantiate, testify** I can vouch for his honesty.

vow *noun* **oath, pledge, promise, assurance, guarantee, affirmation, plight, troth, warranty** The knight took a vow of loyalty to his king. ◆ *verb* **pledge, promise, swear, affirm, declare, assert, contract, undertake, resolve** The wife and husband vowed to love each other always.

voyage *noun* **expedition, journey, trip, cruise, sail, passage, trek, travels, crossing** Captain James Cook discovered the Sandwich Islands on his third voyage to the South Pacific. ◆ *verb* **cruise, sail, traverse, journey, cross, travel, navigate, go, fly** My family is going to voyage to Australia this summer.

vulgar *adjective* **1. common, popular, everyday, vernacular, plebeian, general, proletarian, commonplace** The vulgar name for *Lycopersicon lycopersicum* is "tomato." **2. crude, coarse, ill-mannered, uncouth, brassy, gross, boorish, uncultivated, tasteless** "Bottom" is the name of a vulgar character in William Shakespeare's *A Midsummer Night's Dream.* ➡ **Antonyms: 2. mannerly, tasteful, polished**

wad *noun* **mass, ball, clump, packet, heap, roll, tuft, lump, filler, stuffing** I used a wad of cotton batting to stuff the pillowcase I made. ◆ *verb* **compress, crush, press, roll, squeeze, mash, crumple, fold** I wadded my sweater into a ball and stuffed it into my backpack.

waddle *verb* **sway, rock, totter, swing, roll, toddle, reel** The ducks waddled down the bank and into the water.

waft *verb* **float, drift, fly, blow, glide, sail, transmit, move, breeze** The smell of baking bread wafted through the house.

wag *verb* **swing, shake, switch, wave, lash, wiggle** My dog wags his tail whenever he's happy. ◆ *noun* **shake, swing, toss, bob, nod, jiggle, jerk, flourish** The horse flicked away a fly with a wag of its tail.

wage *noun* **compensation, earnings, pay, salary, fee, payment, stipend, remuneration** My brother will receive a higher wage at his new job. ◆ *verb* **carry on, conduct, make, pursue, undertake, practice, maintain, manage** The senator waged a campaign for reelection.

> ## Word Group
>
> A **wagon** is a four-wheeled, usually horse-drawn vehicle with a rectangular body. **Wagon** is a general term with no true synonyms. Here are some types of wagons:
>
> **baggage wagon, brougham, buggy, caravan, chariot, Conestoga wagon, covered wagon, farm wagon, hackney, hay wagon, milk wagon, prairie schooner**

wail *verb* **bawl, cry, howl, moan, sob, weep, lament, bemoan, shriek** In many cultures, it is traditional to wail aloud when mourning. ◆ *noun* **shriek, howl, whine, cry, moan, lament, plaint, lamentation, keening** We heard the loud wail of the ambulance.

wait *verb* **linger, remain, stand by, stall, stay, delay, dally, dawdle** I waited by the bus stop for my friends to arrive. ◆ *noun* **delay, pause, postponement, interval, break, lull, rest, deferment** There was a long wait before the doctor was able to see me.

wake¹ *verb* **awake, awaken, waken, rouse, arouse, stir, activate** My alarm clock wakes me every day at 6:30 a.m.

wake² *noun* **aftermath, path, track, trail, course, vestige, train** The tornado left many ruined buildings in its wake.

walk *verb* **amble, hike, march, stride, trek, stroll, traipse, tramp, tread, step, pace** I walk to school every day. ◆ *noun* **1. stroll, hike, jaunt, march, ramble, trek, tramp** He took his dog for a walk in the park. **2. walkway, path, sidewalk, footpath, lane, promenade, track, bypath, boardwalk, trail** This walk leads to the docks.

wallow *verb* **slosh, roll, flounder, splash, tumble, loll, plunge, revel** The seals wallowed playfully in the water.

wan *adjective* **pale, pasty, ashen, colorless, waxen, gaunt, pallid, ghostly, sallow** His face was wan after he heard the terrible news.

wander *verb* **1. amble, ramble, roam, saunter, stroll, meander, rove** My friends and I wandered around the amusement park. **2. drift, stray, shift, swerve, digress, diverge, deviate** The speaker wandered from his subject.

wane *verb* **fade, ebb, decrease, dwindle, decline, abate, weaken, subside** The moon waxes and wanes on a 28-day cycle. ➡ **Antonyms: rise, wax, grow**

want *verb* **1. long, yearn, crave, desire, wish, need, hunger, thirst** He wants to get the lead in the school play. **2. lack, need, require, miss, demand, call for** That soup wants salt. ◆ *noun* **1. desire, craving, wish, need, requirement, demand, necessity** The old hermit had few material wants. **2. lack, need, poverty, dearth, inadequacy, exigency, paucity, shortage, scarcity** Many families have a want of food.

war *noun* **battle, fight, combat, warfare, conflict, struggle, campaign, crusade** The war ended when the leaders called a truce. ➡ **Antonyms: peace, amity, truce**

ward *noun* **1. precinct, zone, bailiwick, borough, department, quarter, district, territory** In some cities voting districts are called wards. **2. wing, hall, section, annex** We finally found the pediatrics ward. ◆ *verb* **repel, block, defend, guard, parry, repulse, fend, foil, deflect, stop** I warded off an overly enthusiastic greeting from my dog.

wardrobe *noun* **clothing, attire, garb, costume, apparel, togs, outfit, garment** Every September I add some new things to my wardrobe.

wares *noun* commodities, goods, merchandise, products, stock, supplies, line, inventory Peddlers used to sell their wares at farms and villages.

warm *adjective* 1. lukewarm, tepid, heated, temperate, hot, sizzling, sultry The recipe said to mix the dry ingredients with a cup of warm water. 2. loving, tender, affectionate, friendly, enthusiastic, hearty, kindly Mom gave me a warm hug when I got home from school. 3. heated, ardent, zealous, earnest, passionate, fervent, fiery, emotional Their warm debate began to make me uncomfortable. ◆ *verb* cook, heat, simmer, warm up, thaw, prepare, fix I warmed some leftovers in the microwave. ➧ **Antonyms:** *adjective* 1. cool, cold 2. aloof, coldhearted

warn *verb* alert, inform, make aware, notify, signal, caution, advise, alarm, counsel Beavers slap their tails on the water to warn others when danger is present.

warning *noun* admonition, notice, notification, alarm, caution, signal, forewarning, caveat Hazardous products contain safety warnings on their labels.

warp *verb* bend, twist, misshape, distort, deform, turn, crook The boards of the old barn had warped from years of exposure to harsh weather. ➧ **Antonym:** straighten

warrant *verb* 1. guarantee, vouch, certify, assure, endorse, back This car is warranted for five years. 2. justify, merit, legitimize, vindicate, validate, sustain, authenticate Does this situation warrant such extreme actions?

warrior *noun* fighter, combatant, soldier, trooper Chief Sitting Bull led his warriors against Custer's Seventh Cavalry in the battle of Little Bighorn in 1876.

wary *adjective* careful, vigilant, watchful, cautious, suspicious, alert, heedful, mindful The birds at the feeder keep a wary eye out for our family cat. ➧ **Antonyms:** reckless, heedless

wash *verb* 1. clean, cleanse, scour, scrub, bathe, launder, shampoo Please wash your hands before dinner. 2. carry, move, convey, transfer, sweep, send, remove The heavy rain washed sand and dirt onto our patio. ◆ *noun* cleaning, cleansing, washing, bath, shower, ablution, scouring My brother's car could use a good wash.

waste *verb* 1. dissipate, lose, squander, throw away, consume, misspend, fritter We wasted two hours trying to find a shortcut. 2. weaken, wither, fade, decline, decrease, diminish, enfeeble, atrophy Certain diseases can cause the body to waste away. 3. raze, destroy, wreck, shatter, demolish, pillage, sack, ravage, loot, plunder The Visigoths wasted Rome in the fifth century A.D. ◆ *noun* 1. misuse, squandering, abuse, mishandling Trying to fix that outdated computer is a waste of both time and money. 2. garbage, refuse, rubbish, trash, debris, litter, junk We take our household waste to the landfill once a week. ➧ **Antonyms:** *verb* 1. conserve, save 2. strengthen

wasteful *adjective* extravagant, lavish, uneconomical, ruinous, careless, wanton, immoderate The young heir was wasteful with his inheritance. ➧ **Antonym:** careful

wasteland *noun* badlands, barrens, desert, veldt, wilds, wilderness, tundra With proper irrigation, the wasteland of California's central valley became good farm land.

watch *verb* 1. gaze, look, observe, see, view, notice, examine, regard Our whole school went to the air base to watch the space shuttle land. 2. attend, tend, guard, mind, care for, look after, oversee Would you mind watching my jacket while I go get some popcorn? ◆ *noun* 1. guard, lookout, vigil, surveillance, attention, observation, vigilance, patrol The mare kept a close watch over her newborn foal. 2. timepiece, wristwatch, clock, pocket watch The digital watch was developed in the 1970s.

watchful *adjective* alert, attentive, vigilant, observant, aware, wary, cautious The border collie kept a watchful eye on the flock of sheep. ➧ **Antonyms:** inattentive, distracted

water *verb* irrigate, sprinkle, dampen, moisten, wet, saturate, soak In dry weather we have to water the vegetable garden every day.

wave *verb* 1. flutter, ripple, flap, sway, beat, shake, fluctuate The tall grass waved in the prairie breeze. 2. gesture, motion, signal, flag, beckon, gesticulate I waved at my friends to get their attention. ◆ *noun* 1. swell, breaker, comber, roller, ripple, surf, billow, ridge, white cap A huge wave almost capsized the rowboat. 2. gesture, motion, movement, signal, sign, salutation, flourish The crossing guard gave us a wave of his hand when it was safe to cross the street.

waver *verb* 1. totter, sway, reel, wobble, swing, stagger, careen, weave The old dog wavered from side to side as he walked. 2. hesitate, vacillate, falter, balk, dilly-dally, pause, demur, vary, hedge I wavered between which of the two dresses to buy. ➧ **Antonyms:** 2. decide, resolve

wax¹ *noun* polish, lubricant, gloss, varnish This wax helps to protect the finish of our wood furniture. ◆ *verb* buff, polish, furbish, burnish, varnish I waxed the kitchen floor.

wax² *verb* **grow, increase, balloon, enlarge, dilate, develop, expand** The moon waxes and wanes each month. ◆ **Antonyms: wane, shrink, decrease**

way *noun* **1. course, path, route, trail, direction, road, lane, track** Do you know the way to the main library? **2. manner, style, method, system, technique, mode, means, procedure** My friend taught me a new way to braid my hair. **3. choice, desire, preference, will, wish, fancy, pleasure** How come you always get your way? **4. distance, length, span, stretch, space, measure** My uncle's farm is a long way from here. **5. aspect, feature, detail, point, respect, particular, characteristic** The reproduction is the same in every way as the original.

weak *adjective* **1. faint, feeble, frail, spent, shaky, enervated, debilitated, unsteady** I felt weak because I skipped breakfast. **2. breakable, brittle, insubstantial, fragile, delicate, flimsy** Bones become weak if they do not receive enough calcium. **3. powerless, ineffective, incapable, helpless, irresolute, timorous, impotent** The small band of soldiers was too weak to hold off the attack. ◆ **Antonyms: 1. strong, vigorous 2. sturdy, steady 3. capable, effective**

weaken *verb* **dwindle, flag, decline, wane, fade, droop, sap, debilitate, enervate** The hurricane weakened as it moved inland.

wealth *noun* **1. assets, capital, fortune, money, riches, treasure, estate, property, goods** The man accumulated his wealth by investing in the stock market. **2. affluence, luxury, prosperity, opulence, fortune, riches, means** My grandmother grew up in great wealth. **3. abundance, lot, profusion, plenty, bounty, store, plentitude** This encyclopedia contains a wealth of information. ◆ **Antonyms: 2. poverty, want, destitution 3. lack, scarcity, shortage**

wealthy *adjective* **affluent, prosperous, rich, well-off, moneyed, flush** The wealthy family gave lots of money to our youth center. ◆ **Antonyms: destitute, poor**

wear *verb* **1. don, sport, dress in, have on, put on, wrap, bear** I wore an African dress to school one day during Black History Month. **2. show, exhibit, affect, display, assume, brandish** She always seems to wear a smile. **3. abrade, erode, rub, wear away, gnaw, corrode, eat** I wore a hole in the elbow of my favorite sweater. **4. last, endure, resist, hold up, stand, bear up, remain** I bought this pair of gloves because I think they will wear well. ◆ *noun* **1. apparel, attire, clothes, clothing, garments, togs, outfit, habiliment, raiment** This store specializes in children's wear. **2. damage, wear and tear, abrasion, corrosion,**

disintegration, erosion The stone steps to the ancient temple show a lot of wear. **3. service, use, utilization, employment, application, function** You certainly have gotten a lot of wear out of those skates.

weary *adjective* **1. drained, exhausted, fatigued, tired, worn-out, spent, beat, sleepy** My brother always feels weary when he gets home from football practice. **2. dreary, tedious, tiresome, wearisome, boring, dull, humdrum, monotonous** It's been a long, weary winter. **3. impatient, fed up, sick, tired, disgusted, annoyed, discontented** My mother said she was weary of picking up after me. ◆ *verb* **tire, drain, exhaust, fatigue, wear out, tax** The long trip wearied my whole family.

weather *noun* **climate, temperature, elements, clime, atmosphere** Arizona is known for its warm weather. ◆ *verb* **1. age, toughen, wrinkle, bleach, dry, season, tan** The old sailor's face was weathered. **2. endure, survive, withstand, deal with, surmount, come through, resist, brave** The President thinks that his administration can weather the current crisis.

weave *verb* **1. braid, knit, lace, plait, spin, twist, interlace, intertwine, entwine** Navajo women weave colorful rugs and blankets from homespun wool. **2. incorporate, fuse, merge, combine, mix, mingle, blend** I will weave these two separate incidents into one feature for the school paper. **3. wind, zigzag, twist, wander, meander, snake, turn, curve** We had to weave our way through the crowd to get to our seats.

web *noun* **1. netting, mesh, webbing, screen, network, net, fabric, cobweb, snare, gossamer** We stretched a web made of plastic over the cherry tree to keep birds from eating the fruit. **2. morass, snarl, knot, jumble, maze, labyrinth, tangle** A web of confusion surrounded the situation.

wed *verb* **marry, espouse, couple, mate, join, link, unite, tie** My aunt will wed her fiancé next August.

wedge *noun* **chock, block, piece, chunk, shim** I used a wedge of wood to hold open the window. ◆ *verb* **1. hold, lodge, fix, secure, fasten** I carefully wedged open the lid of the trunk. **2. cram, jam, pack, stuff, squeeze, press, ram, crowd** I wedged one more book into my backpack.

weep *verb* **1. cry, shed tears, sob, bawl, wail, snivel, blubber** I began to weep as I read the tragic story. **2. grieve, mourn, lament, sorrow, regret, bemoan, keen** It is natural to weep when one loses a beloved pet.

weigh *verb* **1. ponder, consider, contemplate, examine, deliberate, study, evaluate, calculate** The committee will weigh the advantages of the two different reading programs. **2. signify, tell, count, matter, impress, pull, measure, influence** Your point is a good one and will weigh heavily in the final decision.

weight *noun* **1. heaviness, mass, poundage, tonnage, heft** If your weight is 115 pounds on the earth, it would be 19 pounds on the moon. **2. load, burden, anxiety, millstone, pressure, onus, strain, encumbrance** Her frail health is a weight on my mind. **3. influence, leverage, sway, importance, consequence, clout, pull, significance** The words and deeds of parents have great weight in the lives of their children. ◆ *verb* **1. ballast, weigh down, load, heap, overload** We need to weight the plastic tarp so that it won't blow away. **2. burden, oppress, stress, tax, saddle, encumber, worry, vex** Many successful people were weighted with responsibility while still very young.

weird **abnormal, irregular, curious, bizarre, odd, peculiar, strange, unorthodox, eccentric** Mom took her car to a mechanic because it was making weird noises. ➡ **Antonyms: normal, conventional**

welcome *adjective* **agreeable, favorable, nice, pleasant, satisfying, amiable, pleasurable** Sunny weather will be a welcome change after all of this rain. ◆ *noun* **greeting, reception, salutation, hello, acceptance, ovation** I always receive a warm welcome at my best friend's house. ◆ *verb* **hail, greet, meet, receive, accept, admit, salute** Mother went to the front door to welcome the guests to her party.

welfare *noun* **well-being, health, happiness, fortune, prosperity, advantage, good** It is the duty of parents to watch out for the welfare of their children.

well[1] *noun* **hole, pit, shaft, pipe, chasm, depression, abyss, bore, pump** The rancher dug a well to provide water for his livestock. ◆ *verb* **stream, flow, pour, spurt, jet, gush, issue, surge, ooze, spout** Oil welled up as the giant drill penetrated the earth.

well[2] *adverb* **1. agreeably, favorably, nicely, satisfactorily, excellently, laudably, splendidly, happily** She is getting along well at her new school. **2. skillfully, proficiently, adroitly, deftly, adeptly, smoothly, effectively, easily** She bakes bread very well. **3. sufficiently, adequately, satisfactorily, suitably, amply, plentifully, abundantly** I studied well for the big test. **4. favorably, kindly, sympathetically, enthusiastically, approvingly, warmly, highly** We think well of our neighbors. **5. closely, intimately, personally, deeply, considerably** I know him well. ◆ *adjective* **1. good, fortunate, right, fitting, favorable, happy, auspicious** It is well that we decided to come home early. **2. fit, healthy, all

right, hale, sound, satisfactory, strong** I was sick last week, but I'm feeling well now. ➡ **Antonyms:** *adverb* **1. unsatisfactorily, badly 2. clumsily, awkwardly** ◆ *adjective* **1. bad 2. ill, sick**

wet *adjective* **1. drenched, soaked, damp, moist, sodden, soggy, sopping** You will get wet if you don't take an umbrella. **2. rainy, stormy, drizzly, showery** The forecast is for another week of wet weather. ◆ *verb* **dampen, moisten, drench, saturate, soak, water, douse** I have to wet my hair before I can style it properly. ➡ **Antonym: dry**

wharf *noun* **dock, jetty, pier, marina, quay, landing, berth, port, harbor** I like to go down to the wharf and watch while the ships are loaded and unloaded.

wheel *noun* **round, circle, ring, hoop, disk, cylinder** We bought a wheel of cheddar cheese. ◆ *verb* **rotate, turn, pivot, spin, swivel, whirl, twist, orbit, revolve** The bull wheeled around and charged the rodeo clown.

wheeze *verb* **gasp, puff, pant, hiss, gasp, whistle** My cold caused me to sneeze and wheeze. ◆ *noun* **gasp, hiss, huffing, puffing, rasp, whistle** The wheeze of the old furnace was a comforting sound.

whet *verb* **1. hone, sharpen, edge, grind, file, strop** Mom needs to whet the paring knife before cutting tomatoes for the salad. **2. stimulate, arouse, excite, pique, stir, rouse, awaken, inflame, intensify** This descriptive menu whets my appetite.

whiff *noun* **1. gust, draft, puff, breath, zephyr, waft** A whiff of air put out the candle. **2. trace, hint, trifle, touch, dab, suggestion** The sauce had just a whiff of garlic in it.

whim *noun* **impulse, desire, fancy, idea, inclination, notion, wish, urge** I bought this game on a whim.

whimper *verb* **cry, whine, moan, sob, sniffle, blubber, fuss, mewl** My dog whimpered to be let outside. ◆ *noun* **sob, cry, moan, whine** My little brother gave a whimper of disappointment when Dad told him that he couldn't go.

whine *verb* **1. fuss, whimper, complain, cry, mewl, wail, snivel** Little children often whine when they get tired. **2. complain, grumble, gripe, grouse** I told my sister not to whine so much about having to walk home.

whip *verb* **1. lash, thrash, beat, strike, switch, flog, wallop, scourge** It was common in Colonial times for teachers to whip disobedient students. **2. crush, defeat, overcome, rout, trounce, vanquish, clobber, conquer, beat** The winning team whipped their opponents by a score of nine to nothing. **3. dart, dash, flash, surge, rush, tear, run, hustle, gallop** The basketball player whipped the ball down the court to his teammate. ◆ *noun* **crop, lash, strap, switch, scourge, bullwhip** The cowboy snapped his whip in the air.

whir *verb* **purr, drone, buzz, hum, whisper, throb, thrum, vibrate** The helicopter whirred as it passed overhead.

whirl *verb* **1. spin, turn, twirl, twist, reel, rotate, swirl, pirouette** I whirled around when I heard a noise behind me. **2. rush, speed, shoot, race, rocket, sail, hustle, zip, zoom** I whirled through my chores so that I could go to the movies with my friends. ◆ *noun* **1. spin, revolution, rotation, turn, twirl, pirouette, swirl** The dancers executed a series of graceful leaps and whirls. **2. bustle, tumult, stir, rush, ferment, whirlwind, uproar** There was a whirl of excitement in our home as we got ready for the holidays.

whisk *verb* **1. brush, flick, sweep, wipe, dust, clean, swish** Dad used a small brush to whisk the dirt out of his car. **2. bustle, hurry, hustle, race, rush, speed, hasten, shoot, dart** When I got a bloody nose, my teacher whisked me off to the nurse's office. ◆ *noun* **flick, swish, brush, sweep, wipe, stroke, movement** She brushed the crumbs from her lap with a whisk of her hand.

whisper *verb* **mutter, mumble, murmur, hiss** Someone is whispering in the back of the classroom. ◆ *noun* **undertone, mumble, murmur, hiss, sigh, buzz** My friend lowered her voice to a whisper when telling me a secret.

white *adjective* **1. pearl, ivory, snow-white, milky, cream** Our white car gets dirty easily. **2. ashen, chalky, pale, sallow, blanched** The driver's face turned white when a car in front of him nearly crashed. **3. silvery, gray, hoary, frosty, faded, snowy, grizzled** Grandpa's hair is turning white. ◈ **Antonyms: 1. black, ebony 2. flushed, rosy**

whittle *verb* **carve, sculpt, shave, trim, hew, pare, form** I enjoyed watching a man whittle small figurines at the fair.

whiz *verb* **rush, dash, zoom, dart, zip, scurry, shoot, scoot, sprint** The cars whizzed along the freeway. ◆ *noun* **genius, master, prodigy, mastermind, adept, wizard, champion** My brother is a whiz in math and science.

whole *adjective* **1. entire, complete, full, total, inclusive** My Dad and I ate a whole bag of chips for a snack. **2. complete, intact, sound, perfect, full, unbroken, entire** This set of encyclopedias is whole. ◆ *noun* **total, aggregate,**

entirety, all, bulk, lot, sum, mass, body We spent the whole of our vacation at the beach. ◈ **Antonyms:** *adjective* **incomplete, partial** ◆ *noun* **part, piece**

wholesome *adjective* **1. healthful, healthy, nutritious, nourishing, invigorating, improving, helpful** A wholesome diet includes plenty of fresh fruits and vegetables. **2. chipper, rosy, healthy, sound, vigorous, hale, hearty, blooming, hardy** You have such a wholesome attitude toward your chores! ◈ **Antonyms: 1. harmful, unhealthy**

wholly *adverb* **entirely, totally, thoroughly, completely, absolutely, fully, utterly** I am wholly committed to getting my ham radio license. ◈ **Antonyms: partially, somewhat**

whoop *noun* **shout, yell, holler, roar, scream, shriek, halloo, bellow, clamor, squawk** We heard the victorious whoops of the fans. ◆ *verb* **holler, shout, cry out, roar, shriek, bellow, yell, clamor, howl** The fans whooped in delight when their team won the game.

wicked *adjective* **1. bad, evil, fiendish, immoral, mean, nasty, corrupt, villainous, contemptible** In "Hansel and Gretel," a gingerbread house is the home of a wicked witch. **2. roguish, impish, sly, rascally, mischievous, devilish, incorrigible** She has a wicked sense of humor. **3. severe, intense, serious, terrible, troublesome, distressing, difficult, extreme** I have a wicked headache. ◈ **Antonyms: 1. good, moral 2. obedient, proper 3. mild**

wide *adjective* **1. large, vast, broad, extensive, ample, full, voluminous** I tossed some confetti into the air, and the wind scattered it over a wide area. **2. inaccurate, off, distant, far, remote, amiss, askew** I aimed at the center of the target, but my shot was wide. ◆ *adverb* **completely, entirely, fully, totally, thoroughly, utterly** The dentist asked me to hold my mouth wide open. ◈ **Antonyms:** *adjective* **1. narrow, small 2. accurate, close** ◆ *adverb* **partially, barely**

width *noun* **breadth, measure, size, wideness, distance, scope, span, girth, diameter** Standard typing paper has a width of 8½ inches.

wield *verb* **1. handle, ply, shake, flourish, brandish, work, operate, employ** I wielded the feather duster energetically. **2. exert, apply, exercise, command, manage, use** I wielded enough pressure on my brother to make him loan me five dollars.

wife *noun* **spouse, mate, partner, helpmate, bride, companion, consort** Dad says that Mom is the best wife in the world.

wig *noun* **toupee, hairpiece, switch, peruke, front** It was fashionable for men to wear wigs in the 17th century.

wiggle *verb* **wriggle, squirm, worm, flutter, twist, writhe, shake** My dog wiggled under the gate and into our neighbor's yard.

wild *adjective* **1. native, uncultivated, natural, undomesticated, untamed, free** Every summer we go out to the woods to pick wild blackberries. **2. uncivilized, savage, unrefined, rough, crude, barbaric, primitive, rude** Enkidu is a wild man in the *Epic of Gilgamesh*. **3. disorderly, unruly, uncontrolled, undisciplined, reckless, intractable, obstinate, lawless** The camp counselor made it clear that he would not tolerate any wild behavior. ◈ **Antonyms:** *adjective* **1. cultivated, domesticated 2. cultured, civilized 3. orderly, polite**

wilderness *noun* **wasteland, barrens, bush, tundra, steppe, desert, jungle, hinterland, badlands** Knowing how to use a compass is essential for traveling in the wilderness.

wile *noun* **trick, ruse, plan, ploy, device, deceit, snare, stratagem** The fox has many wiles, but the hedgehog only one.

will *noun* **1. volition, choosing, willpower, mind, intention** He joined the Navy of his own free will. **2. determination, drive, resolve, conviction, resolution, decisiveness, dedication** He is a good soccer player in part because he has a strong will to win. **3. testament, legacy, instructions, decree, order, bequest, estate, heritage** According to the terms of the man's will, his wife is to inherit all of his money. ◆ *verb* **1. wish, want, like, decide, choose, resolve, opt, elect, incline** You may have more dessert if you will. **2. command, resolve, induce, influence, enjoin, cause, determine, decree** The marathon runner willed herself to keep going. **3. bequeath, leave, confer, endow, pass, transfer, probate** The wealthy man willed most of his money to charity.

willing *adjective* **agreeable, consenting, ready, happy, delighted, prepared, pleased** Dad is willing to drive us to the concert. ◈ **Antonym: reluctant**

wilt *verb* **1. droop, wither, sag, shrivel, dry up, collapse, wizen** Plants will wilt if they don't get enough water. **2. sag, languish, flag, weaken, ebb, fade, diminish, collapse** We could feel ourselves beginning to wilt in the heat.

wily *adjective* **cunning, sly, crafty, devious, tricky, shrewd, scheming, sneaky** The wily boy was always finding ways to avoid doing his chores. ◈ **Antonyms: open, artless**

win *verb* **1. prevail, triumph, beat, best, conquer, defeat, vanquish, better** My younger brother usually wins when we play checkers. **2. acquire, earn, gain, get, obtain, receive, attain, secure** I won a trophy for being our basketball team's best player. ◆ *noun* **victory, conquest, success, triumph, coup, gain, sweep** Our baseball team has had five consecutive wins so far this season. ◈ **Antonyms:** *verb* **lose** ◆ *noun* **defeat, loss**

wince *verb* **flinch, cringe, grimace, shrink, start, recoil, shudder, quail** I winced when the nurse gave me a shot.

wind¹ *noun* **1. breeze, gust, blow, draft, gale, blast, zephyr, chinook, puff** This wind is perfect for flying a kite. **2. breath, air, respiration** The hard tackle knocked the wind out of me. **3. hint, rumor, clue, suggestion, intimation** She got wind of the surprise party being planned for her.

wind² *verb* **1. coil, loop, roll, twist, reel, wrap, spiral, entwine** Please wind the rope into a coil. **2. meander, snake, turn, wander, weave, bend, corkscrew, zigzag** This road winds through the town and out into the country.

wing *noun* **1. addition, annex, extension, branch, section, sector, arm** The new library wing will be completed this summer. **2. segment, faction, set, clique, group, circle, fraternity, knot** The liberal wing of the Republican party voted with the Democratic president.

winner *noun* **champion, victor, master, medalist, leader, prizewinner** The winner of our school's spelling contest will advance to the citywide competition. ◈ **Antonym: loser**

wipe *verb* **clean, wash, dry, dust, mop, polish, rub, scrub, towel** I used a damp sponge to wipe off the kitchen table.

wire *noun* **1. cable, cord, filament, line, strand, thread, rope, hawser, strand** The rancher used a roll of wire to repair his fences. **2. cable, cablegram, telegram, telegraph, radiogram, radiotelegraph** The wire contained an urgent message. ◆ *verb* **1. lash, tie, bind, fasten, join, lash, secure, attach** When my kite broke, I wired the pieces back together. **2. cable, telegraph, radio, send, dispatch, transmit** My parents wired some money to my brother at college.

wisdom *noun* **knowledge, understanding, intelligence, judgement, common sense, discernment, insight, enlightenment** We often gain wisdom by learning from our own experiences. ◈ **Antonyms: foolishness, stupidity**

wise *adjective* **1. judicious, prudent, sensible, rational, smart, intelligent, sane, discerning** She made a wise decision not to go jogging alone after dark. **2. canny, astute, shrewd,**

sharp, cunning, crafty, tricky, keen, calculating, clever The fox is often portrayed as a wise animal. **Antonyms: 1. imprudent, foolish 2. artless, open**

wish *noun* **1. desire, hope, hankering, longing, want, yearning, need, liking, yen** My secret wish is to become a chef. **2. request, entreaty, suit, plea, petition, behest** The audience quieted down at the emcee's wish. ◆ *verb* **desire, hope, want, choose, fancy, elect, covet, crave** You may go first if you wish.

wistful *adjective* **1. wishful, pining, desirous, longing, yearning, craving** He gave his novel a wistful glance, but started his homework instead. **2. sad, melancholy, low, pensive, downcast** Autumn days make me wistful.

wit *noun* **1. cleverness, comedy, humor, ridiculousness, fun, joke, repartee, satire** Mark Twain's books successfully mix wit and realism. **2. comedian, comic, wag, punster, wag, card, jester, humorist** My brother likes to think of himself as a wit.

witch *noun* **enchantress, sorceress, conjurer, magician** Witches are said to be able to put spells on people.

withdraw *verb* **1. remove, retract, rescind, take away, take back, cancel, void, renege** I withdrew my suggestion when I realized that it wasn't practical. **2. depart, leave, exit, go away, retire, retreat, quit, disappear** The waiter served our dinner and then quietly withdrew. **Antonyms: 1. introduce, submit 2. arrive, appear**

wither *verb* **1. dry up, shrivel, droop, die, fail, sag, wilt, shrink, wizen** Our grass withered during last summer's drought. **2. languish, fade, decline, fail, deteriorate, wane** My interest in sailing withered when I got seasick. **Antonyms: flourish, thrive**

withhold *verb* **curb, reserve, retain, check, restrain, hold, repress** Please withhold your questions until the end. **Antonym: release**

withstand *verb* **bear, endure, tolerate, take, oppose, resist, weather, sustain, abide** Our new camping tent can withstand winds of up to 90 miles per hour.

witness *noun* **1. eyewitness, onlooker, spectator, observer, viewer** There have to be witnesses present in order for a wedding to be legal. **2. sign, evidence, testimony, proof, affirmation, corroboration** Those footprints bear witness that a coyote was in the yard. ◆ *verb* **observe, see, view, watch, notice, spot, note** The police are hoping to find someone who witnessed the accident.

witty *adjective* **amusing, funny, humorous, clever, smart, sharp, droll, quick, entertaining** I laughed out loud when I heard the witty comment. **Antonym: dull**

wizard *noun* **1. magician, sorcerer, enchanter, conjurer** The wizard cast a spell that made the dragon fall asleep. **2. ace, expert, genius, prodigy, master, professional, mastermind, virtuoso, pro** My friend Jeffrey is a computer wizard.

wobble *verb* **rock, totter, teeter, shake, sway, quake, waver, shimmy, quiver** This chair wobbles because one of the legs is loose.

woe *noun* **1. anguish, sorrow, grief, misery, distress, agony, suffering, pain, wretchedness** I tried to comfort my friend in her woe. **2. difficulty, affliction, trial, trouble, adversity, misfortune, hardship, calamity** The fire was a great woe to our family. **Antonyms: 1. happiness, joy**

woman *noun* **lady, female, gentlewoman, matron, gal, girl, maiden** My teacher is a very intelligent woman.

wonder *noun* **1. marvel, sensation, spectacle, curiosity, miracle, phenomenon** One of the Seven Wonders of the Ancient World was the Hanging Gardens of Babylon. **2. awe, fascination, amazement, wonderment, astonishment, surprise, stupefaction** We watched in wonder as our cat gave birth to her kittens. ◆ *verb* **ponder, speculate, question, reflect, meditate, think, inquire, conjecture** I sometimes wonder what my life will be like when I grow up.

wonderful *adjective* **1. amazing, astonishing, fantastic, incredible, marvelous, astounding, fascinating, unique** The splendors of Yosemite Valley are wonderful to behold. **2. terrific, marvelous, great, splendid, excellent, superb, first-rate, smashing, magnificent** I had a wonderful time at your party. **Antonyms: 1. ordinary, routine 2. terrible**

wont *noun* **habit, practice, manner, custom, fashion, way, mode, rule** It is his wont to meditate every day.

woo *verb* **1. court, romance, pursue, pay suit, chase, make advances** My brother tried sending flowers to woo back his ex-girlfriend. **2. entice, lure, solicit, seek, address, flatter, persuade, coax** The restaurant tried to woo new customers by offering coupons.

wood *noun* **1. boards, lumber, planks, timber, logs, clapboard, firewood, kindling** I need some wood to make more bookshelves in my room. **2. forest, timber, timberland, woodland, grove, copse, thicket** My friends and I are going to explore the woods behind my house.

word *noun* **1. term, designation, expression, name, locution** *Gigantic* is a word that means "very large." **2. conversation, discussion, talk, chat, conference, consultation, audience** The principal wants to have a word with us. **3. word of honor, pledge, promise, vow, assurance, guarantee, warrant, declaration** My friend gave me her word that she would return the money I loaned her. **4. message, news, notice, communication, report, information, tidings, report** Our relatives sent word that they would be arriving a day late. **5. dispute, argument, quarrel, debate, dispute, altercation, row** My brother and I had words over whose need for the car was more urgent. ◆ *verb* **express, formulate, phrase, put, state, term, couch, frame, style** I worded my request carefully.

work *noun* **1. labor, effort, drudgery, toil, exertion, sweat, moil, industry, travail** Mowing a large yard takes a lot of work. **2. career, employment, job, occupation, profession, business, trade, vocation** My sister enjoys her work as a nurse practitioner. **3. chore, task, assignment, duty, project, responsibility, obligation** Mom said that I could go to the mall as soon as I finished my work around the house. **4. accomplishment, feat, achievement, undertaking, deed, act, enterprise, exploit** The construction of the Panama Canal was a great work. **5. creation, piece, product, handiwork, handicraft, composition, opus** This gallery specializes in displaying the works of local artists. ◆ *verb* **1. labor, toil, strive, endeavor, strain, grind, slave, sweat** I worked hard to get the den clean. **2. function, operate, go, run, perform, act, behave, manage** Do you know how a computer works? **3. do, perform, cause, produce, effect, bring about, create, originate, engender, generate** Studies have shown that pets can work wonders for patients recovering from depression. **4. solve, unravel, untangle, crack, answer, decipher, reason, figure out** He finally worked out all the answers to the crossword puzzle.

worker *noun* **employee, operative, laborer, craftsperson, tradesperson, breadwinner, hired hand** My mom is a worker in an automobile factory.

world *noun* **1. earth, planet, globe, sphere, heavenly body, orb, terra firma** Ferdinand Magellan commanded the first expedition to sail around the world. **2. universe, cosmos, creation, macrocosm, nature, existence** How do you believe the world began? **3. humanity, humankind, mankind, human race, everyone, everybody, populace** It felt to me as if the whole world mourned Princess Diana's death. **4. area, domain, field, arena, group, sphere, realm, set, profession, industry** Dr. Michael Gershon is well-known in the world of neurobiology. **5. abundance, wealth, profusion, mass, mountain, heap, sea, multitude, lot, host** A good library contains a world of information.

Word Group

A **worm** is an animal having a soft, long, rounded or flattened body and no backbone. **Worm** is a specific term with no true synonyms. Here are some common worms:

angleworm, earthworm, flatworm, nematode, pinworm, roundworm, tapeworm, trematode

---

worrisome *adjective* **annoying, irksome, irritating, bothersome, distressing, provoking, troublesome, galling, nagging** Your negative attitude is worrisome.

worry *verb* **1. concern, trouble, distress, fret, disturb, upset, dread, despair, agonize** I'm worried that I might not pass tomorrow's math test. **2. annoy, torment, agitate, vex, harass, badger, pester, tease, perturb** Try not to worry your sister while she's studying. ◆ *noun* **care, concern, anxiety, apprehension, trouble, burden, difficulty, grief** My cousin acts as if he doesn't have a worry in the world. ◈ **Antonyms:** *verb* **2. comfort, soothe, calm**

worship *noun* **veneration, reverence, devotion, exaltation, adulation, homage** The worship of the Egyptian goddess Isis was widespread in the ancient world. ◆ *verb* **1. revere, glorify, idolize, honor, praise, magnify, celebrate, sanctify, venerate, adulate** The ancient Greeks worshiped many different gods and goddesses. **2. love, esteem, adore, like, admire, respect, cherish** My grandmother worships my sister's new baby. ◈ **Antonyms:** *verb* **1. blaspheme, mock, dishonor 2. hate, detest**

worth *noun* **1. importance, value, merit, usefulness, significance, virtue, use** She proved her worth to the team when she hit two home runs in one game. **2. value, price, cost, caliber, quality** An appraiser was called in to establish the worth of the furniture. ◈ **Antonym: 1. insignificance, irrelevance**

worthless *adjective* **good-for-nothing, insignificant, unimportant, useless, inconsequential, meaningless, trivial** This is just a worthless piece of junk mail. ◈ **Antonyms: valuable, worthwhile**

worthwhile *adjective* **good, important, useful, valuable, worthy, laudable, beneficial** Helping to feed the homeless is a worthwhile cause. ◈ **Antonym: worthless**

worthy *adjective* **deserving, commendable, fitting, excellent, good, worthwhile, meritorious, praiseworthy** Your plan for organizing our fundraiser is a worthy one. ◈ **Antonym:** *adjective* **useless**

wound *noun* **1. injury, sore, cut, abrasion, lesion, contusion, scratch, hurt** Our first-aid instructor showed us how to bandage a wound. **2. blow, insult, affront, offense** Her cold remark was a wound to my self-esteem. ◆ *verb* **1. injure, hurt, harm, cut, stab, scratch, lacerate, bruise** A police officer was wounded in the shootout. **2. insult, offend, outrage, affront, grieve, vex, distress, hurt, pique** I wounded my younger sister's feelings when I ignored her. ✎ **Antonyms:** *verb* **2. soothe, calm, appease**

wrap *verb* **1. package, gift-wrap, bind, cover, enclose, fold, bundle, encase** I wrapped my mom's present in bright paper. **2. enfold, envelop, shroud, veil, cloak, swathe, surround, conceal, sheathe** The early morning sun was wrapped in clouds. ◆ *noun* **shawl, mantle, cape, cloak, jacket, coat, wraparound, stole** Elise brought a wrap in case the evening cooled off. ✎ **Antonyms:** *verb* **2. reveal, expose, uncover**

wrath *noun* **anger, fury, ire, rage, rancor, furor** I was filled with wrath when my computer crashed before I had saved my work. ✎ **Antonym: pleasure**

wreath *noun* **garland, circlet, bouquet, festoon, laurel, crown, loop** We hung a wreath of dried flowers and vines on the door.

wreathe *verb* **festoon, decorate, encircle, surround, ring, entwine, adorn, twist, wind, twine** Every holiday season, my mom wreathes our banister with pine boughs.

wreck *noun* **accident, crash, smashup, smash, pileup, destruction, disaster, ruin** Fortunately, no one was hurt in yesterday's train wreck. ◆ *verb* **ruin, demolish, destroy, damage, shatter, smash, spoil, devastate** Dad accidentally wrecked my bike when he backed the car over it.

wrench *verb* **1. jerk, pull, snatch, tug, twist, wring, rip, force, wrest** My dog wrenched his toy out of my hand. **2. sprain, strain, turn, twist, overstrain, pull, tear** I wrenched my back when I lifted a pumpkin that was too heavy for me.

wrest *verb* **wrench, twist, wring, grab, force, usurp, seize, steal, exact, appropriate** History is filled with examples of people wresting power from others.

wrestle *verb* **grapple, struggle, fight, battle, scuffle, contest, joust, combat, compete** My sister and I wrestle constantly with the problem of sharing a room.

wretched *adjective* **1. depressed, sad, unhappy, dejected, forlorn, woeful, despondent** I am wretched because my best friend is mad at me. **2. dreadful, horrid, lousy, miserable, rotten, terrible, awful, nasty** We've had wretched weather all summer long. ✎ **Antonyms: 1. happy, cheerful 2. excellent, wonderful**

wring *verb* **1. squeeze, compress, force, twist, press, push** I had to wring the water out of my wet towel. **2. coerce, force, extract, wrench, wrest, extort, exact, compel, pressure** The Spanish Inquisition used torture to wring false confessions from many innocent people.

wrinkle *noun* **fold, crease, line, furrow, crinkle** Mom ironed the wrinkles out of her skirt. ◆ *verb* **crease, crinkle, crumple, furrow, pucker, rumple** Doing the dishes took so long that the water wrinkled my hands.

write *verb* **1. inscribe, record, jot down, note, scrawl, scribble, scratch** Please write your name and the date in the upper right corner of the page. **2. draft, compose, author, create, produce, originate, invent, formulate, pen** I have to write a lab report for my chemistry class.

writer *noun* **author, novelist, journalist, poet, essayist, columnist, reporter, editor** John Steinbeck is one of my favorite writers.

writhe *verb* **twist, squirm, wiggle, turn, contort, toss** The kitten writhed in my arms, trying to get free.

wrong *adjective* **1. false, inaccurate, incorrect, mistaken, untrue, erroneous, faulty** I had only one wrong answer on my vocabulary test. **2. bad, immoral, sinful, evil, wicked, dishonest, criminal, vicious, corrupt, base** It is wrong to tell lies about other people. **3. improper, inappropriate, unsuitable, awkward, unseemly, unacceptable** High-heeled shoes are the wrong thing to wear when playing racquetball. **4. amiss, defective, faulty, askew, inoperative, broken, imperfect** There's something wrong with Dad's car. ◆ *adverb* **incorrectly, erroneously, mistakenly, badly, inaccurately, improperly** Most people pronounce my name wrong. ◆ *noun* **misdeed, crime, evil, offense, sin, injury, trespass, injustice** "Two wrongs don't make a right" means that it is not proper to seek revenge. ◆ *verb* **mistreat, harm, hurt, injure, cheat, persecute, abuse, offend, outrage** I wronged my friend when I revealed her secret. ✎ **Antonyms:** *adjective* **1. correct, true 2. good, moral 3. appropriate, proper 4. right** ◆ *adverb* **accurately, correctly**

wry *adjective* **1. ironic, dry, sarcastic, satiric, funny, sardonic, droll, amusing, caustic** My class enjoys our teacher's wry sense of humor. **2. twisted, distorted, warped, deformed, crooked, askew, bent, contorted** He made a wry face when he heard the corny joke.

Xx Yy Zz

x-ray *noun* **radiograph, diagnostic picture, medical photograph** The doctor examined the x-rays of my injured ankle. ◆ *verb* **radiograph, photograph, film** The dentist x-rays my teeth once a year.

yank *verb* **jerk, pull, tug, wrench, snatch, draw, pluck, wrest** I was yanked off my feet during a game of tug of war. ◆ *noun* **jerk, pull, tug, wrench, snap, pluck, jolt, snatch, grab** I gave the stuck door a good hard yank. ● **Antonyms: push, shove**

yard *noun* **lawn, back yard, grounds, lot, courtyard, court, enclosure** We set up the net and had a game of volleyball in the yard.

yardstick *noun* **criterion, standard, test, measure, mark, benchmark, gauge** Popularity is not a valid yardstick of a person's worth.

yarn *noun* **1. spun wool, fiber, strand, thread, filament** Carol is knitting a sweater out of green yarn. **2. anecdote, story, tale, fable, tall tale, reminiscence, account, narrative** We enjoy it when Dad tell us yarns about his days in the navy.

yawn *verb* **gape, expand, open, spread, stretch out, gap** The entrance to the huge copper mine yawned before us.

year *noun* **ages, eon, eternity, forever, time, epoch** It's been years since I've seen him.

yearn *verb* **ache, desire, long, want, wish, crave, hanker, pine** My grandmother yearns to see her sister in Japan.

yell *verb* **bellow, call, cry, scream, shout, holler, halloo, roar, howl, whoop** My friend yelled that he would be with me in a minute. ◆ *noun* **call, cry, scream, shout, holler, bellow, shriek, screech, halloo** Firefighters rescued the girl after they heard her yells for help.

yelp *verb* **bark, cry out, yap, yawp, yip, squeal, howl, squeak** The puppy yelped when the veterinarian gave him a shot. ◆ *noun* **squeal, yap, yawp, yip, bark, cry, howl, shriek** My dog gave a yelp when I accidentally stepped on his tail.

yen *noun* **craving, longing, wish, desire, itch, yearning, appetite, hunger, thirst** I have a yen for Mexican food tonight.

yes *adverb* **all right, aye, agreed, absolutely, definitely, indeed, certainly** Yes, we can all go out for Mexican food tonight. ● **Antonyms: no, nay**

yesterday *noun* **days of old, the past, olden times, yesteryear, yore, bygone days** Grandfather likes to reminisce about the automobiles of yesterday.

yet *adverb* **1. as yet, so far, thus far, heretofore, before, previously, earlier** Dad has not gotten home yet. **2. eventually, finally, someday, sometime, even, ultimately, still** If the rain stops, we may yet go camping. **3. anyway, regardless, nonetheless, nevertheless, notwithstanding, still** Despite the rain, we might go camping yet. ◆ *conjunction* **but, however, nevertheless, nonetheless, still, though** I was pretty full, yet I had another slice of pizza.

yield *verb* **1. bear, give, produce, provide, supply, generate, furnish** The tree in our back yard yielded more than a hundred oranges last year. **2. earn, pay, bring in, clear, gave, gain, gross, net, return, realize** My savings account yields five percent interest every year. **3. bow, buckle, give in, capitulate, submit, succumb, surrender, fold** Mark yielded to temptation and had another cookie. **4. cede, hand over, give, relinquish, abandon, renounce, concede, resign, abdicate** The owner yielded control of the company to his son. ◆ *noun* **crop, harvest, output, gain, production, return, profit** We had a good yield from our garden this summer. ● **Antonyms:** *verb* **3. resist, withstand 4. keep, retain**

yoke *noun* **1. pair, brace, couple, duo, twosome, team, span** The wagon was pulled by a yoke of oxen. **2. burden, tie, weight, bondage, slavery, servitude, enslavement, bond** In 1783, the American colonies finally freed themselves from the yoke of British imperialism. ◆ *verb* **harness, hitch, attach, connect, couple, join, link, bind, tie** I'm so busy writing my report that I feel as if I'm yoked to my computer. ● **Antonym:** *verb* **detach**

yonder *adjective* **yon, distant, faraway, remote, far-off** I'll race you to yonder tree and back. ● **Antonyms: near, nearby**

yore *noun* **olden times, past, yesterday, yesteryear, bygone days** In days of yore, pirates roamed the high seas.

young *adjective* **immature, juvenile, youthful, underage, new, undeveloped** Dad was joking when he said that he is too young to watch horror movies. ◆ *noun* **1. youths, kids, juveniles, children, youngsters, adolescents** This TV series has special appeal for the young. **2. babies, offspring, progeny, issue, family, brood, litter** Mother bears are known for keeping a close watch over their young. ⏺ **Antonyms:** *adjective* **mature, old** ◆ *noun* **1. adults, grownups 2. parents**

youngster *noun* **child, juvenile, youth, kid, moppet, tot, adolescent, boy, girl** Grandpa says that he didn't have TV to watch when he was a youngster. ⏺ **Antonyms: adult, grownup**

youth *noun* **1. adolescence, childhood, boyhood, girlhood, minority, youthfulness** Our neighbor has lived in this town since his youth. **2. adolescent, juvenile, teen, teenager, minor, youngster, child, boy, girl** Dad started working when he was just a youth of 17. ⏺ **Antonyms: 1. adulthood, maturity 2. adult, grownup**

youthful *adjective* **adolescent, juvenile, young, childish, immature, teenage, boyish, girlish** This movie was meant to entertain a youthful audience. ⏺ **Antonyms: old, elderly**

yowl *verb* **caterwaul, howl, screech, wail, cry, scream, shout, yell, moan, bay** I was awakened by two cats yowling in the alley. ◆ *noun* **cry, howl, moan, scream, screech, shout, wail, yell, bay, caterwaul** I let out a yowl of pain when I hit my thumb with a hammer.

zany *noun* **clown, comedian, joker, jester, jokester, comic, humorist, buffoon** Some zany put a fake fly in my soup. ◆ *adjective* **ludicrous, clownish, absurd, comical, amusing, humorous, funny, silly** The audience laughed at the clown's zany stunts.

zeal *noun* **ardor, passion, enthusiasm, eagerness, zest, fervor, fire, devotion** He pursues his interest in tennis with great zeal. ⏺ **Antonyms: apathy, indifference**

zealot *noun* **devotee, fanatic, enthusiast, addict, fan, buff, disciple, follower** My aunt has recently become an exercise zealot.

zealous *adjective* **ardent, fervent, enthusiastic, devoted, passionate, keen, fanatical** Reg is a zealous collector of basketball cards. ⏺ **Antonyms: apathetic, unenthusiastic**

zenith *noun* **acme, apex, height, climax, crest, peak, pinnacle, summit, top** At the zenith of his career, the actor starred in three movies in one year. ⏺ **Antonyms: nadir, low point**

zero *noun* **nothing, nil, naught, nought, none, null, cipher** Five subtracted from five equals zero.

zest *noun* **1. pungency, spice, tang, flavor, savor, taste, smack, piquancy** Dad puts salsa on his scrambled eggs to give them zest. **2. relish, gusto, pleasure, enjoyment, eagerness, enthusiasm, passion, delight** He ate the sushi with zest. ⏺ **Antonyms: 2. apathy, ennui**

zestful *adjective* **exciting, thrilling, stimulating, energetic, dynamic, forceful, spirited** The gospel choir gave the audience a zestful rendition of "Swing Low, Sweet Chariot."

zigzag *verb* **wind, snake, meander, weave, twist, spiral, curl** The river zigzagged through the valley.

zing *verb* **zip, zoom, whiz, buzz, rush, dash, fly, race** I heard a wasp zing past my ear.

zip *noun* **energy, vim, vigor, vitality, liveliness, spirit, pep, sprightliness** The playful kittens were full of zip. ◆ *verb* **1. zoom, whiz, flash, rush, fly, race, dart, dash, hasten** Elma zipped around the corner on her bicycle. **2. fasten, close, shut, secure, button, snap** I put my books in my backpack and zipped it closed.

Word Group

A **zipper** is a fastener that is closed or opened by a sliding tab. **Zipper** is a specific term with no true synonyms. Here are some other fasteners:

belt, cinch strap, drawstring, elastic band, hook and eye, strap, tie, Velcro

---

zippy *adjective* **active, brisk, dynamic, energetic, lively, sprightly, spirited, vigorous** The polka is a zippy dance.

zone *noun* **area, district, locality, neighborhood, quarter, region, territory** Our town has only a small business zone. ◆ *verb* **designate, set aside, subdivide, district, apportion, divide, section, partition** This district is zoned for agricultural and residential use.

zoo *noun* **menagerie, animal farm, game preserve, wildlife preserve** We went to the zoo to see giant pandas.

zoom *verb* **1. zip, whiz, dart, dash, flash, race, speed, streak, tear, sprint** The cyclists zoomed around the track during the final lap of the race. **2. climb, soar, rise, ascend, swoop, fly, rocket** The fighter plane zoomed off the aircraft carrier's deck.